McGRAW-HILL YEARBOOK OF
Science & Technology

2003

McGRAW-HILL YEARBOOK OF
Science &
Technology

2003

Comprehensive coverage of recent events and research as compiled by the staff of the McGraw-Hill Encyclopedia of Science & Technology

McGraw-Hill
New York   Chicago   San Francisco   Lisbon   London   Madrid   Mexico City   Milan
New Delhi   San Juan   Seoul   Singapore   Sydney   Toronto

The **McGraw·Hill** Companies

Library of Congress Cataloging in Publication data

McGraw-Hill yearbook of science and technology.
1962–   . New York, McGraw-Hill.

    v. illus. 26 cm.
    Vols. for 1962–   compiled by the staff of the
McGraw-Hill encyclopedia of science and technology.
     1. Science—Yearbooks.   2. Technology—
Yearbooks.   1. McGraw-Hill encyclopedia of
science and technology.
Q1.M13   505.8   62-12028

ISBN 0-07-141062-7
ISSN 0076-2016

1 2 3 4 5 6 7 8 9 0   DOW/DOW   0 9 8 7 6 5 4 3

This book was printed on acid-free paper.

*It was set in Garamond Book and Neue Helvetica Black Condensed by
TechBooks, Fairfax, Virginia. The art was prepared by TechBooks.
The book was printed and bound by RR Donnelley, The Lakeside Press.*

Contents

Editing, Design, & Production Staff

Consulting Editors

Dr. John Timoney. *Department of Veterinary Science, University of Kentucky, Lexington.* VETERINARY MEDICINE.

Dr. Gordon E. Uno. *Department of Botany and Microbiology, University of Oklahoma, Norman.* PLANT PHYSIOLOGY.

Dr. Sally E. Walker. *Associate Professor of Geology and Marine Science, University of Georgia, Athens.* INVERTEBRATE PALEONTOLOGY.

Dr. Nicole Y. Weekes. *Pomona College, Claremont, California.* NEUROPSYCHOLOGY.

Prof. Mary Anne White. *Killam Research Professor in Materials Science, Department of Chemistry, Dalhousie University, Halifax, Nova Scotia, Canada.* MATERIALS SCIENCE AND METALLURGIC ENGINEERING.

Prof. Thomas A. Wikle. *Head, Department of Geography, Oklahoma State University, Stillwater.* PHYSICAL GEOGRAPHY.

Prof. W. A. Williams. *Professor Emeritus, Department of Agronomy and Range Science, University of California, Davis.* AGRICULTURE.

Dr. Gary Wnek. *Department of Chemical Engineering, Virginia Commonwealth University, Richmond.* CHEMICAL ENGINEERING.

Dr. James C. Wyant. *University of Arizona Optical Sciences Center, Tucson.* ELECTROMAGNETIC RADIATION AND OPTICS.

Article Titles and Authors

The 2003 *McGraw-Hill Yearbook of Science & Technology* provides a broad overview of important recent developments in science, technology, and engineering as selected by our distinguished board of consulting editors. At the same time, it satisfies the nonspecialist reader's need to stay informed about important trends in research and development that will advance our knowledge in the future in fields ranging from agriculture to zoology and lead to important new practical applications. Readers of the *McGraw-Hill Encyclopedia of Science & Technology*, Ninth Edition (2002), also will find the *Yearbook* to be a valuable companion publication, supplementing and updating the basic information.

In the 2003 edition, we continue to document the advances in such areas as anthropology and archeology, astronomy, biomedical sciences, chemistry, computing and information technology, communications, earth and environmental sciences, forensic science, materials science and engineering, nanotechnology, and theoretical and experimental physics, among other topics.

Each contribution to the *Yearbook* is a concise yet authoritative article authored by one or more authorities in the field. We are pleased that noted researchers have been supporting the *Yearbook* since its first edition in 1962 by taking time to share their knowledge with our readers. The topics are selected by our consulting editors in conjunction with our editorial staff based on present significance and potential applications. McGraw-Hill strives to make each article as readily understandable as possible for the nonspecialist reader through careful editing and the extensive use of graphics, much of which is prepared specially for the *Yearbook*.

Librarians, students, teachers, the scientific community, journalists and writers, and the general reader continue to find in the *McGraw-Hill Yearbook of Science & Technology* the information they need in order to follow the rapid pace of advances in science and technology and to understand the developments in these fields that will shape the world of the twenty-first century.

Mark D. Licker
PUBLISHER

A–Z

ABC lipid transporters

ABC transporters belong to a large, diverse super-family of adenosine triphosphate–binding cassette (ABC) transporter transmembrane proteins. The latter translocate a variety of molecules, including proteins, ions, sugars, and lipids, across extracellular and intracellular membranes using energy derived from adenosine triphosphate (ATP). ABC transporters are characterized by ATP-binding cassettes (catalytic regions) that contain the amino acid sequence patterns known as Walker A and B motifs, which are found in all ATP-binding proteins, and an intervening signature C motif found specifically in ABC transporters (see **illus.**). The transmembrane domains contain six transmembrane helices and confer substrate specificity. The ABC transporters are classified either as full transporters, containing two ATP-binding cassettes and two transmembrane domains, or as half-transporters which, having only one of each domain, are thought to dimerize (form a pair) with another

half-transporter to create a functional transporter. Based on phylogenetic analysis, the ABC transporter superfamily is subdivided into seven subfamilies (ABCA, ABCB, ABCC, ABCD, ABCE, ABCF, and ABCG), which are functionally as well as morphologically distinct.

ABC transporters in general have been implicated in drug resistance, cystic fibrosis, and a variety of metabolic diseases. In particular, the recent discovery of ABC lipid transporter gene defects in lipoprotein metabolic diseases may have important implications for the treatment of atherosclerosis.

Atherosclerosis and reverse cholesterol transport. Cholesterol accumulation in macrophages and foam cells (lipid-laden macrophages) in the peripheral arterial vasculature promotes atherosclerosis and cardiovascular disease, the major cause of mortality in industrialized nations. Cholesterol absorbed from the diet or secreted from the liver is packaged into lipoproteins, such as chylomicrons, very low density lipoprotein (VLDL), and low-density lipoprotein

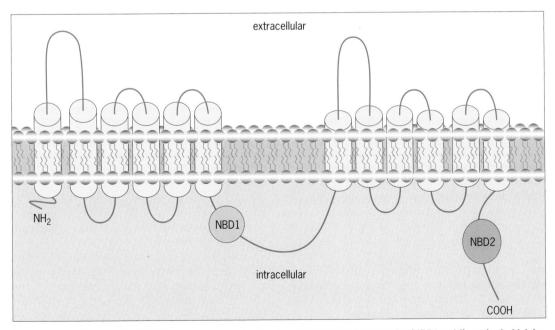

Membrane topology model of ABCA1 contains two cytoplasmic nucleotide-binding domains (NBD1 and 2), each of which is composed of a Walker A and Walker B ATP-binding domain interspersed by an ABC transporter signature motif.

(LDL), along with other lipids for transport to peripheral tissues (tissues other than the liver). To prevent accumulation of cholesterol in the periphery, excess sterols from peripheral cells are packaged into high-density lipoproteins (HDL) and transported back to the liver through a mechanism termed reverse cholesterol transport. The liver, the only organ that can remove excess cholesterol from the body, can then excrete the excess sterols into the bile either as free sterols or, after modification, as bile acids. ABC lipid transporters in the ABCA and ABCG subfamilies are believed to play a key role in reverse cholesterol transport and secretion of excess sterols into the bile.

ABCA1. ABCA1, a member of the ABCA subfamily of ABC transporters, is a full transporter containing two ATP-binding cassettes and two transmembrane domains (see illus.). It exhibits a highly complex intracellular trafficking pattern, shuttling between the plasma membrane and intracellular late endocytic vesicles. This suggests an important role for ABCA1 in the movement of cholesterol between these two cellular compartments. ABCA1 is synthesized by most tissues but is most abundant in the liver, testes, and adrenals and moderately abundant in the small intestine, lung, and adipose.

Tangier disease. The gene coding for ABCA1 has been identified as the primary defective gene in patients with Tangier disease. This rare genetic disorder is characterized by near-complete absence of circulating HDL, decreased levels of LDL, moderately increased levels of triglycerides, orange tonsils, and increased risk of coronary artery disease. Patients with Tangier disease are unable to remove excess cholesterol and phospholipids from cells, and accumulate cholesteryl esters in many tissues, including tonsils, lymph nodes, liver, spleen, and intestine. ABCA1 apparently functions in the efflux (removal) of intracellular cholesterol and phospholipid to extracellular apolipoprotein acceptors, such as apolipoproteins AI and E, initiating the process of reverse cholesterol transport in which excess cholesterol from peripheral tissues is transported to the liver for excretion.

Studies in ABCA1 knockout and transgenic mouse models support this concept. Like human patients with Tangier disease, ABCA1 knockout mice (mice without the ABCA1 gene) have virtually undetectable plasma concentrations of HDL, reduced levels of LDL-cholesterol, significant accumulation of lipid-laden macrophages in various tissues, and enhanced aortic atherosclerosis when crossed with hyperlipidemic mice. Conversely, overexpression of ABCA1 in mice raises plasma HDL and significantly reduces diet-induced aortic atherosclerosis. Thus, changes in ABCA1 gene expression in mice markedly alter not only the plasma concentrations of the antiatherogenic HDL but also atherogenic risk. These findings identify ABCA1 as a target for the development of therapeutic agents for the treatment of low-HDL syndromes and cardiovascular disease.

ABCA1 gene expression. ABCA1 gene expression is highly regulated by a variety of agents including cholesterol, retinoic acid, oxysterols, fatty acids, cyclic adenosine monophosphate (cAMP), and cytokines such as interferon. As might be anticipated from ABCA1's role in facilitating the efflux of cellular lipids, cholesterol loading markedly enhances the accumulation of ABCA1 messenger ribonucleic acid and protein, whereas removal of cellular cholesterol by incubation with HDL down-regulates (decreases) ABCA1 gene expression. Recent reports have demonstrated that lipid X/retinoid X nuclear receptor heterodimer (LXR/RXR)–responsive elements (specific DNA sequences that bind agonists to activate gene transcription) in the proximal promoter of the ABCA1 gene mediate retinoic acid– and oxysterol-dependent activation of ABCA1 and confer the observed induction of ABCA1 during lipid loading. An alternative promoter in the first intron of the ABCA1 gene that mediates liver-specific LXR/RXR-dependent ABCA1 expression has also been identified. Furthermore, peroxisome proliferator-activated receptor α (PPARα) has been shown to up-regulate ABCA1 expression indirectly through an interaction with several peroxisome proliferator response elements (PPREs) in the LXRα promoter. Multiple other factors related to lipid metabolism and other cell-specific functions regulate ABCA1 gene expression. Unsaturated fatty acids have been shown to enhance the intracellular degradation of ABCA1. Analogs of cAMP stimulate ABCA1 transcription in fibroblasts and macrophages, whereas interferon-γ reduces ABCA1 mRNA and cholesterol/phospholipid efflux to apolipoprotein A1 (apoA1) in macrophages and foam cells, indicating that inflammatory cytokines may modulate cellular cholesterol efflux by changing ABCA1 gene expression.

ABCG1. ABCG1 belongs to the ABCG subfamily that has been shown to be involved in the regulation of lipid-trafficking mechanisms in macrophages, hepatocytes, and intestinal mucosa cells. ABCG1 is a half-transporter that contains a single nucleotide-binding domain at the amino terminus, followed by six transmembrane domains. The half-transporter that dimerizes with ABCG1 to generate a functional transporter has not been identified; thus, it is unclear whether ABCG1 functions as a homodimer or heterodimer. ABCG1 is predominantly localized in intracellular compartments and is associated with the endoplasmic reticulum and Golgi membranes.

The human ABCG1 gene spans more than 97 kilobase pairs comprising 20 exons. It contains two separate promoters, upstream of exons 1 and 5, respectively. Although ubiquitously expressed, it is present mainly in the liver, macrophages, lung, and heart. Cholesterol loading enhances ABCG1 gene expression in human macrophages, and ABCG1 mRNA levels are increased after stimulation of the LXR/RXR pathway, suggesting a potential role for ABCG1 in macrophage cholesterol homeostasis. However, neither the molecules transported by ABCG1 nor its function is known. Because of its potential role in cholesterol metabolism, the ABCG1 gene may also prove to be a useful target for the development of antiatherogenic therapies.

ABCG5/ABCG8. The genes coding for ABCG5 and ABCG8 have been identified as the defective genes in patients with β-sitosterolemia, an autosomal, recessive metabolic disease characterized by accumulation of sterols, including those from plants and shellfish. Patients with β-sitosterolemia have enhanced absorption of these sterols as well as cholesterol and inefficiently eliminate excess sterols through the bile, resulting in development of xanthomas (cholesterol accumulation under skin causing yellowish discoloration) and premature cardiovascular disease. Thus, ABCG5 and ABCG8 are believed to participate in biliary excretion of plant and shellfish sterols and exclusion of plant and shellfish sterols from gut absorption.

ABCG5 and ABCG8, like ABCG1, are members of the ABCG half-transporter subfamily of ABC transporters. The human genes coding for ABCG5 and ABCG8 each have 13 exons and 12 introns. Interestingly, the genes are located in a head-to-head orientation with only 372 base pairs separating the translational start sites. The ABCG5 and ABCG8 genes are transcribed in the liver and small intestine and, to a lesser degree, in the colon. High-cholesterol feeding of mice can induce the hepatic and intestinal mRNA expression of the genes for ABCG5 and ABCG8. The coordinate regulation of the two genes by cholesterol, their shared promoter, their similar tissue distribution, and the similar phenotypes of patients with defects in the genes encoding ABCG5 and ABCG8 suggest that these half-transporters likely form functional heterodimers that regulate dietary sterol absorption as well as biliary sterol excretion. Thus, ABCG5 and ABCG8 represent attractive targets for the development of therapeutic agents that might modulate both intestinal sterol absorption and biliary sterol excretion.

Summary. Investigation into ABC lipid transporters has yielded major advances in understanding the mechanisms by which excess cholesterol and other sterols are removed from the body. Future research may reveal new pathways involved in cholesterol transport and should provide novel therapeutic agents for cardiovascular disease.

For background information *see* ARTERIOSCLEROSIS; CHOLESTEROL; GENE; LIPID METABOLISM; LIPOPROTEIN; LIVER; PROTEIN in the McGraw-Hill Encyclopedia of Science & Technology.

Justina Wu; Charles Joyce; Federica Basso;
Silvia Santamarina-Fojo

Bibliography. G. Assmann, A. von Eckardstein, and H. Bryan Brewer, Jr., Familial ananphalipoproteinemia: Tangier disease, in *The Metabolic and Molecular Bases of Inherited Disease*, McGraw-Hill, New York, 2001; M. Lee, K. Lu, and S. Patel, Genetic basis of sitosterolemia, *Curr. Opin. Lipid.*, 12:141–149, 2001; J. F. Oram, Molecular basis of cholesterol homeostasis: Lessons from Tangier disease and ABCA1, *Mol. Med.*, 8:168–73, 2001; S. Santamarina-Fojo et al., Regulation and intracellular trafficking of the ABCA1 promoter, *J. Lipid Res.*, 42:1339–1345, 2001; G. Schmitz, L. Langmann, and S. Heimerl, Role of ABCG1 and other ABCG family members in lipid metabolism, *J. Lipid Res.*, 42:1513–1552, 2001.

Acoustic phonetics

The discipline of acoustic phonetics can be narrowly defined as the study of the acoustic output of the vocal tract for speech, but ultimately it encompasses much more. Acoustic phonetics makes direct contact with, and in many cases is the foundation of, areas of study such as speech synthesis, machine recognition of speech, speech perception, phonology, and speech pathology.

Source-filter theory. There is a well-articulated theory of acoustic phonetics, the source-filter theory, where the source is the input to the system and the filter is the resonator. It is easiest to introduce the theory by first discussing vowels, the kinds of speech sound for which the theory is best known.

Source. More specifically, the source is the energy produced by the vibrating vocal folds (**Fig. 1**), which are set into motion by a combination of muscular forces that close the vocal folds as well as raise the pressure in the trachea relative to the pressure above the vocal folds. When the tracheal pressure overcomes the resistance offered by the closed vocal folds, the latter are blown apart and will continue to oscillate, by virtue of a delicate interplay of aerodynamic and mechanical forces, as long as the pressure differential exists. The nearly periodic vibration of the vocal folds can be characterized in either the time domain (as a waveform) or frequency domain

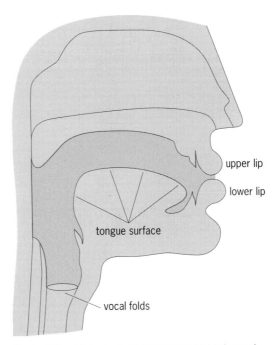

upper lip

lower lip

tongue surface

vocal folds

Fig. 1. Midsagittal schematic view of vocal folds (source) and vocal tract (filter, colored area).

(as a spectrum); most models of the vibration focus on parameters of the time-domain representation and their relationship to the spectral composition of the vibration. Vibration of the vocal folds generates a consecutive-integer harmonic spectrum, with greatest energy at the fundamental frequency (F0), or lowest-frequency component, and decreasing energy across the higher harmonics at the frequencies 2F0, 3F0, 4F0, 5F0, ... The time-domain models show how subtle changes in the temporal parameters result in systematic frequency-domain changes. The frequency-domain representation, also called the glottal source spectrum, can be associated very directly with the perception of voice quality (encompassing harshness, breathiness, and so forth).

Filter. The glottal source spectrum can be considered as the input to the filter, which in anatomical terms is the vocal tract. The vocal tract is the length of airway running from the vocal folds, in the larynx, to the lips (Fig. 1). The vocal-tract filter has the characteristics of a resonating tube, with one end closed. The closed end is at the vocal folds because the acoustic energy generated there excites the vocal-tract filter each time the vocal folds close during their vibratory cycles. The open end is at the lips because vowel sounds are produced with the mouth open to varying degrees, depending on the vowel. A tube resonator with a closed end and uniform cross-sectional area from end to end has multiple resonant frequencies determined by the tube's length. For such

a tube having a length of 17 cm (6.7 in.), a typical length for the adult male vocal tract, the resonant frequencies are determined by the quarter-wavelength rule, given by the equation below,

$$f_r = \frac{(2n - 1)\,c}{4l}$$

where f_r is a resonant frequency, $n = 1, 2, 3, \ldots$, c is the constant speed of sound in air (35,400 cm/s), and l is the length of the tube. This formula gives an odd-integer series of resonant frequencies at approximately 520 Hz, 1560 Hz, 2600 Hz, and so forth. These resonant frequencies can be thought of as peaks in a theoretical spectrum (where "theoretical" means calculated from theory, rather than being measured empirically), which have noninfinite amplitude as a result of both energy loss within the vocal tract and sound radiating from the lips. The overall shape of the theoretical spectrum can be thought of as the resonance curve or filter function of the vocal tract.

Output signal. The filtering effect of the vocal tract can be thought of in another way, that of the vocal-tract filter function shaping the source harmonic energy generated by the input, or vibrating vocal folds. The output signal thus represents the combined effect of the source and filter (**Fig. 2a–c**). The peaks in the output spectrum are referred to as formants, and the frequency locations of the first three formants (F1, F2, and F3, the first three resonances of the tube) are a function of the configuration of

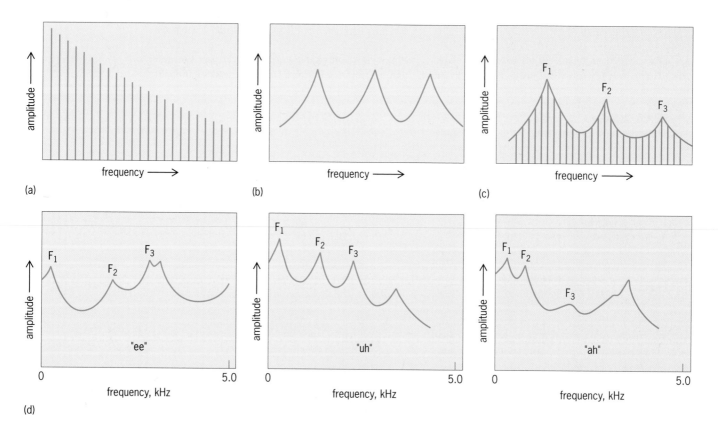

Fig. 2. Production of output spectrum of the vocal tract. (*a*) Source spectrum produced by vibrating vocal folds. (*b*) Resonance curve (filter) of vocal-tract tube having uniform cross-sectional area. (*c*) Output spectrum from combined source and filter. (*d*) Output spectra for vowels "ee," "uh," and "ah."

the vocal-tract tube, which is to say of the vowel articulation. The resonant frequencies predicted by the quarter-wavelength rule—when the tube has a uniform cross-sectional area from end to end—are changed in systematic ways that depend on the location of constrictions relative to the standing-wave patterns of pressure and velocity within the tube. Thus a vowel such as the "ee" in the word "heat," for which the vocal tract tube shape is constricted toward the front (that is, toward the lips) and wide open toward the back (that is, toward the vocal folds) is associated with a resonance curve, and therefore with an output spectrum, substantially different from the case of the tube without any constrictions (as for the first vowel "uh" in the word "about"); on the other hand, a vowel like the "ah" in "father" constricts the tube toward the back and leaves the front wide open, yielding a different kind of deviation from the quarter-wavelength resonances of an unconstricted tube (Fig. 2d).

Although a tube resonator has, in theory, an infinite series of resonance peaks, only the first three formant frequencies have critical phonetic importance in the sense of distinguishing acoustically among the vowels of a language. Not surprisingly, these same three formant frequencies have been shown to be of critical importance in the perception of vowel categories.

Consonants and nasals. The model of a source spectrum shaped by a vocal-tract filter or resonator also applies to consonants such as stops (such as p, b), fricatives (such as s, z), and affricates (such as ch, j), but in these cases the sources are likely to involve aperiodic (inharmonic) spectra generated by impulse or turbulent air flows. For some sounds (such as b, z, j) the aperiodic sources are combined with the periodic source described above. Another class of sounds, the nasals (such as m, n), require a theory for parallel resonating tubes where one of the tubes has a dead end and therefore traps energy at its resonant frequencies. In this case the theoretical and empirical spectrum will have reverse peaks or antiresonances, indicating frequencies at which the combination of source and filter results in little or no output energy. Antiresonances are also found in the spectra of the stops, fricatives, and affricates.

Properties of speech sounds. The last half-century has seen an enormous amount of research on the temporal and spectral properties of speech sounds. This work has been critical to the design of speech synthesizers and algorithms for computer recognition of speech, and in some cases to the design of hearing aids and processing schemes for cochlear implants; the data have also proven useful in understanding speech disorders. The standard representation of speech sounds in acoustic phonetics research is the spectrogram (**Fig. 3**), which shows the formant frequencies of the vocal-tract signal as a function of time, with intensity coded in a gray scale (or, in more modern computer applications, by a color scheme). Measurement conventions have been established for the correspondence between temporal intervals and

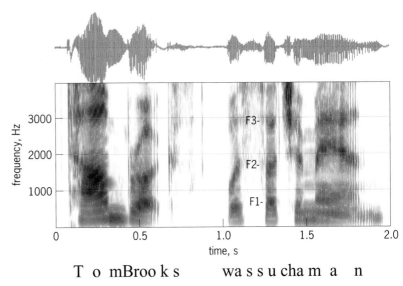

Fig. 3. Spectrogram of the utterance, "Tom Brooks was such a man." Intensity is coded by the gray scale. The speech waveform (amplitude over time) is at the top of the plot. Letters beneath the plot show the approximate locations of the sounds. First three formants, F1, F2, and F3, are indicated for the vowel "uh" in "such."

certain sound categories, as well as for the spectral characteristics of speech sound categories. A large amount of data has been generated for naturally spoken vowel and consonant durations and spectra, and these have been used, for example, to design high-quality speech synthesizers. The very high intelligibility of sophisticated speech synthesizers, whose algorithms are based on these measurements, is strong evidence for the high quality of acoustic-phonetics research.

Factors affecting speech sounds. A largely predictable characteristic of any spectral measurement of vocal-tract output is its dependence on the age and gender of the speaker. Because the vocal tract resonates like a tube closed at one end with tube length being a scaling factor for the resonant frequencies, the formant frequencies of a particular sound spoken by men, women, and children will be quite different as a result of their general size differences, which are mirrored by differences in vocal-tract length. More generally, the acoustic characteristics of any speech sound, including their durations and spectra, are affected by many factors including (but not limited to) age, gender, speaking rate, dialect, linguistic stress (for example, *re*bel versus re*bel*), and phonetic context (the sounds surrounding the sound of interest). This means that the acoustic characteristics of a given sound cannot be considered as fixed or templatelike. One challenge of research in acoustic phonetics is to account for the factors that can affect the acoustic representation of speech sounds, and to relate these factors to speech synthesis, automatic speech recognition, speech perception, phonological theory, and clinical application in the diagnosis and understanding of speech disorders.

For background information *see* SOUND; SPEECH; SPEECH PERCEPTION; SPEECH RECOGNITION;

VIBRATION; VOICE RESPONSE in the McGraw-Hill Encyclopedia of Science & Technology.   Gary Weismer

Bibliography. G. Fant, *Acoustic Theory of Speech Production*, rev. ed., Mouton de Gruyter, The Hague, 1970; J. L. Flanagan, *Speech Analysis, Synthesis, and Perception*, 2d ed., Springer-Verlag, Berlin, 1972; K. Forrest et al., Statistical analysis of word-initial voiceless obstruents: Preliminary data, *J. Acous. Soc. Amer.*, 84:115–123, 1988; J. Hillenbrand et al., Acoustic characteristics of American English vowels, *J. Acous. Soc. Amer.*, 97:3099–3111, 1995; D. H. Klatt and L. C. Klatt, Analysis, synthesis, and perception of voice quality variation among female and male talkers, *J. Acous. Soc. Amer.*, 87:820–857, 1990; K. N. Stevens, *Acoustic Phonetics*, MIT Press, Cambridge, 1998.

Advanced glycation end products

Sugars serve as energy sources and building blocks for macromolecules, making them indispensable to living organisms. Yet, there is also a negative side to the actions of sugars. They fuel nonenzymatic glycation, a spontaneous posttranslational modification of proteins in vivo that results in the formation of advanced glycation end products (AGEs), which adversely effect biochemical, biomechanical, and cellular function and are implicated in the complications of diabetes and many age-related diseases.

Mechanisms of formation. In the classical view, nonenzymatic glycation is initiated by the spontaneous condensation of reducing sugars, such as glucose, with free amino groups in lysine or arginine residues within proteins. After formation of a covalent bond between the sugar and the protein, subsequent reactions (known as Maillard or brown-

ing reactions) give rise to the formation of AGEs. Some AGEs are adducts (covalently bound chemical groups) to the original protein, whereas others form protein-protein crosslinks (**Fig. 1**). Recently, alternative pathways for the formation of AGEs have been proposed (for example, metal-catalyzed glucose autooxidation and lipid peroxidation reactions), suggesting that there are multiple sources and mechanisms of AGE formation in vivo. Due to the highly diverse reaction pathways leading to AGE formation, AGEs with a variety of chemical structures have been identified (**Fig. 2** and **table**).

Once formed, AGEs are removed only when the protein is degraded. Therefore, although all proteins are prone to AGE formation, AGEs accumulate only in long-lived proteins, that is, proteins with a slow turnover, such as lens crystallins and tissue collagens.

Adverse effects. Accumulation of AGEs results in changes in the chemical and physical properties of proteins and interferes with cellular processes.

Biochemical. Modification of lysine and arginine residues changes the charge distribution of the protein, thereby influencing its tertiary structure (that is, its three-dimensional folded structure) as well as its interactions with other proteins. AGE formation also leads to increased inter- and intramolecular crosslinking of proteins. Functionally, these changes in protein properties contribute to reduced protein solubility and proteolytic degradation, thereby influencing normal tissue turnover and compromising tissue repair. Indeed, a decrease in the susceptibility of extracellular matrix proteins to proteolytic degradation has been reported at elevated AGE levels.

Biomechanical. The accumulation of spontaneously formed AGE crosslinks also adversely affects the mechanical properties of tissues. Accumulation of AGEs is correlated with increased tissue stiffness in the arteries, eye lenses, skin, tendons, and articular cartilage. Moreover, an increase in AGE levels makes tissues increasingly brittle and thus more prone to mechanical damage. This effect has been shown for human lens capsules, cortical bone, and articular cartilage.

Cellular processes. It has been suggested that many of the effects of protein glycation are mediated by interaction with specific cell-surface receptors. The best characterized AGE-binding cell surface molecule is the receptor for AGEs (RAGE), although other AGE-binding receptors have also been reported (for example, class A and B scavenger receptors and galectin-3). AGE receptors are found on numerous cell types, including monocytes, macrophages, endothelial cells, pericytes, podocytes, astrocytes, and microglia. Cell activation in response to binding of AGE-modified proteins results in activation of key cell signaling molecules, such as nuclear factor kappa B (NF-κB), and changes in gene expression. Depending on the cell type, this can be associated with cell proliferation, oxidative stress, or apoptosis (cell death).

AGE-modified proteins also affect the synthesis of matrix components. For example, upon exposure of chondrocytes (cartilage cells) to glycating sugars or

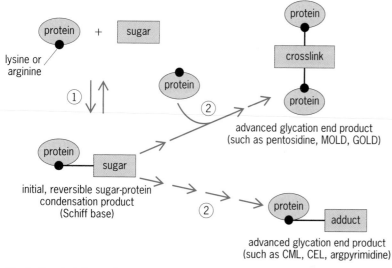

Fig. 1. Classical view of AGE formation. Reducing sugars such as glucose or fructose react spontaneously with lysine or arginine residues in proteins. Initially a reversible condensation product (Schiff base, for example, fructose-lysine) is formed (1). Subsequently, stabilization of the adduct and Maillard browning reactions (2) result in the formation of stable AGEs: some form protein-protein crosslinks, whereas others are protein adducts. MOLD, methylglyoxal-lysine dimer; GOLD, glyoxal-lysine dimer; CML, N^{ϵ}-(carboxymethyl)lysine; CEL, N^{ϵ}-(carboxyethyl)lysine.

glycated matrix, their synthesis of both collagen and proteoglycan is inhibited. These effects of AGEs on matrix synthesis impair the maintenance of tissue integrity and the tissue's capacity to repair damage. In addition to effects mediated by specific AGE receptors, accumulation of AGEs in extracellular matrix proteins may also interfere with cell-matrix interactions or affect cellular function because of changes in the mechanical properties of the matrix. Decreased adhesion to glycated extracellular matrix has been demonstrated for osteosarcoma and fibrosarcoma cells, which is most probably mediated by glycation of the arginine residue in the arginine-glycine-aspartic acid (RGD) recognition sites for integrins.

Genetic. Recently, DNA has been considered as a target for glycation reactions. Sensitive groups within DNA are, for example, the amino groups of adenine and guanine. Unlike proteins, AGE-modified bases in DNA will be excised and replaced, so glycation products themselves are not expected to accumulate in DNA. Nevertheless, since the DNA repair mechanisms are not error-free, future research in this area will likely provide evidence that glycation of DNA leads to a gradual accumulation of mutations.

Aging and diabetes. The adverse effects of AGEs on cell and tissue function have been implicated in changes associated with aging and in the pathogenesis of diabetes. Evidence has accumulated that AGEs contribute to the development of age-related chronic diseases such as osteoarthritis (cartilage degeneration) and Alzheimer's disease. In articular cartilage, the age-related accumulation of AGEs affects the tissue's mechanical properties and chondrocyte metabolism, both of which are important for the maintenance of tissue integrity. Loss of tissue integrity with advancing age eventually leads to the development of osteoarthritis. In Alzheimer's disease, AGEs are thought to play a role in the abnormal accumulation of amyloid aggregates.

Several complications of diabetes, such as cataract, atherosclerosis, neuropathy, and nephropathy, resemble processes that are characteristic of aging, but often occur at an earlier age in diabetes. Prolonged exposure to hyperglycemia has been recognized as the primary causal factor in diabetic complications, and it is conceivable that this is mediated by the formation of AGEs. This hypothesis is further supported

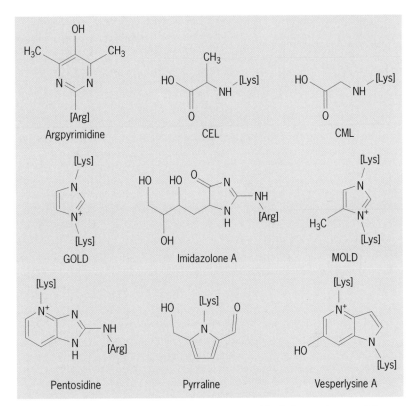

Fig. 2. Chemical structures of AGEs that have been identified in human tissue proteins.

by the finding that the occurrence of diabetes complications is associated with increased levels of RAGE expression and with polymorphisms in the RAGE gene.

In addition to its role in age-related chronic diseases, the rate of protein AGE accumulation in different species was shown to be inversely correlated with the maximal life span of the species. However, whether this reflects a causal relationship or merely a correlation is still subject to debate.

Anti-AGE therapy. Strategies aimed at inhibiting AGE formation and accumulation (**Fig. 3**) have led to the discovery of several promising therapeutic agents, including aminoguanidine, pyridoxamine, tenilsetam, and simple amino acids (for example, lysine or arginine). Some of these agents act by trapping glycating sugars or reactive carbonyl intermediates, thereby blocking the formation of the initial

AGEs identified in human tissue proteins		
AGE	Form	Location
Argpyrimidine	Adduct	Cornea, diabetic kidney
CEL [N^ε-(carboxyethyl)lysine]	Adduct	Lens, articular cartilage
CML [N^ε-(carboxymethyl)lysine]	Adduct	Lens, skin, articular cartilage, brain
GOLD (glyoxal-lysine dimer)	Crosslink	Lens, skin
Imidazolones	Adduct	Diabetic aorta, kidney, diabetic retina
MOLD (methylglyoxal-lysine dimer)	Crosslink	Lens, skin
NFC-1 (nonfluorescent crosslink 1)	Crosslink	Diabetic skin, aorta
Pentosidine	Crosslink	Dura mater, skin, articular cartilage, brain, Bruch's membrane
Pyrraline	Adduct	Kidney
Vesperlysine A (LM-1)	Crosslink	Lens

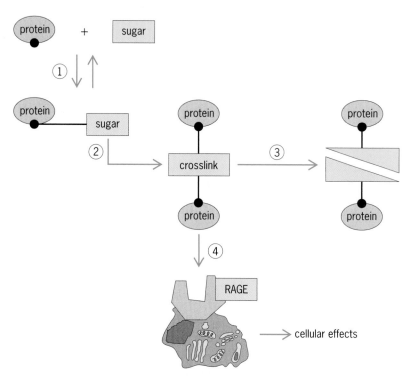

Fig. 3. Potential strategies for anti-AGE therapies. Strategies include (1) inhibition of Schiff-base formation (for example, by aminoguanidine, lysine, or arginine); (2) inhibition of subsequent AGE formation (for example, by aminoguanidine or pyridoxamine); (3) breaking of AGE crosslinks (for example, by PTB or ALT-711); or (4) modulation of cellular effects by blockade of the AGE-RAGE interaction.

and the accompanying impaired cardiac function in dogs. These data from animal models, in combination with the preliminary data from human studies, suggest that ALT-711 has potential as a therapeutic agent to reverse AGE-mediated problems.

Another strategy to interfere with the effects of AGEs on cellular function focuses on the blockade of the AGE-RAGE interaction. Antagonists of RAGE have already been shown to be an effective therapeutic modality in suppressing the development of complications in animal models of diabetes.

Although AGE accumulation is mainly regarded as a process that is detrimental to proteins and tissues, AGEs also seem to have a beneficial physiological function; they act as age markers for proteins and cells, triggering their endocytosis and degradation. AGEs also play a role in the immune system via their interaction with RAGE, which results in cellular activation and generation of key proinflammatory mediators. These beneficial functions of AGEs will have to be considered while studying the applicability of anti-AGE therapy.

For background information *see* AGING; AMINO ACIDS; ALZHEIMER'S DISEASE; CARBOHYDRATE; DIABETES; GLYCOSIDE; MAILLARD REACTION; PROTEIN in the McGraw-Hill Encyclopedia of Science & Technology.
Nicole Verzijl; Jeroen DeGroot; Ruud A. Bank; Johan M. TeKoppele

Bibliography. J. W. Baynes, The Maillard hypothesis on aging: Time to focus on DNA, *Ann. NY Acad. Sci.*, 959:360–367, 2002; J. W. Baynes and S. R. Thorpe, Role of oxidative stress in diabetic complications: A new perspective on an old paradigm, *Diabetes*, 48:1–9, 1999; A. M. Schmidt and D. M. Stern, RAGE: A new target for the prevention and treatment of the vascular and inflammatory complications of diabetes, *Trends Endocrinol. Metab.*, 11:368–375, 2000; P. J. Thornalley, Cell activation by glycated proteins: AGE receptors, receptor recognition factors and functional classification of AGEs, *Cell. Mol. Biol.*, 44:1013–1023, 1998; S. Vasan, P. G. Foiles, and H. W. Founds, Therapeutic potential of AGE inhibitors and breakers of AGE protein cross-links, *Expert Opin. Investig. Drugs*, 10:1977–1987, 2001.

condensation product (see number 1 in Fig. 3). In addition, chelating or antioxidant activity of some of the compounds may be involved in preventing formation of this product. Later in the cascade, compounds such as aminoguanidine and pyridoxamine can inhibit the conversion of the stable sugar-protein adduct to AGEs (see number 2 in Fig. 3) by direct reaction with the protein adduct. The capability of the above-mentioned compounds to prevent AGE-induced protein crosslinking, tissue collagen accumulation, and stiffening of tail tendon, cartilage, or cardiac tissue has been demonstrated in both in vitro studies and animal models.

Until now, only aminoguanidine has been studied in human clinical trials. Aminoguanidine treatment showed a trend in preventing loss of kidney function and a decrease in the progression of retinopathy in diabetes patients. In vivo animal studies suggest that pyridoxamine is an even more potent inhibitor of AGE formation than aminoguanidine, which warrants future clinical evaluation.

Potentially even more promising are the agents that are able to break already-formed AGE crosslinks. These thiazolium derivatives, such as *N*-phenacylthiazolium bromide (PTB) and the more stable phenyl-4,5-dimethylthiazolium chloride (ALT-711), are designed to specifically break dicarbonyl-containing AGEs. ALT-711 has been extensively investigated for its beneficial effects on the cardiovascular system and was shown to effectively reverse diabetes-induced arterial stiffening in rats as well as the age-related increase in cardiac stiffness

Aerosol-climate interactions

Aerosols are suspensions of solid or liquid particles in air. The particles are sufficiently small that their settling due to gravity is minimal, leading to long residence times in the atmosphere. Their atmospheric significance is multifold. For example, they play an important role in polluted urban environments by lowering visibility and leading to health problems in humans. They also catalyze reactions that affect atmospheric chemical composition, leading, for example, to the Antarctic ozone hole.

Although it has long been known that aerosols also affect climate, only in the past few years have aerosol-climate interactions been studied in detail.

The effects arise from direct interactions of the particles with sunlight and from particulate-mediated cloud formation. It is believed that climate change arising from industrial and agricultural activity is affected significantly by changes in the character and abundance of atmospheric aerosols.

Atmospheric aerosols. Atmospheric aerosols arise through both natural and anthropogenic processes. The smallest aerosols, below 100 nanometers in size, are known as nucleation-mode particles. They are formed by processes occurring at the molecular scale when nonvolatile gases and ions aggregate together. An important species is sulfuric acid, formed via the oxidation of sulfur dioxide emitted, for example, during coal combustion. Polar organic molecules, resulting from the breakdown of biologically and industrially released organic precursor species, also form nucleation-mode particles.

Nucleation-mode particles have relatively short lifetimes because they readily coagulate into larger accumulation-mode particles, ranging in size from a hundred nanometers to a few micrometers. Sulfate and organic aerosols are formed in this manner. Other accumulation-mode aerosols include soot particles, which are formed during combustion and are composed primarily of carbon. Accumulation-mode particles can have week-long lifetimes in the atmosphere because they neither rapidly coagulate nor gravitationally settle. Instead, they are lost by deposition to the Earth's surface or by the cleansing action of rain.

Large, coarse-mode aerosols (at least a micrometer in diameter) are formed by wind passing over deserts to generate mineral particles, and over oceans to produce small saline droplets. The atmospheric effects of coarse-mode particles usually occur close to the surface because their gravitational settling rates are high. However, they can occasionally be transported considerable distances by strong winds. For example, crustal aerosols formed from storms over the Gobi and Saharan deserts have been deposited in North America and Europe, respectively.

Climate. Climate is the long-term average of temperature, wind, and precipitation conditions prevailing on either a global or a regional level, whereas weather is the day-to-day variation in these conditions experienced on a local scale. A variety of phenomena maintain the average surface temperature of the Earth at a habitable value. The Sun warms the Earth, supplying electromagnetic radiation at visible and nearby wavelengths. One-third of the solar radiation striking the top of the atmosphere is reflected back to space by clouds, aerosols, and ice-covered regions. The other two-thirds is absorbed by the surface, and then reemitted as infrared radiation in amounts equal to the amount of energy absorbed. Without atmospheric greenhouse gases, which absorb this upwelling infrared radiation, the average temperature of the Earth's surface would be well below 0°C (32°F). However, gases such as carbon dioxide and water vapor absorb the escaping infrared energy and then reemit some of it down-

ward, providing a mechanism for additional surface warming. This is the greenhouse effect, a natural phenomenon prevalent for much of Earth's history. While global climate is so determined, regional climate is also influenced by the redistribution of energy within the earth-atmosphere-ocean system that occurs via ocean currents, wind patterns, and the release of latent heat when water vapor condenses to form clouds.

Direct effects of aerosols on climate. Scattering of atmospheric radiation results from the redirection of light after interaction with either a molecule or a particle. Scattering of solar radiation by air molecules gives rise to the blue color of the sky, but does not significantly lower the amount of energy reaching the Earth's surface. On the other hand, scattering by atmospheric aerosols, particularly accumulation-mode particles, is a significant cooling mechanism by directly reflecting solar energy. City dwellers experience this phenomenon when skies over polluted cities appear whitish, even on cloud-free days. This occurs because incoming solar photons repeatedly scatter before they reach the ground.

Absorption of solar radiation, where the energy of the incoming photon is converted into heat energy, also occurs with some particles, particularly those containing soot. The black color of soot indicates that these particles efficiently absorb visible radiation, leading to a redistribution of energy away from the surface to the atmosphere.

Indirect effects of aerosols on climate. Clouds form when the relative humidity rises above the saturation point, usually as a result of cooling that comes with ascending air motion. The mechanism of cloud droplet formation involves the condensation of water vapor onto accumulation-mode particles called cloud condensation nuclei (CCN). The resulting droplets grow enormously, reaching tenths of millimeters in size. Water-soluble molecules, such as the sulfates, are efficient CCN.

Given the importance of clouds as global cooling agents, aerosols have two indirect effects on climate. First, the number of CCN determines the number of waterdroplets in a cloud. Assuming the amount of liquid water remains constant, more CCN lead to smaller cloud droplets on average. Because the light-scattering efficiency of droplets is proportional to their total surface area, this leads to a brighter, more reflective cloud. Second, if the cloud droplet size is smaller, the cloud precipitates less. This is because there are fewer large droplets available to collide and coalesce with smaller droplets, as is needed to form precipitation. Thus, more CCN lead to longer-lived, more prevalent clouds, reducing the amount of radiation reaching the Earth's surface.

Aerosols and climate change. Concern over climate change arises from the enhanced greenhouse effect driven by humankind's large-scale emissions of greenhouse gases to the atmosphere. Primarily through burning of fossil fuels, atmospheric carbon dioxide levels have increased by a third since preindustrial times. As shown in **Fig. 1**, the resulting

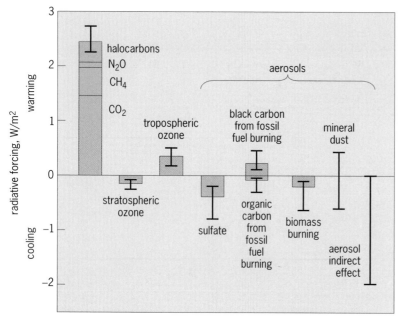

Fig. 1. Global mean radiative forcing of the climate system for the year 2000, relative to 1750. As determined by the Intergovernmental Panel on Climate Change, the estimated changes in the radiative forcing since preindustrial times are due to (1) increases in concentrations of greenhouse gases such as carbon dioxide (CO_2), methane (CH_4), nitrous oxide (N_2O), chlorofluorocarbons and other halogenated gases (halocarbons), and lower atmospheric ozone (tropospheric ozone), and a decrease of upper atmospheric ozone (stratospheric ozone), (2) the direct effect of aerosols on climate, including sulfate, soot (black carbon), organics (organic carbon), biomass-burning-generated particles, and mineral dust; and (3) the indirect effect of aerosols on clouds. The height of the rectangle represents the best estimate of the change in the radiative forcing, and the extent of the vertical lines represent error estimates. No estimate is made for the indirect effect and for the mineral dust direct effect because of large uncertainties. Note that errors associated with aerosol effects are often larger than those associated with greenhouse gas effects. (*Adapted from J. T. Houghton et al., eds., Climate Change 2001: The Scientific Basis, Contribution of Working Group I to the Third Assessment Report of the Intergovernmental Panel on Climate Change, Cambridge University Press, Cambridge, 2001*)

change in the radiative forcing is about $+1.5$ W/m², where the radiative forcing is the amount of energy that warms the lower atmosphere and Earth's surface. Increases in other greenhouse gases have contributed another $+1$ W/m². Most of the temperature rise experienced globally in the past few decades is likely due to increased levels of greenhouse gases.

Changes to the direct aerosol effect, which are smaller but still significant compared to the enhanced greenhouse effect, are also shown in Fig. 1. From fossil fuel burning, it is thought that levels of sulfate, soot, and organic carbon aerosols have increased, leading to cooling (-0.4 W/m²), warming ($+0.2$ W/m²), and cooling (-0.1 W/m²) effects, respectively. In addition, biomass burning that accompanies some agricultural processes and tropical deforestation releases particles that have a negative effect on the radiative forcing (-0.2 W/m²). Estimates in the change of radiative forcing associated with mineral dust in the atmosphere, arising from different land uses and desertification, are highly uncertain.

Evidence that changes in the direct aerosol effect have occurred in the past century comes from comparison of trends in daytime and nighttime temperatures. Because the direct aerosol effect gives rise to cooling and operates only during the day, the average daytime temperatures over land have risen less than those during the night when the full enhanced greenhouse effect is felt. Another feature of the direct aerosol effect is that it is experienced more strongly close to aerosol source regions, where the aerosol abundance is highest. By contrast, greenhouse gases have long lifetimes and are uniformly mixed through the atmosphere. **Figure 2** shows that the strongest effects are felt over continents, particularly regions of

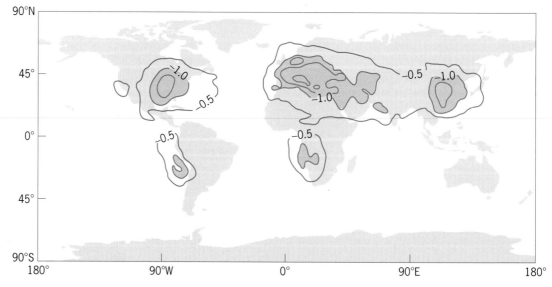

Fig. 2. Annual mean radiative forcing of anthropogenic sulfate aerosols. The estimate of the direct effect of humankind-generated sulfate aerosols is plotted geographically as contours, in W/m². High negative values, representing cooling, are associated with aerosol source regions located over industrialized continents and biomass-burning regions in the tropics. Regions with an effect higher than -1.0 W/m² are shaded. (*Adapted from J. T. Houghton et al., eds., Climate Change 1994: Radiative Forcing of Climate Change, Intergovernmental Panel on Climate Change, Cambridge University Press, Cambridge, 1995*)

high industrial or biomass burning activity. Although the direct effect of aerosols on the change in the global radiative forcing is not as large as that arising from enhanced greenhouse warming, aerosols can have a much larger relative effect over regional distance scales.

Evidence for the indirect aerosol effect comes from satellite and aircraft observations which have recently illustrated that average cloud droplet sizes are smaller in polluted air than in surrounding clouds. However, given the heterogeneity in aerosol types, emission rates, and source locations, and the multistep mechanism that transforms an aerosol particle into a cloud droplet which may or may not precipitate, accurate assessments of the anthropogenic-driven change in the global indirect effect are difficult to make. Indeed, an accurate representation of clouds is one of the greatest challenges to climate modeling. This is reflected by the error bars in Fig. 1 for the contribution of the indirect effect to changes in radiative forcing. Additional uncertainties arise from the potential for natural feedbacks between clouds to exist between clouds, climate, and aerosols. For example, an intriguing suggestion is that the amount of cloud cover and available sunlight in marine environments may be regulated by the photobiological production of dimethyl sulfide. The atmospheric degradation of dimethyl sulfide is the primary source of oxidized sulfur in these regions, and the sulfate aerosols that form as a result act as nuclei for cloud formation, thus giving rise to some degree of climate regulation. This example represents just one of many areas of research currently being performed to better evaluate connections between aerosols and climate.

For background information *see* AEROSOL; ATMOSPHERE; ATMOSPHERIC CHEMISTRY; CLIMATOLOGY; CLOUD; STRATOSPHERE in the McGraw-Hill Encyclopedia of Science & Technology.   Jonathan Abbatt

Bibliography. B. J. Finlayson-Pitts and J. N. Pitts, Jr., *Chemistry of the Upper and Lower Atmosphere*, Academic Press, New York, 2000; J. T. Houghton et al. (eds.), *Climate Change 2001: The Scientific Basis*, Contribution of Working Group I to the Third Assessment Report of the Intergovernmental Panel on Climate Change, Cambridge University Press, Cambridge, 2001; V. Ramanathan et al., Aerosols, climate and the hydrological cycle, *Science*, 294:2119–2124, 2001; J. H. Seinfeld and S. N. Pandis, *Atmospheric Chemistry and Physics*, Wiley, New York, 1998.

Aluminum-accumulating plants

Aluminum is the most abundant metal in the Earth's crust. Although rocks and soils consist of primary and secondary aluminosilicate minerals, the solubility of aluminum in soil solutions is very limited and varies according to soil pH. Trivalent aluminum (Al^{3+}) ions predominate in acid soil solutions and may be detrimental to many plant species, especially some widely cultivated crop plants. Therefore, aluminum toxicity is a well-studied topic in agricultural research all over the world. In contrast, relatively little attention has been paid to plants that tolerate very high aluminum concentrations in their shoot tissues.

Aluminum-tolerant plants include aluminum excluders and aluminum accumulators. Aluminum excluders do not suffer from aluminum toxicity thanks to a wide range of mechanisms that exclude aluminum from their shoots, and aluminum concentrations in their leaves are much lower than external aluminum levels in the soil. The much rarer aluminum accumulators are defined as plants with aluminum concentrations of at least 1000 mg kg^{-1} in their leaf dry matter. Aluminum concentrations above 1000 mg kg^{-1} are also found in wood of the stem and tissues of bark, fruits, and seeds. (Most plants take up an average of 200 mg kg^{-1} of aluminum in all their aboveground tissues.) Aluminum accumulators have mainly been studied from an ecological and physiological point of view because of substantial questions about the possible significance of aluminum accumulation.

Abundance. The highest number of aluminum accumulators are found in the coffee family (Rubiaceae), but the coffee shrub itself (*Coffea* spp.) is an aluminum excluder. The Rubiaceae comprise more than 11,000 species, of which more than 1000 have been recorded to accumulate aluminum, and it is likely that numerous untested species are also aluminum accumulators. Moreover, aluminum accumulation is found to be characteristic of the Rubioideae, one of the three major subgroups within the family.

The second largest number of aluminum accumulators occur in the melastome family (Melastomataceae), one of the most abundant and diversified plant families throughout the tropics (**Fig. 1**).

Fig. 1. Beneficial effect of aluminum on the growth of an aluminum-accumulating plant. A healthy plant of *Miconia albicans* (Sw.) Triana (Melastomataceae) is growing on an acid, aluminum-rich soil at left, and a weak plant of the same age with leaf yellowing is growing on a nonacid, aluminum-poor soil at right.

Fig. 2. *Vochysia thyrsoidea* Pohl (Vochysiaceae), an aluminum accumulator from the cerrado region in central Brazil.

Aluminum accumulators are also abundantly present in its close relatives Memecylaceae and Vochysiaceae (**Fig. 2**).

The most important economic aluminum accumulator is the tea bush (*Camellia sinensis*) in the family Theaceae. Many other members of this family also accumulate aluminum. It has been shown that the uptake of high aluminum concentrations has a beneficial effect on the growth of the tea bush as well as on some other aluminum accumulators (Fig. 1).

Physiology. Aluminum accumulators frequently show thick, leathery, characteristically yellow-green leaves in dried samples of herbarium material, whereas fresh leaves are frequently dark green. A more remarkable correlation exists between the presence of aluminum in abnormal quantities and the blue color of flowers and fruits. It is well known, for instance, that the flower color of the popular French hortensia (*Hydrangea macrophylla*) will change from pink to dark blue when high aluminum levels are accumulated in the aboveground plant organs. Thus in acid soils, this ornamental species shows blue flowers, whereas the color turns pink in a nonacid or calcareous condition. The physiological explanation is that the formation of blue pigments, at least in some aluminum-accumulating plants, is due to the presence of the trivalent aluminum ion. The blue color can be caused by a chemical interaction between an anthocyanin (for instance, delphinidin), aluminum, and a co-pigment. Aluminum is suggested to play a leading role as an ionic stabilizer in the formation of this blue-colored complex. However, not all plants with blue-colored flowers and fruits are aluminum accumulators.

Ecological importance. The majority of aluminum-accumulating plants grow in humid tropics and savannas, where acid soils are highly weathered with low organic matter and nutrient reserves. If we look at the natural vegetation as found, for instance, in the Amazonian tropical forests and savanna woodlands of central Brazil, we find that native species do well in the highly acidic, nutrient-poor soils with high levels of soluble aluminum. Most species are aluminum excluders; however, many are aluminum accumulators and occur widely in native plant communities (Fig. 2).

It is difficult to speculate on the competitive advantage of aluminum accumulators. Aluminum accumulation probably is a successful, but not an essential, adaptive strategy in strongly acid soils. Some aluminum accumulators, however, are able to absorb aluminum from high-pH soils, and plants undoubtedly may choose between different options, allowing them to survive in an extremely acidic, nutrient-deficient soil condition.

Phylogenetic implications. Reconstruction of the evolution of angiosperms (flowering plants) is not yet completed, although considerable progress has been made during the last 10 years. Recent developments in molecular- and morphology-based systematics using powerful computer algorithms for analyzing large datasets in a phylogenetic context, have resulted in a robust (stable) phylogeny. This evolutionary skeleton is used as a tool to evaluate the phylogenetic significance of characters and trends in a more accurate way than ever before.

Plant systematists, who aim to elucidate plant diversity, have paid little attention to aluminum accumulation, probably because they were not fully convinced of the usefulness of this feature in systematics. Although recent phylogenetic insights illustrate that aluminum accumulation has evolved independently in several plant groups that are not necessarily closely related, its distribution is far from being random. About 93% of all known aluminum accumulators belong to the higher angiosperm groups of asterids (45.3%) and rosids (47.8%) [**Fig. 3**]. Within these groups, aluminum accumulation is largely restricted

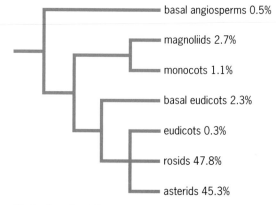

Fig. 3. Hypothesis for relationships among angiosperms based on molecular analyses. Percentages of the total record of aluminum-accumulating plants known are indicated for each group. (*Adapted from P. Soltis et al., Angiosperm phylogeny inferred from multiple genes as a tool for comparative biology, Nature, 402:402–403, 1999*)

to two orders, Myrtales and Gentianales, which consist of several closely related families and account for 42.5% and 35%, respectively, of all known accumulators. Within these derived groups, the character coincides with early or ancient phylogenetic splits rather than shallow or more recent evolutionary pathways. Hence, the most likely explanation is that the feature has developed in a common ancestor and is inherited in a large number of successors, for instance, in many Myrtales and Rubioideae (Rubiaceae).

Aluminum accumulation has been suggested to be a primitive feature in rather derived families of the angiosperms. This hypothesis can now be confirmed based on present evolutionary pathways because aluminum accumulators are most common in rather primitive groups. The evolution of aluminum accumulation, however, is complicated by the occurrence of numerous losses as well as parallel origins among angiosperms. The absence of aluminum accumulation in herbaceous plant groups such as monocots, one of the major traditional groups within the angiosperms, may also be caused by the general absence of this character in herbs, although it is still unclear why herbaceous plants usually do not accumulate aluminum.

In general, aluminum accumulation is a common feature of large taxonomic groups, such as plant families or orders, occurring over very large geographic areas with high biodiversity (for example, tropical rainforests and savannas). There is usually no variation in the presence or absence of the feature between different plants of the same species. Contrary to this, heavy-metal accumulation is typically common at the level of variety or species, since it is more restricted geographically than aluminum accumulation and under the control of different physiological mechanisms.

Future studies. Interest in studying aluminum compounds has increased over recent years due to negative effects of aluminum on the environment and human health. Examples of aluminum's deleterious effects range from the acidification of the soils (for example, by acid rain, intensive farming, and mining of bauxite) and the decline of forests, to the role of aluminum in human neurodegenerative disorders such as Alzheimer's disease. Furthermore, aluminum accumulators have been used for centuries in traditional dyeing technologies because the high aluminum levels provide a mordant (a substance that prevents dyes from fading) instead of alum. A better understanding of aluminum accumulators and their physiological processes may also help to develop more resistant plants that can be used for food. For instance, crops such as pineapple, coffee, tea, and guinea grass can be cultivated in soils with relatively high levels of bioavailable aluminum that would not be suitable for more sensitive plants such as wheat, corn, or soybean. Tobacco and papaya plants have been made aluminum-tolerant by genetic engineering, using genes from the bacterium *Pseudomonas aeruginosa* to enhance citric acid production in the roots. Better knowledge of nutritional plant strategies in different soils is also useful for employing certain species in forest management, soil improvement, or recuperation of degraded lands, especially in tropical rainforests and savannas.

For background information *see* ALUMINUM; COFFEE; MAGNOLIOPHYTA; PHYLOGENY; PLANT EVOLUTION; PLANT MINERAL NUTRITION; TEA in the McGraw-Hill Encyclopedia of Science & Technology.

Steven Jansen; Mundayatan Haridasan; Erik Smets

Bibliography. E. M. Chenery and R. Metcalfe, Aluminum accumulation as a taxonomic character, in C. R. Metcalfe and L. Chalk (eds.), *Anatomy of the Dicotyledons*, vol. II: *Wood Structure and Conclusion of the General Introduction*, pp. 165–167, Clarendon Press, Oxford, 1983; E. M. Chenery and K. R. Sporne, A note on the evolutionary status of aluminum-accumulators among dicotyledons, *New Phytol.*, 76:551–554, 1976; M. Haridasan, Aluminum accumulation by some cerrado native species of central Brazil, *Plant Soil*, 65:265–273, 1982; S. Jansen et al., Aluminum hyperaccumulation in angiosperms: A review of its phylogenetic significance, *Bot. Rev.*, 68:235–269, 2002.

Antarctic ice stream dynamics

Snow that falls on Antarctica is gradually compressed, by the weight of the snow that accumulates above it, into ice. This ice flows toward the coast, where it eventually melts or calves (breaks) off into the ocean as icebergs. Most of the ice flows in the form of a large, continuous, slowly moving ice sheet, but in many places drainage basins occur in the ice sheet that contain faster-moving ice streams and their tributaries. The flow dynamics of these systems can be monitored and the findings used to shed light on many phenomena, including global climate change.

Ice streams. Antarctic ice stream networks are analogous to river systems on other continents and carry as much as 90% of the total ice discharge from the Antarctic ice sheet. Most of the Antarctic ice sheet flows mainly by internal creep (deformation) and slowly, at the rate of tens of meters per year or less. Ice streams and tributaries flow faster, but at differing speeds (**Fig. 1**). Typical ice stream velocities fall in the range of 200 to 2000 m (650 to 6500 ft) per year; this speed is a direct result of the ice sliding over a slippery bed of water or mud. The speed of the tributaries that feed the ice streams falls in a range intermediate between the sliding ice streams and the creeping ice sheet, approximately 50 to 200 m (160 to 650 ft) per year.

Antarctic ice streams are not only fast but large. Their lengths are of the order of hundreds of kilometers and their widths range between approximately 30 and 100 km (20 and 60 mi). The combination of their relatively high speed and large size turns them into efficient conduits for ice discharge. Individual ice streams empty between 10 and 70 km³ of water (2.5 and 17 mi³) per year into the Southern Ocean.

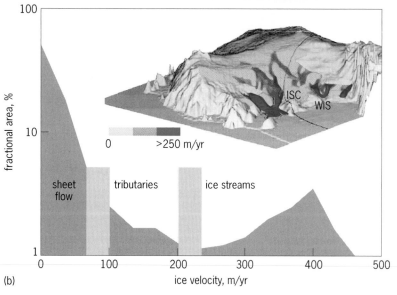

Fig. 1. Antarctic ice flow speeds. (*a*) Satellite image centered on the West Antarctic ice sheet (PIG = Pine Island Glacier). In the inset the areas covered by *a* and *b* are indicated with the larger and smaller square, respectively. (*b*) Histogram displaying percentages of the total area shown in the inset that are moving at different velocities; total velocity range is 0 to 500 m (1650 ft) per year. The vertical scale is logarithmic to emphasize the secondary peak at high velocities. In the inset, light blue corresponds to slow velocities within the creeping ice sheet, medium blue indicates ice stream tributaries, and darker blue denotes the major ice streams. ISC and WIS show locations of Ice Stream C and Whillans Ice Stream. (*Reprinted with permission from J. L. Bamber et al., Science, 287:1248–1250, 2000; copyright 2000 American Association for Advancement of Science*)

For comparison, annual discharge of water from the Missouri River is 72 km³ (18 mi³).

Although the existence of Antarctic ice streams has been recognized for several decades, recently collected satellite data allowed glaciologists to map and analyze the spatial complexity of ice flow in Antarctica. New satellite and ground measurements have also demonstrated that Antarctic ice streams are very dynamic. Large crevasses buried under 150 years of snow accumulation show that Ice Stream C, whose main trunk is now almost motionless, was flowing fast until the middle of the nineteenth century. The motion of the neighboring Whillans Ice Stream has been monitored by scientists since 1974. Between that year and 1997 the flow rate of this ice stream dropped from 500 m (1650 ft) to 400 m (1300 ft) per year. As a result of Ice Stream C stopping and Whillans Ice Stream slowing, the Ross Sea sector of the Antarctic ice sheet is thickening locally at rates up to 1.5 m (5 ft) per year. Meanwhile, the not-too-distant Pine Island Glacier is accelerating, thinning at up to 3.5 m (11 ft) per year, and experiencing fast retreat of its grounding line (where ice becomes thin enough to float) at approximately 1200 m (3900 ft) per year. These observations stress the importance of further research on ice stream dynamics. Improved understanding of ice stream behavior is needed to evaluate the contribution of Antarctica to global sea-level changes in the near future, particularly in the light of the anticipated global climate warming.

Ice stream flow. Antarctic ice streams slide fast because they move over slippery beds lubricated by weak glacial till (mud) or a subglacial water layer. As in the case of water flow in a river channel, ice streams are propelled in the direction of surface slope by the gravitational driving stress τ_d as in Eq. (1), where ρ_i = ice density (900 kg/m³; 56 lb/ft³),

$$\tau_d = \rho_i \, g \, H \sin \alpha \qquad (1)$$

g = gravitational acceleration (9.8 m/s²; 32 ft/s²), H = ice thickness (1000–2000 m; 3300–6600 ft), and α = surface slope (~0.0005 to 0.005). Driving stresses on ice streams range typically between 2 and 50 kilopascals (0.3 and 7 psi), which is low compared to driving stresses acting on common glaciers (50 to 150 kPa or 7 to 20 psi). In the case of ice streams, driving stresses are resisted by a combination of basal stress τ_b and marginal shear stress τ_s (**Fig. 2**). The latter arises in ice stream margins where fast-moving ice rubs against slow-moving ice. Measurements in boreholes drilled to the beds of several ice streams have revealed basal shear stresses with typical magnitudes of about 2 kPa (0.3 psi), while marginal shear stress has been estimated to be about 100 times greater (about 200 kPa or 30 psi). Charles F. Raymond (University of Washington) derived an equation (2) for

$$V_b = \frac{A}{n+1}(\tau_d - \tau_b)^n \frac{W^{n+1}}{(2H)^n} \qquad (2)$$

the sliding velocity V_b of an ice stream moving over a weak bed (such that $\tau_b < \tau_d$) in a rectangular channel with width W and depth equal to ice thickness H. Here A and n are parameters from the nonlinear ice flow law [the temperature-dependent ice viscosity parameter and the stress exponent (typically set to 3) parameter, respectively]. Examination of Eq. (2) reveals that ice stream sliding speed depends nonlinearly on the difference between the driving stress and basal resistance (taken up by the marginal shear stress) and on the aspect ratio of ice stream cross section (Fig. 2b). An ice stream achieves its maximum velocity if the bed is frictionless, $\tau_b = 0$. Its sliding speed drops off rapidly with increasing basal resistance until it reaches zero when $\tau_b = \tau_d$. The influence of the aspect ratio is such as to make wide and thin ice streams move faster than narrow and thick ones. Three examples shown in Fig. 2b demonstrate that Eq. (2) works reasonably well. It provides a useful basis for understanding the physical nature of ice stream flow.

Monitoring ice stream behavior. Glaciologists are interested in ice stream mechanics and dynamics mainly because they want to make reliable predictions about the near-future contribution of ice streams to global sea-level changes. This objective puts special emphasis on variability of ice stream flow over time scales of decades to centuries. Inspection of Eq. (2) shows that ice stream velocity may change due to variability in (1) driving stress, (2) the width-to-thickness aspect ratio, and (3) basal resistance. A variety of ground-, airplane-, and satellite-based techniques are used to monitor the current state of these key parameters and to evaluate their potential for significant change over the coming decades and centuries. Spot measurements of surface velocity and ice thickness changes combined with radar thickness soundings represent the traditional approach to study of ice streams. Increasing use of the Global Positioning System (GPS) over the last decade has made such ice surface investigations much more efficient. At the same time, application of spacecraft-based interferometric synthetic aperture radar (InSAR) and laser altimetry has allowed the generation of ice velocity and topography maps over regions as large as 10^6 km² (400,000 mi²) with spatial resolution of 1 km (0.6 mi) or better.

Observations of ice surface have shown that ice stream width does change over time, with rates as high as 100 m (330 ft) per year at some locations. Local changes in ice thickness and driving stress may be significant as well. However, the two well-documented recent changes in ice stream flow, the stoppage of Ice Stream C and the slowdown of the Whillans Ice Stream, can be explained most easily by changes in basal resistance. This is somewhat unfortunate because basal conditions are difficult to investigate, being hidden under 1 to 2 km (1 mi) of ice. What we know about physical processes at the base of ice streams comes mainly from a decade of borehole drilling and geophysical remote sensing of subglacial conditions. Results of these studies indicate that the magnitude of basal resistance depends very much on the amount of water present beneath an ice stream. For instance, withdrawal of just several centimeters (~2 in.) of water, either through drainage or freezing onto the base of an ice stream, could cause ice stream stoppage. Subtle changes in basal hydrology (water flow) may be the root causes of the observed variations in the behavior of Ice Stream C and the Whillans Ice Stream.

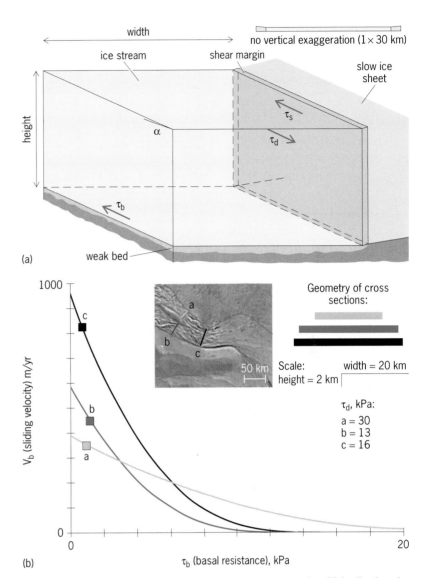

Fig. 2. Stresses acting on an ice stream. (a) Schematic representation. (b) Application of Eq. (2) to cross sections a, b, c on Whillans Ice Stream. The inset shows locations, schematic cross-sectional geometry, and corresponding driving stresses. Curves in the graph show the theoretical dependence of ice stream velocity on basal resistance; squares on curves designate observed velocities for each of the three cross sections.

Global climate change. Because of their potential influence on future sea levels, Antarctic ice streams represent one of the foci of the current scientific effort to evaluate the global impact of anticipated climate warming. The general expectation is that polar ice sheets may respond to the warming by releasing more water into the world ocean.

Equation (2) shows that increased ice stream discharge requires either an increase in ice stream width or additional basal lubrication. The former can result from initiating basal melting beneath the nonstreaming portions of the Antarctic ice sheet (currently frozen to the bed); the latter could be caused by an increase in the amount of available subglacial water which also results from basal melting. In principle, climate warming may cause a widespread increase in basal melting, but only after the surface warming propagates to the bed. For ice that is 1 km (0.6 mi) thick, it takes approximately 10,000 years for surface climate changes to be felt at the base. Furthermore, most of Antarctica (even with significant warming) is too cold for significant surface melting. This is in contrast to the case for some outlet glaciers in Greenland, where meltwater generated at the surface may percolate to the bed and result in an immediate enhancement in flow. Hence, any current global warming is unlikely to increase Antarctic ice stream discharge as a direct response to near-term climate change. Nonetheless, the long response time of ice streams to climate changes means that ice streams, and the surrounding slow-moving ice masses, may still be adjusting to the large climate warming that ended the last ice age, 15,000–20,000 years ago. This past global warming may contribute to widening of ice streams in the future. In addition to climate warming, subglacial volcanic eruptions may provide a highly unpredictable source of basal water. The presence of abundant volcanic rocks, and at least one potentially active volcano, has been inferred beneath the West Antarctic ice sheet.

The most recently discovered mechanism that has the potential to translate global warming into higher sea levels is rapid melting at ice stream grounding lines. There, ice comes in contact with ocean water, which may contain enough heat to melt off a layer of bottom ice up to 40 m (130 ft) thick per year. These bottom melting rates are highly sensitive to the temperature of ocean water, and if the latter increases in the future, mass loss from ice streams may accelerate as well. Although the bottom melting influences directly only the ice-ocean interface, its influence may be propagated upstream as a thinning and retreat of ice streams. This is illustrated by the fact that the highest bottom melting rate (approximately 43 m, or 140 ft, per year) observed around Antarctica occurs at the grounding line of the Pine Island Glacier, which is also experiencing fast inland thinning at rates up to 3.5 m (11.5 ft) per year.

For background information *see* ANTARCTICA; FLUID FLOW; GLACIOLOGY; GLOBAL CLIMATE CHANGE; ICE FIELD in the McGraw-Hill Encyclopedia of Science & Technology.

Slawek Tulaczyk; Ian Joughin

Bibliography. J. L. Bamber et al., Widespread complex flow in the interior of the Antarctic ice sheet, *Science*, 287:1248–1250, 2000; I. Joughin et al., Tributaries of West Antarctic ice streams revealed by RADARSAT interferometry, *Science*, 286:283–286, 1999; I. Joughin and S. Tulaczyk, Positive mass balance of the Ross Ice Streams, West Antarctica, *Science*, 295:476–480, 2002; C. Raymond, Shear margins in glaciers and ice streams, *J. Glaciol.*, 42:90–102, 1996; E. Rignot and S. S. Jacobs, Rapid bottom melting widespread near Antarctic ice sheet grounding lines, *Science*, 296:2020–2023, 2002; A. Shepherd et al., Inland thinning of Pine Island Glacier, West Antarctica, *Science*, 291:862–864, 2001; S. Tulaczyk et al., Basal mechanics of Ice Stream B: II. Undrained plastic bed model, *J. Geophys. Res.*, 105:483–494, 2000.

Antibiotic resistance

Antibiotics are popular weapons to fight bacterial infectious diseases of humans, animals, and plants. In 60 years of application more than 1 million metric tons of antibiotics have been introduced into the biosphere. This enormous selection pressure has resulted in an alarming development of antibiotic resistance in pathogenic bacteria, which has mainly been attributed to the application of antimicrobials in human medicine. The contributions of veterinary medicine and agriculture, however, are increasingly implicated as well.

The veterinary use of antibiotics (that is, use in pets, farm animals, and animals raised in aquaculture) relies on the same antibiotics as human medicine (for example, penicillins, cephalosporins, tetracylines, chloramphenicols, aminoglycosides, macrolides, nitrofurans, nitroimidazoles, sulfonamides, polymyxins, and quinolones). The infectious diseases treated include enteric and pulmonary infections, skin and organ abscesses, and mastitis (inflammation of the mammary gland). Prophylactic application of antimicrobials to prevent these infections in large herds of animals is common practice. In addition, the use of antibiotics at subtherapeutic levels for increased growth and feed efficiencies in farm animals (pigs, cattle, turkeys, and chickens) is an integrated part of modern agriculture. (Although the mechanisms of action of subtherapeutical levels of antibiotics are unclear, it is believed that they increase growth and feed efficiency via inhibition of intestinal microbes, which leaves more nutrients for the animals, or via a hidden antibiotic effect on pathogenic bacteria.) The Union of Concerned Scientists estimated in 2001 that United States livestock producers use 24.6 million pounds of antimicrobials every year in the absence of disease for nontherapeutic purposes. Although the use of antimicrobials for growth promotion has recently been banned in the European Union, the European pharmaceutical industry reported that in 1999 the total sum of antibiotics used in the European Union was 13,126 tons, with 8528 tons for human medicine, 3902 tons for veterinary medicine (80% farm animals, 20 pets), and 786 residual tons for growth promotion.

Resonant bacteria. The continuous and large-scale agricultural use of antibiotics has resulted in the selection and enrichment of resistant bacteria, including pathogens, potential pathogens, and commensals (organisms that benefit from, but do not harm, their hosts), in the microflora of farm animals, shrimp, fish, and certain regularly treated plants such as apple, peach, and pear trees. As a consequence, many food-borne bacteria, including pathogens that cause enteric disorder, such as *Salmonella typhimurium*, *Staphylococcus aureus*, *Campylobacter* species, and enterohemorrhagic *Escherichia coli* O157:H7, have developed multiple antibiotic resistances. There has been a worldwide spread of a type of *Sal. typhimurium* (DT104) that is resistant to ampicillin, chloramphenicol, streptomycin,

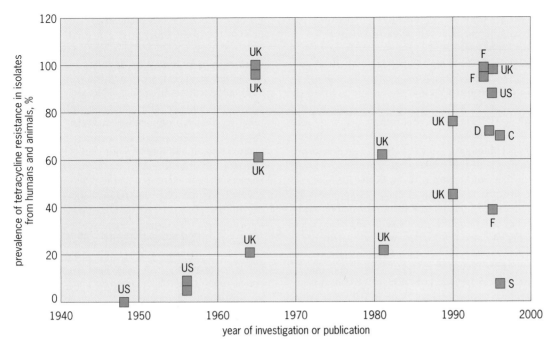

Fig. 1. Time-dependent development of tetracyline resistance in *Salmonella typhimurium* isolated from animals, humans, and food. At the start of tetracycline production in 1948, all investigated strains were susceptible. After 50 years of heavy application in human and veterinary medicine and agriculture, the resistance level in certain countries approaches 100%. (C, China; D, Germany; F, France; S, Sweden; UK, United Kingdom; US, United States).

sulfonamide, and tetracycline. Such multiply resistant strains are now starting to pick up additional resistances against fluoroquinolones and ceftriaxone. For *Sal. typhimurium* there is also suffcient scientific data to demonstrate the time-dependent increase of tetracycline resistance, from 0% in 1948 to nearly 100% in 2000 in some countries (**Fig. 1**). Indiscriminate use of fluoroquinolones in veterinary and human medicine in Spain has resulted in fluroquinolone resistance in 99% of the animal strains and 71% of the human strains of *Campylobacter* species. The spread of such strains by tourists to other European countries has also been demonstrated.

Enterococci and coagulase-negative staphylococci, previously regarded as commensal bacteria of the human body but also as food contaminants of animal origin (intestine and skin, respectively) in meat and raw milk, have become major problems in hospital infections; however, their source is still unknown. These bacteria are notoriously multiply resistant and pose a new risk factor. Erythromycin- and tetracycline-resistance genes have also invaded harmless lactic acid bacteria of the animal and human intestine and in *Bacteroides* species, which make up one-third of the human intestinal microflora.

The raising of shrimp or salmonids (trout and salmon) in aquaculture requires therapeutic and prophylactic applications of antibiotics, such as oxytetracycline and chloramphenicol, that are incorporated into feed pellets, and typical water bacteria such as *Aeromonas hydrophila* isolated from ponds and fresh- and deep-frozen market shrimp, trout, and salmon have been found to carry the corresponding resistance traits. In plant agriculture, streptomycin is

used to fight fire blight diseases of apples, pears, and quinces as well as bacterial leaf and fruit spots of peaches and nectarines. Unfortunately, the responsible infective bacterial agents, *Erwinia amylovora* and *Xanthomonas campestris* pv *pruni*, respectively, have rapidly developed resistance to streptomycin, so oxytetracycline must now be used in addition to streptomycin in the United States. In Chile, Central America, and Mexico, gentamicin has been recently introduced for the same purpose. Compared with the enormous amounts applied in animal agriculture, 39,800 pounds of streptomycin and 26,800 pounds of oxytetracycline sprayed in 1997 in the United States, mostly on apples and pears, seems little, but the application mode contaminates the entire environment of the trees.

Resistance genes. Through the use of modern molecular techniques, scientists have discovered that many antibiotic resistance determinants (genes) found in resistant bacteria from farm animals and food are also found in bacteria present in human pathogenic material. Once a resistance tool has arisen in nature, it is used by many different members of the microbial community if an antibiotic selection pressure occurs. (Examples include resistance determinants for ampicillin, chloramphenicol, streptomycin, tetracyclines, erythromycin, vancomycin, sulfonamides.) Antibiotic resistance genes work by directing the synthesis of enzymes which inactivate the antibiotic (via ampicillin splitting, aminoglycoside modifications), modify the bacterial target sites of the antibiotics (via cell wall biosynthesis, metabolism, protein synthesis) or expel intruding antibiotics from the bacterial interior back into the surrounding medium (via efflux proteins).

Horizontal gene transfer. The almost universal presence of the same or very similar antibiotic resistance determinants in distantly related members of the animal, human, and plant microbial communities is believed to be the result of horizontal gene transfer, the exchange of genetic material in the absence of reproduction. Horizontal gene transfer across genus borders is commonly facilitated by conjugation, a process in which cell-to-cell contact promotes transfer of genetic information usually in the form of conjugative plasmids (small circular deoxyribonucleic acid genetic elements that carry information for resistance and gene transfer by self-transmission) and conjugative transposons (linear genetic elements incorporated into the bacterial chromosome that, like conjugative plasmids, carry resistance and transfer genes but can free themselves from the chromosome and move to other places either in the same cell or into the chromosome or plasmids of a conjugation partner). The prerequisites for conjugation are direct cell-to-cell contacts, which are abundant in densely populated biotopes such as the intestine (10^{11}– 10^{12} bacteria per gram feces), at the mucosal surface of the mouth and throat, and in a fully developed dental plaque which is 300 to 500 cells thick. Optimal conjugation rates in such biotopes (for example,

for enterococci or enterobacteria) have been estimated to be in the order of 10^{-2} to 10^{-3}.

A fully sequenced conjugative multiresistance plasmid from *Enterococcus faecalis* (found in a raw fermented sausage) carries a package of five resistance genes (three for aminoglycosides, one for erythromycin, and one for chloramphenicol) and a highly conserved conjugation machinery previously detected in *Streptococcus agalactiae*, a highly contagious human and animal pathogen (**Fig. 2**). This plasmid was experimentally transferred over genus borders by conjugation to potentially pathogenic bacteria such as other enterococci and *Listeria innocua*, but also to commensal bacteria such as *Lactococcus lactis*, a common lactic acid bacterium of cheese production. Conjugative transfer of resistance genes by one of the mentioned mechanisms has also repeatedly been described for pathogenic enteric bacteria such *Escherichia coli* and *Salmonella* and *Shigella* species.

A worrisome discovery in *Sal. typhimurium* and other pathogenic bacteria is the presence of multiple resistance elements in the form of integrons, mobile genetic elements that, with the help of the enzyme integrase, integrate and accumulate resistance cassettes (transposable DNA segments containing resistance genes) and move them to other places in the chromosome or a (conjugative) plasmid where they

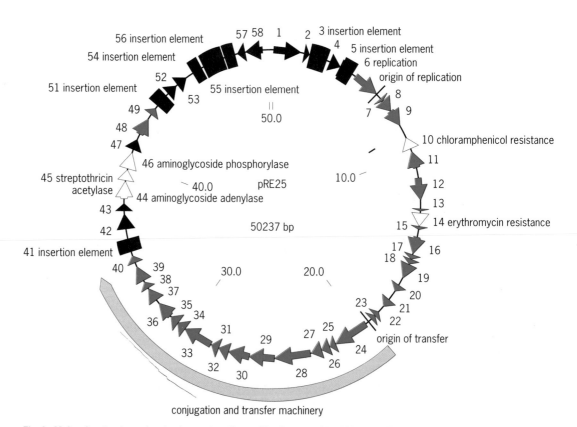

Fig. 2. Molecular structure of a circular, conjugative multiresistance plasmid from an *Enterococcus faecalis* isolated from a raw fermented sausage. The molecule is made up of a part originating from *Streptococcus* (blue symbols) and *Enterococcus* (black symbols). Antibiotic resistance genes are in white; the segment responsible for conjugative resistance transfer is indicated. Insertion elements are shown as boxes: they are potent tools to excise and to insert genes into DNA. A total of 58 potential genes are present. (© *M. Teuber*)

become functional if placed within transposons. In addition, enterococcal transposons which carry the vancomycin resistance assembly (vanA) or the tetracycline resistance gene *tetM* have been isolated not only from human patients but also from animal intestines and food. In this respect, animal and human microbial communities are genetically not isolated.

Spread of resistant food-borne bacteria. It has been unequivocally demonstrated that resistant bacteria, with their multiple resistance gene pools, do contaminate their environment via food produced from infected farm animals and via their waste products. Enterococci, enterobacteria, and some commensal lactic acid bacteria are the main investigated carriers. Raw meat is inevitably contaminated with the resistant intestinal and skin microflora during slaughter, as is raw milk during milking. The resistant flora is purchased at the supermarket if the products are not pasteurized. Some raw milk, cheeses, and raw fermented sausages may even allow proliferation of resistant enterococci, such that a fully ripenened raw milk soft cheese may contain 10^7 resistant enterococci per gram. The transfer of *Ent. faecalis* from a raw milk cheddar into the intestinal microflora of healthy volunteers has recently been shown. In a similar experiment, a vancomycin-resistant *Ent. faecium* from chicken was transiently showing up in high numbers in the intestine of volunteers consuming it together with milk. A resistance transfer between enterococci from food and endogenous human enterococci has not yet been demonstrated directly; however, it is deduced from molecular epidemiological data of vancomycin-resistance transposons from human intestinal isolates. In experimental animals, intestinal conjugative transfer of tetracycline resistance from *Ent. faecalis* to *Lis. monocytogenes* has been achieved. Resistant *Ent. faecalis* isolated from different food items have also been found to contain a high percentage of the same virulence factors as isolates from human patients, including gelatinase (an enzyme that cleaves connective tissue), hemolysine (destroys red blood cells), aggregation factors (induce conjugation), and enterococcal surface proteins (involved in adhesion to host tissues). The isolates also excreted superoxide, a toxic oxygen radical, a novel microbiological source of oxidative stress for the intestinal epithelium that has been linked to intestinal diseases such as colon cancer.

For background information *see* ANIMAL FEEDS; ANTIBIOTIC; BACTERIA; BACTERIAL GENETICS; DRUG RESISTANCE; ESCHERICHIA; STAPHYLOCOCCUS; STREPTOCOCCUS in the McGraw-Hill Encyclopedia of Science & Technology.   Michael Teuber

Bibliography. J. F. Prescott, Antimicrobial drug resistance and its epidemiology, in J. F. Prescott et al. (eds.), *Antimicrobial Therapy in Veterinary Medicine*, 3d ed., Iowa State University Press, Ames, 2000; D. L. Smith et al., Animal antibiotic use has an early but important impact on the emergence of antibiotic resistance in human commensal bacteria, *Proc. Nat. Acad. Sci. USA*, 99:6434–6439, 2002; T. L. Sorensen et al., Transient intestinal carriage after ingestion of antibiotic-resistant *Enterococcus faecium* from chicken and pork. *New Eng. J. Med.*, 345: 1161–1166, 2001; M. Teuber, Veterinary use and antibiotic resistance, *Curr. Opin. Microbiol.*, 4:493–499, 2001; M. Teuber et al., Acquired antibiotic resistance in lactic acid bacteria from food, *Antonie van Leeuwenhoek*, 76:115–137, 1999; A. K. Vidaver, Uses of antimicrobials in plant agriculture, *Clin. Infect. Dis.*, 34(Suppl. 3):S107-S110, 2002.

Ape cognition

The apes are a branch of Old World primates, distinguished from monkeys by their mode of locomotion (arm swinging, rather than quadrupedal walking). It has long been known that humans are more closely related to apes than to other primates. However, the true phylogenetic position of humans has become clear only since the 1960s due to advances in molecular taxonomy. Humans are more closely related to African apes than to Asian apes, and are particularly close to chimpanzees. Dating of these phylogenetic events is problematic due to the scarcity of reliable fossils ancestral to modern apes. However, it is estimated that the ancestors of all African great apes, as well as humans, separated from the orangutan line about 14–16 million years ago (Ma), only about 2 Ma after the great ape line diverged from that of the lesser apes (gibbons). Gorillas diverged next, at around 7–8 Ma. The human and chimpanzee lineages finally separated only about 5–6 Ma. Much more recently, a chimpanzee population south of the Congo River became so distinct (in appearance, behavior, and, to a lesser extent, deoxyribonucleic acid) that it is now classified as a separate species, the bonobo.

Understanding these details in the human family tree has revolutionized interpretation of ape cognition. When it was thought that our direct ancestors, the hominids, had separated from the pongids (a term formerly used to lump together all nonhuman great apes) some 30 Ma, there was little reason to expect close mental similarities; moreover, any pongid species would do as well as any other for comparative purposes. Now, the striking differences between human and ape cognition are revealed to be very recent in origin, and the pattern of differences among living apes will be crucial for reconstructing the evolutionary past of humans. Complex features shared by a related group of living species are most likely to have originated by common descent from a single ancestor population. So by discovering the distribution of cognitive capacities of living apes (and monkeys), scientists can trace back to the mental characteristics of remote human ancestors.

Old World monkeys. Because little is known about gibbon cognition, the Old World monkeys are the most appropriate group to use as a baseline (technically, an outgroup) for applying this process to great apes—hereafter, referred to as "apes." Unlike the white rat, long treated as "the typical animal" by comparative psychology, these monkeys are unusually large-brained for mammals. Under laboratory conditions they show considerable curiosity and rapid learning. However, their cognitive sophistication is most impressively shown in the social arena. Monkeys are so reliant on social support that daughters "inherit" the rank of their mothers (who defend them); they also cultivate the friendship and support of nonrelatives, choosing the most powerful individuals for these alliances. Grooming is used as a trade currency in building up relationships, and with important allies, monkeys will go out of their way to reconcile after aggression.

Patterns of aggressive behavior suggest that monkeys understand the kin relationships of other individuals in their social group. Field experiments have confirmed this and have also shown that monkeys are able to convey in their calls the specific identity of dangerous predators they detect, and can learn to correctly interpret some of the calls of other species of monkeys and birds. Impressive learning is also evident in the many documented cases of deception in social contexts and in the development of distinctive techniques for eating artificially provided foods, techniques that may persist over generations.

Thus Old World monkeys, by comparison with most mammals, are socially complex and socially knowledgeable, able to manipulate their companions, intellectually curious, quick to learn, and dextrous with their hands. The cognitive skills of monkeys seem to be based on rapid learning and may be directly related to neocortical enlargement. However, these differences from other mammals are most likely to be quantitative ones; comparable social complexity and rapid learning ability can be expected in other taxa with large brains, such as carnivores and toothed whales.

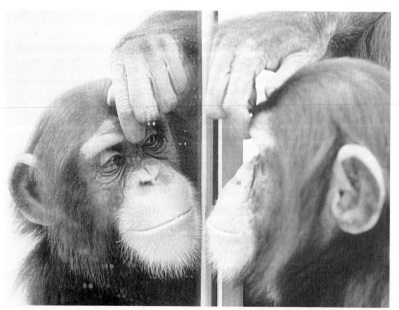

A chimpanzee that has had experience with mirrors behaves in a way that suggests it understands about reflection, and uses the mirror to examine its own face. (*Courtesy of Daniel Povinelli*)

Great apes. In asking how cognition of any ape differs from that of monkeys, scientists are handicapped by the very different research conditions that apply. Apes are comparatively rare species, living naturally in rather remote and often war-torn areas—all are now threatened with extinction. Orangutans and gorillas often do not thrive in captivity; moreover, there is serious debate about whether any of the great apes should be kept for research or entertainment. The best captive studies, chiefly involving chimpanzees, have usually been restricted to a very small number of individuals with heterogeneous backgrounds and have frequently entailed unusual rearing conditions; long-term field studies of wild populations have understandably been more concerned with behavioral ecology than field experimentation.

However, in laboratory tests of learning, few real differences between monkeys and apes have been demonstrated, although attempts to get apes to acquire human language have produced large repertoires of signs and symbols used in a referential way, and understanding of some syntax.

Brain size. The brains of great apes, like their bodies, are larger than those of any monkey. Since brain proportions change allometrically with total size, in apes this difference particularly emphasizes neocortex size, especially of areas not directly linked to sensory or motor systems. The significance of these size differences is not yet well understood, and other species—notably toothed whales—have much larger brains than apes, whether measured in absolute terms or relative to body size.

Social skills. The natural social groupings of apes are not larger or apparently more complex than those of monkeys. Whenever directly comparable data are available, apes show equally sophisticated behavior to monkeys. However, this similarity may be superficial, since there is increasing evidence to suggest that apes have greater, and more humanlike, understanding of their social companions. After learning to take part in a two-role cooperative task, chimpanzees are able to switch to the complementary role without further training, whereas Old World macaque monkeys are not. When given the chance to warn a social companion of an approaching veterinary technician with a dart gun, chimpanzees—but not macaques—distinguished knowledge from ignorance, only giving alarm calls if their companion could not see the danger for itself. Similarly, confronted by a dominant competitor, chimpanzees were found to use the other's ignorance to maximize their own gains, taking account of which food sources the competitor had been able to see. (It should be noted that numerous other experiments have failed to find such capacities in other paradigms; however, interpretation of negative evidence is as problematic here as elsewhere in science, especially so with the small numbers of extensively trained subjects often employed.)

Most intriguingly, all species of great apes give clear evidence that they can learn to recognize their face in a mirror (see **illus.**) and use this to inspect hidden parts of their anatomy (for example, pigment spots on gums and artificially placed marks on brow ridges). Most animals, of course, respond to their mirror image as if it were another individual; but the difference is not simply that apes alone understand how mirrors work, because monkeys have been found able to learn to use mirror (or television) images to guide their hand to otherwise hidden foods. It may be that some concept of oneself as an entity is necessary for mirror self-recognition. Since ape social circumstances seem no more challenging than those of monkeys, the origin of the greater social sophistication of apes should perhaps be sought in the physical environment.

Feeding. Apes show remarkable manual skills in feeding. Chimpanzees use many types of objects as tools, modifying sticks or leaves to suit the purpose. Sometimes tools are carefully selected or made in advance of the need itself, showing that chimpanzees mentally represent the outline specification of a suitable tool. The pattern of tool usage differs from site to site, often in ways that researchers cannot relate to environmental need. With the intriguing exception of one tool-using orangutan population (and the fact that all apes construct beds of branches and leaves to sleep each night), other ape species do not use tools in the wild; the nearest equivalent is to be found in the New Caledonia crow, a bird that makes and uses several types of tools. However, apes may show comparable manual skill in other ways. Mountain gorillas have a repertoire of hierarchically organized, multistage, bimanual techniques for dealing with edible plants defended by stings, spines, or hard casing. These procedures were found to be standardized in the study population, though useful only for plants of very localized distribution. When orangutans and chimpanzees have been studied carefully, similar skills have been found. It seems that all apes are adapted to acquire elaborate manual skills for dealing with their local feeding problems. The original evolutionary pressure that selected for such abilities is likely to have been competition from sympatric (occupying the same range as another species but maintaining identity by not interbreeding) monkeys, whose more efficient (quadrupedal) locomotion, smaller body size, and greater ability to digest leafy material give them inherent advantages in food competition.

The cognitive underpinnings of ape feeding skills bring together the ability to anticipate future needs, the efficiency conferred by structuring actions hierarchically, and the ability to assemble complex programs of actions, partly by social learning. Ape social learning does not appear regularly to include teaching, but rather a form of imitation, in which underlying organization can be perceived in others' behavior. (Apes have also been reported to show neonatal imitation of facial gestures and adult copying of manual gestures, but the cognitive significance of these observations is not yet clear.) It is tempting, on current evidence, to treat the comprehension by apes of the intentions and knowledge of others as a secondary consequence of their ability to perceive organization in behavior, itself an adaptation allowing more efficient feeding by building efficient manual skills. In this scenario, the ability to plan and comprehend hierarchical structures, both in manual action and eventually in language syntax, may relate ultimately to ape foraging skills.

For background information *see* APES; COGNITION; FOSSIL APES; FOSSIL HUMANS; MONKEY; SOCIAL MAMMALS; SOCIOBIOLOGY in the McGraw-Hill Encyclopedia of Science & Technology.   Richard W. Byrne

Bibliography. R. W. Byrne, Cognition in great apes, in A. D. Milner (ed.), *Comparative Neuropsychology*, pp. 228–244, Oxford University Press, Oxford, 1998; R. W. Byrne, *The Thinking Ape*, Oxford University Press, Oxford, 1995; F. B. M. De Waal (ed.), *Tree of Origin*, Harvard University Press, Cambridge, MA, 2001; A. E. Russon, K. A. Bard, and S. T. Parker, (eds.), *Reaching into Thought: The Minds of the Great Apes*, Cambridge University Press, Cambridge, 1996.

Aspect-oriented software development

Progress in programming languages is driven by the discovery of new design methods that provide modularity where existing approaches fail. Aspect-oriented programming introduces a new linguistic mechanism to centralize common code that is scattered among different modules, known as crosscutting concerns (program features). The modular unit that implements crosscutting concerns is called an aspect. For example, security code scattered among different program modules could be located in one place called the security aspect.

Crosscutting concerns. Object-oriented programming focuses on the data items that are being manipulated. The data items are characterized as active entities, that is, objects that perform operations on and for them. System behavior is implemented through the interaction of objects. The objects abstract behavior and data into a single conceptual and physical entity. This methodology works well for software systems where it is possible to decompose the software requirements such that most concerns could be modularized (for example as procedures, objects, or classes). For complex systems, such as concurrent and distributed systems, preservation of modularity is not possible for all concerns.

One special case where a program can fail to preserve modularity is when the implementation of a specific concern cuts across the modular representation of other concerns, as in the example above where the program code for security is repeatedly scattered across different, otherwise modular, components. Other notoriously crosscutting concerns include synchronization, scheduling, fault tolerance, and logging, for which implementation cannot be modularized but must be scattered across the various program components.

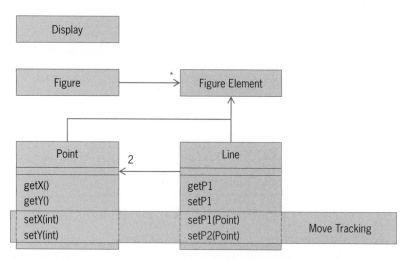

The aspect, Move Tracking, cuts across class modularity. (*Reproduced with permission from Elrad, Kiczales, et al., Discussing aspects of AOP, Commun. ACM, 44(10):33, 2001*)

To clarify the concept of crosscutting concerns, consider the example of a simple figure editor in which there are two concrete classes of figure elements, "points" and "lines" (see **illus.**). These classes manifest good modularity in that the source code in each class is closely related (cohesion) and each class has a clear and well-defined interface. However, consider the concern that the screen manager should be notified whenever a figure element moves. This requires every method that moves a figure element to perform the notification. The "move tracking" box in the figure is drawn around every method that must implement this concern, just as the point and line boxes are drawn around every method that implements those concerns. Notice that the move tracking box fits neither inside of nor around the other boxes in the picture—instead it cuts across the other boxes in the picture.

Code tangling. The implementation of crosscutting concerns, using current programming languages, results in code tangling. Ideally, software engineering principles instruct programmers to modularize software systems such that each module is cohesive in terms of the concerns it implements and the interface between modules is simple. Complying with these principles contributes to software that is easier to produce, naturally distributed among programmers, easier to verify and to test, easier to maintain and reuse, and adaptable for future requirements.

Now consider the impact of implementing a crosscutting concern, such as security, if its implementation is not modularized. In this case, the code must be inserted into a variety of modules, each of which implements an activity requiring security. As a result, cohesiveness is lost and the module interface is complicated. Violating the above software engineering principles results in software that is harder to produce, harder to distribute among programmers, harder to verify and test, harder to maintain and reuse, and less agreeable with the needs for future adaptability. Add to the system other crosscutting concerns, such as scheduling, synchronization, fault tolerance, and logging, and software bugs are inevitable.

The use of aspects solves the problem of modularizing the implementation of crosscutting concerns but introduces a new challenge—the aspect code still needs to be inserted in the right places at runtime. Here is where the aspect-oriented methods provide solutions.

Programming methods. In aspect-oriented programming, a number of different methods are used to compose core functionality with aspects.

Weaving. The process of composing core functionality modules with aspects is called weaving. Weaving can be done statically at compile time or dynamically at runtime.

Join points. Join points are well-defined points (code interfaces) in the execution and flow of the program. Join points are the links between aspects and classes. For example, method calls are used as common join points. A join point model provides a common frame of reference to enable the definition of the structure of aspects.

Pointcut. A set of join points is described by a pointcut designator. A pointcut expression filters out a subset of join points. This is an important feature of aspect-oriented programming because it provides a quantification mechanism. A programmer may designate all the join points in a program where, for example, a security code should be invoked. This eliminates the need to refer to each join point explicitly and, as a result, reduces the likelihood that any aspect code will be invoked incorrectly. A pointcut might also be specified in terms of properties of methods rather than by their names.

Advice. Advice declarations are used to define the aspect code that runs at join points. This, for example, might be the security code itself that runs at every join point filtered out by the security pointcut expression. For a method call (common join points) there are three kinds of advice: (1) before advice, where advice code runs at the moment before the method begins running; (2) after advice, where advice code runs at the moment control returns after the method is completed; and (3) around advice, where advice code runs when the join point is reached and it can check for conditions that may control the selection of advice code. Advice is a method-like mechanism except that there is no explicit call to it at the point where it is executed.

Aspects. An aspect, as previously described, is a modular unit designed to implement crosscutting concerns. An aspect definition may contain some advice and the instructions on where, when, and how to invoke them. It can be defined as a class, and it can contain all intelligent information regarding aspect deployment. An aspect declaration may name the aspect, use pointcut designators to quantify all the possible places where the aspect advices should be invoked, and defines the advice that should run at the designated join points.

Aspect-oriented languages. These are mainly extensions to current languages such as Java, C, and C++.

The first language to capture aspects is Aspect J. It is a seamless, aspect-oriented extension to Java that enables the modular implementation of a wide range of crosscutting concerns. Hyper/J is a language that supports "multidimensional" separation and integration of concerns in standard Java software. Other aspect-oriented programming languages for writing Java programs include DemetrJ and DJ.

Frameworks. Other attempts to realize aspect orientation are language-independent. Composition filters, which are a modular extension to the object-oriented model, allow the modular specification of aspects. In addition, frameworks, such as the Aspect Moderator, JAC, a Java framework for aspect-oriented distributed programming, are used to represent the integration of aspect and components.

Outlook. Separating concerns is a core principle in software engineering, with well-established benefits. The problem of applying this principle is at the heart of ongoing software development. The core issue behind aspect-oriented programming is to expand programmers' ability to capture each concern as a modular software unit. The better the representation of concerns is separated throughout the software life cycle, the more flexible and reusable software becomes. Aspect-oriented software development is a step in achieving these goals.

For background information *see* ABSTRACT DATA TYPES; CONCURRENT PROCESSING; DISTRIBUTED SYSTEMS (COMPUTERS); OBJECT-ORIENTED PROGRAMMING; PROGRAMMING LANGUAGES; SOFTWARE; SOFTWARE ENGINEERING in the McGraw-Hill Encyclopedia of Science & Technology.   Tzilla Elrad

Bibliography. T. Elrad, R. E. Filman, and A. Bader (guest eds.), Special section on aspect oriented programming, *Commun. ACM*, 44(10):29–32, 2001.

Atom interferometer, magnetic waveguide

A magnetic waveguide atom interferometer is a device which creates an interference pattern by coherently splitting a Bose-Einstein condensate (BEC) into two separate parts, guiding each along separate paths using magnetic waveguides, and recombining them at some point later, resulting in interference between the two pieces of the condensate. Such a device is sensitive to the relative atomic phase between the two condensate pieces, and is therefore sensitive to the difference in path lengths traversed by the two condensate parts. A separated-path atom interferometer can detect anything that alters the condensate phase or path traveled, including inertial forces (such as gravity, gravity gradients, and rotation), magnetic fields, electric fields, and relativistic effects. There are a myriad of applications to inertial force sensors, particularly involving the detection of topographical features that have densities different from surrounding areas. Applications include navigation, object avoidance, detection of underground oil and minerals, corrections to the orbits of Global Positioning System (GPS) satellites, detection of subsurface structures such as tunnels, precision tests of general relativity, and searches for new fundamental forces. Atom interferometers are robust and potentially inexpensive devices for these applications, as they have no moving parts and can be built with commercially available technology. Waveguide interferometers add the benefits of extremely high sensitivity coupled with compact size.

Fundamental to the understanding of atom interferometry is an understanding of quantum mechanics. In the framework of quantum mechanics, one can think of an atom as either a particle or a wave, or more precisely, as a small piece of a sinusoidal wave within an amplitude envelope called a wavepacket. It is the phase of the oscillations within the wavepacket, or more typically only changes in this phase, that atom interferometers endeavor to measure. Each independent atom is an independent wavepacket. One of the remarkable properties of a Bose-Einstein condensate is that, due to its extremely low temperature, all of the atoms come together to form one large macroscopic wavepacket, in which every atom acts identically. What actually occurs with an atom (or a Bose-Einstein condensate) in an interferometer is that the atomic wavepacket is split into two wavepackets (or the macroscopic wavepacket is split into two macroscopic wavepackets in the case of a Bose-Einstein condensate), each of which can follow a separate path. Each atom moves as if it were simply a particle; yet when two atomic wavepackets are overlapped, they can interfere with each other like waves. According to quantum mechanics, when the atomic wavepacket is divided in two and separated, the atom is actually in both places at the same time.

Fundamental principles. Atom interferometer inertial force sensors measure the perturbations induced by inertial forces on the trajectories of cold atoms. Atoms are allowed to move in ballistic trajectories, and their resulting motion is characterized with interferometry. At the input of the interferometer, each atom is divided coherently into two wavepackets by an initial beamsplitter. The two wavepackets are then guided through the desired interferometer geometry, using optical, mechanical (gratings), or magnetic forces. After the atoms traverse the interferometer, the wavepackets are recombined with a final beamsplitter. The perturbations to the trajectories (typically due to inertial forces) experienced by the atom in the interferometer determine the probability for the atom to be found leaving a particular output path, or port, of the interferometer. For example, in a gyroscope, the probability of finding an atom leaving by a specific one of the two output ports of the interferometer is given by Eq. (1), where $\Delta\phi$ is the

$$P(\Delta\phi) = 1 - \cos(\Delta\phi) \qquad (1)$$

rotationally induced Sagnac phase shift. The Sagnac phase shift from a rotation Ω experienced by a particle of mass m in the interferometer area A enclosed by the two paths can be written as Eq. (2), where $\hbar$

$$\Delta\phi = \frac{2m\Omega A}{\hbar} \qquad (2)$$

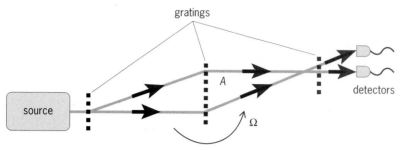

Fig. 1. Atomic beam interferometer with two separated paths, three gratings, and one detector for the output of each port. The interferometer is sensitive to rotations Ω in the plane of the beams, and its sensitivity goes as the area A. The probability of either of the two detectors to see the atom is determined by the trajectories of the atoms (and anything perturbing those trajectories) in each arm of the interferometer. (*Courtesy of T. Kishimoto*)

is Planck's constant divided by 2π. Thus, increasing the area enclosed by the interferometer increases its sensitivity to rotations (**Fig. 1**).

Most previously demonstrated atom interferometer inertial force sensors have relied on pulses of light to manipulate atomic wavepackets. Light-pulse interferometers have proven to be highly sensitive. However, because the light-pulse method uses momentum transfer from the optical fields to the atomic wavepackets, very little momentum is transferred to the wavepackets due to the small momentum imparted by each photon. (In order to understand optical momentum transfer, one must invoke the principle of relativity, in which energy can be converted into mass, and one can think of massless particles such as photons as having momentum.) Because of this small momentum transfer, the paths of the atomic wavepackets are not altered much, and the interferometer paths do not enclose a large area. In order to create large-area sensors, a different method is employed: magnetic waveguiding. *See* OPTICAL MANIPULATION OF MATTER.

Magnetic waveguiding. Magnetic waveguides for atoms can create extremely large-area interferometers, significantly larger than is practically achievable with the light-pulse method. Any atom with a mag-

netic moment μ interacting with a magnetic field **B** experiences an energy shift $E = -\mu \cdot \mathbf{B}$ and a force on the atom proportional to the gradient in the magnetic field. Thus, atoms in weak-field-seeking states (states whose energy is minimized as magnetic field decreases) are attracted to minima in the magnetic field. Small current-carrying wires are used to create a strong magnetic field near their surface. If a uniform external magnetic field $\mathbf{B}_{ext}$ is applied transverse to the wire, then the total magnetic field is the vector sum of the external field and the field produced by the current in the wire; a minimum in this total magnetic field is created just above the surface of the wire all along the length of the wire (**Fig. 2a**). Atoms in weak-field-seeking states will be constrained to propagate along the field minimum by the magnetic field gradient and will flow in a confining channel along the wire, just a small distance above the wire's surface. With appropriate choice of external field and wire current, the gradient at the field minimum can be very steep, which creates strong confining forces for the atoms and restricts the waveguide to allow only a single spatial mode to propagate. The waveguides can be constructed with standard lithographic techniques. Copper or gold wires are deposited on an insulating substrate such as glass or sapphire (preferable for its thermal conductivity). The wires are typically on the order of 100 micrometers square in cross section and can support currents of several amperes. *See* MANIPULATING COLD ATOMS.

In addition to waveguides, beamsplitters can be created with current-carrying wires. By bringing two current-carrying wires sufficiently close to each other, the two minima in the magnetic field overlap and merge (Fig. 2b). Separating the wires again separates the two waveguides, creating two output ports for the beamsplitter. By adjusting the external magnetic field and the current in each wire, atoms entering the beamsplitter from one waveguide can be divided between the two output ports with arbitrary splitting ratio.

Sensor geometry. Magnetic waveguiding technology allows a wide variety of sensors to be created. By changing the layout of the lithographically patterned wires, all manner of sensors for inertial forces and other effects can be constructed. For example, a loop geometry such as in **Fig. 3a** can be used as a gyroscope to measure rotations. The initial beamsplitter splits each atom into two wavepackets, each of which makes a complete loop around the interferometer. When the wavepackets interfere at the beamsplitter again, the probability of the atom exiting the beamsplitter by each of the two exit ports is given by the rotationally induced Sagnac shift as described above. Because each wavepacket makes one complete loop, any systematics such as Zeeman shifts or gravitational shifts will cancel between the two wavepackets. Also, magnetic waveguides can be operated in a dynamic fashion by changing the currents in the wires. This dynamic mode allows the output coupler to be switched on and off. In this

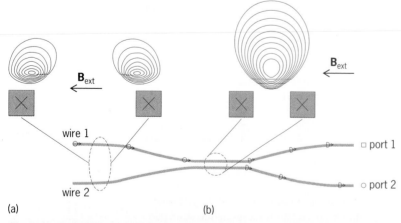

(a)   (b)

Fig. 2. Magnetic field strength above two current-carrying wires with a uniform external field $\mathbf{B}_{ext}$ applied. (*a*) Configuration with separated wires. Atoms are trapped in the waveguide at the field minimum above each wire and propagate through the field minimum along the length of the wires. (*b*) Beamsplitter configuration, showing the magnetic field strength where the waveguides merge. (*Courtesy of T. Kishimoto*)

mode the atoms can traverse the interferometer loop many times before exiting the interferometer, effectively increasing the interferometer area, and thus the sensitivity.

More complex waveguide geometries can be easily patterned as well. A double-loop structure constitutes a gravity gradiometer that is sensitive to spatial changes in gravity along the direction of the loops (Fig. 3b). The rotation signal from each loop cancels, giving a pure gravity gradient signal. With several such devices, all components of the gravity gradient tensor could be measured. Other geometries could be specifically constructed for precision measurements probing other forces and effects.

Use of Bose-Einstein condensates. Condensates are critical for use in magnetic waveguide sensors because of their extremely low temperatures (nearing absolute zero) and small spatial extent. The narrow velocity spread of a condensate is necessary for the atoms to occupy only the lowest-lying transverse spatial mode. Atoms occupying multiple modes act similarly to a white-light interferometer. Such an interferometer is possible, but typically it has poor interference fringe contrast and therefore a low sensitivity to phase shifts. **Figure 4** depicts the coupling of a condensate into a waveguide interferometer.

Additionally, low temperatures mean the condensate cloud remains small for long interaction times, and the size of the condensate is not an issue in the experiment. Also, the small size of the condensate is well matched to the waveguide size, typically on the order of 10–100 μm. Coupling larger atom clouds either would result in large losses due to imperfect mode-matching or would require more difficult coupling methods. Also, Bose-Einstein condensates are intrinsically spin-polarized; no extra manipulation is needed to produce atoms in the desired internal state.

The most powerful advantage of using condensates is the possibility of performing squeezing of the atomic phase to achieve precision limited only by the Heisenberg uncertainty principle. Typically, experiments relying on measuring relative atomic

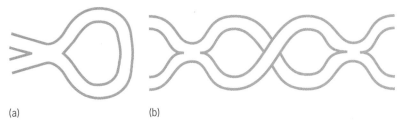

Fig. 3. Interferometer geometries. (a) Sagnac gyroscope geometry. Atoms enter via one of the two paths (or ports) and, after making a complete circuit of the loop, can leave via either of the two ports depending on the rotations experienced during their traversal of the interferometer. In this geometry the atoms enter and leave the interferometer through the same two ports. (*b*) Twisted Mach-Zender interferometer, which is sensitive to gravity gradients in the plane of the interferometer. (*Courtesy of T. Kishimoto*)

phase by essentially counting atom number in a particular state are limited to a phase uncertainty of $1/\sqrt{N}$ for atom number N by the statistical nature of projecting a superposition of two states. However, with a carefully prepared ensemble, called an entangled state, one of a pair of coupled, or conjugate, observables (for example, phase and number) can be detected with a Heisenberg-limited uncertainty, that is, phase measured to an uncertainty of $1/N$, based on the number-phase Heisenberg relation: $\delta\Phi\delta N \geq {}^{1}\!/_{2}$. Squeezing is a phenomenon that has long been understood in electromagnetic fields, and number squeezing has recently been observed in Bose-condensed atoms. An interferometer using the quantum noise properties of a squeezed state would increase the sensitivity to phase shifts (and therefore to inertial forces) by several orders of magnitude by improving the counting statistics. Such a squeezed state can be prepared in an uncondensed cloud, but the macroscopic phase uniformity of a condensate makes the task far simpler.

Sensitivity calculation. The potential sensitivity of these sensors is extremely high. For instance, in the case of the proposed gyroscope, for a flux of 10^6 atoms per second entering the waveguide and making one full loop around a 100-cm^2 interferometer, the sensitivity is 10^{-11} rad/s in 1 s. This sensitivity is two orders of magnitude greater than that of the most sensitive current gyroscopes. Additionally,

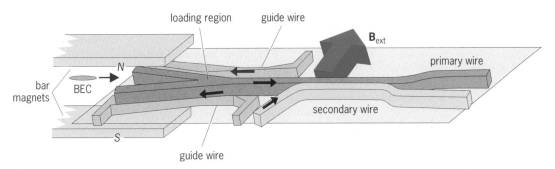

Fig. 4. Representation of the first half of an atom chip interferometer. The direction of Bose-Einstein condensate (BEC) motion is from far left to far right. Two bar magnets, along with two guide wires, guide the condensate into the funnel-shaped loading region (Y-shaped wires). The condensate follows the primary wire and is then split into two wavepackets at the intersection between the primary guide wire and the secondary wire, with a wavepacket following each wire. The large arrow shows the direction of the external bias magnetic field, and the small arrows show the directions of the currents in the wires. Typical dimensions are ∼2.5 cm (1 in.) square. (*Courtesy of T. Kishimoto*)

using a time-varying switching scheme, it is possible to inject atoms clockwise and counterclockwise into the loop, then close the loop and allow the atoms to circulate multiple times before switching them back into the beamsplitter to perform the interferometric readout. Using a ten-loop scheme would provide the precision to test the Lens-Thirring general relativistic frame-dragging effect (one of the most demanding applications) to a high level of precision in a reasonable integration time of several days. *See* GRAVITY PROBE B.

Waveguide interferometers are sensitive to anything that can alter the trajectory of an atom. This sensitivity is a virtue if one wishes to construct an interferometer sensitive to magnetic fields, for instance. However, for designing an interferometer sensitive only to inertial forces (gravitation and rotations), the sensitivity to magnetic fields is a serious drawback. To combat this problem, only a slight alteration is necessary in the geometry of the interferometer. If each of the two wavepackets in a gyroscope makes a complete loop around the interferometer, then each wavepacket will have experienced exactly the same magnetic fields, and any systematic bias due to magnetic fields will cancel out. This design is still sensitive to rotations, however. Similar schemes can be implemented in the measurement of gravity gradients to remove magnetic field effects. In making precision measurements of general relativity or searching for new forces, care must be taken to understand fully the "trivial" inertial phase shifts caused by gravitation and rotation, which are much larger than the quantities to be measured in these precision tests.

Current progress. Progress toward demonstration of a Bose-Einstein-condensate waveguide interferometer has proceeded rapidly on a number of fronts. Recently condensates have been coupled into magnetic waveguides on chips, and condensates have been produced on chips themselves. Several experiments have been performed that demonstrate the crucial property of atomic squeezing which should produce extremely high signal-to-noise ratio sensors. As of yet, no coherent beamsplitter has been demonstrated, but given the rapid progress in waveguide interferometers, working prototypes are expected in the near future.

For background information *see* BOSE-EINSTEIN CONDENSATION; FIBER-OPTIC SENSOR; GRAVITY METER; GYROSCOPE; INTERFERENCE OF WAVES; PARTICLE TRAP; QUANTUM MECHANICS; RELATIVITY; SQUEEZED QUANTUM STATES; UNCERTAINTY PRINCIPLE in the McGraw-Hill Encyclopedia of Science & Technology.   Jeffrey M. McGuirk

Bibliography. P. Berman (ed.), *Atom Interferometry*, Academic, New York, 1997; M. Inguscio, S. Stringari, and C. E. Wieman (eds.), *Bose-Einstein Condensation in Atomic Gases*, Proceedings of the International School of Physics "Enrico Fermi," IOS Press, Amsterdam, 1999; H. J. Metcalf, *Laser Cooling and Trapping*, Springer-Verlag, 1999.

Avian evolution

The genealogical relationship of birds—members of the class Aves—to other vertebrates has been debated throughout the history of evolutionary biology. These days, despite a few poorly substantiated proposals suggesting that birds may be the descendants of a variety of basal archosaurian reptiles (reptiles that predated the dinosaurs), the overwhelming consensus is that Aves are living representatives of the carnivorous theropod dinosaurs. This hypothesis has its roots in the nineteenth century, but in the last decade it has received a great deal of persuasive paleontological support. Despite disagreement regarding the specific theropod taxon that can be placed closest to birds (candidates include the sickle-clawed dromaeosaurids, parrot-headed oviraptorids, and ostrichlike ornithomimids), studies in areas as disparate as osteology (bones), behavior, oology (eggs), and integument (skin) converge to sustain the origin of birds within the maniraptoriform theropods, no longer leaving any reasonable doubt that extant birds are indeed short-tailed, feathered dinosaurs. In addition, the great amount of fossil information discovered over the last 20 years has revealed that the avian taxa that have evolved since their origin are much more diverse than had been expected.

Basal birds. Birds include more species than any other group of living land vertebrates, and the origins of their lineage can be traced back more than 150 million years to the *Archaeopteryx* from the Late Jurassic Period of Germany. Although it was described nearly 150 years ago, *Archaeopteryx* is still the oldest recognized bird and for a long time was one of very few fossils from which the early phases of avian evolution could be inferred. Over the last two decades, however, more and more fossil information has come to light, revealing an unexpectedly large diversity of primitive birds that existed throughout the last half of the Mesozoic Era (the geologic time interval that ranges from 245 to 65 million years ago). In fact, the number of new species of Mesozoic birds discovered and described over the last 10 years more than triples those known for much of the last two centuries. Newly discovered taxa span the large temporal gap between *Archaeopteryx* and modern birds and testify to the presence of a number of diverse (but now extinct) lineages that radiated (that is, evolved and diversified) during this time (**Fig. 1**).

Among these newly discovered fossils are some of the most primitive birds yet known, *Jeholornis* and *Rahonavis*, from the Early Cretaceous in China and the Late Cretaceous in Madagascar, respectively. These taxa had long bony tails similar to those of *Archaeopteryx* and nonavian theropods but had developed more advanced shoulder girdles and wings. Additional evolutionary innovations of the flight apparatus are seen in the Enantiornithes, a diverse and cosmopolitan group of Mesozoic birds, with more

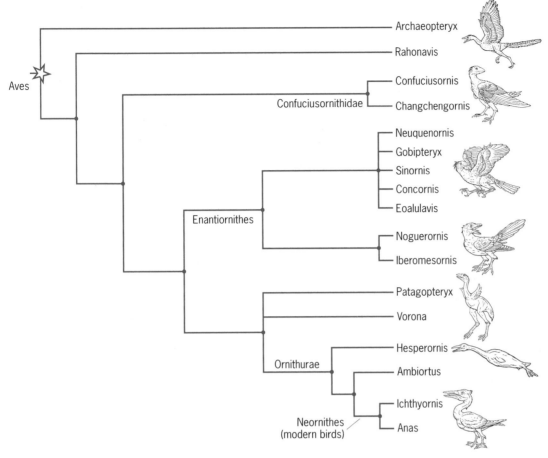

Fig. 1. Cladogram depicting the relationships among the various Mesozoic avian taxa.

than 20 species reported to date. Representatives of this lineage are well known throughout the Cretaceous, especially from Early Cretaceous lake deposits in Spain and China. While some of these birds had teeth (like *Archaeopteryx*), some did not (*Gobipteryx*), and they ranged from sparrow size (*Eoalulavis*) to taxa with wingspans of almost 1 meter (*Enantiornis*). The anatomy of these fossils demonstrates that Enantiornithes were proficient fliers (similar to living birds), and provides some of the earliest evidence for perching (based on the morphology of their feet) seen in avian evolution. Although fossil remains of these birds have mostly been recovered from inland deposits, enantiornithines also occupied littoral (shoreline) and marine environments, and are even known to have extended into polar regions.

Some other taxa (for example, *Patagopteryx, Apsaravis*) represent evolutionary intermediates between the enantiornithine radiation and the divergence of a second major avian group, Ornithurae. *Patagopteryx* from the Late Cretaceous of Argentina documents the earliest known experiment toward flightlessness in a lineage of land birds, whereas the Mongolian Late Cretaceous *Apsaravis* is important because it provides new anatomical

data relating to the evolution of the modern avian wing.

Ornithurae contains the immediate relatives of all living birds (Fig. 1). In spite of their having teeth, the early members of this radiation are essentially modern in morphology. However, until recently the fossil record of these birds was limited to just the flightless, loonlike *Hesperornis* and its kin (Hesperornithiformes), and *Ichthyornis* (Ichthyornithiformes), known since the nineteenth century from Late Cretaceous marine rocks of the Northern Hemisphere. *Hesperornis* was a specialized sea diving bird that had extremely abbreviated forelimbs and was about the size of an Emperor penguin, whereas *Ichthyornis* was much smaller and was able to fly. Significant recent additions to the Mesozoic fossil record of ornithurine birds include the Early Cretaceous *Yanornis* and *Yixianornis* from China, which may be the oldest and most primitive ornithurines discovered to date.

Modern birds. Modern birds—Neornithes—is the group that includes the more than 10,000 living species. Although Neornithes is diverse and cosmopolitan today, the evolutionary history of modern birds is far from well understood. Debates have centered on the question of when the major lineages

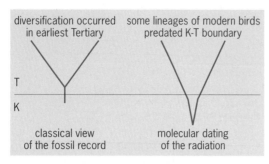

diversification occurred   some lineages of modern birds
in earliest Tertiary   predated K-T boundary

T

K

classical view   molecular dating
of the fossil record   of the radiation

Fig. 2. Diagram of the two extreme hypotheses to explain the pattern of radiation of modern birds (Neornithes) across the Cretaceous-Tertiary (K-T) boundary.

of Neornithes (that is, the extant orders and families) originated—specifically, whether or not these taxa differentiated prior to the Cretaceous-Tertiary (K-T) extinction event 65 million years ago and, if so, how far back in the Cretaceous (**Fig. 2**). The fossil record of putative modern birds from the Cretaceous is scant—a few fossil specimens have been described, but most of them are single bones that lack clear diagnostic features of the extant lineages. However, in the earliest Tertiary the fossil record of modern birds improves dramatically—hundreds of fossils (in many cases complete skeletons, often with feathers and other soft tissue impressions) are known from localities of Paleocene and Eocene age (60–55 million years old). This abundance of fossil birds clearly modern in their anatomy has led some workers to propose that the bulk of the evolutionary radiation of Neornithes occurred rapidly in this small window of time immediately after the K-T extinction event, and to speculate that perhaps the extinction itself allowed the repatriation of avian ecological niches previously occupied by more archaic birds during the Cretaceous.

However, this literal interpretation of the fossil record to explain the pattern of the radiation has been challenged recently by a number of other lines of evidence, notably the genealogic interpretation of living birds based on gene data. By considering the number of differences between aligned DNA sequences (both nuclear and mitochrondrial) of living birds and by use of either a fossil of known systematic position or a well-dated continental split as a calibration point back in time—the so-called molecular clock—new ideas about the timing of the divergence of the major lineages of living birds have been developed (Fig. 2). Such divergence estimates have been made for a number of groups of living birds and in all cases have led to proposals arguing that the radiation of Neornithes occurred much earlier than inferred from the known fossil record. Molecular clock estimates vary but have led to a consensus that the majority of the major lineages of living birds predate the K-T boundary, originating sometime in the Cretaceous. It has further been argued that these hypotheses, although currently receiving little support from the known fossil record,

agree with what is known about the pattern of breakup of the continental landmasses during the Mesozoic. A causal correlation between the breakup of landmasses and the differentiation of certain groups of extant birds has been proposed, and there is a general agreement among molecular systematists that the initial radiation of Neornithes likely occurred on the Southern Hemisphere during the Mesozoic.

At the root of this ongoing debate regarding the pattern of radiation of modern birds is a clear discrepancy between the results of studies founded on molecular data and the apparent pattern seen in the fossil record. Despite a large number of exceptional fossil-bearing deposits from the Late Cretaceous, especially in the Northern Hemisphere, convincing remains of modern birds have yet to be found. Opinions about the apparent absence of these birds vary: While some have proposed that it likely reflects a real evolutionary pattern (fossils of other small vertebrates, such as mammals and lizards, are well known from the Cretaceous), others have suggested that perhaps paleontologists have simply not been looking in the right place (relatively little collecting effort has so far been focused in the Cretaceous rocks of the Southern Hemisphere). What is clear is that existing records of Cretaceous modern birds should be treated with extreme caution: The earliest neornithine bird fossils that are complete enough to be informative for cladistic analyses (analyses of evolutionary relationships among various groups), and hence potentially informative for estimating the temporal divergence of the extant lineages, come from rocks that are roughly 55 million years old, deposited some 10 million years after the end of the Cretaceous.

Summary. Paleontological evidence uncovered in the last decade has cemented the notion that birds are the living descendants of carnivorous dinosaurs. Exceptional new finds have also documented a remarkable diversity of avian lineages that thrived and diversified during the Mesozoic. Yet the time of divergence of the major lineages of extant birds remains unclear. More well-preserved fossils combined with a better understanding of the relationships of these birds will be required to unravel the temporal divergence of these living dinosaurs.

For background information *see* ANIMAL SYSTEMATICS; AVES; DINOSAUR; FOSSIL; GEOLOGIC TIME SCALE in the McGraw-Hill Encyclopedia of Science & Technology.   Gareth J. Dyke; Luis M. Chiappe

Bibliography. S. Chatterjee, *The Rise of Birds*, Johns Hopkins Press, Baltimore, 1997; L. M. Chiappe and G. J. Dyke, Mesozoic radiations of birds, *Annu. Rev. Ecol. Sys.*, 33:91–124, 2002; L. M. Chiappe and L. M. Witmer, *Mesozoic Birds: Above the Heads of Dinosaurs*, University of California Press, Berkeley, 2002; A. Feduccia, *The Origin and Evolution of Birds*, 2d ed., Yale University Press, New Haven, 1999; K. Padian and L. M. Chiappe, The origin and early evolution of birds, *Biol. Rev. Camb. Phil. Soc.*, 73:1–42, 1997.

Bacterial transformation of fungi

During the last two decades, the natural ability of a common soil bacterium, *Agrobacterium tumefaciens*, to transfer deoxyribonucleic acid (DNA) to plants has been modified by scientists for use in the genetic engineering of many crop species into improved sources of food, fiber, and ornamentation. A scientific milestone in the genetic transformation of organisms occurred in recent years with the discovery that this bacterium can be manipulated to shuttle genes into fungi as well. The ease with which a rapidly increasing number and diversity of fungal species lend themselves to *Agrobacterium*-mediated transformation promises that genetically enhanced fungi will play a prominent role in a wide variety of novel industrial processes and applications.

Crown gall–assisted gene delivery. *Agrobacterium tumefaciens* causes a disease known as crown gall in hundreds of woody and herbaceous plant species, but most commonly in pome and stone fruits, brambles, and grapes. The bacterium induces the formation of tumorlike growths (galls; **Fig. 1**), often in association with wound sites on the plant stem near its interface with the soil line (crown). Virulent strains of *A. tumefaciens* contain, in addition to the chromosomal DNA, a separate, smaller ring of DNA referred to as the tumor inducing (Ti)-plasmid, so named because of its involvement in gall formation. Within the Ti-plasmid is a defined

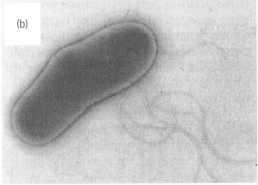

Fig. 1. Bacterial crown gall disease. (*a***) Characteristic galls developing on a euonymus plant following infection by *Agrobacterium tumefaciens* (*Pennsylvania State University*). (***b***) *Agrobacterium tumefaciens* (*Cornell University*).**

region termed the T-DNA, which is transferred during the normal infection process from the bacterium to the chromosomal DNA of the plant. The transferred T-DNA contains a group of genes for the biosynthesis of the plant hormones auxin and cytokinin and opine amino acids (condensation products of amino acids with keto-acids or sugars, a synthesis unique to tumor cells). Expression of these bacterial genes by the cellular machinery of the plant results in the synthesis of the hormones, which leads to the neoplastic growths, and the opines, which provide a food source and are consumed exclusively by the bacterium for reproduction. Thus, the galls represent food factories for the mass production of *A. tumefaciens*. Bacteria that are shed from the galls can be spread by various agents to nearby healthy plants and can initiate new infection cycles.

The realization that *A. tumefaciens* might be used to transfer genes to plants came with the understanding that the T-DNA genes do not participate in the transfer process itself. Rather, low-molecular-weight phenolic compounds exuded from plant wounds serve as biochemical signals that activate a cluster of virulence genes (*vir* genes) also located on the Ti-plasmid, but apart from the T-DNA region. The protein products of the *vir* genes, working in concert with proteins encoded by genes located on the bacterial chromosomal DNA, carry out a complex series of steps leading to the stable integration of the T-DNA in the plant chromosome. Scientists soon learned the hormone and amino acid biosynthetic genes could be removed and replaced by other genes if the short regions of DNA flanking the T-DNA, called the border sequences, remained in place. These disarmed bacterial strains were incapable of inducing galls but retained the ability to transfer DNA, in fact, any DNA. In essence, a natural biological process was modified to create a bacterial delivery system for moving genes into plants.

Transformation of fungi. Fungi are microscopic, spore-bearing organisms that lack chlorophyll and therefore derive nourishment by colonizing dead or dying organic matter. There are the yeast fungi, having single-celled ovoid bodies, and the filamentous fungi, whose bodies consist of masses of threadlike filaments known as mycelium (**Fig. 2**). In the life cycle of most filamentous fungi, the mycelium produces spores that are borne on various microscopic structures or sizable, fleshy structures commonly referred to as mushrooms.

Although *A. tumefaciens* and a plethora of fungi have most certainly coinhabited the same soil environments for eons, fungi are not considered natural hosts of the bacterium. Success in experimentally extending the host range of *Agrobacterium* from the plant kingdom to the realm of fungi arose from detailed knowledge of the molecular basis of the gene transfer process in the bacterium-plant interaction. Fungi do not produce the phenolic compounds that cue the bacterium to the presence of a susceptible plant host, launching the gene transfer mechanism. However, by providing the bacterium with a

Fig. 2. Vegetative and reproductive bodies of yeast and filamentous fungi. (*a*) Baker's yeast, *Saccharomyces cerevisiae* (*from the home page of A. Wheals; www.bath.ac.uk/bio-sci/wheals2.htm*). (*b*) Filamentous green mold, *Trichoderma* spp. (*G. Samuels, U.S. Department of Agriculture*). (c) Common cultivated mushroom, *Agaricus bisporus* (*Pennsylvania State University*).

supplemental source of a signaling phenolic compound, *A. tumefaciens* can be "tricked" into sensing a fungus as a susceptible plant. For example, treating the bacterium with the signaling molecule acetosyringone activates the *vir* genes, leading to the cascade of events culminating in the transfer of DNA into the fungal chromosome.

The precise mechanism by which gene shuttling takes place in fungi is the subject of ongoing scientific investigation, but it is likely to be similar to that disclosed for plants. In plants, attachment of the bacterium to the host cell surface, possibly via receptor sites, is required for DNA transfer. It is unclear if fungi possess the same putative specific receptors or if their physical association with the bacterium is more casual. However, it is known that strains of *A. tumefaciens* commonly used for gene transfer in plants operate efficiently with fungi. Further, the protein products of certain bacterial *vir* genes functioning in the transfer process itself are essential or stimulatory for shuttling DNA into fungi, whereas plant host range factors encoded by other *vir* genes are not important to the mechanism.

Gene transfer to diverse fungal species. Biochemically disguising fungi to become the targets for *Agrobacterium*-directed gene transfer is proving to be highly effective for an increasing number of species, many of which have been recalcitrant to more traditional methods of transformation. *Agrobacterium*-mediated transformation in fungi

was first demonstrated for baker's yeast, *Saccharomyces cerevisiae*, and was subsequently extended to numerous filamentous fungi, ranging from the common *Aspergillus* black mold to the cultivated button mushroom *Agaricus bisporus*. (Interestingly, the interkingdom delivery of genes by *Agrobacterium* is not restricted to fungi, since the mechanism was recently shown to function with human cells.) Evidently, the bacterium is so highly promiscuous at gene shuttling that it is reasonable to suggest that this transformation method will be applicable to most, if not all, fungi.

Gene transfer protocol. The experimental protocol for *Agrobacterium*-mediated genetic transformation of different fungal species is fundamentally similar. Typically, the gene being transferred is joined to regulatory DNA sequences derived from the targeted fungus in order for it to be expressed efficiently following integration into the fungal chromosome. Next, a disarmed bacterial strain carrying a plasmid with the gene inserted between the T-DNA border sequences is cocultivated on a nutrient medium with yeast cells or with mycelium, spores, or mushroom tissue of filamentous fungi. The bacterium is then treated with acetosyringone so that during cocultivation the *vir* genes are activated and the gene transfer process ensues.

For experimental applications, a marker gene conferring a selectable trait, for example, resistance to an antibiotic such as hygromycin, is generally used as the DNA to be transferred. In this manner, fungal cells receiving the gene from the bacterium, referred to as transformants, become marked by the resistance trait and can be selected for the ability to grow on a hygromycin-amended nutrient medium. Fungal transformants growing on the antibiotic medium show the stable integration of the resistance gene in their chromosomes and pass the gene on to their offspring like a normal cellular gene. In actual applications, the antibiotic-resistance gene would be replaced or complemented by a gene intended to alter the traits of the fungus in some desired manner.

Advantages over traditional methods. *Agrobacterium*-mediated genetic transformation offers several distinct advantages over traditional transformation methods (such as direct uptake of DNA and DNA delivery by gene gun): (1) the highly reproducible and efficient transformation of diverse fungal species, (2) the transfer of relatively large genes, (3) uniform gene expression in fungal tissues, and (4) high-frequency integration of single copies of genes into the fungal chromosome, leading to a lower likelihood of gene silencing and instability. Aside from its utility in genetically engineering fungi, *Agrobacterium*-mediated transformation represents a powerful research tool to explore the genetic basis of biological processes. By T-DNA insertional mutagenesis, *Agrobacterium* can, by random chance, insert the transferred DNA into any fungal gene, thereby disrupting its function. Since a single copy of the gene is most frequently transferred to the chromosome, fungal transformants can be screened for altered traits and then steps taken to pinpoint the disrupted gene controlling the trait.

Practical applications. Considering the prominent role that fungi play in a wide array of environmental and industrial applications, the availability of a facile and robust genetic transformation scheme has significant practical implication. Fungi are instrumental in the production of bread, beer, wine, cheese, soy sauce, edible mushrooms, animal feed, biopesticides, and biofertilizers, and in wastewater management and the detoxification of chemically contaminated environments. Also, fungi are valued commercially for the large-scale biosynthesis of organic acids, vitamins, enzymes, penicillin and cephalosporin antibiotics, cyclosporin immunosuppressant, and the statin class of anticholesterol drugs. Moreover, only 5% of an estimated 1.5 million species of fungi in existence have been characterized. As such, fungi are viewed as a vast unexplored resource for new pharmaceuticals, agrochemicals, and industrial products. The genetic manipulation of fungi using *Agrobacterium*-mediated transformation will undoubtedly serve to increase the efficiency of existing commercial processes and enable the transfer of the genetic apparatus required for a broad spectrum of new applications.

For background information *see* BACTERIAL GENETICS; BIOTECHNOLOGY; CROWN GALL; FUNGI; GENE; GENETIC ENGINEERING in the McGraw-Hill Encyclopedia of Science & Technology.   C. Peter Romaine

Bibliography. P. Bundock et al., Trans-kingdom T-DNA transfer from *Agrobacterium tumefaciens* to *Saccharomyces cerevisiae*, *EMBO J.*, 14:3206–3214, 1995; X. Chen et al., A fruiting body tissue method for efficient *Agrobacterium*-mediated transformation of *Agaricus bisporus*, *Appl. Environ. Microbiol.*, 66:4510–4513, 2000; M. J. A. De Groot et al., *Agrobacterium*-mediated genetic transformation of filamentous fungi, *Nat. Biotechnol.*, 16:839–842, 1998; T. Kunik et al., Genetic transformation of HeLa cells by *Agrobacterium*, *Proc. Nat. Acad. Sci. USA*, 98:1871–1876, 2001; E. D. Mullins et al., *Agrobacterium*-mediated transformation of *Fusarium oxysporum*: An efficient tool for insertional mutagenesis and gene transfer, *Phytopathology*, 91: 173–180, 2001; W. Ream and S. B. Gelvin (eds.), *Crown Gall: Advances in Understanding Interkingdom Gene Transfer*, American Phytopathological Society, St. Paul, MN, 1996; J. Sheng and V. Citovsky, *Agrobacterium*-plant cell DNA transport: Have virulence proteins, will travel, *Plant Cell*, 8:1699–1710, 1996.

Biocatalysis

Biocatalysis refers to the use of isolated enzymes or whole cells as catalysts for the synthesis of organic molecules. Enzymes are protein catalysts that accelerate chemical transformations inside a living organism. As essential components of all living systems, they catalyze the chemical transformations in cellular metabolism and are responsible for the creation of a large number and many types of molecules required for life. Biocatalysis, by exploiting nature's catalysts, offers exciting opportunities to capture nature's enormous catalytic power and synthetic diversity in chemical synthesis.

In many ways, enzymes are better catalysts than their synthetic counterparts. They have evolved over many millions of years to near perfection in serving their particular physiological roles in biological systems. They display three types of selectivity unmatched by synthetic catalysts. The first is chemical selectivity (chemoselectivity). Enzymes usually act on only one type of functional group, leaving even related or more active functional groups untouched. When a molecule has more than one functional group of the same type, enzymes are capable of differentiating this positional difference and acting only on the functional group in a particular position. This second type of selectivity is called regioselectivity. The third type is stereoselectivity, or enantioselectivity. This refers to the ability of the enzyme to recognize the chirality within a molecule and to create chiral molecules from prochiral substrates.

In addition to superior selectivity, enzymes are very efficient in terms of the rate of acceleration of the reactions they catalyze. An acceleration factor of 10^{12} or even higher is possible, which is several orders of magnitude higher than synthetic catalysts achieve. Moreover, unlike most synthetic processes, which require high pressure, high temperature, and organic solvents, enzymes are remarkable in that they achieve their exquisite selectivity and high efficiency under very mild conditions, typically in aqueous solution, close to neutral pH, at room temperature, and at atmospheric pressure. Mild working conditions, together with high selectivity, minimize side reactions and thus reduce by-product formation. Hence enzymes often lead to high-yielding processes with low downstream processing requirements. Enzymes are also environmentally friendly catalysts. They are completely biodegradable and pose no risk to the environment. Using mild conditions in enzyme-catalyzed reactions also means lower energy utilization and less emission of greenhouse gases. These attributes make enzymes particularly attractive catalysts. Often, biocatalysis is not only the more environmentally friendly alternative but also the more cost-effective alternative.

Biocatalyst preparation. Enzymes used in biocatalysis are derived from living systems such as bacteria, yeast, fungi, animal organs or tissues, and plant materials. By far the most common sources are microbial cells. They are cultivated typically in a bioreactor (also called a fermentor), which provides a controlled environment favorable to cell growth and the desired enzyme production. After cultivation, extracellular enzymes are recovered from the growth medium by removing cell biomass. Recovery of intracellular enzymes requires cell breakage to release the enzymes. Enzymes recovered from the fermentation process can be used directly as crude preparations either in powders or in liquid form. If purified enzymes are required, a purification process can be designed. Common purification processes includes salt or solvent precipitation followed by one or more chromatography steps. In many industrial applications, crude preparations with little or no purification steps are adequate for use in catalysis.

Many enzymes of interest to organic chemists exist in minute quantity in their native biological system or reside in organisms that are not conveniently accessible with conventional technology. This had been a major hurdle until recently; however, recombinant deoxyribonucleic acid (DNA) technology has changed the situation dramatically. Genes coding for enzymes can be cloned from their native organisms and inserted into *Escherichia coli*, yeast, or other easy-to-grow microorganisms. Fermentation of the recombinant cells containing the cloned genes will then provide access to large quantities of enzymes at markedly reduced cost. This has enabled many biocatalysis applications previously limited by the availability of enzymes.

In many applications, more than one enzyme is required. In order to avoid tedious multiple isolations of the required enzymes, whole-cell systems are used instead. The choice between whole cells and isolated enzymes depends on a number of factors. Major considerations are whether the presence of other enzymes in the whole-cell system affects the reaction of interest and whether the enzyme-catalyzed transformation requires expensive cofactors, which are easily replenished if whole-cell systems are used.

Recombinant DNA technology in concert with modern fermentation technology has drastically reduced the cost of biocatalysts; however, the cost of enzymes in most biocatalysis applications is still dominant. Multiple uses of enzymes and microbial cells are almost always desirable. This can be achieved by immobilizing enzymes or cells on solid supports through covalent or noncovalent attachment. The immobilized enzymes can be recovered easily from the reaction medium after the reaction by filtration for repeated use. Multiple use of the biocatalysts effectively reduces cost.

Applications. Successful examples of the application of biocatalysis in organic synthesis are abundant, with many having reached industrial scale. Production of high-fructose corn syrup (used as a sweetener in food and beverages) using glucose isomerase is an example involving a single isolated enzyme. 2-Keto-L-gulonate, a precursor of L-ascorbate (vitamin C), is made from glucose with two types of microbial cells, and more recently with a recombinant bacterium, *Erwinia herbicola*, carrying the necessary genes for the enzymes from *Corynebacterium* spp.

Despite many successful examples, biocatalysis is far from reaching its potential as a prevailing technology and an indispensable synthetic tool in the arsenal of organic synthesis. It is still viewed by many as a tool of last resort and is considered only when there is no other choice. There are a number of reasons for this. In the past, the cost of enzymes and their stability under technical conditions had been major obstacles, but the advent of recombinant DNA technology and recent advances in applied enzymology have made these two issues less of a concern as they are generally considered solvable. The requirement of expensive cofactors for many enzymes also has been a major factor hindering the use of this technology in organic synthesis. It has been addressed with varied success. In-situ regeneration of nicotinamide adenine dinucleotide (NAD/NADH), common cofactors required in many oxidoreductase-catalyzed reactions, has been demonstrated on a commercial scale in the production of a nonnatural amino acid, tert-leucine, although success with certain other cofactors, such as S-adenosyl methionine in enzymatic methyl transfer reactions, has yet to be attained. Another challenge in the use of large-scale enzyme technology is that enzyme activity frequently is inhibited by the products formed during the reaction. As a consequence, such an enzyme-catalyzed reaction would stop at a very low product concentration, resulting in a very inefficient process.

In addition to these technical factors, two other factors play a role in limiting the application of biocatalysis. A lack of widespread recognition of the potential of enzymes to serve as catalysts in organic synthesis is a major one. Additionally, biocatalysis development requires a much longer time frame compared with other synthetic reactions (because the understanding of the structure and mechanism of enzymes is not adequate to predict possible substrates and optimal conditions for enzymatic reactions); this puts biocatalysis at a competitive disadvantage, as the development of many processes, especially for pharmaceuticals, is extremely time-sensitive.

Prospects. So far about 3000 enzymes have been characterized. This represents about 10% of all the enzymes believed to exist in nature. Only about 300 are commercially available. By far, most of the catalytic power in nature remains untapped. Much scientific and technological progress has set the stage for rapid growth of the application of biocatalysis over the next decade. First, the availability of the genome sequences of many microbes and higher organisms is making the discovery and cloning of enzymes much easier and less time-consuming. Novel enzymes are being discovered at a much faster rate than in the past. Enzymes from extremophiles, that is, microorganisms that are active in extreme conditions such as high temperature, high pressure, high pH, and high salt concentration, are being discovered, and more and more are being exploited in various applications. Furthermore, recent progress in nonaqueous enzymology has expanded the application of enzymes from their natural milieu to organic solvents, which allows a wide range of organic compounds to be accessible to enzymes. In addition, protein engineering, either rationally based (utilizing available protein structure for guidance) or directed evolution (relying on random mutagenesis and subsequent screening), has emerged as a powerful tool to tailor the various attributes of enzymes for specific applications. Protein engineering and metabolic engineering are being used to address the previously formidable problems of cofactor regeneration and product inhibition. High-throughput screening technology, though still too expensive for an ordinary biocatalysis laboratory, is being used increasingly in almost all aspects of biocatalysis development, from enzyme discovery, cloning, and protein engineering to biocatalysis process research, with the potential to greatly shorten the development cycle of a biocatalytic process. Finally, explosive progress in biocatalysis research is leading to increased awareness of the possibilities of enzyme catalysis by the organic chemistry community. As a result, many universities are incorporating biocatalysis in the chemistry curriculum, and several outstanding textbooks have been written specifically for organic chemists entering this interdisciplinary field.

At present, about 80% of chemical synthesis reactions are catalyzed by synthetic catalysts. Since for almost every type of organic reaction there is an equivalent enzyme-catalyzed process, biocatalysis is expected to reshape the landscape of chemical synthesis in the future.

For background information *see* CATALYSIS; ENZYME; FERMENTATION; GENETIC ENGINEERING in the McGraw-Hill Encyclopedia of Science & Technology.

Ruizhen Chen

Bibliography. M. W. Adams, F. B. Perler, and R. M. Kelly, Extremozymes: Expanding the limits of biocatalysis, *Bio/Technology*, 13:662–668, July 1995; F. H. Arnold, Combinatorial and computational challenges for biocatalyst design, *Nature*, 409:253–257, January 11, 2001; K. Faber, *Biotransformations in Organic Chemistry*, 4th ed., Springer-Verlag, Berlin, 2000; A. Schmid et al., Industrial biocatalysis today and tomorrow, *Nature*, 409:258–267, January 11, 2001; C.-H. Wong and G. M. Whitesides, *Enzymes in Synthetic Organic Chemistry*, Pergamon, Trowbridge, 1994.

Bioluminescence in insects

The phenomenon of bioluminescence—visible light emitted by organisms—is rare on land compared with its diverse manifestations in the oceans. Most of the terrestrial representatives are insects, followed by bioluminescent fungi and a few earthworms, millipedes, centipedes, and snails. Beetles (Coleoptera) make up the majority of the bioluminescent insects, with more than 2000 reported species, mostly tropical in distribution.

Some Collembola (small, wingless soil arthropods that many researchers classify as insects) appear to glow faintly, but it is unknown whether this is due to the Collembola themselves, to symbiotic bacteria, or to glowing fungi or bacteria upon which they feed. The remaining 10 or 11 reported insects that glow are true flies (Diptera) of the mycetophilid (fungus gnat) subfamily Keroplatinae. Probably the best known is the glowworm *Arachnocampa luminosa*, which draws tourists to the Glowworm Cave at Waitomo, New Zealand. A second species, *Orfelia futoni*, behaves similarly, but is found under shallow rock outcrops throughout the Ozark plateau in the central highlands of the United States. The chemistry of bioluminescence in these fungus gnats is based on an enzyme and substrate unique among luminous insects.

Bioluminescent beetles include the genera *Pyrophorus* and *Pyrearinus* among click beetles (family Elateridae), which are only distantly related to all remaining bioluminescent beetles. The photic enzymes of the click beetles are nonetheless cross-reactive with those of the families Lampyridae (fireflies) and Phengodidae (railroad worms), indicating that the beetle systems must be rather similar chemically, even if they have distinct evolutionary origins.

The expression of bioluminescence in widely disparate groups of organisms, with significant differences in light organ morphologies and chemistries, indicates a pattern of convergent evolution and illustrates the selective advantages afforded by light emitters.

Light production. In insects, bioluminescence is produced in specialized light organs or fat bodies that can occur anywhere on the body. Any or all of the life stages (egg, larva, pupa, adult) or sexes can glow. The light-producing mechanism typically involves the oxidation of the substrate luciferin by catalytic enzymes called luciferases in the presence of the energy source adenosine triphosphate (ATP). The by-products of the reaction are oxyluciferin, carbon dioxide, and light.

Firefly luciferase varies from species to species, but apparently it originated through a modification of a common enzyme, ligase, that ordinarily functions in deoxyribonucleic acid (DNA) repair and replication. The rapid flashing produced by many adult fireflies is achieved through regulation of the oxygen supply to a firefly's photic (light) organ. Mitochondria in the photic organs use up the free oxygen in the photic organ quickly, so little is available for the light-producing reaction. When a firefly produces a flash, a neural impulse initiates the production of nitric oxide, which shuts off the mitochondria and allows oxygen to be delivered from the ends of tiny air tubes, past mitochondria, to the regions of the photocyte containing luciferin and ATP.

Bioluminescent beetles. The most elaborate and best-studied bioluminescent systems occur in the true fireflies (family Lampyridae) found worldwide and the family Phengodidae (also commonly called glowworm beetles or railroad worms). Other closely related families that glow are more obscure, such as the Asian Rhagophthalmidae or European Omalisidae. These families are united in a group of beetles that includes many diurnal species that do not glow, such as the common families Cantharidae,

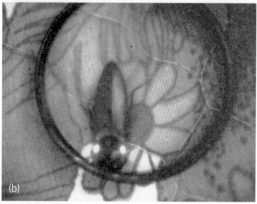

Fig. 1. Fire beetle (Coleoptera: Elateridae: Pyrophorini) at rest on a leaf. The beetle pictured is approximately 30 mm in length. (*a*) The two spots visible on the prothorax are light organs. (*b*) At night the light organs glow a brilliant green and are quite spectacular. (*Prof. J. Lloyd, University of Florida*)

Lycidae, and Omethidae. All beetles of this general group are at least partly toxic and protected by defensive compounds. Some of these compounds, called lucibufagins, are steroids that are chemically related to the protective compounds found in toads. The ingestion of *Photinus* fireflies has been found to be lethal to Australian lizards of the genus *Pogona* and the Australian tree frog *Litoria caerulea*. The ingestion of a single firefly appears to be enough to cause death in *Pogona* lizards.

Lampyridae. In all of the luminous species that have been studied, larvae produce light that seems to serve as a warning to potential predators. Lizards that eat fireflies reject them and vomit, whereas some have been known to turn black and die. Laboratory mice learn to avoid glowing, unpalatable items after a single trial, and wild-caught starlings avoid both firefly larvae and adults in daylight. Most fireflies have classical black-and-red or black-and-yellow warning coloration that is visible in daylight, and apparently the primitive condition for the family Lampyridae is that adults are not luminous and are active diurnally.

Phengodidae. Approximately 170 beetle species of the family Phengodidae are light emitters. They occur mainly in neotropical regions and are specialist predators of millipedes. A good example is the

railroad worm *Phrixothrix* of Brazil. In this genus, wingless females and larvae possess two head lanterns that emit red light while the insects walk over the ground. Researchers believe these wavelengths are visible to the eyes of *Phrixothrix* but not to its prey, suggesting an illumination function. There are also 11 pairs of yellow-green lateral lanterns along their sides, which are probably used defensively to warn off predators.

Elateridae. In click beetles, bioluminescence appears to play a role in the nocturnal, predatory habit of *Pyrearinus* larvae in species that prey on free-flying, winged termites, which are attracted to the glow emitted from the segment immediately behind the larva's head. It is not clear what role larval luminescence has in *Pyrophorus* species that burrow for prey in dead wood; they possess no distinct photic organ, although the glow is brightest from the membranes between body segments. Adults of *Pyrophorus* (fire beetles) produce light from two glowing spots on the prothorax (**Fig. 1**), which may look like eyespots and shine dorsally, and a ventral region (between the metathorax and the first abdominal segment) that is visible only when the beetle is in flight. These regions produce light as part of courtship displays. Some populations have polymorphisms, with individuals producing either a green-yellow or orange light. The variation in light color is due to a simple amino acid substitution in the luciferase.

Firefly bioluminescent sexual signals. In many fireflies (Lampyridae), the photic organs of adults also serve in sexual communication (**Fig. 2**). In three different lineages, males have enlarged photic organs, presumably increasing visibility to females. In each lineage, males call to females by flashing while in flight. Females apparently no longer release long-distance pheromones to attract mates; rather, they

Fig. 2. *Photinus ignitus* firefly (Coleoptera: Lampyridae) resting on a leaf during the day. The light organs can be seen at the base of the abdomen. (*Prof. J. Lloyd, University of Florida*)

judge among flashing males and respond selectively. After a female responds, a short flashing dialog may ensue until the male lands near the female and mating occurs.

The details of the signal system include a precise number, duration, rate, and pattern of male flashes, often including a distinct flight path as well (an upward J shape in *Photinus pyralis*, common in eastern North America). Females respond with a species-specific signal following a precise time delay after the male extinguishes his light. In some species, females seem to prefer males that can flash at high rates, which is presumably difficult physiologically and may be an indicator of male fitness. Such females express preference for artificial lights flashing at rates higher than those found in nature, indicating strong directional selection upon males. Many species may court simultaneously in the same location, without confusion among them. Although these courtship systems are very similar in general description, careful analysis demonstrates that each of three different lineages developed flashing signal systems independently and convergently.

Aggressive mimicry is known to occur in the females of several species in the firefly genus *Photuris*. In these species, females attract mates by emitting their own species-specific flash patterns following the male's flash pattern. After copulation, the *Photuris* females appear to undergo a behavioral switch, in which they no longer produce their own species-specific flash pattern but mimic the female flash pattern of other species in the same location that are active at the same time of night. These mimics attract males of another species, which are then attacked and eaten by the *Photuris* females. These females may acquire additional amounts of defensive steroids from the males they feed upon, and transfer these protective chemicals to their eggs.

In some cases, the color of the bioluminescent signal seems correlated with the time of evening when courtship occurs to maximize visibility. Dusk-active species that signal when the evening sky is still somewhat light have yellowish emissions that contrast well against greenish light reflected from background vegetation. The species that are active later in the night tend to produce photic emissions that are shifted toward green, which is best seen in deep darkness.

Fungus gnats: Arachnocampa species. In glowworms of the genus *Arachnocampa*, found in bush and caves in New Zealand and Australia, every life stage except for the eggs can emit light, which is blue-green in color. The glowworm light organ consists of the distended tips of the Malpighian tubules. These tubules are associated with the removal of waste (excretion) in insects, and are located at the end of the abdomen in front of a mat of tracheoles, very fine tubes which supply the light organ with oxygen and also function as reflectors of the light.

The larvae of *Arachnocampa* flies are predaceous and construct silk and mucus webs from which hang

Fig. 3. Two larvae of the New Zealand glowworm *Arachnocampa luminosa* (Diptera: Mycetophilidae: Keroplatinae) in their mucus webs suspended from the ceiling of a cave. Hanging from the web are the "fishing lines" coated with evenly spaced sticky droplets used by each larva to ensnare small insects. These larvae are not glowing, but a light organ, pale in color, can be seen in the larva at top. (*P. Dimond, Waitomo Museum of Caves*)

numerous vertical 'fishing lines' studded with sticky droplets. Blue-green light, such as that which the larvae produce, is known to be especially attractive to insects. Insects flying inside a cave or in bush may mistake the nearby glows of these larvae for stars in a night sky, resulting in the spiraling of the insects toward the light, only to find themselves caught in the sticky web (**Fig. 3**).

The hypothesis that glowworms use bioluminescence to attract prey was recently confirmed. Transparent adhesive traps were placed over the larvae, and over areas from where the larvae had been removed, both in a cave and in bush at the cave entrance. It was then possible to count and identify the types of invertebrates attracted to larval bioluminescence and compare them to catches from traps without larvae. Over the 200 trapping days it was found that the traps at both sites with larvae caught significantly more total invertebrates than control traps. Nearly 90% of the invertebrates caught were small flying Diptera. In the bush, traps with larvae caught significantly more total Diptera, and the dipteran families Dolichopodidae, Psychodidae, and Teratomyzidae, but in the cave the numbers of each taxon caught were quite low, so it was not possible to demonstrate any significant differences. However, it seems likely that larval bioluminescence may attract other groups of Diptera, such as Sciaridae, Trichoceridae, Mycetophilidae, Heleomyzidae, and Tipulidae. A few nondipteran invertebrates (such as small spiders, Coleoptera, and Hymenoptera) were also trapped, mostly in the bush, but there were no significant differences in the numbers caught. No *A. luminosa* adults were caught in any of the traps. As the adult males possess chemically sensitive plumose antennae, it seems plausible that the females use pheromones rather than bioluminescence to attract mates, thereby preventing the adults from being caught and devoured by their own larvae.

For background information *see* BIOLUMINESCENCE; COLEOPTERA; COLLEMBOLA; DIPTERA; INSECT PHYSIOLOGY; INSECTA in the McGraw-Hill Encyclopedia of Science & Technology.

Marc A. Branham; R. Adam Broadley; John W. Wenzel

Bibliography. M. A. Branham and M. D. Greenfield, Flashing males win mate success, *Nature*, 381:745–746, 1996; M. A. Branham and J. W. Wenzel, The evolution of bioluminescence in cantharoids (Coleoptera: Elateroidea), *Florida Entomol.*, 84:478–499, 2001; R. A. Broadley and I. A. N. Stringer, Prey attraction by larvae of the New Zealand glowworm, *Arachnocampa luminosa* (Diptera: Mycetophilidae), *Invert. Biol.*, 120(2):170–177, 2001; T. Eisner et al., Lucibufagins: Defensive steroids from the fireflies *Photinus ignitus* and *P. marginellus* (Coleoptera: Lampyridae), *Proc. Nat. Acad. Sci. USA*, 94:9723–9728, 1978; J. E. Lloyd, Bioluminescent communication in insects, *Annu. Rev. Entomol.*, 16:97–122, 1971; J. Sivinski, The nature and possible functions of luminescence in Coleoptera larvae, *Coleopterists Bull.*, 35:167–179, 1981; J. Sivinski, Phototropism, bioluminescence, and the Diptera, *Florida Entomol.*, 81(3):282–292, 1998; J. Sivinski, Prey attraction by luminous larvae of the fungus gnat *Orfelia fultoni, Ecol. Entomol.*, 7:443–446, 1982; B. A. Trimmer et al., Nitric oxide and the control of firefly flashing, *Science*, 292:2486–2488, 2001; V. R. Viviani and E. J. H. Bechara, Bioluminescence and biological aspects of Brazilian railroadworms (Coleoptera: Phengodidae), *Ann. Entomol. Soc. Amer.*, 90(3):389–398, 1997.

Bio-micro-electro-mechanical systems for drug delivery

Biomedical applications of micro-electro-mechanical systems, or BioMEMS, is an emerging field that uses techniques adapted from the microelectronics industry to create devices for sensing and manipulating biological material with a precision not previously possible. For example, microfabrication technology is being applied to create drug delivery systems that allow tight control over physical parameters such as fluid flow rates and pressure, enabling precise delivery of concentrated drug solutions in order to meet dosage specifications of drugs. By integrating microfabricated devices such as microneedles and micropumps, very tight control over injection flow rates at given drug concentrations can be achieved. Drug solutions may be administrated as needed by the patient. Thus, the drug concentration in the body may be controlled to achieve either a constant or time-varying drug concentration profile in the body.

Optical lithography. All microfabricated devices are created by a succession of material deposition and selective removal. In order to selectively remove material, a photosensitive material (photoresist) is added onto a substrate and patterned by optical lithography. By shining light through a patterned photomask, the photoresist is selectively exposed and developed to transfer a pattern from the mask onto the substrate. This procedure is analogous to printing a photograph, with the photomask serving as the negative and the photoresist serving as photographic paper. This technique can reproducibly pattern features smaller than 1 micrometer. The major advantages of optical lithography are the ability to miniaturize devices and to economically produce many identical devices in parallel.

Transducers. Most microfabricated systems incorporate transducers, devices that convert energy from one form to another more useful form. Transducers are classified as either sensors or actuators. Sensors convert an incoming optical, chemical, or mechanical signal into an electrical signal that can be analyzed. Actuators convert an electrical signal into another form of energy (very often mechanical energy). Specific examples of sensors with biomedical utility include pressure sensors for blood pressure monitoring; pH, ion sensitive, and chemical sensors for medical monitoring; and accelerometers used in pacemakers. Actuators are often used in robotic surgical devices. These include piezoelectric (able to produce a mechanical force when a voltage is applied) materials for extremely precise robotic guidance of surgical tools and ultrasonic cutting tools. In addition, investigators have been able to use lithographic patterning of surfaces to create hybrid devices that use biological materials as sensors or actuators. Researchers have been able to selectively treat surfaces to direct cell adhesion, allowing micropatterned cell cultures for cell-based biosensors. Recent studies have focused on using biomolecular motors (for example F_1-ATPase, actin, kinesin) that naturally function in cells to produce useful work in microfabricated devices.

Microneedles. In modern medical applications such as drug delivery, there is a need for very small needles. Currently, the smallest needles commercially available, 30-gauge needles, have a 305-μm outer diameter with a wall thickness of 76 μm. Microneedles, however, can be fabricated in almost any size and geometry since they are made with microfabrication techniques (such as photolithography and reactive ion etching) used in the microelectronics industry for making integrated circuits. As a result, the majority of microneedles are silicon, although there have been some recently reported electroplated metals and polymer microneedle designs (which do not fracture as easily as silicon).

Microneedles are designed to be high-performance, minimally invasive conduits through which drug solutions may pass into the body. In order to be minimally invasive, the needles are designed to be as small as possible. Needles are also extremely sharp, with submicrometer tip radii. This allows the needles to be effectively inserted into the skin. In addition, the small size of the needles cause less compression of the tissue during insertion, which leads to a decrease in pain and discomfort. Many

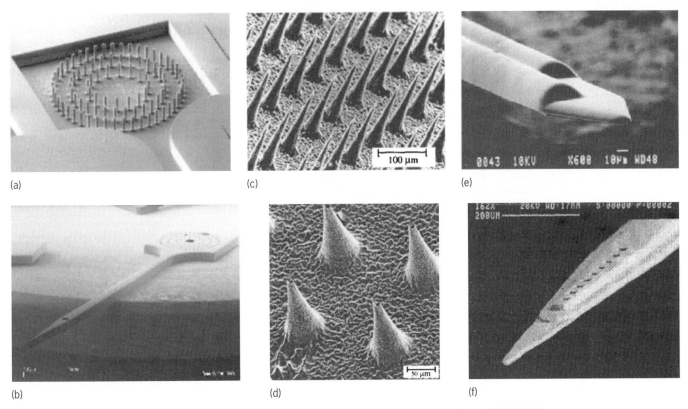

(a)

(c)

(e)

(b)

(d)

(f)

Fig. 1. Various microneedle designs. (*a*) Scanning electron micrograph (SEM) of a polysilicon microneedle mold. (*b*) SEM of the fabricated 6-mm-long microneedle. (*c*) Black silicon microneedles. (*d*) Metal microneedles produced from electroplating SU-8 molds of the black silicon microneedles. (*e*) Microfabricated neural probes with buried channels for selective drug delivery into neural tissue. (*f*) Metal microneedle created from electroplated metal layers. (*All reproduced with permission. a and b from J. D. Zahn et al., 2000; c and d from D. V. McAllister et al., 1999; e from J. D. Chen, 1994; f from J. Brazzle et al., 2000*)

different microneedle designs have been fabricated (**Fig. 1**).

Microneedles have advantages over other approaches to transdermal drug delivery, such as electroporation, ultrasonic delivery, or chemical modifiers/enhancers, that rely on decreasing the permeation barrier of the stratum corneum, the outermost layer of the skin. Microneedles mechanically penetrate the skin barrier and allow the injection of any volume of fluid over time. They can also be precisely inserted at any specified distance below the stratum corneum in order to obtain effective drug absorption into the bloodstream or to stimulate particular clusters of cells in or near the skin. Further, drug delivery via microneedles is independent of drug composition and concentration, and merely relies on the subsequent drug absorption into the bloodstream, which occurs at a much faster rate than permeation of a solution across the skin. This also allows complex drug delivery profiles; since the drug is actively injected into a patient, the dosage may be varied with time. In addition, by using multiple needles or effective fluid control with mixing of solutions, multiple drugs may be injected simultaneously, specific to a patient's personal needs.

Since microneedles allow such compact, potentially portable, and precise delivery of therapeutics, they are well suited for any drug delivery regime in

which a continuous infusion is preferred to a bolus injection (**Fig. 2**). Microneedles are extremely attractive for delivering therapeutics in a portable intravenous drip style fashion, such as the continuous delivery of insulin to a diabetic patient. Microneedles also find tremendous application in chemotherapy, catheterized instrumentation for local vascular

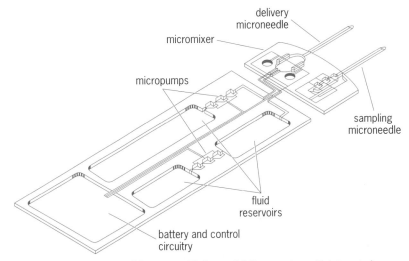

Fig. 2. Proposed integrated drug reconstitution and delivery system with integrated fluidic components; and microvalves, micropumps, micromixer, microneedles, and sensors for feedback-controlled drug delivery.

drug delivery, delivery of antibiotics, and vaccination. The reduced pain is also helpful in improving patient compliance.

Continuous drug delivery increases drug effectiveness and lowers side effects for a large range of therapeutics. It also allows a lower drug dosage to be injected over a longer period of time to maintain a constant blood concentration. A bolus injection, on the other hand, leads to a rapid increase in blood concentration, often to toxic levels, followed by a decay period as the drug is metabolized. This time-varying, high-concentration injection is often responsible for many side effects associated with a large number of therapeutics. By maintaining a constant blood concentration below toxic levels, side effects associated with a high-concentration bolus injection may be reduced.

Sensors and actuators play a major role in interfacing microneedles with biological systems. A precise mechanical actuator may be used for controlling the forces on the needle during insertion to minimize insertion pain. Microfluidic actuators are used for pumping fluid through the needles, and the needles may be integrated with biosensors for biological analysis. Micropumps may be used for fluid extraction through the microneedle simply by reversing the flow direction so that the net pumping is into the device rather than out. Thus, an integrated device could be fabricated to determine glucose levels for diabetics. One needle/pump system could sample interstitial fluid to determine glucose level while a second pump could deliver insulin in a controlled manner as needed by the patient.

Microfluidic devices. Any portable drug delivery device will need a compact means to deliver the correct drug dosages; thus there is active research in compact fluid handling and delivery systems. Several key components for fluid handling are microvalves for rectifying fluid flow, micropumps to deliver fluid through the needles into the body, and micromixers for diluting high-concentration drug solutions to the correct dosages.

The basic physics of fluid mechanics do not change as the transition from macroscale to microscale systems is made. However, a different aspect of physical science becomes important, since decreasing the channel diameter increases the relative surface area of a channel, increasing the viscous drag on a

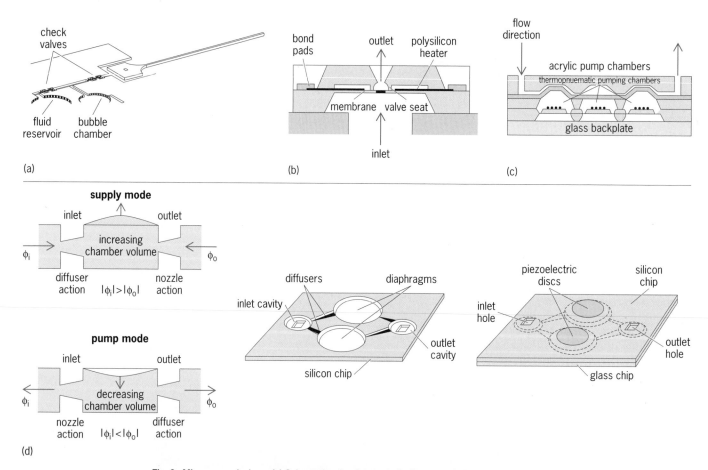

Fig. 3. Micropump designs. (*a*) Schematic of an integrated micropump/microneedle device. (*b*) Batch-fabricated, normally closed microvalve. When fluid is boiled using the polysilicon heaters, it pushes the membrane away from the orifice opening the valve. (*c*) Batch-fabricated micropump based on peristaltic pumping. A flexible membrane performs a sealing function to prevent backflow and a compression function to force fluid forward. Initially a chamber is sealed to prevent backflow, and then the fluid is displaced into the next chamber using thermopneumatic actuation of the membrane. A net pumping is achieved by sequentially actuating membranes in a line. (*d*) Micromachined diffuser nozzle pump. The diffuser is a diverging channel design that increases the resistance to flow in the converging channel over the diverging channel. Thus, when a piezoelectric actuator oscillates in a central chamber, there is a net flow in the device.

fluid within a microchannel. Thus in microfluidics, pressure forces are equally dissipated by drag forces on the fluid, with relatively little inertia. Due to the unique planar processing techniques utilized in microfabrication, flows are generally constrained in a microchannel so that fluid flows only within the plane of the channel.

Microvalves. Microvalves are necessary components to rectify and control fluid flow in any microfluidic device. There have been many valve designs for microfluidic flow control. The designs usually involve a block that is pushed against an etched orifice to stop flow and is pushed away from the hole to allow flow. An active valve usually maintains one state; either open or closed, via activation of an actuator. A constant energy input is required to maintain the current state. A passive valve uses either fluid pressure or viscous drag and a specific geometry to rectify flow. A common example is a flapper valve that is a cantilevered (fixed at one end and hanging free at the other end) beam over an orifice. In the forward flow direction, the beam is deformed away from the orifice by fluid forces allowing flows. During the reverse flow, the beam is pushed the other way to seal the orifice, preventing flow. Bistable valves are neutrally stable in either the open or closed position. Energy is only required to change the valve from one state to the other. Once the valve is in one position, no energy dissipation is required to hold the valve in the current state.

Micropumps and micromixers. In addition to microvalves, several designs for micropumps (**Fig. 3**) have been fabricated. Valves may be integrated with the pumps or the pumps may be valveless, based on the desired type of flow—either peristaltic flow or unidirectional flow based on an asymmetric design. All microfluidic components require an actuation source to produce mechanical force. The most common actuation source is either piezoelectric, pneumatic (in which compressed fluid energy is converted into mechanical energy), or thermopneumatic (in which energy from a liquid-gaseous phase change creates a bubble to force pressure on a component and pushes like a piston). Since flows are constrained within the plane of the channel, three-dimensional flows are difficult to achieve. Most mass transfer is achieved by diffusion. Three-dimensional turbulence or vortical flow fields (stirring) enhances mixing on the macroscale. On the microscale, however, mixing is achieved using pulsed fluid pumping of two fluids to elongate the interface between two fluids and allow a greater surface area for diffusion to occur more rapidly.

For background information *see* BIOMECHANICS; BIOMEDICAL ENGINEERING; DRUG DELIVERY SYSTEMS; MICRO-ELECTRO-MECHANICAL SYSTEMS (MEMS) in the McGraw-Hill Encyclopedia of Science & Technology.

Jeffrey Zahn

Bibliography. J. Brazzle et al., Active microneedles with integrated functionality, *Proceedings of the 2000 Solid State Sensor and Actuator Workshop*, Hilton Head, SC, pp. 199–202, 2000; J. P. Brody et al., Biotechnology at low Reynolds numbers, *Biophys. J.*, 71:3430–3441, 1996; J. Chen and K. D. Wise, A multichannel neural probe for selective chemical delivery at the cellular level, *Proceedings of the 1994 Solid State Sensor and Actuator Workshop*, Hilton Head, SC, pp. 256–259, 1994; P. Gravesen, J. Branebjerg, and O. S. Jensen, Microfluidics: A review, *J. Micromech. Microeng.*, 3:168–182, 1993; M. Madou, *Fundamentals of Microfabrication*, CRC Press, Boca Raton, FL, 1997; D. V. McAllister et al., Three-dimensional hollow microneedle and microtube arrays, *Proceedings of the 10th International Conference on Solid State Sensors and Actuators (Transducers '99)*, pp. 1098–1101, 1999; D. V. McAllister, M. G. Allen, and M. R. Prausnitz, Microfabricated microneedles for gene and drug delivery, *Annu. Rev. Biomed. Eng.*, 2:289–313, 2000; J. D. Zahn et al., Continuous on-chip micropumping through a microneedle, *14th Annual IEEE International MEMS-01 Conference.* pp. 503–506, 2001; J. D. Zahn et al., Microfabricated microneedles for minimally invasive biomedical devices, *Biomed. Microdevices*, 2(4):295–303, 2000.

Body dysmorphic disorder

Body dysmorphic disorder, first described in the medical literature more than a century ago, is a psychiatric illness worldwide. The *Diagnostic and Statistical Manual of Mental Disorders*, Fourth Edition (DSM-IV), defines body dysmorphic disorder as a preoccupation with an imagined defect in appearance; if a slight physical anomaly is present, the person's concern is markedly excessive. The preoccupation must cause clinically significant distress or impairment in social, occupational, or other important areas of functioning. In addition, the appearance concerns are not better accounted for by another psychiatric illness, such as anorexia nervosa.

Although many people are dissatisfied with their appearance, the preoccupation in body dysmorphic disorder differs from normal appearance concerns. Individuals with the disorder are obsessed about how they look, and their concerns cause them much distress or interfere with their functioning (usually both). In more severe cases, the disorder can even lead to severe depression, a need for psychiatric hospitalization, or suicide.

Epidemiology. Body dysmorphic disorder appears to be relatively common compared to other psychiatric disorders. Although studies of its current prevalence in the general population are limited, they have consistently reported a rate of 0.7–2.3%. Its prevalence is higher in certain populations, with studies finding rates of 13% in psychiatric inpatients; 14–42% of outpatients with major depression; 8–37% of outpatients with obsessive-compulsive disorder; 6–15% of people seeking cosmetic surgery; and 12% of people seeking treatment with a dermatologist.

Children as well as adults suffer from body dysmorphic disorder. In fact, the disorder usually begins in early adolescence. If untreated, it appears to persist for years, if not decades, and tends to be unremitting, sometimes worsening over time. Body dysmorphic disorder appears to be as common in men as in women, and the clinical features appear generally similar in both sexes. Most affected people have never been married, and a relatively high percentage are unemployed.

Clinical features. Individuals with body dysmorphic disorder are preoccupied with the idea that some aspect of their appearance is unattractive, deformed, ugly, or "not right," when the perceived flaw is actually minimal or nonexistent. Some individuals describe themselves as looking hideous, repulsive, or like the Elephant Man. Preoccupations usually involve the face or head, most often attributes of the skin, hair, or nose (for example, acne, scarring, pale or red skin, thinning hair, or a large or crooked nose). However, any body part can be the focus, and concern with bodily asymmetry is common. Individuals typically think about their perceived flaws for 3 to 8 hours a day, and the thoughts are usually difficult to resist or control. Before treatment, most individuals have poor or absent insight, not recognizing that the flaw they perceive is actually minimal or nonexistent.

Nearly all persons with body dysmorphic disorder perform repetitive, time-consuming, compulsive behaviors that they use to examine, improve, be reassured about, or hide the perceived defect. Common behaviors are comparing one's appearance with that of others; excessively checking the perceived flaw directly in mirrors or in other reflecting surfaces (for example, windows); excessively grooming (for example, applying makeup or tweezing, styling, or cutting hair); seeking reassurance about the perceived flaw or attempting to convince others of its ugliness; and camouflaging (for example, with hair, a wig, makeup, body position, sunglasses, a hat or other clothing). Related behaviors include dieting, excessive exercising, touching or measuring the body part, buying excessive amounts of beauty products, repeated clothes changing, and seeking surgery or medical treatment.

Nearly all patients with body dysmorphic disorder experience impairment in social, occupational, and academic functioning as a result of their appearance concerns. They may avoid dating and other social interactions, have few or no friends, or get divorced because of their symptoms. Impairment in academic or occupational functioning is common and may be caused by poor concentration due to obsessions, time-consuming related behaviors, or self-consciousness about being seen. People with the disorder also have markedly poor quality of life. In fact, approximately one-quarter of the patients are so distressed that they attempt suicide. However, the severity of the disorder varies, with some people appearing to lead relatively normal lives despite the suffering and interference they experience.

Relationship to other mental illnesses. Body dysmorphic disorder has many similarities to obsessive-compulsive disorder—notably, the presence of prominent obsessions and repetitive compulsive

behaviors. However, there appear to be differences between these disorders; for example, body dysmorphic disorder patients are less likely to be married, have poorer insight, and are more likely to think about suicide or make a suicide attempt. They also have higher lifetime rates of major depression and social phobia than individuals with obsessive-compulsive disorder. In addition, body dysmorphic disorder is more often characterized by shame, embarrassment, humiliation, low self-esteem, and rejection sensitivity—features that it shares with social phobia.

Body dysmorphic disorder has also been postulated to be related to depression. Both disorders often occur together, and both are characterized by low self-esteem, rejection sensitivity, and feelings of unworthiness. However, unlike depression, a core feature of body dysmorphic disorder is prominent obsessional preoccupations and repetitive compulsive behaviors. Many depressed patients focus less on their appearance, even neglecting it, rather than overfocusing on it. In addition, onset of body dysmorphic disorder usually precedes that of major depression, suggesting that body dysmorphic disorder is not simply a symptom of depression.

Body dysmorphic disorder and eating disorders share disturbed body image and a preoccupation with perceived appearance flaws, performance of compulsive behaviors such as mirror checking and body measuring, and a similar age of onset. However, patients with eating disorders tend to dislike their weight, whereas those with body dysmorphic disorder tend to dislike specific body parts. Furthermore, body dysmorphic disorder affects as many men as women (whereas eating disorders affect women more than men). Effective treatments for the two types of disorder differ in some ways. For example, the response of anorexia nervosa patients to serotonin reuptake inhibitors has generally been less frequent and less robust than the response of patients with body dysmorphic disorder.

Etiology and pathophysiology. The cause of body dysmorphic disorder is unknown but is likely multifactorial, with neurobiological, evolutionary, sociocultural, and psychological factors. Family history data, although limited, suggest that the disorder tends to run in families. Furthermore, it may involve pathology in executive functioning (implicating frontal-striatal brain pathology), dysfunction of the orbitofrontal system of the brain, or problems in the temporal and occipital lobes, which process facial images and (along with the parietal lobes) are involved in neurological disorders involving disturbed body image.

Pathology in executive functioning. Pathology of the frontal lobe results in problems with executive functioning, and body dysmorphic disorder pathogenesis may involve executive dysfunction. Neuropsychological studies have shown that individuals with the disorder overfocus on minor and irrelevant stimuli, suggesting that their appearance-related beliefs may arise from overfocusing on minimal appearance flaws (isolated details rather than overall appearance), causing a visual attention bias.

Orbitofrontal system dysfunction. Positron emission tomography studies of obsessive-compulsive disorder have implicated the orbitofrontal cortex (a frontal subcortical neurocircuit) in the pathophysiology of obsessive behavior, which is also a prominent feature of body dysmorphic disorder. The orbitofrontal cortex, in part, mediates empathic, civil, and socially appropriate behavior and takes part in object-affect associations. Increased metabolic activity in this area has been associated with the inability to inhibit intrusive thoughts, the inability of compulsive behavior to satisfy anxiety, and the overengagement in expectancies of future aversive events.

Temporal, occipital, and parietal lobe dysfunction. Subacute sclerosing panencephalitis, a rare and diffuse brain disease, and stroke of the parietal region have been associated with body image disturbances. For example, anosognosia, a neurological problem in which a person is unable to recognize impaired bodily functioning, such as paralysis, may involve a distorted understanding of what the paralyzed limb looks like. Injury to the occipital lobes can impair visual perception of facial images. Damage to the temporal lobe can result in a distorted view of body size.

Other factors. Treatment data indicate that the neurotransmitter serotonin may also play a role in body dysmorphic disorder. Psychological/environmental factors (for example, being teased about one's appearance) are likely to be important as well, although what these factors consist of has received virtually no investigation.

Treatment. Many people suffering from body dysmorphic disorder seek surgical and nonpsychiatric medical treatments (for example, dermatologic, dental) for their appearance concerns. Available data suggest that such treatments are usually ineffective and may even worsen appearance concerns. Occasional dissatisfied patients commit suicide or are even violent toward the treating physician.

In contrast, serotonin-reuptake inhibitors appear to be more effective than other medications for body dysmorphic disorder. These serotonin medications include fluoxetine (Prozac), citalopram (Celexa), fluvoxamine (Luvox), sertraline (Zoloft), paroxetine (Paxil), and clomipramine (Anafranil). Response to medication usually results in improved functioning and decreased appearance-related preoccupations, distress, and behaviors. Treatment response often requires 10–12 weeks and use of relatively high doses. Long-term treatment is often needed, and serotonin-reuptake inhibitors' efficacy for body dysmorphic disorder is usually sustained over time. These medications are usually well tolerated.

Cognitive-behavioral therapy is another promising treatment for body dysmorphic disorder. Studies using exposure (for example, letting the perceived defect be seen in social situations and preventing avoidance behaviors), response prevention (stopping compulsive behaviors such as mirror checking), and cognitive restructuring (for example, changing distorted views about appearance) have found these approaches to be effective for a majority of patients. Whereas some patients respond well to either serotonin-reuptake inhibitors or cognitive-behavioral therapy, others benefit from a combination of these treatments. Research is in progress to better identify and develop effective treatments for adults, children, and adolescents with body dysmorphic disorder.

For background information *see* AFFECTIVE DISORDERS; BRAIN; EATING DISORDERS; OBSESSIVE-COMPULSIVE DISORDER; PSYCHOPHARMACOLOGY; PSYCHOTHERAPY; SEROTONIN in the McGraw-Hill Encyclopedia of Science & Technology.

Jon E. Grant; Katharine A. Phillips

Bibliography. *Diagnostic and Statistical Manual of Mental Disorders*, DSM-IV, 4th ed., American Psychiatric Association, 1994; F. A. Neziroglu et al., Exposure, response prevention, and cognitive therapy in the treatment of body dysmorphic disorder, *Behav. Ther.*, 24:431–438, 1993; K. A. Phillips, *The Broken Mirror: Recognizing and Treating Body Dysmorphic Disorder*, Oxford University Press, 1996; K. A. Phillips, Pharmacologic treatment of body dysmorphic disorder: Review of the evidence and a recommended treatment approach, *CNS Spectrums*, in press; K. A. Phillips et al., Body dysmorphic disorder: 30 cases of imagined ugliness, *Amer. J. Psychiat.*, 150:302–308, 1993; H. G. Pope et al., *The Adonis Complex: The Secret Crisis of Male Body Obsession*, Free Press, New York, 2000.

Burkholderia cepacia complex

The *Burkholderia cepacia* complex is a group of bacteria prevalent in the natural environment that can cause human infections (so-called opportunistic infections) in vulnerable individuals. These microorganisms can colonize a variety of different habitats, including soil (especially at the rhizosphere—the interface between the soil and plant roots), water, polluted environments, and the lungs of patients with cystic fibrosis. Their success as microbial colonizers appears to be dependent on two innate properties: (1) *B. cepacia* complex bacteria can metabolize an enormous range of organic compounds, and (2) they possess considerable resistance to antimicrobial agents and may synthesize antibiotics of their own.

The metabolic diversity of *B. cepacia* complex bacteria has prompted a considerable amount of research into their use as natural bioremediation agents (organisms with the ability to degrade and detoxify human-made pollutants). The organisms also possess plant beneficial properties, and their ability to protect commercially important crops such as peas and maize from attack by fungal and worm pests has led to their commercial development as biological control agents (biopesticides). Another potential use of these microorganisms is their application, outside the United States, in the commercial production of enzymes. However, the striking ability of the

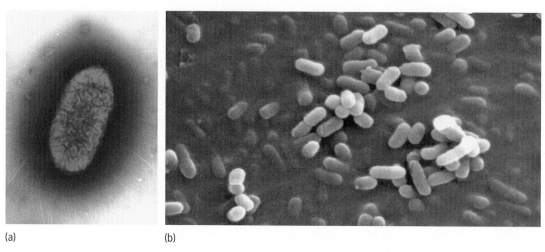

(a)   (b)

Electron micrographs of *B. cepacia* genomovar III strain J2315. (*a*) Transmission electron micrograph showing characteristic rod shape and cable pili. (*b*) Three-dimensional scanning electron microscope. (*Used with the permission of Emma Ralph*)

B. cepacia complex bacteria to produce commercially useful products has been overshadowed by their devastating ability to cause disease and death among vulnerable members of society.

Taxonomy. *Burkholderia cepacia* complex bacteria are gram-negative, aerobic, motile rods (see **illus.**). Understanding the taxonomy of the bacteria is a vital first step in being able to assess the risks of their commercial use. However, problems exist in our ability to speciate this group of bacteria, and over the last decade many changes have been made to the taxonomy of the *B. cepacia* complex. In 1992, the genus *Burkholderia* was created, with *Pseudomonas cepacia*, as it was known then, becoming the *Burkholderia* type species. The application of polyphasic taxonomy (the incorporation of multiple tests to classify an organism, including tests of phenotypic, genotypic, and phylogenetic properties) led to the discovery that at least five further genetically distinct species were present among strains biochemically identified as *B. cepacia*. If a simple diagnostic test was found for a group of related isolates, they were described as a new species; however, if no straightforward tests were available to distinguish strains that were genetically greater than 70% identical, they were described using the taxonomic term "genomovar." In 1997 this led to the description of two new species, *B. multivorans* (formerly *B. cepacia* genomovar II) and *B. vietnamiensis* (formerly *B. cepacia* genomovar V), and three *B. cepacia* genomovars, I, III, and IV. The term *B. cepacia* complex was adopted to describe the group as a collective. The taxonomy has continued to change, with several existing genomovars being formally named and further new species discovered. Currently, there are at least nine species or genomovar members of the *B. cepacia* complex (see **table**).

Identification. Accurate identification of these bacteria requires the performance of several tests. Diagnosis using selective media, conventional biochemical analysis, and commercial assays is usually sufficient to provide a putative identification of an isolate as *B. cepacia* complex. Critical biochemical traits that should be examined for presumptive identification are oxidation of sucrose and adonitol, the presence of lysine and ornithine decarboxylase, oxidase activity, hemolysis, secretion of pigments, and growth at 42°C. Discriminatory assays include whole-genome deoxyribonucleic acid (DNA)–DNA hybridization, whole-cell protein analysis; amplified fragment length polymorphism; whole-cell fatty acid profiling; and polymerase chain reaction assays based on genes such as bacterial 16S and 23S ribosomal ribonucleic acid (RNA) and the *recA* genes. Overall, the performance of multiple tests is recommended to confirm the identification of *B. cepacia* complex bacteria. In addition, several research laboratories for *B. cepacia* complex identification exist in Europe and North America that are operated by members of the International *Burkholderia cepacia* Working Group.

Opportunistic infections. *Burkholderia cepacia* complex bacteria cause problematic infections in patients with cystic fibrosis and chronic granulomatous disease; they are also a common cause of hospital-associated (nosocomial) infection, causing outbreaks of disease in intensive care units and surgical wards. Two traits of *B. cepacia* complex bacteria make infection with these organisms particularly difficult to treat: (1) their innate resistance to many antibiotics and (2) their ability to spread epidemically from patient to patient. The antimicrobial resistance of these organisms is profound. For example, *B. stabilis* strain ATCC 35254 (see table) was isolated as a contaminant growing in an iodine-based disinfectant solution. *Burkholderia cepacia* complex lung infection in patients with cystic fibrosis is rarely eradicated, and constant antibiotic therapy is required to keep infections under control. Cystic fibrosis patients may also die prematurely from virulent *B. cepacia* complex lung disease. Strains of *B. cepacia* genomovar III and *B. multivorans* are the prominent cystic fibrosis pathogens (see table) and are capable of transmitting from patient to patient.

Taxonomy and estimated ecological prevalence of the *Burkholderia cepacia* complex

Species or genomovar	Estimated prevalence in		Comments
	Cystic fibrosis	Natural environment*	
B. cepacia (genomovar I)	Low†	High	Contains the *B. cepacia* type strain ATCC‡ 25416
B. multivorans (genomovar II)	High (>30% of infections)	Not known	Second most predominant cystic fibrosis pathogen; multiple-replicon genome first described in strain ATCC 17616
B. cepacia (genomovar III)	High (>50% of infections)	High	Major cystic fibrosis pathogen; prevalent in the rhizosphere; U.S.-registered biocontrol strain from this genomovar withdrawn from use by the manufacturer
B. stabilis (genomovar IV)	Low	Not known	Species demonstrates limited genomic diversity; strain ATCC 35254 found as a disinfectant contaminant
B. vietnamiesis (genomovar V)	Low	High	Predominant in the rhizosphere and associated with crops such as rice; contains the trichloroethylene-degrading strain ATCC 53617 (also known as strain G4)
B. cepacia (genomovar VI)	Low	Not known	To date, this genomovar contains only isolates from cystic fibrosis infection
B. ambifaria (genomovar VII)	Low	High	Contains the two other U.S. biopesticide-registered strains; extensive biological control uses described; may cause infections in patients with cystic fibrosis
B. anthina (genomovar VIII)	Low	Not known	Contains isolates from human infection and the natural environment
B. pyrrocinia (genomovar IX)	Low	High	Species name *B. pyrrocinia* proposed prior to the discovery that it was a member of the *B. cepacia* complex

*Prevalence in the natural environment is estimated from published reports and analysis of strains within the author's collection, unless not known.
†"Low" indicates that prevalence in cystic fibrosis is generally estimated to be below 5% of total *B. cepacia* complex infections.
‡ATCC = American Type Culture Collection.

Stringent infection control procedures are required to prevent the spread of infection. To date, all the species and genomovars within the *B. cepacia* complex have been found to cause human infections (see table).

Biotechnological potential. The metabolic diversity of bacteria in the *B. cepacia* complex enables them to colonize many different habitats, and several beneficial properties have been identified from these interactions. The most well-known applications for the *B. cepacia* complex are pesticidal in nature. However, in 2002 the U.S. Environmental Protection Agency (EPA) contacted over 100 firms, associations, and researchers (along with searching the academic and patent literature) to determine the extent of nonpesticidal applications of the *B. cepacia* complex. None of the companies stated that they included live *B. cepacia* complex bacteria in their products. One company, however, did list seven fat-dissolving enzymes (lipases) derived from these species. In addition, it was discovered that commercial interests and academics have used these bacteria directly in field tests to degrade hazardous wastes.

Bioremediation. Many *B. cepacia* complex strains have been studied as bioremediation agents. The ability of *B. vietnamiensis* strain ATCC 53617 (see table) to degrade aromatic hydrocarbon pollutants such as toluene and chlorinated solvents such as trichloroethylene has been studied at both the biochemical and molecular levels. Several of the genes involved in degradation are encoded on a large plasmid that can be found in many other bacterial species; however, none to date are as efficient as ATCC 53617 at cooxidizing trichloroethylene. A derivative of ATCC 53617, referred to as *B. cepacia* strain ENV435, has been applied in commercial field tests. Approximately 550 liters of this bacterial strain were injected into a silty-sand aquifer, with the result that chlorinated solvents were reduced by as much as 78%. Another derivative of ATCC 53617 has been used to intercept a trichloroethylene contaminated groundwater plume by loading live bacteria into large cassettes placed in the ground directly in the path of the plume. A field test involving injection of a putative *B. cepacia* isolate was performed to test the ability of this bacterium and others to move through the subsurface.

Although these cases exist in the published or gray (open-source) literature regarding bioremediation applications, it is possible that some companies might introduce *B. cepacia* complex into commercial products without knowing its exact taxonomic composition. There are a number of small companies which make drain cleaners, bioremediation agents, and turf enhancers that use natural isolates (either individual bacterial isolates or consortia) obtained from the environment (such as landfills). Only a careful examination of these products, including appropriate isolation and taxonomic approaches, would confirm the presence of particular *B. cepacia* complex bacteria.

Biopesticides. *Burkholderia cepacia* complex strains demonstrating biopesticidal properties are used commercially in the United States. The use of such naturally occurring biopesticidal agents can replace the application of highly toxic and persistent (long-lasting) chemical pesticides, which are frequently used in modern agriculture. Three strains known as *B. cepacia* Type Wisconsin are registered for use as biopesticides by the EPA and are used in commercial biopesticide products. Analysis of these strains demonstrated that one was a member of *B. cepacia* genomovar III and the other two belonged to the new species *B. ambifaria* (see table). Many of the strains that show the greatest biocontrol potential belong to the recently proposed species *B. ambifaria*. One strain, *B. ambifaria* strain AMMD (which has not been registered by the EPA as a biopesticide), has been extensively researched. In addition to conferring excellent protection for seedling crops, treatment with *B. ambifaria* strain AMMD also significantly increases yield at harvest. Hence, a single biological control strategy can reduce the application of both chemical pesticides and fertilizers, which potentially confer an ecological risk.

Future commercial development. The contrast between the helpful and harmful traits of *B. cepacia* complex bacteria provides a legislative dilemma: how can the government ensure that commercial products containing *B. cepacia* complex are safe? In July 1999, in an attempt to resolve this dilemma, the EPA performed a risk assessment of biopesticide use that highlighted several areas in which further research was needed to understand the possible dangers posed by *B. cepacia* complex as well as other bacterial biocontrol agents related to or known to be human opportunistic pathogens. Areas that were determined to require further study included the fate of the bacteria after release and the factors involved in their virulence and pathogenicity (ability to cause disease). An EPA scientific advisory panel of outside experts urged caution on commercial applications of the *B. cepacia* complex, based in part on these findings. In August 2001, the EPA received a request from the Cystic Fibrosis Foundation that non-pesticide-related manufacturing, commercial distribution, use, and improper disposal of members of the *B. cepacia* complex be prohibited in the United States. The EPA denied this request, but proposed in January 2002 that commercial entities provide risk assessment information on each such *B. cepacia* complex product so that the EPA can review each on a case-by-case basis prior to the products' being marketed in the United States. The EPA has received comments on this regulatory action, and is deciding whether to finalize its decision to review such products.

Without further understanding of the biology, taxonomy, and pathogenicity of *B. cepacia* complex bacteria, it is unlikely that there will be significant commercial development of biopesticidal or bioremedial agents based on this microorganism. Elucidation of the complete genome sequence (genetic code) of several *Burkholderia* species, such as the human pathogens *B. cepacia* genomovar III and *B. pseudomallei* and the bioremediation strain *Burkholderia* species LB400 (taxonomic status currently unknown), will greatly enhance understanding of the genetics and evolution of these organisms. Combined with modern genetic tools, the genome sequence may enable the future identification of biotechnologically useful genes and the attenuation of pathogenic ones. Potentially safe biopesticidal and bioremedial strains may then be constructed using genetic modification.

For background information *see* BACTERIA; BIODEGRADATION; DRUG RESISTANCE; INDUSTRIAL BACTERIOLOGY; MEDICAL BACTERIOLOGY; OPPORTUNISTIC INFECTIONS; PESTICIDE in the McGraw-Hill Encyclopedia of Science & Technology.

Eshwar Mahenthiralingam; Philip Sayre

Bibliography. T. Coenye et al., Taxonomy and identification of the *Burkholderia cepacia* complex, *J. Clin. Microbiol.*, 39:3427–3436, 2001; E. Mahenthiralingam, A. Baldwin, and P. Vandamme, *Burkholderia cepacia* complex infections in patients with cystic fibrosis, *J. Med. Microbiol.*, 51:1–6, 2002; J. Parke and D. Gurian-Sherman, Diversity of the *Burkholderia cepacia* complex and implications for risk assessment of biological control strains, *Annu. Rev. Phytopathol.*, 39:225–258, 2001; R. Steffan et al., Field-scale evaluation of in situ bioaugmentation for remediation of chlorinated solvents in groundwater, *Environ. Sci. Technol.*, 33:2771–2781, 1999.

C-H activation

Petroleum and natural gas, two important energy resources, are both alkanes, C_nH_{2n+2}, having numerous C-H bonds. The conversion of these and related C-H bonds to other, more useful reactive functional groups is known as C-H activation. Conversion is particularly difficult because of the lack of reactivity of alkanes, as indicated by their older name, paraffins (Latin: low affinity).

Activation is a chemical reaction in which a bond, such as an alkane C-H bond, is broken, ideally in a selective way under mild conditions (low temperature and pressure). This normally leads to a functionalization step in which the C-H bond is converted to another chemical group such as C-OH. In C-H activation, metal catalysts are used to mediate the hydrocarbon conversion reactions.

Radical reactions. The earliest C-H activation reactions, dating from the work of H. S. H. Fenton in the late nineteenth century, used iron salts as the catalyst and hydrogen peroxide as the oxidant. In these reactions, a hydrogen atom is abstracted from the hydrocarbon, RH; and then the resulting radical intermediate, R·, reacts with oxygen from air. The role of the metal is to catalytically decompose the resulting peroxide, ROOH, to provide a continuous supply of reactive radicals, such as ·OH, capable of abstracting a hydrogen atom from the hydrocarbon by a chain reaction.

Such radical reactions tend to be both unselective and very inefficient. Improved Fenton chemistry has been developed in recent years, but the selectivity is still poor unless there is only one type of C-H bond that can be attacked. This is the case for *para*-dimethylbenzene, where the CH_3 groups have particularly weak C-H bonds and are preferentially attacked. Commercial processes use Fenton-like conditions that lead to terephthalic acid, an important component of polyester materials.

p-Dimethylbenzene

$+ 2H_2O$

Terephthalic acid

Superacid reactions. Another important reaction involves the abstraction of a hydrogen from the hydrocarbon using a very strong acid (proton source). Most acids are ineffective, but G. A. Olah (Nobel prize, 1994) found that exceptionally strong acids (superacids) could be formed by combining two acidic components, such as hydrofluoric acid (HF) and antimony pentafluoride (SbF_5). These react to give the superacid $HSbF_6$, capable of protonating alkanes. The proton is released after the reaction and so acts catalytically. Only a few such reactions are possible, at least on a commercial scale. These include cracking and reforming reactions that are carried out at high temperature and are therefore unselective. One application of this procedure causes linear, low-octane alkanes typical of petroleum to rearrange to highly branched, high-octane alkanes useful for gasoline. The acid used commercially is a solid superacid, such as an acid clay or zeolite, not $HSbF_6$.

Methane-to-methanol conversion. Only certain reactions are possible using radical and superacid pathways, however, and further methods are currently sought. One such reaction is the conversion of natural gas, largely methane (CH_4), to methanol (CH_3OH). The reaction of methane with air to give methanol would be an application of such a process which, if realized, would simplify the transport of natural gas from remote locations (methanol is easily transported as a liquid).

The first example of this type of process was Shilov chemistry dating from 1970–1980 in the Soviet Union. In this work, platinous salts were found to be capable of breaking alkane C-H bonds under relatively mild conditions (hot aqueous solution). At first,

isotopic substitution was seen (C-H → C-D), but with addition of an oxidizing agent the desired conversion of C-H to C-OH was indeed observed. Unfortunately, the only efficient oxidant found was a very expensive platinic salt, and the rates of reaction were very slow.

R. A. Periana at Catalytica Corporation made the next advance by showing how an inexpensive, regenerable oxidant, sulfuric acid, could be substituted for the platinic salt, and a more efficient platinum-based catalyst,

could be substituted for the simple platinous salt of the original Shilov system. In this work, methane was converted to methyl bisulfate, CH_3OSO_3H, an ester from which methanol can be obtained by hydrolysis. Although a great improvement over the original system, the Periana system was still not economic, so the general problem of direct, practical methane conversion to methanol remains unsolved.

Alkane functionalization. A variety of ML_n fragments, consisting of a metal, M, and its associated ligands, L_n, are capable of reaction with an alkane to give C-H bond breaking as shown in the first step of reaction (1). In principle, it should be possible

$$CH_4 + ML_n \xrightarrow[\text{activation step}]{} \underset{H}{\overset{CH_3}{\diagdown}}ML_n \xrightarrow[\text{functionalization step}]{\frac{1}{2}O_2} CH_3OH + ML_n \qquad (1)$$

to follow this up with a second step to give the functionalized alkane, but this has proved difficult in practice. R. G. Bergman showed as early as 1982 that (C_5Me_5)Ir(PMe_3), formed photochemically, is suitable for the first reaction, for example.

Other cases are known where the first step of reaction (1) is followed by a functionalization reaction. H. Felkin, R. H. Crabtree, and A. S. Goldman independently showed reactions of this type, where the intermediate alkyl hydride decomposes to give alkene and free H_2 or, in the presence of a second alkene as sacrificial oxidant, alkene and hydrogenated sacrificial oxidant [reaction (2)].

$$(2)$$

Y. Saito and M. Tanaka showed that the intermediate alkyl hydride can be trapped by carbon monoxide (CO) to give aldehyde RCHO as final product, and J. F. Hartwig trapped the alkyl with diborane derivatives to give alkyl boronic esters [reaction (2)]. In all of these cases, C-H activation preferentially occurs at the least hindered C-H bond, leading to products that are quite different from those formed in radical and acid pathways, where the most substituted and most hindered C-H bonds are most reactive. Hartwig converted alkanes to alkylboranes. In each case, the reaction requires the presence of an appropriate transition-metal complex as catalyst.

These research findings do not yet form the basis for any practical process but have the great merit of producing terminally functionalized products, much more valuable than the mixtures normally found from other routes.

Finally, enzymes are known that catalyze C-H activation reactions in vivo; for example, methane monooxygenase, a bacterial enzyme, converts methane to methanol.

For background information *see* ALKANE; CHEMICAL BONDING; COORDINATION CHEMISTRY; HYDROXIDE; LIGAND; ORGANIC CHEMISTRY; SUPERACID in the McGraw-Hill Encyclopedia of Science & Technology.

Robert H. Crabtree

Bibliography. R. H. Crabtree, Alkane C-H activation and functionalization with homogeneous transition metal catalysts: A century of progress—A new millennium in prospect, *J. Chem. Soc., Dalton Trans.*, 17:2437–2450, 2001; R. H. Crabtree, The organometallic chemistry of alkanes, *Chem. Rev.*, 85(4): 245–269, 1985; B. Meunier, *Biomimetic Oxidations Catalyzed by Transition Metal Complexes*, ICP, London, 2000; G. A. Olah and A. Molnar, *Hydrocarbon Chemistry*, Wiley, New York, 1995; A. E. Shilov and G. B. Shul'pin, *Activation and Catalytic Reactions of Saturated Hydrocarbons in the Presence of Metal Complexes*, Kluwer, Dordrecht, 2000.

Capability maturity modeling

Capability Maturity Models (CMM[R]) represent a recent step in the evolution of process improvement techniques that enable organizations to repeatably produce high-quality, complex, software-intensive systems faster and within expected costs. The foundations of this work include approaches to improved quality developed by W. Edwards Deming, Joseph Juran, Walter A. Shewart, and Philip B. Crosby, particularly Crosby's quality management maturity grid.

Model structure. CMMs are designed to describe discrete levels of improvement within process areas, measured against specific goals and generic goals. A process area is a group of related practices that are performed collectively to achieve a set of objectives. There are typically 15 to 25 process areas represented in a model, including requirements development, validation, configuration management, and project planning. Each process area has specific goals that describe what must be implemented to satisfy the purpose of the process area. Each specific goal has specific practices that describe the activities expected to result in achievement of the goal. For example, some specific goals of the project planning process area involve establishing estimates, developing a project plan, and obtaining commitment to the plan. The specific practices related to the "establishing estimates" goal involve estimating the scope of the project, establishing estimates of project attributes, defining project life cycle, and determining estimates of effort and cost. Although process areas depict behavior that should be exhibited in any organization, practices must be interpreted using in-depth knowledge of the model, the organization, the business environment, and the specific circumstances involved.

Generic goals apply to all process areas. Achievement of each of these goals in a process area signifies whether the implementation and institutionalization of each process area are effective, repeatable, and lasting. Each generic goal comprises specific generic practices. For example, the generic goal titled "institutionalize a quantitatively managed process" has two generic practices, "establish quality objectives" and "stabilize subprocess performance."

The model does not prejudge which processes are right for any organization or project. Instead, it establishes minimal criteria that processes must meet to be considered capable. A capable process is defined, documented, practiced, supported, maintained, controlled, verified, validated, measured, and able to be improved. Also, the model should allow interpretion and modification as needed to suit an organization's size or business objectives.

Representations. Capability Maturity Models have been architected in two representations, continuous and staged. They provide alternative approaches to process improvement that take advantage of the familiarity of users with either approach. The representations contain the same essential content but are organized differently.

Continuous representation is based on capability within a given process area—the range of expected results that can be achieved by following a process. A low-capability process is improvised and highly dependent on current practitioners; results are difficult to predict, and product functionality and quality are typically compromised to meet schedules. A high-capability process is well controlled, defined, continually improving, supported by measurement, and a basis for disciplined use of technology.

Continuous representation provides organizations with the flexibility to choose which processes to emphasize for improvement and how much to improve each process. Process improvement is measured in six capability levels: (0) incomplete, (1) performed, (2) managed, (3) defined, (4) quantitatively managed, and (5) optimizing. The levels relate to the achievement of specific and generic goals that apply to a process area. For example, an organization can reach capability level 2 of a process area when the specific and generic goals up through capability level 2 are achieved for the process area.

Continuous representation enables selection of the order of process improvement that best meets the organization's business objectives and that most mitigates risk. **Figure 1** illustrates the structure of continuous representation.

Staged representation is based on organizational maturity—the combined capabilities of a set of related processes. Thus, in a highly mature organization the set of organizational processes, taken as a whole, are of higher capability. Organizational improvement is measured in five maturity levels: (1) initial, (2) managed, (3) defined, (4) quantitatively managed, and (5) optimizing. The maturity levels are well-defined evolutionary plateaus on the path to becoming a mature organization. **Figure 2** provides a brief definition of each maturity level.

Staged representation has a recommended order for approaching process improvement, beginning with basic management practices and progressing along a proven path. The Capability Maturity Model for Software (SW-CMM), People Capability Maturity Model (P-CMM), and Capability Maturity Model for Software Acquisition (SA-CMM) use this structure. **Figure 3** illustrates the structure of the staged representation.

Generic practices are grouped by common features in the staged representation. "Commitment to perform" describes practices that relate to creating management policies and securing sponsorship. "Ability to perform" characterizes practices related to establishing and maintaining plans, resources, assigned responsibility and authority, and training. "Directing implementation" comprises measurement, control, and performance practices. "Verifying implementation" comprises practices that ensure implementation and compliance.

Model evolution. In 1987, the U.S. Air Force asked Carnegie Mellon University's Software Engineering Institute (SEI) to identify key practices that a contractor had to perform to deliver software-intensive systems reliably. By 1991, this tracking of practices had matured into the Capability Maturity Model for Software. The success of this model for one discipline led to similar efforts for other elements of the product development community. Interest in such models for systems engineering process improvement led to two models produced in 1994. These were the Software Engineering CMM, created by the Enterprise Process Improvement Collaboration (EPIC), and the Systems Engineering Capability and Assessment Method, created by the International Council on Systems Engineering (INCOSE). These two models were successfully merged into Electronic Industries Alliance (EIA) Interim Standard 731 in 1998 as a result of a collaborative effort of EIA, EPIC, and INCOSE. In 1996, a sister model to cover key practices in software acquisition was created, the Software Acquisition Capability Maturity Model. Concerns about preserving and enhancing the capabilities of developmental engineering staff led to the creation of the People Capability Maturity Model in 1997.

In 1997, work was underway at the Software Engineering Institute to produce an update to the SW-CMM, and also to produce a model that would

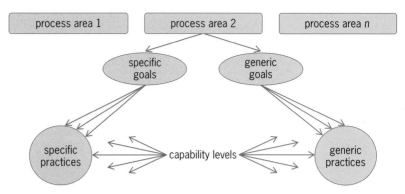

Fig. 1. Capability Maturity Models: the continuous representation.

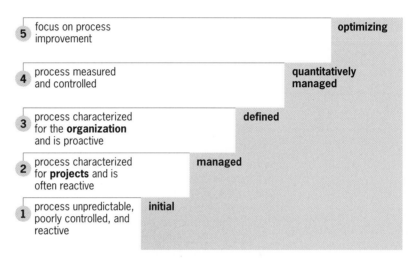

Fig. 2. Organizational maturity levels.

capture concurrent engineering practices in an Integrated Product Development CMM. The Institute's sponsor, the U.S. Department of Defense (DoD), determined that these efforts should be merged into an integrated model, to be called Capability Maturity Model Integration (CMMI). The feasibility of integrating a diverse set of maturity models had been demonstrated earlier that year by the Federal Aviation Administration (FAA), which had developed an integrated capability maturity model (FAA-iCMM V1.0). Due to the widespread focus on integrated product and process development (IPPD) by the DoD and industry, it was decided that the initial focus of the CMMI effort would be integration of systems engineering, software engineering, and IPPD. A more recent CMMI version added guidance for supplier sourcing. **Figure 4** depicts the evolution of the CMMI models.

CMMs in use. Several CMMs are now in widespread use, with some having achieved the status of de facto or recognized international standard, for the assessment and improvement of such areas as software engineering and acquisition practices, work force development practices, and systems security practices, among others.

SW-CMM. The Capability Maturity Model for Software is a model for judging the maturity of the

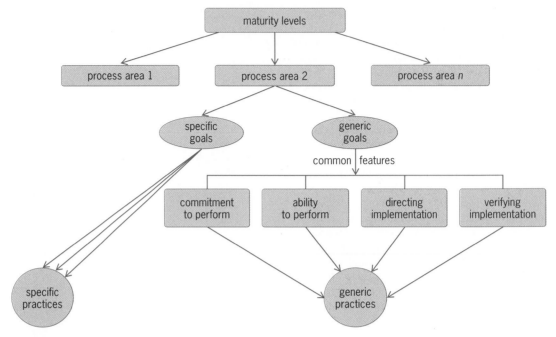

Fig. 3. Capability Maturity Models: the staged representation.

software processes of an organization and for identifying the key practices that are required to increase the maturity of these processes. Used worldwide, the SW-CMM has become a de facto standard for assessing and improving software processes.

SA-CMM. The Software Acquisition Capability Model is used for benchmarking and improving the software acquisition process. The model follows the same architecture as the SW-CMM, but with an emphasis on acquisition issues and the needs of individuals and groups who are planning and managing software acquisition efforts. For example, unique key process areas address contractor tracking and oversight, transition to support, and acquisition risk management.

P-CMM. The People Capability Maturity Model is a framework that helps organizations successfully address people issues. Based on the best current prac-

tices in fields such as human resources, knowledge management, and organizational development, the P-CMM helps organizations characterize the maturity of their work-force practices, establish a program of continuous work-force development, set priorities for improvement actions, integrate work-force development with process improvement, and establish a culture of excellence. Its five maturity levels establish successive foundations for continuously improving individual competencies, developing effective teams, motivating improved performance, and shaping the work force that the organization needs to accomplish its future business plans. By following the maturity framework, an organization can avoid introducing work-force practices that its employees are unprepared to implement effectively.

SSE-CMM. The Systems Security Engineering Capability Maturity Model describes the essential characteristics of an organization's security engineering process that must exist to ensure good security engineering. It is now an emerging international standard (ISO/IEC 21827). The model highlights the relationship between security engineering and systems engineering. It provides a way to measure and improve capability in applying security engineering principles and to address capability-based assurance. Unique process areas include administering security controls; assessing impact, security risk, threat, and vulnerability; and verifying and validating security.

FAA-iCMM. The Federal Aviation Administration developed the FAA-iCMM to increase the efficiency and effectiveness of process improvement by providing a single reference model that integrates engineering, management, and acquisition processes used in developing, managing, acquiring, and maintaining systems. The FAA-iCMM integrates all features and practices of three CMMs that were being used separately

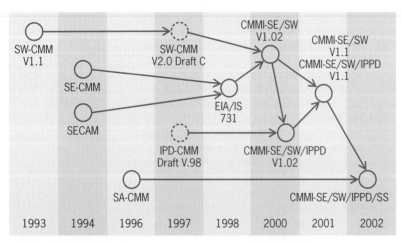

Fig. 4. CMMI model evolution.

in the FAA: the SE-CMM (V1.1), the SA-CMM (V1.01), and the SW-CMM (V1.1).

CMMI. The CMMI includes a common set of process areas that form the core of a model that integrates process improvement guidance for systems engineering, software engineering, and integrated product and process development. The resulting integrated capability models may be adapted to an organization's mission and business objectives. The CMMI Product Suite reduces the redundancy and complexity that can result from the use of separate multiple CMMs, thus improving the efficiency of and the return on investment for process improvement.

For background information *see* ENGINEERING DESIGN; REENGINEERING; SOFTWARE ENGINEERING; SYSTEM DESIGN EVALUATION; SYSTEMS ENGINEERING; SYSTEMS INTEGRATION in the McGraw-Hill Encyclopedia of Science & Technology.   Mike Phillips

Bibliography. D. Ahern, A. Clouse, and R. Turner, *CMMI^{SM} Distilled: A Practical Introduction to Integrated Process Improvement*, Addison-Wesley, Boston, 2001; P. B. Crosby, *The Eternally Successful Organization: The Art of Corporate Wellness*, Mentor Books, 1992; P. B. Crosby, *Quality Is Free*, McGraw-Hill, New York, 1979; J. M. Juran and A. B. Godfrey (eds.), *Juran's Quality Handbook*, McGraw-Hill, New York, 1998; Software Engineering Institute, Carnegie Mellon University, *The Capability Maturity Model®: Guidelines for Improving the Software Process*, ed. by M. C. Paulk et al., Addison-Wesley, Boston, 1995.

Capacitance tomography

Capacitance tomography is a relatively new imaging technique used to visualize the distribution of dielectric materials (that is, electrical insulators) for industrial applications. In the literature, it is often referred to as electrical capacitance tomography (ECT). In principle, ECT is similar to medical computerized tomography (CT), which is commonly used in hospitals for diagnostic purposes. However, there are some major differences between an industrial ECT system and a medical CT scanner (see **table**).

Major differences between an industrial ECT system and a medical CT scanner

	Medical CT scanner	Industrial ECT system
Subject to be imaged	"Static" patient	Dynamic process
Sensor	A single radiation source slowly rotating	Fixed electrodes
Sensing field	Hard-field (no distortion)	Soft-field (distorted by object)
Independent measurements	Many	Limited to a few tens
Imaging speed	A few minutes per image	Up to 100 frames per second
Image resolution	High	Moderate
Cost	Millions of dollars	Thousands of dollars

Electrical capacitance tomography is based on measuring changes in capacitance caused by the change in dielectric material distribution. Capacitance measurements are taken from a multielectrode sensor surrounding an industrial process vessel or pipeline. The cross-sectional distribution of permittivity (that is, electrical constant) is reconstructed from these measurements. The first ECT system was developed in the 1970s by the U.S. Department of Energy in Morgantown, West Virginia, to image the solid-particle distribution supported by up-flowing gas in fluidized beds. Since the late 1980s, ECT techniques have developed rapidly in Europe. The first real-time ECT system was developed at the University of Manchester Institute of Science and Technology (UMIST), United Kingdom, in 1991, based on a charge/discharge capacitance-measuring circuit and Transputers, a type of microprocessor for parallel data processing. This ECT system can collect image data from a 12-electrode sensor at 100 frames per second, and can display 32×32 pixel images at 25 frames per second when four Transputers are used.

Many sensing techniques have been used to develop industrial tomography systems, including nuclear magnetic resonance (NMR), x-ray, γ-ray, positron emission tomography (PET), optical, microwave, ultrasonic, capacitance, inductance, and resistance techniques. ECT has several advantages over other techniques. It is low-cost, has rapid response, and is nonintrusive and robust.

Sensor and system hardware. A typical ECT system consists of three main units: (1) a multielectrode sensor; (2) sensing electronics, that is, a data acquisition system including capacitance-measuring circuits; and (3) a computer for data acquisition and image reconstruction (**Fig. 1**).

A typical ECT sensor has 8 or 12 measurement electrodes. If the length of electrodes is fixed, more electrodes result in smaller capacitance, which may be hard to measure accurately. Fewer electrodes give fewer independent measurements, making image reconstruction more difficult. The measurement electrodes are usually mounted on the outside of an insulating (plastic or ceramic) pipe section, making the sensor both nonintrusive and noninvasive. An externally grounded screen prevents interference from external noise. Interelectrode screens are fitted between the electrodes to reduce the standing capacitance. The capacitance between each electrode pair is measured sequentially. Taking the eight-electrode sensor as an example, an excitation voltage is applied first to electrode 1, and the resultant charge signals on electrodes 2–8 are measured. Next, electrode 2 is energized and measurements are taken from electrodes 3–8, and so on, until finally the capacitance between electrodes 7 and 8 is measured. An eight-electrode sensor gives a total of 28 independent capacitance measurements. In general, an N-electrode sensor gives $N(N - 1)/2$ independent measurements.

Selecting the length of electrodes requires a trade-off between signal bandwidth and measurement

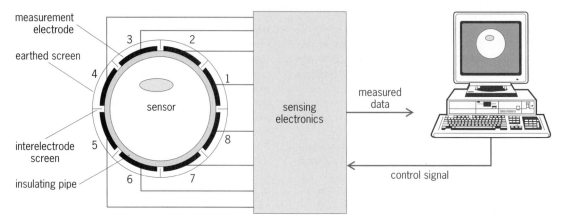

Fig. 1. Typical ECT system with an eight-electrode sensor.

uncertainty. Longer electrodes produce an average signal over a greater axial length. Shorter electrodes may result in capacitance that is too small to be measured accurately. Typically, the electrodes are 10 cm (4 in.) in length, and the interelectrode capacitance is in the range of 0.01–0.5 picofarad (1 pF = 1×10^{-12} F), depending on the electrode combinations. The change in capacitance due to variations in permittivity distribution is extremely small, typically in the range of 0.001–0.1 pF. Therefore, a highly sensitive capacitance measuring circuit has to be used.

While the interelectrode capacitance to be measured is small, the stray capacitance between a measurement electrode and the ground can be relatively large, typically 150 pF. Therefore, the capacitance-measuring circuits used in an ECT system must be stray-immune, that is, insensitive to stray capacitance. Three types of stray-immune capacitance measuring circuits/instruments have been used in ECT systems: (1) a charge/discharge circuit, (2) an AC-based circuit, and (3) an impedance analyzer.

The charge/discharge circuit uses complementary metal-oxide semiconductor (CMOS) switches to control its charge transfer process. The unknown capacitance is charged to a fixed voltage and then discharged to the ground. The charge and discharge currents, which are proportional to the unknown capacitance, are measured. Except for its stray-immunity, an advantage of this circuit is its low cost. Although it was used successfully in the first real-time ECT system, it has two major problems: (1) charge injection currents introduced by the CMOS switches interfere with the measurements, and (2) it is unable to measure true capacitance when conductive material is present.

A new ECT system has been developed that uses an AC-based circuit with direct digital synthesizer (DDS) signal generators, high-frequency (around 1 MHz) sine-wave excitation, and phase-sensitive demodulation (PSD). This circuit can measure both capacitance and loss-conductance by adjusting the reference phase. The DDS signal generators also enable different frequencies to be applied for spectroscopic measurement. Using this circuit, the ECT system showed an improved signal-to-noise ratio (SNR) by a factor of 4 and an increased data acquisition rate by 40%, compared with the previous charge/discharge system.

Since the standing capacitance is much larger than the changes in capacitance (which are used in image reconstruction), the standing capacitance must be offset so that these changes in capacitance can be measured accurately. To accommodate the large dynamic range of capacitance with different electrode combinations, programmable gain amplifiers (PGA) are used. These features have been implemented in both systems and make it possible to measure very small changes in capacitance over a large dynamic range.

For some industrial applications, even higher sensitivity and signal-to-noise ratio are required. To meet this need, an ECT system has been developed, using an impedance analyzer/LCR meter (L, inductance; C, capacitance; R, resistance). This system can provide six-digit readings with a resolution of 0.1 femtofarad (1 fF = 1×10^{-15} F). The disadvantage of this system is that the data acquisition rate is low, about 20 seconds per image.

Image reconstruction. For computation and display purposes, the imaging area is divided into many pixels, typically a 32 × 32 grid, giving about 800 pixels for a circular sensor. Reconstructing the cross-sectional images involves the forward problem and the inverse problem. The forward problem is how to determine the interelectrode capacitance of the sensor from the cross-sectional permittivity distribution, usually using a finite element software package. The inverse problem is how to determine the permittivity distribution from capacitance measurements. However, there are no explicit solutions to this inverse problem.

Finite element techniques are used to compute the capacitance of each electrode pair for a single element of dielectric material placed at each pixel in turn. This gives a sensitivity map for each electrode pair. For an eight-electrode sensor, there are 28 electrode pairs but initially only four different maps because of symmetry. Two typical sensitivity

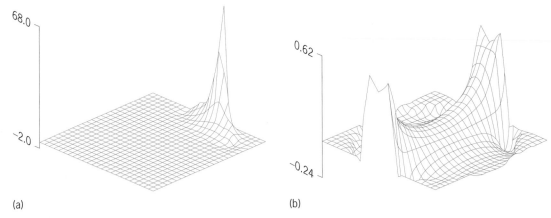

68.0

-2.0

(a)

0.62

-0.24

(b)

Fig. 2. Typical sensitivity maps for (a) an adjacent electrode pair and (b) an opposing electrode pair. The vertical scale is in femtofarads per unit of permittivity.

maps, for an adjacent electrode pair and an opposing electrode pair, show uneven sensitivity distributions (**Fig. 2**).

The most popular image reconstruction algorithm for ECT is linear back-projection (LBP), which was initially developed for x-ray tomography. Linear back-projection uses the sensitivity maps to reconstruct images by linearly superimposing all the capacitance measurements together, using the appropriate sensitivity maps as weighting factors. This is a single-step or noniterative method. It is simple and fast but can produce only low-quality images because of the nonlinear relationship between capacitance and permittivity.

To deal with the nonlinearity, various iterative algorithms have been developed for ECT. The basic principles of all these iterative algorithms are the same. A first estimate of the image is reconstructed using a simple algorithm, for example, linear back-projection. The interelectrode capacitances are computed from the current image, by solving the forward problem, and then compared with the measured capacitances. The difference is used to modify the image in order to reduce the difference. This process is repeated until the difference is acceptably small. It has been confirmed that iterative algorithms can produce high-quality images. However, they require intensive computation, and the iterative process is time-consuming. At present, iterative algorithms can be used only for off-line analysis. The Landweber iteration method was originally designed for solving classical ill-posed mathematical problems. It now has been used successfully as an image reconstruction algorithm for ECT. Images of two plastic rods in air reconstructed using linear back-projection and Landweber iteration, respectively, are shown in **Fig. 3**. Obviously, the Landweber iterative algorithm produces much better images than linear back-projection in terms of image size, shape, and position.

Industrial applications. ECT has been used successfully in a number of industrial research investigations, including the measurement of gas/oil flows in oil pipelines, gas/solids flows in pneumatic conveyors, gas/solids distribution in fluidized beds, flame combustion in engine chambers, dust explosion processes, water hammer, and gas/liquid droplets distribution in gas pipelines. The cross-sectional images produced by ECT systems provide valuable information for process visualization and mathematical model verification and offer the possibility of advanced control systems.

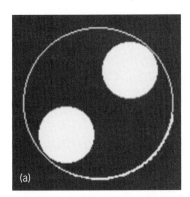 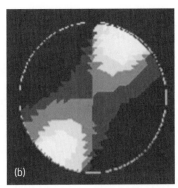 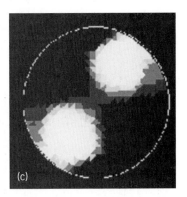

(a)   (b)   (c)

Fig. 3. Reconstructed images of two plastic rods in air: (a) true distribution, (b) by linear back-projection, and (c) by Landweber iteration. White = higher permittivity material, black = lower permittivity material.

Fig. 4. ECT and ultrasonic tomography sensors in an oil pipeline to measure gas/oil/water three-component flows.

Pipeline flows. In the oil industry, multicomponent flow measurement is notoriously difficult. One problem is that existing flow meters are flow-regime-dependent. ECT can provide cross-sectional images, from which concentrations can be derived and flow regimes identified. Therefore, ECT offers a unique opportunity for developing a new type of multicomponent flow meter for use in the oil industry. ECT has been used successfully to measure gas/oil two-component flows in oil pipelines. The first attempt to measure oil/gas/water three-component flows was made using a combination of ECT and ultrasonic tomography (**Fig. 4**). However, some problems remain to be solved, such as the effect of salt content on the capacitance measurements.

Pneumatic conveyors. Pneumatic conveyors are commonly used in the process, food, and power industries to transport bulk or solids materials, such as plastic beads, grains, flour, cement, and coal. Because existing transducers provide little information on solids distribution and flow regime, almost all pneumatic conveying systems are currently "free-running," without flow condition control. To avoid the risk of blockage, they are operated in conservative conditions, involving for example low solids feeding rates and high gas velocities, and hence result in low transportation efficiency, high-energy con-

sumption, and high material and pipeline attrition. ECT has been used successfully to visualize gas/solids flows in pneumatic conveyors for monitoring purposes. The next task is to use tomographic imaging for control, aiming to optimize the running conditions.

Fluidized beds. Fluidized beds are used in the chemical and process industries for grain drying, catalytic cracking, coal combustion, and other heat and mass transfer purposes. Ideally, fluidized beds provide a uniform lift of solids or fluids. However, it is difficult to know exactly what is happening inside these complicated processes because currently no instruments can provide sufficient internal information. ECT is regarded as the most suitable and powerful tool for visualizing the internal behavior of fluidized beds. The cross-sectional images have provided unique and valuable information on the spatial and temporal distribution of gases and solids (**Fig. 5**).

Internal combustion engine. To optimize the design and operation of internal combustion engines, that is, to maximize combustion efficiency and minimize environmental pollution, it is necessary to have precise knowledge of the combustion process inside the engine chambers. ECT has been used to image the combustion flames inside a model engine chamber. A six-electrode sensor was used because of the limited space inside the engine chamber. Preliminary experimental results show that the flame development process can be visualized clearly. A problem similar to combustion flame is to visualize dust explosion (resulting in a confined space from the ignition of fine particles in air), especially the propagation of the flame front. This research will improve the understanding of these processes and facilitate accurate risk assessments.

Water hammer. A water hammer is caused by transient cavitation, that is, gas voids in water, which is formed when the pressure in a water pipeline is suddenly changed. It is important to understand how water hammer develops and how to prevent its happening, because water hammer can damage pipelines. Many mathematical models have been developed to analyze the phenomenon, but a lack of suitable instrumentation makes it difficult to verify these models. ECT has been used successfully to image water hammer, showing the transient process of growth and collapse of gas voids. This research

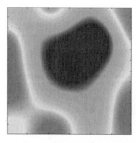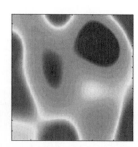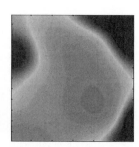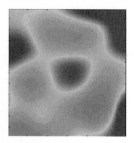

Fig. 5. Reconstructed images of gas/solids distribution in a square circulating fluidized bed in 10-millisecond intervals.

may benefit pumping stations, hydroelectric plants, and nuclear reactors in the power industry.

Liquid component visualization. In the gas industry, it is necessary to separate the liquid components, such as water and hydrocarbons, from the gas streams. An innovative type of separator based on hydrocyclone principles has been designed by a gas/oil company. Computational fluid dynamics (CFD) models have been developed to assist in the design. ECT has been used to investigate the behavior of this type of separator and to verify the computational fluid dynamics models. It has been shown experimentally that liquid droplets distributions of around 100 parts per million (ppm) can be visualized in gas flows, offering the possibility for further development in field operation and control of separators for enhanced separation efficiency.

Outlook. Capacitance tomography is arguably the most developed industrial tomography technique, and further improvements are expected in the near future. For example, iterative algorithms implemented with parallel data processor arrays will enable real-time iterative image reconstruction, and improved circuit design should increase data acquisition rate to 1000 frames per second with a 12-electrode sensor, making investigations of high-speed phenomena possible.

For background information *see* CAPACITANCE; CAPACITANCE MEASUREMENT; COMPUTERIZED TOMOGRAPHY; DIELECTRIC MATERIALS; FINITE ELEMENT METHOD; FLUIDIZATION; PERMITTIVITY in the McGraw-Hill Encyclopedia of Science & Technology.
W. Q. Yang

Bibliography. M. S. Beck et al., Principles and industrial applications of electrical capacitance tomography, *Measurement + Control*, 30:197–200, 1997; T. Dyakowski et al., Applications of electrical capacitance tomography for gas-solids and liquid-solids flow: A review, *Powder Technol.*, 112:174–192, 2000; W. Q. Yang et al., Electrical capacitance tomography from design to applications, *Measurement + Control*, 28:261–266, 1995; W. Q. Yang and L. H. Peng, Image reconstruction algorithms for electrical capacitance tomography (to be published as a Review Article), *Meas. Sci. Technol.*, 2002; W. Q. Yang and T. A. York, New AC-based capacitance tomography system, *IEE Proc. Sci. Meas. Technol.*, 146:47–53, 1999; T. York, Status of electrical tomography in industrial applications, *J. Electr. Imaging*, 10:608–619, 2001.

Carbon isotope discrimination measurement

Plant scientists use carbon isotope discrimination (Δ) to express the relative abundances in plant carbon of the isotopes carbon-12 (^{12}C) and carbon-13 (^{13}C). These stable isotopes are present in carbon dioxide (CO_2) in ambient air. They are incorporated by photosynthetic CO_2 assimilation into plant organic matter, but the two isotopes do not appear in plants in the same proportions as in the air. Carbon isotope discrimination by plants has been studied extensively in agricultural and native species (such as wheat, rice, and crested wheatgrass), often together with plant water-use efficiency and yield.

Drought stress causes yield losses in agriculture throughout the world. Although water-use efficiency has long been known to vary among species and cultivars, breeders have been unable to capitalize on the variability because they have no tool to identify individuals that use water efficiently. For theoretical reasons that have now been supported by experimental verification, Δ has gained attention as a tool for improving the water-use efficiency of C_3 crops. [In general, C_3, C_4, and CAM (crassulacean acid metabolism) plants differ in their use of CO_2 in their photosynthetic pathways. Most crops are C_3 plants; C_4 crops include tropical grasses such as corn, sorghum, and sugarcane; and CAM plants include succulents such as pineapple.]

Determination. The procedure for determining the $^{13}C/^{12}C$ ratio, R, consists of grinding a dry plant sample, typically a few leaves, to a powder, combusting the powder, and releasing the produced purified CO_2 into an isotope ratio mass spectrometer. The R value is converted to a value of carbon isotope composition, $\delta^{13}C$, as shown in Eq. (1). R_{sample} and $R_{standard}$

$$\delta^{13}C = \left(\frac{R_{sample}}{R_{standard}} - 1 \right) \times 1000 \qquad (1)$$

are the $^{13}C/^{12}C$ molar ratios of a plant sample and a

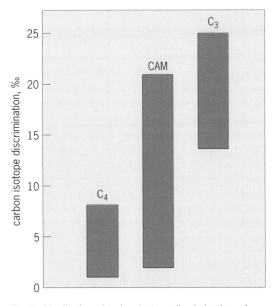

Fig. 1. Distribution of carbon isotope discrimination values among plants. These values are influenced by genetic as well as environmental factors. The large difference between C_3 and C_4 plants reflects the difference in isotope fractionation between the initial photosynthetic carboxylases in the two plant groups, Rubisco and PEP-carboxylase, respectively. Obligate CAM plants also use PEP-carboxylase as the initial carboxylase and have discrimination values as low as C_4 plants. Facultative CAM plants mix the CAM and C_3 metabolisms, and their discrimination values can be indistinguishable from those of C_3 plants.

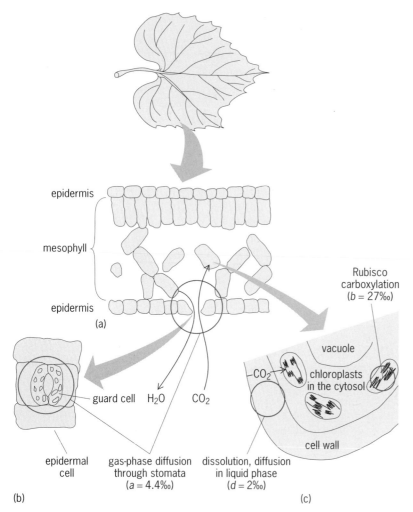

Fig. 2. Fractionation of carbon isotopes at the leaf of a C₃ plant exchanging CO_2 and water vapor with the air surrounding it. (*a*) Schematic cross section of the leaf. (*b*) CO_2 diffuses from the outside air through the stomata and (*c*) into the chloroplasts of the mesophyll cells. The major carbon isotope fractionation occurs in the carboxylation process catalyzed by Rubisco inside the chloroplasts. Fractionation also occurs in the gas-phase diffusion of CO_2 from the outside air to the mesophyll cell wall, and in dissolution of CO_2 in the water of the cell wall and the subsequent liquid-phase diffusion into the chloroplasts. Water vapor diffuses in the opposite direction to CO_2 from the point of evaporation at the mesophyll cell wall, through the stomata, and into the air around the leaf.

standard, respectively. Carbon dioxide in normal air has a $\delta^{13}C_{air}$ value of -8.0 parts per thousand (‰) relative to the common (PeeDee-carbonate) standard. It has become the norm to further convert $\delta^{13}C$ into Δ as shown in Eq. (2).

$$\Delta = \frac{\delta^{13}C_{air} - \delta^{13}C_{sample}}{1 + \delta^{13}C_{sample}/1000} \qquad (2)$$

Major plant groups. Mass spectrometers became available before the mid-1900s and quickly found use among geochemists. Their work inspired determination of $^{13}C/^{12}C$ ratios of plants collected around the world and sometimes stored dry for long periods in herbaria. It became clear that the isotope ratio of plant tissues is depleted in ^{13}C compared to CO_2 in the air, and that the isotope ratio varies among plants by about 20‰ on the Δ scale (**Fig. 1**). Moreover, many plants native to hot and dry habitats tended to have lower Δ than plants from cool and humid environments. The explanation became

clear many years later when it was found that plants belong to one of three groups, each group with a distinctly different photosynthetic pathway. Plants with the C₃ pathway use Rubisco (ribulose bisphosphate carboxylase-oxygenase) as the single photosynthetic carboxylase. They dominate in humid and often mild climates and have high Δ. C₄ plants contain Rubisco in the bundle sheath cells, deep in the leaf, but the initial carboxylation is catalyzed by PEP-carboxylase in the mesophyll, closer to the leaf surface. These plants abound in dry and hot climates and have low Δ. Obligate CAM plants first fix CO_2 at night by PEP-carboxylase and release the fixed CO_2 the following day for immediate refixation by Rubisco. These plants have low Δ. Facultative CAM plants mix in with the CAM metabolism various amounts of initial Rubisco carboxylation; that is, they operate partly as C₃ plants and they have high Δ. The general theory discussed below linking to water-use efficiency applies only to plants with Rubisco as the initial carboxylase, that is, to C₃ plants. (The initial carboxylation in C₄ and CAM plants is catalyzed by PEP-carboxylase that has small isotope fractionation.)

C₃ plants. By the end of the 1960s, it had been established that CO_2 uptake and water loss are coupled at the leaf level. It had also been suggested that carbon isotope fractionation in plants has a diffusion component and a mesophyll-biochemistry component. Soon it was pondered that Δ might be linked to CO_2 fixation and water loss. The seminal model linking Δ to leaf gas exchange, presented by G. D. Farquhar et al. in 1982, remains central to carbon isotope work in plant sciences today.

Of every 100 CO_2 molecules in the air, 99 are $^{12}CO_2$ and one is the heavier $^{13}CO_2$. Due primarily to the difference in atomic mass, several component processes of photosynthesis fractionate the two isotopes as shown in Eq. (3) and **Fig. 2**. The largest fraction-

$$\Delta = a - d + (b - c) \times \frac{c_i}{c_a} \qquad (3)$$

ation (b, 27‰) results from Rubisco carboxylation. This value has been calculated from gas-exchange measurements on leaves, although purified Rubisco has given a slightly greater value. Gas-phase diffusion of CO_2 from the air around the leaf, through the stomata, and into the leaf interior causes further fractionation (a, 4.4‰). Equation (3) also includes a fractionation term (d, ~2‰) that lumps together effects of respiration, dissolution of CO_2 in the water of the cell wall, and liquid-phase diffusion to the site of carboxylation inside the chloroplast. Finally, Δ is affected by c_i/c_a, that is, the ratio of the CO_2 concentrations in the intercellular air spaces of the leaves (c_i) and the air surrounding them (c_a). Among C₃ plants, c_i/c_a is typically close to 0.7 ($c_i = 260$ μmol mol^{-1}), which by Eq. (3) gives $\Delta = 18$‰. This agrees with published Δ values for C₃ plants that range about 14–27‰.

Water-use efficiency. Rates of leaf gas exchange are governed by concentration gradients and the resistances that gas molecules encounter when diffusing between the leaf interior and the outside air. The leaf resistance is normally dominated by the stomatal resistance, but at low wind speed the boundary layer resistance becomes substantial. Equations (4) and (5) describe the rates of photosynthesis, A, and

$$A = \frac{c_a - c_i}{1.6 \times r} \qquad (4)$$

$$E = \frac{e_i - e_a}{r} \qquad (5)$$

respiration, E, in terms of concentration gradients and resistances. Here e_a and e_i are the water vapor concentration in the outside air and the intercellular air spaces, respectively, and r is the leaf resistance to water vapor. Resistance for CO_2 is 1.6 times larger than the resistance for water vapor. By dividing A by E, Eq. (6) is obtained for the instantaneous leaf

$$WUE_{leaf} = \frac{A}{E} = \frac{c_a \times (1 - c_i/c_a)}{1.6 \times (e_i - e_a)} \qquad (6)$$

water-use efficiency, WUE_{leaf}, also called the leaf transpiration efficiency. WUE_{leaf} can be scaled up to long-term, whole-plant water-use efficiency, WUE_{plant}, as shown in Eq. (7), by including two terms that reduce

$$WUE_{plant} = \frac{A}{E} = \frac{(1 - \phi_a) \times c_a \times (1 - c_i/c_a)}{1.6 \times (1 + \phi_w) \times (e_i - e_a)} \qquad (7)$$

the efficiency of water use by the plant below that of the leaf. Here, ϕ_c refers to the fraction of the daily net photosynthetic carbon gain that is lost by leaf respiration at night and respiration of nonphotosynthetic plant parts, and ϕ_w refers to the proportion of the daily water loss that is not in exchange for CO_2. Some water is lost through imperfectly closed stomata and the cuticle at night, for example, and nonphotosynthetic plant parts also lose water. Equation (7) shows that WUE_{plant} increases when c_i decreases. The reason for low c_i could be either large stomatal resistance obstructing entry of CO_2 into the leaf, or large capacity of photosynthesis in the mesophyll achieving a great draw-down of the leaf internal CO_2 concentration. While both mechanisms would increase WUE_{plant}, they would have opposite effects on the rate by which photosynthate (plant carbohydrate) is produced.

Water-use efficiency in C₃ plants. Equations (3), (6), and (7) show that WUE_{leaf} and WUE_{plant} are linked to Δ by a common dependence on c_i/c_a. By combining Eqs. (3) and (7), Eq. (8) is obtained that describes

$$WUE_{plant} = \frac{(1 - \phi_c) \times c_a \times (b - d - \Delta)}{1.6 \times (1 + \phi_w) \times (b - a) \times (e_i - e_a)} \qquad (8)$$

the relationship between WUE_{plant} and Δ. WUE_{plant} is dependent on $e_i - e_a$. Therefore, Δ will be a good measure of differences in WUE_{plant} among plants only if they have the same $e_i - e_a$. This condition is usually not met unless the plants are grown in the same location at the same time or in growth chambers with very precise environmental control. As the terms a,

b, and d relate to enzyme-kinetic and physical properties that are essentially stable, WUE_{plant} should vary in concert with Δ as long as ϕ_c and ϕ_w are reasonably similar among the plants observed. The value of Δ is a productivity-weighted measure of WUE_{plant} over time of growth rather than a point measurement.

Applications. The expectation from Eq. (8) that WUE_{plant} of C₃ plants should be negatively correlated with Δ has now been verified in native as well as agricultural plants. The relationship has held also when WUE_{plant} is multiplied by the harvest index, that is, the proportion of harvestable yield relative to total biomass. The heritability of Δ appears to be sufficiently large to be useful in breeding. However, biomass and yield are not always negatively correlated with Δ, that is, positively correlated with WUE_{plant}. In general, the correlation with Δ has been found to be negative in water-deficient environments but not usually under well-watered conditions. This suggests that efficient water use offers a growth advantage when low water availability causes the growth rate to be slow, but when water is plentiful those plants that use much water and grow fast appear to have a growth advantage. These plants are generally not efficient water users, however. Isotope discrimination should thus be most suitable for improving crops in dry environments.

For background information *see* CARBON; ISOTOPE; LEAF; MASS SPECTROMETRY; ORGANIC GEOCHEMISTRY; PHOTOSYNTHESIS; PHYSIOLOGICAL ECOLOGY (PLANT); PLANT METABOLISM; PLANT RESPIRATION in the McGraw-Hill Encyclopedia of Science & Technology.   Bjorn Martin

Bibliography. A. G. Condon et al., Improving intrinsic water-use efficiency and crop yield, *Crop Sci.*, 42:122–131, 2002; J. R. Ehleringer et al. (eds.), *Stable Isotopes and Plant Carbon-Water Relations*, Academic Press, San Diego, 1993; G. D. Farquhar et al., On the relationship between carbon isotope discrimination and the intercellular carbon dioxide concentration in leaves, *Aust. J. Plant Physiol.*, 9:121–137, 1982; G. J. Rebetzke et al., Selection for reduced carbon isotope discrimination increases aerial biomass and grain yield of rainfed bread wheat, *Crop Sci.*, 42:739–745, 2002.

Ceramic whiskers

Whiskers are elongated single crystals, typically having cross-sectional diameters of 0.1–10 micrometers and lengths of 10–1000 μm. Because they are single crystals, which ideally contain very few dislocations and the same crystallographic orientation throughout, their strength and Young's modulus (stiffness) is expected to be very high; their values do, in fact, approach those predicted from bond strength calculations. Due to their hardness and strength, these whiskers are highly interesting as reinforcing materials in ceramics.

When ceramic materials (compacts or powders) are prepared under conditions close to equilibrium, the product formed tends to have as small area-to-volume ratio as possible (spherically shaped particles). Ceramic whiskers, however, have a nonequilibrium shape (elongated) and must be prepared under nonequilibrium conditions. As a result, a cylindrical whisker with a diameter of 1 μm and a length of 10 μm will have a greater area-to-volume ratio ($\sim$4.2 μm^{-1}) than a sphere of the same amount of material, which would have an area-to-volume ratio of $\sim$2.4 μm^{-1}.

Silicon carbide (SiC) whiskers are commercially available on a large scale and are mainly used as a reinforcing material, for example, in high-performance ceramics such as those used in cutting tools for metal machining, as well as in other wear-resistant applications that need improved toughness and resistance to thermal crack formation. The whiskers reinforce the material by forming crack-deflecting interfaces.

A large number of new whisker materials have been produced by various synthetic methods. The three main reaction mechanism are (1) precipitation from a melt, called the liquid-solid (LS) method; (2) vapor-phase transport of one or more of the whisker constituents to a solid surface from which the whiskers grow, called the vapor-solid (VS) method; and (3) vapor-phase transport of one or more of the whisker constituents to a metal catalyst droplet where the components decompose and dissolve, supersaturating the droplet, whereupon a whisker grows out from the surface, called the vapor-liquid-solid (VLS) method. Chemical vapor deposition, a process in which a thin solid film grows on a crystalline substrate as the result of a thermochemical vapor-phase reaction, is a VLS process that is frequently used for exploring new whisker phases. Another mechanism, namely carbothermal reduction (CTR) in combination with the VLS process, is most commonly used for large-scale production of SiC whiskers. The starting material in this case is often rice husks, which naturally contain silicon dioxide (SiO$_2$), organic material as the precursor for carbon (C), and small amounts of iron (Fe) as the catalyst. The milled husks are stepwise heated to 1500–1600°C (2700–2900°F)—below 1000°C (1800°F) in a carbon monoxide (CO) atmosphere, and above 1000°C in nitrogen or ammonia. The overall reaction is a carbothermal reduction process in which both whiskers and particles are formed. Wet processes are used to separate the whiskers from the particles, and excess carbon is removed by oxidation. SiC whiskers can also be formed from a precursor mixture consisting of SiO$_2$, excess carbon, and a catalyst metal (for example, iron).

In order to optimize the mechanical properties of a whisker-reinforced ceramic, the coefficient of thermal expansion and the chemical properties of the whiskers need to be matched to the corresponding properties of the matrix material. In this context, whiskers having the general composition Me$_{1-x}$Me$'_x$C$_{1-y}$N$_y$ are of interest, where Me and Me$'$ are different transition metals, C is carbon, and N

is nitrogen. The following examples describe the preparation of ceramic whiskers, especially those of transition-metal carbides and carbonitrides, using a carbothermal vapor-liquid-solid process.

CTR-VLS growth mechanism. The synthesis of tantalum carbide (TaC) whiskers is an example where the carbothermal vapor-liquid-solid (CTR-VLS) growth mechanism has proved to be successful. The VLS growth mechanism involves vapor-phase transport of one or more reacting species to a droplet of a metal catalyst in contact with carbon, where they are decomposed. The whisker components (Ta and C) then dissolve in the catalyst, forming a eutectic alloy, and the desired whiskers grow out from the droplet. The VLS mechanism is operative only at temperatures above the melting temperature of the catalyst (that is, the eutectic temperature), which is therefore the lower temperature limit for the whisker synthesis. Nickel has proved to be a good catalyst for TaC. For successful whisker growth, the appropriate gas species have to be formed and transported to the catalyst at a sufficient rate.

The overall reaction mechanism is a straightforward carbothermal reduction of tantalum pentoxide (Ta$_2$O$_5$) [reaction (6) and **Fig. 1a**]. The reactions that actually take place are much more difficult to study. A principal requirement for VLS growth is that the

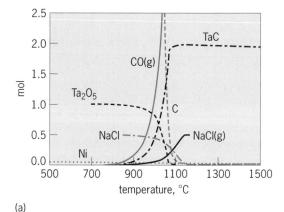

(a)

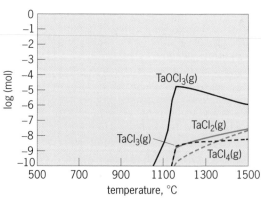

(b)

Fig. 1. Equilibrium calculations showing (*a*) carbothermal reduction of Ta$_2$O$_5$ to TaC; and (*b*) formation of gaseous Ta oxochlorides and chlorides from a starting mixture of 1 mol Ta$_2$O$_5$ + 7 mol C + 0.5 mol NaCl + 0.05 mol Ni.

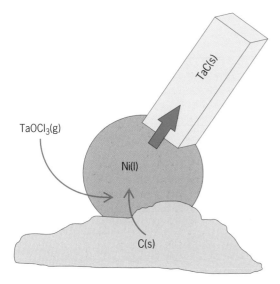

Fig. 2. Simplified sketch of the whisker growth mechanism. Ta oxochlorides are transported in the gas phase to the metal catalyst droplet, which becomes supersaturated and precipitates the TaC whisker.

carbothermal reduction process should be thermodynamically possible, yet kinetically slowed.

In the synthesis, the starting materials typically used are (1) carbon in the form of carbon black, containing a large amount of volatile matter; (2) Ta_2O_5; (3) nickel (Ni) which acts as a catalyst and is able to dissolve both C and Ta; (4) sodium chloride (NaCl) which is partly decomposed to Na(g) and Cl(g) at the reaction temperature (1200–1300°C; 2200–2300°F). The reactions take place in an inert atmosphere (such as argon). Equilibrium calculations have shown that Ta is mainly transported as tantalum oxochloride gas [$TaOCl_3$(g); Fig. 1*b*]. Reactions (1)–(7) or very similar ones are found to represent the actual mechanism in a flowing argon atmosphere, using Cl as the Ta-volatilizing element.

The synthesis begins by forming the Ta-containing gas species [chlorine is mainly present as Cl(g) at the high reaction temperature when NaCl is used as the Cl source].

$$NaCl(l) \longrightarrow Na(g) + Cl(g) \qquad (1)$$

$$Ta_2O_5(s) + 6Cl(g) + 3C(s) \longrightarrow 2TaOCl_3(g) + 3CO(g) \quad (2)$$

The Ta oxochloride must be reduced at the surface of the Ni catalyst (Ni-C-Ta denotes that C and Ta are dissolved in the Ni catalyst).

$$Ni(l) + C(s) \longrightarrow Ni\text{-}C(l) \qquad (3)$$

$$TaOCl_3(g) + C(s) + Ni\text{-}C(l) \longrightarrow$$

$$Ni\text{-}Ta\text{-}C(l) + CO(g) + 3Cl(g) \quad (4)$$

$$Ni\text{-}Ta\text{-}C(l) \longrightarrow TaC(s) + Ni(l) \qquad (5)$$

When the catalyst droplet has become supersaturated, a whisker may precipitate. At the same time, a continuous supply of gas species are transported to the catalyst droplet, such that there is a continuous driving force for whisker formation (**Fig. 2**).

$$Ta_2O_5 + 7C(s) \longrightarrow 2TaC(s) \qquad (6)$$

When all carbon in contact with the catalyst droplet has been consumed, the whisker growth will terminate and the droplet may react with Cl(g). Nickel is transported and recycled by reacting with chlorine gas to form $NiCl_2$(g) [**Fig. 3**].

$$Ni(l) + 2Cl(g) \longrightarrow NiCl_2(g) \qquad (7)$$

A Ni-C alloy can form again when $NiCl_2$(g) makes contact with a new carbon particle. Nickel can be recycled in this way several times during the synthesis.

The properties of the starting materials (for example, their particle size), the procedure for mixing the precursor materials, and the preparative conditions applied are of great importance for obtaining the maximum yield of whiskers. The process described above can give whiskers in a yield of 75–90 vol %, with the remainder of the product being TaC particles (**Fig. 4**). If the heating rate is too low, TaC

Fig. 3. Tunneling electron micrograph showing a whisker terminated with a nickel catalyst droplet. The droplet has started to react with Cl(g), and a part of it has been transported away.

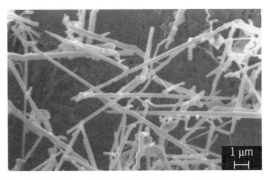

Fig. 4. Tantalum carbide (TaC) whiskers synthesized via the VLS growth mechanism in an estimated yield of 75–90 vol %, and the reminder as TaC particles.

particles will form before the catalyst is activated, resulting in a poor whisker yield. A heating rate of at least $300°C/h$ ($570°F/h$) is required to prevent excessive particle formation. Optimizing the synthesis temperature is a balancing act; it must be high enough to activate the catalyst and allow the formation of Ta oxochlorides. If it is too high, the whiskers will be shorter, and more particulate TaC will form via direct carbothermal reduction of Ta_2O_5. In addition, too high a temperature will cause more Ta oxochloride to form than can be consumed by the catalyst, which implies that this excess will be transported out of the reactor chamber and will thus be removed from the VLS process. The formation rate of Ta oxochlorides at the synthesis temperature depends largely on the Ta_2O_5 particle size. Gas exchange between the reactor and the furnace chamber is necessary in order to remove product gases such as $CO(g)$, $Na(g)$, $Cl(g)$, and volatiles from the carbon source, as well as to allow an inflow of nitrogen or argon. The gas flow rate must not be too high, or the Ta oxochlorides will be flushed from the reaction chamber before they react with the catalyst.

CTR-VLS process for other ceramic whiskers. The CTR-VLS process can be applied also to other types of whiskers by selecting proper starting materials, synthesis temperature, and so on. Titanium carbide (TiC) and niobium carbide (NbC) whiskers can be synthesized starting with the oxides TiO_2 or Nb_2O_5, respectively. In addition, whiskers have been synthesized for (Ti,Ta)C and (Ti,Ta,Nb)C, starting with the oxides Ta_2O_5, TiO_2, and Nb_2O_5. This extension of the CTR-VLS process is of great interest because it provides the possibility of tailoring the coefficient of thermal expansion of the whiskers by varying their chemical composition.

Carbonitrides, for example, Ti(C,N) and (Ti,Ta, Nb)-C,N, can be obtained by performing the synthesis in nitrogen gas. Nitrogen can be taken up either by first dissolving it in the catalyst metal, which then precipitates the carbonitride directly, or by an exchange reaction with carbon in the carbide compound initially formed.

Titanium boride (TiB_2) whiskers have been synthesized by combining TiO_2 and B_2O_3 in the reaction mixture. For this compound, the overall reaction (8)

$$TiO_2 + B_2O_3 + 5C \longrightarrow TiB_2 + 5CO(g) \qquad (8)$$

involves carbothermal reduction of two oxides.

In this synthesis, the gaseous species are formed by reactions (9) and (10), according to equilibrium calculations.

$$TiO_2(s) + 2C(s) + 3Cl(g) \longrightarrow TiCl_3(g) + 2CO(g) \qquad (9)$$

$$B_2O_3(s) + C(s) + 2Cl(g) \longrightarrow 2BOCl(g) + CO(g) \qquad (10)$$

The same process has also yielded boron carbide (B_4C) whiskers, starting with B_2O_3, C, NaCl, and a catalyst metal (nickel or cobalt).

For background information *see* CERAMICS; COMPOSITE MATERIAL; SILICON; SINGLE CRYSTAL; TANTA-LUM; VAPOR DEPOSITION; YOUNG'S MODULUS in the McGraw-Hill Encyclopedia of Science & Technology.

Mats Johnsson; Mats Nygren

Bibliography. D. Belitskus, Fiber and whisker reinforced ceramics for structural applications, Marcel Dekker, New York, 1993; M. Carlsson, M. Johnsson, and M. Nygren, Synthesis and characterisation of $Ta_{0.33}Ti_{0.33}Nb_{0.33}C_xN_{1-x}$ whiskers, *J. Amer. Ceram. Soc.*, 82:1969–1976, 1999; J.-G. Lee and I. B. Cutler, Formation of silicon carbide from rice hulls, *Amer. Ceram. Soc. Bull.*, 54:195–198, 1975; M. Johnsson and M. Nygren, Carbothermal synthesis of TaC whiskers via a vapor-liquid-solid growth mechanism, *J. Mater. Res.*, 12:2419–2427, 1997.

Circadian clock (plants)

Circadian systems are natural phenomena whereby the biological functions of organisms are synchronized with the day-night cycle of their environment, allowing biological processes to anticipate environmental changes. This is thought to provide organisms with an adaptive advantage, and is present in animals, plants, fungi, and cyanobacteria.

Circadian systems. Broadly, a circadian system consists of three modules: an input signal through a receptor (for example, light perceived by an eye), a "central oscillator" (molecular feedback pathways) analogous to that of a clock, and output pathways (such as changing protein levels) which communicate the "clock's" rhythm to control the organism's biological processes (**Fig. 1**). The central oscillator in all the systems deduced so far in cyanobacteria, fungi, insects, and mammals (*Synechococcus, Neurospora, Drosophila*, and mouse, for example), includes a negative feedback loop of molecular signal pathways that oscillates under constant conditions with a period close to 24 h. In the plant species that has been most studied, *Arabidopsis thaliana* (thale cress), a similar oscillator mechanism appears to be present. Compared with other species, there is considerable information about the input photoreceptors in plants but less about the output pathways that impose rhythmicity on biochemical and physiological systems such as gene expression, leaf movement, and hypocotyl elongation (seedling growth). There are added complications; for example, in some cases the clock rhythmically controls the input systems, such as the photoreceptors in *Arabidopsis*, as well as the output.

Plant rhythms. Signals from the central oscillator pass though output pathways to control diverse processes in plants. Diurnal growth rhythms such as petal opening, hypocotyl elongation, and leaf movements were noted by classical scholars and studied by Charles Darwin, among others. Recent DNA microarray experiments have shown that the expression of 2–6% of *Arabidopsis* genes (totaling 1250–1500 genes) is controlled by the circadian clock. Rhythmic changes in gene expression produce fluctuations in many biochemical pathways, which in turn affect the expression of other genes. A few clock-regulated DNA-binding proteins are each thought to control many output genes. One example is a protein related to the mammalian myb protein that is expressed before dawn and activates the expression of about two dozen genes encoding enzymes for phenylpropanoid synthesis. The phenylpropanoids include photo-protectant compounds that act as a type of molecular sunscreen, protecting plant cells from light damage.

The circadian clock is also required for the measurement of day length, which allows photoperiodic regulation. This results in the annual rhythms of many seasonal processes, such as tuber formation, bud dormancy, and flowering. There is therefore a close connection between circadian rhythms and flowering time, which has been a useful tool in the laboratory.

Arabidopsis. The *Arabidopsis* clock will oscillate in constant conditions with a period close to 24 h, like the circadian clocks of all other organisms. In nature, it is entrained through several input pathways which signal environmental changes to synchronize the clock with the day-night cycle. Light and temperature changes are thought to be the most potent signals for entraining the clock, though others exist, such as the hydration of dried seeds.

Photoreceptors. The first circadian photoreceptors to be unequivocally identified were those in plants. Those that have been found to entrain circadian rhythms in *Arabidopsis* include the phytochrome photoreceptors phyA, which responds to low levels of red light, and phyB and phyD, which function at higher intensities of red light. Two cryptochrome photoreceptors, cry1 and cry2, respond to blue light. Plants that lack cryptochromes are still rhythmic so, unlike in mammals, crys are apparently not an essential part of the plant oscillator. The photoreceptor functions overlap in complex ways: phyA is also activated by blue light; cry1 is necessary for phyA signaling in both red and blue light; and phyB is required for cry2 function in white light. This overlap probably contributes to the stability of the clock under changing illumination conditions. Signaling from these photoreceptors also directly affects cell growth by elongation, and the expression of light-regulated genes such as those for the chlorophyll *a/b*-binding (CAB) protein.

How the information passes from the activated photoreceptors to the oscillator is not completely understood. The signaling components downstream of the photoreceptors in the molecular signaling pathway include phytochrome interacting factor 3, PIF3. Red-light-activated phyB can bind to PIF3. In turn, PIF3 binds to the G box DNA sequence (CACGTG) in the promoters of several phytochrome-activated genes, including *Circadian clock associated 1* (*CCA1*) and *Late elongated hypocotyl* (*LHY*). Both are thought to be components of the circadian oscillator, suggesting that the input pathway is short and direct.

Fig. 1. Three-module circadian clock system.

Additional genes whose protein products affect light signaling have been identified through mutant screens (that is, by studying the functioning of individuals that lack these genes). These include the *Early flowering 3* (*ELF3*) and *Gigantea* (*GI*) genes. Both their proteins interact with the phyB photoreceptor and, as the expression of both genes is clock-controlled, they may play a part in circadian regulation of the light signaling pathway.

Circadian oscillator. A negative feedback loop has been implicated in the *Arabidopsis* oscillator, as in other species. However, the molecules with rhythmically changing abundance, which are thought to drive the clock, show little or no amino acid sequence homology to those found in fungi, animals, or cyanobacteria. Three genes, *TOC1* (*timing of CAB expression 1*), *LHY*, and *CCA1*, regulate all circadian rhythms in *Arabidopsis* and are thought to have crucial roles in the central oscillator. Mutant plants with reduced levels of these proteins have shorter circadian periods (21 h in the *cca1-1* mutant, for example) or can be arrhythmic. The current challenges are to determine how the interactions between these genes result in 24-h rhythms, and what additional components, such as a small family of *TOC1*-related genes, contribute. One possible model is shown in **Fig. 2**.

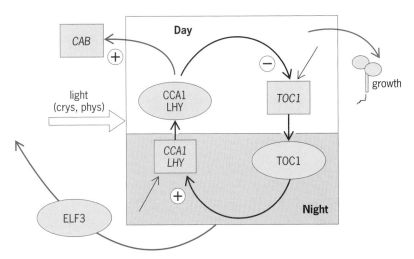

Fig. 2. Model of the *Arabidopsis* circadian clock, showing light input (white arrow), the central oscillator (large box), and output/response (blue arrows). Light signals synchronize the clock via the cryptochromes (crys) and phytochromes (phys). These are regulated by the oscillator, in part by ELF3 protein. The central oscillator is shown with a number of components, indicating the time of peak mRNA (rectangles) and protein (ovals) levels, relative to the day-night cycle (white and shaded areas). CCA1/LHY proteins are thought to activate *CAB* gene expression in the morning but inhibit *TOC1* gene expression, whereas *TOC1* activates *CCA1* and *LHY* expression at night. Other components are likely to participate in these steps (black arrows). Growth typically occurs in the late day, but the output mechanism is poorly understood. (*Adapted from D. Albadi et al., Reciprocal regulation between TOC1 and LHY/CCA1, Science, 293:880–883, 2001*)

CCA1 and LHY. CCA1 and LHY proteins have high sequence similarity and are partially redundant in function. Both are DNA-binding proteins with similarity to the animal myb proteins, and both are rhythmically expressed with a peak at dawn. Their overexpression in transgenic plants produces similar phenotypes (absence of all rhythms and late flowering). At high levels, either protein can prevent transcription from both gene promoters, though the mechanism of this negative feedback is unknown. CCA1 also binds to *CAB* gene promoters, providing a short and direct output pathway from the oscillator to clock-regulated genes.

As in *Drosophila*, both protein phosphorylation and protein degradation by the ubiquitin-proteasome pathway have been implicated in maintaining the pace of the clock. *Arabidopsis* casein kinase II (CK2) phosphorylates CCA1 and LHY proteins, for example. A three-member protein family may link the clock to protein degradation. Rhythmic proteins such as CCA1 must be quickly degraded (destroyed) within each circadian cycle. A family of proteins (named ZTL, FKF, and LKP2) is thought to target some proteins of the plant clock for degradation. Plants that lack ZTL have a 27-h period, for example, as would be expected if a rhythmic protein is too slow to degrade. Each protein of the ZTL family contains a domain which can interact with a component of the widely conserved, ubiquitin-dependent pathway of protein degradation.

TOC1. TOC1 protein has sequence similarity to the response regulator proteins found in bacterial two-component signal transduction systems. However, TOC1 lacks amino acids that are crucial for the bacterial proteins' function; presumably it also has a different biochemical mechanism, so it has been called an *Arabidopsis* pseudo-response regulator (APRR). It is rhythmically expressed with a peak at the end of the day. TOC1 is located in the cell nucleus, like CCA1, LHY, and ELF3. The *Arabidopsis* genome contains at least five related APRR genes, which are also rhythmically expressed. Strikingly, the APRR mRNA levels peak in sequence from dawn (APRR9) to dusk (TOC1), separated by 2–3 h intervals. This pattern suggests that the APRRs could regulate rhythmic processes that peak at any time during the day, though this remains to be tested. Altered expression of TOC1 affects the levels and timing of LHY and CCA1 expression and vice versa, indicating that there are strong links between these components, though the details are still under active investigation (Fig. 2).

For background information *see* BIOLOGICAL CLOCKS; PHOTOMORPHOGENESIS; PHOTOPERIODISM; PLANT GROWTH; PLANT MOVEMENTS; PLANT PHYSIOLOGY; SIGNAL TRANSDUCTION in the McGraw-Hill Encyclopedia of Science & Technology.

Roger Cook; Andrew J. Millar

Bibliography. S. Barak et al., All in good time: The *Arabidopsis* circadian clock, *Trends Plant Sci.*, 5:517–522, 2000; C. R. McClung, Circadian rhythms in plants, *Annu. Rev. Plant Physiol. Plant Mol. Biol.*, 52:139–162, 2001; A. Samach and G. Coupland, Time measurement and the control of flowering in plants, *Bioessays*, 22:38–47, 2000; M. J. Yanovsky and S. A. Kay, Signalling networks in the plant circadian system, *Curr. Opin. Plant Biol.*, 4:429–435, 2001.

Climate change and plant adaptation

The manner and extent to which plant species will respond to ongoing global climate change is of central concern in predicting how the face of the Earth will change in the twenty-first century. Unfortunately, ecological prediction is hindered by a lack of direct experience with global warming of the projected magnitude. As one method of gathering useful information, ecologists have looked to the paleontological record for patterns from which to construct models of vegetation response to the expected changes. Such records reveal that during past episodes of global climate change many plant species responded by shifting their geographical centers of distribution. However, contemporary fragmentation of the landscape makes ineffective many of the dispersal mechanisms (seed and pollen dispersal) that allowed plant species to physically follow the climate during past episodes of change. For a great number of plant species, the coming environmental changes dictate that either they adapt (change genetically) or face extinction. Furthermore, whereas previous climate changes may have involved a degree of change equivalent to that currently projected, the speed of current change is without precedent (at the current rate, a 1–4°C average increase over the next 100 years). The problem therefore is twofold: Can plants adapt to the extent necessary to cope with the degree of environmental change expected, and can they do so within a short time frame?

Although theoretical models have suggested that, in the absence of migration, populations will be able to keep up with their environments only if the speed of environmental change is quite modest, there are examples showing that adaptive response of the sort needed can occur within the requisite length of time. For instance, heavy-metal tolerance and genetic differentiation of plants growing on mine tailings (relative to plants just feet away that are not on tailings) has taken place on the scale of decades. Mounting evidence exists for equally rapid response to air pollutants. However, both past events and contemporary observation of genetic change show response to be species-specific; that is, different species respond differently. Whereas some species may adapt to high pollution or heavy-metal levels, many will not, and this difference is reflected in the relatively low diversity of mine tailing or roadside plant communities. Similarly, in response to the changing conditions brought about by the last ice age, some species shifted their entire distribution, some contracted their ranges, and some expanded them. Studies have been performed more frequently for economic or logistical reasons, and data sufficient to determine whether some types of plants are more likely than others to adapt successfully to climate change are not yet available. Nonetheless, the last decade has yielded a better understanding of basic processes and factors that have the potential to bias those processes, as well as some speculation as to potential general patterns.

Factors affecting adaptive response. Factors affecting a species' ability to respond to climate change are numerous, but they all ultimately depend on the fitness of its genes.

Genetic variation. It is evident that genetic variation differs between species, although the several means of documenting this variation and the relatively small number of species thus far assayed for traits directly relevant to climate change obviate many comparative statements regarding biases by plant type. The clearest pattern yet revealed is that, as a group, aquatic plants show relatively little genetic variation at the level of populations. This is important because the ability of a species to respond adaptively depends fundamentally on the genetic variation within its populations. All else being equal, a population with more genetic variation will be more likely to have successful individuals and so will be better able to respond to selection pressures than a population with less variation. Island populations, isolated populations, and populations on the margins of a species distribution are thought to be relatively low in genetic variability. Genetic variation is itself directly dependent on effective population size (number of viable reproductive adults), and within a similar area plant species with physically larger individuals generally will have a smaller population. Even so, the degree of genetic variation may differ greatly even between tree species of similar size.

Pleiotropy. Pleiotropy refers to a gene's having more than one phenotypic effect (that is, the gene is expressed in various ways). Pleiotropy is commonly used to indicate that change in one character will affect other characters. For example, increases in leaf number and in leaf thickness are advantageous responses to warmer climates in *Chamaecrista fasciculata*, an annual legume; when they occur together, these traits tend not to change individually, suggesting that they are the products of the same rather than different genes. There is overall agreement that pleiotropy is likely to be of special importance in limiting the response to a selective pressure as complex as climate, but there is little indication through either study or theory that there is any particular bias in its occurrence.

Generation time. Species with longer generation times (average time between one generation and the next) show less genetic change over the same period of time than species with shorter generation times. Generation time is correlated with physical size in plants much as it is in animals. The expectation, then, is that weeds and annuals are more likely to be able to adjust in situ to ongoing climate changes than trees and shrubs, and shorter-lived, "weedier" trees and shrubs will show more adaptive change than longer-lived trees and shrubs.

Population structure. An assumption of the study of adaptation is that a reproductive individual is equally likely to mate with any other reproductive individual (of the opposite sex). Deviation from such panmixsa is one aspect of population structure. Probability of mating may be biased by factors such as spatial distribution, the possession of a particular trait, or a combination of factors. Assortative mating occurs when mating pairs are of similar phenotype more often than would occur by chance. If assortative mating is based on a trait not directly relevant to climate change, it may inhibit the speed of adaptive response to climate change. On the other hand, if based on a trait involved with adaptation to climate change, assortative mating will speed the rate of adaptation.

Spatial structure. Spatial structure is ubiquitous in plants, but some sorts will be of more importance than others. For example, populations on north-facing and adjacent south-facing slopes within a ridge system may be genetically differentiated, as in *Pseudotsuga menziesii* (fir) in the Colorado Rocky Mountains. In the same vein, *Betula pendula* (birch) has been shown recently to exist as differentiated cohorts of individuals established in cold versus warm years, apparently as a result of normal year-to-year variation in temperature. Differentiation at a scale that allows this coexistence of climatic "types" will allow cooptation of a site by seeds and seedlings of the better-adapted type at the advent of climatic change, with little or no obvious change in overall species distribution. The existence of such "pre-adapted" genotypes within the population will speed the response to change in much the same manner as assortative mating. Whereas both examples given here are trees, population structure and spatial distribution are factors for all plant forms.

Summary. The pressure to change—selection pressure—will not be experienced equally by all species. Not all species will be equally restricted in area or population size. Individuals of some species will have a greater range of conditions that are experienced as tolerable than others, and will react to the projected climate change without problems. It is argued that if changes are not immediately lethal, long-lived individuals in particular may be able to accumulate enough resources over the years to continue effective seed production in spite of environmental change. The vulnerable point of the life cycle for such species will be at the time of seedling establishment, and recent work with seedlings of tropical deep-forest trees indicates that even seedlings may be less constrained in light and moisture requirements than is indicated by previous research. Even so, tree species consistently show local adaptation when subjected to common garden and transplant experiments, indicating that a change in local conditions will move the habitat away from conditions under which individuals do best, and so will foster a genetic response. Although weed species were previously thought to possess a "general-purpose genotype" (adapted to any climate) at the level of the individual, this opinion is no longer widely held. Hence, this may be another argument that less adaptive change in response to global climate change will be found in tree species than other life forms.

For background information *see* CLIMATE MODIFICATION; ECOLOGY; GLOBAL CLIMATE CHANGE; PHYSIOLOGICAL ECOLOGY (PLANT); PLANT EVOLUTION; PLANT GEOGRAPHY; POLYMORPHISM (GENETICS); POPULATION GENETICS; REPRODUCTION (PLANT) in the McGraw-Hill Encyclopedia of Science & Technology.

Colleen K. Kelly

Bibliography. M. B. Davis and R. G. Shaw, Range shifts and adaptive responses to quaternary climate change, *Science*, 292:673–679, 2001; C. K. Kelly et al., Temperature-based population segregation in birch, *Ecol. Lett.*; Y. B. Linhart and M. C. Grant, Evolutionary significance of local genetic differentiation in plants, *Annu. Rev. Ecol. Systematics*, 27:237–277, 1996; H. A. Mooney and R. J. Hobbs (eds.), *Invasive Species in a Changing World*, Island, Washington, DC, 2000.

Coalbed methane

Coalbed methane reservoirs, which in 2001 supplied 7% of U.S. natural gas, are an economically important and unique petroleum system. A petroleum system typically consists of a sedimentary basin that contains a hydrocarbon source rock and all of the oil and gas related to this source rock. The classical petroleum system consists of a hydrocarbon-generative shale source rock that, with burial and resultant heating, expels oil and gas that are free to migrate to porous reservoir rock such as sandstone or limestone. A coalbed methane system is different in that the coal itself is both source and reservoir. The coal is a hydrocarbon source rock that during burial heating evolves into a substance similar in structure to activated carbon. Activated carbons are organic-based materials that are chemically treated or heat-treated to markedly increase micropores, with

a corresponding increase in the internal surface area and gas sorption capacity. The coal both produces methane gas and develops the storage capacity to hold the gas in place. Migration outside the coalbed is unnecessary.

Methane storage in coal. The amount of methane that can be stored in and recovered from coal depends on a number of factors, including the porosity and composition of the coal and the surrounding temperature and pressure conditions.

Sorption capacity. Sorption is a physical process whereby gas is held by weak electrostatic bonds on the internal pore surfaces of a solid, conceptually like a static electricity–charged balloon that is attracted and held to a wall. All activated carbons are solids with surfaces that are mostly nonpolar and act to hold natural gases such as methane, propane, carbon dioxide, and nitrogen. According to the Langmuir sorption model, increasing pressure acting on coal causes increasing amounts of gas to be held on the pore surfaces. Because the bond is electrostatic, its strength decreases with the square of the distance between the surface and gas molecule, and the strongest bonds are formed with the molecules held in a single layer, or monolayer. The internal surfaces of coal can be visualized as spherical to irregularly shaped pores lined with a monolayer of methane gas (**Fig. 1**) when saturated. Under saturated conditions, sorption is a dynamic system in which as many gas molecules approach the surface as are leaving it. Pores in coal may be near molecular-level size but are mostly less than 300 angstroms in size. As coal burial increases, natural heat-treating causes the pores of less than 12 Å to increase in number and those of greater than 300 Å to decrease in number. The cross section of a methane molecule is 3.7 Å and can easily move within these pores. Proliferation of pores that are smaller than 12 Å during burial heating produces a net increase in coal surface area along with an increase in sorption capacity.

Composition. Coal composition in terms of its plant matter, mineral matter, and moisture content is also an important control on coalbed methane gas storage capacity. There are three main organic constituents of coal, called macerals, which are microscopically identifiable plant components. The vitrinite group is formed from woody plant debris; the liptinite group is from waxy, resinous, and oily plant matter; and inertinite is often composed of fossil charcoal but also includes other altered and oxidized plant matter. Increasing vitrinite content enhances coalbed methane storage capacity and the tendency of the coal to develop fracture permeability. Increasing inertinite content enhances matrix permeability, due to the large open pores of this material, but because it is chemically inert, it decreases gas generation potential and reduces storage capacity.

There are two main inorganic constituents of coal, mineral matter and moisture. Mineral matter has a low surface area and low storage capacity; it consequently reduces gas content in direct proportion to its abundance. Mineral matter also inhibits the formation of natural fractures in the coal, called cleat,

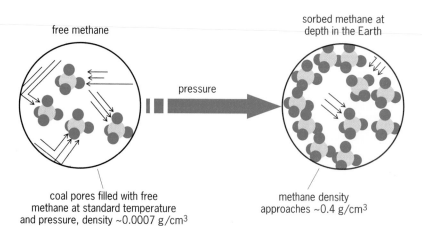

free methane

sorbed methane at depth in the Earth

pressure

coal pores filled with free methane at standard temperature and pressure, density ~0.0007 g/cm³

methane density approaches ~0.4 g/cm³

Fig. 1. Concentration of free gas as a monolayer on the surface of coal pores. Sorbed gas takes on liquidlike densities but does not have other liquid properties such as viscosity because the molecule is not mobile as it would be in a liquid. (*Density data from M. Mavor and C. R. Nelson, 1997*)

because it does lose volatile matter and contract as much as coal does during burial heating. Moisture competes with gases for sorption sites and proportionately reduces the methane storage capacity of a coal.

Temperature and pressure. The gas in coalbeds can be of thermogenic or biogenic origin. In the simplest hydrocarbon generator reaction, burial heating causes thermogenic methane to be freed by cleavage of methyl groups from the coal "molecule." One ton of coal heated to reach an anthracite rank is estimated to produce up to 180 m³ (6400 ft³) of gas. Biogenic gas generation is the result of a methane waste product produced from anaerobic microbial metabolism. As such, biogenic gas generation is restricted to temperatures less than about 90°C (194°F) because higher temperatures sterilize the rock. Biogenic generation can be twofold, occurring during early burial and after exhumation. These coalbed-generated gases are readily sorbed into the coal microporosity. This sorbed gas is usually composed of methane, but coal can also contain carbon dioxide as well as nitrogen, ethane, and longer-chain alkane hydrocarbons.

Coalbed methane has a wide occurrence because it tends to be preserved through burial, and even if lost it can be biogenically regenerated late in burial history when cooler temperatures are reached. Therefore, it is virtually characteristic of coalbeds to contain some methane. The problem is that while the gas is ubiquitous, coals are often impermeable, making the gas inaccessible. Gas must migrate by solid-state diffusion from the coal matrix to open fractures to become the accessible free gas that flows to wells and thus becomes usable. If the natural fractures (cleat) are too widely spaced, the path of solid-state diffusion is so slow that the gas production rate falls below commercial standards (**Fig. 2**). The current geologic paradigm is that coal bed methane production is limited to a 150 m (490 ft) to 2 km (1.2 mi) depth, because at shallow depths low hydraulic pressure causes the coal to retain too little methane, and at depths greater than 2 km coal cleat is generally tightly closed, reducing permeability and making commercial production difficult.

Environmental impact. Coal bed methane was first noticed because it makes the coal mine atmosphere toxic as well as potentially explosive. In fact, early recovery efforts for coalbed methane in the 1930s

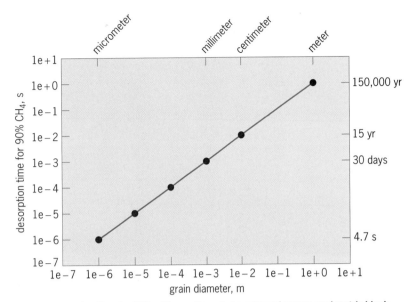

Fig. 2. Desorption time for 90% of the methane to be released versus coal matrix block size. The relationship is determined by the solid-state diffusion path length, which is geometrically related to the coal matrix grain size. (*Data from D. Masszi, 1991*)

focused on mining where methane was an explosion hazard when released underground and an environmental hazard when released aboveground. Coalbed methane is released both when the coalbed is depressurized by pumping water from underground workings and open pits and when the coalbed is broken into lumps during the mining process. It was discovered that this released gas is often natural-gas quality and can be sold directly to gas pipelines. The United States pioneered the drilling of commercially viable coalbed methane wells, drilled solely for energy, in the latter half of the twentieth century. Thus, the environmental effects of coalbed methane can be negative or positive, depending on whether or not the methane is successfully captured and used.

Methane capture. To reduce the hazard from the release of methane during coal mining, the gas may be gathered by wells drilled ahead of the mining face or by ventilation during mining. Residual coalbed methane is also released after mining, during collapse of the mined-out area. All of these methane emissions are environmental hazards in terms of safety, air pollution, and greenhouse heating effects. The modern mining practice of capturing these gases led to a 32% reduction in coal mining-related methane emissions from 1990 to 2000 (**Table 1**). The

TABLE 1. Principal sources of anthropogenic emissions of methane in the United States

Source	1990	2000	1990–2000, percent change	Percent of emissions in 2000
	10⁶ metric tons of methane			
Energy—coal mining	4.2	2.9	−32	10
Energy—other	7.7	8.1	+5	29
Waste management	11.4	8.0	−30	28
Agriculture	8.3	9.1	+9	32
Industrial processes	0.1	0.1	0	1
TOTAL	31.7	28.2	−11	100

*Modified from Energy Information Agency, *Emissions of Greenhouse Gases in the United States 2000: Methane Emissions*, Rep. DOE/EIA-0573(2000), November 2001.

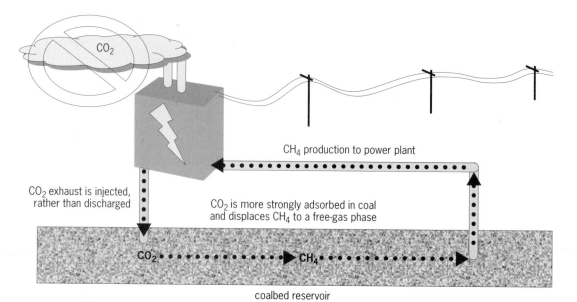

Fig. 3. Zero greenhouse gas emissions during electricity generation in a closed-loop system using CO_2 sequestration. Sequestration involves the injection of power plant CO_2 exhaust to displace methane, which is in turn burned to CO_2 that is injected into the coal seam, and so on.

gas gathered by mining operations is generally commercial quality. However, if only a small percentage of the mine air contains methane after mining, this is an unprofitable source of gas. In any case, environmental concerns may make it important to capture and process as much coalbed methane as is economically feasible.

Methane as an energy source. The advantage of coalbed methane capture for energy is twofold. First, methane burns to carbon dioxide (CO_2) and water with no other pollutants. Thus, methane is a preferred fuel for electricity generation in cities where pollution is a major concern. Second, the combus-

tion process has significant but largely unrecognized environmental benefits, since it removes methane, which is 20 times more potent as a greenhouse gas than CO_2. Given that coal mining contributes 10% of all anthropogenic methane emissions in the United States (Table 1), it is an important part of greenhouse gas mitigation to capture coal mine methane and burn it.

Perhaps the most exciting potential advantage of coalbed methane is related to the fact that CO_2 is more strongly sorbed onto coal surfaces than methane. The possibility exists of being able to inject CO_2 from a power plant into a nearby coalbed

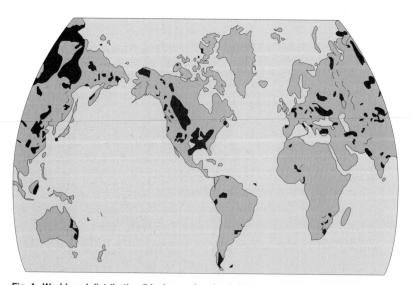

Fig. 4. World coal distribution (black areas) on land. Although coal deposits are distributed worldwide, 60% of the world's recoverable reserves are located in three regions: the United States (25%), former Soviet Union (23%), and China (12%). Australia, India, Germany, and South Africa account for an additional 29%. Thus, seven countries contain a total of 89% of the world's coal resources. The map excludes Antarctica, which contains large coal deposits but is not usable by international convention. (*Map from E. R. Landis and J. N. Weaver, 1993*)

TABLE 2. Coal resource and gas-in-place estimates for 12 countries constituting about 90% of the world's total coal resources

Country*	Coal resource, metric tons	Gas in place, m³
Russia	6.5×10^{12}	6.5×10^{13}
China	4.0×10^{12}	3.3×10^{13}
U.S. coterminous 48 states	4.5×10^{12}	2.1×10^{13}
Alaska	3.6×10^{12}	2.8×10^{13}
Canada	2.3×10^{12}	1.5×10^{13}
Australia	1.7×10^{12}	1.1×10^{13}
Germany	3.3×10^{11}	3.0×10^{12}
U.K.	1.9×10^{11}	2.0×10^{12}
Kazakhstan	1.7×10^{11}	1.0×10^{12}
Poland	1.6×10^{11}	3.0×10^{12}
India	1.6×10^{11}	1.0×10^{12}
South Africa	1.5×10^{11}	1.0×10^{12}
Ukraine	1.4×10^{12}	2.0×10^{12}
TOTAL	2.52×10^{13}	1.8×10^{14} (6500 Tcf)

*Data from V. A. Kuuskraa, C. M. Boyer II, and J. A. Kelafant, Hunt for quality basins goes abroad, *Oil Gas J.*, 90:49–54, 1992; and Potential Gas Committee, *Potential Supply of Natural Gas in the United States*, Colorado School of Mines, 2001. Tcf = trillion cubic feet.

TABLE 3. World proven recoverable conventional energy resources compared to the coalbed methane resource in 1999*

Commodity	World reserve in place	World consumption	Estimated accessible fraction	Indicated producible supply (in years)[†]
Recoverable coal	9.9×10^{11} metric tons	4.3×10^9 metric tons	0.25	58
Recoverable crude oil	1.02×10^{12} barrels	2.73×10^9 barrels	1.0	37
Recoverable natural gas	5150 Tcf	84 Tcf	1.0	61
Recoverable coalbed methane	3250 Tcf	84 Tcf	0.75	30

*Conventional resource data from Energy Information Administration, *International Energy Outlook 1999*, 2000.
[†]Coalbed methane-in-place data in Table 1 is converted to recoverable coalbed methane using a 50% recovery factor. The producible supply remaining is obtained by dividing 1999 reserve by 1999 consumption and multiplying this result by the estimated accessible fraction.

(a process called sequestration), displace coalbed methane, and burn that methane to make more CO_2 for injection plus heat energy that can be converted to electricity (**Fig. 3**).

Coalbed methane may also become a renewable resource. Bench-scale laboratory experiments indicate that anaerobic microbes when injected and nurtured in a coalbed can metabolize coal and release methane as a by-product. This results in a renewable resource (as long as coal supplies last), similar to growing corn as the raw material to make ethanol. The unusual aspect of renewable coalbed methane is that coal is used as the growth medium rather than soil, and the process occurs largely underground with minimal surface disturbance.

Resource base. Coal has the widest distribution of any fossil energy source on land (**Fig. 4**). Given the typical presence of methane in buried coal, coalbed methane is the most widely distributed commercial natural gas source. Coalbed methane should be of particular interest in countries without a pipeline infrastructure because the gas is usable at the wellhead or through a local pipeline system for domestic or industrial use. **Table 2** shows a compilation of estimated coalbed methane in place for the top dozen coal-bearing nations, indicating some 6500 trillion cubic feet (Tcf), or 185 trillion cubic meters, of gas. A comparison of conventional natural gas and coalbed methane resources shows that coalbed methane can produce about one-half of the volume of recoverable conventional natural gas (**Table 3**). To appreciate the magnitude of coalbed methane, consider that the world now consumes 84 Tcf/year. Production experience indicates about 50% of coalbed methane in place is recoverable as free methane, suggesting that if three-quarters of recoverable coalbed methane were economically and geographically accessble, then 6500 Tcf is the equivalent of a 30-year supply for the world. Table 3 also indicates that gas resources will outlast oil resources, and that there is a supply of coal that could be mined for energy use for many years if mining coal deposits can meet global economic and environmental standards. In the future, declining production of conventional oil and gas, along with the increased need to decrease methane emissions, indicates that world production of coalbed methane will markedly rise.

For background information *see* COAL; COAL DEGASIFICATION; COAL MINING; COAL PALEOBOTANY;
METHANE; UNDERGROUND MINING in the McGraw-Hill Encyclopedia of Science & Technology.

Charles E. Barker

Bibliography. R. Gayer and I. Harris, *Coalbed Methane and Coal Geology*, Geological Society, London, Spec. Publ. 109, 1996; D. G. Howell (ed.), *The Future of Energy Gases*, U.S. Geological Survey Prof. Pap. 1570, 1993; B. E. Law and D. D. Rice (eds.), *Hydrocarbons from Coal*, American Association of Petroleum Geologists Studies in Geology, vol. 38, 1993; C. T. Rightmire, G. E. Eddy, and J. N. Kirr (eds.), *Coalbed Methane Resources of the United States*, American Association of Petroleum Geologists Studies in Geology, vol. 17, 1984; B. P. Tissot and D. H. Welte, *Petroleum Formation and Occurrence*, 2d ed., Springer-Verlag, Berlin, 1987.

Connected landscapes

A landscape is considered connected when it has few impediments that restrict the ability of animals to move about, particularly between core areas of habitat. Although natural features such as steep canyons can also restrict animal movement, scientists are increasingly concerned about the rapid expansion of human-related features and activities such as highways, roads, agricultural fields, and urban areas that impede movement between patches of habitat. Habitat fragmentation is commonly cited as one of the leading causes of the loss of biodiversity because it leads to smaller, more isolated populations that have less genetic diversity and are more likely to become extinct.

Factors in fragmentation. Whether a landscape can be considered connected or fragmented often depends on the particular movement abilities of a given animal. A coyote might be able to move about a landscape with ease, while the same landscape would be effectively fragmented into smaller, isolated patches of habitat for a less mobile or more reclusive creature. Much of our understanding about landscape connectivity comes from investigations of large terrestrial mammals, such as grizzly bears and mountain lions, but landscapes may become fragmented for many other groups of animals, such as butterflies, amphibians, birds, or fish. Animals that move poorly or require specific or rare habitat are particularly sensitive to fragmentation, as are animals that have low population densities and require large expanses of habitat (such as forest carnivores).

Another factor in fragmentation is human land-use choices. The Bow River Valley in Alberta, Canada, provides a dramatic example of a region struggling with the ecological consequences of highways and fragmenting land uses. This narrow valley adjacent to Banff National Park contains the Trans-Canada Highway, which carries upwards of 10 million people per year, as well as a number of additional highways, the town of Banff, and the Canadian Pacific Railway. Wildlife movement there has been constrained, and high rates of mortality have been recorded in the past two decades. For example, 771 road kills were found on the Trans-Canada Highway in the summers of 1997 to 1999, including wolves, bears, cougars, and other mammals, as well as birds and amphibians. These road kills have occurred despite the construction of 14 wildlife underpasses and overpasses since 1988 in an attempt to decrease animal mortality and increase connectivity. Use of these under- and overpasses has been documented from 1996 to 1999; nearly 15,000 passes by elk, deer, and sheep, and nearly 4000 passes by coyotes, black bears, cougars, wolves, and grizzly bears have occurred.

Land managers and conservation organizations are challenged to reduce fragmentation and keep connectivity within a landscape. A central question is where are the key locations that might add disproportionately to connectivity. Once these choke points are identified, different strategies can be employed to protect movement corridors there from future harmful land uses, notably urban development and road expansion, or to restore lost connectivity through mitigation measures, such as the construction of underpasses and the removal of obstructions such as dams.

Assessing animal movement. Wildlife biologists have developed numerous techniques to understand animal movement. Road kill data and counts of animal tracks in snow or sand beds have been used to estimate movement at underpasses, bridges, and culverts. A common technique for studying movement across a landscape is to capture and tag many individual animals (marking each with a unique identifier and noting the capture site), release them, and then recapture some of them at a later date (usually at a different location). This technique works well for animals that are small and relatively easy to catch, such as birds and butterflies, but determining their actual path of movement is problematic.

A preferred technique is to capture individuals and outfit each with a radio collar that transmits a unique frequency. Field technicians then follow an individual through a landscape, recording its location. Some collars can now be equipped with Global Positioning System (GPS) devices so that locations are automatically recorded. However, there is a trade-off between how frequently locations are recorded (weekly, daily, hourly) and how long the transmitter lasts (bigger animals can handle heavier batteries).

Modeling corridors of movement. Scientists use models to relate individual movement data to specific features in the landscape, such as vegetation types, ridges, drainages, roads, and urban areas. Models are also needed to represent and test different assumptions about broad, landscape-level movement patterns to inform land managers' decision making. Modeling is a good option when no field data exist, which often occurs when funding is not adequate to mount a field-collection effort, or to inform reintroduction efforts after a species is extirpated from an area.

A number of modeling approaches have recently been developed, most of which use Geographic Information Systems (GIS) as a platform. GIS is a computerized system for the capture (via GPS satellites), storage, retrieval, analysis, and display of spatial data. It can be used to obtain geographic data so that vegetation, elevation, and land use can be incorporated into a model. One simple function of GIS is to capture the spatial continuity of land cover types across a landscape, for example, by identifying the cover type that covers the largest proportion of a landscape. However, simple metrics do not adequately capture the configuration of habitat patches or the extent to which animal movement is impeded between patches, so they cannot by themselves identify the choke points that are key elements of connected landscapes.

Consolidating most-likely movement paths. One solution is to model how an individual animal might move between habitat patches. A landscape is typically represented by a matrix or grid of cells, and the land cover type is noted at each cell. A computer-generated

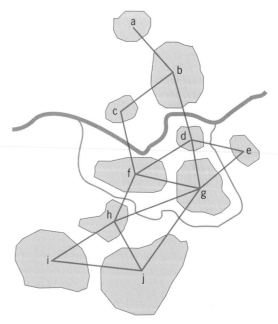

Fig. 1. Hypothetical landscape represented by a graph network. Nodes are enumerated with letters, representing each patch (gray polygons). Edges connect nodes, and some crossroads (thick gray lines). Not all possible edges are shown.

Description of edges shown in Fig. 1

Edge	Nodes connected	Edge-to-edge length	Crosses road?	Distance w/road (if any)
1	a, b	3		3
2	b, c	4		4
3	b, d	3	Yes	4
4	c, f	6	Yes	8
5	d, f	4		4
6	d, g	2		2
7	d, e	4	Yes	5
8	e, g	3	Yes	4
9	f, h	2	Yes	3
10	f, g	1		1
11	g, j	5	Yes	7
12	g, h	8	Yes	10
13	h, i	3		3
14	h, j	3		3
15	i, j	2		2

individual is randomly placed in a cell at the edge of a habitat patch and then moved to one of the seven adjacent cells (an individual cannot move back to the cell it came from). The likelihood of moving to an adjacent cell is proportional to the land cover types of the seven cells, reflecting how an animal selects different types. For example, a lynx might prefer coniferous forest over grassland. By generating thousands of movement paths, each with up to thousands of steps, and stacking them on top of one another, likely corridors of movement on a landscape can be mapped and the degree of connectivity between patches can be calculated.

Least-cost paths. A second approach is to identify corridors by using cost-distance methods. Rather than simply delineating corridors on a map by connecting habitat patches via the straight-line distance, or drawing corridors to follow some ridgeline or drainage feature, the arrangement and quality of land cover types can be interpreted from the animal's perspective. Cover types are differentiated based on preference, and the differences are expressed in terms of cost. Each cell that is considered to be high quality is assigned a cost value of one, whereas low-quality types are assigned a cost greater than one. For example, for a lynx that prefers vegetation that

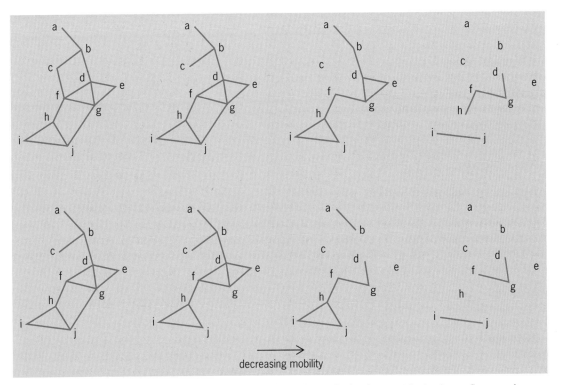

decreasing mobility

Fig. 2. Connectivity declines as mobility declines (left to right). Roads may further fragment the landscape (lower row). Nodes "d" and "h" are key "choke points" in the landscape.

provides cover, forest cells would be assigned a value of one but grassland cells might be assigned a value of three. After all cells in a landscape are assigned a cost, the least-cost path between each pair of patches can be calculated such that moving between patches accrues the lowest possible cost. Least-cost paths then serve as the backbone for corridors.

Graph theory. A third approach is to develop a model based on graph theory, a field of mathematics which is also used for transportation planning, circuitry design, and even the Internet. A graph represents a landscape as a network of nodes located at each habitat patch, connected by edges representing connectivity between the patches (**Fig. 1**). Although theoretically all nodes can be connected to one another, some are better connected than others. Typically, the degree of connectedness is represented using the distance—either physical straight-line distance or least-cost distance—between two nodes, with shorter distances equaling more connectivity (see **table**). The functional length of an edge may be longer than its straight-line distance, particularly if it crosses a feature such as a road or urban area. The degree of connection is often adjusted to incorporate the size of the patches, because the number of dispersing juveniles (young animals that are striking out on their own) is proportional to patch size.

A graph can then be examined to determine at what point the network begins to break down as animal movement capabilities decline. That is, if it is likely that a species can move farther than the longest edge, then the entire landscape is represented by a single, connected graph—all nodes can be reached by following the path of an edge from one node to another. As animal movement capability decreases relative to edge length, the full network begins to break into subgraphs, identifying a transition from a connected to a fragmented landscape. Choke points, or edges that are critical to the overall connectivity of the network, can be identified by iteratively removing each edge, recalculating the graph structure, and prioritizing edges based on whether removing them causes greater isolation of nodes in the graph. Because graphs are a very compact and elegant data structure, simulations can be run very rapidly (**Fig. 2**).

Ecosystem management. The remaining challenge for land-use managers is to move beyond understanding connectivity in terms of individual movement to understanding a whole ecosystem. A greater understanding of how the flow of nutrients such as carbon, ecological processes such as fire, and interactions among different groups of species are modified by the degree of landscape connectivity is needed.

For background information *see* ECOLOGICAL COMMUNITIES; GEOGRAPHIC INFORMATION SYSTEMS; GLOBAL POSITIONING SYSTEM; LAND-USE PLANNING; LANDSCAPE ECOLOGY; POPULATION DISPERSAL; THEORETICAL ECOLOGY in the McGraw-Hill Encyclopedia of Science & Technology.   David Theobald

Bibliography. A. L. Barabasi, *The New Science of Networks*, Perseus Publishing, 2002; W. E. Grant, E. K. Pedersen, and S. L. Marin, Ecology and natural resource management: Systems analysis and simulation, Wiley, New York, 1997; W. Hudson (ed.), *Landscape Linkages and Biodiversity*, Island Press, Washington, DC, 1991; M. G. Turner, R. H. Gardner, and R. V. O'Neill, *Landscape Ecology in Theory and Practice*, Springer-Verlag, New York, 2001.

Contact lenses

The modern contact lens combines state-of-the-art advances in optics, mechanical engineering, and material science to provide correction for a full range of vision problems. It is a comfortable, economical, and healthy option for vision correction.

Conceptually, a contact lens is similar to traditional optical systems in that it has an optical component and a supporting structure. However, with a contact lens, both the optical component and the structure typically are made of the same material in a continuous piece. The lens must be comfortable on the eye and have structural integrity so it can be easily inserted and removed. The lens material must be biologically safe when placed on the eye for extended periods of time.

Human eye. The human eye can be described as an optical system consisting of the cornea, the crystalline lens, and the retina. In the emmetropic eye, light from a distant object is bent, or refracted, by both the cornea and the crystalline lens, and comes to focus on the retina. When an object, such as a book or computer monitor, is closer to the eye, the focus moves to a position behind the retina. The crystalline lens reshapes itself to bring the focus back to the retina. This process, referred to as accommodation, provides the ability to focus over a large range of object distances.

Myopia results when the image of a distant object comes to focus in front of the retina (**Fig. 1***a*). Hyperopia is the condition where the distant image comes to focus behind the retina (Fig. 1*b*). The crystalline lens can only move the image toward the cornea. Therefore, accommodation corrects only hyperopic focus errors. As a human ages, the crystalline lens becomes less flexible, and the ability to accommodate diminishes. This condition, known as presbyopia, commonly becomes noticeable as a person reaches the midforties, and signals the need for bifocal correction.

Astigmatism results in two focal positions, each associated with locations in the eye with different refractive properties (Fig. 1*c*). Corneal astigmatism results from different curvatures in orthogonal axes along the corneal surface. Lenticular astigmatism results from refractive differences along orthogonal axes of the crystalline lens. Astigmatism can exist by itself or in combination with myopia, hyperopia, or presbyopia.

Lens types. Contact lenses are generally divided into hard and soft categories.

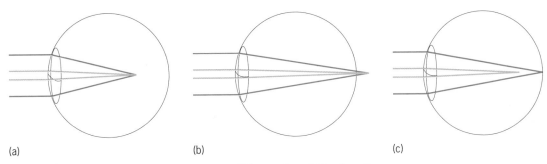

Fig. 1. Common vision problems include (*a*) myopia, (*b*) hyperopia, and (*c*) astigmatism.

Hard contact lenses. The majority of modern hard lenses are rigid gas-permeable (RGP) lenses. Optically, they work by vaulting over the cornea, providing in essence a new corneal surface to interact with light. The natural tear film fills the area between the back of the lens and the cornea, nullifying the optical effects of the patient's cornea. RGP lenses provide excellent vision and are particularly advantageous for patients with very unusual corneal surface conditions, such as keratoconus, an asymmetric bulging of the cornea. Rigid lenses vault over the bulge, effectively masking it. Very large amounts of corneal astigmatism are also routinely masked using rigid lenses. Because of a relatively high modulus, RGPs are easily handled, inserted, and removed from the eye.

RGPs are oxygen-permeable, an important factor in corneal health. Typical RGP materials are fluorosilicone acrylates, perfluoropolyethers, and silicone acrylates copolymerized with polymethylmethacrylate. They tend to be smaller in diameter than the limbus, the junction where the cornea meets the rest of the eye, so lens motion is common, and the lenses are more prone to become dislodged from the eye (**Fig. 2**).

RGPs are very durable, intended for long periods of use. They must be removed each day and subjected to cleaning and sterilization, a regimen necessary for maximum optical performance and health. Because of size and rigidity, patients must acclimate to wearing RGPs over a period of several days. Typically, the lens is worn for 4 hours the first day. An hour is added to each subsequent day until the wearer adjusts to the lens's presence.

Soft contact lenses . These make up the majority of the contact lens market. Soft contact lenses are thinner with a lower modulus that allows them to wrap onto the cornea. Soft lenses are made from hydrogels, hydrophilic polymers such as hydroxy-ethylmethacrylate (HEMA) combined with water. The water content of soft lenses ranges 37.5–79%, depending on manufacturers' formulations and intended wear regimens. They are replaced with a much higher frequency than RGPs, and are commonly referred to as disposable lenses.

Soft lens diameters usually extend beyond the limbus and under the eyelids (Fig. 2). They may have several zones: an optical zone that is positioned over the cornea, stability zones to provide a specific orientation, stiffening zones to retain shape when handled, inserted, or removed, and bevels to provide comfort. Soft lenses require little or no acclimatization and are not easily dislodged. Handling, insertion, and removal can be more difficult than with RGPs.

DK/L is an important measure of the oxygen permeability of any contact lens. *D* is the diffusion coefficient for oxygen movement in the material, *K* is the solubility of oxygen in the material, and *L* is the thickness of the lens. The higher the product *DK* and the thinner the lens, the more oxygen is available to the cornea. These factors combine in soft lenses to allow for choice in replacement schedules.

One-day wear lenses are replaced at the beginning of each day. The water content of these lenses is typically at the low to medium end of the range. Fresh lenses are used each day, so eye health is maximized. Extended wear lenses are typically used in one of two ways. The patient wears them continuously, including periods of sleep, for 1 week, and then the lenses are replaced. Alternatively, the wearer inserts the lenses at the beginning of each day and removes them prior to sleep. The lenses are typically replaced after 2 weeks in this modality. Extended wear lenses are usually high in water content and very thin. Typically, special cleaners and sterilization solutions are not required for extended use; a sterile buffered saline solution is sufficient to maintain the integrity of the lens. Daily wear lenses are typically replaced after 3 months of use, with removal at the end of each day and overnight cleaning and sterilization similar to the regimen used with RGPs.

Lens design. An optical system composed of *n* elements can be described as shown in Eq. (1); *f* is

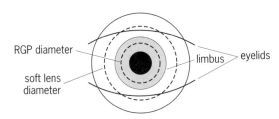

Fig. 2. Relative diameters of RGP and soft lenses.

$$\frac{1}{f_{\text{system}}} = \sum_{1}^{n} \frac{1}{f_n} \qquad (1)$$

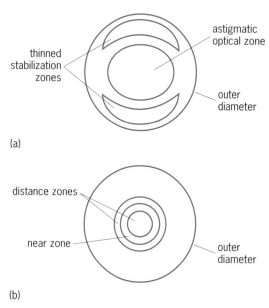

thinned
stabilization
zones

astigmatic
optical zone

outer
diameter

(a)

distance zones

near zone

outer
diameter

(b)

Fig. 3. Schematic of (a) slab-off toric and (b) multifocal bifocal soft lenses.

focal length. For convenience, the ophthalmic field utilizes diopters, or dioptric power, defined as Eq. (2); f is focal length in meters. For example, a

$$D = \frac{1}{f} \qquad (2)$$

2.00 D lens has a focal length of 0.50 m (1.6 ft). Simple substitution yields Eq. (3).

$$D_{\text{system}} = \sum_{1}^{n} D_n \qquad (3)$$

Ocular focus errors. These are corrected by the placement of a lens of the properly prescribed dioptric power in front of the cornea to relocate the position of the focused image. In the case of contact lenses, the lens is placed directly on the corneal surface. Because they do not mask the cornea, soft lens designs must address corneal shape. Because they achieve optical correction by masking the cornea, RGP designs must factor in errors in the crystalline lens.

Myopia and hyperopia. These are corrected using nominally spherical contact lenses. Typical lenses in this category consist of two spherical surfaces separated by an appropriately selected thickness of material.

Astigmatism-correcting lenses. These are called torics, which have two dioptric powers, each power corresponding to the differing refractive zones. Soft lenses have a further complication in that the negating astigmatic correction must be placed onto one or both of the lens surfaces and the lens stabilized to accurately locate it with respect to the cornea. Because they are difficult to stabilize, RGPs are not particularly suited for lenticular astigmatism.

Orientation and stabilization. These are influenced by the interaction of the lens with the eyelids and to some extent by gravity. Lens positioning is addressed by a number of design approaches. Examples are prism ballasting, where the lens has an increasing thickness gradient from top to bottom, and slab-offs, where the lens peripheries are selectively thinned (**Fig. 3a**).

Bifocal contact lenses. All presbyopic designs are a static solution to the loss of the dynamic accommodation process. Simultaneous vision designs are common. In these designs, an object is simultaneously imaged by both near and distance correction zones. The zones may be distinct rings, in multifocal designs; or may be a smooth curve transitioning from one power to another, in progressive designs (Fig. 3b). In many patients, good vision is achieved after an initial period of adjustment to the dual images. Translating designs use separate distance and near zones in a manner similar to bifocal spectacles. The patient learns to position his or her eyes so the appropriate zone is positioned over the cornea. Monovision is a third option. The patient is corrected for distance in one eye and for near in the other. Many patients report satisfaction with this approach. However, a loss in depth perception, or stereopsis, is not uncommon.

Requirements. A number of other factors are used by the eye-care practitioner to determine the suitability and appropriate modality for a contact lens candidate. These include eye diameter, eye health, the topography of the cornea, eyelid conditions, the ability to produce sufficient tears, and the ability to insert and remove lenses.

For background information *see* DIOPTER; EYE (VERTEBRATE); EYEGLASSES AND CONTACT LENSES; EYEPIECE; FOCAL LENGTH; LENS (OPTICS); OPTICAL MATERIALS; OPTICS; VISION in the McGraw-Hill Encyclopedia of Science & Technology.   Russell Spaulding

Bibliography. D. A. Atchison, D. H. Scott, and M. J. Cox, Mathematical treatment of ocular aberrations: A user's guide, *Trends in Optics and Photonics: Vision Science and Its Applications*, 35:110–130, 2000; G. Smith and D. A. Atchison, *The Eye and Visual Optical Instruments*, Cambridge University Press, 1997; H. A. Stein et al., *Contact Lenses: Fundamentals and Clinical Use*, SLACK Inc., 1997; H. A. Stein, B. J. Slatt, and R. A. Stein, *The Ophthalmic Assistant: A Guide for Ophthalmic Medical Personnel*, 6th ed., Mosby-Year Book, Inc., 1994.

CP symmetry and its violation

CP symmetry is the technical name for an almost, but not quite, exact symmetry of the laws of physics. It is the symmetry between the laws of physics for matter and those for antimatter. *CP* violation refers to the very small effects showing that this symmetry is not exact. The symmetry appears to be exact for strong interactions and for electromagnetic and gravitational interactions. Only in a few weak interaction processes is any violation of this symmetry found.

Weak interaction processes, such as those decays in which the quark type or lepton type changes, are rare in comparison to strong and electromagnetic interaction processes with similar energy release. *CP* symmetry-violating effects are an even rarer subset of weak processes. However, *CP* violation can be observed by looking for an effect that would be forbidden if the symmetry were exact. Any observation of such an effect, however rare, is an indication of breaking of the symmetry in the underlying physical laws.

In contrast to the small symmetry breaking in the laws of physics, the world around us has a huge asymmetry: The universe contains matter, which forms all the visible objects in it, but very little antimatter. A major puzzle of modern cosmology is how such an imbalance in the substance in the universe could arise, given the small asymmetry in the laws of interactions.

Theory. To solve this puzzle, it is necessary to understand *CP* symmetry and its violation in detail. The symmetry is an invariance of the laws of physics after the product of two exchanges. The first replaces every particle by its antiparticle (and vice versa); this operation is known as *C* or charge conjugation. The second is an inversion of all spatial directions, known as *P* or parity. The combined operation turns left-handedly spinning neutrinos into right-handedly spinning antineutrinos, for example. It is observed that weak interactions involve both of these types of particles but do not involve right-handedly spinning neutrinos or left-handedly spinning antineutrinos. This feature of weak interactions violates both the *C* symmetry and the *P* symmetry separately, but seems to conserve the combined *CP* symmetry. This was first observed in 1956 and led physicists to the recognition that *CP* is closer to an exact matter-antimatter symmetry than the simple particle-antiparticle transposition of *C* alone. For some time thereafter, it was thought that the *CP* symmetry was an exact, and even perhaps an unavoidable, symmetry of the laws of nature. When effects that prove the symmetry is not exact were first observed in 1964, this was regarded as a major puzzle.

It is now understood that particle theories with a large number of different particle types can allow *CP*-violating effects. The modern theory of particle interactions, known as the standard model, encompasses all particle interactions aside from gravity. The original version of this theory had four quarks and four leptons, including two types of massless neutrino, making up two generations of particles. This theory has no room for *CP* violation, without adding additional particles. However, now it has been observed that there are three generations of quarks and three of leptons. When the standard model is extended in this way, it allows *CP*-violating effects in the pattern of weak decay couplings for the quarks. However, the pattern of these *CP*-violating effects predicted by the standard model has been, until quite recently, one of the least tested aspects of the theory.

Experiments. Recent experimental developments have occurred on two fronts. In the quark sector, measurements of *CP*-violating effects in the decay of *B* mesons have been made. In the lepton sector, recent measurements have shown that neutrinos have very tiny masses, and that the three states of definite mass are not the same as the three states produced by *W* emission from each of the three charged leptons [the electron (*e*), the muon (*μ*), and the tau lepton (*τ*)]. Thus there can be *CP* violation in the pattern of lepton weak couplings (between states of definite mass), just as there is in the quark sector. Exploration of that *CP* violation is an interesting problem for future neutrino experiments. *See* NEUTRINO MASSES AND OSCILLATIONS.

In the quark sector a large *CP*-violating effect in certain rare decays of neutral *B* mesons was recently observed at two facilities, in Japan and in the United States. These facilities were built for the express purpose of studying these effects. They produce millions of pairs of a B^0 (*B*-zero) meson (made from a *d* quark and an anti-*b* quark) and its antiparticle known as an anti-B^0 (*B*-zero-bar) meson (made from a *b* quark and an anti-*d* quark.) By comparing the probability that a B^0 decays to a particular final set of particles to the probability that an anti-B^0 decays to the *CP*-mirror set, one can search for *CP* violation. Any difference between these two is a *CP*-violating effect. Particularly interesting cases to study are those where the final set of particles is identical to its *CP*-mirror set (for example, two oppositely charged pions moving apart with equal and opposite momenta).

A clear *CP*-violating effect has been seen for decays to a final state containing a neutral *K* meson and a ψ meson (J/ψ or one of its close relatives such as ψ' or η_c, all of which are made from a *c* quark and an anti-*c* quark). The result can be interpreted as a measurement of an angle, called β or ϕ_1, which is a parameter that appears in the standard model. The two experiments follow different conventions on the name for this parameter, but they agree, within their statistical uncertainties, on its value. The measured quantity is the sine of twice the angle. If there were no *CP* violation, it would be zero. Combining the results of both experiments gives a value of 0.78 with an uncertainty of plus or minus 0.08, clearly inconsistent with zero. Furthermore, it is consistent with the standard model, that is, within the range predicted based on measurements of other effects that depend on the same set of parameters in the standard model, including the *CP*-violating effects in *K* meson decays. This match suggests that the *CP*-violation effect in quark decays is at least in part described by the standard model parameters.

The experiments are continuing, both to refine this measurement and to measure other similar effects with different final states. The set of many such measurements can further refine the tests of whether the standard model theory correctly describes the *CP* violation in the quark sector, or, alternatively, whether there is need for input from theories that go beyond the standard model.

Extensions of the standard model. Physicists will be much more excited if they find that the predicted patterns are not realized. That would point the way to extensions of the current theory. One reason to seek a breakdown of the theory in the area of *CP* violation is in order to describe the development of an imbalance between matter and antimatter in the history of the universe. Starting from an early period where reactions enforced equality between the population of matter particles and that of antimatter particles, one cannot successfully model evolution to the now-observed universe, using just the standard model theory. One must add speculative extensions to the theory. Many of the possible extensions are in the category of baryogenesis, which means the generation of the matter-antimatter inbalance in the universe by any process which gives an excess of baryons (such as protons or neutrons) over their antiparticles. These extensions would also introduce effects that could be seen in the pattern of CP violations in the B factories. The ongoing experiments at these facilities hope to find some pointers that help distinguish which (if any) of these extensions correctly describes the physics of the universe.

Another type of extension of the standard model theory is needed to incorporate neutrino masses. This adds another set of CP-violating parameters in the neutrino sector of the theory. This would not affect the physics seen at the B factories. However, it does allow a quite different possibility for the development of the matter-antimatter imbalance in the universe, a scenario known as leptogenesis, which means the generation of this imbalance by any process that gives an excess of leptons (such as electrons and neutrinos) over their antiparticles. In addition to the light, weakly interacting neutrino species that are now observed, theories to incorporate neutrino masses introduce some very massive and even more weakly interacting types of neutrinos. These particles would be produced in the hot early universe. Any CP violation in their decays can introduce a matter-antimatter imbalance in lepton populations, which may later lead to a matter-antimatter imbalance in baryons (protons and neutrons and their ilk) as well, via processes known to exist in the standard model theory. Experiments to further delineate the neutrino masses and weak couplings can eventually explore this story further. Unfortunately, some of the parameters in such a theory affect only the very massive and very weakly interacting neutrino types, and are not accessible to any foreseeable experiment.

Both B physics and neutrino mass studies are very active parts of current particle experiments. Eventually they will yield a better understanding of the differences between the laws of physics for matter and those for antimatter, that is, the CP symmetry violation. The hope is that this will lead to a better understanding of the asymmetry of matter and antimatter content in the universe, and of how and when in the history of the universe that asymmetry developed.

For background information *see* ANTIMATTER; ELEMENTARY PARTICLE; MESON; NEUTRINO; PARITY (QUANTUM MECHANICS); QUARK; STANDARD MODEL; SUPERSYMMETRY; SYMMETRY LAWS (PHYSICS); TIME REVERSAL INVARIANCE; WEAK NUCLEAR INTERAC-TIONS; WEAKLY INTERACTING MASSIVE PARTICLE (WIMP) in the McGraw-Hill Encyclopedia of Science & Technology.   Helen R. Quinn

Bibliography. G. P. Collins, SNO nus is good news, *Sci. Amer.*, 285(3):16, September 2001; H. R. Quinn and M. S. Witherell, The asymmetry between matter and antimatter, *Sci. Amer.*, 279(4):50, October 1998.

Crustacean olfaction

Crustaceans, in particular larger crustaceans such as crayfish and lobsters, are among the animal models used to study olfaction, the sense of smell. Although crustaceans as a group are largely aquatic animals, and have their olfactory receptor neurons packaged in sensilla (hairlike sensory structures), the crustacean olfactory organ is functionally similar to noses of other animals and has contributed to common understanding of the sense of smell. The olfactory organ or "nose" of crustaceans has been especially well studied.

Olfactory receptor neurons. The crustacean olfactory organ is borne on the lateral filament of the paired second antenna, called the antennule (see **illus.**). The antennule can be long and filamentous or short and clublike depending on the species. The actual olfactory organ consists of a tuft of up to 1000 or more specialized sensilla called aesthetascs. Up to several hundred modified ciliary bipolar receptor neurons are associated with each aesthetasc. Each receptor cell consists of a cell body (or soma), a dendrite, and an axon. The somata cluster in the lumen of the antennule. The dendrites extend from the somata into the lumen of the sensillum with which the cells are associated. Shortly after entering the sensillum, the dendrites in many species bifurcate repeatedly into an arbor of outer dendritic segments, or cilia. The outer dendritic segments normally extend the full length of the hair and contact the environment through the hair's permeable cuticle. The number of olfactory receptor neurons is impressive. The Caribbean spiny lobster, *Panulirus argus*, for instance, has an estimated 250,000–300,000 olfactory receptor neurons in each of its two olfactory organs (see illus.).

The olfactory receptor neurons, as in other animals, continuously turn over (that is, they die and are replaced) throughout the life of the animal. New aesthetascs proliferate from a region just proximal to the tuft and progressively move along a disto-proximal axis as older aesthetascs are lost at the distal part of the tuft with each successive molt. Functional maturation of the olfactory receptor neurons, however, is not synchronized with molting and may not be completed for many weeks after sensillar emergence. This finding suggests that successive spatio-temporal waves of birth, differentiation, functional maturation, and death of the olfactory receptor neurons move down the antennule as the animal matures.

Olfactory lobe. The axons of the olfactory receptor neurons project to a glomerularly organized synaptic

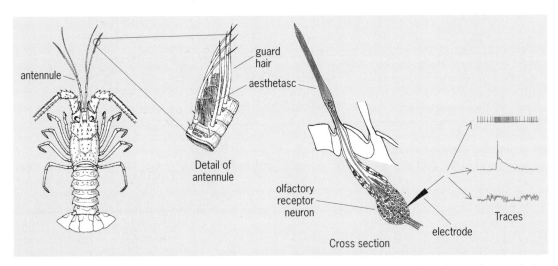

In the Caribbean spiny lobster, the paired antennules constitute the "nose." The enlargement shows the detailed organization of the tuft of antennular olfactory sensilla, called aesthetascs, and their protective guard hairs that constitute the olfactory organ proper. The enlarged cross section of the tuft shows some of the 250–300 primary olfactory receptor neurons associated with each aesthetasc in this species. As shown for one neuron, each neuron extends its dendrite into the hairlike sensillum, where the dendrite branches into multiple outer dendritic segments, or cilia, that bind odorant molecules entering through the permeable cuticle of the sensillum. Patch-clamp electrodes can be used in different configurations to record extracellular trains of odorant-evoked action potentials (top trace), intracellular receptor potentials (middle trace), or unitary currents from single ion channels (bottom trace) from the cells in vivo or after placing the cells in primary culture.

relay in the brain known as the olfactory lobe. The structural and functional organization of this relay is strikingly similar to the first olfactory relay in most animals, from fish to terrestrial vertebrates to insects, and thus the basis for considering the antennule to be an olfactory organ. Nonaesthetasc chemosensory sensilla also occur on the antennule. Although neurons from these sensilla do not project to the olfactory lobe, this pathway has some overlap and redundancy of function with the aesthetasc pathway, for example in complex odorant-mediated behaviors such as learning and discrimination, which are typically associated with olfaction. Exactly how this non-aesthetasc chemosensory input relates to aesthetasc input is an unanswered question.

Odorant binding. The outer dendrites of olfactory receptor neurons are the presumed site of odorant binding. Odorant binding is assumed to activate odorant-specific G-protein coupled receptors, as in other animals; however, these receptors remain to be identified for crustaceans. Odorant binding can activate two distinct intracellular signaling pathways in an odorant-specific manner. One pathway, mediated by phosphinositide signaling, inhibits excitation of the cell. The extent to which each of these pathways is coactivated by a given odorant, which in nature is inevitably a complex mixture of substances, determines the net output of the cell. In other words, the receptor cell can serve as an integrating unit. Activation of the olfactory receptor neuron also involves a novel sodium-activated cation conductance that carries the bulk of receptor current.

Odorant coding. Olfactory receptor neurons are typical "spiking" neurons that encode information in trains of action potentials that propagate to the brain (see illus.), a distance of more than 10 cm in larger species of crustaceans with stalked, fila-

mentous antennules. The temporal profile of the discharge is determined by the kinetics of odorant binding and stimulus access to the receptor. Relatively little is known of the kinetics of receptor binding other than that it is fast, occurring within several tens of milliseconds of stimulus onset. Stimulus onset is actively regulated in most species by a reflex known as antennular flicking. Unstirred (stagnant) layers surrounding each sensillum normally make the tuft relatively impermeant to the odor environment, even though the antennule, which extends well beyond the head of the animal in most species, would appear to be continuously exposed to odorants. Flicking rapidly and transiently increases the velocity of the antennule and, during the downstroke of the flick, the tuft reaches velocities necessary to disrupt the unstirred layer and allow essentially instantaneous access of the stimulus to the receptors within the sensilla. The resulting intermittent exposure of the receptor cells to the odor environment is analogous to sniffing in mammals and temporally synchronizes the discharge of the receptor cells in a manner that potentially could contribute to odorant coding.

Odorant recognition and discrimination. Adequate stimuli for crustacean olfactory receptor cells are largely unknown but inevitably are as diverse as crustaceans themselves, and certainly differ for terrestrial and aquatic species. Adequate stimuli for terrestrial species have yet to be defined, but among the adequate stimuli for the olfactory receptors of aquatic species are low-molecular-weight organic compounds such as amino acids, amines, organic acids, and nucleotides that serve in mixture as feeding cues. Behavioral studies indicate crustaceans rely on social cues (pheromones), but receptor cells specialized for pheromone detection do not appear to exist in crustacean olfactory organs as they do in some insects.

Receptor cells responding to low-molecular-weight organic compounds show various degrees of "tuning," in that some cells show more restricted response spectra, whereas others respond to multiple compounds in complex patterns. In general, the cells do not readily fall into types, suggesting that odorant recognition and discrimination in crustaceans, as in other animals, is based on a combinatorial or distributed code. In this coding strategy, each odorant generates a unique pattern of discharge across the population of receptor cells that becomes the "signature" of that odorant to be deciphered (in some yet unknown way) by the central nervous system.

For background information *see* BIOPOTENTIALS AND IONIC CURRENTS; CHEMORECEPTION; CRUSTACEA; NEUROBIOLOGY; NEURON; OLFACTION; SIGNAL TRANSDUCTION; SYNAPTIC TRANSMISSION in the McGraw-Hill Encyclopedia of Science & Technology.
Barry W. Ache

Bibliography. B. W. Ache and A. Zhainazarov, Dual second messenger pathways in olfaction, *Curr. Opin. Neurobiol.*, 5:461–466, 1995; C. D. Derby, Learning from spiny lobsters about chemosensory coding of mixtures, *Physiol. Behav.*, 69:203–209, 2000; U. Gruenert and B. W. Ache, Ultrastructure of the aesthetasc (olfactory) sensilla of the spiny lobster *Panulirus argus*, *Cell Tissue Res.*, 251:95–103, 1988; J. G. Hildebrand and G. M. Shepherd, Mechanisms of olfactory discrimination: Converging evidence for common principles across phyla, *Annu. Rev. Neurosci.*, 20:595–631, 1997; M. A. Koehl et al., Lobster sniffing: Antennule design and hydrodynamic filtering of information in an odor plume, *Science*, 294:1948–1951, 2001.

Data mining

Data mining is the process of discovering valid, comprehensible, and potentially useful knowledge from large data sources with the purpose of applying this knowledge to making decisions. Although generally driven by competitive business environments, data mining is not specific to any particular industry. In fact, any organization can use data mining to extract information in the form of facts, relationships, trends, or patterns. Data mining can also be used to reveal missing pieces of data, or to discover anomalies or exceptions to assumed relationships between some different pieces of data. For this reason, data mining is sometimes referred to as knowledge discovery in databases (KDD). Data mining and KDD, however, are not synonymous. The KDD concept is generally used to describe the whole process of extracting knowledge, whereas data mining is considered a particular activity within KDD where specific algorithms are used to extract data.

The results of the data mining process may be reported in many different formats, such as listings, graphic outputs, summary tables, and visualizations.

The large data sources necessary for data mining are generally provided by specialized databases called data warehouses that may contain billions of records. In 2000, Wal-Mart's warehouse contained more than 100 terabytes (trillions of bytes) of information. To understand the size of this warehouse, assume that the size of each character of a standard printed page of 8 × 11 in. is a byte. A terabyte then is approximately equivalent to 250 million pages of text. Therefore, if the size of the warehouse in printed pages is measured, Wal-Mart's warehouse would be about 25 billion pages. Due to the vast amount of information that needs to be manipulated and the type of output that is expected from the data mining process, traditional databases or multidimensional analysis techniques generally are not suitable. In both cases, the results that they produce are merely extracted values (in response to ad hoc queries), or an aggregation of values. To make data mining more efficient, the data source should have an aggregated or summarized collection of data.

Process. Data mining is a complex process involving several iterative steps (see **illus.**). The initial step is the selection of data. This data may come from a single warehouse or may be extracted from other data sources. The selected data set then goes through a cleaning and preprocessing stage to format it in a

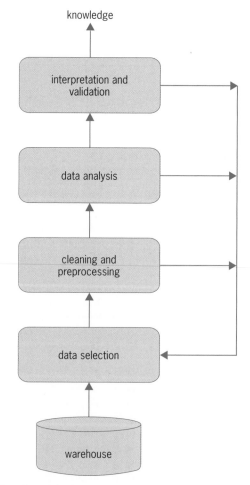

Overview of the data mining process.

convenient way, remove inconsistencies, or reduce its dimensions. This data set is then analyzed to identify patterns or trends which, if considered meaningful, serve as the basis for creating a model of relationships among the data. This model is tested against new sets of data to ensure its validity. That is, new data are run against the model to verify that the discovered relationships still hold among the data. If the validation of the model is successful, the model becomes business knowledge. It is this knowledge that gets translated into a business plan that is used to help the decision makers achieve the goals of the organization.

Technology. Although the term "data mining" may convey the use of a single technology, this is not generally the case. Data mining integrates areas such as database management, data engineering, modern statistics, intelligent information systems, pattern recognition, machine learning, and decision theory, to name a few. There is not a distinct separation of data mining from the collective use of these disciplines. To accomplish its objectives, data mining may make extensive use of tools derived from the fields of neural networks or genetic programming. Some of the tools commonly used are rule induction, data visualization, and decision trees. These tools help to automatically find correlations and groupings of data. In tightly integrated environments, one tool may work in conjunction with others. For example, the exploratory nature of a decision tree may be used to evaluate and explain the results of a neural network.

Goals. In general, the goals of data mining include identification, association, sequence, classification, clustering, forecasting, and optimization. Identification determines the existence of an item, event, or activity from existing data patterns. Association determines if two or more events or characteristics are related or not. Sequence determines if events or characteristics are linked over time. Classification partitions the data so that each record is placed in a group or class with other similar members. Clustering is similar to classification but differs in that no groups have yet been defined. Forecasting estimates the future value of continuous variables based on patterns within the data. Optimization intends to maximize the output variables of the data mining process while making the most efficient use of limited resources such as time, money, space, or materials.

Knowledge discovery. The knowledge discovered during the data mining process can be classified as association rules, classification hierarchies, sequential patterns, patterns with time series, categorization, and segmentation. However, most of the time the knowledge resulting from the data mining process is a combination of several of these types of knowledge. Association rules allow inference of the presence of a set of values from the values of another set. For example, from the information extracted from the mining of the data of a nationwide retail store, it can be inferred that whenever a person buys wrapping paper the same person is likely to buy paper plates. Classification hierarchies create a hierarchy

of classes from values of a given set. For example, insurance companies can classify their customers and set their rates based on the family and health history of individuals. Sequential patterns involve the detection of temporal associations between events. For instance, using information from the Department of Education gathered from schools across the country, the mining process may determine that infants that attend pre-kindergarten and kindergarten classes are more likely to attend and finish college than those students that start at the first grade. Patterns with time series are used to find similarities within particular time frames. Time series have been successfully applied to predict bankruptcy of firms under varied economic conditions. Categorization and segmentation groups data according to some relevant criteria. For instance, e-buyers at a particular Web site can be identified and grouped into categories of more or less likely to buy a new set of products.

Tools. Several commercial tools have "intuitive" user interfaces. These graphical user interfaces (GUIs) let users choose from menus, "fill-in-the-blanks" input boxes, or "point-and-click" icons to produce text reports, spreadsheets, two- or three-dimensional charts, and other types of graphs. Most of these data mining tools make use of the industry standard known as Open Database Connectivity (ODBC) to interact and extract information from data sources including legacy databases. Data exploration, through the use of techniques such as decision trees and graphics, can be deployed via an intranet or the Internet. Data can also be imported from a variety of file formats and analyzed using statistical packages. In well-structured databases, a user can identify a particular table and mine it while the data reside in the database. This is known as "in-place" mining. Data can be mined on a single workstation or remotely. In the latter case, network protocols such as TCP/IP are necessary to communicate between the client machine and its server. Data mining techniques and tools continue to evolve and benefit from the latest research in their traditional supporting fields and other areas such as computer science, statistics, and operation research. At present, the trend is to allow full data mining capabilities through the Internet with expanded capabilities that may include multimedia databases and specialized warehouses.

Solution-based approach. New developments in data mining combined with current databases' ability to accommodate knowledge discovery have resulted in solution-based approaches. That is, each enterprise or company stores only the information necessary to solve an immediate problem at hand. This approach has been successfully applied by credit card companies to detect fraud by keeping track of the purchase behavior of their customers (profiling the customer). This way, if a series of transactions do not fit the customer's normal (past) credit card behavior, or if the transactions do not take place where the card is mostly used, the transactions trigger a statistical outlier event (a deviation from the normal parameters set for a particular individual that generates a warning from the system). For example, if the profile of a particular customer shows that he rarely makes more than five purchases of $50.00 or more in a month, a series of transactions of more than $250.00 over a short period of time will trigger a statistical outlier. In this case, the warning generated by the system will alert the card company to take remedial action. This may requires that the customer be contacted about the validity of the transactions or may result in a refusal to honor the credit card purchase.

For background information *see* ALGORITHM; ARTIFICIAL INTELLIGENCE; DATA MINING; DATABASE MANAGEMENT SYSTEM; DECISION SUPPORT SYSTEM; DECISION THEORY; GENETIC ALGORITHMS; INFORMATION SYSTEMS ENGINEERING; INTERNET; NEURAL NETWORK; STATISTICS in the McGraw-Hill Encyclopedia of Science & Technology.   Ramon A. Mata-Toledo

Bibliography. I. Bose and R. K. Mahapatra, Business data mining: A machine learning perspective, *Inform. Manag.*, 39:211–225, 2001; R. Elmasri and S. B. Navathe, *Fundamentals of Database Systems*, 3d ed., Addison-Wesley, 2000; D. Meyer and C. Cannon, *Data Warehouse*, Prentice Hall, 1998.

Declining amphibians

Declines in the populations of amphibians (frogs, toads, salamanders, newts, and caecilians) were first highlighted internationally in 1989 at the First World Congress of Herpetology (the study of amphibians and reptiles) in Canterbury, U.K. Many researchers had independently noticed that the populations of frogs they studied were greatly reduced in number or had disappeared altogether from locations in which they had previously been abundant. One such location was in the Sierra Nevada mountains of California.

A series of meetings of international amphibian experts found that reports of declining amphibian populations came from a variety of geographically dispersed locations, and a number of different and apparently unconnected species seemed to be affected. Particularly worrisome was that many of these reports came from apparently "pristine" or protected areas. This led to the formation of the Declining Amphibian Populations Task Force (DAPTF) in late 1990. The DAPTF's mission is to determine the nature, extent, and causes of amphibian declines and to promote the means by which declines can be halted or reversed.

Amphibians as environmental indicators. Amphibians are especially vulnerable to subtle environmental changes because of their biphasic life cycle (most species have both aquatic and terrestrial stages). Their skin is very permeable to air, water, and pollutants so that any change in either the aquatic or terrestrial environments of their habitat may affect them significantly. Amphibians are, therefore, important indicators of general environmental health, and declines in their populations may serve as early warning signs of ecological problems in environments that humans perceive as healthy.

Human factor. The declines in amphibian populations have been attributed to many factors, including habitat destruction, global warming, increased ultraviolet light radiation, pollution, and disease. There is mounting evidence that the most significant factor negatively affecting amphibian populations is habitat destruction (or alteration) by humans. This includes activities such as deforestation and urbanization; however, it has been discovered that habitat fragmentation (the separation of suitable pockets of habitat by major roads or other development schemes) is an important factor as well. Amphibian breeding populations are cyclic, that is, they suffer crashes and booms over periods of several years; and amphibians may become locally extinct at certain breeding sites (for example, an individual pond or wetland). Recolonization of such sites then relies on a nearby population to experience a boom period, in which dispersing animals reoccupy the vacant habitat. The separation of habitat pockets by barriers, however, can make this impossible, causing the species to become locally extinct on a permanent basis, even though the habitat may remain suitable.

Pollutants. Pollutant-induced declines are easier to assess than declines in protected or pristine locations. Many studies over the last 10 years have found that various forms of pollution affect amphibians in unexpected ways and at lower levels than might be expected. Heavy metals, pesticides, and sewage runoff find their way into rivers and ponds, and may adversely affect (on their own or in conjunction with other pollutants) amphibian eggs, tadpoles, or adults. A startling recent example is the finding by researchers at the University of California at Berkeley that very low levels of atrazine (which is the most commonly used herbicide in the United States and one of the most commonly used in the world) cause male frogs to become more female: they begin to develop ovaries or their voices (important in attracting a mate) fail to develop properly. Levels as low as 0.1 part per billion (ppb) have been seen to initiate this effect. (The U.S. Environmental Protection Agency currently allows up to 3 ppb of atrazine in drinking water.) The effects of certain other pollutants seem to be increased in conjunction with other environmental changes such as higher ultraviolet light levels (caused by reduced cloud cover in parts of the world and changes in the ozone layer). However, since some amphibian species possess a chemical "sunblock" which protects their eggs from the effects of ultraviolet light, researchers are unsure that high ultraviolet light levels by themselves are causing amphibian declines.

Malformations. Malformed frogs (with extra or missing limbs and eyes or misshapen bodies) were first noticed in large numbers in Minnesota ponds in 1995. Since such frogs have a low survival rate (they feed poorly and may be easily caught by predators), it was thought that malformations may be contributing to the global decline of amphibians. Subsequently, it was discovered that both the usual suspects, pollution and ultraviolet light, do indeed increase malformation rates in frogs, as do certain species of frog parasites (such as trematodes). In addition, these factors have a more adverse effect when they act together, suggesting that the reduced survival of individual frogs caused by malformation could affect the survival of the population as a whole, especially at a time when the population cycle is in a "crash" phase. What is clear, however, is that many factors acting together can contribute to this phenomenon; thus, finding out exactly how any one affects amphibian populations is extremely difficult.

Chytrid fungus. An important development in understanding amphibian declines has been the discovery of new infectious diseases that are killing amphibians in many parts of the world. One breakthrough has been the identification of a previously unknown species of fungus (a chytrid), first found in frogs in Central America and Queensland, Australia. This pathogen has caused some of the most dramatic declines of amphibians that have been observed to date.

In the mid-1990s, there was a mass mortality of frogs in both Central America and Queensland that drew the attention of researchers and prompted urgent investigation. In both locations, the same fungus was found in the skin of dead and dying frogs. After intensive investigation, researchers in both locations independently confirmed it as a previously unknown species of chytrid fungus. Subsequently, the chytrid was found on every continent. It is directly responsible for mortality events in amphibian communities in South, Central, and North America (where it came to attention in connection with population declines of the boreal toad in the Rocky Mountains), Australia, and more recently Europe and New Zealand. It has also been found in wild-caught amphibians being kept as pets.

Two recent findings may have important implications for scientists' understanding of the epidemiology and distribution of the amphibian chytrid fungus. First, the chytrid is increasingly found in museum specimens of amphibians, indicating that it has been around for a while. Second, chytrid infection has been discovered in clawed frogs (*Xenopus*) in South Africa. Intriguingly, although the chytrid fungus is widespread in the populations studied, it has achieved this large-scale distribution without causing any harmful effects. This, in combination with the museum findings, may indicate that chytrid infection has existed in this population long enough for the *Xenopus* to evolve immunological defense mechanisms against it. The frogs in "novel" locations such as Queensland and the Rocky Mountains have not previously encountered this disease and so have not been able to evolve any means of surviving being infected, hence its disastrous effects on their populations. In addition, *Xenopus* has for many years been traded around the globe for use in pregnancy testing, schools, universities, and laboratories; this may

be the means by which the chytrid has found its way to many corners of the world.

The chytrid is only one of the pathogens that have been recorded as causing amphibian mortality. Several other diseases have been found to cause the death of North American salamanders, Israeli toads, and common frogs in garden ponds in England. Researchers are doing everything they can to understand the mechanisms by which these diseases work, how they spread, and, most importantly, what can be done to prevent them from killing more amphibians.

Conclusion. There is no one answer to the question of what has caused the global decline of amphibians. Many diverse factors have been found to play a part. Many questions remain. For example, do novel diseases have a worse effect on isolated populations or on populations in high-ultraviolet-light areas? Is the effect of pollution worsened by increased temperature (global warming) or reduced cloud cover?

The DAPTF runs a network of over 3000 scientists and conservationists that disseminate the results of their research to concerned individuals, institutions, conservation bodies, and legislators around the world. There is a program of small grants which enables promising research corridors to be explored, and it is through this program that many advances leading to breakthroughs in the investigation of amphibian declines have been made. The process of understanding amphibian declines is an ongoing one. This process should lead to a greater understanding of the threats to the world's biodiversity as a whole and ultimately to the means by which the biodiversity of various areas can be protected and conserved.

For background information *see* AMPHIBIA; CHYTRIDIOMYCETES; ECOLOGY, APPLIED; ENDANGERED SPECIES in the McGraw-Hill Encyclopedia of Science & Technology.   John Wilkinson

Bibliography. M. Crump, *In Search of the Golden Frog*, Chicago University Press, 2000; R. Dalton, Frogs put in the gender blender by America's favourite herbicide, *Nature*, 416:665–666, 2002; D. M. Green (ed.), *Amphibians in Decline: Canadian Studies of a Global Problem*, Society for the Study of Amphibians and Reptiles, St. Louis, 1997; M. J. Lannoo (ed.), *Status and Conservation of Midwest Amphibians*, University of Iowa Press, 1998; W. Mara, *The Fragile Frog* (for children), Whitman, Morton Grove, IL, 1996.

Deep-sea squid

In 2001 an unusual squid estimated at 7 m (23 ft) in length was reported for the first time. That such a large animal could have gone undetected for so long seems remarkable. This squid, however, was found in the bathypelagic zone of the deep sea, a region that, because of its large size and inaccessibility, has been poorly investigated. The ocean has about 300 times more living space than exists on land. Over two-thirds of this vast aquatic realm lies in the bathypelagic zone, generally ranging from approximately 1000 m (3280 ft) deep down to the ocean floor.

Deep-sea fauna. The bathypelagic zone is characterized by the absence of sunlight (the only light there being an occasional flash or glow of bioluminescence from organisms), low temperatures (usually below 4°C or 40°F), high hydrostatic pressures (pressure increases by one atmosphere for every 10 m or 33 ft of depth), and the low availability of food (because animals ultimately depend on plants for food, the sunlit near-surface waters are the primary feeding grounds of the ocean). The last results in very low animal abundances. The low temperatures may be an advantage for animals living in this zone, as it decreases metabolic rates and thereby lowers their food requirements. The absence of sunlight also favors a slower lifestyle, as swimming around rapidly in the darkness is an inefficient means of locating food. In this environment stealth is more effective than speed. The high hydrostatic pressures appear to cause few problems as most animals in this zone lack compressible gas spaces (such as swim bladders).

Knowledge of the bathypelagic fauna is limited. The primary inhabitants among the larger organisms are jellyfish, gelatinous worms, fragile shrimps, and some of the most unusual fishes and cephalopods (squids and octopods) known. Typically the cephalopods are gelatinous and neutrally buoyant; they often have eyes that are reduced in size and sometimes virtually nonfunctional. Occasionally squids are found in bathypelagic waters that do not have these common adaptations. Some muscular squids that spend most of their life in upper zones move into bathypelagic depths to spawn, presumably for greater safety from predators. After spawning an egg mass, they hold onto it and brood the embryos. This seems like a good strategy but it has a downside. The low food availability in the bathypelagic zone means that the female must brood without feeding, and the low temperatures slow embryonic development which extends the brooding period to as long as 9 months. Comparable-sized eggs developing in warm surface waters would take about a week to hatch. Few other upper-zone squids have opted for such a trade-off.

New squid. As knowledge of this vast inaccessible environment improves, many new and peculiar animals will be found. The new squid mentioned earlier is one example. Separate sightings of it have occurred in the Atlantic, Pacific, and Indian oceans within the past few years. All sightings have been at depths between 1940 and 4735 m (6365 and 15,535 ft) and from a few meters to 60 m (10 to 200 ft) above the ocean floor. While the low density of animal life in the bathypelagic zone means that little food is available for large animals like this squid, the region near the deep-sea floor is one of the better feeding grounds. Most swimming organisms that die and are not consumed sink to the ocean floor. In addition, fecal matter that has passed through the guts of animals, but still has some food value, also generally sinks. This rain of dead material accumulates on the ocean floor and provides a source of food for animals living there.

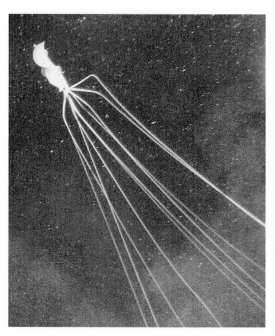

Fig. 1. The new squid photographed from the submersible *ALVIN*, October 2000, at 1940 m (6360 ft) depth in the Gulf of Mexico.

Locomotion. The new squid (**Fig. 1**) is peculiar in several ways. First, it has very large fins. This indicates that its primary means of locomotion is with the fins rather than by jet propulsion, the typical mode of swimming in squids. Videos of the squid show slow undulations of the giant fins. Some other squids have large fins (for example, the diamondback squid), but if fin size is judged by the area of the fins compared to the volume of the body, the fins of this squid are among the largest of any cephalopod. Swimming with fins is more efficient, and requires less energy, than jet swimming but cannot produce the speed attained by the latter method. As mentioned earlier, however, in the dark bathypelagic zone speed is less important than stealth in locating prey. Speed also holds limited value in avoiding predators, as safety may lie only inches away due to the cover of darkness. The new squid does use jet propulsion but it is weak and limited. One video sequence shows the squid, when disturbed, giving a single contraction of its mantle to produce a single jet, followed by strong flapping movements of the fins. The single, brief dart produced by the jet can effectively lose a predator in this environment.

Arms. The second peculiarity of the new squid is its extremely long, highly contractile, slender arms that can extend up to 10 times the body (that is, the mantle) length; these are the longest known arms, relative to body length, of any squid. Photographs show that the arms are held in a peculiar attitude. They first extend at right angles to the body of the squid, directed away from the head like spokes on

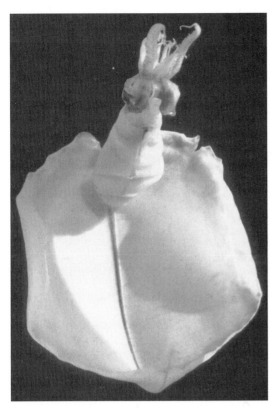

Fig. 2. *Magnapinna pacifica.* Photograph of a preserved 51-mm (2-in.) juvenile.

a wheel, then turn abruptly forward. They appear to be so long and slender that they probably cannot be maneuvered quickly, and this is confirmed by the video tapes. In this attitude, the arms beyond the bases lie parallel to one another surrounding a long cylindrical area of water. The slender arms are probably covered with suckers that are too small to be detected in the video pictures. Another deep-sea squid, known as the whiplash squid, has suckers so small that they can barely be resolved by the human eye; these suckers are found only on the tentacles, which are the modified fourth pair (of a total of five pairs) of arms and are much longer than the other arms. In contrast to the tentacles of shallow-water squids, which have large suckers at the ends and can be quickly extended forward to grab prey, the tentacles of the whiplash squid dangle freely in the water and act like fly paper. Any small animal that bumps into a tentacle is held fast by numerous tiny suckers. In the new squid, the tentacles seem to be similar to the arms and all apparently have the same function. Just how the eight arms and two tentacles are used is uncertain, but they may function similarly to the two tentacles of the whiplash squid. Their long, slender appearance suggests that they are dangling traps like the web of a spider, or more precisely, like the feeding tentacles of a jellyfish.

Relationship to Magnapinnidae. The new squid, never captured and known only from sightings from manned submersibles or ROVs (remotely operated vehicles), has not been identified as belonging to any known species. However, while this large squid is very different from any squid previously seen or captured, the early juvenile of the species may be known. In 1998, a new family of squid, the Magnapinnidae, was described from only three specimens (**Fig. 2**). These were juveniles with mantle lengths of 19 and 51 mm (0.75 and 2 in.). One juvenile was taken from the stomach of a captured fish, and the other in a plankton net in the upper 200 m (650 ft) of the open ocean. *Magnapinna* has the general fin and body shape of the new deep-sea squid. Although the arms and tentacles are very different (they are short and stubby), the tip of each arm and tentacle is a slender filament, a feature that is unique to this species. Possibly the filaments will grow into the long forward-directed portion of the arms and tentacles of the new deep-sea squid. The identity of this large squid, however, will remain uncertain until one is caught, and that is unlikely to be easy or to occur soon.

For background information *see* CEPHALOPODA; DEEP-SEA FAUNA; MARINE ECOLOGY; SQUID in the McGraw-Hill Encyclopedia of Science & Technology.

Richard E. Young

Bibliography. C. F. E. Roper and M. Vecchione, In situ observations test hypotheses of functional morphology in *Mastigoteuthis* (Cephalopoda, Oegopsida), *Vie et Milieu*, 47(2):87–93, 1997; B. A. Seibel, F. G. Hochberg, and D. B. Carlini, Life history of *Gonatus onyx* (Cephalopoda: Teuthoidea): Deep-sea spawning and post-spawning egg care, *Mar. Biol.*, 137:519–526, 2000; M. Vecchione et al., Worldwide observations of remarkable deep-sea squids, *Science*, 294:2505–2506, 2001.

Deuterostome evolution

Our understanding of the early evolution of animals is undergoing radical reappraisals, spurred by new data from molecular biology and remarkable fossil discoveries. These revisions are largely set in the context of the Cambrian explosion, an important evolutionary event in which the advanced animal phyla were assembled and began to diversify. These phyla are characterized by bilateral symmetry (hence their designation Bilateria) and the possession of three embryonic germ layers (hence the descriptor triploblastic). Current evidence points to three bilaterian superclades (very large phylogenetic groupings encompassing several phyla). Respectively, these are the ecdysozoans (notably the arthropods, as well as nematodes and priapulids), the lophotrochozoans (characterized by such phyla as the annelids, brachiopods, and mollusks), and the deuterostomes. The last includes the chordates (the phylum to which humans belong, together with other vertebrates) and echinoderms (such as starfish).

In contrast to the ecdysozoans and lophotrochozoans, which together define the protostomes (a reference to the embryological origin of the mouth, literally "first-mouth"), the earliest diversification of

intestine   segmented tail   gill pouch

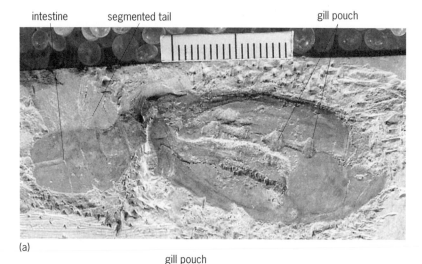

(a)

gill pouch

(b)

gill pouch   segmented tail

(c)

Vetulicola. (*a*) Entire specimen. The anterior with gill pouches on either side is visible: right side on upper surface, left side exposed by excavation; segmented tail with trace of intestine. (Scale bars are in millimeters.) (*b*) Anterior section excavated to show pouchlike gills as seen from the interior side. (*c*) Entire specimen showing gills along lateral midline. The anterior four gills are well preserved; the posterior fifth gill is less clear. The segmented tail is incompletely preserved.

the deuterostomes (literally "second-mouth," again referring to its embryological origins) has remained highly problematic. However, a fossil group known as the vetulicolians may hold a key position in our understanding of the evolution of primitive deuterostomes.

Origins of phyla. While molecular biology is invaluable for defining the three bilaterian superclades and indicating the relative closeness of particular phyla, it is dependent on data from living animals. This source of information is therefore silent about the origin and early history of the various phyla, notably the functional transitions in terms of defense, feeding, and locomotion that must have accompanied the assembly of the various body plans. In principal, however, the fossil record can shed light on these problems. As far as the Cambrian is concerned, the fossils from the Burgess Shale–type faunas are of key importance, as exemplified by the Burgess Shale itself (mid-Middle Cambrian, British Columbia) and the somewhat older Chengjiang assemblage (mid-Lower Cambrian, Yunnan, China). A number of the exquisitely preserved fossils from these faunas appear to represent the so-called stem groups of various phyla, that is, species showing some, but not all, of the major characters of a given phylum. Thus, in principle, these fossils reveal the earliest evolution of a number of body plans, and a number of intriguing fossils appear to shed light on the origins of the ecdysozoans, the lophotrochozoans, and now the deuterostomes. To our eyes the relevant fossils have rather strange, if not bizarre, appearances that bear little resemblance to the various hypothetical (and fanciful) ancestors that are the staple of many textbooks.

Deuterostomes. The extant deuterostome phyla are highly disparate, and in the case of the echinoderms (familiar from starfish and sea urchins) are radically modified by the imposition of a fivefold symmetry. So different are the deuterostome phyla—compare for example a fish with a starfish—that it is difficult to imagine they have a common ancestor. Indeed, apart from certain embryological similarities, the only significant feature the deuterostomes share comprises structures known as the gill slits. These are perforations that connect the pharynx to the exterior, thereby allowing the egress of swallowed seawater. The principal function of the gill slits is respiratory, although they may also serve to sieve the water for food particles. Echinoderms have evidently lost their gill slits, with the exception of some extinct forms known as calcichordates. These fossils have a bipartite body, with a large anterior bearing the gill slits and an elongate segmented tail. Despite being clearly echinoderms, they are otherwise highly problematic, not least because of controversial hypotheses which link them to the origin of other deuterostome phyla. Discoveries from the Chengjiang faunas, in the form of the vetulicolians (effectively equivalent to an extinct phylum), now suggest that the question of deuterostome origins may be close to a resolution.

Vetulicolians. The relevance of the vetulicolians has become apparent only recently, although they were first described in 1987, when the type-taxon *Vetulicola* was interpreted as "a very strange arthropod" (see **illus.**). At first sight such an assignment is not surprising, because the fossils of *Vetulicola* look vaguely similar to the brine shrimp, with a bipartite body consisting of a carapace-like anterior section and a tail with articulated segments. In reality, however, the anterior section consists of four large plates, two dorsal and two ventral, on either side of the midline. This arrangement is unlike any known arthropod, a view reinforced by the absence of evidence for any associated appendages or eyes. The interior of the anterior section was presumably lined by soft tissue, but otherwise appears to have been a voluminous cavity. The most notable structures, however, are five pouchlike units. These are located along the midlateral margins, where the dorsal and ventral plates meet along a narrow zone of flexible tissue. The structure of these pouches is quite complex, but effectively each consists of a chamber containing fine filamentous units with inhalant and exhalant apertures. Apparently, these opened to the interior cavity of the animal and to the exterior, respectively. These pouches evidently represent primitive gills (see illus.).

Judging from its overall shape, the mode of life of *Vetulicola* was that of an active swimmer, propulsion being provided by a muscular tail and stability assisted by a small dorsal fin located near the posterior end of the anterior section. Water would have been drawn into the voluminous anterior cavity, but whether the food captured was small and particulate or was larger prey is uncertain. The active mode of life presumably imposed high respiratory demands that were met by extracting oxygen via filaments in the gill chambers.

The nature of the vetulicolians has also become clearer because of the discovery of an associated series of taxa, also from Chengjiang. These animals, which include the taxa *Didazoon* and *Xidazoon*, have the same bipartite body plan, with a series of gills in the anterior section and a segmented tail that is joined via a waistlike constriction. This body form suggests that in life these other vetulicolians were more sluggish. The apparently simpler structure of the gills, without associated filaments, is consistent with a lower respiratory demand and, in contrast to the cuticularized *Vetulicola*, oxygen probably also diffused through the soft integument. The interrelationships between these vetulicolians are not resolved, but it is possible there is an evolutionary trend toward greater motility in the form of *Vetulicola*.

Evolutionary significance. The possession of gills is a strong indication that the vetulicolians are some sort of primitive deuterostome. On the other hand, their specific structure, not to mention the overall appearance of these animals, is unlike any hypothesized deuterostome ancestor. What is the relationship between these two groups, then? Several clues already exist to help resolve the role of vetulicolians in early deuterostome phylogeny. One is a proposed link to another group of Chengjiang fossils, referred to as the yunnanozoans. These are irrefutably deuterostomes, although their precise position has been controversial. Competing hypotheses have linked them either to the hemichordates or, alternatively and surely less probably, to the fish. The yunnanozoans have a body plan that appears to be derived from a bipartite arrangement, similar to that of the vetulicolians. The yunnanozoan gills, however, are not pouchlike but are more similar to the arrangement seen in such primitive deuterostomes as the acorn worms (hemichordates) and *Branchiostoma* (formerly *Amphioxon*) [cephalochordates]. It thus seems likely that the yunnanozoans represent an important intermediate stage close to the hemichordates and hence the next evolutionary milestone leading to the chordates. The bipartite body plan of the vetulicolians is also reminiscent of the calcichordates, introduced earlier as an enigmatic group of echinoderms with chordate-like characteristics. The similarities between vetulicolian and calcichordate are only approximate, but the origin of the most primitive echinoderms, marked by the acquisition of a characteristic porous calcite skeleton (the stereom), is probably fairly close to a vetulicolian-like animal.

Unsolved questions. Recognition of the vetulicolians is a reminder of two cardinal facts in evolution. First, when available, the fossil record can provide unique evolutionary information; and second, the organisms concerned often have little similarity to hypothetical constructs of ancestral forms. It would be unwise, however, to imagine that in the context of vetulicolians all questions are solved; rather the reverse. Three points need to be made: (1) the preferred hypothesis is that vetulicolians are basal deuterostomes, but alternatives such as their representing ancestral tunicates (and by inference chordates) will also need to be considered; (2) strange-looking relatives, notably the calcichordates and yunnanozoans, will probably play an important part in unraveling further details of deuterostome phylogeny, yet the precise connections between these groups remain tentative; and (3) vetulicolians (and their relatives) obviously evolved from something more primitive, conceivably some sort of protostome animal with segmentation. The nature of this ancestor and the transitional forms leading to vetulicolians are, however, yet to be identified.

It seems likely that the Cambrian vetulicolians hold a key position in our understanding of the evolution of basal deuterostomes. The calcichordates and yunnanozoans may be valuable indicators as to the next steps in deuterostome evolution. It is clear, however, that new fossil finds will be needed to elucidate the evolutionary steps that led ultimately to deuterostomes and higher animals.

For background information *see* ANIMAL EVOLUTION; BURGESS SHALE; CAMBRIAN; CEPHALOCHORDATA; DEVELOPMENTAL BIOLOGY; ECHINODERMATA;

FOSSIL; HEMICHORDATA; METAZOA in the McGraw-Hill Encyclopedia of Science & Technology.

Simon Conway Morris; Degan Shu

Bibliography. N. D. Holland and J.-Y. Chen, Origin and early evolution of the vertebrates: New insights from advances in molecular biology, anatomy, and palaeontology, *BioEssays*, 23:142–151, 2001; T. C. Lacalli, Vetulicolians—Are they deuterostomes? chordates?, *BioEssays*, 24:208–211, 2002; D. Shu et al., Lower Cambrian vertebrates from South China, *Nature*, 402:42–46, 1999; D. Shu et al., Primitive deuterostomes from the Chengjiang Lagerstätte (Lower Cambrian, China), *Nature*, 414:419–424, 2001; D. Shu et al., Reinterpretation of *Yunnanozoon* as the earliest known hemichordate, *Nature*, 380:428–430, 1996; C. J. Winchell et al., Evaluating hypotheses of deuterostome phylogeny and chordate evolution with new LSU and SSU ribosomal DNA data, *Mol. Biol. Evol.*, 19:762–776, 2002.

Diamond electrodes (electrochemistry)

Electrically conducting diamond thin-film electrodes, fabricated by chemical vapor deposition (CVD), are providing researchers with a new material that meets the requirements for a wide range of applications. Many electrochemical measurements involve recording an electrical signal (such as a potential, current, or charge) associated with the oxidation or reduction (redox) of an analyte present in solution, and then relating this signal to the analyte concentration. The oxidation or reduction reaction occurs at an electrode-electrolyte solution interface (the electrochemical reaction zone). Therefore, the electrode reaction kinetics and reaction mechanism are strongly influenced by the structure of this interface, particularly the physical and chemical properties of the electrode material. Important electrode properties include surface cleanliness, microstructure, surface chemistry, and density of electronic states (that is, electrical conductivity). The extent to which any one of these parameters affects a redox reaction depends upon the nature of the analyte. The electrode materials most often used in electrochemical measurements are platinum (Pt), gold (Au), and various forms of sp^2-bonded (trigonal planar) carbon (for example, carbon fibers, glassy carbon, and pyrolytic graphite). A new electrode material, sp^3-bonded (tetrahedral) diamond, offers advantages over graphite electrodes for electroanalysis and electrocatalysis.

Chemical vapor deposition. Diamond thin films can be produced synthetically by several deposition methods, the most popular being hot-filament and microwave-assisted CVD. Proper control of the source gas composition, system pressure, and substrate temperature allows diamond, instead of graphite, to be grown preferentially and metastably. Metastable phases can form from precursors if the activation barriers to more stable phases are sufficiently high. CVD diamond is produced under conditions where graphite is the more thermodynamically stable phase. Both graphite and diamond are in deep potential energy wells with a large activation energy barrier between them. Once diamond is formed, it remains a metastable phase with a negligible rate of transformation unless heated to high temperatures (>1200°C or 2200°F).

Strongly adhering diamond films can be deposited on several different substrates, the most common being silicon, molybdenum, tungsten, platinum, and quartz. Two important considerations when selecting a substrate are (1) tolerance of high deposition temperatures (>600°C or 1100°F) and (2) similarity in the thermal expansion coefficient with that of diamond.

Two general source-gas mixtures are routinely used for deposition, which produce diamond thin films with different morphologies.

Methane/hydrogen. Methane/hydrogen gas mixtures can be used to produce microcrystalline diamond thin films. This film, as seen in the scanning electron micrograph in **Fig. 1a**, possesses a well-faceted, polycrystalline morphology with a nominal crystallite size of ~2 micrometers or greater. Typical growth conditions for such films are a 0.3–1.0% methane/hydrogen volumetric ratio, 35–65 torr (5–9 kPa), and

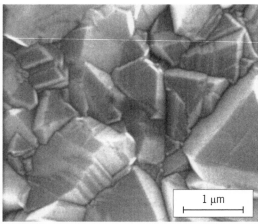

(a)

(b)

Fig. 1. Scanning electron micrographs of (a) microcrystalline and (b) nanocrystalline diamond thin films deposited on silicon substrates.

700–900°C (1300–1650°F). The source-gas mixture is activated by either a plasma (microwave-assisted CVD) or thermal energy (hot-filament CVD) to form reactive radical species in proximity to the substrate surface. These radical species are chemisorbed (taken up and chemically bonded) on the substrate surface, where they react to form sp³-bonded diamond through a complex nucleation and growth mechanism. The surface atoms of the film are terminated by hydrogen, making the surface very hydrophobic.

Methane/argon. Methane/argon gas mixtures can be used to produce nanocrystalline diamond thin films. This film, as seen in the scanning electron micrograph in Fig. 1*b*, possesses a smoother texture with a nominal feature size of ∼100 nanometers or less. The features are actually clusters of individual diamond grains, which are approximately 15 nm in diameter. The smooth, nanocrystalline morphology results from a very high rate of nucleation in the methane-argon gas mixture. Typical growth conditions for such films are a 1.0% methane/argon volumetric ratio, 100–150 torr (13–160 kPa), and 700–900°C (1300–1650°F). The surface atoms of the film are also terminated by hydrogen.

Doping. In order to have sufficient electrical conductivity for electrochemical measurements (<0.1 ohm-cm), diamond films must be doped (an impurity is added) with boron at a concentration of 1×10^{19} cm^{-3} (atoms per cubic centimeter) or greater. (Boron is the most useful dopant at present.) This is most often accomplished by adding controlled amounts of diborane or trimethylboron to the source-gas mixture. Boron atoms substituted for some of the carbon atoms in the growing diamond lattice. These boron atoms function as electron acceptors and, at room temperature, contribute to the formation of free-charge carriers (that is, holes or electron vacancies). The film's electrical conductivity is directly related to the carrier concentration and the carrier mobility.

Basic electrochemical properties. Boron-doped microcrystalline and nanocrystalline diamond thin films possess a number of electrochemical properties that distinguish them from other commonly used sp^2-bonded carbon electrodes, such as glassy carbon, pyrolytic graphite, or carbon paste. These properties are (1) a low and stable voltammetric and amperometric background current, leading to improved signal-to-noise ratios (SNR) and signal-to-bias ratios (SBR); (2) a wide working potential window in aqueous and nonaqueous media; (3) superb microstructural and morphological stability at high temperatures (180°C; 360°F) and current densities (0.1 A/cm², 85% H₃PO₄); (4) good responsiveness for several aqueous and nonaqueous redox analytes without any conventional pretreatment; (5) weak molecular adsorption, leading to improved fouling resistance; (6) long-term response stability; and (7) optical transparency in the ultraviolet, visible, and infrared regions of the electromagnetic spectrum, useful properties for spectroelectrochemical

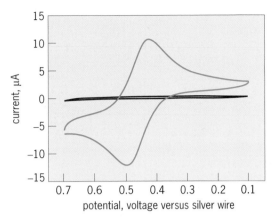

Fig. 2. Cyclic voltammetric curve for 1 mM ferrocene in acetonitrile containing 0.1 M TBAClO₄ at a microcrystalline diamond thin-film electrode. The background current of the supporting electrolyte is also shown for comparison. Scan rate = 0.2 V/s.

measurements. **Figure 2** shows a cyclic voltammetric curve at 0.2 V/s for 1 millimole ferrocene in acetonitrile containing 0.1 mole tetra-*n*-butyl ammoniumperchlorate (TBAClO₄). The background voltammogram at the same scan rate is also presented for comparison. Cyclic voltammetry is a commonly used electrochemical technique in which the potential applied to the working electrode is changed linearly in time from an initial value to a switching value and back to the initial value, and the resulting current is measured. There are two kinds of current: background and faradaic. The background current results from the charging of the electric double layer, electrochemical reactions on the electrode surface, and the electrolysis of adventitious solution impurities. The faradaic current (the one of analytical interest) is associated with the redox activity of the solution analyte. In Fig. 2, a well-defined response is seen at the untreated diamond electrode with a peak potential separation, ΔE_p, of 74 mV. The background current at the same scan rate is very low, leading to a large SBR.

Electroanalytical applications. CVD diamond provides electrochemists with a new type of carbon electrode that meets the requirements of responsiveness, conductivity, and stability for a wide range of applications. Diamond offers advantages over other electrodes, especially sp^2-bonded carbon electrodes, in terms of linear dynamic range (corresponding linear increase in signal detection with concentration), limit of detection, response time, response precision, and response stability.

One of the first demonstrations of diamond's usefulness in electroanalysis was the oxidative detection of the azide anion in aqueous media. Sodium azide has been widely used commercially, particularly as an inflator in automotive airbags. Azide anions are highly toxic and present a health hazard at relatively modest levels, so there is a need for sensitive and stable analytical methods for their detection. Industries producing or using azide generally have

Summary of FIA-EC data for azide at diamond and glassy carbon		
	Diamond	Glassy carbon
Dynamic range (μM)	0.30–3300	1.0–3300
Sensitivity (nA/μM)	33 ± 5	36 ± 7
Detection limit (nM), S/N = 3	8 ± 8 (0.3 ppb)	50 ± 20 (2.1 ppb)
Reproducibility (% RSD)	0.5–5	6–20
Stability (% response loss over 12 h)	5	50

tight controls on the levels of the anion discharged in the water. Moreover, as an ever-increasing number of automobiles containing azide-based inflators in their airbags are retired to salvage yards, the incidence of ground-water contamination is more probable.

Diamond provides a sensitive, reproducible, and stable response for the electrooxidation of azide. A well-defined oxidation peak, E_p^{ox}, is observed in the cyclic voltammogram (pH 7.2 phosphate buffer) at 1100 mV versus Ag/AgCl with a background-corrected peak current, i_p^{ox}, of 88 μA. Most importantly, the oxidation current for azide, at this positive potential, is recorded on a low and unchanging background signal.

Azide anion was also detected by flow injection analysis with electrochemical detection (FIA-EC)— that is, amperometric mode. The **table** shows a comparison of data for diamond and glassy carbon. Diamond outperforms glassy carbon in terms of linear dynamic range, limit of detection, response precision, and response stability.

Electrocatalysis. One technology requiring dimensionally stable and electrocatalytically active electrodes is fuel cells. There is a need to develop new electrodes that can stably function—that is, without microstructural or morphological degradation and lost catalytic activity—at the elevated temperatures (150–200°C or 300–390°F) and in the aggressive chemical environments (for example, acid-doped ionomeric membranes) envisioned for fuel cells. Boron-doped diamond thin films are superb catalyst support/host materials because of their high electrical conductivity ($\sim$0.01 ohm-cm), dimensional stability, and the fact that the catalyst particles can be stably anchored into the surface microstructure during deposition. For example, nanometer-size Pt particles can be incorporated into electrically conducting diamond by a sequential diamond deposition–metal electrodeposition–diamond deposition procedure. The process results in a conductive, dimensionally stable carbon electrode containing Pt particles of controlled composition, size, and catalytic activity. **Figure 3** shows an atomic force micrograph of the electrode, revealing the Pt dispersions over the surface. The advantages of this composite electrode, compared to commercial Pt-impregnated sp^2 carbon electrodes, are (1) the dimensional stability of the diamond support results in a highly stable reaction center, even at high current densities and temperatures; and (2) all the metal catalyst is available at the electrode surface and not inside pores. These electrodes exhibit good performance for the oxidation of methanol and the reduction of oxygen, two important fuel cell reactions.

Outlook. Diamond offers significant advantages over other electrodes (particularly sp^2-bonded carbon electrodes) in terms of linear dynamic range, limit of detection, response time, response precision, and response stability. Some important areas of future work include growth and characterization of diamond films deposited on fibrous substrates of 10-μm diameter or less, and on high-surface-area metal meshes; chemical modification of diamond surfaces to control adsorption and electron-transfer kinetics; and patterning of electrically conductive diamond electrodes into microarray geometries.

For background information *see* CATALYSIS; DIAMOND; ELECTROCHEMISTRY; ELECTRODE; FUEL CELL; GRAPHITE; NUCLEATION; OXIDATION-REDUCTION; VAPOR DEPOSITION in the McGraw-Hill Encyclopedia of Science & Technology.   Greg M. Swain

Bibliography. Q. Chen et al., The structure and electrochemical behavior of nitrogen-containing diamond films deposited from CH$_4$/N$_2$/Ar mixtures, *J. Electrochem. Soc.*, 148:E44, 2001; K. E. Spear and J. P. Dismukes (eds.), *Synthetic Diamond: Emerging CVD Science and Technology*, Wiley, New York, 1994; G. M. Swain, A. B. Anderson, and J. C. Angus, Applications of diamond thin films in electrochemistry, *MRS Bull.*, 23:56, 1998; J. Wang et al., Incorporation of Pt particles in boron-doped diamond thin films: Applications in electrocatalysis, *Electrochem. Solid-State Lett.*, 3:286, 2000; J. Xu et al., Boron-doped diamond thin film electrodes, *Anal. Chem.*, 69:591A, 1997; J. Xu and G. M. Swain, Oxidation of azide anion at boron-doped diamond thin film electrodes, *Anal. Chem.*, 70:1502, 1998.

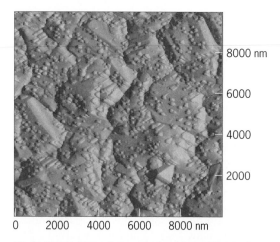

Fig. 3. Atomic force micrograph of a platinum/diamond composite thin-film electrode. The Pt particles range in diameter from 30 to 300 nm with a distribution of about 2 × 10^2 cm^{-2}. Apparent loadings range from 25 to 100 μg/cm^2.

Digital Object Identifier

The Digital Object Identifier (DOI) is an Internet-based global naming and resolution system that provides for the precise identification, retrieval, and trading of digital items in the form of articles, books, images, bibliographies, supporting data, videos, charts, tables, audio, and other electronic files. Development of the DOI system began in 1996 when content creators and technologists jointly recognized that information and entertainment objects could not be commercially distributed on the Internet unless there was a common system of unique identification for those objects. These early stakeholders envisioned an unambiguous, machine-readable identifier that could be used for all electronic communications and transactions involving content throughout its life cycle, including its creation, editing, publication, distribution, and archiving. Such an identifier would be especially critical for commercial transactions, from initial licensing through sales tracking, royalty computation, and financial reporting.

The dominant practice used today by publishers for naming Internet-distributed objects involves referring to their location, using an addressing system known as the uniform resource identifier (URL). URL-only naming fails whenever the resources are moved or reorganized. By contrast, the DOI system introduces a level of indirection that ensures persistent or permanent links to objects by way of a global directory. This level of indirection enables object administrators to update a single, centralized database record for each object, such that requests for the object are automatically and reliably redirected to the object itself, wherever it might be located on the network. The DOI also has a multiple-resolution feature that enables a single DOI to be resolved to locations for related services, transactions, or other information that the object's owner wises to make available.

Unique, persistent identification. In order to discover, retrieve, manage, and trade the vast array of creative works that are becoming available in the digital domain, a way to refer to them unambiguously, by means of unique identifiers, is required. While uniqueness ensures that the identifier will refer to only one object, persistence ensures that if that object is moved or if ownership of the object changes, the identification of that object does not need to change.

Uniqueness and persistence are facilitated if an identifier is designed as an opaque string or dumb number, meaning that no meaning should be inferred from the assigned value of the name or number. This characteristic distinguishes the DOI from many identifier systems that build "intelligence" into the number itself, a feature that might enable the user to deduce something about the entity that is being identified, or perhaps about the person or organization that registered the identifier. In the case of a dumb number like the DOI, the only reliable way to know anything about an identified object is to view the metadata (description of the object) declared at the time of registration. This ensures that even when the ownership of a particular item changes, its identifier remains the same, with the same descriptive information.

Uses. The DOI is a persistent identifier of intellectual property entities, where an "entity" is any object that can be usefully identified, including resources made available on the World Wide Web (WWW). In general, "intellectual property" is defined by the World Intellectual Property Organization (WIPO) and related international treaties such as the Berne Convention.

Typically, the DOI may be used by publishers to identify the various physical objects that are manifestations of intellectual property, including printed books, CD recordings, videotapes, and journal articles. A DOI may also be used to identify less tangible manifestations, especially the digital files that are the common form of intellectual property expression on the Internet. But the power of the DOI goes beyond its ability to identify manifestations—it may also be used to identify performances of intellectual property or the abstractions, including works such as musical scores or lyrics, that are the basis for those manifestations.

Finally, the DOI can be used to route users and applications to multiple services related to the named object, such as bibliographic or transaction services.

Prefix and suffix. A DOI is made up of two components (see **illus.**). The first element, the prefix, is assigned to an appropriate grouping of content such as the publisher, label, or imprint by a registration agency. All prefixes begin with 10, followed by a number designating the organization, publisher, or any rights holder or controller who has obtained that prefix and is responsible for depositing the individual DOIs. Organizations such as publishers might choose to request a prefix for each of their imprints or product lines, or they might use a single prefix.

The second element of a DOI is the suffix, a unique character string assigned by the prefix holder to the specific object being identified. Existing identifier or product numbering systems used within a particular industry, as well as private naming systems used within the corporation, are typically incorporated within the suffix of the DOI. The suffix may be assigned to entities of any size or granularity (such as a book, article, abstract, chart, album, song, or melody) or any file type (such as text, audio, video, image, or software). The prefix holder decides the level or granularity of identification based on the nature of the objects to be distributed or sold electronically.

Digital Object Identifier components.

Resolution. The power of the DOI system is its function as a global routing or resolution system. Since digital content frequently changes ownership and location over the course of its useful life, the DOI system uses a distributed global directory. Whenever a request is made to resolve a DOI (for example, when a user clicks on a DOI link in a Web page), a message is sent to the central directory on a server where the current address associated with that DOI appears. This location is sent back to the user, enabling redirection within the user's browser to this particular Internet address. The user would simply see the content itself, or further information about the object with information on how to obtain it.

When the object moves to a new server or the copyright holder transfers the product line to another company, only one change needs to be recorded in the directory; from this time onward, all users will instantly be sent to the new location. The assigned DOI remains reliable and accurate because the link to the associated information or source of the content is easily and efficiently changed. The underlying technology of the secured global name service, called the Handle System®, has been optimized for speed, efficiency, and persistence.

Metadata. Since there is no intelligence built into the DOI itself, the ability to retrieve descriptive metadata about DOI-named objects and related services is an essential component of the DOI system. Information about an identified object must be created and maintained by the holder of the DOI prefix. The DOI system mandates a minimum level of publicly available structured metadata, known as kernel metadata, which serves a role similar to a telephone directory entry; the data enable users to ensure that the identified entity found is the one sought. Kernel metadata elements include:

Identifier: an identifier associated with the entity from a legacy identification scheme, such as an ISBN.

Title: a name by which the entity is known.

Type: the primary type of intellectual property entity that is being identified (an abstract work, a tangible or intangible manifestation, a performance).

Mode: the sensory mode through which the intellectual property entity is intended to be perceived (visual, audio, and audiovisual).

Primary agent: the identity of the primary agent, normally the first-named creator of the object.

Agent role: the role that the primary agent played in creating the object.

DOI application developers and their user communities may also define specialized metadata structures that further describe the object and enable its use in proprietary ways, such as transaction systems. These structures are known as application profiles, and their data may or may not be publicly available.

Technology. The underlying technology for resolving DOIs on the Internet, the Handle System®, is a distributed, scalable system based on open protocols developed by the Center for National Research Initiatives (CNRI) in the United States. The DOI's metadata system is based on the <indecs> metadata framework, which has also been adopted as the basis of the data dictionary of the MPEG-21 Multimedia Framework. Since both the Handle System® resolution and the DOI metadata components are structured, consistent, and manageable, it is possible to apply DOIs to any form of content and to develop additional tools for content management. Ultimately, the system allows the development of automated agents that can use DOIs to manage entities throughout the transaction life cycle of the object.

Reference linking. Reference linking is a mechanism that easily and accurately takes readers of electronic journals from one document into another. References are the traditional means for authors to establish links between their work and scholarship that preceded it. Reference linking based upon the DOI is a means for making those links immediately actionable across publications and publishers.

In January 2000, a collaborative venture, called CrossRef, was incorporated among 12 of the world's largest scientific and scholarly publishers, both commercial and not-for-profit, to enable cross-publisher reference linking throughout the digital journal literature. With over 150 members, 6700 journals, and 5.1 million articles linked, CrossRef is the most significant and successful application of the DOI.

A researcher clicking on a CrossRef link within a journal article will be connected to a page on the publisher's Website showing a full bibliographical citation of the article, including in most cases the article abstract. The reader then has the option to immediately access the target article; subscribers to the target can typically go straight to the full text, while nonsubscribed users are presented with options for access.

Governance. Since 1998, the controlling authority for the DOI has been the not-for-profit International DOI Foundation (IDF), based in Washington, DC, and Geneva. Members of the IDF may include larger companies from the publishing, music, still-image, broadcast, online news, software, and other content industries; technology providers to these industries; associations representing these industries; Internet technology companies; associations representing stakeholders such as authors, artists, libraries, secondary publishers, and users; government agencies with a mission in a related area; others for whom Internet commerce is a critical business, social, cultural, political, or personal interest.

Future developments. The DOI is currently undergoing a period of rapid development, following the early acceptance of the principles of the system and its adoption in initial applications. As of July 2002, several million DOIs had been issued, with over 200 organizations allocating DOIs; five DOI Registration Agencies had been appointed (with more planned to come); and the DOI had been well integrated into several related standards activities, with many applications actively under development. That development is evident in all aspects of the DOI System—technology, procedure, and policy.

For background information *see* DATABASE MANAGEMENT SYSTEM; INFORMATION MANAGEMENT; INTERNET; MULTIMEDIA TECHNOLOGY; WORLD WIDE WEB in the McGraw-Hill Encyclopedia of Science & Technology.   John S. Erickson

Bibliography. N. Paskin, Toward unique identifiers, *Proc. IEEE*, 87(7):1208–1227, 1999; *Syntax for the Digital Object Identifier*, Z39.84–2000 Document Number: ANSI/NISO Z39.84–2000, National Information Standards Organization Staff and National Information Standards Organization, 2000.

Digital photography

Digital still photography has experienced exponential growth in recent years. This is primarily due to a series of technical improvements and price reductions that have made the technology more appealing to the mass market and professionals alike. Parallel growth has been taking place in digital video, and the most recent cameras can be used to capture high-resolution still images or to make lower-resolution video recordings. In addition, the use of digital photography has been increasing in a host of other imaging applications such as surveillance, astronomy, and medical imaging.

Digital photography has advantages over film photography in productivity, quality control, and profitability. Instead of shooting, processing, printing, and scanning, digital photography allows the capture of images directly as digital files, thus saving time and materials.

Sensors. Digital photography is based on the photoelectric effect of silicon. When photons strike silicon, they excite electrons from the valence band to the conduction band. The number of electrons freed is proportional to the size of the light-sensing element, the amount of light exposure, and the wavelength of the light. Silicon light-sensing elements are arranged in a grid format with each photosite comprising one picture element (pixel). The electrons resulting from light exposure are collected and measured from the pixel array. The charge voltages are converted from analog to digital (A/D) format and amplified to create digital picture files. The cameras have random-access memory (RAM) buffers to hold images while they are being downloaded or recorded on disk.

Two types of sensors—charge-coupled device (CCD) and complementary metal-oxide semiconductor (CMOS)—are used for the image-sensing elements in digital cameras. CCDs were developed by Bell Labs in the early 1970s for use in satellites and astronomy. By 1985 they were starting to appear in consumer products. CMOS sensors were developed soon after CCDs, but the technology was not extensively used until the early 1990s when products with lower noise and leakage current became available.

CCD fabrication relies on older, less efficient metal-oxide semiconductor production methods. Today, CCDs produce higher-quality images and are used in most digital cameras. However, CMOS sensors have inherent size and cost advantages over CCDs and are making inroads on the low end of the image sensor market.

CCD sensors. CCD photosites are light-receptive over most of the pixel surface, with photodiodes collecting electrons based on the intensity of exposure. Electrons are transferred to the adjacent charge transfer cells in the same column with the photosites. For readout, each row of data is transferred to horizontal charge transfer registers. Charged packets for each row are then are read out serially and sensed by a charge-to-voltage conversion and amplifier section.

CCD sensors have wide dynamic ranges and high light sensitivity, and can operate at 30 frames/second for video applications. They have low noise when correlated double sampling (a process by which a pixel's dark or reference output level is subtracted from its light-induced output) is used to cancel offset variations. They also have good uniformity across photosites because all charges are read through a single readout circuit. CCD pixel elements generally range between 9 and 13 micrometers. Larger pixel elements have greater light sensitivity but lower resolution. Arrays of over 2 million pixels are needed to generate 4 by 6 in. (10 by 15 cm) prints that would be evaluated as excellent.

The CCD architecture makes it impractical to integrate other electronics onto the same chip with the light sensor. CCD cameras require supplemental integrated circuits to support the imaging function. For example, they need a separate chip to generate precisely timed multiple phases of a clock to transfer the photon-generated image from the photosites to the amplifier. Other chips are needed to accomplish the A/D conversions or to supply the several bias voltages that CCDs require. CCDs use 15-volt power supplies, while CMOSs use as little as 2.5 volts. In total, CCD cameras typically require five or more supporting chips.

CCDs are sensitive to infrared radiation, which can cause overheating. Thus, an infrared filter is incorporated in the camera design. Even with these filters, CCDs can overheat with long or multiple exposures, which produces blooming, a defect caused by the overflow of electrons to adjacent photosites. To counteract overheating, manufacturers use special alloys, fans, and circuits to cool CCDs.

CMOS sensors. These have the advantage that many imaging functions are manufactured on the same chip with the light-sensing elements. This leads to smaller, less expensive product designs. Each photosite contains a photodiode that converts light to electrons, a charge-to-voltage conversion section, select/reset transistor, and an amplification section. A grid of metal interconnects overlays the sensor to supply timing and readout signals. Also overlaying the sensor is an array of column output signal interconnects.

The column lines connect to a set of decode and readout (multiplexing) electronics that are arranged by column outside the pixel array. Unlike CCDs, CMOS signals from the entire array, subsections, or a single pixel can be read out by an X-Y addressing technique. Also, unlike CCDs, nondestructive readout and random pixel access are possible with CMOS sensors. These techniques allow noise reduction through signal averaging and adaptive exposure. Contrast can be improved by allowing pixel collecting from dark scenes to have longer exposures than other pixels. CMOS cameras produce no smear because the charge stays within each pixel. They also are not prone to blooming, as CCD cameras are, because the CMOS sensor pixel is a diode held in reverse bias and precharged to a set charge. Photons reduce the charge of the pixel; when it reaches zero, it stops (the pixel is white).

CMOS sensors are of two types: active-pixel sensor (APS) CMOS and active-column sensor (ACS) CMOS. APS CMOS sensors use active pixels, where each photosite contains an amplifier that converts the charge to a voltage. This prevents the percentage of photosite that is light-receptive (fill factor) from being 100%, which reduces the magnitude of the output signal in relation to noise. Furthermore, mismatched amplifiers at the photosites cause differences in the responses of pixels. APS CMOS sensors also suffer from the dark leakage of current, which results in a thermally generated charge that contaminates images.

ACS CMOS, a more recent design, uses a unity gain amplifier where only the input element is present at each photosite. This is physically smaller and allows for higher fill factors. The ACS CMOS design provides the same gain for every photosite, thus improving image quality. ACS CMOS sensors do not convert photon-generated charges to voltages to drive column buses; instead they produce high-proportional currents, which allow them to run faster than APS CMOS sensors.

Image capture. The arrangements of CCDs in digital cameras are divided between linear sensors that scan the image plane and area arrays that capture the entire image with a single exposure. Linear arrays are capable of capturing higher-resolution images, but they are restricted to still-life photography and are not compatible with strobe lighting, which is commonly used in photo studios. Area arrays, by contrast, produce lower-resolution images, but they can be used for live action photography and are strobe-light-compatible.

Capturing color images requires that three separate signals (blue, green, and red) be generated from a scene. This is generally accomplished by placing separation filters in the light path during exposure. Three approaches are used: filter wheels, dyed photo sites, and silicon filtering.

Filter wheels. These systems require three successive exposures after blue, green, and red filters have been placed in the image path. They have the advantage that each pixel records an image for each primary color and the disadvantage that capture times are greatly increased and live action cannot be captured.

Dyed photosites. These are systems where each pixel has a filter applied to its surface. When this approach is used with linear arrays, it results in a trilinear array configuration where blue, green, and red linear arrays scan the image plane. This has the advantage that each pixel measures all three primary components of light, but the cost of the sensor is greatly increased because three times as many photosites are required.

When dyed photosites are used with area arrays, each pixel is dyed with a primary color. This is usually done in a Bayer configuration where there are two green pixels for each blue and red pixel. This configuration has the advantage that a color image can be captured with a single exposure, thus making it capable of capturing live action scenes. Dyed photosite area arrays have the disadvantage that each pixel receives exposure from only one of the primary colors, but the image file requires picture information for all three primary colors at each pixel. To provide this missing information, the camera's firmware calculates the missing color values from the responses of neighboring pixels. This causes problems with aliasing in areas of fine detail or image edges, and it also complicates and slows the image processing function of cameras.

Dyed photosite area arrays are the most commonly used configuration in current digital cameras due to their ability to capture images in a single short exposure. The image processing algorithms have improved, and the number of photosites in area array sensors has increased to over 6 million in professional-grade cameras. This improves, but does not eliminate, the aliasing and pixelization problems caused by calculating rather than measuring color values for photosites.

An expensive approach to solving this dilemma is the tri-area array configuration, which uses a prism inside the camera to split the incoming light into three images that are individually filtered and focused on three different area array CCDs. This configuration allows single-exposure image capture where each pixel has measured blue, green, and red values. However, the resulting cameras are large and awkward to use in the field, and the engineering demands are daunting.

Silicon filtering. A solution to the problems of dyed photosites is the use of silicon filtering as implemented in the Foveon X3 sensor, a new CMOS chip design. It has long been known that light will penetrate into a silicon surface to a distance proportional to the wavelength of the light before it creates a hole-electron pair. Longer wavelengths penetrate deeper. A single pixel can capture all three primary colors of light if two critical conditions are met. First, the photodiode needs to be precisely controlled so that it will collect only the desired wavelengths. Second, an optically transparent insulating layer must separate the light-sensing layers. By making a sensor that has three layers of photoreceptive sites at different depths, the Foveon X3 captures blue, green, and red information at each pixel without the need for external filtration. This eliminates the need for complex algorithms to interpolate the color information from neighboring pixels, thus avoiding errors, reducing camera costs, and reducing the click-to-capture time of cameras.

The Foveon sensors are also designed with a unique capability called variable pixel size. The pixels can be instantaneously grouped to form larger sizes that have greater light sensitivity and are desirable for video, auto focusing, and low-light situations. Another advantage of silicon filtering is the reduction of noise, which occurs with dyed photosites due to adjacent pixels having different color filters. Silicon filters are inherently more uniform than dyed photosites because they are precisely grown, flat, crystalline structures. Conventional filters are coated onto the uneven surface of the sensor in the last stages of production and are subject to subsequent fading.

The downside of silicon filtering is that each pixel requires three times the number of support circuits (reset, column access, exposure setting). This increases the size of the pixel, decreases the fill factor, and increases the incidence of defective pixels. Silicon filter designs need to have three separate pixel processing chains including amplifiers and A/D converters.

For background information *see* ANALOG-TO-DIGITAL CONVERTER; CHARGE-COUPLED DEVICES; INTEGRATED CIRCUITS; OPTICAL DETECTORS; PHOTOELECTRIC DEVICES; PHOTOGRAPHY; SILICON in the McGraw-Hill Encyclopedia of Science & Technology.

Anthony Stanton

Bibliography. R. Hanley, The next generation of digital camera technology, *Advanced Imaging*, May 2002; L. A. Hindus, CMOS: The image of the future, *Advanced Imaging*, May 2001; L. A. Hindus, The convergent camera: High value, low response, *Advanced Imaging*, May 2001; D. W. Lake, Silicon filter technology: Is this the future of image sensing?, *Advanced Imaging*, May 2002; J. Larish, Breakthrough design: Fuji delivers a super CCD for digital photography, *Advanced Imaging*, January 2000; T. McMillan, Will CMOS overtake CCDs?, *Electronic Publishing*, June 1997; A. Wilson, CMOS sensors contend for camera designs, *Vision Systems Design*, September 2001; T. Zarnowski and T. Vogelsong, CMOS and CCD sensors contend for imaging use, *Vision Systems Design*, February 2001.

Digital watermarking technology

The use of digital media to create, capture, and store electronic data has grown tremendously in recent years, as has the need to protect owners' intellectual property rights. Digital watermarking is one means of protection, whereby information, such as copyright information, is embedded in a digital file.

The concept of watermarking goes back to the thirteenth century when physical watermarks were added to paper as a means of authentication. The watermark was generally invisible until the paper was held up to the light. Although digital watermarks in image files are sometimes visible, more often they are imperceptible to the human eye. Digital watermarks are not limited to digital images, but can be part of any form of digital media (images, audio, or video), print media, or software applications.

Digital watermarking is a form of steganography, the art of hiding a message inside a medium so that it defies detection. The term derives from Greek, meaning "covered writing." In ancient Greece, writing was often done on wax-covered boards. To avoid detection of a secret message, a person would write on the board, then cover it with wax, so that it looked unused. The person could then record something else on the wax, such that only the sender and recipient would know that there was another message underneath. Steganography, like cryptology, is often associated with covert communication. While cryptology scrambles a message so that it cannot be read, steganography hides the fact that there is a message at all. A message written in invisible ink on paper is a well-known steganographic communication method. Digitally watermarked files are steganographic in that they are made up of two components: the host or cover medium (the image, movie, sound, multimedia file, or application) and the embedded signal or message (the digital watermark).

Applications. Digital watermarks are added to files to solve a number of problems inherent in the digital distribution of data.

Copyright protection. It is very easy for someone who has obtained a digital file to duplicate and redistribute it at will. A watermark embedded into a digital data file can carry information as to who owns the original file. This information can be used to allow a consumer to contact the file creator or distributor to license the file, or to prove ownership in the case of a copyright dispute. It can also be used to trace the source of illegal use or copying of digital files (a process called digital fingerprinting). Copyright protection in watermarked files can extend to physical devices, such as digital video disk (DVD) players/recorders, and instruct them as to whether or not to play or duplicate the host file. For copyrighted data, the embedded signal must be robust enough to survive intentional and unintentional attempts to remove it.

Authentication. Authentication is a data integrity check, much like a digital signature. Unlike applications for copyright protection, authentication data are necessarily fragile in that they would be altered if the file or image were manipulated. This would let the owner know if the file had been tampered with.

Covert communication. The exchange of secret messages is another reason to use digital watermarking. Encrypted files, by the very fact that they are scrambled, draw suspicion to those who are sending and receiving them. The message in a digitally watermarked file, on the other hand, is embedded in an innocent cover file, such as a scanned image or multimedia presentation, and therefore does not raise suspicion that there is a secret message included.

Open communications. Digital watermarks can also be used as a means of open communication, linking different types of media to one another. For example, a digital watermark could be embedded into a bitmap image file that is part of a printed page, for example, in a book or magazine. The watermark would contain a pointer to a Website address (URL), specified by the creator. When the watermark is read by a special device, usually a digital camera attached to a computer system, the Web browser on that computer is launched and opens to the URL indicated in the watermark. This type of watermark is fixed in the deployment medium (the printed piece) and, as long as it survives any variances in the printing process, it is fairly impervious to attack.

Monitoring. A digital watermark can be used as a monitoring tool. For example, an advertiser can use a digital watermark to monitor advertisement airplay (radio or television) by embedding a digital signal into a video or audio ad file and counting the number of times the watermark is broadcast during a given period.

Watermarking techniques. Watermarking techniques have been described in hundreds of technical papers, with dozens of patents applied for or held in watermarking or steganography disciplines. While there is much diversity in how most of the watermarking systems work, there are some basic requirements. In nearly any watermarking scheme, there are three distinct action phases: (1) watermark creation, in which the watermark is produced using an owner "key"; (2) watermark embedding, the placement of the message signal within the host file; (3) watermark detection.

In some watermarking schemes, the original/host signal (file) must be available during the detection process. These are called private or nonblind watermarking schemes. Private systems make for strong watermark signals in that the original image is available for direct comparison to the watermarked image. However, it is often not feasible for the original image to be available during the detection phase such as images made available on removable media, such as a DVD. Conversely, public or blind watermarking schemes do not require the host image to be available during detection. Instead, the owner key is all that is required. Watermark keys can be restricted or unrestricted. Restricted watermark keys can be decoded only by those who have access to a secret key. Unrestricted watermark keys can be decoded by anyone who receives the watermarked file, while only the owner can embed or remove the watermark.

To be successful, digital watermarking schemes must meet certain criteria. In the case of watermarking digital image files, the embedded code must be readily identifiable, yet its insertion should not visibly deteriorate the host image. Generally, the more robust the embedded signal, the more noticeable it is in the host image. An understanding of the human visual system is critical to the development of successful watermarking systems for image files. Noise masking is a property of human vision and refers to the visibility of one visual stimulus when super-imposed over another. For watermarked image files, this is used to judge the "just noticeable distortion," or the largest possible visual image distortion, and "minimally noticed distortion," or the distortion that is less visible than other distortions of the same power. If watermarks are intended to be invisible, the embedding scheme must not introduce too many visible artifacts in the image. Rich media files (music, video, and images) are often distorted by compression, and image files are often rotated, cropped, and scaled. Robust watermarks must be able to survive these distortions. Finally, the security of a watermarking scheme should not rely merely on the assumption that possible attackers are ignorant of how the code was embedded. Once that information is discovered, it will be a simple matter for attackers to render a watermark unreadable.

An example of a common method of embedding information into an image file is a technique called the least significant bit (LSB) insertion. Digital images are usually saved as 24-bit or 8-bit files. For 24-bit multicolor images, pixel variation comes from a combination of three primary colors: red, green, and blue (RGB). Since each primary color is made up of one byte, an RGB pixel is represented by three bytes. Thus, one pixel of an RGB image expressed as binary data could be something like (11000110 10111000 10000100). It would take three pixels to hide one byte of data, such as an alphanumeric character, using the LSB technique. For example, to embed the letter B (binary value 01000010) into three pixels of an image with the values

$$(11000110\ 10111000\ 10000100)$$
$$(11000110\ 10111000\ 10000100)$$
$$(11000110\ 10111000\ 10000100)$$

one would change the LSB (last bit on the right) to

$$(1100011\underline{0}\ 1011100\underline{1}\ 1000010\underline{0})$$
$$(1100011\underline{0}\ 1011100\underline{0}\ 1000010\underline{0})$$
$$(1100011\underline{1}\ 1011100\underline{0}\ 10000100)$$

Reading the last bit of each byte in this group of pixels, one sees the binary value 01000010 (the remaining byte is unused in this case). The principle is that changes made to the last bit are so minute that the resultant change in color would not be detected by the human eye.

Outlook. Because so much business, educational, entertainment, and communication information is now created, stored, and disseminated in digital form, it is critical that digital media be protected. Digital watermarking is one means. Although there has been much effort in the development of digital watermarking systems in recent years, so far none have been proven to be impervious to attack. As newer, more robust watermarking schemes develop, so too can new ways to break them. If successful watermarking schemes are to continue to develop, it is critical that standard protocols, performance benchmarks, and a central regulatory authority be developed as well.

For background information *see* COMPUTER SECURITY; CRYPTOGRAPHY; INTERNET; VISION; WORLD

WIDE WEB in the McGraw-Hill Encyclopedia of Science & Technology.   Julie Shaffer

Bibliography. N. F. Johnson, Z. Duric, and S. Jajodia, *Information Hiding: Steganography and Watermarking—Attacks and Countermeasures*, Kluwer Academic Publishers, Boston, 2000; N. F. Johnson and S. Jajodia, *Exploring Steganography: Seeing the Unseen*, IEEE, 0018-9162, 1998; S. Katzenbeisser and F. A. P. Petitcolas (eds.), *Information Hiding Techniques for Steganography and Digital Watermarking*, Artech House Books, Norwood, MA, 2000; N. Nikolaidis and I. Pitas, Digital image watermarking: An overview, *Int. Conf. Multimedia Comput. Sys. (ICMCS '99)*, 1:1–6, Florence, Italy, June 7–11, 1999; A. Piva, M. Barni, and F. Bartolini, Copyright protection of digital images by means of frequency domain watermarking, in *Mathematics of Data/Image Coding, Compression, and Encryption*, ed. by M. S. Schmalz, Proceedings of SPIE, vol. 3456, pp. 25–35, San Diego, July 21–22, 1998.

Disease-modifying anti-rheumatic drugs

Autoimmune illnesses are characterized by a loss of self-tolerance, whereby the body's own immune defense mechanisms are inappropriately directed against body components, resulting in organ damage or activation of a systemic immune response. Some organ-specific autoimmune illnesses are self-limited, since only one tissue is affected, but the ongoing inflammatory response may interfere with normal organ function. However, multisystem autoimmune illnesses, such as rheumatoid arthritis (characterized by chronic inflammation of the synovium, or the lining membrane, of joints, and surrounding tissue, as well as other body systems) have the propensity to involve multiple organs. If the immune response is not adequately suppressed during times of increased disease activity, then organ failure, death, or permanent disability may result.

The number of effective agents used to treat rheumatoid arthritis has grown substantially in the last 5 years. Many of these medications are in a class of drugs known as disease-modifying anti-rheumatic disease agents (DMARDs). Unlike the other main drug classes used to treat rheumatoid arthritis, nonsteroidal anti-inflammatory drugs (NSAIDs) and corticosteroids, DMARDs do more than just reduce pain and inflammation; they have the ability to reduce disease activity, thereby preventing joint damage or disability.

Anticytokine biologic agents. The most effective therapeutic agents available today for the treatment of rheumatoid arthritis are drugs that specifically inhibit the action of the proinflammatory cytokine tumor necrosis factor alpha (TNF-α). This cytokine is elevated in the plasma and joint fluid of patients with rheumatoid arthritis. It exerts its biologic effect after binding to specific cell-surface receptors, TNF-RI (p55) and TNF-RII (p75), which induce intracellular signaling and alter gene expression leading to the release of other proinflammatory mediators

such as interleukin-1 (IL-1), IL-6, and IL-8. The inflammatory cascade is further amplified by the activation of T cells and the recruitment of neutrophils via an increased expression of endothelial adhesion molecules. Bone and joint destruction result from the release of a variety of degradative enzymes from macrophages and neutrophils and the stimulation of bone osteoclasts.

Etanercept. This drug is produced in Chinese hamster ovary cells using recombinant deoxyribonucleic acid (DNA) technology. It is a fusion product combining the extracellular domain of two human p75 TNF-receptors and the Fc portion (region that is responsible for effector function) of human immunoglobulin G1 (IgG1), which prolongs the half-life of the circulating drug. Etanercept binds soluble TNF-α and -β and prevents activation of cell-surface TNF receptors, thus weakening the inflammatory response within the synovial tissue of the rheumatoid joint. The short half-life of 72 hours requires twice weekly subcutaneous injections of 25 mg. It has also been very efficacious in the treatment of juvenile rheumatoid arthritis, anklylosing spondylitis (arthritis primarily affecting the spine), and psoriatic arthritis (arthritis associated with psoriasis, an inflammatory skin condition characterized by patches of red dry skin).

Infliximab. Another anti-TNF-α agent, infliximab, is a chimeric monoclonal antibody containing a mouse-derived hypervariable region coupled with a human IgG1 Fc heavy chain and partial kappa light chain. This DMARD can bind to circulating TNF as well as TNF-α bound to cellular receptors leading to subsequent cell lysis. Since infliximab has a much longer half-life than entanercept, it needs only to be administered intravenously every 8 weeks after an initial loading dose of three injections within the first 6 weeks. This drug was first approved for the treatment of Crohn's disease and subsequently for rheumatoid arthritis when used in combination with another DMARD, methotrexate. To achieve greater control, the dosing interval may be reduced or the initial infusion dose of 3 mg/kg may be increased to 10 mg/kg. Dosages of 10 mg/kg are associated with increased risk of infections. Although infliximab may be more efficacious than etanercept, a higher risk of allergic reactions due to antimurine (mouse) antibodies and/or a systemic lupus erythematosus–like reaction can be observed. In addition, reactivation of latent tuberculosis (due to the key role of TNF in fighting mycobacterial and other infections) has been observed more frequently than with etanercept.

Anakinra. Anakinra is the third anticytokine biologic agent approved by the Food and Drug Administration for the treatment of rheumatoid arthritis. Anakinra is a competitive inhibitor of the proinflammatory cytokine IL-1 that, like TNF-α, is elevated in the plasma and joint fluid of rheumatoid arthritis patients. IL-1 exhibits a variety of actions that facilitate the local inflammatory response, including activation of B and T cells, induction of other cytokines (Il-6, TNF, and IL-8), and release of destructive enzymes and other inflammatory mediators. IL-1ra (IL-1 receptor antagonist) is a naturally occurring counterregulatory cytokine that increases in response to elevated IL-1 levels and competes for IL-1-β binding to type I IL-1 receptors without possessing any agonist activity on cells expressing those receptors (that is, without inducing the same reaction as IL-1-β binding). Anakinra is a nonglycosylated recombinant human IL-1ra which has been cloned from human monocytes and expressed in *Escherichia coli*. Due to its short half-life of 4–6 hours, 100 mg of anakinra must be administered daily by subcutaneous injections.

Nonbiologic agents. Long before FDA approval of etanercept in 1999 as the first biologic response modifier agent to treat rheumatoid arthritis, multiple nonbiologic DMARDs were available to suppress disease activity. Unlike the biologic agents, which specifically target one proinflammatory cytokine, nonbiologic DMARDs are chemical compounds which usually suppress multiple components of the inflammatory response. The nonselective immunomodulatory activity accounts for their toxicities and often results in an increased risk of infections. However, due largely to their lower cost relative to biologic agents, the more established nonbiologic DMARDs are still popular antirheumatic drugs.

Methotrexate. Methotrexate is now the first-line drug used in the treatment of rheumatoid arthritis in the United States due to its efficacy, excellent safety profile, patient tolerance, and the ability to escalate the dose if the disease progresses. Methotrexate is considered the "gold standard" by which most new drugs are compared. At higher doses, methotrexate interferes with folic acid metabolism by reducing dihydrofolate reductase activity, thus impairing purine biosynthesis. Although its mechanism of action is still unknown, the finding that the concomitant administration of folic acid and methotrexate to rheumatoid arthritis patients reduces its toxicity but not its efficacy indicates that its mechanism of action in suppressing rheumatoid arthritis disease activity must be independent of its action on folate metabolism. The drug is administered 1 day per week orally or via subcutaneous injection at the usual dosage between 7.5 and 25 mg. The most common side effects include elevated levels of liver enzymes; gastrointestinal irritation; reduction in blood counts; and, rarely, lung toxicity, infections, and the development of lymphoma. It frequently leads to spontaneous abortions and is very toxic to the developing fetus; therefore, women of childbearing age must use adequate contraception.

Leflunomide. Leflunomide is the most recent nonbiologic agent approved for the treatment of rheumatoid arthritis. Leflunomide is a prodrug that undergoes hepatic metabolism to the active compound, A77 1726. Leflunomide disrupts cell cycle progression from G1 to S phase by inhibiting dihydroorate dehydrogenase, which interferes with pyrimidine biosynthesis. The daily maintenance dose is 20 mg; however, a loading daily dose of three 100-mg tablets

must be administered during the first several weeks to speed the onset of activity. Leflunomide is approved to treat rheumatoid arthritis and is similar to methotrexate in its efficacy and liver toxicity. However, unlike methotrexate, the dose may not be increased to achieve greater efficacy. Extreme caution is advised with the concomitant use of other drugs with liver toxicity, such as methotrexate.

Sulfasalazine. Sulfasalazine is a less toxic drug used alone to treat mild rheumatoid arthritis or in combination with other DMARDS, due to its excellent safety profile. The drug is a combination of sulfapyridine and 5-aminosalicylic acid, so it cannot be used in patients allergic to sulfa drugs. Tolerance is improved by slowly increasing the oral dose from 0.5 g to 1.5 g twice daily or using the enteric-coated preparation. Monitoring includes periodic blood counts and liver enzyme tests to detect rare but usually reversible toxic reactions.

Hydroxychloroquine. The antimalarial drug hydroxychloroquine is the least toxic among DMARDs and is effective in the treatment of mild rheumatoid arthritis and several other autoimmune diseases, including systemic lupus erythematosus. The exact mechanism of action is unknown, but this slow-acting drug may interfere with the processing of autoantigenic peptides by its action within lysosomes. The usual daily dose is 200–400 mg, and routine monitoring involves only a yearly eye exam to detect the extremely rare occurrence of retinal injury associated with prolonged therapy (more than 10 years) or high daily doses (more than 6.5 mg/kg). Hydroxychloroquine's excellent safety profile makes it an ideal drug to use in combination with other DMARDs.

Other DMARDs. Injectable gold compounds including aurothioglucose and gold sodium thiomalate were the first significant DMARDs used in the treatment of rheumatoid arthritis until methotrexate became available in the 1980s. Significant side effects, including kidney damage, blood count reduction, and skin rashes, made it necessary for one-third of rheumatoid arthritis patients to discontinue use. The exact mechanism of action is unknown. Today gold compounds are rarely used for the treatment of rheumatoid arthritis in the United States, due to the availability of more effective, less toxic noninjectable agents. An oral gold compound, auranofin, is occasionally used (3 mg twice daily) for the treatment of mild rheumatoid arthritis. Although auranofin is less effective than gold compounds, it is less likely to cause renal injury; however, gastrointestinal side effects occur more frequently. The immunomodulatory drug cyclosporine A was first approved for the prevention of transplanted organ rejection in the 1980s, as it was associated with fewer serious infections than prior regimens. It is also effective in the treatment of rheumatoid arthritis and other autoimmune illnesses, but long-term adherence to this drug is difficult due to possible side effects such as hypertension and kidney toxicity. Cyclosporine A inhibits T cell activation by binding to the cytoplasmic protein immunophilin, which subsequently interferes with the activation of IL-2. The usual dose of 2.5–5.0 mg/kg/day may precipitate gout attacks and requires frequent monitoring of blood counts, renal function, and blood pressure. Similar agents such as tacrolimus and sirolimus might be less toxic; however, these newer drugs have not been as extensively studied as cyclosporine A in treating serious autoimmune diseases.

Future directions. Rheumatologists now have a variety of highly effective agents that may be used in combination for enhanced efficacy without additional toxicity. Treatment with highly effective agents early in the course of disease greatly reduces disability and, in many cases, actually halts the progression of disease and prevents joint damage. The effectiveness of anticytokine therapy has confirmed the pivotal role of specific proinflammatory cytokines such as TNF in the pathogenesis of rheumatoid arthritis and psoriatic arthritis. Multiple new anti-TNF drugs are currently undergoing clinical trials; it is hoped that these new drugs will possess fewer side effects and eventually reduce the high cost of current biologic therapeutic agents in the treatment of autoimmune diseases.

Despite the rapid advances in therapeutic agents for rheumatoid arthritis, not all patients respond adequately, indicating that different cytokines may play different roles in the pathogenesis of rheumatoid arthritis and that optimum therapy may need to be individualized. In the future, agents should be investigated which target multiple inflammatory mediators, including different proinflammatory cytokines, cell adhesion molecules, angiogenesis factors, and various degradative enzymes. Continued discovery of effective therapeutic agents by scientists in academic centers and the pharmaceutical industry should allow even more effective, safer agents to halt the progression of autoimmune illnesses.

For background information *see* ARTHRITIS; AUTOIMMUNITY; CELLULAR IMMUNOLOGY; IMMUNITY; IMMUNOSUPPRESSION in the McGraw-Hill Encyclopedia of Science & Technology.   Richard Meehan

Bibliography. W. P. Arend and J. M. Dayer, Cytokines and cytokine inhibitors or antagonists in rheumatoid arthritis, *Arthritis Rheum.*, 33:305–315, 1990; A. Cannella and J. O'Dell, Cytotoxic, imunomodulatory and biologic agents, in S. West (ed.), *Rheumatology Secrets*, Hanley & Belfus, Philadelphia, 2002; Y. Jiang et al., A multicenter, double-blind, dose-ranging, randomized placebo-controlled study of recombinant human interleukin-1 receptor antagonist in patients with rheumatoid arthritis: Radiological progression and correlation of Genant and Larsen scores, *Arthritis Rheum.*, 43:1001–1009, 2000; J. M. Kremer, Rational use of new and existing disease-modifying agents in rheumatoid arthritis, *Ann. Intern. Med.*, 134:695–706, 2001; L. W. Moreland et al., Etanercept therapy in rheumatoid arthritis: A randomized controlled trial, *Ann. Intern. Med.*, 30(6):478–486, 1999.

DNA delivery systems

Deoxyribonucleic acid (DNA) has long been envisioned as a drug for both therapeutic (gene therapy) and prophylactic (vaccination) use. The idea of gene-based medicine is simple and appealing: If a disease is caused by a deficient gene, delivery of a good copy of the gene should correct the defect, making DNA a therapeutic drug. Similarly, delivery of an antigen gene should elicit a specific immune response against the protein encoded by the delivered gene, making DNA a prophylactic vaccine. (Note that delivery of genes is much safer than delivery of proteins because DNA molecules themselves do not elicit immune reactions.) However, after more than a decade of intense research and more than 600 clinical trials, no truly successful gene therapy protocol has been reported, and no DNA vaccination has been approved. The reason is the lack of an efficient and safe gene delivery system.

Viral versus nonviral. Methods of DNA delivery have been studied since the late 1950s, when the technique of introducing exogenous (foreign) DNA into cells was first developed as a tool to study genes. Both viral and nonviral vectors have been explored, resulting in two major classes of DNA delivery methods (see **table**): infection (viral) and transfection (nonviral).

Viruses have evolved over time to deliver and replicate their own genomes in host cells and thus are by far the most efficient way to deliver DNA in vivo, although the efficiency of nonviral transfection is approaching viral infection in vitro. The earliest gene therapy protocols almost exclusively utilized viral vectors; at present about 25% of protocols are through nonviral systems (mostly lipid-based delivery). Recently with growing concerns over the safety and immunogenicity (ability to induce an immune response) of viral-mediated DNA delivery, however, nonviral, synthetic methods are gaining acceptance and popularity as an important alternative.

Delivery barriers. DNA can be delivered into the body via a myriad of routes (for example, orally, intravenously, intramuscularly, and subcutaneously). However, once inside the body, the final destination of all methods of DNA delivery is the cell nucleus, where DNA is transcribed to messenger ribonucleic acid (mRNA), which is ultimately translated to proteins encoded by the delivered DNA. The journey for DNA traveling outside the cell to the inside of the nucleus is not an easy one, as many barriers have to be overcome before reaching the destination. There are three major barriers to nonviral DNA delivery: (1) targeting and uptake: DNA must be delivered to the surface of particular intended cells and be transported across the plasma membrane efficiently; (2) cytosol survival: DNA is generally taken up by cells via endocytosis, a process that will ultimately lyse DNA molecules; therefore, it must escape the endosomal/lysosomal pathways and survive nuclease attacks once released into the cytosol; and

DNA delivery methods		
	Nonviral vectors	Viral vectors

	Chemical
	    Lipid-based (such as lipoplex)
	    Polymer-based (such as polyplex)
	    Other (such as CaPO$_4$)
	Mechanical
	    Microinjection
	    Particle bombardment (such as gene gun)
	    Pressure-mediated
	Electrical
	    Electroporation
	Other
	    Magnetofection
	    Photochemical transfection
	    Sonoporation
		Retrovirus
		Adenovirus
		Poxvirus
		Adeno-associated virus
		Herpes simplex virus

(3) nucleus targeting: from the cytosol, DNA must be able to find the nucleus and enter it through small nuclear pores with high efficiency.

DNA delivery systems. Nonviral delivery systems involve the use of chemical, electrical, mechanical, and other methods to facilitate DNA delivery. Chemical-based DNA delivery is arguably the easiest and most versatile type of DNA delivery system. The basic mechanism involves complex formations between positively charged (cationic) chemicals and negatively charged DNA. Depending on the chemicals used, chemical methods of DNA delivery can be further classified into three major categories: lipid-based, polymer-based, and other [for example, calcium phosphate (CaPO$_4$)].

Lipid-based delivery. Lipid-based DNA delivery is among the earliest reagent methods developed for transfection. It utilizes mostly cationic lipids or cationic lipids mixed with other lipids, such as cholesterol, to encapsulate DNA into liposomes, forming lipid-DNA complexes (lipoplexes). DNA molecules are confined inside the lipoplexes and therefore are protected from degradation. The outside of lipoplexes is usually positively charged, making it easier to interact with the negatively charged cell surface, thus promoting cellular uptake mostly through endocytosis. A variety of cationic lipids with different molecular compositions and structures have been synthesized, and new formulations of mixtures have been tested in hopes of increasing DNA delivery efficiency by overcoming the major delivery barriers. Although the efficiency of in vitro transfection (especially lipid-based transfections) has increased dramatically in recent years, the drawbacks of lipid-based delivery remain: lack of targeting (specific ligands must be conjugated to the liposomes in order to achieve target delivery), clearance in the bloodstream (the half-life of liposomes in the bloodstream is very short; most liposomes are degraded before reaching intended tissues), and the difficulty of correlating in vitro success to in vivo applications.

Polymer-based delivery. Polymer-based DNA delivery is progressing rapidly. As in lipid-based delivery, cationic polymers are utilized to condense DNA molecules, forming transportable complexes called polyplexes. Unlike lipids, however, polymers are relatively easy to modify via conjugation of ligands such as galactose, transferrin, antibody, folate, and growth factor, thus making targeting easier. In addition, in order to increase the stability and biocompatibility of polymer-based (also used for lipid-based) delivery systems, a common strategy is to conjugate polyethylene glycol (PEG) chains onto the polymers because of their high water solubility, nonimmunogenicity, and biocompatibility.

Among the many polymers capable of DNA delivery, several stand out due to their unique features. Poly-L-lysine, a highly positively charged polymer that is able to condense DNA, is the earliest polymer tested for DNA delivery. Some forms of polyethylenimine (PEI) are able to assist endosomal escape and facilitate nuclear entry, making them very powerful DNA delivery tools. Polyamidoamine (PAMAM) dendrimers are highly branched polymers with well-defined molecular architecture. Fractured, higher-generation PAMAM have been shown to increase transfection efficiency 10–100-fold over lipid-based reagents. (Recently, it was observed that PEGylation of lower-generation PAMAM also increased transfection efficiency dramatically.) Poly(D,L-lactide-*co*-glycolide) [PLGA] is a biocompatible and biodegradable polymer that has also been successfully used to encapsulate DNA. DNA can be released continuously from PLGA in a sustained and controlled fashion for up to a year.

Calcium phosphate delivery. Calcium phosphate, one of the earliest chemicals developed for DNA delivery, is a simple and effective transfection reagent that is still widely used. The drawbacks of CaPO$_4$ include high cytotoxicity, difficulty of applying it in vivo, and lack of consistency in transfection efficiencies due to uncontrollable sizes of calcium phosphate–DNA precipitates.

Nonchemical delivery methods. Besides chemical means, many other forces, including mechanical and electrical, can be employed to directly deliver or enhance the delivery of DNA. Direct injection of naked DNA into a cell nucleus (microinjection) is the simplest DNA delivery method, although it is not practical in vivo. Direct injection of DNA into tissues (for example, skeletal muscle) is widely used for DNA vaccination in cases in which low efficiency of delivery is not as limiting as in gene therapy (for example, immune responses are always amplified in vivo). Pressure-mediated DNA delivery, including the hydrodynamic force–based approach (a rapid injection of a large volume of DNA solution into the bloodstream), has also been explored. DNA can also be delivered with a "gene gun," a particle bombardment device that accelerates DNA-coated gold microparticles to an extremely high speed to penetrate cell membranes, thus introducing large amounts of DNA into cells. Electrical force represents a different class of DNA delivery, called electroporation. In this approach, high-voltage electrical pulses (in the millisecond range) are applied to puncture cell membranes transiently, allowing DNA to diffuse into a cell. Although electroporation is one of the most efficient ways of DNA delivery, it is also one of the most toxic methods. Magnetofection represents a relatively new approach. DNA vectors are first associated with superparamagnetic nanoparticles; localized delivery is then achieved by application of a magnetic field. Other interesting methods of DNA delivery include sonoporation, in which DNA delivery is accomplished by ultrasonic cavitation, and photochemical transfection, in which light and photosensitizing compounds are used to direct DNA delivery.

Challenges and the future. It is clear now that there will be no single, universal DNA delivery system that suits all needs; each clinical setting needs a particular delivery method tailored toward the treatment or prevention of that particular disease. The greatest challenge is to develop a nonviral DNA delivery system that has high efficiency and specificity but low toxicity and cost. Thus future DNA delivery may rely on a hybrid system that combines the advantages of both viral and nonviral components, or a modular system that incorporates many currently developed methods to meet the challenge.

For background information *see* DEOXYRIBONU-CLEIC ACID (DNA); GENE; LIPOSOME; PLASMID; VACCI-NATION in the McGraw-Hill Encyclopedia of Science & Technology.   Dan Luo

Bibliography. M. E. Davis, Non-viral gene delivery systems, *Curr. Opin. Biotechnol.*, 13:128-131, 2002; M. A. Kay, J. C. Glorioso, and L. Naldini, Viral vectors for gene therapy: The art of turning infectious agents into vehicles of therapeutics, *Nat. Med.*, 7: 33-40, 2001; F. Liu and L. Huang, Development of non-viral vectors for systemic gene delivery, *J. Control Release*, 78:259-266, 2002; D. Luo and W. M. Saltzman, Synthetic DNA delivery systems, *Nat. Biotechnol.*, 18:33-37, 2000; W. M. Saltzman, *Drug Delivery: Engineering Principles for Drug Therapy*, Oxford University Press, New York, 2001; W. M. Saltzman and D. Luo, *Synthetic DNA Delivery Systems*, Landes Bioscience, in press.

DNA helicases

In all cellular organisms from bacteria to humans, genetic information is locked within a double helix formed by the two antiparallel deoxyribonucleic

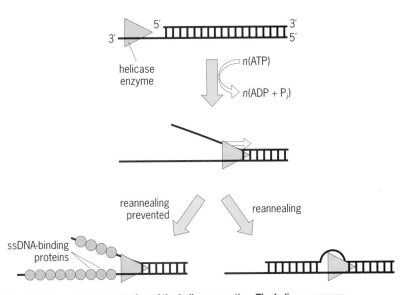

Fig. 1. Schematic representation of the helicase reaction. The helicase enzyme translocates along the DNA molecule and separates the strands. Energy for this unfavorable reaction is provided by the hydrolysis of adenosine triphosphates (ATP) to adenosine diphosphates (ADP) and inorganic phosphate ions (P$_i$). In the presence of a single-stranded DNA binding protein, reannealing of the DNA duplex is prevented. The helicase depicted here displays a $3' \rightarrow 5'$ polarity, tracking unidirectionally along the lower of the two DNA strands in the duplex (the loading strand).

acid (DNA) strands. Although double-stranded DNA (dsDNA) is the form most suitable for secure information storage, hydrogen bonds formed between complementary bases (Watson-Crick base pairing) impair readout of this information by the cellular machinery, which frequently requires a single-stranded DNA (ssDNA) intermediate as a template. The unwinding of dsDNA into ssDNA, a function critical for virtually every aspect of cellular DNA metabolism from DNA replication to homologous DNA recombination, is provided by a ubiquitous class of enzymes called DNA helicases. First identified in the 1970s, DNA helicases are motor proteins that convert chemical energy into mechanical work. Chemical energy is derived from the hydrolysis of adenosine triphosphate (ATP) or other nucleoside triphosphates, and is coupled with mechanical work during at least two important steps within the helicase reaction cycle (**Fig. 1**): (1) the unidirectional translocations along the substrate molecule and (2) the melting of the DNA duplex, which together result in the formation of the ssDNA intermediates essential for vital cellular processes.

Classifications. Helicases are divided into five main superfamilies based on the presence and composition of conserved amino acid motifs (often referred to as the helicase signature motifs). (It is important to note, however, that only a small fraction of these putative helicases have been studied biochemically and, of those proteins, not all have been shown to possess nucleic acid strand separation activity.) Biochemical and structural data have suggested that helicases function as monomers, dimers, and multimers (predominantly hexamers) and that they can also be classified based on a substrate requirement for dsDNA, dsRNA, or DNA-RNA hybrids. To unwind dsDNA efficiently, many DNA helicases need to initiate from an ssDNA region adjacent to the duplex part of the substrate molecule. Based on the requirement for an ssDNA overhang of a certain polarity, helicases are divided into two functional groups: those that utilize a $3'$-terminated ssDNA are designated as $3' \rightarrow 5'$ helicases, whereas enzymes that require a $5'$ overhang are designated as $5' \rightarrow 3'$ helicases.

Directional translocation. It is now generally believed that the observed polarity requirement of helicases is a consequence of a directional bias in translocation on ssDNA. For example, the enzyme depicted in Fig. 1 is a $3' \rightarrow 5'$ helicase. Upon binding to the ssDNA, it starts moving toward the $5'$ end of the loading strand, which brings the enzyme to the ssDNA-dsDNA junction and subsequently through the duplex portion of the substrate.

Evidence for directional translocation on ssDNA was provided by two different approaches. The first examined the dependence of helicase ATPase activity on the length of the ssDNA substrate. The second, based on the ability of many helicases to create sufficient force during ssDNA translocation to disrupt the tight interaction between streptavidin and biotin ($K_d = 10^{-15}$M), measured the ability of the helicase to increase the rate of streptavidin dissociation from DNA substrates biotinylated at either the $3'$ or $5'$ end. This second method was used successfully to determine the directionality of movement of several helicases on ssDNA.

High-resolution structural data suggest that the helicase signature motifs are not essential for the duplex DNA separation per se, but for the ATP-dependent unidirectional motion of the helicases on either single- or double-stranded DNA lattices. Consequently, it was proposed that the helicase signature motifs define a modular structure that functions as the DNA motor, while additional domains, which may vary from one protein to another, may be responsible for the DNA unwinding.

Accessory factors. Once dsDNA unwinding is achieved, spontaneous reannealing of the duplex may be avoided if the nascent ssDNA strands are trapped by single-stranded DNA binding proteins or other "coupling factors" that hand off the intermediates to the next step in a reaction pathway (Fig. 1). Although ssDNA binding proteins have frequently been shown to stimulate helicase activity in vitro, helicase activity can also be stimulated by other accessory factors that increase the rate or processivity of unwinding. The primary replicative helicase of

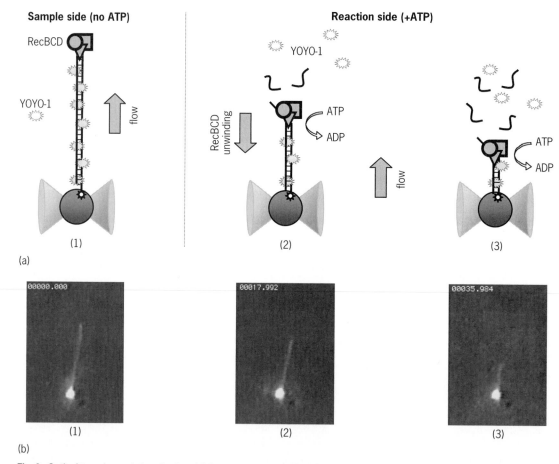

Fig. 2. Optical trapping and visualization. (*a*) Optical trapping method for studying RecBCD helicase/nuclease at the single-molecule level. (1) A polystyrene bead is held in the optical trap with dsDNA (stained with the fluorescent dye YOYO-1) stretched out in the flow behind it. (2) Upon addition of ATP, the helicase begins to unwind and degrade the DNA. (3) Unwinding continues until the helicase reaches the bead or falls off of its DNA track. (*b*) Frames from a movie of DNA unwinding and degradation in the optical trap apparatus. The frames are equivalent to the representation in *a*. (*The original movie of the helicase in action may be viewed in its entirety at http://microbiology.ucdavis.edu/sklab/kowalczykowskilab.htm*)

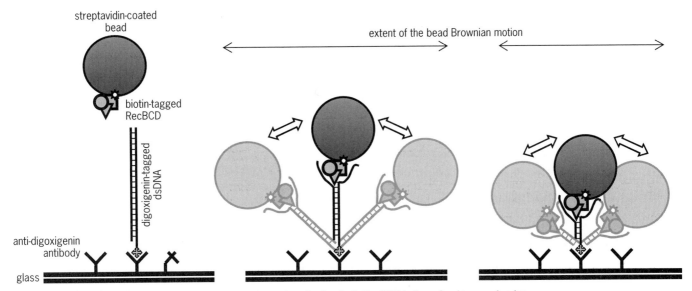

streptavidin-coated
bead

biotin-tagged
RecBCD

extent of the bead Brownian motion

digoxigenin-tagged
dsDNA

anti-digoxigenin
antibody

glass

Fig. 3. Tethered particle motion experiment to study DNA translocation by single RecBCD helicase/nuclease molecules. A dsDNA molecule is attached to a glass surface, and RecBCD molecules are attached to polystyrene beads. As RecBCD tracks along the DNA molecule in an ATP-dependent manner, it gradually draws the bead closer to the glass surface. This translocation results in a decrease in the Brownian motion of the bead that can be measured by light microscopy. (*Adapted from http://www.bio.brandeis.edu/~gelles/movies.html*)

Escherchia coli, DnaB, is a good example of a helicase that acts poorly in isolation from the accessory factors with which the enzyme is intended to operate. As part of the replisome (the DNA synthesis machinery of the cell), the role of DnaB is to separate the DNA strands at the replication fork. It was shown recently that the rate of movement of the replication machinery at the fork is coordinated by an interaction between DnaB and DNA polymerase (enzyme that synthesizes a daughter strand of DNA residues) that is mediated by the τ subunit of the DNA polymerase. The τ subunit bridges the polymerase dimer and the hexameric helicase, inducing a conformational change in DnaB that enhances its translocation rate by almost 30-fold to 1000 base pairs per second. In the absence of τ, the replication machinery is uncoupled, and the polymerase simply follows DnaB as it unwinds DNA at approximately 35 bp/s.

Single-molecule translocation visualization. Until recently, all biochemical data on helicases were derived from conventional bulk-phase techniques, which observe the population-averaged properties of large molecular ensembles. In 2001 two new approaches to visualize translocation by a single molecule of a helicase were reported. These new techniques successfully visualized translocation of a single molecule of RecBCD, a multifunctional heterotrimeric enzyme employed by *E. coli* to initiate homologous recombination at dsDNA breaks. RecBCD is an exceptionally fast helicase that is furnished with all of the processivity and accessory factors it requires. The enzyme has a high affinity for blunt or nearly blunt dsDNA ends, and it can unwind, on average, 30,000 bp of dsDNA per binding event at a rate of 1000 bp/s, while simultaneously degrading the ssDNA products of its helicase activity.

Optical trap visualization. In one approach, a device called an optical trap was used to manipulate in-

dividual, fluorescently labeled DNA molecules and to visualize their unwinding and degradation by the RecBCD enzyme (**Fig. 2***a*). A dsDNA molecule, biotinylated at one end, was attached to streptavidin-coated polystyrene beads. The RecBCD enzyme was then prebound to the free DNA end in the absence of ATP. The bead was caught and held by lasers (the optical trap); buffer flowing through the optical cell caused the DNA to stretch out behind the trapped bead. The dsDNA was visualized by staining with a fluorescent intercalating dye (YOYO-1) and appeared as a bright 15-micrometer rod. Upon addition of ATP, the RecBCD enzyme mediated the unwinding of dsDNA, which was observed as a progressive shortening of the fluorescently labeled DNA molecule (Fig. 2*b*).

Tethered particle motion visualization. An alternative single-molecule approach used light microscopy to follow translocation of a biotin-tagged RecBCD enzyme bound to a streptavidin-coated polystyrene bead. In the tethered particle motion experiment (**Fig. 3**), dsDNA molecules, modified with digoxigenin at one end, were attached to a glass surface coated with antidigoxigenin antibodies. Bead-labeled RecBCD molecules were bound to the free (unmodified) dsDNA ends. Because the DNA acts as a flexible tether, RecBCD translocation was observed as a decrease in the Brownian motion (the irregular motion of small particles caused by the random bombardment by molecules in the surrounding medium) of the bead as it was pulled toward the glass surface.

Combined observations. The two single-molecule experiments are different yet complementary: the tethered particle motion experiment directly measures translocation, whereas the optical trap method (and conventional bulk assays) measures dsDNA unwinding. Therefore, together, the studies provide additional powerful evidence for the coupling of DNA strand separation with movement of the helicase protein on its substrate lattice. Both single-molecule visualization methods show that RecBCD translocates unidirectionally and processively on dsDNA, with each molecule moving at a constant rate (within the limit of experimental detection). Although the average translocation rate is similar to that derived from bulk measurements, considerable variation is observed in the translocation rate of individual RecBCD enzymes. This surprising observation is an example of the kind of information that is accessible only by single-molecule studies.

Conclusion. In the last 10 years, considerable progress has been made in the understanding of the molecular mechanisms of DNA helicases. Although many questions remain, perhaps the next challenge in this field is to understand how these DNA motors are incorporated into and used by large multiprotein complexes, such as the replisome, to orchestrate complex DNA processing events.

For background information *see* ADENOSINE TRIPHOSPHATE (ATP); DEOXYRIBONUCLEIC ACID (DNA); ENZYME; MOLECULAR BIOLOGY; NUCLEOPROTEIN in the McGraw-Hill Encyclopedia of Science & Technology.   Maria Spies; Mark S. Dillingham; Stephen C. Kowalczykowski

Bibliography. B. Alberts et al., *Molecular Biology of the Cell*, 3d ed. (II, Chap. 6), Garland Publishing, New York, 1994; P. R. Bianco et al., Processive translocation and DNA unwinding by individual RecBCD enzyme molecules, *Nature*, 409(18):374-378, 2001; K. M. Dohoney and J. Gelles, χ-Sequence recognition and DNA translocation by single RecBCD helicase/nuclease molecules, *Nature*, 409(18):370-374, 2001; H. Lodish et al., *Molecular Cell Biology*, 4th ed. (Chap. 12), W H Freeman, New York, 2000; P. Soultanas and D. B. Wigley, Unwinding the "Gordian Knot" of helicase action, *TIBS*, 26(1):47-54, 2001.

Dynamic brain atlas

Magnetic resonance imaging (MRI) has become the imaging technique of choice for the diagnosis of many brain disorders. It is also increasingly used to assist diagnosis of psychiatric disorders and dementia, which are characterized by subtle abnormalities in the size and shape of brain structures, instead of the distinct lesions visible in patients with, for example, brain tumors. Unfortunately, these subtle abnormalities are difficult to describe precisely, making diagnosis of individual brain MRI scans difficult. However, the dynamic brain atlas, a new technique for analyzing brain MRI scans, may assist physicians to overcome these diagnostic obstacles.

Brain atlases. In neuroimaging research, brain atlases are widely used to assist in data analysis. Typically, brain atlases are based on brain MRI scans and are generated either by fusing images from multiple subjects or fusing multiple images of a single representative subject. A brain atlas is considered a reference brain with which the brain MRI scan of a specific subject or group of subjects can be compared. Atlases from multiple subjects have the advantage of giving an indication of natural variability in the size and shape of structures.

Static. In today's practice, brain atlases are built statically (that is, all images are fused at once after acquiring the data). Brain atlases can be found in neurological textbooks or, more and more often, in electronic form on the Internet. Although these atlases have been very successful in research applications, they are not so helpful for the diagnosis of individual patient brain MRI scans. For patient diagnosis, it is necessary to have information relevant to the specific patient (that is, relevant to the patient's age, gender, background, and medical history), but static precalculated atlases do not have this property.

Dynamic. The ideal atlas would be dynamic, that is, customized to the current patient by being made up of images from individuals of the same age, gender, background, and medical history as the study subject. This would make the process of identifying subtle or diffuse brain disease (for example, psychiatric disorders and dementia) more straightforward, as slight differences between the current patient and similar normal individuals could be spotted at a glance. Dynamic atlases will be increasingly valuable as hospitals computerize their storing and handling of medical images.

Computational grids. A dynamic brain atlas requires large collections of images from which a subgroup that matches the current patient can be chosen. As digital-image archive systems are becoming more common in hospitals and image data are being incorporated into multimedia patient records, widespread computational analysis of clinical images is becoming possible for the first time. However, the time-consuming fusion of large numbers of images cannot be performed on one standard computer in practical time, and few hospitals are likely to want to invest in expensive supercomputer facilities. The capabilities provided by computational grids, however, could make it possible to use the huge quantity of distributed on-line patient images for decision support in diagnosis. Similar to the document-sharing concept of the World Wide Web, the grid concept is based on the coordinated sharing of computational resources via the Internet. Grid users could have at their disposal distributed high-performance computers that are able to access and process large amounts of data stored in global databases, as well as the appropriate tools to control these resources. By using this grid infrastructure, the task of fusing images is distributed to grid computers that process the data simultaneously, instead of being performed on the local machine. Hence, a task that could last for days on one computer can be processed in a matter of minutes on the grid. Additionally, no local high-performance computer is necessary anymore, because the local machine serves just as a "gateway" to the grid. The task of building a customized brain atlas could even be submitted, for instance, by a low-performance notebook computer.

Prototype of a dynamic atlas. A prototype system has been developed (Hill et al., 2002) that builds near real-time, dynamically configurable atlases that are adjusted to a current subject's brain scan. The image data comprises 180 whole-brain MRI scans of reference subjects aged 18 to 80 years. The database records subject age at scan date, gender, and the network address of the image file, enabling different parts of the dataset to be stored on servers at separate sites. A graphical interface incorporated into an interactive image viewer provides a user-friendly environment to query the database, transfer images using secure grid protocols, and securely launch processing on the distributed computing cluster. Database images are segmented into tissue types, and anatomical structures of interest delineated. The very substantial computation required for these automated analysis stages was carried out on computing hardware distributed across three sites, and the database was automatically populated with the analysis results. Each brain volume was automatically segmented into different brain tissues [(gray matter, white matter, and cerebrospinal fluid (CSF)] using an algorithm called a statistical classifier. The dynamic aspect of the system is the ability to generate an atlas specific to a particular subject in near real time, rather than making use of a precomputed atlas that may not be appropriate.

Example clinical application. A radiologist wishes to diagnose the brain MRI scan of a patient with a subtle brain abnormality (such as in psychiatric conditions or dementia).

Procedure. Armed with a notebook computer with network connection, the radiologist downloads the brain MRI scan from the hospital computer system onto his or her local system and views it. Although there appear to be diffuse abnormalities, the radiologist has difficulty precisely identifying their nature. To assist the diagnosis, the radiologist makes use of a grid application that can dynamically generate a brain atlas customized to the current patient. This brain atlas will show the normal range of size and shape of brain structures of interest for a person of the same age, gender, and past medical history as the current patient. The radiologist selects a pop-up window from his or her viewing software, enters the desired properties of the customized atlas, and launches the analysis.

At this point the grid takes over. The current image is securely uploaded onto the grid application, ensuring patient confidentiality. Simultaneously, images of many reference subjects that have the properties selected by the radiologist are securely accessed by the same grid application. Software then matches each reference subject to the patient. The computing power and image storage needed is distributed around the grid, and the radiologist does not need to be concerned with any of these details. After a few minutes, the results are securely transferred back to

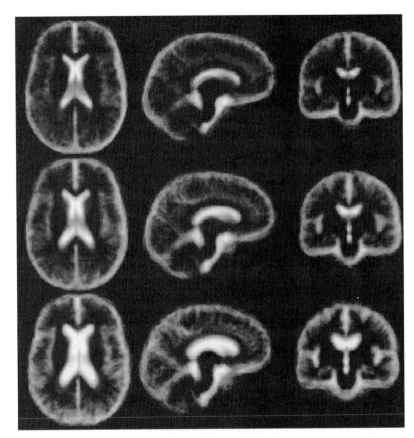

Fig. 1. Fluid CSF maps from three dynamically configured atlases generated for a 25-year-old subject (top), a 45-year-old subject (middle), and a 75-year-old subject (bottom).

the local notebook computer, and the radiologist can see the patient images alongside a customized atlas (**Fig. 1**) or can view the patient images with features from the atlas overlaid (**Fig. 2**), enabling the radiologist to pinpoint the regions of the brain that are abnormal.

Potential result. Figures 1 and 2 illustrate potential results of a dynamic brain atlas system. Figure 1 shows fluid CSF maps from three dynamically configured atlases generated for study subjects of three different ages: For a 25-year-old subject (top), the atlas was generated from images in the database from 30 subjects between 16 and 35 years of age, each aligned to the study subject. For a 45-year-old subject (middle), the process was repeated using database subjects between 35 and 65 years of age, and for a

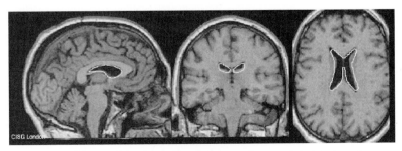

Fig. 2. MRI scan of a study subject with the 50th percentile boundary of the lateral ventricles from a similar-aged group of database subjects overlaid.

75-year-old subject (bottom), the atlas was generated from database subjects over 70 years old. Note the increasing size of CSF spaces with age.

Figure 2 shows a study subject with the 50th percentile boundary of the lateral ventricles from a similar-aged group of database subjects overlaid. This sort of functionality could assist a radiologist in quantifying the degree of abnormality in a patient. Similar overlays could be produced for any delineated structure in the reference image.

Future neuroimaging research applications. In addition to clinical applications, the dynamic brain atlas system has potential utility in neuroimaging research. For instance, a natural extension of the dynamic atlas would be to add a knowledge discovery component. Rather than aligning the images to a study subject, the network application could align the images to one another in order to discover relationships between the data. The value of such a component would increase with increasing numbers of subjects and larger amounts of nonimage information about the subjects, potentially including genetic information. In order increase current understanding of brain development, aging, and pathology, future neuroimaging research will require analysis of much larger cohorts of data in order to increase the sensitivity of detecting differences between subject groups. Such large-scale projects will require better data analysis infrastructure than is provided by the existing World Wide Web and computing facilities at individual laboratories. The dynamic brain atlas prototype system must be the sort of capability that will be needed in such research programs in the future.

For background information *see* BRAIN; INTERNET; MAGNETIC RESONANCE; MEDICAL IMAGING in the McGraw-Hill Encyclopedia of Science & Technology.

T. Hartkens; D. L. G. Hill; J. V. Hajnal; D. Rueckert; S. M. Smith; K. McKleish

Bibliography. M. K. Chung et al., A unified statistical approach to deformation-based morphometry, *Neuroimage*, 14(3):595–606, 2001; C. A. Cocosco et al., BrainWeb: Online interface to a 3D MRI simulated brain database, *NeuroImage*, vol. 5, no. 4, part 2/4, S425, 1997; I. Foster, C. Kesselman, and S. Tuecke, The anatomy of the grid: Enabling scalable virtual organizations, *Int. J. Supercomputer Appl.*, 15(3), 2001; D. L. G. Hill et al., A dynamic brain atlas, *Proceedings of the 5th International Conference on Medical Image Computing and Computer Assisted Intervention (MICCAI)*, in press; S. Sandor and R. Leahy, Surface-based labeling of cortical anatomy using a deformable atlas, *IEEE Trans. Med. Imag.*, 16(1):41–54, 1997; P. M. Thompson et al., Cortical change in Alzheimer's disease detected with a disease-specific population-based brain atlas, *Cerebral Cortex*, 11(1):1–16, 2001; K. van Leemput et al., Automated model-based bias field correction of MR images of the brain, *IEEE Trans. Med. Imag.*, 18(10):885–896, 1999; R. P. Woods et al., Creation and use of a Talairach-compatible atlas for accurate, automated, nonlinear intersubject registration, and analysis of functional imaging data, *Human Brain Map.*, 8(2-3):73–9, 1999.

Dyslexia

Developmental dyslexia is characterized by unexpected difficulty in reading in children and adults who otherwise possess the intelligence and motivation considered necessary for accurate and fluent reading. Dyslexia is one of the most common problems affecting children and adults; in the United States, the prevalence of dyslexia is estimated to range from 5 to 17% of school-age children, with as many as 40% reading below grade level. It is the most common and most carefully studied of the learning disabilities, affecting at least 80% of all individuals identified as learning-disabled. Recent epidemiologic data indicate that, like hypertension and obesity, dyslexia fits a dimensional model—within the population, reading ability occurs along a continuum, with reading disability representing the tail of a normal distribution. Good evidence based on sample surveys of randomly selected populations of children indicates that dyslexia affects boys and girls comparably. (The long-held belief that only boys suffer from dyslexia reflected bias in school-identified samples.) Dyslexia is a persistent, chronic condition that stays with the individual for a lifetime. It is both familial and heritable; about half of children who have a parent with dyslexia, as well as half of the siblings of dyslexics and half of the parents of dyslexics, may have the disorder.

Etiology. Although the causes of dyslexia are not completely understood, current evidence indicates that the central difficulty reflects a deficit within the language system. The language system is conceptualized as a hierarchical series of components: at higher levels are neural systems engaged in processing, for example, semantics (meaning) and syntax (grammar); at the low level is the phonologic module dedicated to processing the distinctive sound elements that constitute language. The functional unit of the phonologic module is the phoneme, defined as the smallest discernible segment of speech; for example, the word "bat" consists of three phonemes: /b/ /ae/ /t/ (buh, aah, tuh). To speak a word, the speaker retrieves the word's phonemic constituents from an internal lexicon, assembles the phonemes, and then utters the word. Conversely, to read a word, the beginning reader must first segment that word into its underlying phonologic elements. Phonemic awareness (the insight that all spoken words can be pulled apart into phonemes) is deficient in dyslexic children and adults. Results from large and well-studied populations with reading disability confirm that in young school children and adolescents a deficit in phonology is the most robust and specific correlate of reading disability.

Reading comprises two main processes, decoding and comprehension. In dyslexia, a deficit at the level of the phonologic module impairs the ability to segment the written word into its phonologic elements. As a result, the reader experiences difficulty in decoding and identifying the printed word. The phonologic deficit is domain-specific; that is, it is independent of other linguistic abilities. In particular, the higher-order cognitive and linguistic functions involved in comprehension (such as general intelligence and reasoning, vocabulary, and syntax) are generally intact. This pattern, a deficit in phonologic analysis contrasted with intact higher-order cognitive abilities, offers an explanation for the paradox of intelligent people who experience great difficulty in reading.

Neurologic basis. Converging evidence demonstrates a disruption in left-hemisphere posterior reading systems (primarily in left temporo-parieto-occipital brain regions) in dyslexic readers, with a relative increase in brain activation in frontal regions in dyslexic compared with nonimpaired readers. These neural systems are part of a widely distributed neural system relating spoken language to the written word.

Dyslexia occurs throughout the world, including countries such as China and Japan where the written language is partially logographic. (Even in these logographic languages there is still a strong phonological component.) Brain imaging studies in dyslexic readers from England, France, and Italy demonstrate the same disruption in posterior reading systems. These studies confirm the findings from clinicians and scientists throughout the world that dyslexia is universal across cultural and linguistic boundaries.

Diagnosis. At all ages, dyslexia is a clinical diagnosis; the clinician seeks to determine through history, observation, and psychometric assessment if there are (1) difficulties in reading that are unexpected for the person's cognitive capacity as shown by his or her age, intelligence, level of education, or professional status, and (2) associated linguistic problems at the level of phonologic processing. There is no single test score that is pathognomonic (pertaining to a diagnostic symptom) of dyslexia. As with any other medical diagnosis, the diagnosis of dyslexia should reflect a thoughtful synthesis of all the available clinical data. Dyslexia is distinguished from other disorders that may prominently feature reading difficulties by the unique, circumscribed nature of the phonologic deficit, which does not intrude into other linguistic or cognitive domains.

Risk factors. In the preschool child, a history of language delay or not attending to the sounds of words (trouble playing rhyming games, confusing words that sound alike, trouble learning to recognize alphabet letters), and a positive family history represent significant risk factors for dyslexia. In the school child, presenting complaints most commonly center on school performance, and often parents and teachers do not appreciate that the reason is a reading difficulty. A typical picture is that of a child who may have had a delay in speaking, does not learn letters by kindergarten, and has not begun to learn to read by first grade. The child progressively falls behind, with teachers and parents puzzled as to why the child may have difficulty learning to read. The reading difficulty is unexpected with respect to the child's ability, age, or grade. Even after acquiring decoding skills, the child generally remains a slow reader. Thus, bright dyslexic children may laboriously learn how to read words accurately but do not become fluent readers; that is, they do not recognize words rapidly and automatically. In an accomplished adolescent or young adult, the level of education or professional status provides the best indication of cognitive capacity; graduation from a competitive college and, for example, completion of medical school and a residency indicate a superior cognitive capacity. In bright adolescents and young adults, a history of phonologically based reading difficulties, requirements for extra time on tests, and current slow and effortful reading (that is, lack of automaticity) are the essential elements of a diagnosis of dyslexia. A history of phonologically based language difficulties, laborious reading and writing, poor spelling, and additional time requirements for reading and taking tests provide indisputable evidence of a deficiency in phonological processing which, in turn, serves as the basis for a reading disability.

Management. The management of dyslexia demands a life-span perspective; early on, the focus is on remediation of the reading problem. As a child matures and enters the more time-demanding setting of secondary school, the emphasis shifts to the important role of providing accommodations.

Remediation. Recently, based on the work of the National Reading Panel, evidence-based reading intervention programs have been identified that provide instruction in the most important elements in reading. Effective interventions used with younger children and even with older children are programs that begin by improving phonemic awareness, that is, the ability to focus on and manipulate phonemes in spoken syllables and words. Next, the beginning reader is taught phonics, that is, how letters are linked to sounds to form letter-sound correspondences and spelling patterns. Effective instruction is explicit and systematic; systematic phonics instruction is more effective than "whole word" instruction that teaches little or no phonics or teaches phonics haphazardly or in a "by-the-way" approach. Last, the focus is on building reading fluency, the ability to read orally with speed, accuracy, and proper expression. The most effective method is a guided repeated oral reading, that is, reading aloud repeatedly to a teacher, an adult, or a peer and receiving feedback. In contrast to teaching phonemic awareness, phonics, and fluency, interventions for reading comprehension are not as well established. In large measure this reflects the nature of the very complex processes influencing reading comprehension. The limited available evidence indicates that the most effective methods to teach reading comprehension involve teaching vocabulary and strategies that encourage a positive interaction between reader and text.

Accommodation. The management of dyslexia in students in secondary school, and especially in college and graduate school, is primarily based on accommodation rather than remediation. High school and college students with a history of dyslexia often present a paradoxical picture; they are similar to their unimpaired peers on measures of word recognition, yet continue to suffer from the phonologic deficit that makes reading more effortful and slow. For these readers with dyslexia, the provision of extra time is essential; it allows them the time to decode each word and to apply their unimpaired higher-order cognitive and linguistic skills to the surrounding context to get at the meaning of words that they cannot entirely or rapidly decode. Although providing extra time for reading is the most common accommodation for people with dyslexia, other accommodations include allowing the use of laptop computers with spelling checkers, tape recorders in the classroom, and recorded books, and providing access to syllabi and lecture notes, tutors to talk through and review the content of reading material, alternatives to multiple-choice tests (for example, reports or orally administered tests), and a separate quiet room for taking tests. With such accommodations, many students with dyslexia are now successfully completing studies in a range of disciplines, including law and medicine.

For background information *see* BRAIN; HEMISPHERIC LATERALITY; LINGUISTICS; PSYCHOLINGUISTICS in the McGraw-Hill Encyclopedia of Science & Technology.   Bennett A. Shaywitz; Sally E. Shaywitz

Bibliography. L. Cohen et al., The visual word form area: Spatial and temporal characterization of an initial stage of reading in normal subjects and posterior split-brain patients, *Brain*, 123:291–307, 2000; E. Paulesu et al., Dyslexia-cultural diversity and biological unity, *Science*, 291:2165–2167, 2001; S. Shaywitz, Current concepts: Dyslexia, *New Eng. J. Med.*, 338(5):307–312, 1998; B. A. Shaywitz et al., Disruption of posterior brain systems for reading in children with developmental dyslexia, *Biol. Psychiat.*, 52:101–110, 2002; S. E. Shaywitz, Dyslexia, *Sci. Amer.*, 275(5):98–104, 1996; S. E. Shaywitz et al., Functional disruption in the organization of the brain for reading in dyslexia, *Proc. Nat. Acad. Sci. USA*, 95:2636–2641, 1998; S. E. Shaywitz et al., Prevalence of reading disability in boys and girls: Results of the Connecticut Longitudinal Study, *J. Amer. Med. Ass.*, 264(8):998–1002, 1990; *Teaching Children To Read: An Evidence Based Assessment of the Scientific Research Literature on Reading and Its Implications for Reading Instruction*, Report of the National Reading Panel, (vol. NIH Pub. 00–4754), U.S. Department of Health and Human Services, Public Health Service, National Institutes of Health, National Institute of Child Health and Human Development, 2000; J. K. Torgesen, *Phonological Awareness: A Critical Factor in Dyslexia*, Orton Dyslexia Society, 1995; R. Wagner and J. Torgesen, The nature of phonological processes and its causal role in the acquisition of reading skills, *Psychol. Bull.*, 101:192–212, 1987.

Electron tomography

Electron tomography is a powerful technique for determining three-dimensional (3D) structure from a series of two-dimensional (2D) images recorded in a transmission electron microscope. Transmission electron microscopy uses high-energy electrons to illuminate specimens at resolutions that in favorable cases surpass 1.0 nanometer (1/25,000,000 of an inch) and can resolve atoms. Resolution is not as great with electron tomography (4–8 nm) but is still much higher than can be achieved by light microscopy or medical imaging methods. However, the weak penetrating power of electrons requires operation under high vacuum and generally limits the technique to specimens less than about 1 micrometer in diameter. The most common application is in biological research to study the 3D architecture of subcellular components such as mitochondria, nerve synapses, the Golgi apparatus, muscle cells during contraction, the arrangement of molecular components in bacterial cells, chromosome fibers, the kinetochore, and other structures. Such studies provide important data for understanding how cellular components carry out their vital functions. Electron tomography is also being used to study the structure of certain inorganic crystals used in the semiconductor industry.

Principles of operation. Transmission electron microscopy provides a translucent interior view of the specimen, analogous to what is seen in an x-ray image, rather than the surface view that we are accustomed to seeing in everyday life. Although this enables the microscopist to see inside the specimen, it has the disadvantage that the image formed is a 2D projection of the 3D object with features from

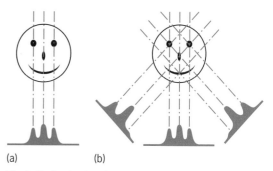

(a)   (b)

Fig. 1. Projection imaging and tomographic reconstruction. **(a)** Formation of one-dimensional (1D) projection of a two-dimensional (2D) smiley face. To form a true projection, the amount of penetrating radiation that strikes a unit length of the recording medium must be a measure of the amount of mass traversed by the beam in its path through the specimen. This is illustrated by the image density graph superimposed upon the 1D projection, and the broken lines that represent the radiation path through areas of maximum density in the specimen (that is, through the eyes or nose plus the mouth of the face). In transmission electron microscopy, true projections are formed as long as the specimen is not thicker than 0.2–0.5 micrometer. **(b)** Tomographic reconstruction of the 2D smiley face. The first step in tomography is to systematically record a series of 1D images from different viewing directions. The density in each 1D image is then projected back into a 2D area by simply distributing the density evenly along the original projection direction. When these "back-projection rays" from the different 1D images are summed, they intersect and reinforce one another only at the points where there was significant mass in the original object. In this way the 2D image is reconstructed from the 1D images. The same strategy is used to reconstruct a 3D image from 2D projection images. (*Adapted with permission from B. F. McEwen and M. Marko, Three-dimensional transmission electron microscopy and its application to mitosis research, Meth. Cell Biol., 61:82–111, 1999*)

different depths superimposed (**Fig. 1***a*). The solution is to reconstruct a 3D image of the original specimen from a series of 2D projections (Fig. 1*b*). This approach is also employed in medical imaging methods such as computerized axial tomography (CAT scanning) and magnetic resonance imaging (MRI).

The series of 2D images required for tomographic reconstructions is obtained by tilting the specimen in the electron beam. This is in contrast to medical imaging in which the patient is kept stationary while the beam source and detector are rotated to provide the necessary views. An important limitation of electron tomography is the inability to collect tilt data over the full 180° range required for complete angular coverage. (A 360° range is not necessary because, in projection imaging, views from the opposite side of the specimen provide the same information.) The difficulty in electron tomography is that typical electron microscope specimens are very thin (50–500 nm) and mounted on a support film that is more than 1000 times wider than the specimen. As a result, images can be recorded only over a limited tilt range of ±60 or 70° (a total range of 120–140°) before the specimen becomes too thick to view. This gives rise to a range of missing angular coverage that produces a well-characterized distortion that must be taken into account when interpreting electron tomographic reconstructions.

Electron tomographic data sets are generally collected with 1 or 2° tilt angle intervals, because the resolution obtained in the resulting reconstruction is dependent upon how finely the angular range is sampled. Thus, a typical tilt series contains 60–140 images. Recording so many images was time-consuming and tedious with older microscopes, but recent improvements to mechanical design, along with incorporation of direct digital recording of the images and computer control of the microscope, have enabled newer microscopes to automatically record a tilt series of 140 images in less than 30 min. These technical developments in electron microscopy, coupled with the rapidly increasing computational power and the disk storage capacity of modern computers, are transforming electron tomography into a high-throughput tool that can be used ever more routinely in research and diagnostic settings.

Volume analysis and sample application. Perhaps the most surprising aspect of electron tomography is that it generally takes longer to analyze an electron tomographic reconstruction than it does to collect the data and compute the reconstruction. The difficulty is that the investigator is faced with displaying a three-dimensional tomographic reconstruction on a two-dimensional computer screen. However, in contrast to the original imaging situation, one now has a 3D image in the computer that can be taken apart and examined from any direction. Usually the

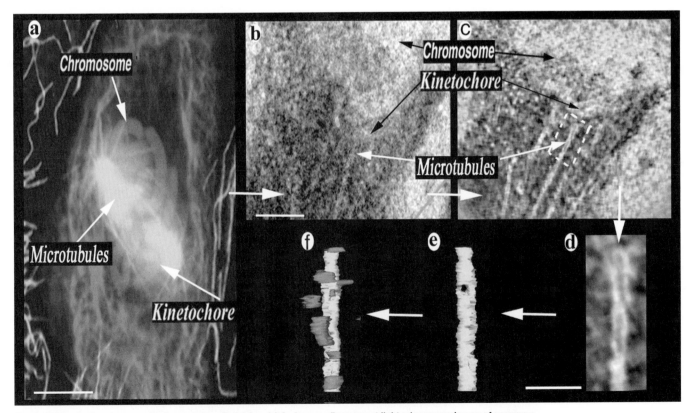

Fig. 2. Using electron tomography to analyze cell division. (*a*) An immunofluorescent light microscopy image of a mammalian cell during cell division. (*b*) Electron microscopy image of a kinetochore from the same type of cell. The kinetochore is the region of the chromosome that attaches to the mitotic spindle. (*c*) Single 2D slice from the 3D electron tomographic reconstruction of the kinetochore in *b*. Note the sharper microtubules in the tomographic reconstruction. (*d*) Single microtubule extracted from the tomographic reconstruction. (*e*) 3D model created by tracing and color-coding (light gray) the microtubule in *d*. (*f*) Same model as in *e* showing kinetochore components (dark gray) that are attached to the microtubule. A full-color version of this figure can be seen online at http://www.wadsworth.org/bms/SCBlinks/mcewen/lab.html.

quickest way to locate components of the structure is to view the reconstruction volume as a sequential stack of thin slices. However, understanding the 3D relationships of component parts and communicating the finding to a larger audience generally require constructing a 3D representation. For complex structures the most common approach is to segment select components away from the rest of the tomographic reconstruction by manual tracing and assignment of a color code.

Figure 2 illustrates the application of electron tomography to the study of the mammalian kinetochore. The kinetochore is a specialized structure that forms at a specific location on chromosomes during cell division. It functions to attach chromosomes to a bipolar spindle, generate chromosome motion, and exert control over the events of cell division. These functions are essential for proper cell division and the viability of the organism. Figure 2*a* is a gray-scale version of an immunofluorescence light microscopy image of a dividing cell, with arrows indicating a chromosome, location of a kinetochore, and microtubules. Microtubules are the chief structural components of the mitotic spindle. In the actual immunofluorescent image, microtubules are stained green, chromosomes blue, and keratin fibers, which form a cage around the spindle, red. One of the crucial yet poorly understood aspects of chromosome alignment is the interaction between the kinetochore and spindle microtubules. It is clear from Fig. 2*a* that the resolution of light microscopy is inadequate to study this interaction. Although single microtubules are visible in an electron microscopy projection image (Fig. 2*b*), details of the microtubule ends become visible only in single slices from the tomographic reconstruction (Fig. 2*c, d*). Manual tracings from trimmed slices such as in Fig. 2*d* were stacked into a 3D image, which are shown as a surface view in Fig. 2*e*. Kinetochore connections to the microtubules were also traced, and are shown in dark gray along with the microtubule in Fig. 2*f*. These and similar 3D models are being used to test current hypotheses on how the kinetochore interacts with microtubule ends.

Future directions and conclusions. Recent technical advances and the inherent versatility of electron tomography have accelerated its use and expanded the range of its applications. In particular, electron tomography is now being used for high-quality frozen-hydrated preparations of biological specimens. These preparations are made by rapidly freezing the specimen to prevent the formation of normal crystalline ice, which severely damages cellular structure. Such preparations are a snapshot of the specimen in its native hydrated environment and, thereby, superior to conventional preparations made by solvent extraction, heavy-metal staining, and plastic embedding. Previously the sensitivity of frozen-hydrated specimens to damage from electron irradiation had precluded such applications.

Electron tomography has been established as an important method for determining the structure of subcellular components and organelles, and the number and range of applications are likely to continue growing rapidly in the near future.

For background information *see* COMPUTERIZED TOMOGRAPHY; ELECTRON MICROSCOPE; FLUORESCENCE MICROSCOPE; OPTICAL MICROSCOPE in the McGraw-Hill Encyclopedia of Science & Technology.
                                    Bruce F. McEwen

Bibliography. W. Baumeister, R. Grimm, and J. Walz, Electron tomography of molecules and cells, *Trends Cell Biol.*, 9:81–85, 1999; B. F. McEwen and M. Marko, The emergence of electron tomography as an important tool for investigating cellular ultrastructure, *J. Histochem. Cytochem.*, 49:553–563, 2001; B. F. McEwen and M. Marko, Three-dimensional transmission electron microscopy and its application to mitosis research, *Meth. Cell Biol.*, 61:82–111, 1999.

Electronic paper

Electronic paper is a display medium that emulates many properties of paper, yet can be reused many times.

Paper has long been the most popular medium for applications such as books, newspapers, magazines, brochures, posters, commercial correspondence, and office documents. Paper has many desirable properties, including low cost and high optical contrast. It is thin and flexible, and can be read in environments having widely different levels of illumination. Energy is required to write on it, but that written information can be stored and generally read without the expenditure of power. Paper also can be rolled up and unrolled many times—an important property for many electronic paper applications.

Most display media, such as cathode-ray tubes (CRTs) and backlit liquid crystals, display information by the spatial variation of light emission. Paper and electronic paper display information by the spatial variation of light reflection. Most papers reflect this light over a large range of viewing angles, a property called Lambertian scattering.

Technologies. A limited number of display media have the collection of properties that make them eligible to be called electronic paper. New display media concepts that have the potential for use as electronic paper are constantly being invented. Technologies currently being developed for electronic paper applications include certain types of liquid crystal displays, modified electrophoretic displays, rotating ball displays, and electrochromic displays.

Liquid crystal displays. In display media, the property of allowing information to be stored and read without the continuous application of power is called bistability. Recently there has been a strong push to develop bistable liquid crystal displays that have a wide viewing angle, suitable for electronic paper applications. Liquid crystal layer thicknesses are less than 5 micrometers, and their allowable thickness variations are tenths of micrometers. This limits the size of these displays and makes it difficult to roll them up. Generally, bistability has been achieved by mixing the liquid crystal materials with polymers or by developing new anchoring layers on the substrates that control the molecular orientation between two stable optical states. There are now bistable versions of nematic, cholesteric, and ferro-electric liquid crystals.

Electrophoretic displays. Electrophoretic displays have been studied for more than 40 years. Early versions of electrophoretic displays consisted of white pigment particles dispersed in a dyed liquid. This suspension was placed between a conductive glass (usually indium-tin oxide–coated glass) window and a rear electrode (**Fig. 1**). When an electrical voltage was placed between the window and the rear electrode, the pigment particles (which have a charge in contact with the dielectric liquid) would drift to the window, causing it to appear white. Reversing the polarity of the voltage caused the pigment particles to drift to the rear electrode, and the appearance of the window became that of the dyed liquid. Recent versions of electrophoretic displays consist of two pigments having contrasting colors and opposite polarities of charge. In one voltage polarity, the dark-colored pigment particles drift to the window, and in the opposite polarity the white pigment particles move to the window. Early attempts to

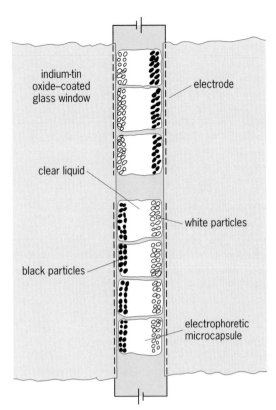

Fig. 2. More recent electrophoretic electronic paper, where there are black and white particles having opposite-polarity electrical charges dispersed in a clear liquid. These particles are placed in microcapsules, and the microcapsules are formed into a single layer. Applying an addressing voltage causes the particles to move in opposite directions, so the cell appears black in one voltage polarity and white in the other. The use of the microcapsules improves long-time stability.

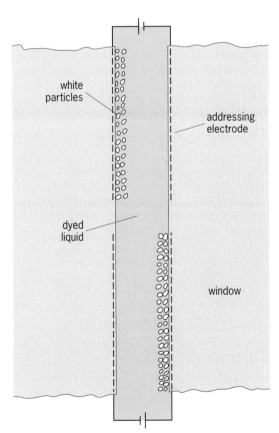

Fig. 1. Traditional electrophoretic display showing two imaging cells. White particles are suspended in a dyed liquid. With the application of a certain polarity voltage across the cells, the white pigment particles move to the viewing window, causing that cell to look white. Reversing the polarity of the applied voltage causes the white particles to move to the rear electrode of the cell, where they are not visible because of the dye in the liquid, making the cell look dark.

commercialize electrophoretic displays were unsuccessful because of the difficulties in maintaining the pigment dispersion. A significant improvement in stability has been achieved by microencapsulating electrophoretic displays, that is, placing the pigment into tiny capsules, limiting pigment settling in the liquid (**Fig. 2**).

Rotating ball displays. The rotating ball display (Gyricon) was invented and briefly worked on at the Xerox Palo Alto Research Center in the early 1970s. In the 1990s, it was revived and further developed. The technology consists of bichromal balls, that is, balls with a white hemisphere and a black hemisphere, each having a different electrical charge when in contact with a dielectric liquid. These balls are contained in a highly transparent silicone elastomer in individual spherical cavities that are about 25% larger than the balls. The spaces between the bichromal balls and the cavity walls is filled with a dielectric oil. Upon application of an external electrical voltage, the bichromal balls move across the cavities, rotating as they do so and exposing either the white or the black hemisphere to a viewer. Upon reaching the opposite wall of the cavity, the bichromal balls stick to the cavity wall, providing bistability and long-term image storage (**Fig. 3**).

Electrochromic displays. Many groups are trying to develop electrochromic displays, which operate on the

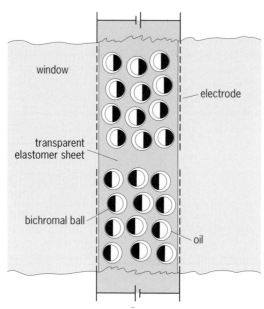

Fig. 3. Gyricon electronic paper consists of 80-micrometer (typically) plastic balls having hemispheres of contrasting colors, commonly black and white. These balls are contained in slightly larger spherical cavities in a highly transparent silicone elastomer. The space between the bichromal ball and the cavity walls is filled with fluid. With application of an external voltage of a given polarity, the white sides of the balls face an observer, while reversing the polarity of the voltage rotates the balls to show their black hemispheres.

principle that electric current causes certain otherwise colorless liquids or solids (placed in front of a white background) to change color, usually taking on a black appearance. These displays have been under intermittent study for at least 40 years. The traditional problem with them has been limited cycle lifetimes due to irreversible chemical changes, although recently announced devices look promising.

Applications. In principle, electronic paper displays can be used to replace paper in most of its information display applications. Thus, proponents of these technologies talk about electronic paper office documents, newspapers, signs, and books. These applications are attractive because of the very low power requirements for these displays and their readability in the same range of lighting conditions as paper.

Signs. It appears that the first applications for electronic paper will be as dynamically changeable signs in places such as department and discount stores. Unlike the paper signs they are replacing, the electronic signs will be addressable by low-power radios (wireless), allowing their messages to be changed and controlled from a remote place and enabling items to be placed on sale with very little advance notice. Because the microprocessors in the signs can be connected to the same database as the store cash registers, an unprecedented degree of accuracy in pricing can be achieved. Such signs will be battery- or solar-cell powered.

Electronic newspapers. This is an especially exciting application for electronic paper because more than

half the cost of putting out a newspaper is in printing and distribution. If each subscriber had an electronic newspaper reader and the Internet were the distribution vehicle, this money would be saved. Such a change is further motivated by the high environmental cost of making the paper, both in the loss of forests and in the pollution associated with papermaking.

An electronic newspaper might be the same size as current newspapers, since the size of advertisements is important to advertisers and because this format is the result of hundreds of years of evolution. The consumer would connect the electronic newspaper reader to the Internet in the morning and download the content to memory within the user interface. The newspaper need be only one page, and the consumer would print successive pages of the downloaded newspaper on that single sheet. Because electronic paper is flexible, it could be rolled up into a cylinder when not being read (**Fig. 4**). The next day the memory would be erased, and a new newspaper could be downloaded. Such a reader would be relatively inexpensive with advances now being made in addressing technology, and over a period of time, very much less expensive than the cost of printing and distributing a newspaper.

Universal document reader. A smaller version of the newspaper reader is called a universal document reader (**Fig. 5**). Here, the sheet of electronic paper could be rolled up into a tube for carrying convenience and unrolled as an 80-in.^{2} (520-cm^2) display. The tube would be small enough to carry easily in a pocket or purse. Information would be downloaded from a cell phone network or an orbiting satellite. This would enable a person to download e-mail and business documents anywhere on the globe. It also

Fig. 4. Simulated electronic newspaper reader. The rolled-up single sheet of electronic paper is stored in a tube with a slit (opening). In one version a linear electrode array is placed along the slit, so that the newspaper is printed as it is pulled through the slit. Retracting the electronic paper into the tube and pulling it out again prints a new page. As low-cost, flexible addressing electronics become available, it will not be necessary to retract the electronic paper into the tube to print each page.

Fig. 5. Document reader, similar to a newspaper reader but small enough to fit into a pocket. It will allow documents such as e-mail, Internet pages, and electronic books to be downloaded from satellites or cell phones and read anywhere.

would provide a convenient book reader, allowing a user to tap into digital libraries.

Limitations. There are many uses of paper that electronic paper will not serve as well. These include wrapping packages and presents, and printing authentication documents such as deeds and licenses. There are also many paper publications that are intended to have a very short lifetime once in the hands of a target customer, such as brochures and mailers. It would be inappropriate to print these on electronic paper.

Outlook. An important application of electronic paper will be in the office. When the personal computer was invented, the prediction was made that it would enable the paperless office. What actually happened was more paper was printed, largely because people did not want to read documents on light-emitting display screens. Most of these printed documents (e-mail, Web pages, and so on) have an intended life of less than one day. If they were printed on sheets of electronic paper that can be reused millions of times, there would be great savings of paper. Such sheets of electronic paper could be 8.5 × 11 in. (22 × 28 cm), and could be handled exactly like paper (that is, they could be arranged on a tabletop, placed in stacks, carried in brief cases, and optically scanned).

Other potential applications of electronic paper include dynamic wallpaper for decoration, billboards, giant screen displays, and even a modified electronic paper, such as an electronic textile from which clothing can be made.

For background information *see* CATHODE-RAY TUBE; ELECTROCHROMIC DEVICES; ELECTRONIC DISPLAY; ELECTROPHORESIS; FLAT-PANEL DISPLAY DEVICE; INTERNET; LIQUID CRYSTALS; PAPER in the McGraw-Hill Encyclopedia of Science & Technology.

Nicholas K. Sheridon

Bibliography. P. Drzaic et al., A printed and rollable electronic display, *SID Digest* (Society for Information Display), pp. 1131–1135, 1998; M. O. M. Edwards et al., Screen-printed electrochromic displays based on nanocrystalline electrodes, *SID Digest*, pp. 1058–1061, 2002; E. Nakamura et al., Development of electrophoretic display using microencapsulated suspension, *SID Digest*, pp. 1014–1018, 1998; T. Pham, N. Sheridon, and R. Sprague, Electrooptical characteristics of the Gyricon display, *SID Digest*, pp. 119–121, 2002; N. K. Sheridon and M. A. Berkovitz, Gyricon—Twisting ball display, *Proc. SID*, 18-3:289–293, 1977; C. Wang et al., A defect free bistable C1 SSFLC, *SID Digest*, pp. 34–36, 2002.

Emergence of vertebrates

The textbook view of early vertebrate evolution posits that although vertebrates were present in the Ordovician and perhaps the Cambrian, they were rare and remained at low diversity until they underwent an explosive radiation during the Mid to Late Silurian. This canonical view has been overturned in recent years with the discovery of an entirely unanticipated diversity of vertebrates in the Cambrian and Ordovician, the reinterpretation of the affinity (phylogenetic relationship) of taxa that were long known but poorly understood, and the incorporation of all these data into new phylogenies.

Affinity of conodonts. One major advance in the understanding of the assembly of the vertebrate bodyplan has arisen through resolution of the affinity of a hitherto entirely enigmatic group of spiny, toothlike microfossils, the conodonts. For over a century, conodonts were known solely from their mineralized skeletal elements, but with the discovery of remains of their soft-tissue anatomy in the 1980s, the anatomy of conodonts has been revealed to be akin to the living amphioxus, hagfishes, and lampreys. As a result, debate over their affinity has been much more constrained but no less heated. The source of contention lies not so much with the interpretation of conodont anatomy but with the phylogenetic significance of the various characters preserved, with some scientists placing greater emphasis on some characters than others and, as a result, arriving at very different conclusions regarding the phylogenetic position of conodonts. In an attempt to resolve the relative importance of the various characters, cladistic analysis, a technique that attempts to resolve phylogenetic relationships through searching for similarities between the anatomical characteristics of organisms, has been employed. Such analysis has revealed that although conodonts share an overall anatomical design with the living invertebrate chordates and primitive jawless vertebrates, they are more closely related to jawed vertebrates. The chief characteristic supporting this is the mineralized component of the skeleton, a feature not encountered in living vertebrates more primitive than jawed vertebrates such as sharks and rays. But this is only a part of the story. Since there are many extinct groups of jawless vertebrates, it is also necessary to resolve more fully their phylogenetic position before the significance of conodonts to assembly of the vertebrate bodyplan can be assessed. These issues notwithstanding, recognition of the vertebrate affinity of conodonts has increased the vertebrate diversity in the early Paleozoic by two orders of magnitude.

New vertebrate fossils. Aside from conodonts, the early evolutionary history of vertebrates has been fleshed out with the discovery of new groups in the Cambrian and Ordovician. This has been achieved primarily through a number of distinct but complementary approaches.

Macrofossil sampling. First, there have been chance discoveries of macrofossils (whole or nearly complete remains) of a number of new forms. These include *Yunnanozoon, Haikouella,* and *Myllokunmingia,* all of which are exclusively soft-bodied forms from the Lower Cambrian Chengjiang Lagerstätte of China. The case for the vertebrate, or even chordate, affinity of some of these taxa is tenuous at best, but *Myllokunmingia* is a good candidate for vertebrate affinity. New, armored, jawless vertebrates have also been discovered, including *Sacabambaspis* and *Arandaspis,* from the Middle Ordovician of South America and Australia, respectively. In addition, there have been chance discoveries of articulated remains of animals, such as *Astraspis,* known until now mainly from isolated scales from the Late Ordovician of North America. Together, these discoveries reveal that the vertebrate fauna of Ordovician seas was dominated by heavily armored jawless vertebrates that lacked the paired appendages common to some Silurian jawless vertebrates and all jawed vertebrates. However, a second, more systematic approach to uncovering the diversity of early vertebrates indicates that this view is extremely biased.

Microfossil sampling. The adoption of systematic sampling for microfossils, disarticulated skeletal elements (such as scales, spines, and teeth) which are more abundant than whole articulated remains and are often species-diagnostic, has provided a much more complete understanding of vertebrate diversity during the Cambrian and Ordovician periods. The discovery of *Anatolepis,* preserved as isolated fragments of skeletal armor composed of dentine and bonelike tissues, has revealed that conodonts were not the only skeletonizing vertebrates in circulation during the Late Cambrian and Early Ordovician. New forms, known only from scales thus far, have also been discovered in the Middle and Late Ordovician. These include *Skiichthys* and a host of other, as yet unnamed, taxa that are the earliest possible records of jawed vertebrates, extending the fossil record of this group several tens of millions of years farther into the geological record than would be indicated by a direct reading of the macrofossil record. Microfossil sampling has also extended the ranges of known groups such as the thelodonts deep into the Ordovician and has provided more reliable stratigraphic ranges for taxa such as *Arandaspis* and *Sacabambaspis,* which have an evolutionary history extending deeper into the Middle Ordovician. Thus, the textbook view of the scarcity of vertebrates in the Cambro-Ordovician must be rejected, and it is likely

that future years will witness many new discoveries in this interval of deep time.

Phylogenetics. Inclusion of the major extinct groups of vertebrates in the phylogenetic analysis used to resolve the affinity of conodonts has revealed that all of the heavily armored jawless vertebrates are more closely related to jawed vertebrates than to conodonts, lampreys, hagfishes, or either of the living invertebrate chordate groups. Thus, conodonts remain the most primitive vertebrates known with a mineralized component of the skeleton. The acquisition of paired fins appears to have occurred prior to the origin of jawed vertebrates in animals such as the osteostracans and, possibly, anaspids and thelodonts. Thus, a number of key anatomical characteristics that, among the living fauna, are found exclusively in jawed vertebrates, appear to have evolved within organisms that are phylogenetic and anatomical intermediates of the living jawless and jawed vertebrates.

Time of emergence. A wealth of new discoveries has extended direct evidence of the existence of vertebrates far deeper into geological time. Thus, beliefs regarding the timing of emergence and radiation of the vertebrates must be revised accordingly. Two analytical approaches suggest that even with the addition of new discoveries, knowledge of early vertebrate evolution remains significantly incomplete.

Phylogenetic tree calibration. Calibration of phylogenetic trees against fossil occurrences in geological time indicates that there are vast gaps in the fossil record of early vertebrates, particularly in the Late Cambrian, the Early-Middle Ordovician, and around the Ordovician-Silurian boundary. Some of the inferred gaps are artifactual, arising from the inability to include many of the fragmentary microvertebrate taxa in the analysis; it is likely that many of the so-called ghost lineages are accounted for by these taxa. But microvertebrates alone cannot account for all of these ghost lineages. Thus, the search for early vertebrates in pre-Silurian rocks must continue; in the interim, it must be accepted that the fossil record alone is an insufficient guide to the precise time of origin of chordates, vertebrates, and jawed vertebrates, although it does provide minimum estimates for the origin of chordates and vertebrates by the Early Cambrian and jawed vertebrates by the Late Ordovician.

Molecular clocks. Molecular clocks provide an alternative and independent approach to inferring the time of origin of groups that have living representatives. Although this method cannot be used to constrain the origin of the extinct conodonts, it can be used to infer the time of origin of chordates, vertebrates, and jawed vertebrates. Molecular clocks work by quantifying the genetic distance between living organisms and calibrating the rate of change using one or more reliable dates from the fossil record for the time of divergence of lineages with living representatives. Such analyses are extremely controversial because of a number of methodological limitations and their consistent failure to corroborate paleontological estimates, or even other molecular clock dates. Estimates for the origin of chordates using this technique range from 1001 to 590 Ma, from 751 to 700 Ma for the origin of vertebrates, and there is a single estimate of 528 Ma for the origin of jawed vertebrates, the clade comprising all living gnathostomes. Although, theoretically, molecular clock estimates are extremely conservative, in practice these dates can safely be accepted as outside limits on the origin of the major chordate clades. In short, attempts to accurately estimate the time of origin of chordates, vertebrates and, jawed vertebrates are very imprecise using the currently available data set.

Conclusion. The discovery of new paleontological data has, paradoxically, led to the rejection of old certainties and to a much more complete, yet uncertain, understanding of the emergence of vertebrates. New data indicate that vertebrates arose much earlier than previously anticipated, but the precise time of their origin remains speculative.

For background information *see* ANIMAL EVOLUTION; CHORDATA; CONODONT; FOSSIL; PHYLOGENY in the McGraw-Hill Encyclopedia of Science & Technology.   Philip C. J. Donoghue;
M. Paul Smith; Ivan J. Sansom

Bibliography. P. C. J. Donoghue, P. L. Forey, and R. J. Aldridge, Conodont affinity and chordate phylogeny, *Biol. Rev.*, 75:191–251, 2000; P. Janvier, *Early Vertebrates*, Oxford University Press, Oxford, 1996; I. J. Sansom, M. M. Smith, and M. P. Smith, The Ordovician radiation of vertebrates, in P. E. Ahlberg (ed.), *Major Events in Early Vertebrate Evolution: Palaeontology, Phylogeny, Genetics and Development*, pp. 156–171, Taylor & Francis, London, 2001; M. P. Smith, P. C. J. Donoghue, and I. J. Sansom, The spatial and temporal diversification of Early Palaeozoic vertebrates, in J. A. Crame and A. W. Owen (eds.), *Palaeobiogeography and Biodiversity Change: The Ordovician and Cenozoic Radiations*, pp. 69–83, Geol. Soc. London Spec. Publ. 194, 2002; M. P. Smith, I. J. Sansom, and K. D. Cochrane, The Cambrian origin of vertebrates, in P. E. Ahlberg (ed.), *Major Events in Early Vertebrate Evolution: Palaeontology, Phylogeny, Genetics and Development*, Taylor & Francis, London, 2001, pp. 67–84.

End-Triassic mass extinction

Past biotic crises, recognized as distinct diversity minima in the marine fossil record, have been a focus of paleontological research for more than 20 years. The Cretaceous/Tertiary (K/T) event garnered the most attention from scientists and the public, followed by the end-Permian, the largest of all extinctions (mass extinctions being the most severe of biotic crises). The crisis that marks the boundary between the Triassic and Jurassic periods also ranks among the five biggest extinction events, but for a long time it remained the least understood among them. Recent research has revealed much new data

suggesting that the Earth underwent a major environmental crisis coupled with ecosystem collapse some 200 million years ago. Discovery of a negative carbon isotope anomaly (a marked decline in the ratio of ^{13}C to ^{12}C isotopes in the ancient ocean and atmosphere) indicates a severe perturbation in the global carbon cycle. There are competing hypotheses about the ultimate trigger of the chain of events leading to the extinction. As did the K/T controversy, the end-Triassic story unfolds as reconstructions are tested against much newly obtained information.

Fossil record. Subdivision of the geological time scale is traditionally based on fossils. The boundary between the Triassic and Jurassic periods corresponds to a major break in the ammonoid fossil record. These fast-evolving marine mollusks, which became key fossils of the Mesozoic Era, only narrowly avoided annihilation at the end of Triassic before eventually succumbing to the K/T event. From diverse Late Triassic ammonoid faunas, including the unusually uncoiled *Choristoceras*, only a single evolutionary lineage is known to cross the boundary, forming the rootstock of a spectacular evolutionary radiation in the Jurassic. Conodonts, the eel-like ancestors of vertebrates known by their hardy, microscopic toothlike structures (fossils of which are abundant in marine Paleozoic and Triassic sediments), were not so lucky; they vanished completely at the close of the Triassic. The rarity of *Misikella*, one of the last conodont genera, may indicate that conodonts were in decline for some time before their final demise.

The shallow, tropical seas of the Late Triassic were home to coral reefs that harbored highly diverse faunas. Best known from the northern Alps, these reefs suddenly disappeared at the Triassic/Jurassic boundary, and a newly compiled global fossil reef database shows that this was one of the worst crises in the history of reef ecosystems. Radiolarians, abundant pelagic microfossils of the open ocean, also show a remarkable turnover from highly evolved, diverse latest Triassic assemblages to impoverished (species-poor) earliest Jurassic ones that consist of simple forms. They provide important evidence that the bottom of the marine food web was severely affected.

The biotic change was also substantial on land. Among the terrestrial vertebrates, there is new evidence that the terminal Triassic extinction of nondinosaurian reptiles opened up the ecological opportunity for theropod dinosaurs. Footprints and skeletal remains suggest that the dinosaurs first attained large sizes and rose to dominance shortly after the beginning of the Jurassic. Evidence for an abrupt end-Triassic floral turnover comes from the pollen record of lake sediments termed the Newark Supergroup in eastern North America. Numerous pollen taxa disappear at the boundary, and the Early Jurassic is characterized by a low-diversity, *Corollina*-dominated pollen assemblage. Curiously, the boundary level is also marked by a transient abundance of fern spores, a pattern similar to the one observed at the K/T boundary. Leaf remains from different parts of the world also reveal a prominent floral change across the boundary. Apart from the turnover of species and higher taxa, the boundary event is also reflected in the anomalously low stomatal density of leaves of fossil Ginkgoales. Stomatal pores are used in the respiration of plants; hence their density is inversely proportional to the ancient atmospheric CO_2 concentration.

The true magnitude of the end-Triassic extinction is not unanimously accepted. An estimated loss of 22% of families, 53% of genera, and a calculated 80% loss of species is based on a single compilation of the global marine fossil record. A marine regression (drop in sea level), also cited as a possible cause of the drop in fossil diversity, is a worldwide feature of the Triassic/Jurassic boundary interval. The exceptionally low stand of sea level is reflected in the lack of marine sediments from this period and a subsequent scarcity of continuous sedimentary sections. Even if the drop in fossil diversity is partly accounted for by the lack of sediments of the right age, however, the evolutionary significance of an end-Triassic

extinction event for several groups of unrelated organisms and habitats is undeniable.

Isotopic signature. Carbon isotope stratigraphy is a useful tool to reveal past perturbations of the global carbon cycle. It was recognized earlier that both the K/T and the end-Permian extinctions are associated with large negative shifts in the $^{13}C/^{12}C$ isotopic ratio of seawater, potentially indicating decreased uptake of the preferred ^{12}C isotope by phytoplankton (that is, a decrease in primary productivity indicating possible ecological disturbance). Recently, three independent studies demonstrated a large negative shift in the $^{13}C/^{12}C$ ratio in marine carbonates as well as marine and terrestrial organic matter at the Triassic/Jurassic boundary. Very similar isotopic curves were obtained from marine rocks in the Queen Charlotte Islands (western Canada), southwest England, and Hungary, as well as lake deposits in east Greenland (see **illus.**). The isotopic spike lends itself to global correlation and attests to a major perturbation of carbon cycle affecting both marine and terrestrial reservoirs. Similar to the case made for K/T boundary, a shutdown of marine primary productivity related to a putative extraterrestrial (comet or

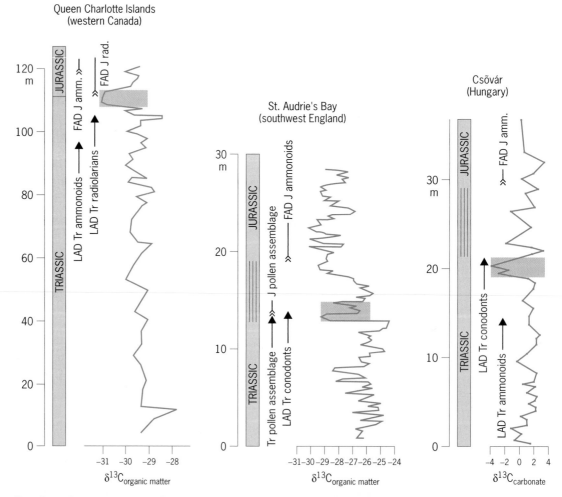

Negative carbon isotope anomaly (tinted) recognized in marine Triassic/Jurassic boundary sections. FAD, first appearance datum; LAD, last appearance datum; Tr, Triassic; J, Jurassic; amm., ammonoids; rad., radiolarians. (*Compiled from P. D. Ward et al., 2001; S. P. Hesselbo et al., 2002; J. Pálfy et al., 2001*)

asteroid) impact was theorized, whereas volcanic emission of large amounts of mantle-derived CO_2 was offered as an alternative explanation. Modeling studies suggest that although both mechanisms result in a negative shift of the carbon isotopic ratio, they cannot fully account for the observed magnitude of the anomaly. Additional input of isotopically light carbon into the ocean-atmosphere system is possible through massive release of methane stored as gas hydrate in continental shelf sediments, if temperature and pressure changes trigger the destabilization and dissociation of gas hydrates. The fossil plant evidence for elevated carbon dioxide (CO_2) levels, a "super greenhouse" event, at the Triassic/Jurassic boundary is consistent with this scenario.

Possible causes of events. The timing and tempo of biotic and environmental changes and their correlation with other events are of paramount importance in developing and evaluating extinction scenarios. Previous geological time scales were inaccurate, as only a few Triassic and Jurassic radioisotopic ages were available. Recently, more relevant data have become available. A volcanic ash layer within marine sediments at the system boundary on the Queen Charlotte Islands yielded a uranium-lead (U-Pb) age of 200 Ma (millions of years ago). Basalts that erupted within a few tens of thousands of years after the pollen turnover in the Newark Basin were dated as 201 to 202 Ma. Recent dating of voluminous basalts in northern parts of South America proved that they erupted 200 Ma. The lava flows and dikes along the eastern seaboard of North America, northeast Africa, and the Iberian Peninsula form the vast Central Atlantic Magmatic Province (CAMP). With an estimated volume of 2.5×10^6 km^3 (600,000 mi^3) of volcanic rocks, the CAMP represents one of the largest volcanic episodes in Earth history, heralding the initial breakup of the supercontinent Pangea. The available isotopic dates suggest an average age of 199.4 ± 2.4 Ma for CAMP rocks. On the basis of paleomagnetic evidence, it is likely that the flood basalt eruptions lasted for less than 1 million years.

Consequences of such short-lived and voluminous volcanism may include short-term cooling and acid rains resulting from sulfur dioxide (SO_2) and halogen emission, although geologic evidence for this is lacking. More important is the subsequent global warming due to the greenhouse effect of CO_2 emission. Sudden warming of deep ocean water may trigger the release of methane from gas hydrates stored in the ocean floor, and positive feedback could lead to runaway greenhouse conditions. The role of gas hydrate dissociation in driving short-term climatic events of the geologic past has only recently been recognized, and it may well be an important factor in the end-Triassic events.

However, there is no consensus about the volcanic causation of the end-Triassic event. The link of the K/T extinction to extraterrestrial impact spurred an intensive search for impact signatures at the Triassic/Jurassic boundary, as the hypothesis of an extraterrestrial cause for all major extinctions is

seriously considered by some researchers. The anomalous abundance of iridium, an element that is normally exceedingly rare in Earth's crust but common in meteorites, was the original proof for the K/T impact, and recently an iridium anomaly was reported from the Triassic/Jurassic boundary in the Newark Basin. Although modest compared to the K/T values, and not reproduced from anywhere else yet, it revitalized the end-Triassic impact theory. However, other impact evidence is meager, and a large impact crater of the right age is missing. (Redating the Manicouagan crater in Quebec, considered a candidate for a time, revealed that it is some 14 million years older than the Triassic/Jurassic boundary.)

Despite the remaining questions, the end-Triassic biotic crisis was undoubtedly related to global environmental change. In the context of modern environmental and ecological issues, it provides a cautionary lesson from Earth history that a large-scale, volcanically induced increase in atmospheric CO_2, perhaps amplified by methane release, played a key role in a major extinction event.

For background information *see* AMMONOIDEA; BIOGEOCHEMISTRY; CARBONATE MINERALS; CHEMOSTRATIGRAPHY; CONODONT; FOSSIL; GAS HYDRATE; GEOLOGIC TIME SCALE; MARINE SEDIMENTS; METHANE; ORGANIC GEOCHEMISTRY; TRIASSIC in the McGraw-Hill Encyclopedia of Science & Technology.

József Pálfy

Bibliography. A. Hallam and P. B. Wignall, *Mass Extinctions and Their Aftermath*, Oxford University Press, Oxford, 1997; S. P. Hesselbo et al., Terrestrial and marine mass extinction at the Triassic-Jurassic boundary synchronized with major carbon-cycle perturbation: A link to initiation of massive volcanism?, *Geology*, 30:251–254, 2002; A. Marzoli et al., Extensive 200-million-year-old continental flood basalts of the Central Atlantic Magmatic Province, *Science*, 284:616–618, 1999; P. E. Olsen et al., Ascent of dinosaurs linked to an iridium anomaly at the Triassic-Jurassic boundary, *Science*, 296:1305–1307, 2002; J. Pálfy et al., Carbon isotope anomaly and other geochemical changes at the Triassic-Jurassic boundary from a marine section in Hungary, *Geology*, 29:1047–1050, 2001; P. D. Ward et al., Sudden productivity collapse associated with the Triassic-Jurassic boundary mass extinction, *Science*, 292:1148–1151, 2001.

Enzyme catalysis (thermodynamics)

Thermodynamics deals with the transformations of matter and energy that occur in chemical reactions. While much of the chemical thermodynamics literature contains the properties and reactions of simple organic and inorganic substances, attention has also turned to reactions that occur in living systems. Many reactions in living systems require the presence of enzymes (catalytic proteins) in order to proceed with sufficient speed. Enzyme-catalyzed reactions make up the majority of the reactions responsible for metabolism and for the

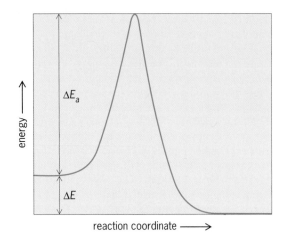

Fig. 1. Potential energy E of a reacting system as a function of the reaction coordinate. ΔE is the change in energy for the reaction, and ΔE_a is the activation energy.

operation of living systems. However, since a true catalyst serves only to lower the activation energy of a reaction and since the catalyst's initial and final states are the same, the thermodynamic quantities that pertain to that reaction are independent of the enzyme used to catalyze it (**Fig. 1**). Should the enzyme be changed as a consequence of the reaction, this change must also be accounted for in any thermodynamic calculations.

Thermodynamics. The most striking feature of enzyme-catalyzed reactions is their complexity,

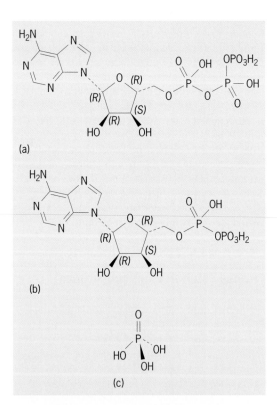

Fig. 2. Structures of (a) adenosine 5′-triphosphate, (b) adenosine 5′-diphosphate (ADP), and (c) phosphate. The binding of protons occurs at the imidazole and phosphate groups; metal ions bind at the phosphate groups.

where the thermodynamic quantities are functions of temperature, pH, pX, and ionic strength. Here, $pX = -\log_{10}[X]$, where $[X]$ is the concentration of an ion or species that binds to one or more of the reactants. This dependency on pH and pX arises because of the multiple states of ionization and metal-ion binding in which the reactant molecules can exist. This concept is illustrated in reaction (1) for the

$$ATP + H_2O = ADP + phosphate \tag{1}$$

primary energy source of living systems—the hydrolysis of adenosine 5′-triphosphate (ATP) to adenosine 5′-diphosphate (ADP) and phosphate (**Fig. 2**). The apparent equilibrium constant K' for this reaction is given by Eq. (2). By convention the concentration

$$K' = \frac{[ADP]_{total}\,[phosphate]_{total}}{[ATP]_{total}} \tag{2}$$

of water has been omitted in the expression for K'. The concentrations used in Eq. (2) are total concentrations of the various ionic and metal bound forms of the reactants and products such as in Eq. (3). If

$$[ATP]_{total} = [ATP^{4-}] + [HATP^{3-}] + [H_2ATP^{2-}]$$

$$+ [H_3ATP^-] + [MgATP^{2-}] + [MgHATP^-]$$

$$+ [MgH_2ATP] + [Mg_2ATP] \tag{3}$$

calcium (or any other divalent metal ion) is present, the analogous Ca-ATP species must be considered. The various forms of a biochemical reactant that differ only in the number of H^+ or X attached to a central reactant are called pseudoisomers. The essential point is that ATP, ADP, and phosphate exist in several ionic and metal bound forms; that is, there is a multiplicity of states for each of these substances. This leads to the aforementioned dependencies of thermodynamic quantities on pH and pX. These dependencies are shown in **Fig. 3**.

The surface plots (Fig. 3) were calculated by using the equilibrium constant for the chemical reference reaction (4) and equilibrium constants for the per-

$$ATP^{4-} + H_2O = ADP^{3-} + HPO_4^{2-} + H^+ \tag{4}$$

tinent H^+ and Mg^{2+} binding constants in reactions (5)–(8). The equilibrium constants K for reactions

$$ATP^{4-} + H^+ = HATP^{3-} \tag{5}$$

$$ATP^{4-} + Mg^{2+} = MgATP^{2-} \tag{6}$$

$$HATP^{3-} + H^+ = H_2ATP^{2-} \tag{7}$$

$$HATP^{3-} + Mg^{2+} = MgHATP^- \tag{8}$$

(4)–(8) pertain to specific chemical species. These chemical reactions must balance both the number of atoms and the charges. While equilibrium constants K depend on temperature and ionic strength, they do not depend on pH or pX as do apparent equilibrium constants K'. Thus, it is important to maintain the distinction between K and K'.

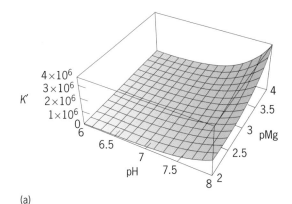

(a)

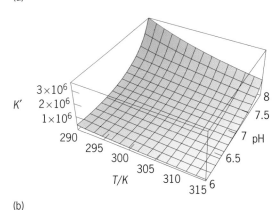

(b)

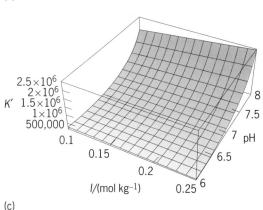

(c)

Fig. 3. Apparent equilibrium constant K' for the hydrolysis reaction (ATP + H_2O = ADP + phosphate) as a function of temperature T, pH, pMg, and ionic strength I. Since it is not possible to represent a five-dimensional surface here, three 3D projections are shown, where appropriate constraints have been applied in calculating each surface. (a) T = 298.15 K and I = 0.25 M. (b) I = 0.25 M and pMg = 3.0. (c) T = 298.15 K and pMg = 3.0.

Values of standard molar enthalpies of reaction $\Delta_r H^0$ can be used to adjust the values of K from one temperature to another over a relatively narrow temperature range. When operating over a wider temperature range, values are needed for the standard molar heat capacity changes $\Delta_r C_p^0$ for the reactions of interest. In general, values of activity coefficients γ have not been experimentally determined for the vast majority of biochemical species. Yet nonideality corrections are needed when adjusting the thermodynamic quantities from one ionic strength to

another. A frequently followed practice is to estimate values of γ by using the extended Debye-Hückel equation (9). Here A is the Debye-Hückel constant

$$\log_e \gamma = \frac{-Az^2 I^{1/2}}{(1 + BI^{1/2})} \qquad (9)$$

(A = 1.1758 $kg^{1/2} \cdot mol^{-1/2}$ at 298.15 K), z is the charge of the species, B is an empirical constant which has often been set at 1.6 $kg^{1/2} \cdot mol^{-1/2}$, and I is the ionic strength.

The principles discussed above provide a basis for the calculation of the results shown in Fig. 3. These calculations depend on having the necessary thermodynamic data available for both the chemical reference reaction and the pertinent H^+ and metal-ion binding constants. The simultaneous nonlinear equations that describe these very complex reaction systems must also be solved. The numerical problem of solving these equations can be handled routinely, using suitable computer algorithms which also permit the calculation of values of molar enthalpy and heat capacity changes pertinent to buffered reaction media as well as the changes in binding $\Delta_r N$ of H^+ and X that occur for overall biochemical reactions such as (1). Additionally, these calculations yield values of the concentrations of all of the species, as well as the concentrations of the biochemical reactants, expressed as sums of concentrations of chemical species. As shown in Fig. 3, these calculations allow one to obtain all of this information as a function of temperature, pH, pX, and ionic strength. Thus, the method outlined above makes it possible to obtain a complete thermodynamic picture of these important reactions. Additionally, by using the mathematical device of Legendre transforms it is possible to treat entire systems of biochemical reactions and metabolic pathways as well as systems that involve electric, gravitational, and magnetic fields and surface effects.

Having a sound thermodynamic framework for dealing with complex reactions is essential. However, reliable results (data) are required for performing practical calculations. A substantial body of experimental results for enzyme-catalyzed reactions has accumulated over many years and has been systematized in review articles and on the Web. Essentially all of the equilibrium data have been obtained by a variety of analytical methods, with chromatography and enzymatic assays being most commonly used. Calorimetry has proven to be an important tool for determining the enthalpies of reaction. The data obtained in such studies are essential for metabolic control analysis and bioprocess engineering calculations (for example, process optimization). However, if data are not available for a specific reaction, it is sometimes possible to calculate the desired quantities using thermochemical cycles (addition and subtraction of chemical equations and of the pertinent thermodynamic state functions), or to estimate the desired quantities using results for chemically similar substances and reactions of interest. Advances in the chemical thermodynamics of enzyme-catalyzed reactions will most likely come from an improved integration of existing databases into thermodynamic networks. This, in turn, will permit the calculation of the formation properties for a wide variety of biochemical species and lead to improved estimation methods. Clearly, many additional experimental results are needed for key reactions. In principle, quantum chemistry can also provide needed values. However, the major hurdle here is the difficulty in accurately treating the hydration of the species. In any case, the relatively recent availability of comprehensive databases and computational tools now makes detailed thermodynamic calculations possible for a variety of biochemical reactions.

Equilibrium thermodynamics. Clearly, living systems are not at equilibrium. However, based upon carefully performed in vivo measurements of metabolite concentrations, it has been observed that many of the reactions of metabolism operate at or near equilibrium. In addition, if a specific metabolic reaction does not operate at equilibrium, the above approach provides a quantitative measure of the extent to which that reaction departs from equilibrium. Thus, equilibrium thermodynamics provides the basic framework upon which irreversible processes are superimposed.

The respective aims of genomics and proteomics are to understand the basis for the operation of genes and proteins. If all issues in these fields were completely resolved and understood, one would still be left with major unanswered questions about the quantitative behavior of the relatively small molecules that provide, via the reactions of metabolism, both the basic structural ingredients and the energy required by living systems. Additionally, differences of metabolite concentrations are implicated in many diseases, such as diabetes, hypertension, arteriosclerosis, malnutrition, cardiac arrhythmias, epilepsy, trauma, and anoxic states. It appears that most, if not all, disease states are associated with abnormal metabolite concentrations. To make metabolism quantitative will require significant effort involving additional kinetic and thermodynamic studies as well as measurements of in vivo metabolite concentrations. Recently, a study was carried out using both thermodynamic and kinetic data, along with metabolic control analysis, to quantitatively assess the effects of different physiological states on the metabolic flux in glycolysis and glycogen metabolism in working perfused rat hearts. In a related study, the gradients of the major inorganic ions across the plasma membrane of a perfused rat heart were also determined. Thus, the thermodynamic information and approach described herein is an essential part of models that aim to calculate the flux of matter and energy in living systems.

For background information *see* ADENOSINE DIPHOSPHATE (ADP); ADENOSINE TRIPHOSPHATE (ATP); BIOORGANIC CHEMISTRY; CHEMICAL DYNAMICS; CHEMICAL EQUILIBRIUM; CHEMICAL KINETICS; CHEMICAL THERMODYNAMICS; ENTHALPY; ENTROPY; ENZYME; FREE ENERGY; KINETIC METHODS OF ANALYSIS;

pH; THERMODYNAMIC PRINCIPLES in the McGraw-Hill Encyclopedia of Science & Technology.

Robert N. Goldberg

Bibliography. D. L. Akers and R. N. Goldberg, BioEqCalc: A package for performing equilibrium calculations on biochemical reactions, *Mathematica J.*, 8(1):86–113, 2001; R. A. Alberty, Legendre transforms in chemical thermodynamics, *Chem. Rev.*, 94(6):1457–1482, 1994; R. A. Alberty et al., Recommendations for nomenclature and tables in biochemical thermodynamics, *Pure Appl. Chem.*, 66(8): 1641–1666, 1994; R. N. Goldberg, Thermodynamics of enzyme-catalyzed reactions: Part 6—1999 update, *J. Phys. Chem. Ref. Data*, 28(4):931–965, 1999; R. N. Goldberg, N. Kishore, and Y. B. Tewari, Thermodynamic studies of enzyme-catalyzed reactions, in T. Letcher (ed.), *Chemical Thermodynamics for the 21st Century*, pp. 291–300, Blackwell Science, Oxford, 1999.

Enzymes of thermophilic fungi

Thermophilic fungi comprise a small assemblage of eukaryotic molds whose optimum growth temperature lies between 40 and 50°C (104 and 122°F). As primary inhabitants of composts of vegetable matter, thermophilic fungi are able to degrade polymeric constituents of biomass. Because of their ubiquitous distribution, ease of isolation and maintenance of cultures, simple nutrition, rapid growth, and secretion of substantial quantities of enzymes, the thermophilic fungi are promising sources of thermostable enzymes for biotechnological applications.

Most species of thermophilic fungi can be grown in media with growth rates and yields comparable to those of mesophilic fungi [fungi that live and grow at temperatures of 20–40°C (68–104°F)]. Some species can grow even at 25–30°C (77–86°F) if spores pregerminated at higher temperatures are used to initiate growth in nutritionally rich media. Hyperthermophilic bacteria are favored as sources of extremozymes, enzymes capable of optimal functioning at 70°C (158°F) and above. However, although at their high growth temperatures extremozymes have optimal conformational flexibility, which is essential for catalysis, they may become too rigid and have low catalytic rates at the operational temperatures of most biotechnological applications (ranging from 50 to 65°C, or 122 to 149°F). Therefore, in most working conditions, the enzymes of thermophilic fungi having moderately high temperature optima and thermostability may be more suitable than the extremozymes from hyperthermophiles.

Secretory (extracellular) enzymes. The large surface area of thermophilic fungal mycelium enables the release of substantial amounts of proteins (secretory enzymes) into the growth medium. Since the mycelium is insoluble, it can easily be removed by filtration, simplifying the task of enzyme purification. Because of their relative abundance and ease of isolation, secretory enzymes of thermophilic fungi have been extensively studied.

Proteases. The need to more easily obtain chymosin (the milk-curdling enzyme, usually obtained from the stomach of suckling calves, used in industrial preparation of cheese; also called rennin) led to an extensive search for a substitute source. Scientists discovered that a soil isolate of the thermophilic fungus *Mucor pusillus*, grown on wheat bran, had strong milk-coagulating activity, identifying it as a potential substitute rennin source. Further investigation confirmed that *M. pusillus* produces an enzyme with a high ratio of milk clotting–to–proteolytic activity, enabling high yields of curds. Subsequently, the *Mucor* rennin was produced by growing the fungus on wheat bran from which it was extracted with water. The rennin is stable at 55°C (131°F) at a pH between 3.0 and 6.0; however, since it has maximal activity at pH 3.7, it is classified as an acid protease.

Mucor rennins have been used as model systems in investigations of the expression of fungal proteins in heterologous host cells (cells of other species), the processing of inactive precursor proteins into active enzymes, the effects of glycosylation on secretion, and the activity and stability of proteins. The *Mucor* rennin gene can be expressed in yeast cells, which secrete the foreign protein at concentrations exceeding 150 mg/liter; removal of the gene's amino-terminus signal sequence by autocatalytic processing at acid pH yields active rennin. Recombinant *Aspergillus oryzae* strains can produce *M. miehei* acid protease in excess of 3 g/liter. A strain of *Penicillium duponti* can produce a highly thermostable acid protease, and *Malbranchea pulchella* var. *sulfurea* and *Humicola lanuginosa* produce thermostable alkaline proteases, or thermomycolases, that can be concentrated without a loss in activity simply by vacuum evaporation of the culture medium at 45°C.

Lipases. Lipases (stable at pH 10–11 and temperatures from 30 to 60°C, or 86 to 140°F) from *H. lanuginosa* and *Rhizomucor miehei* are produced for preparation of detergents. A lipase gene from *H. lanuginosa* was cloned and expressed in *A. oryzae*, and the *R. miehei* lipase was the first lipase whose three-dimensional structure was deduced by x-ray analysis. Although the overall structures of the lipases are quite different, the lipase catalytic center always has the same three amino acids (serine–histidine–aspartic acid) as in the serine proteases. The lipase catalytic site is covered by a short α-helical loop that acts as a "lid" that moves when the enzyme is adsorbed at the oil-water interface, allowing the substrate to access the active site. Mutation of an active-site serine causes an alteration in the motion of the lid, which affects the binding affinity of the enzyme.

α-Amylase and glucoamylase. α-Amylase, an endo-acting enzyme, hydrolyzes bonds within starch to produce maltose and oligosaccharides of various lengths; whereas glucoamylase, an exo-acting enzyme, hydrolyzes bonds from the nonreducing end of starch, producing β-D-glucose. Both enzymes have potential application in the industrial saccharification of starch. *Thermomyces lanuginosus* produces both enzymes simultaneously when grown on starch. However, a strain of *H. grisea* var. *thermoidea* produces 2.5- to 3.0-fold higher yields of glucoamylase in a medium containing maltose rather than starch. Another strain of the same fungus produced an enzyme which was remarkably insensitive to end-product inhibition.

Cellulase. Cellulase refers to a group of enzymes (endoglucanase, exoglucanase, and β-glucosidase) that work together to hydrolyze cellulose. Cellulase enzymes are used in detergent formulations to remove unwanted pill-like balls of fuzz that form on clothes, collecting dirt, due to repeated washing and wearing. The endoglucanases (mol wt ranging from 30 to 100 kilodaltons) of thermophilic fungi are thermostable, and active between 55 and 80°C (131 and 176°F) at pH 5.0–5.5. Their carbohydrate content varies from 2 to 50%. The exoglucanases (mol wt 40–70 kDa) are thermostable glycoproteins that are optimally active at 50–75°C (122–167°F). The molecular characteristics of β-glucosidases are more variable, with mol wt ranging from 45 to 250 kDa, and carbohydrate content ranging from 9 to 50%. Except for the thermostability, the molecular characteristics of cellulase components of thermophilic and mesophilic fungi are similar. Several species of thermophilic fungi degrade cellulose rapidly, but their extracellular cellulase activity is low (suggesting that in addition to the secreted levels of cellulase, hyphal-wall-bound enzymes or oxidative enzymes may be involved in cellulose degradation). A thermophilic fungus, *Thermoascus aurantiacus*, grown on shredded paper and peptone, is an exceptionally good producer of cellulases, as is a strain of *H. insolens* grown on wheat bran.

Xylanase. Xylanases of thermophilic fungi are receiving considerable attention because of their application in biobleaching of pulp in the paper industry. The enzymatic removal of xylan from lignin-carbohydrate complexes in the pulp facilitates the leaching of lignin from the fiber cell wall, obviating the need for chlorine for pulp bleaching in the brightening process. Xylanases also have applications in the pretreatment of animal feed, as they improve its digestibility. Outstanding yields of xylanases, requiring only three- to fourfold purification of culture filtrate protein, have been obtained from some wild isolates of thermophilic fungi, such as strains of *H. lanuginosa*, *Paecilomyces varioti*, and *Thermoascus aurantiacus*. The thermostability of *H. lanuginosa* (*Thermomyces lanuginosus*) xylanase is ascribed to the presence of an extra disulfide bridge that is absent in most mesophilic xylanases and to an increased density of charged residues throughout the protein.

Laccases. Laccases are copper-containing enzymes that catalyze the oxidation of phenolic compounds accompanied by reduction of oxygen to water. The gene encoding laccase of *Myceliophthora thermophila* has been cloned and expressed in *A. oryzae*, and the recombinant enzyme purified from culture broth with two- to fourfold higher yield than the native laccase. The enzyme is optimally active at pH 6.5, and it retains full activity when incubated at 60°C (140°F) for 20 min. A purified laccase from culture filtrates of *Chaetomium thermophilum* polymerized low-molecular-weight, water-soluble organic matter from compost into a high-molecular-weight product, suggesting that the enzyme might be involved in the formation of humus during composting.

Phytases. Phytases catalyze the hydrolysis of phytic acid, the primary storage form of phosphorus in plant seeds. It has potential application in agriculture as a supplement to seed-based poultry and pig feed. Addition of phytase increases the availability of phosphorus, an essential nutrient for pig and chicken growth. When the gene encoding the extracellular phytase from *Thermomyces lanuginosus* is expressed in the mesophilic fungus *Fusarium*, twice as much enzyme is produced.

Cell-associated (intracellular) enzymes. Since the cell-associated enzymes have been difficult to solubilize, they have been less studied. However, among the few enzymes studied, trehalase and invertase are noteworthy.

Trehalase. Trehalase, which catalyzes the hydrolysis of trehalose to glucose, is used for enzymatic estimation of trehalose in biological samples. This enzyme from *T. lanuginosus* was partially solubilized from acetone-butanol treated mycelia. Comparison of the trehalases from the thermophilic *T. lanuginosus* and the mesophilic *Neurospora crassa* indicate that both enzymes are glycoproteins with acidic pH optima (between 5.0 and 5.5). In addition, both trehalase are optimally active at 50°C and exhibit similar thermostability at this temperature. The *T. lanuginosus* enzyme is a monomeric protein (145 kDa), whereas the *N. crassa* enzyme is a homotetramer (subunit molecular mass 92 kDa). The catalytic efficiency and activation energy for thermal inactivation values of *Neurospora* trehalase are higher than the values for *T. lanuginosus* trehalase, indicating that the mesophilic trehalase is a better catalyst than the thermophilic trehalase. (These results, however, cannot be generalized.)

Invertases. Invertases are required biochemical reagents for estimation of sucrose in biological samples. Unusual invertase activity is observed in *T. lanuginosus*. Although invertase activity in the mesophilic fungus *N. crassa* is constitutive and stable, in the thermophilic fungus *T. lanuginosus* invertase activity is inducible and highly unstable in cell extracts. Thiol compounds activate and stabilize *T. lanuginosus* invertase activity, but have no effect on *N. crassa* activity. Moreover, invertase activity in *T. lanuginosus* appears to be localized in the hyphal tips, whereas the enzyme activity in *N. crassa* is associated with the hyphal wall. The unusual behavior of invertase in *T. lanuginosus* suggests that the activity of certain sensitive enzymes in thermophilic fungi may be optimized by substrate-induced synthesis and by their localization in the growing hyphal tips.

For background information *see* BIOTECHNOLOGY; ENZYME; FUNGAL ECOLOGY; FUNGI; GENETIC ENGI-NEERING in the McGraw-Hill Encyclopedia of Science & Technology.   Ramesh Maheshwari

Bibliography. D. G. Cooney and R. Emerson, *Thermophilic Fungi: An Account of Their Biology, Activities and Classification*, W. H. Freeman, San Francisco, 1964; R. Maheshwari, G. Bharadwaj, and M. K. Bhat, Thermophilic fungi: Their physiology and enzymes, *Microbiol. Mol. Biol. Rev.*, 64:461–488, 2000.

Epicuticular waxes (botany)

A plant's cuticle is the boundary layer between the plant and its environment, and is one of the key innovations that occurred during the evolution of land plants. Over the last 400 million years the plant cuticle has evolved to become a complex and multifunctional interface, consisting mainly of insoluble polymers such as cutin (a polyester matrix) and (in some species) cutan, plus polysaccharides such as cellulose. Waxes are a major component of the cuticle that are either embedded into the cutin matrix (intracuticular waxes) or deposited onto the cuticle surface (epicuticular waxes). The major function of the cuticle is to serve as a highly efficient barrier against uncontrolled water loss and to reduce leaching of organic and inorganic substances from the leaf interior, and waxes are the main determinants of these properties.

During the last 30 years cuticular surfaces of plants have been intensively investigated using scanning electron microscopy (SEM). These studies revealed an incredible microstructural diversity. Among the most prominent structural elements are the epicuticular waxes, a general term for various soluble lipids deposited upon the cuticle and therefore representing the plant's outermost barrier. The presence of such waxes causes the glaucousness of many surfaces, that is, the white or bluish appearance of fruits such as grapes, plums, and cabbage leaves. Epicuticular waxes are able to self-assemble into complex three-dimensional crystals, usually between 0.2 and 100 micrometers, that often form dense coverings on the cuticle. Today it is widely accepted that the individual structure of most wax crystals depends mainly on the dominant chemical component. This has been demonstrated by in vitro crystallization of the total wax, isolated fractions of it, and individual components extracted from plant surfaces.

Composition and structure. Plant waxes are complex mixtures of aliphatic (chainlike) and cyclic components, the composition of which is subject to great variability among different plant species, different organs of an individual plant, or during the ontogeny of individual organs. The aliphatic compounds are derived from synthesis of C_{16} and C_{18} fatty acids in the plastids of epidermal cells. The dominant individual components of these complex mixtures are often responsible for the characteristic ultrastructure of epicuticular wax crystals, which are usually self-assembling. Wax tubules have been studied most intensively in this respect. Corresponding to their chemical composition, two types of tubules can be distinguished: (1) those dominated by the secondary alcohol nonacosan-10-ol; these tubules branch at an angle of approximately 90° (**Fig. 1**); and (2) those consisting of various β-diketones; these tubules branch at an acute angle. Another type of wax ultrastructure is transversely ridged rodlets, in which the ketone palmiton is the dominant component (**Fig. 2**).

Epicuticular waxes are able to form films, layers, or complex three-dimensional crystalline structures with great diversity. The most common morphologies are grains, platelets, rodlets, filaments, or tubes. A comprehensive overview, including a classification of 23 different wax types, was published by W. Barthlott et al. in 1998. Atomic force microscopy (AFM) represents a modern tool for the investigation of surfaces at the molecular level, that is, the nanometer scale, and allows real-time documentation of the early stages of wax accumulation and crystal growth on the surface of living plants in a nearly nondestructive way. Thus, applying this method will provide new insights into the dynamic process of three-dimensional structure formation and the organization of supramolecular hydrophobic nanostructures in waxes.

Environmental factors such as light intensity or air humidity may alter the amount of wax crystals on a given surface, but not the individual crystal morphology. As a result, wax crystals are valuable characteristics in systematics and taxonomy, permitting the grouping of plants at ascending taxonomic levels.

Transport of waxes. Waxes are synthesized within living epidermal cells and must cross the nonliving cuticular membrane of those cells in order to reach the cutin matrix, where they may remain or move across the cuticle to be deposited onto its surface. The process by which wax components move from the inside of the epidermal cell to the cuticle surface has been subject to much speculation. Various hypotheses have been published, involving different types of cuticular channels (ectodesmata), organic solvents, and lipid transfer proteins. Although none of these hypotheses have been proven, the movement of wax components in the presence of water or water vapor, similar to the process of steam distillation, was recently proposed and substantiated by a series of experiments using isolated cuticles as well as artificial polymer membranes.

Functional aspects. Epicuticular wax crystals form a regular microrelief covering the cuticular surfaces of many terrestrial plants. Here the crystals serve different purposes, such as increased reflection of solar radiation (reducing photoinhibition of photosynthesis), and reduction of cuticular transpiration as well as the leaching of ions and other substances from inside the leaf. In several plant species epicuticular waxes play an important role in the plants' interactions with animals, such as by providing a slippery

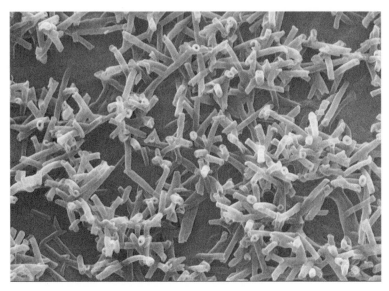

Fig. 1. Nonacosan-10-ol wax tubules on the leaf of *Thalictrum flavum* (Ranunculaceae). Magnification ×15,000.

surface for the traps of the carnivorous genus *Sarracenia*. A number of lipid components in waxes have been found to influence the growth and feeding behavior of the insects that feed on them.

Waxes are hydrophobic and, in conjunction with a microscopic roughness, often form a highly effective water-repellent cuticular surface, causing water droplets to run off even at extremely low tilting angles. In addition, contaminating particles such as dust, spores, or microorganisms stick to the droplet surface and are carried away. At the microscopic level, the basis of this self-cleaning property can be found in the contact areas of contaminating particles. The particles touch only the tips of the wax crystals and, as a consequence, the adhesion forces acting at

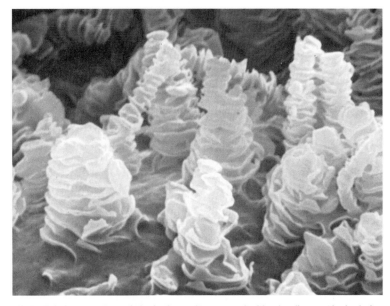

Fig. 2. Palmiton wax crystals in the form of transversely ridged rodlets on the leaf of *Williamodendron quadrilocellatum* (Lauraceae). Magnification ×9000.

these contact areas are extremely small. On the other hand, the adhesion between a water droplet and a particle is larger due to the larger contact area. Consequently, the particle is picked up and sticks to the surface of the water droplet. This self-cleaning mechanism is called the lotus effect because the sacred lotus (*Nelumbo nucifera* Gaert.), which is a symbol of purity in eastern Asian religions, shows this property to perfection. The lotus effect may be the most important function of many microstructured biological surfaces.

The explanation for the evolution of a self-cleaning surface can be found in the negative effects of inorganic contamination on living tissue (including higher surface temperatures under exposed sunlight) and the battle between plants and pathogens. Pathogens are usually deposited on leaves as conidia, spores, or cells (bacteria, algae), transported there either through rain or air. The lotus effect prevents pathogens from establishing themselves on the plant surface because they are washed off with every rainfall. (In the case of a long period without rain, the lack of water obstructs pathogen germination or growth.) The self-cleaning property has been subject to intensive investigation and serves as a fascinating example of the highly effective adaptations of plants interacting with the environment.

Since the lotus effect depends only on the physical and chemical properties of the plant surfaces, this property can be transferred to nonbiological surfaces such as paints, ceramics, and glass, and may find several technical applications. Certain plant waxes are already of commercial interest, such as the wax from the wax-palm *Copernica cerifera*, known as carnauba wax, which is used in the production of numerous polishes and coatings.

For background information *see* EPIDERMIS (PLANT); PLANT PHYSIOLOGY; SCANNING ELECTRON MICROSCOPE; SECRETORY STRUCTURES (PLANT); WAX, ANIMAL AND VEGETABLE in the McGraw-Hill Encyclopedia of Science & Technology.

K. Koch; Wilhelm Barthlott; Christoph Neinhuis

Bibliography. H. Bargel et al., Plant cuticles: Multifunctional interfaces between plant and environment, in A. R. Hemsley and I. Poole (eds.), *Evolutionary Physiology at the Sub-plant Level*, Academic Press, London, 2002; W. Barthlott et al., Classification and terminology of plant epicuticular waxes, *Bot. J. Linn. Soc.*, 126:137–260, 1998; W. Barthlott et al., Epicuticular waxes and vascular plant systematics: Integrating micromorphological and chemical data, *Regnum Vegetabile*, International Association of Plant Taxonomists, 2002; C. E. Jeffree, The cuticle, epicuticular waxes and trichomes of plants, with reference to their structure, functions and evolution, in B. E. Juniper and S. R. Southwood (eds.), *Insects and the Plant Surface*, pp. 22–63, Edward Arnold, London, 1986; J. T. Martin and B. E. Juniper, *The Cuticles of Plants*. Edward Arnold, London, 1970; D. Post-Beitenmiller, Biochemistry and molecular biology of wax production in plants, *Annu. Rev. Plant Physiol. Plant Mol. Biol.*, 47:405–430, 1996.

Evidence of Archean life

During the first 500–600 million years of the Earth's history, the crust was continuously destroyed by convection within the very hot young planet and by meteorite bombardment. This turbulent period is known as the Hadean Era, which is defined as the period from which no geological record exists (no rocks were preserved). The oldest rocks known on the Earth occur in Canada and West Greenland and appeared between 4000 and 3800 million years ago (Ma). They define the beginning of the Archean Era, which gave way to the Proterozoic ("earlier life") Era 2500 Ma. Until recently, no fossils were known from the Archean.

Age of Earth. The question of the antiquity of life on Earth is coupled to the question of the age of Earth itself. Many attempts to date the Earth have been made throughout history, including the biblical estimate of approximately 6000 years by Bishop Ussher in the eighteenth century, and Lord Kelvin's nineteenth-century estimate of approximately 90 million years based on the theory of passive cooling of a once glowing Earth. Lord Kelvin's estimate was long used as an argument against Darwin's theories of the evolution of life through natural selection, because 90 million years was judged too short a time span for such a process to operate. Present understanding of the formation of the Earth indicates that all the planets formed from accumulations of gases and dust during a short time interval about 4550 Ma, and that estimates of the age of the Earth can be constrained by the age of meteorites left over from the accretion of the planets. Modern geological age determinations are based on the analysis of isotopic ratios that change with known rates through time, due to the decay of radioactive isotopes.

Early life. Geological materials that have escaped reworking by the forces of plate tectonics are necessary components in the search for traces of the most ancient life. Traces of life must be sought in rocks that were originally deposited as sediments on the surface of the Earth, or in cracks and veins formed near the surface, where water might have percolated. Relatively well-preserved sedimentary rocks with ages up to approximately 3500 Ma are known from Western Australia, South Africa, and North America. These rocks have been the focus of much attention in the search for early life. Most conspicuously, many of these deposits preserve some layered hummocky structures called stromatolites, which were probably constructed by living organisms that trapped sediment particles on biofilm or perhaps even precipitated carbonate as a part of their activity. In a controversial study of some 3500-Ma rocks from Western Australia, J. W. Schopf reported the presence of microscopic carbon structures that he interpreted as true fossils of organisms similar to cyanobacteria (blue-green algae). Although Schopf's findings have been seriously questioned and true fossils may not be preserved in these rocks after all, it is still generally accepted that life flourished in the oceans 3500 Ma.

Isua supracrustals. To probe deeper into the roots of the tree of life, research has concentrated on the oldest sedimentary rocks known, which occur at Isua approximately 150 km (93 mi) northeast of Greenland's capital, Nuuk.

The Isua supracrustals (rocks originally formed at the surface) form a belt of rocks 35 km (21.7 mi) long and up to 4 km (2.5 mi) wide. The exact age of the Isua rocks is unknown, but they are certainly older than 3700 Ma and were probably deposited during the 3900–3800-Ma time span (**Fig. 1**). These rocks represent a very interesting period, during which the heavy meteorite bombardment that preceded it ceased. Earth stepped out of the Hadean turmoil into a regime more akin to the present. Model calculations have shown that impacts during the heavy bombardment might have boiled off the oceans and sterilized the Earth on several occasions up to the time of deposition of the Isua supracrustals. This time could be the threshold for life on the Earth.

The Isua supracrustals are dominated by amphibolite that was originally deposited as basalt lava and volcanic ash layers. Interleaved with the amphibolites are layers of sediments, including banded iron formation (BIF). This is a peculiar rock type known only from the Archean and the first half of the Proterozoic. It consists of alternating layers of quartz and the iron oxide mineral magnetite. It is believed that BIFs are chemical sediments formed by oxidation and precipitation of iron dissolved in the ocean water. The presence in the oceans of dissolved iron in sufficient quantities to form BIF is possible only when there is no oxygen in the atmosphere. This explains the absence of BIF from the later parts of Earth history when oxygen had started to build up in the atmosphere. It is often assumed that the oxidation and precipitation of iron was caused by the presence of living organisms, but neither the exact mechanism nor any objective proofs of this contention have been established. Like all rocks from 3500 Ma or older, the Isua rocks have been severely affected by metamorphism and deformation during their long geologic history. This means that all mineral grains in the rocks have recrystallized and changed shape several times. Therefore the probability that fossils of any kind could be preserved in these rocks is extremely poor, particularly since it is assumed that life, at best, could have been small, fragile, single-celled organisms.

Chemical fossils. In 1979, the German geochemist Manfred Schidlowski suggested that the search for early life should concentrate on chemical marks that life might have left on the environment. Living organisms selectively consume some chemical components from their surroundings through their metabolic activity. If life were abundantly present, this should leave characteristic and recognizable chemical indicators that might be robust to later geological reworking, called chemofossils. Schidlowski pointed out that the fractionation of carbon isotopes might be the best indicator, because carbon is an essential component of all living organisms, and

Fig. 1. The age of the Isua supracrustals must be older than the age of cross-cutting granite veins. Folded (dark) volcanic rocks are cut by a vein of granite (white), which intruded 3700 Ma.

because most carbon in the oceans and atmosphere is cycled through the biosphere. Carbon has two stable isotopes, carbon-12 (^{12}C) and carbon-13 (^{13}C). On average 98.89% of Earth carbon is ^{12}C and 1.11% is ^{13}C. With few possible exceptions, this ratio would be present in all materials in a lifeless Earth. However, when living organisms form organic molecules to build their cells or fuel their activities, they often process the ^{12}C isotope more efficiently. Organic materials therefore have a small deficit in ^{13}C—usually about 20–25 per mil (parts per thousand)—relative to the global average carbon. The accumulated biomass holds less of the ^{13}C, and consequently the inorganic carbon inventory found as CO_2 in the atmosphere and bicarbonate in the ocean is enriched in this isotope. Therefore limestone formed from ocean water has a small surplus of ^{13}C of approximately 5 per mil relative to average carbon. Such marine carbonate material—specifically, a certain type of skeletal carbonate from fossil squid, called the Pee Dee belemnite (PDB)—is used as reference material when carbon isotopic ratios (^{13}C/^{12}C) are analyzed. This PDB standard has by definition the composition 0 per mil relative to PDB. Average carbon has the composition −5 per mil (PDB), and biogenic materials often have values around −25 to −30 per mil (PDB).

First analysis of Isua samples. Schidlowski and coworkers analyzed a number of Isua samples that contained graphite (crystalline carbon) supposed to be derived from organic material, and carbonate supposed to be derived from marine limestone. It was found that the carbonate had a surplus and the graphite a deficit in ^{13}C, such as could be expected if life forms had metabolized carbon in the ocean and atmosphere. The researchers concluded that the biological carbon cycle was already active at Isua times. However, Schidlowski's study suffered from a rather poor understanding of the complicated Isua geology

Fig. 2. Sediment layers from approximately 3700 Ma at Isua. The layers were originally deposited horizontally. Tectonic forces have tilted the layers, but sedimentary structures are still preserved. The gray layer is a mud flow, and the black layers are carbon-rich clay layers.

Fig. 3. Closeup of the clay layers. The perfect preservation of fine lamina allows a detailed description of the sedimentary environment.

a BIF and which was of approximately the same age as Isua but was found on the small island Akilia approximately 150 km (93 mi) southwest of Isua. In this study S. J. Mojzsis and coworkers used a sophisticated ion microprobe technique to show that this carbon also carried the characteristic low ^{13}C signature of life. This study has met with considerable criticism for the same reason as the pioneering study by Schidlowski et al., namely that the carbon cannot be proven to be primary. It has even been suggested that the Akilia rock was originally a magmatic rock, and that the carbon was introduced much later from an unknown source.

Analysis of sedimentary rocks at Isua. The uncertainty about the source of carbon was overcome in a study by M. T. Rosing, who identified a small outcrop of sedimentary rocks at Isua where the state of preservation was good enough to allow a detailed interpretation of the sedimentary environment (**Fig. 2**). The sediments were deposited in deep water by the slow sedimentation of fine clay suspended in the water, probably depositing a few millimeters every thousand years (**Fig. 3**). For every few centimeters of clay, millimeter-thin layers of volcanic ash carried from distant volcanoes settled almost instantly. At times, this quiet scenario was interrupted by avalanches of mud that came cascading down submarine slopes and dumped sandy layers up to 1 m (3.3 ft) thick on the sea floor. The slowly deposited clay layers contain up to 0.5% carbon in the form of 2–5-micrometer graphite grains (**Fig. 4**). In contrast, the thin volcanic ash layers, which settled rapidly, contain no carbon. This relationship indicates that the carbon in this deposit formed part of the original sediment, and was not introduced later (**Fig. 5**). The carbon in these sediments is depleted in ^{13}C by −20 to −25 per mil relative to PDB. The deposit can be interpreted as having been formed by the slow precipitation of clay particles and dead organisms, probably plankton, raining down from the photic zone near the ocean surface. When the rate of sedimentation was high, as during deposition of the volcanic ash layers, the contribution from the organisms

prevailing at that time, and the samples used were in many cases not derived from ancient sediments but were formed by percolating deep crustal fluids much later in Earth history. The isotopic signal of life could thus most likely have been picked up from the late fluids. The problems of unambiguously relating carbon-bearing materials to the original sedimentary environment have proven to be one of the main obstacles in identifying traces of early life, and are the source of much controversy in the scientific literature.

Analysis of samples from Isua and Akilia. The second major advance toward the documentation of life in the earliest Archean was a study of microscopic carbon inclusions in the mineral apatite found in BIF from Isua and in a layered rock which might once have been

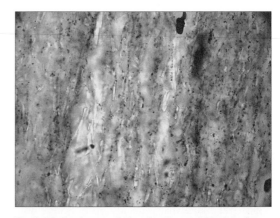

Fig. 4. Photomicrograph showing the small black carbon particles in Isua clay layers. The particles are approximately 2 to 5 micrometers and were formed from organic debris that settled on the ocean floor.

Fig. 5. Photomicrograph of the contact between a carbon-rich clay layer (dark gray) and a millimeter-thin volcanic ash layer (white). There are no carbon particles in the ash layer (the dark specks in the white layer are iron-titanium oxide), which indicates that the carbon in the clay layer was an original component in the sediment.

was insignificant and the layers ended up without appreciable carbon. This study shows that ^{13}C-depleted carbon was deposited in the oceans during the Isua time, and that life had probably already reached a level of sophistication to allow colonization of the open oceans. It represents the best documented evidence for the earliest life on the Earth.

For background information *see* ARCHEAN; CARBON; DATING METHODS; EARTH, AGE OF; GEOCHRONOMETRY; GEOLOGIC THERMOMETRY; GEOLOGIC TIME SCALE; HADEAN; METAMORPHIC ROCKS; PROTEROZOIC; RADIOISOTOPE; ROCK AGE DETERMINATION; SEDIMENTARY ROCKS; SEQUENCE STRATIGRAPHY in the McGraw-Hill Encyclopedia of Science & Technology.   Minik T. Rosing

Bibliography. M. D. Brasier et al., *Nature*, 416:76–81, 2002; S. J. Mojzsis et al., *Nature*, 384:55–59, 1996; M. T. Rosing, *Science*, 283:674–676, 1999; M. Schidlowski et al., *Geochim. Cosmochim. Acta*, 43:189–199, 1979; J. W. Shopf, *Proc. Nat. Acad. Sci. USA*, 91:6735–6742, 1994.

Evolution of Bantu languages

The Bantu language family comprises over 450 languages spoken across most of sub-Saharan Africa south of about 5° North. It belongs to the Niger-Kordofanian phylum (a maximal group of related languages), whose other languages are found mostly in West Africa. The languages spoken in the northwest of the Bantu-speaking region are the most divergent in their vocabulary from other Bantu languages, suggesting that Bantu originated there. The level of diversity within the Bantu languages compared with that of languages for which there are longer historical records, such as Latin and French, suggests that they began to diverge around 5000 years ago.

Language trees and population history. Languages can be a useful source of information about human population history, because languages tend to diverge after populations divide. If a speech commu-

nity (a population speaking a common language) divides, with part of the community migrating to a new area, over time the languages spoken in the separated populations will diverge. Words change gradually over time or are replaced. The process of linguistic divergence gives rise first to separate dialects, which are distinct but mutually comprehensible, and later to mutually incomprehensible languages. The development of two new languages from a common ancestral language is thought to take about 500 years. Over centuries, this process of continued splitting and divergence among languages gives rise to groups of hierarchically related languages. Tree diagrams (language trees) can be constructed to show how languages are related. Linguistic divergence often occurs in tandem with genetic divergence among human populations, resulting in similarities between genetic and linguistic trees.

Linguistic relationships can be reconstructed in detail to a time depth of 5000–10,000 years. During this period the expansion of farming populations, together with the spread of the early farmers' languages, is thought to have given rise to many large language groups that exist today, including the Bantu languages in sub-Saharan Africa. Like many other cultural groups, Bantu-speaking populations lack written records for most of their history. Linguistic reconstruction has provided a crucial source of information about their past population movements and cultural history. Basic linguistic data are available for most Bantu languages. As yet, far fewer Bantu-speaking populations have been studied genetically, but both linguistic and genetic data have enormous potential to increase knowledge of Bantu prehistory.

Constructing language trees. Recently researchers have begun to use tree-building methods developed in evolutionary biology to reconstruct linguistic trees. This is possible because of similarities in the processes of linguistic and biological divergence. The parallels between linguistic and biological evolution were noted by Darwin, who observed: "The formation of different languages and of distinct species, and the proofs that both have been developed through a gradual process, are curiously the same."

Tree-building methods. Linguistic descent groups, or groups of languages sharing a unique common ancestor, are recognized by the presence of shared linguistic innovations. Linguistic innovations are equivalent to the shared derived characters used by evolutionary biologists to construct trees of biological species. New quantitative methods for inferring trees such as maximum-parsimony and maximum-likelihood methods have revolutionized evolutionary biology over the past two decades. (The principle of maximum parsimony, a widely used tree-building method, is to find the tree with the smallest number of evolutionary changes required to explain the observed data.) These new tree-building methods can also be used to construct language trees. Like the "comparative method" traditionally used by linguists to construct language trees, the new tree-building methods

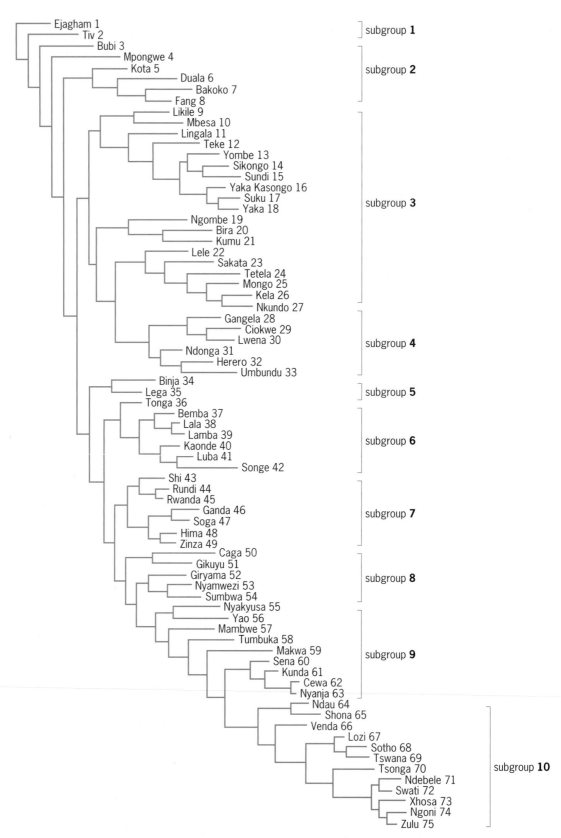

Fig. 1. Weighted-parsimony tree of 75 Bantu languages. Languages are numbered in order to show their geographical location (see Fig. 2). Brackets on the right indicate Bantu subgroups, defined by the language tree and by geography (see Fig. 3). The Bantoid languages (group 1), spoken in modern Nigeria, are not part of the Bantu language group proper but are related to Bantu. Branch lengths are proportional to the number of linguistic changes on each branch.

developed in evolutionary biology define descent groups using shared innovations rather than overall similarity. In addition, they use efficient, computer-implemented algorithms to search for the best tree or trees from the millions of possible trees, according to an explicit optimality criterion. Using the method of weighted maximum parsimony, it was possible to construct a tree of 75 Bantu languages (**Fig. 1**). The geographical locations of these languages are shown in **Fig. 2**.

Vocabulary evolution. Ninety-two items of basic vocabulary were used to construct the Bantu language tree. "Basic vocabulary" refers to the meanings of words such as "man," "woman," "moon," and "cloud" that are present in all languages. (When categorizing words, a distinction is made between a word's *meaning* and its *form*. The meaning is what the word refers to, for example a man or a hoe; the form is the word's sound.) The meaning of a word such as "iron," which is not present in all languages, would not be counted as basic vocabulary. (The meaning of the word "iron" would probably be absent in the language of a pre–Iron Age culture.) Cognates are meanings whose word-form shares a common root in two or more languages; the presence of cognates in two languages indicates that those languages are related. Over time, as languages evolve, word-forms for meanings are gradually replaced; the number of cognates shared by related languages falls and the languages diverge. The basic vocabulary is thought to change more slowly than other vocabulary, being less subject to linguistic innovation or borrowing from neighboring languages, so cognates in the basic vocabulary can reflect linguistic relationships that are several thousand years old. Such shared cognate forms were identified in the 92 items of the Bantu basic vocabulary and used to construct the tree in Fig. 1.

Spread of farming. The Bantu language tree can be compared to archeological evidence for the spread of farming in sub-Saharan Africa, in order to investigate how far the Bantu language tree reflects broader cultural history in this region. It is thought that the first farmers in this region were Bantu speakers, who spread both agricultural technology and Bantu languages across Central and Southern Africa.

The maximum-parsimony Bantu language tree closely matches archeological evidence for the spread of farming across these areas between about 3000 B.C. and A.D. 200. This suggests that the Bantu language tree reflects the population history of Bantu-speaking farmers as they spread across the southern half of the African continent. The brackets in Fig. 1 show Bantu subgroups, defined by geography and the language tree. The geographical location of each subgroup is shown in **Fig. 3**, with arrows indicating the probable direction of the Bantu expansion, based on the maximum-parsimony language tree and archeological evidence for the spread of farming.

Using both archeological evidence and the language tree, the following sequence is hypothesized

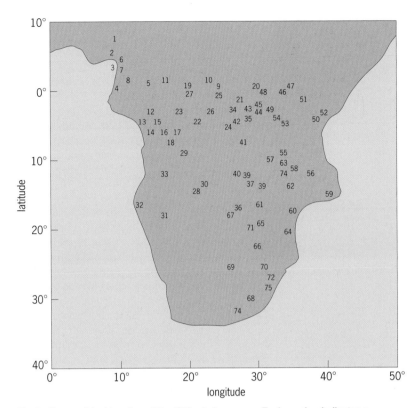

Fig. 2. Geographical location of the 75 Bantu languages. Each number indicates a language (see Fig. 1). Languages 1 and 2 (Tiv and Ejagham) are Bantoid languages. Northwest Bantu languages (3–8) may descend from the earliest Bantu languages.

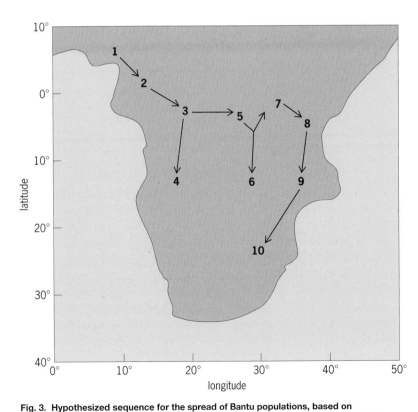

Fig. 3. Hypothesized sequence for the spread of Bantu populations, based on archeological evidence and the language tree (see Fig. 1). Archeological dates for the spread of farming suggest that this expansion occurred between 3000 B.C. (group 2) and A.D. 200 (group 10).

for the spread of Bantu-speaking populations. Dates are based on estimated archeological dates for the earliest farmers in each area. Neolithic farmers entered the region from the northwest around 3000 B.C. (groups 1 and 2). They spread across the forest during the 1st millennium B.C. (groups 3 and 4). During the later 1st millennium B.C., Bantu-speaking populations around Lake Victoria (groups 5 and 7) developed iron technology. They also acquired cereal agriculture and cattle from their non-Bantu neighbors, herders and farmers who probably spoke Cushitic and Nilotic languages. These Early Iron Age populations belonged to an archeological tradition known as Urewe. Early Iron Age farmers, probably speaking Bantu languages, then spread rapidly to Southern Africa by ca. A.D. 200 in two main migrations, the Western stream (group 6) and the Eastern stream (groups 8, 9, and 10).

Linguistic borrowing: trees versus networks. In historical linguistics, tree models are widely used to show how languages are related. However, the validity of tree models has been questioned because it is known that there is some "borrowing" or diffusion of linguistic elements between neighboring languages. How much borrowing occurs between languages? If borrowing is widespread, a net rather than a tree may be a better model to show how languages are related. The extent to which linguistic relationships are treelike or netlike is part of a wider debate in anthropology about the level of interconnection among human cultures.

To assess how well a tree model describes Bantu language evolution, how well the linguistic data fit on the tree can be measured. On a tree, linguistic borrowing will appear to be convergent evolution in different branches, reducing the fit of the linguistic data on the tree. Compared to biological trees of a similar size, the fit of the Bantu language data on the tree was good. A tree model therefore seems to describe Bantu language evolution well. This suggests that, at least for the basic vocabulary, the Bantu languages evolved mainly by a process of splitting and divergence. This is probably because as Bantu-speaking populations spread across this region of Africa, groups separated and spread away from each other. Linguistic divergence (branching) rather than convergence (reticulation) probably predominated throughout most of Bantu history.

There has been widespread diffusion of some Bantu words for meanings such as "iron" (that is, they were borrowed freely by neighboring languages), along with the spread of iron technology, but much less diffusion of the basic vocabulary. The Bantu languages are spoken across the continental landmass of sub-Saharan Africa, and neighboring languages are not geographically isolated from one another. This suggests that social factors rather than geographical barriers were responsible for maintaining distinct speech communities among speakers of the Bantu languages.

For background information *see* ANTHROPOLOGY; ARCHEOLOGY; HUMAN ECOLOGY; LINGUISTICS; PHY-

LOGENY in the McGraw-Hill Encyclopedia of Science & Technology.   Clare Janaki Holden

Bibliography. Y. Bastin, A. Coupez, and M. Mann, Continuity and divergence in the Bantu languages: Perspectives from a lexicostatic study, Tervuren, Musée Royale d'Afrique Centrale, *Annales, Sciences humaines*, vol. 162, 1999; C. Darwin, *The Descent of Man, and Selection in Relation to Sex*, J. Murray, London, 1871; C. Ehret, *An African Classical Age: Eastern and Southern Africa in World History, 1000 B.C. to A.D. 400*, University Press of Virginia, 1998; C. J. Holden, Bantu language trees reflect the spread of farming across sub-Saharan Africa: A maximum-parsimony analysis, *Proc. Roy. Soc. London Ser. B*, 269:793–799, 2002; D. W. Phillipson, *African Archaeology*, 2d ed., Cambridge University Press, Cambridge, 1993; J. Vansina, *Paths in the Rainforests: Toward a History of the Political Tradition in Equatorial Africa*, James Currey, London, 1990.

Exercise and the brain

The salutary effects of physical activity on general physiology (for example, increasing body fitness and endurance) have long been known. Such effects should not be surprising considering the integral aspect that physical activity has occupied in human biological adaptation. Therefore, it is likely that a biological need for exercise has become part of the human gene pool, as suggested by the many studies showing that a lack of exercise is linked to increased incidence of disease. Although exercise has long been perceived as a good predictor of improved neural functioning, its effects on specific functions commanded by the brain and spinal cord have started to be elucidated over the last decade. Indeed, recent developments in the field of molecular biology have brought to light some of the molecular components underlying the effects of exercise on the brain. Scientists are now in a position to start realistically evaluating the mechanisms involved and assessing the capacity of their implementation in therapeutic strategies aimed at harnessing the benefits of exercise. Obvious applications are decreasing or slowing the onset of various neurodegenerative diseases and overcoming the hardship associated with loss of function following brain and spinal cord injury.

Improved neural function. The brain's ability to adapt in response to challenging situations is known as brain plasticity. Several research fronts indicate that exercise can enhance brain plasticity. Studies have also demonstrated the beneficial effects of exercise on improving or maintaining cognition, especially in aged populations. Human studies involving a large number of subjects have shown that a regular exercise regimen reduces the normal decay of cognitive function observed during aging, and may reduce the risk of developing Alzheimer's disease. If fact, the practice of some form of exercise is becoming common in many senior homes, in hope of reducing the risk of developing cognitive impairments. Exercise can increase the quality of life of individuals by raising levels of alertness to various situations. Studies in animals also indicate that exercise increases the efficacy of learning a spatial memory task.

A robust body of evidence indicates that repetitive locomotor activity can improve functional recovery following different types of injuries to the spinal cord in humans and animals. It appears that functional recovery is highly task-specific, such that rehabilitative strategies that simulate walking are particularly effective in promoting the recovery of locomotion. In addition, even minimal exposure to exercise has been shown to markedly improve the quality of life of individuals with reduced mobility. However, the types of exercise routines that accelerate recovery processes are still unknown.

Neurotrophic factors. Recent advances in the field of molecular biology have helped scientists to understand the mechanisms by which exercise promotes functional changes in the central nervous system. It is now known that the effects of exercise on the brain go beyond simply increasing regional blood supply. In fact, exercise has profound effects on specific molecular systems involved in the regulation of neuroplasticity (**illus.** *a*, *b*). The current view is that exercise, as other types of behavioral manifestations, can activate specific neural circuits by modifying the way information is transmitted across cells at the synapse and by influencing the action of specialized molecules. Indeed, neurotrophins—initially defined as a class of proteins important for the survival, growth, and differentiation of neurons—have emerged as crucial regulators of the synaptic transmission under the influence of exercise. This capacity of neurotrophins to modulate transference of information across the synapse implies that these factors have the potential to serve as molecular intermediates of higher-order functions such as learning and memory. In particular, many studies in animals have shown that the brain-derived neurotrophic factor (BDNF) promotes formation of new synaptic contacts and increases synaptic efficacy. In the hippocampus, a brain region important for memory formation and learning, relative contents of BDNF have a direct effect on a type of cellular memory known as long-term potentiation.

Interestingly, voluntary wheel running in rodents elevates levels of BDNF and synaptic proteins in select regions of the brain and spinal cord (illus. *c*). Recent studies evaluating multiple genes using microarray technology have also revealed that exercise can preferentially influence the expression of molecules that help BDNF to maintain synaptic function. For example, exercise and BDNF affect the synthesis and activity of synapsin I, a vesicle-associated phosphoprotein involved in neurotransmitter release and maintenance of the presynaptic structure. Exercise also upregulates the transcription activator cyclic AMP-responsive element binding protein (CREB), whose action is believed to be necessary for learning and memory formation. Although exer-

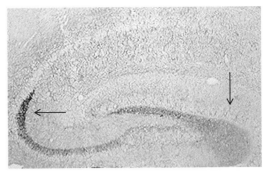

(a)

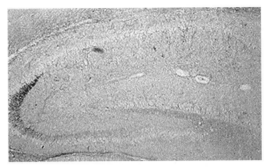

(b)

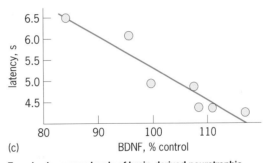

(c)

Exercise increases levels of brain-derived neurotrophic factor, or BDNF, in (a) particular cell groups of the hippocampus (at arrows) relative to (b) sedentary rodents. (c) In order to evaluate the action of BDNF on spatial learning efficiency, animals were tested in a water maze. Proportionally higher levels of BDNF exist in the hippocampus of animals that learn faster.

cise also affects the expression of other neurotrophic factors, according to these multigene studies, BDNF is the only neurotrophic factor found at consistently elevated levels after several weeks of continuous exercise. Studies have also shown that exercise has a selective effect on the synaptic machinery within the hippocampus, and this evidence has provided initial molecular support to previous observations showing the beneficial effects of exercise on cognitive function.

The intrinsic limitation of mature neurons to divide and replace lost neurons has been a dogma in neuroscience until recently. New studies show that there is a significant increase in the number of new neurons in the hippocampal formation of adult rodents in response to voluntary exercise. BDNF also seems to be involved in adult neurogenesis, as BDNF infusion into the brain stimulates neuron formation. Therefore, it appears that exercise is instrumental in activating several mechanisms involved in the maintenance of neural plasticity and health. The capacity of exercise to promote neuronal health can become even more critical under challenging circumstances.

Compensation for diet. There is unequivocal evidence that exercise can provide protection against various diseases such as cancer and diabetes, and the deleterious effects of lifestyle, particularly an unhealthy diet, since dietary factors are considered to be important predictors of the general health of individuals. Recent studies of rodents indicate that a diet rich in saturated fat and refined sugar (HFS), similar in composition to the average diet of members of most industrialized western societies, can threaten neuronal health and reduce the capacity of the brain for learning. These studies have demonstrated that consumption of an HFS diet decreases BDNF, CREB, and synapsin I messenger ribonucleic acid, selectively, in the hippocampus. In addition, the hippocampal expression of the growth-associated protein 43 (GAP-43), important for axonal growth, neurotransmitter release, and learning and memory, is also reduced after consumption of the HFS diet. Furthermore, the HFS diet reduces the capacity of rodents to learn a spatial memory task in a water maze. Interestingly, access to voluntary physical activity for as little as 2 months is sufficient to reverse the effects of the HFS diet. That is, rodents fed the HFS diet that were exposed to exercise did not experience the cognitive decline nor the deficiencies in BDNF, synapsin I, CREB, and GAP-43 seen in sedentary HFS-diet rats. These findings emphasize the value of exercise as a compensatory strategy, functioning to ameliorate the effects of an unhealthy lifestyle on both cognition and neural plasticity.

Spinal cord. Voluntary wheel running and forced treadmill exercise elevate the expression of BDNF and molecules important for synaptic function and neurite outgrowth in the spinal cord and innervated skeletal muscle of rodents. It is likely that neurotrophic factors produced in muscle as a result of exercise can be transported to the spinal cord via motoneuron axons and can help spinal cells. The results of several studies in which BDNF was added to the neural milieu support the possibility that these factors promote survival and growth of brain and spinal cord neurons affected by several types of damage. For example, it has been shown that BDNF administration after midthoracic complete spinal cord transection improves the functional recovery of hindlimb stepping, and these changes appear to be associated with neuronal sprouting at the injury site. Some of the protective effects of exercise on the spinal system recently have been illustrated in the dorsal root ganglion, which can be thought of as a relay station of sensory information going to the spinal cord. In rodent studies, exercising prior to the development of a sciatic nerve lesion has been shown to increase the capacity for regeneration of the severed sciatic nerve. These results have led to cautious speculation that exercise (via neurotrophins) might have the potential to be a suitable therapy to promote functional restoration following injury to the spinal cord in humans.

Conclusions and future research. It is fascinating that in rodents regular exercise can translate into changes in neurotrophic factor expression to help maintain and strengthen neural circuits. Recent advances in the understanding of the mechanisms through which experience can impact neural function can help develop therapies aimed at maximizing the beneficial effects of exercise and neurotrophic factors. Indeed, most of the current therapies, which make use of the ability of neurotrophic factors to help neural function, are based on the exogenous delivery of these factors into the brain or spinal cord. In turn, the induction of neurotrophic factors by physiological means has the advantage of using the intrinsic neurochemistry of brain cells, thereby maximizing physiological effects. For example, the capacity of exercise to compensate for the decrease in hippocampal BDNF levels and poor cognitive function caused by the consumption of a "bad diet" can belong to a general neuroprotective mechanism. Strategies based on neurotrophic factor induction by exercise might one day lead to new treatments for maintaining a healthy brain and facilitating repair processes after trauma or disease.

For background information see ALZHEIMER'S DISEASE; BRAIN; COGNITION; LEARNING MECHANISMS; NEUROBIOLOGY; NEURON; SPINAL CORD in the McGraw-Hill Encyclopedia of Science & Technology.

Fernando Gómez-Pinilla

Bibliography. H. Barbeau et al., Does neurorehabilitation play a role in the recovery of walking in neurological populations?, *Ann. N.Y. Acad. Sci.*, 860: 377–392, 1998; F. W. Booth et al., Waging war on physical inactivity: Using modern molecular ammunition, *J. Appl. Physiol.*, 93(1):3–30, 2002; V. R. Edgerton et al., Retraining the injured spinal cord, *J. Physiol.*, 533.1:15–22, 2001; F. Gómez-Pinilla et al., Exercise up-regulates BDNF mRNA and protein in the spinal cord and skeletal muscle, *Eur. J. Neurosci.*, 13:1078–1084, 2001; F. Gómez-Pinilla et al., Spatial learning and physical activity contribute to the induction of FGF: Neural substrates for increased cognition associated with exercise, *Neuroscience*, 85(1):53–61, 1998; F. Gómez-Pinilla et al., Spatial learning induces trkB and synapsin I mRNAs in the hippocampus, *Brain Res.*, 904:13–19, 2001; F. Gómez-Pinilla et al., Voluntary exercise induces a BDNF-mediated mechanism that promotes neuroplasticity, *J. Neurophysiol.*, 68:2187–2195, 2002; D. Laurin et al., Physical activity and risk of cognitive impairment and dementia in elderly persons, *Arch. Neurol.*, 58:498–504, 2001; R. Molteni et al., A high-fat, refined-sugar diet reduces BDNF, neuronal plasticity, and cognitive function, *Neuroscience*, 112(4): 803–814, 2002; R. Molteni et al., Differential expression of plasticity-related genes in the rat hippocampus after voluntary wheel running, *Eur. J. Neurosci.*, in press; H. Van Praag et al., Neural consequences of environmental enrichment, *Nat. Rev. Neurosci.*, 1:191–198, 2000.

Exotic mesons

In order to properly discuss the exotic mesons, it is necessary to start with a brief account of the standard model of high-energy physics.

Standard model. It was shown early in the twentieth century that, to be consistent with quantum mechanics and the special theory of relativity, the elementary particles must have masses greater than or equal to zero, and that each variety is endowed with a property called spin, which can be either an integer or a half-integer, measured in units of Planck's constant divided by 2π. More specifically, in relativistic quantum mechanics, a one-particle state (or its wave function) has a mass M, with $M > 0$ or $M = 0$, and spin J, where $J = 0, 1/2, 1, 3/2, \ldots$. In addition, the wave function possesses a certain symmetry called parity ($P = \pm 1$) associated with the operation of space inversion through the origin of the coordinate system that has been chosen for use in specifying the wave function. (Space inversion is the simultaneous reflection of all coordinates through the origin, whereby x is replaced by $-x$, y by $-y$, and z by $-z$.) It turns out that the standard model calls for a number of spin-1/2 particles (some with positive parity), all massive, and several spin-1 particles (some with negative parity), both massive and massless. The model is based on a quantum field theory, similar to the quantum theory of electromagnetic interactions (quantum electrodynamics) but extended to encompass a more complex structure. It consists of 12 fields, one for each of the 12 spin-1/2 particles in the model (plus their antiparticle counterparts) and five spin-1 particles (two massless particles—the photon and the gluon—and three massive bosons, W^+, W^-, and Z^0), which interact with the spin-1/2 fields.

Quarks and gluons. Six of the twelve spin-1/2 elementary particles are called quarks, named "up" (u), "down" (d), "strange" (s), "charm" (c), "bottom" (b), and "top" (t) [**Table 1**]. The word "flavor" is used to distinguish one quark from the other. The quarks come with fractional electric charges, measured in units of the electric charge of an electron. For instance, the electric charges Q for u and d are $Q_u = +2/3$, $Q_d = -1/3$. The quark masses vary widely;

the lightest is the up quark at less than 5 MeV; the next lightest is the down quark at less than 10 MeV; and the heaviest is the top quark at around 175,000 MeV. (For comparison, the proton mass is about 938 MeV.)

There is one massless spin-1 particle, called the gluon (g), which interacts with all the quarks and their antiparticle partners through interchange of a property called color charge, analogous to the electric charge which governs the electromagnetic interactions. So each of the six quarks comes in three colors, and its antiparticle partner in three anticolors, while the gluons come in eight combinations of colors and anticolors. The field theory which describes these "strong" interactions is called quantum chromodynamics (QCD).

Hadrons. Five of the six quarks (all of them except the top quark) constitute the building blocks for a class of particles known as hadrons. For instance, protons and neutrons are thought to be bound states of three quarks ($p = uud$ and $n = udd$), and the Λ particle is also a three-quark bound system ($\Lambda = uds$). The bound states of three quarks, such as p, n, and Λ, form a class of hadrons called the baryons (**Table 2**).

Another class of hadrons, called the mesons, are bound states of a quark and an antiquark. Thus, a ρ meson with positive charge is $\rho^+ = u\bar{d}$, while a negative K meson is $K^- = \bar{u}s$. Another example is the J/ψ, which is a bound state of $c\bar{c}$.

All hadrons are unstable, except the proton, which has a mean lifetime greater than 10^{25} years. Let q stand for any of the five quarks u, d, c, s, and b. It is now possible to define precisely two classes of hadrons: a baryon, which is a qqq bound state, and a meson, which is a $q\bar{q}$ bound state.

Energy into mass. If the u and d quarks have masses less than 10 MeV, an obvious question is how the proton, a composite of two u quarks and a d quark, can have a mass of 938 MeV. Likewise, the ρ meson mass of 770 MeV requires explanation. The answer lies in the special theory of relativity in which energy E and mass M are equivalent through Albert Einstein's formula $E = Mc^2$, where c is the speed of light in vacuum. Since a particle has kinetic energy by virtue of its motion, such motion generates mass; moreover, since the particle's kinetic energy depends on the reference frame in which the particle's velocity is measured, so does its mass. In the reference frame in

TABLE 2. Sample baryons

Name	Quarks	Charge	I	J^P	Mass, MeV
p	uud	+1	$\frac{1}{2}$	$\frac{1}{2}^+$	938.27200±0.00004
n	udd	0	$\frac{1}{2}$	$\frac{1}{2}^+$	939.56533±0.00004
Δ^{++}	uuu	+2	$\frac{3}{2}$	$\frac{3}{2}^+$	1230–1234
Σ^+	uus	+1	1	$\frac{1}{2}^+$	1189.37±0.07
Λ	uds	0	0	$\frac{1}{2}^+$	1115.683±0.006
Ω^-	sss	−1	0	$\frac{3}{2}^+$	1672.45±0.29

TABLE 1. Quarks

Name	Charge	I^*	J^P	Mass, MeV
u	$+\frac{2}{3}$	$\frac{1}{2}$	$\frac{1}{2}^+$	1–5
d	$-\frac{1}{3}$	$\frac{1}{2}$	$\frac{1}{2}^+$	3–9
c	$+\frac{2}{3}$	0	$\frac{1}{2}^+$	1150–1350
s	$-\frac{1}{3}$	0	$\frac{1}{2}^+$	75–170
t	$+\frac{2}{3}$	0	$\frac{1}{2}^+$	174,300–5100
b	$-\frac{1}{3}$	0	$\frac{1}{2}^+$	4000–4400

*I refers to isotopic spin, defined in text.

TABLE 3. Sample mesons

Name	Quarks	$I^G\,(J^{PC})$	Mass, MeV	Width, MeV	Major decay
π^+	$u\bar{d}$	$1^-(0^{-+})$	$139.57018-0.00035$	$(2.5284-0.0005)\times10^{-14}$	$\mu^+\nu_\mu$
π^-	$\bar{u}d$	$1^-(0^{-+})$	$139.57018-0.00035$	$(2.5284-0.0005)\times10^{-14}$	$\mu^-\bar{\nu}_\mu$
ρ^+ (770)	$u\bar{d}$	$1^+(1^{--})$	$769.3-0.8$	$150.2-0.8$	$\pi^+\pi^0$
ρ^- (770)	$\bar{u}d$	$1^+(1^{--})$	$769.3-0.8$	$150.2-0.8$	$\pi^-\pi^0$
ϕ (1020)	$s\bar{s}$	$0^-(1^{--})$	$1019.417-0.014$	$4.458-0.032$	$(K\bar{K})^0$
a_2^+ (1320)	$u\bar{d}$	$1^-(2^{++})$	$1318.0-0.6$	$107-5$	$(\rho\pi)^+$
a_2^- (1320)	$\bar{u}d$	$1^-(2^{++})$	$1318.0-0.6$	$107-5$	$(\rho\pi)^-$

which the proton or the ρ is at rest, the quarks (u, d, or $\bar{d}$) are in a state of motion, which generates mass. Moreover, the color field of the gluons g that bind them has its own energy, which is again transformed into mass. The mass shift due to these energies is very large indeed; without it, the proton or the ρ would have masses less than 20 and 15 MeV—instead of 938 and 770 MeV—respectively. It is not surprising, therefore, that the term "strong interactions" is used to describe the physics of quantum chromodynamics.

Role of gluons. So the gluons g play an important role in the makeup of hadrons, but it is a curious experimental fact that gluons remain hidden when the hadrons are studied in their rest frame. Thus, a successful phenomenological model of hadrons has been developed in which the quark masses are replaced by their so-called constituent masses of roughly 300 MeV for both the u and d quarks (and the same mass for their antiparticle partners).

In the "static" limit, in which the hadrons are studied in their rest frames, is it possible that nature allows for a hadron whereby the gluons g play a more active role (valence gluons) and are not hidden (virtual gluons)? To be more specific, can a meson exist whose constituents are ($q\bar{q} + g$) or even ($g + g$)? Or, for that matter, can a four-quark meson ($q\bar{q} + q\bar{q}$) exist? The answer is "yes." There are tantalizing hints that these exotic (or non-$q\bar{q}$) mesons do exist. But much work remains to be done before the nature of the exotic mesons is fully understood.

Quantum numbers I and C. It is necessary to introduce some additional concepts before discussing exotic mesons. Table 1 shows that u and d quarks come with $I = 1/2$, and all others with $I = 0$. The I stands for the isotopic spin, similar to the spin introduced above. (The same I applies to antiparticles.) The simplest way to explain this concept is to state that u and d quarks are each a different manifestation of the single object n_q, and n_q has the isotopic spin $I = 1/2$. This concept is useful because the strong interactions conserve I. Any reaction or decay process mediated by the strong interaction must have the same I in the initial and the final states. In addition, any hadron which is made up of one, two, or three of the doublet $n_q = \{u, d\}$ or $\bar{n}_q = \{\bar{u}, \bar{d}\}$ will be endowed with $I = 0$, 1/2, 1, or 3/2 (Table 2).

Finally, there is the concept of C, the quantum number corresponding to particle-antiparticle conjugation. The wave function for a neutral, unflavored particle is in an eigenstate of the C operation, that is,

$C = \pm 1$. For an unflavored $q\bar{q}$ meson, it is also convenient to define an additional quantity called the G-parity, which may be expressed, for the purpose of this article, by $G = C(-)^I$ where $I = 0$ or 1. The π's are said to have $G = -1$ regardless of their electric charge, whereas the ρ's have $G = +1$. If a particle in a given G decays via the strong interaction, it must decay into a final state with the same G. A few examples of conventional, that is, nonexotic, mesons are given in **Table 3**.

Searches for exotic mesons. The search for exotic mesons, that is, non-$q\bar{q}$ mesons, has a long history. More than a quarter century ago theorists predicted that exotic mesons should exist in the form of a multiquark state ($q\bar{q} + q\bar{q}$) or glueballs ($g + g$ or $g + g + g$; no "valence" quarks). More recently, theorists predicted that there should exist hybrid mesons ($q\bar{q} + g$). The predicted masses range from 1.0 to over 2.5 GeV, which is where most of the conventional mesons are found experimentally. This makes unambiguous identification of the exotic mesons very difficult indeed. It turns out that $q\bar{q}$ mesons cannot come with the combinations $J^{PC} = 0^{--}, 0^{+-}, 1^{-+}, 2^{+-}, 3^{-+}, 4^{+-}$, and so forth, because of certain rules derived from relativistic quantum mechanics. Most recent experimental progress in the search for exotic mesons has been made in this sector of J^{PC}-exotic mesons.

Glueball searches. Experimental glueball candidates exist for $J^{PC} = 0^{++}$ (scalar) and 2^{++} (tensor) mesons. Quantum chromodynamics (based on the lattice-gauge theory) predicts that the scalar glueballs should be the lightest, at a mass of around 1.8 GeV, while the tensor glueballs are higher in mass, at about 2.2 GeV. The problem here is that most conventional mesons of the same J^{PC} will mix with the glueballs (a well-known quantum-mechanical effect), so an unambiguous identification is very difficult. Nevertheless, the scalar mesons listed in **Table 4** may be considered to be a mixture of conventional scalar

TABLE 4. $J^{PC} = 0^{++}$ (scalar) mesons (glueball candidates)

Name	Mass, MeV	Width, MeV	Decay(s)
$f_0(400-1200)$	$400-1200$	$600-1000$	$\pi\pi$
$f_0(1370)$	$1200-1500$	$200-500$	$\pi\pi\pi\pi$
$f_0(1500)$	1500 ± 10	112 ± 10	$\pi\pi$, $K\bar{K}$, $\eta\eta$, $\eta\eta'$, $\pi\pi\pi\pi$
$f_0(1710)$	1715 ± 7	125 ± 12	KK, $\eta\eta$, $\pi\pi$

TABLE 5. $J^{PC} = 2^{++}$ (tensor) mesons (glueball candidates)

Name	Mass, MeV	Width, MeV	Decay
$f_2(2010)$	2011^{+60}_{-80}	202 ± 60	$\phi\phi$
$f_2(2300)$	2297 ± 28	149 ± 40	$\phi\phi$
$f_2(2340)$	2339 ± 60	319^{+80}_{-70}	$\phi\phi$

TABLE 6. $J^{PC} = 0^{++}$ (scalar) mesons (KK states)

Name	$I^G (J^{PC})$	Mass (MeV)	Width (MeV)	Decay(s)
$a_0(980)$	$1^-(0^{++})$	$984.8 - 1.4$	$50 - 100$	$\eta\pi, K\bar{K}$
$f_0(980)$	$0^+(0^{++})$	$980 - 10$	$40 - 100$	$\pi\pi, K\bar{K}$

mesons and the scalar glueball. Some phenomenologists suggest that the $f_0(1500)$ should have the highest glueball content.

Table 5 lists tensor glueball candidates. These states were first seen in the process $\pi\pi \to \phi\phi$. The π is an $n_q\bar{n}_q$ state, whereas the ϕ is thought to be mostly $s\bar{s}$. Therefore, the reaction can occur only through quark-pair annihilation and creation, through two (or more) gluons. In other words, the process $\pi\pi \to g + g \to \phi\phi$ goes through an intermediate state $g + g$, which should be a glueball. It is not understood why there are three candidates; in any event, since ordinary tensor mesons can mix with the glueball, it is unlikely that all three are glueballs. The middle state has recently been seen in the process $\bar{p}p \to \phi\phi$, which may again proceed via a two-gluon intermediate state.

$K\bar{K}$ system. Two additional exotic-meson candidates in the scalar sector are listed in **Table 6**. The most distinguishing characteristic of these two mesons is that both have a prominent decay mode into $K\bar{K}$, with their masses very close to the $K\bar{K}$ threshold. As a result, they have long been considered to be bound states of the $K\bar{K}$ molecule (or a multiquark system, that is, $n_q\bar{n}_q + s\bar{s}$). The strange particles K or $\bar{K}$ have isotopic spin $I = 1/2$, so a $K\bar{K}$ system can occur with $I = 1$ or $I = 0$. This explains the two states listed above.

Exotic hybrid mesons. A meson with the quantum numbers $I^G (J^{PC}) = 1^-(1^{-+})$ has J^{PC} belonging to the exotic series listed earlier, so it cannot be a $q\bar{q}$ state. In addition, since $I = 1$ for the meson, it cannot be a glueball. (A gluon is flavorless; that is, $I = 0$.) So it can be either $q\bar{q} + g$ or $q\bar{q} + q\bar{q}$ but not a conventional $q\bar{q}$ meson. Such a state is called a hybrid meson. Two exotic hybrids have been reported so far. The first to be studied, the $\pi_1(1400)$ at mass 1.4 GeV, decays into $\eta\pi$ and is seen in four data sets (**Table 7**).

The Brookhaven National Laboratory results come from studies of the reaction

$$\pi^- p \text{ (at 18 GeV)} \to \pi_1^-(1400)\, p \to \eta\pi^- p$$

while the Crystal Barrel observations are based on

the reactions

$$\bar{p}n \text{ (at rest)} \to [\pi_1(1400)\pi]^- \to \eta\pi^-\pi^0$$
$$pp \text{ (at rest)} \to \pi_1^0(1400)\pi^0 \to \eta\pi^0\eta^0$$

The analysis techniques involved in these two reactions are so different—to say nothing of the fact that the data sets come from two very different detectors, one at Brookhaven National Laboratory on Long Island, New York, and the other at CERN in Geneva, Switzerland—that the existence of an exotic hybrid, the $\pi_1(1400)$, appears to be firmly established.

Another exotic hybrid, the $\pi_1(1600)$, has also been reported. Again, it is seen in two different experiments, one at Brookhaven National Laboratory and the other at the Vertex Spectrometer (VES) at the Institute for High-Energy Physics in Protvino, Russia. The results are summarized in **Table 8**.

Both experiments see the exotic meson in the decay $\eta'\pi$ very strongly, but its evidence is somewhat weak in the decay $\rho\pi$. There are indications, in addition, that the $\pi_1(1600)$ couples to other decay modes such as $b_1(1235)\pi$ or $f_1(1285)\pi$.

TABLE 7. Parameters for π_1 (1400) $\to \eta\pi$

Experiment	Mass, MeV[*]	Width, MeV[*]
Brookhaven National Laboratory (1994)	$1370 - 16^{+50}_{-30}$	$385 - 40^{+65}_{-105}$
Brookhaven National Laboratory (1995)	1359^{+16+10}_{-14-24}	314^{+31+9}_{-29-66}
Crystal Barrel	$1400 - 20 - 20$	$310 - 50^{+50}_{-30}$
Crystal Barrel	$1360 - 25$	$220 - 90$

[*]The first errors are statistical and the second errors are systematic.

TABLE 8. Parameters for π_1 (1600)

Experiment	Mass, MeV[*]	Width, MeV[*]	Decay
Brookhaven National Laboratory	$1593 - 8^{+20}_{-47}$	$168 - 20^{+150}_{-12}$	$\rho\pi$
Brookhaven National Laboratory	$1597 - 10^{+45}_{-10}$	$340 - 40 - 50$	$\eta'\pi$
Vertex Spectrometer	$1610 - 20$	$290 - 30$	$\rho\pi, \eta'\pi$

[*]The first errors are statistical and the second errors are systematic.

Thus, there are two solid candidates for an exotic hybrid, $\pi_1(1400) \to \eta\pi$ and $\pi_1(1600) \to \eta'\pi$. The discovery of exotic mesons is only beginning, and there is much to learn. A recent quantum chromodynamics calculation (based on the lattice-gauge theory) predicts a mass of 1.9 ± 0.2 GeV for a J^{PC}-exotic gluonic hybrid ($q\bar{q} + g$), but the exotic mesons experimentally are found at 1.4 and 1.6 GeV. It is not yet known if this apparent discrepancy is because of a flaw (calculational or theoretical) in the quantum-chromodynamics predictions or because the current experimental states are of the four-quark variety ($q\bar{q} + q\bar{q}$), in which case a gluonic hybrid at a higher mass is still to be discovered.

For background information *see* ELEMENTARY PAR-
TICLE; GLUONS; I-SPIN; MESON; PARITY (QUANTUM ME-
CHANICS); QUANTUM CHROMODYNAMICS; QUARKS;
RELATIVITY; STANDARD MODEL in the McGraw-Hill
Encyclopedia of Science & Technology.

Suh-Urk Chung

Bibliography. F. E. Close and P. R. Page, Glueballs,
Sci. Amer., 279(5):80–85, November 1998; A. R.
Dzierba, C. A. Meyer, and E. S. Swanson, The search
for QCD exotics, *Amer. Scientist*, 88:406, 2000; Mini-
reviews on "Non-$q\bar{q}$ Candidates" by C. Amsler,
p. 682, and "Scalar Mesons" by S. Spanier and N. A.
Törnqvist, p. 437, Review of Particle Physics, Particle
Data Group, *Eur. Phys. J.*, C15:1, 2000; F. Wilczek,
Mass without mass I, *Phys. Today*, 52(11):11,
November 1999; F. Wilcek, Mass without mass II,
Phys. Today, 53(1):13, January 2000.

Extrasolar planets

The study of extrasolar planets has become one of
the most active fields of research in astronomy since
the discovery in 1995 of several giant planets orbiting nearby stars similar to the Sun. There have been
many unexpected results, and the progress has been
remarkable. More than 100 planets are now known,
many of them in systems of two or more bodies orbiting the same star. In one case it has even been
possible to detect the atmosphere of the planet as it
transits between us and its star.

Indirect versus direct detection. Someday it may be
possible to produce direct images of planets using
space missions now in the conceptual design phase.
This is beyond current technical capabilities because
planets are so much fainter than their parent stars.
All of the recent planet detections have been indirect, relying on the slight motion induced in the
parent star by the gravitational pull of the unseen
planet. Nearly all of the discoveries have relied on
very precise measurements of the star's motion back
and forth along the line of sight, using spectrographs
to measure the Doppler shifts. So far there is only
one convincing case, Gliese 876, where the star's
orbital motion in the plane of the sky, across the
line of sight, has been accurately measured. Called
astrometry, this approach holds great promise for
the future, after space missions now being designed
are launched. The Doppler technique is most sensitive for planets in short-period orbits close to their
parent stars, while astrometry is better suited for
studies of planets with longer periods in wider orbits.
Thus, the two techniques complement each other.

Orbital inclination and planetary masses. A major advantage of astrometry is that it can determine the inclination of the planet's orbit, namely how much the
plane of the orbit is tilted compared to the line of
sight. In contrast, the orbital inclination cannot be
derived from Doppler shifts alone. As a result, there
is a fundamental ambiguity for nearly all the planets
discovered so far: Their masses are not known. We
can say what the minimum mass of the planet would
be if the orbit happens to be viewed edge-on, but it

could also be a much more massive planet in an orbit
that is viewed nearly face-on. This is why the discovery of the first transiting planet was so significant.
Because the planet orbiting the star HD 209458 was
seen to pass in front of the star, its orbit was known to
be almost exactly edge-on. The transit observations
showed that at least one of the planets discovered
using Doppler shifts was indeed a giant planet rather
similar to Jupiter, but in an entirely different orbit
very close to its parent star.

Unexpected results. When only one planetary system was known, namely that of the Sun, it was natural to suppose that other systems would resemble
ours. The large gas giants would have wide outer
orbits, because they could form only far from the parent star, where it was cold enough for vast amounts
of planetary material to condense out. All the planets
would have nearly circular orbits as observed for our
system, presumably because they formed in a flattened disk; and the largest planet could not be much
larger than Jupiter. Thus, the first planet candidate
discovered using Doppler shifts was viewed with
widespread skepticism when it was announced in
1989. With a period of 84 days it was impossibly close
to its parent star, HD 114762; its orbit was much too
elongated; and it was at least 10 times more massive
than Jupiter. Then in 1995 numerous new planets
began to be reported, starting with the discovery of
a planet orbiting 51 Pegasi with a 4-day period. Extrasolar planets are now known that are more massive,
have more elongated orbits, and are much closer to
their parent stars than the one orbiting HD 114762.

Orbital migration. To explain how some of the
giant planets end up orbiting so close to their parent stars, most experts favor the idea that gas giants
must form much farther out, in the ice condensation zone, and thus they must migrate inward after
they form. One way to accomplish migration is a
gravitation drag between the newly formed planet
and the remains of the disk that it formed: the drag
causes the planet's orbit to spiral inward. Another
possible mechanism is to form several planets in the
ice condensation zone, with gravitational encounters, almost like billiard balls, sending one of the
planets close to the parent star while flinging others into more distant orbits. A mystery that remains
is why the known planets tend to pile up at periods
of 3 or 4 days, with none shorter.

Systems of planets. The first planets to be discovered were the easiest. They induced large Doppler
shifts in the spectra of their parent stars because they
were big and had orbits with short periods. Planet
hunters pay special attention to stars where the easiest planet has already been discovered. The goal is to
find additional planets orbiting the same star and to
learn more about planetary systems. Several systems
of two and even three planets have been discovered,
but so far none of them bear a close resemblence to
our own solar system. For example, the three planets
orbiting upsilon Andromedae have periods of 4.6,
241, and 1266 days, and all have masses similar to
Jupiter. This does not leave any room in the star's
habitable zone for a small planet like the Earth. The

Doppler technique has now improved, and the time spanned by the observations has lengthened to the point where it is possible to pick up extrasolar planets truly like Jupiter, not only in mass but also with an orbital period similar to Jupiter's 12 years. The recent detection of a massive outer planet in the 55 Cancri system with a period of 14 years is a good example.

Toward finding Earths. Although the number of detected extrasolar planets continues to grow at a steady rate, the frequency is still fairly low. Only a few percent of the stars surveyed so far are known to have planets. Presumably this fraction will continue to rise as search techniques improve and we extend the detections to smaller planets and wider orbits. But Doppler spectroscopy cannot be expected to detect Earth-like planets orbiting in the habitable zones of solar-type stars. Effects such as convective motions near the surface of the star, or star spots combined with stellar rotation, can cause spurious Doppler shifts much larger than the Earth would induce. Remarkably, a system of Earth-sized planets has already been discovered in orbit around a pulsar, the remnant of a supernova explosion, using the extraordinarily precise timing of the radio pulses to deduce the displacement of the spinning neutron star induced by the planets. Of course, there is much more interest in finding habitable planets orbiting stars like the Sun. Perhaps the most promising technique for finding other Earths is to search for transiting systems.

Transiting planets. The orbits of extrasolar planets are thought to be randomly oriented in space; it is therefore uncommon for the Earth to lie very near a planet's orbital plane. But if it does, then once during each planetary orbit the planet crosses the disk of its parent star, blocking out some of the star's light. These events are called transits. They play an important role in studying extrasolar planets, because they make it possible to measure properties, such as the planet's size, that are otherwise unobservable.

The likelihood of an orbital alignment that allows transits increases with decreasing orbital radius. For planets such as the one orbiting the solar-type star 51 Pegasi, the chance of a good alignment is about 1 in 10; for a planet orbiting at the Earth's distance, it is only 1 in 200. The fraction of a star's light blocked by its transiting planet depends on the relative sizes of the star and the planet; a hypothetical distant observer watching Jupiter pass in front of the Sun would see a brightness dip of about 1%, whereas the Earth would yield only 0.01%.

HD 209458. Just one transiting extrasolar planet is known—that circling the star HD 209458. The planet was first detected using radial velocity observations, and soon after was found by two independent teams to show the brightness dips that characterize transits. The observed transits decrease the star's brightness by 1.6%, last for 3 hours, and occur every 3.52 days. The transit signal is strong enough that one of the detections was performed with a telescope of only 4-in. (0.1-m) aperture, and transits of

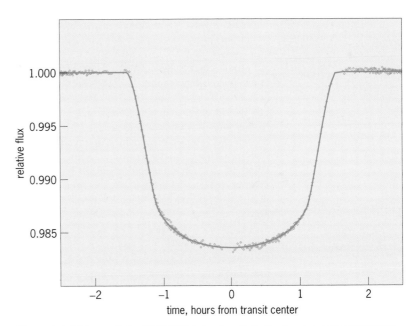

Change in brightness of star HD 209458 during transits by its planet, measured in yellow light (wavelength near 600 nm) using the Hubble Space Telescope.

HD 209458 have now been observed by several amateur astronomers, also using small telescopes.

Precise brightness measurements with the Hubble Space Telescope allow important characteristics of the planet to be inferred with considerable accuracy (see **illus.**). The orbital inclination may be determined from the shape of the light variation, so that radial velocity wobble measurements can yield the planet's true mass, relative to the parent star. The fractional dimming of starlight during the transit gives the planet's radius. Knowing these two quantities, the planet's density can be calculated, which in turn implies something about its composition and history. Finally, during the transit a small portion (less than 0.1%) of the star's light passes through the outer parts of the planetary atmosphere. Atoms and molecules found there absorb the star's light at some wavelengths but not at others, imprinting a signal on the light that carries information about conditions in the atmosphere.

For the planet of HD 209458, the transit data imply that the planet's mass is 0.69 Jupiter mass, its radius is 1.35 times Jupiter's, and its density is just 0.35 times that of water. This density is much less than that of Saturn, which is the least dense planet in our solar system. This probably means that it is composed almost entirely of hydrogen and helium, and that its interior never cooled from the high temperatures that prevailed just after the planet formed. For this to be so, the planet must have reached its present orbital distance, 0.05 astronomical unit from its parent star, within a few million years after its formation. The spectrum of light transmitted through the planet's atmosphere reveals small amounts of sodium vapor. Sodium is commonly observed in the outer layers of Sun-like stars; its presence in the planet is consistent with the idea that extrasolar planets are composed of a starlike mix of elements. Using similar methods but observing compounds such as water, methane, and carbon monoxide, prospects are good for a more complete characterization of the planet's atmosphere.

Searching for habitable planets. Besides helping to characterize planets found by other methods, transits provide an efficient way to detect new planets. Present-day imaging detectors make it possible to measure the brightness of tens or hundreds of thousands of stars at once, taking one reading every few minutes for months at a time. Stars with transiting planets may then be recognized by the presence of repetitive short-lived dips in their apparent brightness. Several ground-based transit search experiments are now using this technique to search for Jupiter-sized planets in small-radius orbits. These experiments are ultimately limited by the Earth's atmosphere, which compromises the accuracy of the brightness measurements, and hence makes small planets unobservable. Telescopes in space would have no such limitation; several space missions to detect Earth-sized planets in Earth-like orbits are now in the planning stages. The most ambitious of these is NASA's Kepler mission, which aims to observe about 100,000 stars continuously for 4 years. If planets like the Earth are common around Sun-like stars, this mission should identify dozens of them during its lifetime. This mission and others like it will likely provide the first clues as to whether solar systems like our own are common or rare in our part of the Milky Way Galaxy.

For background information *see* PLANET; SOLAR SYSTEM in the McGraw-Hill Encyclopedia of Science & Technology.   David Latham; Timothy Brown

Bibliography. L. R. Doyle, H.-J. Deeg, and J. M. Jenkins, Discovering worlds in transit, *Astronomy*, 29(3):38–43, March 2001; B. G. Levi, Sodium detected in the atmosphere of an extrasolar planet, *Phys. Today*, 55(4):19–21, April 2002; J. I. Lunine, The occurrence of Jovian planets and the habitability of planetary systems, *Proc. Nat. Acad. Sci. USA*, 98(3):809–814, January 30, 2001.

Far-ultraviolet astronomy

The *Far Ultraviolet Spectroscopic Explorer* (*FUSE*) is studying a wide range of astronomical problems in the 90.5–118.7-nanometer wavelength region through the use of high-resolution spectroscopy. The *FUSE* bandpass forms a nearly optimal complement to the spectral coverage provided by the Hubble Space Telescope, which extends down to about 117 nm. The photoionization threshold of atomic hydrogen (91.1 nm) sets a natural short-wavelength limit for the far ultraviolet. *FUSE* was launched in June 1999 from Cape Canaveral, Florida, on a Delta II rocket into a 768-km (477-mi) circular orbit. Scientific observations started later that year.

FUSE uses several unique design features (**Fig. 1**). Instead of a single telescope mirror, *FUSE* has four mirror segments to reflect the light to a focus. The instrument has two nearly identical halves, and in

each half one mirror is coated with silicon carbide and the other with aluminum and lithium fluoride in order to optimize the instrument's performance over the entire *FUSE* bandpass. The focused light from each mirror passes through a small aperture at the focal plane and is then reflected by a diffraction grating that spreads the light out into a spectrum that is recorded by a special electronic detector.

The spectral region studied by *FUSE* is extremely rich in spectral diagnostics of astrophysical gases over a wide range of temperatures (100 K to over 10^7 K). Important strong spectral lines in this wavelength range include those of neutral hydrogen, deuterium, nitrogen, oxygen, and argon (H I, D I, N I, O I, and Ar I), molecular hydrogen (H_2), five-times ionized oxygen (O VI), and several ionization states of sulfur (S III–S VI). These elements are essential for understanding the origin and evolution of the chemical elements, the formation of stars and the solar system, and the structure of galaxies, including the Milky Way Galaxy.

FUSE is one of the National Aeronautics and Space Administration's (NASA) Explorer missions and a cooperative project of NASA and the space agencies of Canada and France. These missions are smaller

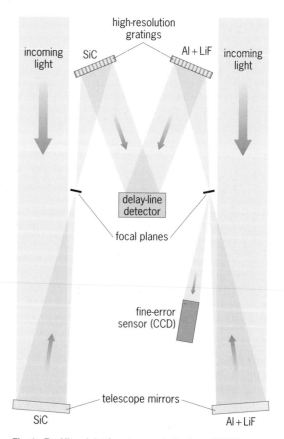

Fig. 1. *Far Ultraviolet Spectroscopic Explorer* (*FUSE*) instrument. It has two nearly identical halves, one of which is shown. One mirror is coated with silicon carbide (SiC) and the other with aluminum (Al) and lithium fluoride (LiF). The fine-error charge-coupled-device (CCD) sensor views light reflected from the focal plane to perform target acquisition and maintain precision pointing during the observations.

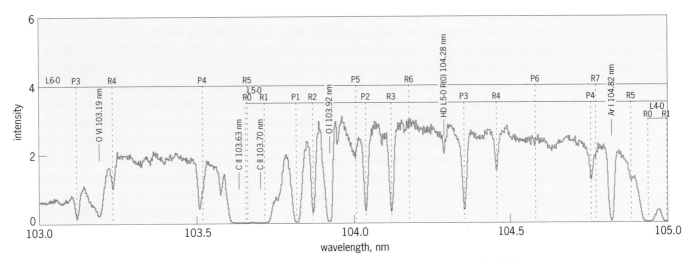

Fig. 2. Part of the *FUSE* spectrum of the star HD 93222, a very hot massive star in the constellation Carina, about 2400 parsecs (7500 light-years) from the Earth. All of the absorption features are due to gas in the interstellar medium between the Earth and the star, illustrating the richness of the far-ultraviolet spectrum for studying interstellar gas over a wide range of temperatures, from O VI (at 500,000 K) to molecular hydrogen (at 100 K). Vertical broken lines mark approximate locations of the lines of molecular hydrogen (H_2). The most important atomic feature is the O VI line at 103.19 nm. Other strong atomic lines (C II, O I, Ar I) and a line of the HD molecule are indicated.

and more scientifically focused than the larger observatories such as Hubble and Chandra. *FUSE* was designed, built, and operated for NASA by the Department of Physics and Astronomy at Johns Hopkins University. Hundreds of astronomers worldwide are using *FUSE* for a wide range of scientific research.

Most of this research uses absorption spectroscopy to investigate the properties of clouds of gas in the Milky Way Galaxy and beyond. This technique detects the gas using a more distant star or other object as a background light source. The foreground material imposes its own spectroscopic signature on the far-ultraviolet spectrum of the background object (**Fig. 2**). This signature can reveal information about the chemical composition of the gas, its temperature, density, and motion toward or away from the observer. *FUSE* observations are capable of distinguishing motions as small as 10 km/s (6 mi/s).

Hot gas in galaxies. The O VI ion is an essential diagnostic of hot gas in many astrophysical plasmas. It is most abundant at temperatures of about 3×10^5 K, but may be present in significant quantities up to 10^6 K. Because oxygen is the most abundant element in the universe after hydrogen and helium, spectral lines of O VI are often much stronger than those of similar ions of carbon or nitrogen.

The presence of a halo of hot gas surrounding the Milky Way Galaxy was predicted in the early 1950s and first detected in the 1980s. However, observations of O VI absorption toward over 100 distant stars and extragalactic sources such as quasars have revealed this halo as never before. A distribution of highly ionized gas is found extending several thousand light-years above and below the plane of the Galaxy. Hot gas traced by O VI is present in virtually all directions studied. This hot gas is detected flowing out of the Milky Way in some directions and

falling into the Galaxy in others. This halo of hot material is direct evidence that supernovae, the explosions of massive stars, heat the interstellar medium of the Galaxy, expelling material away from the Galaxy, where it cools and then falls back. The amount of hot gas in the galactic halo is extremely irregular, with large variations in its concentration over angular scales as small as $0.1°$.

From the analysis of *FUSE* spectra of many distant quasars and active galactic nuclei, astronomers have also discovered a second, more distant reservoir of hot gas associated with the Milky Way Galaxy and nearby galaxies. O VI absorption associated with the high-velocity clouds implies the existence of a galactic corona extending over 100,000 light-years from the Sun. These clouds are moving at high speeds, over 150 km/s (90 mi/s) relative to the Sun. For example, the Magellanic Stream is a trail of tidal debris torn from the Magellanic Clouds, two satellite galaxies of the Milky Way, with a distance of over 100,000 light-years from the Sun. A high-velocity cloud in the northern sky known as Complex C is at least 30,000 light-years from the Sun. Gas in the high-velocity clouds is primarily neutral or singly ionized, far too cool for O VI to be produced internally. Analysis shows that O VI is being produced by the collision of these clouds with a hot, very rarefied gas far from the Milky Way Galaxy, in the same way as a streak of a meteor is created when a small particle collides with the Earth's upper atmosphere. The galactic corona may be associated with a very extended galactic corona or hot intergalactic gas associated with the Local Group of galaxies, left over from their formation billions of years ago.

FUSE observations of many hot, massive stars in the Magellanic Clouds show how the rate of star formation, mass, metallicity, and other properties of a galaxy influence their hot interstellar gas content.

(Metallicity refers to the proportion, relative to hydrogen, of elements heavier than hydrogen and helium that are present in a particular object or cloud of gas.) The hot gas in the Large Magellanic Cloud, the nearest galaxy to the Milky Way, has properties similar to those of the Milky Way, even though the Large Magellanic Cloud's oxygen abundance is about 40% that of the Sun. Hot gas in the Large Magellanic Cloud is extended vertically, perhaps very similar to that found in the Milky Way halo. The hot gas in the Small Magellanic Cloud appears to be present in greater concentrations than the average of the Milky Way halo, even though the Small Magellanic Cloud's oxygen abundance is only about 20% that of the Sun. Unlike the Large Magellanic Cloud, which exhibits strong O VI over the entire Galaxy, the production of hot gas in the Small Magellanic Cloud is strongly dominated by star-forming regions.

Deuterium. Hydrogen, deuterium, helium, and some lithium were the only elements formed in the big bang. Stars derive their energy from nuclear fusion reactions that convert lighter elements to heavier ones, for example hydrogen to helium. In the process of this hydrogen burning, deuterium, an isotope of hydrogen, is also converted to helium. This process is so efficient that all the deuterium initially present in a star is destroyed. Therefore, there are no appreciable sources of deuterium other than the big bang. This makes deuterium a nuclear fossil of the early universe and a sensitive indicator of the degree to which a given amount of gas has been affected by stellar nuclear processing. Understanding the abundance ratio of deuterium relative to hydrogen (D/H) in the Milky Way Galaxy is one of the primary objectives of the *FUSE* mission. The D/H ratio is very uniform with an abundance of about 15 deuterium atoms per million hydrogen atoms in the interstellar medium within about 300 light-years of the Sun, a region referred to as the Local Bubble. However, based on the *FUSE* measurements combined with other high-quality D/H measurements from the Hubble Space Telescope and earlier missions, the D/H ratio beyond about 300 light-years appears to be highly variable. Stellar nuclear processing that destroys deuterium also creates oxygen, so an anticorrelation between deuterium and oxygen might be expected. However, no such correlation was found. The contrast between the homogeneity in D/H in the Local Bubble and its nonuniformity outside it highlights the need for better understanding of element production, dispersal, mixing, and evolution of interstellar gas inside the Milky Way Galaxy.

Molecular hydrogen. The molecule H_2 is the most abundant molecule in the Milky Way Galaxy and the primary raw material for the formation of new stars. *FUSE* measurements of H_2 are providing a detailed picture of previously undetected cold molecular gas in the galactic halo. The detection of H_2 in high-velocity clouds is correlated with the presence there of interstellar dust. Without the surfaces of dust grains, H_2 cannot form in appreciable quantities. This is because the reaction $H + H \rightarrow H_2$ is exothermic,

and is therefore very unlikely to occur as a gas-phase collision in interstellar space. The dust content of the clouds is, in turn, determined from their iron abundance. In interstellar gases with sufficient metallicity, iron is systematically used in the formation of new dust grains, but there is insufficient iron and other elements to form dust grains in very low metallicity gas. In particular, clouds with elemental abundances of oxygen greater than 30% of that of the Sun have observable amounts of H_2 and interstellar dust. On the other hand, Complex C has very low metallicity (oxygen abundance 10% that of the Sun) and has no detectable H_2 or dust.

Planets and proto-planetary systems. The young star Beta Pictoris is well known for its large circumstellar disk of dust and gas, 3×10^4 km (2×10^4 mi) in diameter, that has given hints that planets may be forming (or recently formed) deep within. *FUSE* observations of the star revealed two surprises. First, O VI emission close to the star indicates that very energetic phenomena are taking place. Second, the *FUSE* spectrum of Beta Pictoris lacked any evidence for H_2 absorption in the far ultraviolet from the gas in the circumstellar disk. This absorption was expected because carbon monoxide (CO), a molecule much less abundant than H_2, was detected in Beta Pictoris by Hubble. The absence of H_2 along the sight line through the Beta Pictoris disk suggests that the H_2 and CO are locked in a reservoir of comets. As the comets swarm around the star, their frozen gases are warm enough to release CO, but not H_2, which remains locked up as water ice.

FUSE observations made the first detection of H_2 in the atmosphere of Mars, a critical molecule for understanding the history of water on that planet. The H_2 measurement, combined with an analysis of other properties of the Martian atmosphere, determined the quantity of Martian water lost to space and provided an estimate of the amount of water on the planet shortly after its formation. These analyses indicate that, if the initial quantity of water on Mars could have been evenly distributed across the planet, it would have been equivalent to a global Martian ocean at least 1.25 km (0.78 mi) deep. This is 1.3 times more water per unit mass than the Earth.

FUSE observations of comets have revealed over 60 new spectral features, including the first detections of H_2, N I, and O VI in comets. *FUSE* is an extremely sensitive probe of CO and Ar I, both of which bear critically on the formation environment of comets early in the history of the solar system, as well as the role played by cometary bombardment on the volatile inventory of the terrestrial planets.

For background information *see* ASTRONOMICAL SPECTROSCOPY; COMET; INTERSTELLAR MATTER; LOCAL GROUP; MAGELLANIC CLOUDS; MARS; MILKY WAY GALAXY; SPACE TELESCOPE, HUBBLE; ULTRAVIOLET ASTRONOMY in the McGraw-Hill Encyclopedia of Science & Technology.   George Sonneborn

Bibliography. J. C. Green, E. Wilkinson, and S. D. Friedman, Design of the *Far Ultraviolet Spectroscopic Explorer* spectrograph, *Proc. SPIE*, 2283:12–19,

1994; H. W. Moos et al., Abundances of deuterium, nitrogen, and oxygen in the local interstellar medium: Overview of first results from the FUSE Mission, *Astrophys. J., Suppl. Ser.*, 140:3–17, 2002; H. W. Moos et al., Overview of the *Far Ultraviolet Spectroscopic Explorer* Mission, *Astrophys. J. Lett.*, 538:L1–L5, 2000; D. J. Sahnow et al., Design and predicted performance of the *Far Ultraviolet Spectroscopic Explorer*, *Proc. SPIE*, 2807:2–10, 1996; K. R. Sembach, The *Far Ultraviolet Spectroscopic Explorer*: Mission overview and prospects for studies of the interstellar medium and high-velocity clouds, in B. K. Gibson and M. E. Putman (eds.), *ASP Conf. Ser.*, 166:243, 1999; G. Sonneborn and H. W. Moos, Joint discussion 11: First results from the FUSE Mission, in H. Richter (ed.), *Highlights of Astronomy*, vol. 11, *ASP Conf. Ser.*, in press.

Forensic arson investigation

Laboratory-based arson investigation is usually limited to the chemical analysis of fire debris, which is used to support field investigators who determine whether a fire is intentional (arson) or accidental. A gap has existed between the field investigators, most of whom have practical experience but a limited understanding of scientific principles, and the scientists and engineers who perform laboratory experiments to verify the hypotheses of the field investigators. This gap, however, is gradually narrowing.

Disproved field indicators. Over the last 20 years, as the "indicators" upon which field investigators base their determinations have been subjected to scientific scrutiny, the value of some of these indicators has been called into question or completely disproved. Prior to 1992, for example, crazed glass (glass with numerous, tightly spaced and random cracks) was considered an indicator of rapid heating which, according to some publications, suggested the presence of burning ignitable liquids (**Fig. 1**). It has since been shown that crazing of glass occurs only because of rapid cooling of glass that has been heated to a temperature in excess of 120°C (248°F), well within the normal range for fires. Likewise, flame temperature itself was once considered an indicator of the presence of ignitiable liquids. It has been shown, however, that the temperature of a well-ventilated wood fire can exceed the temperature of a well-ventilated gasoline fire.

Since heat rises, it was easy for fire investigators to believe that burn marks on the floor indicated that the fire had "help." However, studies carried out by the National Institute of Standards and Technology (NIST) Center for Fire Research, and others, have shown conclusively that in a "compartment" fire, heat does not rise indefinitely. Upon encountering an obstruction, a hot gas layer is formed beneath the ceiling of a compartment, and as the fire burns, that hot gas layer acquires more and more energy, which it radiates in all directions, including downward. When the hot gas layer has accu-

Fig. 1. Crazed glass was once considered to be evidence of rapid heating. This piece of glass was slowly heated to 450°C (842°F), held at that temperature for 30 min, and then sprayed with water in the upper left corner. Despite proof that only rapid cooling will cause crazing of glass, some fire investigators still cite the presence of crazed glass as evidence of an accelerated fire.

mulated sufficient energy and the radiant heat flux exceeds 2 W/cm² (0.3 W/in.²), any combustible materials (such as furniture, floor coverings, wall coverings, and so on) are likely to burst into flames almost instantaneously, resulting in irregular burns on the floor, even in the absence of ignitable liquids. In the 1980s and early 1990s, fire investigators began to understand the impact of a phenomenon known as flashover on the artifacts that remain after a fire. The progress of a typical compartment fire, from the free-burning stage to the postflashover stage, is shown in **Fig. 2**.

Laboratory analysis. Of the over 500,000 structure fires that occur annually in the United States, about 15% are declared to be suspicious. In classifying these fires, there are many opportunities for error. Compounding the problems of field investigators relying on unreliable indicators are laboratories that misidentify background materials and pyrolysis products (partially decomposed organic materials produced by burning of polymers, wood, and so on) as ignitable liquid residues. For example, there have been instances in which laboratories that test for BETX (benzene, ethylbenzene, toluene, and xylene) to quantify the presence of gasoline in soil at sites of known spills have identified gasoline elsewhere where none was present using the same test. All of the components of BETX are normally produced in the decomposition of household polymeric materials, such as nylon, and it requires careful analysis and judgment on the part of the forensic scientist to make a distinction between burned carpeting and

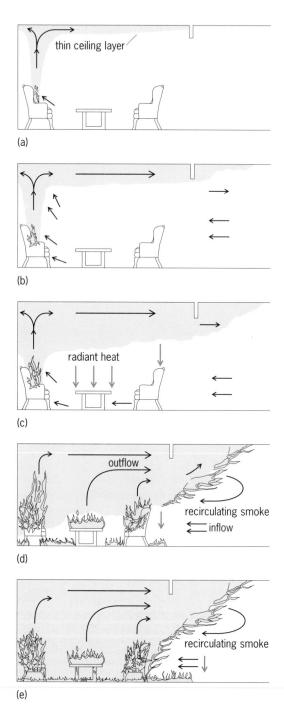

(a)

(b)

(c)

(d)

outflow

recirculating smoke
inflow

(e)

recirculating smoke

Fig. 2. Typical compartment fire. The ceiling causes fire to behave in a manner unfamiliar to most people. The hot gas layer eventually radiates sufficient heat downward to ignite the floor, even in areas initially protected by the "shadow" of tables and chairs. (*a*) Early development. This free-burning stage reflects the experience of most people with campfires and brush fires. (*b*) Ceiling layer development. The hot gas layer acts as a blackbody, which absorbs radiant heat and hot gases, and continues to gain energy from the burning fuel. (*c*) Preflashover conditions. Downward arrows represent radiant heat, which increases the temperature of fuels below the hot gas layer. (*d*) Flashover conditions. As the radiant heat flux reaches 2 W/cm^2, all combustible fuels ignite almost simultaneously. (*e*) Postflashover conditions. As the fire extends to other rooms, the fire in the compartment of origin continues to burn, igniting even fuels in protected areas. (*Reprinted with permission from Guide for Fire and Explosion Investigations, NFPA 921, Copyright © 2001, National Fire Protection Association, Quincy, MA 02269*)

weathered (evaporated) gasoline. The guidance for making this distinction and others is found in the standard test methods developed by American Society for Testing and Materials (ASTM) Committee E30 on Forensic Sciences for fire debris analysis.

Wrongful prosecutions. In a 1982 case, an Arizona man escaped from a nighttime fire in his mobile home, while his wife and daughter perished in the fire. Fire investigators found burn marks on the floor of the trailer and crazed glass on the sliding glass door, at floor level, which was interpreted (incorrectly) as evidence of flammable liquids at floor level. Despite the fact that the laboratory analysis of samples collected from the scene failed to reveal the presence of any ignitable liquid residues, the man was convicted of arson. After the man had served 8 years of a life sentence, the judge ordered a new trial based on the state fire investigator's 1983 testimony that only flammable liquids could have caused the burn patterns seen after the fire. By 1991, there was a greater understanding about the artifacts normally expected in a fire that had attained flashover (Fig. 2). As a result, the convicted man was freed.

A more recent case involved a couple in Ohio whose child died in a fire and who were jailed for arson and homicide, based on the fact that there were suspicious "burn patterns" in their living room. Their story about how the fire started did not at all match the fire investigators' interpretation. Samples sent to the laboratory came back positive for the presence of turpentine. The forensic scientists in this case failed to advise the investigators that houses built out of coniferous (pine and fir) wood contain terpenes, compounds that are currently indistinguishable from commercial-grade turpentine. The state intended to prosecute with the theory that the parents had purchased turpentine (though there was no evidence of this) and used it to ignite their house and kill their son, despite the fact that there was no apparent motive. Faced with a growing body of evidence that the turpentine was a natural background finding, and that the fire was electrical, the prosecutor dropped the case.

Standardization. The National Fire Protection Association published in 1992 NFPA 921, *Guide for Fire and Explosion Investigations*, which addressed many of the misconceptions about fire investigation that had resulted in incorrect determinations of fire cause. With each succeeding edition, the participation of the fire investigation community has increased, as has the acceptance of the document by major organizations of fire investigators. While it is still labeled as a "guide," many courts have agreed that this document represents the standard for fire investigations.

Concurrently, the International Association of Arson Investigators (IAAI), through its forensic science committee, produced a standard for gas chromatographic analysis of ignitable liquid residues in fire debris samples. Endorsement of this standard has led to the adoption of its methods by many laboratories. The IAAI standard is actually a restatement of a classification system for ignitable liquids developed jointly by the Bureau of Alcohol, Tobacco and Firearms and the National Bureau of Standards (now NIST) in the early 1980s. In 1990, ASTM Committee E30 on Forensic Sciences adapted the IAAI standard into ASTM format and produced five standard practices on the separation of ignitable liquids and one standard test method for the identification via gas chromatography. These ASTM standards were adopted quickly by forensic scientists, and since then an additional standard for gas chromatography/mass spectrometry (GC/MS) fire debris analysis has been adopted. These standards are subject to a 5-year revision, and most of them are now in their third edition.

New frontiers. In both the investigation of fire scenes and the chemical analysis of fire debris, new developments promise to improve the accuracy. Computer modeling, pioneered by the Building and Fire Research Laboratory at NIST and generally offered free to the public, allows investigators to input data about a structure and fire to simulate the development of the fire. The initial models used a "zone" concept, which divided each compartment of interest into two layers, upper and lower. The models, while crude, provided useful information about the predicted development of a fire, and the resulting concentrations of certain gases.

A more sophisticated model, called a field model, is based on computational fluid dynamics. It breaks each compartment up into hundreds, thousands, or millions of elements and simultaneously predicts the conditions in each element. Field models require powerful computers and days or weeks of computer time to process the numbers, but their output is more accurate. In all cases of computer modeling, it is best to compare what the model predicts to the artifacts at the scene, and see if the computer output is useful for testing hypotheses.

In the laboratory analysis of fire debris, the identification of certain biomarkers (compounds left over from the dead life forms that became crude oil) used in tracking the source of environmental oil spills may one day help to identify a sample of weathered fuel recovered from a fire scene as coming from a particular source. Such a capability is not currently available in the field of fire debris analysis, though it is quite advanced in environmental analysis.

Another prospect for the more discriminating analysis of fuels is two-dimensional gas chromatography, currently being studied under a National Institute of Justice grant at the U.S. Coast Guard Academy. In two-dimensional gas chromatography, two columns are coupled via an interface, which periodically (every few seconds) sends the effluent from the first column through a second column, where it is further separated. The second column is typically chemically different from the first, and is heated in a separate oven. Combining this two-dimensional gas chromatography with mass spectrometry may also help with the individualization of weathered fuel samples as well as a more certain identification of ignitable liquid residues.

The prime motivation for fire investigators to update the approach to their job comes from the courts, which have demanded in recent years that the opinions expressed by all experts be demonstrably reliable.

For background information *see* COMBUSTION; FIRE; FLAME; FORENSIC CHEMISTRY; GAS CHROMATOGRAPHY; MASS SPECTROMETRY in the McGraw-Hill Encyclopedia of Science & Technology.   John J. Lentini

Bibliography. *ASTM Annual Book of Standards*, ASTM E-1387, ASTM E-1618, ASTM International, West Conshohocken, PA, 2001; D. L. Faigman et al., *Science in the Law: Forensic Science Issues*, pp. 338–354, West Publishing, St. Paul, MN, 2002; *Guide for Fire and Explosion Investigations*, NFPA 921, p. 30, National Fire Protection Association, Quincy, MA, 2001; J. J. Lentini, Behavior of glass at elevated temperature, *J. Forensic Sci.*, vol. 37, no. 5, September 1992; *State of Arizona v. Ray Girdler*, Yavapai County, Case # 9809, 1982.

Forensic microscopy

Edmond Locard (1877–1966) stated that every contact leaves a trace. This is known as the Locard exchange principle, the basis for much of forensic microscopy. Since the early 1800s, the microscope has been used to help solve crimes. Today, it remains one of the most used tools in the crime laboratory. Criminal evidence ranging in scale from micrometer-sized particles to hair and paint chips can be found and removed to a laboratory for microscopic analysis, where its history may be deduced to help solve the crime. Microscopy can provide insight into the identity and origin of a material, what has happened to it and when, and the routes it may have taken between a crime victim, suspect, and crime scene (**Fig. 1**).

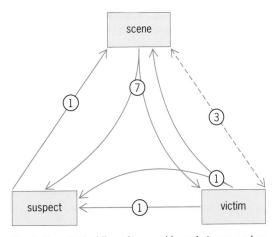

Fig. 1. Hypothetical flow of trace evidence between a crime scene, victim, and suspect. Seven types of trace evidence were transferred from the crime scene to both the suspect and victim. Three types of trace evidence were found at both the crime scene and on the victim. One type of trace evidence was transferred from the victim to the suspect and the crime scene. One type of evidence was transferred from the victim to the suspect. One type of evidence was transferred from the suspect to the crime scene.

Stereomicroscope. The low-powered stereomicroscope is probably the most used microscope in the crime lab. The magnification typically ranges from 7× to 40×, and the image is upright (not reversed) and three-dimensional. With additional lenses, the magnification can range from below 3× to above 100×. This type of microscope can be used with a variety of lighting techniques such as transmitted, fluorescence, diffuse, coaxial, and oblique illumination.

The stereomicroscope is used in drug analysis to help identify marijuana and to evaluate powders and chunks of material that may need to be separated before analysis. In examining firearms and tool marks, it is used to evaluate striations or imprint marks, look for trace evidence, evaluate bullet holes for muzzle blast, and search for unburned gunpowder particles. In addition, when a bullet passes through an object, some of that object may be transferred to the bullet and detected microscopically. In forensic biology the stereomicroscope is used to find and measure small bloodstains, to evaluate a bloodstain to determine if it came from the inside or outside of a garment, and to remove stains from hidden places. When examining documents, it can be used to evaluate typefaces, examine strikeovers and ink lines that cross over, and find erasures or alterations. For trace evidence, the stereomicroscope is the tool of choice for finding and characterizing hairs, fibers, paint, glass, soil, and building material.

Biological microscope. The biological microscope is used for examining biological fluids, human tissue, hairs, fibers, drug crystals, food, and other stains. A typical biological microscope has 4×, 10×, 20×, and 40× objectives on a revolving nosepiece. It is normally equipped with 10× eyepieces giving a final magnification of from 40× to 400×. Many additional lenses can be added to this style of microscope to increase the range of magnification from less than 20× to greater than 1500×. In addition, these microscopes can be modified to include darkfield, phase contrast, fluorescence, dispersion staining, darkfield epi-illumination, and reflected coaxial illumination. When darkfield epi-illumination or reflected coaxial illumination is used, the biological microscope is transformed into a metallurgical microscope, which can be used to examine surface detail and opaque objects.

A forensic pathologist typically uses the biological microscope to examine tissue samples from injuries to determine if the injuries occurred before, during, or after death. In the forensic biology section of the laboratory, the microscope is typically used to identify sperm in rape cases. This process involves differential staining and examining the slide at greater than 200×. When sperm are identified from samples collected from a victim, this is proof that sexual activity has taken place. The legal issue of consent is not addressed by the presence of sperm. Other body fluids such as vaginal secretions, saliva, and feces might have been mixed with semen, and microscopy can give vital clues as to the origins of these other body fluids.

Some crime labs use crystal tests to identify drugs such as phencyclidine, amphetamines, cocaine, barbiturates, heroin, morphine, and codeine. In a typical crystal test, a small amount of the drug and a liquid reagent are placed on a microscope slide. After a short time, unique crystals for that drug can be recognized at 100× with a biological microscope.

Polarized light microscope. The polarized light microscope is a biological microscope with special modifications, including a polarizer, analyzer, rotating stage, accessory slot, Bertrand lens, and a flip-up condenser. This microscope is typically used to

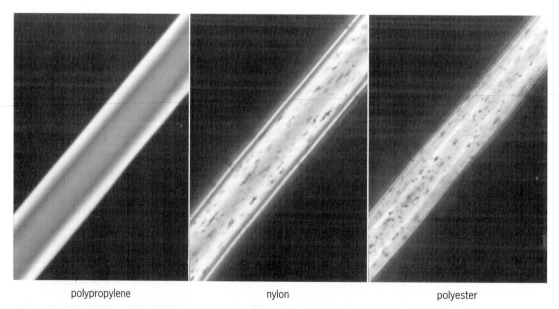

polypropylene   nylon   polyester

Fig. 2. Crossed polarizers showing interference colors (represented here in black and white) of three colorless synthetic fibers. These interference colors can be used to calculate the birefringence, which is an optical property used to identify these fibers. The birefringence of polyepropylene is medium, nylon is high, and polyester is very high.

identify synthetic fibers, minerals, glass, starch, and many other types of particles. It has the advantage of measuring optical properties without altering the sample. Six major synthetic fiber types (acrylic, acetate, rayon, olefin, nylon, and polyester) can be quickly differentiated with the polarized light microscope (**Fig. 2**). A significant amount of training and experience, as well as reference standards, is necessary to master the use of this instrument, since most universities do not teach this subject. The McCrone Research Institute in Chicago has trained many forensic scientists in the use of the polarized light microscope.

Comparison microscope. A comparison microscope consists of two identically equipped compound microscopes joined together with an optical bridge, giving a split-screen image. The comparison microscope is used to compare bullets, cartridge cases, and toolmarks. This microscope normally uses low-powered objectives and reflected, diffused, or oblique illumination. The comparison microscope is also used to compare trace evidence such as hairs and fibers. It uses the same range of magnifications as the biological microscope.

One such case illustrating the comparison of hair, as well as DNA analysis, involved an elderly male victim who was stabbed in a robbery at a hamburger stand. Clumps of long dark hair that appeared to have been pulled out during a struggle were found in several locations at the crime scene. Microscopic examination of that hair showed more than 50 anagen roots. Anagen roots are those still attached to the scalp with a blood vessel and a nerve, indicating that the clumps of hair were forcibly removed during the struggle. The hair from the crime scene had a maximum length of 17 in. The maximum length of the victim's gray hair was less than 1 in. The police collected and the crime lab compared hair from several long-haired suspects with negative results. Finally, a female drug user was identified by a relative as the murderer. A hair sample was collected and submitted to the hair examiner, who testified that the hairs from the crime scene probably came from the suspect. A blood sample from the suspect along with 15 roots from the crime scene hairs were submitted to a DNA laboratory (**Fig. 3**). The DNA matched, and the suspect was convicted. This case became the first California DNA case to successfully get through the Appeals Court.

Scanning electron microscope. The scanning electron microscope with energy dispersive x-ray spectrometer (SEM/EDX) is routinely used to identify the elemental content of very small samples. The most common sample analyzed with the SEM/EDX is gunshot residue. This is done by dabbing the shooter's hands with sticky tape attached to an SEM stub (a substrate for mounting specimens). The stub is then examined for gunshot residue (GSR) particles (usually 1–6 micrometers) that contain lead, barium, and antimony. Many of the SEM/EDX microscopes are connected to computers that have programs that can search automatically for GSR particles.

Fig. 3. Fifteen anagen hair roots sent for DNA typing.

Digital forensic microscopy. Most microscope systems can be modified to capture digital images, which can be sent by e-mail to forensic scientists for examination and comment. An automated system for glass refractive index measurement uses a phase-contrast microscope, hot stage, video system, and computer to compare glass samples. The National Integrated Ballistics Identification Network (NIBIN), sponsored by the Federal Bureau of Investigation (FBI) and Bureau of Alcohol, Tobacco and Firearms (ATF), uses digitally captured images (through the microscope) of cartridge cases or bullets to link shooting incidents with guns taken from suspects in distant jurisdictions.

The infrared spectrophotometer with a microscope attached is a common tool in crime laboratories. It is used to perform spectrophotometric analysis on very small samples such as paints, plastics, fibers, and many other substances. The microspectrophotometer is used to measure the spectrum of the visible colors, ultraviolet radiation, and fluorescence that are present in microscopic objects. An automated version of the microspectrophotometer using a remote control stage and computer can search tape lifts taken from suspects, victims, and crime scenes. First a fiber is chosen and entered into the apparatus. The tape lifts are then searched for that target fiber.

Another digital system is a portable microscope with fiber-optic cables that is used to acquire high-quality microscopic images such as a paint transfer on a bumper or hood of a vehicle without dismantling.

For background information *see* BIREFRINGENCE; CRIMINALISTICS; FLUORESCENCE MICROSCOPE; FORENSIC BIOLOGY; INTERFERENCE MICROSCOPE; MICROSCOPE; OPTICAL MICROSCOPE; PHASE-CONTRAST MICROSCOPE; POLARIZED LIGHT MICROSCOPE; REFLECTING MICROSCOPE; SCANNING ELECTRON MICROSCOPE in the McGraw-Hill Encyclopedia of Science & Technology.   Edwin L. Jones, Jr.

Bibliography. P. De Forest, Foundations of forensic microscopy, in R. Saferstein (ed.), *Forensic Science Handbook*, Prentice Hall, Upper Saddle River, NJ, 2002; B. Fisher, *Techniques of Crime Scene Investigation*, CRC Press, Boca Raton, 1993; J. Houde, *Crime Lab: A Guide for Nonscientists*, Calico Press, Ventura, CA, 1999; S. Palinik, Microscopy, in J. A. Siegal et al. (eds.), *Encyclopedia of Forensic Sciences*, Academic Press, San Diego, 2000; R. Saferstein, *Criminalistics: An Introduction to Forensic Science*, Prentice Hall, Upper Saddle River, NJ, 2001.

Forensic mitochondrial DNA analysis

Deoxyribonucleic acid (DNA) is found in two locations in all human cells, except in red blood cells. Nuclear DNA (nuDNA), inherited from both parents, makes up 23 pairs of chromosomes in the nucleus of somatic cells. Mitochondrial DNA (mtDNA), inherited only from the mother, is located in the mitochondria, the peanut-shaped cytoplasmic organelles that generate cellular energy. The coding region of mtDNA contains 37 genes encoding proteins involved in cellular respiration, transfer ribonucleic acid (RNA), and ribosomal RNA. The full complement of nuDNA has about 3 billion of the four chemical bases of DNA (adenine, guanine, thymine, and cytosine, abbreviated A, G, T, and C; also known as nucleotides), in a linear array within the chromosomes. Mitochondrial DNA contains 16,569 of these same chemical bases within a circular molecule (**Fig. 1**). Whereas each cell contains two copies of nuDNA, there are hundreds to thousands of mtDNA molecules within dozens to hundreds of mitochondria per cell, depending on the particular tissue. With some exceptions, all tissues in an individual are homogeneous for a single mtDNA type.

Mitochondrial DNA is a valuable forensic tool in certain cases. The sequence of nucleotides differs so much among individuals, particularly in two "hypervariable" sections of the molecule, that the likelihood of choosing two people at random with the same mtDNA sequence is very low. Mitochondrial DNA recovery from small or degraded biological samples is greater than nuclear DNA recovery due to its high copy number and because the molecule's circular structure may protect it from damage by heat, humidity, acidity, and ultraviolet light. Therefore, degraded muscle, bone, hair, skin, blood, or other body fluids often provide enough material for mtDNA typing. In addition, the pattern of maternal inheritance means that in situations where an individual is not available for a direct comparison with a biological sample, his or her maternal relative may provide a comparison sample.

Related applications. While mtDNA is useful for forensic examinations, it also has been studied extensively in medicine and molecular anthropology. Many serious human diseases, such as Leber's hereditary optic neuropathy (LHON), and mitochondrial myopathy, encephalopathy, lactic acidosis, and stroke-like episodes syndrome (MELAS), are caused by deleterious mutations in gene-coding regions of the mtDNA molecule. In addition, molecular anthropologists have been using mtDNA for more than a decade to examine the genetic variation in and ancestral relatedness of worldwide human populations. Because of its unique mode of maternal inheritance, mtDNA can reveal ancient population histories, which might include migration patterns, expansion dates, and geographic homelands. In 1997 mtDNA was extracted and sequenced from a Neanderthal skeleton. The sequence results allowed anthropologists to conclude that modern humans do not share a close evolutionary relationship with Neanderthals.

Laboratory methods. An mtDNA analysis begins when total genomic DNA is extracted from a biological material, such as a tooth, blood sample, or hair. The polymerase chain reaction (PCR) is then used to copy the two mtDNA hypervariable regions, each of which contains about 350 (single-strand) or 700 (double-strand) nucleotides. Oligonucleotide primers, or small sequences of known DNA, are attached to the ends of the region that one wishes to copy, and then a thermal cycling process produces, after several hours, millions of copies of the starting material. Sequencing reactions then use each PCR product as a template to create a new complementary strand of DNA in which each A, T, C, and G is labeled with fluorescent dye. The strands created in this stage are separated according to size by an automated sequencing machine that uses a laser and camera to "read" the sequence of the nucleotides. The sequences of both hypervariable regions are determined on both strands of the double-stranded mtDNA molecule and assembled in a computer file, which an analyst evaluates for the quality

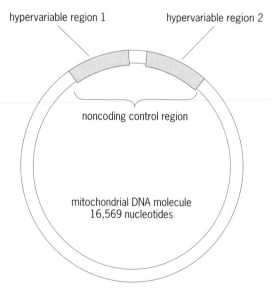

hypervariable region 1   hypervariable region 2

noncoding control region

mitochondrial DNA molecule
16,569 nucleotides

Fig. 1. Diagram of the closed, circular mitochondrial DNA molecule showing the location of the hypervariable regions typically sequenced in a forensic analysis. The remaining portion of the molecule codes for a number of genes.

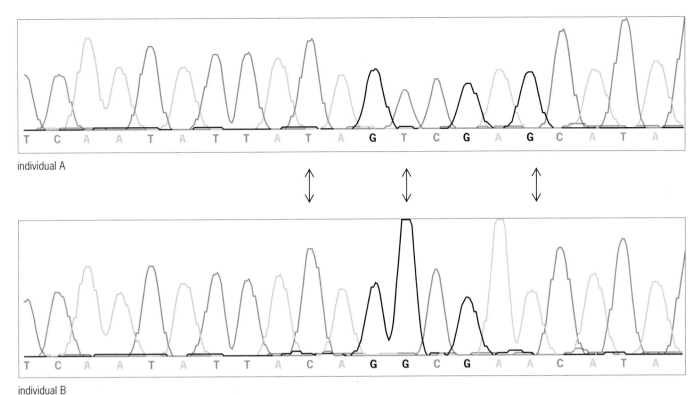

Fig. 2. Analysis by electrophoresis. This electropherogram of a short stretch of DNA shows the sequence of each A, C, T, and G. Individuals A and B differ at three nucleotide positions in this short region.

of the data. The entire laboratory and analytic process is then repeated with a known sample, such as blood or saliva collected from a known individual. The sequences from both samples are compared to determine if they match (**Fig. 2**). Several outcomes of this comparison are possible: (1) inclusion—the sequences share a common nucleotide at every location along the DNA sequence, meaning that the contributor of the known sample, or his or her maternal relatives, cannot be excluded as the contributor of the questioned sample; (2) exclusion—there are two or more different nucleotides between the samples, meaning that the contributor of the known sample and his or her maternal relatives are excluded as the contributor of the questioned sample; or (3) inconclusive—there is a single difference between the two sequences, meaning that no conclusions can be drawn about the contributors. (A single difference is inconclusive because it cannot be known whether it is indicative of different source individuals or of a single base mutation between samples from the same individual.) In the event of an inclusion, a forensic mtDNA database, maintained by the FBI, is searched for the mitochondrial sequence in the case. The number of observations of this type in the database allows a frequency estimate of this type in the population.

Forensic mtDNA database. The current FBI forensic mtDNA database has around 4800 typed sequences. The database is made up of samples from blood banks, FBI personnel, crime labs, family reference samples from the Armed Forces DNA Identification

lab, population studies, and so on. It is assumed to be representative of the population of North America and random with respect to the mtDNA types in it. In the case of an inclusion, the purpose of a database search is to count the number of times that the observed type is in the database. A population frequency estimate is calculated from this number, but a 95–99% confidence interval is placed around the frequency to account for the inherent uncertainty in the frequency calculation. While most types appear to be rare or at least infrequent in each of the ethnic subdatabases (African or African-origin, Asian or Asian-origin, Caucasian or European-origin, Hispanic, and Native American), there is one type that is present in around 7% of Caucasians. However, about two-thirds of newly typed samples have novel mtDNA sequences with respect to the database, so all human mtDNA variation has not yet been observed. In general, the pattern observed in most populations around the world is that most sequences are uncommon, and relatively few types are present at frequencies greater than 1% (**Fig. 3**). As a result, it is possible to exclude greater than 99% of a population as contributors of a sample in most cases, except where one is dealing with a more "common" type.

Advantages and disadvantages. Mitochondrial DNA has advantages and disadvantages as a forensic marker, especially compared to forensic nuDNA markers. Because mtDNA is maternally inherited, all maternally related individuals will share the same sequence. This is especially useful in missing

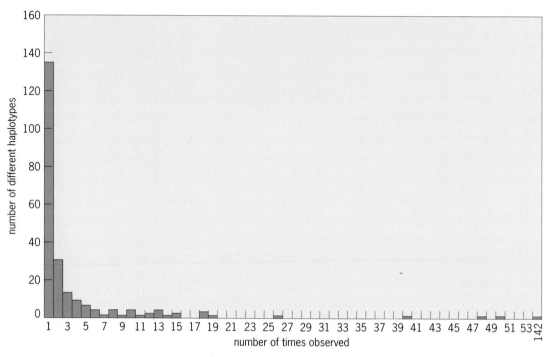

Fig. 3. Classic distribution of mtDNA types, showing that within most sampled populations there are a high number of types that occur one time only, and many fewer types that occur more than once. This is an indication of the high diversity levels in most populations, which exceed 0.96, where 1.0 would mean that each individual is different.

person cases where skeletal remains need identification, and a mother, a sibling, or even a very distant maternal relative can provide a comparison sample. Because of meiotic recombination and the diploid (bi-parental) inheritance of nuDNA, the reconstruction of a nuDNA profile from even first-degree relatives of a missing individual is rarely this straightforward. On the other hand, the maternal inheritance pattern of mtDNA is problematic. Because all individuals in a maternal lineage share the same mtDNA sequence, mtDNA cannot be considered a unique identifier of a questioned sample. In fact, apparently unrelated individuals might share an unknown maternal relative in the past. Therefore, source attribution of a questioned sample is not possible with mtDNA. Instead, an estimate of the frequency of a type provides an idea of how often this type might be chosen at random. In contrast, an nuDNA profile provides superior discriminatory power such that a particular sample may be attributed to a particular known individual.

Because mtDNA typing cannot provide the resolution of individuality that nuclear typing can, it should be reserved for samples for which nuclear typing is not possible. The best candidates for mtDNA analysis are hairs with no robust root, degraded skeletal material, and stains or organ tissue that has been unsuccessfully typed for nuDNA.

Current applications. In addition to the successful analysis of Neanderthal remains, mtDNA testing has been applied to many other historical mysteries, including the identification of the 75-year-old remains of Czar Nicholas, Czarina Alexandra, and their children. In addition, mtDNA testing confirmed the identities of the outlaws Jesse James and Wild Bill Longley, and proved that Anna Anderson was not a surviving Romanov, the Grand Duchess Anastasia. The Armed Forces DNA Identification Laboratory in Rockville, Maryland, has been using this technique for over 10 years to identify military dead from World War II and the Korean and Vietnam wars; it identified the individual in the Vietnam Tomb of the Unknown Soldier. More recently, mtDNA testing has been used to identify victims of the 2001 World Trade Center terrorist attacks in conjunction with nuclear DNA profiling.

Because of the advantages and in spite of the limitations mentioned above, mtDNA analysis has found a place in the forensics arena, and is used in many other countries besides the United States. Dozens of criminal cases have been tried in U.S. and international courts using mtDNA evidence to augment traditional forms of evidence, and several postconviction exonerations have been obtained in cases where microscopically examined hairs used originally as trial evidence were reanalyzed for mtDNA. In cases where nuclear DNA testing is not possible, mtDNA typing can provide additional information about the relationship of an individual to a biological sample.

For background information *see* CRIMINALISTICS; DEOXYRIBONUCLEIC ACID (DNA); FORENSIC BIOLOGY; GENE AMPLIFICATION; GENETIC CODE; MITOCHONDRIA in the McGraw-Hill Encyclopedia of Science & Technology.   Terry Melton

Bibliography. S. Anderson et al., Sequence and organization of the human mitochondrial genome. *Nature*, 290:457–465, 1981; J. M. Butler, *Forensic DNA*

Typing, Academic Press, San Diego, 2001; R. L. Cann, M. Stoneking, and A. C. Wilson, Mitochondrial DNA and human evolution, *Nature*, 325:31-36, 1987; R. N. Lightowlers et al., Mammalian genetics, heredity, heteroplasmy and disease, *Trends Genet.*, 13: 450-455, 1997; T. Melton and G. Sensabaugh, Mitochondrial deoxyribonucleic acid, in J. A. Seigel (ed.), *Encyclopedia of Forensic Sciences*, Academic Press, San Diego, 2000.

Frozen light

Ultraslow light was first observed by L. V. Hau and her colleagues in 1998. Light pulses were slowed in a Bose-Einstein condensate of sodium to only 17 m/s (38 mi/h), more than seven orders of magnitude lower than the light speed in vacuum. In later experiments, light pulse velocities as low as 50 cm/s (1.1 mi/h) were observed. This method was brought to its logical extreme when light pulses were completely stopped and stored in an atomic medium for up to several milliseconds. Associated with the dramatic reduction factor for the light speed is a spatial compression of the pulses by the same large factor. A light pulse, which is 2-3 km (1-2 mi) long in vacuum, is compressed to a size of about 50 micrometers, and at that point it is completely contained within the condensate.

Experimental procedure. The extremely low light speeds, and stopped light, are obtained in a new optical medium created by illuminating ultracold atoms with laser beams. Atoms are cooled to nanokelvin temperatures with a combination of laser and evaporative cooling, where the latter part of the process takes place with the atoms trapped in a magnetic field. At the end of the cooling process, the de Broglie wavelengths of the atoms become comparable to the distance between the atoms, and Bose-Einstein condensates are formed. The condensates are typically 0.1-0.2 mm long, cigar-shaped, and 0.05 mm in diameter.

The experimental setup and the energy levels used to create slow light are shown in **Fig. 1**. The atom cloud, trapped in the magnetic field, is first illuminated from the side with a "coupling" laser beam resonant with the transition between quantum states |2> and |3>. The laser field creates a coupling between these states, and it is no longer possible to treat the atoms isolated from the coupling laser; it is necessary to consider the total system, the mixture of atoms and laser light. The single energy level corresponding to the energy of quantum state |3> splits into two close-lying levels, and the splitting is proportional to the square root of the intensity of the coupling laser.

Next a "probe" laser pulse, which is nearly resonant with the |1>-|3> transition, is sent into the atom cloud in a direction parallel to its long axis. (Both laser beams have a wavelength of approximately 589 nanometers and corresponding frequency of about 509,000 GHz; their frequency separation is only 1.7 GHz.) The atom-coupling laser system creates a very unusual refractive index profile for the probe field. Right on |1>-|3> resonance, which corresponds to tuning of the probe laser right in between the two new, split energy levels, the refractive index is one, exactly what it is in free space. A way of understanding this is to model the system as two coupled harmonic oscillators with slightly different oscillation frequencies. These frequencies correspond to the energy differences between state |1>

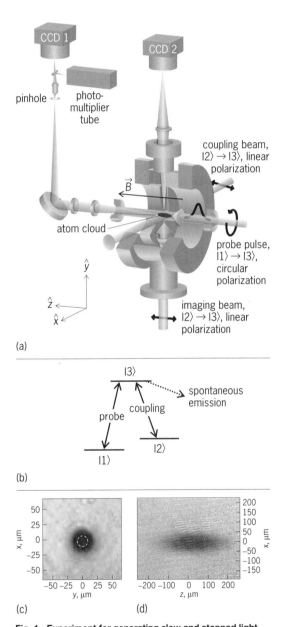

(a)

(b)

(c)   (d)

Fig. 1. Experiment for generating slow and stopped light. Arrows indicate polarization of laser beams and the direction of the magnetic field $\vec{B}$. (*a*) Experimental setup. (*b*) Three-level atomic system of interest. (*c*) Absorption shadow of the atom cloud created in the probe beam and recorded on the charge-coupled-device camera CCD 1. (*d*) Absorption shadow of the atom cloud created in the imaging beam and recorded on CCD 2. (*Reprinted with permission from L. V. Hau et al., Nature, 397:594–598, 1999; copyright 1999 Macmillan Magazines Limited*)

and the two split energy levels. The probe laser field drives the oscillators, and with the probe laser on resonance, the oscillators are driven at a frequency midway between their two oscillation frequencies. The result is that the oscillators are driven 180° out of phase and their excitations cancel, leaving no net effect, that is, no net polarization of the atom.

Mechanism of slowing light. Thus, light is not slowed down by creating a large refractive index. Rather, a very steep slope of the refractive index as a function of probe laser frequency is created around the resonance. The propagation speed of a light pulse, the group velocity, is inversely proportional to that slope. The steepest slope, and the lowest light speed, is obtained by minimizing the distance between the energy levels of the mixed atomlight system, that is, by applying very weak coupling laser fields. For very cold atoms, there is no smearing of the atomic energy levels from Doppler effects, and the split energy levels can indeed be brought together very closely without overlapping. It is important that the refractive index stays very close to one for all the frequency components in the pulse. If slow light were obtained by creating a very large refractive index, a perfect reflection of the light pulse at the boundary of the atom cloud would result and it would be impossible to get the pulse into and through the cloud. The fact that the refractive index stays close to one also means that the wavelength of the light pulse and its peak electric field strength are the same inside and outside the medium.

Electromagnetically induced transparency. It is important to discuss the transmission of the probe pulses through the atom clouds. In the absence of the coupling laser, a cloud would be completely opaque to the resonant probe laser pulses. However, in the presence of the coupling laser, the medium becomes transparent. This effect is called electromagnetically induced transparency, first observed in the early 1990s by S. E. Harris and his colleagues. The transparency comes about because a quantum-mechanical interference is created in the system. Absorption out of the probe pulse should be thought of as a two-step process: with the atom in state $|1>$, a probe photon can be absorbed, and the atom then spontaneously reemits from state $|3>$ into a random direction. That final state can be reached in another way: with the atom in state $|2>$, a coupling laser photon can be absorbed, followed by spontaneous emission. Quantum-mechanically, the total transition rate to the final state is obtained from a sum of the transition amplitudes for the two paths. With the atoms in a very particular superposition state, where they are partly in state $|1>$ and partly in state $|2>$, the two transition amplitudes cancel exactly, with the result that there is no absorption of either probe pulse or coupling laser. The superposition state is termed a "dark" state, in which the atoms do not interact with the light fields. (The ratio of the atomic population amplitudes for states $12>$ and $11>$ is deter-

mined by the electric field of the probe laser relative to the coupling laser field.) This quantum interference is also responsible for the fact that the steep refractive index profiles are retained in the presence of spontaneous radiation damping from state $|3>$.

In the experiment, all atoms are initially in their (internal) ground state $|1>$ (the magnet acts as a filter). By first turning on the coupling laser, which does not interact with atoms in this state, the system is made to start out in a dark state. When the probe pulse arrives, the atoms in state $|1>$ are coupled to state $|2>$ via a coherent two-photon process, and the atomic population of state $|2>$ increases with probe intensity. However, if the probe pulse is turned on at a slow enough rate, the "magic" superposition state will also change so that the atoms remain dark and neither beam is absorbed.

Pulse compression. Associated with the tremendous slowing down of a light pulse is an equally impressive compression of its spatial dimension. When a light pulse enters an atom cloud, the front edge of the light pulse slows down, and the back edge, still in free space and traveling at the normal vacuum light speed, catches up; that is, the pulse starts to compress. At the center of the cloud, where the atomic density is the greatest, the speed and spatial extent of the light pulse are minimized. The pulse is spatially compressed by the same factor as it is slowed down. Since the peak electric field amplitude of the pulse stays the same, as noted above, energy is clearly missing in the pulse. Part of that "missing" energy is temporarily stored in the atoms, but mostly it has been transferred to the coupling laser field through stimulated emission. When the pulse leaves the medium, the energy is transferred back to the light pulse— no energy is lost—and the pulse regains the shape

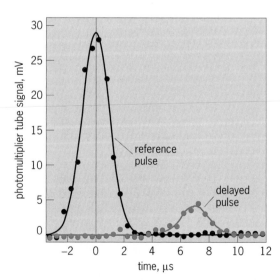

Fig. 2. Ultraslow light. A light pulse that has propagated through a 0.2-mm-long cloud of cold atoms (temperature of 450 nanokelvins) is delayed by 7 μs, corresponding to a light speed of 32 m/s (72 mi/h). A reference pulse recorded with no atoms is also shown to set the zero point for the time axis.

it had before it entered the medium; however, it is significantly delayed. As the light pulse propagates slowly through the medium, at any given time, the atoms within the compressed, localized light-pulse region will be prepared in dark superposition states. The spatial distribution of the dark states mimics the shape of the probe pulse; that is, the light pulse creates an imprint in the atoms and that imprint follows the pulse as it propagates through the cloud.

Observation of ultraslow light. A photomultiplier is used to measure the delay and transmission of the probe pulse. The size of the condensate is determined with a third laser, the imaging beam, which is sent into the system from a direction perpendicular to both the coupling and probe beams. The atom cloud's absorption shadow, created in the beam, is recorded on a charge-coupled-device (CCD) camera (CCD 2 in Fig. 1*a*); a typical image is shown in Fig. 1*d*.

Figure 2 shows the detection of a light pulse after it has propagated through an atom cloud. In this case, the light pulse is delayed by more than 7 microseconds in a cloud that is only 0.2 mm long, corresponding to a light speed of 32 m/s (72 mi/h). By varying the coupling laser intensity, the light speed and the light pulse delays can be controlled. To obtain such large optical delays in an optical fiber would require miles of such fiber. In the first experiments, light speeds of 17 m/s (38 mi/h) were obtained for light pulses propagating in almost pure Bose-Einstein condensates. These experiments exploited the extremely low temperature and large density of condensates.

Stopped light. With this ability to slow light pulses down to bicycle speeds—and at the same time spatially compress them so that they are completely contained within atom clouds—it is possible to go further. A light pulse has been completely stopped by turning off the coupling laser when the pulse is at the center of a cloud. The light pulse comes to a halt and turns off, but the imprint, following the pulse, is stored in the atom cloud as if a hologram had been written onto the atoms. When later the coupling laser is turned back on, the light pulse can be regenerated and sent back on its way. Light pulses have been stored in the medium for a long time, up to several milliseconds. During that time, a light pulse at normal speed would travel hundreds of kilometers.

The observation of stopped light is shown in **Fig. 3**. An experiment similar to that of Fig. 2 is shown in Fig. 3*a*. The arrow indicates the time when the light pulse is slowed down and compressed at the center of the atom cloud. At this point the pulse is contained completely within the cloud. Figure 3*b* shows the same experiment except that the coupling laser is turned off when the probe pulse is at the center of the cloud, and no pulse comes out. When the coupling laser is turned back on 40–50 μs later, the light pulse is regenerated, sent back on its way, and detected. Its shape and intensity are exactly the same

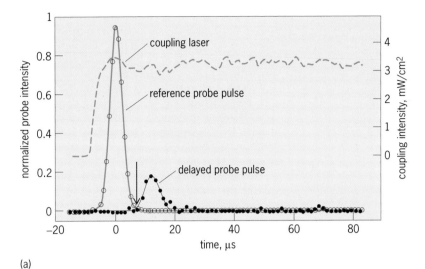

(a)

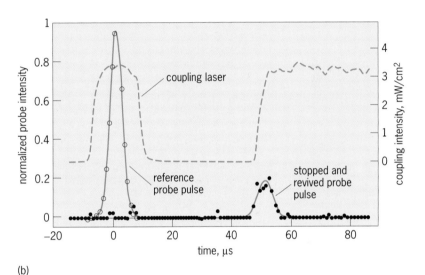

(b)

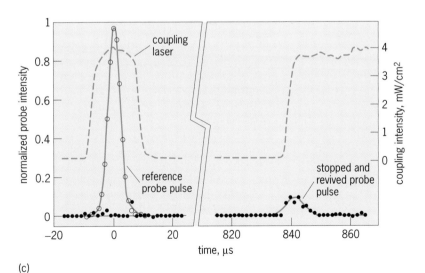

(c)

Fig. 3. Stopped light. (*a*) Experiment similar to Fig. 2. The arrow indicates the time when the light pulse is slowed down and compressed at the center of the atom cloud. (*b*) Same experiment except that the coupling laser is turned off when the probe pulse is at the center of the cloud, and turned back on 40–50 μs later, so that the pulse is stored in the medium during this time interval. (*c*) Same experiment except that the probe pulse is stored for close to 1 ms. A break in the time axis is needed to show the regenerated light pulse.

as those of the pulse in Fig. 3*a* that was delayed but not stopped in the atom cloud. Figure 3*c* shows the same experiment except that the pulse is stored for close to 1 ms, requiring a break in the time axis to show the regenerated light pulse.

Outlook. Ultraslow and stopped light could form the basis for creation of dynamically controllable optical delay lines and for controlled optical information storage. Optical information could be stored in extremely compressed form in three-dimensional patterns. Atom-atom interactions during the storage time could be used for processing of the stored information that could subsequently be read out through revival of light pulses. This could potentially be of extreme importance for optical data manipulation in connection with optical communication, for example. Furthermore, with a recent extension of this method, the light roadblock, light pulses have been compressed from 3 km (2 mi) to only 2 μm. This system has been used to generate extremely localized defects and dramatic excitations in Bose-Einstein condensates and directly reveal the superfluid nature of the condensates. Superfluid shock waves have been generated that result in the creation of solitons and quantized vortices. The vortices are produced far from equilibrium, in pairs of opposite circulation, and the dynamics of this system are extremely rich.

For background information *see* ABSORPTION OF ELECTROMAGNETIC RADIATION; BOSE-EINSTEIN CONDENSATION; GROUP VELOCITY; LASER; LIGHT; OPTICAL PULSES; QUANTIZED VORTICES; QUANTUM MECHANICS; REFRACTION OF WAVES; SOLITON in the McGraw-Hill Encyclopedia of Science & Technology.

Lene Vestergaard Hau

Bibliography. Z. Dutton et al., Observation of quantum shock waves created with ultra-compressed slow light pulses in a Bose-Einstein condensate, *Science*, 293:663–668, 2001; S. E. Harris, Electromagnetically induced transparency, *Phys. Today*, 50(7):36, July 1997; L. V. Hau, Frozen light, *Sci. Amer.*, 285(1):66–73, July 2001; L. V. Hau, *Proceedings from the Workshop on Bose-Einstein Condensation and Degenerate Fermi Gases*, JILA-University of Colorado, February 10–12, 1999; L. V. Hau, Taming light with cold atoms, *Phys. World*, pp. 35–40, September 2001; L. V. Hau et al., Light speed reduction to 17 metres per second in an ultracold atomic gas, *Nature*, 397:594–598, 1999; C. Liu et al., Observation of coherent optical information storage in an atomic medium using halted light pulses, *Nature*, 409:490–493, 2001.

Gamma-ray imaging

Gamma-ray imaging attempts to capture the distribution of radioactive decays within a body or from a distant source by detecting the emitted gamma rays. Unlike conventional x-ray or magnetic resonance imaging, gamma-ray imaging in humans and animals requires the introduction of a radioactive source into the body through injection, inhalation, or oral administration. The principal advantage of gamma-ray imaging over more conventional methods is that specially designed radiotracers can follow physiological pathways in the body. A number of chemicals are absorbed by specific organs. For example, the thyroid gland takes up iodine and the brain consumes glucose. With this knowledge, radiopharmacists are able to attach various radiotracers to biologically active substances such as iodine or glucose. In more conventional imaging such as transmission x-ray imaging, the anatomy of the patient is revealed, whereas gamma-ray imaging reveals the functional dynamics of processes in the body through so-called functional imaging.

Gamma-ray imaging is a means to gather medical information that may otherwise be unavailable, require surgery, or necessitate more expensive diagnostic tests. While great progress has been made in processing and reconstructing the data taken from gamma-ray imaging systems, the recent key advances in medical gamma-ray imaging have been in radiotracer development.

Gamma-ray detectors. Common methods of detecting gamma rays include scintillation cameras and solid-state detectors. Scintillation detectors use crystal scintillators that emit low-energy, often visible photons when struck by a high-energy charged particle. The incident gamma rays produce charged particles in the crystal that, in turn, produce visible light. The light emitted by the crystal is subsequently collected by photomultiplier tubes.

Solid-state detectors use advanced semiconductor materials and potentially offer better energy resolution, less noise, and better spatial resolution than the standard scintillators. As with scintillation detectors, solid-state detectors rely on photoelectric ionization of the material by the gamma ray. Instead of electron-ion pair creation that occurs in scintillators, electron-hole pairs are created in the semiconductor material and are subsequently detected.

Recently, semiconductor materials such as cadmium zinc telluride (CdZnTe, or CZT) and germanium have been extensively studied for use as gamma-ray detectors. CZT detectors offer excellent stopping power for a wide range of gamma-ray energies and can be operated at room temperature, unlike many solid-state detectors. CZT detectors are, however, difficult to produce in large wafers without significant defects arising, and they are still more expensive than scintillation crystals.

Imaging systems. Planar imaging, single photon emission computed tomography (SPECT), and positron emission tomography (PET) constitute the most common gamma-ray imaging procedures performed on humans. Planar imaging involves placing a detector and a collimator near the patient and using the collimator to restrict the angles of emitted radiation that will be incident on the detector. Thus, a planar imaging system takes a single two-dimensional projection image of the three-dimensional emitted activity distribution. Both SPECT and PET take images around the patient and then reconstruct three-dimensional slices through the patient; that is, they are tomographic imaging systems. SPECT systems image the directly emitted photons and generally require a collimator in front of the detector plane to focus the radiation. PET systems are used to image the distribution of positron-emitting radiotracers. The injected tracer decays to produce positrons. These positrons travel a short distance and are annihilated by electrons, producing two 511-MeV photons per positron. Because the photons are traveling in opposite directions and detected by opposing detectors, there is no need to place a collimator in front of the detector surfaces.

Collimators impose a physical constraint in SPECT imaging that ties together the detector sensitivity and spatial resolution in an inverse relationship. To overcome this sensitivity-resolution trade-off, a great effort has been put forth to develop electronically collimated cameras or Compton cameras. A Compton camera works by having two detector planes: one for the incident gamma rays and one for the Compton-scattered gamma rays. The incoming gamma ray Compton-scatters off an electron in the first detector and is subsequently absorbed in the second detector. The position and energy deposited are recorded in both detectors. This information provides an angular range from which the original gamma ray may have originated just as physical collimation does. Recent studies have shown that Compton cameras can obtain much better sensitivity for the same resolution at certain gamma-ray energies.

Cancer studies. Gamma-ray imaging has become a valuable, although still rarely used, tool in the diagnosis of breast cancer. The majority of breast lumps are benign. Hence, the challenge is to distinguish between the malignant and benign tumors. Out of the 1 million breast biopsies performed annually in the United States, approximately 80% are benign. This large fraction of women undergo unnecessary testing for beast cancer and are caused stress due to the potential diagnosis and the invasiveness of a biopsy. Nuclear medicine techniques can play an important role in improving this situation. Studies have shown that the uptake of the radiotracer sestamibi is significantly higher in invasive breast tumors than in the normal breast tissue. The reasons, however, are not completely understood. It is generally thought that sestamibi collects in cells with high metabolic activity (cancer cells have a substantially higher metabolic rate than that of normal cells) or that membrane changes in cancerous cells contribute to the increased uptake. It has been recently determined that the use of sestamibi to distinguish between malignant and benign tumors has a sensitivity (the percentage of malignant tumors correctly identified as malignant) of 90% and a specificity (the percentage of benign tumors correctly identified as benign) of 87%. The use of sestamibi or thallium-201 (Tl-201) in conjunction with conventional x-ray mammography yields a high specificity of 90% and sensitivity of 97% for the diagnosis of breast

cancer. That is, using x-ray mammography along with gamma-ray imaging allows radiologists to both detect abnormalities and to correctly identify those abnormalities as being either malignant or benign.

Rapidly proliferating tumor cells use more glucose than do normal cells. Thus, a high glucose uptake may indicate breast cancer. PET imaging with a fluorine-labeled glucose tracer may be used to gauge the effectiveness of chemotherapy and may also be used to detect the degree to which the cancer has spread.

Brain imaging. One of the most successful uses of PET has been in the area of brain imaging. With various tracers, PET can be utilized to image cerebral blood flow, oxygen utilization, and glucose metabolism in the brain. The organization of the brain undergoes changes between birth and adulthood. These changes can be viewed with PET imaging by studying the pattern of glucose utilization as a function of age. PET imaging can also help diagnose and explain the causes of epilepsy.

One active area of medical research is in understanding and treating Parkinson's disease. PET imaging is not required to diagnose this disease; however, the presence of a deficit of brain activity, its pattern, and the conservation of dopamine can assist in the diagnosis. The uptake of fluorine-18-labeled dopamine (FDOPA) provides an in vivo index of the integrity of the dopamine terminals. FDOPA is increasingly used to monitor the effects of Parkinson's disease treatments such as transplanted dopamine-producing tissues. The use of PET has demonstrated a substantial increase in FDOPA in patients following human fetal nigral grafts. PET imaging has also recently been used to monitor the effects of neuroprotective therapies or surgery such as deep-brain stimulation. Recent studies using a different radiolabeled compound suggest the correlation of Parkinson's disease with the presence of an ongoing inflammatory process in the brain.

PET continues to be the best imaging modality for cognitive brain studies. These studies have typically analyzed cerebral blood flow, a measure that provides the most reliable index of moment-to-moment brain function. A standard cognitive PET study consists of several consecutive scans per subject, measuring blood flow changes in the brain that take place while the subject is engaged in some kind of cognitive task such as reading or speaking. By comparing the activation pattern associated with different conditions, it is possible to identify brain areas showing a differential response in relation to a specific cognitive performance. Recently PET imaging has been used extensively to study the performance of magnetic resonance imaging (MRI) cognitive studies. MRI cognitive studies are less expensive, but the results are not as clear as in PET imaging.

Small animal imaging. Many dramatic advances in biological research in recent years have focused on the molecular basis of how systems of the body function. PET and SPECT imaging permit noninvasive

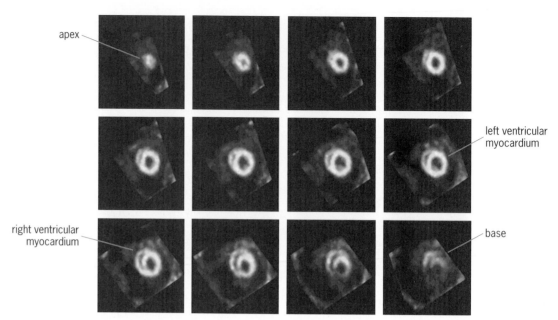

Fig. 1. Sestamibi study of a normal rat heart performed on the FASPECT imaging system at the University of Arizona, showing consecutive (left to right) reconstructed slices of a normal myocardium after 99mTc-MIBI injection. The images are displayed from apex to base of the heart with 1-mm (0.04-in.) spacing. The left ventricular and right ventricular myocardium can be identified. (*Courtesy of G. Kastis*)

molecular imaging of cellular function in the living subject. It is advantageous to use small animals such as mice and rats to perform such functional studies because they can be imaged in large numbers and under strict controls. However, SPECT and PET have generally been considered to lack the necessary resolution to image such small animals. Recently PET and SPECT systems have been designed and successfully used to image small animals. Two such

systems, the microPET system and the FASTSPECT system, have an approximate resolution between 1 and 2 mm.

To design PET systems for small animal imaging, researchers had to minimize the overall size of the system and use high-resolution detectors. For SPECT systems, researchers have replaced the traditional parallel-hole or fan-beam collimators with pinhole collimators placed near the mouse to magnify the projection images at each tomographic projection angle. In addition, it is advantageous not to rotate the detectors but to use a set of fixed detectors and pinhole collimators placed around the animal and a fixed set of angles.

PET and SPECT imaging allows the time course and biodistribution of a molecular probe to be determined in a single living animal. Furthermore, because the same animal is used at each time point, variability caused by interanimal differences is removed. These modalities also provide the opportunity to quickly perform the same experiment in both mice and humans, facilitating direct comparison and unification of basic and clinical research. An example is rat myocardial imaging with technetium-labeled sestamibi to image the infarct or dead regions of the heart (**Figs. 1** and **2**).

Imaging gene expression. Gene expression refers to the extent to which the protein encoded by the gene is successfully produced in a cell. An area attracting considerable interest is the merger of molecular imaging with molecular biology to create methods to measure the expression of a reporter gene (a gene that is known to encode a specific, detectable protein) in vivo with PET and SPECT. A PET or SPECT reporter gene encodes a protein that is able to trap or bind a radiolabeled probe. The location, magnitude

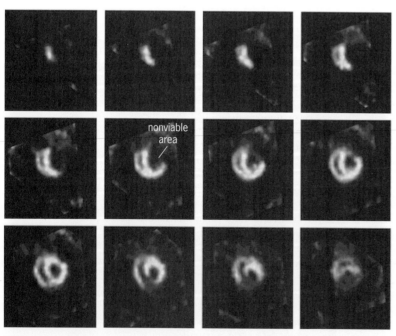

Fig. 2. Consecutive (left to right) reconstructed slices of a rat myocardium that contain nonviable tissue due to temporary blockage. The tracer was sestamibi. (*Courtesy of G. Kastis*)

of expression, and time course of expression levels of any gene that is introduced into a mouse can be monitored in vivo. Conventional methods of detecting reporter gene expression are limited by their inability to noninvasively determine the location and magnitude of gene expression in living animals.

For background information *see* COMPTON EFFECT; COMPUTERIZED TOMOGRAPHY; GAMMA-RAY DETECTORS; GENE; MEDICAL IMAGING; MOLECULAR BIOLOGY; SCINTILLATION COUNTER in the McGraw-Hill Encyclopedia of Science & Technology.

Matthew A. Kupinski

Bibliography. P. Berghammer et al., Nuclear medicine and breast cancer: A review of current strategies and novel therapies, *Breast*, 10:184–197, 2001; R. Cabeza and A. Kingstone (eds.), *Handbook of Functional Neuroimaging of Cognition*, MIT Press, Cambridge, 2001; A. F. Chatziioannou, PET scanners dedicated to molecular imaging of small animal models, *Mol. Imag. Biol.*, 4(1):47–63, 2002; S. S. Gambhir et al., Assays for noninvasive imaging of reporter gene expression, *Nucl. Med. Biol.*, 26:481–490, 1999; J. W. LeBlank et al., C-SPRINT: A prototype Compton camera system for low energy gamma-ray imaging, *IEEE Trans. Nucl. Sci.*, 45(3):943–950, 1998; M. E. Phelps, Positron emission tomography provides molecular imaging of biological processes, *Proc. Nat. Acad. Sci.*, 97(16):9226–9233, 2000.

Genetic diversity in nature reserves

A major objective of conservation is to maintain biological diversity by promoting long-term persistence of species as part of native ecosystems. Biological diversity includes genetic diversity within populations, within species, and within natural assemblages or communities of different species. These types of diversity are interdependent. For example, genetic diversity is known to promote species persistence, and species depend on the communities to which they belong. At the same time, if a species is lost, so too is its genetic diversity, and the diversity of the community of which the species was a part is diminished.

Because the greatest threat to biodiversity is habitat loss and fragmentation, much attention has focused on establishing reserves and reserve networks to maintain habitat and to slow rates of loss. As it is not possible to commit all potential sites to conservation purposes, it is necessary for conservation practitioners to decide both how many and which sites are necessary to conserve biological diversity.

Ecological conservation. Despite the role that genetic diversity plays in promoting persistence of populations and species, most reserve selection and design efforts focus on ecological characteristics (for example, habitat requirements and demography of a species), species distribution patterns, or natural community diversity. Ecological conservation approaches are advocated because ecological and an-

thropogenic factors typically pose more immediate extinction threats to species than do genetic factors and because populations that are ecologically secure are typically genetically secure. However, how well ecological conservation approaches actually maintain genetic diversity depends on the aspect of genetic diversity considered.

Genetic conservation. Two aspects of genetic diversity are important in conservation: (1) preventing excessive levels of inbreeding (mating among close relatives) within populations to ensure that genetic factors do not increase species extinction probabilities, and (2) maintaining the range of diversity in a species to provide future evolutionary potential.

Inbreeding prevention. Increased levels of inbreeding can reduce survival and reproduction (called inbreeding depression), but it is a concern only in extremely small populations and in populations that have decreased substantially in size over a short period of time. Preventing excessive inbreeding within populations can typically be accomplished by managing for ecological characteristics that facilitate large population sizes (that is, by providing sufficient habitat area or resources). In all but extreme cases, preventing inbreeding does not require specific manipulation of genetic diversity.

Capturing species diversity. Capturing a species' natural diversity within a reserve in order to provide future evolutionary potential is more problematic. Most conservation scientists agree that maintaining genetic variation that allows individuals to adapt to current and future environments is important. However, determining how best to measure and conserve such variation remains the subject of extensive debate. Additionally, there is no scientific evidence regarding the proportion of genetic diversity in a species that is necessary to maintain future evolutionary potential.

Measuring genetic diversity. Often, genetic diversity in a population or species is represented by the number of alleles sampled from the deoxyribonucleic acid (DNA) or allozymes (different forms of the same protein) of a number of individuals and by estimates of the frequency of heterozygotes versus homozygotes. This information can also be used to quantify how differentiated populations are from one another. This type of diversity is relatively easy to measure and has been used as an index of overall genetic variation in a species. In this context, it has been used extensively to identify high-priority populations and to set genetic conservation goals. For example, the Center for Plant Conservation recommends having a 90–95% probability of conserving alleles that occur at a frequency greater than 0.05. Others recommend conserving examples of all alleles.

Unfortunately, patterns based on DNA or allozymes are not always correlated with patterns of physical characteristics. Because physical characteristics are more likely to be the result of natural selection, many researchers advocate measuring genetic diversity based on these characteristics directly.

Physical characteristics are challenging to quantify because they are the result of interactions between many genes and the environment, and removing environmental effects requires specialized experimental and analytical techniques. Determining which physical characteristics are adaptive is even more difficult. Further, diversity patterns for multiple physical characteristics often are not correlated, indicating that reserves established based on variation in one physical characteristic would not reflect others.

Very recently it has been suggested that rather than conserving patterns based on current physical characteristics, conservation scientists should target variation in alleles at all the gene loci affecting the physical traits of interest. There is theoretical evidence that genetic diversity measured using allozymes and DNA is correlated with allelic diversity at these other gene loci and, therefore, may, under certain circumstances, in fact provide good estimates of adaptive potential after all.

Other indicators of genetic diversity. The best way to capture genetic diversity in a subset of populations is to base conservation decisions on known levels and patterns of diversity. Unfortunately, such data are lacking for most species; and due to limited time and funding, genetic diversity patterns likely remain uncharacterized. Therefore, it is important to understand how much diversity is likely to be captured when conservation decisions are based on other criteria. For example, in an empirical study based on four endangered plant species, protecting 53–100% of the populations was necessary to represent allelic richness in a species when different populations were chosen with no prior knowledge of genetic diversity. It was necessary to conserve 20–64% of populations to be within ±10% of species-level heterozygosity estimates. Numbers of populations needed to meet diversity goals were similar, regardless of whether the populations were chosen randomly or based on ecological criteria, indicating that the proportion of populations conserved is a good indicator of the likelihood that genetic diversity is represented. These results are likely to be broadly applicable to rare species that occur in patchy populations with moderate to high interpopulational dispersal.

Conserving rare species. There is little information on the proportion of populations of individual rare species that are included in reserves, so it is difficult to assess the adequacy of current reserve networks for conserving genetic diversity. Historically, lands have been conserved for a variety of nonbiological reasons, resulting in some species and natural communities being overrepresented in protected areas (those in mountainous areas), whereas others (mostly those in low elevation and coastal areas) are poorly represented or not represented at all. Clearly, if species are not included in reserve networks or are included only at a few sites, a great deal of genetic diversity will not be captured. Since the mid-1980s, researchers have been developing methods that maximize the number of communities or species included in regional reserve networks by selecting sites that best complement sites that have already been selected for protection. Although these methods ensure representation of all species and communities of concern, it is still necessary for practitioners to decide how many examples of each species should be included in reserve networks to capture genetic diversity.

A number of general conservation intensities (number or proportion of populations conserved) have been suggested and applied; however, only one targets genetic diversity. The Center for Plant Conservation suggests that sampling from five rare plant populations is sufficient to conserve most of the evolutionarily significant genetic variation (as represented by allozyme alleles) for conservation in captivity. The World Conservation Union recommends protecting 10–12% of the total land area or of each ecosystem in a nation or region in order to maintain general species diversity. Others have considered rare plant species to be adequately represented if 10–12% of the populations are protected. The Nature Conservancy suggests conserving at least 10 viable populations of species distributed throughout as much of each regional planning area in which the species occurs. Some Nature Conservancy planning regions have based conservation intensities on the regional species distributions, conserving larger numbers of populations for species with more limited distributions.

Given the empirical results discussed above, reserve designs based on most of these suggested conservation intensities will result in substantial loss of genetic diversity. The Nature Conservancy recommendations are likely sufficient for species with less than 20 populations, but genetic diversity in species with larger numbers of populations could still be underrepresented.

Clearly, losing any populations of a rare species will have genetic consequences. Although conserving all populations of all rare species is not feasible, there is no scientific evidence indicating how much genetic diversity can be lost before future evolutionary potential is significantly diminished. Thus, reserve networks should include as many populations as possible, ideally at least 60–70% of those populations. Conserving larger proportions of populations would also reduce stochastic (random or unpredictable) extinction threats and provide a more realistic chance of maintaining processes that help perpetuate diversity over time.

For background information *see* BIODIVERSITY; ECOLOGY, APPLIED; ENDANGERED SPECIES; GENETICS; POPULATION VIABILITY in the McGraw-Hill Encyclopedia of Science & Technology.　　Maile Neel

Bibliography. Center for Plant Conservation, Genetic sampling guidelines for conservation collections of endangered plants, in D. A. Falk and K. E. Holsinger (eds.), *Genetics and Conservation of Rare Plants*, pp. 225–238, Oxford University Press, New York, 1991; C. Groves et al., *Designing a Geography of Hope*, Nature Conservancy, Arlington, VA, 2000;

M. E. Soulé and J. Terborgh, *Continental Conservation: Scientific Foundations of Regional Reserve Networks*, Island Press, Washington, DC, 1999.

Genetics of flower morphology

The evolution of flower morphology is beginning to be understood through research on the genetic mechanisms of reproductive development in angiosperms (flowering plants). The model organism *Arabidopsis thaliana* (thale cress) has figured prominently in these studies. Although *Arabidopsis* was the first plant completely sequenced (in 2000), earlier genetic studies of *Arabidopsis* (beginning in the late 1980s) paved the way for evolutionary interpretations of the molecular processes underlying floral diversity.

Genes directing flower development. Many of the most central genes controlling flower development were discovered in the earliest stages of *Arabidopsis* mutant analysis.

MADS-box genes. In 1990, the genes representing the *deficiens* and *agamous* mutants were cloned from *Antirrhinum* and *Arabidopsis*, respectively. The protein products of *DEFICIENS (DEF)* and *AGAMOUS (AG)* were found to be similar to each other as well as to protein products of the serum response factor (*SRF*; from humans) and mini-chromosome maintenance-1 (*MCM1*; from yeast) genes. All four genes encode transcription factors (regulators of the expression of other genes) and contain the same deoxyribonucleic acid (DNA)–binding, 56-amino-acid domain known as the MADS box (named after the first letter of each gene: *MCM1, AG, DEF,* and *SRF*); these are known together as the MADS-box genes.

ABC model. It had already been hypothesized from mutant phenotypes that the *DEF* and *AG* genes controlled floral organ identity in a combinatorial, whorl-specific fashion; that is, floral organs arise in four concentric rings (whorls), with sepals in the outermost whorl, followed by petals and stamens and finally carpels in the central whorl. An A function was envisioned to direct sepal identity, a B function together with A to specify petals, B plus a C function to designate stamens, and C alone to promote carpel development. This is the so-called ABC model for floral organ specification (**Fig. 1**). The *DEF* and *AG* gene products were assigned to the B and C functions, respectively.

Non–MADS-box regulators. Other principal, non-MADS-box regulators of flower development were discovered early as *Arabidopsis* mutants. The *APETALA2 (AP2)* gene was shown to confer the A function along with *APETALA1 (AP1)*. *AP1* was cloned first and shown to be a MADS-box gene, but *AP2* was found to encode a putative transcription factor from a hitherto unknown protein family. Likewise, the *LEAFY (LFY)* gene, which was shown to control the entire floral developmental program, was also found to code for a previously unknown type of transcriptional regulator.

Limitations of ABC model. Researchers are discovering that the ABC model may need to be revised, as the model alone cannot explain certain observed complexities of floral developmental genetics, such as digressions in the conservation of A function, redundant control over the ABC system, and partitioning of genetic function.

Incomplete A function conservation. Through molecular evolutionary and gene exchange studies, sequence and functional homologies were found between *AG* and *LFY* and genes present in *Antirrhinum*. However, even though an *AP1*-like gene has been cloned from *Antirrhinum* based on mutant phenotype (*SQUAMOSA*), the product of this gene appears to operate in a manner distinct from the A function. Indeed, no A-function gene has so far been reported from *Antirrhinum*. Although *AP1*- and *AP2*-like genes are known from a diversity of plants, including

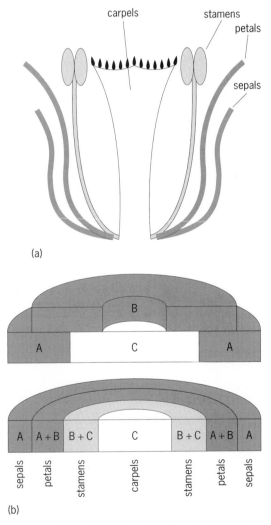

Fig. 1. Regulation of floral organ fate based on the ABC model. (*a*) Cross section of a mature flower, indicating the four types of organs forming the central gynoecium. (*b*) Half section of an early flower primordium with the domains of ABC homeotic gene activities, which generate four unique combinations that specify organ fate. (*Adapted from Detlef Weigel, Plant development, 1999 McGraw-Hill Yearbook of Science & Technology, McGraw-Hill, New York, 1998*)

Gerbera (Asteraceae), *Petunia* (Solanaceae), and maize (Poaceae), none of these appear to code for A-function proteins. Therefore, the existence of a conserved A function in angiosperm flower development is questionable. Instead, it is possible that different genes take on the A function in different groups of flowering plants, or that the ABC model is too simple to accommodate all cases of sepal and petal determination.

Based on the presence of B- and C-function MADS-box genes in flowerless gymnosperms, it has been hypothesized that determination of flower organ identity is secondary to a more basic role of these genes in sex determination. It has also been hypothesized that "true" sepals of the kind expressed by *Arabidopsis* and *Antirrhinum* are a relatively recent evolutionary innovation, since lower dicots and monocots characteristically lack discrete sepals and petals and bear only one type of organ, tepals (usually petallike).

Redundant control. A more recently recognized class of MADS-box genes, the three *SEPALLATA* (*SEP*) genes of *Arabidopsis*, provide redundant control over the ABC system. These genes were identified through their sequence similarity to *AG* rather than through individual mutant phenotypes. Triple-null mutants of *SEP1-3* produce "flowers" consisting only of sepallike organs, which has indicated to some investigators that these leaflike structures represent the "ground state" for floral parts. However, research on other organisms such as *Gerbera* has shown that *SEP*-class homologs play divergent roles in development of the condensed, disklike asteraceous inflorescence as well as in the different floral forms that are borne on it.

Partitioning of genetic function. Specifically, one *SEP*-like gene of *Gerbera* controls the C function only in the staminal whorl of flowers borne at the inflorescence periphery, whereas another *SEP* homolog (the probable duplication partner of the first) appears to control the C function only in carpels of inner flowers. This partitioning of genetic function has probably had morphological evolutionary consequences since the outer flowers of *Gerbera* inflorescences are male-sterile and highly asymmetrical, with fused elongate petals, whereas the inner flowers are bisexual and nearly symmetrical with nonelongate petals. In its totality, the *Gerbera* inflorescence looks much like a single flower and probably attracts pollinating insects in the same capacity.

Evolutionary genetics. The greater genetic complexity now recognized behind flower development indicates that the ABC model is in need of revision. For example, it was once believed that explaining the homeotic evolution of a second corolla (fused petal) whorl in the Hawaiian lobelia genus *Clermontia* (Campanulaceae) would be a simple issue of demonstrating expression of B-function genes in the first, normally sepalar whorl (**Fig. 2**). However, with the generality of A function now in question, the mechanistic basis for the double-corolla phenotype in *Clermontia* might be other than simply out-of-place B-function gene expression. It might be that the naturally occurring mutation could be within a B-function coding sequence or perhaps in its transcriptional promoter, which might have elements that fine-tune spatiotemporal expression. It could equally well be that a dysfunctional gene that normally excludes B-function genes from the first whorl of *Clermontia* could be the culprit.

Analyzing this problem genetically will not be a simple task, since *Clermontia*, unlike weedy *Arabidopsis*, is a small tree that is much less tractable to genetic studies requiring progeny analysis. Such

(a)

(b)

Fig. 2. Clermontia species. (*a*) *Clermontia montis-loa*, from the island of Hawaii, has an extra whorl of petals substituted for sepals. Two-thirds of the naturally occurring species of this endemic genus have this homeotic phenotype. (*b*) A comparison of preserved flowers and buds from "wild type" *Clermontia* species with those showing the double-corolla phenotype. *Clermontia arborescens* and *C. tuberculata* have short, true sepals; *C. clermontioides* subsp. *rockiana* has long sepals; and *C. kakeana* shows complete sepal-to-petal conversion. (*Courtesy of M. Weinerman*)

"forward" genetic studies, starting with a phenotypically recognizable mutation and ending up with the gene linked to it, may be difficult to accomplish outside of model plant species. Therefore, investigators are turning more to "reverse" genetic approaches that start with a gene sequence that is suspected to have a particular function (for example, through molecular evolutionary relationship to genes of known function) and work backwards to establish this function through transgenic experiments that overexpress and/or underexpress the protein product of the gene. It is in this way, for example, that the *Gerbera SEP*-like genes were characterized.

A large-scale effort of this type to identify genes specific to flower development and those linked with floral diversification, the Floral Genome Project, is under way. The Floral Genome Project is sequencing genes expressed during the earliest stages of floral development in diverse lineages of angiosperms, particularly putatively primitive taxa such as *Amborella* (the sister group to the rest of flowering plants), water lilies (Nymphaeales), other members of the ANITA grade (such as *Illicium*), tulip tree (Magnoliaceae), avocado (Lauraceae), and *Acorus* (a basal monocot). Genes in common or distinct to these species should provide valuable molecular tools for the next generation of plant evolutionary developmental research.

For background information *see* DEVELOPMENTAL GENETICS; FLOWER; PLANT EVOLUTION; PLANT GROWTH; PLANT MORPHOGENESIS in the McGraw-Hill Encyclopedia of Science & Technology.

Bibliography. E. Coen, *The Art of Genes: How Organisms Make Themselves*, Oxford University Press, Oxford, 1999; Q. C. B. Cronk, R. M. Bateman, and J. A. Hawkins (eds.), *Developmental Genetics and Plant Evolution*, Taylor & Francis, London, 2002; S. H. Howell, *Molecular Genetics of Plant Development*, Cambridge University Press, Cambridge, 1998.

Geothermal energy

Earth is an extraordinarily hot planet. The center of Earth, which on average is 6371 km (3982 mi) below the surface, is as hot as the surface of the Sun—around 6273 K (6000°C; 10,800°F). The source of this heat is the radioactive decay of long-lived isotopes of potassium (^{40}K), thorium (^{232}Th), and uranium (^{238}U); without the heat generated from these decaying isotopes, Earth would have cooled since its formation to a cold solid mass. That Earth's surface is livable with such high temperatures in its interior is due mainly to the low thermal conductivity of most crustal rocks. In some places, however, very high temperatures are present right at Earth's surface. Volcanic eruptions can bring molten lava to the surface, while in other locations geysers, fumaroles, and hot springs are strong reminders of Earth's internal heat. Such heat, produced from Earth's natural processes

whether at the surface or at depth, is the source of the sustainable energy supply known as geothermal energy.

Accessing Earth's heat. The median global heat flow through Earth's surface is around 60 mW m^{-2}. This figure is small in comparison to the energy from mean global insolation (the solar radiation received by the Earth's surface at any given point), which is around 1400 W m^{-2}. However, the temperature in Earth's crust increases with depth at an average rate of about 17–30°C/km (50–87°F/mi). This means that temperatures high enough to produce energy are quite accessible in many places.

To utilize this subsurface heat, a "working fluid" is needed to extract the heat and bring it to the surface where it can be used to operate a power station. This working fluid is usually water or steam that is heated when percolating ground water encounters magmatically heated rocks. **Figure 1** shows a conventional geothermal field in cross section. The essential elements are an aquifer bringing ground water into proximity to a deep heat source and an overlying impermeable cap rock. This cap retains the steam and hot water and allows useful pressures to develop. Continual water recharge is necessary to maintain the hydraulic state. These elements occur together in only a very restricted range worldwide, which is why geothermal power is used only in a limited number of countries at present.

In February 2000, geothermal power plants operated in 21 countries including Iceland, Italy, New Zealand, Japan, the Philippines, Indonesia, the United States, Mexico, and some countries in Central America. The total generating capacity was 7974 MW, which was a 16.7% increase over 1995 levels.

Conventional power plants. The first modern geothermal power plant was built at Lardarello, Italy, in 1904. This plant and later ones built on the site use naturally occurring steam to power turbines and generate electricity. "Vapor-dominated" geothermal fields such as Lardarello and The Geysers in California are at the high-enthalpy end of a spectrum of geothermal resources. More common are medium-enthalpy geothermal fields such as Sumikawa and Yanaizu-Nishiyama in Japan, which produce both steam and high-pressure hot water. The lowest-enthalpy fields, producing primarily hot water, are generally for "direct-use" applications such as heating of buildings, greenhouses, and public facilities, though electricity may also be generated.

Enthalpy level differences. Different geothermal power station technologies have been developed for each enthalpy level. In high-enthalpy fields dominated by natural steam, "dry steam" power plants are operated by feeding steam directly into a turbine. The steam is garnered from boreholes drilled into the rock mass. In medium-enthalpy fields, the boreholes deliver a mixture of steam and high-pressure hot water to a "flash steam" power plant. The high-pressure hot water is piped into a lower-pressure "flash unit" where a proportion of the water rapidly

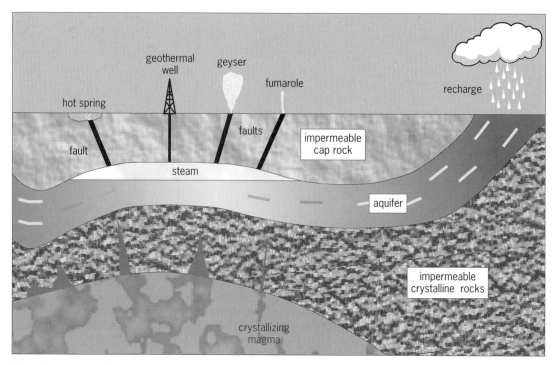

Fig. 1. Cross section of a conventional geothermal field. Water enters the system in the recharge zone and is heated by contact with a buried magmatic source. The cap rock retains the steam and hot water except where faults and wells cut it.

vaporizes (flashes) to steam. This steam is combined with the primary vapor produced from the borehole, and both are again fed into a turbine to generate electricity. The hot water may be flashed several times if sufficient energy remains. In the lowest-enthalpy-level geothermal fields, a technology known as binary power generation is used to generate electricity. In this case, low-enthalpy fluids with temperatures sometimes below 100°C (212°F) are passed through a heat exchanger that transfers the energy to a low-boiling-point fluid such as iso-pentane or a refrigerant. This fluid is vaporized and used to operate a turbine before being condensed back to a liquid for reuse.

Future capacity. Continued growth in conventional geothermal power generation is expected, with generating capacity predicted to reach 11,400 MW in 2005. Most of this growth is anticipated to occur in countries already actively generating power from geothermal energy, notably Indonesia, Kenya, the Philippines, Turkey, Nicaragua, and the United States. This distribution owes more to geological factors than to business or politics. The majority of worldwide geothermal generating capacity adjoins tectonic plate boundaries such as the Pacific Ring of Fire, which are regions of concentrated volcanic activity and subsequent high heat flow.

HDR technology. Conventional geothermal energy is limited by its particular need for cap rock, an aquifer, and a magmatic heat source. The heat of the Earth is very much more widespread, but without a working fluid it is impractical to extract the energy. More extensive use of the Earth's abundant geothermal energy requires an engineered solution.

This tantalizing prospect is called hot dry rock (HDR) geothermal energy.

In a region where rocks with temperatures in the range 200–300°C (392–572°F) occur at depths of less than 5 km (3.1 mi), heat can be extracted by pumping water through an engineered heat exchanger connecting two or more wells (**Fig. 2**). This heat exchanger is a volume of hot dry rock with its permeability enhanced by hydraulic stimulation. This involves pumping high-pressure water into the preexisting fracture system that is present in all rocks to varying degrees. The high-pressure water opens the stressed natural fractures and facilitates micro-slippage along them. When the water pressure is released, the fractures close once more, but the slippage that occurred prevents them from mating perfectly again. The result is a permanent million-fold increase in permeability along the fracture systems.

In a typical HDR system, an initial borehole is sunk into the hot rock mass and a hydraulic stimulation is performed. A three-dimensional microseismic array deployed on the surface and in nearby wells is used to record acoustic emissions from the slipping fractures. In this way the progress of the stimulation is monitored over several weeks, and the shape and size of the growing heat exchanger is mapped. A second well is then drilled into the margin of the heat exchanger about 500 m (1640 ft) distant from the first well. Water can then be pumped between the two wellheads through the underground heat exchanger. The superheated water returned to the surface can have its energy extracted and then be reinjected to repeat the process.

More than $500 million has been spent in the United States, Europe, Japan, and Australia on HDR research since the concept was first proposed at the Los Alamos National Laboratory, New Mexico, in 1973. To date, no HDR power stations have been built, but a number of very promising research tests have recently been completed. The signs suggest that HDR is a technology on the point of maturing.

HDR resources. One problem with HDR is the lack of physical manifestation of the energy sought. Unlike conventional geothermal energy, there is often no outward sign of the presence of suitable high-temperature rock masses. No geysers, fumaroles, or hot springs occur, because of the lack of natural fluid. Exploration for HDR resources requires a different approach.

In Australia, for example, there are signs of current volcanism. The last volcanic activity occurred in the southeast around 5000 years ago, and there is little remaining heat associated with this episode. However, Australia has a huge HDR geothermal energy resource (**Fig. 3**). The origins of the heat are large granite bodies that crystallized more than 300 million years ago. The original heat is lost, but many of these granites are highly fractionated with unusually elevated levels of ^{40}K, ^{232}Th, and ^{238}U. This causes them to generate above-average quantities of heat. With much of the Australian continent covered by sedimentary basins full of shales, coals, and siltstones of low thermal conductivity, many high-heat-producing granites are covered in a thick insulating blanket. The combination of a high heat source and good insulation has produced high temperatures. Buried granites with temperatures as high as 253°C (487°F) have been located by drilling through the sediments to depths as shallow as 3.5 km (2.2 mi).

One method that shows promise for HDR exploration under sedimentary basins is gravity surveying. The highly fractionated target granites are lower in density than most rocks. Their presence causes a small but detectable mass deficit which is reflected in lower-than-average values of gravity. With the cost of wildcat drilling for geothermal energy too high to be economical, a reliable remote sensing technique such as gravity surveying may turn out to be very important in the future of HDR geothermal energy.

Outlook. There are many locations worldwide where relatively high temperatures occur in the subsurface at drillable depths. Conventional geothermal power generation will continue to grow and flourish in those places where naturally occurring steam and hot water result. Elsewhere, the HDR approach to geothermal energy production holds the promise of abundant renewable energy for a much wider cross section of humanity.

For background information *see* EARTH, HEAT FLOW IN; EARTH INTERIOR; ELECTRIC POWER GENERATION; ENERGY CONVERSION; ENERGY SOURCES; ENTHALPY; GEOLOGIC THERMOMETRY; GEOPHYSICAL EXPLORATION; GEOTHERMAL POWER; HEAT TRANSFER;

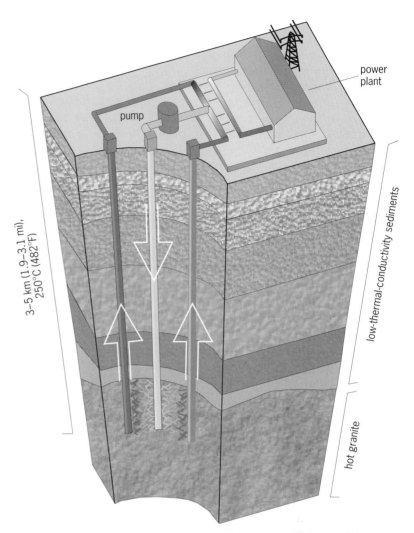

Fig. 2. Heat-exchange system for extracting hot dry rock geothermal energy. This involves pumping cold water down a 3–5-km-deep (1.9–3.1-mi) central well and recovering it as superheated water from wells on either side.

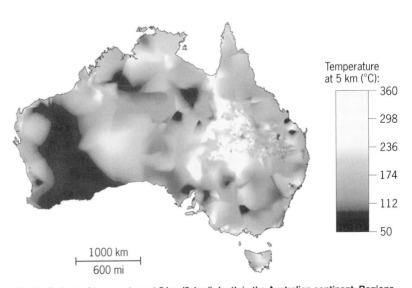

Fig. 3. Estimated temperature at 5 km (3.1 mi) depth in the Australian continent. Regions of high temperature are shown in light shades of gray. (*After D. Swenson, P. Chopra, and D. Wyborn, Initial calculations of performance for an Australian hot dry rock reservoir, Proceedings of the World Geothermal Congress 2000, Kyushu-Tohoku, Japan, pp. 3907–3912, May 28–June 10, 2000*)

MAGMA; VOLCANOLOGY in the McGraw-Hill Encyclopedia of Science & Technology.   Prame Chopra

Bibliography. W. B. Durham and B. Bonner, Self propping and fluid flow in slightly offset joints at high effective pressure, *J. Geophys. Res.*, 99:9391–9399, 1994; G. W. Huttrer, The status of world geothermal power generation 1995–2000, *Proceedings of the World Geothermal Congress 2000, Kyushu-Tohoku, Japan*, pp. 23–37, May 28–June 10, 2000; D. Swenson, P. Chopra, and D. Wyborn, Initial calculations of performance for an Australian hot dry rock reservoir, *Proceedings of the World Geothermal Congress 2000, Kyushu-Tohoku, Japan*, pp. 3907–3912, May 28–June 10, 2000.

Global warming and atmospheric ozone

Stratospheric ozone depletion was arguably the most important global-scale environmental problem of the twentieth century, and global warming may be the greatest for the twenty-first century. Since these two phenomena are largely caused by emissions of different gases, they have usually been thought of as independent. Recently, scientists have realized that these two may be more connected than was believed.

Depletion of the Earth's protective stratospheric ozone layer has been caused by human production and release of halocarbons, both chlorofluorocarbons (CFCs) and bromine-containing gases. These compounds decompose in the stratosphere, releasing the halogens chlorine and bromine, which chemically destroy ozone. In polar regions, the depletion chemistry is quite sensitive to temperature, with extremely cold conditions leading to severe ozone destruction. This has been seen most dramatically over Antarctica, where more than 35% of the ozone layer has been destroyed each year since 1985 during the Southern Hemisphere springtime (September and October) when the region is sunlit (activating the chlorine) but the air is still cold and isolated from midlatitude air by a strong polar vortex. In addition to the halogens, reactive molecules containing nitrogen or hydrogen can also destroy ozone. The abundance of these gases in the stratosphere has increased, but this is not believed to have contributed very much to ozone losses up to the present.

Trends. The buildup of greenhouse gases in the atmosphere has resulted in global warming. While CFCs are greenhouse gases and have therefore contributed to global warming over the past few decades, their contribution has been small (16%) compared to that from carbon dioxide (CO_2), methane (CH_4), and nitrous oxide (N_2O) [**Fig. 1**]. Ozone is also a greenhouse gas, so changes in its abundance affect global warming as well. Stratospheric ozone depletion has reduced the strength of the greenhouse effect, but this effect is even weaker than the warming influence of the halocarbons (which it partially offsets). The net effect of the halocarbons (as a greenhouse gas) and the resulting ozone loss has been to contribute an additional 9% to the greenhouse effect.

The net climate forcing (often referred to as the net greenhouse effect) results from addition of several individual terms. The largest positive term is the impact of greenhouse gases, which has been about $+2.5$ W/m^2 since 1750. However, particulates in the troposphere have had a substantial negative forcing, offsetting most of that. As a result, the net forcing (those two plus several others small terms) has been about $+0.5$ W/m^2. The importance of halocarbons depends upon how the picture is presented. Compared to greenhouse gases, they are small (9%). But compared to the net forcing of all the terms, the $+0.5$ W/m^2, they are quite large (30–40%).

Concern over ozone depletion has led to an international agreement limiting emissions of halocarbons (the Montreal Protocol and its amendments). Decreased halogen abundance is expected to lead to a recovery from the present depletion during the next several decades. However, the anticipated recovery will be complicated by effects other than halogen-induced destruction. The ozone response to climate change is complex, encompassing the many direct and indirect ways in which greenhouse gases affect the atmosphere.

Areas outside the polar regions are subject to several effects. There, greenhouse gas increases cool the stratosphere, which slows the chemical reaction rates of ozone depletion, indirectly leading to more ozone. Increases in methane directly affect ozone

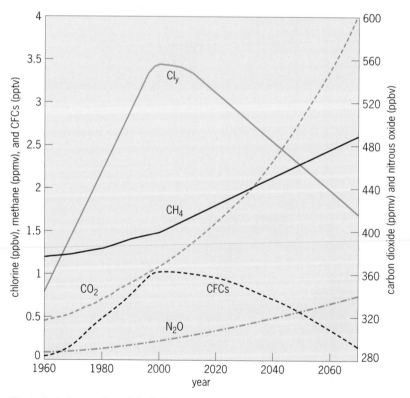

Fig. 1. Emission trends for CO_2, N_2O, CH_4, CFCs, and chlorine (Cl_y). Projected lower stratospheric chlorine loading is based on the trend derived from the 1992 Copenhagen revisions to the 1987 Montreal Protocol. Greenhouse gas emissions are based on observations through the 1980s, and subsequently are similar to the projections of the 1992 Intergovernmental Panel on Climate Change. The exception is CFCs, for which a steady reduction after 2000 has been assumed, consistent with their expected phase-out and with the chlorine trends.

chemistry by removing chlorine from reactive, ozone-depleting species into stable molecules, again leading to ozone increases. However, increased methane also causes ozone destruction by enhancing the production of water vapor, which is a by-product of methane oxidation. Water vapor in the stratosphere alters local temperatures, and is a source of hydrogen oxides, molecules which catalytically destroy ozone. Circulation changes, water vapor increases in the lower atmosphere, or a warming of the tropopause (the boundary between the lower atmosphere and the stratosphere) may also increase the amount of water vapor entering the stratosphere; this has recently been observed but remains poorly understood. Increases in nitrogen oxides, released from N_2O in the stratosphere, also lead to small amounts of additional chemical ozone destruction.

Model simulations. It is expected that emissions of greenhouse gases will continue to grow in the future. While many teams of researchers have examined the potential impacts on climate, due to the complexity and computational expense of including chemistry in a global climate model, only a few have recently investigated the potential impacts on stratospheric ozone. The existing model results are somewhat uncertain, especially in the lowermost stratosphere where the bulk of the ozone layer is located. In that region, models have had only limited success in reproducing past trends as observed by ground-based and satellite instruments. Additionally, models exhibit considerable differences in the predicted temperature response to increasing greenhouse gases in the lowermost stratosphere. Though the radiative influence of these gases is fairly straightforward for most of the atmosphere, in this region dynamics plays a significant role as convection in the lower atmosphere influences the temperature of the tropopause. In some climate models, future greenhouse gas increases lead to warming not only in the troposphere but also in the lower stratosphere, resulting in ozone decreases there. In others, however, increased greenhouse gases lead to a colder lowermost stratosphere and, hence, more ozone. Additional uncertainties arise because observations show large increases in water vapor in this region during recent decades, but models cannot accurately simulate those changes. Models with a warmer tropopause do show increasing water vapor amounts, but this seems to be for the wrong reason as observations do not show a warmer tropopause. The largest effects are seen in models with a warmer tropopause and lower stratosphere, which probably give an idea of the upper limit of the greenhouse gas impact on ozone. In these models, both temperature changes and water vapor increases lead to significant ozone depletion, augmented by small additional depletion due to increased methane and N_2O. Future projections show that initial changes in ozone during the 2000–2010 decade arise primarily from greenhouse gases (**Fig. 2**). The total impact from climate exceeds that from halogens by the 2020s. Though the uncer-

tainties are large, those simulations indicate that the total ozone recovery may perhaps take roughly a decade longer than it would in the absence of climate change. The eventual recovery of stratospheric ozone will lead to a reversal of its climate impacts. Thus stratosphere ozone will go from having a weak surface cooling effect to a weak warming one, while the net effect of halocarbons will go from a weak surface warming to a weak cooling.

Upper stratosphere. Some scientists have instead examined the future of ozone in the upper stratosphere, where dynamics is not very important and where models can accurately reproduce past trends. Though there is less ozone there, it provides a guide to the potential impact of greenhouse gases on stratospheric ozone. In that region, chlorine-catalyzed depletion accounts for nearly all the twentieth-century trend, but this is not predicted to be the case in the twenty-first century. Initial recovery during the current decade is almost exclusively due to climate change, as chlorine amounts hold relatively steady. In subsequent decades, chlorine decreases and climate change combine to increase ozone amounts. By the 2030s, the impact of stratospheric cooling surpasses that of chlorine, so that there is more ozone than in 1979 despite significant remaining chlorine-induced depletion. Overall, the chlorine signal diminishes during the twenty-first century, approaching zero in the 2040s, while the climate change signal grows. Such results suggest that greenhouse gas emissions may indeed have a significant impact on future ozone levels.

Polar regions. In the polar regions, where ozone depletion has been the most severe, again climate

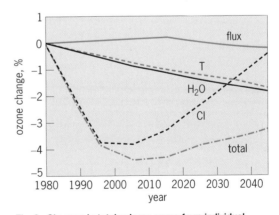

Fig. 2. Changes in total column ozone from individual factors in a model simulation with increasing water vapor. Changes are due to chemical interactions with chlorine and bromine (Cl) and water vapor (H_2O), cooling induced by increasing greenhouse gases (T), and changes in the flux of solar radiation resulting from ozone changes at higher altitudes. The last factor is affected by both halogens and greenhouse gases. The total change includes the negative feedback resulting from ozone changes themselves (increases heat the atmosphere, increasing the reaction rates of the chemistry which destroys ozone, reducing ozone amounts). Ozone changes due to methane and nitrous oxide are extremely small, so are not shown. (*From D. T. Shindell and V. Grewe, Separating the influence of halogen and climate changes on ozone recovery in the upper stratosphere, J. Geophys. Res., vol. 107, DOI 10.1029/2001JD000420, 2002*)

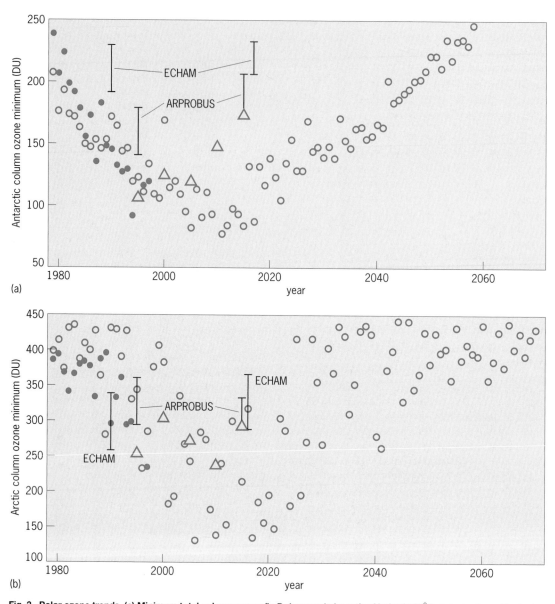

(a)

(b)

Fig. 3. Polar ozone trends. (*a*) Minimum total column ozone (in Dobson units) south of latitude 65°N, averaged over the last three days of September, as seen in satellite observations (filled circles), and in various global climate-chemistry models [GISS (open circles), UKMO (triangles), ARPROBUS (bars give range), ECHAM3/CHEM (bars give standard deviation)]. (*b*) Minimum column ozone north of latitude 65°N, averaged over the last three days of March, as seen in satellite data and in the four models. (*Adapted from World Meteorological Organization, Scientific Assessment of Ozone Depletion: 1998, Rep. 44, Geneva, 1999*).

models provide conflicting predictions about the future response of atmospheric dynamics to increasing greenhouse gases (**Fig. 3**). The largest observed depletion, so far, has been over Antarctica, where strong circumpolar winds confine air within a vortex over the polar cap, allowing it to become very cold during the winter. This extreme cold exacerbates ozone depletion, which responds nonlinearly to temperature. In fact, ozone depletion has been less severe over the Arctic because the temperature of the stratosphere there is typically a few degrees warmer than its Antarctic counterpart. In the Northern Hemisphere circulation is more dynamically active, leading to a less confined airmass over the pole and, hence, slightly warmer temperatures, such that

the conditions necessary to keep chlorine activated are no longer present in March when the Sun returns over the polar cap. Some climate models predict that increasing greenhouse gases may increase the stability of the Arctic vortex, allowing Antarctic-type depletion to occur in the Northern Hemisphere. Though some models do not find an increase in stability, the stratospheric cooling from greenhouse gases takes place in all the models, so that the overall conclusion from all the models is that a delay of about a decade in the onset of ozone recovery in the Arctic is likely. Longer delays and enhanced Arctic ozone depletion depend on the stability enhancement of the Arctic vortex, which is uncertain due to difficulties in simulating global-scale atmospheric waves in climate models. In the Antarctic, the models indicate that the ozone hole may increase in size due to the cooling effect of greenhouse gases, but that in the central portion of the ozone hole it is already so cold that further cooling does little to enhance ozone depletion. Antarctic recovery will likely begin within the next few years, although year-to-year variability may make it difficult to definitively detect for around a decade.

Tropospheric ozone. Greenhouse gas emissions do not have a profound influence on tropospheric ozone, other than emissions of methane, which plays an important role in chemical ozone formation. Global warming changes chemical reaction rates in the troposphere, and increases the abundance of water vapor through increased evaporation. Additionally, ozone changes in the stratosphere affect the amount of radiation reaching the troposphere, impacting photochemistry there. All these influences are thought to be quite small compared with the emissions of pollutants such as nitrogen oxides and carbon monoxide. Those emissions have led to a very large increase in tropospheric ozone since the industrial revolution which has contributed an additional 16% to the forcing of climate change from CO_2, CH_4, and N_2O.

For background information *see* ATMOSPHERIC GENERAL CIRCULATION; ATMOSPHERIC OZONE; CLIMATE MODELING; GLOBAL CLIMATE CHANGE; GREENHOUSE EFFECT; HALOGENATED HYDROCARBON; OZONE; STRATOSPHERIC OZONE in the McGraw-Hill Encyclopedia of Science & Technology.

Drew Shindell

Bibliography. J. E. Rosenfield, A. R. Douglass, and D. B. Considine, The impact of increasing carbon dioxide on ozone recovery, *J. Geophys. Res.*, vol. 107, DOI 10.1029/2001JD000824, 2002; D. T. Shindell and V. Grewe, Separating the influence of halogen and climate changes on ozone recovery in the upper stratosphere, *J. Geophys. Res.*, vol. 107, DOI 10.1029/2001JD000420, 2002; D. T. Shindell, D. Rind, and P. Lonergan, Increased polar stratospheric ozone losses and delayed eventual recovery due to increasing greenhouse gas concentrations, *Nature*, 392:589–592, 1998; S. Solomon and J. S. Daniel, Impact of the Montreal Protocol and its amendments on the rate of change of global radiative forcing, *Climatic Change*, 32:7–17, 1996; World Meteorological Organization, *Scientific Assessment of Ozone Depletion: 1998*, Rep. 44, Geneva, 1999.

Glycoprotein synthesis

Glycoproteins, that is, proteins with covalently attached sugars, are important in a myriad of biological processes and materials, including the determination of blood type, the resilience of cartilage, and virus infection. Glycoproteins may remain within the cells in which they are produced, attach to the cell surface, or be secreted. They have a diverse range of functions, including intercellular recognition, modulation of biological activity, and alteration of protein stability. The understanding of glycoproteins has lagged behind the study of other biomolecules such as DNA and RNA due to difficulties in working with glycoproteins. Biological systems produce glycoproteins as heterogeneous mixtures, and this presents practical problems in the purification of glycoproteins and the characterization of their biological effects. Currently, much research is focused on developing methods for glycoprotein synthesis that would offer access to homogeneous glycoproteins for biological and biophysical studies.

Biosynthesis. Biosynthesis of glycoproteins occurs via protein glycosylation (the addition of chains of sugar units, or oligosaccharides, to proteins). Protein glycosylation is a group of complex co- and posttranslational modifications that occur through the function of many enzymes working together in the endoplasmic reticulum (ER) and Golgi apparatus. Oligosaccharides can be attached to proteins through a variety of linkages, with the two most common linkages being N-linked and O-linked glycosylation.

N-linked glycosylation. In N-linked glycosylation, large oligosaccharides are linked to proteins through the side-chain nitrogen of the amino acid asparagine. The N-linked glycosylation process starts with the assembly of a lipid-linked oligosaccharide in the ER (**Fig. 1**). A series of glycotransferases add monosaccharides such as glucose and mannose to the lipid dolichol pyrophosphate to yield a large dolichol-linked oligosaccharide. Then the enzyme oligosaccharide transferase (OST) transfers the entire dolichol-linked oligosaccharide to a nascent polypeptide chain cotranslationally. OST recognizes a consensus sequence in the nascent polypeptide chain that consists of asparagine-X-serine or asparagine-X-threonine, where X can be any amino acid except proline. When the N-linked glycoprotein has been translated, a series of enzymes act on the polypeptide in the ER to ensure that the protein is folded correctly. Once the glycoprotein is correctly folded, it is targeted for transport to the Golgi apparatus.

In the Golgi apparatus, the N-linked glycoproteins are processed by a series of glycosidases (enzymes that cleave bonds between sugar units) and glycotransferases (enzymes that transfer sugar units) that trim and add new monosaccharides to the N-linked glycoprotein to form a wide variety of final structures. The processing step is the result of many glycosidases and glycotransferases working simultaneously, with some having competing activities. The net result is that an N-linked glycoprotein with the same amino acid sequence can have several different oligosaccharides attached to it; these oligosaccharide variations are known as glycoforms.

O-linked glycosylation. O-linked oligosaccharides are attached to glycoproteins posttranslationally in the Golgi apparatus. The O-linked glycans are attached to the proteins through the hydroxyl oxygen of serine or threonine; and unlike N-linked oligosaccharides,

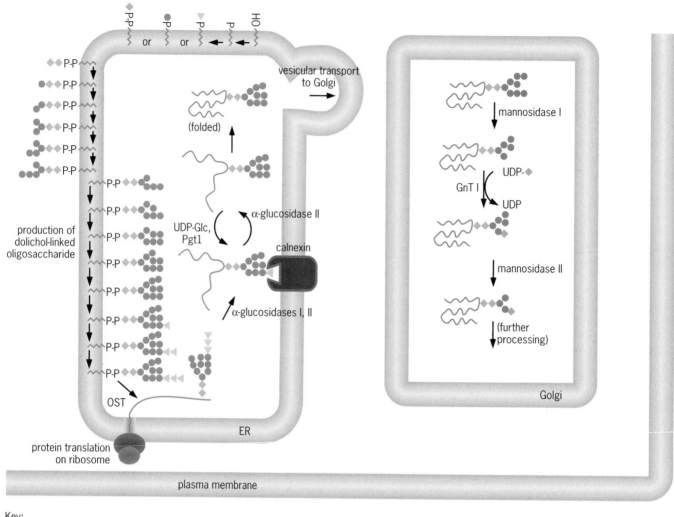

Fig. 1. N-linked glycoprotein biosynthesis. A large lipid-linked oligosaccharide is constructed and then transferred to a protein cotranslationally by OST. Then a series of enzymes—including glycosidases that remove sugar residues (alpha-glucosidase I and II), protein chaperones that aid in protein folding (calnexin), and glycotransferases (Pgt 1) that transfer sugar residues from activated sugar-nucleotides (UDP-Glc)—act on the polypeptide in the ER to ensure that it is folded correctly. Once folded, the glycoprotein is transported to the Golgi apparatus, where additional processing occurs. UDP-Glc = uridine 5′-diphosphoglucose; Pgt 1 = glycoprotein (glucosyltransferase) 1; GnTI = N-acetylglucosaminyltransferase 1; UDP = uridine 5′-diphosphate; UMP = uridine 5′-monophosphate.

there is no simple consensus sequence on the protein for initiation of O-linked glycosylation. O-linked glycosylation is most often initiated in the Golgi by transfer of N-acetylgalactosamine (GalNAc) to serine or threonine by GalNAc transferase. More complex O-linked glycans are then built up from GalNAc one monosaccharide at a time by multiple glycotransferases. Transfer of N-acetylglucosamine (GlcNAc) to serine or threonine can also occur in the cytoplasm and nucleus, and is a dynamic protein modification similar to phosphorylation that is important in regulation of protein function. As with N-linked glycoproteins, O-linked glycoproteins are heterogeneous with many different glycoforms produced for a single glycoprotein.

Chemoenzymatic synthesis. For many studies of the function of glycosylation in producing glycoproteins, it is desirable to have a homogeneous glycoprotein to study rather than the mixture of glycoforms that is produced by biosynthesis. Chemical and enzymatic synthesis (chemoenzymatic synthesis) has been used in order to produce glycoproteins with homogenous glycoforms. The basic strategy that has been most often applied involves incorporating a homogeneous core glycan (oligosaccharide) into a glycoprotein through a variety of methods, and then further extending the core glycan, if desired, with the use of glycotransferases. This allows a well-defined glycan to be produced in the context of a complete glycoprotein.

Glycosidase treatment. The simplest solution for obtaining a glycoprotein with a homogeneous glycoform is treatment of glycoproteins produced biosynthetically with glycosidases that can cleave bonds between oligosaccharides preferentially (that is, only between specific units). While glycoprotein biosynthesis produces heterogeneous oligosaccharides attached to proteins, there is often a core oligosaccharide that is common to all of the oligosaccharides of a given type. For instance, all N-linked oligosaccharides have a core that consists of two N-acetylglucosamine (GlcNAc) residues and three mannose residues attached to asparagine (Fig. 1). In addition, O-linked glycoproteins often have a common core of a single GalNAc or GlcNAc sugar that is attached to serine or threonine. Treatment of heterogenous glycoproteins with specific glycosidases that cleave only within the common core can remove the heterogenous residues producing a homogenous glycoform. For example, this method has been demonstrated with RNase B, which is an N-linked glycoprotein with a single N-linked glycosylation site. Digestion of the heterogeneous RNase B with endoglycosidase H, which cleaves N-linked glycans between the two GlcNAc residues in the core oligosaccharide, produces a homogeneous glycoform of RNase B that has a single GlcNAc. While this approach has the advantage of being straightforward, the types of homogeneous glycoforms produced are limited to the naturally occurring common core oligosaccharides.

Extension with glycotransferases. Once homogeneous core oligosaccharides have been incorporated into glycoproteins, they can be made into more complex oligosaccharides using glycotransferases (**Fig. 2**). This can be used to make more complex glycoproteins from common-core oligosaccharides obtained by glycosidase treatment, and also serves to extend the size of oligosaccharides that can be obtained by chemical glycopeptide synthesis. An example is the use of glycotransferases to extend a single GlcNAc residue on RNase B, obtained by glycosidase treatment, to the tetrasaccharide sialyl Lewis X. A large number of glycotransferases have been cloned and expressed, many of which are now commercially available, offering a wide range of glycotransferase reactions that can be used to extend glycan cores.

Ligation methods. Some methods of glycoprotein synthesis do not begin with a biologically produced oligosaccharide. Solid-phase glycopeptide synthesis can be used to produce glycopeptides of approximately 30–50 amino acids in length, depending on the sequence. However, loss of product due to incomplete coupling at each sequential step limits the length of glycopeptides that can be synthesized. To produce larger glycopeptides and glycoproteins, researchers have combined peptide synthesis with techniques that allow the joining (ligation) of two peptide fragments (**Fig. 3**). This allows small, synthetic glycopeptide fragments to be ligated to larger nonglycosylated protein fragments that were produced biologically.

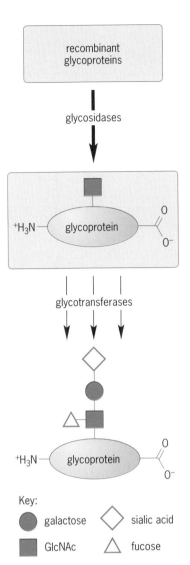

Fig. 2. Synthesis of homogeneous glycoprotein via glycosidase treatment and extension with glycotransferases to form the tetrasaccharide sialyl Lewis X.

One technique that has been used to ligate glycopeptide fragments together is protease-catalyzed fragment condensation. Proteases usually cleave proteins into fragments, but by placing them under the proper conditions they can be used to do the reverse—to condense smaller fragments into proteins. One way to accomplish this is by removing water from the protease reaction. When proteases cleave proteins, they convert the initial protein and a water molecule into two protein fragments. Replacing part of the water in the reaction with a water-miscible organic solvent, such as dimethyl sulfoxide (DMSO) or dimethylformamide (DMF), allows the protease reaction equilibrium to be driven toward fragment condensation.

A second technique for protease-catalyzed ligation is to activate one of the fragments to be condensed as an ester. This results in a competition between two protease-catalyzed reactions: hydrolysis of the ester with water, and aminolysis of the ester with the N-terminus of the other peptide fragment. Organic

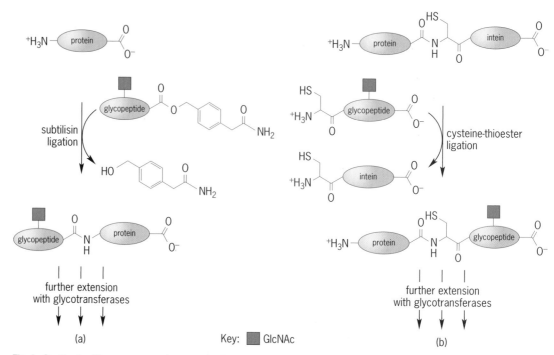

Fig. 3. Synthesis of homogeneous glycoprotein via ligation. (*a*) Protease-catalyzed subtilisin (condensation) ligation. (*b*) Cysteine-thioester ligation. The products of both types of ligation may be further extended by treatment with glycotransferases as shown in Fig. 2.

cosolvents can also be used in this method to favor fragment condensation. The serine protease subtilisin has been used in this condensation technique to ligate many glycopeptides together (Fig. 3*a*), and the glycopeptide substrate specificity for subtilisin has been mapped out to aid in planning future condensation reactions. In addition to natural proteases, existing proteases can be altered so that they have more favorable qualities for fragment condensation.

Another method for joining glycopeptide and protein fragments together is to use chemoselective cysteine-thioester ligations such as expressed protein ligation (EPL). Cysteine-thioester ligations are spontaneous chemical reactions between two unprotected peptide or protein fragments, one with an N-terminal cysteine and another with a C-terminal thioester. The net effect of a cysteine-thioester ligation is to join two peptide or protein fragments together with a cysteine at the junction between them. EPL is a cysteine-thioester ligation that uses an intein-fusion protein to produce an activated C-terminal thioester protein fragment (Fig. 3*b*). Inteins are sequences capable of cleaving peptide bonds and forming thioesters in the process of splicing proteins. Mutated inteins have been produced that form only the thioester intermediate, and some are commercially available. These mutated inteins are used in EPL to produce thioesters from expressed proteins so that synthetic peptides can be ligated to the expressed protein fragments. This is very useful for increasing the size of glycoproteins that can be synthesized, since large protein fragments can be expressed in bacteria and then ligated to small synthetic glycopeptides. This approach has been used to ligate a short 2-amino-acid glycopeptide to the 392-amino-acid maltose-binding protein.

Outlook. Methods for glycoprotein synthesis should lead to a better understanding of glycobiology. Access to homogeneous glycoforms of glycoproteins will facilitate biochemical and structural studies, which will help characterize the functions of glycosylation in glycoproteins. In addition, many human therapeutic proteins such as antibodies are glycoproteins, and methods for controlling and altering glycosylation of those glycoproteins could potentially improve the use of these compounds in medicine.

For background information *see* AMINO SUGAR; BLOOD GROUPS; CARBOHYDRATE; ENDOPLASMIC RETICULUM; ENZYME; GLYCOPROTEIN; GLYCOSIDE; GOLGI APPARATUS; INFLUENZA; MONOSACCHARIDE; OLIGOSACCHARIDE; PROTEIN in the McGraw-Hill Encyclopedia of Science & Technology.

Thomas J. Tolbert; Chi-Huey Wong

Bibliography. P. Sears, T. Tolbert, and C.-H. Wong, Enzymatic approaches to glycoprotein synthesis, *Genetic Eng.*, 23:45–68, 2001; T. J. Tolbert and C.-H. Wong, Intein-mediated synthesis of proteins containing carbohydrates and other molecular probes, *J. Amer. Chem. Soc.*, 122:5421–5428, 2000; K. Witte, P. Sears, and C.-H. Wong, Enzymic glycoprotein synthesis: Preparation of ribonuclease glycoforms via enzymic glycopeptide condensation and glycosylation, *J. Amer. Chem. Soc.*, 119:2114–2118, 1997; K. Witte, O. Seitz, and C.-H. Wong, Solution and solid-phase synthesis of N-protected glycopeptide esters of the benzyl type as substrates for subtilisin-catalyzed glycopeptide couplings, *J. Amer. Chem. Soc.*, 120:1979–1989, 1998.

Graft copolymers

Two different polymers blended together rarely are miscible and, due to repulsive interactions, exhibit macroscopic phase separation (that is, they may separate into two distinct phases). Chemically different polymer chain segments connected by covalent bonds, called block copolymers, do not undergo macroscopic phase separation. As a result, diblock (AB) and triblock (ABA) copolymers (**Fig. 1**) have been of great interest in academia and industry for decades. Block copolymers, however, exhibit phase separation on the nanoscale into well-ordered structures (morphologies of polymer blocks A and B), with feature sizes of the order of 10–50 nanometers. Industrially such nanophase-separated materials have been exploited as thermoplastic elastomers, toughened plastics, and compatibilizers for polymer blends. Today much attention is focused on using nanophase-separated block copolymers in applications such as the confined growth of nanoparticles and in nanolithography.

Graft copolymers are a subclass of block copolymers where the backbone is composed of one type of polymer (A), and another polymer (B) is attached pendent to this backbone as one or more side chains (Fig. 1). Until recently most of the fundamental understanding of the structure-morphology-property relationships for nanophase-separated copolymer systems was derived from studies of linear diblock and triblock copolymers. This is due to the straightforward synthesis of model diblock and triblock structures having controlled block lengths and overall narrow molecular weight distributions. In contrast, graft copolymers with controlled block lengths and molecular weight distributions are much more difficult to synthesize.

Three classical strategies have been used for graft copolymer synthesis: (1) "grafting from," where reactive sites are created on the polymer backbone followed by addition of monomer; (2) "grafting onto," where the preformed side chains are end-functionalized so that they may react with reactive sites on the preformed polymer backbone; and (3) "grafting through," where a "macromolecular monomer" having a polymerizable group at one end of the chain is copolymerized with a conventional monomer to create a graft copolymer. None of these classical strategies controls all the required variables for making model graft copolymers, such as the molecular weight of each branch, the number of branches per molecule, and branch placement along the backbone. However, model graft copolymers with precisely tailored architectures (and properties) recently have been synthesized by new techniques.

Synthesis of model graft copolymers. The synthetic approach involves first making the polymer backbone segments and branches with the desired molecular weight and narrow polydispersity (molecular weight distribution) by using a combination of living (termination-free) anionic polymerization and chlorosilane linking chemistry. The segments have reactive anions at one or both chain ends and are connected together into the desired architecture via substitution reactions with multifunctional chlorosilanes. For example, the simplest graft copolymer architecture is one having a single branch centrally located on a polymer backbone (single-graft or A_2B miktoarm star in Fig. 1). This material, having a polyisoprene (PI) backbone and polystyrene (PS) branch, is synthesized by reactions (1)–(4). In (1) and (2),

$$sec\text{-BuLi} + styrene \rightarrow PS^- Li^+ \qquad (1)$$

$$sec\text{-BuLi} + isoprene \rightarrow PI^- Li^+ \qquad (2)$$

$$PS^- Li^+ + CH_3SiCl_3 \text{ (large excess)} \rightarrow$$
$$PSSi(CH_3)Cl_2 + LiCl + CH_3SiCl_3\uparrow \qquad (3)$$

$$PSSi(CH_3)Cl_2 + 2PI^- Li^+ \rightarrow PSSi(CH_3)PI_2 + LiCl \qquad (4)$$

living polystyrene and polyisoprene segments are made using anionic polymerization, typically with benzene as solvent. The molecular weights of these polymer segments are controlled through the ratio of monomer to initiator. In (3) the living side-chain styrene polymer ($PS^- Li^+$) is reacted with an excess of methyltrichlorosilane to endcap all the polystyrene chains with dichlorosilane functionality [$PSSi(CH_3)Cl_2$]. A large excess of chlorosilane is

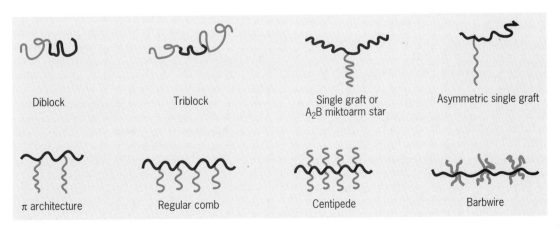

Diblock   Triblock   Single graft or A_2B miktoarm star   Asymmetric single graft

π architecture   Regular comb   Centipede   Barbwire

Fig. 1. Block and graft copolymer architectures.

needed to avoid coupling of the polystyrene chains. The remaining methyltrichlorosilane is then removed under vacuum. Pure solvent (usually benzene) is then reintroduced into the reactor to dissolve the $PSSi(CH_3)Cl_2$ prior to adding the living isoprene polymer (PI^-Li^+) in (4). Reaction (4) is slow due to the low concentration of reactive sites and steric hindrance. The addition of a polar additive, such as tetrahydrofuran (THF), will accelerate this process. More complex architectures have been prepared by extensions of these techniques.

Recently the synthetic strategies described above have been used for the synthesis of graft copolymers having multiple, regularly spaced branch points such as the regular comb, centipede, and barbwire architectures shown in Fig. 1. To create these structures, a combination of anionic polymerization and step-growth (condensation) polymerization is used. The basic strategy is to create a dichloro-functionalized species that contains one, two, or four polystyrene side chains connected to it (using CH_3SiCl_3, $SiCl_4$, and $Cl_3SiCH_2CH_2SiCl_3$, respectively). Reaction of these species with a slight excess of polyisoprene having anionic sites at both chain ends constitutes a step-growth polymerization, and the number of branch points incorporated may be controlled through the reaction stoichiometry. The scheme for centipede synthesis is summarized in reactions (5)–(7).

$$PS^- Li^+ + SiCl_4 \text{ (excess)} \rightarrow PSSiCl_3 + LiCl + SiCl_4 \quad (5)$$

$$PSSiCl_3 + PS^- Li^+ \text{ (titration)} \rightarrow (PS)_2SiCl_2 + LiCl \quad (6)$$

$$(PS)_2SiCl_2 + Li^+ {}^-PI^-Li^+ \text{ (slight excess)} \rightarrow$$

$$(PI\text{-}Si(PS)_2)_n + LiCl \quad (7)$$

In (7), n depicts the number of repeating sequences incorporated into the polymer chain. Materials having more then 12 branch points have been synthesized for the centipede architectures, while up to 90 branch points have been achieved with the regular comb structure (where steric hindrances to linking are reduced). A limitation of this method is a consequence of the step-growth process used to build the final multigrafts: the raw products exhibit heterogeneity in terms of number of branch points (or overall chain length). However, these products may be fractionated to yield specimens with narrow distributions in terms of the number of branch points. The key strength of the method is the capacity to control precisely branch length, functionality of the branch point, and the placement of branch points along the backbone.

Morphology. In order to optimize the performance of nanophase-separated materials, one needs to be able to control the size, shape, symmetry, and overall volume fraction of nanoscale-separated domain structures independently. This independent control, however, is not possible with conventional linear block copolymers for which the nanophase-separated morphology (which forms spheres, cylinders, cubic bicontinuous, or lamellae) is tied directly to the relative volume fractions of the two block materials. For example, if an application demands a material with phase-separated nanometer-length-scale cylinders in which the component comprising the cylindrical domain makes up over 50 volume percent of the material, linear block copolymers would not be useful. Or suppose one needs an alternating layered structure on a similar length scale in which the layers differ considerably in thickness, that is, thick layers alternating with thin layers. The lamellar structures formed by linear block copolymers would not suffice in this case since they are formed only when volume fractions are near 50/50.

A way to uncouple block copolymer morphology from its rigid dependence on component volume fractions is to vary molecule architecture. A large number of the possible variations can be represented by a single molecular asymmetry parameter, ε, introduced by Scott Milner. For miktoarm star architectures of A_nB_m architecture, $\varepsilon = (n/m)(l_A/l_B)^{1/2}$. Here n/m is the ratio of arm numbers of the two block types and represents the asymmetry due to the architecture. The conformational asymmetry between the two block materials is expressed by the ratio, $(l_A/l_B)^{1/2}$, where l_i is the ratio of segmental volume to the square of statistical segment length for the block material I (that is, l_i represents l_A for segment A, and l_B for segment B). In other words, l_A is the ratio of the segmental volume to the square of statistical segment length for block A; l_B is this same ratio for block B. At $\varepsilon = 1$, the Milner diagram models linear, conformationally symmetric, AB diblock behavior with symmetric morphology windows around $\phi_B = 0.5$, meaning that around 0.50 volume fraction (roughly 0.35–0.65 volume fraction) of one component in a linear diblock, a lamellar morphology is observed. If one component is present at >0.50 volume fraction, a nonlamellar morphology such as spheres or cylinders will be observed. If one is dealing with a diblock and $\varepsilon = 1$, this will occur over a composition range that is symmetrical about 0.5. However, as one increases the number of arms of one species relative to the other, the morphological behavior can become strongly asymmetric with respect to volume fraction. This allows the sought-after uncoupling of morphology from volume fraction; that is, the morphology can be varied independently of volume fraction by adjusting the molecular architecture.

Milner's theory is not strictly applicable to more complex, multiple graft copolymer materials. However, it has been shown that complex graft copolymer architectures with multiple grafting points (such as the comb architecture in Fig. 1) can be understood morphologically by analogy to the fundamental building blocks defined as the average structure per junction or the constituting block copolymer. For a graft copolymer with a backbone of A and blocks of B joined to the backbone at trifunctional branch points, the constituting block copolymer is an A_2B single graft copolymer (Fig. 1). It has generally been found that the morphology observed for multiple graft materials is the same as that found for its constituting block copolymer.

Long-range order. Within each morphological classification (spheres, cylinders, and so on), samples display a range of degrees of long-range order. Long-range order is the degree of perfection of the lattice symmetry and orientation, and the extent of material over which this symmetry and orientation persists. For example, at the local scale (range of hundreds of nanometers), a particular type of morphology is observed (such as hexagonally packed cylinders of component A in a continuous phase of matrix B). Locally the cylinders will be oriented in a particular direction in a three-dimensional space. If in a bulk specimen ($1 \times 1 \times 1$ in.) all the cylinders are oriented in the same direction in 3D space, there is perfect long-range order (such as in a single crystal). In block or graft copolymer morphologies, this perfect order is not found. There are regions with locally perfect order, then "defect regions" (called grain boundaries) and other areas of the sample that exhibit the same morphology but, for example, have the cylinders pointing in a different direction.

Previous work has shown that the degree of long-range order decreases with increasing molecular weight and with increasing complexity of molecular architecture. Nitash Balsara and coworkers pioneered methods based on depolarized light scattering and digital analysis of transmission electron micrographs which provide a means to quantify long-range order in nanophase-separated block copolymer materials. Application of this type of analysis to lamellar forming multigraft copolymers with multiple tetrafunctional branch points per molecule has shown that long-range order (correlation length) decreases as approximately $n^{-2.0}$, where n is the number of junction points per molecule.

Mechanical behavior. Recent work on the mechanical properties of multigraft copolymers has demonstrated that, in comparison to other thermoplastic elastomers, excellent mechanical properties can be obtained and that these properties are tailorable over a broad range through changes in molecular architecture. Parameters such as the number of graft points, the functionality of the graft points (that is, whether one, two, or more grafts are attached at each point), and the molecular weights of the grafts were found to have a profound influence on mechanical behavior.

Figure 2 shows the stress-versus-strain behavior of three model graft copolymers and a commercial thermoplastic elastomer (Kraton D1101). The curve labeled PI-g-PS$_2$ corresponds to a multigraft copolymer with regularly spaced, tetrafunctional branch points. It has a polyisoprene backbone, and two polystyrene arms per junction point (centipede polymer). The overall polystyrene volume fraction was 21%. It forms a morphology of weakly ordered polystyrene cylinders in a polyisoprene matrix and has a much lower long-range order than Kraton. The combination of two branches at each branch point, combined with the large number of branch points per molecule, allows the elastic polyisoprene backbone to couple into a large number of reinforcing polystyrene domains, resulting in huge elasticity combined with a high tensile strength. As a result, the

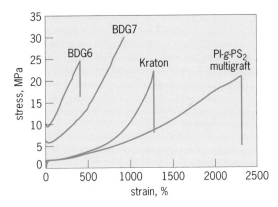

Fig. 2. Stress-strain curves for Kraton D1101 versus PI-g-PS$_2$ (multigraft copolymer with nine junction points; the branch molecular weight is 13,000 g/mol), BDG6 (nine junction points; the branch molecular weight is 14,000 g/mol), and BDG7 (three junction points; the branch molecular weight is 32,800 g/mol).

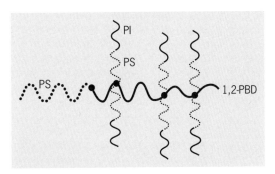

Fig. 3. Block double graft molecular architecture, where PI = polyisoprene, PS = polystyrene, and 1,2-PBD = 1,2-polybutadiene.

material could be strained over 2000% before breaking, and sustained a high stress of 19 megapascals at the breaking point. The two other curves in Fig. 2, labeled BDG6 and BDG7, illustrate the mechanical behavior of block double graft copolymers with molecular architectures as shown in **Fig. 3.** These materials are based on a backbone which is a polystyrene-polybutadiene (PS-PBD) diblock. The PBD part of the backbone has polystyrene-polyisoprene (PS-PI) diblocks grafted to it, two per junction point, in which the PS end is attached to the backbone. Clearly, graft copolymers allow variables such as the number of grafts per branch point and the number of branch points to be used in the design of thermoplastic elastomers and other multiphase polymer systems.

For background information *see* BRANCHED POLYMER; COPOLYMER; POLYMER; POLYMERIZATION; POLYSTYRENE RESIN; RUBBER in the McGraw-Hill Encyclopedia of Science & Technology.

Jimmy W. Mays; Samuel P. Gido

Bibliography. F. L. Beyer et al., Graft copolymers with regularly spaced, tetrafunctional branch points: Morphology and grain structure, *Macromolecules*, 33:2039–2048, 2000; H. Iatrou et al., Regular comb polystyrenes and graft polyisoprene/polystyrene copolymers with double branches ("centipedes"), *Macromolecules*, 31:6697–6701, 1998; S. T. Milner,

Chain architecture and asymmetry in copolymer microphases, *Macromolecules*, 27:2333–2335, 1994; D. J. Pochan et al., Morphologies of microphase-separated A₂B simple graft copolymers, *Macromolecules*, 29:5091–5098, 1996; R. Weidisch et al., Tetrafunctional multigraft copolymers as novel thermoplastic elastomers, *Macromolecules*, 34:6333–6337, 2001.

Gravity Probe B

The purpose of the Gravity Probe B (GP-B) experiment is to test two effects predicted by the general theory of relativity. This theory, established in 1916 by Albert Einstein, provides a geometrical framework for gravity, one of the four known forces in the universe. This view of gravity uses a metric to describe the curvature of space and time. Far from massive bodies, this metric reduces to that for euclidean space. In 1960, Leonard I. Schiff, using the general theory of relativity, predicted two new relativistic effects which cause an orbiting gyroscope to slowly precess. The first effect, known as the geodetic effect, is caused by the orbital motion of a gyroscope about the static mass of the Earth. The second effect, known as the frame dragging or gravitomagnetic effect, is caused by the rotation of the massive Earth. Frame dragging causes a slow rotation of the Earth's local space-time framework. The Gravity Probe B experiment will measure the size of these two deviations from flat space-time.

Gravity Probe B uses a unique space vehicle in a specific orbit about the Earth, a nearly circular polar orbit at an altitude of 650 km (400 mi), to perform its mission (**Fig. 1**). While the vehicle orbits the Earth, the spin axis direction of a nearly perfect gyroscope will be measured relative to fixed inertial space. The fixed inertial reference is provided using a tracking telescope to lock on to a distant reference star. The position of the star is known to high precision relative to extragalactic reference stars. Any change in the gyroscope's spin axis direction can thus be referenced to inertial space. For a gyroscope in a polar orbit about the Earth, the two gravitational effects are orthogonal to one another. A single gyroscope can therefore measure both effects. The geodetic effect has a predicted size of 6.6 arc-seconds per year, and the frame dragging effect has a predicted size of 0.042 arc-second per year. The challenge of the Gravity Probe B experiment is to measure the relativistic gyroscope drift rates to better than 0.5 milli-arc-second per year, or equivalently, to better than 10^{-16} radian per second. For comparative purposes, 0.5 milli-arc-second is the angle subtended by the width of a human hair when viewed from a distance of about 30 km (20 mi).

Experiment configuration. The Gravity Probe B science instrument is operated at cryogenic temperatures (**Fig. 2**). The cryogenic environment allows for improved control of classical gyroscope torques, a SQUID (superconducting quantum interference device)–based spin-axis readout system, and improved mechanical stability of the science instrument. A 2300-liter (600-gallon) liquid helium storage dewar provides an on-orbit cryogen lifetime of more than 18 months at a temperature of 1.8 K. There are four gyroscopes to provide independent measures of the gravitational effects and to provide redundancy for enhanced mission reliability. The tracking telescope is a folded cassegrainian design. It is important that the gyroscope and telescope readouts remain fixed relative to one another. This stability is achieved by using a quartz block to minimize relative mechanical drift. An on-board Global Positioning System (GPS) receiver is used to give precision position and velocity information of the space vehicle.

Gyroscope. The Gravity Probe B flight gyroscope assembly comprises three primary parts; a rotor and two housing parts (**Fig. 3**). A spherical rotor, with a diameter of approximately 4 cm (1.5 in.), is the spinning test mass. It is fabricated out of fused silica and is coated with a superconducting niobium thin film. The superconducting film provides a magnetic marker for measurement of the spin axis direction. This magnetic marker, the London moment, arises in rotating superconductors. The orientation of the London moment is aligned with the spin axis of the rotor so that changes in spin-axis orientation are reflected in orientation of the London moment. The superconducting coating also allows for the use of a capacitive readout system to measure and control the rotor's position.

The portion of the gyroscope's drift rate associated with nonrelativistic drifts must be limited to less than 0.3 milli-arc-second per year. This newtonian drift

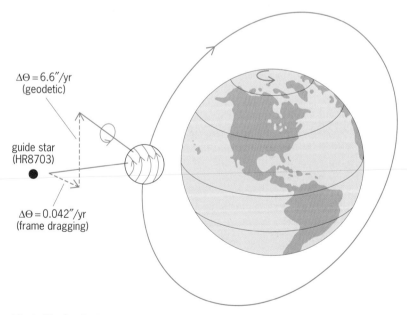

$\Delta\Theta = 6.6''/\text{yr}$
(geodetic)

guide star
(HR8703)

$\Delta\Theta = 0.042''/\text{yr}$
(frame dragging)

Fig. 1. **The Gravity Probe B mission. The spacecraft is placed in a nearly circular polar orbit at an altitude of 650 km (400 mi). The space vehicle is locked onto the guide star HR8703. The two orthogonal relativistic effects are then measured over the course of the 18-month mission using four nearly perfect gyroscopes. The solid arrow pointing at the guide star is the starting orientation of the gyroscope spin axis; the two broken arrows are the precessions in two orthogonal directions; and the remaining solid arrow, which is the vector sum of the first three vectors, is the direction of the gyroscope spin axis at the conclusion of the experiment.**

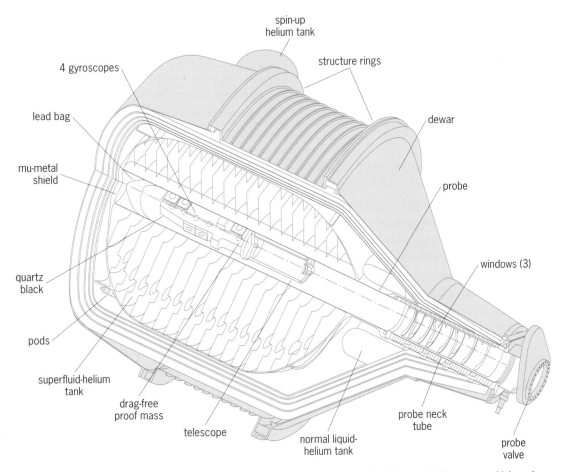

spin-up
helium tank

structure rings

4 gyroscopes

dewar

lead bag

probe

mu-metal
shield

windows (3)

quartz
black

pods

superfluid-helium
tank

drag-free
proof mass

telescope

normal liquid-
helium tank

probe neck
tube

probe
valve

Fig. 2. Gravity Probe B experiment configuration. The science instrument is located at the heart of the space vehicle and consists of the gyroscopes, one of which is drag-free; the quartz block; and the telescope. The probe supports the science instrument and includes the neck tube, valves, and windows. The dewar holds the superfluid helium and includes a lead bag, a mu-metal shield, pods, structural rings, and spin-up gas tanks. Not shown is the spacecraft support structure and the electronics required to operate the science instrument and spacecraft.

rate is a function of imperfections in the rotor and external forces acting on the rotor. Rotor imperfections are therefore controlled with rotor sphericity and homogeneity requirements of better than one part in a million.

External forces acting on the gyroscope are dramatically reduced by operating the gyroscope in orbit about the Earth. The size of the remaining forces are further reduced by employing a drag-free technique whereby the location of one of the four rotors is capacitively monitored and the spacecraft is forced to fly about this rotor. In this way residual spacecraft disturbances such as atmospheric drag and solar wind are eliminated. The resulting residual average acceleration on the gyroscope is of order 3×10^{-11} m/s^2 (10^{-10} ft/s^2).

The two halves of the gyroscope housing, which hold the rotor, are also fabricated with fused silica. After assembly the gap between the rotor and the housing is approximately 25 micrometers (0.001 in.). This small gap requires that the gyroscope be kept nearly perfectly clean during the mission.

The gyroscope housing supports (1) London moment spin-axis direction readout, (2) rotor position measurement and control, (3) rotor spin-up, and

(4) rotor charge control. The rotor's spin-axis signal is coupled to a pickup loop located on one of the housing halves. The signal coupled to this pickup loop is thus a measure of the gyroscope spin direction relative to the gyroscope housing (and spacecraft) reference frame. Three pairs of orthogonal electrodes located on the housing allow for a capacitive measurement of the rotor position relative to the

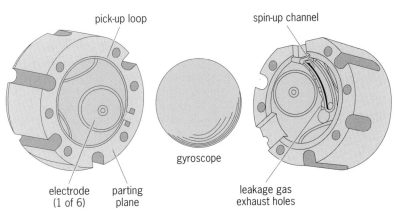

pick-up loop

spin-up channel

gyroscope

electrode
(1 of 6)

parting
plane

leakage gas
exhaust holes

Fig. 3. Gravity Probe B gyroscope.

housing. Electrostatic forces, resulting from voltages applied to these electrodes, control the location of the three non-drag-free rotors. Rotor spin-up to approximately 150 Hz occurs when helium gas flows through a channel located directly above the rotor's surface in one of housing parts. Ultraviolet light delivered to the rotor and an adjustable biasing electrode allow for bidirectional electrical discharging of the rotor.

A number of cryogenic and ambient space temperature electronic systems are required to support these gyroscope operations. The rotor's London moment spin signal is delivered from the pickup loop via a superconducting cable to a SQUID. The SQUID amplifies the gyroscope spin direction signal. Ambient temperature electronics are used to operate the SQUID and to measure the spin-axis signal. Additional gyroscope support electronics are used to measure and control the gyroscope location, control the gyroscope's electrical charge, and operate the spin-up gas supply system.

Telescope and spacecraft attitude control. The spacecraft attitude control system uses the output of the tracking telescope to maintain an inertially fixed pointing direction for the duration of the experiment. Pointing control authority is provided by the boil-off gas from the experiment's liquid-helium dewar. The telescope is an all-quartz construction. A novel bonding technique is used to assemble the telescope's quartz components and to bond the telescope to the adjacent gyroscope quartz block. The star light is split within the telescope to provide a two-axis readout of the position of the star relative to a null output. Cryogenic photodiodes detect the starlight signal. The output from these photodiodes is delivered to the spacecraft attitude control system to maintain the telescope output at the null point; that is, it keeps the telescope pointed at the star.

The star that will be tracked is HR8703. It was chosen because its proper motion has been accurately measured and because it is adequately bright. This star is also a radio-frequency source, and therefore its proper motion can be cross-checked on the ground to very high precision using radio-frequency-based, very long baseline interferometry (VLBI).

Ground-based tests. Many tests have been performed on the hardware in preparation for launch. All of these tests have been successful. The four gyroscopes have been levitated and spun. The gyroscope readout and ultraviolet systems have been successfully operated. An artificial star simulating the real star has been successfully used to test the telescope and telescope readout electronics. The dewar has been kept full with liquid helium for the past 5 years. Test and analysis confirms an expected on-orbit liquid-helium hold time of greater than 18 months. Combining all of the test and analysis results gives an overall experimental prediction of an on-orbit drift rate error of 0.21 milli-arc-second per year for one gyroscope or 0.12 milli-arc-second per year when the results of the four gyroscopes are combined.

Mission plans. The plan is to complete space vehicle environmental testing, ship the vehicle to Vandenberg Air Force Base in California, and launch it in early 2003. Once on-orbit, the first 40 to 60 days will be spent setting up the experiment. The electronics will be turned on, the attitude control system will lock on to the star, the orbit will be adjusted to the correct orientation, and the gyroscopes will be spun. Following this setup phase, science data will be collected for approximately 14 months. One month of post-science tests will be performed following the science data phase. The post-science phase of the experiment will end when the liquid helium in the main tank is fully depleted. The collection and analysis of the data will culminate the 35-year effort to perform this experiment.

For background information *see* GYROSCOPE; RADIO ASTRONOMY; RELATIVITY; SQUID; SUPERCONDUCTIVITY; TELESCOPE in the McGraw-Hill Encyclopedia of Science & Technology.   Barry Muhlfelder

Bibliography. C. W. F. Everitt, in J. D. Fairbank et al. (eds.), *The Stanford Relativity Gyroscope Experiment: History and Overview, in Near Zero*, pp. 587–639, W. H. Freeman, New York, 1988; T. Piran (ed.), *Proceedings of the 8th Marcel Grossmann Meeting on General Relativity*, World Scientific, Singapore, 1999; L. I. Schiff, Possible new experimental test of the general theory of relativity, *Phys. Rev. Lett.*, 4:215–217, 1960; J. P. Turneaure, C. W. F. Everitt, and B. W. Parkinson, The Gravity-Probe-B relativity gyroscope experiment: Approach to a flight mission, in R. Ruffini (ed.), *Proceedings of the 4th Marcel Grossmann Meeting on General Relativity*, pp. 411–464, Elsevier Science Publishers B.V., 1986.

Hepatitis C

Hepatitis C is a disease of the liver caused by the hepatitis C virus (HCV). Although the incidence of new HCV cases is declining, the number of patients with complications of chronic HCV continues to rise. The prevalence of HCV infection worldwide is 3% (170 million people), with infection rates in North America ranging from 1 to 2% of the population. The impact of HCV is being felt in the offices of primary care physicians, hepatologists (specialists in liver disease), and liver transplant programs. A simulation analysis estimated that in the period from 1998 to 2008 there will be an increase of 92% in the incidence of cirrhosis of the liver, resulting in a 126% increase in the incidence of liver failures and a 102% increase in the incidence of hepatocellular carcinoma (HCC), all attributed to HCV, placing an increasing burden on the health care system.

Hepatitis C virus can be transmitted only by blood-to-blood contact. Prior to 1990, the major source of infection was through contaminated blood or blood products. With the institution of screening of blood, intravenous drug use has become the major source of transmission in North America. Approximately 89%

of people who use intravenous drugs for one year become infected with HCV. Other routes of transmission include transfusion (1 in 100,000 risk), nondisposable needles and syringes, vaccination practices, tattoos, body piercing, and cocaine snorting. The rate of sexual transmission is estimated to be approximately 4% among monogamous heterosexual couples. A higher risk is associated with homosexual relationships, multiple sexual partners, and the presence of sexually transmitted diseases. Vertical transmission from mother to infant is approximately 6% and is related to viral load. It is also affected by route of delivery (vaginal versus cesarean section). Viral load, the amount of virus present in the blood, has been traditionally measured as the number of copies of virus per milliliter of blood. More recently it is being reported as international units (IU) per liter. There is no direct relationship between the two units.

Natural history. The natural history of HCV is important, since treatment varies with the progression of the disease. The initial acquisition of HCV is infrequently diagnosed, since the clinical manifestations are nonspecific, with the majority of patients having no symptoms at all. When present, symptoms consist of malaise, nausea, and jaundice. Fulminant hepatitis (a severe, rapidly progressive form of hepatitis), though reported, is extremely rare. During the acute phase of the virus, clinical symptoms, if they occur, are manifested usually within 7 to 8 weeks. Approximately 15 to 30% of infected individuals spontaneously clear the virus; 70 to 85% will progress to chronic infection, which is usually an asymptomatic period defined as elevation in alanine aminotransferase (ALT) for greater than 6 months.

It is believed that fibrosis of the liver in the immunocompetent HCV-infected individual develops linearly over decades following acquistion. Though data are mainly retrospective, studies show that the rate of progression to cirrhosis is approximately 20% in 20 years. This rate can be accelerated by factors such as male gender, obesity, alcohol use, coinfection with HIV, and age at the time of acquisition of HCV, with those infected after 40 having a more progressive course (**Fig. 1**). Once cirrhosis has developed, the rate of developing HCC is approximately 1 to 4% per year. In contrast to hepatitis B, where development of HCC can precede the onset of cirrhosis, HCC in hepatitis C is exceedingly rare in those without cirrhosis. Once cirrhosis is established, the survival probability depends on whether there have been complications of impaired liver disease. Without complications in HCV-cirrhotic patients (compensated), the 5-year survival is approximately 90%. Once complications develop, 5-year survival drops dramatically to 50%. Although the natural history of HCV is protracted and the majority of patients do not develop cirrhosis, the prevalence of the disease is so high that the number of patients with complications from hepatitis C is staggering. As such, management strategies must be implemented safely, quickly, and effectively.

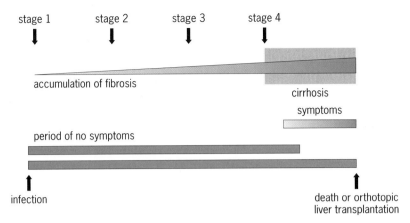

Fig. 1. Natural history of chronic hepatitis C. It is presumed that liver fibrosis progresses in a linear course from the time of acquisition of the infection to the development of cirrhosis. Stages of fibrosis are from the METAVIR scoring system: stage 1 = portal tract expansion; stage 2 = fibrous septation; stage 3 = bridging fibrosis; stage 4 = cirrhosis (bridging fibrosis and nodular regeneration).

Management. Treatment of HCV has changed dramatically over the last decade, from controlling symptoms and complications to the ability to completely eradicate the virus. Management strategies can be divided into three main areas: surveillance of patients with chronic HCV infection who have not developed cirrhosis; surveillance of patients with established cirrhosis; and strategies to eradicate HCV.

In the first instance, it is critical to determine the stage of disease, as cirrhosis is a bad prognostic indicator of outcome to treatment. The only method to definitively confirm the diagnosis of cirrhosis is a liver biopsy; thus, it is recommended that such a biopsy be performed prior to initiating therapy. A second principle in the management of these patients is to eliminate any factors which may contribute to progression of HCV disease. Specifically, patients should be advised to stop drinking, normalize their body weights, avoid potentially toxic drugs, and where appropriate be vaccinated against hepatitis A and B. In patients with established cirrhosis, it is

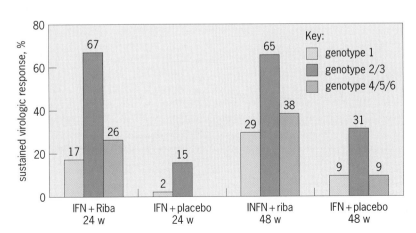

Fig. 2. Results of treatment of patients with hepatitis C who received interferon (IFN) as monotherapy (IFN + placebo), or in combination with ribavirin (IFN + Riba) for either 24 or 48 weeks. Combination therapy of IFN and Riba appears to increase sustained virologic response rates for all genotypes compared with IFN monotherapy. Longer treatment of 48 weeks versus 24 weeks appears to improve response rates in those patients with genotype 1 HCV.

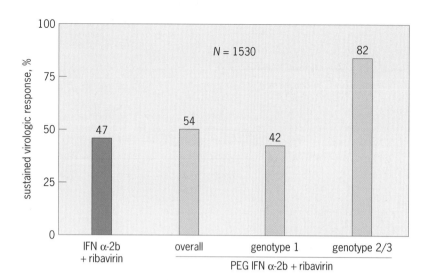

Fig. 3. Peginterferon alpha-2b/ribavirin weight-based dosing. The sustained virologic response is improved overall and by genotype in patients who received pegylated interferon in combination with ribavirin for 48 weeks, in comparison with patients who were treated with interferon alpha-2b in combination with ribavirin for 48 weeks. (*After M. P. Manns et al., Lancet, 358:958–965, 2001*)

recommended that they enter a screening program for the development of HCC.

Eradication therapy has changed dramatically over the last 10 years. Antiviral therapy varies depending on whether treatment is addressing acute or chronic hepatitis C infection. For chronic HCV there are five main goals of antiviral therapy: viral clearance; delaying decompensation; preventing HCC; slowing progression of fibrosis; and preventing HCV recurrence after liver transplantation. Patients with chronically elevated serum transaminases (greater than 1.5 times the upper limit of normal over 3 months) may be considered for antiviral therapy. Factors that determine long-term benefit include age, duration of disease, severity of fibrosis, intercurrent illness, and the likelihood of response to therapy. Successful treatment is defined as a sustained biochemical and virologic response, that is, both normalization of liver enzymes and no detectable HCV ribonucleic acid (RNA) in the blood 6 months posttreatment.

The two mainstays of treatment are interferon and ribavirin. Interferon has both antiviral and immune modulating effects. When it is used alone, the sustained virologic response (SVR)—that is, complete eradication of the HCV virus—is seen in less than 20% of patients. Ribavirin is a nucleoside analog with primarily immunomodulatory activity and poor antiviral properties. When it is used alone, it gives a transient biochemical response with no significant virologic response, and patients continue to be HCV-RNA positive. The combination of interferon and ribavirin has resulted in marked improvements in sustained response rates: approximately 29% in genotype 1 patients and 65% in genotype 2/3 (**Fig. 2**).

Recently, a long-acting interferon, pegylated interferon, has been developed through the attachment of polyethylene glycol to interferon alpha. This extends the half-life and duration of the therapeutic activity of interferon alpha, and thus pegylated interferon need be given only once a week. The use of pegylated interferon and ribavirin for the treatment of HCV has again resulted in a marked improvement in sustained virologic response rates. Genotype 1 patients have a 42% sustained response rate, and genotype 2/3 have an 82% sustained response. Overall, due to the increased frequency of genotype 1 HCV, the sustained response rate is 54% (**Fig. 3**). Genotype 2/3 HCV patients are treated for 24 weeks, whereas other genotypes are treated for 48 weeks. At 24 weeks if patients still have detectable HCV-RNA, treatment is considered to have failed. Studies have shown with a sustained response to treatment, there is persistent, undetectable HCV-RNA and normalization of liver enzymes in 97% even after 10 years. Studies have also shown regression of fibrosis with viral clearance. Factors that predict a favorable response to treatment are viral genotype, a viral load less than 2 million viral copies per milliliter of blood, female gender, age less than 40, and little or no fibrosis. A greater number of favorable factors corresponds to an increased sustained response rate.

The rate-limiting step in the treatment of HCV is the side-effect profile of interferon and ribavirin. With careful follow-up of symptoms and investigations,

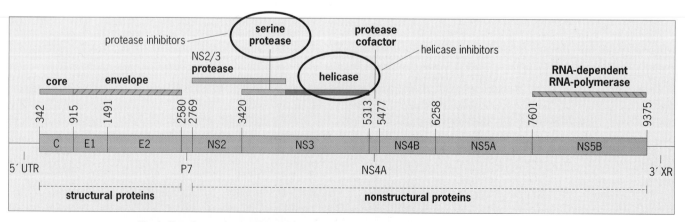

Fig. 4. Based on understanding of the genomic structure of HCV, additional therapies, including serine protease inhibitors, helicase inhibitors, and RNA polymerase inhibitors, are being developed.

most patients can continue treatment; however, some patients may need adjustment or even discontinuation of treatment due to serious side effects. Though less likely to respond and complete treatment, patients with compensated cirrhosis have fairly good sustained response rates. It is contraindicated to treat patients with decompensated cirrhosis.

Treatment of acute HCV has recently been shown to prevent the development of chronic HCV infection. Most patients with acute infection were treated for 24 weeks with interferon monotherapy. The study found approximately 98% of patients had a sustained response with a 24-week course of treatment. This suggests that early treatment of patients will lead to better long-term results. For those patients who have decompensated liver disease or have already developed small hepatocellular carcinomas, liver transplantation remains an option; today HCV infection remains the most common indication for liver transplantation. A 5-year survival rate of 80% is seen in patients with transplants due to HCV, although recurrence of infection is universal and in some patients disease recurrence can be quite rapid and progressive. Use of interferon or combination therapy appears to be less effective in liver transplant recipients.

Future direction. Although tremendous progress has been achieved, there is a need for the development of additional therapeutic agents as many patients still are ineligible or unresponsive to current treatments. The genetic sequencing of HCV has allowed scientists to speculate on novel targets for antiviral therapy. Today protease inhibitors, helicases, and additional immunomodulatory agents are being studied for their potential effectiveness. It is anticipated that these agents will be introduced in the foreseeable future. For example, in a small study interleukin-10 was shown to have beneficial effects on liver abnormalities. With better characterization of the replicative cycle of HCV, drugs that target virus-specific inhibitors will be developed (**Fig. 4**). Potential targets include HCV proteases, helicase and polymerase, and internal ribosomal entry sites. HCV vaccination is also being sought aggressively.

For background information *see* ANIMAL VIRUS; HEPATITIS; INTERFERON; LIVER in the McGraw-Hill Encyclopedia of Science & Technology.

Naveen Arya; Nigel Girgraph; Gary Levy

Bibliography. E. J. Heathcote et al., Peginterferon alpha-2a in patients with chronic hepatitis C and cirrhosis, *NEJM*, 7;343(23):1673–1680, 2000; E. Jaeckel et al., Treatment of acute hepatitis C with interferon alpha-2b, *NEJM*, November 15, 2001; K. L. Lindsay et al., A randomized, double blind trial comparing pegylated interferon alpha-2b to interferon alpha-2b as initial treatment for chronic hepatitis C, *Hepatology*, 34(2), August 2001; J. G. McHutchison et al., Interferon alpha-2b alone or in combination with ribavirin as initial treatment for chronic hepatitis C, *NEJM*, vol. 339, 1998; X. X. Poynard et al., Randomized trial of interferon alpha 2b plus ribavirin for 48 weeks or 24 weeks versus interferon alpha 2b plus placebo for 48 weeks for treatment of chronic infection with hepatitis C virus, *Lancet*, vol. 352, October 31, 1998; S. Zeuzem et al., Peginterferon alpha-2a in patients with chronic hepatitis C, *NEJM*, 7;343(23):1666–1672, 2000.

High-brightness light-emitting diodes

High-brightness light-emitting diodes (LEDs) emit visible light at efficiencies competetive with conventional incandescent and fluorescent lamps. The levels of radiant efficiency for conventional white light sources (5–7% for incandescent lamps and 28% for fluorescent ones) are unlikely to increase significantly because of the limits of the underlying physical processes. In contrast, LEDs have the potential for close to 100% power-to-light conversion (theoretically, the effective conversion efficiency could be even higher than 100%, since the LED could take some energy out of the environment). LED lamps are more efficient, longer-lived (100,000 h and more), environmentally friendlier (mercury-free), and more shock-resistant than conventional light bulbs and fluorescent tubes. In addition, LED technologies offer more versatility in the design of lighting fixtures, and digital control of color and light intensity. Over the next 20 years, LEDs are predicted to gradually replace conventional lamps in much the same manner as solid-state circuits replaced vacuum tubes years ago.

Materials. Materials for fabrication of high-brightness LEDs must satisfy certain requirements. Only direct-band-gap semiconductors are suitable for efficient light generation. And the band gap of the semiconductor (the energy separation between the valance band and the conduction band) must match the wavelengths of the visible or near-ultraviolet range. The crystal must resist defect generation under intense light and sustain high current densities. It also must be possible to fabricate heterostructures, and both p- and n-type materials must be available. At present, there are three semiconductor materials systems that meet these requirements and are used in LED lamps. They are ternary $Al_xGa_{1-x}As$ alloys for red LEDs, emitting at wavelengths above 650 nm; quaternary $(Al_xGa_{1-x})_{0.5}In_{0.5}P$ alloys for red to amber LEDs, emitting at wavelengths above 570 nm; and AlInGaN (ternary $In_xGa_{1-x}N$ and $Al_xGa_{1-x}N$ and quaternary $Al_xIn_yGa_{1-x-y}N$) for green to near-ultraviolet LEDs.

Another promising technology is LEDs made of organic materials (OLEDs), including small molecules or polymers. Organic LEDs contain relatively inexpensive materials that can be deposited over large, flexible substrates (lighting wallpaper). However, reduced longevity and brightness are obstacles for their wider application.

Efficiency. Compared to conventional LEDs, new LED lamps have improved external quantum efficiency, that is, a higher ratio of the number of

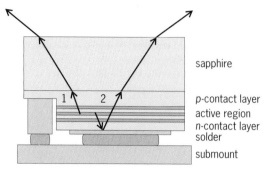

Fig. 1. Schematic cross section of an AlInGaN flip-chip LED. The light-emitting structure (the multiple-quantum-well active region clad between contact layers) is grown over sapphire. Light ray 1 undergoes no total internal reflection and escapes through the sapphire substrate. Light ray 2 is totally internally reflected from the bottom surface. However, the reflected ray can escape through the substrate. Eventually, about 30% of generated light can be extracted.

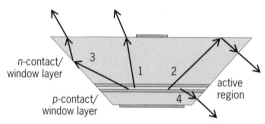

Fig. 2. Schematic cross section of an AlGaInP/GaP truncated-inverted-pyramid LED. The AlGaInP double heterostructure (active region) is clad between transparent GaP contact/window layers. The sidewalls of the chip are slanted with respect to the vertical. Light rays 1 and 4 escape directly without total internal reflection. Light rays 4 and 3 are first totally internally reflected and then escape on the second pass. The structure features light extraction efficiency up to 80%.

photons emitted to the number of the electrons passed through the LED. External quantum efficiency is the product of injection efficiency, internal quantum efficiency, and light extraction efficiency.

Injection efficiency. Injection efficiency is the fraction of electrons passed through the LED that are injected into the active region, where radiative recombination takes place. Generally, because of low injection efficiency, conventional *p-n* junctions are no longer used in LED lamps. Instead, to facilitate injection efficiency close to unity, electrons and holes are injected into a lower-band-gap active region clad by wider-band-gap *n*- and *p*-contact regions. Owing to lower band-gap energy, the active region confines the carriers (electrons and holes). This is achieved by using double heterostructures or quantum wells. To prevent carrier leakage from the active region, additional layers, such as electron blocking layers, multiple quantum wells, and multiple quantum barriers, are used.

Internal quantum efficiency. Internal quantum efficiency is the ratio of the number of electron-hole pairs that recombine radiatively, to the total number of pairs that recombine in the active region (both radiatively and nonradiatively). To reduce nonradiative recombination, the semiconductor is fabricated with fewer defects that trap carriers. To increase the rate of

radiative recombination, the active layer is undoped, and intrinsic band-to-band transitions are used. The internal quantum efficiency of LED lamps can be 80% or higher.

Light extraction efficiency. Light extraction efficiency is the most critical issue for new LED lamps. The main physical impediment to light extraction is internal reflection due to the large ratio of the refractive indices of the semiconductor to that of the surrounding medium. This limits the fraction of light extracted through one surface of a rectangular-parallelepiped chip that is encapsulated in a plastic dome to 4% in AlGaAs- and AlGaInP-based LEDs and to 9% in AlInGaN LEDs. The light extraction through two surfaces is achieved by using a transparent substrate. By using a thick "window" layer over the active region, light extraction is possible through up to six surfaces. In AlInGaN LEDs, the lower value of the refractive index of the sapphire substrate helps improve the light extraction. This approach is implemented in a flip-chip (FC) LED (**Fig. 1**). However, the most advanced structures are based on nonrectangular geometries that help deflect rays of light in appropriate directions. The best values for light extraction efficiency (~80%) are attained in a truncated-inverted-pyramid LED (**Fig. 2**). Similar light extraction efficiencies can be attained by using randomly nanotextured surfaces for scattering the photons' trajectories (nonresonant-cavity LED). The ultimate approach that, in principle, offers 100% light extraction efficiency is to use photonic crystal structures. In a photonic crystal, light generation can be facilitated for favorable propagation directions (that is, perpendicularly to the surface) and impeded for the unfavorable directions (**Fig. 3**).

White LED lamps. There are two ways to produce white light from LEDs. One approach is to mix light of different colors using different chips (multichip LED) or a single chip. On a single chip, different colors can be produced by stacking semiconductor layers with different band-gap energies or by using a mixture of different molecules in an organic LED. A second approach is to convert the emission from a blue or near-ultraviolet LED to a longer-wavelength light using phosphors, called a phosphor conversion

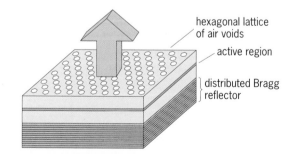

Fig. 3. Future LED lamp based on a photonic crystal. The chip is patterned with a lattice of vertical air voids. The lattice (photonic crystal) allows generation of light that propagates in the vertical direction and inhibits generation in lateral directions. Since the generated light undergoes no total internal reflection, light extraction efficiency can attain values close to unity.

LED. The wavelengths of the primary LEDs and phosphors are optimized to maximize the response of the human visual system (luminous efficacy) and the ability to properly reproduce the colors of illuminated objects (color rendering).

A multichip LED requires at least two primary LEDs (for example, yellow and blue; dichromatic LED). However, dichromatic LEDs suffer from poor color rendering. Improved color rendering is achieved in a trichromatic LED (red-orange/green/blue). Based on AlGaInP and AlInGaN chips, trichromatic LEDs can have power conversion efficiency almost equal to that of fluorescent lamps. Quadrichromatic (red/yellow-green/cyan/blue) and quintichromatic (red/yellow-green/green/cyan/blue) multichip LEDs can provide "deluxe" color rendering that meets most lighting needs.

Common phosphor conversion LEDs use a partial conversion of blue light from an InGaN chip and a yellow-emitting phosphor (yttrium aluminum garnet doped with Ce^{3+} ions). However, this structure is deficient in color rendering. Advanced phosphor conversion LEDs contain multiphosphor blends excited by an ultraviolet LED (the idea was adopted from fluorescent lamps). In general, phosphor conversion LEDs have lower efficiency than their multichip counterparts, since a portion of the exiting photon energy is inevitably lost in the down-conversion process. Present phosphor conversion LEDs exhibit luminous efficiency twice that of incandescent lamps, with the potential to catch up to fluorescent lamps in the future.

Applications. Inherently, high-brightness LEDs are efficient, highly reliable, and long-lived sources of colored light. For instance, advanced AlGaInP LEDs are 20 or more times as efficient as red-filtered incandescent lamps. As a result, most applications have been for power signage (traffic lights, automotive signage, all kinds of beacons and security lights, airport runway and taxiway lighting). Another important application of new LED lamps is alphanumeric and full-color video displays that can be viewed at large distances or in direct sunlight. In this application, high-brightness LED-based large-area displays have replaced cathode-ray-tube display technology.

Due to their high fluxes of (almost) monochromatic light, LED lamps are useful for photochemical processes. Typical applications are phototherapy for neonatal jaundice (photoinduced decay of excess bilirubin in newborns), photodynamic therapy (photoactivation of toxic pigments for destruction of tumor cells and viruses), and photobiostimulation (wound healing). In addition, LED lamps have started replacing halogen bulbs in light curing units for the photopolymerization of dental composites. And power-efficient LED illumination for photosynthesis in plants and phototrophic microorganisms (algae) has been demonstrated.

LED lamps generate fluxes of light that are sufficient for fluorescence excitation. Because of their high stability, small dimensions, possibility of high-frequency modulation, and short-pulse generation, high-brightness LEDs have found numerous applications in chemical and biological fluorescence sensors, and for cost-efficient fluorescence lifetime measurements on the nanosecond time scale.

The most challenging application of LED technology is, in fact, general lighting. Today, 21% of electric energy use is in lighting, and perhaps half of this energy could be saved by switching to efficient, cold, solid-state lighting sources. Cumulative financial savings from LED lighting could reach $115 billion by the year 2020. Colored and white LEDs are already used in decorative, landscape, and automotive interior lighting, as well as spotlighting in retail stores, museums, and galleries.

At present, LED-based residence, office, and street lighting has been demonstrated. But widespread use of solid-state lighting is still a few years away.

For background information *see* COLOR; ELECTROLUMINESCENCE; ELECTRON-HOLE RECOMBINATION; FLUORESCENCE; FRANCK-CONDON PRINCIPLE; ILLUMINATION; LASER PHOTOBIOLOGY; LIGHT-EMITTING DIODE; LUMINESCENCE; PHOTOSYNTHESIS; SEMICONDUCTOR; SEMICONDUCTOR HETEROSTRUCTURES in the McGraw-Hill Encyclopedia of Science & Technology.   Artūras Žukauskas; Michael S. Shur; Remis Gaska

Bibliography. M. R. Krames et al., *Appl. Phys. Lett.*, 75:2365, 1999; G. Mueller (ed.), *Semiconductors and Semimetals*, vol. 64: *Elecroluminescence I*, 2000; S. Nakamura and S. F. Chichibu (eds.), *Introduction to Nitride Semiconductor Lasers and Light Emitting Diodes*, 2000; G. B. Stringfellow and M. G. Craford (eds.), *Semiconductors and Semimetals*, vol. 48: *High Brightness Light Emitting Diodes*, 1997; J. J. Wierer et al., *Appl. Phys. Lett.*, 78:3379, 2001; A. Žukauskas, M. S. Shur, and R. Gaska, *Introduction to Solid-State Lighting*, 2002.

High-intensity focused ultrasound

An important goal of medicine is to provide patients with minimally invasive medical procedures. With such procedures infection and blood loss are minimized, procedure and recovery times are shortened, and procedures can be offered on an outpatient basis. High-intensity focused ultrasound (HIFU), also known as focused ultrasound surgery (FUS), is emerging as a modality for minimally invasive therapy, and is gaining clinical acceptance as an alternative to surgical procedures.

Applications. The history of ultrasound as a therapeutic modality dates back to the midtwentieth century—much earlier than when ultrasound was first used as a diagnostic tool in the 1970s. In 1942, J. G. Lynn and colleagues demonstrated the potential of HIFU for therapeutic effects. HIFU lesions, or areas of localized tissue necrosis, were produced deep within the bovine liver without damaging surrounding tissue. In the late 1950s, William Fry and Frank Fry, and others, developed a HIFU device that was used to produce lesions in brains of patients with hyperkinetic and hypertonic disorders. HIFU

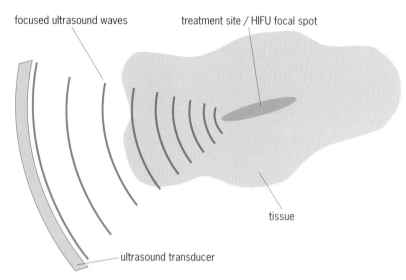

focused ultrasound waves

treatment site / HIFU focal spot

tissue

ultrasound transducer

Fig. 1. Focusing of ultrasonic radiation for localized treatment in high-intensity focused ultrasound.

is currently in clinical use in Europe and Japan and is undergoing clinical trials in the United States for the treatment of prostate cancer and benign prostatic hyperplasia, as well as in clinical trials for benign breast fibroadenomas and a variety of primary and metastatic cancer tumors of the kidney, liver, and ovaries. Researchers in China have used HIFU to treat thousands of patients with liver cancer, breast cancer, malignant bone tumor, and soft tissue sarcoma. Applications in hemostasis (arrest of hemorrhage) in trauma, vascular and gastrointestinal bleeding, and treatment of uterine and brain tumors are being investigated. Along with investigations into

new applications for HIFU, researchers are developing innovative devices and test equipment for exploring HIFU. HIFU devices have emerged that are optimally designed for specific treatments, have a variable, electronically controlled focal pattern, and combine ultrasound imaging and therapy.

Generation. HIFU can be used to treat tissues located deep within the body without surgical exposure. Ultrasound energy generated using a piezoelectric transducer can be focused to a small spot, similar to the manner in which a magnifying glass focuses light energy. The focal intensity (power density) of HIFU is upward of 1000 W/cm^2, which is 4 to 5 orders of magnitude greater than that of diagnostic ultrasound systems ($\sim$0.1 W/cm^2), leading to localized heating and tissue disruption. The size of the HIFU focal spot volume is similar to the size of a grain of rice, up to 2 mm (0.08 in.) in width and 5 to 15 mm (0.2 to 0.6 in.) in length. Since HIFU effects are localized at the focus, intervening and surrounding tissues remain unaffected, resulting in precise localized treatment (**Fig. 1**).

HIFU transducers operate at frequencies between 1 and 10 MHz. A focused propagating ultrasound wave is generated when an amplified electrical waveform activates either a curved piezoceramic crystal, a flat piezoceramic crystal attached to an acoustic lens, or a phased array of piezoceramic crystals. Although the first two designs are the most simple, the HIFU focal distance and focal spot size are fixed. In a phased-array design, each crystal is driven by a separate signal, allowing the focal distance and shape to be electronically controlled.

Thermal and mechanical mechanisms. The mechanisms behind HIFU-induced biological effects during treatment are primarily temperature increase and cavitation. HIFU energy is converted to heat mainly by absorption and viscous shearing effects. Lesions formed solely due to thermal effects are associated with relatively low intensities (below 1000 W/cm^2). HIFU exposures are usually short because HIFU can induce rapid temperature increases at the focus, up to 100°C (180°F), in less than a few seconds. The short exposure times combined with a steep decline in temperature outside the focus (approximately 10°C per millimeter or 450°F per inch) result in localized perfusion-independent treatments.

At higher intensities, acoustic fields stimulate bubbles into motion, resulting in cavitation. Cavitation refers to the dynamic behavior of gas bubbles due to pressure changes in a medium, as a result of regions of compression and rarefaction caused by a propagating ultrasound wave. The degree of cavitation due to HIFU exposure is dependent on HIFU intensity and frequency. Cavitation can be classified as stable or inertial. Stable cavitation refers to the cyclic expansion and contraction of bubbles already present in the medium without collapse. Gas bubble oscillations may produce high shearing forces, causing tissue damage. Inertial cavitation refers to the nucleation (inception) of bubbles, and the rapid growth and violent collapse of these bubbles. Bubble collapse

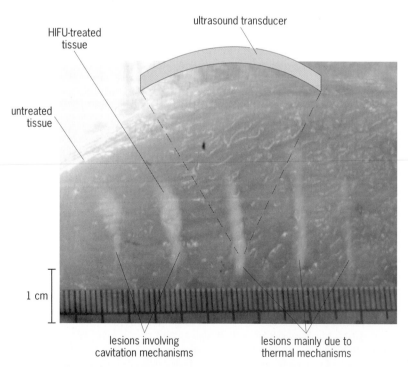

HIFU-treated tissue

ultrasound transducer

untreated tissue

1 cm

lesions involving cavitation mechanisms

lesions mainly due to thermal mechanisms

Fig. 2. Turkey breast tissue that has been treated with high-intensity focused ultrasound. The influence of the HIFU mechanism (thermal or mechanical) on lesion dimension can be seen.

is associated with high-energy concentrations causing high acoustic pressure (20,000–30,000 bars or 2000–3000 megapascals), high temperatures (1000–20,000 K or 1300–35,500°F), propagation of a shock wave, and high fluid velocities resulting in mechanical tissue destruction.

Biological effects. The extent of tissue necrosis due to the mechanisms of HIFU depends on HIFU intensity, frequency, and exposure time. Histological analyses of HIFU-treated areas reveal a sharp demarcation between viable and necrotic HIFU-treated tissue. Biological effects of HIFU include coagulative necrosis, protein denaturation, nuclei damage, membrane disruption and leakage, and apoptosis. On a macroscopic scale, tissue treated by HIFU appears blanched or "cooked" (**Fig. 2**). Lesion dimension is influenced by the mechanism of HIFU (thermal or mechanical) that is responsible for lesion formation. Lesions mainly due to thermal mechanisms are cigar-shaped elongated ellipsoids, and are generally thinner in width than lesions that involve cavitation, which are tadpole-shaped. Studies investigating long-term effects of HIFU treatment have discovered no harmful effects due to HIFU within 2 months after treatment. Phagocytes remove HIFU-damaged tissue, and dense collagen deposition at the treatment site and scarring often result during the healing of the HIFU-treated area.

Image-guided HIFU. During HIFU treatment, it is crucial to have some means of assessing the treatment location, tracking the position of the focal volume, verifying that power is being delivered to the proper location, and ascertaining whether tissue destruction has occurred. This feedback allows lesion formation to be controlled and confined to areas of desired tissue destruction. Methods currently in use and under investigation include visual monitoring, x-ray imaging, magnetic resonance imaging (MRI), and diagnostic ultrasound.

Visual monitoring is the most elementary method of HIFU therapy guidance and is often used when the treatment site can be visually observed. An example would be intraoperative acoustic hemostasis, where blood vessels and other sources of bleeding are surgically exposed for HIFU treatment. X-ray imaging was the earliest form of guidance for HIFU therapy, and is currently used for catheter-delivered ultrasound therapy methods such as ultrasonic thrombolysis. MRI provides tissue contrast for localization of the target volume, and can characterize diffusion, perfusion, flow, and temperature, thus enabling the detection of tissue damage induced by HIFU. Diagnostic ultrasound can also be used to map the treatment area and to indicate the progress of HIFU treatment. These treated regions appear as hyperechoic images in real time in the ultrasound scan (**Fig. 3**). Additionally, tissue characteristics such as elasticity and temperature have been quantified using ultrasound imaging.

Potential. HIFU is emerging as a promising and valuable modality for the treatment of many medical conditions and has the potential to provide a nonin-

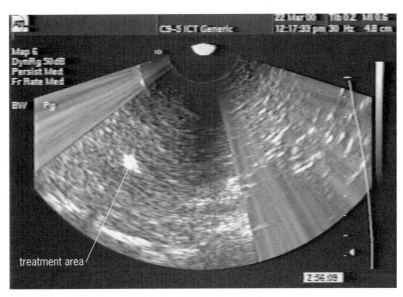

Fig. 3. Real-time ultrasound scan of porcine liver tissue treated by high-intensity focused ultrasound. The image was taken during treatments immediately after the onset of lesion formation. Treated region appears as the bright white spot.

vasive alternative to conventional surgery. For example, HIFU may be used to treat a symptomatic uterine fibroid, thus obviating the need for hysterectomy (surgical removal of the uterus). With its potential to treat internal bleeding and to prevent blood loss from severe organ trauma, HIFU units placed in ambulances or rescue helicopters could be used to quickly control bleeding from a person involved in an automobile accident, a soldier wounded on the battlefield, or an injured mountain climber or surfer—scenarios where hospital facilities are not readily available. In fact, HIFU devices may one day become as common as a defibrillator in first-aid stations and on airplanes. HIFU also has the potential to be used in many new fields such as dentistry, cosmetic surgery, and veterinary medicine. The growing clinical acceptance and research interest shows promise that HIFU may change the future of minimally invasive therapy.

For background information *see* BIOMEDICAL ULTRASONICS; CAVITATION; MEDICAL IMAGING; ULTRASONICS in the McGraw-Hill Encyclopedia of Science & Technology.   Arthur H. Chan; Shahram Vaezy; Lawrence A. Crum

Bibliography. A. Gelet et al., Transrectal high-intensity focused ultrasound: Minimally invasive therapy of localized prostate cancer, *J. Endourol.*, 14(6):519–28, 2000; K. Hynynen et al., MR imaging-guided focused ultrasound surgery of fibroadenomas in the breast: A feasibility study, *Radiology*, 219(1): 176–85, 2001; N. T. Sanghvi et al., Noninvasive surgery of prostate tissue by high intensity focused ultrasound: An updated report, *Eur. J. Ultrasound*, 9(1):19–29, 1999; G. ter Haar, Therapeutic ultrasound, *Eur. J. Ultrasound*, 9(1):3–9, 1999; S. Vaezy et al., Image-guided acoustic therapy, *Annu. Rev. Biomed. Eng.*, 3:375–90, 2001; F. Wu et al., Pathological changes in human malignant carcinoma treated with high-intensity focused ultrasound, *Ultrasound Med. Biol.*, 27(8):1099–1106, 2001.

High-speed train aerodynamics

The aerodynamics of trains has much in common with that of other vehicles, but there are important differences. Airplanes also involve streamlined bodies, but trains operate near the ground, have much greater length-to-diameter ratios, pass by structures and other trains, are more subject to crosswinds, and operate at lower speeds. Trains are affected by phenomena that arise as they enter and exit tunnels. Automobiles and trucks also operate near the ground, pass each other, and are subject to crosswinds, but trains have much greater length-to-diameter ratios and higher speeds. As with other types of transportation systems, fluid resistance to train motion has been increasingly important as speeds have increased over the years (**Fig. 1**). At lower speeds, other types of resistance such as that from wheels on the track are relatively more significant.

Drag. A critical quantity is train aerodynamic resistance, R, or drag. For streamlined trains at 250–300 km/h (155–186 mi/h), 75–80% of the total resistance is external aerodynamic drag. This is subdivided as 30% skin friction; 8–13% pressure drag at the nose and tail of the train; 38–47% drag from bogies (the trucks or axles that support the cars), including "interference" drag, which is due to the downstream effect of the bogie on skin friction; and 8–20% drag from pantographs (which pick up electric power from overhead wires) and roof equipment. Clearly, for higher-speed trains, such as magnetic levitation (maglev) trains or other advanced concepts, external aerodynamics is a major consideration.

The drag is given by Eq. (1), where C is constant,

$$R = CV_A^2 = {}^1/_2\rho V_A^2 S C_D \qquad (1)$$

V_A is train speed relative to the air, ρ is the air density, S is the frontal area of the train, and C_D is the drag coefficient. The coefficient C_D ranges from about 1 for streamlined trains to 10–15 for freight trains.

Further, the drag coefficient can be written as the sum in Eq. (2), where C_{DL} is the leading-car drag

$$C_D = C_{DL} + C_B + \lambda_T(l_T - l_L)/S^{1/2} \qquad (2)$$

coefficient, C_B is the base drag at the tail, λ_T is the "friction" coefficient along the train (including bogies, wheels, interference, underbelly effects, and so forth), and l_T and l_L are the length of the total train and the lead car. Typical values of these parameters are given in the **table**. For comparison, modern automobiles have drag coefficients of 0.2–0.4 and trucks have values of 0.7–1.0. Trains are much longer than automobiles or trucks, so they have larger friction drag.

Crosswind velocity combined with train velocity produces a yaw angle, β, and a drag coefficient correction that is given by Eq. (3), where β is measured in degrees.

$$C_D(\beta) = C_D(1 + 0.02\beta) \qquad \text{for } \beta < 30° \qquad (3)$$

Effects of tunnels. The aerodynamic consequences of train operation in tunnels center on two interdependent phenomena, namely generation of pressure waves and an increase in drag. In long tunnels drag increase is the most important effect, while in short tunnels pressure pulses generated at the tunnel entrance and exit cause the most problems. The aerodynamic drag of a train in a tunnel can exceed that for the same train in open air by a substantial margin. The effect is dependent primarily on the area blockage ratio of the train in the tunnel (the ratio Q of the area blocked by the train to the cross-sectional area of the tunnel), the tunnel and train lengths, the nose and tail shapes, the presence of air shafts and cross-connections in the tunnel, and the presence of other trains in the tunnel. The ratio C_D(tunnel)/C_D is found to decrease with increasing train length, but to be nearly independent of tunnel length and train speed in the usual range of $Q = 0.1$–0.2. As for any vehicle, the drag is a combination of pressure drag and skin friction drag, but here the magnitudes of the two are altered compared to operation in the open. Significant pressure waves are generated at the tunnel entrance and exit, and longitudinal pressure gradients develop along the train in the confines of a tunnel. Clearly, the flowfield around the train is altered. In particular, any separation zones just downstream of the nose or on the tail will be strongly affected, which influences nose and tail drag.

Testing. The aerodynamic resistance formulas are based on full-scale track data and subscale wind tunnel, water tunnel, towing tank, or test track data. The coasting technique, in which the deceleration of the train is measured as it coasts without power, is often used to determine the total resistance, as is also done for automobiles. Since this method measures the total resistances, it is necessary to subtract an estimate of other sources of resistance in order to calculate the aerodynamic resistance. In addition to high cost, there are numerous problems with open-air, full-scale testing, especially crosswind effects.

Subscale testing. Most experimental studies on the aerodynamics of high-speed trains are conducted at subscale in laboratories. The Reynolds number (Re) is a measure of viscous effects, the Mach number

Fig. 1. Lead car of a modern high-speed train. (*Federal Railroad Administration, U.S. Department of Transportation*)

Typical drag and friction coefficients for trains

Train type	C_D	S, m^2	l_T, m	l_L, m	C_B	C_{DL}	λ_T
Advanced Passenger Train (APT-P)	2.05	8.05	300	13	0.11	0.2	0.0172
High-speed Train (HST)	2.11	9.12	300	17.4	0.11	0.2	0.0192
Conventional passenger train, MKII	2.75	8.8	300	20	0.11	0.3	0.0248
Container train, 80% loaded	6.5	8.8	300	20	0.11	0.5	0.0624
Shinkansen 200	1.52	13.3	300	24.5	0.11	0.2	0.0160
InterCity Express (ICE)	0.69	10.2	115	20.9	0.12	0.2	0.0125

(Ma) is a measure of the effects of air compressibility, and both should be matched between test-scale and full-scale conditions. If wave propagation phenomena are not important and $M < 0.2$ for full-scale conditions, it is necessary only that $M < 0.2$ for the scale model. If the air speeds relative to the train are approximately the same in the two scales, the laboratory Reynolds number will be much less than the full-scale number, as with other vehicle testing. Trains have particular problems with subscale testing because of drag-producing small-scale items like bogies, pantographs, and gaps between cars.

Ground-plane simulation. A problem for wind and water tunnel tests of ground vehicles is simulation of the nearby ground plane or track. In the real case, the ground and air are at rest and the vehicle moves. In wind tunnels, the ground and the vehicle model are at rest and the air moves past. By far the most satisfactory method is to employ a moving tunnel wall in the form of a belt. The belt speed must match the tunnel speed, and for high-speed train testing that is more challenging than it is for automobile testing.

Some of these problems can be alleviated with a moving vehicle on a track. A towing tank used for ship model testing can be used. In air, rubber-band launchers are used to propel models, and when they reach the end of the test section, a hook engages a cable for braking.

Testing with crosswinds. This presents more problems. Blockage effects of a long model in a wind tunnel are greater if it is at yaw. If a moving belt simulation of the ground plane is employed, a question arises as to whether the moving belt should be yawed as well. That procedure leads to complexity and a disturbance produced by the exposed edge of the moving belt. Matters are more complex for simulation of the so-called ground plane, since the most troublesome locations for crosswinds are on exposed embankments or viaducts.

Boundary-layer simulation. Further problems arise in properly simulating the atmospheric boundary layer (in particular, its nonuniform velocity approach profile) on a laboratory scale. These considerations have led to wind tunnel test approaches at two extremes. The first is a relatively large-scale model at yaw in a wind tunnel placed on a fixed, elevated ground board. This gives a reasonable Reynolds number level, but the moving ground plane and the atmospheric boundary layer are not represented. The second extreme has a small-scale model set on a fixed floor exposed to an elaborately simulated atmospheric boundary layer.

A different idea is to launch a model along a track on a ground surface in a wind tunnel over which there is a simulated atmospheric boundary layer flowing. The ground plane and the crosswind are properly simulated relative to the moving train model. There are new test problems that focus on the need to have a smooth, accurately aligned track to assure smooth motion of the model, or the instrument that measures loads on the model will have difficulty distinguishing the aerodynamic loads on the model from dynamic inertia forces fed up from the track.

Effects of crosswinds and lift. Data on the effects of a crosswind on not only drag but also lift, side force, and moments are very important for assessing vehicle stability. Interest in this subject has increased recently with the introduction of unpowered, lightweight, high-speed vehicles placed in the lead position of a train. Strong gusts cause a deloading of the wheels on the windward side. A particularly difficult situation arises if a train encounters a gust just as it leaves a tunnel. Aerodynamic lift is also important for maglev trains, since lift changes with speed, and this variation must be taken into account in the design of the levitation system.

Pressure waves. There are other aerodynamic issues besides overall forces and moments. As a train passes through a tunnel, a series of compression and expansion waves are formed which propagate along the tunnel at approximately the speed of sound. These waves cause a number of problems in the areas near the tunnel entrance and exit and for the passengers. The limiting acceptable pressure change is in the range of 1–4 kilopascals (0.01–0.04 atm or 0.15–0.6 lbf/in.^{2}) for a pulse length of 4–10 s, and modern train operations approach these limits. The pressure waves also put a load on the structure of the cars. When trains pass each other, the relative speeds can be quite high, and pressure waves can form between them. Obviously, the situation is aggravated when the trains are passing within the confines of a tunnel.

Theoretical treatment. Experimental information can be supplemented by theoretical treatments at differing levels of complexity and fidelity. There are relatively simple analytical models that can treat some

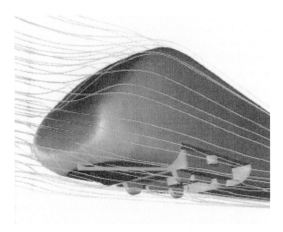

Fig. 2. Computer simulation of the air flow over the tail of an ICE2 railroad car. The contours on the surface indicate the pressure distribution, and the lines are streamlines in the flow. (*From G. Matschke et al., Numerical simulation of the flow around a six-coach high speed train, in World Congress of Railroad Research, Railway Technical Research Institute, 1999*)

situations reasonably well, but they involve restrictive assumptions such as neglecting viscous effects. The best simulations (**Fig. 2**) are achieved with elaborate computational models. These models are based upon the full Navier-Stokes equations for three-dimensional, turbulent, and sometimes unsteady flows. They require sophisticated, approximate representations of the effects of turbulence. Calculations with such models require large and complicated computer codes running on very large computers for very long run times.

For background information *see* AERODYNAMIC FORCE; BOUNDARY-LAYER FLOW; COMPUTATIONAL FLUID DYNAMICS; MAGNETIC LEVITATION; RAILROAD ENGINEERING; STREAMLINING; TURBULENT FLOW; WATER TUNNEL; WIND TUNNEL in the McGraw-Hill Encyclopedia of Science & Technology.

Joseph A. Schetz

Bibliography. J. A. Schetz, Aerodynamics of high-speed trains, *Annu. Rev. Fluid Mech.*, 33:371–414, 2001; H. Sockel, The aerodynamics of trains, in J. A. Schetz and A. E. Fuhs (eds.), *Handbook of Fluid Dynamics and Fluid Machinery*, pp. 1721–1741, Wiley, New York, 1996.

Historical ecology

Even as we continue to destroy vast amounts of natural habitat, we are attempting to restore areas of degraded habitat to their past conditions. Unfortunately it is often unclear what the past conditions of the area were and, therefore, what the goal of habitat restoration should be. Historical ecology explores what a region or ecosystem looked like during different points in history. It can therefore aid us in setting goals for restoration projects and help us predict how our actions will affect the ultimate appearance of the land.

Historical ecology is interdisciplinary, relying on methods from anthropology, cultural ecology, and environmental history. Yet, historical ecology remains a unique discipline. What sets it apart is its tenet that not only has the environment influenced human history but human history has also altered the environment. The focus of historical ecology, therefore, is the ongoing interplay of humans and their environment through which the two constantly influence one another. Historical ecology explicitly recognizes that the relationship between humans and their environment has never been static. The goal of historical ecology is, therefore, not to define the natural state of a region but to understand the interactions between the environment and its human inhabitants.

One reason why historical ecology is gaining popularity is that the dynamic equilibrium between people and the environment is increasingly dysfunctional; humans today extract more resources than the environment can sustainably produce. In an attempt to restore degraded ecosystems, ecologists are working with anthropologists, historians, and geologists as well as native locals to determine the best ways to restore specific sites and sustain ecosystems. This is not an easy task. However, through careful research and dedication, it is feasible to understand how an ecosystem has changed over time and responded to human activities. The following case studies provide examples of projects that have relied on historical ecology to attain their goals.

Case studies. Historical ecology combines investigations of a region's past ecology with studies of historical patterns of land use by humans. Records of land use and alteration by human populations may be culled from written documents, including personal letters from early settlers, journals kept by explorers, paintings, and hand-drawn maps. Studies of more recent land-use patterns may rely upon old photographs, interviews of elderly locals, and city records. Information regarding the composition of historical plant and animal communities, as well as historical disturbance regimes, can be gleaned from the sources mentioned above, but also from analysis of tree rings, soil cores, pollen, and fossils.

Greater Grand Canyon Region. From a quick glance at old photographs and the journals of early explorers, it is apparent that the ecology of the Grand Canyon has changed dramatically over the last 150 years. Much evidence points to the fact that biodiversity in the region has decreased over this time period. Fires, aggressive species such as snakeweed and sagebrush, and disease have diminished the abundance of many native plant species.

Although it is clear from photographs that the shrub and tree communities have changed, it is less obvious how the community of grasses and small forbs has been altered. A large effort in historical ecology has recently been undertaken to determine exactly what the plant communities of the Greater Grand Canyon Region looked like before European settlement (around 1870). The project focused on identifying which species once thrived in the understories of three plant communities: ponderosa pine, pinyon-juniper, and sagebrush grassland. Aside from comparing old documents with lists of plants currently extant in the Greater Grand Canyon Region, scientists used pollen analysis, plant and animal remains, packrat middens (preserved debris left by packrats), and fossilized human feces to identify plant species.

The project found that 30 species formerly in the Greater Grand Canyon Region are no longer present. In addition, plant biodiversity in the three communities has dropped by over 90%. The next steps for this project are to identify reference conditions for a restoration project and determine if the 30 "missing" species can be found elsewhere, perhaps one day to be reintroduced to the Greater Grand Canyon Region.

San Francisco Area. The San Francisco Estuary Institute (SFEI) has attempted to recreate what the region looked like as far back as 1769, prior to European settlement. Obviously, the San Francisco Bay landscape has changed dramatically as wetlands have been transformed into a major metropolitan city. But many endemic, threatened, and endangered species, including the snowy plover, the San Francisco garter snake, the California clapper rail, and several salmon species still exist in the region. Thus, there is great interest in determining what ecosystems once occurred in the area and how to maintain the vigor of native animal and plant communities.

SFBEI set out to gather as much information as possible about the Bay Area. Most of the data came from old maps, photos, drawings, journals, mission texts, and interviews with elders. Many of the sources were scattered about in places ranging from museums and city archives to people's basements. No two sources used the same methods of documentation, and very few were complete records. Experts in local history documents, including many local agency staff and some professional historians, were essential early on; geomorphologists and ecologists provided the final interpretations and analysis by correlating the historical reports with pollen and tree ring analyses. Maps and sketches were digitized and compiled into a geographic information system (GIS) database called the San Francisco Bay EcoAtlas.

SFBEI found that 97% of the area's natural ponds and high-tide marshes have disappeared but low-tide marsh areas have increased by 300%. Some ecosystems, such as sand beach barriers to lagoons, have been completely destroyed. Also, many creeks that now flow into the bay once flowed into inland wetlands. The San Francisco Bay EcoAtlas has been used to assist in regional planning and development. It has become a valuable resource for environmental groups in their efforts to protect species and habitats. In addition, knowing where rivers and creeks once ran, where railroad tracks were first laid, and which hills were logged first has helped city planners and engineers to interpret current environmental phenomena such as erosion and flooding.

Valle del Mazquital. The Valle del Mazquital is located 60 mi (97 km) north of Mexico City, and the Otomi people have lived there for nearly 500 years. Although the rivers of the Valle del Mazquital have become informal water treatment plants for Mexico City, the local traditions, language, and culture of the people remain strong and distinct from those of other Mexican regions. Historians have long been curious about why the Otomi people were able to remain so distinct when the majority of other native tribes blended with the Spanish in the late sixteenth and early seventeenth centuries. Also, the land of this region is ecologically distinct in that the soil is remarkably infertile. Is the difference in fertility because of poor agricultural practices by the Otomi, or because of early and current land-use practices by others in the surrounding areas? Historical ecology was used to explore the roots of these cultural and ecological differences.

Historical ecologists relied on oral histories and records from early Spanish missionaries to discern how the land-management techniques used by the Otomi evolved in response to the Spanish invasion. Historical documents tell how the Otomi initially conformed to the new Spanish practices such as sheep herding. However, as the Spanish and other native Mexican tribes replaced sheep with more land-degrading grazers such as cows, the Otomi continued to raise sheep because they provided a source of food and warm clothing. The Spanish also began extensively irrigating the land and implementing pastoralism, allowing animals to graze in all surrounding lands, not just the owners' land. The Otomi continued to practice minimal herding and farming for the sustenance of their village—not for exporting. As more water was extracted for irrigation of the surrounding land, traditional farming became more difficult in the Otomi valley. These locally distinct patterns of land use set the stage for a degree of political separation for the Otomi that has allowed them to remain culturally distinct. The disparity in land use has also led to the differences in soil health and production that are evident today. This example illustrates not only how history affected ecology but also how ecology alters history.

Outlook. Historical ecology provides much more than interesting stories about the past. A clear understanding of how humans have altered landscapes can uncover dramatic cautionary tales of irreversible changes we may want to avoid in the future. In addition, accurate depictions of what once occupied a landscape helps identify fundamental geological and climatological factors that may constrain our designs for future restoration or land management. Perhaps most important, historical ecology integrates explicitly human activities into the examination of ecological processes, and does so in a way that should motivate careful thought about their impact.

For background information *see* ECOLOGY; ECOSYSTEM; EXTINCTION; HUMAN ECOLOGY; LAND-USE CLASSES; LAND-USE PLANNING; LANDSCAPE ECOLOGY; SYSTEMS ECOLOGY in the McGraw-Hill Encyclopedia of Science & Technology.   Christine Dindia

Bibliography. W. Balee, *Advances in Historical Ecology*, Columbia Press, 1998; L. J. Bilsky, *Historical Ecology: Essays on Environment and Social Change*, Kennikat Press Corp., 1980; C. L. Crumley, *Historical Ecology: Cultural, Knowledge and Changing Landscapes*, School of American Research Press, 1994; D. Egan and E. A. Howell, *The Historical Ecology Handbook*, Society for Ecological Restoration, Island Press, 2001.

Homocysteine

Homocysteine is a sulfur-containing amino acid that is structurally and metabolically related to the essential amino acid methionine. Discovered by Vincent du Vigneaud in 1932, homocysteine is found in both

prokaryotic and eukaryotic organisms. It is a sensitive marker of nutritional status, vitamin deficiency, and kidney function.

It has been known since the 1960s that elevated levels of homocysteine and homocystine (the disulfide form of homocysteine) are found in the blood and urine of children with certain hereditary diseases of methionine metabolism. Clinical features of these rare diseases include skeletal deformities, abnormalities of the lens of the eye, mental retardation, abnormal blood clots, and premature death. Recent interest in homocysteine has been stimulated by emerging evidence that elevated blood levels of homocysteine are linked to coronary heart disease, stroke, Alzheimer's disease, and birth defects.

Homocysteine metabolism. Unlike most amino acids, homocysteine is not incorporated into polypeptide chains during protein synthesis but functions as a key intermediate in the metabolism of methionine (see **illus.**). Methionine is derived from dietary protein and is the direct precursor of the ubiquitous methyl donor, *S*-adenosylmethionine (SAM). By donating one-carbon methyl groups to hormones, neurotransmitters, nucleic acids, phospholipids, proteins, and other substrates, SAM serves an essential function in mammalian homeostasis. Homocysteine is produced as a by-product of SAM-dependent methyl transfer reactions.

Homocysteine occupies a critical branch point in the methionine metabolic cycle. Depending on the metabolic need for methionine and SAM, homocysteine either can serve as a substrate for the regeneration of methionine or can be diverted from the methionine cycle to produce cystathionine and, ultimately, cysteine (see illus.). The major pathway for the regeneration of methionine from homocysteine in most tissues is catalyzed by the enzyme methionine synthase (MS). The MS reaction requires two B

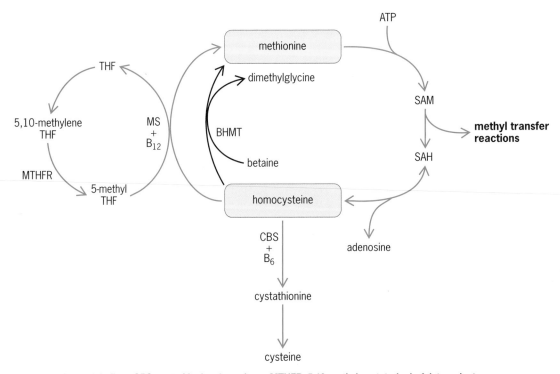

Homocysteine metabolism. CBS, cystathionine β-synthase; MTHFR, 5,10-methylene tetrahydrofolate reductase; MS, methionine synthase; BHMT, betaine:homocysteine methyltransferase; SAM, *S*-adenosylmethionine; SAH, *S*-adenosylhomocysteine; 5-methyl THF, 5-methyltetrahydrofolate; 5,10-methylene THF; 5,10-methylene tetrahydrofolate; B_6, vitamin B_6; B_{12}, vitamin B_{12}. Black arrows indicate an alternate pathway that does not require B vitamins.

vitamins, methylcobalamin (a form of vitamin B_{12}) and 5-methyl tetrahydrofolate (a form of folate). 5-Methyl tetrahydrofolate, in turn, is produced by the enzyme 5,10-methylene tetrahydrofolate reductase (MTHFR). An alternative pathway for the regeneration of methionine from homocysteine is catalyzed by the enzyme betaine:homocysteine methyltransferase (BHMT), which transfers a methyl group from betaine to homocysteine. BHMT is found mainly in the liver and kidney and does not require B vitamins.

The rate-limiting reaction in the conversion of homocysteine to cysteine is catalyzed by the enzyme cystathionine β-synthase (CBS), which requires pyridoxal phosphate (a form of vitamin B_6). Thus, the level of homocysteine in a given tissue is determined by the amount of methionine in the diet, the bioavailability of B vitamins, and the relative activities of the enzymes MS, MTHFR, BHMT, and CBS.

Hyperhomocysteinemia. Homocysteine contains a free thiol (SH) group, but only a small fraction (<2%) of the total homocysteine in blood is found in this (aminothiol) form. The remainder is a mixture of disulfide derivatives, including homocystine, homocysteine-cysteine mixed disulfide, and protein-bound disulfides. These various forms of homocysteine in blood are all derived from homocysteine that has been exported from the liver and other tissues. Sensitive and reliable methods for measurement of total homocysteine in blood have become widely available during the past decade. The normal concentration of total homocysteine in blood plasma is 5–15 μmol/L. Levels of total homocysteine tend to increase with age and are higher in men than in women.

Severe hyperhomocysteinemia. The term "hyperhomocysteinemia" refers to elevation of the blood level of total homocysteine above 15 μmol/L. Severe hyperhomocysteinemia, which is defined as a total homocysteine concentration greater than 100 μmol/L, occurs classically in patients with a homozygous defect of the gene that encodes CBS. Because these patients also have elevated levels of total homocysteine in their urine, they are said to have hereditary homocystinuria. Severe hyperhomocysteinemia also can be caused by hereditary defects in vitamin B_{12} metabolism or deficiency of vitamin B_{12} due to pernicious anemia.

Moderate hyperhomocysteinemia. Moderate hyperhomocysteinemia is defined as a blood level of total homocysteine between 15 and 100 μmol/L. This moderate degree of elevation of total homocysteine can be caused by genetic defects in CBS or MTHFR, kidney failure, or dietary deficiencies of folate or vitamin B_{12}. Moderate hyperhomocysteinemia also can be produced by drugs that interfere with the bioavailability of B vitamins, including certain medications used for the treatment of cancer, epilepsy, infections, asthma, and Parkinson's disease.

Hereditary homocystinuria. Hereditary homocystinuria (severe hyperhomocysteinemia) is quite rare, occurring in approximately 1 in 100,000 live births. The classic form of this disease, homozygous CBS deficiency, is the most prevalent of the genetic disorders that cause hereditary homocystinuria. CBS deficiency, produces defective transformation of homocysteine to cysteine, leading to accumulation of high blood levels of both homocysteine and methionine. When untreated, patients with homozygous CBS deficiency may develop skeletal deformities, dislocation of the lens of the eye, mental retardation, and premature death due to blood clots in the arteries or veins. Treatment with pharmacological doses of vitamin B_6, vitamin B_{12}, and folate, in conjunction with methionine restriction and supplemental betaine, lowers the plasma concentration of total homocysteine in most patients and markedly decreases their risk for vascular complications.

Hereditary homocystinuria also can be caused by genetic defects in the transport or metabolism of vitamin B_{12} or folate. Like homozygous CBS deficiency, these disorders cause markedly elevated levels of total homocysteine in the blood and urine, but levels of methionine are usually lower than normal. The clinical features of these disorders are very similar to those of homozygous CBS deficiency and include a high rate of cardiovascular events. It was the observation that vascular disease is a characteristic feature of homocystinuria caused by distinct metabolic defects that led the pathologist Kilmer McCully to postulate in 1969 that homocysteine may be a causative agent in atherosclerosis.

Birth defects and pregnancy complications. Moderate hyperhomocysteinemia is associated with an increased risk for birth defects resulting from incomplete closure of the neural tube during early embryogenesis. Although the overall prevalence is low (approximately 1 per 1000 live births), over 400,000 children are born each year with neural tube defects worldwide, and many of the cases are disabling.

The risk of a neural tube defect can be decreased by oral supplementation with folic acid during pregnancy, but only if the supplement is started before pregnancy or near the time of conception. To help prevent neural tube defects, all cereal and grain products in the United States have been fortified with folic acid since 1998.

Moderate hyperhomocysteinemia also has been implicated as a possible risk factor for other complications of pregnancy, including intrauterine growth retardation, severe preeclampsia, birth defects other than neural tube defects, and premature separation of the placenta from the wall of the uterus. It is not yet known, however, whether treatment with folic acid or other homocysteine-lowering therapies will protect pregnant women from these complications.

Vascular disease. The hypothesis that homocysteine may cause cardiovascular disease was proposed over 30 years ago by McCully, who observed advanced vascular lesions in children with hereditary homocystinuria. McCully's pioneering observations were confirmed in 1985 by an analysis of over 600 patients with severe hyperhomocysteinemia due to CBS deficiency. By the age of 30, approximately half of these patients had suffered from a cardiovascular event (stroke, myocardial infarction, or abnormal blood clots). It is now known that the risk of cardiovascular events in patients with hereditary homocystinuria can be markedly reduced by homocysteine-lowering therapy.

The mechanisms by which elevated levels of homocysteine predispose to vascular pathology are incompletely understood. Homocysteine appears to damage the endothelial cells that line the surface of blood vessels, interfering with their ability to regulate blood flow and prevent blood clots and inflammation. Homocysteine also may produce an oxidative stress that leads to atherosclerosis through the generation of oxidized lipoproteins.

Although severe hyperhomocysteinemia is a proven risk factor for adverse vascular events, the importance of moderate hyperhomocysteinemia as a cardiovascular risk factor is still undefined. Since the 1980s, a large number of epidemiological studies have suggested that moderate hyperhomocysteinemia may be a very prevalent risk factor, occurring in approximately 30% of patients with stroke, myocardial infarction, poor circulation in the arteries, or blood clots in the veins. In fact, some recent epidemiological studies suggest that blood levels of total homocysteine within the high-normal range (10–15 μmol/L) may confer an increased risk of cardiovascular disease.

A statistical association between moderate hyperhomocysteinemia and future cardiovascular events also has been observed in prospective studies, although a few prospective studies have failed to demonstrate this association. It is still uncertain, therefore, whether moderate hyperhomocysteinemia is an independent risk factor for cardiovascular disease or simply a marker for (that is, associated with) another factor. Nevertheless, because total homocysteine in blood can be lowered by oral administration of folic acid or combinations of B vitamins, there is growing enthusiasm for treatment of moderate hyperhomocysteinemia as a strategy for prevention of cardiovascular disease and its complications. This approach is currently being evaluated in several large clinical trials.

Current guidelines from the American Heart Association emphasize that it is not yet known whether reduction of blood levels of total homocysteine through increased intake of folic acid or other B vitamins will decrease cardiovascular risk in patients with moderate hyperhomocysteinemia. Until the results of controlled clinical trials become available, widespread treatment of moderate hyperhomocysteinemia for this purpose is not recommended.

Neurological disease. Regulation of homocysteine metabolism appears to be especially important in the central nervous system, presumably because of the critical role of methyl transfer reactions in the production of neurotransmitters and other methylated products. Abnormal accumulation of homocysteine in the brain may lead to increased levels of *S*-adenosylhomocysteine (see illus.), which can inhibit methyl transfer reactions. Another metabolite

of homocysteine, homocysteic acid, may directly damage the brain by activating a specific receptor on neurons.

It has been known for decades that mental retardation is a feature of severe hyperhomocysteinemia due to hereditary homocystinuria. It also is well known that impaired cognitive function can result from pernicious anemia, which causes hyperhomocysteinemia due to deficiency of vitamin B_{12}. Hyperhomocysteinemia also may be linked to several other neurological disorders, including depression, schizophrenia, multiple sclerosis, and dementia (including both Alzheimer's disease and other types of dementia).

The strongest evidence for a role for homocysteine in dementia comes from a recent prospective study in which moderate hyperhomocysteinemia was found to predict for the future development of Alzheimer's disease in elderly subjects. The predictive value of hyperhomocysteinemia was demonstrated for both Alzheimer's disease and non-Alzheimer's dementia. Thus, it is possible that metabolic abnormalities that produce hyperhomocysteinemia also lead to cognitive decline in elderly persons. However, no controlled treatment trials have been performed to determine whether homocysteine-lowering therapies prevent the development of dementia. Further research is needed to address this important question.

For background information *see* ALZHEIMER'S DISEASE; AMINO ACIDS; CONGENITAL ABNORMALITIES; METABOLIC DISORDERS; NERVOUS SYSTEM DISORDERS; VASCULAR DISORDERS; VITAMIN in the McGraw-Hill Encyclopedia of Science & Technology.

Steven R. Lentz

Bibliography. R. Carmel and D. W. Jacobsen (eds.), *Homocysteine in Health and Disease*, Cambridge University Press, Cambridge, 2001; R. Clarke and J. Armitage, Vitamin supplements and cardiovascular risk: Review of the randomized trials of homocysteine-lowering vitamin supplements, *Semin. Thromb. Hemost.*, 26:341–348, 2000; J. Selhub, Homocysteine metabolism, *Annu. Rev. Med.*, 19:217–246, 1999.

Hubble Space Telescope

The Hubble Space Telescope (HST) Servicing Mission 3B is currently the best example of NASA's ability to maintain, repair, and improve satellites in orbit. Actually, the genesis of this mission occurred more than 30 years ago. In the late 1960s and early 1970s, during the early development phase of the space shuttle, NASA was experiencing a 20–30% failure rate of its satellites due to either launch vehicle or satellite problems. Designers at NASA's Goddard Space Flight Center realized that a modular spacecraft could be repaired or serviced in orbit by spacewalking astronauts, so they developed an astronaut-friendly modular spacecraft concept that could be serviced by an extravehicular-activity (EVA) crew from the space shuttle. This concept featured ease of integration and testing during ground processing, and it proved to be less expensive and more reliable than competing "throwaway" concepts, in which equipment in space is discarded when it is no longer operable.

The first satellite to be repaired in orbit was the *Solar Maximum Mission* (*SMM*) observatory. This fully modular spacecraft pioneered the concept of in-orbit servicing via the shuttle and astronauts. After the success of this repair mission, astronauts serviced several commercial communication satellites by using various early capabilities, tools, and hardware support systems. But not until the First Servicing Mission of the Hubble Space Telescope in 1993 did the full complement of engineering ingenuity, astronaut skills, and shuttle capabilities come to fruition (**Fig. 1**).

Design features. The Hubble Space Telescope's design took advantage of the modular and astronaut-friendly design features of the *Solar Maximum Mission*. Such servicing features as the *Solar Maximum Mission* avionics and equipment carriers were incorporated into the Hubble mission. The Hubble team took advantage of NASA's mature processes, techniques, and tools for servicing, repairing, and improving spacecraft. Building on this expertise, they demonstrated that new technologies could be rapidly infused into a large space program in time spans of 3 years or less. NASA's valuable space assets would no longer have to suffer technological obsolescence as they languished through 6–10-year development cycles on the ground, followed by 3–5 years of degradation from in orbit radiation. In 1990, the Hubble Space Telescope was launched with a variety of servicing capabilities, from handrails and guiderails to upgradable components and new, replaceable science instruments.

The Hubble Space Telescope is NASA's most productive and recognizable scientific mission. Hubble's high discovery rate is due in large part to its ability to take advantage of rapidly evolving new technologies, and to use the space shuttle and its astronauts to place them into orbit in 3-year cycles. The serviceability minimizes technology obsolescence, maintains high productivity, and consistently yields a high return on scientific investment. NASA now can make major science discoveries while paying to develop and launch new spacecraft and telescope infrastructure much less often.

Early servicing missions. The wisdom of incorporating in-orbit servicing capabilities became apparent in 1993 during HST Servicing Mission 1 (Fig. 1). NASA's ability to service the Hubble dramatically reversed the disaster of a major optical fabrication flaw, called spherical aberration, by enabling astronauts to infuse the telescope with new, corrective optics technology. In 1997, Servicing Mission 2 added two next-generation scientific instruments and gave the telescope a 10-fold increase in observing power for each new instrument. During Servicing Mission 3A in 1999, astronauts installed six new ultraprecision gyroscopes and replaced Hubble's main computer.

Fig. 1. Astronauts repairing the Hubble Space Telescope during Servicing Mission 1 in December 1993. One astronaut is riding on the end of the space shuttle's Remote Manipulator System arm to a location on the telescope, while another, standing in the shuttle's cargo bay, is taking tools from a storage locker in preparation for instrument change-out. (*NASA*)

These improvements added life-extending capabilities to Hubble, and the new main computer provided 100 times as much computing power as its predecessor, while being stable and "hardened" against the radiation environment of space.

Servicing Mission 3B. In 2002, the fourth visit to the Hubble Space Telescope raised the standards and expectations for future in-orbit servicing missions. Designated HST Servicing Mission 3B, this 10-day mission involved the unprecedented complete changeout of the power generation system; improvements to the telescope's pointing and control system; incorporation of an advanced scientific camera with 12 times greater discovery power than its predecessor; and the development of a unique cooling technology, specifically designed to revive a dormant onboard camera. This new, closed-cycle, nondepletable cryogenic cooler renewed the telescope's infrared science observation capability.

Spacewalks 1 and 2. The Hubble Space Telescope's winglike solar arrays convert sunlight directly into electricity to run its scientific instruments, computers, and radio transmitters. The first spacewalk began the replacement of the Hubble's flexible arrays with ultraquiet, rigid arrays (**Fig. 2**). Although 33% smaller than the first two pairs, the new arrays produce 25% more power and significantly less pointing jitter. Over the course of 2 days, astronauts replaced both arrays and added a refurbished

Fig. 2. Astronauts at the completion of the installation of new solar panels on the Hubble Space Telescope during Servicing Mission 3B in March 2002. One astronaut (near center) stands with feet anchored to the end of the space shuttle's Remote Manipulator System arm, holding in his hand a highly precise microprocessor-controlled power tool. The other astronaut is standing on a fixed platform. (*NASA*)

reaction wheel assembly, which is an important component of the telescope's pointing control subsystem. The Hubble's four reaction wheel assemblies spin at 3000 revolutions per minute to produce the

Fig. 3. Dynamic responses of the Hubble Space Telescope during vehicle disturbance tests before and after the replacement of the old solar arrays with new ones with vibration dampers during Servicing Mission 3B in December 2002. Thermal gradients in the old arrays produced oscillations which were transmitted to the spacecraft, especially when it entered and left the Earth's shadow (end of day and end of night). The new arrays produce significantly less pointing jitter. (*NASA*)

rotational or angular torque needed to slew the telescope from one target to another, and to keep it stable once the target is acquired. The telescope's pointing stability is so steady that it can focus on the face of a dime over 5000 km (3000 mi) away (**Fig. 3**). After completing these major tasks, the astronauts had enough time to repair torn insulation and adjust a door hinge on the telescope's aft shroud.

Spacewalk 3. The most critical spacewalk of this mission was the changeout of the telescope's power control unit, which controls and distributes electricity from the solar arrays and batteries to other parts of the telescope. Engineers completely powered down Hubble for the first time since its launch in 1990. After astronauts replaced the original 12-year-old unit, the telescope was carefully powered up again and its vital signs returned to normal.

Spacewalk 4. Of the mission's five spacewalks, the installation of the Advanced Camera for Surveys (ACS) was the one most anticipated by astronomers. The telescope's most powerful instrument yet, this state-of-the-art imager has twice the field of view, five times more sensitivity, and at least ten times more discovery power than the instrument it replaced. Astronomers now use ACS to study weather on other planets, conduct new surveys of the universe, and gain more insight as to how the universe evolved. ACS, which sees in wavelengths ranging from visible to far-ultraviolet, has three different channels with specialized capabilities. The Wide Field channel conducts vast sky surveys to study the nature and distribution of galaxies. The High Resolution channel takes extremely detailed pictures of the inner regions of galaxies and searches neighboring stars for planets and planets-to-be. The Solar Blind channel blocks visible light to enhance Hubble's vision in the ultraviolet. The ACS detectors consist of 16 million light-gathering semiconductors and represent a major breakthrough in space visible detectors. The camera's sensitivity and spatial resolution are comparable to standing in Washington, DC, and both seeing and being able to distinguish two fireflies in Japan that are 2 m (6 ft) apart.

Spacewalk 5. The mission's final spacewalk restored Hubble's near-infrared capability by returning the Near Infrared Camera and Multi-Object Spectrometer (NICMOS) to full operation. The sensitive infrared detectors in NICMOS must operate at very cold temperatures, $-200°C$ or 73 K ($-328°F$). The NICMOS instrument had been dormant since 1999 after its supply of solid nitrogen cryogen was expended. A new system, called the NICMOS Cryocooler (NCC), was installed to restore the cooling originally provided by the solid nitrogen ice. The system successfully recooled the detectors by pumping ultracold neon gas through the internal plumbing of the instrument.

The NICMOS Cryocooler operates on principles similar to those of a home refrigerator (**Fig. 4**). At its core are three miniature, precisely machined turbines that spin at rates up to 430,000 revolutions per minute, which is more than 50 times the operating speed of a typical automobile engine. Two of these turbines implement a reverse-Brayton-cycle cryocooler, while the third turbine circulates cold gas through the NICMOS instrument. The turbines operate at such high speeds that exquisite balancing is necessary to eliminate the devastating effect of vibration on the telescope. NICMOS was able to preserve Hubble's extremely demanding pointing

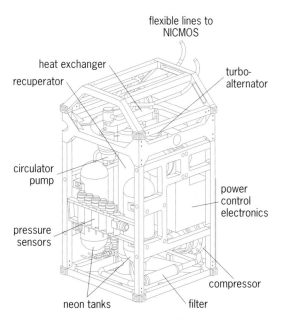

Fig. 4. Mechanical layout of the NICMOS Cryocooler. (*Ed Cheng, NASA/Goddard Space Flight Center*)

stability. The restored NICMOS is allowing scientists to see back billions of years in time, when the first galaxies were born.

Earthly benefits. The rapid infusion of technologies for servicing the Hubble Space Telescope has benefits outside the space program. Hubble's imaging needs were the impetus for the development of an ultrasensitive, low-noise, charge-coupled device, which found a use in the medical field before it ever flew on Hubble. This advanced visible and ultraviolet detector became the digital imaging device in a new procedure called the stereotactic large-core needle biopsy. It enabled the first widespread use of a less invasive type of nonsurgical biopsy.

The Hubble team also partnered with a private-industry manufacturer to produce a tough, slippery, diamond-hard coating that covers tiny parts on the NICMOS Cryocooler. Called UltraC Diamond™, this filmlike coating is approximately 1/100 the thickness of a human hair, yet virtually eliminates wear and tear on moving parts. It has applications in space, and anywhere else that requires an environment free of wear debris. This includes precision high-speed micromachines, semiconductor wafer processing equipment, and prosthetic biomedical implants. *See* MICRO-OPTO-ELECTRO-MECHANICAL SYSTEMS.

Finally, a sophisticated, highly precise power tool designed for use by spacewalking astronauts in servicing Hubble (Fig. 2) has many potential commercial uses. Called the pistol grip tool, it is especially suited for manufacturing and surgical procedures where mechanisms must be turned to critical specifications.

For background information *see* SPACE FLIGHT; SPACE SHUTTLE; SPACE TECHNOLOGY; SPACE TELESCOPE, HUBBLE in the McGraw-Hill Encyclopedia of Science & Technology.   Frank J. Cepollina

Bibliography. M. Henderson, Hubble coldly goes where no man has gone before, *New York Times*, Late Edition, sec. A, p. 2, col. 5, June 8, 2002; M. Livio, *The Accelerating Universe, Infinite Expansion, the Cosmological Constant, and the Beauty of the Cosmos*, Wiley, New York, 2000; C. C. Petersen and J. C. Brandt (contributors), *Hubble Vision: Astronomy with the Hubble Space Telescope*, Cambridge University Press, Cambridge, January 1996; C. C. Petersen and J. C. Brandt, (contributors), *Hubble Vision: Further Adventures with the Hubble Space Telescope*, 2d ed., Cambridge University Press, Cambridge, November 1998; R. Schwolksy, The right stuff, *Hanley-Wood's Tools of the Trade*, p. 36, March/April 2002.

Human origins

The combined evidence from molecular systematics, comparative morphology, and primatology has established that the African great apes—gorillas and chimpanzees—are more closely related to humans than they are to the Asian orangutan and other extant primates. Since our closest primate relatives are restricted today to Equatorial Africa, it can be deduced (as Charles Darwin and Thomas Huxley did more than a century ago) that humans are descended from a last common ancestor that also lived in Africa. Using a "molecular clock" model, in which the time scale of genetic change is calibrated against the fossil record, and based on the degree of genetic similarity between humans and chimpanzees (we share about 98% of our genomes), scientists can infer that humans diverged from the African apes about 6–7 million years ago (Ma).

Paleontologists searching for the fossil remains of human ancestors or hominins (that is, the taxonomic group to which modern humans and all extinct members of the human lineage belong) have been extraordinarily successful in piecing together the early stages of human evolutionary history. The fossil evidence shows that a diverse group of primitive hominins, comprising at least six species belonging to the genera *Australopithecus* and *Kenyanthropus*, were present in Africa 4–2 Ma. After 2.5 Ma, following climatic and ecological changes, more specialized hominins appeared in Africa, better adapted to exploiting drier, more seasonal habitats. These new kinds of hominins, belonging to the genera *Paranthropus* and *Homo*, replaced *Australopithecus* and *Kenyanthropus*. *Paranthropus* eventually became extinct 1.4 Ma, leaving *Homo erectus* (sometimes referred to as *Homo ergaster*) as the sole surviving hominin in Africa, and this eventually gave rise to our own species—*Homo sapiens*.

Australopithecus. One consequence of these discoveries is that scientists have been able to partially reconstruct the initial evolutionary steps taken by humans subsequent to their divergence from the last common ancestor with chimpanzees. Hominins 3–4 Ma, belonging to *Australopithecus*, were much more apelike than modern humans in many regards, but they had already acquired a suite of specialized characteristics unique to humans: (1) There is a slight increase in relative brain size (judging from the capacity of the braincase of the cranium, which is large in relation to that of chimpanzees, but less than one-third of an average modern human braincase). (2) The upper and lower canines are reduced in size compared with great apes and have a tip-to-tip bite pattern, functionally more similar to incisor teeth (whereas great apes have large tusklike canines, in which the upper canine slices down the outer side of the lower canine and the first lower premolar so that with wear they maintain sharp edges), and the canines are much less sexually dimorphic (that is, the sexes have canines that do not differ much in size, as in humans, whereas in all great apes the canines of males are much larger and more projecting than those of females). (3) The skeleton exhibits numerous distinctive specializations, especially of the hip, hindlimb, and foot, indicating that *Australopithecus*, when on the ground, traveled in an upright posture on two legs, similar to the striding bipedal gait of modern humans (whereas extant great apes are more specialized for arboreal activities, and primarily move along the ground quadrupedally, using all four limbs).

Fossil hominids. However, pertinent fossils from 5–7 Ma, the crucial time period for documenting the earliest representatives of the human lineage, have proved frustratingly elusive. Fossil hominids (the taxonomic group to which the great apes and humans belong) are extremely rare in Africa during the late Miocene (10–5 Ma). In fact, the fossil record of chimpanzees and gorillas, in contrast to that of humans, is entirely unknown. A large hominid, *Samburupithecus*, known only from a single upper jaw fragment from the site of Namurungule in Kenya (dated to 8–9 Ma), may represent a stem member of the African ape-human lineage. Until recently, a few isolated teeth of fossil hominids from the late Miocene sites of Lukeino and Lothagam in Kenya (dated at 5.0–6.5 Ma) were all that were available to document the earliest known occurrence of the human lineage prior to 5 Ma, but the remains were too fragmentary to be confident about their phylogenetic affinities or tell us much about their anatomy. Then, beginning in the mid-1990s, intrepid paleontologists working in Ethiopia, Kenya, and Chad made some remarkable discoveries that have helped to fill this critical gap in the fossil record (see **illus.**).

Ardipithecus ramidus. In 1994, Tim White and colleagues described important new fossil hominids from the early Pliocene site of Aramis in the Middle Awash region of Ethiopia. The specimens consist of a mandible fragment of an infant, an associated

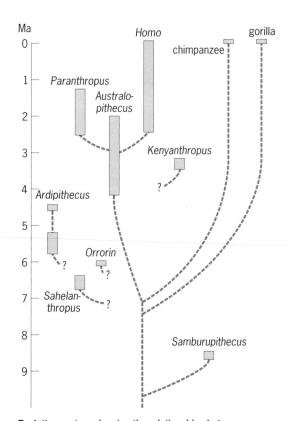

Evolutionary tree showing the relationships between humans, African great apes (chimpanzees and gorillas), and fossil hominids from the late Miocene onward. Bars depict the known time range of each genus. Broken lines represent inferred relationships. Question marks indicate uncertain relationships.

dental series, some isolated teeth, cranial fragments, and several bones of the forelimb. The material, reliably dated to 4.4 Ma, was described as a new genus and species of hominin—*Ardipithecus ramidus*. White and colleagues suggested that *Ardipithecus* was the earliest known hominin and a member of the stem group from which all later hominins were derived. *Ardipithecus* is certainly more primitive than *Australopithecus*, but it does share several specialized features that link it with these later hominins. For example, the canines are relatively small and more incisiform, and they exhibit reduced sexual dimorphism compared with those of great apes. *Ardipithecus* also has a more forward-positioned foramen magnum (the large aperture in the base of the cranium that connects the spinal cord and brain), and this indicates perhaps a more upright posture than is typical of extant apes. Unfortunately, hip and hindlimb bones, which are critical for confirming whether or not *Ardipithecus* was bipedal, have not yet been described from the site.

More recently, Yohannes Haile-Selassie reported *Ardipithecus* specimens from several sites in the Middle Awash that are significantly older than those from Aramis, being dated to 5.2–5.8 Ma. These finds share the same tendency toward small, incisiform lower canines as the Aramis material, but since they differ in other details of their dental anatomy, Haile-Selassie recognized them as a separate subspecies, *Ardipithecus ramidus kadabba*. One of the new specimens is a toe bone that is strongly curved as in apes, but the joint surface for articulation with the metatarsal is orientated in a fashion that resembles that seen in later bipedal hominins.

Orrorin tugenensis. In 2000, a French-Kenyan team directed by Brigitte Senut and Martin Pickford resumed work at sites in the Lukeino Formation of the Tugen Hills of Kenya that had previously yielded an isolated tooth of a hominin dated to 6 Ma. They recovered additional finds that formed the basis for the description of a new genus and species of hominin—*Orrorin tugenensis*. The teeth are generally similar to those of middle and late Miocene apes from Africa and Eurasia, with no dental specializations that link the species uniquely with hominins. Although the forelimb bones suggest that *Orrorin* was a good arboreal climber like modern apes, Senut and colleagues have argued that the structure of the upper part of the femur (the thighbone) indicates that it was a terrestrial biped. The discoverers suggest that *Orrorin* is a direct ancestor of *Homo*, with *Australopithecus* being an earlier evolutionary offshoot, whereas *Ardipithecus* is relegated to the ancestry of the African great apes. Critics, however, question the interpretation that *Orrorin* was bipedal, preferring instead to view it as an ape, possibly a primitive member of the African ape-human lineage.

Sahelanthropus tchadensis. The most recent, and arguably the most spectacular, contender for the title of the earliest hominin is *Sahelanthropus tchadensis* from the wind-swept deserts of northern Chad in central Africa. The fossils, from the late Miocene locality of Toros-Menalla, dated to 6–7 Ma, were recovered in 2001–2002 by a team of scientists led by French paleontologist Michel Brunet. The best specimen, a crushed but relatively complete cranium, is characterized by a short face, an ape-sized braincase, widely spaced eye sockets, a broad nasal aperture, a thick bony bar that runs across the top of the eyes (as in gorillas, but even more pronounced), and a small crest along the midline of the rear of the cranium for the attachment of large chewing muscles. The teeth of *Sahelanthropus* are generally apelike, although it does have relatively small canines with tip-to-tip wear as in later hominins. Unfortunately, no postcranial bones of *Sahelanthropus* have been recovered, so it is not possible to deduce anything about its locomotor behavior. Brunet and colleagues proposed that *Sahelanthropus* is the oldest and most primitive known hominin, very close to the divergence of the human and chimpanzee lineages, although other scientists have suggested that it may be a stem member of the African ape-human lineage.

Conclusion. It is evident from preliminary assessments of the evolutionary relationships of these new fossil finds that it will take some time to resolve ongoing debates about their hominin status. Part of the difficulty is that the further back in time the human lineage is traced, the fewer humanlike specializations would have been accrued by human ancestors, and these could well have been quite subtle anatomical and behavioral shifts initially, not easily recognizable based on fragmentary fossils. Nevertheless, the recent fossil hominid remains discovered from the late Miocene and early Pliocene of Africa certainly offer tantalizing clues to suggest that aspects of their anatomy foreshadow the more specialized pattern seen in later hominins. Even so, given the fragmentary nature of the available fossil record and the inherently mosaic fashion in which characters evolve, it is possible that at least some of these contenders may eventually turn out to be fossil apes rather than hominins. Regardless of the final outcome, researchers agree that these exciting discoveries contribute an important new dimension to the understanding of early hominid diversity, one that will profoundly influence the way in which scientists perceive and interpret the critical events and factors that led to the origin and subsequent divergence of the human lineage.

For background information *see* AUSTRALO-PITHECINE; EARLY MODERN HUMANS; FOSSIL APES; FOSSIL HUMANS; PHYSICAL ANTHROPOLOGY in the McGraw-Hill Encyclopedia of Science & Technology.

Terry Harrison

Bibliography. E. Delson et al., *Encyclopedia of Human Evolution and Prehistory*, 2d ed., Garland Publishing, New York, 2000; A. Gibbons, In search of the first hominids, *Science*, 295:1214–1219, 2002; R. G. Klein, *The Human Career: Human Biological and Cultural Origins*, University of Chicago Press, Chicago, 1999; B. Wood, Hominid revelations from Chad, *Nature*, 418:133–135, 2002.

Hyperspectral remote sensing

"Hyperspectral" refers to the many wavelength bands that are characteristic of a remote sensing spectral data set. With earlier remote sensing systems, data were acquired in four to seven spectral bands. Airborne and space-borne hyperspectral systems, or imaging spectrometers, can simultaneously acquire data in hundreds of spectral bands. Because of the increased information content of the data acquired by hyperspectral systems, many more applications can be addressed by this remote sensing technique.

The technology is unique because hyperspectral systems can acquire a complete reflectance spectrum for each pixel in the image (**Fig. 1**). The reflectance spectrum in the region from 400 to 2500 nm can be used to identify a large range of materials on the Earth's surface that cannot be identified with broadband, low-resolution imaging systems such as the *Landsat TM* remote sensing satellite.

Many materials on the Earth's surface have diagnostic spectral absorption features that are 20 to 40 nanometers wide at half the band depth (**Fig. 2**). Hyperspectral imaging systems, which acquire data in contiguous bands that are 10 nm or less in width, can produce data with sufficient resolution for the direct identification of those materials with diagnostic spectral features.

Early hyperspectral systems were airborne, such as the Airborne Imaging Spectrometer and the subsequent Airborne Visible Infrared Imaging Spectrometer, both developed and operated by the National Aeronautics and Space Administration (NASA) and Jet Propulsion Laboratory (JPL). As these systems evolved and improved, design and development of space-borne systems occurred. The culmination was the launch of NASA's *Earth Observing 1 (EO-1)* satellite with the Hyperion hyperspectral imager on board.

Airborne Imaging Spectrometer. Initial hyperspectral remote sensing research was conducted with data acquired by the Airborne Imaging Spectrometer (AIS). The first test flight of the AIS was conducted in November 1982 aboard a NASA/Dryden C-47 aircraft. The AIS was designed as an engineering test bed for use with prototype detector arrays of the type that would be flown in space.

The AIS system collected 128 bands of data, each approximately 9.3 nm wide. In its "tree mode," the AIS collected data in contiguous bands between 400 and 1200 nm. The AIS also had a "rock mode," where it collected data between 1.2 and 2.4 micrometers. The AIS was operated from a U2 aircraft, typically from an altitude of 4200 m (13,800 ft) above the terrain. With a ground pixel size of approximately 8×8 m (26×26 ft), this altitude yielded a swath that was 32 pixels wide beneath the flight path for AIS-1 (64 pixels wide for AIS-2).

The AIS system operated in a push-broom mode; that is, it did not use a scanning mirror. Light passed from the foreoptics through a slit that defined the cross-track footprint on the ground. In the spectrometer the light was dispersed with a diffraction grating and focused on a mercury cadmium telluride detector array located inside a dewar containing liquid nitrogen for detector cooling. To acquire 128 hyperspectral images, the grating was tilted through four positions as the aircraft moved forward.

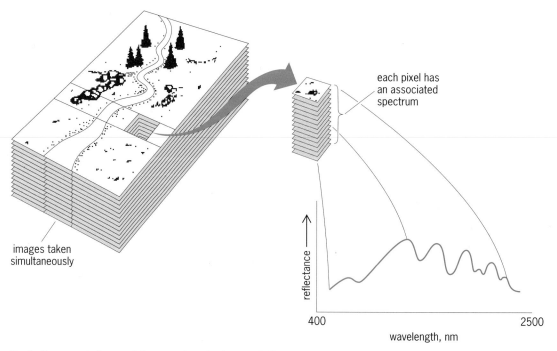

Fig. 1. **Hyperspectral concept. Images taken simultaneously (for example, in 200 or more spectral bands) are inherently registered. Each pixel has an associated, continuous spectrum that can be used to identify the surface materials.** (*After G. Vane, High spectral resolution remote sensing of the Earth, Sensors, no. 2, pp. 11–20, 1985*)

AVIRIS. The Airborne Visible-Infrared Imaging Spectrometer (AVIRIS) is capable of collecting data in 224 spectral bands. These contiguous spectral bands are approximately 9.6 nm wide and are located in the visible/near-infrared portion of the spectrum between 400 and 2450 nm. AVIRIS uses a scanning mirror to sweep back and forth (in whisk-broom fashion), producing 614 pixels for the 224 detectors each scan. When the AVIRIS system is flown on NASA's ER-2 research aircraft at an altitude of 20 km (12 mi), the swath width is approximately 10 km (6 mi). At this elevation, the AVIRIS system has a ground pixel resolution of approximately 20 m (65 ft). AVIRIS is also flown in a Twin Otter turboprop aircraft at 4 km (2.5 mi) above ground level, resulting in a narrow swath and better ground pixel resolution. AVIRIS has collected hyperspectral remote sensing data in North America, Europe, and portions of South America.

The main objective of the AVIRIS project is to identify, measure, and monitor constituents of the Earth's surface and atmosphere based on molecular absorption and particle scattering signatures. Research with AVIRIS data is predominantly focused on understanding processes related to the global environment and climate change.

Hyperion. Hyperion was launched in November 2000 aboard NASA's *Earth Observing 1* satellite and is NASA's first hyperspectral imager to become operational in space. *EO-1* is the first satellite in NASA's New Millennium Program Earth Observing series. The focus of *EO-1* primarily is on developing and testing instruments that are smaller, less expensive, and more capable than existing instruments.

Hyperion provides a high-resolution hyperspectral imager capable of resolving 220 spectral bands (from 400 to 2500 nm) with a 30-m (100-ft) ground pixel resolution. The instrument can cover a 7.5 × 100 km (4.7 × 62 mi) land area per image and provide detailed spectral mapping across all 220 channels with high radiometric accuracy. Hyperion is a push-broom instrument, with one visible/near-infrared (VNIR) spectrometer and one short-wave infrared (SWIR) spectrometer. The VNIR and SWIR spectrum overlap from 900 to 1000 nm and will allow cross calibration between the two spectrometers.

Hyperion, aboard *EO-1*, is in an orbit that allows it to, in effect, fly in formation with other remote sensing satellites, such as *Landsat* 7. The *EO-1*/Hyperion orbit matches the *Landsat* 7 orbit within 1 minute and collects nearly identical images for subsequent comparison. Hyperion will routinely collect images hundreds of kilometers long.

Future systems. The U.S. Navy, with private industry, has developed the *Naval Earth Map Observer* (*NEMO*) satellite program, which includes the Coastal Ocean Imaging Spectrometer (COIS). This hyperspectral instrument acquires data in 210 spectral bands over the range from 400 to 2500 nm. The *NEMO* system will have 60 spectral bands over the 400–1000-nm range and 150 bands over the 1000–2500-nm range, respectively. *NEMO* will collect

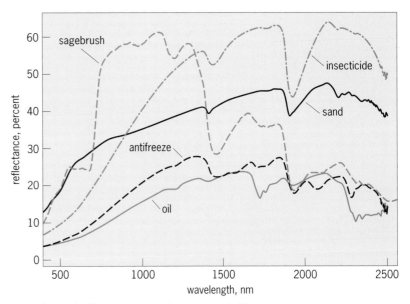

Fig. 2. **Spectral reflectance curves of common materials.**

hyperspectral data at ground resolutions of either 30 or 60 m (100 or 200 ft), over a 30-km (19-mi) swath width.

A number of other countries besides the United States have plans to launch and operate hyperspectral satellite systems. The *Australian Resource Information and Environmental Satellite* (*ARIES*) is an example. The nominal specifications for *ARIES* include a hyperspectral imager with up to 105 bands located between 400 and 2500 nm. Although *ARIES* was designed primarily for mineral exploration, it will collect data that will support applications ranging from agriculture and forestry to wetland mapping and environmental monitoring.

Japan is also planning to launch a 36-band sensor aboard its *ADEOS II* platform. Japan's Global Imager (GLI) has 250–1000-m (820–3280-ft) resolution and a 1600-km (1000-mi) swath width.

Image processing and exploitation. The light curve of the Sun and the absorption features of the atmosphere dominate the general shape of the spectrum from a hyperspectral system. The light curve for the Sun peaks in the green wavelengths but decreases toward longer and shorter wavelengths. The atmosphere absorbs light at wavelengths that correspond to the absorption characteristics of the constituent gases, such as nitrogen, oxygen, carbon dioxide, and water vapor.

The peaks and valleys of a spectrum not due to the Sun or the atmosphere reveal information about the chemical composition of the spectrum being examined. Since every material has a unique spectrum, an analyst can look for diagnostic features from hyperspectral data. For example, the chlorophyll in vegetation absorbs visible light from the Sun but reflects the infrared portion. This infrared reflection can be seen in the spectra at the transition from red light (700 nm) to the infrared.

Hyperspectral sensors offer a wealth of information about the physical and chemical composition of materials on the Earth's surface. While most visible/near-infrared optical sensors are capable only of discriminating among various surface features, hyperspectral sensors can potentially identify and determine many of their characteristics. The disadvantages of hyperspectral sensors are the large data volume and the need to incorporate atmospheric correction algorithms. Also, with hyperspectral systems, the signal-to-noise ratio tends to decrease because the incoming radiance is distributed over more spectral bands.

Image processing and exploitation techniques must address the issue of atmospheric correction, and rely more on physical and biophysical models rather than on purely statistical techniques. After a hyperspectral image has been corrected for the effects of atmospheric absorption and scattering, a reflectance signature can be produced for each pixel. This hyperspectral signature can be compared to reference spectra consisting of previously acquired spectra of known material types. Spectral libraries of reference spectra, representing primarily minerals, soils, and vegetation types, have been collected in the laboratory and in the field.

Applications. Hyperspectral imaging has wideranging applications in mining, geology, forestry, agriculture, and environmental management. For example, detailed classification of land assets will enable more accurate remote mineral exploration and better predictions of crop yield.

For the Hyperion system, a broad range of applications research is addressing the use of hyperspectral data for assessing land cover/land use, mineral resources, coastal processes, and other earth and atmospheric processes. NASA has selected a total of 31 science teams with worldwide representation to evaluate applications of Hyperion data.

For background information *see* INFRARED IMAGING DEVICES; REMOTE SENSING in the McGraw-Hill Encyclopedia of Science & Technology.

Marcus Borengasser

Bibliography. J. B. Campbell, *Introduction to Remote Sensing*, Guilford Press, 2002; T. M. Lillesand and R. W. Kiefer, *Remote Sensing and Image Interpretation*, Wiley, 2000; NASA/JPL, *Proceedings of the Airborne Imaging Spectrometer Data Analysis Workshop*, JPL Publ. 85-41, 1987; NASA/JPL, *Summaries of the 7th JPL Airborne Earth Science Workshop*, HPL Publ. 97-21, vol. 1, 1998; G. Vane, High spectral resolution remote sensing of the earth, *Sensors*, no. 2, pp. 11-20, 1985.

Inhibin

Inhibin is an endocrine hormone made by the ovary and testis that is secreted into the bloodstream to control (inhibit) the secretion of follicle stimulating hormone by the pituitary gland (**Fig. 1**). It is thus an important part of an endocrine feedback loop. There are two functional forms of inhibin, A and B. Inhibin A has two protein subunits, an α subunit and a βA

subunit, whereas inhibin B has an α subunit and a βB subunit. In both forms, the two subunits, of almost the same size, are held together by covalent linkages.

Although the existence of inhibin had been suggested as early as 1932, it was not until inhibin A was purified from bovine ovarian follicular fluid around 1985 by researchers at Monash University in Melbourne and the genes encoding it were cloned that real progress was made. The Monash researchers established a radioimmunoassay method for measuring the concentrations of the hormone in blood, which was widely used from 1986 to 1992. However, it was gradually realized that this assay could not distinguish between inhibin A and B, nor between these functional forms and free α subunit forms that were present in large amounts in body fluids. This problem was solved in 1994 with the development of a specific assay for inhibin A followed by a similar assay for inhibin B, enabling scientists to discover their distinct physiologic effects and clinical applications.

Physiology and clinical applications in women. During the normal menstrual cycle, inhibin A is secreted by the granulosa cells of the dominant egg follicle as it grows, causing blood inhibin A levels to gradually increase toward midcycle, with the main peak occurring after ovulation during the luteal phase of the cycle (**Fig. 2**). By contrast, inhibin B is produced by small follicles at the start of the cycle, with minimal secretion during the luteal phase. It has been subsequently shown subsequently that as women age they use up their reserve of egg follicles, which is reflected by a decrease of circulating inhibin B levels in the follicular phase of the cycle. This explains why follicle stimulating hormone levels rise at this time of the cycle as women approach menopause.

Ovarian reserve. Some researchers have proposed the use of inhibin B as a marker for ovarian reserve (reproductive potential), since it has been successfully used to identify women who have few eggs remaining and are thus close to menopause. (In fact, it is claimed that a fall in circulating inhibin B is the earliest endocrine warning of oncoming menopause.) Women with low inhibin B on day 3 of the menstrual cycle have been reported to be less successful in achieving pregnancy through in vitro fertilization procedures. Other researchers have reported that even if women with low inhibin levels decide to undergo in vitro fertilization treatment, measurement of inhibin B levels soon after the start of treatment can identify women who are responding poorly and thus are unlikely to produce usable oocytes.

Down syndrome. Currently, the major clinical application of inhibin A is in prenatal screening for Down syndrome. Conventionally, this screening is done at 12-16 weeks' gestation with the so-called triple test (the measurement of the maternal serum concentrations of three substances: human chorionic gonadotrophin, estriol, and α fetoprotein). It has been shown that adding inhibin A into this second trimester screening (the quad test) detects about 7% more of the babies with Down syndrome, which might otherwise have been missed, while keeping the false positive rate at 5%. Other researchers have kept their detection rate the same but used inhibin A to lower the false positive rate. Since false positives may lead to unnecessary amniocentesis, which could cause the loss of a pregnancy, a low rate of false positives is highly desirable. Currently, a Food and Drug Administration-approved form of the inhibin A assay is being marketed in the United States, and about 15-20% of pregnancies are being screened using inhibin A.

Ovarian cancer. Although for most research and clinical studies the more specific inhibin A and B assays are most useful, there is one application in women which seems to require assays able to measure the totality of inhibin forms. This is the suggested use of inhibin as a screening marker for ovarian cancer. Although the CA125 marker normally used is good for the detection of many ovarian cancer types, it is poor for granulosa cell cancers and mucinous epithelial tumors. Since these tumors secrete inhibin, it is believed that CA125 screening can be combined with total inhibin assays to give a useful clinical tool that is able to detect more types of ovarian cancer than either method alone.

Inhibin has been reported to be particularly useful in women with granulosa cell cancers of the ovaries. Such cancers comprise about 5-10% of all ovarian cancers and are very slow growing, requiring monitoring for many years after a lump has been removed. Since in postmenopausal women any inhibin B detected in the blood is from the cancer, it is likely that measurement of inhibin B blood concentrations can detect some recurrences before new symptoms appear.

Physiology and clinical applications in men. Although men do not appear to use inhibin A, inhibin B has proved a useful circulating marker for spermatogenesis. In fact, it is the only substance measurable in a man's blood which correlates with his ability to make sperm. Inhibin B is made by the Sertoli cells, which surround and nourish the developing sperm. In healthy men, there is a high correlation between blood inhibin B levels and sperm density and testicular volume. For this reason, it was thought at one time that blood levels of inhibin B might also be used to predict the success with which sperm might be retrieved surgically from the testis to use for direct injection into the partner's oocytes. However, although men with very low blood inhibin B will typically have a low sperm count, it is also possible for men with normal inhibin B levels to have very low sperm count because of the presence of an obstruction. In addition, since successful sperm retrieval can be achieved even with very low numbers of sperm, inhibin B is not a useful predictor of unsuccessful sperm retrieval.

Blood inhibin B measurements are, however, useful in population studies of male fertility as an alternative to sperm counts. They have also been used to assess the gonadotoxicity of chemotherapy regimes in patients with cancer, and the inhibin B assay has been used in vitro to detect the possible

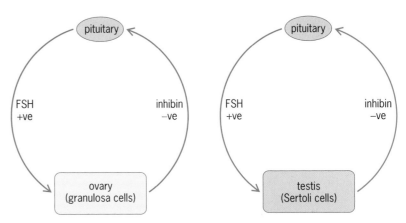

Fig. 1. Endocrine roles of inhibin in women and men; +ve signifies stimulation, and −ve signifies inhibition.

effects of environmental toxicants on Sertoli cell function.

Future applications. Because of the large amount of research currently being done on inhibin, it is likely that other clinical applications for the measurement of inhibin will emerge.

Preeclampsia risk. Blood concentrations of inhibin A are highly elevated in women in the second trimester of pregnancy, during which the serious complication of preeclampsia (a condition characterized by increased blood pressure, swelling, and protein in the urine) can develop. Thus, researchers are investigating the use of an inhibin assay as part of a prenatal screening program to identify women at risk. However, recent data suggest that inhibin A is more directly correlated with intrauterine growth restriction (which often accompanies preeclampsia) than with preeclampsia itself. Further work is needed to determine how blood inhibin A determinations might be used diagnostically.

Pregnancy viability. Inhibin A might also be useful in assessing the viability of pregnancies. If a pregnancy is viable, blood inhibin A levels should rise as the fetoplacental unit develops; however, if the embryo is dead, inhibin A levels would decline.

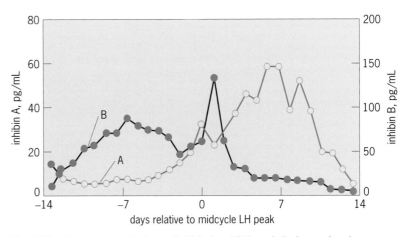

Fig. 2. Blood serum concentrations of inhibin A and B through the human female menstrual cycle. Menstruation is represented on the left of the cycle (−14 to −7) and ovulation on the day marked 0. LH = luteinizing hormone.

Gynecological malignancy. Other recent research suggests the potential application of a blood inhibin A assay in the detection of the rare gynecological malignancy known as hydatidiform mole, particularly in confirming its successful surgical removal. In this application (as well as in pregnancy viability detection), one advantage of inhibin might be its short serum half-life, enabling it to reflect current events more closely than conventional markers. However, only after rigorous clinical assessment would it be appropriate to replace established markers with inhibin.

Abnormal gonad development. Inhibin A and B are also likely to be increasingly used in monitoring abnormal gonad development in boys and girls. Prior to puberty, for example, there is little correlation between blood inhibin and follicle stimulating hormone levels. However, in boys undergoing normal puberty, a negative relationship is established between blood inhibin B and follicle stimulating hormone, consistent with the role of inhibin as a negative regulator of follicle stimulating hormone levels. Thus, blood inhibin profiles in childhood may give early warning of potential problems that might affect an individual's fertility later in life.

For background information *see* ENDOCRINE SYSTEM (VERTEBRATE); OVARY; PITUITARY GLAND; REPRODUCTIVE SYSTEM; REPRODUCTIVE TECHNOLOGY; TESTIS in the McGraw-Hill Encyclopedia of Science & Technology.   N. P. Groome

Bibliography. S. Bhasin and D. D. de Kretser, Measurement of circulating inhibin levels: Revisiting the inhibin hypothesis, *J. Clin. Endocrinol. Metab.*, 81:1318–1320, 1996; H. G. Burger et al., The ageing female reproductive axis, *Novartis Foundation Symposium*, 242:161–167, 2002; N. P. Groome and L. W. Evans, Clinical uses of inhibin assay, *Ann. Clin. Biochem.*, 37:419–431, 2000; S. Muttukrishna and W. Ledger, *Inhibin and Activin in Human Reproductive Physiology*, Imperial College Press, 2001; D. M. Robertson et al., Inhibins/activins as markers of ovarian cancer, *Mol. Cell. Endocrinol.*, 191:97–103, 2002.

Inner-core anisotropy and hemisphericity

The Earth is divided into crust, mantle, and core, with the core further divided into the inner and outer portions. The inner core, discovered by Inge Lehmann in 1936, has a radius of 1220 km (758 mi) and a density about 13 g/cm³. It represents about 1.7% of the mass of the Earth. The inner-core boundary represents a phase transition from liquid iron in the outer core to solid iron in the inner core. Despite its size, the inner core plays an important role in the Earth's dynamical system. For example, scientists believe the solidification of the outer-core materials, that is, the growth of the inner core, drives the convection in the outer core and powers the geodynamo, a physical process that generates the Earth's magnetic field. Most knowledge about the inner core (its discovery, radius, and density) has come from the study of seismic waves, or seismology. Recently, much has been learned by studying variations in seismic waves due to the direction in which they are propagated (anisotropy) and the part of the inner core in which they travel (hemisphericity).

Seismology. Seismology plays a vital role in deciphering the physical processes in the inner core. An earthquake radiates seismic energy, which is transmitted through the Earth's body and is recorded by seismometers around the globe. Many earthquakes are powerful enough that their radiated seismic waves visit the inner core and come back to the Earth's surface with enough energy remaining that the waves can be detected and measured.

Seismic properties. Seismic properties, such as wave speed, attenuation, and anisotropy, provide crucial information about the deepest part of the Earth. Seismic speed can be measured by dividing the path length of seismic waves by the time the waves spend in the inner core. Seismic attenuation, a measure of a material's ability to dissipate seismic energy, can be measured by the energy lost by a seismic wave during its visit to the inner core. Seismic anisotropy describes the phenomenon in which seismic wave speed depends on the direction of the wave's propagation through a medium (lack of such dependence is called isotropy); it is studied by comparing the speeds of seismic waves traveling in different directions through the same medium. Seismic speed is influenced by many factors: intrinsic wave speed of the material, temperature, melt inclusion, and alignment of anisotropic crystals in the material. For anisotropic crystals, seismic speed varies with direction because, within the atomic framework of the crystals, the neighboring atom distances and interactions are closer together in some planes through the material than in others. Seismic attenuation is sensitive to temperature, melt volume, and melt geometry. Seismic anisotropy (in a solid-state medium) requires two conditions: (1) that the crystals composing the medium (in the case of the inner core, mostly iron) are anisotropic, and (2) that there is a physical mechanism (or mechanisms) to preferentially align the fast speed axes of the anisotropic crystals in certain directions. Thus, the seismic speed, attenuation, and anisotropy inferred from seismology provide crucial constraints on the presumed composition, thermal status, and physical mechanisms in the inner core.

Seismic wave analysis. Most knowledge about seismic structures in the inner core comes from a seismic compressional (P) wave transmitted through the inner core known as PKIKP (**Fig. 1**). In order to use PKIKP to study the inner core, it is imperative to address the effect on the waves of the mantle, another place where PKIKP waves spend a major portion of time. Often, rather than directly correct for the mantle contribution, which is not an easy task, scientists use other core waves, or phases, whose ray paths are similar to PKIKP's in the mantle as reference phases, and use the differential travel time and relative energy between PKIKP phases and the reference phases to infer seismic speed and attenuation structure in the inner core. The most commonly used reference phases are PKiKP, the compressional wave reflected off the inner-core boundary, and PKPbc, a compressional wave traveling in the lower part of the outer core (Fig. 1). Because PKIKP, PKiKP, and PKPbc phases are so close together in the mantle, they experience similar alterations there. Using the differential travel time and relative energy between the phase pairs effectively eliminates the mantle alterations, and therefore variations in their differential travel time and relative energy are indicative of variations of seismic speed and attenuation in the inner core. Scientists collect these phase pairs from seismometers around the globe and measure their differential travel times and relative energy. They then track the observations back to the contributing paths in the inner core, translate them into seismic speed and attenuation, and analyze the geographic, depth, and directional variations of these seismic properties.

Inner-core observations. To their surprise, scientists discovered that in the top (that is, outermost) part of the inner core seismic speeds are faster in the "eastern" hemisphere (40°E–180°E) than in the "western" (180°W–40°E). They also noticed that the seismic waves traveling through the faster eastern hemisphere emerged at their endpoints with less energy, indicating a higher attenuation (energy loss)

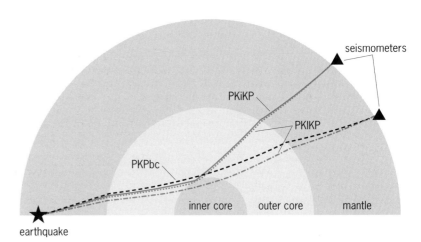

Fig. 1. Ray paths of some compressional waves through a cross section of the Earth. PKIKP (colored dashed traces) is a wave propagating through the inner core and is the primary source of information about seismic structures in the inner core; PKiKP (colored trace) is the wave reflected off the inner-core boundary; and PKPbc (black dashed traces) is a wave in the lower portion of the outer core.

rather than the lower attenuation that commonly accompanies faster speeds. The hemispherical variation in speed is best demonstrated from the residuals (difference between measured and predicted values) of PKiKP–PKIKP differential travel time (**Fig. 2**). In this dataset, PKIKP phases sample the top 80 km (50 mi) of the inner core based on computer

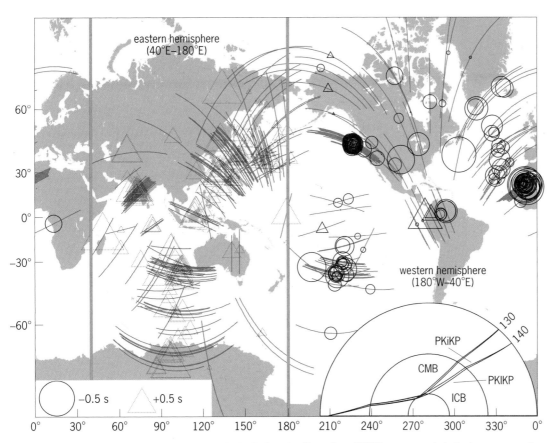

Fig. 2. Map view of PKiKP–PKIKP travel time residuals displayed as lines along PKIKP ray segments in the inner core and symbols at the turning point, the deepest point that a seismic ray travels inside the Earth where it begins its return to the surface. Circles and triangles represent negative and positive residuals, respectively. The size of the symbols is proportional to the absolute value of residuals. Ray paths of PKiKP and PKIKP are shown in the inset, where ICB is the inner-core boundary and CMB is the core-mantle boundary. (*Courtesy of Fenglin Niu*)

modeling. The residuals are obtained by subtracting the PKiKP-PKIKP time separations predicted by the Preliminary Reference Earth Model (PREM) from what is observed in the seismic data. A positive residual means that PKIKP phase spends less time in the inner core than predicted by the model, and thus suggests higher wave speed in the inner core. A negative residual indicates the opposite. The differential PKiKP-PKIKP travel time residuals are systematically larger in the eastern hemisphere than in the western. When these travel time residuals are translated into seismic compressional speed variations in the top portion of the inner core, the eastern hemisphere is about 1% faster than the western. Scientists find no dependence of wave speed on the direction in which seismic waves sample this portion of the inner core, suggesting anisotropy is nonexistent in the top of the inner core.

When scientists analyzed the PKPbc-PKIKP observations recorded at larger distances (distances that allow PKIKP to tap deeper into the inner core), they discovered that seismic waves start to travel faster when they pass through the inner core at an angle closer to the Earth's rotation axis; that is, wave speed is anisotropic. They further noticed that rather than having a simple and uniform form, this anisotropy emerged at different depths and had different magni-

tudes, again, between the eastern and western hemispheres. This anisotropy and hemisphericity is best viewed form the residuals of PKPbc-PKIKP differential travel times (**Fig. 3**). Again, positive and negative residuals suggest faster and slower wave speeds in the inner core, respectively. Note that the polar residuals (triangles) are larger than their equatorial counterparts (circles), indicating faster speed when seismic ray angles are closer to the Earth's rotation axis. It is also evident that the polar-equatorial difference is much smaller and the onset of the difference starts deeper in the eastern hemisphere than in the western. These travel time residuals suggest that anisotropy emerges at about 50-150 km (31-93 mi) below the inner-core boundary with a magnitude about 5-8% in the western hemisphere, and at about 200 km (124.3 mi) with a magnitude about 0.4-0.8% in the eastern. PKIKP phases lose their reference phases, as they penetrate 400 km (248.6 mi) deeper into the inner core (Fig. 1). As a result, studying the deepest part of the inner core becomes difficult. But PKIKP observations alone suggest that the anisotropy likely extends deep into the inner core.

Summary. The inner core has a top isotropic layer overlying an anisotropic deeper part (**Fig. 4**). Both the top isotropic speed and the deep anisotropy

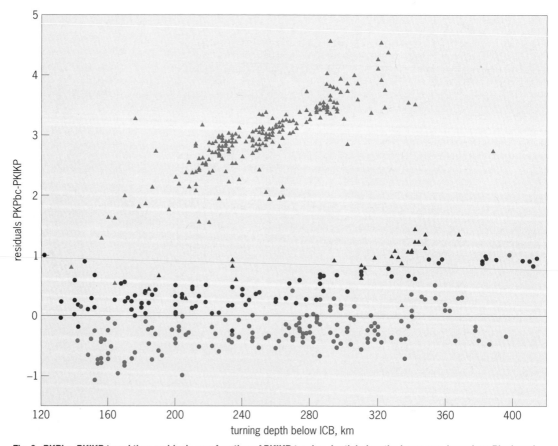

Fig. 3. PKPbc–PKIKP travel time residuals as a function of PKIKP turning depth below the inner-core boundary. Black and colored symbols represent observations sampling the eastern and western hemispheres, respectively. Triangles and circles represent polar and equatorial data, respectively. Polar data are a collection of seismic observations whose PKIKP ray angle in the inner core is within 35° of the Earth's rotational axis (others are defined as equatorial data). [*West-polar data (colored triangles) are from J. Creager, Geophys. Res., 104:23,127–23,139, 1999; figure by Wen-che Yu*]

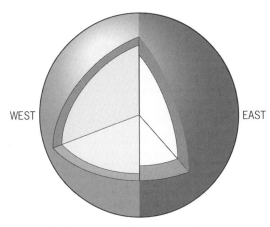

Fig. 4. Seismic structure of the inner core. The inner core has an isotropic layer at the top overlying an anisotropic inner part. In the top isotropic layer, the eastern hemisphere (colored) is about 1% faster and attenuates seismic energy more than the western. The deep anisotropy has a fast direction approximately parallel to the Earth's rotation axis. The anisotropy has a magnitude of 5–8% (that is, speed is about 5–8% faster along the polar direction than along the equatorial direction) and emerges at 50–150 km (31–93 mi) depth in the western, and a magnitude of 0.4–0.8% and an emerging depth of about 200 km (124.3 mi) in the eastern. (*Courtesy of Masayuki Obayashi and Fenglin Niu*).

exhibit a hemispherical pattern. In the top isotropic layer, the eastern hemisphere is faster (about 1%) and attenuates seismic energy more than the western hemisphere. The deep anisotropy, while it appears to have a fast direction close to the Earth's rotation axis, is also hemispherically different in both magnitude and emerging depth.

The cause of the top isotropic layer and its hemispherical variations remains speculative. The correlation between fast speed and high attenuation is opposite to what would be predicted by temperature effects. One possible explanation is the existence of melt pockets that differ in shape between the two hemispheres. Still, it is not known why the outer core solidifies to form the inner core differently in the two hemispheres. Scientists are also searching for the cause of the deep anisotropy. Studies have shown iron crystals to be anisotropic under the pressure and temperature conditions of the inner core. Proposed mechanisms to generate such anisotropy include convection, preferential growth along the equator of the inner core, forces due to the Earth's magnetic field acting on the inner core boundary, and texturing during solidification. It is frustrating, but exciting, that none of the proposed physical mechanisms would seem to be able to preferentially align the fast axes of iron crystals close to the Earth's rotation axis and yet do so differently in the two hemispheres.

For background information *see* EARTH INTERIOR; GEODYNAMO; IRON; MAGNETIC FIELD; SEISMOLOGY in the McGraw-Hill Encyclopedia of Science & Technology. Lianxing Wen

Bibliography. F. Niu and L. Wen, Hemispherical variations in seismic velocity at the top of the Earth's inner core, *Nature*, 410:1081–1084, 2001; F. Niu and L. Wen, Seismic anisotropy in the top 400 km of the inner core beneath the "eastern" hemisphere, *Geophys. Res. Lett.*, 29, 10.1029/2001GL014118, 2002; A. Ouzounis and K. C. Creager, Isotropy overlying anisotropy at the top of the inner core, *Geophys. Res. Lett.*, 28:4331–4334, 2001; L. Wen and F. Niu, Seismic velocity and attenuation structures in the top of the inner core, *J. Geophys. Res.*, 10.1029/2001JB000170.

Inner ear development

The inner ear is a complex sensory organ that allows us to hear and to maintain a sense of balance. It consists of the fluid-filled cochlea, which transforms sound waves into nerve impulses, and the semicircular canals, which provide a sense of orientation and balance. From the evolutionary perspective, it is the most ancient component of the ear, and it is a conserved feature of all vertebrates. For such a complex organ, it is perhaps surprising that the inner ear has a seemingly simple embryonic origin, arising from the otic placodes, paired thickenings of the embryonic ectoderm which form during early development alongside the hindbrain (see **illus.**). These thickenings subsequently invaginate to form the otic cup, the edges of which then come together and close, forming the otic vesicle, which then pinches off from the ectoderm. The otic vesicle undergoes a series of complex developmental processes to generate the intricately patterned inner ear. Given the obvious importance of the inner ear, there has been long-standing interest in understanding the first crucial step in its development, the formation of the otic placode. Recent studies have begun to identify the molecular basis of this process.

The otic placode forms in a stereotypical position in all vertebrates, suggesting that the cues that

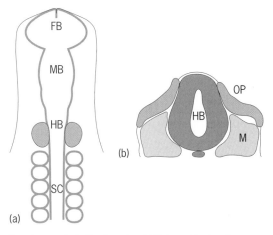

Development of otic placodes. (*a*) Schematic showing a dorsal view of a 10-somite chick embryo. The paired otic placodes, which develop on either side of the hindbrain (HB), are highlighted. The other major subdivisions of the nervous system are: FB, forebrain; MB, midbrain; and SC, spinal cord. (*b*) The otic placodes (OP) shown in section, revealing their relationship to the hindbrain (HB) and the mesoderm (M).

direct its formation are conserved among species, and indeed studies on a variety of vertebrate embryos support this assertion. These studies demonstrated that the induction, or formation, of the otic placodes is a complex process involving cues from both the mesoderm and hindbrain lying in proximity to the site of placode formation. The mesoderm signal seems to act first, exerting its effect on the overlying ectoderm to render this tissue competent to initiate placode development. Soon thereafter the hindbrain signals to this ectoderm to induce the formation of the otic placode. It also has been shown that ectoderm from other regions of the head which normally would not form an otic placode can be directed to do so when recombined with these tissues, suggesting that the signals from the mesoderm and the hindbrain are acting in an instructive manner upon seemingly naive ectoderm.

Signaling molecules. There has been great interest in identifying the signaling molecules that mediate the induction of the otic placode, and in recent years a number of studies have shown that the fibroblast growth factors (FGFs) seem to play a pivotal role. The fibroblast growth factor family comprises about 28 members, all of which are structurally related proteins with a molecular mass of 20–30 kilodaltons. FGFs are secreted signaling molecules that bind to transmembrane tyrosine kinase receptors, of which there are four, and they have been implicated in a diverse range of developmental processes. The first studies implicating FGFs showed that *fgf-3* (gene encoding the protein FGF-3) displays an expression pattern that would be consistent with its playing a role in otic placode induction, being expressed in the central hindbrain region adjacent to the site of induction. Furthermore, ectopic expression of *fgf-3* in the ectoderm (that is, in tissue where it is not normally expressed) was found to promote the formation of small extra otic vesicles. However, mutational studies in mice did not reveal an absolute requirement for the *fgf-3* gene. In animals lacking a functional version of this gene the inner ear still formed and exhibited a largely normal morphology, suggesting that FGF-3 alone could not be responsible for the induction of the otic placode.

Analysis in the chick further suggested that otic placode induction does involve FGF signaling, but that it is a different fibroblast growth factor, FGF-19, that directs the earliest events. This molecule is expressed in the mesoderm that underlies the presumptive otic placode and is known to induce otic placode formation. At slightly later stages, *fgf-19* begins to be expressed in the central hindbrain, which also is known to possess inductive activity. However, in vitro studies showed that FGF-19 on its own had little effect upon cranial ectoderm, and in fact it could promote otic development only if neural tissue was included with the ectoderm, suggesting that it directs its effect on the neural tissue, which in turn acts upon the ectoderm to induce the placode. Moreover, it was found that FGF-19 treatment resulted in the induction of the expression of the signaling molecule wnt-8c in the neural tissue, possibly suggesting that

this factor was also involved in placode induction. Indeed, it was shown that FGF-19 and wnt-8c could act together to induce otic placode development directly in cranial ectoderm in the absence of neural tissue. Treatment with wnt-8c alone, or with FGF-19, resulted in the induction of *fgf-3* expression, which could then have also acted to help promote the formation of the otic placode.

Mutational studies. Definitive proof that FGFs are involved in otic induction requires more than the demonstration that these factors can elicit the formation of the otic placode; it must be shown that in the absence of their activity the otic placode fails to develop. While mutational studies in mice did not find a requirement for *fgf-3* in the induction of the otic placode, more recent studies in the zebrafish have shown that it does play a role in otic placode induction but that it functions together with another fibroblast growth factor, FGF-8. During very early stages of zebrafish development, prior to initiation of otic placode development, both *fgf-3* and *fgf-8* are expressed in the central hindbrain region adjacent to the presumptive otic placode territory, which would be consistent with both being required for otic placode induction. Subsequently, and in keeping with the data from mice, it was found that inhibiting either *fgf-3* or *fgf-8* function separately in the zebrafish embryo did not interfere with otic placode induction, although in both cases a reduction in the size of the otic vesicle was noted. However, if the genes for both FGFs are inhibited simultaneously, there are dramatic consequences for the development of the inner ear, with the otic vesicles never forming. Indeed, detailed molecular studies have shown that inhibiting both *fgf-3* and *fgf-8* interferes with the earliest steps in the development of the otic placode, and in the absence of these factors the ectoderm alongside the hindbrain never initiates placodal development, as shown by its failure to express the very earliest otic placode markers, transcription factors pax 2.1 and dlx-3.

Inhibition of signaling receptors. Further proof that the development of the otic placode requires FGF signaling was provided by experiments in which zebrafish embryos were incubated with an inhibitor of the FGF receptors, SU5402, which acts by binding to and inhibiting the kinase domain of the receptor. In embryos treated with this reagent, the otic placode fails to develop, as evidenced by absence of pax 2.1 expression. Embryos can also be treated with this reagent at fixed time points, which allows determination of the time at which the FGF signal is required for otic placode development. This study has shown that otic placode induction requires the FGF signal during the period when *fgf-3* and *fgf-8* are coexpressed in the hindbrain adjacent to it. FGF signaling is not required at the later stages of development when *fgf-3* alone is expressed in the hindbrain.

Collectively, these studies demonstrated that FGFs are required for the induction of the otic placode, and it does seem that FGF-3 is likely to play a role in all vertebrates but that it acts in concert with another fibroblast growth factor, FGF-8, in fish and possibly FGF-19, or FGF-4, which is also expressed close to the otic placode, in chicks and mice. It appears to be quite significant that the major source of these FGFs is the hindbrain, and it is likely that it is this tissue and not the mesoderm which is the primary player in inducing the otic placode. The role of the mesoderm in otic placode induction may in fact be indirect, acting by inducing the otic placode signals, the FGFs, in the hindbrain. This is supported by studies in the chick. The fact that the hindbrain is likely the major inducer of the otic placode is also of great anatomical significance, as it is within this region that the auditory and vestibular nuclei, which receive the sensory impulses from the inner ear, develop. Thus, in functional terms, the formation of sensory apparatus, the inner ear, is induced by the signal transduction apparatus. It has also been shown that inhibiting *fgf-3* and *fgf-8* function in the zebrafish also severely perturbs the development of this region of the brain. Thus, it would seem that these FGFs are in fact directing the coordinated development of the inner ear and the central hindbrain area.

For background information *see* EAR; EMBRYONIC INDUCTION; GROWTH FACTOR; HEARING (VERTEBRATE); NERVOUS SYSTEM (VERTEBRATE); VESTIBULAR SYSTEM in the McGraw-Hill Encyclopedia of Science & Technology.   Anthony Graham

Bibliography. R. K. Ladher et al., Identification of synergistic signals initiating inner ear development, *Science*, 290:1965–1967, 2000; S. L. Mansour, J. M. Goddard, and M. R. Capecchi, Mice homozygous for a targeted disruption of the proto-oncogene int-2 have developmental defects in the tail and inner ear, *Development*, 117:13–28, 1993; H. Maroon et al., Fgf3 and Fgf8 are required together for formation of the otic placode and vesicle, *Development*, 129: 2099–2108, 2002; B. T. Phillips, K. Bolding, and B. B. Riley, Zebrafish fgf3 and fgf8 encode redundant functions required for otic placode induction, *Dev. Biol.*, 235:351–365, 2001; M. Torres and F. Giraldez, The development of the vertebrate inner ear, *Mech. Dev.*, 71:5–21, 1998; V. Vendrell et al., Induction of inner ear fate by FGF3, *Development* 127:2011–2019, 2000; D. G. Wilkinson et al., Expression of the FGF-related proto-oncogene int-2 during gastrulation and neurulation in the mouse. *EMBO J.*, 7:691–695, 1988.

Inorganic and organometallic polymers

Inorganic polymers are macromolecules that contain metals (for example, iron and cobalt), metalloids (for example, boron and silicon), or other elements (for example, phosphorus and sulfur). The inorganic element may lie along the polymer backbone where it is covalently bonded to the adjacent atoms (**Fig. 1***a, e*); the inorganic element may be ligand-coordinated (Fig. 1*b, c*); or the inorganic element may be pendant to the polymeric chain (Fig. 1*d*). Organometallic polymers are a special class of inorganic polymers in which the metal, metalloid, or other element is covalently bonded to carbon (Fig. 1*d–f*).

Many examples of inorganic polymers are found in nature having important physiological functions such as respiration, photosynthesis, energy transfer, and metal-ion storage. Small proteins called metallothioniens store metals such as copper and zinc in higher animals. For example, cd$_7$-metallothionein-2 is a rat protein rich in cysteine that is bonded to four zinc atoms through sulfur-containing amino acids. Ferrodoxins are bacterial proteins containing up to eight iron-sulfur complexes that are responsible for biological oxidation-reduction and electron transfer reactions. In addition, mammalian ferritin (a high-molecular-weight protein containing approximately 4500 iron atoms) is essential for the storage and transfer of Fe(II) and oxidation to Fe(III).

Synthetic inorganic and organometallic polymers were developed in the early part of the twentieth century. One of the first useful inorganic coordination polymers was prepared by impregnating a plastic film with dithiooxamide (a tetradentate ligand), and treating the film with a solution of Cu(II) or Ni(II) salts. The resulting linear polymer [reaction (1)] had

Dithiooxamide   Poly(nickel(II) dithiooxamide)   (1)

light-polarizing properties. In the 1960s, new developments in synthetic methods led to a number of polymers that contain main-group, transition, and inner transition elements. Many of these materials were designed to withstand high temperatures and resist erosion, while maintaining desirable attributes such as oxidative stability, elasticity, electric conductivity or resistivity, optical properties, fire retardancy, catalytic properties, low density, high tensile strength, and inertness to chemicals.

Classification. Inorganic and organometallic polymers may be classified in terms of morphology (chains, sheets, and networks) or backbone elemental composition (homoatom and heteroatom).

Chain polymers. A chain polymer is a one-dimensional (1D) macromolecule composed of linear repeating units that lack inter- or intrachain crosslinks. Examples are poly(dialkylstannane) (structure **1**) and polythiazyl (**2**). Under certain circumstances, the

(1)   (2)

ends of linear chains connect to form macrocyclic structures. Thus, cyclic poly(methylhydrosiloxane)

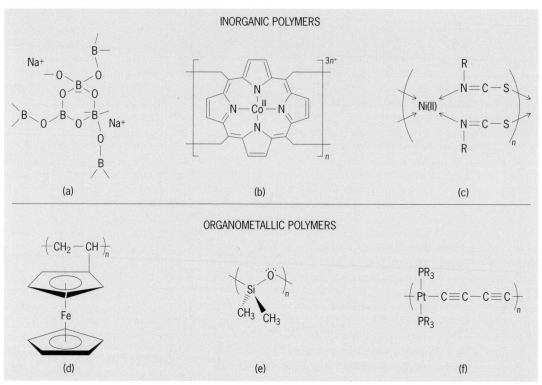

Fig. 1. Inorganic polymers: (*a*) borate polymer (metalloid in the backbone), (*b*) cobaltoporphyrin polymer (ligand-coordinated metal), and (*c*) nickel(II) dithiooxamide polymer (ligand-coordinated metal). Organometallic polymers: (*d*) ferrocene polymer (metalloid in backbone), (*e*) poly(dimethylsiloxane) (metalloid in backbone), and (*f*) platinum-diacetylene polymer (metal in backbone).

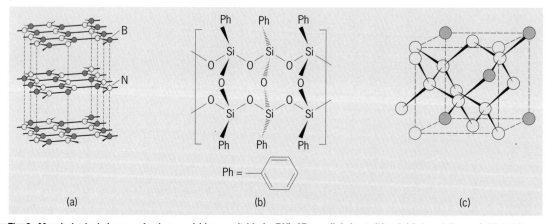

Fig. 2. Morphological classes of polymers: (*a*) boron nitride (α-BN), 2D parallel sheet; (*b*) poly(diphenylsiloxane), 2D ladder; and (*c*) silicon dioxide (silica), 3D network.

with as many as 50 —CH$_3$SiH— repeat units is known. Cyclic chains with a relatively small number of repeat units (oligomers) are very common. Some well-known cyclic oligomers are octamethylcyclotetrasiloxane, (Me$_2$SiO)$_4$ (**3**), and several allotropic forms of sulfur, for example, S$_8$ (**4**). Linear 1D chain polymers are also known to assume random coil, helical (proteinlike), and rigid rod structures.

Sheet polymers. Sheet polymers are two-dimensional (2D) macromolecules in which the primary valences of the metal/metalloid atoms are satisfied by covalent bonds. Boron nitride (α-BN) is an example of a 2D sheet polymer (**Fig. 2a**) in which each atom is bonded to three other atoms in the same layer. The stacked layers (lamellae) interact through van der Waals forces. Another variation of a 2D sheet occurs if two chains are crosslinked at regular intervals to give a ladder structure such as the crosslinked siloxane polymer (Fig. 2*b*). Ladder polymers are unusually high-melting solids with oxidative, hydrolytic, thermal, and chemical stability.

Network polymers. Network polymers are highly crosslinked materials in which the metal/semimetal atom valences are satisfied by bonds that result in a three-dimensional (3D) structure. Such polymers are usually difficult to characterize because of their refractory (ceramic-like) nature. Network polymers are often hard, infusible, and insoluble substances such as silicon dioxide and silicon nitride (Fig. 2*c*). These materials are added to organic polymers to enhance their strength and thermal stability.

Homoatom polymers. Poly(diphenylsilane), $(Ph_2Si)_n$, is an example of a homoatom polymer because it contains only silicon atoms along the backbone. Some metalloid anions have homoatomic polymeric structures. For instance, metal borides of formula M_xB_y contain the anion as chains, ladders, 2D sheets, or 3D networks (**Table 1**). These anionic polymers possess high thermal stability, excellent chemical resistance, and potentially useful electrical properties.

Certain elements, such as phosphorus, prefer to aggregate as low-molecular-weight oligomers. For example, white phosphorus is a tetramer (P_4) with phosphorus atoms at the corners of a tetrahedron. Black phosphorus, which is obtained by heating P_4 under pressure [200°C (390°F), 12,000 atm (1220 MPa)] with a catalyst, is a sheet polymer with each phosphorus atom bound to three neighbors in double layers. This giant molecule consists of stacked double layers, analogous to the boron nitride lamellae. In addition, black phosphorus is a good electrical conductor. Red phosphorus is made by heating P_4 at 400°C (750°F) in a sealed vessel. One crystalline form of red phosphorus has a linear, tubular arrangement of eight phosphorus atoms in a pentagonal wedge structure.

Elemental sulfur is also a polyatomic and polymorphic substance. Oligomeric sulfur rings consisting of 6, 7, 8, and 12 sulfur atoms have been identified. The orthorhombic α-S_8 form is the most thermodynamically stable and consists of eight-member puckered rings in a crown conformation stacked together in "crankcase" fashion. The chain polymer form of sulfur (catena or plastic sulfur) is obtained by quenching molten S_8 in water. If stretched, catena sulfur has a helical structure. Selenium forms similar polymers.

Heteroatom polymers. Heteroatom polymers contain a metal or semimetal in addition to one or more other atoms (such as oxygen, sulfur, nitrogen, phosphorus, and carbon) in the backbone. In general, polymer stability and inertness increases when the heteroatom is electron-rich. Presumably, such atoms serve as electron sources toward low-lying vacant orbitals on the

TABLE 1. Polymeric metal boride structures

Formula	Metal	Morphology	Anion structure
MB	Fe, Ni	Zigzag chains	
$M_{11}B_8$	Ru	Branched chains	
M_3B_4	Cr, Ta	Ladder	
MB_2	Mg, Ti, Zr, Gd	Sheet	
MB_4	La	Network (octahedron)	

M = metal; B at each vertex of octahedra

metal or metalloid (structure **5**). The resulting back-

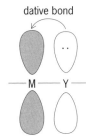

dative bond

M = metal, semimetal
Y = heteroatom with a
lone pair of electrons

(5)

bonding (dative bond) generally decreases the electrophilicity of the metal or metalloid and reduces the susceptibility of the polymer to attack by Lewis bases. In addition, the interaction tends to stabilize the polymer toward thermal degradation and aids in the regulation of structure, chain mobility, and interchain forces that enhance its dynamic and mechanical properties.

Synthetic methods. A number of methods have been developed to synthesize inorganic and organometallic polymers. Representative examples of the more important and commonly used preparative techniques include step-growth (condensation) polymerization, ring-opening polymerization, chain-growth (addition) polymerization, and reductive (Wurtz-type) coupling polymerization.

Step-growth polymerization. In step-growth polymerization, two molecules combine with the evolution of a small molecule such as water, ammonia, or a salt (for example, hydrogen chloride). For example, dihydroxymetallophthalocyanine [prepared from a metalloid halide such as silicon tetrachloride ($SiCl_4$) or germanium tetrachloride ($GeCl_4$) and phthalocyanine followed by hydrolysis] undergoes dehydration under vacuum at elevated temperatures to give a linear, 1D "shish-kebab" polymer with an —M—O—M—O— chain backbone [reaction (2)]. This material has excellent thermal and chemical stability, solubility in strong acids, interesting magnetic and optical properties, as well as electrical (semiconducting) properties when doped with iodine.

Another step-growth polymerization uses an inorganic or organometallic compound that contains a difunctional organic ligand. For example, diiodoferrocene reacts with a dilithioferrocene [reaction (3)]

1. MCl_4 (M=Si, Ge)
2. H_2O, py

Dihydroxymetallophthalocyanine

vacuum
270–360°C

Poly(metalloxyphthalocyanine)

(2)

−LiI

(3)

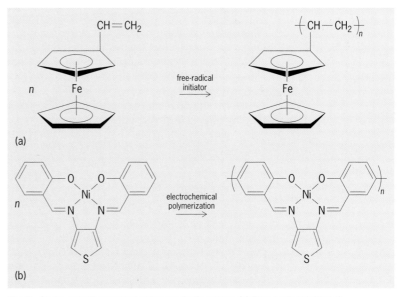

$$\text{(CH}_3)_2\text{SiCl}_2 \xrightarrow[\text{condensation}]{\text{H}_2\text{O (— HCL)}}$$

Cyclic trimer and
tetramer oligomers

$$\xrightarrow[\substack{\text{ring-opening}\\\text{polymerization}}]{\substack{100°C\\ \text{acid or base}}} \quad \text{HO}\!\left(\!\!\begin{array}{c}\text{CH}_3\\ |\\ \text{Si}\!-\!\text{O}\\ |\\ \text{CH}_3\end{array}\!\!\right)_{\!n}\!\!\text{H} \qquad (5)$$

Poly(dimethysiloxane)

to give a polyferrocene. The driving force for the reaction is the precipitation of the salt, lithium iodide. Similarly, condensation with bridging difunctional reagents, such as the sodium salt of an organic diol, can produce metal-containing polymers [reaction (4)].

Ring-opening polymerization. Ring-opening polymerization is a principal method of preparing inorganic and organometallic polymers. The method is convenient and usually requires heat, light, or a catalyst. The reaction yields high-molecular-weight polymers without condensation products. An example of a ring-opening polymerization is the synthesis of polysiloxanes (silicones), which have many industrial and consumer applications, including:

Insulators	Masonry additives
Dielectric materials	Surfactants
Heat-exchange fluids	Paper release coatings
Seals and gaskets	Coupling agents
Caulking agents	Water repellants
Emulsifying agents	Lubricants
Surgery implants	Hydraulic fluids
Mold-forming agents	Ceramic composites
Antifoaming agents	Pressure-sensitive adhesives

The industrial process involves the hydrolysis of dimethyldichlorosilane followed by acid- or base-catalyzed ring-opening polymerization [reaction (5)] to give poly(dimethylsiloxane). The ring-opening polymerization method permits excellent control of molecular weight and polydispersity (molecular-weight distribution). **Table 2** summarizes other examples of rings and polymers that can be prepared by ring-opening polymerization.

Chain-growth polymerization. Chain-growth polymerization is initiated with free radicals, which may be generated chemically, thermally, photochemically, electrochemically, as well as with ions (cations or anions) or coordination complexes (for example, Ziegler-Natta or ferrocene catalysts). Invariably, chain-growth polymerization requires that the monomer contain an unsaturated functionality, usually an olefin. As a result, the polymers contain carbon in the chain backbone. Some examples of chain-growth polymerization that incorporate metals or metalloids into the polymer are given in **Fig. 3**.

Fig. 3. Chain-growth polymerization synthetic routes. (*a*) Free-radical initiated. (*b*) Electrochemical polymerization.

TABLE 2. Some rings and polymers formed by ring-opening polymerization

Ring	Polymer	Name
	$(N=P)_{3n}$ with Cl substituents	Polyphosphazene
		Poly(diorganosilyl ferrocene)
		Poly(diorganosilane)
		Poly(diorganocarbosilane)

Reductive (Wurtz-type) coupling polymerization. Reductive coupling polymerization uses active metals (such as sodium or potassium) in a reaction with difunctional, halogen-containing organometallic compounds (for example, organosilanes, organogermanes, organostannanes, carbometallanes, and ferrocenes). Typically, the reactions are carried out at a temperature that melts the alkaline metal and disperses it in a nonreactive solvent such as toluene or tetrahydrofuran. Alternatively, the reducing agent is made soluble with a chelating (complex-forming) agent such as crown ether.

For background information *see* BORON; COORDINATION COMPLEXES; GERMANIUM; INORGANIC POLYMER; LIGAND; METALLOID; NONMETAL; ORGANOMETALLIC COMPOUND; POLYMER; POLYMERIZATION; SILICON; SULFUR in the McGraw-Hill Encyclopedia of Science & Technology.   Martel Zeldin

Bibliography. F. W. Amon, Jr., and M. W. Kane, U.S. Pat. 2,505,085, April 15, 1950; R. D. Archer, *Inorganic and Organometallic Polymers*, Wiley-VCH, New York, 2001; I. Bertini et al. (eds.), *Bioinorganic Chemistry*, University Science Books, Mill Valley, CA, 1994; J. E. Mark, H. R. Allcock, and R. West, *Inorganic Polymers*, Prentice Hall, Englewood Cliffs, NJ, 1992; C. U. Pittman, Jr., et al. (eds.), *Metal-Containing Polymeric Materials*, Plenum Press, New York, 1996.

Intelligent completion technology

The incorporation of flow-control equipment and reservoir monitoring (pressure, temperature, flow rate, fluid composition, and so on) at remotely accessed petroleum reservoirs is known as intelligent completion technology. Intelligent completion technology (also called smart well technology) includes the downhole equipment, as well as the interfacing for controlling subsea systems and acquiring and manipulating data for reservoir management. It allows operators to control (remotely) downhole flow-control devices, and to obtain real-time data with which improved decisions can be made regarding reservoir optimization and field development.

Over the last 5 years, intelligent completion technology has emerged in the petroleum industry, changing the way the industry views the downhole drilling and completion market, just as coiled tubing and horizontal drilling did earlier. The future of intelligent completion technology is the full automation of all these systems such that the analyzed reservoir information is fed directly back to the flow-control system to optimize reservoir performance, possibly eliminating the human interface.

Economic justification. In the deepwater and ultra-deepwater environments of the Gulf of Mexico,

Brazil, and West Africa, the use of new well technology is paramount to the economic justification for the development of some projects. Where each well is highly leveraged and the total cost of the projects ranges from $300 million to several billion dollars, reliable new technologies are incorporated to ensure economic project completion and implementation.

The value of intelligent completion technology can be realized in a number of different scenarios, for example, in eliminating planned well intervention, shutting off zones of high water or gas production, controlling the injection of fluids to displace hydrocarbons in long heterogeneous intervals (layers of rock), optimizing production profiles in a long horizontal section, or maximizing long-term reservoir performance based on pressure depletion throughout the reservoir.

The most fundamental economic benefit is in eliminating planned well intervention. In deepwater and ultradeepwater environments, well intervention costs can exceed $10 million for recompleting a second interval. Intelligent completion technology can eliminate this intervention by allowing the operator to complete multiple zones at one time and leave them shut-in (closed off) until needed. Remote actuation capability allows the zones to be turned on when required.

Technical justification. In many cases, it is not known how much or to what extent water or gas encroachment is going to occur in the life of a producing well. Platform processing and pipeline design often limit the amount of gas or water production that is acceptable. With intelligent completion technology, when gas or water encroaches the offending zone (whether it is deep or shallow in the well), this zone can be shut off while the other zones remain productive.

For reservoirs produced by secondary methods (in which hydrocarbons are displaced with a sweeping fluid, typically water or gas), sweep efficiency can be an issue for long intervals. Large permeability streaks or fractures in the rock can allow specific areas to receive more injection than is desired. Remote-actuated flow-control equipment can allow the operator to inject the appropriate flow volumes at specific intervals, maximizing sweep efficiency.

In long horizontal wells, it has been recognized through production logging and flow testing that the heel portion of the well often produces more than the toe (**Fig. 1**). In addition, the introduction of water or gas in an isolated area can hinder the performance of the entire well and make it inoperable. Flow-control equipment and monitoring technology can identify areas of water or gas encroachment prior to "losing the well." Through choking (flow

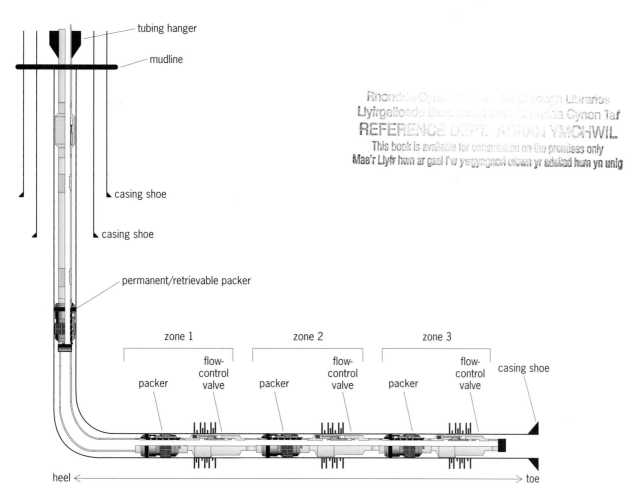

Fig. 1. Multizone horizontal well with intelligent completion monitoring and control.

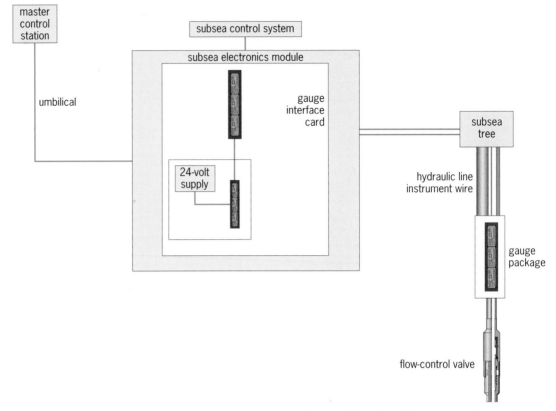

Fig. 2. Subsea control system layout. The gauge package is used to obtain real-time downhole pressure and temperature for enhanced reservoir management capability.

restriction) mechanisms, various portions of the horizontal section can be choked back to equalize the pressure drop across the length of the horizontal, allowing all the intervals to be produced equally.

Reservoir management on a full field basis can be greatly enhanced by intelligent completion technology. As more knowledge is obtained throughout the reservoir's producing life, the reservoir can be managed more effectively. Production decisions range from the simple, such as whether to choke a specific interval to decrease inflow from that particular part of the field, to the complex, such as whether to cancel plans for additional wells because the reservoir is fully exploited with the existing production/injection configuration.

The ultimate benefit of intelligent completion technology is the application of intelligent fields. An intelligent field is a field produced and optimized in all aspects, such as production, injection, workover timing, and simulation modeling, through the use of intelligent completion technology. Some of the wells may require a fully integrated control and monitoring system with full choking capability, while others may require only permanent downhole gauges for pressure analysis. The combination of intelligent requirements in association with field configuration is determined by reservoir connectivity, pressure response, well count, sweep efficiency, and so on.

Technology. Oil and gas wells have traditionally been completed as follows: (1) drill the well and run intermediate casings (protective steel tubing), (2) run production casing and liner, or leave as an open hole, (3) perforate single or commingled producion/injection intervals, (4) perform stimulation or sand control (sand-exclusion techniques) as required, (5) run production tubing, (6) set the production/injection packer (inflatable wellbore seal), and (7) produce/inject the well.

This single zone completion can be modified to complete multiple intervals during the initial completion phase (Fig. 1). In wells in which multiple zones are completed, steps need to be taken to ensure that all productive intervals are produced effectively. To assist, productivity-flow-control equipment is installed to individually control these zones.

System requirements. In subsea offshore projects, requirements vary depending on the complexity of both the subsea control system and the intelligent completion system. Downhole equipment interfacing can be incorporated into the subsea control system, or the subsea control system can be used as a "pass-thru modem" providing the physical link between the systems without controlling and manipulating equipment or data. This decision is largely dependent on the control system and the intelligent completion provider.

In deepwater and ultradeepwater environments, subsea wellheads and subsea control modules are required to provide power (electrical and/or hydraulic) and communication from producing platforms on the ocean surface to downhole equipment. Electric and hydraulic umbilicals are run between the producing vessel (offshore production facility) and the subsea control system. The umbilical can be required to transmit power and communication farther than 50 mi (80 km) in some instances.

The subsea control system is used to control functions on the subsea tree, and provide power and control to downhole equipment. Accumulators (energy storage devices) in the subsea control system provide continuous hydraulic pressure ranging 3000–10,000 psi (20.7–68.9 MPa) depending on the system requirements. Electrical communication is provided through the use of interface cards allowing communication from the subsea control system to the downhole system. Power is provided by the subsea control system to both the interface card and the downhole equipment (**Fig. 2**).

Not all deepwater projects use subsea control systems. In projects in which the wells are located around a relatively central location or close to the production vessel, and have moderate power requirements, it may be more economical to run separate umbilicals to independent wellheads or templates servicing multiple wellheads. This decision is most often made based on project economics.

Downhole control requirements are less complex than those of the surface and subsea system. Traditionally the intelligent completion supplier provides all the equipment which needs to be interfaced. This includes the flow-control equipment, the downhole monitoring (which may be integrated with the flow-control functionality), the hydraulic/electrical flat-packs (power and communication conduits) run downhole, and all required connections. The constraints on the system are similar to those of other downhole equipment constraints and include the casing size, minimum restriction due to sand control equipment where applicable, reservoir pressure, reservoir temperature, reservoir depth, and flow rate.

Case studies. Close to a hundred wells have been completed globally using intelligent completion technology. As a greater number of fields are discovered and developed at greater water depths, the number of intelligent completions run subsea will increase greatly.

Fifteen subsea wells have been completed in the Gulf of Mexico. The wells completed by one supplier range in water depth from 2000 ft (610 m) to greater than 7000 ft (2134 m). The majority of these have been direct hydraulic applications with nonintegrated reservoir sensing installed to eliminate future well interventions or water encroachment problems. When the Canyon Express field began production in 2002, it contained eight intelligent completions out of nine wells (**Fig. 3**).

Brazil is another area of growth for subsea applications in deepwater and ultradeepwater. By the end of 2002, two subsea wells were expected to begin production in the Campos Basin in approximately 3300 ft (1000 m) of water. The applications are in-

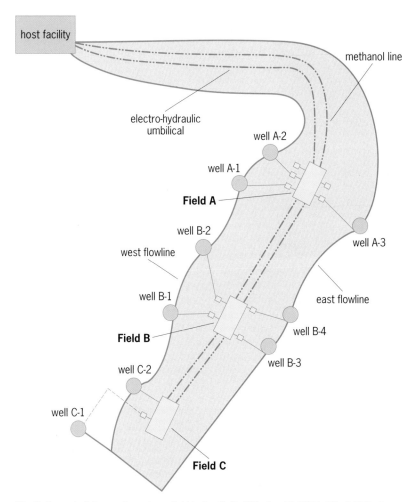

Fig. 3. Layout of deepwater subsea field in the Gulf of Mexico. Field C is 53 mi (85 km) from the host platform. The methanol line is used to inject methanol in the production string to mitigate the risk of gas hydrate formation.

tegrated systems in which the full control equipment is actuated by the hydraulic/electric or electric downhole system. This fully integrated system is the most advanced intelligent completion technology currently available.

West Africa is the third major deepwater basin in the world. Work is being done on fields in both Nigeria and Angola with the first installation off the coast of Nigeria scheduled to be completed in the fall of 2002. Again, this will be a fully integrated system using the most advanced technology.

Outlook. As reliability increases and perceived risk decreases, intelligent completion technology will become more widely acceptable in land, platform, and subsea applications. The economic benefits are multifold, ranging from the elimination of planned well intervention to the enhancement of reservoir performance.

For background information *see* OIL AND GAS, OFFSHORE; OIL AND GAS WELL COMPLETION; OIL AND GAS WELL DRILLING; PETROLEUM ENGINEERING; PETROLEUM ENHANCED RECOVERY; PETROLEUM RESERVOIR ENGINEERING; WELL LOGGING in the McGraw-Hill Encyclopedia of Science & Technology.

Victoria B. Jackson Nielson

Bibliography. S. M. Erlandsen, Production experience from smart wells in the Oseberg Field, *2000 Annual Technical Conference and Exhibition* (Dallas), Pap. SPE 62953, October 1–4, 2000; V. B. Jackson and T. R. Tips, Case study: First intelligent completion system installed in the Gulf of Mexico, presented at the *2000 Offshore Technology Conference* (Houston), Pap. OTC 11928, May 1–4, 2000; V. B. Jackson Nielsen et al., Aconcagua, Camden Hills, King's Peak Fields, Gulf of Mexico employ intelligent completion technology in unique field development scenario, presented at the *2001 Annual Technical Conference and Exhibition* (New Orleans), Pap. SPE 71675, September 30–October 3, 2001; J. Oberkircher et al., Intelligent multilaterals: The next step in the evolution of well construction, *2002 Offshore Technology Conference* (Houston), Pap. OTC 14253, May 6–9, 2002; S. Rester et al., Application of intelligent completion technology to optimize the reservoir management of a deepwater Gulf of Mexico field—A reservoir simulation case study, *1999 Annual Technical Conference and Exhibition* (Houston), Pap. SPE 56670, October 3–6, 1999.

International GPS Service

The Global Positioning System (GPS) provides unprecedented potential for precise ground- and space-based positioning, timing, and navigation anywhere in the world. Extremely precise use of GPS, particularly for earth sciences applications, stems largely from activities of the International GPS Service (IGS). More than 200 organizations in 75 countries contribute daily to the IGS, which is dependent upon a cooperative global tracking network of over 300 GPS stations. Data are collected continuously and archived at distributed data centers. Analysis centers retrieve the data and produce the most accurate GPS data products available anywhere. IGS data and data products are made accessible to users, reflecting the organization's open data policy. The IGS, a scientific service of the International Association of Geodesy, is a highly successful scientific federation and a model of international cooperation.

History. A number of factors led to the formation of the IGS. By the late 1980s many geodynamics and geodetic organizations recognized the potential uses of this affordable technology for scientific research (such as earthquake studies, fault motion, and plate tectonics) as well as other applications. The motivating goal for the earth sciences was millimeter-level positioning anywhere in the world. However, a single civil organization could not assume the capital investment and recurring operations costs to install and maintain a globally based system. At this point, international groups considered entering into joint partnerships for collecting data, making observations, developing cooperative approaches, and defining standards to ensure that future activities would be driven by science requirements.

The idea for an international GPS service began to crystallize at the 1989 International Association of Geodesy (IAG) Scientific Assembly in Edinburgh, United Kingdom. It was here that people recognized that a standardized civilian system for using GPS would be universally beneficial. Subsequently, a planning committee was established within IAG to transform this recognition into action.

In 1991 a Call for Participation was organized by this IAG Planning Committee, seeking participants to form a demonstration campaign to help develop the "proof of concept" for an international service. It requested interested groups to assume the roles of station operators, networks, data centers, analysis centers, and a Central Bureau for coordination. The pilot activity took place from June to September 1992 and was highly successful, demonstrating IGS viability. The IGS was officially established as an IAG international service on January 1, 1994.

The IGS, as a completely voluntary organization, continues to operate the global civilian GPS tracking system for science and research. Since the pilot project in 1992, the network has grown from approximately 30 permanent GPS stations to more than 300 and the accuracy of the IGS orbits has improved an order of magnitude, from 50 cm (20 in.) to less than 5 cm (2 in.). The IGS continues developing and improving traditional products such as orbits, clocks, station positions, and velocities, as well as fostering projects and working groups that produce additional data products, such as precipitable water vapor (a valuable input into weather forecasting), and total electron content (useful for ionospheric space weather research). Some current IGS projects and working groups are shown in the **table**.

How the IGS works. The IGS functions via a global complex of tracking stations, data analysis centers, working (research) groups, projects, and administrators.

Network of tracking stations. All components of the IGS are critically dependent on the global network of precise GPS tracking stations. Recognizing the fundamental requirement for consistent, coordinated, and high-quality network operations, where different receivers are fielded by more than 100 organizations, a Network Coordinator position resides within the Central Bureau. The IGS network includes over 300 stations that operate continuously, delivering data hourly or daily to the data centers. After a lengthy test and validation period initiated in 1999, in early 2002 the IGS network was expanded to include over 30 GLONASS tracking stations.

Data centers. Since the inception of the IGS, the archives of the data centers have been increasingly important to a wide range of scientific and research applications. The distributed nature of the data flow supporting the IGS has been the key to the successful archiving and availability of both IGS data and products. A hierarchy of data centers (operational, regional, and global) exchanges data from the network of tracking stations. This scheme provides for efficient access and storage of GPS and ancillary data, thus reducing network traffic and providing a level of

IGS science applications	
Projects and groups	Purpose
Precise Time and Frequency Transfer Project	Global subnanosecond time transfer; joint with the Bureau International des Poids et Mésures (BIPM)
Low Earth Orbiter (LEO) Pilot Project	Orbit determination of LEO satellites that carry on-board precise GPS receivers (CHAMP, SAC-C, GRACE, Jason, etc.)
International GLONASS Service Pilot Project (IGLOS-PP)	Includes data from the Russian GLONASS system into the IGS processes, producing GLONASS orbits, clocks, station positions, etc.
Tide Gauge Benchmark Monitoring Project	Monitors long-term sea-level change; attempt to decouple crustal motion/subsidence at coastal sites from tide gauge records
IGS Reference Frame Working Group	Global reference frame; Earth orientation; station positions and velocities determined by GPS
Ionospheric Working Group	Ionospheric science research; global ionospheric maps
Atmospheric Working Group	Water vapor in the atmosphere can be estimated from the propagation delay encountered by the GPS signal; useful parameters for weather forecasting
Real-Time Working Group	Investigates methods for IGS real-time network operations
Global Navigation Satellite Systems (GNSS)	Determine actions necessary for IGS to incorporate new GNSS. European Union Galileo system

redundancy for security of the data holdings. There are three global data centers, five regional data centers, and 23 operational data centers.

Analysis centers, analysis coordinator, and associate analysis centers. The eight analysis centers are the scientific backbone of the IGS. They provide, based on the available tracking data of the whole IGS network, a consistent set of high-quality products such as precise satellite orbits, station and satellite clock information, station coordinates, Earth rotation parameters, and atmospheric information. Besides their routine work, the analysis centers are asked to continue developing improved models for GPS observations, and these activities are the driving forces of the success of the IGS.

Analysis center personnel work with the analysis coordinator, who ensures that the IGS objectives are carried out. Specific responsibilities of the coordinator include quality control, performance evaluation, and continued development of appropriate analysis standards. The coordinator is also responsible for the appropriate combination of the analysis centers products into a single set of official IGS products.

Associate analysis centers are organizations that produce specialized products, such as ionospheric information or station coordinates and velocities for a global or regional subnetwork, and are generally linked to an IGS pilot project or working group. There are more than 20 associated centers.

Working groups and pilot projects. Working groups focus on selected topics related to the IGS components according to goals and a schedule specified in a charter. Pilot projects aim to develop particular products or services relying on the IGS infrastructure.

Central Bureau. The Central Bureau is the executive arm of the IGS Governing Board and is responsible for the general management, coordination, and communications of IGS activities and external affairs consistent with the directives, policies, and priorities set by the Governing Board.

Governing Board. The principal roles of the Governing Board are to set policy and to exercise broad oversight of all IGS functions and components. It also controls general activities of the IGS that are appropriate to maintain efficiency and reliability, while taking full advantage of advances in technology and theory.

Summary. Through the IGS contributing organizations, its associate members, hundreds of participating scientists and engineers, and the many respective sponsoring agencies, the IGS operates a collective system that has provided geodetic reference data and related products of enormous benefit to earth science research. The IGS has accomplished much as a fully voluntary, global, decentralized, self-governing organization, without any central source of funding. Financial support is provided through the various member organizations and the agencies around the world that sponsor them.

Building upon its record of achievement, the IGS continues to establish objectives consonant with emerging technological and scientific trends. Technological advances will include improvements to GPS in the form of next-generation GPS and other next-generation Global Navigation Satellite Systems (GNSS), such as Galileo and modernized GPS. For science and research, there will be a host of next-generation low earth orbiting (LEO) satellite missions driven by a broad range of scientific objectives such as weather forecasting, climate monitoring, upper atmosphere monitoring, space weather prediction, and interdisciplinary Earth system studies such as the relationships between ultrasensitive gravity measurements in space and hydrological parameters at the Earth's surface. Use of GPS technology is expanding rapidly and is playing an increasing role in many arenas, including transportation, navigation, agriculture, and geographical information systems. Users of a wide variety of scientific as well as civilian applications have a need for increasingly accurate, reliable, and timely GPS data and products from existing and, in some cases, specialized networks. The IGS, with its breadth of expertise and geographic diversity, is well positioned to serve many of these users. The IGS will respond to these needs and opportunities by broadening its range of services to science and will seek to serve society better through establishing appropriate strategic alliances and collaborations.

[The success of the IGS is solely due to the dedicated contributors and their sponsors worldwide. This article was provided through the courtesy of NASA/Jet Propulsion Laboratory, home of the IGS Control Bureau.]

For background information *see* GEODESY; GEOGRAPHIC INFORMATION SYSTEMS; NAVIGATION; SATELLITE; SATELLITE NAVIGATION SYSTEMS in the McGraw-Hill Encyclopedia of Science & Technology.

Ruth E. Neilan

Bibliography. G. Beutler, *IAG Services in the Current Framework of the International Association of Geodesy*, Geodesy Beyond 2000—International Association of Geodesy Symposia 121, Springer-Verlag 2000; *IGS 2000 Annual Report*, IGS Central Bureau, Jet Propulsion Laboratory, 2001; R. Neilan, W. Melbourne, and G. Mader, *The Development of a Global GPS Tracking System in Support of Space and Ground-based GPS Programs*, International Association of Geodesy Symposia 102, Springer-Verlag, 1989; J. Ray et al., Progress in carrier phase time transfer, *GPS Solutions*, vol. 4, no. 4, Spring 2001; C. Reigber et al., Water vapor monitoring for weather forecasts, *GPS World Mag.*, January 2002; J. Slater and P. Willis, The International GLONASS Service Pilot Project, *GPS Solutions*, vol. 4, no. 4, Spring 2001.

Invasive species impacts

Invasive species are organisms that have expanded their geographic ranges and become established in new habitats. Although species invasions have occurred throughout evolutionary history, human activities have greatly increased their frequency and scope, particularly in the last 200 years. Although only a fraction of species introductions result in established, invasive populations, successful invasions can cause profound negative changes in recipient ecosystems and the human societies dependent upon those ecosystems. Ecologists, economists, resource managers, and policymakers devote considerable energy to studying and minimizing the negative impacts of species invasions.

Impacts on other species. Invasive species negatively affect individual native species in many ways. If an invader is more efficient than a native species in acquiring limited resources, such as food, water, light, or space, the native population may decrease, depending on the importance of the resource to both species' ecology. Grazing or predation by invaders has negative effects on many species. Well-known cases include the brown tree snake, which extirpated most of Guam's forest birds; the gypsy moth, which can defoliate vast tracts of eastern North American forests during outbreaks; and the Nile perch, which ate 150–200 species of cichlids into extinction in Africa's Lake Victoria. The interbreeding of closely related invasive and native species has

many potential consequences: the native's genetic information could be swamped by the invader's; the native's reproductive output may be lowered because of production of infertile hybrids; or the hybrid may constitute a new species with invasive characteristics, as has happened with some plants and insects. Diseases borne or caused by invasive species can devastate organisms that have not coexisted with and adapted to the introduced pathogens.

Impacts on communities and ecosystems. Invasive species often have broad impacts on whole communities or ecosystems. They can alter food web structure in complex, unpredictable ways. For example, a small shrimp that invaded Flathead Lake, Montana, in the 1980s outcompeted kokanee salmon for food resources while avoiding salmon predation. The salmon population collapsed, and populations of eagles, bears, and other animals that relied on spawning salmon as a food source also declined. Invaders, especially plants, can drastically change cycles of water, carbon, nitrogen, and other materials in an ecosystem. Saltcedar (*Tamarix* spp.), for example, uses more water than native plants in the western United States, annually costing the region 1.4–3 billion cubic meters of water. Plant invaders sometimes increase the frequency and intensity of large-scale disturbances, including fire, erosion, and flooding. Finally, some studies suggest that certain communities, including islands, communities that experience frequent disturbances, and communities that have been invaded previously, are more vulnerable to species invasions and their impacts.

Economic impacts. Invasive species profoundly affect human economies. Invasive species are estimated to cost the United States several billion dollars annually, mostly due to invasive weeds and insects that affect agricultural and forest resources. Most money is spent controlling nuisance species that might otherwise inflict much greater losses to forests, crops, fisheries resources, infrastructure such as hydropower and canals, and recreational interests. For example, roughly $10 million is spent annually to control sea lamprey that have gotten into the North American Great Lakes via shipping canals; unchecked, sea lamprey could cause 50 times as much economic loss by preying on commercially valuable native fish.

Assessment methods. Once established, invasive species are difficult to remove. Control efforts have largely focused on holding invaders at acceptable levels or preventing invasions altogether. Minimizing invasive species impacts requires first defining and measuring those impacts.

Before-after and presence-absence comparisons. Most assessments of invasive species impacts involve comparing pre- and postinvasion conditions in a habitat (before-after study) or comparing an invaded community to a similar community without the invader (presence-absence study). Comparisons focus on variables such as population trends of indicator species, biodiversity indexes, primary production rates, cycling rates of water, or fire frequencies.

Technological advances, including satellite imaging, instruments that continuously sample environmental parameters, and naturally occurring chemical tracers, have greatly increased the information that such studies can yield. However, before-after and presence-absence comparisons have limitations. Before-after studies may require years or even decades of data to produce reasonable conclusions, and such data are often unavailable for the preinvasion period. Presence-absence studies carry the sometimes faulty assumption that the two communities, except for the presence of the invader, are essentially the same.

Field experiments. A powerful alternative to comparison studies is to conduct experiments in which populations are actively manipulated in the field to identify and quantify the effects of invaders. One experimental method is to manipulate densities of an invader in defined areas and to measure key environmental variables in those areas as well as in control areas where the invader remains at ambient densities. In one such experiment, an invasive periwinkle (a marine snail) was removed from areas of New England rocky coastline. Periwinkle-free areas experienced rapid sediment accumulation compared with adjacent control areas where periwinkles remained (**Fig. 1**). Subsequently, biomass of algae, marsh grass, and mud-dwelling invertebrates increased compared with control areas, which retained organisms such as barnacles that are adapted to bare rock. This experiment demonstrated the invasive periwinkle's ability to structure coastal habitat and community composition. Another experimental procedure is to create disturbances and measure ecological responses, including those of invasive species. For example, terrestrial ecologists use controlled burning, grazing, or mowing of plots to determine the role of invasive plants in plant community succession following different types and intensities of disturbance.

Laboratory experiments. Laboratory experiments are often run to compare characteristics of invasive or hybrid species against native species. Such characteristics may include growth rates, tolerances to different climate conditions, feeding preferences, aggressive behavior, or production of offspring, any one of which might confer an advantage to the nonnative species in the wild. Researchers must exercise care, however, when extrapolating laboratory results to natural situations, where many other factors influence native and invasive species biology.

Computer modeling. A critical tool in assessing invasive species impacts is computer modeling. Models synthesize large amounts of information, such as data collected from comparative and experimental studies, and simulate the effects of invasive species in the model system. For example, some models are designed to predict when and where a species is likely to invade next, based on its dispersal capabilities, the presence of natural dispersal corridors, human activities, and the presence of suitable habitat to invade. These models help resource managers decide where resources are most needed to contain the spread of an invader. Other models describe the structure of food webs into which invaders have become integrated. These models synthesize information on abundances, diets, production rates, and death rates of different organisms at different times

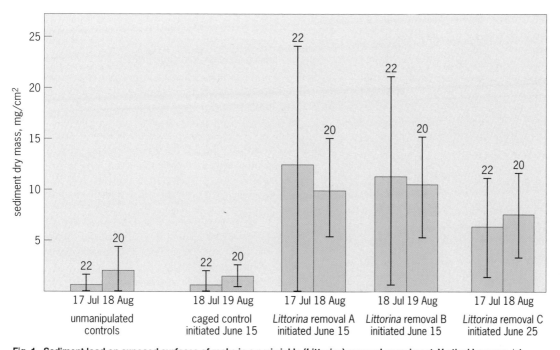

Fig. 1. Sediment load on exposed surfaces of rocks in a periwinkle (*Littorina*) removal experiment. Vertical bars are ±1 standard deviation, and sample sizes are given over the error bars. Removal of periwinkles caused significant increases in sediment load compared with control areas. (*After M. D. Bertness, Habitat and community modification by an introduced herbivorous snail, Ecology, 65:370–381, 1984*)

and life stages. The models can then be used to identify what species are most negatively affected by invaders, and also to test how the food web would respond if the invader's abundance or production rates were to increase or decrease. Predictions from these and other models can be compared with conditions observed in nature to help clarify the ecological processes at work in a species invasion, to improve the models' predictive abilities, and to identify areas where further research is needed.

Economic analysis. Careful economic damage analysis is a central part of invasive species impact assessment because resources for controlling invasive species are limited and therefore need to be used effectively. The societal benefits of controlling an invader must be weighed against the cost of controlling or eradicating the invader. Cost-benefit analysis is difficult because it is not easy to assign monetary value to some environmental commodities. For example, an economic analysis of saltcedar impacts in the western United States included costs of water losses experienced by municipalities, farms, and hydroelectric dams; lost recreational opportunities; damages associated with increased flooding; and public valuation of wildlife (saltcedar thickets are very poor habitat for native birds, reptiles, and mammals, and they deplete water tables that maintain desert fish habitat). Most cost estimates have large ranges because alternate sources of water, electrical power, and recreation have inherently different values, and valuing wildlife is highly subjective. Furthermore, currently unidentified impacts cannot be included in the analysis (this underscores the need to study the roles of invaders in host communities, as described above).

A telling economic analysis is a hypothetical comparison of the cost of preventing invasions altogether, controlling invasions before they become explosive, or ignoring them until they have become major problems (**Fig. 2**). With effective prevention, exotic species cause no damage, and costs are limited to prevention programs. With early control, the

invaders cause some damages, but the damages no longer accumulate once the exotic species are controlled and effective prevention is instituted. However, failure to control exotic species until it is too late (and major invasions have developed) can result in exponentially increasing economic losses, which can be further compounded by native species extinctions.

Looking to the future. Ultimately, the most effective and inexpensive means of minimizing invasive species impacts will be prevention or rapid control of the invasions. In cases where invaders become established, impact assessment will require effective combinations of comparative studies, large-scale and long-term experiments, simulation models, and cost-benefit analyses. Human activities (such as trade, agriculture, fishing, forestry, and urbanization) and global climate change will undoubtedly interact with changes caused by invasions, and distinguishing the impacts of invasions from these other impacts is critical to minimizing the ecological and economic effects of invasive species.

For background information *see* ECOLOGICAL COMMUNITIES; ECOLOGICAL COMPETITION; ECOLOGICAL METHODS; ECOLOGICAL MODELING; ECOLOGICAL SUCCESSION; POPULATION ECOLOGY in the McGraw-Hill Encyclopedia of Science & Technology.

Chris Harvey

Bibliography. C. S. Elton, *The Ecology of Invasions by Animals and Plants*, Methuen, 1958; H. A. Mooney and R. J. Hobbs, *Invasive Species in a Changing World*, Island, 2000; Office of Technology Assessment, *Harmful Non-Indigenous Species in the United States*, U.S. Government Printing Office, 1993; M. Williamson, *Biological Invasions*, Chapman and Hall, 1996.

Knowledge management

It has long been common practice to distinguish between data, information, and knowledge. Information is data arranged in meaningful patterns such that it is potentially useful for decision making. Knowledge is something that is believed, and is true, effective, and reliable. Knowledge is necessarily associated with an experiential context, and so is generally more valuable than information. However, knowledge is much harder to assimilate, understand, transfer, and share than information.

Many organizational scholars, seeking enhanced performance approaches, have begun to investigate and advocate the initiation of knowledge management efforts. Many organizations are acquiring systems to enable the sharing, exchange, and integration of knowledge. Knowledge, which is created in the mind of the individuals, is often of little value to an enterprise unless it is shared. Managers are rapidly learning that just because technology exists, knowledge will not necessarily flow freely throughout an organization. Cultural issues are regularly cited as one concern of those implementing knowledge management initiatives. The benefit of knowledge

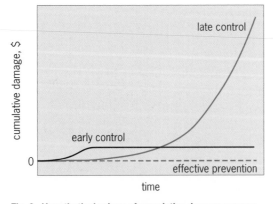

Fig. 2. Hypothetical values of cumulative damage over an extended time period with three invasive species control strategies. With late control, the value of damages might rise indefinitely if irreversible losses in biodiversity occur. (*After R. L. Naylor, The economics of alien species invasions, in H. A. Mooney and R. J. Hobbs, eds., Invasive Species in a Changing World, pp. 241–259, Island, 2000*)

management initiatives will not be realized unless the associated cultural, management, and organizational elements are aligned.

Schools of thought. There are two primary contemporary schools of thought on knowledge management: one that focuses on existing explicit knowledge, and one that focuses on the building or creation of knowledge. The first school focuses almost entirely upon information technology tools, whereas the second focuses on knowledge management as a transdisciplinary subject with major behavioral and organizational, as well as technology, concerns. Literature in the fields of computer science and artificial intelligence often focuses primarily on explicit knowledge and associated tools and technology. It is not uncommon in this school to have enterprise knowledge management defined as the formal management of resources to facilitate access and reuse of knowledge that is generally enabled by advanced information technology. Works in the second school of thought generally focus on generation and creation of knowledge. There is a major environmental context associated with this knowledge. Knowledge is generally thought to be a powerful source of innovation. In this school, knowledge management is viewed from a holistic point of view that encompasses both tacit and implicit knowledge.

The Nonaka and Takeuchi theory of knowledge creation is representative of the typically Eastern philosophy that stresses the complimentary nature of the intuitive (tacit) and the analytical (explicit). The theory comprises four knowledge-conversion stages: socialization, externalization, combination, and internalization. The conversion takes place in five phases: sharing of tacit knowledge, creating concepts, justifying concepts, building an archetype, and cross-level knowledge. Critical to this theory is the concept of levels of knowledge: individual, group, organizational, and interorganizational. Sharing primarily occurs during the socialization, externalization, and combination stages. During the socialization stage, sharing occurs primarily at the individual and group levels. In the externalization stage, knowledge is codified and shared at the group and organizational level. In the cross-leveling-of-knowledge phase, an enterprise shares knowledge both intra- and interorganizationally.

Knowledge sharing. Knowledge sharing is not necessarily a natural phenomenon within the context of an enterprise. Often, practices are embedded in organizational culture, processes, and strategies that inhibit this process. In addition, technological support may be insufficient to enable knowledge sharing, even when other organizational support is present. There is potential for knowledge sharing in three of the four knowledge-conversion states (all but internalization). Knowledge sharing can be accomplished with an internal audience of knowledge sharers or with an external audience. Decision making relative to what knowledge to share is very important. For example, one can share "know how," "know what," and best practices. One can also share "know why" (knowledge principles) or "know when" (knowledge perspectives). Knowledge-sharing systems that enable sharing future perspectives may allow for new and potentially innovative notions that have not been shown to be fully trustworthy and reliable and that, in the philosophical sense, may not even fully be considered knowledge. Generally, knowledge sharing is an evolutionary and emergent phenomenon. It may be accomplished through the sharing of collections or repositories of knowledge, or through a knowledge-connections dimension that recognizes that knowledge is embodied both in humans and in the relationships between humans and organizations. All of this can be accomplished at the level of knowledge-oriented products, such as an Internet-based electronic encyclopedia, and at the level of knowledge-oriented processes, such as software and human usage of this product to enable implementation of a process to create the Internet encyclopedia product noted above, and this process level can be driven by knowledge-oriented strategic policy considerations.

Contextual awareness interrogatives. The distinction between data, information, knowledge, and potentially wisdom are important. Data represent points in space and time that relate to particular aspects. Information is data that are potentially relevant to decision making; it relates to description, definition, or outlook. Generally, information is responsive to questions that relate to "what," "when," "where," or "who." Knowledge is information imbedded in context and may comprise approach, method, practice, or strategy. Generally, knowledge responds to questions that relate to "how." It is sometimes desirable to distinguish wisdom as an even higher-level construct that represents insights, prototypes or models, or principles which would be responsive to questions concerning "why." If the distinction is not made, knowledge is expected to respond to "why" questions as well as "how." These six important questions or concerns might be collectively called contextual awareness interrogatives.

Each of these six questions is important and is needed to be responsive to broad-scope inquiry in modern transdisciplinary endeavors. Systems engineering, one such endeavor, is concerned with developing appropriate relationships between the major groups associated with engineering large systems. These groups are represented by the rows in the **illustration**, which is a two-dimensional framework for information and knowledge that is derived from an adaptation of the Zachman architectural framework. The framework can be associated with any of the phases associated with the engineering of a system. The rows of this illustration represent the perspectives or views of the many stakeholders to a large issue such as sustainable development: policy makers, planners, enterprise owners, life-support systems engineers and architects, life-support system builders, and the public impacted by the resulting systems. Information and knowledge relevant to each cell in this framework must be present in any constructive effort to engineer solutions to large issues.

		Information			Knowledge	
		Entities (What)	Time (When)	Locations (Where)	People (Who)	Activities (How)	Motivation (Why)
Stakeholders	Policy makers						
	Planners						
	Enterprise owners						
	Systems engineers/ architects						
	Builders						
	Impacted public						

Knowledge management perspectives of systems engineering stakeholders.

Information transformation. Knowledge can be viewed as transformation of information in the context of a contingency task structure and experiential familiarity. This allows information to have value in such activities as planning and decision making. Knowledge management refers to management of the environment associated with the transformation of data to information, and information to knowledge, such that these transformations are effective and efficient. This requires that particular attention be paid to the contextual awareness and environmental facets of the contingency task structure associated with knowledge acquisition and use. Several observations and principles follow from this. The most important of these is that knowledge management flourishes when there is appropriate encouragement of knowledge diversity, which in turn requires understanding the relevant facets of organizational activities and the broader context and environment in which the organization operates. Knowledge management should be ubiquitous throughout the organization. Knowledge workers should be empowered through enhancements associated with competence, commitment, communications, collaboration, and courage. Thus, two-way communication with knowledge workers is required to cultivate an intelligence that empowers all and encourages bilateral transitions between explicit and tacit knowledge. Knowledge management is critically dependent upon a proper focus on people and knowledge behavior: All relevant aspects of the knowledge environment must be considered in a continuous learning effort that makes knowledge acquisition cycles and processes visible throughout the organization.

Practical applications. Organizations are beginning to realize that knowledge is the most valuable asset of employees and the organization. This recognition must be converted into pragmatic action

guidelines, plans, and specific approaches. Effective management of the environmental factors that lead to enhanced learning and the transfer of information into knowledge requires organizational investments in terms of financial capital for technology and human labor. It also requires knowledge managers to facilitate identification, distribution, storage, use, and sharing of knowledge. Other issues include incentive systems and appropriate rewards for active knowledge creators, as well as the legalities and ethics of knowledge management. In each of these efforts, it is critical to regard technology as a potential enabler of human effort, not as a substitute for it.

For background information see SYSTEMS ENGINEERING in the McGraw-Hill Encyclopedia of Science & Technology.   Andrew P. Sage

Bibliography. J. S. Brown and P. Duguid, *The Social Life of Information*, Harvard Business School Press, Boston, 2000; S. D. N. Cook and J. S. Brown, Bridging epistemologies: The generative dance between organizational knowledge and organizational knowing, *Organization Sci.*, 10(4):381–400, July–August 1999; I. Nonaka and H. Takeuchi, *The Knowledge-Creating Company: How Japanese Companies Create the Dynamics of Innovation*, Oxford University Press, New York, 1995; M. Polonyi, *The Tacit Dimension*, Doubleday, Garden City, NY, 1996; L. Prusak and T. Davenport, *Working Knowledge: How Organizations Manage What They Know*, Harvard Business School Press, Boston, 1998; A. P. Sage and W. B. Rouse (eds.), *Handbook of Systems Engineering and Management*, Wiley, New York, 1999; G. Von Krough, K. Ichijo, and I. Nonaka, *Enabling Knowledge Creation*, Oxford University Press, New York, 2000; J. Zachman, A framework for information systems architecture, *IBM Sys. J.*, 26(3):84–92, 1987.

Laser-controlled chemical reactions

Lasers can be used both to initiate chemical reactions and to control their rates and product distributions. The frequency, intensity, and phase properties of a laser beam are used to great advantage in controlling the motion of nuclei and electrons. For example, infrared radiation is used to excite specific vibrational modes of a molecule, whereas visible radiation and ultraviolet radiation are used to induce electronic transitions. The tunability and narrow bandwidth (that is, sharp wavelength) of a laser permit very precise selection of the desired transition. The high intensity achievable with pulsed lasers promotes multiphoton or overtone transitions. Finally, the phase coherence of a laser exploits the quantum-mechanical properties of matter in ways that are inaccessible by conventional methods.

There are three general methods of controlling chemical reactions with lasers: (1) Mode-selective control uses one or more lasers to increase the number of molecules in a particular state (referred to as "populating" the state), which then undergo a unimolecular or bimolecular reaction unique to that state. (2) Wave packet control involves a superposition of states excited by a short laser pulse. This superposition state evolves in time until another pulse, or a later part of the original pulse, projects the wave packet into a desired reaction channel. (3) Coherent phase control involves two competing excitation paths which interfere constructively so as to enhance a particular product channel. The latter two methods are inherently nonclassical in that they exploit the wave properties of matter.

Mode-selective control. The underlying idea in mode-selective control is to use a laser to energize the bond that is to be broken. Activation of the bond might be achieved, for example, by excitation of a vibrational eigenstate of the molecule (the state or level that a molecule remains in that is unchanged until it interacts with another particle). The vibrationally excited molecule may subsequently absorb a visible or ultraviolet photon that promotes it to an electronically excited state, where it reacts to form the products of interest (**Fig. 1**).

The bond-specific reactions of partially deuterated (isotopically labeled) water (HOD) studied by F. Crim are an example of mode-selective control. Excitation of HOD with a laser pulse having a wavelength of 722.5 nanometers induces a transition to an overtone state with four vibrational quanta in the OH bond. Because the excited molecule is in a stationary eigenstate, it remains in that state indefinitely until it interacts with another photon or particle (or emits a photon), resulting in selective rupture of the OH bond. For example, if the energized molecule

absorbs a 266-nm photon, the molecule dissociates into the products H + OD. If instead the molecule collides with a chlorine atom, it undergoes the bimolecular reaction (1).

$$HOD(4\nu_{OH}) + Cl \rightarrow HCl + OD \qquad (1)$$

A more complex example of vibrational mode-selective chemistry is the collision of ammonia ions with neutral ammonia molecules, studied by R. Zare and coworkers. They found that excitation of the umbrella mode of the ammonia ion primarily induces the proton transfer reaction (2).

$$NH_3^+(\nu_2) + ND_3 \rightarrow NH_2 + ND_3H^+ \qquad (2)$$

Electronic modes can also be used to promote bond-specific reactions. One example, studied by L. Butler, is the photodissociation of CH_2IBr. Excitation of the molecule at 248.5 nm promotes primarily a nonbonding iodine electron into an antibonding orbital, producing 60% CH_2Br + I and 40% CH_2I + Br. In contrast, at 210 nm a nonbonding bromine electron is excited, and only CH_2I + Br is formed.

Mode-selective control depends on the coupling of a chromophore to specific vibrational or electronic degrees of freedom. Unfortunately, such energy localization does not occur in every molecule. Typically, a normal vibrational mode of a molecule is a linear combination of stretches or bends of more than one bond. Similarly, an excited orbital need not be localized on a single bond. The techniques described in the following two sections exploit the quantum-mechanical properties of molecules in order to overcome these limitations.

Wave packet control. In this type of control, very short laser pulses are used to excite a superposition of states, known as a wave packet, and to steer it into a desired product channel. The wave properties of light require that the spectral width of a light pulse varies inversely with its temporal duration. Consequently, pulses shorter than ~100 femtoseconds have a wavelength range that is broad enough to excite more than one vibrational state of a molecule. For example, an excitation (pump) pulse promotes the molecule to an electronically excited state in which several vibrational eigenstates are populated (**Fig. 2**). Such a coherent combination of states is spatially localized and evolves in time on the excited potential energy surface. After a suitable delay, a stimulation (dump) pulse transfers the population to some other electronic state, where the desired reaction occurs. This method, developed by S. Rice and D. Tannor, has been applied to a number of simple reactions. One example, demonstrated by G. Gerber and coworkers, is the ionization of Na_2. By varying the pump-dump delay, they were able to produce selectively Na_2^+ or Na + Na^+ products.

In a generalization of this method pioneered by H. Rabitz, an optimally shaped pulse may be used to guide the wave packet to the desired products.

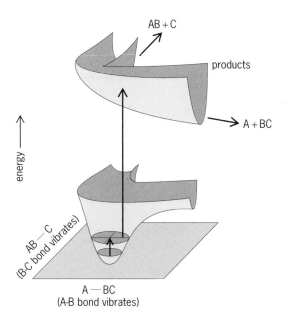

Fig. 1. Mode-selective control. A triatomic molecule, ABC, absorbs one or more low-energy photons causing the A-B and B-C bonds to vibrate. Subsequent absorption of an energetic photon promotes the molecule to a repulsive potential energy surface on which the bond breaks to yield the products A + BC and AB + C.

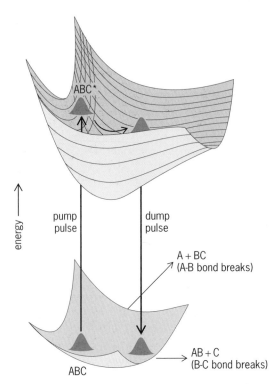

Fig. 2. Wave packet control. A triatomic molecule, ABC, is promoted to an electronically excited state by the pump pulse. A vibrational wave packet evolves on the excited surface until a dump pulse returns it to the ground electronic state in a region where the A-B or B-C bond breaks.

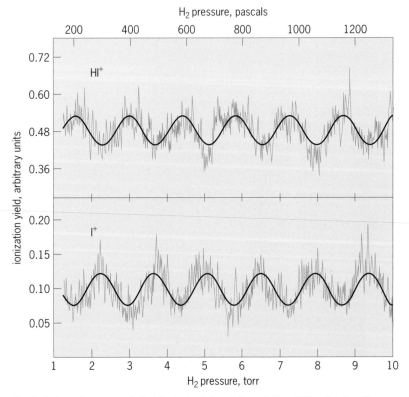

Fig. 3. Coherent phase control of the ionization and dissociation of HI molecules. The molecules are excited with one photon at a wavelength of 118 nm and three photons at 354 nm, with the relative intensities adjusted so that the ionization rates from the two processes are equal. (The dissociation product, I, absorbs additional photons to produce the I^+ ion.) The oscillatory signals are produced by varying the relative phase of the two beams by passing them through a cell containing H_2 gas. The phase lag between the two signals is evidence of control of the branching ratio.

A shaped (tailored) pulse is one in which the amplitude, phase, and polarization are varied in a predetermined way during the pulse. A pulse may be tailored by first dispersing its frequency components with a grating. The dispersed components are then passed through one or more filters known as spatial light modulators. These modulators are typically an array of liquid crystals, which can be programmed to adjust the properties of each frequency component of the beam. The various components are finally recombined by a second grating to form the desired shaped pulse.

The optimally shaped pulse for producing a particular product may be predicted if one knows the complete Hamiltonian. For complex reactions, such detailed information in unavailable, and calculation of the optimal pulse is a formidable task. An empirical solution may be achieved, however, by introducing a feedback loop, allowing the laser to "learn" from the product distribution how to improve the pulse characteristics. This process is implemented by a genetic algorithm in which the voltages applied to each pixel in the spatial light modulator are treated as the elements of a genetic code. Reproduction, mutation, and crossover of the "genes" in successive generations allow the system to seek the optimal pulse for a desired reaction product. An application of this method reported by R. Levis is the photo-induced reaction of acetophenone ($C_6H_5COCH_3$) using shaped Ti:sapphire (800 nm, 60 fs) laser pulses. Employing a closed feedback loop, he selectively enhanced the relative yields of $C_6H_5CO + CH_3$, $C_6H_5 + COCH_3$, and $C_6H_5CH_3 + CO$. The last set of products is especially noteworthy because they involve a complex rearrangement mechanism.

Coherent phase control. A different approach, pioneered independently by P. Brumer and M. Shapiro, uses the interference between competing quantum-mechanical processes. It was shown by T. Young 200 years ago that two coherent light waves emerging from a pair of slits produce an undulatory interference pattern on a distant screen. The oscillatory pattern is a consequence of the property that the combined intensity of two beams is equal to the square of the sum of the amplitudes of the individual waves. The same principle applies in quantum mechanics, where the combined probability for two competing processes linking the same initial and final states is given by the square of the sum of the probability amplitudes for each process. An example of two such competing processes is the excitation of a molecule by either one photon of frequency ω_3 or by three photons of frequency ω_1, where $\omega_3 = 3\omega_1$. If the probability amplitude (the transition matrix element) for the first process is denoted by f_3, and the probability for that process is given by $P_3 = |f_3|^2$, and the corresponding quantities for the second process are given by f_1 and P_1, then the total transition probability is shown in Eq. (3), where the asterisk

$$P = |f_1 + f_3|^2 = P_1 + P_3 + f_1 f_3^* + f_1^* f_3 \qquad (3)$$

denotes the complex conjugate.

If in addition the phase of the light wave that induces the one-photon transition is denoted by ϕ_1, and the phase of the second beam by ϕ_1, then it is not difficult to show the total transition probability between two bound states as in Eq. (4), where

$$P = P_1 + P_3 + 2\sqrt{P_1 P_3}\cos\phi \qquad (4)$$

$\phi = \phi_3 - 3\phi_1$. The transition probability oscillates with the relative phase of the two paths, just as in Young's two-slit experiment. The transition probability can be controlled by varying ϕ in passing the two laser beams through a cell containing a gas that has a different index of refraction at the two wavelengths.

This method may be generalized to chemical reactions, where the upper state is unbound, as in Fig. 1. One important difference between the bound-bound and bound-continuum cases is that in the latter an additional phase appears in the interference term that has its origin in the continuum properties of the molecule. The different sets of products are labeled by the superscript S (for example, $S_1 = A + BC$ and $S_2 = AB + C$). It is shown in this case that the products also contribute a phase, δ_{13}^S, to the interference term, as shown in Eq. (5). The important point

$$P^S = P_1^S + P_3^S + 2P_{13}^S\cos\left(\phi + \delta_{13}^S\right) \qquad (5)$$

to notice is that this "molecular phase" depends on the product, so that the two products oscillate out of phase, and that by varying ϕ it is possible to control the product branching ratio. This result is illustrated in **Fig. 3** for the reaction of HI, studied by R. Gordon, to produce either HI^+ by photoionization or $H + I$ by photodissociation of the parent molecule.

Outlook. Laser-controlled chemistry has provided a wealth of fundamental knowledge about chemical reaction dynamics and the interaction of light with matter. Recent developments in laser technology offer the hope that lasers may also have practical applications in controlling the product distributions of chemical reactions.

For background information *see* CHEMICAL DYNAMICS; LASER; LASER PHOTOCHEMISTRY; PHOTON; QUANTUM MECHANICS; ULTRAFAST MOLECULAR PROCESSES; WAVE PACKET in the McGraw-Hill Encyclopedia of Science & Technology.   Robert Gordon

Bibliography. D. L. Andrews, *Lasers in Chemistry*, Springer-Verlag, 1997; P. Brumer and M. Shapiro, Laser control of chemical reactions, *Sci. Amer.*, 272: 56–63, 1995; F. F. Crim, Vibrational state control of bimolecular reactions: Discovering and directing the chemistry, *Acc. Chem. Res.*, 32:877–884, 1999; R. J. Gordon and S. A. Rice, Active control of the dynamics of atoms and molecules, *Annu. Rev. Phys. Chem.*, 28:601–641, 1997; R. J. Gordon, L. Zhu, and T. Seideman, Using the phase of light as a photochemical tool, *J. Phys. Chem. A*, 105:4387, 2001; R. J. Levis, G. M. Menkir, and H. Rabitz, Selective bond dissociation and rearrangement with optimally tailored, strong field laser pulses, *Science*, 292:709–713, 2001; S. A. Rice and M. Zhao, *Optical Control of Molecular Dynamics*, Wiley, New York, 2000.

Laser-driven x-ray sources

Ever since the invention of the microscope, one of the great trends of modern science has been toward resolving ever-finer detail in the study of matter. Since small objects generally move quickly (which simply follows from the dependence of inertia on mass), high spatial resolution alone is not sufficient to image such objects (for example, to take a magnified photograph of them with a camera). A short-duration flash of light (or fast shutter) is also necessary to prevent blurring of the image. While the millisecond duration of an ordinary camera is sufficient to freeze the action of a person running (meter-scale length), a strobe light with ultrashort pulse duration (1 femtosecond or 10^{-15} s) is required in order to resolve a moving atom (10^{-10}-m-scale length).

For this reason, the study of ultrafast molecular dynamics did not begin until the development of femtosecond-duration optical lasers in the late 1970s. However, direct time-domain measurements with femtosecond temporal resolution could be made with only micrometer-scale spatial resolution because of the relatively long wavelength (~1 micrometer) of optical light. Alternatively, direct measurements with atomic-scale spatial resolution could be made with x-rays from synchrotrons, but with only nanosecond temporal resolution, because of the relatively long duration of these sources. Now, with the development of a new generation of tabletop-size laser systems, it is feasible to generate femtosecond-duration x-ray pulses, which will allow high resolution to be achieved simultaneously in both space and time.

What makes these lasers so promising is that they can deliver both short pulses and high peak power. Because power is energy divided by time, when only a joule of energy is released over femtoseconds, it can produce a terawatt of power. This power can produce the highest light intensities on Earth, 10^{21} W/cm^2, by focusing the light to a spot size of the laser wavelength. Associated with these extreme power densities are the largest electric and magnetic fields ever produced, of the order of 10^{12} V/cm and 10^5 tesla (10^9 gauss), respectively. What permits solid-state lasers to generate such high fields is the chirped-pulse-amplification technique, invented in 1987. In order to prevent damage to the amplifiers, the laser light is first stretched in time, then amplified as a pulse with long duration, and thus with lower power, and lastly compressed to a short duration after the energy has been increased. Fields of this high strength can accelerate electrons to relativistic energies, which can then be used to convert light to short pulses of x-rays.

Electron motion in laser fields. Light is a wave with transverse electric and magnetic fields oscillating at the same frequency. At low laser power, electrons oscillate along the light's electric field (E) with a velocity (v) which is always very small compared to the speed of light (**Fig. 1a**). This motion is described by the equation $m(d\mathbf{v}/dt) = -e\mathbf{E}$, where m is the electron mass and e is the magnitude of its

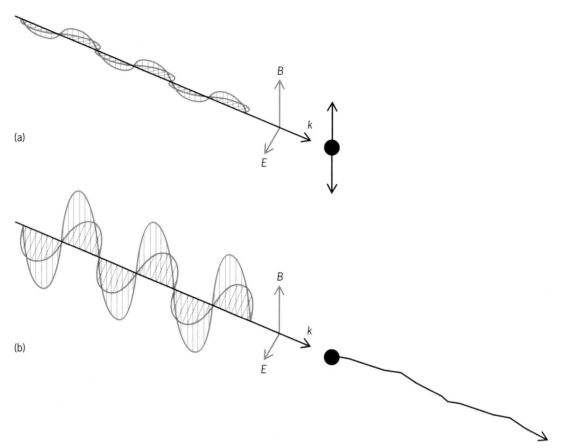

Fig. 1. Motion of an electron in a light wave. (*a*) In classical optics, the amplitude of the light wave is small, electrons oscillate in the direction of the electric field, *E*, at the light's frequency, and there is no displacement along the light's propagation direction, *k*. Only the electric field acts on the electron, and the electron-oscillation velocity is very small compared with the speed of light. (*b*) In relativistic optics, the amplitude of the light wave is very large, the light's magnetic field becomes important, and the combined action of the electric and magnetic fields pushes the electron forward. In this case, the electron velocity becomes close to the speed of light.

charge. At higher laser intensities, the electron velocity in a laser focus can reach close to the speed of light (*c*) and its mass (*m*) will increase due to relativistic effects. In this relativistic regime, one must also include an additional term in the equation of motion, which then becomes $m(d\mathbf{v}/dt) = -e[\mathbf{E} + (\mathbf{v}/c) \times \mathbf{B}]$. Thus, the light's magnetic field (*B*) will act to bend the electrons in the direction of light propagation, perpendicular to both *E* and *B* (Fig. 1*b*). With this additional force, the electron traces a figure-8, oscillating twice in the direction of the light wave for every single oscillation along the polarization direction (along *E*). This oscillating motion is then superimposed upon a steady drift in the direction of the light wave. Thus the motion is increasingly longitudinal as the light intensity is increased.

Laser focusing on solid targets. One way to make x-rays is by focusing an intense laser onto a solid target. When the relativistic electrons collide with the ions of the solid, they rapidly accelerate, causing the emission of bremsstrahlung radiation in the x-ray spectral region. This is just like a conventional x-ray tube, such as found in a dentist's office, except it is the laser's short-duration electromagnetic field that accelerates the electrons instead of the continuous

electrostatic field between the anode and cathode of the x-ray tube. One of the problems with these x-rays is that they are produced in all directions simultaneously (4π steradians), and so their intensity decreases with the square of the distance from the source. They are also incoherent and deliver relatively long pulses, picosecond in duration. However, because of the simplicity of the method used to produce them, these x-rays have been used to study picosecond processes such as shock formation or melting by means of either x-ray absorption or diffraction.

Laser focusing on gaseous targets. Another way to make x-rays is to focus an intense laser onto a gaseous-density target. The highly nonlinear but periodic motion discussed above will result in nonlinear scattering. For instance, when the strength of the light field approaches the Coulomb field binding electrons to nuclei, extremely high order harmonics can be observed, culminating in the recent observation of the 501st harmonic of 800-nanometer laser light. The mechanism responsible for this is scattering of the electron from the atomic nucleus. At larger light field strengths, the atoms become ionized, producing plasma, which disrupts phase matching and prevents the efficient generation of higher harmonics. In even larger fields, the electron will no longer even collide with the nucleus due to acceleration in the direction of the light wave. But when the field is increased yet further, the free electrons in the plasma begin to oscillate with relativistic velocities, and the nonlinear motion (discussed above) can produce harmonics. The usefulness of this nonlinearly Thomson scattered light, however, is limited, owing to the fact that the harmonics are scattered at large angles. Also, because the oscillation frequency is reduced, so too is the scattering efficiency into high harmonics.

Fortunately, at high laser intensities a directed beam of relativistic electrons is also produced in the direction of the laser light by laser-driven plasma waves. Lasers have been shown to accelerate greater than 10^{10} electrons to energies well above 1 MeV in low-divergence ($<10°$ angle) beams at repetition rates of 10 Hz. The acceleration gradient is greater than 1 GeV/cm, 10^4 times greater than that of conventional radio-frequency accelerators. Recent experiments have shown that Compton scattering by such a co-propagating electron beam produces a collimated beam of high-order harmonics, also in the direction of the laser light (**Figs. 2** and **3**). Unlike Thomson scattering from low-velocity electrons, which produces only harmonics, Compton scattering from relativistic electron beams also results in a Doppler shift, which (in the case of counterpropagating beams) can further upshift the energy of the scattered light to the hard x-ray region of the spectrum. For example, electrons with only 100-MeV energy can boost a 1-eV energy photon to 50 keV. This opens up the possibility of an all-optically-driven "tabletop" hard x-ray source, which is of interest not only as a probe with atomic-scale spatial resolution but also as a medical diagnostic tool because of the large penetration of such energetic light through matter.

Other x-ray sources. There exist other means to generate x-ray sources, such as synchrotrons and

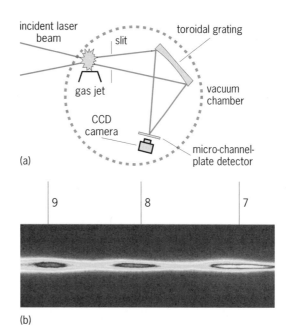

(a)

(b)

Fig. 3. Experimental study of nonlinear Compton scattering. (*a*) Apparatus. (*b*) Output of the charge-coupled-device (CCD) camera of the spectrometer, showing light at the 7th through 9th harmonics of the laser frequency.

free-electron lasers. They rely on conventional (radio-frequency) accelerators to generate an electron beam, but because of their low field gradients (0.1 MeV/cm) they are usually quite large (tens to hundreds of meters in length). Long sets of magnets (tens of meters) are required to wiggle the electrons. Laser-Compton sources, by contrast, accelerate electrons in millimeter distances, and the electrons are wiggled in a millimeter-long interaction region by the magnetic field of the laser pulse. Consequently, laser-Compton sources will be much more affordable, thus potentially permitting their operation at university, industrial, and hospital laboratories. The latter will also provide better temporal resolution (femtoseconds instead of tens of picoseconds). There are proposals to build a short-pulse x-ray free-electron laser, but this will require a 50-GeV-energy electron beam conventionally accelerated in a 3-km-long (2-mi) tunnel to be passed through a 50-m-long (150-ft) set of wiggler magnets. Free-electron lasers do have the advantage over Compton sources that the electrons become tightly bunched, improving coherence and x-ray power.

Compton scattering has also been used to produce x-rays from electron beams that are conventionally accelerated. But besides being much larger, radio-frequency accelerators produce picosecond-duration electron bunches, which are mismatched with the femtosecond duration of the laser pulse, limiting their efficiency. This problem is mitigated with laser-accelerated electron beams, which can produce laser-synchronized femtosecond electron pulses.

Another laser-driven x-ray source is an x-ray laser, which is driven by electronic transitions in highly stripped ions. X-rays lasers do have the best

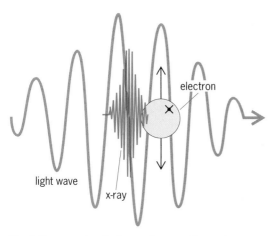

Fig. 2. Process whereby harmonic generation and a relativistic Doppler shift can upshift the frequency of visible radiation from a laser that Compton-scatters from an energetic electron beam to the x-ray region of the spectrum. Colliding a laser with 100-MeV-energy electron beams from a tabletop laser accelerator can produce 50-keV x-rays.

coherence properties and are currently the brightest monochromatic sources in the extreme-ultraviolet region of the spectrum, but they do not scale to the hard x-ray regime. Although they produce shorter pulses than synchrotrons, their pulses, several picoseconds in duration, are still relatively long compared with laser-Compton sources.

Improved electron beams. One of the challenges for the future of laser-Compton x-ray sources is to find ways to produce more monoenergetic laser-driven electron beams in order to increase the number of scattered photons per unit bandwidth. A potential solution is optical injection of plasma electrons into laser-driven plasma waves. Higher-energy electron beams, gigaelectronvolts instead of megaelectronvolts, will dramatically increase the scattered power. A means to achieve this would be to increase the acceleration length by means of optical guiding of the intense light in preformed plasma channels or the use of multiple acceleration stages.

Applications. Laser-driven ultrafast x-rays can provide the requisite temporal resolution for the study of ultrafast processes such as conformational changes in ultrafast biology and chemistry, inner-shell electronic processes in atomic systems, and phase transitions in materials science. One problem they might help solve is the determination of protein structure. They are also useful in the study of photo-initiated processes, such as photosynthesis, because in this case the optical pump and x-ray probe are absolutely synchronized with each other, being derived from the same laser. Also, significant absorption of the x-ray probe pulse (such as occurs in the in vitro imaging of live biological cells) can destroy a sample or at least cause it to move. Thus, in order to acquire an image before the occurrence of blurring from this heat-induced motion, a single-shot pump-probe measurement with ultrashort-duration and high-peak-power x-rays is required. Low-repetition-rate, laser-produced x-ray sources are also best suited for studies of processes that are irreversible, and in which the sample must be moved between shots. Tunable x-rays that have energy near 50 keV can also be used in medicine for applications such as either differential absorption or phase-contrast imaging.

For background information *see* BREMSSTRAHLUNG; COMPTON EFFECT; ELECTRON MOTION IN VACUUM; LASER; NONLINEAR OPTICS; OPTICAL PULSES; PARTICLE ACCELERATOR; PLASMA (PHYSICS); SCATTERING OF ELECTROMAGNETIC RADIATION; SYNCHROTRON RADIATION; X-RAY TUBE in the McGraw-Hill Encyclopedia of Science & Technology.

Donald Umstadter

Bibliography. F. Hartemann, *High-Field Electrodynamics*, CRC Press, Boca Raton, 2001; G. A. Mourou, C. P. J. Barty, and M. D. Perry, Ultrahigh-intensity lasers: Physics of the extreme on a tabletop, *Phys. Today*, 51(1):22, January 1998; D. Umstadter, Physics and applications of relativistic plasmas driven by ultra-intense lasers, *Phys. Plasmas*, 8: 1774–1785, 2001; D. Umstadter, Terawatt lasers produce faster electron acceleration, *Laser Focus World*, pp. 101–104, February 1996; D. Umstadter and G. Mourou, Extreme light, *Sci. Amer.*, 286(5):81–86, May 2002.

Leech evolution

The facility of leeches for extracting blood from living organisms has long been known to human society. That influential ancient physicians such as Nicander of Colophon (ca. 200 B.C.), Wang Chung (ca. A.D. 30), and Kunja Lal Sharma (ca. A.D. 50) described therapeutic uses for leeches indicates that medical use of leeches was widespread in the ancient world. However, application of leeches in Europe for relief of a myriad of ailments such as headaches, insomnia, ulcers, and obesity did not reach its acme until the 1800s, when exploitation in France exceeded 50 million leeches per year. Today, legitimate use of medicinal leeches includes hematoma treatment after microsurgical reattachment procedures. There has also been an increase in understanding of the anticoagulation components of leech salivary secretions. Thorough understanding of the evolutionary relationships of leeches provides a means for targeting other therapeutically useful species and permits the elucidation of patterns in the evolution of blood feeding from their common ancestor to the present.

Anatomy of blood feeding. Leeches are oligochaetes; however, unlike other members of the Oligochaeta, such as the earthworms, leeches have special anatomical adaptations for blood feeding. Principal among these is the muscular caudal sucker composed of the posterior seven somites (body segments) and controlled by as many neural ganglia. The sucker is critical for maintaining position on a host and often doubles as a powerful swimming fluke. The anterior six somites are likewise modified into a region with a ventral sucker surrounding a mouth pore. The negative pressure applied by this anterior sucker aids in attachment and promotes upwelling of blood from the bite wound. Blood-feeding leeches are equipped with a large branched stomach (crop) permitting great expansion during feeding episodes; some leeches consume up to six times their unfed body weight. That all blood-feeding leeches have these features suggests they also were properties of the ancestral leech.

Leeches are subdivided into groups based on anatomical variations in blood-feeding mechanisms. The large wormlike Arhynchobdellida, of which *Hirudo medicinalis* (the "medicinal leech") is typical, have three muscular jaws (**Fig. 1**). Each of these possesses a row of teeth, creating a serrated edge for puncturing through skin into capillary-rich tissues. The Rhynchobdellida have a muscular proboscis to effect blood-feeding from vascularized subdermal tissues. The giant Amazonian leech, *Haementeria ghilianii*, which grows to 16 in., has a proboscis that is nearly half its body length (Fig. 1).

Arhynchobdellids. Blood-feeding arhynchobdellids include the aquatic Hirudinidae and the terrestrial Haemadipsidae ("jungle leeches"). In the humid forests of tropical zones, the latter are more common than their aquatic cousins. Both of these groups are equipped with a parabolic arc of 10 eyespots that detect movement in three dimensions. Terrestrial leeches, however, have the additional adaptation of respiratory auricles near their sucker, permitting gas exchange without excessive loss of fluid, and well-developed sensory systems for detecting vibrations, carbon dioxide, and heat.

Rhynchobdellids. The two groups of proboscis-bearing Rhynchobdellida have pairs of centrally arranged eyespots that sense two-dimensional movement. The small fish leeches, or Piscicolidae, exhibit a form of parental care that enables their offspring to obtain an early blood meal. Rather than abandoning a secreted cocoon, as the arhynchobdellids do, the piscicolids cement dozens of egg cases to the surface of shrimp or crabs. When that crustacean is eaten, young leeches jump off, attaching to the buccal surfaces or migrating to the gills of the fish (predator) to acquire a blood meal. The Glossiphoniidae, like *Haementeria ghilianii,* are broad and flattened, normally feeding on turtles or amphibians. Glossiphoniids secrete a membranous bag to hold their eggs on their underside. Covering their eggs, adults will fan the brood until they hatch. The brood then will turn and attach to the venter (underside of the abdomen) of their parent and, when the parent finds its next blood meal, they are carried to their first.

Non-blood-feeding leeches. Many leeches do not feed on blood at all. Glossiphoniids, such as species of *Helobdella* and *Glossiphonia,* feed on aquatic oligochaetes and snails. The jawless Erpobdellidae feed on chironomid (two-winged fly) larvae, and the jawed Haemopidae consume whole earthworms, shredding them over jaws with two rows of large teeth. Typically it is assumed that non-blood-feeding varieties are more primitive than those with the advanced behavior of blood feeding.

Chemistry of blood feeding. The specifics of finding and acquiring a blood meal is only part of how these worms adapted exquisitely to their task. Vertebrate blood has a range of clotting factors, making it necessary for leeches to be equipped with mechanisms for preventing the activation of this system. Usually a wound as small and inconspicuous as a leech bite will clot in seconds, yet most leeches need to feed for 20 to 40 min. If ingested blood coagulated in their gut, leeches would become as immobile as a block of cement.

The extent to which leeches have circumvented this problem is seen in relation to the mammalian coagulation pathway in **Fig. 2.** The significant end points of this cascade (in capitals) include crosslinkage of platelets (that is, the formation of a matrix of platelets that stick to each other), thrombin's conversion of fibrinogen to fibrin to produce a fibrin matrix, and the crosslinking of fibrin and platelets into a hard clot. Activated clotting factors (for example,

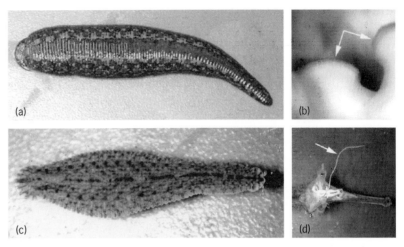

Fig. 1. Leeches are subdivided into two groups: the Arhynchobdellida, such as (*a*) the European medicinal leech, *Hirudo medicinalis,* (*b*) which possess serrated jaws for cutting skin; and Rhynchobdellida, such as (*c*) the giant Amazonian leech, *Haementeria ghilianii,* (*d*) which use a proboscis to pierce into blood-filled tissues.

Xa) repeatedly catalyze activation of their substrates (for example, prothrombin to thrombin); thus the conversion of a single prekillikrein peptide to killikrein, for example, can produce millions of fibrin molecules in the cascade.

Hirudin, from *Hirudo medicinalis,* was the first anticoagulant to be isolated from a leech. This potent thrombin inhibitor is the principal reason that victims bleed for several hours from the bite of the European medicinal leech. Several hirudin homologs

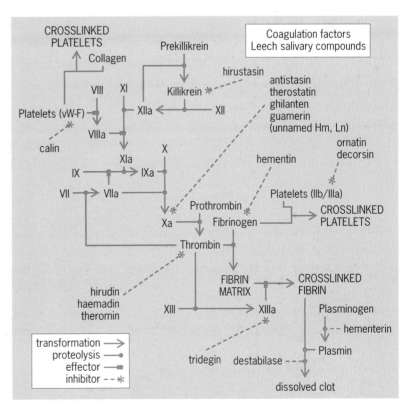

Fig. 2. Diagrammatic representation of the mammalian coagulation cascade, which results in clots from the crosslinkage of fibrin (a fibrous, insoluble protein) and platelets. Leeches have evolved numerous salivary compounds (in italics) that interrupt coagulation.

are known, such as haemadin from haemadipsids and theromin from duck-parasitic *Theromyzon* species. There are at least seven different points in the coagulation cascade blocked by leech salivary compounds, many of which are protease inhibitors (Fig. 2). *Hirudo medicinalis* also has a platelet aggregation inhibitor, calin, that works by blocking von Willebrand's factor, whereas the platelet inhibitors from North American species of *Macrobdella* and *Placobdella* (decorsin and ornatin, respectively) prevent aggregation by interfering with glycoprotein IIb/IIIa. The most frequently encountered protease inhibitors block factor Xa, preventing conversion of prothrombin to thrombin.

Beyond simply blocking the formation of clots, the giant Amazonian leech, *Haementeria ghilianii*, has also evolved ways to break them down, such as by preventing fibrin crosslinking (by tridegin) and promoting the production of the fibrin-digesting enzyme plasmin (by hementerin). There are even known anti-inflammatory agents, such as eglin, bdellin, and cytin, in the leech pharmacopoeia.

Phylogeny and evolution of blood feeding. Prior to the 1990s, consideration of the evolution of leeches was limited to speculations about which characteristics were primitive in leech diversity. Currently, there is considerably more information available in the form of morphological character data and several deoxyribonucleic acid (DNA) sequences from all major lineages. **Figure 3** highlights results of cladistic analysis of all of these data (including two nuclear ribo-

somal genes, as well as mitochondrial genes encoding ribosomes, cytochrome *c* oxidase, and nicotine adenine dehydrogenase) for 10 families of leeches (with a breakdown to genera for the Glossiphoniidae). Using this tree, it is possible to make a variety of parsimonious inferences (that is, hypotheses that minimize the total amount of evolutionary change required to explain the distribution of traits at the tips of the phylogenetic tree) about the evolution of blood feeding.

The closest relative of leeches, the Branchiobdellida, are tiny worms that feed on the surface of freshwater crayfish. Because the branchiobdellidans also have suckers, it is clear that this organ did not originate in conjunction with the origin of blood feeding. Nonetheless, there does appear to have been a single origin of sanguivory in the ancestral leech. As a consequence, there must have been at least five independent occasions in which leeches gave up blood feeding in favor of predation of invertebrates. This runs counter to early notions that absence of parasitism must be the primitive condition.

With respect to anatomical specializations for blood feeding, the cladogram in Fig. 3 suggests that the ancestral leech had a proboscis that was lost with a move to the terrestrial environment prior to the evolution of jaws. Interestingly, aquatic medicinal leeches in Hirudinidae and Macrobdellidae have terrestrial ancestors. Corroborating this inference is their tendency of depositing egg cases on shore. Branchiobdellidans and piscicolids cement their egg cases to the surfaces of crustaceans; thus it can be inferred that the ancestral leech did this as well. This behavior later evolved into the specialized brooding parental care described for the Glossiphoniidae.

Few leech species have been examined for the presence of anticoagulants. However, it is already clear from the cladogram that three coagulation inhibitors must have been inherited from the common ancestor. Beyond being an indication that there are undiscovered bioactive compounds in uninvestigated species, there is a startling secondary inference from the foregoing. If such a broad range of leeches have all inherited from the ancestral leech the genes coding for the anti-Xa, antithrombin, and antiplatelet factors, then perhaps so too have many of the lineages that later gave up blood feeding. Already this has been corroborated by the discovery of anti-Xa guamerins in the non-blood-feeding haemopid, *Whitmania edentula*. What lies undiscovered in other non-blood-feeding groups remains an exciting prospect.

For background information *see* ANNELIDA; BLOOD; FIBRINOGEN; HIRUDINEA; OLIGOCHAETA; PHYLOGENY in the McGraw-Hill Encyclopedia of Science & Technology.   Mark E. Siddall

Bibliography. C. M. Halton, *Those Amazing Leeches*, Silver Burdett, 1990; M. L. Ives, A leech and his leeches, *Natural History*, December 1938; K. H. Mann, *Leeches (Hirudinea): Their Structure, Physiology, Ecology and Embryology*, Pergamon, New

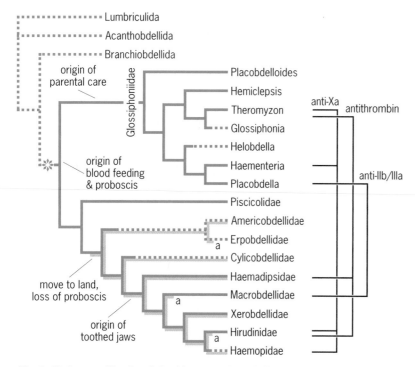

Fig. 3. Cladogram of leeches derived from use of morphological character data and DNA sequences from the nucleus and mitochondrion. This cladogram implies that the ancestral leech was a blood feeder using a proboscis and that the aquatic medicinal leeches returned to water (a) from a terrestrial ancestry (tinted lines). Parasitism on vertebrate blood has been lost several times in the evolution of leeches (broken lines). Known distributions of some anticoagulants are outlined to the right of the tree.

York, 1961; J. McClintock, Blood suckers, *Discover*, December 2001; R. T. Sawyer, *Leech Biology and Behaviour*, Clarendon Press, Oxford, 1986; W. Wordsworth, *The Leech Gatherer*, Wood and Innes, London, 1807.

Light rail and transport policies

There are many different definitions of light rail. Typically, a light rail system is defined as an urban electric railway that operates on its own right-of-way, not generally shared by other vehicles and pedestrians. The definition proposed by the European Conference of Ministers of Transport (ECMT), and used in this article, is: "A rail-borne form of transportation which can be developed in stages from a modern tramway to a rapid transit system operating its own right-of-way, underground, at ground level, or elevated. Each stage of development can be the final stage, but it should also permit development to the next higher stage."

Technically, a tramway is an earlier, sometimes lower-capacity form of light rail. It often shares the road space with other users. However, for the purposes of many studies, including the one described here, the terms light rail, tramway, and streetcar are used interchangeably.

The construction and extension of light rail today are among the most active public transportation issues that are being considered by many cities throughout the world. As a result, the use of international comparisons has become important in light rail policy development.

Comparing light rail and buses. When discussing new light rail systems or light rail extensions, there is disagreement whether other public transportation modes (such as buses) are as good or even better. The arguments are hardly ever value-free, and the strongest argument in favor of buses has been that they are cheaper and more flexible than light rail. A 2000 study by the author concluded that both bus and light rail transportation systems can increase ridership if high-density and high-quality service is provided, and if buses throughout the town have their own right-of-way. In addition, car parking has to be limited in the city center, and other car use restrictions have to be in place. Despite the similarity between bus and light rail the choice in Europe often has been in favor of trams (light rail vehicles) despite their higher costs and inflexibility, because other factors, such as design quality and redesign of the

Study cities or transport regions					
City	Country	Population in city (transport area), $\times 10^3$	Track-km of the total light rail systems in 1999 or 2000	Network density, track-km/pop., $\times 10^4$	Ranking
Europe					
Basel	Switzerland	192 (453)	88	1.9	3*
Birmingham/West Midlands	U.K.	966 (2,600)	20	0.1	22*
Bremen	Germany	544	63	1.2	14
Den Haag	Netherlands	564	130	2.3	15*
Dresden	Germany	467	131	2.8	12
Düsseldorf	Germany	569	145.5	2.6	7
Essen	Germany	605	70	1.2	13
Freiburg	Germany	201	27.5	1.4	1
Göteborg	Sweden	470	82	1.8	11
Greater Manchester	U.K.	415 (2,500)	37	0.4	22*
Hannover	Germany	523	114	2.2	6
Cologne	Germany	966	186	1.9	3*
Leipzig	Germany	517	153	3.0	20
Newcastle/Tyne and Wear	U.K.	273 (1,100)	56	0.5	18
Rouen	France	106 (390)	14	0.4	8*
Saarbrücken	Germany	190 (360)	20[†]	0.6	15*
Strasbourg	France	264 (451)	25[‡]	0.8	5
Zurich	Switzerland	361	68.5	1.9	2
North America					
Calgary	Canada	842	29	0.3	8*
Dallas	U.S.	1,904	34	0.2	24
Portland[¶]	U.S.	1,172	53	0.5	10
Sacramento[§]	U.S.	1,224	29	0.2	21
San Diego	U.S.	1,400 (2,000)	75	0.4	17
Australia					
Melbourne	Australia	3,417	220	0.6	19

*Two cities tied.
[†]Since October 2001: 28 km.
[‡]Of which 12.2 km opened in October 2000.
[¶]Oregon.
[§]County.

A tram in Strasbourg.

to population in a city or transport region, (2) the ratio of public transport passengers to population in a city or transport region, (3) growth in light rail use, (4) growth in public transport use, (5) the ratio of light rail passengers to total system track (km), (6) the ratio of annual light rail passenger trips (km) to total system track (km).

Results. Of the 24 cities or transport areas, seven cities were at the top of the ranking list, 10 in the middle, and 7 at the bottom (see table). There was only one modern tram system in the top list, Strasbourg in France (see **illus.**). All the others were traditional light rail systems, with most of them located in Switzerland and Germany. The probable reasons for the greater success of the traditional light rail systems are that car restriction measures have been in place longer in these cities, and the integration of the light rail and bus systems is also more advanced.

Many of the cities ranked near or at the bottom are suffering from fragmentation and deregulation of their rail transportation systems as a result of privatization in the mid-1980s. They also lack integrated ticketing. The most successful of the United States transport areas was Portland, Oregon, which ranked 10th. In general, establishing new public transport systems has been much harder in the United States than in Europe, as reliance on car use has been greater in the United States.

Analysis. After ranking, an attempt was made to explain the ranking according to a range of operational factors such as headway (trains per hour), average speed, fares, park and ride spaces, percentage of passengers using monthly passes, as well as demographic factors such as the population density along the light rail routes in 300- and 600-m (1000- and 2000-ft) corridors. In addition, "hard" complementary factors, such as the scale of car traffic restrictions, and the number of public car parking spaces in the city center, were studied. Finally, the "soft" complementary measures, such as the percentage of modern to traditional light rail vehicles, were analyzed.

The available data allowed the effects of nine different influences to be examined, using correlation and multivariate regression methods. Of those, four factors seemed to have had a significant effect on whether a light rail network was successful in terms of attracting public transportation passengers. They were (1) a high level of monthly pass use, (2) a low monthly fare relative to the country's gross domestic product per capita, (3) a large pedestrian area in the city center, and (4) a high population density along the light rail corridor.

These four factors often reinforced each other. In many cases, cities with large pedestrian areas have high population densities along the light rail corridors and high rail pass use. Both high rail pass use and low monthly fares through large carrestricted areas are purely political decisions adopted by local public transportation and land-use planners.

Interpretation. The spatial structure and geographical nature of a city influence the likelihood of success of any new light rail investment, and as a

city center and arterial streets, appear to be more important. That is, the modern design of the trams (including features such as large glass windows and doors) and the redesign of the city center (less space for cars through the light rail corridor, or car restriction zones where only cyclists and public transportation are allowed) are considered improvements that are worth their extra cost.

International study of 24 cities. As a continuation of the 2000 study, an analysis was made of public transportation and light rail systems in 24 cities worldwide (see **table**). Most of these cities are located in Europe, while four are in the United States, and one each in Canada and Australia.

About half of the cities or transport areas had traditional light rail systems. That is, the networks were built at the end of the nineteenth century and had been in continuous use since. However, most of them had been modernized during the last 20–30 years. The remaining half of the cities or transport areas had modern light rail systems, most of which had been built during the last 10–20 years. One (Tyne and Wear in the United Kingdom) was completed in 1984, and is more of a metro (underground) style than a light rail system.

Only cities which had light rail and no underground were included (cities with both underground and light rail, or cities that have only underground, were excluded). All the cities studied had an additional network of buses, and most of them also had a suburban rail network.

Criteria. The goal of this study was to explain and clarify why some light rail systems were more successful than others. Success was measured by passenger use and growth in passenger numbers, and was achieved in a number of ways. The six main indicators of light rail and public transport use were: (1) the ratio of the number of light rail passengers

result systems should be designed to follow the greatest population densities where this is practical. Consistent complementary measures, especially in relation to car traffic restrictions and the level of integration of public transportation, are likely to be more important. It was especially striking that higher monthly pass use led to more successful public transportation operation. A relatively low-priced multiple trip pass supported high use, in effect through making extra journeys free.

For overall strategic approaches, seven cities emerged as being particularly useful as light rail models, namely, Freiburg, Zurich, Basel, Cologne, Strasbourg, Hannover, and Düsseldorf, together with the top-ranked cities in the second group, Rouen and Calgary. Still, there are other examples of success in quite different circumstances, so that cities need not be discouraged if their circumstances differ from these cases. For example, French cities are starting to provide the most appropriate models for urban design, new light rail investment, and car traffic restriction.

Further statistical methods (factor analysis in grouping and weighting of dependent and explanatory variables, and factor scores in regression analysis) were used, but the basic findings did not change. They reinforced the conclusion that the technical performance of light rail seemed to play a very little role in either the accumulated level of public transportation and light rail performances or its recent growth. Successful and intensively used public transportation requires car traffic restraint and integrated transportation policies.

For background information *see* BUS; RAILROAD ENGINEERING; SUBWAY ENGINEERING; TRANSPORTATION ENGINEERING in the McGraw-Hill Encyclopedia of Science & Technology.   Carmen Hass-Klau

Bibliography. C. Hass-Klau et al., *Bus or Light Rail: Making the Right Choice*, ETP, Brighton, 2000; C. Hass-Klau and G. Crampton, *Future of Urban Transport: Learning from Success and Weakness: Light Rail*, ETP, Brighton, 2002; *Light Rail Transit Systems*, ECMT, Paris, 1994; T. Pattison (ed.), *Jane's Urban Transport Systems 2000-2001*, Coulsdon, Surrey, 2000.

Loran

Loran is a ground-based radionavigation system, with signals that propagate along the surface of the Earth (groundwaves) and reflect off the ionosphere to return to the Earth's surface (skywaves). Groundwaves and skywaves impinge on a receiver, together with other noise present in the spectrum at frequencies around 100 kHz (such as noise from nearby power lines or lightning). In general, groundwaves are useful for navigation purposes, but skywaves contribute unwanted noise and distort groundwaves. In order to resolve the most useful groundwaves accurately and to reduce noise introduced by skywaves, less useful groundwaves, and other interference sources, a

modern Loran receiver must track, separate, and process all these signals simultaneously to achieve the performance now possible.

A modern Loran system can operate as an independent backup to the global positioning satellite system (GPS) in all modalities (aviation, marine, terrestrial, and timing applications), and the systems are synergistic. For example, GPS can be used to generate ground conductivity correction factors that greatly enhance Loran's absolute accuracy, and Loran can be used to transmit differential GPS corrections and integrity messages to improve GPS performance.

Loran services in the United States are operated by the Department of Transportation, and Loran support was to be discontinued in 2000. However, due to numerous studies on GPS vulnerabilities and national security concerns regarding dependence on a sole-means GPS system, the Department of Transportation has extended Loran operations for the foreseeable future.

Meanwhile Loran receiver technology made major advances over the last decade, largely due to contemporary digital signal processing (DSP) hardware and software. However, Loran is a system composed of the transmitter-control infrastructure and the individual receiver, and Loran receiver performance is currently limited by an antiquated infrastructure. Fortunately, the United States Loran infrastructure modernization will be completed in a few years, and results discussed here will improve when that modernization is complete.

Modern Loran receivers. Older Loran receivers were typically hybrid analog-digital devices with little processing power. Most tracked only 5-7 Loran stations and had limited signal-resolution and noise-handling capabilities. In contrast, modern Loran receivers are DSP-based and all-in-view, meaning they track up to 40 stations simultaneously and use DSP technology to enhance useful signals and remove or reduce unwanted noise.

All-in-view capability. Tracking all these stations might appear to be overkill, but in fact is necessary. Loran's relatively low-frequency signals travel great distances with little attenuation, so a receiver can track distant as well as nearby stations. Moreover, signals from distant transmitters are often significantly stronger than those from nearby transmitters, and those signal levels can vary rapidly, depending on topography, weather, time of day, transmitter power levels, and so forth. Identifying, quantifying and, in some cases, removing other Loran signals, plus other background noise, is a complex process requiring sophisticated software and hardware.

Data from an all-in-view receiver illustrate this point. **Table 1** shows data from 6 of 35 stations across the United States and Canada tracked simultaneously in Madison, Wisconsin. Signals from the Caribou, Maine, transmitter, 1076 mi (1731 km) distant, and the Nantucket, Massachusetts, transmitter, 1000 mi (1609 km) distant, have signal-to-noise ratios that differ by 15 dB (a factor of about 6), despite transmission paths that are only 76 mi (122 km) different. **Table 2** shows just a few of the skywave

TABLE 1. Data from 6 of 35 stations simultaneously tracked by an all-in-view receiver in Madison, Wisconsin

Chain/station*	Location	Distance from receiver, mi†	Signal-to-noise ratio, dB	Time of arrival‡
5930Y	Cape Race, Canada	1775	−13	32510363
7980Y	Jupiter, FL	1224	−5	47121889
9610W	Searchlight, NV	1462	−15	31890672
9960W	Caribou, ME	1076	−11	16173428
9960X	Nantucket, MA	1000	4	28933526
9960Z	Dana, IN	245	23	55068549

*The four digits are the chain's group rate interval (GRI), and the letter is the station identifier.
†1 mi = 1.609 km.
‡Time difference between the master station and identified station.

and groundwave signals that can be received at Fairbanks, Alaska. Here, groundwaves from Shoal Cove, Alaska, 862 mi (1387 km) from Fairbanks, are 17 dB μV/m (that is, the magnitude of the electric field vector is 17 decibels above the reference level of 1 μV/m); but skywaves from Ejde, Norway, 3441 mi distant, are 44 dB μV/m. Since Shoal Cove signals are more important to the Alaskan user than Ejde signals, the all-in-view receiver must be able to remove the much larger Ejde signal without distorting the smaller but essential Shoal Cove signal.

Processing capability. All-in-view receivers address this fundamental problem by removing background noise and resolving nearby Loran signals much more effectively than older receivers. Effective signal-to-noise ratios are improved by about 24 dB (a factor of about 16) for the closest 10–15 Loran signals most important to navigation. This is a huge improvement and enhances Loran accuracy, dynamics, reliability, coverage, and so forth. Representative DSP processes include:

1. *Crossrate interference cancellation.* Groundwaves from distant Loran stations generate crossrate interference, and since crossrate is predictable, it can be digitally identified and removed.
2. *Adaptive skywave compensation.* Loran skywaves vary rapidly and fluctuate greatly in size, frequency, and range in a manner that is not a simple function of transmitter power and distance. Special DSP techniques adapt to these changes in real time and compensate for skywave distortion of groundwaves.
3. *Adaptive digital filtering.* Strong, time-variant noise from non-Loran sources must be identified and removed, eliminating approximately 24 non-Loran interferers.
4. *Impulse noise blanking.* Impulsive noise emanates from a variety of sources, most commonly lightning, and can be digitally blanked. This information is processed so quickly that receiver recovery is virtually instantaneous, leaving the navigation function unaffected.

Performance. The overall performance improvement from all-in-view, DSP-based receivers is dramatic, as exemplified by two comparisons with older-technology receivers. All-in-view receivers are linear devices, which accurately resolve the time differences used to calculate receiver position to 1 nanosecond. Older receivers were hard-limited devices, only able to resolve time differences to 100 nanoseconds. Higher, more accurate time-difference resolution improves receiver accuracy, and in fact, all-in-view receivers identified the need for more accurate control of the Loran infrastructure. (Previously, monitoring receivers based on the older

TABLE 2. Data from a few of the Loran transmitters tracked by an all-in-view receiver located in Fairbanks, Alaska

Group rate interval (GRI)/Chain name	Station*	Distance from receiver, mi†	Signal level‡
7960 / Gulf of Alaska	TOK (M)	185	78 (G)
	Narrow Cape (X)	533	54 (G)
	Shoal Cove (Y)	862	17 (G)
8290 / North-Central U.S.	Havre (M)	1774	44 (S)
	Baudette (W)	2225	48 (S)
	Gillette (X)	2162	31 (S)
	Williams Lake (Y)	1268	54 (S)
	Port Clarence (Z)	555	54 (G)
7970 / Norwegian Sea	Ejde (M)	3441	44 (S)
	Bo (W)	3188	33 (S)
	Sandur (Y)	3055	41 (S)
	Jan Mayen (Z)	2872	30 (S)

*The letter (M, W, X, Y, Z) is the station identifier.
†1 mi = 1.609 km.
‡Maximum signal level (in decibels above 1 μV/m) reached during a 24-hour recording period. G indicates groundwave and S indicates skywave signals.

technology had masked these control problems.) Another useful comparison is envelope-to-cycle difference (ECD), which a receiver uses to determine the correct zero crossing of the Loran pulse for the time-difference measurement. All-in-view receivers have improved ECD noise by a factor of 6 or more, meaning they need to average only 1/36 as many samples as older-technology receivers. In practice, this advance means that dynamic receiver perfor-

mance is greatly improved, and cycle slips (that is, identification of an incorrect zero crossing) are virtually nonexistent in modern receivers.

Flight test data. Some performance improvements seen with all-in-view technology are shown in data obtained by the Federal Aviation Administration's Technology Center (FAATC) during flight tests comparing all-in-view receiver performance with GPS and legacy Loran receiver performance (**Fig. 1**). In

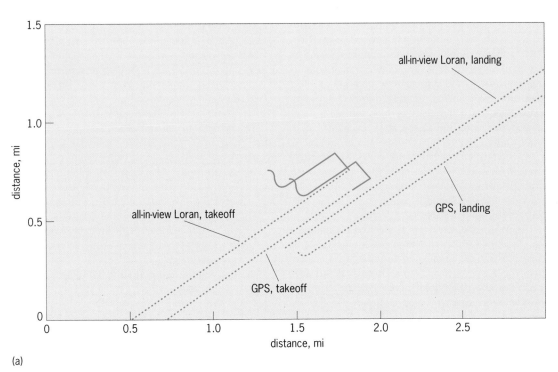

(a)

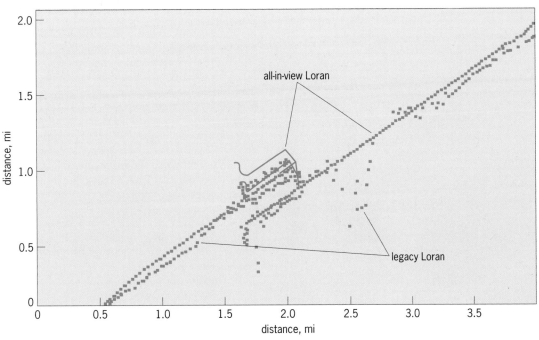

(b)

Fig. 1. Takeoff and landing data from Sacramento, California, airport taken during flight tests conducted to compare GPS, all-in-view Loran, and legacy Loran receivers. A computer logged data from each receiver once every second, and these data are plotted as points showing the aircraft locations given by the receivers at 1-s time intervals on a map covering the area of the airport. (*a*) All-in-view Loran and GPS data. (*b*) All-in-view Loran and legacy Loran data only.

an 8-day trial in August 2001, the FAATC flew northern and southern routes over the continental United States, including a leg to Anchorage, Alaska. A computer logged data from each receiver once every second, and representative data from the takeoff and landing at Sacramento, California, are graphed. It is immediately evident that the all-in-view and GPS data are quite similar except for a consistent offset in positions generated by the two receivers (Fig. 1a).

This offset is largely due to Loran signal propagation delays caused by land, which are a function of the conductivity of the land path between the Loran transmitters and the receiver. Additional secondary factor (ASF) corrections are introduced to compensate for these delays; they are analogous to the ionospheric and tropospheric corrections used to improve GPS accuracy. Since ground conductivity tends to vary slowly, mostly as the result of seasonal cycles, individual time delays between transmitters and specified geographic positions can be measured periodically to form a map of ASF corrections, which an all-in-view receiver can apply in real time. The Federal Aviation Administration and U.S. Coast Guard are currently developing a plan to produce an ASF map for the United States.

The most salient feature of the two data sets in Fig. 1a is their remarkable similarity in form. If ASF corrections were applied to the all-in-view Loran data, these points would superimpose on the GPS track. For contrast, simultaneous data from an all-in-view and a legacy receiver are shown in Fig. 1b with GPS data removed for clarity. The performance improvement provided by all-in-view technology is obvious, even ignoring ASF corrections. Subsequent flight data, collected and processed with ASF corrections included, show that the all-in-view Loran solution can be within 5–10 m (15–30 ft) of a GPS

solution corrected by the Wide Area Augmentation System (in terms of the cross-track difference, the horizontal difference between the parallel Loran and GPS tracks).

Modern Loran antennas. Loran receiver performance is highly dependent upon antenna performance, and technology has mainly advanced in magnetic, or H-field, antennas. The primary reason for developing H-field antenna technology is that magnetic antennas are immune to precipitation-static (P-static) noise that can occur on an airplane during stormy weather. Under these conditions, ionized particles accumulate on an airplane's skin, often generating potentials in the 20,000–40,000-volt range. The spontaneous discharge of these high potentials disrupts reception by Loran E-field antennas; thus, H-field antennas have a distinct advantage in aviation.

H-field antennas also have several other important advantages:

1. Theoretically, they have an inherent 3-decibel advantage in signal-to-noise ratio over E-field antennas, which can be significant, particularly in marginal situations.
2. They produce lower ECD values, so identification of the correct zero crossing is more rapid and reliable.
3. They require no grounding, which means H-field antennas are easier to install and will operate closer to the ground.
4. H-field antennas can be quite small; they can be integrated with a GPS antenna into a single unit (**Fig. 2**).

The advantages of an H-field antenna come with a price, mainly in the demands that the antenna places on the associated receiver. For example, the antennas are polarized, which requires the receiver to "steer" them in some manner. Fortunately, DSP-based receivers have the processing power to meet these demands, and both receiver and antenna technologies have advanced overall Loran system performance.

Tests on a combined GPS/Loran H-field prototype antenna (Fig. 2) have demonstrated that neither GPS nor Loran reception is compromised by the presence of the other antenna. Thus, GPS and Loran are synergistic systems that complement one another. A combined system provides performance advantages over any single system and eliminates sole-means vulnerabilities. Loran receiver technology will continue to advance, and integrated GPS/Loran systems will be demonstrated in 2003.

For background information see ANTENNA (ELECTROMAGNETISM); LORAN; RADIO-WAVE PROPAGATION; SATELLITE NAVIGATION SYSTEMS in the McGraw-Hill Encyclopedia of Science & Technology.

G. Linn Roth

Bibliography. J. D. Last and P. Williams, Loran-C for European non-precision aircraft approaches, *Proceedings of the 30th Annual Convention and*

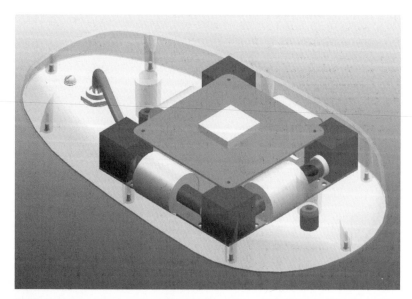

Fig. 2. Mechanical drawing of a combined GPS and Loran H-field (magnetic) antenna. The combined unit has been mounted in a certified radome to expedite aviation tests, and the GPS microstrip patch antenna is positioned in the center of the Loran antenna. The dimensions of the H-field antenna are 130 × 130 × 50 mm (5 × 5 × 2 in.).

Technical Symposium of the International Loran Association, October 2001; B. Peterson et al., Integrated GPS/Loran: Structure and Issues, *Navig., J. Inst. Navig.*, 45(3):183-194, Fall 1998; G. L. Roth, The case for Loran, *J. Air Traf. Control*, 41(3):24-28, 1999; G. L. Roth et al., Performance of DSP-Loran/H-field antenna system and implications for complementing GPS, *Proceedings of the National Technical Meeting of the Institute of Navigation*, January 2002; G. L. Roth and P. W. Schick, New Loran capabilities enhance performance of hybridized GPS/Loran receivers, *Navig., J. Inst. Navig.*, 46(4):249-260, Winter 1999.

Magnesium diboride superconductors

Magnesium diboride, MgB_2, superconducts below a critical temperature of 39 K (−389°F). It is a simple binary compound made of two of the more abundant elements in the Earth's crust. Although the compound has been known for decades, superconductivity in MgB_2 was discovered only in 2001. Since then, MgB_2 has become one of the most promising superconducting materials because of its high critical temperature, low normal-state resistivity, and relatively high critical field and critical current density, which can be further increased by the addition of impurities.

BCS theory. In order to understand the significance of MgB_2, it is important to review some of the basics of the Bardeen-Cooper-Schrieffer (BCS) theory of superconductivity. According to this theory, the superconducting state occurs due to an attraction between conduction electrons that is mediated by lattice vibrations, that is, phonons. As one electron moves through the crystal, it distorts the positively charged ions that make up the lattice. This much slower moving distortion, with its net positive charge, will then attract a second electron. This attractive interaction between electrons leads to the formation of the superconducting state below a critical temperature, T_c.

One of the most important predictions of the BCS theory is given by the equation

$$k_B T_c = 1.13\hbar\omega_D \, \exp[-1/VN(E_F)]$$

where ω_D is the characteristic frequency of the lattice vibrations, V is proportional to the strength of the coupling between the electrons and the lattice vibrations, and $N(E_F)$ is the density of electronic states at the Fermi surface, which, for the purposes of this discussion, can be taken as a measure of the number of electrons able to participate in the superconducting state; k_B and $\hbar$ are the Boltzmann constant and Planck's constant divided by 2π, respectively. Within this simple model, T_c increases [linearly with ω_D and exponentially with V and $N(E_F)$] if the value of any these three parameters increases.

This equation contains within it the prediction of an isotope effect: the shift of the value of T_c with

the isotopic mass of the elements used to make the compound. If the lattice is modeled as a collection of masses (the atoms) connected by springs (the bonds), the characteristic frequency ω_D is inversely proportional to the square root of the atomic masses, that is, $\omega_D \propto 1/\sqrt{M}$. Within this simple model, T_c will increase as the isotopic masses of the elements decrease. Historically, the experimental determination of the isotope effect was a clear demonstration that lattice vibrations were involved in the formation of the superconducting state and this was one of the key experiments that originally motivated the formulation of the BCS theory.

Isotope effect in MgB_2. When superconductivity with $T_c \sim 40$ K was discovered in MgB_2, a question was whether this was conventional BCS superconductivity similar to that found in the A15 materials (such as Nb_3Sn) and other intermetallic compounds, or another example of the exotic, as yet poorly understood superconductivity found in the high-T_c oxides. Experiments on isotopically pure samples of $Mg^{11}B_2$ and $Mg^{10}B_2$ (**Fig. 1**) showed that there was a large isotope effect, fully consistent with the BCS theory. These measurements as well as subsequent

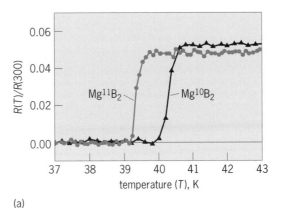

(a)

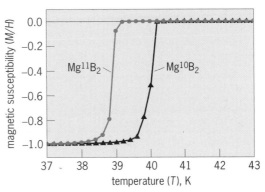

(b)

Fig. 1. Temperature-dependent properties of isotopically pure $Mg^{11}B_2$ and $Mg^{10}B_2$ sintered pellets made by diffusing magnesium vapor into ^{11}B and ^{10}B powders. These data show a 1.0-K shift in the critical temperature T_c, with the lighter $Mg^{10}B_2$ having the higher superconducting transition temperature. (*a*) Ratio of electrical resistance, $R(T)$, to $R(300)$, the resistance at 300 K (80°F). (*b*) Magnetic susceptibility (the ratio of magnetization M to applied magnetic field H). °F = (K × 1.8) −459.67.

experimental and theoretical work have firmly placed MgB$_2$ as an extreme example of phonon-mediated BCS superconductivity.

Extreme example of BCS superconductivity. The remarkably high value of T_c in MgB$_2$, combined with the fact that it has a relatively small value of $N(E_F)$, indicates that one way to search for other extreme examples of BCS superconductivity is to try to optimize the electron-phonon coupling parameter, V, and characteristic lattice vibration frequency, ω_D, without too much concern about $N(E_F)$. This is a very different approach from many of the historical searches that emphasized optimizing $N(E_F)$ and ω_D first. Deemphasizing the importance of $N(E_F)$ allows many classes of compounds that do not contain transition-metal elements to become viable candidates for high-T_c intermetallic superconductors. Whether other intermetallic superconductors with comparable or higher values of T_c can be found remains to be seen.

Normal-state resistivity of MgB$_2$. The temperature-dependent resistivity of a dense MgB$_2$ wire segment is shown in **Fig. 2**. The resistivity (particularly just above T_c) is remarkably low, especially given the very high value of T_c for this compound. This goes against the general trend that good superconductors generally have poor normal-state conductivities. This rare combination of a high value of T_c and a low normal-state resistivity stems from the fact that there are two distinct conduction bands, each with its own electron-phonon coupling, which take turns acting as electrical shorts for each other.

Critical fields and current densities. The physical properties of MgB$_2$ are both promising and intrigu-

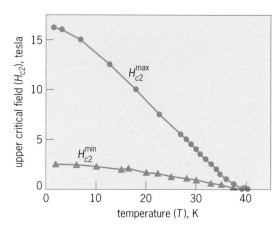

Fig. 3. Superconducting upper critical field, H_{c2} (T), for high-purity MgB$_2$. The upper critical field is anisotropic, and the curves H_{c2}^{min} and H_{c2}^{max} represent H_{c2} for grains that have the magnetic field aligned parallel and perpendicular to the crystallographic c axis, respectively.

ing. The upper critical field, H_{c2}, is shown as a function of temperature in **Fig. 3**. The upper critical field is the applied magnetic field above which the (bulk) superconductivity vanishes. The upper curve is the value of H_{c2} measured on a pure, polycrystalline sample of dense wire, using zero resistivity as the criterion for determining $H_{c2}(T)$. The upper critical field of MgB$_2$ is actually anisotropic, with the lower curve in Fig. 3 showing the value, H_{c2}^{min}, of the upper critical field for grains that have the applied field aligned parallel to the crystallographic c axis. The upper curve represents the value, H_{c2}^{max}, of the upper critical field both for polycrystalline samples and for grains that have the applied field aligned perpendicular to the crystallographic c axis, that is, for the field applied in the hexagonal basal plane of the unit cell. This anisotropy is thought to arise from the highly anisotropic nature of the electronic bands in this material.

The critical current density, J_c, of dense, high-purity MgB$_2$ wire reaches 10^6 A/cm^2 at low temperature and low magnetic field ($T = 5$ K, $H = 0$). For reference the critical current density of Nb$_3$Sn (one of the classic A15 intermetallic superconductors) at $T = 4.2$ K and $H = 1$ T is about 4×10^5 A/cm^2, whereas for MgB$_2$ it is about 10^5 A/cm^2. While the critical current density of high-purity MgB$_2$ is lower than that of Nb$_3$Sn, this parameter can be increased by judicious addition of impurities, as will be discussed below. Moreover, the critical current density of MgB$_2$ is nearly as high as that of Nb$_3$Sn at low fields and low temperatures and, of course, is much larger that that of Nb$_3$Sn for temperatures near or above 20 K (because Nb$_3$Sn becomes a normal metal at this temperature).

Promise of MgB$_2$ as a superconductor. The temperature dependencies of many of the material properties of a superconductor tend to saturate for temperatures below $\frac{1}{2}T_c$. Therefore, a superconductor just needs to be cooled to about $\frac{1}{2}T_c$ in order to

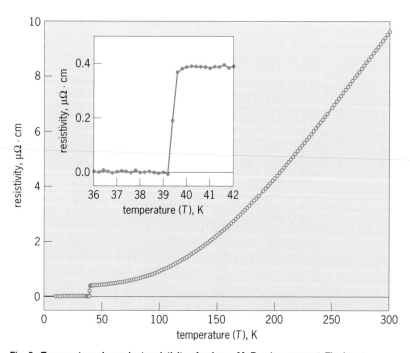

Fig. 2. Temperature-dependent resistivity of a dense MgB$_2$ wire segment. The inset shows the resistivity for temperatures near T_c. $^\circ$F = (K × 1.8) − 459.67.

have near-optimal performance. For the A15 compounds this temperature ends up being very close to the boiling point of helium (4.2 K or $-452°$F), and such cooling generally requires the use of liquid helium as a cryogen. On the other hand, using this $\frac{1}{2}T_c$ criterion, MgB_2 needs to be cooled to only about 20 K ($-424°$F). This is a temperature readily achieved by closed-cycle refrigerators (often referred to as Displex systems). The fact that MgB_2 can be a useful superconductor at temperatures provided by a simple closed-cycle cooling system is one of the primary reasons that it is such a promising practical superconductor.

Another reason is its very low normal-state resistivity. The relatively high values of normal-state resistivity generally associated with high values of T_c have led to the need to encase high-current-density superconducting wires in low-resistivity, nonsuperconducting metal sheaths to protect them against resistive heating in case of a sudden reversion to the normal state (for example, due to a loss of cooling power). In the case of MgB_2, the remarkably low normal-state resistivity just above T_c, about 0.5 $\mu\Omega$-cm, is comparable with that of copper wire, and means that there will be very little need to protect the superconducting wire against resistive heating in the normal state (a very serious problem with A15 as well as the high-T_c superconductors).

Finally, both H_{c2} and J_c are materials properties that often can be readily changed by the addition of impurities. There are indications that H_{c2} may be increased by factors of 2, and J_c values of up to 10^7 A/cm^2 have been observed in MgB_2 thin films.

Synthesis of MgB$_2$. Magnesium diboride has been synthesized in the form of sintered pellets, thin films, and wire. In addition, there have been successes in growing small (much smaller than 1 mm^3) single crystals. One of the easiest ways of synthesizing MgB_2 is by reacting elemental boron (in powder, film, or filament form) with magnesium vapor, generally at temperatures near 950°C (1740°F). This gives rise to MgB_2 powders, films, or wire segments (**Fig. 4**).

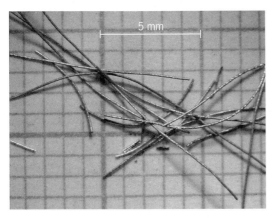

Fig. 4. MgB$_2$ wire segments photographed with a 1-mm grid. These wire segments are about 200 micrometers in diameter and were synthesized by reacting a boron filament with 950°C (1740°F) magnesium vapor.

Recent reports indicate that meter-length, multifilament MgB_2 wires can be synthesized via conventional, powder-in-tube techniques with critical current densities high enough to allow the construction of a 3-tesla solenoid that would operate at 20 K. This is precisely the field range of interest for medical imaging magnets and is close to the field range of interest for the next generation of particle accelerator magnets. In both of these cases, the lighter weight and higher operating temperature of MgB_2 make it a potentially appealing replacement material for Nb_3Sn or other currently used intermetallic superconductors.

There have also been substantial advances in the synthesis of thin films of MgB_2. These efforts give rise to the strong possibility that MgB_2 will also be a useful material for the synthesis of superconducting devices such as SQUIDs and radio-frequency filters. Both of these applications require relatively small cooling power, and therefore the fact that MgB_2 can be cooled via closed-cycle refrigeration makes it an attractive material.

For background information *see* A15 PHASES; BAND THEORY OF SOLIDS; FERMI SURFACE; LATTICE VIBRATIONS; MEDICAL IMAGING; PARTICLE ACCELERATOR; PHONON; SUPERCONDUCTING DEVICES; SUPERCONDUCTIVITY in the McGraw-Hill Encyclopedia of Science & Technology.   Paul C. Canfield; Sergey Bud'ko

Bibliography. S. L. Bud'ko et al., Boron isotope effect in superconducting MgB_2, *Phys. Rev. Lett.*, 86:1877–1880, February 26, 2001; P. C. Canfield et al., Superconductivity in dense MgB_2 wires, *Phys. Rev. Lett.*, 86:2423–2426, March 12, 2001; J. Nagamatsu et al., Superconductivity at 39 K in magnesium diboride, *Nature*, 410: 63–64, March 1, 2001.

Manipulating cold atoms

It is now routine for scientists to use laser light for cooling clouds of alkali atoms to temperatures in the range 1–100 microkelvins, and for subsequent evaporation in the dark to lower these temperatures by a further factor of 100. When held in sufficiently small traps and guides, atoms this cold can no longer be considered as classical particles following Newton's laws of motion. Instead, they behave as quantum waves that diffract and interfere with each other. It is now possible to hold cold atoms magnetically in microscopic traps or guides formed above a surface. This suggests a technology based on the controlled flow and interaction of cold atoms which may use the laws of quantum mechanics to accomplish new feats of measurement or computation. These devices are known as atom chips. At present, the chips are quite primitive, but even so they are generating great excitement because the idea has immense potential.

Miniature magnetic guides. Alkali atoms have an odd, unpaired electron and are therefore magnetic.

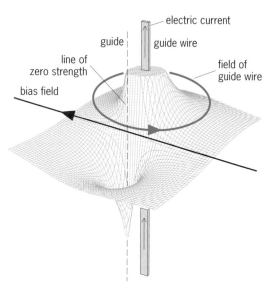

electric current

guide   guide wire

line of
zero strength

field of
guide wire

bias field

Fig. 1. The magnetic field circulating around a current-carrying guide wire can be canceled by adding a constant bias field. The total magnetic field strength (mesh) has a line of zero strength parallel to the wire which makes a guide for weak-field-seeking atoms.

When prepared with their magnetic moments pointing opposite to a magnetic field, they are attracted to the place where the field is weakest. This allows cold alkali atoms to be manipulated magnetically. To make an atom guide, a thin wire typically 10 micrometers in width can be fabricated on a semiconductor substrate such as silicon or on a dielectric such as glass using the standard lithographic techniques of microelectronics. With a current of 0.25 A flowing in the wire, the magnetic field 50 μm away from the surface is 1 millitesla parallel to the surface (**Fig. 1**). Farther away than this the field is weaker, and closer to the surface it is stronger. In order to form an atom guide, a uniform bias field of 1 mT is applied in the opposite direction, canceling the wire field to make a line of zero field 50 μm away from the surface. Cold atoms placed near this line are guided along it. An atom passing through the line of zero field experiences a sudden reversal of the field direction, which its magnetic moment is unable to follow. This leaves the atom magnetized parallel to the field instead of antiparallel, and the magnetic force then expels it from the guide. However, the addition of a small field of 10–100 μT along the guide allows the net field to change direction less abruptly across the center, and avoids this loss.

An atom held in this guide is free to move along the length of it, but any movement away from the center is counteracted by a restoring force, which causes the atom to oscillate from side to side at a frequency f of roughly 10 kHz. This frequency determines the characteristic energy E of quantum-physics effects in the guide through the relation $E = hf$, where h is Planck's constant. The side-to-side motion of the atom is restricted by quantum mechanics to specific quantum states that have the particular energies E,

$2E$, $3E$, and so forth. In a gas at 1 μK the energy available for transverse vibration is almost the same as E. (The temperature of a gas is a measure of how much energy it has in any particular motion.) This means that a gas much colder than 1 μK traveling in the guide could only be in the lowest vibrational quantum state with little possibility of higher-energy motion because the atoms do not have the energy hf needed to jump up to the first excited state. Once the transverse motion is frozen out in this way, the only freedom of movement the atoms have is along the length of the guide. This single-mode operation is closely analogous to the propagation of light in a single-mode optical fiber or microwaves in a transmission line.

A strong gradient of magnetic field in the guide makes the oscillation frequency of atoms high enough for quantum effects to become important. The large field gradient of 20 T/m in the guide described here is achieved by its being close to a narrow wire. Doubling the bias field to 2 mT would roughly halve the distance between the current-carrying wire and the guide, and would give a four times higher transverse oscillation frequency. This scaling works as long as the width of the wire is much smaller than the distance away from the wire. Miniaturization is therefore the key. Magnetic recording media offer an alternative way to achieve strong confinement. For example, miniature magnetic patterns recorded on videotape have been used to make atom guides with frequencies approaching 1 MHz.

Atom chips. The idea of using miniaturization to achieve strong field gradients came independently and almost simultaneously from several origins. In 1995, E. Hinds and his colleagues used miniature patterns on videotape to make strong field gradients to reflect cold atoms. In the same year, K. Libbrecht and J. Weinstein pointed out that microscopic wires on a chip could also produce very tightly confining traps and guides. Following this, many groups started fabricating microscopic wires on sapphire, ceramic, and semiconductor substrates and learning how to pass high currents through the wires without blowing them up.

By the end of 2000, several groups had succeeded in making and demonstrating atom chips. An example from the group of J. Reichel and T. Hänsch is shown in **Fig. 2**. The chip is used in a high vacuum, where atoms from a pulse of rubidium vapor are laser-cooled and collected in a magneto-optical trap several millimeters above the surface. Current in the U-shaped loop at the bottom left of the chip pulls the atoms magnetically down to the surface, where they are passed into the magnetic traps and guides formed by the thinner wires. The main guide is made by flowing current along the central wire and adding a bias field. Two end wires perpendicular to this make a field along the main guide that can be used to push atoms away from the ends so that the guide becomes a trap. The two square-wave patterns of wire form a

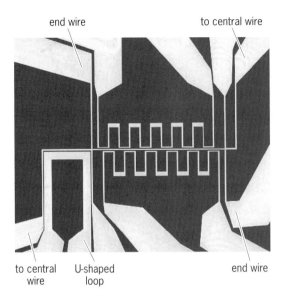

end wire   to central wire

to central   U-shaped   end wire
wire   loop

Fig. 2. Chip for manipulating cold atoms.

miniature motor used to transport atoms along the main guide. Alternating currents that are $90°$ out of phase with each other push the atoms to the left or right depending on which wire has the leading phase.

Chips such as this and chips based on microscopic patterns of permanent magnets have been able to perform a wide variety of manipulations: splitting clouds of atoms into two or more smaller clouds, transporting the smaller clouds to various different sites, and shooting them at each other to observe collisions. Recently it has become possible to reach the low temperatures of single-mode propagation where transverse vibrations are suppressed. This has brought the goal of building quantum circuits, using cold atoms that flow and interact within the guides and traps of an atom chip, close to realization.

Quantum circuits with atoms. An example of a simple quantum circuit is the atom interferometer. An atom guide splits into two, thus splitting the quantum wave that describes each atom. The two parts propagate separately for a while before the double guide once again becomes one and the parts of the wave are recombined. The final state of each atom depends on the phase difference accumulated by the quantum waves along the two paths. If no phase difference is accumulated while the wave function is split, recombination returns the atoms to the ground state of the guide, but a phase shift of π leaves them vibrationally excited. Recent studies show that this kind of atom interferometer on a chip could be spectacularly sensitive to gravity and rotations, and could become a powerful tool in fields ranging from mineral prospecting to navigation. *See* ATOM INTERFEROMETER; MAGNETIC WAVEGUIDE.

A more extreme example of quantum circuits with atoms is the concept of a quantum computer. The idea is that each atom floating above an atom chip can store a quantum bit, or qubit, that has the ability to represent logical values 0 and 1, both at the same time. If n of these atoms form an array of qubits, they jointly have the capacity to store any or all of the numbers between 1 and 2^n simultaneously. These complicated many-particle quantum states—entangled states—are at the heart of quantum computing. They give the quantum computer immense power by allowing it to perform a very large number of calculations at the same time. With this in mind, many research groups are working to load arrays of miniature traps with a single atom in each trap rather than a cold cloud. The detailed architecture of such a computer is still far from clear, but the present techniques for preparing atoms with nanokelvin temperatures and confining them on the nanometer scale are already sufficient to make this degree of quantum control a possibility.

For background information *see* INTEGRATED CIRCUITS; INTERFERENCE OF WAVES; MAGNETIC RECORDING; MAGNETISM; OPTICAL FIBERS; PARTICLE TRAP; QUANTUM MECHANICS; WAVEGUIDE in the McGraw-Hill Encyclopedia of Science & Technology.

Edward A. Hinds

Bibliography. C. S. Adams and E. Riis, Laser cooling and trapping of neutral atoms, *Prog. Quant. Electr.*, 21:1, 1997; W. Hänsel et al., Bose-Einstein condensation on a microelectronic chip, *Nature*, 413:498–500, 2001; E. A. Hinds, Magnetic chips and quantum circuits for atoms, *Phys. World*, 14(7):39–43, July 2001; E. A. Hinds and I. G. Hughes, Magnetic atom optics: Mirrors, guides, traps and chips for atoms, *J. Phys. D*, 32:R119–R146, 1999; E. A. Hinds, C. J. Vale, and M. G. Boshier, Two-wire waveguide and interferometer for cold atoms, *Phys. Rev. Lett.*, 86:1462–1465, 2001.

Materials processing

Materials processing is the preparation and treatment of materials in order to obtain products with desired properties and characteristics. Raw materials, such as metals, glass, and plastics, are often transformed into useful shapes and configurations, or partially finished products are obtained through various processing techniques. The **table** lists some important materials processing operations, along with a few examples. Many materials processing techniques are based on the changes in the material characteristics resulting from the flow and temperature history to which the material is subjected. Processes such as extrusion, heat treatment, coating, optical-fiber drawing, crystal growing, plastic injection molding, and powder metallurgy are included in this area, which is generally referred to as thermal processing.

In recent years, there has been increased interest in specialized materials in fields such as medicine,

Common materials processing methods

Processes	Examples
Crystal growing	Czochralski, floating-zone, Bridgman
Polymer processing	Extrusion, injection molding, thermoforming
Reactive processing	Chemical vapor deposition, food processing
Powder processing	Powder metallurgy, sintering, sputtering
Glass processing	Optical-fiber drawing, glass blowing, annealing
Coating	Thermal spray coating, polymer coating
Heat treatment	Annealing, hardening, tempering, surface treatment, curing, baking
Forming operations	Hot rolling, wire drawing, metal forming, extrusion, forging
Cutting	Laser and gas cutting, fluid-jet cutting, grinding, machining
Bonding processes	Soldering, welding, explosive bonding, chemical bonding
Casting	Ingot casting, continuous casting
Others	Composite materials processing, microgravity materials processing, rapid prototyping processes

energy, biotechnology, transportation, telecommunications, and electronics. New materials, such as ceramics, composites, and a wide range of polymers, have replaced traditional materials such as metals and alloys in many applications. Growing international competition has led to advances in the methods for fabricating both traditional and new materials, in order to optimize existing processing techniques with respect to cost and product quality, and to develop new techniques.

Crystal growth. This is an important process since most semiconductor devices are fabricated from single crystals (same crystallographic orientation throughout) grown from the vapor phase or from molten material. The Czochralski method, in which the crystal is grown from the melt by gradually moving the solidified crystalline material away from the solid-liquid interface, has dominated the production of single crystals for microelectronics (**Fig. 1**). The fluid-flow phenomena involves buoyancy-driven convection in the melt due to temperature and con-

centration gradients, forced and mixed convection because of moving surfaces and materials, thermocapillary flows because of surface tension gradients, phase change, and thermal and mass transport processes.

The flows that arise in crystal growing can strongly affect the quality of the crystal and resulting semiconductor. Therefore, it is important to understand these flows and develop methods to minimize their effects. A proper control of the thermal process, particularly of the rate of cooling, is essential to maintain high crystal quality. Flow oscillations arise in many cases, and are prevented by process control. Though silicon crystals have been of particular interest in the fabrication of electronic devices, there has been growing interest in gallium-arsenide, indium-phosphide, and other such compounds because of their use in various electro-optic applications. In addition, three-dimensional effects, continuous growth systems, effects of thermal boundary conditions, and convection in high-pressure liquid-encapsulated Czochralski crystal growth have been investigated.

Several other crystal growth techniques, such as Bridgman crystal growth in which the furnace has an upper zone at temperatures above the melting point and a lower zone at temperatures below the melting point, have been developed.

Chemical vapor deposition. The deposition of thin films onto a solid substrate has become an important technique for the fabrication of microelectronic circuits, optical and magnetic devices, high-performance cutting and grinding tools, and solar cells. Though a relatively new method for materials processing, thin-film deposition has attracted the interest of many researchers because of the high quality of material generated, good control of the process, and overall efficiency of the process. In chemical vapor deposition (CVD), thin films are deposited from a gas phase onto a solid surface, and a chemical reaction takes place during the deposition process. The products of the reactions form a solid crystalline or amorphous layer on the substrate. The activation energy needed for the chemical reactions involved is provided by an external heat source. After material deposition on the surface, the

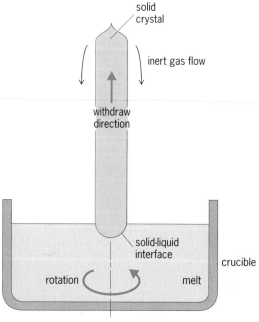

Fig. 1. Czochralski method for crystal growth.

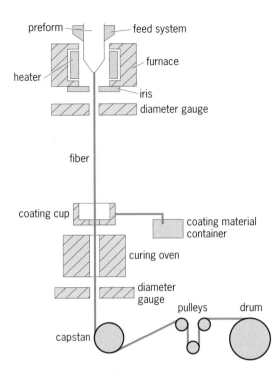

Fig. 2. Typical optical-fiber-drawing process.

Optical fibers. Optical-fiber drawing and coating processes have become critical for advancements in telecommunications and network communications.

Drawing. In this process, a cylindrical rod, which is specially fabricated to obtain a desired refractive index variation and which is called a preform, is heated and drawn into a fiber (**Fig. 2**). The diameter changes substantially, from several centimeters to about 125 micrometers, in a distance of only a few centimeters. The main interest in this process lies in obtaining high-quality optical fibers, as indicated by low concentration of process-induced defects, desired variation of refractive index, low tension, high strength, and other important measures, at high draw speeds. In recent years, the industry has been moving toward higher draw speeds and larger preform diameters, on the order of 20 m/s (65 ft/s) and 10 cm (4 in.), respectively, placing very stringent demands on the process. The quality of the fiber is largely determined by the flow and temperature history of the glass in the "neck-down" region, where the large reduction in diameter occurs; it is important to understand the underlying mechanisms in this region. For a given fiber and preform diameter at a given draw speed, the fiber must be drawn at a specific furnace wall temperature distribution. If the furnace temperature is not high enough, the fiber will break due to lack of material flow, a phenomenon that is known as viscous rupture. Therefore, a region where drawing is feasible, as determined largely by tension and material flow, must be obtained.

Coating. In a typical fiber-drawing process (Fig. 2), the fiber is cooled as it moves toward the coating section, where it is coated with a jacketing material for protection against abrasion, for reduction of stress-induced microbending losses, and for increased strength. The upper temperature at the coating section is limited by the properties of the coating material used. For commercial curable acrylates, this temperature generally cannot exceed 150°C (300°F).

by-products of the reactions are removed by carrier gases. Silicon films have been extensively fabricated using this process. Film thicknesses range from a few nanometers to tens of micrometers. The quality of the film deposited is characterized in terms of its purity, composition, thickness, adhesion, surface morphology, and crystalline structure. The level of quality needed depends on the intended application, with electronic and optical materials having the most stringent demands. Uniform film thickness and composition are obtained by proper control of the process conditions. Many different types of CVD reactors have been developed and used for various applications.

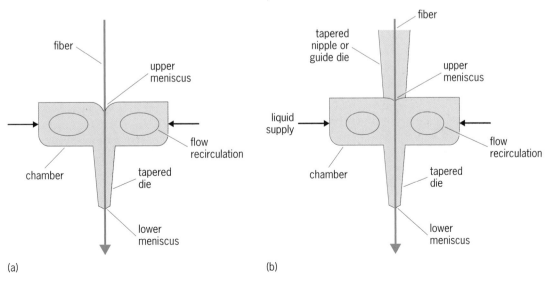

Fig. 3. Coating applicators: (*a*) open cup, and (*b*) pressurized.

The wet coating is then cured by ultraviolet radiation, and finally the fiber is spooled.

The coating process involves drawing the fiber through a reservoir of coating fluid, and then the fiber is passed through a die that may be used to control the thickness and the concentricity of the coating layer. Coating thickness may also be controlled by metering the flow rate, while a flexible exit die may be used for centering the fiber. **Figure 3** shows typical coating applicator and die systems. Viscous shear due to the moving fiber results in a circulatory fluid motion within the fluid. A balance between surface-tension, viscous, gravitational, and pressure forces results in an upstream meniscus at the cup entrance. A downstream meniscus at the die exit results primarily from a balance between viscous and inertia forces, the surface tension being a relatively small effect. Centering forces within the tapered die contribute to the positioning of the fiber at the die exit center. Successful coatings are concentric, of uniform thickness, and free of particle inclusions or bubbles.

Additional techniques. There has been considerable interest in materials processing under microgravity conditions. Such an environment would be obtained, for instance, in laboratories orbiting in space and would allow the processing of materials to be carried out with reduced effects of the terrestrial gravitational field. This reduces the buoyancy-driven flow, for instance, in the melt of a crystal-growing system, which affects the quality and characteristics of the crystal. Similar considerations arise in other processes such at chemical vapor deposition and coating. Gravity plays an important role in determining the shape of the meniscus in the optical-fiber-coating process and in the neck-down profile in optical-fiber drawing. Controlling the gravitational force could influence flow, and the resulting process and product.

Another area that has received considerable attention as a viable process for manufacturing near-net-shape (final-shape) structured materials is thermal sprays. Sprays containing droplets of the desired deposition material are directed at a chosen substrate and deposited by rapid solidification. The process is fast since many processing steps are eliminated, and rapid solidification eliminates macrosegregation, which weakens traditionally cast materials. Superior properties associated with fine-grained microstructures and nonequilibrium phases are usually obtained. A wide variety of materials, such as aluminum, tin, and various alloys, have been used in the droplet-based manufacturing process. Plasma spraying is used for fabricating ceramics, particularly nanostructured ceramics, and various other materials. Much of the effort in this area has focused on rapid solidification because the properties of the final product are strongly dependent on this process.

For background information *see* CERAMICS; CRYSTAL GROWTH; OPTICAL FIBERS; SINGLE CRYSTAL; SPACE PROCESSING in the McGraw-Hill Encyclopedia of Science & Technology.   Yogesh Jaluria

Bibliography. T. Altan, S. I. Oh, and H. L. Gegel, *Metal Forming: Fundamentals and Applications*, American Society of Metals, Metals Park, OH, 1971; A. Ghosh and A. K. Mallik, *Manufacturing Science*, Ellis Horwood, Chichester, U.K., 1986; Y. Jaluria, *Design and Optimization of Thermal Systems*, McGraw-Hill, New York, 1998; Y. Jaluria and K. E. Torrance, *Computational Heat Transfer*, Taylor and Francis, Washington, DC, 1986; S. Kou, *Transport Phenomena and Materials Processing*, Wiley, New York, 1996; D. Poulikakos (ed.), *Transport Phenomena in Materials Processing*, Advances in Heat Transfer, vol. 28, Academic Press, San Diego, 1996; V. Prasad, H. Zhang, and A. P. Anselmo, Transport phenomena in Czochralski crystal growth and processes, *Adv. Heat Transfer*, 30:313–435, 1997; J. Szekely, *Fluid Flow Phenomena in Metals Processing*, Academic Press, New York, 1979; Z. Tadmor and C. Gogos, *Principles of Polymer Processing*, Wiley, New York, 1979.

Medical geology

Medical geology, an emerging field of cooperative research, focuses on the interactions between earth materials and processes with human and animal health. It links geologists and other earth scientists with plant and animal biologists, as well as medical, dental, and veterinary specialists, to resolve local and global health issues.

The basis of medical geology is that individuals and populations are products of their environment, and their well-being depends on their intimate association with their physical and chemical surroundings. For example, the sources of some diseases, as well as some beneficial relationships, can be identified by combining information from environmental geochemistry (the study of the distribution of elements, gases, and mineral materials in specific geologic/geographic areas) with medical or dental abnormalities. The combination of such disparate areas of science and expertise can provide more precise diagnosis of some human disorders and possibly uncover mechanisms for their treatment. The goal of researchers in this field is to identify the environmental causes of disease to alleviate human suffering. Earth scientists with sensitive detection techniques are engaged in preparing maps on which they can plot the worldwide distribution of the many elements in soils, water, and plants. As a result, geoscientists, medical practitioners, and government personnel can now identify potentially hazardous habitats in a variety of environments.

Nutrition (essential elements). The human body regularly requires over 30 elements in addition to water. Carbon, nitrogen, oxygen, and sulfur are the basic elements of all the molecules that make up our soft tissues and organs. Calcium and phosphorus are elements essential to the formation of the mineral portion of the human skeleton, while sodium, potassium, and magnesium are necessary for maintaining the chemical balances in the fluids and cells required for bodily functions. Of the remaining elements, most, such as zinc, have special roles in the cascade of biochemical processes that take place every moment of our lives. The source of these elements are the food and fluids we ingest, which come to us via the agricultural products that grow on the soils produced by the weathering of rocks. If there are appropriate amounts of all the elements in the plants, animals, and humans, they have come from the ultimate source, the geoenvironment, modulated by their bioavailability up the food chain. There are places, especially in poor countries, where the inhabitants are not able to obtain the necessary nutrients due to deficiencies in their soil.

A well-known example of the connection of health and the geological environment involves the element iodine. Iodine is concentrated and bioavailable in the ocean, and the fish and plants that live there are good sources of the element. Low iodine concentrations are typical of mountainous terranes that often contain a complex of igneous and metamorphic rocks. The minerals typical of these rocks may contain small amounts of iodine, but the element is usually not readily available (that is, is not chemically removed from the rock very easily). The soils generated from these rocks, where the inhabitants grow their grains, are therefore depleted of iodine. There is an early historical record of disease related to such iodine deficiency. Chinese screens depicting daily life in the central mountainous portions of continental Asia show some people with thick necks, and other who appear to be retarded. Indeed, geochemical data coupled with epidemiological studies have shown that insufficient iodine in the diet, especially in early childhood and during development, causes goiter and cretinism. (The addition of iodized salt or iodine-enhanced cooking oil to food can ease this shortfall. There are, however, populations at risk in midcontinent China and in Sri Lanka in spite of the identification of the symptoms, the geological association, and the relative simplicity of correcting the deficit.)

Hazards. The transport and distribution of earth materials and the geologic processes that control them characterize much geologic research. Such research can shed light on how medical hazards can be spread by normal geologic processes.

Airborne hazards. Noxious gases generated by volcanic eruptions are airborne hazards obviously related to a normal geologic process. To mitigate the immediate health impact of volcanic gases, seismic detectors can be installed in susceptible areas throughout the globe to allow evacuation of communities when necessary. However, in addition to the immediate gas explosion, volcanoes generate particles of mineral materials that may become globally distributed, staying in suspension in the atmosphere for years with possible health effects that may not be immediate or obvious.

Mineral dusts such as the silica dusts or loess (sand) generated in arid areas can be significant hazards.

In the past, the problem of blowing sand has had no obvious solution, other than moving the population. Although there is little opportunity for altering weather patterns or providing a physical diversion for blowing sand, advances in technology may succeed in detecting the wind speed that permits fine particles to become airborne. Plotting the normal track of particle movement and monitoring changes in areas with airborne particulates could avert future health problems.

The naturally occurring and industrially important asbestos minerals pose another potential airborne hazard. Disease related to asbestos inhalation, usually originating in occupational settings, may not arise until tens of years after exposure. Because of the susceptibility of lung disease arising from asbestos exposure, the use of asbestos has been outlawed and its removal mandated.

In regions of China with fluoride-rich coal deposits, the indoor burning of this coal for heating, cooking, and food drying without adequate ventilation has resulted in a high rate of dental fluorosis among the residents (see **illus.**). Dental fluorosis, the observable effect of overexposure to fluoride in childhood when the teeth were developing, is characterized by discolored (brown-black) or chalky-white teeth. It is irreversible and no treatment exists.

Waterborne hazards. The addition of manufactured chemicals such as phthalates (estrogen disruptors) consumed by individuals and discharged from sewage treatment plants has caused abnormal shapes and other unwanted characteristics in the fish in some estuaries. Endocrine disruptors are newly created chemicals that also make their way into waterways and should be considered as potential hazards. A classic case of waterborne poison occurred in 1956 in Minimata, Japan, where industrial mercury compounds were discharged into Minimata Bay and taken up by fish that were eventually eaten by humans. The resulting poisoning and deaths in Japan became a major concern, and alerted investigators to look for mercury in other environments.

Many health hazards occur over a period during which there are few, if any, overt expressions of disease. For example, skin lesions in a population in Bangladesh were diagnosed in the 1980s and confirmed in the 1990s as being related to intake of elevated amounts of arsenic. The arsenic was present in water, used for domestic purposes and irrigation, from shallow wells that had been dug increasingly since the 1970s. The people not only drank the arsenic-contaminated water but also grew their vegetables and fed their animals with plants containing it. The ingestion of high levels of arsenic over many months and years led to dermatologic lesions and death, symptoms which continue to this day. This human disaster began rather innocently with the wish to provide the population with pure (microorganism-free) ground water rather than contaminated surface water (from cisterns), but the arsenic level of the wells was not tested. With hindsight it can be said that integration of hydrological

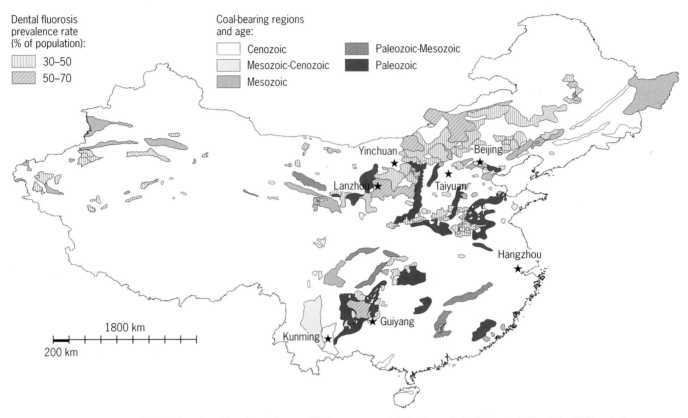

Dental fluorosis
prevalence rate
(% of population):

30–50

50–70

Coal-bearing regions
and age:

Cenozoic

Mesozoic-Cenozoic

Mesozoic

Paleozoic-Mesozoic

Paleozoic

Yinchuan

Beijing

Lanzhou

Taiyuan

Hangzhou

Guiyang

Kunming

1800 km

200 km

Distribution of coal-bearing regions and the occurrence of dental fluorosis in the People's Republic of China. In these regions, the population uses coal containing a high concentration of fluorine-bound clay for their domestic fuel, compounding their exposure to an already high concentration of fluorine in their drinking water. (*Open File Report #01-318 USGS, compiled by A. W. Karlsen et al.*)

information for this basin environment should have been obtained before the wells were dug.

The importance of testing and monitoring water supplies coupled with the coordination of medical and governmental personnel will undoubtedly become much more regularized in the future as a result of the arsenic problem in Bangladesh. We are becoming more appreciative of the dependence of humans on their environment, and have identified a few of the environmental factors that are hazardous to health. Such coordination may also have financial benefits. The methods available for treatment of overexposure to arsenic, especially for large populations, are expensive; the possibility of locating alternative potable water sources through subsurface geological mapping of the aquifer may prove economically preferable in the long term when the health costs are factored in.

For background information *see* ARSENIC; AS-BESTOS; ENVIRONMENTAL GEOLOGY; IODINE; LOESS; MERCURY (ELEMENT); NUTRITION; STREAM TRANSPORT AND DEPOSITION; THYROID GLAND; TOXICOLOGY; VOLCANOLOGY; WEATHERING PROCESSES in the McGraw-Hill Encyclopedia of Science & Technology.

H. Catherine W. Skinner

Bibliography. R. M. Cohn and K. S. Roth, *Biochemistry and Disease: Bridging Basic Science and Clinical Practice*, Williams & Wilkins, Baltimore, 1996; A. G. Darnley et al., *A Global Geochemical Database for Environmental and Resource Management: Recommendations for International Geochemical Mapping*, Earth Sci. Rep. 19, UNESCO, Paris, 1995; R. B. Finkelman, H. E. Belkin, and B. Zheng, Health impacts of domestic coal use in China, *Proc. Nat. Acad. Sci. USA*, 96:3427–3431, 1999; J. P. Gratton, The toxicology of volcanic gases, their historical impact and their potential role in contemporary European environments, in J. Rose (ed.), *Environmental Toxicology*, pp. 109–120, Gordon Breach, Amsterdam, 1998; B. S. Hetzel, *The Story of Iodine Deficiency*, Oxford University Press, Oxford, 1989; J. Lag, *Geomedicine*, CRC Press, Boca Raton, FL, 1990; H. C. W. Skinner, In praise of phosphates or why vertebrates chose apatite to mineralize their skeletal elements, *Int. Geol. Rev.*, 42:232–240, 2000; H. C. W. Skinner, M. Ross, and C. Frondel, *Asbestos and Other Fibrous Materials: Mineralogy, Crystal Chemistry and Health Effects*, Oxford University Press, New York, 1988.

Mesoscopic mechanical systems

Mesoscopic mechanical systems originated from a need to create new machines that are "a sugar cube to a fist" in size for applications ranging from controlling the environment (air, water, or temperature) for people, to generating moderate amounts (1–100 W) of electricity to power small systems. The challenge is that shrinking normal-scale machines to these sizes often has serious problems. These machines can be inefficient, too complex to manufacture with standard fabrication methods, or simply unfeasible due to mismatched scales. Moreover, microscopic machines that are on the order of micrometers to millimeters, such as micro-electro-mechanical systems (MEMS), are just too small for many of these applications. As a result, machines that were sized in the middle, that is, mesoscopic, were born of necessity to provide the technologies desired.

Mesoscale. There is more to mesoscopic machines than simply being sized in the middle. Physics defines a mesoscale system as one whose size matches a length scale associated with a phenomenon of interest. Examples of phenomenological length scales are the thermal diffusion length, δ_{th}, for transient conduction heat transfer; the wavelength of light, λ, for optics; the Debye length, λ_D, for shielding of electric charges; the hydrodynamic boundary layer thickness, δ_b, for fluid mechanics; and the mean free path, L_{mfp}, for collisions between gas particles. There are hundreds of such phenomenological length scales in biology, chemistry, engineering, and physics.

An important quality of mesoscopic systems is that when phenomenological length scales match the physical size of a system, strong coupling between different physical fields can occur. For example, electrostatics (one physical phenomenon) can strongly affect the bending of a cantilevered metal beam (another physical phenomenon) when a voltage is applied between the beam and a metal surface some distance away. As the beam deflects (mechanically strains) toward the surface due to the electrostatic attraction, the attractive force becomes larger due to the beam now being closer, which in turn makes the electrostatic force even stronger (that is, the fields are now coupled). If the physical distance is on the order of the electrostatic decay length, this coupling can become very strong and the beam will pull toward the metal surface until they touch, hence closing the circuit. If the gap is too large or the beam is too stiff, they will never touch. So, whether or not the fields can become strongly coupled depends on the phenomenological length scale of the beam/surface system, compared to the physical distance. When machines are designed to exploit the mesoscale from the micrometer to centimeter length scales, significant enhancements in functionality or performance can occur, as the example below demonstrates.

Mesoscopic heat pumps. Normal-scale mechanical vapor-compression heat pumps are used extensively in refrigeration, air-conditioning, and heating systems. They use the reverse Rankine refrigeration (RRR) cycle, where refrigerant vapor is (1) compressed (compressor), (2) condensed into a liquid by transferring heat to a lower-temperature heat bath (condenser), (3) expanded (orifice), and (4) evaporated by heat transferred from a low-temperature heat bath (evaporator).

The RRR heat pump has compelling advantages over competing methods. For small temperature differences between heat baths, it is as efficient as any other method and can move many times more heat energy, Q, than the work, W_{in}, needed to compress the vapor, giving a coefficient of performance, $COP = Q/W_{in} \gg 1$. RRR systems proportionally move more Q with increase in W_{in}, and provide robust control over wide operating conditions. In addition, RRR machines are mechanically simple, heat flow direction can be easily reversed, and refrigerants exist that are environmentally safe.

If RRR systems are so compelling, then why is it that tiny RRR heat pumps do not exist? Two of the required components, the condenser and evaporator, can be provided by microchannel heat exchangers that greatly increase heat transfer rates. However, tiny systems are thwarted by the lack of efficient compressors, due primarily to key physical constraints. Piston-, impeller-, and rotor-type compressors use the relative motion of a mechanical actuator to compress the vapor. Sliding and relative motion creates frictional and viscous losses, which do not scale well as the dimensions are shrunk. At the microscale, the losses can exceed the work done on the fluid, making these types of compressors very inefficient.

Recently, an RRR system was developed that uses mesoscale physics to create efficient mesoscopic heat pumps. **Figure 1** shows a flexible RRR heat pump system developed at the University of Illinois at Urbana-Champaign that is only 2.5 mm (<0.1 in.) thick and can be joined together to form a larger system, designed to cool soldiers in hot environments where protective clothing from biological and chemical hazards is needed. The demands on a total soldier system are daunting. It has to be very lightweight, <2 kg (4 lb), tough, flexible, and very energy efficient (COP>4). The total system needs to

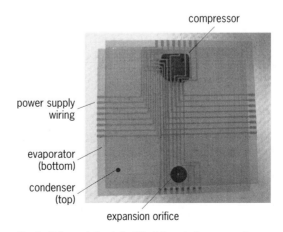

Fig. 1. Fully contained, flexible, integrated mesoscopic cooler circuit, which is 100 mm (4 in.) square and 2.5 mm (0.1 in.) thick and weighs 14 g. Its layered construction has all the components to execute the RRR cycle, including two polyimide 250-μm microchannel heat exchangers, an electrostatically driven compressor, a 30-μm-diameter sapphire orifice, and nanoporous insulation between the heat exchangers.

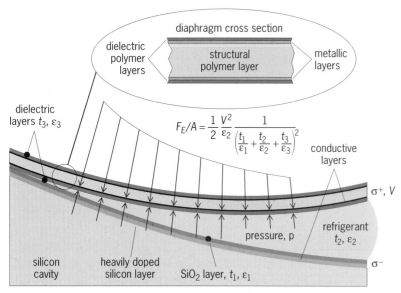

diaphragm cross section

dielectric polymer layers → structural polymer layer ← metallic layers

dielectric layers t_3, ε_3

$$F_E/A = \frac{1}{2}\frac{V^2}{\varepsilon_2}\frac{1}{\left(\frac{t_1}{\varepsilon_1}+\frac{t_2}{\varepsilon_2}+\frac{t_3}{\varepsilon_3}\right)^2}$$

conductive layers

σ^+, V

refrigerant t_2, ε_2

pressure, p

σ^-

silicon cavity   heavily doped silicon layer SiO_2 layer, t_1, ε_1

Fig. 2. Concept of electrostatic attraction of a movable diaphragm that comes into contact with a cavity, as when a voltage is applied between a conductive plane in the diaphragm and one in the silicon cavity. The high compression is achieved by the very high electrostatic force per unit area that occurs as t_2 goes to zero, and by having a very large area diaphragm per unit volume of refrigerant to be compressed.

transfer 300 W of sensible heat, which is about the capacity of a large refrigerator. If the RRR system of a refrigerator weighing over 40 kg (88 lb) were proportionally shrunk to 2 kg to move 300 W of heat at the same evaporator temperature, the condenser temperature would have to be much hotter, and high-velocity air would have to cool the condenser. The combination of both factors would make this size of RRR system extremely inefficient to operate with

a COP<0.1. Thermoelectric and other competing heat pump technologies, such as the absorption cycle, would be a better choice.

In contrast to shrinking a normal RRR system, a mesoscopic heat pump that is electrostatically actuated with electrical energy recovery can compress vapor efficiently (>80%), if it can provide (1) sufficient force to raise the vapor pressures high enough, and (2) enough energy to overcome the pressure volume work of the vapor compression. To achieve both, two length scales are used. Electrostatic compression is best illustrated with parallel plate actuators. The force between two closely spaced plates of distance d apart is proportional to $\varepsilon AE^2 = pA$, where E is the electric field strength and ε is the permittivity of the space between the plates of area A, which is balanced with the vapor pressure, p. The energy required to compress the vapor between the plates, as with a piston in a normal compressor, is proportional to $\varepsilon AE^2 \cdot d$. The problem is that force and energy must both be in balance at equilibrium. For $E = V/d$, they can be in balance only when d is very large (hence the pressure is very low), or d is very small (hence the pressure is very high). There is not enough electrostatic energy present to reach the high-pressure point, if the compressor moves rigidly.

One solution to this problem is to generate two length scales for the electromechanics of the plate: one with high forces at small d at the microscale, and the other at the normal scale with sufficient electrostatic energy to compress the volume of vapor desired. The first scale matches the electrostatic decay length to the distance between the conductive layers, and the second the characteristic length for the average electrostatic energy per unit of pressure. **Figure 2** shows this principle, with a diaphragm that comes into contact with another surface (without sliding that generates friction). A voltage is applied across the two conductive planes which pulls them toward each other by electrostatic attraction, at a force per unit area, F_E/A (Fig. 2), that varies quadratically with the sum of the distances t_1, t_2, and t_3. The electrostatic force is highest near the contact point, which pulls the diaphragm toward the cavity. Provided the diaphragm is laterally stiff enough as it is pulled in, the diaphragm nearest the contact is brought closer, increasing the electrostatic force at that point. The process continues until it zips closed, compressing the refrigerant between the diaphragm and cavity as it does. Several things can prevent full zipping of the diaphragm, such as a bubble mode of the diaphragm, too much strain energy in the diaphragm caused by the zipping, or the conduction of electrical charge through the dielectric layers. The desired high electrostatic force is achieved by carefully designing and fabricating the cavity and diaphragm. If the area of the diaphragm is sufficiently large with respect to the volume being compressed, there will be enough energy per unit pressure to compress the vapor. The result of matching these two length scales with the phenomenological scales is the mesoscopic compressor shown in **Fig. 3**.

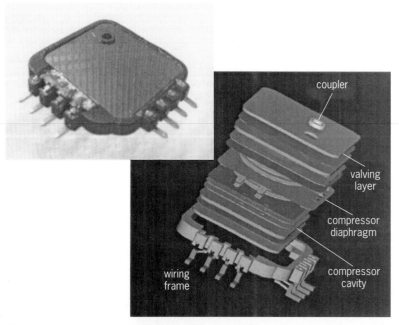

coupler

valving layer

compressor diaphragm

wiring frame

compressor cavity

Fig. 3. Electrostatic compressor in Fig. 1 with an exploded view showing multiple layers of silicon, oxides, polymers, metals, and plastic frame. It measures 22 mm (0.9 in.) square by 2 mm (0.08 in.) thick, and operates by the principle shown in Fig. 2, with double-action compression on both sides of the compressor diaphragm.

The design of this compressor uses multiple layers that span submicrometers to centimeters in size and are etched, molded, and bonded together to create valves, pumps, and flow channels at the mesoscale.

Other mesoscopic systems. There are many other examples of machines that exploit the physics of the mesoscale, such as pumps, motors, internal combustion engines, fuel cells, robots, and even airplanes and rockets. Pumps at the normal scale usually are powered by impellers and pistons; but at the mesoscale, diaphragm, bubble, and electrokinetic fluid pumps couple fields more effectively, and are more often found. Electric motors at the normal scale use wire windings carrying electric current, but resistance losses begin to dominate as such motors are shrunk, so electrostatic and piezoelectric motors tend to dominate at the mesoscale. Gas turbine engines with dimensions and physics that are about the size of two stacked quarters have been made, but the individual components' dimensions are vastly different than if a jet engine was simply shrunk to this size. In fact, the combustor is 40 times larger than it would be if designed for a normal-scale engine. Other mesoscopic mechanical and chemical systems are being developed to generate power and motion, from fuel cells to rotary engines. These systems use microcombustors, micro-heat exchangers, reactors, pumps, and valves, creating in effect a whole chemical plant, but with vastly different sizes and physics governing the process. In each of these examples, shrinking the equivalent normal-scale systems is not sufficient. Careful sizing of the phenomenological and physical length scales is needed to develop systems that span the micro- to normal scale. By exploiting the physics of the mesoscale, the variety of mesoscopic machines that can be developed is limited only by the imagination of scientists and engineers creating this new field.

For background information *see* HEAT PUMP; MICRO-ELECTRO-MECHANICAL SYSTEMS (MEMS); REFRIGERATION; REFRIGERATION CYCLE; THERMOELECTRICITY; VAPOR CYCLE in the McGraw-Hill Encyclopedia of Science & Technology.   Mark A. Shannon

Bibliography. A. S. Dewa, Mesoscopic systems: Bridging from micromachined devices to macroscopic systems, *Mechatronics*, 8(5):521–534, August 1998; A. H. Epstein et al., Power MEMS and microengines, *Tranducers 97: 1997 International Conference on Solid-State Sensors and Actuators*, Digest of Technical Papers (Cat. no. 97TH8267), IEEE Part, vol. 2, pp.753–756, 1997; A. Mehra et al., A six-wafer combustion system for a silicon micro gas turbine engine, *J. Microelectromech. Sys.*, 9(4):517–527, December 2000; M. A. Shannon et al., High-temperature microcombustion-based ammonia microchemical hydrogen generator reactors for PEM fuel cells, *Technical Digest of the Solid-State Sensor, Actuator, and Microsystems Workshop*, pp. 27–30, Hilton Head Island, SC, June 2–6, 2002; M. A. Shannon et al., Integrated mesoscopic cooler circuits (IMCCs), *Technical Digest of 1999 ASME International Mechanical Engineering Congress and Exhibition*, AES vol. 39, pp. 75–82, 1999.

Meteor storms

Meteor storms are spectacular events which occur rarely—only a few were observed in the twentieth century. The problem of reliably predicting them has occupied solar system scientists since the unexpected and astonishing Leonid meteor display of 1833. Advances in understanding the phenomenon, with determinations of exactly when and from which parts of the world displays would be visible, allowed a number of storms to be widely observed recently in the years following the latest return of the Leonids' parent comet 55P/Tempel-Tuttle.

Recent Leonid displays. In 1999, from Middle Eastern and European longitudes, and in 2001, when the activity curve peaked over North America and again some hours later as viewed from East Asian longitudes, spectacular Leonid displays were seen by many observers in moonless skies (**Fig. 1**). Scientific meteor observations are conventionally normalized to a zenithal hourly rate (ZHR), corresponding to essentially ideal conditions (cloudless skies so dark that

Fig. 1. Wide-field view of the 2001 Leonid meteor storm viewed from Uluru (Ayers Rock), Australia. Trails of dozens of the brightest Leonid meteors are captured in this 72-min composite made from eight 9-min exposures using a 16-mm full-frame fisheye lens. To the lower-right the meteor shower radiates from the sickle-shaped string of stars in Leo. Trails of two bolides (fireballs) are visible in Taurus (center left) and near the Large Magellanic Cloud (top right). (© *2001 by Fred Espenak*)

stars are visible down to a limiting magnitude of 6.5, with the meteor radiant at the zenith) for a single average visual observer, and to the observer's field of view. A peak zenithal hourly rate above 1000 commonly defines a storm. In 1999 and 2001, not only the zenithal hourly rate but also, for many meteor watchers, the observed rates were well above this value. The twentieth century's finest storm, the 1966 Leonids, was an order of magnitude higher. The 1998 display was well below a storm-level zenithal hourly rate but notable for the high number of bright fireballs.

Sporadic meteors, showers, and storms. As the Earth continuously moves through the sporadic meteoroid background in interplanetary space, a few meteors an hour can be seen on any clear, dark night. Particles down to a millimeter or so in size (less than 0.1 in.) impacting the atmosphere at tens of kilometers per second (tens of miles per second) can produce visual meteors.

The inner solar system contains several coherent streams, each consisting of particles released from a given parent object, generally an active or formerly active comet. Each time a periodic comet returns to perihelion and the temperature is sufficiently warm, ices at the cometary surface sublimate and the expanding gases drag small grains out with them, allowing these solid meteoroid particles to escape from the comet nucleus. The velocities (relative to the nucleus) imparted to the meteoroids during the ejection process cause them to have slightly different orbits from the comet, and the meteoroids disperse over millennia to form a stream or tube of material all the way around the comet's orbit. A meteor shower occurs if and when the Earth passes through the stream. For example, Leonids are observable (usually at a low level) every November. As particles in a single stream are traveling on similar paths to each other when they hit the Earth, the meteors appear to radiate from a single point in the sky, for example, in Leo for the Leonids. Some annual meteor showers reach a zenithal hourly rate of 100.

Over very narrow regions of space, generally within streams, are much denser concentrations of particles. Occasionally the Earth chances to encounter one of these, and a sharp meteor outburst or storm results. The dense regions take the form of long trails, particles remaining for some centuries in these compact structures before dispersing into their respective streams. Trails, streams, and the sporadic background represent an evolutionary sequence in the zodiacal meteoroid complex.

Formation of narrow trails. When meteoroids are ejected over a range of orbital periods, particles of shorter and longer period progressively get farther ahead and behind respectively in their orbit; in this way a trail is formed, and it lengthens with time. Ejection speeds and orbital geometry vary from comet to comet, but lengths can extend to a significant fraction of the $360°$ around an orbit within a century.

The range of orbits present after ejection also determines a trail's width. Orbital geometry implies that the width varies with heliocentric distance; of relevance to meteor storms is the width near the Earth's distance from the Sun. Standard equations of celestial mechanics show that the same size of ejection velocities that soon allow trails to become extremely long (several times 10^8 km) can nevertheless yield trail widths that are only of the order of 10^5 km or a few to several times the Earth's diameter. Therefore, in three dimensions, most trails miss the Earth's orbit by a distance much greater than the trail's width. Solar radiation pressure slightly increases the orbital periods and trail widths that result from ejection velocities.

Apart from manifesting themselves as meteor storms, dust trails have been observed remotely. Among the many dense, narrow trails discovered by the *Infrared Astronomical Satellite* were those associated with comets 10P/Tempel 2 and 2P/Encke.

Perturbations and trail predictability. Orbits precess when acted on by gravitational perturbations of planets. Immediately after ejection, trail particles are usually on orbits that comfortably miss Earth, but the possibility exists of precisely the right perturbation occurring to bring them to Earth intersection at some time. Achieving Earth intercept can be easier for comet orbits closer to the Earth's orbit, since the required perturbation is smaller. However, the condition for a storm is that the orbits of trail particles, regardless of the comet, intersect the Earth.

Storms are predictable because, over short enough time scales, before the effects of chaotic dynamics become significant, gravitational perturbations can be calculated precisely. The only requirement is an accurate knowledge of the comet's orbit at the time of meteoroid ejection, to give initial conditions.

Perturbations are a function of a particle's continuously varying position relative to each planet. As a trail is much longer than it is wide, position depends on location along the trail rather than on location within the trail cross section. The stream's parent comet is itself perturbed between successive returns to perihelion, and creates a separate trail on each return. Perturbations subsequently vary along the length of each trail, and between trails.

How far ahead or behind a particle is along a trail depends on the particle's orbital period (although as the period itself is continuously perturbed, position along a trail eventually ceases to be a monotonic function of the instantaneous period). Therefore, until motion becomes chaotic, perturbations are a precise function of the orbital period immediately after ejection. Varying this single parameter gives a method of accurately determining positions of particles all the way along any given trail that does not require great computational power.

Ejection velocities and radiation pressure imply the existence of a trail width, but planetary perturbations and radiation pressure do not impose any progressive further widening during the first several revolutions of a trail's evolution. The seasonal Yarkovsky effect due to the nonisotropic reradiation of energy from meteoroids can cause some widening

Parameters of selected encounters with Leonid trails

Observed peak time, Greenwich Mean Time	Longitude observed from	Trail created	Trail age, revolutions	Miss distance, astronomical units	ΔP, years	Observed peak zenithal hourly rate
1866 Nov 14.05	Europe, Middle East	1733	4	−0.0004	+0.31	8,000
1867 Nov 14.40	North America	1833	1	−0.0002	+1.83	4,500
1966 Nov 17.50	W. North America	1899	2	−0.0001	+0.83	90,000
1999 Nov 18.08	Europe, Middle East	1899	3	−0.0007	+0.69	3,700
2000 Nov 18.30	E. North America	1866	4	+0.0008	+0.57	500
2001 Nov 18.44	North America	1767	7	−0.0004	+0.41	1,600
2001 Nov 18.73	E. Asia, Australia	1699	9	+0.0001	+0.22	1,000
2001 Nov 18.76	E. Asia, Australia	1866	4	+0.0002	+0.71	2,500

over centuries. Overall, trails remain narrow except when the particles at certain locations along the trails make a fairly close approach to a planet and are widely scattered. In this way, the chaotic nature of planet crossing orbits eventually breaks up a trail and disperses it into its background stream. Within centuries, this process typically prevents dynamical evolution from being predictable, although, for example, the 1998 Leonid fireball outburst was due to material ejected several centuries ago.

Application to known streams. The storm prediction technique has been successfully applied to associate outbursts in the Leonid, Andromedid, Draconid, June Boötid, and Ursid streams with meteoroids from specific returns of the respective parent comets. The Leonids produced the majority of big displays in the past two centuries, although the Andromedids in the nineteenth century and Draconids in the twentieth century also yielded storm-level activity. Observations usually match within minutes the calculated peak times of close encounters with young trails. In a few cases, discrepancies of a few tens of minutes have been significantly reduced by allowing for subtle effects due to radiative forces.

In its simplest form, the technique comprises varying the orbital period of particles ejected at a given return of a comet and determining the period that results in particles reaching the ecliptic at a given later date. For the Leonids, dates of interest would be mid-November of various years as the Earth traverses the Leonid stream in that month. The location of the ecliptic crossings of these particles is then determined. (Because perturbations vary along a trail, particles in the trail that reach the ecliptic at other times will have different ecliptic crossing points.) If an ecliptic intersection is found within a trail's width of the Earth's orbit, a meteor outburst is expected; the longitude of the ecliptic crossing is related to the peak time of the outburst. As trails are narrow compared to the scale of the inner solar system, most ecliptic crossings are distant from Earth, but, for example, in November 2001 there were multiple encounters with Leonid trails (**Fig. 2**). The occurrence versus nonoccurrence of outbursts at different miss distances is a powerful indirect method of determining ejection speeds from a cometary nucleus, since ejection speeds are closely related to trail widths.

The peak zenithal hourly rate reached during a storm depends on various parameters of the trail encounter. The **table** lists parameters of selected encounters with Leonid trails. The difference in heliocentric distance of the Earth relative to the nominal trail center is shown; for comparison the Earth's diameter is a little under 0.0001 astronomical unit. Encounters within a few Earth diameters produce major meteor outbursts. As the spatial density of meteoroids is expected to increase toward trail centers, smaller miss distances tend to give higher zenithal hourly rates. Along a trail, meteoroids are concentrated at preferential values of the orbital period; basically particles concentrate near the comet's period, but solar radiation pressure introduces a bias toward slightly higher periods. The parameter ΔP is the orbital period relative to that of the comet immediately after ejection; the number of Leonid meteoroids of sizes that produce visual meteors may reach a maximum around values approaching $\Delta P = +1$ year. Any trail's density is also diluted with age (shown in revolutions in the table) as the trail

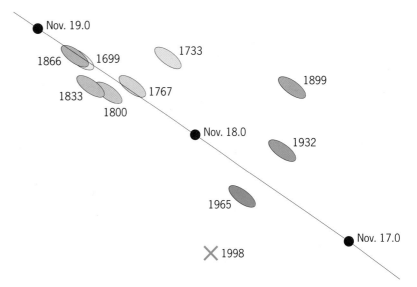

Fig. 2. Cross sections in the ecliptic of Leonid trails created over the past 300 years, labeled by when they were formed. (Comet Tempel-Tuttle returns roughly every 33 years, most recently in 1998.) The cross sections plotted are for particles that crossed the ecliptic in November 2001. When the Earth, whose position at 1-day intervals is shown, passed through the Leonid stream in 2001, it encountered trails created around the 1866, 1767, and 1699 returns of the comet.

progressively stretches along its length. All these dependences of the zenithal hourly rate on various factors are qualitatively similar but quantitatively different for different comets and streams. Precise details of the zenithal hourly rate profile depend on cometary ejection processes, and are therefore harder to calculate than peak times, the latter depending on well-established, accurate techniques for evaluating gravitational perturbations.

Preferred observing locations. Most trails are so narrow that the Earth crosses them within hours. Sometimes activity is well below the maximum even a half hour on either side of the peak. In November Leo is above the horizon roughly after local midnight, depending on latitude, constraining the region of the Earth's surface from where a Leonid storm can be viewed. When the fractional part of the Greenwich Mean Time date is 0.1, 0.4, and 0.8, European, American, and East Asian longitudes, respectively, are well placed.

For background information *see* CELESTIAL MECHANICS; COMET; METEOR; SOLAR SYSTEM in the McGraw-Hill Encyclopedia of Science & Technology.

David J. Asher

Bibliography. P. Brown, The Leonid meteor shower: Historical visual observations, *Icarus*, 138:287–308, 1999; M. Littmann, *The Heavens on Fire: The Great Leonid Meteor Storms*, Cambridge University Press, 1998; J. Rao, Leonids 2001: The saga continues, *Sky Telesc.*, 102(5):109–115, November 2001; B. Warmbein (ed.), *Proceedings of the Meteoroids 2001 Conference*, ESA SP-495, European Space Agency, Noordwijk, 2001.

Methane clathrate

Methane clathrate, also known as methane hydrate, is a crystalline inclusion compound (a compound in which a guest species is spatially confined within another species, the host) which is stable only at high pressures or low temperatures. Gas hydrates are composed of water molecules linked together by hydrogen bonds to form polyhedral water cages (hosts) which trap the guest molecules. There are at least three classes of natural gas hydrates: structures I, II, and H, which differ in the type of water cages present. I and II have cubic structures which can occur with guest molecules as large as 0.55 and 0.65 nanometer, respectively. H has a hexagonal structure which can occur with guest molecules as large as 0.9 nm. In general, the type of gas hydrate structure formed depends on the size of the guest species. Methane clathrate is a structure I gas hydrate. Scientists began studying the composition and physical properties of gas hydrates around 1810, when they were considered to be merely a scientific oddity. Since 1934, when the occurrence of gas hydrates in pipelines was established, the structure, phase equilibria, thermodynamics, and kinetics of these compounds have been studied. It is now recognized that gas hydrates, particularly methane

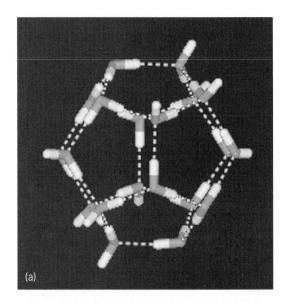

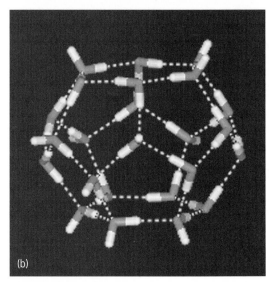

Fig. 1. Methane clathrate water cages: (*a*) small (5^{12}) cage and (*b*) large ($5^{12}6^2$) cage.

clathrate, are important in a wide range of scientific and engineering fields and have a number of important industrial applications.

Crystal structure. The methane clathrate structure is composed of two types of water cages: a small cage of radius about 0.395 nm, which is commonly represented by the symbol 5^{12} (twelve pentagonal water rings form the faces of this small cage; **Fig. 1***a*), and a large cage of radius about 0.433 nm, commonly given the symbol $5^{12}6^2$ (twelve pentagonal water rings plus two hexagonal water rings form the faces of this large cage; Fig. 1*b*).

The crystal structure of methane clathrate has been determined from powder x-ray and neutron diffraction. It has a primitive cubic crystal structure (space group $Pm3n$), with two small water cages and six large water cages per unit cell, and a total of 46 water molecules per unit cell (a unit cell is the smallest repeat unit of a crystal which when translated along parallel lines will generate the entire crystal structure). Only one methane molecule can be accommodated per water cage. Single cage occupancy is assumed for all gas hydrates, although recently there has been evidence of double occupancy in the large cage in nitrogen clathrates (structure II hydrate). However, not all cages in the lattice need to be occupied for the clathrate structure to be stable. Hence, gas hydrates are nonstoichiometric compounds (x-ray and neutron diffraction measurements give an empirical formula of $CH_4 \cdot 5.75\ H_2O$). The typical occupancy of methane in the clathrate lattice is around 90%.

New energy supply. Methane clathrate is of interest to the oil and gas industries and energy agencies. This is because huge quantities of naturally occurring methane clathrate deposits have been located in the marine sediments (at depths of a few hundred meters or more) on continental margins worldwide (for example, the Middle America Trench off Costa Rica; Japan Sea; Gulf of Mexico; Crimea, Ukraine, Black Sea in Russia; Mackenzie Delta in Canada) and permafrost regions (such as the North Slope of Alaska) where deposits contain gas hydrate and ice. The location and extent of methane clathrate deposits in ocean environments have been determined from seismic reflection surveys (Bottom Simulating Reflector, or BSR, measurements), and more directly by deep-ocean drilling. However, the location of methane clathrate present in permafrost regions cannot be established from seismic BSR measurements, since the latter cannot easily distinguish between ice and gas hydrate.

Current estimates of methane clathrate in oceanic and permafrost deposits range widely from 1×10^{15} to $7 \times 10^{18}\ m^3$ (3.5×10^{16} to $2.5 \times 10^{20}\ ft^3$). Clearly, the volume of methane stored in these clathrate deposits is significant: $1\ m^3$ ($35.3\ ft^3$) of methane clathrate (90% methane occupancy) contains $156\ m^3$ ($5500\ ft^3$) of methane gas at standard temperature and pressure. The methane content of these deposits has been estimated to be twice the amount of the total fossil fuel resources (coal, oil, gas) that the world has available. Therefore, as an energy resource, methane clathrate presents a very attractive, clean alternative to coal and oil supplies. Industry and energy sectors are currently focusing much of their efforts on developing strategies for extracting methane from these natural deposits in a safe and environmentally friendly manner, since uncontrolled release of significant amounts of methane, a greenhouse gas, into the atmosphere must be avoided during extraction. *See* COALBED METHANE.

Industrial problem. Natural gas hydrates (where methane is the major guest component) can also form in subsea gas and oil pipelines at certain temperature and pressure conditions. The formation of these gas hydrates can lead to blockages of the pipelines and often to catastrophic consequences, both in terms of the safety of personnel working on these facilities and huge economic losses. For example, a critical safety issue arises if a gas hydrate plug

acts as a projectile and erupts from the pipeline. In order to prevent these blockages or to dissociate them once formed, chemical inhibitors, such as methanol, are commonly used by the industry, although the costs associated with methanol addition are substantial.

Pressure-temperature dependence. Efficient extraction of methane from methane clathrate deposits as well as the prevention of gas clathrate formation in pipelines requires knowledge of the effects of pressure and temperature on the equilibrium:

$$CH_4\ (g) + nH_2O\ (l) \ \leftrightarrow\ CH_4 \cdot nH_2O\ (crystalline)$$

This system has two components which can be varied at will, CH_4 and H_2O, and three phases, methane vapor (g), liquid water (l), and gas hydrate. Hence, from the phase rule, $F = C - P + 2 = 1$, where $F =$ the number of degrees of freedom at equilibrium, $C =$ the number of components, and $P =$ the number of phases. This indicates univariance: For any given pressure P there is a fixed temperature T, and vice versa. Strictly speaking, there is always water vapor present with CH_4 (g), but it is commonly ignored because its partial pressure is always negligible. Its presence changes neither C nor the number of phases P, so F remains 1. The P-T dependence of methane clathrate has been extensively studied (**Fig. 2**).

To prevent methane clathrate formation, or to melt the gas hydrate crystal, an inhibitor can be added to the system. This brings C to 3 and hence F to 2. The choice is now clearly to be able to choose any pair from P, T, and inhibitor concentration. Once the latter is fixed, the system is again univariant. If the inhibitor is effective, the new P-T curve will be at

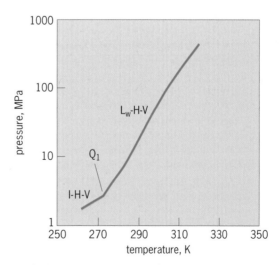

Fig. 2. Pressure-temperature phase diagram for methane clathrate based on published experimental data from several sources. The three-phase line labeled L_w-H-V is the phase boundary of liquid water-hydrate-vapor; the three-phase line labeled I-H-V is the phase boundary of ice-hydrate-vapor. Methane clathrate is stable only in the regions above and to the left of each of these three-phase lines. Q_1 is the lower quadruple point where four phases, I-L_w-H-V, coexist. $°F = (K \times 1.8) - 459.67$.

higher P and lower T throughout. If at fixed P and T, gas hydrate is formed from H_2O (l) and CH_4 (g), ΔG (the Gibbs free energy) must be negative, since this is the condition required for a phase transformation to occur, that is, for CH_4 (g) and H_2O (l) to be converted to gas hydrate. If on addition of an inhibitor no gas hydrate is formed, ΔG must now be positive, that is, no phase transformation has occurred. $\Delta G = \Delta H - T\Delta S$, and it has been found that ΔH does not significantly change with T, P, or the presence of an inhibitor. Therefore, ΔG will be governed by the entropy, ΔS. Hence, the change in ΔG is due entirely to the change in ΔS, whose magnitude must have changed. In molecular terms, it could be inferred that this change in ΔS is caused by changes in the hydrogen bonding between water molecules, making it more difficult to form gas hydrate cages.

Measuring phase equilibria. Much work has been performed on the phase equilibria of methane clathrate, mainly involving macroscopic pressure-temperature measurements on water/methane mixtures without and with inhibitors. The heat capacity and enthalpy of dissociation of methane clathrate has been measured using calorimetry ($\Delta H = 54.2$ kJ mol^{-1}). Molecular-level techniques have been more recently applied to study the structure and dynamics of the gas hydrate phase. Solid-state nuclear magnetic resonance (NMR) and Raman spectroscopies have been used to determine the guest occupancy and hydration number (number of water molecules per guest) of methane clathrate. The former can also be determined from x-ray and neutron diffraction measurements. The occupancy of methane in small and large cages as a function of temperature and pressure is an important question in terms of determining the detailed structure and stability of the clathrate, as well as in determining more accurate estimates of the energy content of methane clathrate deposits.

Calculating phase equilibria. Methane clathrate phase equilibria can be calculated using the van der Waals and Platteeuw (vdWP) model, which is based on statistical thermodynamics. The vdWP method takes into account both the gas hydrate composition and fractional occupancy of guest molecules in each cavity. The main assumptions of the vdWP model are: only one guest is held per cavity; guest motion is independent of the number of types of guests present; only weak van der Waals interactions are present between guest and host molecules; and finally, there is no lattice distortion by the guest. In essence, the vdWP method is based on the Langmuir model for gas adsorption on a solid, in which guest occupancy is related to the Langmuir constant (a measure of the attractiveness of the cavity for a guest molecule) and the vapor pressure (or fugacity) of the gas. The chemical potential of water in the gas hydrate phase is assumed to depend on the concentration of guest molecules in the two types of gas hydrate cavities.

Although the vdWP method was developed in 1959, nearly all thermodynamic models used to predict gas hydrate phase equilibria are still based on this model. Extensions to the vdWP model have been made to improve the accuracy of the predictions of phase equilibria, for example, by accounting for lattice stretching due to large guests being present. Despite the shortcomings of the vdWP-based models, the results obtained give reasonably good agreement with experimentally measured data for simple gas hydrates, such as methane clathrate.

Future developments. In view of the important technological applications of methane clathrates, future studies will focus on studying the kinetics and thermodynamics of methane clathrate formation and decomposition using both macroscopic and molecular-level techniques. Future research will also be directed toward measurements on the phase equilibria and kinetics of methane clathrate formation and decomposition in the presence of porous materials, similar to porous sediments in which methane clathrate is naturally found. Better control of methane clathrate crystallization will be important for its use as a fuel for vehicle transportation, as well as preventing blockages in gas/oil subsea pipelines.

For background information see CLATHRATE COMPOUNDS; HYDRATE; NATURAL GAS; PHASE EQUILIBRIUM; PHASE RULE; THERMODYNAMIC PRINCIPLES in the McGraw-Hill Encyclopedia of Science & Technology.   Carolyn Ann Koh

Bibliography. P. Englezos, Clathrate hydrates, *Ind. Eng. Chem. Res.*, 32:1251–1274, 1993; G. D. Holder and P. R. Bishnoi (eds.), Gas hydrates: Challenges for the future, *Ann. N.Y. Acad. Sci.*, vol. 912, 2000; C. A. Koh, Towards a fundamental understanding of natural gas hydrates, *Chem. Soc. Rev.*, 31:157–167, 2002; E. D. Sloan, *Clathrate Hydrates of Natural Gas*, 2d ed., Marcel Dekker, New York, 1998.

Microbial enhanced oil recovery

Standard oil recovery methods typically extract only one-third of the oil originally present in a reservoir. The physical reasons for this have driven the development of many chemical processes to enhance recovery. Most of these methods rely on relatively expensive additives, making field implementation economically unattractive. Introducing microbes into the reservoir in order to produce recovery-enhancing chemicals in situ could reduce costs, but taking advantage of this potential requires great improvements over the current performance of microbial systems.

Recovery processes. Oil reservoirs are found in layers of sedimentary rock hundreds to thousands of meters below the surface of the Earth. Primary oil recovery is the process of allowing oil to flow through wells to the surface, driven by forces such as expansion of oil as pressure declines. Secondary recovery is implemented when primary production rates fall below some economic threshold. The usual secondary recovery process is waterflooding (injecting water into selected wells to push oil toward production wells). At the economic limit of a waterflood (when operating costs exceed revenue from

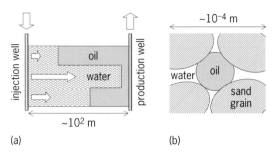

Fig. 1. Physical factors limiting oil recovery. (*a*) Oil reservoirs exhibit highly varying flow properties, so that injected fluids tend to flow preferentially in certain rock layers. (*b*) In the tiny pores of sedimentary rocks, capillary forces are much stronger than viscous or gravity forces and can trap droplets of oil.

oil sales), only about one-third of the oil originally contained in the reservoir has been produced.

Waterflooding leaves oil in the reservoir for two reasons. First, all reservoirs exhibit spatially variable flow properties, reflecting the variability in the geologic processes that formed the reservoir. Inevitably, injected water finds the path of least resistance between an injection and a production well, and such a path sweeps out only a fraction of the reservoir volume (**Fig. 1***a*). Second, reservoir fluids reside in tiny pores, 10–100 micrometers in diameter, between the grains making up the rock. At this length scale the phenomenon of capillarity becomes important: The curvature of the interface between oil and water induces pressures large enough to break the oil phase into isolated droplets. The viscous forces exerted on a droplet by flowing water are much smaller than the capillary forces resisting droplet displacement. These trapped droplets, typically constituting one-third of the oil originally contained within the pore, are collectively referred to as residual oil (Fig. 1*b*).

Enhanced oil recovery (EOR) processes. Traditional primary and secondary oil recovery extracts one-third of the oil in the reservoir. The remaining two-thirds constitutes an enormous potential resource, and this oil is the target of chemical and microbial EOR processes.

Chemical EOR technology. Chemical EOR technologies address one or both of the recovery-limiting factors affecting waterflooding (**Fig. 2**). For example, dissolving a polymer (such as polyacrylamide) into the injected water increases its viscosity, causing it to sweep a larger volume of the reservoir. Adding surfactant to the injected water reduces the capillary forces between oil and water, enabling displacement of residual oil. Although field trials have demonstrated the technical feasibility of chemical EOR, most processes are uneconomical.

Microbial EOR (MEOR) technology. Microbial metabolic products include chemicals functionally equivalent to those used in chemical EOR. This observation, combined with the discovery of microbes that remain viable at the temperatures and pressures of oil reservoirs, has motivated investigation of MEOR for several decades. Typically MEOR has been

envisioned as a chemical EOR process, implemented by establishing bioreactors within the reservoir. (Many microbial species have been studied for this purpose, including *Bacillus licheniformis* (ATCC 39307), *Clostridium pasteurianum*, *Leuconostoc mesenteroides*, and *Rhodococcus qurantiacus* 80001.) These in situ bioreactors are usually created by injecting specially cultured microbes that colonize the reservoir in the vicinity of injection wells, though some reservoirs contain indigenous microbes that can be stimulated. The microbes feed on nutrients (such as dissolved oxygen, nitrate, phosphate, and a carbon source such as molasses) dissolved into the injected water, and among their metabolic products are biosurfactants and biopolymers (**Fig. 3**).

Many instances of well stimulation via microbes have been reported in which the objective was to increase production rates by removing organic deposits or reducing oil viscosity in the rock surrounding production wells. This objective differs from that of EOR, and it is an unfortunate source of confusion that the literature commonly refers to these treatments as MEOR. Current literature documenting field trials of bona fide MEOR depict results that have not been encouraging. In two trials reported in sufficient detail to permit analysis, a contributing factor to their poor performance was the failure to satisfy reactor/reservoir engineering constraints.

Current MEOR research. Studies on MEOR have largely aimed at demonstrating the ability to establish active microbial populations within samples of porous rock and documenting their depth of penetration. Little information is available on the rate or extent of conversion of carbon source and nutrients to useful chemical products. Levels of incremental oil recovery are usually low in these experiments (for example, 10% of the oil remaining after waterflood versus 50% recovered by chemical EOR processes) and are often obtained only after injecting many pore volumes of water through the rock sample. Further, these recoveries involve oil contained within the bioreactor itself, whereas in the industry the target is the massive amount of residual oil lying outside the bioreactor.

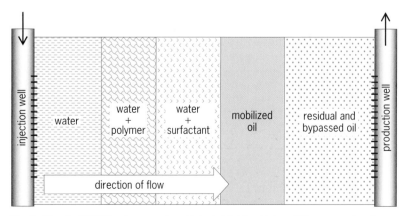

Fig. 2. Chemical EOR involves a series of injected fluids which mobilize unswept and residual oil, yielding an oil bank that is pushed toward production wells.

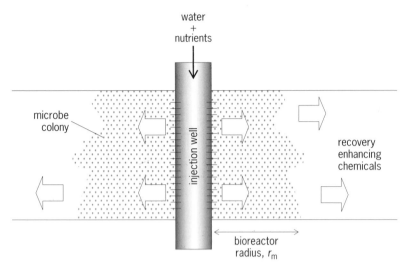

Fig. 3. Microbial EOR seeks to establish and operate bioreactors within the oil reservoir. These bioreactors create recovery enhancing chemicals corresponding to those used in chemical EOR. In some processes, the objective is to favor multiplication of microbes already present within the reservoir.

An emerging trend is to use microbes for profile modification (redirecting injected water to push oil from previously unswept regions of the reservoir). The simplest version of this type of MEOR seeks only to stimulate microbe growth, without regard to their metabolic products. As the microbes reproduce, they fill the pore space within the rock, effectively blocking flow through that rock. This process appears ideally suited to reservoirs containing indigenous microbes, as the feasibility of colonizing a reservoir across interwell distances (hundreds of meters) remains an open question.

Reservoir bioreactor operation. As described above, the MEOR process involves establishing an active microbial population (a bioreactor) within the reservoir rock around injection wells. Of particular interest is the use of residual oil as a carbon source. This would eliminate the cost and logistical complexity of supplying a carbon source such as molasses from the surface. To be compatible with reservoir operational requirements, however, the microbial system for such a process would have to meet a variety of performance constraints. These constraints are best understood by applying the principles of reaction engineering to the reservoir bioreactors.

Reactant conversion to EOR chemicals. In order to be effective, biosurfactants and biopolymers, like any EOR chemical, must be produced above a minimum concentration. The chemical concentration in the water exiting the bioreactor depends on the rate of the biotransformation and the residence time of water within the bioreactor. Clearly, the residence time must not be less than the reaction time required to reach the desired product concentration (**Fig. 4**). This requirement defines a quantitative relationship between reservoir parameters (injection rate and depth of microbe placement, r_m) and microbial parameters (such as required product concentration and reaction rate). The need to maintain high rates of water injection and the difficulty in establishing large bioreactors place a premium on microbes capable of rapidly transforming nutrient into EOR chemical. Most laboratory studies, however, suggest that the time scale for polymer/surfactant production is a few days.

Experience shows that successful EOR requires large volumes of water containing the EOR chemical, approximately 10% of the fluid volume in the reservoir. Accomplishing this is a challenging objective, as typical bioreactors (with r_m of approximately a few meters) contain a relatively small volume of carbon source. While large bioreactors would allow production of larger total volumes of EOR chemicals, establishing and sustaining deeper microbe penetration is increasingly difficult as r_m increases. Thus an important measure of the efficiency of an MEOR process is the selectivity and degree to which nutrients and residual oil are converted to the active chemical species.

Nutrient supply. The amount of nutrient that can be delivered to the bioreactor is limited by its aqueous solubility. A potential operating constraint is that sparingly soluble nutrients could be entirely consumed within the bioreactor. This poses practical limits on the ability to establish and maintain a large bioreactor. It may also make it difficult to maintain injectivity, as the highest density of microbial colonies are likely to form where nutrient concentrations are highest (near the wellbore).

Bioreactor size. The ability to extend a bioreactor to great distances within the reservoir rock is not well documented, and presents a number of technical challenges such as selective microbe retention (avoiding filtration and consequent plugging of the rock near the wellbore). If it is possible to stimulate a microbial population indigenous to the reservoir, the bioreactor size would be that of the reservoir, overcoming constraints on residence time and the volume of chemical that could be produced. Another possibility is to develop a growing or mobile reactor that progressively contacts a larger portion of the reservoir volume, though the operational challenges here appear to be even greater than those to establish a fixed bioreactor.

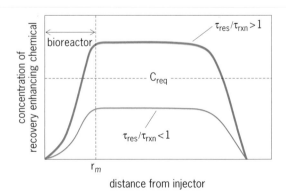

Fig. 4. The concentration of recovery enhancing chemical produced depends on the residence time (τ_{res}) of nutrient in the bioreactor and the time required for complete reaction (τ_{rxn}). To be effective, the reaction yield within the bioreactor must exceed the minimum required product concentration C_{req}.

Outlook. An MEOR process that utilizes residual oil as its carbon source would dramatically change the business of oil production, especially in mature fields, because in principle it could yield much higher oil recoveries while costing marginally more than a waterflood. A viable MEOR process based on a fixed bioreactor must overcome considerable challenges, however. In large part, the problem is to establish and maintain a sufficiently large bioreactor to produce the required volume and concentration of EOR chemicals. A necessary element of future work is to determine the reaction engineering parameters of MEOR processes. Another key question is the feasibility of microbially mediated mobility control, which adjusts the viscosity of injected fluids so as to increase the stability of the EOR displacement process.

For background information *see* BIOPOLYMER; FLUID FLOW; OIL AND GAS FIELD EXPLORATION; PETROLEUM ENGINEERING; PETROLEUM ENHANCED RECOVERY; PETROLEUM MICROBIOLOGY; PETROLEUM RESERVOIR MODELS in the McGraw-Hill Encyclopedia of Science & Technology.   Thomas P. Lockhart;
Steven L. Bryant

Bibliography. S. L. Bryant and T. P. Lockhart, *Reservoir Engineering Analysis of Microbial Enhanced Oil Recovery*, Society of Petroleum Engineers Annual Technical Conference and Exhibition (Dallas), SPE Pap. 63229, October 1–4, 2000; E. Donaldson, G. Chilingarian, and T. Yen (eds.), *Developments in Petroleum Science, 22. Microbial Enhanced Oil Recovery*, Elsevier, Amsterdam, 1989; L. Lake, *Enhanced Oil Recovery*, Prentice Hall, Englewood Cliffs, 1989; T. Yen, *Microbial Enhanced Oil Recovery: Principle and Practice*, CRC Press, Boca Raton, 1990; J. Zajic and E. Donaldson (eds.), *Microbes and Oil Recovery*, vol. 1, *International Bioresources Journal*, 1985.

Microgravity

The microgravity environment, that is, the condition of weightlessness, offers unique possibilities for the study of thermodynamic phenomena. Some important results have already been obtained, and many more can be expected when the International Space Station becomes operational.

Under microgravity conditions, the mass density of a body becomes an irrelevant quantity, and consequently, density differences play no role. Fluids are the most sensitive of the thermodynamic phases of matter to a gravitational force. This force causes an acceleration of all masses toward the center of gravitation; it makes bodies fall and fluids flow downward. In an inhomogeneous fluid system at rest, sedimentation will result. In combination with a temperature or concentration gradient, gravity can also induce convective flows. In the absence of gravity, no container is needed to position a fluid, and there is no sedimentation, no hydrostatic pressure, and no buoyancy-driven convection.

Microgravity conditions have been exploited to study a large number of different phenomena in the materials and life sciences. This includes short-duration experiments of the order of 1–10 seconds, which can be conducted during free fall in a drop tube or drop tower, or on board an airplane performing parabolic flight trajectories, as well as long-duration experiments carried out in space. Thermodynamic research has been carried out in the areas of phase transitions and transport phenomena.

Phase transitions. First- and second-order phase transitions have been studied, namely solidification, boiling, and critical phenomena. Whereas the absence of convection is the main reason to study first-order phase transitions in microgravity, critical phenomena can be investigated with greater accuracy in microgravity due to the absence of hydrostatic pressure. Supercritical fluids have a high compressibility which diverges at the critical point. The critical point itself is a singular point in the phase diagram and is realized when all the thermodynamic variables of the system attain their critical values, that is, the critical temperature T_c, the critical density ρ_c, and the critical pressure p_c. A compressible fluid under the action of gravity displays a density profile, with the density increasing in the direction of the gravity vector. Therefore, if a fluid of nominal critical density ρ_c is filled into a container, only an infinitely thin layer will have this density. Consequently, a very small amount of the substance is critical, and the critical behavior predicted by modern theories, such as the renormalization group theory, will be masked by the noncritical behavior of the major part of the test substance. Successful microgravity experiments have been performed and are planned on superfluid helium-4 (^{4}He) at the λ-point to experimentally verify the predictions of the renormalization group theory.

First-order phase transitions are characterized by a discrete rather than a continuous change of the phase and are accompanied by a discontinuity in the corresponding Gibbs energy of the system. The features of a first-order phase transition are the existence of an interface of finite thickness, metastable states and hysteresis effects, and nonzero enthalpy of transition. For liquids, the surface or interfacial tension becomes the dominant force in the absence of gravity, and capillarity effects determine their shape and behavior.

Metastable states are associated with first-order phase transitions because the new phase is distinctly different from the old phase, and a barrier must be overcome before the thermodynamically stable new phase can develop. In solidification, this barrier is due to the energy required to establish a solid-liquid interface. Although this nucleation process is not gravity-dependent, the possibility of working in a containerless environment in microgravity helps to reduce potential nucleation sites and therefore allows the study of metastable states, in particular undercooled liquids, their nucleation, and the subsequent growth of the solid phase.

Transport phenomena. The dynamics of a first-order phase transition are of course closely dependent upon the heat and mass transport processes occurring at the phase boundary. For example, if a binary liquid is solidified, both latent heat and solute are released at the solid-liquid interface. Usually a larger concentration of solute can be accommodated in the liquid phase than in the solid phase, which leads to the rejection of solute by the solid and a pile-up of solute ahead of the solidification front in the liquid phase. Therefore, both a temperature gradient and a concentration gradient are created at the solid-liquid interface. In the presence of a gravitational force, these gradients lead to thermal, solutal, or coupled thermo-solutal convection. This is an extremely complex problem which cannot be solved generally and which may lead to unpredictable and undesired variations of the growing solid phase. On the other hand, heat and mass transport in microgravity are accomplished by mass diffusion and heat conduction, which can be described by the corresponding transport equations, namely Fick's law and Fourier's law.

Many microgravity experiments have been performed dealing with solidification of metals or of semiconductors, all trying to avoid or suppress convection and to produce homogeneous materials, free of defects. Some of these experiments suffered from the fact that the absence of gravity does not necessarily imply convection-free circumstances. If there are liquid-vapor surfaces, as in many crystal growth experiments, such as in zone melting, and if there are temperature or concentration gradients along the surface, there is Marangoni convection. Fluid flow develops along the surface toward regions of higher surface tension, leading to convection rolls very similar to those of buoyancy-driven convection. This phenomenon has been overlooked by many of the early crystal growth experiments in space and has given rise to unexpected, and disappointing, results.

In the framework of linear irreversible thermodynamics, flow of heat or mass is linearly dependent on generalized thermodynamic forces such as temperature or concentration gradients through the Onsager coefficients. Common examples for such linear relations are Fick's diffusion equation, which relates mass flow to a concentration gradient via the diffusion constant D, and Fourier's law for heat conduction, where heat flow is related to a temperature gradient via the thermal conductivity λ. For simple geometries, these partial differential equations can be solved analytically, and the experiment can be compared to the theoretical prediction. However, under terrestrial conditions convection dominates heat and mass transport and destroys these diffusive solutions. Under microgravity the analytical solutions can be verified experimentally, and the diffusion constant D and thermal conductivity λ can be measured with great precision. For example, it was shown that the diffusion constant of a specific element depends on its atomic mass; that is, there is an isotope effect. Such an effect is predicted by atomistic theories of diffusion. Furthermore, it turned out that the dependence of the diffusion constant on the thermodynamic temperature T is quadratic, that is, $D \propto T^2$, in contradiction to the generally assumed Arrhenius behavior, $D \propto \exp(-E/kT)$, where k is Boltzmann's constant. The latter is based on the assumption that diffusion is an activated process requiring an activation energy E, while the quadratic temperature dependence can be explained on the basis of a collective model.

The Onsager relations can be written in matrix form, where a matrix consisting of the Onsager coefficients connects the generalized forces to the fluxes. The two examples discussed above represent diagonal elements linking fluxes to their conjugate forces. However, the Onsager matrix can have nondiagonal elements, describing for example mass flow originating from a temperature gradient. Such an effect is called the Soret effect. Based on the properties of the Onsager coefficients, the Soret effect was predicted to exist in liquid mixtures. Under terrestrial conditions it is nearly impossible to measure the Soret coefficient S of a liquid because unavoidable convection counteracts this very weak effect. In microgravity, however, it was possible to prove its existence and to determine the Soret coefficient of a liquid cobalt-tin alloy.

Transport phenomena also play a major role in the area of combustion. Combustion is an exothermic chemical reaction. A flame can burn if enough oxygen is supplied, and if the reaction products, in particular soot, are transported away from the flame. On Earth, this transport is accomplished by convection in the surrounding gas. Therefore, it was thought originally that a flame would extinguish under microgravity conditions because diffusive transport would not be sufficient. In contrast to this assumption, the flame persists in microgravity, but it is weaker and it has a nearly spherical shape. Combustion has become a very active research field in microgravity. Most of the related experiments are of short duration and can be carried out conveniently in drop towers, but combustion experiments have also been performed on board the space shuttle.

Containerless processing. Containerless processing techniques have been developed for terrestrial applications. Positioning is accomplished by acoustic, electric, or electromagnetic fields. The most widely used of these techniques is electromagnetic levitation. It is restricted to metallic samples and is based on the Lorentz force for positioning and on ohmic losses for heating. Terrestrial levitation techniques provide a containerless environment at the expense of strong forces acting on the sample. These forces have detrimental side effects which must be tolerated when applying levitation on Earth. Under microgravity conditions, these forces can be minimized to a negligible amount, and a unique opportunity exists to study a sample not in contact with any material container and free of external forces.

Such an environment allows the study of under-cooled liquids, their nucleation, and subsequent solidification. For example, the dependence of the solidification velocity can be determined as a function of undercooling for a large temperature range. Undercoolings of more than 20% have been achieved in electromagnetic and electrostatic levitators. Also, by repeating the identical undercooling experiment many times, the statistical nature of the nucleation process itself can be probed and different nucleation theories can be tested.

Containerless processing not only provides ultra-pure conditions necessary for undercooling and nucleation studies, but also allows the handling of highly aggressive materials for which no suitable container exists. Therefore, it is used to study high-temperature (metallic) melts. Due to the experimental difficulties, the thermodynamic and thermophysical properties of these melts are only poorly known. The potential of electromagnetic levitation for measurement of thermophysical properties of liquid metals was recognized in the 1960s, when the first experiments were conducted to determine the density and surface tension of liquid copper and nickel. Such measurements require, in addition to container-less positioning and heating, noncontact diagnostics. For example, the density is determined by reconstructing the volume of the levitated drop from photographic images. The surface tension can be derived from the frequency of surface oscillations of the drop. This is due to the fact that surface tension is the restoring force for such oscillations. For a force-free spherical liquid drop, this relation is particularly simple. Such a situation is realized only in microgravity, whereas gravity and the levitation field deform the liquid drop in terrestrial experiments, rendering the simple equation inapplicable. Consequently, the first precise surface tension measurements of liquid metals applying the oscillating drop technique were carried out in space in 1994. The surface oscillations are damped by the viscosity of the liquid. Therefore, the oscillating drop method can also be used to measure the viscosity of liquid metals by observing the damping of the surface oscillations. Again, this is possible only under microgravity conditions because on the ground the electromagnetic levitation fields disturb the measurement.

In addition to density, surface tension, and viscosity, the heat capacity and the electrical conductivity can be measured by noncontact methods. For the heat capacity, the heat input into the sample is modulated sinusoidally, and the corresponding temperature response is recorded. If the modulation frequency is chosen correctly, a simple algebraic expression for the heat capacity can be derived. Finally, the electrical conductivity is determined inductively by measuring the impedance of a coil surrounding the sample.

For background information *see* ACOUSTIC LEVITATION; CONDUCTION (HEAT); CRITICAL PHENOMENA; DIFFUSION; LIQUID HELIUM; PHASE TRANSITIONS; SPACE PROCESSING; SURFACE TENSION; WEIGHTLESS-NESS in the McGraw-Hill Encyclopedia of Science & Technology.
                                            Ivan Egry

Bibliography. S. Chandrasekhar, *Hydrodynamic and Hydromagnetic Stability*, Oxford University Press, Oxford, 1961, reprint, Dover Publications, 1981; I. Egry and C. Nieto de Castro, Thermodynamics and microgravity—What can we learn, in *Chemical Thermodynamics*, ed. by T. M. Letcher, pp. 171–186, Blackwell, Oxford, 1999; M. Velarde and Ch. Normand, Convection, *Sci. Amer.*, 243(1):92–108, July 1980; H. Walter (ed.), *Fluid Sciences and Materials Sciences in Space*, Springer, Berlin, 1987.

Micro-opto-electro-mechanical systems

Micromachines, such as micro-electro-mechanical systems (MEMS) and micro-opto-electro-mechanical systems (MOEMS), are beginning to affect almost every area of science and technology. In areas as diverse as the chemical, automotive, aeronautical, cellular, and optical (light-wave) communications industries, silicon-based micromachines are becoming the solution of choice for many problems. Devices such as optical switches, variable attenuators, active equalizers, add/drop multiplexers, optical cross-connects, gain tilt equalizers, and data transmitters are finding application in advanced light-wave systems.

Light-wave systems. The capacity of light-wave systems, using optical fibers, is exploding as a function of time. Driven by the growth of the Internet, the rate of progress surpasses even Moore's law, the observation that the number of transistors on a microprocessor doubles every 18 months. For light-wave systems, the capacity-doubling time for an optical fiber is 6–9 months. Therefore, light-wave system architects must quadruple system capacity every year, while increasing costs by only a factor of 2. The current record for opticalfiber transmission capacity is more than 10 terabits per second of information, or roughly a billion phone calls in a single fiber. Keeping up with this trend is quite a feat. MOEMS for light-wave systems will help solve this capacity problem.

Advantages. MOEMS offer a number of advantages for optical designers. They are made using integrated circuit batch-processing techniques, so although fabrication may consist of a complicated multistep process, the devices are economical to produce because many are made simultaneously. In addition, designers and manufacturers can exploit the extensive

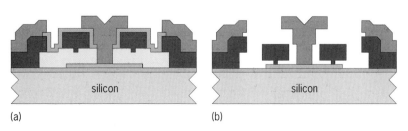

Fig. 1. Silicon-fabricated MEMS device (a) before the release step, and (b) after the release step.

(a)

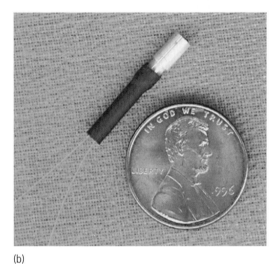

(b)

Fig. 2. Optical modulator: (a) trampoline structure, and (b) packaged device.

capabilities of the integrated circuit fabrication industry and profitably use previous-generation equipment. In an era in which an integrated circuit factory costs a billion dollars and is obsolete in less than 5 years, the ability to reuse the equipment for a new class of products is very appealing.

Integrated circuit fabrication techniques also allow designers to integrate micromechanical, analog, and digital microelectronic devices on the same chip, producing multifunctional integrated systems. Contrary to intuition, MOEMS have proven to be robust and long-lived—especially ones whose parts flex without showing microscopic wear points. Research in this area has been extremely active over the last decade. It is believed that the scale at which these machines work makes them a particularly good match for optics problems, where the devices, structures, and relevant wavelengths range in size from one to several hundred micrometers. In addition, the devices are small, cheap, and fast, and operate at low power.

Device fabrication. Starting with a silicon wafer (substrate), MOEMS are built by patterning and depositing various materials using integrated circuit

fabrication techniques known as very large scale integration (VLSI). Typical materials are alternating layers of polycrystalline silicon and silicon dioxide glasses. As in VLSI, the structures and patterns can have submicrometer features. After fabrication, the devices can have a quite complicated three-dimensional structure (**Fig. 1***a*). Unlike VLSI, after all the materials are patterned and deposited, parts of the device are etched away, leaving parts that are free to move (Fig. 1*b*). Typically, the oxides are etched away, leaving the silicon structures. MOEMS consist primarily of silicon with other materials, such as nitrides and metals, used as insulators and wires, where needed. Clearly, while quite simple, the fabrication techniques are very powerful in that very complex devices can be built. After fabrication, MOEMS are packaged in ways similar to those used to package silicon integrated circuits.

Light-wave network applications. MOEMS are actuated (made to move) using electrostatic forces. For example, the membrane device shown in **Fig. 2***a* is made to move by applying a voltage between it and the substrate, which pulls it down like a trampoline. Typical MOEMS devices, such as optical modulators, variable attenuators, switches, add/drop multiplexers, active equalizers, and optical cross-connects, manipulate light in some way, usually involving optical fibers as both inputs and outputs.

Optical switch. A micrograph of a 1 × 2 MOEMS switch is shown in **Fig. 3**. An optical switch is used to switch light from one optical fiber to another in much the same way an electrical switch is used to switch electrons from one wire to another. The mirror reflects the light from the optical fiber on the left to the fiber at right angles to it, or moves out of the way to allow the light to go straight through into the other fiber. In other words, it switches the light from one input fiber to either of two output fibers. The mirror itself is attached to a seesaw structure that can lift it up and out of the way. When no voltage is applied, the mirror is in the position shown. When a voltage is applied, it moves up, allowing the light to

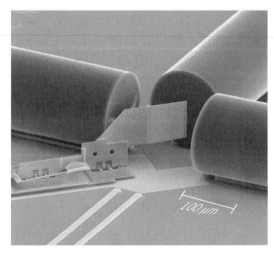

Fig. 3. A 1 × 2 optical switch. The structure between the three optical fibers is the mirror.

Fig. 4. Mirror for a variable optical attenuator.

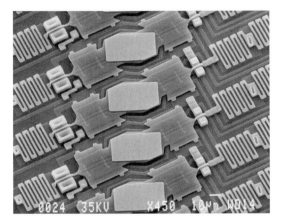

Fig. 5. Array of micromirrors for use in an add/drop multiplexer.

go straight to the other fiber. Such switches can be small, fast, and inexpensive.

Variable attenuator. **Figure** 4 shows a micromirror used in a variable attenuator. A variable attenuator is the optical equivalent to a rheostat. It is used to adjust the intensity of the light in a network in an analog mode. For the attenuator shown, light from a fiber at right angles to the mirror is reflected to an output fiber. The amount of coupling between the fibers is determined by the angle of the micromirror with respect to the input mirror. Imagine being in a room with light streaming in one window while you are holding a mirror. By adjusting the angle of the mirror the amount of light reflected out another window is controlled. In the device in Fig. 4, by applying a voltage to the left side of the mirror its angle can be adjusted and the optical coupling between two fibers is controlled.

Optical modulator. High-speed optical modulators are used to turn light on and off quickly in order to encode data on a fiber as a series of ones and zeros. The device works like a microscopic trampoline (Fig. 2*a*). Packaged devices can be orders of magnitude smaller than with previous technologies (Fig. 2*b*). Typical response times are 50 nanoseconds for such modulators.

Add/drop multiplexer. An add/drop multiplexer is a more complicated optical switch than the one shown

in Fig. 3. In operation, each wavelength of light in an optical fiber is spatially demultiplexed by a grating (which works as a prism) and lands on its own mirror to be correctly routed to an appropriate output port. An array of mirrors, such as shown in **Fig. 5**, can then route many beams of light in a complicated three-dimensional pattern.

Cross-connect. A cross-connect is a very large optical switch that can route light from hundreds of input fibers to hundreds of output fibers. Unlike the mirrors in Figs. 3, 4, and 5, which rotate on one axis, these mirrors can route light in two directions, allowing complex switching functions to be accomplished. **Figure 6** shows a two-axis micromirror for use in an all-optical cross-connect. Such mirrors have been used to build large, MOEMS-based optical cross-connects with a petabit/s capacity (1000 terabits/s).

Outlook. **Figure 7** shows a research device. Built for fun, it is a fully functional optical microscope (hundreds of which could fit on the head of a pin). In operation, light comes in through a tapered optical fiber (the pencil-looking object), and the sample is moved by a three-axis (x, y, z) stage (seen as the complicated structure below the fiber). Clearly, the possibilities for novel optical devices and functions are endless.

Fig. 6. Two-axis micromirror for use in an optical cross-connect.

Fig. 7. Fully functional micro-microscope.

For background information *see* ELECTRONIC PACKAGING; INTEGRATED CIRCUITS; MICRO-ELECTRO-MECHANICAL SYSTEMS (MEMS); MICRO-OPTO-ELECTRO-MECHANICAL SYSTEMS (MOEMS); OPTICAL COMMUNICATIONS; OPTICAL FIBERS in the McGraw-Hill Encyclopedia of Science & Technology.

David Bishop

Bibliography. V. Aksyuk et al., Micromechanical "trampoline" magnetometers for use in large pulsed magnetic fields, *Science*, 280:720–722, 1998; D. Bishop et al., The little machines that are making it big, *Phys. Today*, October 2001; D. Bishop et al., The rise of optical switching, *Sci. Amer.*, 284(1):88, 2001; C. Bolle et al., Observation of mesoscopic vortex physics using micromechanical oscillators, *Nature*, 399:43–46, May 1999; H. Chan et al., Quantum mechanical actuation of microelectromechanical systems by the Casimir force, *Science*, 291:1941–1944, 2001; Special Issue on Microelectromechanical Systems: Technology and Applications, *MRS Bull.*, vol. 26, no. 4, April, 2001.

Migration and navigation (vertebrates)

The periodic movement of a population of animals, or a part of it, away from a region and their subsequent return to that region is termed migration. Migratory movements may be daily, as with fishes that move upward and downward in the water column; annual, as with many birds and mammals; or irregular, as with some salmon and fresh-water eels that may require a lifetime to complete their migration.

Some species migrate only short distances. This local, or microgeographic, migration is typical of some salamanders, frogs, house mice, and some snakes. Some species that live in mountainous regions, such as dark-eyed juncos, Carolina chickadees, and many elk, move between higher and lower elevations. These movements are known as altitudinal migration. The best-known migrators, however, are the macrogeographic, or long-distance, migrators such as Pacific salmon, ducks, geese, swans, swallows, thrushes, sea turtles, some bats, whales, fur seals, and sea lions. These species may cover several thousands of kilometers annually.

Many migrating animals travel either at regular times during the year or at a particular time during their lives. Some travel to avoid cold or hot weather, some to find a steady food supply, and others to reach breeding sites or special places to produce their young. Many species travel in groups (for example, Canada geese, caribou, elephants, elephant seals, and whales), whereas others travel alone (for example, ruby-throated hummingbird, sea turtles, and red bats).

Donald W. Linzey

Birds

The migratory habits and navigational mechanisms utilized by birds during their annual migrations are the best known and, in many cases, the most spectacular in the animal kingdom. Migration in birds is found to involve a variety of cues linked together by learning processes. The first migration is guided by the innate migration program; during later migrations, however, this program is largely replaced by experience-based mechanisms, which may involve additional cues.

Innate migration program. Young birds beginning their first migration face the task of starting at the right time and reaching an unknown region, where their population stays during the winter. The onset of migration is controlled by an inner calendar, an endogenous annual cycle that is synchronized by the decreasing day length in autumn. This innate program determines the direction and distance to be traveled. Distance is controlled by the amount of nocturnal migratory activity, which has been found to be closely related to the migration distance of a population; under normal circumstances, there will be just the right amount of migratory activity to reach the population-specific wintering area. Direction is controlled by a spontaneous tendency to prefer a certain compass course. Translated into human terms, the migration program tells young birds something equivalent to "fly for six weeks toward southwest." Cross-breeding experiments with conspecifics from different populations clearly show that both the amount of migratory activity and the migratory direction are innate and passed genetically from one generation to the next.

To convert the genetically coded information on direction into an actual compass course, birds use two reference systems: the geomagnetic field and celestial rotation, with the latter derived from the apparent rotation of the pattern of polarized light around the celestial pole during the daytime and of the stars at night. Experiments with hand-raised passerine (songbird or perching bird) migrants suggest that both systems interact to establish the migration course. The interaction has been analyzed in garden warblers (*Sylvia borin*) from Central Europe, a population that starts migrating on a southwesterly course. Celestial rotation seems to provide a reference direction away from its center, which corresponds to geographic south; the population-specific tendency toward southwest is coded with respect to the geomagnetic field, namely as a deviation from the reference direction (**Fig. 1**). The processes establishing the migration course take place in summer during the premigratory period so that the course is available when migration begins.

First migration. Once the young migrants start, their main navigational task is to locate their course at the beginning of each flight.

Compass mechanisms. Birds have several compass mechanisms at their disposal. A magnetic compass is provided by their ability to perceive the direction of the magnetic field lines. The other compass mechanisms are based on celestial cues. The star compass derives directions from the configuration of the stars with respect to the celestial pole, similar to the way that humans are able to find north by the Big Dipper (Ursa Major) regardless of its position. This makes the star compass immune to the movements of the stars and, more importantly, to the birds' own movements across geographic latitudes. Another set of cues providing nocturnal migrants with directional information at sunset are factors associated with the setting sun; here, the typical pattern of polarized light is most important.

In contrast to the magnetic compass, the celestial compass mechanisms are learned. Experiments with hand-raised birds suggest that a first-star compass is established during the premigratory period, with celestial rotation serving as reference. During migration, however, both the star compass and the sunset cues are controlled by the magnetic compass (Fig. 1). This is indicated by numerous experiments with magnetic and celestial cues giving contradictory information. Birds usually follow magnetic information, which has proved to be dominant over stars as well as sunset cues. Celestial cues are not simply ignored but are recalibrated according to magnetic north. This way, the birds solve the conflict between cues, and all compass mechanisms again provide the same directional information. Interestingly, this recalibration of celestial cues seems to be valid only for the time of day during which the birds experienced the conflicting cues; in birds migrating during twilight hours, recalibration of the sunset cues at dusk was found not to affect the response to the corresponding cues at dawn.

Directional changes. Many bird species migrate along routes that are not straight in order to avoid ecological barriers such as mountains, seas, or deserts. This means that they have to change course during migration. In some species, such directional changes are controlled by the migration program alone via the internal calendar; other species, however, seem to need external triggers to perform the respective shift. For example, pied flycatchers (*Ficedula hypoleuca*) change direction only when they experience the magnetic intensity and inclination of the region where the shift normally occurs; specific local values of the geomagnetic field serve as triggers to induce the directional change.

Later migrations. The return migration to the breeding grounds and all later migrations are no longer controlled by the innate migration program alone. Now the goal is familiar, and the birds can make use of the experience obtained during the previous trips. Largescale displacement experiments have shown that experienced migrants can modify their course to compensate for the displacement, heading directly toward their goal. This requires mechanisms of true navigation, similar to the ones employed by homing pigeons and other displaced birds. What additional cues may be involved in determining the course to the goal is not entirely clear. The compass mechanisms, however,

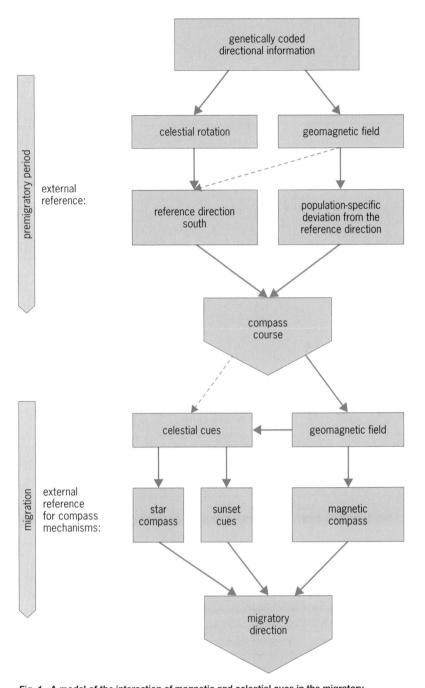

Fig. 1. A model of the interaction of magnetic and celestial cues in the migratory orientation of young birds during their first migration. Solid arrows show the normal pathways; broken arrows indicate pathways that became evident in specific experimental situations. (*After W. Wiltschko, P. Weindler, and R. Wiltschko, Interaction of magnetic and celestial cues in the migratory orientation of passerines, J. Avian Biol., 29:606–617, 1998*)

are the same as the ones used during the first migration.   Wolfgang Wiltschko; Roswitha Wiltschko

Sea Turtles

The migrations of sea turtles involve remarkable feats of orientation and navigation. Hatchlings that have never before been in the ocean swim directly away from land to the open sea without any assistance or guidance from other turtles. Juveniles of several species migrate across enormous expanses of seemingly featureless sea, sometimes crossing entire ocean basins. Finally, as adults, many turtles migrate considerable distances from feeding grounds to nesting beaches located in the same general area where they themselves hatched.

The longest and most astonishing migrations of sea turtles are made by young loggerhead turtles (*Caretta caretta*). During their vast migrations, these turtles travel for years along migratory routes that stretch across entire oceans and back. Young loggerheads in the North Atlantic cover more than 15,000 km before returning to the North American coast. Those in the Pacific travel even farther. Recently, considerable progress has been made toward understanding how young loggerheads guide themselves across the Atlantic Ocean and back.

Migratory path. Hatchling loggerhead turtles leave their natal beaches along the east coast of Florida and migrate east to the Gulf Stream, a major oceanic current that sweeps northward along the southeastern United States coast. This offshore migration from the beach to the Gulf Stream is believed to help the small, defenseless turtles survive by getting them away from shallow inshore waters, where predatory birds and fish are particularly abundant. Most loggerheads complete this journey during their first few days in the ocean.

During the next several years, the young loggerheads complete a much longer transoceanic migration. The offshore migration ends as the turtles enter the Gulf Stream current, but the Gulf Stream itself is part of the North Atlantic gyre, the circular current system that flows around the Sargasso Sea (**Fig. 2**). The warm waters of the North Atlantic gyre provide young turtles with a favorable habitat for growth and development. During this time, the turtles circle the

Fig. 2. North Atlantic gyre, the circular current system that flows around the Sargasso Sea. Currents of the gyre are represented by arrows, with the North Atlantic Drift current branching off from the northeastern corner of the gyre.

North Atlantic, crossing to the eastern side before returning as large juveniles to feeding grounds along the North American coast.

Navigational cues in offshore migration. Florida loggerheads appear to use three different sets of navigational cues sequentially during offshore migration (**Fig. 3**). On the beach, hatchlings crawl seaward by orienting toward the low, bright, oceanic horizon. Once they enter the ocean, the turtles initially head offshore by swimming into waves. Because waves are refracted in shallow coastal areas until they approach land directly, swimming into waves in the wave refraction zone reliably leads turtles seaward.

In deeper water farther from land, waves can move in any direction relative to the coastline and may no longer indicate offshore direction. Nevertheless, tracking studies suggest that hatchlings continue

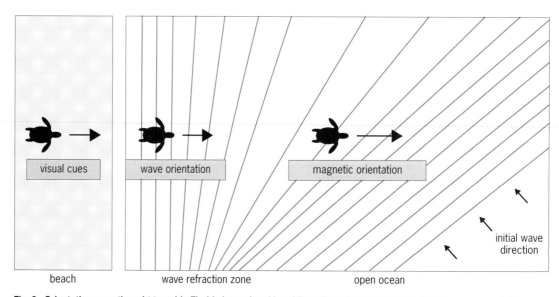

Fig. 3. Orientation cues thought to guide Florida loggerhead hatchlings from their nests to the Gulf Stream current. The beach is to the left and progressively deeper water is to the right. Lines represent oceanic waves moving toward the beach; as they enter shallow coastal areas, waves refract (bend) until they approach the beach directly. Visual cues guide hatchlings from their nests to the sea. Nearshore, turtles orient into refracted waves, which provide a reliable cue for swimming seaward. In deeper water, waves no longer provide a consistent cue for offshore orientation, and hatchlings are hypothesized to transfer their seaward courses to their magnetic compasses.

offshore even after they have left the wave refraction zone. Other experiments show that, while swimming into waves, hatchlings can learn the magnetic direction of their courses and then use their internal magnetic compasses to maintain those headings. Thus, the third step of the offshore migration seems to be a switch from wave orientation to magnetic orientation.

Navigating the Atlantic Ocean. For young loggerheads, straying beyond the latitudinal extremes of the gyre can be fatal. Along the northeastern edge of the gyre, the east-flowing current divides. The northern branch continues past Great Britain, and the water temperature drops rapidly. Loggerheads caught in this current soon die from the cold. In the south, turtles straying out of the gyre risk being swept into the South Atlantic current system and carried far from their normal range.

Recent experiments suggest that young loggerheads avoid straying out of the gyre by detecting subtle differences in the magnetic fields that exist in different parts of the ocean, and thus use these magnetic fields as navigational markers. In one crucial experiment, hatchling loggerheads were placed into tiny harnesses and tethered so that they swam in place in a pool of water in the laboratory. The turtles were then exposed to magnetic fields replicating those found in three widely separated locations along their migratory path. The turtles responded by swimming in directions that would, in each case, help keep them within North Atlantic gyre and facilitate movement along the migratory pathway. These results demonstrate that sea turtles can use the Earth's magnetic field not only as a source of directional or compass information but also as a source of positional information.

Kenneth J. Lohmann;
Catherine M. F. Lohmann

Elephant Seals

Northern elephant seals (*Mirounga angustirostris*) and southern elephant seals (*M. leonina*) make one or more long-distance seasonal migrations each year between small isolated breeding sites on land and distant, widely dispersed marine foraging areas. Among northern elephant seals, there are clear differences between the migratory routes and foraging destinations of adult males and adult females. Those differential migratory patterns become established around puberty in males. There may also be differences in the migratory patterns of southern elephant seals according to sex, though substantial variability among individual seals has made any differential migratory behaviors less clear. Recent studies of southern elephant seals have suggested that juveniles and adults, either male or female, migrate to different foraging areas.

Migratory patterns and behavior. Adult northern elephant seals make at least two round-trip migrations each year while traveling over vast areas of the North Pacific Ocean. During the 8 to 10 months each year that the adults are at sea, they cover at least 18,000 km (females) to 21,000 km (males). Adult

southern elephant seals also cover several thousand kilometers or more during their migrations; in contrast to northern elephant seals, however, they do not all return to the breeding colony sites to molt after spending several months at sea feeding after the breeding season. Consequently, some southern elephant seals may make only a single round-trip migration from breeding colonies each year, with a stopover to molt at a distant site near where they are foraging.

Typically, seals of both species dive without interruption during these migrations. They are submerged for around 85–90% of the time at sea and spend most of that time at depths of 200–2000 m. They spend only 1–3 min at the surface breathing between dives, the duration of which vary from 15 min to 2 h. Nonetheless, their movements between terrestrial haul-out sites and ocean foraging areas are relatively quick and direct, which raises challenging questions about how these seals orient and navigate between the two areas and how they orient and find food during each dive, particularly when actively migrating, and keep on a true course between origins and destinations.

Navigational ability. Telemetry and tracking studies have demonstrated that adult and juvenile elephant seals have remarkable navigational abilities. Studies have indicated that pups are capable of orienting, navigating, and migrating in marine environments when they first enter the ocean at only several months of age. During the first 3 weeks after birth, elephant seal pups are attended to constantly by their mothers on land. The mothers then wean and, almost simultaneously, abandon their pups on land and abruptly return to the sea to forage for several months. The pups remain mostly on land for the next 1–2 months and then also depart for foraging sojourns at sea lasting several months. Since elephant seals appear to travel and forage alone, there are probably few, if any, opportunities for young naive seals to learn from others about appropriate migratory routes and behaviors or favorable foraging locations. Arguably then, basic abilities to orient and navigate must be innate, perhaps modified by later direct experience.

Navigational cues. As yet, it is not known what physical, chemical, or biological cues might be used by elephant seals to orient and navigate during migration, nor what sensory mechanisms they might have for detecting and processing them. It is possible that the search for good foraging areas after departure from terrestrial breeding and molting sites simply involves movement along increasing gradients of prey density or direct following of migrating prey species or assemblages. However, the very accurate navigation back to small remote islands and beaches from distant foraging areas suggest that other mechanisms and factors are involved.

Innate map and compass. Northern and southern elephant seals spend much of their lives at great ocean depths, far from land. Consequently, navigation from maps established by prior experience and learning about geophysical characteristics is unlikely to be a significant factor in navigation, though it could influence orientation and homing behaviors near particular shallow nearshore sites. Nonetheless, the extensive data on elephant seal migration demonstrate that these seals have some kind of map, evidently an innate one. Moreover, the distinct differential migratory patterns of male and female northern elephant seals suggests that there may be differences in these maps according to sex and perhaps a change in a common map in young seals as males and females mature sexually. There has been increasing evidence for the use of large-scale variations in the Earth's magnetic field as a general map by a number of animals. However, there is no evidence for a mechanism of magnetic sensing or cognitive mapping in elephant seals.

The highly directional and accurate migrations of elephant seals also suggest that these seals have an innate compass, which would be crucial for the constant evaluation of their locations relative to features on their innate or experientially modified map. Celestial map navigation by the Sun or other celestial bodies has been suggested or demonstrated for some animals; however, it is likely to be of minor use by elephant seals, as they are at the ocean surface for only a few minutes every hour during their 8–10 months at sea each year.

For background information *see* AVES; BEHAVIORAL ECOLOGY; CHELONIA; MAGNETIC RECEPTION (BIOLOGY); MIGRATORY BEHAVIOR; PINNIPEDS in the McGraw-Hill Encyclopedia of Science & Technology.

Brent S. Stewart

Bibliography. P. Berthold, A comprehensive theory for the evolution, control and adaptability of avian migration, in N. J. Adams and R. H. Slowtow (eds.), *Proceedings of the 22nd International Ornithological Congress, Durban, Ostrich 70*, pp. 1–11, 1999; H. Bornemann et al., Southern elephant seal movements and Antarctic sea ice, *Antarctic Sci.*, 12:3–15, 2000; D. R. Brillinger and B. S. Stewart, Elephant seal movements: Modelling migration, *Can. J. Statistics*, 26:41–443, 1998; A. Carr, Rips, FADS, and little loggerheads, *BioScience*, 36(2):92–100, 1986; A. Carr, *The Windward Road*, University Presses of Florida, Tallahassee, 1979; F. C. Jonker and M. N. Bester, Seasonal movements and foraging areas of adult southern female elephant seals, *Mirounga leonine*, from Marion Island, *Antarctic Sci.*, 10:21–30; B. McConnell et al., Movements of naive, recently weaned southern elephant seal pups, *J. Animal Ecol.*, 71:65–78; B. S. Stewart, Ontogeny of differential migration and sexual segregation in northern elephant seals, *J. Mammalogy*, 78:1101–1116, 1997; B. S. Stewart and R. L. DeLong, Double migrations of the northern elephant seal, *Mirounga angustirostris*, *J. Mammalogy*, 76:196–205, 1995; R. Wiltschko and W. Wiltschko, *Magnetic Orientation in Animals*, Springer-Verlag, Berlin, 1995; W. Wiltschko, P. Weindler, and R. Wiltschko, Interaction of magnetic and celestial cues in the migratory orientation of passerines, *J. Avian Biol.*, 29:606–617, 1998.

Mine seismology

Seismology, the study of ground tremors in the Earth's crust, has been used extensively to monitor earthquakes and other natural phenomena. For the last 20 years, seismology has been used in the mining industry to monitor disturbances in rock caused by underground excavations. In mining, the scale of the recorded seismic activity is several orders of magnitude smaller than in earthquake seismology. Seismic information is used to understand how the rock mass responds to mining activity, in order to predict or characterize the risk potential for larger, more damaging seismic events.

In the mining industry, the seismic source is often only tens of meters away from the infrastructure and workers. Seismic tremors attenuate with distance, so the proximity to the source plays a large role in the potential damage caused by an event. Small-magnitude events may pose as great a hazard as larger ones if their source is close to an excavation.

Research efforts have focused on predicting large seismic events in mines, but with only modest success. Recent efforts are concentrating more on risk assessment, and rock mass characterization using seismic data. In a mine, a seismic network consists of an array of sensors (known as geophones or accelerometers) distributed throughout the underground workings. The sensitivity of the network is directly related to the density of sensor placement. Typical North American or Australian mine networks have sensors spaced a few hundred meters apart. This type of array can record very small tremors and locate their source to within a few meters, which may originate from intact rock cracking or small weaknesses in the rock.

Seismic mechanisms. Seismic waves are emitted from rock when the rock's stress state exceeds the strength of the rock mass, causing fractures to occur, or when dynamic displacement occurs on a preexisting geological feature (such as a fault). Stress in the mining context is the natural pressure in the rock, often caused by the weight of the rock above the excavation, and increases with depth. In many mines, residual stresses from ancient tectonic activity (the process that drives earthquakes) or from other sources, such as past glaciation, can cause significant increases in the local stress field. In Canadian Shield (Laurentian Plate) mines, for example, it is common to have horizontal stresses double the vertical stress.

Stress increases locally around an excavation, much like water flowing around a large rock in a stream. Voids interrupt the stress flow especially around the excavation opening (**Fig. 1a**). This process may cause fracturing around the opening, which is often the source of underground failures. Seismic waves are emitted and recorded as events (date, time, three-dimensional location, and magnitude). A detailed study of the resultant seismic events provides insight into the extent of induced damage around an opening.

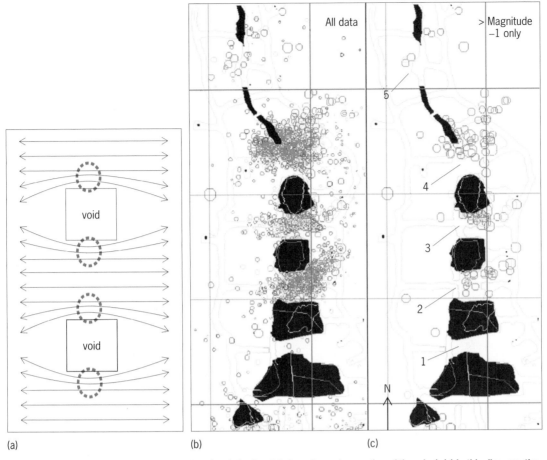

Fig. 1. Stress flow around an opening, in plan view (a horizontal plane through a portion of the mine). (*a*) **In this diagram, the dotted circles indicate the areas of highest stress concentration; the principal stress flow in this case is horizontal.** (*b*) **Seismic events around mined-out excavations (shown in black), using all data, and** (*c*) **using only >magnitude −1 data.**

In Fig. 1*b*, the seismic plot shows all the events for a one-year period (4568 events). Numbering the rock pillars from south to north, pillar 1 is seismically quiet. In this mine the highest stress direction is horizontal in the east-west direction. Pillar 1 is thus the slenderest with respect to the stress direction, and is adjacent to the largest mined-out areas. It has effectively failed, with the rock being sufficiently fractured that it no longer generates significant seismic activity. The pillars become broader relative to the high east-west stress flow going south to north due to the narrowing of the ore zone. Pillars 2, 3, and 4 are highly stressed and seismically very active. However, after several years of seismicity they are also starting to show signs of failure. A seismic gap (lack of seismic activity) occurs along the southern edge of pillar 4. If this area were solid rock, it would be the highest point of stress flow (similar to the fast water current around the rock in the stream). The seismic plot (Fig. 1*c*) shows only moderate-sized events (338 greater than local Richter magnitude −1). The seismic gaps here are more clearly visible, as damaged rock generally cannot store enough energy to be released as large events. Pillar 5 is in the narrowest portion of the zone, and thus is very squat, and strong. In addition, less volumetric mining has occurred next to it. The moderate seismicity in this case reflects the

fact that the pillar is in the earlier stages of damage, rather than the advanced state inferred in pillar 1.

In hazard or risk terms, the highly stressed, seismically active areas may be prone to rockbursting (described below) while the damaged zones are more prone to gravity-driven failures.

Rock bursting. Stress buildup around an opening may not cause excessive fracturing, but may be stored as strain energy in the rock. In extreme situations, this can lead to a mining phenomenon known as rock bursting (**Fig. 2**). A rock burst is a violent expulsion of material. Designing support systems to combat rock bursting is exceptionally difficult. In deeper mines or extensively mined-out deposits, rock burst potential is a serious safety problem. Mine seismology plays a critical role in engineering solutions, as bursts are usually seismic sources or are triggered by a seismic event.

Fault slip events. The other common group of mining-induced seismicity comes from slippage on preexisting geological features such as faults. In general, the largest events recorded in mines have a prominent geological feature as the source. Creating voids that intersect a fault allows room for the rock masses to move, and this additional degree of freedom may promote large-magnitude events. In addition, the mining creates local stress increases which may drive the

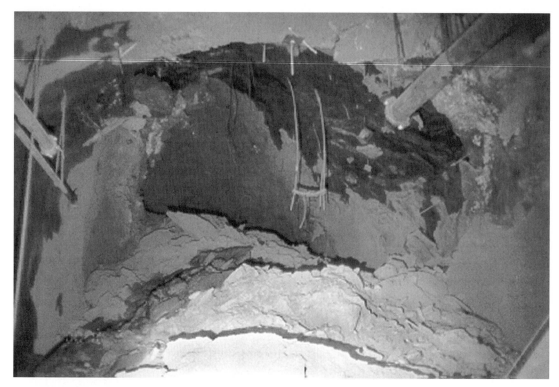

Fig. 2. A rockburst, in which the original 4.5-m-high (15-ft) tunnel sustained a roof collapse that peaked as much as 5 m (16 ft) above the original profile. A large seismic event, measured as a local Richter magnitude 2.7 by the mine's seismic network, was chiefly responsible for the damage.

structures to move. When the displacement is hindered, it can build up forces on the structural surface, which are released violently. Even the ground motion caused by a fault slip can trigger a rock burst in a tunnel that has a high stress concentration around it. Tremors from large events are commonly felt on the surface, even when the source is a few kilometers below surface.

In **Fig. 3** the event locations, indicated by circles scaled to the event magnitude, are projected onto the level plan, with the large events all located close to major geological features. A dike is an intrusive rock unit that has a weak contact with the surrounding rock, allowing movement to occur. The central features are inclusions of weak, laminated material within a massive, competent (solid) rock type. The

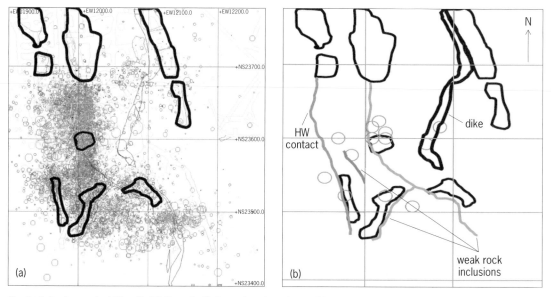

Fig. 3. Seismic events ±30 m (±100 ft) vertically from plan view shown. (a) Using all data. (b) Using events greater than local Richter magnitude 2 only. Major grid spacing is 100 m (330 ft). Mined-out regions are highlighted in black. HW = hanging wall.

hanging wall contact is a contact between a weak rock type and a much stronger rock. All these geological structures have significant planar area (in the hundreds of square meters) and can build up sufficient stresses to cause sudden, violent movement. Small-magnitude seismic activity has a broader scatter because the source mechanisms vary from intact rock cracking, to slip on both minor and major geological structures. In this example, the major stress direction is horizontal east-west which causes both lateral and vertical displacements on the structures.

Fault creep. Faults can also creep (undergo gradual displacement over time) without emitting seismic waves that are detected by a typical mine array. Seismic prediction relies on precursory activity, and if the fault is moving "quietly," there may not be any precursors to the big event. Other types of displacement monitoring can be used, but there is no other practical way to monitor a large three-dimensional mining region without the use of seismology.

Remediation. Many different parameters can be derived from seismographs. For example, the apparent stress (the ratio of seismic energy to seismic moment) multiplied by a rock property constant, is useful for interpreting the high stress portions in a mine which will have characteristically high apparent stress events (**Fig. 4**). Areas that have expected high stress conditions, such as isolated pillars, but show characteristically low apparent stress events are likely to be damaged by rock fracturing.

For large events, simply knowing the accurate location and time of the source helps direct required remedial measures, which vary from possible rescue efforts for excavation failures to proactive closures of portions of the mine.

The rock burst in Fig. 2 occurred on October 17, 2000, without any significant precursory activity. However, a previous burst had occurred on October 13, with 4 hours of small events serving as a warning (**Fig. 5**). The increase in local seismic activity prompted mine officials to close off the

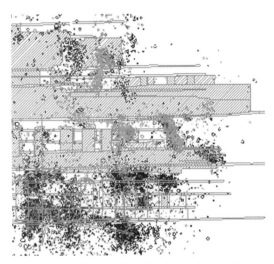

Fig. 4. Apparent stress of events in the northern portion of a mine. The view is a longitudinal section looking west. High apparent stress areas are shown in black, low apparent stress in gray. Mined-out regions are shown by cross-hatching.

affected area before this rockburst, and the general region was kept closed until a better understanding of the episode and the risks could be developed. A few days later the second burst occurred. The mine subsequently changed the mining strategy for the zone and improved the tunnel support systems to mitigate future risk.

For background information *see* FAULT AND FAULT STRUCTURES; ORE AND MINERAL DEPOSITS; ROCK BURST; ROCK MECHANICS; SEISMOLOGY; UNDERGROUND MINING in the McGraw-Hill Encyclopedia of Science & Technology.   Brad Simser

Bibliography. S. J. Gibowicz and A. Kojko, *An Introduction to Mining Seismology*, Academic Press, New York, 1994; A. J. Mendecki (ed.), *Seismic Monitoring in Mines*, Chapman & Hall, London, 1997; A. J. Mendecki and G. van Aswegen, Seismic monitoring in mines: Selected terms and definitions, in G. van Aswegen et al., (eds.), *Proceedings of the*

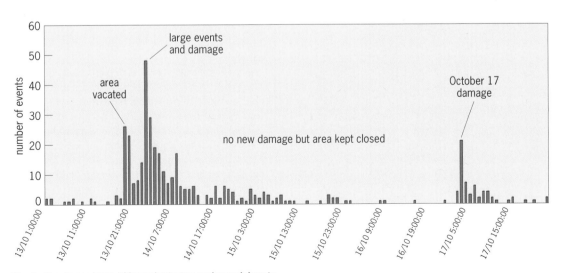

Fig. 5. Events per hour ±30 m prior to two major rock bursts.

5th International Symposium on Rockbursts and Seismicity in Mines, pp. 563–570, Symposium Series S27, South African Institute of Mining and Metallurgy, Johannesburg, 2001.

Mobile communications

Fourth-generation (4G) mobile communications concepts and technologies are beginning to evolve. In the simplest form, 4G consists of an evolution beyond the third-generation (3G) cellular communication systems now at or near deployment worldwide. Cellular communications has evolved from the original analog formats, called 1G, to the digital formats now in use and labeled 2G, to 2.5G and 3G. Most treatments of 4G involve a much more expansive view of the wireless services that are possible, and often encompass a vision of seamless, ubiquitous connectivity with cellular networks, wireless local area networks (WLANs), and wireless personal area networks (WPANs, wireless networks that cover a very short distance, and may be used to interconnect devices on one's person or very close vicinity), as well as the connections into fixed wireless and wired networks. Applications and services available through any network are also made available on any other wireless network. The wireless world, a term first used by the Wireless World Research Forum (WWRF) in its *Book of Visions* to describe 4G, would be a fundamentally better wireless communications and networking system than those currently in use or in deployment.

3G mobile communications. 3G technologies for cellular and mobile communications were set into standards in late 1999 and are being built in vari-

ous versions, including WCDMA (Wideband Code Division Multiple Access) and CDMA2000. Predecessors to it are labeled 2.5G and have been in use since 2001. 2.5G and 3G aim to make the cell phone an Internet and multimedia digital experience, with services enabled by higher data rates and an Internet-like always-on connection. The 4G viewpoint is that 3G, tied to the telephony-based circuit switched infrastructure, will not do enough and will be too expensive.

Evolution and paradigm shift. 4G was still not well defined in 2002, but there was an acceleration of the interest and work on this concept. Economic pressures for less expensive networks and services than those emerging in 3G, and the hope of more useful data applications, are driving the technical search for a more efficient end-to-end fully packet switched wireless network, for radio access anywhere anytime, and for higher data rates. 4G is envisioned as a paradigm shift allowing seamless wireless connectivity over heterogeneous networks, with interconnections to wireline networks, higher data rates (up to 100 megabits per second for mobile users and 1 gigabit per second for fixed or local users), and high but flexible and application-dependent quality of service (**Fig. 1**). The WWRF and other forums are planning on 4G systems becoming operational soon after 2010. The International Telecommunications Union (ITU) has organized a working group, Working Party 8F (WP8F), to define and prepare specifications for mobile communications beyond 3G. While most of the work of WP8F involves near and midterm evolutionary improvements to 3G—called 3G+ —there has also been work on a vision for more advanced systems. Meanwhile, market attempts to interface WLANs to cellular networks, and indeed to use them as wireless wide-area networks (WWANs), are under way, and other market trials of 4G-like concepts involving various access networks and interconnections are likely before 2010.

4G technologies. Various technologies and architectures are considered possible 4G candidates. Innovations in radio communications and wireless access, including adaptive air interface and smart radio, in wireless networks, and in spectrum allocation and utilization, encompass some of the key technologies.

Adaptive air interface. New radio communications and wireless access technologies are the engine for possible change by providing the means for high efficiency and seamless access. The air interface, including the modulation, coding, and multiple-access schemes, will need to accommodate efficiently the higher data rates, the multiple-access networks, and a greater number and variety of users and qualities of service. There is a consensus that the core technology will need to change from the dominant 3G code-division multiple-access (CDMA) techniques to a very flexible form of orthogonal frequency-division multiplexing (OFDM) in 4G.

OFDM digitally implements multiple optimally spaced subcarriers, with information bits encoded

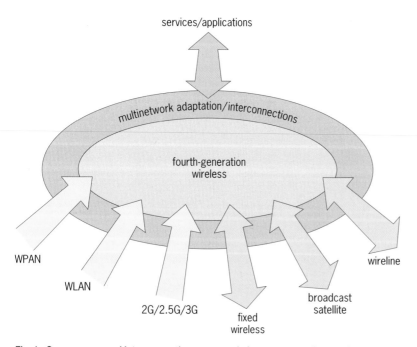

Fig. 1. Convergence and interconnections across wireless access and network technologies.

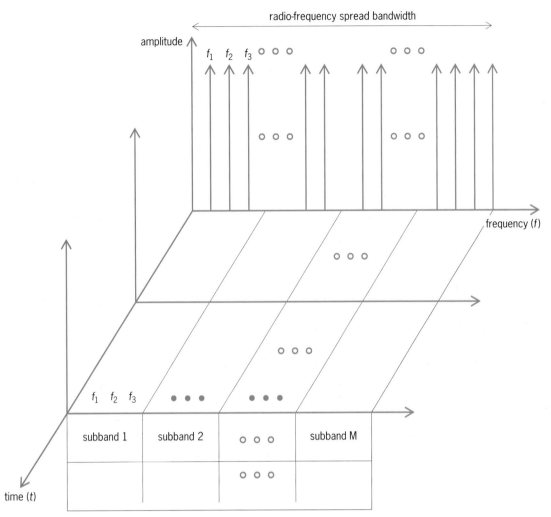

Fig. 2. Orthogonal frequency-division multiplexing (OFDM) and multichannel code-division multiple access (MC-CDMA).
The vertical arrows represent the OFDM subcarriers, distributed over a frequency range and over time. The subcarriers can
be modulated to bear the information bits, and spread as in MC-CDMA.

across the multiple subcarriers (**Fig. 2**). It is already used on higher-data-rate systems such as IEEE standard 802.11a for WLANs, at up to 54 megabits per second. At high data rates the channel is technically wideband and yields a larger number of resolvable, but random, multiple paths. OFDM can handle this wideband multipath more efficiently than CDMA. Also, because it allows a great deal of flexibility in the subcarrier modulation, data rate, coding, spacing, and other parameters, OFDM can be optimized to the channel conditions and to a variable wireless environment and its uses, for mobile as well as fixed users. Each subcarrier can also be spread as in multicarrier CDMA (MC-CDMA) to optimize performance, or minimized or eliminated to fit spectrum or interference constraints. Channel and error coding can also be varied and adapted to the link needs. A high degree of adaptation in all the physical-layer parameters is key to the efficiencies and service qualities expected in 4G.

Another element of the air interface that will involve adaptation is the multiple-access method.

Current mobile systems use frequency-division multiple access (FDMA), time-division multiple access (TDMA), or CDMA. Spatial separation, the basis of space-division multiple access (SDMA), is an extension of cellular sectoring and is currently being considered by network operators as a way to increase capacity inexpensively in hot spots of current cellular networks. With the flexibility inherent in the various OFDM forms, the multiple-access scheme can evolve in 4G to a set of hybrid schemes that permit a multidimensional selection in frequency, time, power, space, and code. Using frequency and code or power involves FDMA/CDMA combinations, and time slots or spatial selectivity can also be used to separate users. Channels formed in this multidimensional space can then be assigned in various modes, from relatively fixed to highly variable. Dynamic channel assignment can be optimized to deal with the varying numbers of users, data rates, and qualities of service.

Smart radio. Networks that may be accessed by multiple device types, or devices that may access multiple types of networks, will probably be needed to make seamless access possible. Software radio and a more evolved form called smart radio technology are being developed to permit radio operations that are spread across multiple frequency bands and use a variety of air interfaces and protocols. Frequencies from about 600 to 3000 MHz include most current or projected terrestrial mobile coverage, with the addition of the 5.5-GHZ region for WLANs. Radio-frequency technologies, including those based on silicon, germanium, and silicon carbide, as well as radio-frequency micro-electro-mechanical systems (MEMS), are evolving to cover these frequency regions with single components, and to make dynamic selections to the bands of interest. Advances in analog-to-digital converters and application specific integrated-circuit (ASIC) technology will allow greater processing, and digital signal processors (DSPs), field-programmable gate arrays (FPGAs), and other forms of programmable high-speed processing will permit flexibility in baseband processing. These form the basis for the move to software radio. As greater intelligence is built into devices and systems, it will permit them to adapt to the wireless link, to the network, and to the application, and thus evolve to smart radio. These software or smart radios will likely be used first as part of the infrastructure, as base stations and access points. As the technology evolves, it will be possible to employ them for the user devices. Topology and architectural issues, as well as economic factors, will help determine the extent to which these smart radio concepts are adopted, as opposed to more uniform and restricted 2- or 3-mode radios, such as the 2/3-mode and 2/3-band handsets used to provide 2G and 2.5G services in European as well as the American cellular bands.

Wireless networks. Wireless network technologies are also evolving quickly. Almost certainly a fuller evolution toward an all-IP (Internet Protocol) or packet-switched form will ocur. Market trials of 802.11 and IP interconnections for WWANs have been undertaken. The quality-of-service issues for voice over IP (VoIP) still remain in dynamic or heterogeneous networks but efforts are under way to resolve them. The cellular architectures, with a centralized base station in each cell, are likely to evolve in 4G toward hybrid and multilayered architectures, with combinations of large, medium, and small cells; pico cells, which may be indistinguishable from WLANs; and even smaller cells functioning as WPANs. Some level of technology and service convergence with fixed wireless networks can also be expected.

For each scale and mobility level, point-to-point, centralized, and ad hoc architectures can coexist, or one form may dominate. Ad hoc networks, defined as having no centralized controller or access node, are of interest in 4G because they can exist without fixed infrastructures and are therefore promising in environments requiring flexibility in the topology, access, and capacity. Ad hoc technologies can be designed to eliminate totally the base stations or access points, or used to make them highly reconfigurable. Besides being investigated for 4G, these technologies are already being used for WPANs in Bluetooth and for the military. (Bluetooth is an example of a WPAN, which can be used, for instance, to interconnect a cell phone to an ear set and microphone such that a wire is not needed to make hands-free cellular calls.)

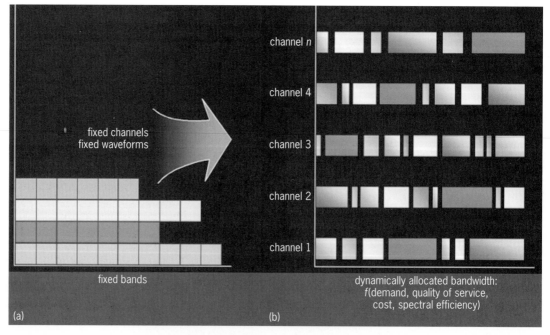

Fig. 3. Evolution of spectrum and bandwidth assignment from (*a*) current fixed allocation to (*b*) dynamically assigned and used spectrum. (*From R. Berezdivin, R. Brienig, and R. Topp, Next-generation wireless communications concepts and technologies, IEEE Commun. Mag., pp. 108–116, March 2002, © 2002 IEEE*)

Bluetooth is a wireless ad hoc network technology, sometimes also labeled as a WLAN, but having a very short range, requiring no access point, and allowing Bluetooth-enabled devices to be automatically recognized when they enter a small area.)

Reconfigurable base stations or radio access points (the terms may merge) will include hardware and software that adapt to the available spectrum, channel conditions, and network protocols. These, and the user terminals, will use software radio and other smart radio technologies to implement truly multimode and multiband capabilities. Reconfigurabilty is also highly likely in the internetwork connectivities, and indeed at all layers of the communications stack and all levels of scalability. Both the radios and the networks may thus be reconfigurable. The control and optimization of reconfigurable systems in a highly complex and variable user and wireless environment is one of the key issues in 4G.

Dynamic spectrum assignment and utilization. Spectrum assignment and utilization are key issues in wireless usage because spectrum is a limited and normally regulated resource. Better spectral efficiencies (both in terms of the basic unit, bps/Hz, and in more complex network terms such as equivalent connections per square kilometer) are needed and are evolving with better physical layer schemes, better link layer protocols and system controls, and smart antennas. 4G will do more. Adaptive spectrum and bandwidth assignment, where spectrum is both dynamically assigned and utilized to satisfy market and traffic needs, is being studied (**Fig. 3**). The Federal Communications Commission (FCC) is looking at ways to allow spectrum resources to be managed flexibly and quickly in response to market conditions. Smart and reconfigurable radios and networks, and new technologies to flexibly control spectrum across multiple users can be designed to implement flexible spectrum assignments and thus provide greater spectrum efficiency, greater capacity, and better quality of service.

For background information *see* ELECTRICAL COMMUNICATIONS; INTERNET; LOCAL-AREA NETWORKS; MOBILE COMMUNICATIONS; MULTIPLEXING AND MULTIPLE ACCESS; WIDE-AREA NETWORKS in the McGraw-Hill Encyclopedia of Science & Technology.
Robert Berezdivin

Bibliography. R. Berezdivin, R. Breinig, and R. Topp, Next-generation wireless communications concepts and technologies, *IEEE Commun. Mag.*, pp. 108–116, March 2002; H. Holma and A. Toskala (eds.), *WCDMA for UMTS: Radio Access for Third Generation Mobile Communications*, Wiley, Chichester, 2000; W. W. Lu and R. Berezdivin (eds.), *IEEE Wireless Commun.*, Special Feature: Technologies for Fourth Generation Mobile Communications, April 2002; A. F. Molisch (ed.), *Wideband Wireless Digital Communications*, Prentice Hall PTR, 2001; World Wireless Research Forum, *The Book of Visions 2000—Visions of a Wireless World, v.1.0*, IST Wireless Strategic Initiative, November 2000.

Modeling languages

A model represents something and includes some but not all qualities of what it represents. For example, an architect's model of a new development area concentrates on the physical appearance, while an aircraft designer's wind-tunnel model concentrates on aerodynamic qualities. When models are used in systems and software engineering, their important qualities are structure, behavior, communication, and requirements. To build the models, graphical or textual languages are used to describe the qualities concerned.

Need for models. Systems and software engineering are both characterized by a combination of large information content with a need for different people with different backgrounds and interests (system stakeholders) to understand at least some system aspects. During the development of systems, developers can see only a small part of the complete system at a time. They will then need models to assist them in understanding the context of their own work and the requirements on it. Models are useful prior to system development to study requirements and design alternatives, and to ensure that all stakeholders have a common understanding of why a system should be built or modified. They are also useful during and after development of a system to assist developers and users to navigate the system's structure and to understand the system's behavior. Finally, models are essential for communication between different participants in projects and as a "corporate project memory."

Systems and software engineering. Systems engineers work with a collection of operator roles (people), software modules, and hardware modules, which are combined to complete one or more missions. Thus, they work in a systems engineering work space with three dimensions (**Fig. 1**): the activity dimension (what they work with), the object category dimension (what kind of object they work with), and

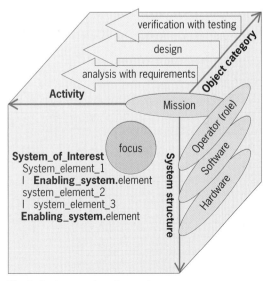

Fig. 1. Systems engineering work space.

Usage of UML diagrams

Diagram	Qualities supported			
	Require-ments	Structure	Communi-cation	Behavior
Use Case	X			
Class		X		
Sequence			X	
Collaboration			X	
Package		X		
State				X
Activity				X
Deployment		X		
Component		X		

the structure dimension (where they work in the system).

It is normally not humanly possible to retain an overall understanding of the system together with a deep insight into the system's details, so there is a need to focus somewhere in this space. A complete system model will then be useful to navigate the system and to ensure that the part that is focused on is consistent with its environment.

Obviously, software is a subset of systems engineering. However, since building the right software requires a correct understanding of the software's environment, it is advisable to include this environment in software engineering models.

Unified Modeling Language diagrams. Recently, the Unified Modeling Language (UML™) has emerged as a standard for software engineering. This standard includes a set of diagrams:

Use Case diagram. This diagram shows the interaction between a user and a software system. This is basically a dependency relation where the user depends on the system.

Class diagram. This diagram is basically an enhanced entity-relationship diagram where the entities are classes with names, attributes, and actions. A "software class" can be seen as a "template" from which instances are created to implement the software. The diagram includes relations such as generalization, association, and aggregation. The diagram can be used for conceptual modeling, for specification, and for documenting a software solution.

Sequence diagram. Message sequence charts have a long tradition for visualizing the interaction between concurrent processes communicating by way of messages. These charts are included in the UML as Sequence diagrams.

Collaboration diagram. This diagram resembles a block diagram with its boxes and arrows. It basically contains the same information as the Sequence diagram.

Package diagram. This diagram shows dependencies between major system components.

State diagram. This diagram visualizes behavior.

Activity diagram. This diagram is a development from flow charts.

Deployment diagram. This diagram shows the distribution of software objects on hardware nodes.

Component diagram. This diagram shows dependencies between components and can also be drawn to show aggregation (components included in other components).

The qualities of a software system that are primarily modeled by the UML are requirements, communication, structure, and behavior. The **table** shows how the diagrams support different qualities.

Extension of UML to systems engineering. At present there is a trend in the systems engineering community toward extended use of the UML for systems engineering. This trend is based on the fact that the UML views software as composed of modules called "classes" or "objects" characterized by their having (1) an offered interface, which contains services offered by the object, (2) an internal behavior, and (3) a required interface, with services required from other objects to complete the internal behavior.

This view is not limited to software, but can be extended to systems engineering when one includes not only software objects but also hardware and operator objects. An example of this extended use is a UML Component diagram (**Fig. 2**) which models a simple system to control the windows in a car.

Figure 2 shows that the car driver requires services from a switch bank and a button to control the car's windows. Further, these hardware control devices depend on software in the car's central computer and in the car's local computers, one in each door. The software in the local computer in the door depends in turn on a set of hardware devices in the door to complete the driver's commands.

Other modeling languages. While the UML is the emerging standard for modeling languages, there are several alternatives, including mathematical formal languages, petri nets, and formalized natural language.

Mathematical formal languages are used in so-called formal methods, with the main advantage

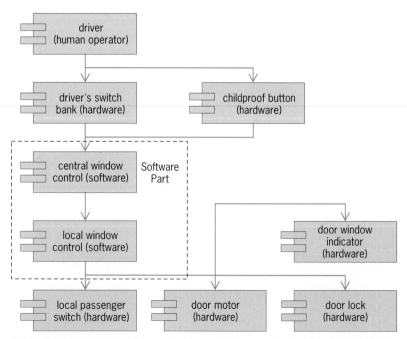

Fig. 2. Component diagram for car window control. The small rectangles signify that this is a component diagram.

being that these languages can be used to create formal specifications, which can then be checked automatically for compliance with a completed software system. The main disadvantage is that the mathematical language used can be difficult to understand for some stakeholders.

Petri nets give a graphical model of how concurrent processes communicate and influence each other through the transmission of "tokens."

A formalized natural language is obtained by simplifying a programming language for modeling use while keeping the "reserved words" and including variables of defined types. An example with part of the behavior for the software module "central window control" in Fig. 2 is:

```
begin
    case direction_up is
        when true =>
            send up_message (window_concerned)
            -- send message to move window
                -- upwards to the local control
            -- software for the concerned window in
                -- the car (driver,
            -- other_front, rear_left or rear_right)
        when false =>
            send down_message (window_concerned)
    end case
end
```

Tailoring of standards. The table shows how various diagrams in the UML address different aspects of modeling, and also shows that some aspects are covered by multiple diagrams. The obvious conclusion is that the standard needs tailoring prior to efficient use. Such tailoring should result in a set of modeling languages, some of which may be taken from within the UML, possibly modified, and some of which may be taken from outside the UML. Using a good set of modeling languages can be a blessing for a project, while careless selection, for example through uncritical acceptance of a "proven toolkit," may result in confusion.

An example of tailoring concerns a systems engineering project with the following requirements on the modeling languages used:

1. The system's missions shall be clearly seen.
2. Objects of categories Operator, Software, and Hardware shall be distinguished in the model.
3. The system's "deep dependency structure" shall be clearly seen.
4. System structure and behavior shall be modeled.
5. Stakeholders, without previous systems or software engineering experience, shall be able to understand the models immediately.

It may seem that the UML cannot satisfy much of these requirements, but tailoring can help. The Component diagram in Fig. 2 really shows a dependency structure with objects of different categories. The diagram can be modified by keeping only the

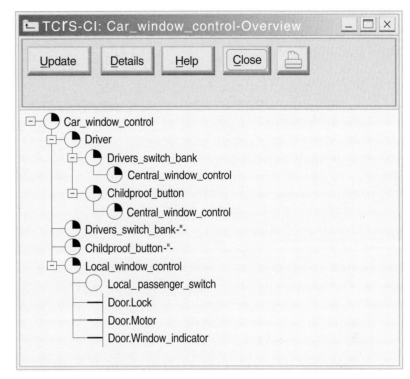

Fig. 3. Example of deep dependency structure.

objects, ordered according to how they depend on each other, and introducing a new "Mission" object at the top to state the mission "Car window control." The result is the diagram in **Fig. 3**, which is known as the deep dependency structure of the system.

This modified Component diagram has only one component (object) on each line, and each component depends on the components below and one step indented. The "little clocks" indicate completion status for the components, and the quotation marks indicate repeated parts of the diagram, when an object appears a second time. The result is that a way has been found to satisfy the requirements for structural models.

The next step is to construct behavioral models, where the UML diagrams have difficulties with ignorant stakeholders. A possible solution is then to select a text-based modeling language, as described above. Thus, it is possible to find a limited set of modeling languages that can be used for communication between stakeholders with minimum education.

For background information *see* MODEL THEORY; OBJECT-ORIENTED PROGRAMMING; PROGRAMMING LANGUAGES; SOFTWARE ENGINEERING; SYSTEMS ENGINEERING in the McGraw-Hill Encyclopedia of Science & Technology.   Ingmar Ogren

Bibliography. E. Best, R. Devillers, and M. Koutny, *Petri Net Algebra*, Springer-Verlag, 2001; M. Fowler and K. Scott, *UML Distilled*, 2d ed., Addison-Wesley, 1999; C. Larman, *Applying UML and Patterns*, 2d ed., Prentice Hall, 2001; I. Ogren, On principles for model-based systems engineering, *Sys. Eng.*, 13(1):38–49, 2000; I. Ogren, Possible tailoring of the UML for systems engineering purposes, *Sys. Eng.*, 3(4):212–224, 2000.

Monoclonal antibodies

In response to either infection or immunization with a foreign agent, the immune system generates many different antibodies that bind to the foreign molecules. Individual antibodies within this polyclonal antibody pool bind to specific sites on a target molecule known as epitopes. Isolation of an individual antibody within the polyclonal antibody pool would allow biochemical and biological characterization of a highly specific molecular entity targeting only a single epitope. Realization of the therapeutic potential of such specificity launched research into the development of methods to isolate and continuously generate a supply of a single lineage of antibody, a monoclonal antibody (mAb).

Hybridoma technology. In 1974, Wolfgang Köhler and César Milstein developed a process for the generation of monoclonal antibodies. In their process, fusion of an individual B cell (or B lymphocyte), which produces an antibody with a single specificity but has a finite life span, with a myeloma (B cell tumor) cell, which can be grown indefinitely in culture, results in a hybridoma cell. This hybridoma retains desirable characteristics of both parental cells, producing an antibody of a single specificity that can grow in culture indefinitely.

Generation of monoclonal antibodies through the hybridoma process worked well with B cells from rodents but not with B cells from humans. Consequently, the majority of the first monoclonal antibodies were from mice. When administered into humans as therapeutic agents in experimental tests, the human immune system recognized the mouse monoclonal antibodies as foreign agents, causing an immune response. This human antimouse antibody (HAMA) response was sometimes severe, even causing patient death in some cases. Although encouraging improvements in disease were sometimes seen, the HAMA response made murine (mouse) antibodies unacceptable for use in humans with a functional immune system.

Due to their immunogenicity in humans, the high hopes for the therapeutic utility of monoclonal antibodies went unmet for the first two decades after their isolation. However, fueled by advances in molecular biology and genetic engineering in the late 1980s, efforts to engineer new generations of monoclonal antibodies with reduced human immunogenicity have come to fruition. Today there are 11 monoclonal antibodies approved for human therapeutic use in the United States (see **table**). With hundreds more in clinical trials or in laboratory testing, therapeutic monoclonal antibodies are at the cutting edge of drug discovery.

Antibody engineering. Characterization of the structure of antibodies and their genes laid the foundation for antibody engineering.

Antibody structure. In most mammals, each antibody is composed of two different polypeptides, the immunoglobulin heavy chain (IgH) and the immunoglobulin light chain (IgL), with the former being a mu (IgM), gamma (IgG), alpha (IgA), epsilon (IgE), or delta (IgD) heavy chain and the latter being a kappa (Igκ) light chain or a lambda (Igλ) light chain. Comparison of the protein sequences of either heavy or light antibody chains reveals a portion that typically varies from one antibody to the next, the variable region, and a portion that is conserved, the constant region.

A heavy and a light chain are folded together in an antibody to align their respective variable and

Monoclonal antibodies approved for therapeutic use in humans in the United States				
Name	Target	Type	Disease	Year approved
OKT3 (muromonab-CD3)	CD3	Mouse	Organ transplant	1986
Reopro (abciximab)	gpIIb/IIIa	Chimeric	Acute myocardial infarction	1994
Rituxan (rituximab)	CD20	Chimeric	Non-Hodgkin's lymphoma	1997
Zenapax (daclizumab)	CD25	Humanized	Organ transplant	1997
Simulect (basiliximab)	CD25	Chimeric	Organ transplant	1998
Synagis (palivizumab)	Respiratory syncytial virus	Humanized	Infectious disease	1998
Remicade (infliximab)	TNF-α	Chimeric	Rheumatoid arthritis, Crohn's disease	1998
Herceptin (trastuzumab)	Her-2/neu	Humanized	Breast cancer	1998
Mylotarg (gemtuzumab ozogamicin)	CD33	Humanized, toxin-conjugated	Acute myeloid leukemia	2000
Campath-1H (alemtuzumab)	CD52	Humanized	Chronic lymphocytic leukemia	2001
Zevalin (ibritumomab tiuxetan)	CD20	Mouse, radio-conjugated	Non-Hodgkin's lymphoma	2002

constant regions. The unique shape of the cofolded heavy- and light-chain variable domains creates the variable domain of the antibody, which fits around the shape of the target epitope and confers the binding specificity of the antibody. In the total population of antibodies circulating in a human, there may be billions of different variable region shapes, enabling an incredibly diverse recognition of target epitopes.

Chimerization. Chimeric antibodies, part mouse and part human, represent the first new class of engineered antibody therapeutics. The process of chimerization starts with identification of a mouse monoclonal antibody that has the desired binding characteristics and biological activities. Next, the deoxyribonucleic acid (DNA) encoding the variable regions of the mouse monoclonal antibody are cloned and conjoined with DNA encoding the human antibody constant region. These engineered chimeric heavy- and light-chain genes are then expressed in cells in tissue culture to produce a recombinant antibody. Because chimeric antibodies possess a variable region that is completely of mouse origin, they can elicit an immune response, a human antichimeric antibody (HACA) response, against the monoclonal antibody in humans. Nevertheless, several chimeric antibodies have been approved for use as therapeutics in humans (see table).

Humanization. The process of antibody humanization further reduces the amount of mouse-derived amino acids to 5–10%. Like chimerization, the humanization process begins with the cloning of the mouse heavy- and light-chain variable region domain DNA for a monoclonal antibody of interest. Using molecular biology techniques, mouse DNA sequences nonessential for antibody activity (for example, regions that are of relatively low variability, called framework regions, that lie between regions of relatively high variability, called complementarity-determining regions) may be swapped for their human counterparts. Reassembly of an antibody with the desired characteristics may require many rounds of molecular engineering. Currently, several humanized monoclonal antibodies are approved human therapeutics (see table).

Antibody display. Scientists skilled in molecular biology and antibody engineering use a technique called antibody display to isolate human antibody fragments that bind to targets. In antibody display, genetically engineered viruses, yeast, or ribosomes synthesize artificial collections of human variable regions on their surface. Like a nineteenth-century gold prospector, a twenty-first-century scientist "pans" a variable region display library and keeps the variable regions that bind to the target molecule. These variable-region polypeptides are physically linked to the DNA or ribonucleic acid (RNA) encoding them, allowing the variable genes to be isolated. Typically, isolation of monoclonal antibodies with therapeutic activity requires many rounds of enhancement through recombinant DNA and screening processes. If a complete antibody is needed, a molecular biologist combines the engineered variable-region DNA

with human constant-region DNA for production in cells in tissue culture.

Transgenic mice. Mice genetically engineered to produce fully human antibodies allow the use of established hybridoma technology to generate fully human antibodies directly, without the need for additional engineering. These transgenic mice contain a large portion of human DNA encoding the antibody heavy and light chains. Inactivation of the mouse's own heavy- and light-chain (generally the Igκ light chain) genes forces the mouse to use the human genes to make antibodies. Current versions of these mice generate a diverse polyclonal antibody response, thereby enabling the generation and recovery of optimal monoclonal antibodies using hybridoma technology. More recently, Abgenix, Inc. introduced all of the human light-chain genes into its XenoMouse® strains of transgenic mice, in addition to large portions of the heavy-chain and Igκ light-chain genes, thereby more faithfully recapitulating the complete diversity of the human antibody repertoire. These genetically engineered mice are a ready source for generating therapeutic-grade fully human antibodies.

Therapeutic mechanisms of action. Disease areas that currently are especially amenable to antibody-based treatments include cancer, immune dysregulation, and infection. Depending upon the disease and the biology of the target, therapeutic monoclonal antibodies can have different mechanisms of action. A therapeutic monoclonal antibody may bind and neutralize the normal function of a target. For example, a monoclonal antibody that blocks the activity of protein needed for the survival of a cancer cell causes the cell's death. Another therapeutic monoclonal antibody may bind and activate the normal function of a target. For example, a monoclonal antibody can bind to a protein on a cell and trigger a suicide signal. Finally, if a monoclonal antibody binds to a target expressed only on diseased tissue, conjugation of a toxic payload (effective agent), such as a chemotherapeutic or radioactive agent, to the monoclonal antibody can create a guided missile for specific delivery of the toxic payload to the diseased tissue and reducing harm to healthy tissue.

Challenges for the future. A challenge in the development of therapeutic monoclonal antibodies is to find and validate additional targets associated with disease. Typical targets for therapeutic monoclonal antibodies include extracellular proteins, either lodged in the cell membrane or secreted by cells, and infectious microorganisms, such as viruses and bacteria. If the target is also present in normal tissue, the activity of the antibody could have deleterious side effects. In such a case, the therapeutic utility of the monoclonal antibody depends upon a number of factors, including the importance of the normal tissue in which the target is expressed, the activity of the antibody, the amount of antibody needed for activity against the disease tissue, and how life-threatening the disease is. For example, the receptor for epidermal growth factor is present on many solid tumors and in many normal tissues, including skin. At therapeutic dose levels, blocking epidermal growth factor function with some neutralizing monoclonal antibodies against epidermal growth factor can lead to the death of tumor cells, while the only prevalent side effect is an acnelike skin rash that disappears without scarring after discontinuing treatment. In contrast, some antibody-based treatments for autoimmune disease can cause susceptibility to infection or lymphoma, limiting their use to only the more severe cases.

Although they have many superior qualities, antibody–based therapeutics remain expensive compared with small-molecule drugs. A full regimen of treatment using an antibody against cancer will likely cost over $10,000. Much of the cost is in the manufacturing of the antibody. Industrial-scale culture of antibody-producing cells is performed in 2000–20,000-liter fermentation tanks. Subsequent purification of the antibody involves a series of concentration and chromatography steps, all performed under careful Food and Drug Administration–monitored conditions of quality control. New technologies that may increase the yield and consequently lower the cost of bulk antibody production include manufacture of monoclonal antibodies in transgenic plants such as tobacco and corn, in the milk of transgenic goats or cows, or in the eggs of transgenic chickens. A remaining challenge is to lower the cost of the recovery and purification of material suitable for administration to humans.

For background information see ANTIBODY; ANTIGEN; GENETIC ENGINEERING; IMMUNOLOGY; MONOCLONAL ANTIBODIES in the McGraw-Hill Encyclopedia of Science & Technology.   Larry Green

Bibliography. J. A. Berzofsky, I. J. Berkower, and S. L. Epstein, Antigen-antibody interactions and monoclonal antibodies, in W. E. Paul (ed.), *Fundamental Immunology*, 4th ed., pp. 75–110, Raven Press, New York, 1998; H. R. Hoogenboom and P. Chames, Natural and designer binding sites made by phage display technology, *Immunol. Today*, 21:371–378, 2000; M. Little et al., Of mice and men: Hybridoma and recombinant antibodies, *Immunol. Today*, 21:364–370, 2000; C. Milstein, With the benefit of hindsight, *Immunol. Today*, 21:359–364, 2000.

Nanoparticles

In recent years, there has been intense interest in the synthesis and characterization of nanoparticles, which range 1–100 nanometers in diameter. Semiconductor nanoparticles around 1–20 nm in diameter are often called quantum dots, nanocrystals, or Q-particles. These particles possess short-range structures that are essentially the same as the bulk semiconductors, yet have optical or electronic properties that are dramatically different from the bulk properties. The confinement of electrons within a semiconductor nanocrystal results in a shift of the band gap to higher energy with smaller crystalline size. This effect is known as the quantum size effect. In the strong confinement regime, the actual size of the semiconductor particle determines the allowed energy levels and thus the optical and electronic properties of the material.

Due to their finite, small size and the high surface-to-volume ratio, nanoparticles often exhibit novel properties. These properties can ultimately lead to new applications, ranging from catalysis, ceramics, microelectronics, sensors, pigments, and magnetic storage, to drug delivery and biomedical applications. Research in this area is motivated by the possibility of designing nanostructured materials that possess novel electronic, optical, magnetic, mechanical, photochemical, and catalytic properties. Such materials are essential for technological advances in photonics, quantum electronics, nonlinear optics, and information storage and processing.

Synthesis. A wide range of scientifically interesting and technologically important nanoparticles have been produced by both chemical and physical methods.

Colloidal. The synthesis of nanocrystals by colloidal methods involves nucleation (the initial formation of the appropriate semiconductor bond), growth (the formation of a highly crystalline core), and passivation of the nanocrystal surface. The passivation step is important in stabilizing the colloid and controlling the growth of the nanoparticles, preventing the agglomeration and fusing of the particles, and allowing the solubility of the nanoparticles in common solvents. A common approach is to use polymeric surfactants (for example, sodium polyphosphate). The polymer attaches to the surface of the growing particles, usually electrostatically, and prevents their further growth. Another passivation approach is to use capping agents such as thiolates.

In the liquid phase, particle size is controlled by confining the growing particles within micelles or reversed micelles, polymer films, glasses, or zeolites. In the case of micelles, the micellar reagent (for example, dihexadecyl phosphate or dioctadecyldimethylammonium) creates a physical boundary, that is, a well-defined region where the semiconductor is precipitated. In reversed micelles, a small amount of water is mixed with a large amount of an organic solvent and surfactant. The surfactant molecules tend to collect on the surface and stabilize the water drop. The size of the water droplets is directly related to the ratio of the water to the organic phase. Smaller droplets result in smaller nanoparticles. Nanoparticle formation occurs by the reaction of two reagents (one which is soluble only in water and another which is soluble only in the organic solvent). Many nanoparticles have been produced by reverse micelles such as cadmium sulfide, selenide, and telluride, lead sulfide and selenide, and zinc and titanium oxides.

Vapor-phase. The common chemical synthesis of metallic and intermetallic nanoparticles includes the decomposition of organometallic precursors, such as metal carbonyls (by thermal, photochemical, laser pyrolysis, and ultrasonic methods), to yield the respective elements or alloys, and the reduction of inorganic or organometallic precursors by reducing agents. Different sources of energy can be used to decompose the precursor such as microwave plasma, laser pyrolysis, laser photolysis, and flame combustion. The size of the nanoparticle is determined by the particle residence time, temperature of the chamber, pressure, and precursor composition. Low-temperature flames can also be used to supply the energy to decompose the precursors. Flame synthesis is most common for the production of oxides. Pure metal particles are best produced by gas condensation.

The vapor-phase synthesis of metallic nanoparticles involves evaporation of the material of interest, followed by the condensation of clusters and nanoparticles from the vapor phase. The vapor may be generated with laser or electron beam heating methods. Laser vaporization provides several advantages, including the production of a high-density vapor of any metal, the generation of a directional high-speed metal vapor from a solid target (which can be useful for directional deposition of the particles), control of the evaporation from specific spots on the target, as well as the simultaneous or sequential evaporation of several different targets.

A technique that combines the advantages of pulsed laser vaporization with controlled condensation (LVCC) under well-defined conditions of temperature and pressure has been developed. It allows the synthesis of a wide variety of nanoparticles of metallic, intermetallic, oxides, and carbides of controlled size and composition.

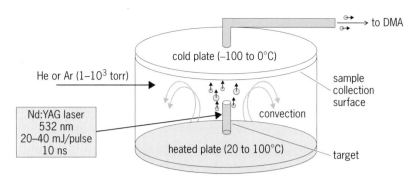

Fig. 1. Experimental setup for the synthesis of nanoparticles by the laser vaporization controlled-condensation method coupled with a differential mobility analyzer (DMA) for the size selection of the nanoparticles.

The LVCC method consists of pulsed laser vaporization of a metal or an alloy target into a selected gas mixture in a convective atmosphere created by a temperature gradient between two plates separated by a glass ring (**Fig. 1**). A pure carrier gas such as helium or argon, or a mixture containing a known composition of a reactant gas (for example, oxygen for the synthesis of oxides, methane for carbides, and so on) can be used. A high-energy pulsed laser (532-nm Nd:YAG laser) with an intensity flux of about 10^6-10^7 W/cm^2 is focused on the target of interest. The resulting plasma causes highly efficient vaporization, and the temperature at the focusing spot can exceed 10,000 K (17,500°F). This high temperature can vaporize all known substances so quickly that the surrounding vapor stays at the ambient temperature. Typical yields are 10^{14}-10^{15} atoms from a surface area of 0.01 cm^2 in a 10^{-8} s pulse. The large temperature gradient between the bottom

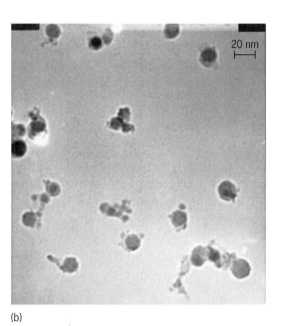

(a)   (b)

Fig. 2. Transmission electron micrographs. (*a*) Iron aluminide (FeAl) nanoparticles prepared with the laser vaporization controlled-condensation method with no size selection. The inset showed electron diffraction. (*b*) 20-nm-diameter FeAl nanoparticles selected by the differential mobility analyzer.

and top plates results in a steady convection current which moves the nanoparticles away from the nucleation zone (once condensed out of the vapor phase) before they can grow into larger particles. The nanoparticles are deposited as weblike aggregates on the top cold plate (**Fig. 2***a*), or transferred in a helium flow to a differential mobility analyzer (DMA) for size selections (Fig. 2*b*). Since the LVCC method produces a significant portion of charged nanoparticles (as ions or free electrons), the DMA classifies and separates the charged nanoparticles based on their electrical mobility in the presence of an electric field.

Assembly of nanoparticles in electric fields. The assembly of nanoparticles into filaments and fibers, which retain the unique properties of the nanoparticles, holds promise for the development of novel functional materials and the engineering of a variety of nanodevices and sensors. The nanoparticles can be assembled into long-chain filaments (**Fig. 3***a*) and fibers (Fig. 3*b*) by applying an electric field during their synthesis by the LVCC method. The filaments can be few centimeters long, and tangle together with neighboring wires to form bundles. Silicon nanoparticles have a tendency to form dendritic structures with unique fractal patterns (Fig. 3*c*, *d*).

The effect of the electric field on the formation of the chain aggregates acts through the polarization of the charges on the nanoparticles' surface. For larger particles the effect of the electrostatic charge is overpowered by gravity, but for nanoparticles the electrostatic forces are dominant. The nanoparticles' surfaces have a mixture of positive and negative charges, and some of the nanoparticles may have net charges. The dipole force is very strong near the surface of the particle, while farther away from the surface the net charge or monopole force becomes important. These two effects, when combined, may lead to the sticking together of particles of the same net charge.

Properties and applications. Semiconductor nanoparticles have technological applications in many areas of optoelectronics such as light-emitting diodes, solid-state lasers, and optical switches. Silicon nanostructures have stimulated much interest due to their unique properties, including single-electron tunneling, nonlinear optical properties, and visible photoluminescence. A transmission electron micrograph and electron diffraction pattern of silicon nanocrystals prepared by the laser vaporization with controlled condensation method are shown in **Fig. 4**. Because of its indirect band gap, bulk

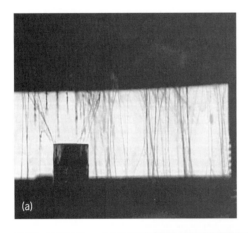

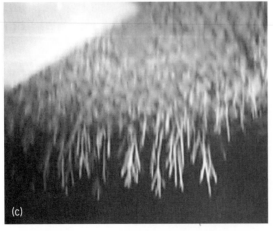
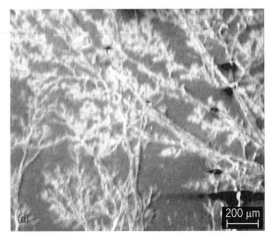

Fig. 3. Photographs of nanoparticle filaments of (*a*) iron aluminide (FeAl), (*b*) titanium aluminide (Ti₃Al), and (*c*) silicon, grown with the application of electric fields during the LVCC synthesis. (*d*) Scanning electron micrograph of a silicon nanoparticle dendritic assembly.

silicon does not exhibit visible photoluminescence. The higher energy shift in the photoluminescence of silicon nanocrystals is attributed to the three-dimensional quantum size effect.

The incorporation of silicon nanocrystals in polymer films may lead to the development of novel materials which combine several properties such as the visible photoluminescence and elasticity. Polymer films containing silicon nanocrystals exhibit the photoluminescence characteristic of the pure polymer and of the suspended silicon nanocrystals (**Fig. 5**). This may have interesting applications in the design of new materials for optical display and for silicon-based devices in optoelectronics.

Nanoparticles have important applications in catalysis and photocatalysis. The large number of surface and edge atoms provides active sites for catalyzing surface reactions. Highly nonstoichiometric oxide nanoparticles such as CeO_{2-x} provide a high oxygen-vacancy concentration, and active superoxide surface species. These nanoparticle oxides enable catalytic activation at significantly lower temperatures for the reduction of sulfur dioxide and oxidation of carbon monoxide. Other nanoparticles such as cadmium sulfide and zinc sulfide are efficient photocatalysts for generating hydrogen from water.

Molybdenum and tungsten trioxides are photochromic materials that change color upon oxidation from one state to another by the absorption of light. The photochromic effect is stronger in the nanoparticles than in the bulk material. The photochromic materials have potential practical applications in areas such as displays, imaging devices, "smart windows," and solar energy conversion.

In general, nanostructured materials possess smoother surfaces and enhanced mechanical properties as compared to conventional-grain-size materials. Nanostructured ceramics possess increased ductility since they do not contain many dislocations, and nanoparticles can diffuse fast into the materials' cracks once they are formed. Consolidated intermetallic materials based on nanoparticles show enhanced plasticity; that is, they exhibit significantly better elongations as compared to cast and powder processed components. The filamentlike and tree-like assemblies of the nanoparticles may have some special applications as fillers (additives) to increase the elastic modulus (stiffness) and tensile strength (maximum stress before breaking) of low-strength oils and polymeric materials.

Nanoparticles and functionalized nanostructured materials may have a significant impact in biological and biomedical applications. In drug delivery, nanoparticles could be used to deliver drugs where they are needed, avoiding the harmful side effects that often result from potent medicine. Prolonged residence times in blood have been achieved by nanoparticles, allowing the carriers to reach sites throughout the body without premature clearance. Because of the size of the nanoparticles, they can leave the vascular system, especially at sites of

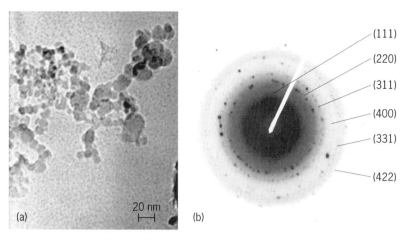

Fig. 4. Silicon nanoparticles. (*a*) Transmission electron micrograph; average particle diameter, 5–6 nm. (*b*) Electron diffraction pattern, showing diffraction rings corresponding to the planes of the randomly oriented nanocrystals.

disease (such as tumors). Since nanoparticles are much smaller than cells, there is the possibility of subcellular targeting, that is, third-order drug targeting. This is key for gene delivery, where nuclear uptake is a requirement. Since nanoparticles have similar dimensions to natural carriers (for example, lipoproteins and viruses), they may serve as structural models for natural carriers.

Nanomedical technology is opening new avenues in medical diagnostics and disease therapy. Since the size of a quantum dot determines the color it emits after exposure to light, different sizes of dots attached to different biological molecules can be used to track the activities of many tagged molecules simultaneously. Magnetic nanoparticles have been investigated as a potential alternative treatment for cancer. The hyperthermic effect (heat produced by relaxation of the magnetic energy of the magnetic nanoparticles exposed to an alternating magnetic

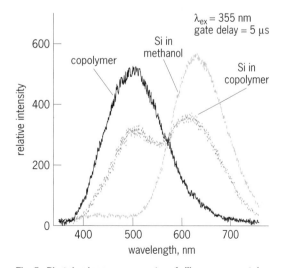

Fig. 5. Photoluminescence spectra of silicon nanocrystals suspended in methanol, sulfonated styrene-ethylene/ butylenes-styrene triblock copolymer film, and triblock copolymer film containing the silicon nanocrystals.

field) can be used to effectively destroy tumor tissue.

For background information *see* ATOM CLUSTER; BAND THEORY OF SOLIDS; CATALYSIS; COLLOID; DRUG DELIVERY SYSTEMS; ELECTRIC FIELD; LASER; MESOSCOPIC PHYSICS; MICELLE; NANOSTRUCTURE; PHOTOLUMINESCENCE; POLYMER; SEMICONDUCTOR; SURFACTANT in the McGraw-Hill Encyclopedia of Science & Technology.   M. Samy El-Shall

Bibliography. M. S. El-Shall et al., Synthesis and photoluminescence of weblike agglomeration of silica nanoparticles, *J. Phys. Chem.*, 99:17805, 1995; M. S. El-Shall et al., Synthesis of nanoscale metal oxide particles using laser vaporization/condensation in a diffusion cloud chamber, *J. Phys. Chem.*, 98:3067, 1994; M. S. El-Shall and S. Li, Synthesis and characterization of metal and semiconductor nanoparticles, in M. A. Duncan (ed.), *Advances in Metal and Semiconductor Clusters*, vol. 4, chap. 3, pp. 115–177, JAI Press, London, 1998; S. Li and M. S. El-Shall, Synthesis and characterization of photochromic molybdenum and tungsten oxide nanoparticles, *Nanostruc. Mater.*, 12:215, 1999; S. Li, S. Silvers, and M. S. El-Shall, Surface oxidation and luminescence properties of weblike agglomeration of silicon nanocrystals produced by laser vaporization—Controlled condensation technique, *J. Phys. Chem. B.*, 101:1794, 1997; I. N. Germanenko et al., Effect of atmospheric oxidation on the electronic and photoluminescence properties of silicon nanocrystals, *Int. J. Pure Appl. Chem.*, 72:245–255, 2000; I. N. Germanenko, S. Li, and M. S. El-Shall, Decay dynamics and quenching of photoluminescence from silicon nanocrystals by aromatic nitro compounds, *J. Phys. Chem. B.*, 105:59–66, 2001; Y. B. Pithawalla et al., Synthesis of magnetic intermetallic FeAl nanoparticles from a non-magnetic bulk alloy, *J. Phys. Chem. B.*, 105:2085–2090, 2001; W. Wang, I. N. Germanenko, and M. S. El-Shall, Room temperature synthesis and characterization of nanocrystalline CdS, ZnS and $Cd_xZn_{1-x}S$, *Chem. Mater.*, 14:3028–3033, 2002.

Nanowire nanocircuits

The rapid miniaturization of electronics to the submicrometer scale has led to remarkable increases in computing power while enabling reductions in cost. However, as the microelectronics industry advances toward ever-smaller devices, it is believed that both physical and economic factors of current top-down (small structures created from larger components) silicon technology may soon limit further advances. Revolutionary breakthroughs rather than current evolutionary progress could enable computing systems to go beyond these limits and fuel the projected increase in computing demands. A bottom-up approach, where functional electronic structures are assembled from chemically synthesized, well-defined nanoscale building blocks, has the potential to go far beyond the limits of top-down technology by defining key nanometer-scale metrics through synthesis and subsequent assembly. This will require conceptually new device architectures and fundamentally different fabrication strategies, but it could provide unparalleled speed, storage, and size reductions, with the promise of powering computers and other miniaturized electronic devices that may outperform existing devices and open up totally new technologies.

Previous studies have led to a broad range of proof-of-concept nanoscale devices, including diodes and transistors based on individual organic molecules, carbon nanotubes, and semiconductor nanowires. However, these studies of individual nanodevices represent only an initial step toward nanoelectronic circuits. To advance from a single device level to the functional circuit level has been a great challenge due to the lack of device-to-device reproducibility, and the lack of reliable methods for efficiently assembling and integrating the building blocks into device arrays and circuits. To jump to this critical level of complexity and achieve integrated nanocircuits requires three fundamental advances, including (1) the development of rational strategies for the assembly of building blocks into increasingly complex structures, (2) the demonstration of new nanodevice concepts that can be implemented in high yield by assembly approaches, and (3) the development of new device architectures that are amenable to integration via self- or directed-assembly.

Nanoscale building blocks. One-dimensional (1D) nanostructures represent the smallest-dimension structure that can efficiently transport electrical carriers, and thus are ideally suited to the critical and ubiquitous task of moving and routing charges, which constitute information in nanoelectronics. In addition, 1D nanostructures can be exploited as both the wiring and device elements (electronic or photonic structures) in future architectures for functional nanosystems. In this regard, two material classes—semiconductor nanowires and carbon nanotubes—have shown particular promise. Single-walled nanotubes have been used to fabricate field-effect transistors (FETs), diodes, and, recently, logic circuits. However, the inability to control whether nanotube building blocks are semiconducting or metallic and the difficulties in manipulating individual nanotubes have made device fabrication largely a random event, posing a clear barrier to achieving nanocircuits.

Semiconductor nanowires have controlled diameters ranging from <2 to >20 nanometers, and lengths extending up to tens of micrometers (**Fig. 1**). In contrast to nanotubes, semiconductor nanowires can be rationally and predictably synthesized in single-crystal form, with all key parameters controlled such as chemical composition, diameter, and length, as well as doping/electronic properties. As a result, semiconductor nanowires represent the best-defined class of nanoscale building blocks. The ability to control, precisely, their key variables has correspondingly enabled a wide-range of devices and integration

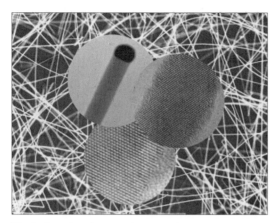

Fig. 1. Scanning electron microscopy image of as-synthesized semiconductor nanowires. The insets show higher-resolution transmission electron microscopy images of the nanowires.

strategies to be pursued. For example, silicon (Si), gallium nitride (GaN), and indium phosphide (InP) semiconductor nanowires have been assembled in parallel into nanoscale FETs, *pn* diodes, light-emitting diodes, and bipolar junction transistors.

Assembly of nanowires. To obtain highly integrated nanowire circuits requires techniques to align and assemble these nanostructures into regular arrays with controlled orientation and spatial location. To this end, a powerful assembly approach based on fluidics has been developed. In this approach, nanowires of gallium phosphide (GaP), GaN, InP, and Si can be readily aligned in one direction over a millimeter-scale area by flowing a nanowire suspension through a channel on a substrate (**Fig. 2**). The space between such nanowire arrays can be precisely controlled using a chemically patterned surface as the substrate, where one component of the chemical pattern is designed to bind selectively to the nanowire surface. Crossed-nanowire arrays have also been obtained by changing the flow direction in a layer-by-layer assembly process. An important feature of this sequential assembly scheme is that each layer is independent. As a result, a variety of homo- and heterojunction configurations can be obtained simply by changing the composition of the nanowire suspension used for each flow step, such as by flowing Si nanowires in the first layer, and then GaN nanowires in a second crossed layer. The crossed nanowire matrix represents an important geometrical configuration for nanocircuits, where each crossing point can function as an independently addressable nanoscale device element.

Crossed-nanowire devices. Direct assembly of highly integrated functional electronic circuits based on nanowires requires the development of new device concepts that are scalable. The crossed-nanowire matrix represents an ideal configuration since the critical device dimension is usually defined by the cross point and can be readily scaled down to the nanometer level, enabling the possibility of

massive system integration. Moreover, the crossed-nanowire matrix is a versatile structure that can be configured to a variety of critical device elements, such as diodes and transistors. For example, a *pn* diode can be obtained by simply crossing *p*- and *n*-type nanowires as demonstrated in the cases of *p*-Si/*n*-Si, *p*-InP/*n*-InP, and *p*-Si/*n*-GaN materials. Electrical measurements of such *pn* diodes show clear current rectification (**Fig. 3a**). Such *pn* diodes have been prepared in >95% yield, and multiple crossed-nanowire *pn* diode arrays can be easily assembled (Fig. 3b).

Nanoscale FETs can also be achieved in a crossed-nanowire configuration using one nanowire as the conducting channel and a crossed nanowire as the gate electrode (Fig. 3c). The three critical FET device metrics are naturally defined at the nanometer scale in the assembled crossed-nanowire FETs, and include (1) a nanoscale channel width determined by the diameter of the active nanowire ($\sim$2-20 nm depending on the chosen nanowire), (2) a nanoscale channel length defined by the crossed gate nanowire diameter ($\sim$10 nm), and (3) a nanoscale gate dielectric thickness determined by the nanowire surface oxide ($\sim$1 nm). These distinct nanoscale metrics lead to greatly improved device characteristics such as high gain, high speed, and low power dissipation. For example, the conductance modulation of a nanowire FET is much more significant with the nanowire gate ($>10^5$) than that with a global back gate (<10) [inset in Fig. 3d]. In addition, local nanowire gates enable independently addressable FET arrays and highly integrated nanocircuits.

Nanoscale logic gates and computational circuits. High-yield assembly of crossed-nanowire *pn* diodes and crossed-nanowire FETs from *p*-type Si and *n*-type GaN materials enables more complex functional electronic circuits, such as logic gates, to be produced. Logic gates, which can be assembled from diodes or transistors, are critical blocks of hardware in computing systems. Both diode- and FET-based nanologic have been demonstrated from nanowire circuits. For example, a two-input logic OR gate was realized using a 2(*p*) × 1(*n*) crossed-nanowire *pn* diode array. When either of the input to the *p*-type nanowire is high, a high output is obtained at the

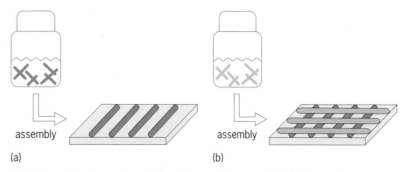

Fig. 2. Assembly of nanowires. (*a*) Parallel-nanowire arrays obtained by passing a nanowire solution through a channel on a substrate. (*b*) Crossed-nanowire matrix obtained by rotating the flow direction 90° in a sequential flow alignment step.

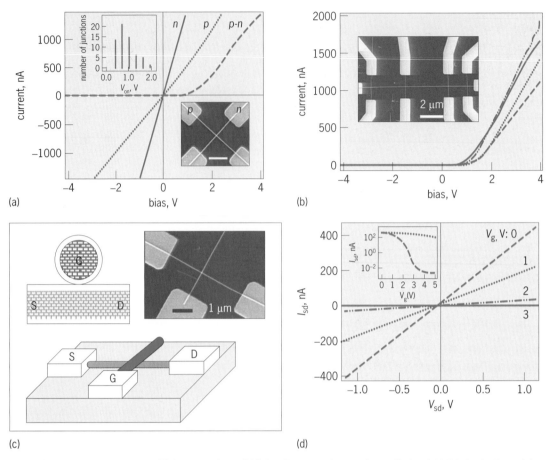

Fig. 3. Crossed-nanowire devices. (*a*) Current-voltage (*I-V*) data for crossed-nanowire *pn* diodes. (*b*) I-V behavior for a 4(*p*) × 1(*n*) multiple junction array. (*c*) Schematics of the crossed-nanowire FET concept. (*d*) Gate-dependent *I-V* characteristics of a crossed-nanowire FET formed using a *p*-type nanowire as the conducting channel and an *n*-type nanowire as the local gate. The curves in the inset show I_{sd} vs. V_{gate} for *n*-type nanowire (lower curve) and global back (upper curve) gates when V_{sd} is set at 1 volt. The FET conductance modulation is much more significant with the nanowire gate ($>10^5$) than with a back gate (<10).

n-type nanowire, and thus achieves the same function as a conventional logic OR gate (**Fig.** 4*a*, *b*). A logic AND gate was also assembled from two *pn* diodes and one crossed-nanowire FET (Fig. 4*c*, *d*), and a logic NOR gate with gain over 5 was assembled from three crossed-nanowire FETs in series (Fig. 4*e*, *f*). Importantly, logic OR, AND, and NOR gates form a complete set of logic elements, and enable the organization of virtually any logic circuit.

Programmable nonvolatile memory. Logic circuits represent critical components for information processing and computation, while memory arrays are essential elements for information storage in future nanocomputer systems. One particularly interesting example of a new concept for a nonvolatile memory device, which is capable of storing information, is based upon molecule-gated nanowires. The new nanoelement consists of nanowire FETs configured from InP or Si nanowire materials and functionalized with redox active molecules, where the redox species can store charge and thereby switch the nanowire FETs to a logic *on* or *off* state with high or low channel conductance, respectively. Experi-

ments demonstrate individual nanowire devices with *on/off* ratios exceeding 10^4 and retention times over 20 min. Integrated parallel arrays in which each device is independently addressable have also been realized (**Fig.** 5*a*, *b*). Lastly, a highly scalable memory device and device architecture has been assembled using a crossed-nanowire matrix assembled from Si and GaN materials (Fig. 5*c*), where each cross point functions as an independently addressable memory element. Significantly, the critical device dimensions in these memory elements can be as small as 10 × 10 nm, and thus could potentially approach an integration density of $10^{12}/cm^2$ (terabyte), which is more than 10,000 times denser than that available with current technology.

Prospects. Overall, the demonstration of integrated nanoscale logic and memory circuits represents critical steps toward realizing nanocomputers. A variety of novel device concepts based on scalable crossed-nanowire configuration with critical device dimension on the order of 10 × 10 nm and improved device characteristics could provide unparalleled speed, storage, and size reduction in future nanocomputer systems. In particular, in a crossbar

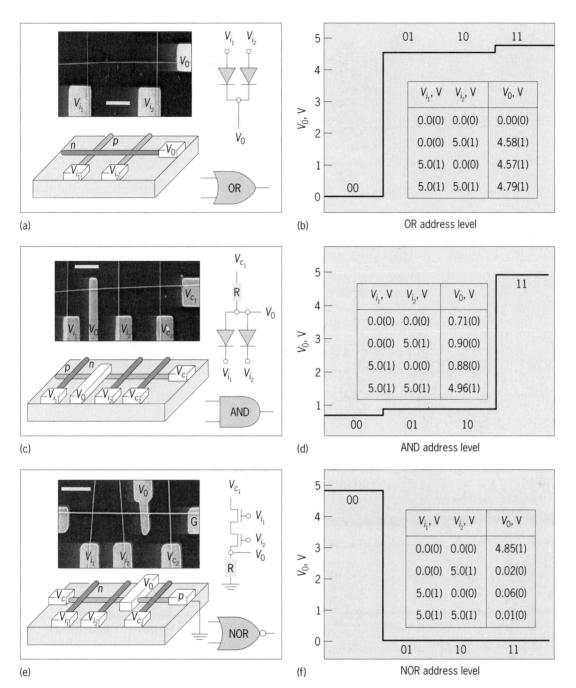

(a)

(b) OR address level

V_{i_1}, V	V_{i_2}, V	V_O, V
0.0(0)	0.0(0)	0.00(0)
0.0(0)	5.0(1)	4.58(1)
5.0(1)	0.0(0)	4.57(1)
5.0(1)	5.0(1)	4.79(1)

(c)

(d) AND address level

V_{i_1}, V	V_{i_2}, V	V_O, V
0.0(0)	0.0(0)	0.71(0)
0.0(0)	5.0(1)	0.90(0)
5.0(1)	0.0(0)	0.88(0)
5.0(1)	5.0(1)	4.96(1)

(e)

(f) NOR address level

V_{i_1}, V	V_{i_2}, V	V_O, V
0.0(0)	0.0(0)	4.85(1)
0.0(0)	5.0(1)	0.02(0)
5.0(1)	0.0(0)	0.06(0)
5.0(1)	5.0(1)	0.01(0)

Fig. 4. Nanoscale logic gates. (a, b) Schematic and measured output vs. address level for a logic OR gate assembled from two crossed-nanowire *pn* diodes. The insets in *a* show the SEM image and the equivalent electronic circuit of the device. The inset in *b* shows the experimental truth table for the nano-OR gate. **(c, d)** Schematic and measured output vs. address level for a logic AND gate assembled from two diode and one crossed-nanowire FET. The inset in *d* shows the experimental truth table for the nano-AND gate. **(e, f)** Schematic and measured output vs. address level for a logic NOR gate assembled from three crossed-nanowire FETs. The inset in *f* shows the experimental truth table for the nano-NOR gate.

array with 5-nm-diameter nanowires, it may be possible to achieve device densities approaching $10^{12}/cm^2$, which is beyond the present semiconductor roadmap for top-down manufacturing.

The bottom-up assembly approach to functional electronics can be easily employed in a layer-by-layer assembly fashion, and thus fundamentally changes the nature of integration from two-dimensional (2D) to three-dimensional (3D). The move to 3D structures could enormously increase future computational power and storage density. Achieving this goal of bottom-up manufacturing will require substantial work (for example, in developing much greater sophistication in assembly and further improving materials synthesis), but is well within the realm of our current understanding and thus suggests a bright future for this approach to integrated nanoelectronics and, perhaps soon, nanocomputers.

(a)

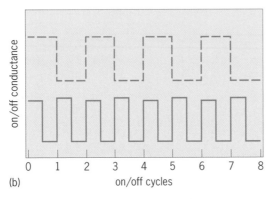

(b)

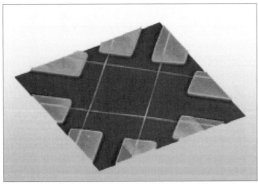

(c)

Fig. 5. Programmable nonvolatile memory array. (*a*) Image of a parallel nanowire memory device array. (*b*) Electrical measurements show independent switching of two neighboring devices. (*c*) Crossed-nanowire memory array. In such an array, each cross point can function as an independently addressable memory element and thus could enable terabyte integration.

For background information *see* ELECTRONICS; INTEGRATED CIRCUITS; LOGIC CIRCUITS; NANOTECHNOLOGY; SEMICONDUCTOR; SEMICONDUCTOR DIODE; SEMICONDUCTOR MEMORIES in the McGraw-Hill Encyclopedia of Science & Technology.

Xiangfeng Duan; Yu Huang; Charles M. Lieber

Bibliography. Y. Cui and C. M. Lieber, Functional nanoscale electronic devices assembled using silicon nanowire building blocks, *Science*, 291:851, 2001; X. Duan et al., Indium phosphide nanowires as building blocks for nanoscale electronic and optoelectronic devices, *Nature*, 409:66, 2001; X. Duan et al., Nonvolatile memory and programmable logic from molecule-gated nanowires, *Nano Lett.*, 2:487, 2002; Y. Huang et al., Directed assembly of one-dimensional nanostructures into functional networks, *Science*, 291:630, 2001; Y. Huang et al., Logic gates and computation from assembled nanowire building blocks, *Science*, 294:1313, 2001.

Natural aerodynamic devices

Large terrestrial walkers, such as humans, are rarely concerned with air movement; yet for many other organisms few factors matter more than fluid motion. The ways these organisms deal with flow help us to see how varied and potent are the possible devices.

Air and water exert a force on any object moving through them. This force opposite the direction of motion is called drag. Air and water also exert drag in the direction of their own motion when moving across a stationary object. In addition, on objects of almost any shape other than those symmetrical about the direction of flow, they exert a cross-flow force. This force perpendicular to flow is called lift, no matter what its orientation is with respect to the Earth. In addition to these simple forces, moving air has structure—spatial and temporal nonuniformities such as vortices and velocity gradients. These forces and phenomena provide opportunities for nature while constraining the design and behavior of successful organisms.

Drag. Drag presents severe problems for trees, which may be uprooted or broken in high winds. These organisms extend high vertically while rooted in soil that has minimal tensile strength, and get their energy by exposing a great amount of surface to the sky. Since wind direction is variable, streamlining (that is, rounding the upstream and extending the downstream ends of a structure) offers trees no obvious escape from drag. The most common solution consists of arranging the shape and mechanical behavior of leaves—a tree's main source of drag—so that they reconfigure in quite specific ways in potentially hazardous winds. Thus, broad leaves with long leaf stems (such as maples) typically curl up into cones; leaves with leaflets on either side of a leaf stem (such as walnuts) curl up into tight cylinders; the leaf stems of stiff holly leaves on a branch bend so the individual leaves stack one against another, and so forth. As a result, at high wind speeds leaves often experience no more than a tenth the drag of flexible flags of the same surface area.

Conversely, drag becomes a virtue for something falling earthward while being dispersed by winds. For such an object, such as a seed, spore, pollen grain, spiderling, or gypsy moth caterpillar, the greater its drag the slower it falls, and the farther it will be carried. The smallest of these have little problem, so great is the ratio of their surface areas to their volumes or weights, and they deviate little from spheres. A fungal spore (as from a puffball or mushroom) falls at around a millimeter (0.04 in.) per second; a pollen grain around 25 mm (1 in.) per second. But windborne seeds such as those of milk-weeds and dandelions, much larger than spores and pollen, equip themselves with all manner of drag-increasing fibrous coats—commercial cotton exhibits one version. Spiderlings extend long, dragging threads into the air after climbing up some available vegetation; they release themselves into auspicious winds (the thread seems to serve as a wind strength and direction monitor before release); and they may be carried astonishing distances—Darwin noted a mass descent of spiderlings on the ship *Beagle* when it was 100 km (60 mi) off South America.

Lift. Lift can present specific hazards, although more for flows of water than air. An animal on a rock in a current forces water to go up and around it, similar to the airflow over an airplane wing and similarly lift-producing. (Cars encounter the same problem, with racing cars often using devices to reduce lift even at the expense of increasing drag.) And for nonmoving (sessile) animals, such as sea anemones, sponges, and mussels, detachment due to lift may be fatal. It has become clear in recent years that lift can be a worse problem than drag for such organisms; a limpet on an intertidal rock may be peeled upward by lift at lower currents than it might be moved downstream by drag. Flounder, lying on sand beneath flows, face the same problem, which they deal with by digging deeper into the sand when flows get high enough to put them at risk of lift-off. Where flow comes from a specific direction, some marine snails (periwinkles) choose the only orientation in which their lift is directed downward toward their attachment.

The fluffy seeds that slow their descent by maximizing drag may be larger than pollen grains, but they rarely exceed 50 milligrams (0.002 ounce). Quite a few groups of plants have independently evolved larger seeds (really, small fruits) that slow their descents by generating lift; the seeds consist of gliding airfoils that produce respectable amounts of lift relative to their drag. A very few seeds glide in straight paths, and so maximize the distance they travel. One of these, the seed-leaf of the Javanese cucumber tree of the high forests of tropical southeast Asia, provided a model for at least one early airplane. Most larger seeds autogyrate downward along helical trajectories, and are not ordinarily recognized as gliders. Maple seeds may be the best known; but pines, some leguminous trees, some relatives of walnuts, and others use the same autogyrating, lift-producing device. Rather than gliding for distance, they simply slow a vertical descent and count on the same wind that dislodged them from the tree to transport them horizontally. Several of these autogyrating seeds, those of tulip poplar, tree-of-heaven, and ash in particular, do not glide in the familiar way; instead they autorotate lengthwise as they autogyrate downward in their helical paths. A similar mechanism makes an index card, flipped so it rotates lengthwise, descend in a

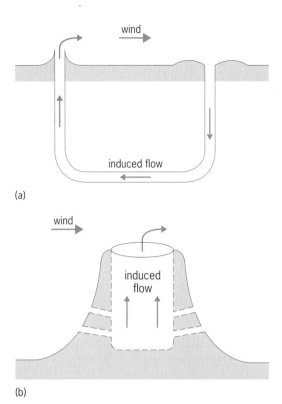

Fig. 1. Ventilatory flow. (*a*) Wind across a pair of openings at opposite ends of a burrow induces a flow through the burrow, from the less protruding end to the more protruding end. (*b*) Wind across an elevated structure can draw air in through low holes (or porous areas) and out through the apex.

steep glide; it is also what allows a thrown baseball or sliced golf ball to travel in a curve.

Flight, whether active or gliding, depends on lift; less obvious are some of the other uses of lift. For instance, a mound protruding from the ground (in the form of a flounder or limpet, for example) forces wind to flow more rapidly across it than along the rest of the ground. That more rapid flow, largely according to Bernoulli's principle, reflects itself in locally lowered pressure. Thus, air will flow through an underground pipe from an opening elsewhere to one on the top of a mound; the direction of the internal flow remains unchanged, whatever that of the wind above. The arrangement can maintain a ventilatory flow through burrow systems with asymmetrical openings such as those of prairie dogs (**Fig. 1***a*) and through the elaborate colonial mounds of some African termites (Fig. 1*b*). It is occasionally put to use in self-ventilating buildings.

Vortices. Vortices provide a range of opportunities for natural devices. Wind across land or ocean creates rolling vortices (**Fig. 2***a*), the passage of which is sometimes noticed as intermittent puffs. On one side of a rolling vortex, air continuously ascends; there an organism can stay aloft while continuously falling through the air immediately around it. That is almost certainly how the spiderlings Darwin observed made their long flight—no thread would slow descent sufficiently for one to go 100 km (60 mi) in

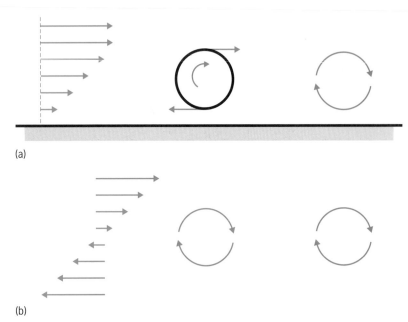

(a)

(b)

Fig. 2. Vortical flow. (*a*) Air blowing across a surface always generates a velocity gradient. An object moving just above the surface rotates; similarly, the air itself often forms rolling vortices. (*b*) Similar vortices can form high up in the atmosphere, wherever wind above moves in a different direction from wind below.

uniformly moving air. Many insects appear to take similar advantage of atmospheric structures, probably vortices in nighttime inversion layers between 30 and 300 m (100 and 1000 ft; Fig. 2*b*). They may be active fliers, but their flights take them much farther than they could go in still air on the fuel they contain. Wind over oceanic waves generates additional, more local vortices; it has recently been shown that albatrosses can exploit these to stay aloft for long periods without beating their wings—in addition to their larger-scale soaring up and down through the velocity gradient in the lowest few hundred feet of the atmosphere over the ocean.

Wind need not be involved in generating vortices. Where a patch of ground heats up more than its surroundings, such as a newly plowed field encircled by vegetation, bubbles of warmer air periodically break loose and ascend like hot-air balloons. Unlike balloons, though, they quickly take on a toroidal form, with air rising on the inside of the torus and descending on the outside. So an animal that can make sufficiently tight gliding circles to stay in the inside of the toroidal ring can descend relative to the air around itself and yet stay within, and thus rise with, the torus. The scheme—thermal soaring—is widely practiced among hawks, vultures, and other large birds. Characteristic of such birds are wing-tip feathers that splay outward like fingers, in sharp contrast with the longer and singly pointed wings of marine soarers. The splayed feathers appear to enable tighter turning, as needed for thermal soaring, with minimal sacrifice in basic gliding performance.

Every possible aerodynamic scheme of nature may still not be recognized. Quite likely these devices, along with the ones mentioned here, hold useful lessons for human technology.

For background information *see* AERODYNAMIC FORCE; AERODYNAMIC WAVE DRAG; AERODYNAMICS; AIR; AIRFOIL; BERNOULLI'S THEOREM; FLIGHT; JET FLOW; LAMINAR FLOW; TURBULENT FLOW; VORTEX; WIND STRESS in the McGraw-Hill Encyclopedia of Science & Technology.   Steven Vogel

Bibliography. M. W. Denny, *Air and Water: The Biology and Physics of Life's Media*, 1993; D. B. Dusenbery, *Life at Small Scale*, 1996; J. S. Turner, *The Extended Organism: The Physiology of Animal-Built Structures*, 2000; S. Vogel, *Life in Moving Fluids: The Physical Biology of Flow*, 2d ed., 1994.

Naval surface ship

From the largest navy, that of the United States, to the navies of newly emergent maritime powers, the end of the Cold War continues to drive radical change in surface ship design in that ship designs are being based less on superpowers conflict and more on varied operational scenarios. Notable trends in naval ship design are described below.

Weapons systems. Current and probable future imperatives in naval operations suggest that surface combatants are likely to require a combination of a relatively large missile silo (in both size and the number of missiles housed) and a provision for several easily installed, close-in or short-range missile systems and small-caliber guns for low-intensity (policing) operations. Ship survivability would be enhanced by splitting up the silo and dispersing it into at least two well-separated locations. When the possible advances in antimissile systems are considered, an obvious technology (development of which is already underway) is that of directed-energy weapons, which replace projectile or guided-missile delivery of ordnance with bursts of intense energy. Ensuring that ship designs can accommodate such systems will remain problematic until the physical demands of the systems are clearer. However, it is likely that directed-energy weapons will require very short bursts of massive and virtually instantaneous packages of energy, not easily provided with current power systems in conventional warships.

Power systems. Although current plans by the U.S. Navy and the Anglo-French Electric Ship Development Programme hold out the possibility of a power system architecture that should be amenable to enhancement, integrated full electric propulsion (IFEP) systems will encompass the total power generation on board. This will enable the designers to significantly reduce the number of prime movers (diesel engines, turbines, or fuel cells) and eliminate the classical design constraint on the ship's internal architecture imposed by the propulsion train of boost and cruise engines, gear box, and shaft. At a minimum this implies just the electric motor and shaft ahead of the propulsor, with the future option, following cruise ship practice, of electrically driven podded drives. In electrically driven podded drives, propellers are fitted to pods containing electric motors and installed below the hull; this creates a better flow regime than occurs with conventional propellers, which are fitted to shafts connected to the machinary installed inside the hull.

Sensor systems. Ongoing growth in the capacity of ship sensors (radars, sonars, and communication systems) and ever greater levels of integration within a warship are anticipated, together with a growing emphasis on the warship as an information node in network centric warfare. Multifunctional sensor systems, provided adequate growth is built in, should enable future designs to cope with further demands through life. A related technological and operationally expanding field is the CNN syndrome, in which ships require not only enhanced military communications capacity but also provision for on-board media personnel and their facilities. There will be further implications of the new broader defense posture, in which future warships must be responsive to a range of potential threats including terrorists and rogue states.

Sonar systems are particularly difficult to accommodate in ships and are major design and cost drivers. First, sonars are likely to be required to be fitted in specific locations (for example, on the underside of the hull well forward, or towed from gantries over the stern), constraining the design. Second, to operate effectively, both the underwater form and ship propulsors, as well as the noise of the machinery on the ship, has to be designed or mounted to ensure the sonar performance is not degraded.

Stealth. In addition to underwater signatures, the abovewater signatures of ships due to radar cross section and infrared technologies have to be accounted for in the structural shape and machinery system design, respectively. For designers in a heavily cost constrained environment, sensible provisions need to be made by ensuring that equipment is not shoehorned in and ship services, such as electrical power and air conditioning, have generous margins on their capacities of power and flow rates to meet future stealth demands. Thus in addition to extra equipment, features such as noise treatments may require allowances for enhancements such as mounting of equipment to reduce noise transmissions to the sea.

Aviation facilities. Another feature which has a large impact on surface combatant ships is that of aviation facilities. Modern helicopters, if carried and fully supported on the ship, place major demands on the design of a frigate-sized ship. The aviation impact is not just in the requirement for substantial flight decks and hangars but also for extra fuel, weapons, maintenance stores, and personnel borne on board. These extensive facilities must accommodate future upgrades of current aircraft as well as new aircraft and systems such as unmanned air vehicles.

Personnel. Given that the cost of running warships is dominated by personnel costs, future ship designs will focus on reducing the number of personnel needed to operate the ship, the U.S. Navy's target of 95 personnel for the DD21 (now DDX) destroyer being the most ambitious declaration to date.

However, this does not mean that navies can restrict the facilities associated with accommodating and supporting personnel to just the minimal complement required to fight. In order to be able to operate effectively in diverse peacekeeping and other roles, additional accommodation and services will have to be provided for passengers, who may range from Special Forces, to humanitarian personnel, to boarding parties for antidrug and antipiracy operations.

Hull forms. Warship architecture must be designed to enable future role changes and insertion of new technologies throughout the life of the ship. There is more to an adaptable architecture than just the modularizing of the combat suite, although this is important. Given that future technology is likely to require locations high in the ship (with the notable exception of hull-mounted sonar fits), a ship designer would preferably provide generous space in prime locations, both on the upper deck and on the main deck below, especially amidships. Neither of these are easily achieved in the conventional monohull without considerable growth in ship size. There are two other important design considerations, survivability and producibility (designing the ship so that it can be quickly and economically assembled). A counter to the growth in hull size, and the consequential reduction in the number of hulls produced, is a renewed interest in small, fast, unconventional vessels; these would provide the numbers of warships previously achievable only by corvettes with low endurance and reduced survivability relative to larger surface combatants. The **table** qualitatively reviews hull configurations that might be appropriate for modern combatants. It shows eight configurations compared with the monohull for nine aspects considered historically to be the basis for comparing different hull forms for warships. Clearly the choice of aspects is debatable and, in any particular new design, those most relevant to its emerging operational concept and acquisition constraints will determine the assessment of the relative merits. What might seem remarkable is the very impressive score of the trimaran configuration, even compared to the monohull, which has been the invariable choice for all except the most operationally specific naval vessels. This latter fact is due to the monohull being an inherently mission-flexible hull form able to undertake most naval roles with more than reasonable capability. The trimaran is essentially a relatively minor departure from the monohull. Unlike the other configurations in the table, it has many features in common with the monohull and largely draws on the technology applicable to monohull warships, minimizing the risk in departing from the proven technology.

Specialist warships. In the case of both the major specialist warships, aircraft carriers and amphibious vessels, there are distinctions to be drawn between the very largest examples, which are operated only by the U.S. Navy, and the medium and smaller vessels that are more widely used. The debate on whether to use nuclear power for future U.S. supercarriers, rather than adopting smaller conventionally

Qualitative assessment of different hull forms*

Aspects	Monohull	Catamaran	Air cushion vehicle (ACV)	Surface effect ship (SES)	Hydrofoil	Small-waterplane-area twin-hull (SWATH)	Hydrofoil small waterplane-area ship (HYSWAS)	Wing in ground (WIG)	Trimaran
Speed, power and endurance	G	G†	VG‡	G	VG‡	G	G	VG	G
Space and layout	G	G	A	G	P	VG	P	P	VG
Structural design and weight	VG	A	P	P	VP	A	P	VP	G
Stability	G	G	G	G	G§	G	G	P	VG
Maneuverability	G	A	P	G	G	A	G	P	G
Noise, radar, and magnetic signature	G	A	G	G	G	VG	G	G	VG
Weapon placement and effectiveness	G	A	A	A	P	G	A	P	VG
Construction costs and build time	VG	H	VH	H	VH	G	H	VH	G
Through-life costs	G	A	VH	H	VH	A	H	VH	VG

*G—good; VG—very good; P—poor; A—average; VH—very high.
†Performance poor in deep ocean seaway.
‡Slow in seaway and endurance-poor.
§Degraded by wave effects in deep ocean.

powered vessels, appears to be resolved with the transition program from the Nimitz Class CV 77 to the new nuclear-powered CVX 1 and 2. However, with France's *Charles de Gaulle* and the projected two Royal Navy CVF medium-sized carriers in combination with the Joint Strike Fighters short takeoff/vertical landing (JSF STOVL) aircraft seen as being possibly a cheaper but still effective combination relative to a conventional fixed-wing takeoff aircraft and carrier solution, the debate may not be over given the colossal cost of the nuclear-powered supercarriers. Smaller navies are fully dependent on current STOVL aircraft if they are to contemplate sea-based naval air power.

Amphibiosity has received a boost in prominence with the emphasis on power projection from the sea. The U.S. Navy, with a fleet of large amphibious ships able to carry the very fast air cushion vehicle (ACV) assault craft, dwarfs other navies' ships in size and numbers. Most navies have modest amphibious lift capabilities (the ability to embark troops and equipment and subsequently send them ashore in an amphibious landing as part of expeditionary warfare). The Royal Navy is completing a large reequipment of its amphibious fleet, which is designed both for war and for worldwide peace-keeping—but noticeably without high-speed ACV assault craft and with the adoption of a significant level of mixed naval and merchant ship engineering standards.

For background information *see* AIR-CUSHION VEHICLE; ELECTRONIC WARFARE; MISSILE; NAVAL ARMAMENT; NAVAL SURFACE SHIP; OCEANOGRAPHIC VESSELS; RADAR; RADAR INTERFEROMETRY; SHIP DESIGN; SHIP POWERING, MANEUVERING, AND SEAKEEPING; SHIP STRUCTURAL DESIGN; SONAR in the McGraw-Hill Encyclopedia of Science & Technology.

David Andrews

Bibliography. D. J. Andrews, Adaptability—The key to modern warship design, *RINA Warship Conference—Future Surface Warships*, London, June 2001; D. J. Andrews, Trends in future warship design, *Naval Platform Technology Seminar 2001*, IMDEX Asia, Singapore, May 2001; B. Bender, A sea change in ship size, *Jane's Defence Weekly*, April 19, 2000; M. Hewish, Shaping tomorrow's big stick, *Jane's International Defence Review*, December 2001; F. Kelso, From the sea: Preparing the Naval Service for the 21st century, *U.S. Naval Institute Proceedings*, November 1992; T. McCoy and M. Benatmane, The all electric warship: An overview of the US Navy's Integrated Power System Development Programme, *International Conference on the Electric Ship*, Instanbul, September 1998; J. M. Newell and S. S. Young, Beyond electric ship, *IMarE*, October 24, 2000; *RINA International Conference: R. V. TRITON Solent Conference*, Southampton, April 2000; *RINA Warship Conference 2000: Warships for Amphibious Operations & Minewarfare*, London, June 2000; S. Scarborough, Network-centric warfare meets the laws of the Navy, *U.S. Naval Institute Proceedings*, May 2001; S. C. Truver, Tomorrow's U.S. Fleet, *U.S. Naval Institute Proceedings*, March 2000.

Neural model of depression

Feeling depressed is a common human experience, occurring most often as a normal response to external events or personal loss. However, a major depressive episode, whether of unknown origin or a part of a defined neurological disorder, is a pathological condition. Depression is characterized as one of the major affective disorders, all of which share a primary dysregulation in mood. It is diagnosed not only by the presence of persistent negative mood but also by pronounced and unrelenting disturbances in attention, motivation, motor and mental speed, sleep, appetite, and libido. These symptoms occur in combination with sustained anhedonia (that is, the inability to experience pleasure), excessive or inappropriate guilt, recurrent thoughts of death with suicidal ideations, and in some cases suicide attempts.

Epidemiology. Depression has an average lifetime prevalence of about 15%, with a twofold greater prevalence in women than in men. Major depressive disorder generally begins after age 20 and before age 50. A later age at onset is associated with a higher incidence of structural brain lesions, including strokes and subcortical white-matter changes. Single episodes are not rare; however, depression is generally considered a chronic, relapsing, remitting illness. Furthermore, although periods of clinical normality are seen throughout the natural course of the disorder, recurrences happen with higher frequency and with greater intensity if episodes are not treated.

Treatment options. An untreated major depressive episode generally lasts 6–13 months. However, treatment can significantly reduce this period. Treatment options include pharmacological (that is, with medication) as well as nonpharmacological strategies. For patients with mild to moderate depression, medication and cognitive therapies have been shown to be equally effective in treating depressive symptoms. Empirically, it is well recognized that patients with a poor or incomplete response to one form of treatment often respond well to another. Others will respond to treatment augmentation or combination strategies using different drugs with complementary pharmacological actions; combined drug and cognitive behavioral therapy; or, in medication-resistant patients, electroconvulsive therapy. Such resistance to treatment is reported to occur in 20–40% of cases. More rarely, patients with high resistance to traditional therapies are treated neurosurgically by the placement of precise lesions in target brain structures, most commonly specific white-matter tracts. (Interruption of dysfunctional neural pathways linked by these fiber tracts is the presumed mechanism for response to this treatment. A similar type of surgery, targeting a different brain location, is used to treat severe Parkinson's disease.) Categorizing patients into different subtypes for the purpose of treatment selection has been attempted, but has yet to prove successful. Neither are there clinical, neurochemical, or imaging markers that can identify which patients will have a protracted disease course. Progress toward these obvious clinical goals is slowed by the absence of clear, definitive etiological models (models of origin).

Etiological models. Although definitive models of origin for depression have yet to be identified, theories implicating focal brain lesions, specific neurochemical and neuropeptide systems, genetic factors, as well as temperament and environmental factors have been proposed. Each theory is supported by clinical and basic empirical studies (**Fig. 1**). The theory of primary dysregulation of specific neurochemicals and neuropeptides is supported by abnor-

malities in blood, spinal fluid, and postmortem brain samples. Definitive links, however, have not yet been made to disease onset. Family, adoption, and twin studies suggest a genetic component to depression, given the high degree of reported heritability. A specific genetic marker has yet to be identified. Biological mechanisms for the increased vulnerability of women relative to men or for the relative constancy in the age of onset are unknown. The influence of environmental factors is equally complex. Although no correlations between depression and socioeconomic status, education, cultural background, or specific lifestyle have been demonstrated, stress is often seen as a precursor. Recent studies provide further evidence that early life trauma and stress may also contribute to an increased vulnerability to developing various types of affective disorders, but causal relationships between stress, disease vulnerability, and precipitation of an acute depressive episode are far from clear. The association of stress-provoking events with the onset of a major depressive episode does, however, appear to be stronger for the first episode of depression than for subsequent episodes.

Neurological disease. Although depression is generally thought of as a primary psychiatric disorder, it is also commonly seen with a variety of neurological and medical illnesses. Such cases further suggest the involvement of specific neural mechanisms. Clinical studies demonstrate that certain disorders are more likely to be associated with a major depression than are others. These include (a) discrete brain lesions as seen with trauma, surgery, stroke, tumors, and certain types of epilepsy; (b) neurodegenerative diseases with regionally confined pathologies such as Parkinson's disease, Huntington's disease, and Alzheimer's disease; (c) disorders affecting diffuse or multiple random locations such as multiple sclerosis; and (d) system illness with known central nervous system effects such as thyroid disease, lupus erythematosus, cancer, and acquired immune deficiency syndrome (AIDS). These studies most consistently show involvement of the frontal and temporal cortex and the basal ganglia. Interestingly,

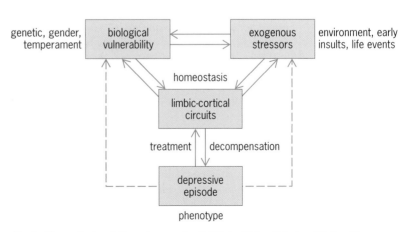

Fig. 1. Diverse factors influencing ongoing limbic-cortical activity in patients with depression.

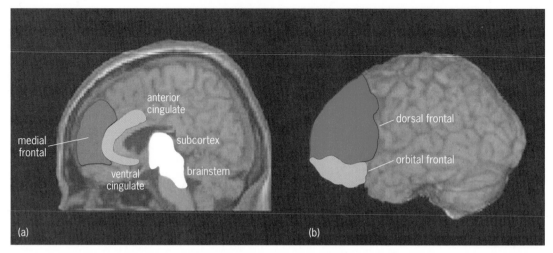

Fig. 2. Gross location of critical brain regions implicated in depression. (*a*) Midsagittal view of brain. (*b*) Lateral view of brain. Dorsal and medial frontal regions are superimposed in dark color; limbic regions, including orbital frontal and ventral and anterior cingulate, are in light color; subcortical and brainstem regions are in white.

primary injury to limbic structures such as the amygdala, hippocampus, and hypothalamus are not associated with primary depressive symptoms, despite their fundamental involvement in critical aspects of motivational and emotional processes. This apparent contradiction suggests that these key regions of the brain share a much more complex organizational structure than that revealed by the classic specific region–specific function approaches.

These brain-behavior associations described in patients with neurological disorders and depression are complemented by parallel experiments of specific cognitive, motor, circadian, and affective behaviors mapped in healthy volunteers, which together suggest that depression might be better seen as a neural *systems* disorder, affecting discrete but functionally linked pathways involving specific cortical, subcortical, and limbic sites and their associated neurotransmitter and peptide mediators.

Integrative depression model. To take all of these various factors into account, depression might be further conceptualized as not only the end result of selective brain regional or neurological pathway dysfunctions but also the failure of the remaining system to maintain emotional balance (homeostasis) in times of increased psychological or physical stress (Fig. 1). Genetic vulnerability, affective temperament, developmental insults, and environmental stressors would be considered likely contributors to this failure, although specific mechanisms are not yet established. Nonetheless, treatments for depression could be similarly viewed within this limbic-cortical framework, where modulation of distinct neural targets by different interventions facilitates a variety of complementary chemical and molecular adaptations and homeostatic effects that reestablish a normal mood state. In testing such a hypothesis, areas of the frontal lobe (cortical regions), ventral cingulate and hippocampus (limbic regions), and the brainstem and basal ganglia (subcortical regions) are considered to be most critical based on observations in

patients with neurological disorders and depression and pharmacological studies of antidepressant medication sites of action (**Fig. 2**).

Imaging studies. Structural and functional neuroimaging methods, including x-ray computed tomography (CT), magnetic resonance imaging (MRI), positron emission tomography (PET), and single-photon emission tomography (SPECT), provide a critical platform for investigating these hypotheses. They facilitate the examination of relationships between genetics, biochemistry, anatomy, functional neurocircuitry, and systems-level behaviors in living human subjects, thus extending findings from postmortem studies and experimental animal models. Studies to date have emphasized the identification of disease markers and treatment effects using PET and SPECT measures of regional cerebral blood flow and glucose metabolism. The use of functional and structural imaging technologies to examine brain-behavioral relationships in primary depression is the natural evolution of the long tradition of symptom localization in patients with brain disorders previously described.

Findings. Early PET studies of patients with neurological disorders and depression of varying etiologies identified consistent metabolic abnormalities involving frontal, cingulate, and temporal cortices. Parallel studies of patients with primary depression have also reported frontal and cingulate and, less commonly, temporal and basal ganglia abnormalities, in general agreement with the pattern seen in neurological depressions. Across studies, the most robust and consistent finding is decreased frontal-lobe function (**Fig. 3**). In addition to frontal changes, limbic (cingulate, amygdala), paralimbic (anterior temporal, insula), and subcortical (basal ganglia, thalamus) abnormalities have been identified, but the findings are more variable. Differences among patient subgroups as well as heterogeneous expression of clinical symptoms, such as illness severity, cognitive impairment, anxiety, and psychomotor slowing, are thought to

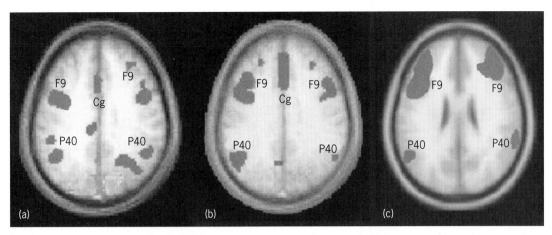

Fig. 3. Common cortical metabolic abnormalities. The image shows areas of frontal cortex hypometabolism (in gray) in three different patients groups: (*a*) unipolar depression, (*b*) bipolar depression, and (*c*) depression with Parkinson's disease. Also seen are additional areas of hypometabolism affecting the anterior cingulate (Cg), prefrontal cortex [Brodmann area 9] (F9), and the inferior parietal cortex (P40).

contribute to this variance in regional metabolism. However, there is not yet a consensus on the specific nature of the relationship between these findings.

Changes with treatment. Changes in regional metabolism and blood flow with recovery from a major depressive episode can also be measured. Studies of this type consistently report normalization of many regional abnormalities identified in the pretreatment state. Changes in cortical (prefrontal, parietal), limbic (cingulate, amygdala, insula), and subcortical (basal ganglia, thalamus, brainstem) areas have been described following various treatments including medication, psychotherapy, sleep deprivation, electroconvulsive therapy, repetitive transcranial magnetic stimulation, and ablative surgery. However, the specific metabolic changes mediating clinical recovery have not been determined, nor have definitive distinctions been made between the specific metabolic changes that accompany different modes of effective treatment. Normalization of frontal abnormalities is the best-replicated finding. **Figure 4** il-

lustrates the effects of the antidepressant fluoxetine (Prozac) on brain metabolism. In addition to metabolic increases in the frontal lobe, successful treatment also decreases metabolism in other regions, including limbic (ventral cingulate, anterior insula) and subcortical (basal ganglia) areas. These effects are thought to be the result of adaptive changes in previously "normal" functioning regions. This combination of reciprocal frontal increases and limbic decreases seen with clinical response following active medication, and also placebo, suggests that changes in these regions might be especially critical for clinical recovery across various treatments (**Fig. 5**). Although these findings appear compelling, recent studies contrasting pharmacological and cognitive therapies suggest a more complex interaction between pretreatment findings and specific treatment effects. This is a focus of ongoing research.

Limbic-cortical dysregulation model. In an attempt to synthesize the findings just described, regions with known anatomical interconnections that also show consistent changes across studies of

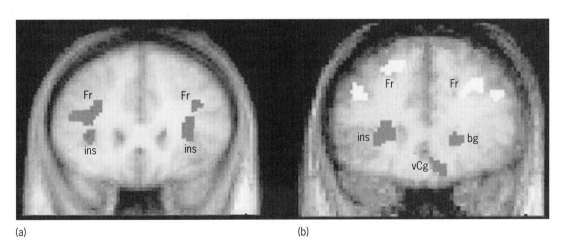

(a)   (b)

Fig. 4. Frontal and limbic changes with antidepressant treatment. (*a*) Frontal abnormalities, displayed in coronal orientation (Fr in gray). (*b*) Increases in frontal metabolism with successful treatment using Prozac for 6 weeks (Fr in white). In addition to increases in the frontal lobe, treatment decreases limbic (ventral cingulate: vCg; anterior insula: ins) and subcortical (basal ganglia: bg) metabolism (these effects are shown in gray).

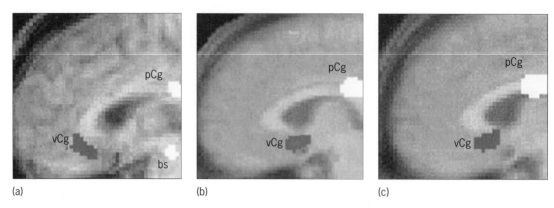

(a)   (b)   (c)

Fig. 5. Images in sagittal orientation showing common changes with different antidepressant treatments. Metabolic decreases in specific brain regions (in this case in the ventral cingulate, vCg, in gray) are present in both. (a) Prozac-treated patients and (b) placebo-treated patients showing a clinical improvement at 6 weeks. Increases in two other brain regions, the posterior cingulate (pCg) and the brainstem (bs), are shown in white. (c) This pattern persists long-term, as illustrated by the findings based on a separate group of previously depressed patients studied in full remission on maintenance antidepressant medication for 18 months.

depression are summarized in **Fig. 6**. Failure of this regional network is hypothesized to explain the combination of clinical symptoms (that is, mood, motor, cognitive, sleep, appetite) seen in depressed patients. Regions are grouped into three main compartments or levels: cortical, subcortical, and limbic. The frontal-limbic (dorsal-ventral) segregation additionally identifies those brain regions where an inverse relationship is seen across the different PET experiments. Both sadness and depressive illness are associated with metabolic decreases in cortical regions and relative metabolic increases in limbic areas. The model, in turn, proposes that illness remission occurs when there is appropriate modulation of dysfunctional limbic-cortical interactions—an effect facilitated by various forms of treatment. It is further postulated that initial modulation of unique target regions by specific treatments facilitates adaptive changes in particular pathways necessary for reestablishing network balance and resulting clinical recovery. Certain frontal and cingulate regions are sep-

arated from their respective compartments in the model to highlight their primary role in giving external emotional events personal meaning—a phenomenon exaggerated in the depressed state.

This model potentially accommodates the multidimensional perspective of depression shown in Fig. 1. Namely, the functional state of the depressed brain reflects both the initial insult or "functional lesion" and the ongoing process of attempted self-correction or adaptation influenced by such factors as heredity, temperament, early-life experiences, and previous depressive episodes. For instance, if frontal hyperactivity is seen, it might be interpreted as an exaggerated and maladaptive compensatory process, manifesting clinically as psychomotor agitation and rumination, whose purpose is to override, at the cortical level, a persistent negative mood generated by abnormal chronic activity of limbic-subcortical structures. In contrast, frontal hypometabolism would be seen as the failure to initiate or maintain such a compensatory state, with resulting apathy, psychomotor

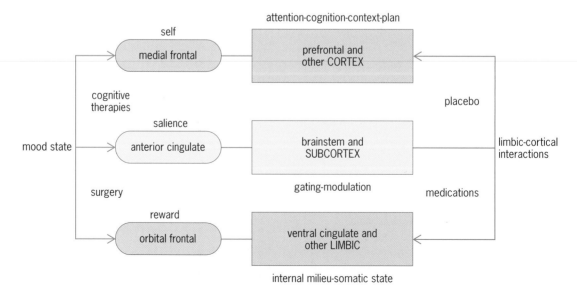

Fig. 6. Limbic-cortical dysregulation model of depression.

slowness, and impaired executive functioning common with increasing depression severity.

In this context, different interventions with varying primary mechanisms of action should be equally effective if there is preserved functional integrity of pathways within the depression circuit overall. This might explain the comparable clinical efficacy of pharmacological and cognitive treatments conducted in mildly to moderately depressed patients. Similarly, increasingly aggressive treatments needed to relieve symptoms in some patients may reflect poor adaptive capacity or an actual disintegration of network connections in these patient subgroups. In further support of the hypothesis, medication responders show preserved or increased pretreatment metabolic activity in the anterior cingulate, whereas medication nonresponders show a dysfunctional, hypometabolic pattern. Although speculative, these findings suggest that a specific metabolic signature may ultimately provide a therapeutic road map for optimal treatment selection based on known patterns of differential change with different treatment interventions.

Although such a network approach is an oversimplification, it provides a means to systematically consider additional contributing variables, such as heredity, temperament, and early life experiences, in the pathogenesis of depression. Continued development of imaging and other strategies that optimally integrate these factors will be a critical next step in fully characterizing the depression phenotype at the neural systems level. These strategies may also lead to the development of routine brain-based clinical approaches that optimize diagnosis and treatment of individual depressed patients.

For background information *see* AFFECTIVE DISORDERS; BRAIN; MEDICAL IMAGING; NERVOUS SYSTEM DISORDERS; PSYCHOPHARMACOLOGY in the McGraw-Hill Encyclopedia of Science & Technology.

Helen Mayberg

Bibliography. M. Fava and K. S. Kendler, Major depressive disorder, *Neuron*, 28:335–341, 2000; E. Frank and M. E. Thase, Natural history and preventative treatment of recurrent mood disorders, *Annu. Rev. Med.*, 50:453–468, 1999; K. S. Kendler, L. M. Thornton, and C. O. Gardner, Genetic risk, number of previous depressive episodes, and stressful life events in predicting onset of major depression, *Amer. J. Psychiat.*, 158:582–586, 2001.

Neurogenesis

During most of the twentieth century, it was thought that the adult human brain was completely incapable of generating new neurons. However, in the last decade the development of new techniques has resulted in an explosion of new research showing that (1) neurogenesis, the birth of new neurons, is not restricted to embryonic development but normally also occurs in at least two limited regions of the adult mammalian brain; (2) there are significant numbers of multipotent neural precursors in many parts of the adult mammalian brain; and (3) it is possible to induce neurogenesis even in regions of the adult mammalian brain, such as the neocortex, where it does not normally occur, via manipulation of endogenous multipotent precursors in situ to replace lost neurons. In the neocortex, recruitment of small numbers of new neurons can be induced in a region-specific, layer-specific, and neuronal-type-specific manner, and newly recruited neurons can form long-distance connections to appropriate targets. This suggests that elucidation of the relevant molecular controls might allow the development of neuronal replacement therapies for neurodegenerative disease and other central nervous system injuries that may not require transplantation of exogenous cells.

Adult mammalian multipotent precursors. Neurogenesis is normally restricted mainly to two specific regions of the adult mammalian brain: the subventricular zone, which provides the olfactory bulb with neurons, and the dentate gyrus of the hippocampus. If adult multipotent precursors were limited to these two neurogenic regions of the adult central nervous system, it would severely limit the potential of neuronal replacement therapies based on manipulation of endogenous precursors in situ (without transplantation). However, adult multipotent precursors have been isolated and cultured in vitro from several other regions of the adult mammalian brain, including caudal portions of the subventricular zone, spinal cord, septum, striatum, neocortex, optic nerve, and retina (see **illus.**). The precursors derived from all these regions can self-renew and differentiate into

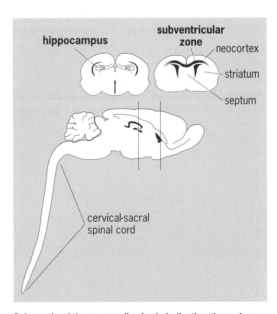

Schematic of the mammalian brain indicating the regions which exhibit persistent neurogenesis throughout life (hippocampus and subventricular zones) and from which growth-factor-expanded cells have been isolated. Multipotent progenitors have been isolated from the nonneurogenic regions such as the septum, striatum, spinal cord, neocortex, optic nerve, and retina. (*Adapted from L. S. Shihabuddin and F. H. Gage, Neurogenesis, McGraw-Hill Yearbook of Science & Technology 2001, p. 269*)

neurons, astroglia, and oligodendroglia (the three main cell types of the brain) in vitro. In nonneurogenic regions of the mature brain, it is thought that adult multipotent precursors normally differentiate only into glia or die. Cells from each region have different requirements for their proliferation and differentiation. Understanding the similarities and differences between the properties of multipotent precursors derived from different regions of the brain will be instrumental in developing neuronal replacement therapies based on manipulation of endogenous precursors.

Cell replacement therapies. Neural cell replacement therapies are based on the idea that neurologic function that is impaired due to injury or neurodegenerative disease can be improved by introducing new cells to replace the function of lost neurons. Theoretically, the new cells can do this in one of two general ways. New neurons can anatomically integrate into the host brain, becoming localized to the diseased portion of the brain, and function by integrating into the microcircuitry of the nervous system. Alternatively, newly introduced cells (introduced by transplantation or by inducing neuronal differentiation from endogenous precursors) simply could secrete neurotransmitters into local central nervous system tissue or could be engineered to produce growth factors to support the survival or regeneration of existing neurons. Growing knowledge about the normal role of endogenous neural precursors, their potential differentiation fates, and their responsiveness to a variety of cellular and molecular controls suggest that neuronal replacement therapies based on manipulation of endogenous precursors either in situ or ex vivo (outside the body) may be possible.

Endogenous versus transplanted neural precursors. Neuronal replacement therapies based on the manipulation of endogenous precursors in situ may have advantages over transplantation-based approaches, but they may have several limitations as well. The most obvious advantage is that there is no need for external sources of cells. Cells for transplantation are generally derived from embryonic tissue, nonhuman species (xenotransplantation), or cells grown in culture. The use of embryo-derived tissue aimed toward human diseases is complicated by limitations in availability and political and ethical issues. Xenotransplantation of animal cells carries potential risks of introducing novel diseases into humans and poses questions about how well xenogenic cells will integrate into the human brain. In many cases, cultured cells need to be immortalized by oncogenesis, increasing the risk that the cells may become tumorigenic (tumor-forming). In addition, transplantation of cells from many of these sources risk immune rejection and may require immunosuppression.

However, there are also potential limitations to manipulating endogenous precursor cells as a neuronal replacement therapy. First, such an approach may be practically limited to particular regions of the brain, since multipotent neural precursors are densely distributed only in particular subregions of the adult brain (for example the subventricular zone and the hippocampal subgranular zone). In addition, the potential differentiation fates of endogenous precursors may be too restricted to allow reconstruction of different regions of the brain. It may also be difficult to provide the precise combination and sequence of molecular signals necessary to induce endogenous precursors to precisely proliferate and differentiate into different types of neurons appropriate for specific regions of the brain.

Manipulation of an inhibitory environment. The fact that new neurons are born only in very restricted areas of the adult mammalian brain, even though neural precursors are found ubiquitously in the adult central nervous system, suggests that precursors from different regions may have different potentials. Alternatively or additionally, local environments may differ in their ability to support or allow neurogenesis from these precursors. Data from several laboratories have shown that multipotent precursors from several regions of the adult brain have a broad potential and can differentiate into at least the three broad cell types of the brain given an appropriate in vitro or in vivo environment. This led to the exploration of the fate of multipotent precursors in an adult cortical environment, which does not normally support de novo neurogenesis.

It has previously been shown that cortex undergoing synchronous apoptotic degeneration (programmed cell death) of projection neurons (neurons with long axons that form long-distance connections with distant parts of the adult mammalian brain) forms an instructive environment that can guide the differentiation of transplanted immature neurons or neural precursors. Immature neurons or multipotent neural precursors transplanted into targeted cortex can migrate selectively to layers of cortex undergoing degeneration of projection neurons, differentiate into projection neurons, receive afferent synapses, express appropriate neurotransmitters and receptors, and re-form appropriate long-distance connections to the original contralateral targets of the degenerating neurons in adult murine (mouse) neocortex. Together, these results suggest that cortex undergoing targeted apoptotic degeneration could direct endogenous multipotent precursors to integrate into adult cortical microcircuitry.

In agreement with this hypothesis, researchers found that endogenous multipotent precursors, normally located in the adult mammalian brain, can be induced in situ to differentiate into cortical neurons, survive for many months, and form appropriate long-distance connections in the adult mammalian brain. The same microenvironment that supports the migration, neuronal differentiation, and appropriate axonal extension of transplanted neuroblasts and precursors also supports and instructs the neuronal differentiation and axon extension of endogenous precursors. Thus, the normal absence of constitutive cortical neurogenesis does not reflect an intrinsic limitation of the endogenous neural precursors' potential, but more likely results from a lack of appropriate microenvironmental signals necessary for neuronal differentiation or survival. Elucidation of these signals could enable central nervous system repair in the future.

Conclusion. Recent data suggest that neuronal replacement therapies based on manipulation of endogenous precursors may be possible in the future. However, several questions must be answered before such therapies become a reality. The multiple signals that are responsible for endogenous precursor division, migration, differentiation, axon extension, and survival must be elucidated in order for such therapies to be developed efficiently. These challenges also exist for neuronal replacement therapies based on transplantation of precursors, since donor cells, whatever their source, must interact with the mature central nervous system's environment in order to integrate into the brain.

In addition, scientists still do not know whether potential therapies manipulating endogenous precursors in situ would be limited to portions of the brain near adult neurogenic regions. However, even if multipotent precursors are not located in very high numbers outside neurogenic regions of the brain, it may be possible to induce them to proliferate from the smaller numbers that are more widely distributed throughout the neuraxis. Further, it may be possible to induce the repopulation of diseased mammalian brain via specific activation and instructive control of endogenous neural precursors along desired neuronal lineages.

Although scientists are just beginning to understand the complexities of neurogenesis, the coming decades promise to offer significant insight into the cellular and molecular controls that are critical to this and related processes.

[This work was partially supported by grants from the NIH (NS41590, NS45523, HD28478, MRRC HD18655), the Alzheimer's Association, the Human Frontiers Science Program, and the National Science Foundation to J. D. Macklis. P. Arlotta was supported by a Wills Foundation fellowship. S. S. Magavi was partially supported by an NIH predoctoral training grant and fellowships from the Leopold Schepp Foundation and the Lefler Foundation.]

For background information *see* BRAIN; NERVOUS SYSTEM (VERTEBRATE); NEUROBIOLOGY; NEURON in the McGraw-Hill Encyclopedia of Science & Technology.   Paola Arlotta; Sanjay S. Magavi; Jeffrey D. Macklis

Bibliography. P. Arlotta et al., Molecular manipulation of neural precursors *in situ*: Induction of adult cortical neurogenesis, *Exp. Gerontol.*, in press; A. Bjorklund et al., Cell replacement therapies for central nervous system disorders, *Nat. Neurosci.*, 3:537-544, 2000; F. H. Gage et al., Multipotent progenitor cells in the adult dentate gyrus, *J. Neurobiol.*, 36:249-266, 1998; S. Magavi et al., Induction of neurogenesis in the neocortex of adult mice, *Nature*, 405:951-955, 2000; R. McKay, Stem cells in the central nervous system, *Science*, 276:66-71, 1997.

Neuromusicology

The emerging field of neuromusicology, the scientific study of the effects of music on the brain, is rooted in the ancient cross-cultural belief that music has a therapeutic effect on the mind and body. In the past 50 years, based on social science concepts of music's influence and role in human life and society, some forms of music therapy have gained acceptance for the treatment of behavioral problems. The therapeutic value of music is generally believed to stem from music's cultural role in facilitating social learning and emotional experiences. More recently, however, the growing adaptation of brain research methods for the study of musical cognition has encouraged research into biomedical applications of music. New findings suggest that music can stimulate complex cognitive, affective, and sensorimotor processes in the brain, which can be generalized and transferred to nonmusical therapeutic purposes.

Biomedical research in music concentrates on areas such as motor therapy, speech, autism, pain management, memory, and attention. Studies show that the rhythmic entrainment of motor function can actively facilitate the recovery of movement in patients afflicted with neurologic disorders such as stroke, Parkinson's disease, or traumatic brain injury. The rhythmic sounds are believed to act as sensory timers, entraining brain mechanisms that control the timing, sequencing, and coordination of movement. Recovery of speech functions can also be facilitated with music, the strong timing mechanisms of which are believed to entrain oscillatory speech circuits in the brain. A small body of research suggests that music may facilitate perception and organization of behavior in autistic children. The use of music in pain therapy has been widely reported, although the actual effectiveness and potential mechanisms underlying the effect of music on pain are not clear. New biomedical frontiers in music research include the effect of music and rhythm on critical aspects of timing in learning, attention, and memory. The current neuroscientific applications are standardized in neurologic music therapy.

Theoretical basis. The study of the neurobiological basis of music ability is inherently linked to the study of music's influence on brain function. In other words, the brain that engages in music is changed by it. Although much has been learned in the last decade about the effect of music on brain structure and function, a transformational framework theory is needed to explain how musical responses can be transformed into nonmusical therapeutic responses. Neuromusicology has moved away from earlier concepts that explained the therapeutic effect of music by simply drawing analogies between musical and nonmusical behavior. The current scientific model searches for the therapeutic effect of music by studying if and how music stimulates and engages parallel or shared brain function in cognition, motor control, and emotion. For example, rhythmicity, a universal function in the control of movement, can be effectively accessed and regulated with music in patients with movement disorders. Temporal organization and appropriate arousal, universally important functions in perception, attention, memory, and problem solving, can be modulated by music in patients with traumatic brain injury or dementia. Appropriate emotional experiences may be important elements in counseling or psychotherapy, experiences which can be effected by musical mood induction techniques.

Neurobiological foundations. One of the most important recent discoveries supporting the therapeutic use of music for movement disorders is the profound effect of musical sounds on the motor system. Sound can arouse and raise the excitability of spinal motor neurons mediated by auditory-motor neuronal connections at the brainstem and spinal cord level. This priming effect sets the motor system in the brain in a state of readiness, facilitating the execution of planned movement. Rhythmic sounds also entrain the timing of muscle activity, thereby cueing the timing of movements. These data illustrate the close connection between the auditory and motor systems. Furthermore, the auditory system is a very fast and precise processor of timing information since it must capture and extract meaning from sensory information that is present only temporally in dynamic waveform patterns with rapid time decay. The mechanically sensitive hair cell channels of the auditory system are stunningly fast, responding within microseconds compared to milliseconds needed by biochemically activated channels such as in the visual system. Thus, the projections of temporal information that the motor system receives from the auditory pathway are based on extremely fast and precise biological processing mechanisms.

Important information for the therapeutic understanding of rhythm has come from rhythmic synchronization studies. Auditory rhythms entrain tightly coupled motor responses within one or two presentations of the rhythmic pattern. When changes are introduced into the tempo of the rhythm, the motor response adjusts rapidly to the new tempo, even when the tempo modulations are so small that they are not consciously perceived. Brain wave data obtained from magnetoencephalographic (MEG) studies have shown that the changes, in millisecond ranges, are represented by precise amplitude decreases and increases of the auditory brain wave patterns. The amplitude scaling, relative to interval duration, occurs around 100 ms after the stimulus and is generated in Heschl's gyrus (the primary auditory cortex). These data show that rhythm perception in the auditory system is based on interval perception and that the motor system has access to this information at levels below conscious perception. Data from brain imaging studies using positron emission tomography (PET) and functional magnetic resonance imaging (fMRI) show that the brain regions subserving rhythmic synchronization are widely distributed cortically and subcortically and consist mainly of primary cortical sensorimotor areas, the basal ganglia, the cerebellum, and the auditory cortex.

Biomedical applications. Neurobiological findings have been the basis for extensive clinical research showing that rhythmic entrainment of motor function can significantly improve recovery of mobility in patients with neurological disorders such as stroke, Parkinson's disease, traumatic brain injury, and cerebral palsy. Clinical research trials of the effect of rhythmic stimulation in stroke patients have shown substantial functional improvements in the control of arm and walking movements over sustainable periods of time when compared with other therapies. In Parkinson's disease, rhythmic stimulation has been shown to decrease bradykinesia (slowness of movement) and akinesia (freezing of movement), and to increase stability of movement. Rhythmic training has also been shown to improve the consistency in which motor neurons are recruited during cyclical movements such as walking or sequential arm reaching. The finding that rhythmic motor synchronization is primarily based on frequency entrainment suggests that rhythm facilitates the recovery of motor function by providing a continuous time reference or template across the total duration of the movement. This time reference not only facilitates the anticipatory timing of the movement but also helps to optimize the control of the movement trajectories and the appropriate scaling of muscle force.

Speech rehabilitation. In speech rehabilitation, the effect of music and rhythm has been documented in several applications related to neurogenic disorders of speech. Singing and rhythm, as used in melodic intonation therapy, have been shown to facilitate significant functional recovery of speech in expressive aphasia (impairment in the use of expressive language) and verbal apraxia (impaired planning of speech motor movements). The current rationale for melodic intonation therapy is based on an assumed hemispheric transfer of speech function from the damaged left hemisphere to the right hemisphere due to singing's role in encoding speech. However, the exact neuroanatomical basis of melodic intonation therapy awaits further research confirmation. Music and rhythm have also been shown to be useful in improving speech control in disorders of fluency and dysarthria (impaired articulation). The neurophysiological assumption is that, similar to rhythmic entrainment of movements, the strong timing functions in music entrain oscillatory speech circuits in the brain and provide a sensory-based template to overcome intrinsic neurological control deficits due to brain injury.

Music cognition and learning. Music cognition and learning is an evolving area of neurobiological research with potential biomedical application. For example, a small behavioral research base shows that music can facilitate memory and attention. The ABC song, in which a child sings the letters of the alphabet to facilitate learning, is an easily understood illustration. The organizing element of chunking, a critical element in memory coding, is continuously represented in all musical patterns as a necessary form-building element through melodic and rhythmic phrasing. Therefore, music can be an excellent memory template for nonmusical declarative or procedural learning. Little is known about the underlying neurobiology of this process. However, studies of memory disorders, such as Alzheimer's disease, frequently show retention of musical information in patients (for example, remembering old songs) that is out of proportion to their concurrent general memory loss. Such data suggest that neuronal memory traces built through music are deeply ingrained and—at least to some extent—more resilient to neurodegenerative influences. The nature of music as a temporally over-structured language of sound patterns may play a critical role in such effective memory formation. Recent research has shown that neuronal oscillations, which build rhythmic patterns in networks and ensembles of neurons, form the neurobiological basis of perception and learning. The precise synchronization of neuronal activation patterns is a crucial element in building such tightly coupled networks underlying effective learning.

Another contributor may be the strong emotional value of music. The effect of mood and emotion on memory is well documented in research. Neurotransmitter release associated with learning may be enhanced by music-facilitated learning, thereby strengthening synaptic network formation underlying memory. The exact neurobiological mechanisms as well as confirmations of a functional cognitive effect in dementia therapy through music, however, await further research.

For background information *see* BRAIN; MEMORY; MOTOR SYSTEMS; NERVOUS SYSTEM (VERTEBRATE); PARKINSON'S DISEASE; SPEECH DISORDERS in the McGraw-Hill Encyclopedia of Science & Technology.

Michael Hugo Thaut

Bibliography. P. Belin et al., Recovery from nonfluent aphasia after melodic intonation therapy, *Neurology*, 47:1504–1511, 1996; D. Deutsch, Organizational processes in music, in M. Clynes (ed.), *Music, Mind and Brain*, pp. 119–131, Plenum Press, New York, 1982; K. M. Stephan et al., Conscious and subconscious sensorimotor synchronization: Prefrontal cortex and the influence of awareness, *NeuroImage*, 15:345–352, 2002; M. H. Thaut et al., The connection between rhythmicity and brain function: Implications for therapy of movement disorders, *IEEE Eng. Med. Biol.*, 18:101–108, 1999; R. J. Zatorre and I. Peretz (eds.), The biological foundations of music, *Ann. N.Y. Acad. Sci.*, vol. 930, 2001.

Neutrino masses and oscillations

Neutrinos are elementary, subatomic particles, first postulated by W. Pauli in 1930 and first detected by F. Reines and C. L. Cowan in 1956. They carry no electric charge and interact with other particles only via the weak force. Neutrinos come in three flavors, as distinguished by the weak force. The three flavors are electron neutrino, muon neutrino, and tau neutrino. Other known elementary particles, such as quarks and charged leptons, also come in three flavors that are successively heavier in mass; however, the situation for neutrinos is less definitive. Until recently, all that was known about neutrino mass was that neutrinos must be very light if they had any mass at all. Theoretically, within the standard model of particle physics, neutrinos were even considered to be massless.

Recent experimental observations have revolutionized the understanding of neutrino masses and flavors. Those observations are that solar neutrinos change flavor en route to Earth, and that atmospheric neutrinos traveling up through the Earth are not as numerous as those traveling down from the atmosphere. These observations are explained by a phenomenon known as neutrino oscillations. The recent discovery of neutrino oscillations indicates that neutrinos have nonzero mass, a fact which has consequences for particle theories and cosmology.

A finite, nonzero neutrino mass allows an interesting phenomenon to occur. Quantum mechanics permits a neutrino flavor state to be a mixture of different mass states (and conversely, a neutrino mass state to be a mixture of different flavor states). When a neutrino is born during a weak interaction, it is produced in a pure flavor state. For example, positron beta decay produces pure electron neutrinos. These electron neutrinos may actually be composed of different mass states, if such quantum-mechanical mixing occurs. Each of the mass states propagates through space and time with its own wavelength, or phase, as governed by quantum mechanics. After traveling some distance, the mass states will be out of phase with respect to the original mixture (**Fig. 1**). The neutrino wave function (the mixture of mass states) at that point may more closely resemble the mixture characteristic of a muon neutrino (or a tau

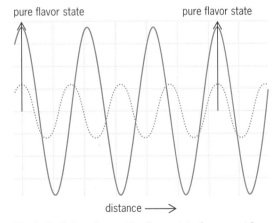

distance ⟶

Fig. 1. Evolution of a neutrino flavor state. A pure neutrino flavor state may be composed of different mass states that propagate with different phases. As the neutrino propagates, the phase of the mass states varies with position, resulting in some probability to detect the neutrino as another flavor when the mass states are out of phase. The neutrino returns periodically to its pure flavor state; the end result is oscillating detection probability as a function of distance traveled.

neutrino). Thus, there will be some probability that the particle, born as an electron neutrino, will be detected as a muon neutrino (or a tau neutrino). As the neutrino wave function propagates through space, the relative phases of the states oscillate back and forth, and the probability of detecting the neutrino in a specific flavor state will increase and decrease periodically. This behavior is known as neutrino oscillations.

Solar neutrinos. The Sun is a copious source of neutrinos, produced in the nuclear fusion reactions that supply its energy. Solar neutrinos have been studied for over 30 years, and during this time the solar neutrino problem emerged. The problem was that the measured flux of solar neutrinos from experiments has always been significantly lower than model predictions; the experimental deficits ranged from 40 to 70%. Over the past three decades, solar astronomical observations have confirmed the physical principles underlying the solar models. Meanwhile, five solar neutrino experiments increased the precision of their measurements across the solar neutrino energy spectrum. It became difficult to explain the different experimental deficits observed by postulating inadequacies in the calculations or experiments, or by suggesting modifications to the solar models.

Neutrino oscillations were proposed as a possible explanation for the solar neutrino deficit. The reactions in the Sun produce only electron neutrinos. Three of the solar neutrino experiments can detect only electron neutrinos, and the other two are predominantly sensitive to electron neutrinos. If neutrino oscillations occur, perhaps solar neutrinos, upon arriving at Earth, are at a phase for which the detection probability of the electron neutrino flavor is at a dip in the oscillations. The solar neutrinos would still all be there, their electron neutrino flavor content simply being replaced by other flavors, a situation that would manifest itself as flux deficits observed by the experiments that do not see those other flavors. Neutrino oscillations can also naturally accommodate an energy-dependent detection probability, explaining the range of deficits observed in the different solar neutrino experiments.

In 2001 and 2002, a new solar neutrino experiment reported results. The Sudbury Neutrino Observatory (SNO) is a neutrino detector containing 1000 tons of pure heavy water and is located 2070 m (6800 ft) underground in a nickel mine near Sudbury, Ontario, Canada. Heavy water contains deuterium (an isotope of hydrogen). Two distinct neutrino-deuterium reactions were studied. Charged-current reactions (in which a neutrino is captured by deuterium and an electron is produced) were observed; around six interactions (or events) of this type per day were detected, compared to 18 events per day predicted by solar models. The charged-current reaction is sensitive only to electron neutrinos, and the Sudbury Neutrino Observatory observes a flux deficit with these events, like the previous experiments. Separately, neutral-current neutrino-deuterium reactions (in which an incoming neutrino

dissociates a deuterium nucleus, producing a free neutron) were also studied; approximately two such events per day were detected. This event rate is roughly three times greater than what should have been seen if the electron neutrinos that were precisely monitored via the charged-current reaction were all that were present in the solar neutrino flux. The neutral-current reaction is equally sensitive to all neutrino flavors; thus, the excess event rate observed in the Sudbury Neutrino Observatory constitutes a discovery that neutrino flavors other than electron neutrinos are also arriving from the Sun, as might be the case if neutrino oscillations occur.

The Sudbury Neutrino Observatory results find that the solar electron neutrino flux is $(35 \pm 2)\%$ of the solar model predicted value while the total neutrino flux of all active flavors, deduced from the neutral-current interaction rate, is $(101 \pm 13)\%$ of the same predicted value. The difference between the two measurements is more than five standard deviations of the experimental uncertainties. When all flavors are examined, the Sun is seen to produce all of the neutrinos that the models predict and there is no flux deficit. Solar neutrinos, initially produced as electron neutrinos, oscillate in flavor as they travel to Earth such that (for the Sudbury Neutrino Observatory measurement) only 35% of the flavor content is electron neutrino and the other 65% is muon neutrino or tau neutrino upon arrival (**Fig. 2**). Neutrino flavor oscillations thus provide the solution to the 30-year-old solar neutrino problem.

The good agreement between the Sudbury Neutrino Observatory measurements and solar model neutrino flux calculations also provides confirmation that the inner workings of the Sun are well

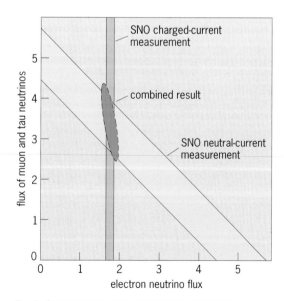

Fig. 2. Solar neutrino fluxes measured by the Sudbury Neutrino Observatory (SNO). Two separate neutrino-deuterium reactions were employed to measure the electron neutrino flux and the total solar neutrino flux. The combined result reveals that muon neutrinos, tau neutrinos, or both are coming from the Sun. Neutrino fluxes are measured in units of 10^6 neutrinos per square centimeter per second.

understood. In fact, the Sudbury Neutrino Observatory results can be interpreted as providing a measurement of the central temperature of the Sun, using neutrinos, to better than 1% accuracy.

All solar neutrino experimental data can be used to constrain how neutrino mass and flavor states give rise to solar neutrino oscillations. A detailed analysis indicates that the electron neutrino is made up of roughly 75% of one mass state and 25% of a second, heavier mass state. The heavier state weighs about 0.007 electronvolt more than the lighter mass state (for comparison, an electron weighs 511,000 eV), and it is this mass difference that is responsible for solar neutrino oscillations. In this analysis, it is also found that the propagation of solar electron neutrinos through the dense matter of the Sun enhances the intensity of the oscillations, driving the conversion of electron neutrinos into other flavors. This additional aspect is known as the MSW effect (after S.P. Mikheyev, A. Yu. Smirnov, and L. Wolfenstein).

Atmospheric neutrinos. High-energy particles from outer space, known as cosmic rays, continuously strike the Earth's atmosphere and produce showers of secondary particles. Neutrinos are produced in these cosmic-ray showers. Both muon neutrinos and electron neutrinos are produced (and much more rarely tau neutrinos); the expected ratio is roughly 2:1. However, as early as 1988, measurements of this flux ratio revealed it to be anomalously low. The atmospheric muon neutrino–to–electron neutrino ratio is measured to be 1.2:1 instead.

In 1998, the Super-Kamiokande experiment presented conclusive evidence for neutrino oscillations using data from atmospheric neutrinos. Super-Kamiokande, located in the Kamioka mine in Japan, detects neutrino interactions using 50,000 tons of water. In addition to confirming the anomalous flux ratio, Super-Kamiokande studied the direction of the zenith-angle distribution of the atmospheric neutrinos it detected. The cosmic rays which produce atmospheric neutrinos are isotropic and uniform around the Earth. Spherical symmetry arguments then guarantee that the atmospheric neutrinos passing through a detector should be up-down symmetric in direction. Super-Kamiokande observed that the direction of electron neutrinos is indeed fairly symmetric. However, the observed zenith-angle distribution for the direction of muon neutrinos is highly asymmetric. The upward-going muon neutrino flux is roughly one-half of the downward-going flux. This fact alone is sufficient to signal that something unusual is happening to muon neutrinos as they travel up through the Earth from their production point to the detector.

Upward-going atmospheric muon neutrinos disappear because they oscillate into tau neutrinos that are not registered in the detector. This oscillation hypothesis explains the atmospheric neutrino observations and is supported by detailed fits to the Super-Kamiokande data. Atmospheric neutrinos coming up through the Earth (neutrinos are not absorbed by the Earth) have traveled 13,000 km (8000 mi). In contrast, those coming down from the atmosphere above the detector have traveled only 10 km (6 mi). Downward-going muon neutrinos are unaffected by oscillations since a longer travel distance is required to allow the neutrino mass states to propagate significantly out of phase, in order to alter the neutrino flavor detection probability. More detailed analyses find that two neutrino mass states, differing by 0.05 eV, produce the oscillations between muon neutrinos and tau neutrinos. The mass states contain equal mixtures of muon and tau neutrino flavor.

Neutrino mass hierarchy. Combining the information gleaned from solar and atmospheric neutrinos, the following picture of neutrino masses and mixing can be constructed (**Fig. 3**). Three neutrino mass states can exist in a successively heavier mass hierarchy, resembling the mass hierarchy of other elementary particles (quarks and leptons). The mass difference between the lightest two states is responsible for solar neutrino oscillations; the mass difference between the two heavier states produces atmospheric neutrino oscillations. Currently, the mixing between the heaviest mass state and the electron neutrino is unknown, though it is restricted to be very small from experiments that study neutrinos from nuclear reactors. Otherwise, the mixing of flavors in the neutrino mass states is found to be large. This is quite unlike the small flavor mixing found in quark mass states. These facts pose interesting new questions for particle physics theories.

The present understanding of neutrino mass is still limited. Though mass differences are now known, the absolute scale for neutrino mass is not. Neutrinos could still be nearly massless, with only the heaviest state (0.05 eV) having significant mass. Alternatively, all neutrino states could have the same sizable mass, with the observed mass splittings small compared to the overall scale. Experiments searching for evidence of neutrino mass in tritium beta decay limit this scale to less than 2.2 eV. Between these two extremes, the total energy density of neutrinos in the universe can be bounded between 0.1 and 14% of the critical

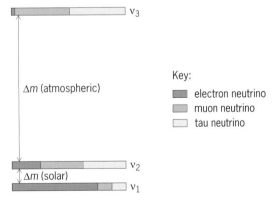

Fig. 3. Present understanding of the neutrino mass hierarchy. Three neutrino mass states, ν_1, ν_2, and ν_3, have been identified; their mass differences, Δm (solar) and Δm (atmospheric), are responsible for solar and atmospheric neutrino oscillations. The flavor composition of the three neutrino mass states is shown. The electron neutrino component in ν_3 is not known but is believed to be small.

density. Thus, neutrinos contribute at least as much to the energy density of the universe as all the visible stars and can play an important role in cosmology.

For background information *see* COSMIC RAYS; COSMOLOGY; ELEMENTARY PARTICLE; NEUTRINO; QUANTUM MECHANICS; SOLAR NEUTRINOS; STANDARD MODEL; WEAK NUCLEAR INTERACTIONS in the McGraw-Hill Encyclopedia of Science & Technology.

Mark Chen

Bibliography. Q. R. Ahmad et al., Direct evidence for neutrino flavor transformation from neutral-current interactions in the Sudbury Neutrino Observatory, *Phys. Rev. Lett.*, 89:011301-1 to 011301-6, 2002; Q. R. Ahmad et al., Measurement of day and night neutrino energy spectra at SNO and constraints on neutrino mixing parameters, *Phys. Rev. Lett.*, 89: 011302-1 to 011302-5, 2002; J. N. Bahcall, *Neutrino Astrophysics*, Cambridge University Press, 1989; F. Boehm and P. Vogel, *Physics of Massive Neutrinos*, 2d ed., Cambridge University Press, 1992; Y. Fukuda et al., Evidence for oscillations of atmospheric neutrinos, *Phys. Rev. Lett.*, 81:1562–1567, 1998.

Nitric oxide biosensors

The definition of a nitric oxide (NO) biosensor is complicated by the fact that the term "biosensor" is often applied to (1) sensors that incorporate a biological entity (such as an enzyme or antibody) as a fundamental part of the recognition element, and (2) sensors that measure a particular analyte in a biological environment. In this article, NO biosensor refers to sensors capable of measuring NO in a biological environment.

For several decades, NO, a highly reactive and potentially toxic radical, was studied extensively for its role in atmospheric chemistry related to air pollution. Since the discovery that NO is a vasodilatory agent and its identification as an endothelium-derived relaxing factor in the late 1980s, the study of NO in biological systems has accelerated significantly. For example, NO has been found to be an important signaling molecule that regulates a broad range of physiological processes and is involved in a number of pathological processes. In 1998, R. F. Furchgott, L. J. Ignarro, and F. Murad received the Nobel Prize in Medicine for their work concerning NO as a signaling molecule in the cardiovascular system.

The physiological importance of NO has resulted in increased interest in the development of methods for detecting and monitoring it. Designing appropriate sensors, however, has been a challenge due to the difficulties associated with NO's low concentration (micromolar to nanomolar), high reactivity with various endogenous components (for example, free radicals, transition-metal ions, and oxygen), and short half-life (<10 s) in biological environments. Moreover, the complexity and size constraints of biological samples (for example, cells, tissue, and blood) significantly hinder the detection

of NO. Traditional techniques for measuring NO are indirect, relying on the determination of a secondary species such as L-citrulline (a coproduct of NO synthesis), nitrite (NO_2^-), or nitrate (NO_3^-) [oxidation products of NO]. Indirect methods often fail to accurately reflect the spatial and temporal distribution of NO in biological environments. Of the feasible approaches to overcome such limitations, electrochemical (for example, amperometric) and optical (for example, chemiluminescence and fluorescence) biosensors represent the most promising devices for detecting NO. Such sensors not only provide direct, real-time measurement of NO in vitro and in vivo, but also are relatively inexpensive and readily microfabricated.

Electrochemical NO sensors. Common electrochemical methods for measuring NO in situ include the use of bare and modified electrodes to electrochemically reduce or oxidize NO. Such sensors afford fast response times (∼2–3 s) and reasonable limits of detection (∼0.5×10^{-9} mol/L). Perhaps the most straightforward electrochemical method for measuring NO is to reduce it at a bare-metal (for example, platinum, gold) or carbon electrode. Traditionally, the most common reaction for the reduction of NO is (1).

$$2NO + 2e^- \rightarrow N_2O_2^{2-} \qquad (1)$$

The current, which is monitored using an ammeter, is proportional to the amount of NO in the sample. Bare-metal electrodes necessitate large reduction potentials (−0.9 to −1.2 V versus a silver/silver chloride reference electrode) due to extraordinarily slow reaction kinetics. Molecular oxygen is also reduced at these potentials, rendering the detection of only NO at bare-metal electrodes extremely challenging, particularly for biological applications. Recently, researchers have modified electrodes with polymers containing transition-metal complexes, such as $[Cr(v\text{-tpy})_2]^{3+}$, where the ligand v-tpy is 4′-vinyl-2,2′, 6′,2″-terpyridyl, so that lower reduction potentials could be employed. At such potentials, the reduction of molecular oxygen is no longer a concern. An example of a modified electrode is given later.

Bare-metal electrodes can also be used to oxidize NO. The electrochemical oxidation of NO is governed by reactions (2) and (3). In reaction (2), an

$$NO \rightarrow NO^+ + e^- \qquad (2)$$

$$NO^+ + HO^- \rightarrow (HNO_2) \rightarrow H^+ + NO_2^- \qquad (3)$$

electron is transferred from NO to the electrode. Since the product, nitrosonium ion (NO^+), is a strong Lewis acid, it is readily converted to NO_2^- in the presence of OH^- [reaction (3)]. NO_2^- is further oxidized to nitrate (NO_3^-) [reaction (4)]. In total, three

$$(HNO_2) + H_2O \rightarrow NO_3^- + 3H^+ + 2e^- \qquad (4)$$

electrons are transferred to the electrode, and measured as a current. The working potential is a potential applied to the working electrode to generate the current flowing between it and a counter electrode, and is related to the concentration of the analyte. Because the direct oxidation of NO requires a relatively high working potential (+0.7 to +1.0 V versus a silver/silver chloride electrode), its detection is hindered by the presence of other readily oxidizable biological species, including nitrite, ascorbic acid, uric acid, acetaminophen, and dopamine. Current strategies for measuring NO via oxidation are based on Clark-style electrodes and surface-modified electrodes.

Clark-style NO electrodes. Clark-style electrodes are fabricated by placing the working (platinum) and pseudo-reference (silver wire) electrodes into a micropipette filled with an internal electrolyte solution (such as potassium chloride). The micropipette is subsequently sealed at the end that will be introduced into a sample with a gas-permeable membrane. As shown in **Fig. 1**, platinum and silver wires are placed in proximity to this gas-permeable membrane. Due to a small tip diameter (~10 micrometers), the electrode can be used to measure NO in tissue and cells with relatively high spatial resolution. Several gas-permeable membranes have been used to achieve high selectivity for NO over the aforementioned interfering species, including collodion (nitrocelluloge), chloroprene, polystyrene, Nafion (perfluorinated polymer), cellulose acetate, and silicone rubber. Clark-style sensors, however, are limited by low sensitivity and comparatively slow response times relative to the rate of physiological changes in NO levels.

Surface-modified NO electrodes. Surface-modified electrodes are fabricated by coating various electrodes (for example, platinum, glassy carbon, and carbon fiber) with catalytically active molecules such as metalloporphyrins (for example, Ni-, Fe-, and Mn-porphyrins), o-phenylenediamines, or metal phthalocyanines to lower the working potential by about 0.3 V relative to unmodified electrodes. In this respect, interfering species are not as readily oxidized. Bare electrodes are typically modified via electrochemical polymerization by either entrapping the catalytic compounds during polymerization of a

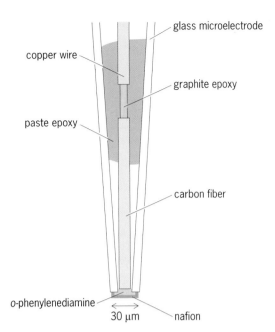

Fig. 2. Schematic of a surface-modified NO microelectrode. (*After S. M. Kumar et al., Nerve injury induces a rapid efflux of nitric oxide (NO) detected with a novel NO microsensor, J. Neurosci., 21:215–220, 2001*)

given monomer, or using monomers that have covalently linked electrocatalysts. Sensitivity and selectivity can be fine-tuned by controlling the polymer thickness. Such electrodes can be further modified with other membranes (such as Nafion and cellulose acetate) to reduce additional interference by size exclusion or electrostatic repulsion. The design of a surface-modified NO microelectrode is shown in **Fig. 2**. For this particular design, a carbon fiber is coated sequentially with monomeric tetrakis (3-methoxy-4-hydroxyphenyl) porphyrin (Ni-TMPP), o-phenylenediamine, and finally Nafion. The tip diameter (after coating) is about 30 micrometers.

Optical NO sensors. The reaction of NO with either ozone or luminal (3-aminophthalhydrazide) and hydrogen peroxide (H_2O_2) is central to chemiluminescence-based optical NO sensors. Optical sensors represent a promising alternative to electrochemical methods. Current optical sensors exhibit excellent detection limits (~10^{-13} mol/L), but only for large sample sizes. Recently, the chemistry associated with optical NO sensors has been combined with fiber-optic technology, significantly reducing the sample size requirement. Consequently, the limit of detection for fiber-optic sensors has been significantly reduced to about 1×10^{-6} mol/L. A standard fiber-optic NO sensor for a luminol-H_2O_2 system is shown in **Fig. 3**. Briefly, NO (from a sample) diffuses through a gas-permeable silicone rubber membrane into an internal solution of H_2O_2 and luminol. The NO reacts with H_2O_2 to form peroxynitrite ($ONOO^-$), a strong oxidant, that further reacts with luminol to generate light ($h\nu$). A fiber-optic probe collects the light and directs it to a photomultiplier tube for detection.

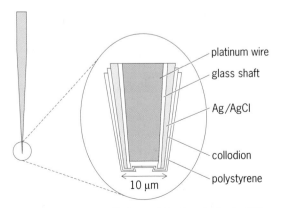

Fig. 1. Schematic of a Clark-type NO microelectrode. (*After Y. Kitamura et al., Microcoaxial electrode for in vivo nitric oxide measurement, Anal. Chem., 72:2957–2962, 2000*)

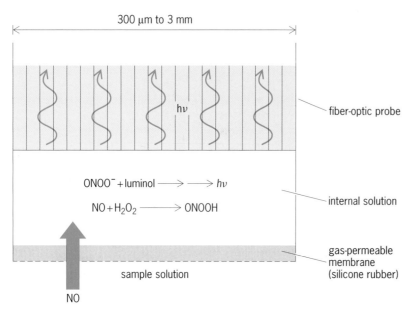

Fig. 3. Membrane phases and reaction chemistry for a chemiluminescent NO fiber-optic sensor. (*After X. Zhou and M. A. Arnold, Response characteristics and mathematical modeling for a nitric oxide fiber-optic chemical sensor, Anal. Chem., 68:1748–1754, 1996*)

Enzyme/protein NO sensors. A number of enzyme- and metalloprotein-based electrochemical and optical biosensors have been developed. Such sensors are based on the formation of a product that generates light or is electrochemically active. In the presence of NO, a lower signal (electrons or photons) is detected. The signal reduction is due to the harmful interaction of NO with the protein, thereby lessening product formation. Nitric oxide is known to inactivate both enzymes and metalloproteins via S-nitrosylation and sulfhydril-oxidation reactions. Because modifying electrodes with enzymes and detecting changes in the formation of product upon introducing a substrate is reasonably straightforward, several electrochemically based biosensor systems have been proposed.

Fiber-optic-based fluorescent sensors using metalloproteins such as cytochrome c' and soluble guanylate cyclase are equally capable of detecting and monitoring NO. For example, cytochrome c' can be labeled with a fluorescent spectator dye and immobilized onto the end of a fiber-optic probe. In the presence of NO, the quantum yield (ability to fluoresce) of the dye molecule decreases proportional to the concentration of NO. Enzyme/protein sensors may represent the future of NO biosensors since they offer the greatest selectivity for NO in a complex environment; other interfering species do not influence the enzyme-product formation.

For background information *see* BIOSENSOR; ELECTRODE; ELECTRODE POTENTIAL; FIBER-OPTIC SENSOR; NITRIC OXIDE; NITROGEN OXIDE; OXIDATION-REDUCTION; REFERENCE ELECTRODE in the McGraw-Hill Encyclopedia of Science & Technology.

Jae Ho Shin; Mark H. Schoenfisch

Bibliography. S. L. R. Barker et al., Ratiometric and fluorescence-lifetime-based biosensors incorporating cytochrome c' and the detection of extra- and intracellular macrophage nitric oxide, *Anal. Chem.*, 71:1767–1772, 1999; F. Bedioui, S. Trevin, and J. Devynck, Chemically modified microelectrodes designed for the electrochemical determination of nitric oxide in biological systems, *Electroanalysis*, 8:1085–1091, 1996; E. Kilinc, M. Ozsoz, and O. A. Sadik, Electrochemical detection of NO by inhibition on oxidase activity, *Electroanalysis*, 12:1467–1471, 2000; X. Zhang et al., Nanometer size electrode for nitric oxide and S-nitrosothiols measurement, *Electrochem. Commun.*, 4:11–16, 2002.

Nobel prizes

The Nobel prizes for 2001 included the following awards for scientific disciplines.

Chemistry. The chemistry prize was awarded in two parts for the development of catalytic asymmetric synthesis, with William S. Knowles and Ryoji Noyori sharing half for their work on chirally catalyzed hydrogenation reactions, and K. Barry Sharpless receiving half for his work on chirally catalyzed oxidation reactions.

Asymmetric synthesis results in the predominant or exclusive formation of a single enantiomer. Enantiomers, also called chiral molecules, are molecules with the same structure that are nonsuperimposable mirror images of each other designated as *R* and *S*.

Almost all molecules in biological systems, such as in DNA or RNA, enzymes, and receptors, occur as single enantiomers and interact differently with different enantiomers. In terms of biological interactivity, *R*- and *S*-enantiomers may have different smell, different taste, and, in the case of drugs, different physiological action. It is important to be able to produce pure, single-enantiomer drugs, because one form may be therapeutically active while the other may be inactive or dangerous.

A catalyst is a substance that speeds up a chemical reaction without being consumed. In 1968, Knowles discovered that chiral molecules could act as catalysts for hydrogenation reactions, preferentially producing one of the two possible enantiomers in excess and, often, in large quantity. In the reaction, a molecule of hydrogen (H_2) is added to the carbon-carbon double bond of an olefin. The side of a double bond on which the two hydrogen atoms are added will determine the resulting product's chirality. Knowles found that catalysts made from a transition metal linked to chiral ligands were able to insert hydrogen in a controlled manner. This was the first catalytic asymmetric synthesis, the preferential formation in a chemical reaction of one enantiomer over the other because of the influence of a chiral feature in the catalyst.

Over the next few years, Knowles refined this technique using transition-metal complexes of rhodium (Rh) with phosphine ligands (with chiral phosphorus atoms) as catalysts, leading to the synthesis of the amino acid L-dopa (in >95% enantiomeric excess) which is used to treat Parkinson's disease. This L-dopa synthesis has been used as a commercial process since 1974.

Chiral catalysts work by a mechanism such that the chiral component is involved in the transition state, with two possible pathways for producing enantiomers of which the lower-energy one is more likely to occur. The greater the difference between the energies of the transition states, the greater the enantiomeric excess. This is the basis of asymmetric synthesis and Noyori's research. Noyori developed catalysts for highly enantioselective hydrogenation of olefins, as well as catalysts for hydrogenation of α,β- and α,γ-unsaturated carboxylic acids which are used, for example, to produce the anti-inflammatory agent (S)-naproxen in 97% enantiomeric excess.

The oxidation of olefins is important scientifically and industrially because the reaction adds a functional group to a molecule which may be used to build more complex molecules. In 1980, Sharpless discovered the use of chiral titanium-tartrate complexes for the asymmetric oxidation of allylic alcohols (the olefin) to chiral epoxides in high enantiomeric excess. These chiral epoxides are important compounds for the synthesis of chiral molecules such as glycidol, which is used to produce heart medicines known as beta-blockers.

For background information see ASYMMETRIC SYNTHESIS; CATALYSIS; COORDINATION COMPLEXES; LIGAND; ORGANIC CHEMISTRY; ORGANOMETALLIC COMPOUND; STEREOCHEMISTRY in the McGraw-Hill Encyclopedia of Science & Technology.

Physiology or medicine. Leland H. Hartwell of Fred Hutchinson Cancer Research Center in Seattle and R. Timothy Hunt and Paul M. Nurse of Imperial Cancer Research Fund in London were jointly awarded the Nobel Prize for Physiology or Medicine for their identification of key regulators of the cell cycle in eukaryotic organisms.

The cell division cycle is the succession of events that culminates in the asexual reproduction of a cell. The eukaryotic cell cycle is divided into two main parts: interphase and mitosis. Interphase, during which the cell grows and replicates its chromosomes, is subdivided into three phases: gap phase 1 (G1), synthesis (S), and gap phase 2 (G2). Interphase is followed by mitosis (nuclear division) and cytokinesis (cell division).

Coordination of cell cycle events is crucial; if the different phases are not completed in the correct order or if one phase fails to finish before the following phase begins, chromosomal defects can result. By identifying key regulators of the cell cycle, these three prize winners have made significant contributions to our understanding of the underlying molecular mechanisms of this vital biological process.

Thirty years ago, Hartwell conducted a series of studies of the genetic basis of cell division in baker's yeast (Saccharomyces cerevisiae) that led to the discovery of more than 100 members of a class of genes specifically involved in cell cycle regulation, the cell cycle division (CDC) genes. Hartwell found that one gene (known as CDC28 or "start") controls the first step in the progression through the G1 phase of the cell cycle. In addition, he documented the existence of cell cycle checkpoints, control mechanisms that coordinate the exact timing of cell cycle transitions and halt the cell cycle in order to repair damaged deoxyribonucleic acid (DNA).

In the mid-1970s, Nurse discovered another gene involved in cell cycle control, the cdc2 gene, which controls the transition from G2 to mitosis in fission yeast (Schizosaccharomyces pombe). He found that cdc2 also controls the transition from G1 to S and was thus identical to the "start" gene that Hartwell had isolated from baker's yeast. Nurse went on to discover the corresponding gene in humans, cyclin-dependent kinase 1 (CDK1), which encodes an enzyme (a cyclin-dependent kinase) that drives the cell cycle via phosphorylation (addition of phosphate groups) of other proteins.

In the early 1980s, building on Nurse's research, Hunt discovered a novel class of proteins involved in cell cycle regulation. Using the sea urchin Arbacia as a model system, he found that this protein, which he named cyclin, is degraded right before cell division. This was a key finding, as protein degradation has proved to be a general principle in cell cycle regulation. Hunt went on to find that cyclins regulate the activity of CDKs; cyclins bind to CDKs, activating them to phosphorylate key molecules in the cell cycle. He has since discovered the existence of cyclins in other species. To date, 10 human cyclins have been identified.

The contributions made by these Nobel laureates in the area of cell cycle regulation may one day lead to diagnosis and treatment of diseases resulting from uncontrolled cell growth, such as cancer. A growing body of knowledge indicates that cyclins, CDKs and CDK inhibitors, and other critical cell cycle proteins are targets for genetic change in the development of cancers, or that they may be disrupted during tumor development. Future advances will likely include the discovery of new members of the cyclin-dependent kinase and cyclin-dependent kinase inhibitor families and elucidation of their roles in cancer development and progression.

For background information see CANCER (MEDICINE); CELL (BIOLOGY); CELL CYCLE; CELL DIVISION; MITOSIS in the McGraw-Hill Encyclopedia of Science & Technology.

Physics. Eric A. Cornell, National Institute of Standards and Technology, Boulder, and University of Colorado; Carl E. Wieman, University of Colorado; and Wolfgang Ketterle, Massachusetts Institute of Technology, were awarded the prize for producing Bose-Einstein condensation in low-density vapors of alkali atoms, and for fundamental studies on the properties of the condensates.

In 1924, the Indian mathematician and physicist Satyendra Nath Bose developed statistical rules for describing the quantum-mechanical behavior of photons. After difficulties in getting this work published, he corresponded with Albert Einstein, who recognized its importance, used his influence to have it published, and then generalized it to include gases consisting of molecules—the so-called Bose-Einstein statistics. Bose-Einstein statistics predicted that the atoms of a gas, if cooled below a critical temperature, would undergo a phase transition where they would occupy the lowest-energy quantum state of the system (the ground state) and gather into a coherent matter wave, effectively behaving as a single "super-atom." This phenomenon became known as Bose-Einstein condensation (BEC). Soon after Einstein's work, it was shown that Bose-Einstein statistics apply only to particles having integer quantum spin and not subject to the Pauli exclusion principle—particles subsequently termed bosons (for example, photons and other particles mediating the fundamental forces of nature, alpha particles, and atomic nuclei having even mass number). Bose-Einstein condensation should thus be limited to bosonic gases.

The temperatures required to demonstrate the existence of this fifth state of matter are so low—less than a millionth of a degree above absolute zero—that Bose-Einstein condensation remained unrealized until 1995. Methods for using lasers to cool and trap atomic gases had already been developed (and were recognized with the Nobel Prize in Physics in 1997) but were inadequate for the task until the team led by Wieman and Cornell employed the technique of laser cooling of alkali atoms in a magneto-optical atom trap followed by evaporative cooling to produce a condensate, using rubidium atoms as the bosonic gas. Wieman had outlined an approach utilizing infrared light beams from lasers to slow down and then trap atoms of rubidium gas. The streams of photons were so aligned that the atoms of the low-density gas were struck from all directions and slowed to the point where their temperature had cooled to about 10 millionths of a degree above absolute zero; the atoms were then held in place by a magnetic field. The final drop to critical temperature was achieved by evaporative cooling, which kicked the most energetic atoms out of the system, and trapping of the remaining coldest atoms by an improvement to the magnetic trap devised by Cornell called a time-averaged orbiting potential trap. The BEC they produced consisted of about 2000 rubidium atoms and lasted 15 s, yet could be viewed with a video camera.

Ketterle, working independently of Wieman and Cornell, reported large Bose-Einstein condensates of sodium atoms and performed fundamental experiments confirming their properties and opening new avenues for the application of BECs. For example, his group demonstrated the existence of the predicted coherence by producing two condensates, releasing them from the trap, and allowing them to interfere with one another. The interference fringes could be visualized and typically showed a spacing of 15 micrometers, a huge length for matter waves. He also was able to produce a stream of coherent matter from the condensate: the first atom laser. Such atom lasers have the potential for application to tasks such as precision measurement of fundamental constants,

atom optics, and precision deposition of atoms on surfaces. *See* ATOM INTERFEROMETER.

For background information *see* ATOM LASER; BOSE-EINSTEIN CONDENSATION; BOSE-EINSTEIN STATISTICS in the McGraw-Hill Encyclopedia of Science & Technology.

Nuclear decay

The atomic nucleus is kept together by a strong nuclear attractive force, while the Coulomb (electrostatic) force tends to blow it apart. The nuclear force acts between the constituents of the nucleus—protons (p) and neutrons (n)—and the Coulomb force only between the protons. The relative size of these two opposing forces is dictated by the relative abundance of protons and neutrons in the nucleus. The Coulomb force becomes more dominating only for nuclei which have a much larger proton-to-neutron ratio than the stable nuclei, which are present in nature. If this ratio becomes large enough, it is indeed possible for the nucleus to emit a proton spontaneously, a process referred to as proton radioactivity. Single-proton radioactivity generally occurs in nuclei with an odd number of protons. For nuclei with an even number of protons, a strong nuclear force component which favors pairs of protons sticking together produces a scenario where the emission of two protons simultaneously is favored. This process of simultaneous two-proton emission was only recently observed in the laboratory.

Radioactive nuclei. Much of the present knowledge of the nucleus is derived from studies of its decay modes. Most nuclei in nature are stable, and the only way to study them is to artificially excite them using nuclear reactions. Some nuclei that are naturally occurring and many more that have been produced artificially at reactors and particle accelerators emit some kind of radiation; these nuclei are called radioactive and have the characteristic that the emission occurs from the lowest-energy state called the ground state. Nuclei of mass below mass number 50 mostly emit electrons or positrons [called beta (β) radiation] and gamma (γ; electromagnetic) rays. At heavier masses, the emission of alpha (α) particles is also common, and recently it has been shown that artificially produced nuclei with a large proton-to-neutron ratio also emit protons. In very heavy nuclei with mass numbers around 240, decay by spontaneous fission with the simultaneous release of neutrons has been observed. A typical example of a light radioactive nucleus is carbon-14 (^{14}C), and a heavy radioactive nucleus is uranium-235 (^{235}U).

The current description of the nucleus assumes that the protons and neutrons are arranged in orbits described by the shell model; therefore, it is important to study how heavier particles can be emitted. There must be correlations within the nucleus that cause clusters of nucleons (such as ^{4}He, $2p$, or $2n$) to be emitted by a radioactive nucleus. Alpha radioactivity—the emission of a helium-4 (^{4}He)

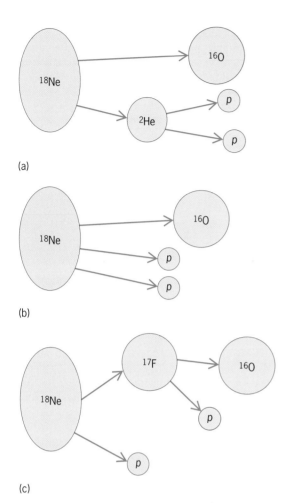

Fig. 1. Possible ways in which two protons (*p*) could be emitted from neon-18 (^{18}Ne). (*a*) Decay of the two protons in a correlated nucleus (^{2}He). (*b*) Simultaneous, uncorrelated emission of two protons (democratic decay). (*c*) Sequential decay of two protons (ruled out experimentally).

nucleus—is a common case that occurs in heavy nuclei such as those of uranium and plutonium, but two-proton (2*p*) or two-neutron (2*n*) radioactivity, while long predicted, has not been observed. Several theoretical calculations predict the possibility of two-proton radioactivity for nuclei around mass 50, and experimental groups are actively searching for such radioactivity in this mass region.

Decay of excited nuclear states. One can also learn about the structure of nuclei by studying their excited states and the decay of these excited states to lower excited states or other nuclei by emission of a particle. An efficient way to produce nuclei in excited states is via a nuclear reaction, and it is in this way that the simultaneous emission of two protons was seen for the first time in 2000. For medium-mass and light nuclei the primary decay mode from excited states is by β, γ, *p*, *n*, and α. For years these decay modes have been used to study the structure of nuclei. With the appearance of radioactive beams, it has become possible to generate nuclear reactions that produce excited nuclei where the numbers of protons exceed the number of neutrons. (Stable nuclei have more neutrons than protons or the same

number of neutrons and protons.) For the experiment that observed the first simultaneous two-proton emission, neon-18 (^{18}Ne) with 10 protons and 8 neutrons was produced in excited states via the fusion of a radioactive fluorine-17 (^{17}F) beam with a proton target.

Excited-state 2p decay. The possible ways in which two protons could be emitted from ^{18}Ne are shown in **Fig. 1**. Figure 1*a* depicts decay by the emission of a correlated pair of protons, called helium-2 (^{2}He). In this situation, the two protons are emitted simultaneously in time. Figure 1*b* depicts the situation, known as democratic decay, in which the two protons are uncorrelated, although their emission is still simultaneous. The distinction between these two decay modes requires a very precise measurement of the energies and emission angles of the two protons. Figure 1*c* depicts the most common decay of two protons, that of sequential decay, in which the two protons are totally uncorrelated in time and space. The present experiment, performed at the Holifield Radioactive Ion Beam Facility at Oak Ridge National Laboratory, ruled out the sequential emission possibility. Many other experiments detecting two-proton emission have been reported, but in all cases the experimental data are consistent with the sequential decay mechanism.

The target in the experiment to detect the two-proton simultaneous emission (**Fig. 2**) consisted of polypropylene (CH_2), which is rich in hydrogen (that is, protons). The ^{17}F nucleus fused with a proton to form a ^{18}Ne nucleus in an excited state where the emission of two protons is energetically allowed. The two protons were detected in a silicon array consisting of 256 pixels distributed in a square measuring 5×5 cm (2×2 in.). Upstream from the target, there was a microchannel plate (MCP), a timing detector which was used to count the particles in the beam and to establish time coincidence between those particles and the reaction products, specifically the two protons. The basic physical quantities that were extracted were the relative angle and kinetic energies of the two protons. With these quantities, in principle, the decay mechanism can be determined. However, in this experiment, the angular opening

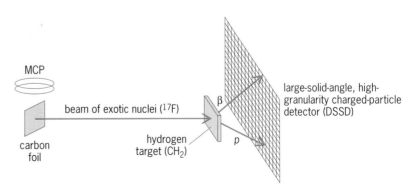

Fig. 2. Experimental setup used to detect the simultaneous emission of two protons. The microchannel plate (MCP) is a timing detector that is used to eliminate beta emission from the data. Passage of beam particles through the carbon foil produces electrons detected by the MCP.

of the detector (30°) was not large enough to distinguish between the various processes depicted in Fig. 1, although it was proven that the two-proton emission was simultaneous. Groups of researchers are actively pursuing two-proton decay studies to determine the emission mechanism in the two-proton decay of ^{18}Ne.

Ground-state 2p decay. In 2002, a study at GSI (Gesellschaft für Schwerionenforschung) in Darmstadt, Germany, revealed the two-proton decay of the nuclear ground state of iron-45 (^{45}Fe). This very exotic isotope of iron (proton number 26) has only 19 neutrons, which is 9 fewer that the lightest stable isotope of iron, ^{54}Fe. It was produced by the fragmentation of a 37.7-GeV nickel-58 (^{58}Ni) beam when impinging on a beryllium target. The resulting fragments near mass 45 were passed through the Fragment Recoil Separator at GSI and deposited in a series of silicon detectors at the focus of the separator which determined the energy of the energetic incident fragment. The different nuclides were unambiguously identified by use of the magnetic field settings, the time of flight through the spectrometer, and the energy of the detected implant in the silicon detectors. The same silicon detector in which the ^{45}Fe nuclide stopped was used to register decay by charged-particle emission. Four events were detected in which low-energy protons were observed that were interpreted as the two-proton radioactivity of the ^{45}Fe ground state (and one event that appeared to be another decay mode). The total decay energy of the 2 protons emitted in the decay of ^{45}Fe is 1.1 MeV, and the measured total half-life for the decay of the ground state is about 3 ms. The two-proton radioactivity of ^{45}Fe was confirmed in a separate experiment carried out at GANIL (Grand Accelerateur National d'Ions Lourds) in Caen, France.

For background information *see* NUCLEAR REACTION; NUCLEAR STRUCTURE; RADIOACTIVE BEAMS; RADIOACTIVITY in the McGraw-Hill Encyclopedia of Science & Technology.

Jorge Gómez del Campo; Carrol Bingham

Bibliography. J. Giovinazzo et al., Two-proton radioactivity of ^{45}Fe, accepted for publication in *Phys. Rev. Lett.*; J. Gomez del Campo et al., Decay of a resonance in ^{18}Ne by simultaneous emission of two protons, *Phys. Rev. Lett.*, 86:43–47, 2001; M. G. Mayer and J. H. D. Jensen, *Elementary Theory of Nuclear Shell Structure*, Wiley, New York, 1955; M. Pfützner et al., First evidence for the two-proton decay of ^{45}Fe, *Eur. Phys. J. A*, 14:279–285, 2002; P. Woods and C. Davids, Nuclei beyond the proton drip line, *Annu. Rev. Nucl. Part. Sci.*, 47:541–590, 1997.

On-press plate imaging

In conventional print media production, the production flow is divided into prepress (film and plate making), press (printed page/sheet production), and postpress/finishing (production of the final print media, such as a book or magazine). Today, digital print production systems may have integrated prepress, press, and postpress, such as a computer-to-press/direct-imaging printing system with on-press plate making.

Since 2001, there have been around 10 direct imaging printing systems introduced in the market (different sizes, design concepts, and imaging systems). These printing systems are available for conventional and waterless offset printing, especially for short-run color printing (500–20,000 prints per job).

Printing technology. Since 1965, offset lithography has been the leading printing technology for economically producing high-quality, multicolor printed media. Lithographic printing uses a printing plate, a smooth/flat surface that has been imaged with fixed content, as a master for the production of multiple copies (prints). Lithographic printing is based on chemical surface effects for inking the imaged area of the plate to be printed. A flow of dampening solution (mainly water plus some additives) is required in conventional offset printing to prevent the ink from adhering to the background (nonimage area) of the plate. In offset lithography, the inked printing plate's image is transferred to an intermediate image carrier (that is, a cylinder covered with a rubber blanket) before it is transferred to the paper. In waterless offset, a special plate material in combination with a special ink allows for elimination of the dampening solution.

Screening and multicolor printing. The content—the image on the plate or the final print—consists of different tone values that are built up as an assemblage of small dots with different sizes and possibly different shapes (to simulate the continuous tone of an original via halftone screening). In digital imaging, individual analog halftone dots may be created as a cluster of many smaller dots [amplitude-modulated (AM) screening]. Alternatively, in stochastic or frequency-modulated (FM) screening, the dot size is very small, and it is identical for all dots. The dots are not clustered to form larger halftone dots. Instead, the dot-to-dot distance is changed to simulate a continuous tone.

In multicolor printing, four color separations are used to image four individual plates for printing sequentially the process colors cyan, magenta, yellow, and black onto the paper. In traditional prepress production, photomechanical techniques and halftone screens are used to create analog halftone dots on films that are used to image the printing plates.

Digitalization. Around 1990, digitalization within the graphic arts industry began to spread faster. It has progressed to the point where all the content (text and graphics) of a printed page is defined with one digital file, including color separation, screening, resolution (specified in dots per inch), screen ruling (lines per inch), attainable gray levels (as a result of resolution and chosen screen ruling/screen frequency), and screening algorithm (AM or FM).

All the different computer to technologies as shown in **Fig. 1** are based on the digital page. The

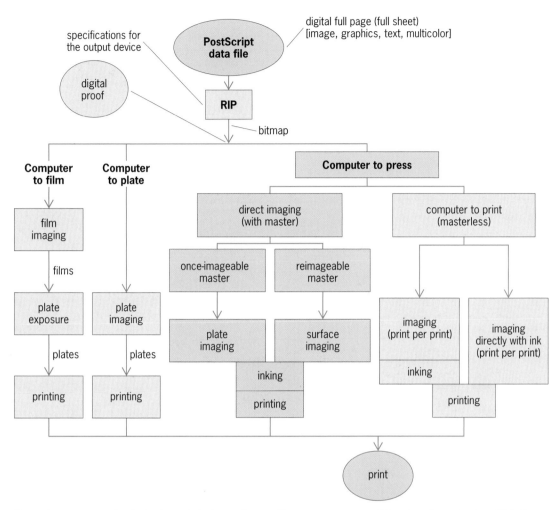

Fig. 1. Computer to technologies for digital print production. The computer-to-press/direct-imaging technology (digital printing with on-press plate imaging) is highlighted with the versions using once imageable master/plates or a reimageable master.

differences between the systems are the increasing levels of digitalization and the integration of prepress and printing processes, as well as the change from mechanical (plate/press) printing to electronic printing systems (with variable images, print-by-print) such as electrophotography and ink jet printing.

In computer-to-film (available since 1990) and computer-to-plate (available since 1995) systems, digital prepress production, that is, full-page film making or plate making, is possible. The advantage of computer-to-film equipment is that the manual assembling (stripping) of multiple film pieces to a full-page film is eliminated. In addition, analog reproduction techniques for creating halftone images are replaced by digital techniques for building up halftone dots with single picture elements (pixels/dots). In computer-to-plate systems, the plate is imaged directly (for example, with a raster image processor, or RIP), eliminating the film. For imaging, lasers are used with special-wavelength light and beam intensity optimized for the plate materials.

On-press imaging. In 1991 on-press plate production was introduced, with the computer-to-plate technology installed within the printing press itself.

For multicolor printing, each printing unit of a four-color offset press is equipped with its own plate imaging system to allow the simultaneous imaging of the four printing plates (**Fig. 2**).

The advantages of the on-press imaging system compared to an off-line (separate from the press) computer-to-plate system is that it is closer to a completely digital workflow. The prepress operation is integrated in the print production system, and conventional (chemical) plate processing is eliminated. Another advantage is that color registration (for multicolor high-quality printing, the accurate positioning of all the plates with the color separations onto the paper) is automatically adjusted and electronically controlled. Once a plate is fixed on the press (cylinder), the operator does not have to adjust the color registration. This leads to shorter start-up times and reduces waste of ink and paper, resulting in faster change-over times between jobs and more economical production of short-run-length, high-quality print jobs.

Most of the plates used are in sheet form and are reapplied to the cylinder after each job. Another possibility is the use a roll of polyester base material

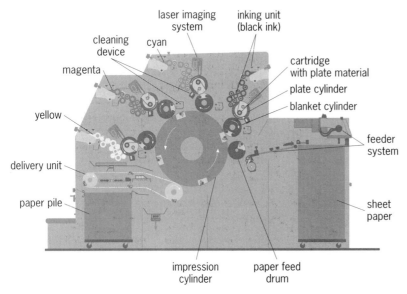

Fig. 2. Cross section of computer to press/direct imaging digital printing system (on-press imaging) for multicolor waterless offset printing in satellite design. (Quickmaster DI 46-4, Pro Heidelberg)

as the plate, where the roll is installed as a cartridge. The cartridge contains enough plate material for imaging about 35 plates automatically before replacement (Fig. 2).

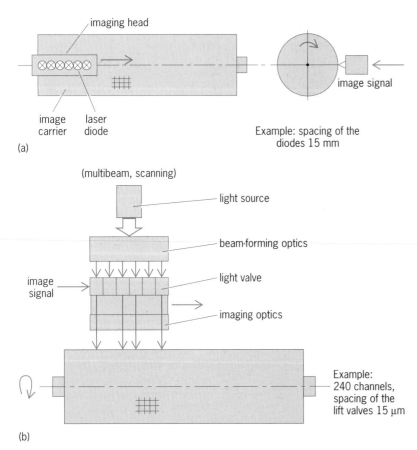

Fig. 3. Design concepts for on-press plate imaging. (*a*) Multibeam imaging system (scanning) with independently controllable laser diodes. (*b*) Multibeam imaging system (scanning) with a single light source and a light-valve array.

Imaging systems. In computer-to-plate and computer-to-press systems, two types of imaging heads generally are used: one with multiple discrete laser diodes (**Fig. 3***a* and **Fig. 4***b*), and the other with a single laser source with an independently controlled light valve (Fig. 2*b*). In both systems, the imaging head has to move in an axial direction while the plate cylinder is revolving. In the single-diode design, mostly the imaging head is wider, and the moving path is shorter than the more compact head design using light-valve technology.

Printing plates. In computer-to-press/direct imaging digital printing systems, waterless offset plates are used most often. The advantage for press design is that there is more room around the plate cylinder for assembling the imaging system. In addition, the operator can concentrate on the flow of ink and does not need to attend the flow of the dampening solution. However, plates and inks for waterless offset have been more expensive than for conventional offset printing. Also, the waterless plate's surface is more sensitive to mechanical damage such as scratches.

Figure 4*a* shows the plate design for waterless offset, using a laser ablation (thermal) imaging technique. Thermal laser diodes (wavelength around 830 nanometers; power approximately 1 watt) selectively ablate the silicone (ink-repelling) layer on top of the plate, creating ink-receptive areas that form the image, dot by dot. The carrier material for the image-forming layers is mostly anodized aluminum, but polyester is also used. An enlarged microscopic section of a thermal plate is shown in Fig. 4*c*. The advantage of thermally sensitive plates is that imaging can take place in daylight environments. No safelight systems are required.

Rewritable plates. A challenge for future development in on-press plate imaging is making a plate material system where, after imaging and printing, the image can be erased and the plate imaged again. In this case, no plate change or removal of a used plate or material section on the plate surface is necessary. Currently under development is the concept for a plate material known as a switchable polymer, with reversible surface characteristics, varying from ink-repelling to ink-accepting and vice versa.

The first commercial printing system to use a rewritable system was introduced in 2001. It is based on conventional offset printing in which a metallic plate sleeve is imaged on-press with an ink-receptive polymeric material via thermal laser imaging (melt deposition and solidification of the polymer on the sleeve surface). After printing, the image is removed by a physical and chemical process.

Other on-press plate imaging system. Since 1988, a small monochrome or spot-color printer has been in the market, especially for office applications. This printer is based on in-line stencil/screen printing. A stencil is imaged using a thermal head with microresistors as heat sources for burning small holes/openings in a special fiber foil material, with resolution up to 600 dots per inch. After imaging, the stencil is automatically affixed to a carrier, that is, a

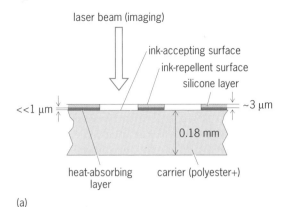

(a)

(b)

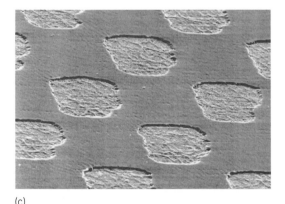

(c)

Fig. 4. On-press plate imaging for waterless offset printing with thermal laser ablation technology. (*a*) Printing plate (thermal plate) structure for waterless offset and thermal ablation process. (*b*) Principle of the imaging head as used for plate imaging in the system shown in Fig. 2. (*c*) Scanning electron microscope shot of the imaged plate surface of the plate shown in *a*.

hollow cylinder with a homogeneous screen surface and an internal ink supply for feeding ink through the open meshes onto the paper.

State of the art. On-press plate imaging continues to be an evolutionary process based on the development of new imaging technologies and systems, including new kinds of plate materials for offset printing. The first direct-imaging system was launched in 1991 for waterless offset printing. By 2002, an eight-page, B-1 size (700 × 1000 mm or 28 × 40 in.) sheetfed press for conventional multicolor offset was available. Computer-to-press/direct-imaging digital printing systems with on-press plate imaging now are available for a range of sheet sizes as well as for web printing. As a result, on-press plate making is an economical production technique for high-quality multicolor printing, and applications cover a high variety of print media products.

For background information *see* COMPUTER GRAPHICS; INK; LASER; PAPER; PRINTING; SILICONE RESINS in the McGraw-Hill Encyclopedia of Science & Technology. Helmut Kipphan

Bibliography. H. Kipphan, Digital multicolor printing: State-of-the-art and future challenges, *Proceedings*, vol. 2413 (Conference: Color Hardcopy and Graphic Arts IV), pp. 7–31, International Society for Optical Engineering, Bellingham, WA, 1995; H. Kipphan, Direct imaging in theory and practice—Computer to press vs. computer to print, *Proceedings of the 48th Annual Conference*, pp. 589–612, Technical Association of the Graphic Arts, Rochester, NY, 1996; H. Kipphan (ed.), *Handbook of Print Media—Technologies and Production Methods*, Springer, Heidelberg, 2001; H. Kipphan, The power of print—Evolution of print media production through digitalization, innovations, electronic media and market demand, *Proceedings of the NIP 17 Conference*, pp. 2–21, Society for Imaging Science and Technology, Springfield, VA, 2001; H. Kipphan, Status and trends in digital multicolor printing: Technologies, materials, processes, architecture, equipment and market, *Proceedings of the NIP 13 Conference*, pp. 11–19, Society for Imaging Science and Technology, Springfield, VA, 1997.

Ontology markup languages

In computing, an ontology is a formal specification of a topic. It is used to define a common terminology for a specific subject or domain (for example, e-commerce, medical guidelines, chemistry). Ontologies can be implemented in varied languages. Some of these languages were created, during the 1990s, specifically for implementing ontologies. Other general languages were also used for that task. Recently, a new generation of ontology markup languages has appeared in the context of the Semantic Web, an extension of the World Wide Web in which information is given well-defined meaning, better enabling computers and people to work in cooperation. Ontologies play a key role in the Semantic Web as a way of representing the semantics of documents and enabling the semantics to be used by Web applications and intelligent agents (for example, Web-searching software).

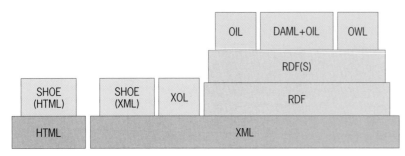

Fig. 1. Ontology markup languages.

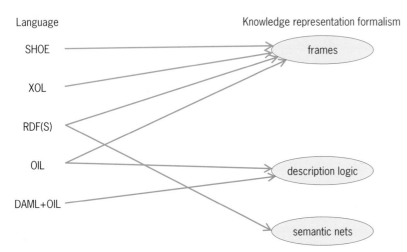

Fig. 2. Knowledge representation formalisms of ontology markup languages.

The languages. The growth of the Internet has led to the creation of ontology languages that exploit the characteristics of the Web. Such languages are usually called Web-based ontology languages or ontology markup languages. These languages and the relationships between them are shown in **Fig. 1**. In 1996, Simple HTML Ontology Extension (SHOE) was built as an extension of Hypertext Markup Language (HTML). It used tags that were different from those of the HTML specification, allowing the insertion of ontologies in HTML documents. SHOE

combines frames (objects, classes, and relations) and interference rules. Following the creation of XML (Extensible Markup Language), which has been widely adopted as a standard language for exchanging information on the Web, SHOE syntax was modified to use XML, and other ontology languages were built based on the XML syntax. The XML-based Ontology Exchange Language (XOL) was developed as a small XML-based subset of primitives (basic operations) from the Open Knowledge Base Connectivity protocol (OKBC), called OKBC-Lite. The Resource Description Framework (RDF) was created by the World Wide Web Consortium (W3C) as a semantic-network-based language to describe information on the Web. Finally, the RDF Schema language was built by the W3C as an extension of RDF with frame-based primitives. The combination of RDF and RDF Schema is known as RDF(S).

These languages are the basis of the Semantic Web. In this context, two additional languages have been developed as extensions of RDF(S): the Ontology Interchange Language (OIL) and DAML+OIL (where DAML stands for DARPA Agent Markup Language). OIL adds frame-based knowledge representation primitives to RDF(S), and its formal semantics is based on description logics. DAML+OIL adds richer modeling primitives to RDF(S).

In 2001, the W3C created the Web-Ontology (Web-Ont) Working Group. The aim of this group was to create a new ontology markup language for the Semantic Web, called the Web Ontology Language (OWL). The working group has already published the first version of the OWL specification, which is currently a W3C working draft.

The **table** summarizes the expressiveness and reasoning mechanisms of the ontology markup languages that have been described in this section, except for OWL.

Implementing an ontology. One key decision in the ontology development process is to select the language (or set of languages) in which the ontology will be implemented. Not all of the existing languages permit implementing the same knowledge, nor do

Expressiveness and reasoning capabilities of ontology markup languages*					
	XOL	SHOE	RDF(S)	OIL	DAML+OIL
Knowledge representation					
Concepts	+	+	+	+	+
Concept attributes	+	+	+	+	+
Relations	−	−	+	+	+
Functions	−	−	−	+	+
Axioms	−	−	−	−	−
Instances	+	+	+	−	+
Reasoning					
Inference engine	−	−	+	+	+
Automatic classification	−	−	−	+	+
Exception handling	−	−	−	−	−
Simple inheritance	+	+	+	+	+
Multiple inheritance	+	+	+	+	+
Constraint checking	−	−	−	−	−

*+means "supported feature" and − means "unsupported feature."

they reason in the same way. As a result, most of the following questions should be answered in selecting an ontology language: What expressiveness does the ontology language have in representing knowledge in a natural way? What are the inference mechanisms attached to the ontology language? Do any ontology development tools support the language? Is the language appropriate for exchanging information between different applications? Does the language ease the integration of the ontology in an application? Is the language compatible with other languages used to represent knowledge and information on the Web? Does the application require integrating existing ontologies that were already implemented in different languages? Are there translators that transform the ontology implemented in a source language into a target language?

Figure 2 shows the knowledge representation paradigms underlying some ontology implementation languages, and reinforces the importance of selecting the correct language in which the ontology will be implemented. For example, a knowledge representation formalism may be very appropriate for a specific task but not for other tasks carried out in the same application.

Therefore, before coding the ontology it must be determined first what is needed in terms of expressiveness and reasoning, and second which languages satisfy such requirements. For this task, the use of an evaluation framework is strongly recommended. Such a framework allows the programmer to analyze and compare the expressiveness and reasoning capabilities of ontology markup languages. The table is based on one such framework, and **Fig. 3** shows an example of the definition of a class Travel in DAML+OIL. Travel is documented as a "journey from place to place," with attributes for the departure and arrival dates, names of the companies that are in charge of it, and its single fare.

Applications. The use of this framework and case studies available from the literature provide guidance on the use of languages for different ontology-based applications. Two such areas are e-commerce and the Semantic Web.

Electronic commerce. In e-commerce applications, ontologies are typically used for representing products and services that are offered in e-commerce platforms (software) and are given to users in catalogs they can browse. Representational needs, such as concepts, their attributes, and relations between concepts, are not too complex. However, reasoning needs are usually higher. Automatic classifications can be useful if the platform offers a high number of products or services (in this case, languages based on description logics are extremely important). Efficient query answering is also important in this environment and is provided by most of the existing languages.

Semantic Web. In the context of the Semantic Web, and for exchanging ontologies between applications, languages based on XML are easily read and managed

```
<daml:Class rdf:ID="Travel">
    <rdfs:comment>A journey from place to place</rdfs:comment>
    <rdfs:subClassOf>
        <daml:Restriction daml:cardinality="1">
            <daml:onProperty rdf:resource="#arrivalDate"/>
            <daml:toClass rdf:resource="&time;Date"/>
        </daml:Restriction>
        <daml:Restriction daml:cardinality="1">
            <daml:onProperty rdf:resource="#departureDate"/>
            <daml:toClass rdf:resource="&time;Date"/>
        </daml:Restriction>
        <daml:Restriction>
            <daml:onProperty rdf:resource="#companyName"/>
            <daml:toClass rdf:resource="&xsd;string"/>
        </daml:Restriction>
        <daml:Restriction daml:maxCardinality="1">
            <daml:onProperty rdf:resource="#singleFare"/>
            <daml:toClass rdf:resource="&units;currencyQuantity"/>
        </daml:Restriction>
    </rdfs:subClassOf>
</daml:Class>
```

Fig. 3. Definition of class Travel coded in DAML+OIL.

since standard libraries for the treatment of XML are freely available. However, it is not difficult to adapt traditional languages to XML syntax, which could make use of the same kind of libraries. The main advantage of RDF(S), OIL, and DAML+OIL is the strong support that they receive from other communities besides the ontology community, and this means that more tools are available for editing, handling, and documenting the ontologies.

For background information *see* ARTIFICIAL INTELLIGENCE; INFORMATION MANAGEMENT; INTERNET; OBJECT-ORIENTED PROGRAMMING; WORLD WIDE WEB in the McGraw-Hill Encyclopedia of Science & Technology.   Oscar Corcho; Asunción Gómez-Pérez

Bibliography. T. Berners-Lee, *Weaving the Web: The Original Design and Ultimate Destiny of the World Wide Web by Its Inventor*, Harper, San Francisco, 1999; T. Berners-Lee, J. Hendler, and O. Lassila, The Semantic Web, *Sci. Amer.*, May 2001; O. Corcho and A. Gómez-Pérez, A roadmap to Ontology Specification Languages, *12th International Conference in Knowledge Engineering and Knowledge Management, Lecture Notes in Artificial Intelligence*, pp. 80–96, Springer-Verlag, Berlin, October, 2000; A. Gómez-Pérez and O. Corcho, Ontology Specification Languages for the Semantic Web, *IEEE Intellig. Sys. Their Appl.*, 17(1):54–60, 2002; R. Gruber, *A Translation Approach to Portable Ontology Specification*, Knowledge Acquisition #5, pp. 199–220, 1993; R. Studer, V. R. Benjamins, and D. Fensel, Knowledge engineering: Principles and methods, *IEEE Trans. Data Knowl. Eng.*, 25(1–2):161–197, 1998.

Optical manipulation of matter

The microscope allows the observation of single cells, the building blocks of life. Since its invention, the resolution, and particularly the contrast, of the instrument has been continually refined. During most of its evolution, however, the microscopist has remained a passive observer. With the recent development of optical manipulation techniques, this situation has completely changed.

It has long been known that light carries momentum; that is, light can exert a force on a material object. Johannes Kepler first proposed that light pushes the tail of a comet away from the Sun. This radiation-induced force is, however, too small to play a role in daily life. It took great experimental skills to perform the first laboratory experiment to demonstrate existence of the force with a traditional light source. The advent of lasers changed the situation dramatically. The laser is a powerful, unidirectional light source which can easily be focused to a small spot. If a laser beam is focused on a micrometer-sized object, a force can be produced that far exceeds the force of gravity. This phenomenon has been used in the design of optical traps for atoms. Laser light can be used to manipulate micrometer-sized objects at the same time as they are being observed under a standard microscope. This effect was first demonstrated by Arthur Ashkin and coworkers in 1971. It turned out to be a very powerful scientific tool, particularly in the field of microbiology.

Optical levitation. **Figure 1a** shows a small drop falling toward a focused, vertically aligned laser beam. A small fraction of the light is reflected from

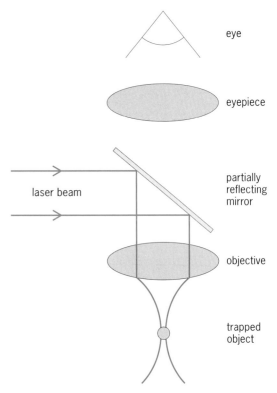

Fig. 2. Set-up of an optical tweezers.

the surface of the drop. The radiation pressure force causes the drop to decelerate. As the drop moves downward, the intensity of the light that the drop encounters increases. At some point the pressure force exerted by the light balances the gravitational force and the drop will remain levitated. Furthermore, the drop has a tendency to stay centered within the laser beam. This stability results from the way the light is transmitted through the drop. As a light beam passes through the drop it is refracted, and the change in direction of the light causes the drop to recoil. Figure 1b illustrates how two light beams of unequal intensity are refracted through a drop, and the magnitudes and directions of the recoil forces are indicated with arrows. The recoil force from the more intense beam at the right of the figure is larger. Hence, the net force on the drop is to the right. Consequently, the drop seeks that part of the laser beam with the highest intensity. It moves horizontally until it is centered within the laser beam. It has been shown, for example, that an oil drop with a diameter of 10 μm can be suspended by a laser beam for several hours.

Optical tweezers. The simplest way to trap particles using laser light is to use a conventional microscope (**Fig. 2**). The objective and eyepiece form an image on the retina of the observer's eye. The laser beam used for trapping is directed downward through the objective by means of a semitransparent mirror. This mirror should ideally reflect all the laser light, while it transmits the light used to observe the sample. Typically, the objective focuses the laser beam to an area smaller than 1 μm^2. A transparent object coming into the focal region is pulled in and

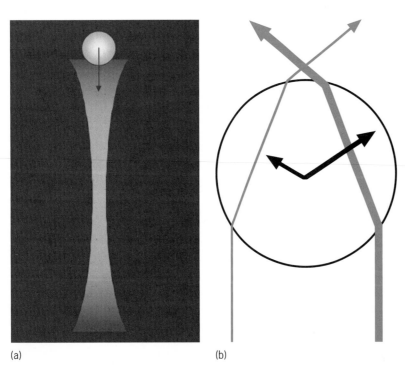

(a)   (b)

Fig. 1. Physics of an oil drop in a laser beam. (a) An oil drop falling toward a vertically aligned laser beam. (b) Optical rays refracted through a transparent drop. The arrows indicate the recoil forces caused by the two optical rays.

trapped by the laser light since it is seeking the region of highest light intensity. A trapped particle can be moved in the horizontal plane by minute changes in the angular direction of the semitransparent mirror. The position of the object in the vertical direction can be adjusted by changing the divergence of the laser beam. This device, which allows nonintrusive manipulation of any transparent object while it is being observed under the microscope, has been named the optical tweezers or the laser trap. It can be used to trap transparent particles up to sizes of tens of micrometers. By directing several laser beams at slightly different angles toward the semitransparent mirror, a system with multiple tweezers can be designed.

Applications in biology. The optical tweezers has turned out to be an extremely useful device in cell biology and microbiology. It allows the biologist to observe and manipulate individual cells instead of large populations, as has been the case in traditional methods. A single cell in a solution can be selected from a large population and isolated for further studies. In principle any cells smaller than 100 μm can be trapped. The cells include, for instance, bacteria, yeast cells, blood cells, and sperm. Cells can be placed in arrays by forcing them onto a surface where they get stuck due to attractive forces between the cell membrane and the surface. Such an array of cells can then, for instance, be screened for a fluorescence signal using standard microscopic techniques. **Figure 3**a shows 37 *Escherichia coli* bacteria that have been placed on a glass plate to form the symbol @. Cell-cell communication can be investigated by placing two cells in contact with each other, and subcellular objects can be moved without breaking the cell membrane. Furthermore, forces between two cells, or a cell and a surface, can be measured by determining the laser power needed to pull them apart.

The main advantage of the optical tweezers is that objects observed under the microscope can be manipulated without using any mechanical parts. By definition, the optical tweezers is a sterile device since only a beam of light is involved in the manipu-

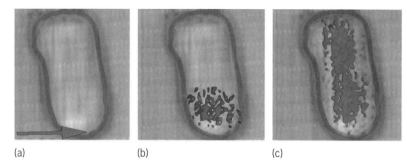

Fig. 4. Diffusion of a dye into an *E. coli* bacterium. (*a*) Bacterium at the time when a 200-nm hole is drilled in the cell membrane at the point indicated by the arrow. (*b*) Bacterium after 4 s, showing diffusion of dye. (*c*) Bacterium after 8 s, showing further diffusion.

lation. The choice of the wavelength of the trapping light is, however, of vital importance. Although the intensity of the laser beam needed to build an optical tweezers is fairly low, the energy per unit time and unit area in the focal plane can be very high. This means that only a minute amount of absorption has a significant effect on the trapped particle. By using light in the near-infrared wavelength region, it is possible to trap particles in the micrometer-sized range, yet still be more than two orders of magnitude below the damage threshold for living cells, which colloquially has been called optocusion.

Laser scalpels. The powerful effect of laser light on trapped particles can, under certain circumstances, be advantageous. For example, a single cell in a more complex organism can be heated by directing a focused infrared laser beam onto it. Furthermore, by using a pulsed, high-intensity ultraviolet laser, it is possible to damage a cell or ultracellular object without heating the sample. The pulse length should then be in the nanosecond range or shorter. Small holes can be drilled in membranes, and intracellular objects can be destroyed. **Figure 4**a shows an *E. coli* bacterium in which a 200-nanometer-diameter hole is drilled in the cell membrane, and successive frames show the diffusion of a dye into the cell. It is even possible to destroy a subcellular object without harming other parts of the cell. When the laser light passes through the cell membrane, it is spread over a finite area. Due to the reduced intensity, the laser light will not damage the organism. It is only at the focal region that the intensity is sufficiently high to cause damage. Thus, by carefully directing the laser beam, it is possible to conduct a rudimentary form of intracellular surgery.

Manipulation of molecules. The optical tweezers can further be used to trap particles much smaller than the highest optical resolution obtainable with visible light. In this case, however, it is not possible to determine whether a single particle or multiple particles have been trapped. A solution to this problem is to attach a transparent bead to the particle under investigation. Steven Chu showed, for example, how a single DNA molecule could be manipulated by attaching it to a micrometer-sized latex bead. **Figure 5** shows two latex beads attached to each end of a

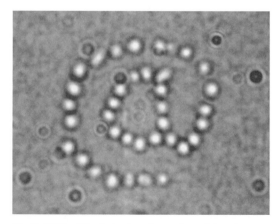

Fig. 3. 37 *E. coli* bacteria placed on a glass plate using an optical tweezers.

Fig. 5. DNA molecule attached to two latex beads.

DNA molecule. By using a dual optical tweezers the molecule can be stretched and positioned in any orientation.

Optical rotation. The optical tweezers is based on the fact that light carries linear momentum; that is, it can exert a linear force on an object. Circularly polarized light is characterized by a rotation of the electric field vector as the light travels through space. Such light can be produced by passing a laser beam through a calcite crystal. If circularly polarized light is used to trap particles in an optical tweezers, it is possible to transfer angular momentum associated with the rotation of the laser light to the trapped particle, causing it to rotate. The speed of the rotation can be several hundred revolutions per second. This mechanism might be used in the future to produce micrometer-sized, optically driven engines and pumps.

For background information *see* LASER; MICRO-ELECTRO-MECHANICAL SYSTEMS (MEMS); OPTICAL MICROSCOPE; PARTICLE TRAP; POLARIZED LIGHT; RADIATION PRESSURE in the McGraw-Hill Encyclopedia of Science & Technology.   Dag Hanstorp; Jonas Enger;
Mattias Ericsson

Bibliography. K. O. Greulich, *Micromanipulation by Light in Biology and Medicine*, Birkhäuser-Verlag, 1999; M. P. Sheetz (ed.), *Methods in Cell Biology*, vol. 55: *Laser Tweezers in Cell Biology*, Academic Press, 1998.

Orbicules (plant anatomy)

In the flowers of many plant species, pollen sacs contain tiny granules (mostly smaller than 4 micrometers) called orbicules, or Ubisch bodies, along with the pollen. The orbicules are sometimes in close contact with the pollen grains and can be dispersed into the atmosphere when the pollen is released from the flower's anthers. Although their function in the plant remains unknown, orbicules may prove useful as phylogenetic markers, and recent studies suggest that they may play a role in allergic reactions associated with pollen.

Development. Figure 1 shows the relationship of orbicules to various structures within flowers, especially the pollen-producing microsporangia (pollen sacs) of the anther. Orbicules develop simul-

taneously with the pollen grain walls, and both are composed of sporopollenin, a complex and durable biopolymer. The progenitors of orbicules, called pro-orbicules, are produced as little vesicles within the tapetum cells, which line the microsporangia and provide the various nutrients needed for pollen grain development. During early pollen development the spherical pro-orbicules are extruded through the walls of the tapetum cells. At the stage of pollen wall formation, sporopollenin is deposited not only on the growing pollen wall but also on the pro-orbicule, giving rise to the mature pollen and orbicule wall.

Potential as phylogenetic and taxonomic markers. Orbicules are considered to be a general feature of species characterized by a tapetum of secretory type, which is considered to be the most primitive tapetum type. They do not occur, however, in every taxon with such a tapetum. The presence of orbicules has also been recorded in some fossil seed plants, which may indicate that this is a primitive feature of seed plants. Species with an amoeboid tapetum type (in which tapetum cells change position and shape during the plant's development), the more recently evolved type, never produce orbicules.

In higher plants, the ornamentation of the pollen wall and that of the orbicule wall often show striking similarities. For example, species with a spiny pollen wall often possess orbicules with similar spines on their wall. Since the great variety of ornamentation types found in pollen walls are useful traits for taxonomic classification, orbicules might have similar taxonomic value (**Fig. 2**). On the basis of such variations in morphology and observations of transverse sections of orbicules, an orbicule typology has been worked out. No intraspecies variations have been observed: all specimens of one species are indeed characterized by the same orbicule type. Apart from studies in the families belonging to the order Gentianales, the taxonomic usefulness of orbicule characters has been studied in the genus *Euphorbia* and the Chloanthaceae, now included in the Verbenaceae.

Proposed functions. During the past 20 years, different hypotheses have been suggested as to the function of orbicules, none of which have been satisfactorily proven. Some researchers have even suggested that orbicules have no specific function, and that they are nothing more than a by-product of tapetal cell metabolism.

Source of sporopollenin. It has been suggested that the orbicule wall could serve as a source of sporopollenin during pollen wall formation. During pollen wall development, sporopollenin derived from the orbicule wall would be transported to the growing pollen wall, resulting in an erosion of the orbicule wall. This hypothesis was based on the observation of thin strands of sporopollenin connecting the spines on orbicules and adjacent pollen walls during pollen wall development in different grass species. However, orbicules are neither eliminated nor eroded during pollen wall growth. In addition, orbicules are not universally present, not even in all

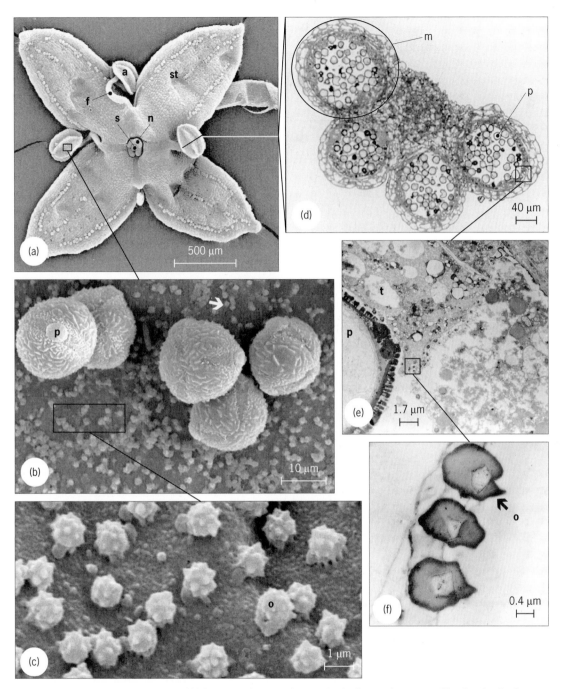

Fig. 1. Orbicules and related structures. (*a*) Scanning electron micrograph of a flower of crosswort (*Cruciata laevipes*). Indicated are the sterile parts (sepals and petals) of the flower (st); the anther (a) supported by the filament (f); the style upon the ovary (s); and the nectary surrounding the style (n). (*b*) Pollen grains (p) lying on the inner wall of the microsporangium (pollen sac) of an Arabian violet (*Exacum*) which is covered by many orbicules (arrow). (*c*) Orbicules (o) in barley (*Hordeum vulgare*) anthers. (*d*) Light microscopic view of a cross section of an anther of a flame flower (*Ixora chinensis alba*). One of the four microsporangia (m) is indicated, in which the pollen grains (p) are produced. (*e*) Transmission electron microscopic observation of a part of a pollen grain (p) in close contact with the tapetum cells (t) of a flame flower (*Ixora chinensis alba*) anther. Orbicules can be seen as little dots (see rectangle) on the walls of these tapetum cells. (*f*) Transmission electron microscopic detail of a cross section of three orbicules (o) present on the inner wall of an *Usteria guineensis* microsporangium. (Enlarged images resemble but are not actual reproductions of the areas shown in blow-up boxes.)

species with the secretory type of tapetum, and thus cannot have a function as general as pollen wall construction.

Storage of pollen components. Orbicules could play a role as a temporary storage place for pollen components such as proteins and polysaccharides before these are transported into the microsporangia for pollen development. The sporopollenin wall of the orbicules may function as an effective barrier against enzymes which may degrade the materials.

Pollen detachment. A function in pollen release has been proposed for orbicules. Just before pollen is

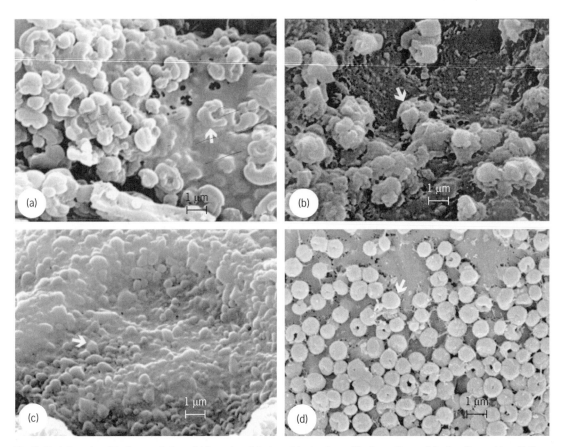

Fig. 2. Variations in orbicule morphology. (*a*) Irregular globular orbicules (arrow) in the anthers of *Acokanthera oblongifolia*. (*b*) Irregular orbicules (arrow) composed of little fragments of sporopollenin, in the anthers of Arabian violets (*Exacum*). (*c*) Many-sided, slightly embedded orbicules (arrow) in the anthers of gentian (*Gentiana acaulis*). (*d*) Spherical orbicules (arrow) in anthers of tea shrub (*Camellia japonica*). Some orbicules are doughnut-shaped.

dispersed, the anther tissue shrinks. This shrinkage draws the orbicules closer together, creating a more continuous layer. This layer forms a nonwettable surface from which pollen can detach easily.

Tapetum degradation. Some researchers suggested that orbicules may contain enzymes which actively participate in the degradation of the tapetum cells at the end of pollen development. This was based on the observation in the species *Lilium henryi* that the tapetum cytoplasm adjacent to the orbicules is the first to degenerate after pollen development.

Support of pollen grains. Excess sporopollenin precursors passing from the tapetum cells to the developing pollen grains are deposited on the growing orbicule walls. This mechanism may prevent the collapse of the developing pollen grains due to high concentrations of sporopollenin precursors in the anther cavity.

Allergenic nature. In the past, allergy research was focused on studying the presence of allergens in pollen grains. However, most pollen grains are too large to reach the smallest structures in the human lungs. Recent studies have supplied evidence that allergenic activity in small particles (a few micrometers or less) present in the atmosphere may play an important role in causing allergic reactions. Orbicules, if emitted from allergenic species, might fall into this category. Notably, hay-fever-inducing seed plants are characterized by having the secretory tapetum type and may produce orbicules in their anthers.

One of the first proofs for the allergenic nature of orbicules was supplied by H. Miki-Hirosige and colleagues in 1994. They found that the major substance shown to be responsible for allergic reactions against Japanese cedar (*Cryptomeria japonica*) is also present in the orbicules of this species. In another study, on the size distribution of particles emitted from the flowers of important allergenic plants in Japan, scanning electron microscopy revealed that 99% of the micronic particles released from the anthers of the Japanese cedar were orbicules. The results of both studies indicate that, in the case of the Japanese cedar, the orbicules can act as very effective vectors to bring allergens to susceptible individuals. A 2001 study on the presence of orbicules in 15 European allergenic species found that orbicules were present in the anthers of 12 of the species (see **table**). Orbicules were absent in ragweed, mugwort, and olive specimens investigated. Orbicules attached to the emitted pollen grains of birch, hazel, black alder, goosefoot, and pellitory; and all grass species studied had diameters of approximately 0.23 to 1.50 μm, well within the range of efficient allergen vectors (**Fig. 3**). H. I. M. V. Vithanage

Orbicule presence or absence in allergenic species

Family	Species	Orbicule size range,* μm	Orbicule shape	Orbicules attached on the pollen wall
Asteraceae	*Ambrosia coronopifolia*[†] (ragweed)	—	—	—
	Artemisia vulgaris[†] (mugwort)	—	—	—
Betulaceae	*Alnus glutinosa* (black alder)	0.50–(0.69)–1.00	Spiny	Yes
	Betula pendula (birch)	0.50–(0.73)–1.00	Spiny	Yes
	Corylus avellana (hazel)	0.38–(0.83)–1.00	Spiny	Yes
Chenopodiaceae	*Chenopodium ambrosioides* (goosefoot)	0.75–(1.19)–1.50	Spiny	Yes
Fagaceae	*Castanea sativa* (sweet chestnut)	0.13–(0.29)–0.50	Spherical	No
	Quercus robur (oak)	0.25–(0.51)–0.75	Granular-spherical	No
Oleaceae	*Olea europaea*[†] (olive)	—	—	—
Poaceae	*Cynodon dactylon* (Bermuda grass)	0.38–(0.54)–0.75	Spiny	Yes
	Dactylis glomerata (cock's foot)	0.38–(0.51)–0.75	Spiny	Yes
	Lolium perenne (rye grass)	0.38–(0.59)–0.88	Spiny	Yes
	Phleum pratense (Timothy grass)	0.23–(0.38)–0.46	Spiny	Yes
Polygonaceae	*Rumex acetosa* (sorrel)	0.75–(0.91)–1.25	Spiny	No
Urticaceae	*Parietaria diffusa* (pellitory)	0.38–(0.58)–1.00	Irregular	Yes

* Mean size is in parentheses.
[†] This species lacks orbicules.
SOURCE: Data from S. Vinckier and E. Smets, 2001.

and coworkers found Group 1 allergen in the orbicules and in the anther cavity of rye grass. (Group 1 allergens are those that have biochemical properties, such as molecular size and amino acid sequence, similar to those of the first identified allergen from rye grass.)

In the species which disperse orbicules along with pollen into the atmosphere, the number of orbicules is well in excess of the number of pollen grains, and they are small enough to penetrate into the small-est regions of the lungs. Because of their small size, they may remain in the air for a long period and can be present even after the end of the pollen season. Besides offering an explanation for bronchial asthma symptoms in susceptible patients, a practical implication of these studies is that the traditional pollen count may be misleading as an index of outdoor allergen exposure. In fact, the pollen count technique consists of the microscopic examination of pollen grains collected in volumetric pollen traps

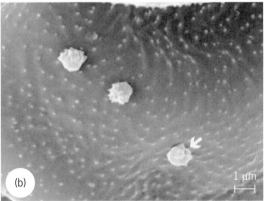

Fig. 3. Orbicules in allergenic species. (*a*) General view of an emitted pollen grain of hazel (*Corylus avellana*) during the pollen season. One orbicule (arrow) is attached to the pollen wall. (*b*) Detailed observation of three spiny orbicules (arrow) attached to the spiny pollen wall of a pollen grain of hazel.

and the determination of their concentration per cubic meter of air, whereas immunochemical methods are required to identify the allergens carried by micrometer-sized particles in the atmosphere such as orbicules. It would be interesting to quantify atmospheric variations in these and other biologic aerosols and their allergenic activity, in an attempt to establish correlations with clinical symptoms and to estimate the different risks they pose for asthma and hay fever sufferers sensitive to pollen allergens.

For background information *see* ALLERGY; ANTHER; FLOWER; PLANT ORGANS; PLANT TAXONOMY; POLLEN in the McGraw-Hill Encyclopedia of Science & Technology.   Stefan Vinckier

Bibliography. S. Huysmans, G. El-Ghazaly, and E. Smets, Orbicules in angiosperms: Morphology, function, distribution, and relation with tapetum types, *Bot. Rev.*, 64:240–272, 1998; H. Miki-Hirosige et al., Immunocytochemical localization of the allergenic proteins in the pollen of *Cryptomeria japonica, Sexual Plant Reprod.*, 7:95–100, 1994; S. Vinckier and E. Smets, The potential role of orbicules as vector of allergens, *Allergy*, 56:1129–1136, 2001; H. I. M. V. Vithanage et al., Immunocytochemical localization of water-soluble glycoproteins, including Group 1 allergen, in pollen of ryegrass, *Lolium perenne*, using ferritin-labelled antibody, *Histochem. J.*, 14:949–966, 1982.

Ordovician radiation

The Ordovician biodiversification event, or radiation, of 500 million years ago (mya) was one of the most significant events in the history of life, and in fact involved a greater increase in diversity at the family and genus level than did the more popularly known Cambrian radiation, which occurred 540 mya. (Recall that families comprise genera, which in turn comprise species.) During the Ordovician radiation the diversity of marine families nearly tripled, and those groups of animals that came to dominate the next 250 million years were established.

The animals that dominated during the Ordovician Period include familiar forms such as echinoderms (sea lilies and sea stars) and corals as well as groups not common today such as brachiopods and bryozoans. Brachiopods are invertebrate animals that superficially resemble clams in that they have two valves that enclose soft parts, but in fact are unrelated to clams. Unlike clams, brachiopods have a coiled feeding organ called a lophophore; their symmetry is also quite different. Bryozoans are common today as encrusters on seaweed and shells and are often referred to as lace animals or moss animals. Groups such as clams (bivalves) and snails (gastropods) also diversified but to a lesser extent; the major radiation of these groups did not occur until around 250 mya.

Diversity patterns. The great increase in marine biodiversity from the Cambrian to the Ordovician was recognized as early as 1860. The magnitude of Ordovician diversification was not fully appreciated, however, until the late 1970s and early 1980s. J. J. Sepkoski's compendium of marine families (1979) revealed a threefold increase in family-level diversity between the Late Cambrian and the Late Ordovician (**Fig. 1**). This expansion followed on the heels of an apparent Late Cambrian diversity plateau. The subsequent diversity plateau established in the Ordovician was roughly maintained (despite significant short-term fluctuations) until the catastrophic Permo-Triassic extinction 250 mya. Following the end-Permian extinction and subsequent Triassic recovery, familial diversity began a steady increase which has apparently continued up to the Recent epoch.

The increase in biodiversity during the Ordovician radiation was not gradual through the Ordovician (approximately 35 million years long) but was concentrated over approximately 10 million years, and the pattern of diversification had a strong and complicated biogeographic component— that is, it was the composite result of processes operating at a variety of taxonomic and geographic levels. Studies have shown that the timing, rate, and magnitude of diversification differed considerably among paleocontinents, and among individual basins within continents. It has been proposed that the differential diversification dynamics among regions and among clades (related groups of species) can, in part, be explained by temporal and geographic variation in plate tectonic activity, which has been tentatively correlated with diversity.

Ecosystem complexity. The Ordovician radiation was an ecological event of extreme magnitude. With a near tripling of biodiversity, significant ecological changes were inevitable, including changes in ecosystem structure and complexity.

The Ordovician radiation largely occurred in the marine ecosystem. However, evidence from spores and terrestrial trace fossils (preserved trails of animals moving through mud) suggests that the initial radiation of complex life onto land also occurred in the Ordovician.

There were numerous large-scale changes within all established ecosystems in the marine realm. One of the most significant changes occurred with the development of hardground and reeflike communities that were to dominate ecosystems for the subsequent 200 million years. Changes were also occurring in the soft-substrate environment of the continental shelves.

Hardground development. Hardgrounds are hardened sea floors that result from cement precipitation from seawater. They are not common today but were widespread in the Ordovician. In the Early Ordovician, hardgrounds were a major factor in the initial diversification of crinoids (stalked echinoderms, such as sea lilies) as well as encrusters and other fauna. A variety of bryozoan clades and functionally similar animals as well as boring sponges and worms diversified on hardground surfaces. The end result was a complex hardground ecosystem. The diversification

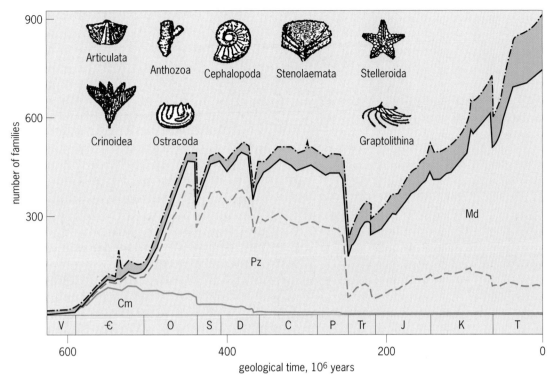

Fig. 1. Marine family diversity during the Phanerozoic eon (540 mya to present). The tinted area indicates diversity contributed by poorly preserved groups. Faunas characteristic of different time periods are indicated as follows: Cm, Cambrian; Pz, Paleozoic; Md, modern. Time periods are V, Vendian; ₵, Cambrian; O, Ordovician; S, Silurian; D, Devonian; C, Carboniferous; P, Permian; Tr, Triassic; J, Jurassic; K, Cretaceous; T, Tertiary. (*After J. J. Sepkoski, Jr., 1979*)

in this habitat was so pronounced that it has been termed the hardground revolution.

Reef complexity. The Ordovician radiation also resulted in a significant increase in reef complexity. Middle Ordovician and later Paleozoic reefs contain a variety of sponges as well as encrusting organisms such as bryozoans. During the Middle Ordovician new framework organisms were added to the reef community. Framework organisms are those that give the reef its three-dimensional structure that rises above the sea floor. Examples include corals and skeletonized sponges known as stromatoporoids. The Ordovician advent of stromatoporoid reefs was of considerable significance as these dominated the reef ecosystem through the Devonian.

Adaptive strategies. Another way of examining ecological change is to look at adaptive strategies—how were animals making a living? Richard Bambach considered this for the Ordovician, using mode of life and feeding type as parameters to distinguish megaguilds (groups of organisms sharing the same adaptive strategy) [**Fig. 2**]. Bambach documented an increase in the number of megaguild occupations after the Cambrian. In fact, all of the adaptive strategies used by multicelled organisms living on or near the sea floor (benthic metazoans) for the remainder of the Paleozoic were in place by the end of the Ordovician. In particular, new general benthic adaptive strategies added to the Cambrian ensemble included mobile suspension feeders and mobile carnivores as well as infaunal (living beneath the sediment) shallow passive suspension feeders and deep active deposit feeders. The major addition was epifaunal (living on top of the sediment) suspension feeders, such as brachiopods, echinoderms, and corals (Fig. 1). These major groups were still present, and the composition of the guilds changed very little, in the post-Ordovician, in spite of two mass extinctions.

Dominance. Another measure of ecological change is dominance—which group is the most important taxonomically and which is the most abundant? In the Ordovician marine ecosystem, there was a switch from taxonomic dominance by trilobites to dominance by brachiopods and, to a lesser extent, crinoids. That is, there were more different kinds of brachiopods and crinoids than trilobites. This change was accompanied by a shift in actual physical dominance or abundance. That is, there were larger numbers of brachiopods and echinoderms than trilobites in the Ordovician. Brachiopods and echinoderms remained the most abundant kinds of animals in the marine realm until the Late Permian mass extinction. If one were to walk along the beach in the Ordovician, the beach would be littered with brachiopods and crinoid bits and pieces and very few trilobites.

Potential causal mechanisms. Compared to Cambrian ecological radiations, relatively little work has been done to explore the causal factors underlying the Ordovician diversifications. Recently, researchers have tended to view the diversifications as resulting

	Suspension	Deposit	Herbivore	Carnivore
Mobile	Bivalvia	Gastropoda Ostracoda MONOPLACOPHORA TRILOBITA	Echinoidea Gastropoda Ostracoda Malacostraca MONOPLACOPHORA	Cephalopoda Malacostraca Stelleroidea Merostomata
Attached Low	Articulata Edrioasteroida Bivalvia Anthozoa Stenolaemata Sclerospongia INARTICULATA			
Attached Erect	Crinoidea Anthozoa Stenolaemata Demospongia Blastoidea Cystoidea Hexactinellida EOCRINOIDEA			
Reclining	Articulata Hyolitha Anthozoa Stelleroidea Cricoconarida			

	Suspension	Deposit	Herbivore	Carnivore
Shallow Passive	Bivalvia Rostroconchia			
Shallow Active	Bivalvia INARTICULATA	Bivalvia POLYCHAETA TRILOBITA		Merostomata POLYCHAETA
Deep Passive				
Deep Active		Bivalvia ?		

Fig. 2. Distribution of Ordovician taxa among benthic megaguilds defined by mode of life and feeding type. Those animals that were present in the Cambrian are capitalized. (*After R. K. Bambach, 1983*)

from a complex mix of intrinsic biological and extrinsic physical factors.

For example, it has been noted that Cambrian oceans appear to have been characterized by mesotrophic-eutrophic (nutrient-moderate to nutrient-rich) conditions and that many Cambrian taxa were sessile (anchored rather than mobile), passive suspension feeders well adapted for such conditions. The diversification of animals in the Cambrian may have created more oligotrophic (nutrient-poor) conditions, thus leading to the rise, diversification, and dominance of the mobile, active-filtering Paleozoic fauna. A shift toward oligotrophic conditions may also have been key in setting the stage for the radiation of calcified algae.

Another body of speculation holds that the Ordovician radiations may be related to increasing continental nutrient flux resulting from increasing tectonism and volcanism. One suggestion is that the two major phases of diversification in the Phanerozoic oceans (Cambro-Ordovician and Mesozoic-Cenozoic) were

generally correlated with intervals of elevated tectonism, which may have produced changes in substrate (changes from mud to sand or carbonate or vice versa), greater primary productivity (that is, production of complex organic molecules from inorganic compounds), and increased habitat partitioning leading to increased speciation. A tentative correlation between diversity and proximity to orogenic (mountain-building) belts has also been reported. These hypotheses and others will be tested in future years to provide a much better understanding of the potential causes of the Ordovician radiation.

For background information *see* BRACHIOPODA; BRYOZOA; DEEP-SEA FAUNA; ECHINODERMATA; ORDOVICIAN; PALEOECOLOGY; PALEOZOIC; REEF in the McGraw-Hill Encyclopedia of Science & Technology.
Mary L. Droser

Bibliography. M. L. Droser, D. J. Bottjer, and P. M. Sheehan, Evaluating the ecological architecture of major events in the Phanerozoic history of marine invertebrate life, *Geology*, 25:167–170, 1997; M. L. Droser, R. A. Fortey, and X. Li, The Ordovician radiation, *Amer. Scientist*, 84:122–131, 1996; T. E. Guensburg and J. Sprinkle, Rise of echinoderms in the Paleozoic fauna: Significance of paleoenvironmental controls, *Geology*, 20:407–410, 1992.

Organic catalysts

The use of organic molecules to catalyze chemical reactions is emerging as a useful method in organic synthesis. The catalytic activity of nitrogen-containing aliphatic and heterocyclic organic compounds has been exploited since the early days of chemistry, for example, in acylation reactions, hydrocyanations, aldol condensations, cycloaddition reactions, hydroborations, and phase-transfer reactions. The application of organic catalysts to asymmetric synthesis, where the reaction predominantly leads to the formation of one of the two possible enantiomers (L or D), is much less common. Enantiomers that are not superimposable on their mirror images are called chiral.

Early synthetic developments. Somewhat paradoxically, asymmetric organocatalytic reactions were developed prior to chiral metal-complex-mediated asymmetric transformations. In the late 1920s, M. M. Vavon and R. Peignier, and independently R. Wegler showed that optically active chiral alkaloids, such as brucine and strychnine, were able to induce enantiomeric enrichment either by esterification of meso (symmetric, optically inactive molecules) dicarboxylic acids or by the kinetic resolution (separation) of secondary alcohols. The enantioselectivity of these early systems was disappointingly low. The breakthrough in the use of efficient enantio-selective organocatalytic methods is related to the L-proline-mediated asymmetric Robinson annulation (ring cyclization reaction) discovered in the early 1970s. The Hajos-Parrish-Wiechert reaction is an intramolecular aldol reaction that permits access to a number of key intermediates for the synthesis of natural products (**Fig. 1**). This L-proline-mediated reaction received a considerable amount of synthetic and mechanistic interest. It has been demonstrated that other amino acids, such as L-phenylalanine, could replace L-proline. The scope of the catalytic process was considerably broadened by demonstrating that L-proline can mediate a number of related transformations such as the enantioselective intermolecular cross-aldol reaction of aldehydes, as well as Michael and Diels-Alder type transformations in solution and on solid supports.

A further development of organocatalytic reactions was the use of diketopiperazines in asymmetric hydrocyanation reactions, developed by Inoue in the late 1970s and early 1980s. These reactions, along with the enantioselective oxidation of enones using polyamino- or resin-bonded polyamino acid, and the Diels-Alder reaction catalyzed by chiral amines, paved the way for efficient asymmetric organocatalytic reactions.

In the above examples, small organic molecules offer distinct preparative advantages over metal-complex- or enzyme-mediated catalysts. Reactions catalyzed by inexpensive organic molecules can be performed in an aerobic atmosphere. In terms of stability, they are more robust than enzymes or other bioorganic catalysts. Environmentally, there is no risk of metal leakage, and no expensive recovery process is required in the waste treatment. In addition, organic molecules are more conveniently immobilized and reused than their organometallic or bioorganic analogs.

Catalysts. Although the first catalysts were naturally occurring molecules containing a rigid backbone, organocatalytic reactions have evolved from the ligand chemistry of organometallic reactions. Ligands, that is, molecules with the affinity to bind to a second atom or molecule, are usually considered as a source of chirality without realizing the benefits of the presence of the catalytically active functionalities. The large array of ligands developed for metal-mediated enantiocatalytic reactions are still among the best-performing organocatalysts (**Fig. 2**).

The main advantages of synthetic molecules over natural ones are their readily available enantiomers and easily tunable structure. Moreover, compound classes having no naturally occurring analogs can be attained. While there is no naturally occurring source of phosphorus-containing chiral compounds for enantiocatalytic use, there is understandably intense synthetic activity to close the gap. Beside the potential complexation abilities of the phosphorus atom, particular advantages of this type of compound are the ability to act as a nucleophilic site as well as a stereogenic center.

Along with purely synthetic compounds, natural-product-derived molecules represent a complementary pool of catalysts. Many alkaloids have been tested, but few have proved useful. One limiting factor is that few of them possess a naturally

occurring enantiomeric counterpart, which is required for their convenient use in enantioselective synthesis. The readily available and inexpensive cinchona alkaloids having pseudoenantiomeric forms such as quinine and quinidine (**Fig. 3**) represent an exception. Both of these natural products and derivatives have been seen in enantiocatalytic reactions to give impressive results.

Amino-acid-based catalysts, which fold into defined secondary structures in organic or aqueous

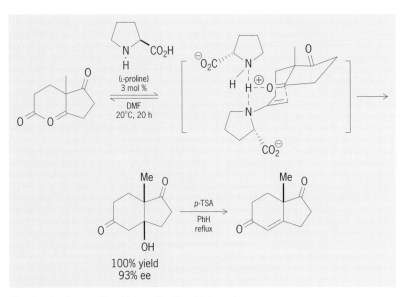

Fig. 1. L-Proline-mediated intramolecular aldol reaction.

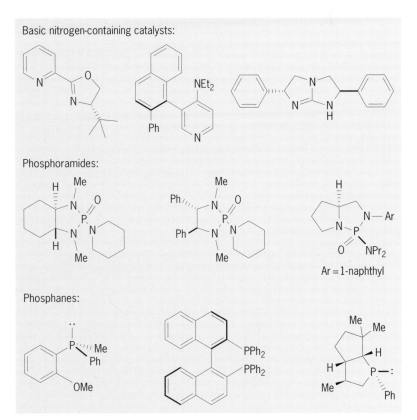

Fig. 2. Some selected organic catalysts of synthetic origin.

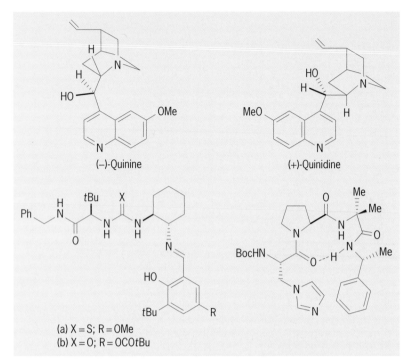

Fig. 3. Some natural-product-derived molecules used as organic catalysts.

(a) X = S; R = OMe
(b) X = O; R = OCO*t*Bu

(–)-Quinine

(+)-Quinidine

ders easier the mechanistic investigations. (3) The flexibility of the method is of great use. It is easy to prepare a peptide sequence that can produce the opposite enantiomer or its epimer (an isomer differing at only one of several chiral centers), a process hardly amenable with enzymes.

The development of novel classes of catalysts has a lot in common with the methods used in ligand chemistry. Along with the most commonly used "try-and-see" method, there are two other major approaches—diversity-driven and mechanism-based—to obtain a new generation of catalysts. Diversity-driven research generates a large number of potential candidates and selects the best-performing ones. This approach is particularly useful for preparing peptide-based catalysts. In contrast, the mechanism-based approach produces a single molecule that corresponds best to the supposed structure of the covalently bonded complex in the transition state. In the rational design of a chiral catalyst, the eternal dilemma arises from the relative positions of the active center and the chiral environment, that is, selectivity versus reactivity. If the reaction center cannot be rendered chiral, the most straightforward approach is to introduce the stereogenic (chiral) center in proximity to the active site. This leads to steric hindrance of the chiral center and often reduces the reactivity of the catalyst. Another approach relies much more on enzymelike structures. The strategy consists of building a simplified version of a complex chiral environment around the catalytic site, much as found in enzymes, where the chiral center is distant from the active site. Such artificial enzymes may comprise a short oligopeptide sequence including an active site (such as imidazole), and a basic secondary structure (for example, a fold).

Mechanisms. Organic molecules may promote chemical reactions either by forming reactive intermediates via a covalently bonded activated complex or by allowing contact between molecules of isolated phases (usually liquid/liquid or liquid/solid phases) by a phase-transfer process. A third application of organic molecules in catalysis is in electron transfer reactions; however, these type reactions are in early development.

Reactive intermediates. Catalysts may play typically a metal-associated Lewis acid/Lewis base role. Amine catalysts, for example, may give rise to immonium intermediates, which is the synthetic equivalent of a Lewis acid activation; this is the case in the Hajos-Parrish-Wiechert reaction (Fig. 1). While the use of nitrogen-based catalysts is common, the use of phosphanes is more recent (Fig. 2). A particular advantage of the phosphane catalyst is its ability to act as a nucleophilic site toward the transferable function as well as a chiral center in the asymmetric transformation. Among the number of organic reactions, typical examples are aldol-type condensations, hydrocyanations, conjugate additions, cycloadditions, and allylation reactions.

The concept of molecular-cavity-accelerated transformations, where the catalyst may select between

solution, are probably the most dynamically growing catalyst class. Although simple amino acids, such as L-proline and L-phenylalanine, have been used for a long time, the use of oligopeptide (peptides with 4 to 10 amino acids bonded together) enzyme mimics is recent. The oligopeptide approach has some distinct advantages: (1) The efficiency of the catalyst can be improved by varying the nature of the amino acids using combinatorial synthetic methods. (2) The structural simplicity of the oligopeptides contrasts with the complexity of the enzymes and thus ren-

Oxone
MeCN-DMM-H$_2$O
0°C, 1.5 h

10 mol %

66%

Fig. 4. Preparation of a key intermediate in the synthesis of (−)-glabrescol using enantiocatalytic epoxidation. Oxone = 2KHSO$_5$ · KHSO$_4$ · K$_2$SO$_4$.

competing substrates depending on size and structure criteria, is a special case of Lewis acid/Lewis base activation. The molecular cavity can be tailored either by using cyclic oligomers having polar groups, such as cyclodextrins, or by using conveniently functionalized polymers. The rate acceleration of the given reaction is similar to the Lewis acid/Lewis base activation and is the consequence of a simultaneous action of different polar functions. The chiral-cavity-accelerated asymmetric transformation is the closest analogy to enzyme catalysis. This analogy goes further than it does with simple organic molecules, as not only the recognition process but also the mode of action—that is, creation of transition-state analogs—are reminiscent of enzyme activity. When polymers are used as the support (molecular imprinting), they are called plastic enzymes.

In addition to the typical Lewis acid/Lewis base rules, organic molecules may promote reactions as true reagents. In these transformations, the catalyst is consumed. In order to preserve the catalytic nature of the process, the consumed reagent is regenerated in a parallel cycle. An example is the oxidation of olefins using chiral ketones in the presence of a co-oxidant such as hydrogen peroxide (H_2O_2) or oxone ($2\ KHSO_5 \cdot KHSO_4 \cdot K_2SO_4$) [**Fig. 4**]. The reaction generates in situ a catalytic amount of chiral dioxirane, the actual oxidizing agent in the process. Other examples are asymmetric ylide reactions such as epoxidation, cyclopropanation, aziridination, or catalytic enantioselective protonation.

Phase-transfer reactions. The basis of this type of catalysis is an extraction, where the catalyst forms a host-guest complex with the substrate and shuttles between an organic solvent and a second phase (that is, a solid, aqueous, or fluorinated solvent phase, where the reaction takes place). Among the major class of purely organic phase-transfer catalysts, quaternary ammonium salts have been extensively developed. Although most polar reactions are described under phase-transfer conditions, the asymmetric variant of this type of transformation is far less common. Among the chiral quaternary ammonium catalysts employed, cinchona-derived catalysts are the most commonly used. In the best-performing cases, the catalyst forms a well-ordered contact ion pair with the substrate in the organic phase, shielding one face of the substrate, thus directing the selectivity of the reaction. In these reactions, both the structure of the catalyst and the nature of the solvent have important effects on the selectivity, as nonpolar solvents provide usually higher stereo- and enantioselectivity (more of the desired product) than polar solvents. Enantioselective alkylations, Michael-type additions, aldol and related condensations, 1,2-addition reactions, oxidations, and asymmetric reductions are among the most developed reactions.

For background information *see* ASYMMETRIC SYNTHESIS; CATALYSIS; DIELS-ALDER REACTION; ELECTRON-TRANSFER REACTION; ENANTIOMER; ENZYME; LIGAND; OPTICAL ACTIVITY; ORGANIC SYNTHESIS; PHASE-TRANSFER CATALYSIS; STEREOCHEMISTRY

in the McGraw-Hill Encyclopedia of Science & Technology.   Peter I. Dalko

Bibliography. P. I. Dalko and L. Moisan, Enantioselective organocatalysis, *Angew. Chem. Int. Ed. Engl.*, 40:3726–3748, Wiley-VCH, 2001; H. Gröger and J. Wilken, The application of L-proline as an enzyme mimic and further new asymmetric syntheses using small organic molecules as chiral catalysts, *Angew. Chem. Int. Ed. Engl.*, 40:529–532, Wiley-VCH, 2001; E. N. Jacobsen, A. Pfalz, and H. Yamamoto (eds.), *Comprehensive Asymmetric Catalysis, I–III*, Springer, Heidelberg, 1999; E. R. Jarvo and S. J. Miller, Amino acids and peptides as asymmetric organocatalysts, *Tetrahedron* 58:2481–2495, Pergamon, 2002.

Origins of symbolism

When considering the origins of art or symbolism, one must bear in mind the fundamental problem that many art forms—song, dance, music, body painting or scarification, hairstyles, and so forth, as well as any artwork involving most organic materials—leave no trace in the early archeological record. Consequently, one has to reconstruct events on the basis of a highly skewed and tiny database—that is, the small sample of what originally existed which has survived, and the minute fraction of this which has been recovered, recognized, and published by archeologists. In addition, there is the simple fact that the further back one goes in time, the less chance there is of art objects surviving.

Until recently, the generally accepted view of prehistory was that symbolism or art—however one wishes to define them—arose around 35,000 years ago, at the beginning of the Upper Paleolithic period (Old Stone Age), and was associated with anatomically modern humans, *Homo sapiens sapiens*. For a long time, many scholars believed that art was invented in Eurasia, or even in southwestern France, during this period. Although some long-known clues suggested otherwise—for example, sporadic examples of art from earlier sites occupied by Neandertals—only in relatively recent years have increasing quantities of evidence made it clear that the origins of symbolism stretch much further back in time.

Earliest evidence. The earliest clue to some kind of esthetic sense, or at least evidence of the awareness of a human likeness, is a red ironstone cobble found in the South African cave of Makapansgat in 1925; some australopithecines (hominids that lived from about 4.4 to 1 million years ago in Africa) had brought this stone to the cave, about 3 million years ago, from at least 20 mi (32 km) away, presumably because of the extraordinary resemblance to a human face on one side (**Fig. 1**). The object is entirely natural, with no trace of human modification, but was probably brought into the site because this resemblance was observed and recognized, and because the face attracted the curiosity of the australopithecines in

Fig. 1. Makapansgat cobble.

some symbolic manner; one can therefore see in it a trace of the roots of art.

Lower Paleolithic. Many scholars have pointed out that the symmetry and beauty of many Lower Paleolithic stone handaxes, hundreds of thousands of years old, went far beyond what was technically required of the tool, whatever its uses; and in fact some specimens are known from England and France in which fossil shells, embedded in the flint, were carefully preserved in the stone as the tool was shaped.

There are also numerous instances of a very early use of ocher in many parts of the world, although one cannot be sure its usage was always for artistic purposes. Pieces of hematite or ocher appear to have been carried into sites in South Africa as far back as 800,000 or 900,000 years ago; a small ocher crayon appears to have been used on rock at Hunsgi, southern India, between 300,000 and 200,000 years ago; and pieces of pigment have also been recovered from Zimbabwean rock-shelter deposits of more than 125,000 years ago. The site of Terra Amata, in southern France (ca. 300,000 B.C.), contained 75 bits of pigment ranging from yellow to brown, red, and purple. Most of them have traces of artificial abrasion and, since they do not occur naturally in the vicinity, must have been brought into the site by the occupants.

Increasing numbers of bones and stones from the Lower Paleolithic are now being found to bear series or patterns of deliberate and nonfunctional incisions—for example, 12 horse bones from the French rock shelter of Abri Suard (Charente), and several bones from Bilzingsleben (Germany), of about 300,000 B.C., with series of parallel incisions which seem to have nothing to do with cutting or working.

The real breakthrough in this domain, however, came in the 1980s with the discovery of a seem-ingly insignificant, tiny (3.5 cm, or 1.4 in., high) piece of volcanic tuff in the site of Berekhat Ram, Israel, dating to between 233,000 and 800,000 years ago. It bears a resemblance to a female figure, and has grooves around its "neck" and along its "arms" (**Fig. 2**). Studies with both a conventional microscope and scanning electron microscope have shown independently that these grooves were humanly made and thus this was an intentionally enhanced image. It is even possible that the whole thing was carved by humans, but it is so eroded that one cannot be sure. Nevertheless, this is unquestionably an art object.

Middle Paleolithic. The Middle Paleolithic period, associated with Neandertals, has produced a wide range of art objects: for example, a limestone block from the French site of La Ferrassie, decorated with pairs of cupmarks and lying over a child burial site; a pebble from Axlor, in the Spanish Basque country, with a central groove and two cupules on it; and a piece of flint from the Israeli site of Quneitra, dating to 54,000 years ago, which is carefully incised with four semicircles and other lines. (Cupmarks and cupules are small, circular hollows pecked or ground into rock.) There are also numerous incised bones from this period, such as at Prolom II cave in the Crimea, which yielded a horse canine marked with five parallel engraved lines, and the phalanx (finger or toe bone) of a saiga antelope bearing a fanlike engraved motif. The Bulgarian cave of Bacho Kiro has

Fig. 2. Berekhat Ram figurine showing the carved bent arm. (*Courtesy of Alexander Marshack*)

a bone fragment, dating to 47,000 years ago, with a zigzag motif.

The most striking piece of Neandertal art, however, has only recently been studied and published, despite having been found more than a quarter century ago. It is a masklike object from La Roche-Cotard (Indre-et-Loire, France) that consists of a piece of flint, flaked and shaped to something like a face, 10.5 cm (4.1 in.) high and 9.8 cm (3.9 in.) across; it has a natural nose with a horizontal hollow behind it. A piece of bone was inserted into this hollow and wedged into place with small flint pieces, so that the overall effect is that of a stone face with bone eyes. This is a remarkable and sophisticated piece of sculpture, a protofigurine, which probably dates to between 50,000 and 70,000 years ago.

Of even greater age—around 77,000 years—are the recent discoveries, at Blombos Cave in South Africa, of abstract representations engraved on at least two pieces of ocher, recovered from layers that contain more than 8000 pieces of ocher. In Australia, used blocks of red and yellow ocher and ground hematite have been found in occupation layers at rock shelters dating to around 60,000 years ago. In Eurasia, usage of ocher also grew markedly in the Neandertal period, with pigments being increasingly frequent and abundant not only in occupation deposits but also in burials which occurred for the first time during this period.

In addition, recent technological studies have shown beyond doubt that the rich array of ornaments from the French cave of the Grotte du Renne at Arcy-sur-Cure (Yonne)—including wolf and fox canines made into pendants by incising a groove around the top, at least one sawed reindeer incisor, a bone fragment with a wide carved hole, a marine fossil with a hole bored through its center, and a fossil shell with a groove cut around the top—can safely be attributed to Neandertal craftsmen; they come from a layer of approximately 34,000 years of age containing a Neandertal bone. It had traditionally been assumed that the Neandertals had stolen or copied these objects from the Cro-Magnons (anatomically modern humans) who had entered western Europe, since ornaments of this kind abound in Cro-Magnon culture. However, it is now clear that the Neandertals produced the material using their own long-developed techniques. The problem remains of why Neandertals and modern humans should both—on present evidence—have begun to produce ornaments at about the same time; and it has reasonably been concluded that it was triggered by their encountering each other, and perhaps served to reinforce group identities.

Both groups clearly produced art or symbols in earlier periods—Neandertals (at, for example, La Roche-Cotard and Quneitra), and modern humans (Blombos); the evidence is sparse on both sides but does exist in a wide variety of forms. It is clear therefore that there was no great or sudden explosion of art around 35,000 years ago or with the arrival of modern humans in Europe.

Upper Paleolithic. Nevertheless, on present evidence there is a growth of art and symbolism—and especially of figurative imagery—during the Upper Paleolithic period, from about 35,000 to 10,000 years ago. Among the earliest images from this time are a series of remarkable ivory figurines from southwest German caves such as Vogelherd, Geissenklösterle, and a large ivory carving, half human and half feline, from Hohlenstein-Stadel: all of these date to more than 30,000 years ago, some of them up to 37,000 years, and they display such sophistication in technique and conception that it is difficult to imagine that they could suddenly have arisen from nothing. The above evidence points clearly to a very long development of artistic expression, not just in Eurasia but all over the world. Similarly, the art of the Ice Age is by no means restricted to Europe—although this is the area where it has been known longest and studied most fully—but is found in some form on every continent.

Cave and rock art also appear to emerge during the Upper Paleolithic, although they may well have existed earlier (although claims for some Lower Paleolithic petroglyphs in India have been refuted recently). So far, about 300 decorated caves and rock shelters have been found in Eurasia which appear to date to the last Ice Age, together with increasing numbers of discoveries of open-air rock art from the period. At present, the earliest dated cave art is that of the Chauvet cave in southern France, where some charcoal from several animal figures has yielded radiocarbon dates of more than 30,000 years. However, many factors, including the extreme sophistication of this cave's art and certain of its motifs, are causing increasing numbers of specialists to question the accuracy of this dating, and to attribute much of the cave's art to later phases of the Ice Age.

Nevertheless, Ice Age art—both the parietal (caves, shelters, and rocks) and the portable (thousands of images on such items as bone, stone, antler, and ivory)—constitutes the first great body of art and symbolism that survives in the archeological record, and provides our first clear insights into the minds and motivations of our ancestors.

For background information *see* ARCHEOLOGICAL CHRONOLOGY; ARCHEOLOGY; AUSTRALOPITHECINE; FOSSIL HUMANS; NEANDERTALS; PALEOLITHIC; PREHISTORIC TECHNOLOGY in the McGraw-Hill Encyclopedia of Science & Technology.   Paul G. Bahn

Bibliography. F. d'Errico et al., Neanderthal acculturation in western Europe?: A critical review of the evidence and its interpretation, *Curr. Anthropol.*, 39(suppl.):S1–S44, 1998; F. d'Errico and A. Nowell, A new look at the Berekhat Ram figurine: Implications for the origins of symbolism, *Cambridge Archaeol. J.*, 10:123–167, 2000; C. S. Henshilwood et al., Emergence of modern human behavior: Middle Stone Age engravings from South Africa, *Science*, 295:1278–1280, 2002; J.-C. Marquet and M. Lorblanchet, Le "masque" moustérien de La Roche-Cotard, Langeais (Indre-et-Loire), *Paléo*, 12:325–338, 2000; A. Marshack, The Berekhat Ram figurine: A late

Acheulian carving from the Middle East, *Antiquity*, 71:327–337, 1997; A. Marshack, A Middle Paleolithic symbolic composition from the Golan Heights: The earliest known depictive image, *Curr. Anthropol.*, 37:357–365, 1996.

Pathogen detection

Due to the threats they pose to the health of humans, animals, and plants, it is crucial to detect and identify pathogenic (disease-causing) bacteria reliably and rapidly. This is true in the medical and veterinary setting, as well as in safety investigations of food, water, pharmaceuticals, and personal care products.

A pathogen detection system has to be specific for a certain microorganism, sensitive enough to detect small amounts of targeted cells, not too expensive, and preferably fast enough to allow a rapid response. Especially in clinical microbiology, a specific identification of the disease-causing (etiologic) agent—that is, the microorganism or its toxin—is essential for successful therapy. Rapid diagnostic methods shorten this process from 48 h to 1–2 h, or sometimes even minutes. Speed of reporting is often essential to subdue an infection at the onset, particularly in nosocomial (hospital-acquired) infections of newborns and human immunodeficiency virus (HIV) patients, and increasing attention is being given as well to the immediate detection and identification of pathogens in bioterrorism and biowarfare.

Traditional versus molecular-based diagnostics. The goals of pathogen diagnosis are to detect the pathogen in a biological sample, confirm a possible etiological diagnosis, and control bacterial infection. Traditional methods such as staining, microscopy, and cultivation are often relatively slow and inconclusive. While traditional microbiology uses mostly phenotypic factors (observable traits of the organism) to identify pathogens, molecular-based diagnostics target genotypic factors which are based on the nucleic acids of an organism. New molecular tools are constantly being integrated and adapted to the area of diagnostic microbiology.

Nucleic acid–based methods of pathogen detection are rapid, sensitive, highly selective, and can often be automated. This rapid detection and identification of the pathogen in a clinical setting permits faster selection of the most effective antibiotic agent; allows public health authorities to contain the infection within a small population and instigate proper protective measures; and permits the selection of an appropriate antibody for passive immunization, if applicable. Another important advantage over conventional culturing methods is that the often difficult process of culturing the pathogen is not necessary (for example, the isolation of single pathogens in complex, nonsterile samples, such as *Mycoplasma pneumoniae* in sputum).

Nucleic acid–based diagnostics are particularly advantageous when slow-growing pathogens (for example, *Mycobacterium tuberculosis* and *Neisseria gonorrhoeae*) must be detected or their culture confirmed; when the location of the pathogen within a tissue sample has to be determined; when the pathogen grows only within the host cell and not by standard cultivation methods such as on agar plates or in liquid growth medium (for example, *Chlamydia trachomatis*); or when the biochemical behavior of a pathogenic strain resembles that of other nonpathogenic strains of that species (for example, harmless *Escherichia coli* versus enterotoxin-producing *E. coli*).

Nucleic acid–based diagnostics may also prove crucial in addressing epidemiologic questions arising from acts of bioterrorism and biowarfare, enabling the identification of the route of distribution of pathogens and the infectious reservoir. This type of diagnostics can identify pathogens that cannot be cultivated, pathogens that undergo certain problematic metabolic states (for example, states in which they are viable but not culturable), or pathogens from dead cell material.

Fast and sensitive nucleic acid detection methods will not make conventional culture and serological techniques obsolete, but will complement them. Nucleic acid–based methods are limited because they can rarely show the viability of a potential pathogen or if the potential pathogen was actually involved in an infectious disease process.

Nucleic acid hybridization. Nucleic acid–based detection methods use hybridization, the formation of a double-stranded piece of nucleic acid by complementary base pairing between two nucleic acid strands. This base pairing is independent of the source of nucleic acid. Diagnostic methods can thus use a single strand of nucleic acid of a known, specific base sequence as a probe to find the exact complementary partner in clinical or environmental samples. To enable hybridization between the probe and the target sequence, the target nucleic acid in the sample has to be made single-stranded by appropriate sample preparation (by the addition of harsh chemicals or by heating the sample close to the boiling point of water). Nucleic acid probes can range from ten to several thousand bases in length. To visualize successful hybridization, one of the partners in this joining reaction has to be labeled to report its location. This is achieved by linking it to a reporter molecule, such as a radioisotope, fluorescent marker molecule (fluorochrome), or enzyme that can be subsequently detected.

The relative chemical stability of nucleic acid is of great advantage, as it allows successful extraction from most samples, the construction of artificial deoxyribonucleic acid (DNA) sequences (probes), and the detection of potentially pathogenic organisms that are already dead.

Conventional hybridization techniques. In conventional hybridization techniques, the nucleic acid of a pathogen is detected with a complementary nucleic acid probe. Hybridization is commonly performed on either solid supports or in liquid. In blotting techniques, DNA is extracted from target cells and the double strand is separated into single strands, which are then fixed onto a nitrocellulose or nylon membrane. Next, the membrane is submersed in hybridization solution with the nucleic acid probe. After hybridization of probe molecules to their targets on the membrane, the excess free probe is washed off and the remaining hybrids analyzed.

Alternatively, a free target-probe interaction can be achieved by direct hybridization in solution, in which the single-stranded DNA is not affixed to a solid support but is combined together in solution. After this faster type of hybridization reaction, the nonbound reporter probe is removed by enzymatic digestion of all single-stranded nucleic acid molecules. The remaining double-stranded hybridization product is then selectively removed with ion-exchanger columns or by chemical precipitation.

In situ hybridization. In situ hybridization allows the localization of pathogens within the infected tissue, as well as yielding quantitative information about its abundance. The in situ hybridization technique requires that intact tissue samples be chemically and mechanically fixed without losing structural integrity, while making the pathogen cells accessible for probe penetration. Another challenge is that the number of identifiable target nucleic acid sequences is limited.

A specialized form of in situ hybridization with fluorescently labeled short probes is called fluorescent in situ hybridization (FISH). In this application, a group- or species-specific probe enters bacterial cells (previously made permeable through the addition of harsh chemicals such as formaldehyde) to bind to a signature sequence of a universal marker gene, the gene for the ribosomal RNA (rRNA). Each of the cell's thousands of ribosomes carries copies of this rRNA, and after successful hybridization the entire cell fluoresces under epifluorescence microscopy or laser confocal microscopy. This technique is limited in that inactive cells frequently contain insufficient rRNA to visualize clearly by hybridization. To bypass this problem for the direct detection of pathogens, which are often under conditions of starvation and thus low in ribosomes, signal amplification is achieved using either multiple probes for different target sequences; more intense fluorochromes; multiple reporter molecules bound to one probe; electronic photointensifiers; or catalyzed reporter deposition (CARD). In the CARD-FISH assay, an enzyme (usually horse radish peroxidase) is attached to the probe. If the fluorochrome-labeled substrate tyramide-F is added, this phenolic compound attaches to the enzyme during processing, resulting in multiple fluorochromes at the probe hybridization site, thus intensifying the signal.

Polymerase chain reaction. The polymerase chain reaction (PCR) technique employs a heat-stable polymerase to complete unfinished double-stranded DNA. The incomplete double-stranded DNA is created by solution hybridization of a short nucleic acid probe of defined sequence and the DNA template (that is, the pathogen DNA made single-stranded by previously heating the solution to $95°C$). The small size of the probe relative to the template, as well as its abundance, ensures that the probe binds to the single-stranded DNA before the partner strand. If the polymerase encounters the incomplete double strand, it is primed to start the completion reaction at the site of the small nucleic acid probe (thus also called primer). For each of the two strands of the original DNA template a specific primer is synthesized and added in excess. The two small nucleic acid probes are added to frame a selected sequence region of the double-stranded template. In subsequent polymerase reactions the extension products of the forward primer can serve as a template for the reverse primer in the following reaction. If this exponential duplication reaction is repeated 30 times, then about 2^{31} (or ~2 billion) copies have theoretically been formed. This amount of identical specific DNA product is sufficient for further characterization experiments.

PCR is so specific and efficient that it can be used to amplify small amounts of template DNA of specific pathogens in a sample, even in nonsterile and complex samples. This technique is therefore the method of choice for intracellular infections (for example, *Chlamydia trachomatis*), but also for many viral infections (for example, HIV). PCR can even be employed on RNA when this single-stranded molecule is first translated into double-stranded DNA using an enzyme called reverse transcriptase. PCR is now used widely in clinical, food, and environmental laboratories. However, PCR is so sensitive that contamination of a sample could easily lead to false positive results. In addition, reaction inhibitors can hide the presence of a pathogen. The addition of multiple experimental and reagent controls to a test are essential for the interpretation of the results.

Ribotyping. Ribotyping is a molecular fingerprinting technique that permits relatively fast identification of bacteria at the species and subspecies (strain) level. The universal marker gene for 16S rRNA is found in all bacteria. This universal genetic element is about 1500 base pairs long and has the unique characteristic of harboring highly conserved regions as well as highly variable regions. Its base pair sequence is highly conserved within species, and often different between strains within a species. Therefore, when DNA from a specific bacterium is digested with site-specific restriction enzymes, the resulting fragments can be separated by gel electrophoresis to create a unique molecular fingerprint. Variations in both position and intensity of the gel bands are used for identification. If an imaging computer is used to compare this fingerprint pattern with a reference database of known ribosomal RNA patterns, specific identification can be rapidly achieved. This technique has found widespread application from clinical labs (to separate toxic strains from other nontoxic strains within the same species) to the food industry (for example, to detect *Salmonella* contamination). Multiple other types of molecular fingerprinting technique that combine PCR-based amplification with genomic information are available for the characterization of bacterial pathogens. These include terminal restriction fragment length polymorphism (t-RFLP) analysis, pulsed field gel electrophoresis (PFGE), and random amplification of polymorphic DNA (RAPD). *See* PATHOGEN DETECTION, FOOD-BORNE.

Biosensors and microarrays. Highly sensitive, specific, and fast environmental monitoring of pathogens is essential for public health, epidemiologic investigations, and investigations of biowarfare and bioterrorism. PCR detection is highly sensitive and specific. However, to increase the detection speed using PCR, new methods have been developed that are fast and universally applicable. One example is a hybridization-based biosensor known as the quartz-crystal microbalance (QCM) biosensor. The QCM vibrates under electric current, and a change in its mass due to the addition of any compound to its surface can be detected by a decrease in the frequency of its vibration. When nucleic acid probe is attached to the surface of a QCM biosensor and then exposed to complementary PCR product, a hybrid forms causing the resonance frequency of the QCM biosensor to decrease dramatically. If this system is combined with fast PCR techniques, the time it takes for specific environmental detection of pathogens, from sampling to identification, is close to 1 hour.

Oligonucleotide microarrays. A potentially very powerful type of pathogen detection system that is currently under development for diagnostics is the use of microarrays. Microarrays are a large assembly of short nucleic acid probes (oligonucleotides) that are linked to a solid surface. The array and internal arrangement of probes is designed to cover a range of template specificity, such that at least some of the probes within a microarray will be specific for the template encountered. Even extensive microarrays find enough room for hundreds or thousands of probes on a single microscopic glass slide, which allows the rapid evaluation of PCR products without time-consuming sequencing. Recent research efforts are focused on developing a technique that applies microarray technology without the need for PCR, which could enable the real-time detection of pathogens in instances of biowarfare. However, multiple internal controls and expensive reporter molecule signal readers are necessary, which would make this technique rather costly. Another potential future application is a universal hospital chip carrying a hybridization microarray specific for many commonly found species and strains of infectious pathogens.

For background information *see* CLINICAL MICROBIOLOGY; DEOXYRIBONUCLEIC ACID (DNA); ELECTROPHORESIS; GENE AMPLIFICATION; MOLECULAR PATHOLOGY; PATHOLOGY; RESTRICTION ENZYME in the McGraw-Hill Encyclopedia of Science & Technology.   Klaus Nüsslein

Bibliography. R. I. Amann et al., Phylogenetic identification and in situ detection of individual microbial cells without cultivation, *Microbiol. Rev.*, 59:143–169, 1995; N. A. Saunders and J. P. Clewley, DNA amplification: General concepts and methods, in N. Woodford and A. P. Johnson (eds.), *Molecular Bacteriology: Protocols and Clinical Applications*, Humana Press, Totowa, NJ, 1998; J. Small et al., Direct detection of 16S rRNA in soil extracts by using oligonucleotide microarrays, *Appl. Environ. Microbiol.*, 67:4708–4716, 2001; Y.-W. Tang and D. H. Persing, Molecular detection and identification of microorganisms, in P. R. Murray (ed.), *Manual of Clinical Microbiology*, 7th ed. American Society of Microbiology Press, Washington, DC, 1999.

Pathogen detection, food-borne

The presence of microorganisms in food is a natural and unavoidable occurrence. Cooking generally destroys most harmful bacteria, but undercooked foods, processed ready-to-eat foods, and minimally processed foods can contain harmful bacteria that are serious health threats. Meat, dairy, and poultry products are important reservoirs for many of the food-borne pathogens, including *Salmonella, Campylobacter, Listeria*, and *Escherichia coli* O157:H7. Animal by-products, such as feed supplements, may also transmit pathogens to food animals (for example, *Salmonella* and bovine spongiform encephalopathy). Seafood is another potential source of food-borne pathogens, such as *Vibrio, Listeria*, and Hepatitis A. Infectious doses of many of these pathogens are very low (~10 bacterial cells), increasing the vulnerability of the elderly, infants, and people with immunological deficiencies or organ transplants.

Researchers are continuously searching for sensitive tools that are fast, accurate, and ultrasensitive. In recent years, there has been much research activity in the area of sensor development for detecting pathogenic microorganisms.

Conventional microbiological methods. Conventional culture methods remain the most reliable and accurate techniques for food-borne pathogen detection. Conventional methods include blending of the food product with a selective enrichment medium to increase the population of the target organism; plating onto selective or differential agar plates to isolate pure cultures; and examining the cultures by phenotypic analysis or metabolic fingerprinting (monitoring of carbon or nitrogen utilization). A major drawback is that these methods are labor-intensive and take 2–3 days for results, and up to 7–10 days for confirmation. To avoid delays, many of the modern detection tools use a conventional method along with an automated or semiautomated DNA, antibody, or biochemical-based method (**Fig. 1**). These methods allow detection in 3–4 days. *See* PATHOGEN DETECTION.

Antibody methods. The basic principle of antibody-based detection (immunoassay) is the binding of antibodies to a target antigen, followed by the detection of the antigen-antibody complex. Antibodies are produced by the body in response to a specific invading pathogen. Experimentally, these molecules are produced in laboratory animals against a specific antigenic component of the pathogen or toxin. The most important characteristic of an antibody is its ability to recognize only the target antigen in the presence of other organisms and interfering food components. In addition, the successful use of antibodies to detect pathogens depends on the stable expression of target antigens in a pathogen, which are often influenced by temperature, preservatives, acids, salts, or other chemicals found in foods.

In a direct immunoassay, antibodies are immobilized onto a solid support and then test samples are added. Once specific antigen-antibody binding takes place, the complex is detected. The most common detection method is to use another antibody (sandwich format of antigen between two antibodies) conjugated to an enzyme or a fluorescent dye specific for the antigen. When enzyme activity is quantified by using a substrate that produces a colored product, the assay is called an enzyme-linked immunosorbent assay, or ELISA (**Fig. 2**). A spectrofluorometer or an epifluorescence microscope is used to measure emission of fluorescence when a fluorescent-labeled antibody is used. The sensitivities of these methods are in the range of 10^4-10^7 bacterial cells, and the assays take about 3–4 h to complete.

Another antibody-based method is the lateral flow device (Fig. 2). Bacterial cells or antigens are detected by a double-antibody sandwich format on a

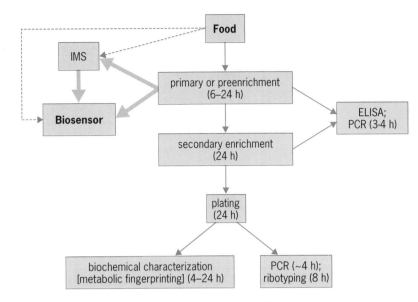

Fig. 1. Flow diagram showing the steps in food-borne pathogen detection. A heavy arrow indicates a realistic step for biosensor application, and a dotted arrow is a desirable step. IMS = immunomagnetic separation; PCR = polymerase chain reaction; ELISA = enzyme linked immunosorbent assay.

membrane. When a sample is introduced, it binds to antibody-gold conjugates. This antigen-antibody complex migrates on the absorbing membrane and binds to another antibody (antigen-specific) resulting

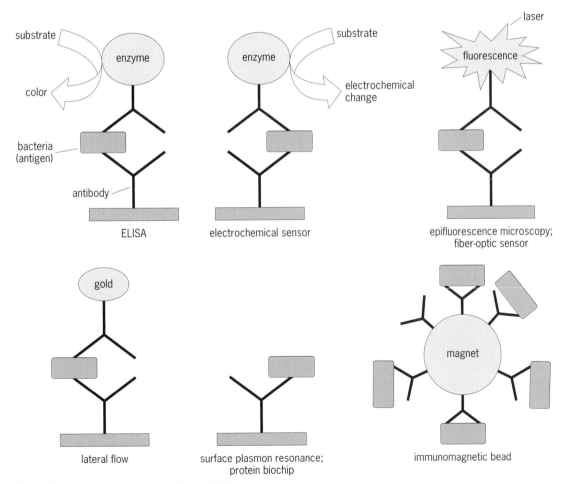

Fig. 2. Various antibody-based detection schemes.

in a visible band. This type of assay is very fast and simple, and results can be obtained in 10–15 min. The assay, however, requires a large number of cells (10^7–10^9 cells) and may lack specificity. Another key development in the antibody-based detection technology is the use of antibody-coated magnetic beads (Fig. 2), which are able to capture and concentrate bacterial cells from complex food matrices. These captured bacterial cells are then detected by various methods, including biosensors.

Biosensors. Biosensors are devices that detect biological or chemical complexes in the form of antigen-antibody, enzyme-substrate, or receptor-ligand. Most biosensors that have been developed for pathogens have been tested only with pure bacterial cultures. For such applications, the pathogens are first separated from the food and then applied to the sensor. Very few studies have actually attempted to detect bacteria directly from food. Food is extremely complex material consisting of fats, proteins, carbohydrates, chemicals, and preservatives, as well as different acidities, salt concentrations, and colors. The application of nanotechnology (interrogating nano-size particles on sensors) to detect pathogens from complex food systems is an incredible challenge. Moreover, the populations of target microorganisms are often extremely small compared with the indigenous ones. Consequently, clever strategies need to be used to detect such low numbers of pathogens directly from food (Fig. 1).

Fiber-optic biosensor. The use of optical fiber is being investigated for the real-time detection of biological agents (such as bacterial cells, toxins, or spores) in the air, soil, or environment. The fiber-optic biosensor operates by covalently linking a specific antibody to the fiber-optic cable, binding a target antigen to the antibody, and then detecting the antigen-antibody complex by means of a secondary antibody conjugated to molecules that can be stimulated to emit fluorescent light which is measured by a laser detector. Antibody-coupled fiber-optic biosensors are being developed for the detection of botulinum toxin, staphylococcal enterotoxin, *E. coli* O157:H7, *Listeria*, and *Salmonella*.

Surface plasmon resonance sensor. A surface plasmon resonance sensor is an optical sensor that is capable of characterizing the binding event of biomolecules in real time (few seconds to minutes) without the need for labeling molecules, by detecting differences in the intensity of light reflecting off a sensing surface. Antibodies or receptors for detection of food-borne pathogens or toxins are immobilized in a biolayer attached to a sensing surface. When binding takes place, it alters the angle of light reflected off the medium, resulting in a signal. If the compound cannot be accommodated within the boundaries of the biolayer, it will not provide a strong signal. Although this system has been used for detection of whole cells of *E. coli* O157:H7, *Salmonella*, and *Listeria* at variable concentrations, it showed strong signals with small toxin molecules, such as staphylococcal or botulinum.

Electrochemical immunosensors. Electrochemical immunosensors are based on conventional antibody-based enzyme immunoassays. In these applications, catalysis of substrates by an enzyme conjugated to an antibody produces products (ions, pH change, or oxygen consumption) capable of generating an electrical signal on a transducer. Potentiometric, capacitive, and amperometric transducers have been used for such applications. In amperometric detection, alkaline phosphatase conjugated to an antibody hydrolyzes nitrophenyl phosphate to produce phenol, which could be detected by voltammetry. In light-addressable potentiometric sensors (LAPS), urease attached to the antibody hydrolyzes urea, resulting in the production of carbon dioxide and ammonia, causing a change in the pH of the solution. A silicon chip coated with a pH-sensitive insulator and an electrochemical circuit detects the alternating photocurrent from a light-emitting photodiode on a silicon chip. These sensors are very sensitive and have been used to detect *Salmonella* and *E. coli* O157:H7 in 30–90 min.

Microfluidic biochips. Biochips are microelectronic or microfabricated electronic devices (such as semiconductor chips) that are used for monitoring the activities of biomolecules. Biochips have been used for monitoring eukaryotic or prokaryotic cell growth and DNA hybridization. Microbial growth on a biochip is measured by an impedance analyzer on a microscale level. The microbial metabolism of sugars or other substrates produces acids and ionic species. If the electrical property of the medium is monitored over time, the conductance and the capacitance increases while the bulk impedance decreases. A concentration level of 50–100 cells per nanoliter can be detected on a chip. In its current setup, the specificity of this type of sensor depends on the specific growth medium used. Alternatively, a specific antibody can be used to capture a target bacterium on the chip.

Cell-based sensor. One key feature of pathogenic bacteria is that they interact with eukaryotic cells as part of the infectious process (**Fig. 3**). A gross change in the eukaryotic cell structure by a pathogen can be observed microscopically. However, if a sensor can be used to measure the change occurring at a single cell, the sensitivity of the detection is greatly enhanced. In principle, the compartments of a cell are separated from the surrounding medium by a cell membrane, which consists mainly of highly structured electrically insulating phospholipids. The electrical properties of the biological membrane can be modeled as a resistor and capacitor network. These membrane properties affect the conductivity of the cell system at alternating-current frequencies. Any external factors, such as live bacteria or active cytotoxins that affect the integrity of the membrane, alter the conductivity and provide a signal. The signal (impedance of the cells) can be measured with an interdigitated microsensor electrode. This type of sensor shows great promise for detecting potential pathogenic food-borne microorganisms and toxins.

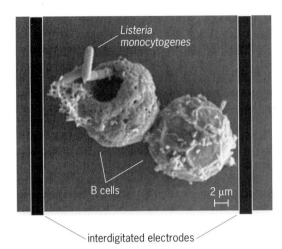

Fig. 3. Interaction of mouse B lymphocytes (B cells) with *Listeria monocytogenes*. The B cell on the left is damaged. (*Courtesy of Jennifer Wampler and Arun Bhunia*)

Piezoelectric (PZ) biosensors. These sensors detect changes in the mass on the surface of a quartz crystal. Antibodies are used for specific binding of the analytes, which increase the mass of the crystal while the resonance frequency of the oscillation decreases proportionately. *Salmonella* and *Listeria* have been detected with this system. A variation of the piezoelectric system called quartz crystal microbalance consists of a thin quartz disc with implanted electrodes.

For background information *see* BIOELECTRONICS; BIOSENSOR; CLINICAL MICROBIOLOGY; FOOD ENGINEERING; FOOD MANUFACTURING; FOOD MICROBIOLOGY; TRANSDUCER in the McGraw-Hill Encyclopedia of Science & Technology.

Arun K. Bhunia; Amanda Lathrop

Bibliography. A. Bhunia et al., Impedance spectroscopy and biochip sensor for detection of *Listeria monocytogenes*, *Proc. Soc. Photo Optical Instrum. Eng.*, 4206:32–39, 2001; *Food and Drug Administration Bacteriological Analytical Manual*, 8th ed., Revision A, AOAC International, Gaithersburg, MD, 1998; R. Gomez et al., Microfluidic biochip for impedance spectroscopy of biological species, *Biomed. Microdevices*, 3(3):201–209, 2001; D. Ivnitski et al., Biosensors for detection of pathogenic bacteria, *Biosensors Bioelectr.* 14:599–624, 1999; P. S. Mead et al., Food-related illness and death in the United States, *Emerging Infect. Dis.*, 5:607–625, 1999; B. Swaminathan and P. Feng, Rapid detection of food-borne pathogenic bacteria, *Annu. Rev. Microbiol.*, 48:401–426, 1994; T. Vo-Dinh and B. Cullum, Biosensors and biochips: Advances in biological and medical diagnostics, *Fresenius J. Analyt. Chem.*, 366:540–551, 2000.

Phanerozoic marine diversity

The Phanerozoic Eon, the period of time between the end of the Precambrian and today, encompasses a half-billion years of Earth history. During this time marine diversity has increased from very few species to the hundreds of thousands (perhaps millions) of species that live in the oceans today. Thirty years ago the path by which this increase in marine diversity occurred was strongly debated. Hypotheses ran from one contending that there had been an order-of-magnitude (tenfold) increase in diversity in the last 260 million years alone, to one arguing that the rate of diversification was nearly constant after the Cambrian Explosion 540 to 500 million years ago and that the apparent lack of diversity in rocks older than 260 million years was due to the loss of geological record through time (from erosion and the collision of tectonic plates). However, the remarkable similarity in the patterns of diversity change shown by several detailed databases developed in the 1970s led to a consensus view of the history of marine diversity. According to this consensus, first published by J. J. Sepkoski, Jr., and colleagues, diversity first increased in two phases over the interval between 543 and 452 million years ago. After these early Paleozoic radiations, diversity fluctuated for 200 million years without trending toward increase or decrease. The catastrophic end-Permian extinction that occurred 250 million years ago, which may have killed off 90% of all marine species living at that time, marked the break from the Paleozoic diversity plateau to the post-Paleozoic interval of renewed diversity increase. The consensus view is that diversity has increased during the last 250 million years and is now two to four times greater than its Paleozoic average. However, several new studies have raised questions about this view.

Studies suggesting overestimation. Although the early Paleozoic episodes of diversification have not been questioned, two important new analyses have reopened the debate about the pattern of change in marine diversity during the last 250 million years (beginning in the Mesozoic). One is a study by J. Alroy and others that evaluates the effect of sampling standardization on estimates of marine diversity. The other is a study by S. Peters and M. Foote that revisits the important issue of how variations in the completeness of the geologic record affect estimates of diversity.

Sampling standardization. The Alroy group study points out that the synoptic databases—databases that collect data from all groups of organisms on a global scale—used in past diversity studies were not developed with any standardization of sampling. The Alroy group study uses data from the new, actively growing Paleobiology Database (currently housed at the National Center for Ecologic Analysis and Synthesis in Santa Barbara, California), in which occurrences of genera are recorded from faunal lists (lists of taxa from particular collections or sets of collections from specific rock units, usually at specific localities) and abundance data are recorded when available. Because geologic preservation of species is not reliable, most large-scale studies of marine diversity through time use either genera (groups of species) or families (groups of genera) as a proxy for species. With several species in a genus the likelihood that one or another will be preserved is greater than the likelihood that any single species will be recorded. From many comparative studies it has been determined that the change over time in the number of genera or families will be less dynamic than that of species, but the general pattern of change is similar. Unlike the synoptic databases, which range through taxa from first to last occurrence (that is, they assume a taxon is present consistently between its first and last occurrence), the Paleobiology Database reports a taxon present only if it has actually been collected from rocks in a particular time interval. Also, every occurrence of a taxon is recorded, along with all the taxa that occur with it at each locality. The Paleobiology Database permits evaluation in several standardized modes so that potential biases in the record can be accounted for, including collecting intensity (number of specimens collected), geographic variability in collecting, and, for taxa with abundance data, issues related to commonness and rarity.

The Alroy group study used several standardization techniques to evaluate estimated diversity levels for the mid-Paleozoic (460 to 300 million years ago) and the late Mesozoic through early Cenozoic (164 to 24 million years ago). The geographic spread of the data was restricted primarily to North America and Europe because data from other areas are not yet sufficient. In all four standardized analyses the diversity levels in the Cretaceous and early Cenozoic were similar to those in the Paleozoic. In three of the four analyses diversity in the second interval did rise above Paleozoic levels, but not as dramatically as in previous synoptic compilations and, in one analysis, early Cenozoic diversity was no higher than in the Paleozoic.

Geologic record variations. The Peters and Foote analysis calculates the variation in amount of rock available from different time intervals (at the epoch level), using the number of rock formations of different ages in the United States as a proxy for global pattern, and compares that with the diversity estimates from a major database on global genus diversity. The correlation of rock availability and sampled diversity is strong, suggesting that apparent changes in diversity may be, at least in part, artificial. Peters and Foote emphasize that the correlation does not mean all change is simply an artifact of the variability of available record, but they note that the change seen in synoptic data may be influenced by the reliability of the record. This is clearly the case for short-term change. For example, a study by P. Kier showed that the diversity of echinoids (sea urchins, a group related to starfish) rose and fell in sawtooth fashion on an epoch scale over the last 150 million years. The high points were all times of known high sea level (with abundant marine rock deposited on flooded areas), and the low points were all times of known low sea level.

Other studies. The Alroy group study and the Peters and Foote studies suggest that the consensus view of a significant increase in marine diversity in the Mesozoic and Cenozoic may be an overestimate. Both raise the possibility that the apparent rise in diversity is primarily an artifact of variable sampling and variability in availability of rock to sample. But two other new studies suggest that the more extreme conclusions of these new evaluations may not be the last word. M. Powell and M. Kowalewski published an analysis comparing alpha diversity (the number of taxa collected in single samples) in the Paleozoic with that from the Cenozoic, and J. Jackson and K. Johnson have argued that the fossil record has been misrepresented by latitude-related changes in the sampled rocks. One study supports the consensus view, while the other suggests all prior estimates of diversity increase are far too low.

Alpha diversity. Powell and Kowalewski concluded that for samples standardized to the same size (something not done in making synoptic databases), taxon richness within collections is about 2.4 times greater in the Cenozoic than in the Paleozoic. Coincidentally, this was the same increase found in a 1977 study of within-habitat diversity, one of the studies used in formulating the consensus view of diversity change. Powell and Kowalewski found that the difference in alpha diversity was largely because Paleozoic collections are commonly dominated by a few taxa, whereas Cenozoic collections are more even in abundance distribution. Thus for Paleozoic samples it is less likely that the rarer taxa will be sampled and diversity will appear low. However, there are rare taxa in modern ecosystems, too. At any sample size, there will be taxa left uncollected in the modern as well as in ancient rocks. Increased alpha diversity thus implies that total diversity has increased, unless provinciality (regional differences in diversity) has decreased. A study comparing provinciality at different times in the late Paleozoic suggests that when using a standardized definition, provinciality has remained nearly constant. Therefore, it is unlikely that diversity differences between regions have decreased, and the increase in alpha diversity does imply that global diversity has increased.

Latitudinal changes. Jackson and Johnson point out that the preponderance of many sampling efforts have been in temperate latitudes, and miss diversity differences related to the generally higher diversity of the tropics. For example, aspects of higher tropical diversities in molluscan faunas have been documented, and it has been shown that tropical diversity is commonly three to four times that of temperate areas. Since North America and Europe were in the tropics during most of the Paleozoic but plate tectonics moved them into temperate latitudes in the early Mesozoic, it is possible that the Alroy group study, which is based predominantly on North American and European data, is affected by the change in climate zones of these continents. If comparable tropical data for the Cenozoic were compared with the tropical data for the Paleozoic, the diversity increase recorded might be considerable rather than slight.

Future direction. New methods for evaluating diversity are still being developed. Each of the standardizing methods used in the Alroy group study has properties that limit its applicability under particular circumstances. But these new methods, properly applied to adequate data, will soon give a better picture of diversity through time. For instance, some methods assume patterns of species abundance do not change over time, which means they incorrectly adjust for change in alpha diversity, and some assume there is little difference in species occurrence between regions, thus not accounting correctly for provinciality. But these methods, when properly applied to data, will eventually give a better picture of diversity through time.

For background information *see* CENOZOIC; FOSSIL; PALEOECOLOGY; PALEOZOIC in the McGraw-Hill Dictionary of Science & Technology.

Richard Bambach

Bibliography. J. Alroy et al., Effects of sampling standardization on estimates of Phanerozoic marine diversification, *Proc. Nat. Acad. Sci. USA*, 98:6261–6266, 2001; J. B. C. Jackson and K. G. Johnson, Measuring past biodiversity, *Science*, 293:2401–2404, 2001; S. E. Peters and M. Foote, Biodiversity in the Phanerozoic: A reinterpretation, *Paleobiology*, 27:583–601, 2001; M. G. Powell and M. Kowalewski, Increase in evenness and sampled alpha diversity through the Phanerozoic: Comparison of early Paleozoic and Cenozoic marine fossil assemblages, *Geology*, 30:331–334, 2002; J. J. Sepkoski et al., Phanerozoic marine diversity: A strong signal from the fossil record, *Nature*, 293:435–437, 1981.

Pharmacogenomics

The study of interactions among drugs, the genome (the complete set of genes in an organism), and the proteome (the complete set of proteins encoded by an organism's genome) is known as pharmacogenomics.

General Principles and Applications

The effective use of pharmacogenomics should enhance the safety and effectiveness of treatment selection and assist in avoiding adverse drug reactions. It is believed that pharmacogenomics will also foster the creation of drugs exquisitely designed to treat specific biochemical defects. Pharmacogenomics is redefining the drug development process. The human genome is being searched diligently for candidate genetic targets related causally to specific maladies. Traditional laboratory investigation and proteomic studies are being performed concurrently to evaluate interaction between gene products, or expression, and other cellular constituents. Validated targets lead to the synthesis or discovery of exquisitely specific therapeutics; and these new drug candidates are subjected to computer modeling and other initial trials. These coordinated studies are aimed at shortening the drug development cycle and bringing revolutionary new treatment modalities more rapidly to bear on patient care.

Polymorphisms and drug response prediction. When specific genetic variations appear consistently in a population with a frequency of 1% or more, such variations from wild type are termed polymorphisms. Clinically important polymorphisms have been identified for many drug-metabolizing enzymes (see **table**).

Thiopurine methyltransferase. Among the best-characterized genetic polymorphisms are those related to thiopurine methyltransferase, an enzyme which catalyzes the metabolism of thiopurine drugs such as azathioprine, mercaptopurine, and thioguanine. About 1 of every 300 Caucasians are homozygous for polymorphisms, resulting in profound deficiency of thiopurine methyltransferase. Because thiopurine drugs cannot be eliminated adequately from leukocytes in these individuals, severe leukopenia (abnormal leukocyte reduction) can develop, with liver toxicity, pancreatitis, or myelosuppression (suppression of bone marrow activity). There is also evidence that metabolites of such drugs may predispose children to a second malignancy. Patients identified as homozygous for a thiopurine methyltransferase deficiency-inducing polymorphism might be given 5–15% of the normal dose of thiopurine drugs.

Ten percent of Caucasians show an intermediate level of thiopurine methyltransferase function—a much higher rate of occurrence than would be predicted based on allelic frequencies alone or on the number of patients heterozygous for a deficiency-inducing thiopurine methyltransferase polymorphism. This phenomenon serves to emphasize how genomics itself (the process of defining genetic influences—often by more than one gene—on the production of cellular constituents), unless carefully correlated with proteomics (the process of characterizing biochemically and biophysically the product of a human gene), enzyme quantitation, drug levels, and traditional surrogate tests for end-organ damage, is not a panacea for avoiding adverse drug reactions. Pharmacogenomics has proven, however, to be a powerful adjunct to optimizing pharmacologic therapy and avoiding undesired drug side effects.

Cytochrome P-450. The context in which knowledge of enzymes and their respective polymorphisms is to be applied on patients' behalf is one of daunting complexity. If a patient is to receive only one drug, the clinician would like to know whether (1) the patient has any genetic polymorphisms that could significantly affect metabolism of the candidate drug; (2) there are features of the patient's pathophysiology, diet, lifestyle, or environment that might alter the expression of genes relevant to metabolism of the candidate drug; (3) there are reasonable means available to monitor the drug's use and correct for undesirable drug levels in patients identified as at risk for an adverse event. For example, at least two polymorphisms of a P-450 enzyme named CYP2C9 have been identified that result in slowed inactivation and elimination of warfarin (an anticoagulant) and signal a need to reduce starting and maintenance dosages. Among patients who have impaired liver function, the P-450 polymorphism-based potential for slowed metabolism of warfarin might be exacerbated. The common use of aspirin (which acts as

---

Selected examples of clinically important polymorphisms*

Polymorphism	Drug	Reported clinical outcome
Metabolism		
Phase 1 (oxidation) enzymes		
CYP2C9	Warfarin	Stable dose requirement, bleeding risks
CYP2C19 (PM)	Omeprazole	Gastric pH, *Helicobacter pylori* and ulcer cure rates
	Proguanil	Efficacy of malaria prophylaxis
CYP2D6 (PM)	Codeine	Inadequate pain management
	TCAs	Increased adverse effects, increased cardiotoxicity risk
	Venlafaxine	Cardiovascular adverse events
CYP2D6 (UEM)	TCAs	Efficacy (nonresponder)
Dihydropyrimidine dehydrogenase	Fluorouracil	Neurotoxicity
Phase 2 (conjugation) enzymes		
Atypical pseudocholinesterase	Succinylcholine	Succinylcholine-induced apnea
NAT2 (slow acetylator)	Isoniazid	Peripheral neuropathy
	Hydralazine	Risk of drug-induced lupus, hypotension
UGT1A1	Irinotecan	Severe neutropenia, chemotherapeutic adverse effect
GST	D-Penicillamine	Efficacy in rheumatoid arthritis
TPMT	Azathioprine, mercaptopurine	Leukopenia, death
Receptors or drug targets		
ACE	Captopril, enalapril	Hypertension and antiproteinuric effects
β_2-adrenergic receptor	Albuterol	Airway responsiveness to albuterol
5-HT2A	Clozapine	Efficacy in patients with schizophrenia
Other		
P-glycoprotein	Digoxin	Drug absorption, plasma concentration
G6PD	Many	Hemolytic anemia
APOE ε4	Tacrine	Poor response in Alzheimer's disease
5-HTT	Fluvoxamine	Efficacy in delusional depression
eNOS	Phenylephrine	Vascular tone

*ACE = angiotensin-converting enzyme
APOE = apolipoprotein E
CYP = cytochrome P-450
eNOS = endothelial nitric oxide synthetase
G6PD = glucose-6-phosphate dehydrogenase

GST = glutathione S-transferase
5-HT2A = serotonin 2A receptor
5-HTT = serotonin transporter
NAT = N-acetyltransferase
PM = poor metabolizer

TCAs = tricyclic antidepressants
TPMT = thiopurine methyltransferase
UEM = ultraextensive metabolizer
UGT1A1 = uridine 5-aliphosphate glucuronosyltransferase 1A1

SOURCE: With permission from R. M. Rusnak et al., *Mayo Clin Proc.*, 76:299–309, 2001.

---

a blood thinner) and other substances further confounds attempts to predict warfarin dosage appropriate to an individual patient. Genetics is not enough; pharmacogenomics is not enough. In the final analysis, a search for P-450 polymorphisms will help anticipate problems, but only an effective regular monitoring of warfarin activity will make such therapy manageable. It is expected that polymorphism searches will be used regularly in the near future to enhance the safety of anticoagulant therapy. The widespread application of P-450 analysis toward enhancing efficacy of antidepressant therapy can also be anticipated. Patients with some CYP2D6 polymorphisms are found to be resistant to some antidepressants but responsive to others. Pharmacogenomics will aide in optimizing selection of antidepressant medications.

Multiple drug therapy. If it is difficult to consider the combinations and permutations of issues related to prescribing one anticoagulant or one antidepressant, it can be impossible to consider all variables, including pharmacogenomic parameters, in the design of multiple drug therapy. The use of more than one drug is increasingly the norm rather than the exception, and as drug combinations are employed, drug selection and dosage are complicated in at least two ways: (1) drugs may interact directly with other drugs; and (2) drugs can interact with the patient to alter the metabolism, action, or transport of other drugs.

Bioinformatics. The advance of genomics and pharmacogenomics has depended largely on an expansive bioinformatics infrastructure. Similarly, any reasonable application of pharmacogenomics to the care of patients receiving multiple medications will require unprecedented medical informatics support. Genomics alone does not assure safety in the use of one drug. Successful use of pharmacogenomics in the care of people receiving multiple drugs will require integration of genomic information with traditional objective information (laboratory tests, imaging, electrocardiogram, weight, blood pressure) and medical history and physical examination. A bioinformatics system loaded with information by experts is likely to integrate an enormous number of variables and highlight situations in which decisions should be made with exceptional caution. The successful application of pharmacogenomics to the care of sick people will require even better-informed judgment.

Hypertension treatment. The treatment of patients with hypertension serves as a useful model for how the discipline of pharmacogenomics might be employed daily in the use of multiple drugs (see **illus.**).

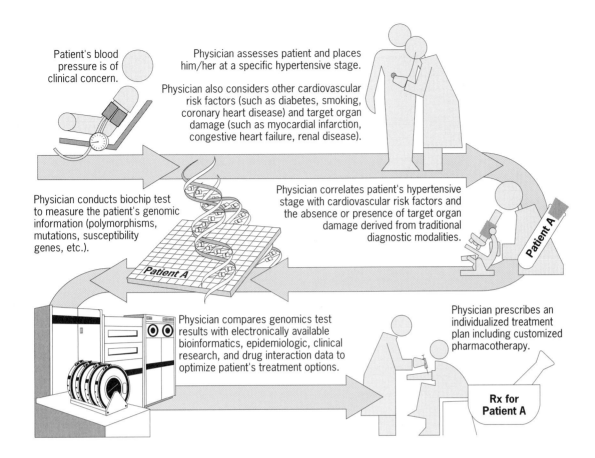

High blood pressure affects more than 50 million Americans, and sequelae (aftereffects) include congestive heart failure, stroke, kidney failure, and myocardial infarction. It is uncommon for physicians to treat based on the patient's blood pressure alone. Before a decision is made to use drugs, the patient must be evaluated for the presence of disorders that frequently accompany hypertension and that significantly affect the selection of optimal therapy, such as previous heart attack, congestive heart failure, hyperlipidemia, diabetes, history of stroke, and impaired kidney function.

The menu of drug groups that might be offered is long, and each group in the menu contains a long list of drug treatment options, including complex formulations containing more than one drug.

In the past, selection of the treatment regimen typically rested largely on the physician's familiarity with choices and past experiences with certain drug combinations. Although these factors will continue to influence any decision, future considerations will include evaluation of patient genomic information for additional hints. This genomic information will need to be intergrated with proteomic information, such as how the patient's genomic information is actually being expressed under current circumstances, as well as other basic laboratory information (such as levels of potassium and creatinine, and liver function). Such integration will require assistance from powerful medical informatics systems prepared to respond instantly to input about the patient and pro-

vide specific reminders aimed at refining therapeutic decisions. As with warfarin, careful monitoring will be needed, not only to assure safety but also to encourage compliance with prescribed treatment. Similarly, as with antidepressent therapy, careful observation of the patient with periodic objective measurements will be needed to document effectiveness of treatment.   Robert Kisabeth

Psychopharmacology Applications

So far, clinicians have not been successful in predicting which individuals with complex disorders will respond favorably to a particular intervention. Therefore, individual treatment consists to a great extent of an educated gamble of unpredictable and uncertain outcome. In this context, the emergence of pharmacogenomics has been particularly auspicious. Pharmacogenomics enables not only the prediction of drug responses and the identification of new targets for treatment but also the dissection of polygenic contributions to disease predisposition. Pharmacogenonics is of particular relevance to psychiatric disorders, which are common and complex disorders of unknown cause for which prediction of treatment response, identification of the biological basis of treatment effects, and identification of new targets for therapeutics are of crucial importance.

Pharmacogenomic approaches to psychiatric disorders offer the possibility of mapping out a network of genes that may underlie the mechanisms of psychotropic drugs, and the possibility of identifying groups of individuals who are more likely to respond to specific drugs or to suffer from side effects. Such efforts will lead to novel therapeutic targets for drug development and to the individualization of treatment, maximizing the likelihood of positive outcomes.

Pharmacogenomics is particularly relevant in psychiatry, because the clinical pharmacology of psychiatric disorders is not straightforward and cannot be dissected by simple measures such as the assessment of drug levels in the plasma. Moreover, it has been shown that the measurement of the plasma level of a psychotropic drug is not often a good index of its effectiveness. Therefore, approaches such as pharmacogenomics are needed for the prediction of treatment effectiveness.

Schizophrenia. Schizophrenia is a severe disorder with a lifetime prevalence of 1%. There are 300,000 episodes of acute schizophrenia per year in the United States, with direct and indirect costs greater than $33 billion. Pharmacogenetic approaches in schizophrenia have tried to achieve two goals: prediction of positive treatment outcome and identification of groups with particularly high risk for adverse drug reactions.

Treatment outcome prediction. The work of Schaffer and colleagues conducted in Germany addressed the pharmacogenetics of antipsychotic response using the commonly prescribed butirophenone antipsychotic haloperidol. The researchers found that the Taq 1 polymorphism of the dopamine receptor D2 (DRD2) gene was associated with antipsychotic response: heterozygous patients showed a better response to acute (28-day) haloperidol treatment. M. J. Arranz and colleagues in the United Kingdom have studied the genetics of clozapine treatment response, demonstrating that in 200 patients a combination of six polymorphisms with the strongest association response had a 77% prediction rate of positive treatment outcome. However, this work has had two nonreplications, indicating that heterogeneous groups of patients studied in different centers in various countries may have different genetic substrates for their complex phenotypes such as atypical antipsychotic response.

Adverse drug reaction prediction. The genetics of adverse drug reactions in schizophrenia has been addressed by candidate gene approaches (that is, studies testing genes that are believed to be associated with a specific process or condition). Because of the clinical importance of tardive dyskenesia, an important complication of neuroleptic (antipsychotic) treatment, efforts have been made to dissect this pharmacogenomic phenotype. Tardive dyskenesia is irreversible and occurs in 20% of patients treated with typical neuroleptics. It is disabling and stigmatizing, and represents a major shortcoming of neuroleptic treatment. Clinically, patients have involuntary movements of orofacial musculature, tics, chorea, and athetosis. A logical candidate gene for identification of patients susceptible to tardive dyskenesia is the dopamine receptor D3 (DRD3) because (1) the

DRD3 messenger ribonucleic acid and protein are localized in the striatum, an area of the brain involved in motor control; (2) DRD3 activity inhibits locomotor activity; and (3) DRD3 knockout mice are hyperactive. Moreover, data from postmortem studies of schizophrenic patients show a 50% increase in DRD3 number. DRD3 has a functional single-nucleotide polymorphism that affects affinity for dopamine. Three independent associations studies conducted in Norway, Canada, and Israel showed there is a 30% higher risk for tardive dyskenesia in subjects with this polymorphism. However, there has been one nonreplication of this work. Further areas of investigation in the genetic prediction of adverse drug reactions in schizophrenia include the genetic predisposition to weight gain in patients taking atypical neuroleptics.

Manic depressive illness (bipolar disorder). Lithium has been a major therapeutic strategy for bipolar disorder. It prevents the dramatic oscillations in mood towards mania or depression that are the highlight of this disorder. Researchers studying the genetics of the clinical response to lithium as a phenotype in large French-Canadian bipolar pedigrees completed a whole genome scan using 378 markers. They found that a locus on chromosome 15q14 appears to be implicated in the etiology of bipolar disorder, whereas a marker on chromosome 7q11.2 appears to be relevant for lithium response. These results show that the systems involved in the causation of psychiatric disorders may be different from those responsible for treatment effects.

Depression. Depression is a major health problem worldwide. It costs the United States economy over $50 billion per year in direct costs plus loss of productivity. It affects about 10% of men and 20% of women nationwide at some period in their lives. Depression is ideal for pharmacogenetics because the response to treatment requires 4–8 weeks of daily medication use. Moreover, the average drug has a 60% positive response. Common side effects, such as sexual side effects with selective serotonin reuptake inhibitors (SSRIs), are highly problematic. However, there are no clinical indicators of treatment response or side effects.

SSRI treatment outcome prediction. The serotonin transporter is of great relevance to antidepressant treatment; it is the initial site of action for selective serotonin reuptake inhibitors, such as fluoxetine and paroxetine. The gene encoding the transporter has a functional polymorphism in the upstream transcriptional regulatory region. The polymorphism is associated with the response to serotonin reuptake inhibition and has been associated with the response to SSRIs and to sleep deprivation.

Adverse drug reactions. Pharmacogenomic approaches are also being used to predict adverse drug reactions in depression. M. Kennedy and colleagues in New Zealand conducted a long-term clinical trial examining patterns and predictors of remission, response, recovery, relapse, and recurrence following an initial randomization to either fluoxetine or nortriptyline (a tricyclic antidepressant) as their first antidepressant. They chose as the outcome phenotype nortriptyline-induced postural hypotension (a consequence of treatment with tricyclic antidepressants). As a candidate gene they chose the multiple drug resistance (MDR1a) gene, which encodes an MDR1 P-glycoprotein that is expressed on the luminal surface of cerebral endothelial cells and is a key element of the blood-brain barrier, contributing to drug entry and elimination in the central nervous system.

Schinkel and colleagues found that MDR1a-knockout mice have blood-brain barrier deficiency and increased sensitivity to many drugs. Uhr and colleagues showed that there is decreased penetration of tricyclic antidepressants (but not SSRIs) into the brain in MDR1a-knockout mice. This gene has also been shown to have a functional single-nucleotide polymorphism (3435 C>T) that is correlated with expression levels and function in vivo. Moreover M. Kennedy and colleagues found a significant association between nortriptyline-induced postural hypotension and the 3435 C>T single-nucleotide polymorphism in the MDR1a gene. Specifically, they found that 3435T homozygosity is a risk factor for nortriptyline-induced hypotension.

Drug development. A key area of research in pharmacogenomics is the identification of new targets for drug development. Emerging work in the pharmacogenomics of antidepressants can illustrate this approach. The effects of antidepressants on monoamine systems is rapid. However, the antidepressant effect takes weeks to occur. Additionally, antidepressants of various classes have the same final antidepressant effects. It has been hypothesized that the therapeutic effects of antidepressants of various classes are mediated by the expression of a common set of genes after chronic treatment. Researchers have found that chronic treatment with the selective serotonin reuptake inhibitor fluoxetine or with the tricyclic antidepressant desipramine elicits patterns of gene expression in the brain that are different from those caused by chronic saline injection. Those differentially expressed genes would be logical candidates for pharmacogenomic association studies and would also represent novel targets for drug discovery. Work in progress around the world is aimed at identifying new genes that are expressed in response to psychotropic medications with the goal of obtaining new insights into the fundamental biology of psychiatric disorders.

[The work of Julio Licinio and Ma-Lai Wong has been supported by NIH grants GM61394, DK58851, HL04526, RR16996, RR017611, HG002500, MH062777, and by awards from NARSAD and the Dana Foundation. The article section is based in part on plenary lectures given to the American Society for Clinical Pharmacology and Therapeutics (2001) and the Italian Society of Biological Psychiatry (2002).]

For background information *see* AFFECTIVE DISORDERS; DOPAMINE; GENE; GENE ACTION; PHAR-MACOLOGY; POLYMORPHISM (GENETICS); PSYCHO-PHARMACOLOGY; SCHIZOPHRENIA; SEROTONIN in the McGraw-Hill Encyclopedia of Science & Technology.   Julio Licinio; Ma-Li Wong

Bibliography. V. S. Basile et al., Association of the MscI polymorphism of the dopamine D3 receptor gene with tardive dyskinesia in schizophrenia, *Neuropsychopharmacology*, 21:17–27, 1999; W. Kalow and D. R. Gunn, The relationship between dose of succinylcholine and duration of apnea in man, *J. Pharmacol. Exp. Ther.*, 120:203–214, 1957; R. L. Roberts et al., A common P-glycoprotein polymorphism is associated with nortriptyline-induced postural hypotension in patients treated for major depression, *Pharmacogenomics J.*, 2:191–196, 2002; J. M. Rusnak et al., Pharmacogenomics: A clinician's primer on emerging technologies for improved patient care, *Mayo Clin. Proc.*, 76:299–309, March 2001; F. J. Simoons, *Plants of Life, Plants of Death*, University of Wisconsin Press, Madison, October 1998; E. Smeraldi et al., Polymorphism within the promoter of the serotonin transporter gene and antidepressant efficacy of fluvoxamine, *Mol. Psychiat.*, 3:508–511, 1998; V. M. Steen et al., Dopamine D3-receptor gene variant and susceptibility to tardive dyskinesia in schizophrenic patients, *Mol. Psychiat.*, 2:139–145, 1997; G. Turecki et al., Mapping susceptibility genes for bipolar disorder: A pharmacogenetic approach based on excellent response to lithium, *Mol. Psychiat.*, 6:570–578, 2001; R. M. Weinshilboum and S. L. Sladek, Mercaptopurine pharmacogenetics: Monogenic inheritance of erythrocyte thiopurine methyltransferase activity, *Amer. J. Human Genet.*, 32:651–662, 1980.

Phosphorus cycle

Phosphorus is indispensable to life on Earth, as it is involved in the passage of genetic information, energy transfer, and the construction of plant cells. Despite this, the amount of phosphorus available for biological uptake is relatively small, so productivity in many terrestrial and aquatic ecosystems is often limited by phosphorus availability. As a result, human interference in the phosphorus cycle can have severe environmental consequences. For example, phosphorus pollution of water bodies by sewage effluents and drainage from agricultural land can contribute to the growth of toxic blue-green algae, fish deaths, and a drastic reduction in the quality of affected water bodies.

The phosphorus cycle differs markedly from other nutrient cycles (carbon, nitrogen, oxygen, and hydrogen), because phosphorus has no significant gaseous phase and, therefore, no major atmospheric component to its cycle. "Phosphorus cycle" refers to the biological, physical, and chemical processes involved in the cycling of phosphorus in the environment. The cycle comprises a geological (long-term) cycle and a biological (short-term) cycle, the latter with both terrestrial and aquatic components.

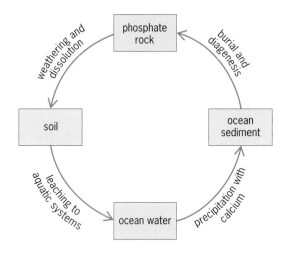

Fig. 1. Simplified geological phosphorus cycle.

Geological cycle. In the natural environment, phosphorus usually exists as fully oxidized phosphate. While the phosphorus cycle has only a negligible atmospheric component, the input of phosphorus from the atmosphere can be significant in some nutrient-poor (oligotrophic) ecosystems.

The generalized geological phosphorus cycle is shown in **Fig. 1**. It begins with the slow weathering and dissolution of phosphate minerals (mainly apatite) in the terrestrial environment. In the short term the released phosphorus is involved in the soil-plant-animal system (the terrestrial biological cycle), but in the long term it leaches slowly from the soil

and is transported by rivers to the oceans. There it can be taken up by phytoplankton and then enters the aquatic biological cycle, or it can precipitate with calcium to form insoluble calcium phosphates, which are deposited onto the ocean floor. The sediments are converted to sedimentary rock by burial and diagenesis (chemical and physical changes) over millions of years, and subsequently uplifted, whereby the process begins again.

An alternative path in the cycle results in the deposition of phosphorus as guano following movement through the marine food chain (phytoplankton–fish–birds). Notable guano deposits exist on Pacific coastal regions and islands, although these are being rapidly depleted by mining.

Biological cycle. The slow release of phosphorus from mineral sources means that the biological demand for phosphorus far exceeds the amounts available for biological uptake. As a result, the availability of soil phosphorus plays a central role in determining the ecology of terrestrial ecosystems.

The biological phosphorus cycle in the terrestrial environment is shown in **Fig. 2**. Plants take up phosphorus from the soil solution as inorganic orthophosphate, but the availability of this compound in soil is typically low. In the early stages of pedogenesis (soil formation), phosphorus is released slowly by the weathering and dissolution of apatite. However, inorganic phosphorus reacts strongly in the soil, forming precipitates with calcium, iron, and aluminium, and becoming adsorbed on the reactive surfaces of clay minerals. This means that the amount of

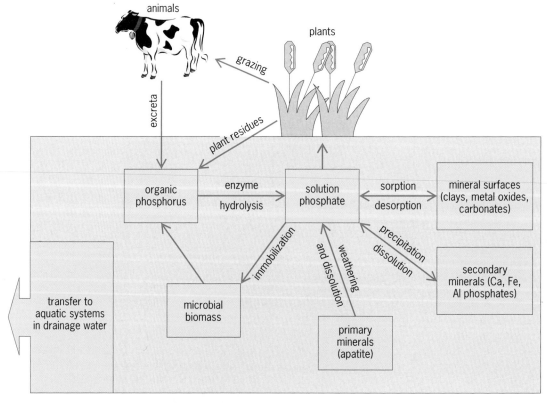

Fig. 2. Phosphorus cycle in the soil-plant-animal system.

soluble phosphorus in soil solution is typically only a minute fraction of that present in the whole soil. In a kilogram of soil, for example, no more than 0.0001 g of phosphorus will typically be dissolved in the soil solution, whereas approximately 1 g will be contained in the solid soil. This does not mean that plants cannot access phosphorus from the soil, because as they deplete inorganic orthophosphate from the soil solution, it is replenished from the solid phase, thus maintaining relatively constant, albeit low concentrations of phosphorus available to plants. The extent to which solid-phase phosphorus is available to plants can be determined by extraction using a variety of chemicals, including water, sodium bicarbonate (Olsen's reagent), and various acids.

After uptake from the soil, plants convert inorganic orthophosphate to organic forms of phosphorus (phosphorus in combination with carbon structures), such as nucleic acids and phospholipids. Therefore, phosphorus is returned to the soil in plant residues as organic phosphates. These organic compounds often represent the major soil phosphorus fraction in natural systems, so it is not surprising to find that many organisms possess complex mechanisms for accessing phosphorus from them. In particular, they are hydrolyzed by enzymes called phosphatases, released by plants and microorganisms in response to a deficiency in phosphorus. The conversion of organic phosphorus to inorganic forms (mineralization) is, therefore, a key stage in the biological phosphorus cycle.

Phosphorus availability also frequently limits biological productivity in natural fresh-water systems, as elegantly demonstrated by whole lake experiments in North America during the 1970s. In these experiments, lakes were fertilized with various nutrients required by algae. Lake sections receiving phosphorus experienced considerable increases in algal productivity compared to areas fertilized with nitrogen, because algae could access carbon and nitrogen from the atmosphere. The dominant algae also tended to be blue-green species, which are often the most objectionable from a water quality standpoint.

The situation is somewhat different in estuarine environments, which tend to be limited more by nitrogen availability, while marine systems can be either phosphorus- or nitrogen-limited. In the oceans, there can be significant differences in phosphorus concentrations with depth; biologically productive surface layers generally contain smaller phosphorus concentrations than the deeper waters.

Phosphorus in plant tissues. Prokaryotic and eukaryotic cells require a certain concentration of phosphorus for normal function. This cellular phosphorus is required for the synthesis of deoxyribonucleic acid (DNA), ribonucleic acid (RNA), proteins, carbohydrates, lipids, and energy transfer. However, a clear distinction must be made between cellular and stored phosphorus when considering the role of plants in the phosphorus cycle. Plant leaf tissues, which typically have no reproductive function, contain between 1 and 10 mg of cellular phosphorus per

gram of dry tissue. Since basic structure and function is essentially similar for all cells, concentrations of cellular phosphorus under normal circumstances typically do not vary more than an order of magnitude. Cellular phosphorus in plants varies in response to the biological availability of soil phosphorus and to the genotype of the plant. Genetic factors include variations in the plant's genetic background (genome), and allelic variation in specific genes that affect phosphorus uptake and distribution throughout the plant. Long-lived plants such as perennials are often adapted to survive on soils containing small concentrations of biologically available phosphorus, and have evolved strategies to retain phosphorus following uptake, called retentive strategies. In contrast, short-lived plants such as most annual grain and legume crops are adapted to soils with greater concentrations of available phosphorus, and have evolved (or been selected for) an acquisitive strategy. Stored phosphorus can exceed the concentration of cellular phosphorus by several times during certain stages in plant growth. Prokaryotic cells (such as bacteria) synthesize linear-chain polyphosphates, whereas eukaryotic cells (such as those in developing plant seeds) synthesize and store phosphorus as a compound called phytic acid (**Fig. 3**). Synthesis and breakdown of stored phosphorus may also maintain relatively constant cellular phosphorus concentrations, a process called phosphorus homeostasis. Whereas nonreproductive tissues may accumulate between 1 and 5 mg of phosphorus per gram of tissue, reproductive tissues, such as mature seeds, may accumulate between 5 and 20 mg.

Strategies of plant phosphorus acquisition. Terrestrial plants acquire phosphorus from the soil through their roots, which are adapted to the complexities of phosphorus availability in soils. Roots take up mineral nutrients directly but also access them via symbiotic partnerships with bacteria or fungi. In the case of phosphorus, roots can take up only soluble inorganic orthophosphate, but frequently form symbiotic relationships with mycorrhizal fungi, which grow into the roots from the soil, thus increasing the total volume of soil from which plants can obtain phosphorus. The fungus receives a labile carbon substrate in return. While a small number of plant species form bacterial symbioses important for nitrogen fixation, the majority of terrestrial plants form symbioses with mycorrhizal fungi that increase

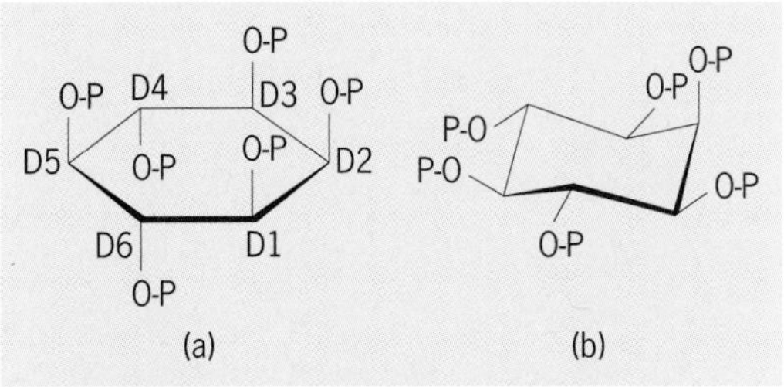

Fig. 3. Chemical structure of phytic acid (*myo*-inositol hexakisphosphate). P = PH$_2$O$_3$. (*a*) Hayworth projection. (*b*) Chair conformation.

their uptake of phosphorus, reflecting the importance of phosphorus in most terrestrial environments. Other strategies that increase phosphorus uptake from the soil include the secretion of enzymes that liberate phosphorus from organic compounds, the extrusion of protons and organic acids that acidify the soil and solubilize both inorganic and organic phosphorus, and the alteration of the kinetics of root plasma-membrane phosphorus transporters to enhance the ability of roots to take up phosphorus. However, these strategies are often employed by specialist species, such as those that invade disturbed sites, whereas mycorrhizal symbiosis is common to plant species inhabiting mature soils throughout the world.

Phosphorus storage in plants. The limited availability of phosphorus in the environment means that plants have evolved strategies to conserve phosphorus once it has been acquired from the soil. These include the ability to translocate phosphorus from older tissues to younger or reproductive tissues. Most agricultural production involves the cultivation of seed crops such as cereal grains and legumes. A significant fraction of the phosphorus taken up by these annual plants is ultimately stored in seeds, of which about 75% occurs as phytic acid. This single compound, therefore, represents a major bottleneck in the flux of phosphorus in the agro-ecological phosphorus cycle. Indeed, phytic acid in seeds

represents a sum equivalent to more than half of the total amount of phosphorus fertilizer applied annually in world agriculture. Phytic acid is only a small fraction of the total phosphorus returned to the soil in plant residues, but it reacts strongly in most soils and accumulates relative to other forms of soil organic phosphorus. As a result, phytic acid is the single most abundant soil organic phosphorus compound, and can also be important in some aquatic systems.

Human impact on global cycle. As with almost all natural element cycles, humans have interfered significantly in the global phosphorus cycle (**Fig. 4**). Phosphorus is mined from phosphate rock and guano deposits (although the latter are rapidly being depleted) and is used for a wide range of purposes, including the manufacture of detergents, fertilizers, and food additives.

In agricultural systems, phosphorus is removed from the soil in crops and animal products, so must be replaced to avoid phosphorus deficiency. Phosphorus deficiency is widespread on a global scale, notably in Australia, South Africa, and parts of South America. To maintain soil phosphorus at levels required to maintain crop yields, mineral phosphate fertilizer is applied to the land, along with other essential plant nutrients including nitrogen and potassium. Only a small proportion of the applied phosphorus fertilizer becomes available for crop uptake

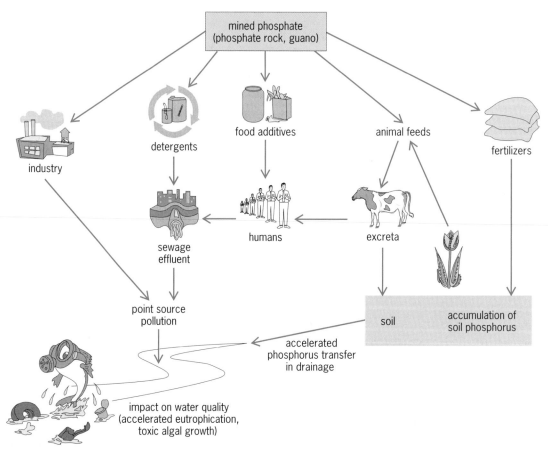

Fig. 4. **Human impact on the global phosphorus cycle.**

in any one year, so phosphorus must be continually applied to maintain yields. In the long-term, however, phosphorus accumulates in the soil to levels that exceed those required by the crop. This is likely the case where animal operations import additional phosphorus into the system via feed products.

The accumulation of phosphorus in soil has severe environmental implications, because it accelerates the rate at which phosphorus leaks into aquatic systems through drainage water. The transfer of soil phosphorus in land drainage is rarely significant relative to the large quantities of phosphorus in the soil, and was considered agronomically unimportant for many years. However, even small amounts of phosphorus can dramatically alter the trophic status of water bodies, because the availability of phosphorus frequently limits the biological productivity of such systems. Phosphorus in effluents from sewage treatment works and industrial sources (point sources) also contributes to phosphorus pollution of aquatic systems, but such sources are relatively easily isolated and abated. For example, modern sewage treatment plants in sensitive catchments now involves tertiary treatment to remove nutrients from the effluent. The result is that phosphorus transfer in drainage from agricultural land (diffuse pollution) is currently the major source of phosphorus pollution to aquatic environments.

Phosphorus pollution of aquatic systems can contribute to serious health problems for both animals and humans, and can be extremely costly in financial terms. While phosphorus is not directly toxic, phosphorus pollution can accelerate the process of eutrophication in receiving water bodies. This process is associated with such undesirable consequences as the growth of toxic blue-green algae (cyanobacteria), oxygen depletion, and fish deaths. A phosphorus-polluted water body is often foul-smelling, the water is expensive to treat for potable supply, and its quality is severely reduced. Concerns over human health include potential neurological damage from the dinoflagellate *Pfiesteria piscidia*, notably in the Chesapeake Bay area of the eastern United States. Diffuse nutrient pollution and associated eutrophication are among the greatest threats to global water quality, and many developed countries now suffer acute effects of eutrophication in major water bodies. Notable examples of eutrophication linked to diffuse phosphorus pollution have been documented in the United States (Chesapeake Bay and Lake Okeechobee), Australia (Gippsland Lakes and Murray-Darling river system), as well as many parts of Europe, such as the Netherlands, where intensive livestock operations have caused extreme accumulation of phosphorus in the soil.

Role of phytic acid. There is currently much interest in seed phytic acid (Fig. 3) from an agronomic perspective, in terms of both human and environmental health. Humans and nonruminant farmed animals (poultry, swine, and fish) do not efficiently digest and absorb phosphorus from phytic acid present in grain- and legume-based foods and feeds. Dietary phytic acid forms strong complexes with minerals such as calcium, iron, and zinc while passing through the digestive tract, and also complexes with proteins. These salts, which are largely excreted, have potentially negative outcomes in both human nutrition and animal production. In terms of human nutrition, phytic acid can contribute to iron and zinc depletion and deficiency, especially in populations that depend on cereal crops and legumes as staple foods. To put this in context, iron deficiency anemia is among the most significant public health problems throughout the world. Reducing the intake of dietary phytic acid could help alleviate iron and zinc deficiency.

In the context of livestock production, the excretion of feed phytic acid by nonruminants means that >50% of the total phosphorus in the feed is not utilized but ultimately ends up in animal manures. Since phosphorus is an important nutrient, feeds must be supplemented with a more readily available form. The phytic acid that ultimately ends up in the feces represents a significant environmental problem, because the high phosphorus concentrations can contribute to eutrophication if it escapes from the soil in runoff water. To put this aspect of the phytic acid problem in perspective, about 80% of all maize (corn) grown in the United States is used in livestock feeds, and about 50% of that is used in poultry and swine feeds. Since phytic acid constitutes about 75% of the phosphorus in maize grain, around 30% of all phosphorus in maize grain is excreted and can potentially contribute to water pollution.

Remediation of phosphorus pollution. Remediation of the effects of phosphorus pollution is a complex problem. Point sources of phosphorus, including sewage and industrial effluents, can be effectively isolated and abated, but diffuse pollution is much more difficult to control. Remedial efforts are often thwarted by processes occurring within the affected water body, because phosphorus remaining in lake sediments can sustain elevated concentrations of phosphorus in the water column for many years following reductions in phosphorus pollution from the surrounding catchment.

In recent decades, a large research effort has been devoted to understanding the process of phosphorus transfer from the soil system. However, the complexity of phosphorus movement in the landscape means that there is still no definitive understanding of the process. Problems include differences in the relative biological availability of the variety of chemical and physical forms of phosphorus, transformations that occur during transport, and difficulties involved with scaling-up information on processes active in small-scale studies to those controlling phosphorus dynamics in the watershed.

Sustainable farming systems involve minimal or no use of mineral fertilizers by emphasizing the use of organic manures and the recycling of nutrients. Such systems are attractive from an environmental standpoint because they minimize the accumulation of soil phosphorus that can contribute to the pollution of aquatic systems. However, such practices are

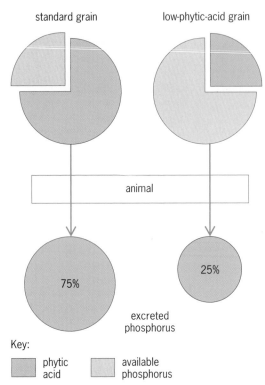

standard grain   low-phytic-acid grain

animal

75%   25%

excreted
phosphorus

Key:

phytic   available
acid   phosphorus

Fig. 5. Impact of low-phytic-acid grains on phosphorus excretion in animal manures. The areas of the circles are in proportion to the amounts of phosphorus at each stage of the process.

difficult to implement on a large scale in an economically viable way.

An approach to remediate phosphorus pollution from agricultural land in the United States is the Phosphorus Index. This simple procedure involves the determination of an index value for individual fields based on the risk of phosphorus transfer to a stream or river. The index values are based on parameters such as phosphorus concentration in the soil, landscape factors related to the likelihood of water movement to streams, and the rate of fertilizer and manure application. Remedial action, such as reducing fertilizer application, conservation tillage practices, or construction of buffer strips, can then be taken for fields most at risk of contributing to phosphorus pollution.

Animal manures have been implicated as a major source of diffuse phosphorus pollution, illustrated by the fact that several European nations, the United States, and Canadian provinces now require that livestock producers deal with phosphorus in animal manures, including regulations that require a 40% reduction in waste phosphorus. Two main approaches are used to achieve these reductions. Phytase enzymes are currently produced industrially as a feed supplement to degrade phytic acid in the gut. This can increase phosphorus uptake by the animal by up to 50% with minimal side effects. An alternative strategy uses plant genetics and breeding to develop crops that produce low concentrations of phytic acid, called low-phytate or low-phytic-acid crops. Single-gene, low-phytic-acid mutations of maize,

barley, wheat, rice, and soybean have been isolated, which contain from 50 to 90% less phytic acid in their seeds than the original varieties. Total phosphorus in the seed remains unaffected, so phosphorus that nonruminants can absorb and utilize is increased from approximately 25% to more than 75% of seed phosphorus (**Fig. 5**). Phosphorus excretion from animals fed low-phytic-acid grains is reduced by about 50%, which can be further reduced by combining the low-phytic-acid grains and legumes with phytase supplements.

For background information *see* APATITE; BIOGEO-CHEMISTRY; DIAGENESIS; ECOSYSTEM; EUTROPHICA-TION; FERTILIZER; MYCORRHIZAE; NUCLEIC ACID; PHOSPHATE METABOLISM; PHOSPHATE MINERALS; PHOSPHOLIPID; PHOSPHORUS; PLANT CELL; RHIZO-SPHERE; SEWAGE TREATMENT in the McGraw-Hill Encyclopedia of Science & Technology.

Benjamin L. Turner; Victor Raboy

Bibliography. H. Brinch-Pedersen, L. D. Sørensen, and P. B. Holm, Engineering crop plants: Getting a handle on phosphate, *Trends Plant Sci.*, 7:118–125, 2002; D. E. C. Corbridge, *Phosphorus 2000: Chemistry, Biochemistry & Technology*, Elsevier, New York, 2000; F. E. Khasawneh, E. C. Sample, and E. J. Kamprath, *The Role of Phosphorus in Agriculture*, ASA, CSSA, SSSA, Madison, WI, 1980; J. N. A. Lott et al., Phytic acid and phosphorus in crop seeds and fruits: A global estimate, *Seed Sci. Res.*, 10:11–33, 2000; J. P. Lynch and J. Deikman (eds.), Phosphorus in plant biology: Regulatory roles in cellular, organismic, and ecosystem processes, *Curr. Top. Plant Physiol.*, vol. 19, American Society of Plant Biologists, Rockville, MD, 1998; H. Tiessen (ed.), *Phosphorus in the Global Environment: Transfers, Cycles and Management (Scope 54)*, Wiley, New York, 1995; H. Tunney et al., Phosphorus loss from soil to water, *CAB Int.*, Wallingford, U.K., 1997.

Photodynamic therapy

Photodynamic therapy (PDT) is a technique for destroying targeted tissues or organisms with light and a photosensitizer in the presence of oxygen. A photosensitizer is a light-absorbing substance that initiates a photochemical or photophysical reaction in another substance but is not consumed in the reaction. In PDT, the photosensitizer is injected or topically applied to the abnormal or target tissue. Upon exposure to light, the photosensitizer reacts with oxygen to produce reactive oxygen species (cytotoxic agents) that destroy the tissue or organism. PDT using a form of porphyrin as the photosensitizer has regulatory approval in the United States, Canada, The Netherlands, France, Germany, and Japan for treating cancers of the lung, digestive tract, and urinary tract. PDT is also being evaluated for treating cancers of the head and neck region and for treating pancreatic cancer, as well as a possible therapy against Karposi's sarcoma and cancers of the brain, breast (both primary and metastatic), skin, and abdomen.

While PDT has been primarily used as a treatment for cancer, it is also being used as a treatment for psoriasis and for age-related macular degeneration. PDT is also currently used as an ex vivo procedure for viral decontamination of freshly frozen blood plasma units.

Mechanism. Light with wavelengths ranging 600–900 nanometers is potentially useful for PDT. Human tissue is transparent to red light, that is, wavelengths longer than 600 nm. At shorter wavelengths, light is rapidly absorbed by biological molecules (hemoglobin and histidine residues, for example). At wavelengths longer than 900 nm, water in the body converts light energy into heat.

When the photosensitizer absorbs a photon, it reacts with oxygen in two different ways. In the first reaction, the ground state (lowest energy state) photosensitizer, ^0S, absorbs a photon to produce the excited singlet state, ^1S, of the photosensitizer; that is, one electron of the photosensitizer is promoted to a higher-energy orbital, resulting in two unpaired electrons with opposite spin (see **illus.**). The ^1S state can transfer an electron to ground-state oxygen ($^3O_2$) to produce a superoxide radical anion (oxygen is reduced by the excited photosensitizer) and an oxidized form of the photosensitizer [reaction (1)].

$$^1S + {}^3O_2 \longrightarrow S^{\ddagger} + O^{\bar{\cdot}}\ \text{(superoxide)} \qquad (1)$$

Superoxide then acts as the cytotoxic agent. In the second reaction, the ^1S state of the photosensitizer can intersystem-cross; that is, the excited electron in the ^1S state inverts its spin to produce the triplet state, ^3S, of the photosensitizer, which then reacts with ground-state oxygen, which is also a triplet, $^3O_2$. The net result of this interaction returns the photosensitizer to its ground state while producing singlet oxygen, $^1O_2$, through spin inversion of an electron [reaction (2)]. Singlet oxygen then acts as a powerful

$$^3S + {}^3O_2 \longrightarrow {}^0S + {}^1O_2\ \text{(singlet oxygen)} \qquad (2)$$

cytotoxic agent. In order to produce $^1O_2$, the ^3S state of the photosensitizer must have sufficient energy to react with $^3O_2$, which limits PDT to photosensitizers that absorb light from 600 to 830 nm.

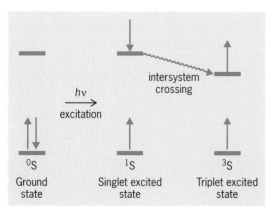

Photoexcitation and spin states for a photosensitizer used in photodynamic therapy.

Light delivery. Several different light sources can be used in PDT. Gallium-arsenide diode lasers emit light from 780 to 830 nm, the range at which penetration of light into tissue is optimal. However, not all photosensitizers absorb photons at these wavelengths. Dye lasers can be tuned to wavelengths compatible with a variety of photosensitizers, and have more power than the diode lasers. In addition, white-light sources, such as a xenon lamp, can be used with appropriate filters to deliver the appropriate wavelength of light. With any of these sources, light is delivered from the source to the treatment area using fiber-optic cables. Often a diffusion tip is used to spread light over a larger area with uniform intensity.

The light source can be of varying intensity, as well as continuous or pulsed. In addition, the wavelength of light can be optimized for the photosensitizer or for the tissue being treated. Many photosensitizers bleach (decrease in absorbance intensity) when exposed to intense light. This process can be reversible or irreversible depending upon the photosensitizer. Irreversible photobleaching can be minimized with lower light intensities, while reversible photobleaching may use pulsed irradiation to allow the photosensitizer to increase in absorbance between pulses.

The selective delivery of light to only the area of treatment localizes the effect of PDT. Ideally, the photosensitizer in vivo has its highest concentration in or around the tumor. In addition, the photosensitizer is administered at a concentration that has little intrinsic toxicity for the patient, which is a major advantage of PDT, compared with conventional chemotherapy or radiation therapy.

Photosensitizers. The ideal photosensitizer should have the following characteristics: (1) chemical purity and known composition, (2) toxicity only in the presence of light, (3) preferential uptake or retention in the target tissue, (4) rapid excretion following treatment, (5) low systemic toxicity, (6) high quantum yield for the photochemical process (high triplet yields and long triplet lifetimes to generate singlet oxygen and other reactive oxygen species), and (7) strong absorbance with a high molar absorption coefficient in the 600–830-nm range where tissue penetration of light is at a maximum while still being energetic enough to produce singlet oxygen.

The first photosensitizer to receive regulatory approval, known as porfimer sodium or hematoporphyrin derivative (HpD), has been shown to be effective against a number of malignancies. However, it is not the "ideal" photosensitizer. HpD and most other porphyrin-related sensitizers have weak absorbance in the red region of the spectrum (that is, ≥600 nm). HpD also induces long-lasting skin photosensitivity (2–3 months) due to retention of porphyrin moieties in cutaneous tissue. Because HpD is not a well-defined, single agent, it is difficult to modify chemically for investigation of structure versus activity relationships. These limitations have stimulated research efforts toward the development of sensitizers for PDT that better fit the definition of an ideal sensitizer.

Protoporphyrin IX (structure **1**) has been found to be an effective photosensitizer and can be induced to form in the body through the administration of 5-aminolevulinic acid [ALA] (**2**). As with other porphyrin deriviatives, protoporphyrin IX suffers from weak absorption of wavelengths of light greater than 600 nm. However, ALA-induced generation of protoporphyrin IX has minimal skin photosensitization (1–2 days) and has been accepted as a treatment for actinic keratosis (precancerous skin lesions). PDT with ALA-induced generation of protoporphyrin IX is not as general a treatment as PDT with HpD since not all tissues produce protoporphyrin IX.

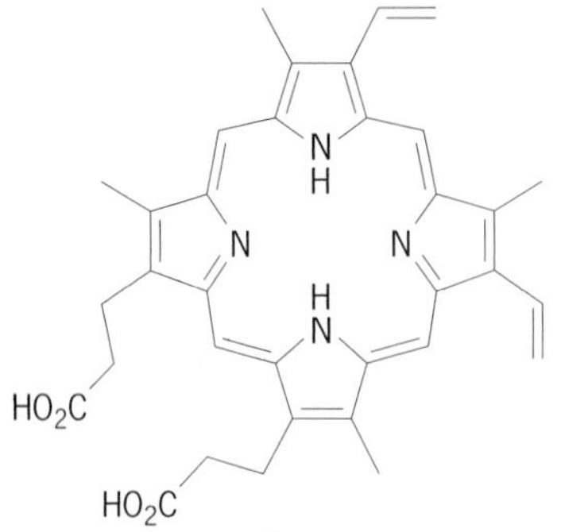

Chlorin molecules (**3**) are produced by saturating one of the carbon-carbon bonds in a pyrrole ring of a porphyrin derivative. The resulting molecules absorb red light more intensely than the corresponding porphyrin derivative, and they absorb light of longer wavelengths. However, simple chlorin analogs have a tendency to oxidize to the porphyrin ring. A chlorin-related structure [benzoporphyrin derivative (**4**)] has been approved for the treatment of age-related macular degeneration. It absorbs 690-nm light with a molar absorption coefficient of 35,000 M^{-1} cm^{-1}, shows limited skin photosensitization (3–5 days), has a narrow treatment window 0.5–2.5 h postinjection, and is rapidly cleared from tissues, which is a desirable characteristic for the treatment of age-related macular degeneration.

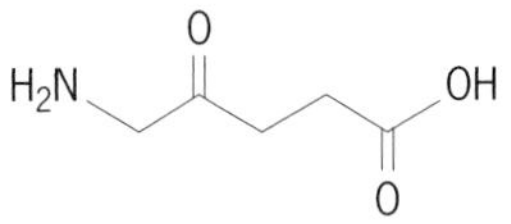

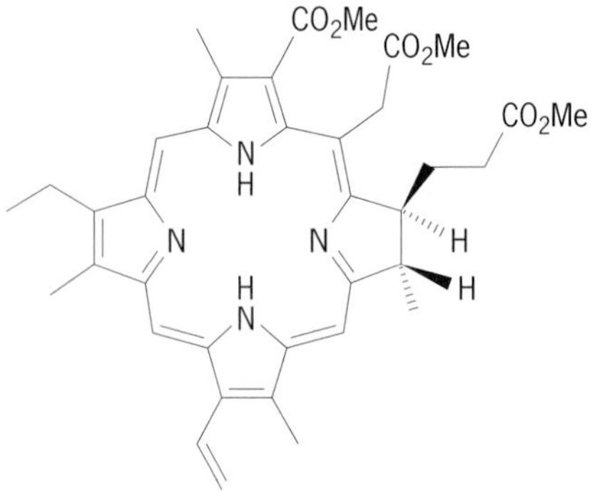

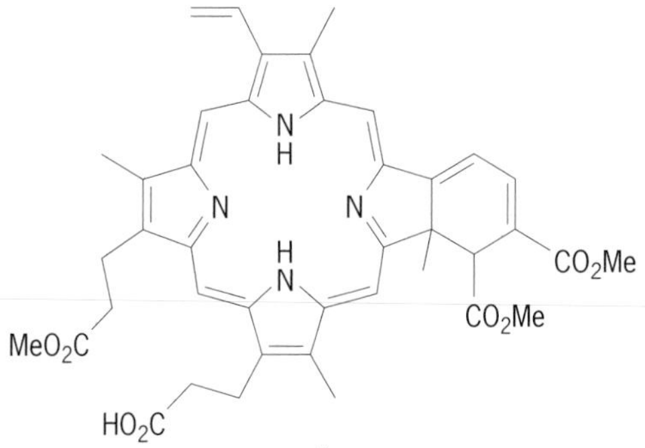

The treatment of recurrent breast cancer and related skin metastases with PDT is an active area of research. Clinical trials have recently been completed with lutetium texaphyrin (**5**) as a photosensitizer for recurrent breast cancer. Texaphyrins are related to porphyrins in structure but have five nitrogen atoms in the central core. Lutetium texaphyrin has shown minimal skin photosensitivity due to rapid clearance, but one consequence of rapid clearance is a narrow treatment window 4–6 h postinjection. A major advantage to using lutetium texaphyrin is its strong absorbance deeper in the red region of the spectrum, with a long-wavelength absorption maximum of 732 nm and a molar extinction coefficient of 42,000 M^{-1} cm^{-1}. In addition to clinical studies for recurrent breast cancer, lutetium texaphyrin and its derivatives have been found to be useful for treating ocular disorders such as age-related macular degeneration, and for the diagnosis of ocular disorders through fluorescence imaging.

Phthalocyanines (**6**) and naphthalocyanines absorb more strongly in the red region of the spectrum

(**1**)

(**2**)

(**3**)

(**4**)

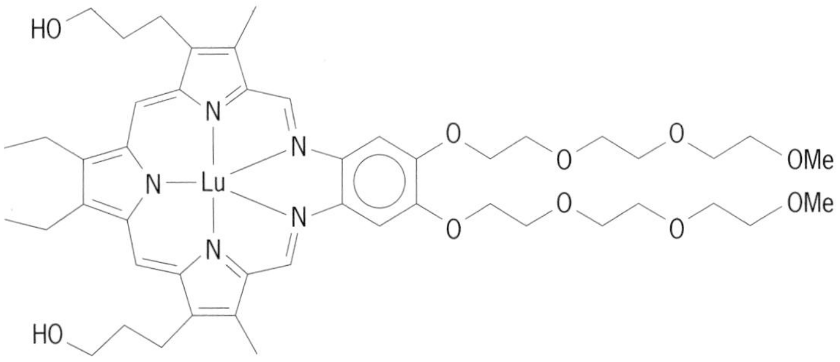

(**5**)

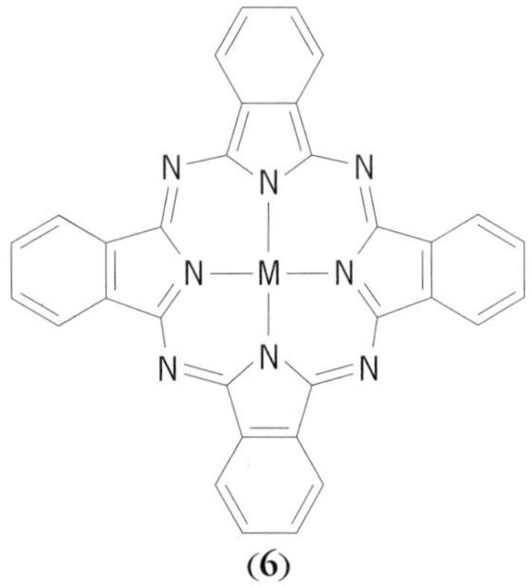

(**6**)

than either chlorin or texaphyrin derivatives. The phthalocyanine derivatives have long-wavelength absorption maxima of 670–780 nm and molar extinction coefficients $\geq 100{,}000 \; M^{-1} \; cm^{-1}$. The phthalocyanines and naphthalocyanines have shown promising results as photosensitizers in early clinical evaluation. One general difficulty with the use of phthalocyanines is finding an appropriate delivery vehicle, since these molecules have limited solubility.

Methylene blue (**7**) is a compound representative

(7)

of the cationic dyes that are useful as photosensitizers for PDT. Methylene blue has low toxicity toward humans and is currently used as an ex vivo procedure for the treatment of methemoglobinemia (excessive conversion of hemoglobin to methemoglobin, which is incapable of binding and carrying oxygen).

While the blood supply in industrialized nations is reasonably safe, blood-borne viral pathogens pose a major medical risk in developing countries for any procedure involving blood transfusions. PDT with methylene blue is effective at destroying viral agents while minimizing damage to red blood cells.

Outlook. PDT has found numerous applications in the treatment of various cancers, age-related macular degeneration, and psoriasis, and in the cleansing of the blood supply. Further advances in the technique will be derived from the design of photosensitizers that are more tissue-specific and that have optimal physical and photophysical properties. The study of the structure versus activity of photosensitizers helps target the desired tissues. Photosensitizers also are being developed that are conjugated to other biomolecules (such as small peptide sequences) that increase the selectivity of photosensitizer delivery. Other structural modifications include the incorporation of heavy atoms in the photosensitizer structure, which produce longer-wavelength photosensitizers with higher quantum yields of cytotoxic agents.

For background information *see* ABSORPTION OF ELECTROMAGNETIC RADIATION; CANCER (MEDICINE); LASER; LASER PHOTOBIOLOGY; LIGHT; ONCOLOGY; PHOTOCHEMISTRY; PHOTON; PORPHYRIN; SPIN (QUANTUM MECHANICS) in the McGraw-Hill Encyclopedia of Science & Technology.   Michael R. Detty

Bibliography. M. R. Detty, Photosensitisers for the photodynamic therapy of cancer and other diseases, *Expert Opin. Ther. Patents*, 11:1849–1860, 2001; T. J. Dougherty et al., Photodynamic therapy, *J. Nat. Cancer Inst.*, 90:889–905, 1998; B. W. Henderson and T. J. Dougherty, How does photodynamic therapy work?, *Photochem. Photobiol.*, 55:145–157, 1992; D. G. Hilmey et al., Water-soluble, core-modified porphyrins as novel, longer-wavelength-absorbing sensitizers for photodynamic therapy, II. Effects of core heteroatoms and *meso*-substituents on biological activity, *J. Med. Chem.*, 45:449–461, 2002; J. L. Sessler and R. A. Miller, Texaphyrins—New drugs with diverse clinical applications in radiation and photodynamic therapy, *Biochem. Pharmacol.*, 59:733–739, 2000; W. M. Sharman, C. M. Allen, and J. E. van Lier, Photodynamic therapeutics: Basic principles and clinical applications, *Drug Discovery Today*, 4:507–517, 1999.

Phylogeny and speciation processes

The living world comprises a dazzling variety of species. Explaining the origins of this diversity is a key goal of evolutionary biology. The process behind diversification is speciation, whereby a single species splits into two or more descendant species. But how can evolutionary biologists study a process that occurs over thousands to millions of years, when the fossil record is often too coarse to follow speciation in detail? The answer is to reconstruct phylogenetic trees, branching diagrams depicting the evolutionary relationships among living species. The growth of molecular phylogenetics, combined with new statistical methods for analyzing the resulting phylogenetic trees, is leading to new understanding of the patterns and processes of speciation.

Phylogeny reconstruction. Phylogenetic studies of speciation focus on reconstructing species-level phylogenies, namely the relationships among species in a higher taxonomic group, such as a genus (**Fig. 1**). The splits in the tree, referred to as nodes, reflect speciation events; evolutionary biologists thus know the closely related pairs of species and, ideally, the timing of those events. However, there is no record of speciation events involving species that later went extinct (and extinctions can affect the shape of the tree) because reconstruction is based on living species.

Phylogenetic reconstruction relies on extracting the historical signal of past phylogeny from the present-day morphological or molecular attributes of species. Molecular markers, particularly deoxyribonucleic acid (DNA) sequences, are becoming the characters of choice for evolutionary studies. Markers for speciation studies need to evolve fast enough to resolve relationships among closely related species. Many DNA markers used for higher-level taxa evolve too slowly for the species level; however, methods are being developed for targeting faster-evolving regions of the genome, for example sequencing DNA fragments that overlap introns (regions of DNA that do not code for proteins and therefore are free to evolve faster than protein-coding regions).

Taxonomic versus evolutionary species. For an accurate view of speciation, it is important to sample most, if not all, of the species from a chosen group. Missing species reduce the sample size of speciation events and can introduce bias (for example,

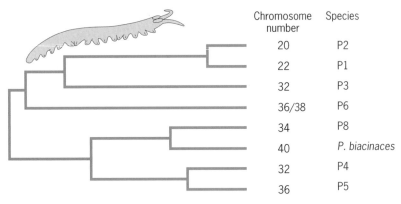

Chromosome number	Species
20	P2
22	P1
32	P3
36/38	P6
34	P8
40	P. biacinaces
32	P4
36	P5

Fig. 1. Phylogenetic tree (based on deoxyribonucleic acid data) of *Planipapillus*, a group of velvet worms from Australia, showing chromosome numbers for each species. (Only one species has been formally described, hence the use of codes.) Consistent with the widespread idea that changes in chromosome number promote speciation, recently diverged species differ in number. An alternative explanation is that chromosome changes evolve rapidly but with no link to speciation, in which case scientists would still tend to observe differences between close relatives. Ultimately, it might be impossible to rule out this explanation using traditional phylogenetic data alone. (*Based on M.V. Rockman et al., Episodic chromosomal evolution in Planipapillus (Onychophora: Peripatopsidae): A phylogenetic approach to evolutionary dynamics and speciation, Evolution, 56:58–69, 2002*)

removing speciation events involving rare species). Using a phylogenetic tree to study speciation assumes that taxonomic species reflect separate evolutionary entities; however, taxonomic opinions can vary, and a number of factors, such as hybridization, can blur species boundaries.

More detailed sampling of individuals with multiple inherited DNA markers, so-called genealogical or phylogeographical studies of speciation, can provide more precise information on species' histories. To date, time and expense have forced a compromise between sampling a large number of species at a broad scale and sampling in more detail at the individual level. However, as molecular methods become less expensive and faster, the need to compromise is decreasing. In lieu of detailed sampling, taxonomic species are perhaps best regarded as hypotheses of evolutionary species.

Estimating speciation rates. One advantage of using DNA sequences for reconstructing phylogenetic trees is that they can be used to establish a time scale for speciation events on the tree. If DNA changes occur randomly over time, molecular distances between species will be roughly proportional to the time elapsed. Although underlying DNA rates vary among organisms, several methods are available for estimating the relative ages of nodes on the tree. However, fossil or geological data are still needed to calibrate the molecular dates in millions of years.

Dated trees can be used to estimate speciation rates. In the simplest case, where speciation rates have been constant over time and there has been no extinction, the average speciation rate is simply the number of nodes on the tree (number of speciation events) divided by the sum of the branch lengths (amount of evolutionary time). This has been used to estimate net diversification rates in an endemic

group of Hawaiian plants, the silversword alliance. Using a DNA tree (a phylogenetic tree based on DNA data) calibrated with geological data, silverswords were found to have diversified at a rate comparable to the fastest rates observed among continental taxa, supporting the idea that radiations occur quickly on islands.

Modeling speciation and extinction. In addition to estimating net speciation rates, it is possible to distinguish alternative scenarios for the buildup of species within a group. Different evolutionary models lead to different predictions for the distribution of node ages on the tree. For example, if speciation rates have declined over time, there should be an excess of relatively older nodes in the tree, with few speciation events nearer the present. Conversely, if rates have increased toward the present, an excess of recent nodes is expected.

Processes other than speciation can affect the distribution of node ages. For example, background extinction (intervals of lower extinction intensity between mass extinctions) leads to a pattern similar to the pattern generated by an increase in speciation rate; that is, the lag between formation of new species and their chance of being lost by extinction leads to an excess of young nodes. Mass extinction, however, leads to an excess of nodes since the date of extinction. Statistical methods are available to test alternative models, comparing the likelihood of observed branching times and estimating relevant parameters, such as speciation and extinction rates. However, because different processes can have similar effects on tree shape, in practice scientists can only rule out some scenarios of speciation and extinction, rather than pick a single best scenario.

Testing hypotheses about speciation rates. Molecular phylogenetic methods are now being used to evaluate long-standing ideas about how speciation rates vary over time and among taxonomic groups and geographic regions. One example is a recent study of the evolutionary causes of the hypothesis that species richness is positively correlated with island area. Using a DNA tree of *Anolis* lizards found throughout the Caribbean, the study found that within-island speciation, indicated by close relationships of species on the same island, occurred only on islands above 3000 km². Moreover, comparison of the statistical likelihoods of alternative models concluded that the increase in slope of species-area relationship above this threshold was explained by the effects of area on speciation, not extinction, thus supporting the idea that speciation rates are higher on larger islands.

Another example used a DNA tree of North American tiger beetles to evaluate the idea that speciation rates increased during the Pleistocene Epoch because of the effects of ice ages on range shifts and fragmentation. The dates of speciation events on the tree were best explained by a model in which speciation rates doubled 1 million years ago, consistent with the Pleistocene hypothesis. However, the results were sensitive to the absence of species in the DNA tree, stressing the need for a nearly complete sample of species. Nonetheless, the study ruled out the alternative hypothesis that speciation rates in tiger beetles declined during the Pleistocene, a possibility raised by some researchers.

Causes of speciation. The traditional approach for identifying the causes of speciation was to look at the morphological and behavioral characteristics of recently diverged species. For example, the view that geographic isolation is the most common cause of speciation arose from observations that closely related species tend to occupy close but separate geographic regions. However, DNA trees allow more precise evaluation of these hypotheses because relationships are more accurately known and information on the timing of speciation allows scientists to focus on the most recent events. The difficulty for both methods, however, is that changes can occur since the time of speciation. The characteristics of present-day species might be the outcome of independent evolutionary histories rather than being indicative of the forces promoting speciation (Fig. 1). Nonetheless, molecular phylogenetic studies are providing new insights into speciation processes.

Sexual selection. Sexual selection has long been thought to promote speciation because of the direct effects of mate choice on reproductive isolation. The prediction is that sexual traits should differ greatly between even recently diverged species. For example, in the spectacular radiations of cichlid fish in the African Great Lakes, phylogenetic analysis based on molecular, morphological, and physiological data has confirmed that closely related species tend to differ in male and female color preferences. Ecological differences, such as specialization for different food types, are found only between more distantly related species, ruling out their role in speciation.

Cichlids have attracted interest because of their rapid speciation rates, but perhaps also because of the visual bias of taxonomists. Clear conditions in African lakes favor obvious visual signaling in cichlids, but many organisms rely on other senses, which can be undetectable by humans. For example, recent research led to the discovery of a previously unknown species flock of electric fish in African rivers. The fish use electricity instead of visual cues for sexual signaling and to navigate murky rivers at night. Based on analysis of DNA, morphological characters, and electric discharge measurements, the study discovered 38 species, only four of which were previously recognized. Closely related species of this fish differed in electrical discharge patterns, indicating a possible role for electrical signaling in speciation (**Fig. 2**). The clear water of African lakes favor visual signaling in cichlids, but perhaps the higher diversity in lakes compared to rivers results as much from our own perceptual biases as from any real difference in speciation rates.

For background information *see* ANIMAL EVOLUTION; ANIMAL SYSTEMATICS; ORGANIC EVOLUTION;

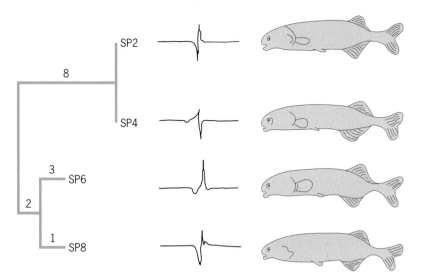

Fig. 2. DNA tree and electric discharge patterns of electric fish species from Gabon. The tree was reconstructed from 1140 base pairs of cytochome *b*, a mitochondrial gene. The number of DNA changes occurring on each branch is shown; the four species shown are closely related and similar in morphology, but they differ in electric discharge patterns. (*Adapted from J. P. Sullivan et al., Discovery and phylogenetic analysis of a riverine species flock of African electric fishes (Mormyridae: Teleostei), Evolution, 56:597–616, 2002*)

PROTEINS, EVOLUTION OF; SPECIATION in the McGraw-Hill Encyclopedia of Science & Technology.

Timothy G. Barraclough

Bibliography. J. C. Avise, *Phylogeography: The History and Formation of Species*, Harvard University Press, Cambridge, 2000; T. G. Barraclough and S. Nee, Phylogenetics and speciation, *Trends Ecol. Evol.*, 16:391–399, 2001; H. Hollocher, *The Genetics of Speciation*, Academic Press, New York, 2002; E. Mayr, *Animal Species and Evolution*, Harvard University Press, Cambridge, 1963.

Phylogeny of early land plants

Land plants, or embryophytes (the plants that produce embryos), include familiar forms such as liverworts, mosses, ferns, gymnosperms, and angiosperms, as well as several obscure groups such as hornworts, lycopods, horsetails, and whiskferns. They evolved about 480 million years ago from some green algae that resemble today's charophyte algae. Their evolution was one of the major events in the history of life on Earth. It led to major changes in the Earth's environment (for example, reduced atmospheric carbon dioxide levels, lower surface temperature, and production of soil), initiated development of the entire modern terrestrial ecosystem, and set the stage for the evolution of other land-dwelling organisms, including humans. Despite efforts (morphological, ultrastructural, chemical, and cytological) by botanists over the last several hundred years, our understanding of the sequence of evolutionary events surrounding the alga–land plant transition remained intuitive and fragmentary. However, the massive infusion of molecular biology techniques into systematics over the last 15 years has significantly enhanced botanists' knowledge of the evolutionary history (that is, phylogeny) of land plants. As a result, for the first time in history, botanists have a fairly good understanding of the origin and early evolution of land plants.

Charophytes. Charophytes represent the closest algal relatives of land plants. They are a small group of predominantly fresh-water green algae, with six orders containing over 5000 species. The orders—Mesostigmatales, Chlorokybales, Klebsormidiales, Zygnematales, Coleochaetales, and Charales—exhibit tremendous morphological diversity, ranging from unicellular, to filamentous, to complex multicellular forms. The first line of evidence that indicated an evolutionary link between these algae and land plants came from the studies of cell division by J. D. Pickett-Heaps in the 1970s. He discovered that unlike other algae, which form a phycoplast (a cytokinetic microtubular system in which microtubules are arranged in parallel to the plane of cell division during mitosis), charophytes are similar to land plants in forming a phragmoplast (the microtubules are oriented perpendicular to the plane of cell division). Numerous molecular studies, on both genomic structural features and deoxyribonucleic acid (DNA) sequences, carried out over the past decade have confirmed this relationship. Consequently, charophytes and land plants together are recognized to compose a major clade of green plants named streptophytes (see **illus.**). Most other green algae are placed in the other major clade called chlorophytes. A few taxa such as *Nephroselmis* may occupy basal positions of the entire green plant clade.

Four interrelated questions regarding the charophytes have been pursued over the last 15 years:

naturalness of the group (that is, whether the group evolved from one or several ancestors); relationships among their lineages; identity of the first species on the evolutionary branch leading to charophytes, and identity of the group most closely related to land plants. Several phylogenetic studies of morphological and molecular characters, in particular one on a multigene data set, have provided the first answers to these questions. All studies clearly indicate that charophytes gave rise to the land plants; that is, they include all but one (land plants) descendant lineages from an immediate common ancestor. Surprisingly, a unicellular green alga, *Mesostigma viride*, which was thought to represent an early branch of the entire green plant clade based on analyses of complete plastid and mitochondrial genome sequences, is identified as the most basal lineage of charophytes (and streptophytes as well). *Chlorokybus atmophyticus*, the only species of Chlorokybales and a sarcinoid alga (having several cells in a three-dimensional packet, an intermediate growth form between unicellular and multicellular forms), comes next in the phylogeny. Klebsormidiales, which now include both *Klebsormidium* and *Entransia* (the latter used to be included in Zygnematales), mark the beginning of multicellularity in streptophyte evolution, as they are the first filamentous lineage in this clade of green plants. Zygnematales, the order that accounts for more than 95% of charophyte diversity, are placed between "lower" and "higher" charophytes. Coleochaetales were identified in morphological cladistic analyses as the closest relative of land plants, but this position is now replaced by Charales based on multigene analyses. Both these lineages have rather complex structural organizations. In particular, Charales have achieved the level of organization of land plants in several aspects, for example, stems, antheridia, and oogonia.

Bryophytes. Bryophytes represent the first level of land-plant evolution. Despite their ancientness, they still possess a moderately large diversity, with three major lineages—liverworts, mosses, and hornworts—containing 8000, 10,000, and 330 species, respectively. They occur in a wide variety of habitats, from rocks, to bark, logs, leaves, and soils. Some grow in dry habitats, whereas others are found in moist places. There are also aquatic species. Early molecular studies produced all kinds of relationship patterns among the three bryophyte lineages; even the naturalness of liverworts and mosses was brought into question. With extensive taxon and gene sampling, however, the emerging consensus is that all land plants were unquestionably derived from a single ancestor, and that the three bryophyte lineages are all natural groups, and that they form the first several branches at the base of land plant phylogeny.

One central question regarding bryophyte phylogeny has been which extant lineage represents the earliest land plants. Some morphological analyses have concluded that liverworts might be

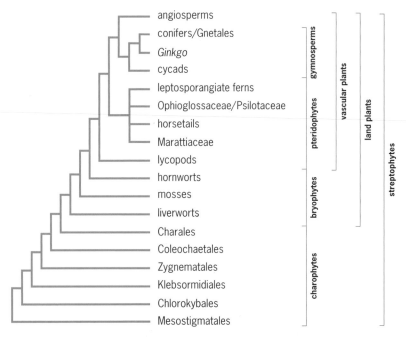

Cladogram showing the relationship of land plants and charophytes based on data synthesized from recent multigene sequence analyses.

descendants of the first branch of land plant evolution, but only a few characteristics could be identified to support such a conclusion. Furthermore, hornworts were placed in this position by some morphological and molecular studies. Recently, however, investigations of mitochondrial genome organization and auxin conjugation patterns throughout land plants have independently uncovered intron gains and auxin conjugation in mosses, hornworts, and land plants (but not in liverworts), supporting liverworts as the first branch of land plants. A large-scale multigene sequence analysis with extensive taxon and gene sampling has now also provided clear evidence for the "liverworts basal hypothesis."

In early sequence studies, *Takakia, Sphagnum,* and *Andreaea* did not group with other mosses, thus raising the issue of naturalness of the moss clade. In the multigene analysis, all these taxa are firmly placed in the moss clade, with *Takakia* being sister to all other mosses.

The isolated position of hornworts has long been recognized, and some authors have even argued that they evolved from a different algal ancestor than other land plants. Now the multigene sequence analysis clearly places them as a sister group of vascular plants. This phylogenetic position can potentially revive an argument of the early twentieth century that a suite of morphological characters (semiindependent sporophytes, embedded sex organs, vascular elements in the columella of sporangia, stomata on sporophytes, and continued intercalary growth of sporophytes) links the group with early vascular plants such as psilophytes. More developmental studies of these features in hornworts may help botanists to understand the origin of vascular plants.

Pteridophytes. The pteridophytes, together with the seed plants (gymnosperms and angiosperms), make up the vascular plants group. The pteridophytes evolved shortly after land plants originated and were instrumental in establishing the early land flora. Their abundance in the fossil record once misled paleobotanists to believe that they were the first land plants. Their modern diversity of less than 10,000 species represents a tiny fraction of their previous diversity. Four groups of pteridophytes have been recognized: lycopods, horsetails, whiskferns (Psilotaceae), and ferns, but molecular studies have now significantly altered this classification.

Lycopods have long been contenders for the position of the basalmost vascular plants along with the whiskferns, which bear some similarities to extinct early pteridophytes, the psilophytes. An investigation of plastid genome structural changes and numerous DNA sequence analyses have unambiguously established that the lycopods occupy this position within the vascular plants. Horsetails and whiskferns were both treated as representatives of early vascular plant lineages, but now multigene sequence analyses put them together with eusporangiate ferns, such as Marattiaceae and Ophioglossaceae, at the base of the fern clade. At present, whiskferns are sister to the

adders' tongues/moonworts (Ophioglossaceae); and Psilotaceae-Ophioglossaceae, Marattiaceae, horsetails, and leptosporangiate ferns form a polytomy in a clade that is sister to seed plants (see illus.). This topology provides a new perspective from which to investigate the origin of seed plants.

Gymnosperms. Gymnosperms, the dominant plant group from the late Paleozoic to mid-Mesozoic eras, are an important, perhaps transitional group between early land plants and angiosperms, the group that dominates modern vegetation. They are the smallest group of extant land plants, with only about 800 species surviving, and over 600 of them are conifers, the rest being cycads, *Ginkgo,* and Gnetales.

Reconstructing the gymnosperm phylogeny is extremely important for botanists to understand the origin of angiosperms. The last several years have seen tremendous progress on this front. It has been debated for more than a century whether angiosperms evolved from seed ferns, to which cycads may be related, or Gnetales, with which angiosperms share several features, including vessels, net-veined leaves, and double fertilization. Morphological studies in the 1980s and 1990s unanimously reached the conclusion that the angiosperms are related to Gnetales. Yet, molecular studies have failed to recover this pattern, and instead almost always place Gnetales with conifers, a relationship proposed in the early twentieth century. In the late 1990s several research groups simultaneously obtained the same clear results using extensive multigene analyses, showing that extant gymnosperms form a monophyletic group, with Gnetales placed as a sister to Pinaceae, and angiosperms as sister to the entire gymnosperm clade. Among gymnosperms, cycads branched out first, followed by *Ginkgo* and the expanded conifer clade including Gnetales (see illus.). This result just adds more uncertainty to Darwin's "abominable mystery"—the origin of angiosperms. Future studies utilizing more molecular markers will be needed to resolve this and other issues in land plant phylogeny.

For background information *see* BRYOPHYTA; CHAROPHYCEAE; LYCOPHYTA; LYCOPSIDA; PALEOBOTANY; PLANT EVOLUTION; PLANT KINGDOM in the McGraw-Hill Encyclopedia of Science & Technology.

Yin-Long Qiu

Bibliography. L. E. Graham, *Origin of Land Plants,* Wiley, New York, 1993; K. G. Karol et al., The closest living relatives of land plants, *Science,* 294:2351–2353, 2001; P. Kenrick and P. R. Crane, *The Origin and Early Diversification of Land Plants: A Cladistic Study,* Smithsonian Institution Press, Washington, DC, 1997; P. Kenrick and P. R. Crane, The origin and early evolution of plants on land, *Nature,* 389:33–39, 1997; K. M. Pryer et al., Horsetails and ferns are a monophyletic group and the closest relatives to seed plants, *Nature,* 409:618–622, 2001; Y.-L. Qiu et al., The gain of three mitochondrial introns identifies liverworts as the earliest land plants, *Nature,* 394:671–674, 1998.

Polymer thermodynamics

Polymers are versatile materials of great importance. Like other materials, the bulk properties of polymers are determined by their chemical structure, but unlike many other classes of engineering materials, the range of properties that can be obtained is extremely wide. This is a consequence of the chemical and structural diversity of polymeric molecules.

Structure. Polymers are formed by linking together monomers (small molecules) to form chains of various "architectures," of which the linear chain is one example. Polymers formed from a single monomer species are called homopolymers, while those formed by the polymerization of more that one monomer species are called copolymers. In the copolymerization of two types of monomer species into a linear polymer, there are three key molecular features that may be varied independently: (1) the sequence in which the monomer units are joined, (2) the molecular weight distribution of the polymer, and (3) the tacticity (stereoregularity) of the polymer.

Possible sequences include block copolymers such as AAABBB, alternating copolymers such as ABAB, and random copolymers, such as ABBAABA, where A and B denote the two different monomers. The manner in which polymers are synthesized invariably leads to a distribution of molecular weights which are typically characterized by an average value and a quantity called the polydispersity (the width of the distribution). The tacticity of a polymer describes the orientation of functional groups attached to the backbone of the molecule. For example, the groups may be attached to one side only (isotactic); or they may alternate (syndiotactic); or they may be orientated randomly (atactic).

Phase behavior. Polymeric molecules typically have negligible vapor pressure and exist only in solid or liquid forms. However, the distinction between these phases is less clear than it is in typical substances composed of small molecules. Some polymers form a regular crystalline solid with a well-defined melting temperature T_m. However, irregularities of molecular size and structure typically lead to solid phases that are amorphous or, at most, semi-crystalline. Thermodynamic studies on such materials reveal a gradual transition from an amorphous glassy phase to a viscoelastic liquid as the temperature is raised above the glass-transition temperature T_g (the temperature above which the polymers becomes flexible). Above either T_m or T_g, the viscosity drops very rapidly with increasing temperature.

Miscibility of blends and solutions. Polymers are frequently blended in order to obtain materials with desired properties. In addition, polymers may be synthesized or processed in solution. In all these situations, the thermodynamics of mixing are of considerable importance. The most important issue is whether or not the components are miscible, and the key to understanding this is the behavior of the

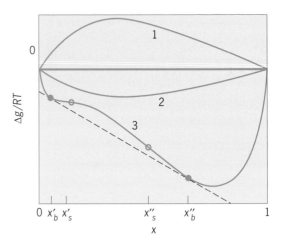

Fig. 1. Three possible forms of Δg for a binary-liquid mixture shown as a function of the mole fraction x of one component at constant temperature T and pressure p. (R = gas constant.) Solid curves show Δg for (1) a totally immiscible system, (2) a totally miscible system, and (3) a partially miscible system. On curve 3, filled circles identify the binodal points at mole fractions x_b' and x_b'', while open circles identify the spinodal points with mole fractions x_s' and x_s''. The broken line is the common tangent which connects the binodal points on curve 3.

Gibbs free energy G of the system. For a system containing fixed amounts of the components under constant temperature T and pressure p, the fundamental thermodynamic criterion governing the number of phases present at equilibrium is that G should be minimized. Thus, a mixture held at constant T and p will split into different phases only if this leads to reduction in G. It follows that the phase behavior of a two-component (binary) mixture may be determined by examining the change of the molar Gibbs free energy upon mixing, Δg, as a function of the mole fraction x of one component. The fundamental criterion requires that, for stability as a single phase, $\Delta g(x)$ must be negative and have positive curvature with respect to the mole fraction x. Three possible scenarios are illustrated in **Fig. 1**. Curve 1 represents a system (for example, polymer A + polymer B or polymer + solvent) which is totally immiscible in all proportions: $\Delta g(x) \geq 0$ for all x. Curve 2 represents a system which is totally miscible in all proportions: $\Delta g(x) \leq 0$ and $(\partial^2 \Delta g / \partial x^2)_{T,p} \geq 0$ for all x. Curve 3 represents a system which is partially miscible, such that the two conditions for phase stability are satisfied only for $x \leq x_s'$ and $x \geq x_s''$, where x_s' and x_s'' are known as the spinodal compositions. Whenever this type of behavior is encountered, a miscibility gap exists within which a single homogeneous phase is not possible. Application of the fundamental criterion (that is, minimization of G) to this case shows that the miscibility gap spans the wider region $x_b'' \leq x \leq x_b'$ between the two binodal points. These are the points joined by a common tangent bounded from above by $\Delta g(x)$. A mixture prepared with overall composition such that $x_b'' \leq x \leq x_b'$ will, at equilibrium, exist as two separate phases with compositions x_b' and x_b''.

The molar Gibbs free energy change upon mixing is related to the corresponding changes Δh in molar enthalpy and Δs in molar entropy by the equation $\Delta g = \Delta h - T\Delta s$, where T is thermodynamic temperature. The entropy change is generally positive, and it does not vary greatly with molecular size. Thus the term containing Δs favors mixing, especially as the temperature is raised. The enthalpic term may be positive or negative, and its magnitude typically increases with molecular size so that, in systems containing polymers, Δh is important in determining the phase behavior. When considering how miscibility changes with temperature, a number of interesting possibilities arise (**Fig. 2**). As with mixtures of many ordinary liquids, the miscibility gap (that is, $x_b'' - x_b'$) may narrow with increasing temperature and eventually vanish at an upper critical solution temperature (UCST) above which the components are fully miscible (Fig. 2*a*). This is typical of systems in which both Δh and Δs are positive and only weakly dependent upon T. Alternatively, the gap may narrow with decreasing temperature and vanish at a lower critical solution temperature (LCST; Fig. 2*b*). This situation is usually a consequence of specific interactions between the molecules (such as hydrogen bonding) which lead to negative values of Δh at low temperatures. In some cases, these two kinds of behavior combine, leading to a miscibility gap which first narrows with increasing temperature and then widens again without reaching a critical solution point (Fig. 2*c*). Occasionally, the binodal compositions define a closed loop within which the system is immiscible and one then has both a UCST and an LCST (Fig. 2*d*).

The phenomenon of partial miscibility is of course not unique to polymer blends and solutions. Many binary liquid mixtures exhibit a UCST if the system does not first freeze. The interesting features for polymer systems are that (1) partial miscibility is so common, and (2) both UCST and LCST behavior are frequently observed.

The actual process of dissolution in a polymer-solvent mixture is itself interesting. A lump of polymer immersed in the solvent usually first swells as the solvent is absorbed. Sometimes the mutual solubility is slight and the process stops there with a gellike polymer-rich phase, containing some solvent, coexisting with a solvent-rich phase which may contain only a vanishingly small concentration of polymer. In a miscible system, the polymer typically proceeds to dissolve after an initial period of swelling. Often the process is very slow, even with vigorous agitation.

Vapor-liquid equilibrium. Although polymers have negligible vapor pressure, situations of vapor-liquid equilibrium arise when polymers are dissolved in low-molecular-weight solvents. The question to be addressed in this case is the value of the saturated vapor pressure p_σ of the solvent above a polymer solution of specified concentration. This quantity varies smoothly from the vapor pressure of the pure solvent through to zero as the weight fraction of the

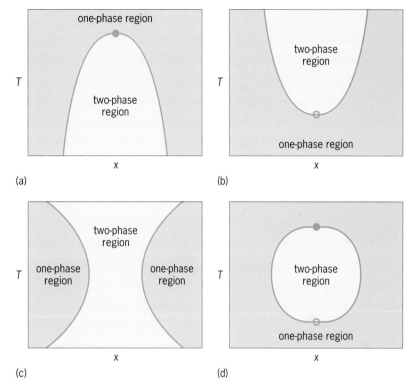

Fig. 2. Typical liquid-liquid miscibility diagrams for a binary mixture. (*a*) System with upper critical solution temperature (UCST). (*b*) System with lower critical solution temperature (LCST). (*c*) System without a critical solution point. (*d*) System with both a UCST and an LCST.

polymer is increased. However, the relation is found to deviate greatly from the ideal-solution theory of elementary thermodynamics.

Thermodynamic models. Because of the huge number of possible blends and solutions of polymers, much of modern polymer thermodynamics is concerned with modeling the liquid-liquid and vapor-liquid equilibrium and other properties of such systems. The goal is to develop models that can predict the properties of mixtures containing polymers based on a minimum set of experimental data. Thermodynamic models fall into two broad categories: excess Gibbs free energy models and equation of state theories. The former seek to relate Δg to temperature, pressure, and composition and may be used to predict phase equilibrium, whereas the latter express the system pressure in terms of temperature, density, and composition. Equation-of-state theories also lead to Δg (and hence to predictions of phase behavior). They also permit other thermodynamic properties, such as compressibility and thermal expansivity, to be predicted.

For background information *see* COPOLYMER; ENTHALPY; FREE ENERGY; GLASS TRANSITION; POLYMER; POLYMERIZATION; THERMODYNAMIC PRINCIPLES in the McGraw-Hill Encyclopedia of Science & Technology.   J. P. Martin Trusler

Bibliography. F. W. Billmeyer, Jr., *Textbook of Polymer Science*, 3d ed., Wiley, Chichester, 1984; H.-G. Elias, *An Introduction to Polymer Science*, VCH,

New York, 1997; J. I. Kroschwitz, *Concise Encyclopedia of Polymer Science and Engineering*, Wiley-Interscience, New York, 1990; F. Rodriguez, *Principles of Polymer Systems*, 4th ed., Taylor & Francis, Washington DC, 1996; S. I. Sandler, Models for thermodynamic and phase equilibria calculations, Dekker, New York, 1994.

Prospecting (metallogenic trends)

Economic deposits of minerals (ore deposits) in the Earth's crust are commonly formed by the transport of dissolved ore-forming materials in fluids (hydrothermal fluids or magmas), with ore deposition occurring at sites of fluid cooling or chemical change. Because of this dependence on fluid mobility, ore deposits are commonly located in areas of relatively high permeability, where fluid flow has been focused. Such zones may be formed by high-permeability sedimentary or volcanic horizons or layers (such as conglomerates, sandstones, or vesicular lavas) or by faulting (that is, fracturing) of otherwise impermeable rocks. Major fault zones and permeable stratigraphic horizons are large-scale crustal features that can be recognized over wide areas, and may even be extrapolated beneath areas where younger geological materials have covered their traces. This geologic evidence provides a powerful tool for mineral exploration, particularly in areas of poor exposure or in covered terrains. Because much of the world's easily accessible land area has now been explored, and easily identified (that is, exposed) ore deposits have already been discovered, modern mineral explorers seek to locate previously hidden deposits. Extrapolation of regional-scale prospective zones beneath cover is one method for selecting early exploration targets.

The relationship of many types of ore deposit to specific stratigraphic horizons or zones of structural disturbance has long been recognized, and some of the best-known gold mining districts, such as the Witwatersrand (South Africa) and Abitibi greenstone belt (Ontario and Quebec, Canada), are localized by regionally extensive sedimentary units or fault zones (**Fig. 1***a, b*). Similarly, major gold deposits in the Carlin district of Nevada lie along linear trends, and large porphyry copper deposits (associated with shallow-level magmatic intrusions) are found in curvilinear belts within volcanic arc terrains at destructive plate margins (that is, above subduction zones; Fig. 1*c, d*).

In the cases of Witwatersrand and Abitibi, the association of localized mineralization with stratigraphy and transcrustal fault zones, respectively, is clear, even if the origin of the Witwatersrand deposits is debated. [Models for formation of the Witwatersrand gold deposits include deposition of gold particles from rivers during filling of the sedimentary basin (placer model), and later introduction of gold by hydrothermal fluids flowing through the permeable sedimentary rocks (hydrothermal model).]

In the case of the Carlin deposits, the cause of the linear array is less clear, but a likely explanation lies in the focusing of heat, magma, or hydrothermal fluid flow along structures in the crystalline basement rock underlying the sedimentary host rocks. Similarly, many intrusive-related ore deposits in volcanic arcs appear to be located above deep-seated basement structures, which serve to focus or channel the ascent of subduction-related magmas rising from depth (that is, from the mantle or lower crust).

Structurally favorable zones. Whereas extrapolation of prospective stratigraphic horizons beneath cover is relatively straightforward, recognition and extrapolation of structural domains, and the controls they exert on ore formation, are more complex. Many major, deep-seated structural discontinuities in the Earth's lithosphere [the crust plus the rigid, upper part of the mantle; upper 100–200 km (62–124 m) of the Earth] are not represented by large, single-fault planes at the surface, but by wide zones [commonly tens of kilometers wide] of smaller structures that can be hard to recognize at a local scale. Such structural corridors are most easily recognized as lineaments—linear arrays of geological and geomorphological features such as igneous intrusions and volcanoes as well as faults—identified on regional-scale maps or remotely sensed images (for example, Landsat or RADARSAT). At this scale, extrapolations may be made between collinear segments of lineament zones separated by tens to hundreds of kilometers where younger cover or poor exposure limits direct observation.

The identification of a single lineament, or the structure that defines it, is insufficient in itself to constrain prospective exploration targets. Such lineaments may be many hundreds of kilometers long and tens of kilometers wide, representing "target" areas measured in thousands of square kilometers and therefore offering little exploration advantage over blind searching. These structural corridors are not uniformly permeable, however, in either space or time, and this inhomogeneity may be used to limit the search area. Specific loci along a fault, such as at bends or intersections with other structures, will provide zones of anomalously high permeability; similarly, the changing tectonic stresses experienced by the crust over geological time may result in extensional strain across a fault (which increases permeability) during specific, discrete tectonic events. Therefore, a refinement of the lineament approach to mineral exploration requires an understanding of the dynamic (state of stress) and kinematic (sense of movement) history of three-dimensional structural frameworks within the crust.

Optimal locations for fluid flow (including magmas) and ore formation are frequently found in regions of oblique compression, where strain in the crust is partitioned into contractional zones (fold and thrust belts) and oblique-slip shear zones (strike-slip faults). Contractional deformation under compressional stress is not generally conducive to

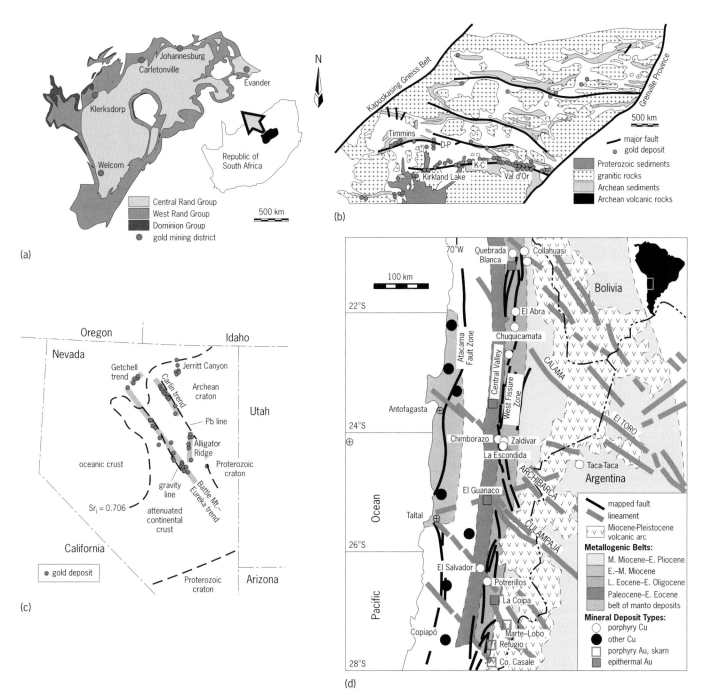

Fig. 1. Geological maps. Witwatersrand Basin, 2.7–2.5 billion years old, showing the distribution of major stratigraphic units. Gold deposits are hosted mainly by conglomeratic units within the Central Rand Group (*modified from Phillips and Law, 2000*). (*b*) Geology and distribution of gold deposits in the Abitibi greenstone belt, Canada (*modified from Ludden et al., 1986*). D-P = Destor-Porcupine fault; K-C = Kirkland Lake–Cadillac fault. (*c*) Distribution of Carlin-type gold deposits in Nevada in relation to lithospheric boundaries, as defined by Sr and Pb isotopic domains, and gravity gradients (*modified from Hofstra and Cline, 2000*). (*d*) Distribution of porphyry copper and epithermal gold deposits in relation to magmatic belts and structural lineaments in northern Chile and northwestern Argentina (*modified from Richards et al., 2001*).

large-volume fluid flow because many potential flow paths are squeezed shut; but where an element of shear strain also exists, discrete high permeability flow paths may be generated. Strike-slip faults are never perfectly linear, but feature bends and structural intersections where partitioning of strain becomes more complex. Consequently, localized zones of contraction (contractional jogs) and extension

(pull-apart zones) form at these bends or offsets along the length of the structure (**Fig. 2**). Maximum permeability in a vertical plane is achieved within extensional pull-apart zones, which may connect deep crustal or even mantle reservoirs of fluids to the surface. This relationship may be seen in the locations of some active arc volcanoes (for example, along the Great Sumatran Fault Zone), and may be inferred

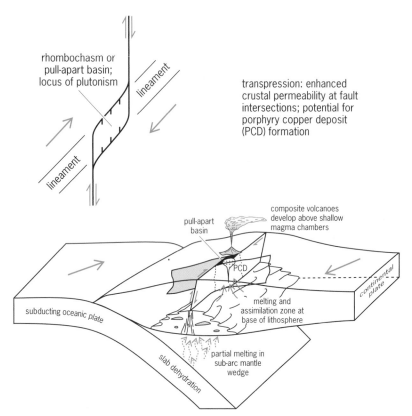

Fig. 2. Formation of extensional pull-apart zones at jogs on strike-slip faults during transpressional deformation (*modified from Richards, 2000, and Tosdal and Richards, 2001*). A sense of movement of plates and fault blocks is shown with large arrows, and fluid (magma) flow with small curved arrows.

in some fossil magmatic systems and associated ore deposits (for example, the early- to mid-Cenozoic volcanic arcs of northern Chile; Fig. 1*d*). Thus, although magma ascent and fluid flow may occur almost anywhere in the crust, enhanced fluid flow and consequent optimization of ore-forming potential will occur in these zones of maximum permeability.

Target areas. Recognition of lineament intersections or offsets in lineament trends is thus an important step in refining target selection for first-pass exploration. However, the identification of such structurally favorable zones is still insufficient to define a prospective target area—a source of magma or hydrothermal fluid must also be present in the area, and this activity must coincide with the time of local extensional deformation. In other words, permeability alone does not cause fluid flow; a source of fluids must also exist. Constraining this aspect of the model requires detailed knowledge of the tectonic history of the region in question, often involving global-scale analyses of plate motions (which provide information on plate convergence rates and geometries at destructive margins) and precise geochronological studies of associated igneous and metamorphic rock suites. Although much of this information already exists in the literature or in data compiled by geological surveys, assembling and integrating such data is a new challenge for the exploration geologist, and is

often best conducted using geographic information systems (GIS).

When integrated with structural interpretations derived from regional mapping and remotely sensed data, lineament analysis can provide a discerning tool for selecting early-stage or first-pass exploration targets. Nevertheless, it is important to recognize that such targets may constrain exploration only to within a relatively large area, perhaps several tens to a few hundred square kilometers (a typical area across which reconnaissance geochemical, geophysical, and geological exploration may readily be conducted). The precise location of a mineralized zone within this area will depend on many local factors, including the distribution of local rock types and the detailed geometry of the structural framework, which cannot accurately be predicted from the regional scale of analysis used for initial target selection. In the past, this failure of a perfect fit (at the kilometer or subkilometer scale) between lineament intersections and the locations of ore deposits has led many to reject the validity of the method. Similarly, the not uncommon discovery of ore bodies well away from any obvious lineaments or their intersections has cast doubt on the usefulness of lineament analysis for mineral exploration. However, given that the model is meant to identify loci of enhanced probability, rather specific and exclusive sites of ore formation, these apparent failures of the model are more a reflection of misguided expectations than inherent flaws in the model itself.

For background information *see* CONGLOMERATE; FAULT AND FAULT STRUCTURES; GEOGRAPHIC INFORMATION SYSTEMS; ORE AND MINERAL DEPOSITS; PLATE TECTONICS; PORPHYRY; PROSPECTING; REMOTE SENSING; SHEAR; STRAIN; STRATIGRAPHY; STRUCTURAL GEOLOGY; SUBDUCTION ZONES; VOLCANO in the McGraw-Hill Encyclopedia of Science & Technology.

J. P. Richards

Bibliography. O. Bellier and M. Sébrier, Relationship between tectonism and volcanism along the Great Sumatran Fault Zone deduced by SPOT image analysis, *Tectonophysics*, 233:215–231, 1994; A. H. Hofstra and J. S. Cline, Characteristics and models for Carlin-type gold deposits, *Rev. Econ. Geol.*, Society of Economic Geologists, 13:163–220, 2000; J. N. Ludden, C. Hubert, and C. Gariepy, The tectonic evolution of the Abitibi greenstone belt of Canada, *Geol. Mag.*, 123:153–166, 1986; G. M. Phillips and J. D. M. Law, Witwatersrand gold fields: Geology, genesis, and exploration, *Rev. Econ. Geol.*, Society of Economic Geologists, 13:439–500, 2000; J. P. Richards, Lineaments revisited, *Soc. Econ. Geol. Newsl.*, no. 42, pp. 1, 14–20, July 2000; J. P. Richards, A. J. Boyce, and M. S. Pringle, Geological evolution of the Escondida area, northern Chile: A model for spatial and temporal localization of porphyry Cu mineralization, *Econ. Geol.*, 96:271–305, 2001; R. M. Tosdal and J. P. Richards, Magmatic and structural controls on the development of porphyry Cu±Mo±Au deposits: *Rev. Econ. Geol.*, Society of Economic Geologists, 14:157–181, 2001.

Protein drug delivery

Therapeutic proteins represent a special and powerful class of drugs. Unlike low-molecular-weight drugs, proteins are very large molecules and possess a complex internal architecture that defines their unique biological functions. Creating new blood vessels in ischemic tissues of the heart, regenerating bone in large fractures, and enhancing recovery after back injury are only a few of the possibilities on the horizon with the use of protein drugs. These functions most often cannot be duplicated with small-molecule drugs such as aspirin or antacids. Over the last 10 to 20 years, advances in recombinant deoxyribonucleic acid (DNA) technology have resulted in an explosive increase in the number of protein molecules being developed for therapeutic use.

Despite their unique biological properties, there are two key features of proteins that make their delivery to the body problematic. First, proteins have difficulty crossing biological barriers such as the intestinal mucosa with minimal metabolism, which severely limits protein entry into the bloodstream; smaller molecules have this ability, making possible their noninvasive delivery (for example, the routine swallowing of an ibuprofen tablet at the first sign of a headache). Second, proteins have a short half-life in the bloodstream and thus must be injected frequently, often by the patient, which can cause significant discomfort, psychological distress, and poor compliance (see **table**). However innovative changes to the protein molecule have been made, such as the attachment of polyethylene glycol chains, which can increase protein half-life in blood. In addition, several minimally invasive protein delivery systems are under development, which may play a pivotal role in the success and scope of therapy possible with the current drugs completing clinical trials. Current delivery system options include (1) advanced inhalation aerosols, (2) implantable pumps, (3) micromachined microneedles, (4) supersonic powder injectors, and (5) membrane (skin and intestinal mucosa) penetration-enhancing strategies. However, one of the most advanced systems is injectable controlled-release depots.

Injectable controlled-delivery. Injectable controlled-release depots involve the injection of protein encapsulated in a polymer, which slowly releases the protein for weeks or more when placed in the body.

Polymer configuration. In order for the polymer to be easily implanted in the body, it must be processed into a configuration small enough to be injected through a syringe needle. The most common injectable configuration consists of millions of microspheres, spherical polymers between 1 and 100 micrometers in size. (Less common polymer configurations studied include larger cylindrical implants of similar size to a mechanical pencil lead, and in situ–forming polymers that are injected in a liquid form and rapidly gel or harden to form the polymer matrix once in contact with body fluids.) Each microsphere is a tiny polymer matrix, which has even smaller protein-containing particles dispersed throughout the entire polymer. Since the protein is released very slowly at a dosing rate that maintains therapeutic protein concentrations in the body, injections can be performed much less frequently (for example, once a month), making the therapy far less cumbersome. Additionally, for indications that require site-specific or regional therapy (for example, bone regeneration), polymers may be implanted directly at the site where the drug is required.

Nondegradable polymers. The first type of polymers to be studied for protein delivery, such as polydimethylsiloxane (silicone rubber) and poly(ethylene-co-vinyl acetate) [EVA], were nondegradable in the body, generally requiring surgical removal after drug release. Nondegradable polymers commonly release protein by diffusion out of the polymer matrix via a network of pores formed by gradual dissolution of the encapsulated protein particles. Today, polymers used for controlling the release of proteins are often biodegradable; they slowly lose their mass for weeks or months after implantation so that surgical removal is not required.

Biodegradable polymers and bioerosion. The most commonly used polymers for controlled release of proteins are the copolymers of lactic and glycolic acids (PLGAs), which is the same polymer type used in the manufacture of resorbable sutures. The polymer is water-insoluble and therefore does not dissolve initially in the body. Instead, the polymer matrix absorbs water from the physiological surroundings, initiating nonenzymatic hydrolysis of the polymer. In

---

Injecton frequency of several marketed protein drugs

Protein drug	Administration route[*]	Half-life in bloodstream	Dosing frequency
Coagulation factor IX	i.v.	19.5 h	1–2 times/day
Erythropoietin	s.c. or i.v.	4–13 h	3 times/week
Granulocyte colony stimulating factor (G-CSF)	s.c. or i.v.	3.5 h	Once a day
Growth hormone (hGH)	s.c.	20 min	Once a day
Interferon-β	s.c.	8 min–4.3 h	3-4 times/week
Interferon-γ	s.c.	2.9–5.9 h	3 times/week
Interleukin-11	s.c.	7 h	Once a day

[*]i.v. = intravenous; s.c. = subcutaneous.
SOURCE: *Physician's Desk Reference*, 2002.

a process known as bioerosion, the polymer's ester bonds are slowly degraded, or cleaved, by the hydrolysis to form low-molecular-weight, nontoxic water-soluble products that dissolve and are released into the body. Unlike controlled release from nondegradable polymers, because the polymer itself is eventually broken down during bioerosion, the release of proteins from a PLGA does not require formation of a pore network by the protein or other nonpolymer components of the polymer-protein system.

Encapsulation. Before a protein can be delivered by a polymer, it must be encapsulated. Early encapsulation techniques to prepare microspheres were those that had been successful for smaller peptides, often less than 10 amino acids. In-liquid drying, coacervation, and spray drying were the techniques most commonly used. Prior to or during each of these techniques, the bulk protein-containing phase is micronized to a size much less than that of the final microspheres. The polymer is dissolved in an organic solvent such as methylene chloride, and tiny droplets of the solution are formed by (1) atomizing into a carrier gas (spray drying and spray congealing), (2) emulsifying into an immiscible solvent (in-liquid drying), or (3) phase separation on addition of a phase inducer (coacervation). The tiny droplets become microspheres upon removal of the organic solvent. During such processing, a large interfacial area (for example, liquid/liquid, solid/liquid, liquid/gas) is created because of the high number of tiny particles of polymer and protein.

Stabilizing encapsulated proteins. After scientists began encapsulating proteins in polymers such as the PLGAs, they observed that the protein would become damaged between the time of encapsulation and its subsequent release from the polymer matrix. Today this difficulty is regarded as the single biggest obstacle to development of polymer dosage forms to deliver proteins. For example, an exceptionally common and frustrating observation when studying PLGAs is that due to insoluble protein aggregation within pores of the polymer matrix, an appreciable fraction of encapsulated protein becomes unreleasable from the polymer by the end of the release interval.

Studies of encapsulating model proteins and a vast knowledge of proteins, particularly enzymes, drawn from several neighboring scientific disciplines, have provided drug delivery researchers with valuable insight into the cause of the protein instability mechanism. During encapsulation, damage to proteins can be caused by the following deleterious stresses: (1) the presence of water, which makes the protein flexible and reactive; (2) dispersal of the protein in form of a microparticulate or an emulsion, which exposes the protein to a large hydrophobic interfacial area, enabling the protein to unfold and aggregate; (3) the presence of denaturants in the protein phase; and (4) drying, which also induces unfolding. During release, damage frequently occurs when the protein is between the solid and dissolved states at physiological temperature, which often triggers moisture-induced aggregation; and there is a common lowering of pH in aqueous pores containing the protein, which can induce several deleterious reactions such as unfolding/aggregation and hydrolysis.

The type of protein damage, or instability mechanism, resulting from the aforementioned stresses is strongly dependent on the specific protein in question. For example, some proteins are particularly susceptible to aggregation, whereas others may be easily hydrolyzed and deamidated (conversion of an amino acid residue with an amide side chain, such as asparagine, to the corresponding carboxylic acid–containing residue, such as aspartic acid, with simultaneous liberation of ammonia). Several techniques have been developed to overcome protein damage during processing, storage, and release from the polymer. The most successful approaches are those elucidating the specific instability pathway, consisting of encapsulation as well as release stresses and mechanisms. With this knowledge, specific techniques can be readily devised to inhibit the mechanism directly or to remove the damaging stress.

Preventing protein unfolding. The first successful PLGA delivery system to display both desirable release kinetics and excellent protein stability for one month in primates was a microsphere formulation for human growth hormone. This formulation incorporates several important principles useful in protein stabilization. First, the protein solution is micronized by rapid spray freeze–drying into cold liquid nitrogen to minimize unfolding at the large aqueous/gas interface. Second, the micronized protein particles are encapsulated in the polymer at very low temperature in the absence of water, which minimizes conformational flexibility and the possibility that the protein will unfold when in contact with the organic solvent used to dissolve the PLGA. Third, the protein is combined with zinc to form a water-insoluble complex (mimicking the natural storage of the hormone in the pituitary gland) before encapsulation. This complex appears to immobilize the protein, protecting it from unfolding due to micronization before encapsulation, local pH changes, and small amounts of water in the polymer during release of the growth hormone.

Inhibiting drops in pH. Promising strategies to inhibit the lowering of pH in the polymer pores include coencapsulation of a poorly soluble base (for example, an antacid); reduction of the degradation rate of PLGA (which produces a molecule of acid for each ester bond hydrolyzed) by increasing the lactic acid–to–glycolic acid ratio of the polymer; and blending polyethylene glycol with the PLGA to increase the release rate of water-soluble, acidic degradation products. Using such techniques, several proteins have been stabilized in PLGAs for periods exceeding the one-month benchmark.

For background information *see* BIOMEDICAL CHEMICAL ENGINEERING; DRUG DELIVERY SYSTEMS; PHARMACOLOGY; PROTEIN; VACCINATION in the McGraw-Hill Encyclopedia of Science & Technology.

Steven P. Schwendeman

Bibliography. J. L. Cleland et al., *Pharm. Res.*, 14: 420–425, 1997; J. L. Cleland and R. Langer (eds.), *Formulation and Delivery of Proteins and Peptides*, ACS Symp. Ser., vol. 567, 1994; S. Cohen and H. Bernstein (eds.), *Microparticulate Systems for the Delivery of Proteins and Vaccines*, Dekker, New York, 1996; T. E. Creighton (ed.), *Protein Function: A Practical Approach*, Oxford University Press, Oxford, 1989; M. Donbrow (ed.), *Microcapsules and Nanoparticles in Medicine and Pharmacy*, CRC Press, Boca Raton, 1991; K. Fu, A. M. Klibanov, and R. Langer, Protein stability in controlled-release systems, *Nat. Biotech.*, 18:24–25, 2000; O. L. Johnson et al., A month-long effect from a single injection of microencapsulated human growth hormone, *Nat. Med.*, 2:795–799, 1996; H. Okada and H. Toguchi, Biodegradable microspheres in drug delivery, *Crit. Rev. Ther. Drug Carr. Sys.*, 12:1–99, 1995; S. D. Putney and P. A. Burke, Improving protein therapeutics with sustained-release formulations, *Nat. Biotech.*, 16:153–157, 1998; S. P. Schwendeman, Recent advances in the stabilization of proteins encapsulated in injectable PLGA delivery systems, *Crit. Rev. Ther. Drug Carr. Sys.*, 19:73–98, 2002; G. Zhu, S. R. Mallery, and S. P. Schwendeman, Stabilization of proteins encapsulated in injectable poly(lactide-co-glycolide), *Nat. Biotechnol.*, 18:52–57, 2000.

Radio-frequency lighting

Electrically powered light sources can be divided into three broad classes: (1) solid materials heated to high temperature such as incandescent lamps, (2) direct-conversion solid-state devices such as light-emitting diodes, and (3) gas-discharge systems such as fluorescent and metal halide lamps. Gas-discharge lamps operated at radio frequencies are efficient sources with interesting properties, whereas there is no advantage in operating incandescent or solid-state light sources at radio frequencies. Radio frequencies range from about 10 kHz to 30 GHz.

Gas-discharge lighting. The most common gas-discharge light source is the linear fluorescent lamp. This is a cylindrical glass tube with an electrode mounted inside each end. Voltage applied between the electrodes creates an electric field that accelerates free electrons in the gas. These electrons absorb energy from the electric field and transfer that energy to gas atoms via collisions. A fraction of these collisions result in excitation of the gas atoms. The excited atoms release the absorbed energy as photons. In fluorescent lamps, the majority of these photons are in the ultraviolet region of the spectrum. A phosphor coating on the interior wall of the lamp converts the ultraviolet photons into visible-light photons. Other discharge lamps, such as metal halide or sulfur lamps, are designed so that most of the photons emitted by the gas are in the visible region of the spectrum.

The best fluorescent and metal halide lamps produce almost 100 lumens of visible light per watt of power drawn from the power line. This quantity, 100 lm/W, is known as the lamp system efficacy. In contrast, the efficacy of common 60–100-W incandescent lamps ranges 14.8–16.9 lm/W. The use of halogen gas and infrared coatings can increase the efficacy of incandescent lamps to about 30 lm/W, but this potential efficacy gain is usually traded off for longer lamp life in commercial products. The high efficacy and long life of fluorescent and other discharge lamps makes them attractive replacements for incandescent lamps.

Fluorescent lamps have been in use for over 60 years. However, electrodes have limited the design and operation of such lamps because (1) electrodes wear out (limiting the life of the lamp), and (2) a transition region exists between the discharge and the electrodes that uses power but does not produce any light. To make an efficient lamp, the voltage drop in the positive column (the part of the discharge that produces light) must be made high compared to the voltage drop in the electrode transition region. This requires that discharge lamps using electrodes have the familiar long, thin shape. (3) In addition, using electrodes inside the lamp limits the gases to those that will not react with metals. All three of these limitations are removed when lamps are operated at radio frequencies.

Radio-frequency operation. All discharge lamps are driven by electric fields. Radio-frequency operation provides three methods for generating this field without immersing the electrodes in the discharge. In the first method, electrodes placed outside the nonconductive discharge tube create electric fields inside the discharge tube through capacitive coupling (**Fig. 1**). In the second method, a time-varying magnetic field is used to create an electric field in the discharge (**Fig. 2**). The root-mean-square voltage V_{RMS} developed in such inductively coupled

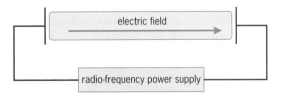

Fig. 1. Capacitively coupled RF lamp.

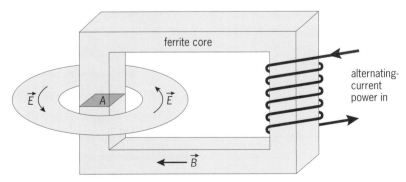

Fig. 2. Inductively coupled, closed-core, radio-frequency, electrodeless discharge lamp, where $\vec{E}$ = electric field, $\vec{B}$ = magnetic flux density, and A = area.

discharges is given by Faraday's law,

$$V_{RMS} = \sqrt{2} * f * B_p * A$$

where f is the frequency in hertz, B_p is the peak magnetic field in tesla, and A is the area of the region containing the magnetic field in square meters. The third method uses a radio-frequency resonant cavity, that is, a box, cylinder, or sphere with conducting walls that supports coupled electric and magnetic fields in resonant modes in which the electric field is zero on the conducting walls. The electric field present in the cavity will pass through the nonconductive lamp envelope and drive the discharge.

Radio-frequency lamps. Of the three types of radio-frequency lamps, only inductively coupled lamps are able to use fill materials that interact with metal electrodes, eliminate electrodes as a life-limiting mecha-

nism, and change the long, thin discharge tube shape. In fact, the physics of inductively coupled lamps strongly favors short, "fat" discharge tubes. This feature of inductively coupled lamps led to their commercialization. Even before the energy crises of the mid-1970s, scientists and engineers were working on high-efficacy replacements for the incandescent lamp. The natural choice was the fluorescent lamp, but its long, thin shape dictated by electrodes made conventional fluorescent lamps unsuitable replacements for the incandescent lamp. While some engineers worked on ways to fold a long discharge into a small space, others recognized that if the requirement for long, thin shapes was driven by use of electrodes, then the solution was to remove the electrodes and use inductive coupling to create the electric field.

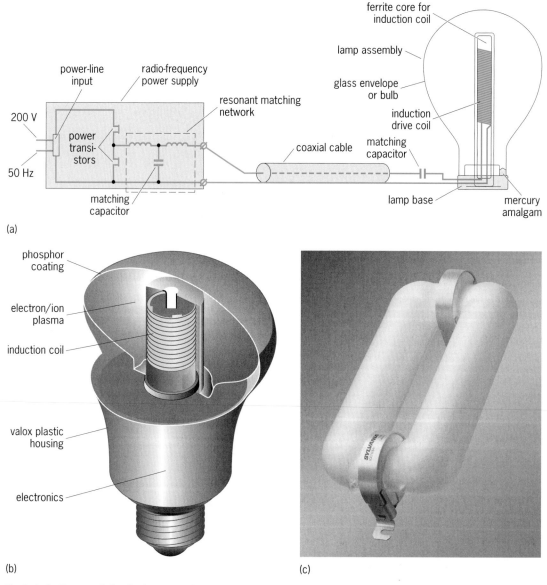

Fig. 3. Induction-coupled radio-frequency electrodeless fluorescent lamps. (a) Philips QL ferrite-rod lamp. Coaxial cable carries radio-frequency power to the lamp. Inner surface of the glass envelope is coated with a phosphor that converts ultraviolet photons to visible light. The mercury amalgam is used to control mercury pressure (*U.S. Patent 6,373,198*). (b) General Electric ferrite-rod lamp (*General Electric Company*). (c) Osram Sylvania Icetron® closed-core lamp (*Osram Sylvania, Inc.; Photographic Illustrators Corp.*).

Induction-coupled radio-frequency fluorescent lamp products

Type	Model	System watts	Initial lumens	System efficacy, lm/W*	Rated life, hours	Dimensions, mm†			
						Diameter	Length	Width	Height
Philips QL‡	QL 55W	55	3,500	63.6	100,000	85	—	—	140
	QL 85W	85	6,000	70.6	100,000	111	—	—	180
	QL 165	165	12,000	72.8	100,000	130	—	—	210
GE Genura®§	EL23/R25	23	1,100	47.8	15,000	81	—	—	126
Osram Sylvania	70/QT100	82	6,500	79.3	100,000	—	313	139	72
Icetron®¶	100/QT100	107	8,000	74.8	100,000	—	313	139	72
	100/QT150	157	11,000	70.1	100,000	—	313	139	72
	150/QT150	157	12,000	76.4	100,000	—	414	139	72

*Efficacy calculated as initial lumens divided by system watts.
†1 mm = 0.04 in.
‡Dimensions do not include external ballast/power supply. Available in 2700 K, 3000 K, and 4000 K color temperatures.
§Dimensions include lamp, integral ballast/power supply, and base. Available in 2700 K and 3000 K color temperatures.
¶Dimensions do not include external ballast/power supply. Available in 3500 K and 4100 K color temperatures.

A U.S. Patent issued to J. M. Anderson in 1970 shows an inductively coupled electrodeless fluorescent lamp designed to replace standard incandescent lamps. Two products that were introduced over 20 years later are similar to Anderson's proposed lamp. In 1992, Philips introduced the QL lamp (**Fig. 3a**), and one year later the General Electric Company introduced the Genura® lamp (Fig. 3b). Both lamps use a ferrite rod instead of the closed ferrite core configuration (Fig. 2) and operate near 2.5 MHz in a frequency band set aside for radio-frequency lighting applications. The QL lamp uses a separate lamp and power supply, and is designed to replace metal halide lamps. The Genura® lamp integrates the lamp and power supply into a single unit and is provided with an Edison screw base so it can replace conventional incandescent reflector lamps. The **table** shows performance data for these lamps.

In 1998, Osram Sylvania introduced the Icetron® lamp (Fig. 3c and table). This lamp uses a configuration similar to that shown in Fig. 2. Advantages of this design include the ability to operate at lower frequency and less radiated electromagnetic interference. The disadvantage is higher manufacturing cost.

A lamp identified with radio-frequency (RF) lighting is the microwave-powered sulfur lamp developed by Fusion Lighting. Microwave-powered electrodeless lamps were developed in the early 1970s and are now widely distributed for use as high-power industrial ultraviolet sources. The microwave oven established the magnetron as an inexpensive source of 2.45-GHz power that could deliver between 500 and 6000 W to bulbs placed in resonant cavities one or two wavelengths in size (13–26 cm; 5–10 in.).

For visible-light applications, Fusion Lighting's lamps use a microwave-excited sulfur discharge (**Fig. 4**). In this lamp, a magnetron generates about 850 W of microwave energy that is transferred through a waveguide into a cavity formed by a conducting and reflective metal mesh. There the energy is coupled into a 28-mm (1.1-in.) spherical fused silica bulb that contains sulfur or selenium and various gases. The radio-frequency electric field accelerates free electrons, which in turn transfer energy to the desired radiating species via collision. Molecular emission of light resulting from transitions between vibrational states has proven to yield high-quality visible light with a continuous spectrum. The sulfur spectrum closely matches the human scotopic response, but the light appears to have a greenish tint when compared to most conventional sources. Key features are the absence of ultraviolet radiation and mercury, and very low infrared content.

Seventy percent of the microwave energy can be converted to visible light in a sulfur bulb, yielding efficacies as high as 170 lumens per RF watt along

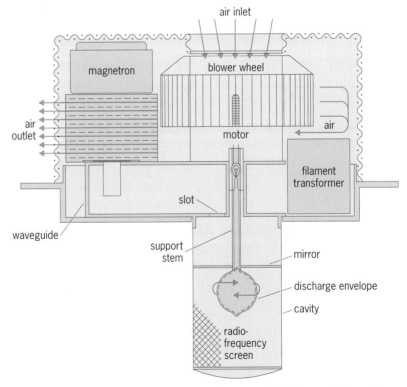

Fig. 4. Fusion Lighting microwave-cavity radio-frequency electrodeless sulfur lamp. The bulb is composed of a discharge envelope and a support stem. The motor rotates the bulb and the cooling blower wheel. The radio-frequency screen forms the microwave cavity. The waveguide couples the energy from the magnetron to the cavity via the slot. (*U.S. Patent 5,811,936*)

with a high quality of light. However, losses associated with the magnetron, the magnetron power supply, and radio-frequency containment screens reduce the efficacy to 85 lm/W. This is high compared to many sources, but not as high as the best metal halide and fluorescent lamps.

The promise of exceptionally long lamp life, very rapid starting and restarting, relatively small source size (allowing for good light control), and high efficacy, coupled with good color rendition, are the main features. The lack of color shift, even when the lamp is dimmed, and the ability to operate at temperature extremes give an advantage for certain uses. These lamps will be most useful in industrial applications, road and parking lot illumination, and other areas requiring high-power light sources.

The future of high-power sulfur lamps (which are not being marketed at this time but are in active development) and other microwave-powered lamps will be assured if the efficacy and reliability can be improved to justify their relatively high price. The same technology can be extended to lower-power lamps, but the need for very reliable high-efficiency, inexpensive, solid-state microwave power sources will be a limiting challenge to the future implementation of this light source.

Various other radio-frequency lamps have been proposed but not yet developed. These include a very high efficacy electrodeless metal halide lamp developed by General Electric and Toshiba Lighting; an incandescent liquid metal cluster lamp developed by Philips; a small, high-brightness inductively coupled projection lamp developed by Fusion Lighting; and a microwave cavity projection lamp developed by Matsushita.

For background information *see* ELECTRIC FIELD; ELECTROMAGNETIC INDUCTION; FLUORESCENT LAMP; GAS DISCHARGE; ILLUMINATION; INCANDESCENT LAMP; LIGHT; LUMINOUS EFFICACY; MAGNETRON; METAL HALIDE LAMP; MICROWAVE; PHOSPHORESCENCE; VISION; WAVEGUIDE in the McGraw-Hill Encyclopedia of Science & Technology.

Victor D. Roberts

Bibliography. J. M. Anderson, *High Frequency Electrodeless Fluorescent Lamp Assembly*, U.S. Patent 3,521,120, July 21, 1970; W. H. Hayt, Jr., *Engineering Electromagnetics*, McGraw-Hill, 1958; D. A. Kirpatrick, Aperture lamps, *9th International Symposium on the Science and Technology of Light Sources*, Ithaca, NY, 2001; J. Schlejen, Inductively coupled fluorescent lamps: The QL lighting system, *6th International Symposium on the Science and Technology of Light Sources*, Budapest, 1992; R. Scholl, B. Weber, and C. Weijtens, New light generation mechanism: Continuous radiation from clusters, *6th International Symposium on the Science and Technology of Light Sources*, Budapest, 1992; C. N. Stewart et al., Inductively coupled HID lighting system, *6th International Symposium on the Science and Technology of Light Sources*, Budapest, 1992; F. Terman, *Electronic and Radio Engineering*, McGraw-Hill, 1955.

Reconstructing environmental history

Most knowledge of past environments has come from the study of the physical, chemical, and biological remains found in the stratigraphic record. The modern environment also plays a key role in the interpretation of such remains. For this reason, the reconstruction of past environments has its foundations in the principle of uniformitarianism and the application of analogical reasoning.

Uniformitarianism (the present is the key to understanding the past) suggests that physical, chemical, and biological processes acting on modern landscapes have taken place during the entire history of the Earth, although their intensity has varied. This principle was first outlined by James Hutton in the late 1700s and developed by Charles Lyell in the early 1800s. Two centuries later, uniformitarianism remains the basis of all paleoenvironmental reconstructions. The difference today is that technological advances permit more accurate methods of reconstruction.

Analogical reasoning in the reconstruction of past environments implies the use of modern analogs that are grounded in uniformitarianism. However, this practice may pose some problems when the environments in the past have no analogs in the present. In this case, earth scientists have devised a series of quantitative methods to measure the direction and rate of change.

Methods. The methods used in paleoenvironmental reconstruction vary depending on the geological period and the type of information used. The reconstruction of environments of recent geological periods relies more on modern analogs because their environments are more similar. If, for example, we compare the Cretaceous (141.5–65 million years ago) with the Pliocene (5.2–1.65 million years ago), we find that the distribution of landmasses, seas, climate zones, and biotic communities in the Pliocene resemble their modern counterparts more than those of the Cretaceous. Also, a large number of plants and animals of the Cretaceous have disappeared through extinction. When this is the case, paleontologists have devised several methods to reconstruct the characteristics of extinct organisms based on the characteristics of their living descendants.

The information used in paleoenvironmental reconstruction comes from a variety of sources (biological, physical, and chemical). Fossils have been the most important source of biological information used for determining past living conditions (for example, climate, ecosystems, and food chains) and for dating past environments. The physical and chemical properties of sediments are also useful sources of information. Trace elements and chemical compounds in rocks, sediments, and fossils are used as indicators of specific environmental conditions, which may not be evident through the study of fossils alone. The physical properties of sediments and rocks, such as their grain size and arrangement (bedding), are often used to determine their mode of deposition

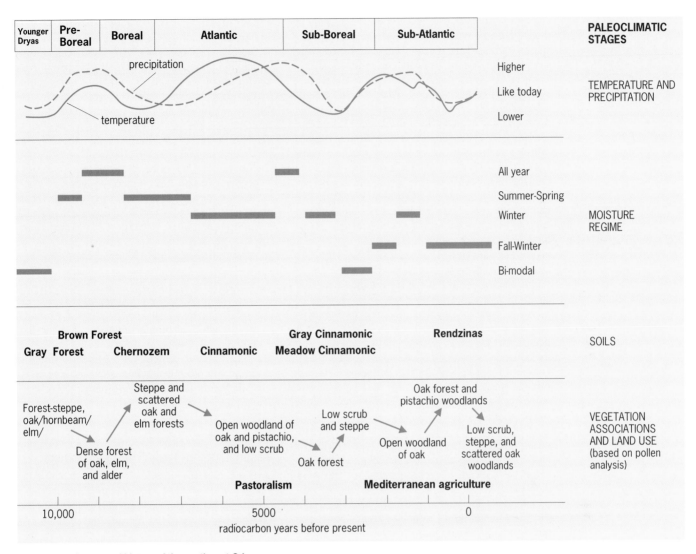

Holocene environmental history of the southwest Crimea.

and, subsequently, the environmental conditions at the time of deposition. Sands, for instance, which are usually transported by water or wind, are deposited in different ways in dunes, beaches, and river beds. Most environmental reconstructions of the Tertiary period or earlier grew out of petroleum and mineral prospecting. For example, petroleum is known to have formed in lacustrine (lake), paludal (marsh), and marine environments with abundant plants and animals.

Applications. The geographical scale of environmental reconstructions is as important as the temporal scale. Thus, reconstructions at the local, regional, and global scale vary in levels of resolution and purpose.

Reconstructions at a local scale. Vegetation is a good indicator of environmental change because most plants react relatively quickly to climatic fluctuations, both in their physiology and in their population dynamics. Reconstruction of past vegetation relies on fossil pollen and spore analyses as well as fossil macroremains (for example, leaves and seeds). Soils are sources of paleoenvironmental information because

they mirror the climatic conditions and vegetation around them.

An example of paleoenvironmental reconstruction using pollen analysis and soil development can be shown in the reconstruction of late Quaternary environments in the southwest part of the Crimean Peninsula, on the northern shores of the Black Sea (see **illus.**). This reconstruction of temperature, precipitation, and moisture regime (rain seasonality) during the last 11,000 years was based on the presence and frequency of pollen from various plants. The development of soil was studied from stratigraphic sections in the region. Pollen assemblages suggest the presence of a dense forest of oak, hornbeam, and elm in the region, indicating that conditions 9000 years ago were wetter than today. Soils at that time were mostly of the brown forest type. Analogs of this type of forest and soil exist today in the Crimean Peninsula at higher elevations, where annual rainfall is more abundant.

A change in the landscapes of the southern Crimea occurred between 7500 and 5000 years ago because of a global warming phase known in Europe as the

Atlantic stage. Pollen data show an assemblage of vegetation with taxa adapted to warm and relatively dry conditions. This pollen assemblage suggests the presence of two types of plant communities: woodlands of oak and pistachio, and low scrub formed by aromatic plants. Modern analogs of this type of vegetation exist in warmer areas farther south in the Mediterranean region. The typical soils formed during this stage are the cinammonic, typical of regions with wet and mild winters and dry summers. This helps to confirm the Mediterranean character of the climate already evidenced by the pollen assemblages. In addition, the presence of certain taxa in the low scrub vegetation suggests that livestock grazing (pastoralism) affected the area at that time. These plants include taxa of the mint family (Labiatae), which are avoided by livestock.

In the last 5000 years, a series of other environmental changes linked to human disturbance occurred (see illus.). The most obvious was the reduction of arboreal vegetation due to agricultural development and livestock grazing. Another change in the pollen data is the presence of crops, which marked the introduction of Mediterranean vegetation by Greek colonists about 2500 years ago. Pollen data suggest that the species cultivated at this time were mostly grape, and to a lesser degree cereals and walnut trees.

Simulation models. A recent trend in paleoenvironmental reconstruction has been the integration of local paleoecological records to create simulation models as a means of reconstructing past environments at regional and global scales. The BIOME project is a model used to reconstruct biomes (for example, tropical rainforests, savannas, tundra, and taiga) for the late Quaternary period based on fossil pollen data. This model evolved from earlier simulation models such as CLIMAP (Climate Mapping Analysis and Prediction) and COHMAP (Cooperative Holocene Mapping Project).

The BIOME project was formally initiated in 1994 with the reconstruction of the biomes at 6000 years before present (BIOME 6000). Additional projects included reconstructions at 18,000 years (Last Glacial Maximum) and at other points in time (for example, 12,000 and 9000 years ago). In these models, the reconstruction of paleoclimates relies on modern bioclimatic limits (such as minimum and maximum temperature tolerated) of plant functional types (PFT). Thus, each PFT contains a group of plant taxa that can be used as reliable modern analogs for each of the world's biomes. For example, the PFT for the boreal biome includes *Betula* (birch), *Alnus* (alder), *Populus* (aspen), and *Salix* (willow). In North America today, this biome extends mostly within Canada, but pollen data show that during the Last Glacial Maximum (18,000 years ago) this type of forest existed as far south as the central Appalachian region in the United States.

Paleoclimate and atmospheric circulation models have been built based on chemical and physical analyses of cores from deep within the ice sheets of Greenland and Antarctica. Models for reconstruct-

ing ocean water paleotemperatures have been based on studies of isotopes from deep-ocean sediments. In addition, global models of past temperature, precipitation, and evaporation in the continents have been attempted using data on lake level fluctuations.

The application of these simulation models has broadened understanding of present climatic trends and predictions for the future. This knowledge of past warm periods and their consequences may provide a clue to understanding the trends and possible effects of global warming in the future.

For background information *see* BIOME; DATING METHODS; DEPOSITIONAL SYSTEMS AND ENVIRONMENTS; GEOLOGICAL TIME SCALE; HOLOCENE; PALEOCLIMATOLOGY; PALEOSOL; PALYNOLOGY; RADIOCARBON DATING; SOIL; STRATIGRAPHY in the McGraw-Hill Encyclopedia of Science & Technology.
Carlos E. Cordova

Bibliography. P. J. Brenchley and D. A. T. Harper, *Palaeoecology: Ecosystems, Environments and Evolution*, Chapman & Hall, London, 1998; J. Kutzbach et al., Climate and biome simulations for the past 21,000 years, *Quaternary Sci. Rev.*, 17:473–506, 1998; C. Prentice and D. Jolly, Mid-Holocene and glacial-maximum vegetation geography of the northern continents and Africa, *J. Biogeog.*, 27:507–519, 2000.

Reconstructing temperature variations

Documenting the large-scale surface temperature changes of the past millennium is necessary in order to place recent climate change in an appropriate long-term context. Because the fundamental boundary conditions on the climate (the parameters of the Earth's orbit in relation to the Sun, and global patterns of vegetation and continental ice cover) have not changed appreciably, the major variations in climate over this time frame are representative of the range of natural climate variability that might be expected in the absence of any human influence on climate. Placing global warming of the twentieth and twenty-first centuries in this longer-term context can aid in our ability to determine the role of anthropogenic factors, such as increases in greenhouse gas concentration produced by humans, in past and future climate change.

Theoretical and empirical approaches. Meteorological instrumental measurements document climate changes on a widespread basis only about one century back in time. Relatively few instrumental records are available from times prior to that. However, a number of distinct approaches exist for describing climate variations as far back as a millennium. One approach is to use theoretical models of the climate system that are driven with estimated changes in external parameters or forcings, such as greenhouse gas concentrations and solar output, which tend to warm the climate when they increase, and the frequency and intensity of explosive volcanic eruptions, which cool the climate by injecting reflective sulfate aerosol into the atmosphere. This approach to reconstructing the past temperature history is limited by the imperfectly known history of these changes in forcing, which are typically estimated indirectly from trapped gas, radioisotopes, and volcanic dust signals left behind in ice cores. Moreover, the reconstruction is limited by any uncertainties in the model's representation of actual climate processes and responses. Since the approach indicates only the forced component of climate change, it cannot estimate the possible role of internal dynamics (such as natural changes in ocean circulation) in the actual climate changes in past centuries.

Human documentary evidence provides another approach for reconstructing climate in past centuries. Records of frost dates, droughts, famines, the freezing of water bodies, duration of snow cover, and phenological evidence (for example, the dates of flowering of plants, and the ranges of various species of plants) can provide insight into past climate conditions. Human accounts of mountain glacier retreats and advance during past centuries, widespread historical documentation of weather conditions, and even a handful of several-centuries-long thermometer measurements are available in Europe for several centuries back in time. Plentiful human documentary evidence is limited, however, to those regions (primarily Europe and eastern Asia) where a written tradition existed. As a result, human accounts are not useful for documenting hemispheric or global-scale climate variations several centuries into the past. In addition, human documentary records must be interpreted with caution, as they are not equivalent in their reliability to actual instrumental measurements of meteorological variables. Typically, these records provide indirect and potentially biased snapshots in time of potentially climate-related phenomena.

We must turn to more widespread, quantifiable measures of climate to document the large-scale climate variations of past centuries. Geological evidence from terminal glacial moraines, indicating the advance of mountain glaciers in past centuries, can provide inferences into past climate changes. However, due to the complex balance between local changes in melting and ice accumulation, and the effects of topography, all of which influence mountain glacier extents, it is difficult to ascertain the true nature of temperature changes simply from this evidence. Both increased winter precipitation and cooler summer temperatures can lead to the growth of a glacier, and large or even moderate glaciers respond slowly to any underlying climate changes. Estimates of long-term ground temperature trends from temperature profiles retrieved from terrestrial borehole data over the Earth can also provide complementary large-scale information regarding ground surface temperature trends in past centuries. But impacts of changes in seasonal snow cover, land surface changes, and other factors unrelated to atmospheric temperature changes, which may complicate the interpretation of these data, have not yet been confidently determined.

Proxy climate reconstruction. A more quantifiable source of information on climate changes in past centuries is provided by proxy indicators (natural archives of information which, by their biological or physical nature, record climate). Certain proxy indicators, including most sediment cores, ice cores, and preserved pollen, do not have the capability to record climate changes at high temporal resolution, and are generally not useful for reconstructing climate changes over the past several centuries. However, high-resolution (annually resolved) proxy climate records, such as growth and density measurements from tree rings, laminated sediment cores, annually resolved ice cores, and isotopic information from corals, can be used to describe year-to-year patterns of climate in past centuries (**Fig. 1**). These indirect measurements of climate change vary

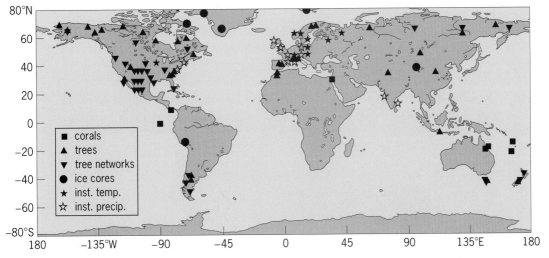

Fig. 1. Natural proxy and historical/instrumental indicators used in large-scale annual surface temperature reconstructions back to the year 1400. Data are increasingly sparse back in time. inst. = instrumental. (*Adapted from M. E. Mann, R. S. Bradley, and M. K. Hughes, Global scale temperature patterns and climate forcing over the past six centuries, Nature, 392:779–787, 1998*)

considerably in their reliability as indicators of long-term climate (varying in the degree of influence by nonclimatic effects, the seasonal nature of the climate information recorded, and the extent to which the records have been verified by comparison with independent data). When taken together, and, particularly when combined with historical documentary information and the few long-term instrumental climate records available, proxy climate records can provide a meaningful annually resolved documentation of large-scale climate changes in past centuries, including patterns of surface temperature change, drought, and atmospheric circulation.

Global assemblages of such high-resolution proxy indicators can be related to the modern instrumental surface temperature record and then used to yield reconstructions of large-scale surface temperature patterns over several centuries. The detailed spatial patterns of these reconstructions can often provide insights into the underlying governing factors. For example, the year 1816 was colder than average for the Northern Hemisphere, most likely due to the injection of large amounts of radiation-reflecting sulfate aerosol into the stratosphere following the April 1815 volcanic eruption of Tambora, Indonesia. The spatial variations in temperature were great, however, with some areas (such as Europe) cooling significantly, and other areas actually warming (**Fig. 2**). This relative pattern of warming and cooling is consistent with the North Atlantic Oscillation or Arctic Oscillation pattern of atmospheric circulation variability, which has an important influence

on regional patterns of temperature in the Northern Hemisphere from year to year, particularly in the winter. In addition, other patterns of climate variability, associated with the global impact of the El Niño/Southern Oscillation phenomenon, have a significant but complex influence on year-to-year global temperature patterns. The complexity of regional variations in temperature trends shows that it is perilous to draw conclusions regarding hemispheric or global temperature trends from isolated regional information.

Hemispheric or global mean surface temperature estimates can be derived by spatially averaging estimates of past large-scale patterns of surface temperature change. It is most appropriate to estimate the average surface temperature changes for the Northern Hemisphere, where considerably more widespread past data are available. Using different sources of proxy data, different estimates of Northern Hemisphere temperature changes over the past millennium have been made, some of which are representative of the full Northern Hemisphere, and others of which are more indicative of extratropical regions of the Northern Hemisphere (**Fig. 3**). Ground temperature changes estimated from boreholes are in disagreement with both the available instrumental record prior to the twentieth century, and the other reconstructions in Fig. 3, probably because of complications in these data discussed earlier.

The various proxy and model-based hemispheric temperature estimates, taken overall, indicate relatively modest variations in temperature over the past

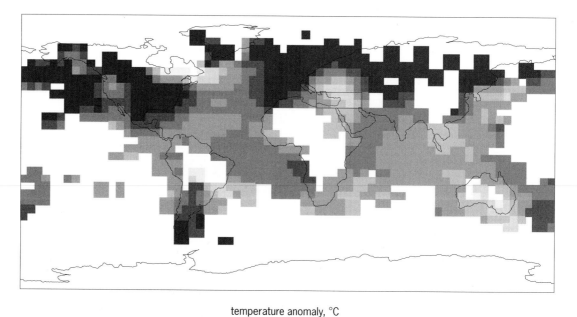

temperature anomaly, °C

−0.75   −0.45   −0.15   0.15   0.45   0.75

Fig. 2. Spatial pattern of surface temperature anomalies (relative to "normal" temperatures of 1902–1980 for the "year without a summer" of 1816. Although temperatures were cold for the Earth overall, note that certain areas (such as Europe and the southeastern United States) were significantly colder than average, while other areas (such as the Middle East) were actually warmer than normal.

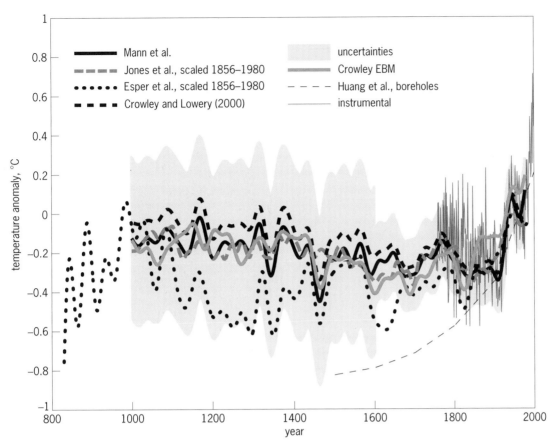

Fig. 3. Comparison between various estimates of Northern Hemisphere temperature changes in past centuries. Included are estimates of annual mean Northern Hemisphere surface temperature reconstructed from proxy data and estimated from theoretical energy balance models as well as estimates of warm-season, extratropical Northern Hemisphere temperature trends which have been scaled to match the full Northern Hemisphere annual temperature record from 1856 to 1980 for appropriate comparison. The reconstructions have been smoothed to highlight variations on time scales greater than 40 years, and the uncertainties (95% confidence interval) in the smoothed Mann et al. reconstruction are shown. Also shown is the instrumental Northern Hemisphere temperature record available back through the mideighteenth century, and independent estimates of ground surface temperature changes from terrestrial borehole data. (*Data from M. E. Mann, R. S. Bradley, and M. K. Hughes, Northern Hemisphere temperatures during the past millennium: Inferences, uncertainties, and limitations, Geophys. Res. Lett., 26:759–762, 1999; T. J. Crowley and T. Lowery, How warm was the medieval warm period?, AMBIO, 29:51–54, 2000; T. J. Crowley, Causes of climate change over the past 1000 years. Science, 289:270–277, 2000; P. D. Jones et al., High-resolution palaeoclimatic records for the last millennium: Interpretation, integration and comparison with general circulation model control run temperatures, Holocene, 8:477–483, 1998; J. Esper, E. R. Cook, and F. H. Schweingruber, Low frequency signals in long tree-ring chronologies for reconstructing past temperature variability, Science, 295:2250–2253, 2002; S. Huang, H. N. Pollack, and P.-Y. Shen, Temperature trends over the past five centuries reconstructed from borehole temperature, Nature, 403:756–758, 2000*)

1000 years, prior to the marked twentieth-century warming. At the full hemispheric scale, temperatures appear to have been slightly warmer (several tenths of a °C) during the period 1000–1400 relative to a later, colder period, 1400–1900, with no previous comparable interval approaching in warmth the latter twentieth century. Some extratropical temperature reconstructions suggest wider swings in temperature, including greater cooling during the seventeenth to nineteenth century, than is evident in the instrumental, model, or proxy-based estimates. The greater variability in this case probably arises from the emphasis on extratropical continental regions. For example, unlike European temperatures, which indicate a distinct cold phase from the seventeenth to nineteenth century, the hemispheric trend shows a steadier, long-term cooling. It is probable that the greater cooling during the Little Ice Age in regions such as Europe was associated with the enhancement of temperature variations by changes in patterns of atmospheric circulation, such as the North Atlantic Oscillation. Recent evidence suggests that the North Atlantic Oscillation can be altered by changes in the Sun's output. Such changes may have led to enhanced cooling in Europe during the eighteenth century. Solar output at this time may have favored greater exposure of Europe to cold, dry Siberian air masses through a negative impact on the North Atlantic Oscillation.

Outlook. Recent work highlights the importance of taking into account regional variation in properly reconstructing the changes in Northern Hemisphere mean temperature in past centuries. This principle clearly holds true for glacial/interglacial climate variations that occur over many thousands of years, wherein temperature changes in the tropics were probably quite small (3°C or so), leading to global mean temperature variations of only about 4°C, even though temperature variations in polar regions may have been considerably larger (10–20°C). Reconstructions of temperature changes in past centuries, for example, have confirmed other (human-documented) evidence of a cooling of 1–2°C in the winter during the Little Ice Age of the seventeenth to nineteenth century in Europe, but do not support the existence of a continuous period of cooler Northern Hemisphere temperature that is of similar magnitude to, or synchronous with, these cold conditions in Europe. The best current estimates of Northern Hemisphere temperature changes in the past, and their relationship between changes in other external factors, such as volcanic and solar influence, support a moderate sensitivity of the climate system to past and continued anthropogenic influences.

For background information see CLIMATE MODIFICATION; CLIMATOLOGY; GLACIOLOGY; GLOBAL CLIMATE CHANGE; SOLAR CONSTANT; UPPER-ATMOSPHERE DYNAMICS; VOLCANO in the McGraw-Hill Encyclopedia of Science & Technology.   Michael E. Mann

Bibliography. R. S. Bradley, Paleoclimatology: Reconstructing climates of the Quaternary, Harcourt, Academic, San Diego, 1999; T. J. Crowley, Causes of climate change over the past 1000 years, Science, 289:270–277, 2000; C. K. Folland et al., Observed climate variability and change, in J. T. Houghton et al. (eds.), Climate Change 2001: The Scientific Basis, pp. 99–181, Cambridge University Press, Cambridge, 2001; T. M. L. Wigley, M. J. Ingram, and G. Farmer, Past climates and their impact on man: A review, in T. M. L. Wigley et al. (eds.), Climate and History, Cambridge University Press, Cambridge, 1981.

Rhizosphere ecology

Photosynthesis is the primary conduit for energy transfer from the Sun to the Earth. Hence, the vast majority of all metabolic processes on the planet are fueled by the capacity of plants to capture the energy from sunlight and use it to reduce carbon dioxide (CO_2) to carbohydrates. Although photosynthesis begins aboveground, approximately 50% of net primary productivity in terrestrial systems is translocated below the soil surface through root growth and activity. The rhizosphere, the region of soil immediately surrounding the plant root [usually extending 1–2 mm (0.04–0.08 in.) from the root] is directly influenced by root growth and activity. This region is characterized by huge inputs of plant carbon that stimulate microbial growth and activity. Thus, the rhizosphere is a major interface for plant and microbial interactions. It is in the rhizosphere that symbiotic relationships form to enhance plant growth and survivability. Pathogenic organisms also exert their negative influence on plants via the rhizosphere. The positive and negative feedback loops between plants and microbes strongly influence terrestrial productivity, ecosystem processes, and global biogeochemical cycles.

Carbon flow. In their natural environment, plants grow in a variety of mineral and organic soils that provide water, nutrients, and physical support. Rhizodeposition, the transfer of carbon from the plant to the surrounding soil matrix, in turn provides energy for the growth and maintenance of symbiotic microorganisms. Thus, the continuous transfer of carbon from the plant to the soil helps create a favorable habitat for microorganisms while also benefiting the plant through maintenance of soil physical and chemical characteristics that promote plant growth.

Types of rhizodeposition. Soil biologists divide the types of rhizosphere carbon deposition into four categories: gases, secretions, lysates, and exudates. Carbon dioxide gas is produced in large quantities through respiration and released into the rhizosphere. The release of CO_2 from the root to the rhizosphere can have a large impact on rhizosphere chemistry and biology. Other gases (for example, ethylene) make up a small proportion of the total carbon flow from plant to the rhizosphere but can have significant influence, especially as regulators of plant growth.

Secretions are composed of polysaccharides and enzymes and other proteins released from the plant root as a result of metabolic processes. For most organisms, these organic materials are slightly more difficult to metabolize. Compounds derived from cell walls, root cells, and eventually whole roots are called lysates. Due to their chemical complexity and the type of chemical bonds that are found in many lysate compounds, these molecules are generally more difficult to decompose than other rhizodeposits.

Exudates are typically water-soluble compounds excreted from the root without the direct use of metabolic energy. Exudates come in a variety of forms but are dominated by amino acids, organic acids, and simple sugars. The enzymes for degrading simple sugars and amino acids are found as constitutive components of most microbial cells, meaning that the majority of microorganisms carry the enzymatic machinery to metabolize these molecules. Hence, exudates are a readily available energy supply for the microbial community found in the rhizosphere.

Role of exudation. While approximately 40–60% of all plant carbon is transferred belowground and eventually deposited in the rhizosphere, 5–20% of net photosynthate is exuded or secreted from roots. Despite this large movement of carbon from the plant, the factors that control carbon flow in the rhizosphere are not well known. However, it has been shown that the addition of microorganisms to the root zone of plants stimulates exudation and secretion compared with sterile root conditions. Exudation may benefit the plant through the attraction of microbial mutualists. Compounds released by the plant roots may serve as signals of host recognition in microorganisms. The elongation of mycorrhizal hyphae has been stimulated by soluble exudates; however, exudation has also been shown to attract zoospores of *Pythium*, a plant pathogen.

Rhizosphere:soil value. The high influx rate of carbon and nutrients in the rhizosphere favors fast-growing microorganisms with short generation times. A means of expressing the feastlike conditions in the rhizosphere compared with the faminelike conditions in the bulk soil is through a ratio, the rhizosphere:soil (R:S) value. R:S values for bacteria typically range from 10 to 100, whereas organisms such as fungi, actinomycetes, protozoa, and microfauna are described by more modest values of 1 to 5. Bacteria in the rhizosphere tend to be larger than in bulk soil (probably reflecting better carbon and nutrient availability), indicating that bacteria R:S values based on biomass are even greater than R:S values based on numbers of individuals.

Symbiotic interactions. Because the rhizosphere is an interface for plants and microorganisms, it is a region characterized by many symbiotic interactions. A symbiosis is a relationship between two dissimilar organisms living in close association with one another. Symbiotic interactions can be described as mutualistic, commensalistic, or antagonistic (parasitic). More often than not, an interaction between organisms does not fit neatly into one of these three symbiotic definitions. Yet, these categories are still useful descriptors of the overall interaction between two organisms living in close association with each other.

Mutalistic. In many ecosystems nitrogen availability limits plant growth, so the capacity to form a mutualistic relationship with an organism capable of acquiring and reducing atmospheric nitrogen gas (N_2) can be beneficial. In fact, root-microbe relationships are common in many plant species. A mutualism between plants and N_2-fixing microorganisms is an important and common interaction in nature that begins in the rhizosphere. Certain secretions from plants attract gram-negative bacteria called Rhizobia that then form nodules on the roots of leguminous plants. The plant benefits from this relationship by obtaining reduced nitrogen from the Rhizobium, whereas the Rhizobium presumably receives several benefits, including reduced carbon (food) and refuge from predators. Some type of actinomycetes are capable of forming an analogous symbiotic relationship with certain species of nonleguminous trees (such as *Alnus* and *Ceanothus*).

Another symbiotic relationship that begins in the rhizosphere is the mutualism between certain types of fungi and most types of plants. Known as mycorrhizae, this plant-fungus interaction provides the plant with nutrients, especially phosphorus, that are in limited supply, while the plant supplies the fungus with carbon. Up to 4% of the carbon converted to organic matter by plants can be transferred to the fungus. Like many fungi, the fungal symbiont forms an extensive hyphal network through the soil, providing a huge surface area important for nutrient acquisition. Plants in nutrient-stressed environments benefit the most from this symbiosis.

Commensalism. When two types of dissimilar organisms are associated, sometimes one benefits while the other organism is largely unaffected. Though this type of interaction is difficult to document, commensalism may be widespread within the rhizosphere. Because the rhizosphere is a zone of high plant and microbial respiration, carbon dioxide concentrations can be 10 to 1000 times greater than the surrounding soil and atmosphere. Many free-living autotrophic organisms utilize CO_2 as a carbon source to build biomass. *Nitrosomonas* is an example of an autotroph that would benefit from the high concentrations of CO_2 in the rhizosphere if both NH_4^+ and O_2 are also readily available.

Antagonistic. Though many mutualistic types of symbiosis take place, the rhizosphere is a war zone with many types of antagonisitic interactions. Fungal hyphae trap and digest nematodes, while amebas engulf and dissolve bacteria. These alterations influence which microorganisms dominate and thus the ecology and chemistry of the rhizosphere. Microorganisms are responsible for the production of phytotoxins, antibiotics, and growth regulators that further influence the habitat of the rhizosphere. Antibiotic production by bacteria, actinomycetes, and fungi can provide a selective advantage over competitors sensitive to these antibiotics. Growth regulators and phytotoxins, in turn, influence the survival and growth rate of plants.

Plant pathologists have noted that soil-borne pathogens are less virulent to plants when surrounded by an active microbial community. This indicates that microorganisms can inhibit the infection of the plant tissue by the pathogen. Disease reduction could result from the direct competition between the pathogens, or antagonism of the pathogen by the rhizosphere microbes. The utilization of carbon through competition or the production of antibiotics by the rhizosphere community (antagonism) could serve as mechanisms controlling pathogen infectivity.

Potential applications. Through research, the capacity to reduce the number and activity of plant pathogenic organisms and increase plant growth–promoting rhizobacteria could greatly benefit agriculture through greater crop productivity and reductions in pesticide applications. In addition, research on how microbial communities influence nutrient dynamics in the rhizosphere could benefit sustainable agriculture by reducing the need for fertilizer applications.

Because more than half of the organic carbon contained in the terrestrial biosphere is contained within the soil, some ecologists believe that rhizodeposition may be a key method to reduce the rising concentration of atmospheric CO_2 and thus the potential for global warming. Certain types of plants can be used for promoting the growth of rhizosphere microbial communities. In turn, these microorganisms remediate soils that are polluted by hydrocarbons and other organic contaminants. Excess nitrogen from agricultural run-off and leaching can be remediated by fast-growing *Populus* spp. that quickly incorporate nitrogen into plant biomass. (Excess nitrate pollutes water resources, causing methemoglobinemia, or blue baby syndrome, in newborn babies.)

Finally, a thorough understanding of rhizosphere ecology might allow for direct management of plant-rhizosphere systems without the need of genetic modification of plants (in which pathogen-suppressing genes from bacteria are inserted into plants). Though there is no direct evidence that genetically modified crops are harmful to the environment or humans, some researchers and environmentalists are concerned about the potential negative consequences of genetic engineering. Hence, elucidating the complex ecological web of the rhizosphere and plant-microbe interactions is still considered an important research area for biocontrol of plant pathogens.

For background information *see* CARBON; CARBON DIOXIDE; CARBON-NITROGEN-OXYGEN CYCLES; PHOTOSYNTHESIS; RHIZOSPHERE; SOIL ECOLOGY in the McGraw-Hill Encyclopedia of Science & Technology.

Mark A. Williams

Bibliography. J. M. Lynch, *The Rhizosphere*, Wiley, Chichester, 1990; R. L. Tate, *Soil Microbiology*, Wiley, New York, 1995; Y. Waise, A. Eshel, and U. Kafkafi, *Plant Roots: The Hidden Half*, Marcel Dekker, New York, 1996.

RNA editing

One emerging feature of the study of mammalian gene expression is the apparent complexity involved in the production of more than 300,000 different proteins from perhaps just 60,000 genes. There are many different mechanisms that permit amplification of the host genetic repertoire from the four-letter code embedded in its chromosomal sequence. These include the ability of genes to undergo regulation by using alternative transcription initiation sites; to alter the patterns of splicing of intronic (noncoding) regions, thereby giving rise to different splice products; to be regulated through the use of alternative polyadenylation sequences that in turn regulate stability and translation of the mature transcript; and to undergo regulation through mechanisms by which the sequence of the ribonucleic acid (RNA) transcript is itself altered. This latter form of gene regulation, RNA editing, is defined as a process introducing a nucleotide alteration in the sequence of the nuclear transcript so that it differs from that encoded in the genomically templated version.

A to I and C to U editing. Two forms of RNA editing are encountered in mammals. In the first, adenosine is deaminated (an amine group is removed) to form inosine, which in turn is read as guanosine by the translational apparatus. Adenosine to inosine (A to I) RNA editing is mediated by a family of enzymes referred to as adenosine deaminases acting on RNA (ADARs) and requires the presence of double-stranded RNA, usually presented in the form of an intron-exon duplex. (In this context, RNA duplex formation refers to a double-stranded confirmation reminiscent of that in DNA.) There is a range of substrates for A to I editing, mostly expressed in brain and neural tissue. The best-studied include the RNA encoding the calciumgated glutamate receptor channel (GluR-B) and a specific subtype of G-protein-coupled receptor for 5-hydroxytryptamine (5HT-2c). ADARs are modular enzymes (enzymes containing multiple catalytic units); they contain an active deaminase motif (amino acid sequence encoding a specific protein structure and function) as well as a double-stranded RNA recognition motif (RRM) that mediates target binding.

A second form of RNA editing is associated with enzymatic deamination of cytosine to uridine. The prototype for this form of C to U editing is the mammalian apolipoproteinB (apoB) transcript. C to U editing of apoB messenger RNA (mRNA) occurs in the small intestinal enterocyte (absorptive epithetical cell) of all mammals, and it results in production of a truncated protein that is required for the absorption of fat and its transport in plasma.

C to U editing of apoB mRNA. ApoB is an abundant gene expressed in the small intestine and liver of all mammals, where it plays an essential role in adapting the products of complex lipid (complexes of cholesterol or glycerol with fatty acid molecules) synthesis, predominantly cholesterol esters and triglycerides, into a form that can be transported in the aqueous medium of blood. A single structural *APOB* gene generates two distinct protein species, referred to as apoB100 and apoB48. ApoB100 contains 4536 amino acids, is synthesized and secreted by liver cells, and is the form of apoB associated with the major cholesterol carrier in blood, known as low-density lipoprotein (LDL; **Fig. 1**). However, a different form of apoB is synthesized in the small intestine as a result of C to U RNA editing of the nuclear apoB transcript. A single cytidine nucleotide (out of ~14,000 nucleotides) is enzymatically deaminated to form a uridine, thereby changing a CAA (glutamine) codon into a UAA (translational stop) codon. The edited apoB mRNA undergoes translational termination resulting in production of a protein (apoB48) containing 2152 amino acids (approximately 48% the size of apoB100). ApoB48 is secreted from the intestine, from which it transports the products of dietary lipid absorption, in the form of a chylomicron particle (an extremely small droplet consisting mostly of triglycerides), to the liver (Fig. 1).

Lipid transport. The production of two distinct forms of apoB in mammals is linked to the presence of different transport pathways for the products of dietary (exogenous) and newly synthesized (endogenous) lipids. As detailed in Fig. 1, hepatocytes secrete lipoproteins containing apoB100, and these particles are eventually internalized through LDL receptors expressed at the cell surface. Virtually all cells have the capacity to acquire cholesterol from circulating LDL by virtue of their expression of LDL receptors, and this endogenous pathway of hepatic lipid

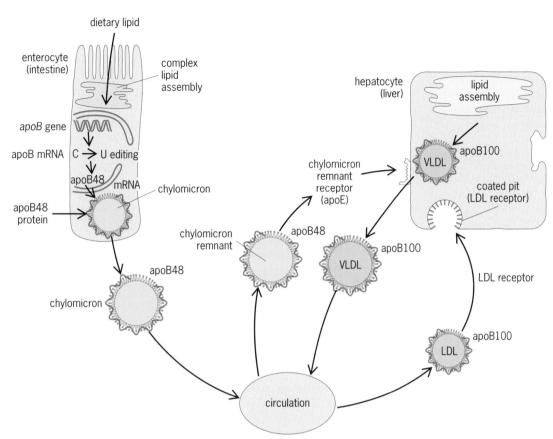

Fig. 1. Tissue-specific expression of apolipoproteinB (apoB) resulting from C to U RNA editing. Hepatocytes secrete apoB100 in association with very low density lipoproteins (VLDL) which are metabolically converted into low-density lipoproteins (LDL), the major cholesterol carrier in humans. Intestinal cells secrete apoB48 following the absorption of dietary lipid and produce large lipoprotein particles called chylomicrons. Both forms of apoB are required for lipid transport. However, apoB100 contains the domains that are required for interaction of lipoprotein with the LDL receptor, whereas this domain is missing from apoB48. As a result, chylomicrons are directed to a different receptor pathway (chylomicron remnant receptor) which recognizes apolipoproteinE (apoE).

secretion and delivery facilitates lipid homeostasis and ensures delivery of cholesterol to these cells. By contrast, secretion of chylomicron particles from the intestine in association with apoB48 is more closely tied to the rapid delivery of dietary lipid to the liver for use as an energy source.

Lipoprotein binding to the LDL receptor requires a domain present in the carboxyl terminus of apoB100; this domain is eliminated from apoB48 as a result of its truncation. The net result is that lipoprotein particles containing apoB48 are directed to a different receptor, the chylomicron remnant receptor or LDL receptor-related protein, which is expressed predominantly in the liver (Fig. 1). This receptor-ligand interaction is mediated by another protein, apoE (Fig. 1). The advantage of this adaptation is that dietary lipid is rapidly (minutes to hours) delivered to the liver through its transport in association with apoB48. By contrast, lipids produced by the liver circulate in association with apoB100 and participate in the fine regulation of plasma lipid levels with an average residence time of 2 days.

RNA target selection. C to U editing of apoB RNA involves the selection of a single cytidine from a transcript of more than 14,000 nucleotides. A number of important sequence elements and two protein

factors regulate the exquisite specificity of this process.

Sequence elements. C to U RNA editing requires a region of about 150 nucleotides flanking the targeted base. This region of apoB RNA is presumed to contain most of the sequence information required for this process in vivo. (Supporting this presumption is the fact that if the DNA encoding the 150-nucleotide region is inserted into another gene, the RNA transcribed from this chimera is edited at the correct site, that is, the same cytidine in the chimera is edited as encountered in the naturally occurring RNA.) Several features of this 150 nucleotide region are important. First, there is an abundance of adenosine and uridine nucleotides (approximately 70% of the region; **Fig. 2**). This abundance of A and U residues likely imparts specificity to the region through the tendency of these residues to fold into ordered structures. Within this 150-nucleotide region are contained distinct functional elements that modulate editing efficiency. Another required sequence element is an 11-nucleotide cassette (a linear sequence of nucleic acids) located 5 nucleotides downstream of the edited C. It is particularly critical, as virtually all mutations within this cassette have been shown to abolish C to U RNA editing (Fig. 2). This region is

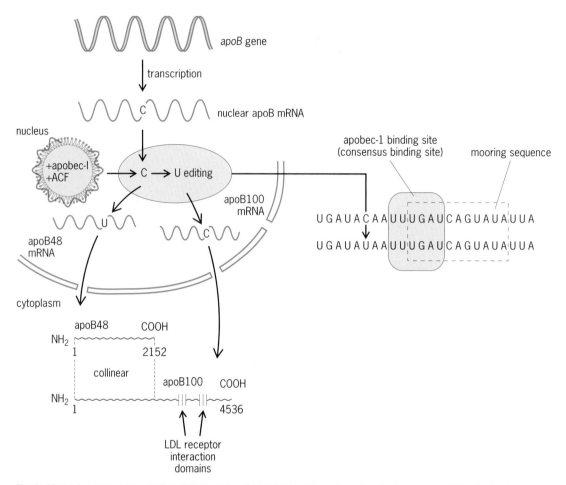

Fig. 2. Molecular mechanisms of C to U RNA editing. C to U RNA editing takes place in the nucleus of intestinal enterocytes. The region flanking the edited base is ~70% A + U rich and contains two important elements in immediate proximity to the targeted cytidine. These include an 11-nucleotide region downstream of the edited base referred to as the "mooring sequence." A second region, spanning the mooring sequence and immediately downstream of the edited base, contains a consensus binding site for apobec-1, the catalytic deaminase which, along with ACF, is responsible for C to U conversion. Following C to U editing of the nuclear transcript, apoB48 RNA is transported into the cytoplasm for translation, giving rise to a protein of 2152 residues that is collinear with the amino terminal half of apoB100 (4536 residues). The physiologically important domains required for binding to the low-density lipoprotein receptor are indicated, within the carboxyl terminus of apoB100.

also required for apoB RNA binding by cell extracts, hence its designation as a mooring sequence. Placement of the mooring sequence either closer or farther than 5 nucleotides from the targeted base alters the efficiency of C to U editing. Finally, within the region between the edited base and the mooring sequence is a consensus binding site (UUUGAU) for the catalytic deaminase (apobec-1), one of the proteins responsible for C to U editing of apoB (Fig. 2). The interaction of the various sequence elements and their spacing relative to the targeted base (cytidine) is one key to the specificity of C to U editing.

Protein factors. C to U editing of apoB RNA is mediated by a multicomponent protein complex containing a core of two proteins, apobec-1 and apobec-1 complementation factor (ACF). There is no firm consensus concerning the size of the native complex or its composition, but it is likely to include proteins that participate in RNA splicing and other forms of posttranscriptional regulation of gene expression. The native editing enzyme has been referred to as

an editosome (analogous to the spliceosome, which contains factors responsible for RNA splicing). Current information indicates that the two core proteins are indispensable; however, the requirement for other candidate proteins is not established.

Apobec-1 is an RNA-specific cytidine deaminase. As with all cytidine deaminases, apobec-1 functions as a higher-order multimer (that is, two, four, or six molecules of apobec-1 are required for function), most likely a dimer (requiring two molecules of apobec-1 per complex). In addition, apobec-1 is an RNA-binding protein whose consensus binding site is located close to the edited base (Fig. 2). In humans, apobec-1 is expressed only in cells of the gastrointestinal tract, as would be predicted from its function in truncating the intestinal apoB gene product. Human liver, by contrast, does not express apobec-1 and as a consequence does not contain edited apoB mRNA. (Interestingly, introduction of apobec-1 into human liver-derived cells results in apoB RNA editing, suggesting that human liver contains all the protein factors necessary for C to U RNA editing, except apobec-1.)

The second required protein component, ACF, most likely functions to position apobec-1 in an appropriate configuration relative to the targeted cytidine. ACF binds to apobec-1 and apoB RNA. Both functions, RNA binding and apobec-1 binding, are required for C to U editing activity of ACF. A defining characteristic of the protein components of the apoB C to U editing enzyme is their partitioning between the nucleus and cytoplasm. C to U RNA editing takes place in the nucleus, yet apobec-1 is distributed largely in the cytoplasm. Translocation of apobec-1 into the nucleus may require its interaction with other protein components of the editing enzyme complex. The expression of proteins involved in C to U RNA editing as well as their distribution and activity within the cell may be relevant to the physiological regulation of RNA editing in vivo.

For background information *see* ENZYME; GENE; LIPID METABOLISM; LIPOPROTEIN; NUCLEOTIDE; PROTEIN; RIBONUCLEIC ACID (RNA) in the McGraw-Hill Encyclopedia of Science & Technology.

Nicholas O. Davidson

Bibliography. S. Anant and N. O. Davidson, Molecular mechanisms of apolipoproteinB mRNA editing, *Curr. Opin. Lipidol.*, 12:159–165, 2001; N. O. Davidson, The challenge of target sequence specificity in C → U RNA editing, *J. Clin. Invest.*, 109: 291–294, 2002; S. Maas and A. Rich, Changing genetic information through RNA editing, *BioEssays*, 22:790–802, 2000.

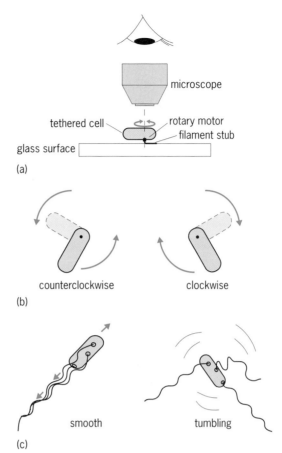

Fig. 1. Tethering experiment demonstrating rotation of the bacterial rotary motor. (*a*) Flagellar filaments are shortened by shearing, and the filament stubs are attached to a stationary surface. Rotation of the flagellar motor causes the cell body to rotate, which can be observed in the light microscope. (*b*) Appearance of a rotating, tethered cell. In wild-type (normal) cells, rotation in both the clockwise and counterclockwise direction is seen, with reversals occurring about once per second. (*c*) Corresponding behavior of freely swimming cells. When motors rotate counterclockwise, the cells swim smoothly; however, when one or more motors turn clockwise, the cells tumble. Because wild-type motors turn both clockwise and counterclockwise, wild-type cells execute a random walk consisting of smooth runs of about a second punctuated by tumbling events that reorient the cell. In the presence of stimuli such as chemical attractants, cells modulate their motor reversals to bias this random walk in a desired direction.

Rotary motors (bacterial)

Soon after the first microscopic observations of bacteria, it was noted that many kinds of bacteria can swim. Their swimming ability is remarkable; for example, *Thiovulum majus*, the current speed-record holder, has been clocked at 600 micrometers per second, a scale speed equivalent to a human swimming 100 m in 1.5 s. The motility of bacteria is even more impressive when one considers the special challenges faced by organisms so small. Since the drag force on a bacterial cell is enormous relative to its momentum, bacteria cannot coast—a cell that ceases actively swimming will lose its forward momentum in less than a microsecond. Also, due to their small size, bacterial cells undergo rapid thermal movements that randomize their orientation every few seconds. Thus, bacterial cells cannot maintain fixed trajectories and must make frequent adjustments to their swimming pattern to maintain progress in a desired direction.

Flagella. Most motile species of bacteria swim by means of flagella. Although it was initially assumed that bacterial flagella generate thrust by a whiplike motion, it was discovered in the early 1970s that they are actually helical propellers turned by rotary motors. Proof of a rotary mechanism came from experiments in which shortened flagellar filaments were tethered to a stationary surface, causing the entire cell body to rotate for prolonged periods (**Fig. 1**). The motors can turn clockwise or counterclockwise, and reversals in motor direction dictate the pattern of swimming. In *Escherichia coli* and *Salmonella*, for example, counterclockwise rotation produces forward movement that is relatively steady, whereas clockwise rotation causes a rapid somersaulting motion termed tumbling. The cells regulate clockwise-counterclockwise motor switching in response to various environmental stimuli to direct their movement toward chemical nutrients or other environmental factors (temperature, pH) that favor survival.

Motor physiology and genetics. The flagellar rotary motors are inserted through the cell membrane (or through both the inner and outer membranes in gram-negative species). The energy for rotation comes from a membrane gradient of ions, either protons (H⁺) or sodium ions (Na⁺), depending on the species and also on the circumstances. Whether H⁺ or Na⁺, the ions have a higher potential energy on the outside of the cell than on the inside. This provides impetus for the ions to move through the motor from the outside to the inside, and this ion movement is harnessed to drive rotation by a mechanism not yet fully understood. The motor uses a large amount of ion fuel, as each revolution requires several hundred ions.

Due to the complexity and membrane location of the flagellar motor, it has not yet been possible to study its function in vitro, and functional studies have mainly examined motors in living cells. The rotation rate and torque of individual flagellar motors can be measured by a variety of methods. Motors turning tethered cells (Fig. 1) operate against a large viscous load; thus a tethering experiment measures motor performance in a high-load, low-speed regime. More

sophisticated optical methods can monitor rotation of the thin flagellar filaments, or small beads attached to flagellar stubs, probing performance in the low-load, high-speed regime. Rotation is very fast when the load is light: Proton-driven motors can turn at speeds approaching 18,000 rpm, and sodium-driven motors as fast as 102,000 rpm. Rotation rate is limited at least in part by rates of ion movement, judging from the greater speed of the sodium-driven motors and from a significant hydrogen-isotope effect (H_2O versus D_2O) on the rotation rate of proton-driven motors.

Much experimental work on the flagellar motor has focused on the relationship between energy input (the magnitude of the ion gradient) and mechanical output (torque and speed). In certain *Streptococcus* species, the membrane ion gradient can be eliminated by starvation, and artificial ion gradients of known magnitude can be applied. Measurements of such artificially energized cells showed that when the motor is turning relatively slowly (as in a tethered-cell experiment), its torque is directly proportional to the energy provided by the proton gradient. These and other measurements of artificially energized cells provide evidence that proton flow is tightly coupled to rotation, with each revolution requiring a fixed number of protons.

A bacterial flagellum contains about two dozen different proteins and is thus a fairly complex structure. Genetic mutations have been invaluable for elucidating the functions of the various components. Most proteins in the flagellum have structural roles or contribute to the process of assembly. Only five proteins are directly involved in rotation: MotA, MotB, FliG, FliM, and FliN. They are distinguished by the fact that they can be mutated to give flagella that are paralyzed, that is, structurally normal but unable to rotate.

Flagellar motor structure. Electron micrographs of flagella from *Salmonella* show a structure at the base that consists of rings of different sizes mounted on a central rod (**Fig. 2**). The ring/rod assembly has a maximum diameter of 45 nanometers and a length of about 50 nm. In overall appearance, it resembles components that might be found in a macroscopic electric motor. Most (if not all) of this basal structure rotates when the motor is working, making it the rotor. The basal structure is attached to an approximately 55-nm-long, hook-shaped segment that functions as a flexible coupling. The hook is, in turn, joined to the long helical filament that functions as propeller.

The innermost and largest ring of the flagellar base is termed the C-ring, reflecting its location in the cytosol. A ring in the cytoplasmic membrane is called the MS-ring. Two outer rings, termed L and P, form a bushing that allows the flagellum to pass through the outer membrane of the cell, presumably helping to maintain the integrity of the outer membrane while minimizing resistance to rotation. Three of the proteins that function in rotation, FliG, FliM, and FliN, form a large complex at the base of the structure.

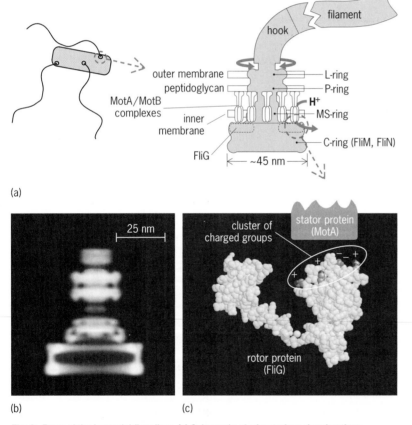

(a)

(b)   (c)

Fig. 2. Base of the bacterial flagellum. (*a*) Schematic of a bacterium showing three flagella, and a detailed view of the base. The stator proteins MotA and MotB are not located with the rest of the structure. (Their location is based on electron micrographs of membranes.) In the action of the motor, ions flow through the MotA/MotB complexes, and this flow is harnessed to drive rotation by a mechanism that is not fully understood (*after P. N. Brown, C. P. Hill, and D. F. Blair, Crystal structure of the middle and C-terminal domains of the flagellar rotor protein FliG, EMBO J., pp. 3225–3234, 2002*). (*b*) Electron micrograph of the flagellar basal structure of *Salmonella typhimurium* (*after N. R. Francis et al., J. Mol. Biol., 235:1261–1270, 1994*). (*c*) Enlarged view of the interface between the stator (the MotA protein) and the rotor (the FliG protein). A part of the FliG protein structure is known from x-ray crystallography. A striking feature of FliG is a cluster of charged, functionally important groups. These groups are known to be at the interface with the stator.

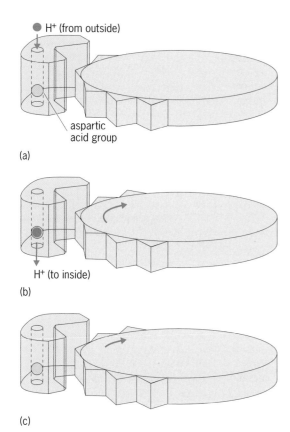

H+ (from outside)

aspartic
acid group

(a)

H+ (to inside)

(b)

(c)

Fig. 3. Hypothetical mechanism for motor rotation. The model is based on experiments showing that ions flow through the stator and do not contact the rotor directly, and that protonation of a critical aspartic acid residue in MotB will cause conformational changes in the stator. Steps are illustrated for a single stator complex; the flagellar motor actually contains about eight stator complexes that produce torque independently. (*a*) In an initial state, the critical aspartic acid group in the stator is deprotonated. (*b*) A proton enters from the periplasm and binds to the aspartic acid group, causing a conformational change in the stator that applies force to the rotor, driving movement. (*c*) The proton leaves the aspartic acid group for the inside of the cell, causing another conformational change that drives further rotor movement. Shapes of the proteins are schematic only; the essential feature is that movements in the stator can somehow engage the rotor to drive rotation.

FliM and FliN form most or all of the C-ring, whereas FliG is positioned at the junction between the C-ring and MS-ring. FliG is especially important for rotation, and contains electrically charged groups that interact with charges on the stator (the stationary part). An atomic structure determined by x-ray crystallography shows that these charged groups in FliG are clustered on a prominent ridge of the protein. This charged ridge appears to be important for rotation, but its precise function is unknown (Fig. 2).

The stator is formed from MotA and MotB, membrane proteins that form a complex with probable composition [MotA]$_4$[MotB]$_2$. Each motor contains several MotA/MotB complexes (at least eight in *E. coli*), which function independently to generate torque. The complexes are not part of the basal structure that has been studied by high-resolution electron microscopy, but have been seen in micrographs of membranes, as arrays of particles surrounding the basal body. MotB contains a segment believed to bind peptidoglycan, anchoring the complexes to the cell wall. The MotA/MotB complexes function to conduct ions across the membrane and appear to have a major role in coupling ion flow to rotation.

The self-assembling ability of the flagellum is as notable as the flagellar structure itself. The growing discipline of nanotechnology seeks to build useful machines with dimensions measured in nanometers; the flagellar motor represents a fully realized example of a self-assembling, highly refined machine on this scale. Assembly of the flagellum proceeds basically from the inside (the cytoplasm-proximal end) toward the outside. Many of the components in the structure reach their destinations by being exported through a channel through the middle of the structure. The flagellum thus contains an apparatus at its base that can identify the needed components and promote their export. This export apparatus is the subject of intense study, as it is evolutionarily related to the type-III export systems that pump virulence factors from pathogenic species into host cells.

Mechanism. The mechanism of rotation of the bacterial motor is not understood in detail. Evidence suggests that ions flow through the MotA/MotB complexes, moving on and off a particular aspartic acid residue in MotB to cause structural changes in the stator protein that apply force to the rotor (**Fig. 3**). A better understanding of the mechanism will require knowledge of the atomic structures of the proteins involved, particularly the MotA and MotB proteins that execute the ion-driven "power stroke" driving rotation. Atomic structures have been solved for only a few flagellar proteins, but efforts are under way to determine more.

ATP synthase. For several years, it was thought that the bacterial rotary motor represented the only true example of rotary motion in biology. In the 1990s, however, it was found that another proton-powered machine, the ATP synthase, also employs a rotary mechanism. This enzyme produces adenosine triphosphate (ATP), the chemical "currency" used to drive most energy-requiring processes in cells. The size, protein composition, and overall organization of the ATP synthase are quite different from the flagellar motor. Ion-driven rotary machines thus appear to have arisen on at least two independent occasions in the course of evolution.

For background information *see* BACTERIA; CELL (BIOLOGY); CELL MOTILITY; CHEMIOSMOSIS; CILIA AND FLAGELLA; MITOCHONDRIA in the McGraw-Hill Encyclopedia of Science & Technology.

Seiji Kojima; David Blair

Bibliography. H. C. Berg and D. A. Brown, Chemotaxis in *E. coli* analysed by three-dimensional tracking, *Nature*, 239:500–504, 1972; N. R. Francis et al., Isolation, characterization and structure of bacterial flagellar motors containing the switch complex, *J. Mol. Biol.*, 235:1261–1270, 1994; S. Kojima and D. F. Blair, Conformational change in the stator of the bacterial flagellar motor, *Biochemistry*, 40:13041–13050, 2001; R. M. Macnab, Flagella and motility, in

F. C. Neidhardt et al. (eds.), *Escherichia coli and Salmonella: Cellular and molecular biology*, 2d ed., pp. 123–145, ASM Press, Washington, DC, 1996; M. Silverman and M. Simon, Flagellar rotation and the mechanism of bacterial motility, *Nature*, 249:73–74, 1974.

Ryegrass

Ryegrass is one of the most important cool-season forage and turf bunchgrasses grown in North America. The perennial species *Lolium perenne*, mainly used for winter turf for recreational sports, and the annual species *L. multiflorum*, mainly used for winter forage and grazing, are largely marketed in the southeastern United States. However, newer cultivars and management techniques have dramatically increased ryegrass's region of adaptability to irrigated pastures in the west and colder midwest and northeast climates. Ryegrasses are grown from coast to coast in Canada, and more than 50% of the world's ryegrass seed is grown in the Pacific Northwest. Various attributes make ryegrass one of the most useful grass species in North America and around the temperate world: they support the livestock industry by providing high yields and quality of forage; enhance the environment through nutrient uptake; and provide esthetically pleasing and important turf for sport and home lawn use.

Background. Perennial ryegrass is thought to be indigenous to Europe, Asia, and northern Africa. In early literature (dating back over 325 years) it is referred to as English ryegrass, and is described as the most desired pasture crop in England. Annual ryegrass, also called Italian ryegrass and thought to be indigenous to Italy, has gained popularity more recently. A type of annual ryegrass, Westerwolds (*L. multiflorum* var. Westerwoldicum), indigenous to the Westerwolde region of the Netherlands, is a highly productive forage crop. Throughout England, Ireland, Europe, Australia, and New Zealand, perennial ryegrass is widely used for pasture, hay, and silage. In the United States, perennial and annual ryegrasses have been recommended as forage for over a century in the maritime, coastal environment of the Pacific Northwest. Since the 1930s warm-season perennial grass sods in the southeast have been overseeded with perennial ryegrass for winter turf or with annual ryegrass for winter forage.

Plant characteristics. Ryegrasses are generally known for rapid establishment, excellent forage yields and quality, and excellent turf characteristics. They have shallow root systems, are able to tolerate water-logged and acid soils, and undergo rapid regrowth after use, but are somewhat intolerant of high temperatures and unable to tolerate droughty conditions. Perennial ryegrass is normally shorter, with narrower leaves that are folded in the bud, while annual ryegrass is taller, with longer leaves rolled in the bud. Perennial ryegrass seedheads are induced in the fall, followed by winter vernalization (exposing seedlings to low temperatures to induce flowering at maturity) for grass seedhead emergence in the spring, while annual ryegrass requires only an 11-hour photoperiod and no fall induction. Following a normal, season-long 35-day silage harvesting schedule, perennial ryegrass produces one major crop of seedhead tillers (seedhead growth units) followed by many crops of vegetative tillers (growth units consisting mostly of leaves). Annual ryegrass produces multiple seedhead tiller crops season-long. Seedheads of perennial ryegrass often are awnless (lacking stiff bristles) with fewer seeds per spike than the awned annuals.

Genetics. Diploid perennial ryegrass and annual ryegrass ($2n = 2x = 14$) are self-incompatible, but can be crossed to develop hybrid ryegrass (*L. hybridum*) or crossed with meadow fescue (*Festuca pratense*, $2n = 2x = 14$) to develop festuloliums (*Festulolium loliaceum* when crossed with perennial ryegrass and *Festulolium braunii* when crossed with annual ryegrass). Cultivars released from a tall fescue (*Festuca arundinacea*, $2n = 6x = 42$) crossed with an annual ryegrass cross appear more like the tall fescue than the ryegrass parent or a festulolium which is distinctly different than either parent. Hybrid ryegrasses, referred to as short rotation ryegrass, are naturally occurring. Theoretically, they should represent the best of both parents but usually express characteristics of one parent more than the other. In turfgrass, hybrid ryegrasses are commonly called intermediate ryegrass. The process for human-made, intermediate turf ryegrass development has recently been patented. Only a few forage festulolium cultivars have been released, none of which are for turfgrass use. Festuloliums incorporate characteristics from both genotypes, such as higher palatability, darker, softer leaves, and rapid establishment from the ryegrass female parent. From the male fescue parent comes greater persistence, drought tolerance, disease resistance, wear tolerance, and growth during hot summers—characteristics that have not been achieved through traditional breeding methods for each grass species.

Using colchinine, a harsh chemical that induces polyploidization, breeders have doubled ryegrass chromosome numbers and developed tetraploid ($2n = 4x = 28$) genotypes. Tetraploid cultivars are available for perennial, annual, and hybrid ryegrasses. Simply doubling the chromosomes of the best diploid genotypes does not ensure that they will be the best tetraploids. Compared with diploid ryegrasses, tetraploids have higher short-term yields (with mechanical harvesting but not always with grazing animals). Tetraploids are taller and have larger leaves and stems, which compete well with taller legumes; have fewer leaves per plant, leading to a more open canopy and stand; and have higher percentages of sugars and digestible forage, which are desirable for livestock. However, tetraploid ryegrasses do not always translate into greater animal performance. Tetraploid ryegrasses are less winter-hardy and less tolerant to environmental stresses than diploid ryegrasses. Newer tetraploid varieties are phenotypically more like diploids, and newer diploids have improved quality over older genotypes.

Uses. About 80–95% of perennial ryegrass seed grown in the Pacific Northwest is utilized as turf. This represents about 200 million pounds of seed. About 75% of the perennial ryegrass turf seed market is used to overseed warm-season bermudagrass (*Cynodon dactylon*) to winterize sports fields and golf courses. (The role of perennial ryegrass when overseeded is to provide a dark green, uniform cover during the winter and early spring, and then to die, leaving the bermudagrass sod strong and healthy for summer use.) The remaining 25% of turf-type perennial ryegrass seed is mixed with Kentucky bluegrass (*Poa pratensis*) and fine fescues for permanent turf. Five to twenty percent of perennial ryegrass seed is grown for forage on irrigated western pastures and rain-fed pastures across Missouri and the Ohio Valley, or as grass silage in the coastal areas of Oregon, Washington, British Columbia, Maryland, and New York. As a turf, perennial ryegrass cultivars exhibit quick germination and sprout emergence, cold tolerance, wear tolerance, dark green color, fine texture, and a pleasing appearance.

Because of its greater height, broad leaves, open canopies, and lighter green color, annual ryegrass is seldom used for turf. Much research has been conducted to identify the contamination percentage of the highly cross-pollinated annual ryegrass seed from perennial ryegrass seed. One test is the seedling root fluorescence (SRF). When viewed under ultraviolet light, annual ryegrass seedlings grown on white filter paper produce an alkaloid that fluoresces. Generally, perennial ryegrass seedlings do not. Unfortunately, some perennial cultivars do fluoresce and some annuals do not.

About 235 million pounds of annual ryegrass seed is grown annually with about 85% used as forage. The remaining amount is included in other grass seed mixes. As a forage crop, ryegrass is much sought out by the dairy and livestock industry.

Recommended forage seeding rates for ryegrasses have increased because producers lack the time to develop a weed-free, finely prepared seedbed. Producers perform one or two tillage operations, then plant. It is recommended that perennial or annual ryegrass be planted at 30 pounds per acre. Soil fertility must remain high for nitrogen-phosphorus-potassium-sodium and water stress must be avoided to produce excellent yields, high-quality forage, and enduring stands.

For background information *see* COVER CROPS; FORAGE CROPS; LAWN AND TURF GRASSES in the McGraw-Hill Encyclopedia of Science & Technology.
Steven C. Fransen

Bibliography. M. D. Casler et al., Natural selection for survival improves freezing tolerance, forage yield and persistence of festulolium, *Crop Sci.*, 42:1421–1426, 2002; D. J. Floyd, Stable Intermediate Ryegrass Varieties, U.S. Patent 6,444,880 BI, 2002; D. J. Floyd and R. E. Barker, Change of ryegrass seedling root fluorescence expression during three generations of seed increase, *Crop Sci.*, 42:905–911, 2002; D. Hannaway et al., *Annual ryegrass*, PNW Bull. 501, 1999; D. Hannaway et al., *Perennial ryegrass*, PNW Bull. 503, 1999; B. Hunter, *Forage-crop practices in Western Oregon and Western Washington*, USDA Farmer Bull. 271, 1906; G. A. Jung et al., Ryegrasses, in L. E. Moser et al. (eds.), *Cool Season Forage Grasses*, Agronomy 34, American Society of Agronomy, Madison, WI, 1996; F. M. Rouquette, Jr., and L. R. Nelson, *Ecology, production, and management of Lolium for forage in the USA*, Special Publ. 24, Crop Science Society of America, Madison, WI, 1997; B. Young, Seed production, *Oregon State Univ. Crop Soil News/Notes*, vol. 12, no. 5, 1998.

Sailing craft

Evidence of early boat and ship structures beyond the level of log canoes and rafts indicates that they shared comparatively simple shapes across cultures, time, and geography. From Egyptian (ca. 2400 B.C.), Roman, or East Asian (reported during the Dark Ages) times to present, there is a basic geometry of bottoms that are flat across and curved up fore and aft (that is, parallel to the midline of the boat) and sides vertical to flaring outwards 30° or more. These simple shapes typically did not reflect an absence of understanding of how to build more complex shapes, but allowed for more affordable ships that could be built quickly.

During the colonial days in North America, exploration and economic interests frequently required ad hoc solutions in order to travel the waters in this largely unmapped territory. Settlers often had just basic carpentry skills to build a boat as quickly as possible, and simple shapes were prevalent. In those early days of virgin forest, the ready availability of wide planks enabled boats such as the flat-iron skiff (**Fig. 1**) to be built by springing planks around one or more spreaders to a point at the bow, and nailing planks across the (upside down) side planks to form the bottom. While this method was often crude, careful location of the spreaders, angling of the sides to the bottom, and curving of the edges

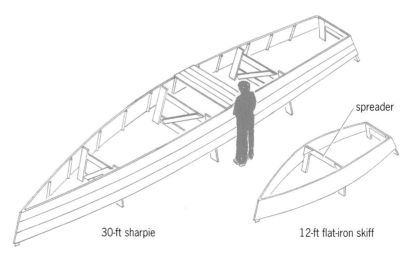

Fig. 1. Sharpie and flat-iron skiff hull forms shown inverted and partially completed. (*Copyright 2002 Phil Bolger & Friends, Inc.*)

of the side planks could result in graceful overall shapes. Sharpies were eventually built on the same principle in lengths up to 60 ft (18 m), using multiple side planks and spreaders, to serve a variety of inshore (at sea but close to the shore) commercial purposes.

Emergence of plywood. Later, boats with simple shapes were built faster, sturdier, and larger by using emerging plate materials such as steel, aluminum, and eventually plywood. The plywood manufacturing process has evolved into peeling a thin veneer off the outside of a rotating log, producing large sheets which are then flattened out and glued together to form standard sheets. Since knotholes and variations in the grain of the wood can leave core voids that often weaken the panel and may induce rot, care in patching these holes and in fitting the edges of the veneers together is the principle criterion of the quality of plywood. As glue became more reliable, it was seen to have advantages for large flat components like bulkheads (the vertical partitions separating boat compartments) and decks, and eventually even hull skins (that is, the outside of the main body of the vessel).

In the late 1930s, C. Raymond Hunt did seminal work in adapting plywood to production boats, emphasizing efficient use of the material. The designs were notable in that they were styled to emphasize rather than minimize the shapes and proportions due to the sheet material. These boats were popular but also criticized as "not looking like boats." Between March 1939 and May 1940, Charles G. MacGregor published a series of articles and designs for *Rudder* magazine, arguing that boats with respectable performance and unexceptionable looks could be built of sheet plywood.

In February 1940, C. P. Burgess published the first popular explanation of developable surfaces, the use of calculated segments of cylinders and cones to form certain boat shapes around the properties of reasonably stiff sheet material like plywood. Burgess showed how the shape that a curved or twisted sheet of plywood naturally assumes could be reliably predicted and defined on paper. In August, Chauncey Parsons reported that practical experiments had produced the shapes that Burgess predicted. However, the advent of World War II slowed the development of pleasure craft and boat design using plywood.

Time-effective one-off construction. Since the early 1900s, a small industry has offered frame kits to amateur builders for conventional boat construction. Following World War II, the use of plywood panels allowed the process to be carried much further, with the complete boat broken down and packaged for shipment. Many popular classes of plywood small boats were introduced, such as the children's trainer boat Optimist, designed by Clark Mills. In the United Kingdom, Jack Holt designed high-performance sail boats, available as plans and kits.

In the mid-1960s, Philip C. Bolger, in collaboration with H. H. Payson, introduced instant boats in lengths ranging from 6 to 31 ft (2 to 9 m). Supplying dimensioned diagrams of all the components of a boat obviated both the shipment of physical materials for the kit boat and the knowledge and skill needed to work from standard boatbuilding plans. These diagrams could be laid directly on the plywood sheets and the components cut out and assembled in the specified order, rapidly producing the correct shape of boat (**Fig. 2**). The 12-ft (4-m) row and sail boat Teal used two 4 by 8 ft (1 by 2m) sheets of plywood, with an assembly time of less than 2 hours.

Complex shapes out of plywood. As sheet plywood constructions improved, free-form hulls of lapstrake construction (having the external planks overlapping, like the clapboards on a house) were developed that used plywood for the comparatively narrow strakes of planking. This began in Great Britain and spread with the availability of good plywood and epoxy glues (developed during World War II). The original object was to eliminate the tendency of natural lapstrake planks to split along mechanical lap fastenings, but it was soon discovered that these boats did not need any framing beyond minimal webs and brackets. The resulting clean interior was widely welcomed. This process was an excellent way to build a light free-form boat; these boats were called "boneless" in England. Several American production builders of lapstrake outboard motor boats used plywood planking, but never eliminated the conventional framing.

Virtues of simple shapes. A portion of the boat design community has claimed the superiority of wading draft boats for all cruising purposes. First successfully demonstrated by Ralph Munroe in the late 1800s, the principle maintains that flat-bottomed, keelless boats (the keel being a long piece of wood or steel along the bottom of a boat that helps to keep the boat balanced in the water), given adequate freeboard (that is, vertical distance from the surface of the water to the upper edge of the boat's sides) and adequately ballasted, could have seaworthy stability and in all other respects be fit for unlimited open sea passages. Compared to conventional cruising boats, these boats are incomparably more useful and safer in coastal waters and more affordable.

Advanced bow shapes. The bow, or forward part, of a boat is an important aspect of its design. While under sail and with the sharp-bowed hull heeling (tilting away from the wind), the flat-bottomed sharpie bow becomes a soft vee. This shape has notorious vices such as pounding all night in choppy water at anchor and while running upright under power. Incorporation of significant curvature from bow to stern (the back part of the boat), or upgrades to even older designs with free-form designs shaped out of plywood, were added forward to calm down the bows at night. This enabled several types of quiet, rough-water-capable bow modifications for sailing and power hulls of all sizes and weights while retaining the desirable pure flat-bottom shapes in the middle and back parts of the boat.

Steel ballast-clad hull bottoms. Flat bottoms of plywood laid in multiple layers and to comparatively

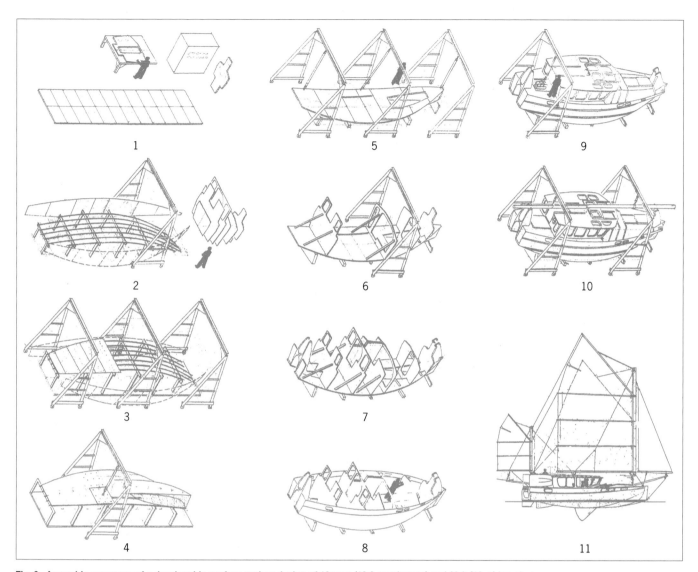

Fig. 2. Assembly sequence of a developable-surface cruiser design of 13 tons (13.2 metric tons) and 39 ft (12 m) length, a live-aboard sailing craft for global itinerary. (*Drawings of Fiji—design #662, courtesy of Phil Bolger & Friends, Inc.*)

massive thickness can be effective, resulting in stout bottoms and near-frameless bottom construction. Previously placed inside these hulls, ballast is now often bolted to the underside of the bottom in the form of thick steel (optionally copper or bronze) plates, which protect the hull bottom in groundings and collisions with submerged objects. This allows purposeful beaching of the boat for hull examination and also makes accessible secluded waters not crowded by boats with deeper hulls and more vulnerable construction.

Superior thermal performance in cruisers. Compared with metal or fiberglass, plywood has good thermal (heat-retaining) qualities, and this is even more true of thicker laminations. Using these advanced simple shapes, superior insulation can be achieved with minimum labor by adding stock insulating foam panels, allowing residence onboard in all seasons.

Quick construction. When properly designed, these boats can be constructed by amateurs—without profound experience of boatbuilding in any size—

while offering professional builders clear advantages in the marketplace as well. Panels and structural members are diagrammed for prefabrication, and large-scale surfacing to final finish is also accomplished at the prefabrication stage. Every structural member is assembled and surfaced separately to full size, and the total number of components is comparatively small. Apart from providing shelter for the building site, elaborate and costly up-front engineering is not necessary. Even global-capable designs can be "home-built." And competitive commercial work as well as custom wish lists can be directed to small segments of the market, since long production runs of single models are no longer economically essential to build even large craft economically.

Outlook. Through the use of proven designs, simple flat panel shapes including plywood can be crafted into watercraft of surprisingly sophisticated capability. These craft often require only very shallow water, and thus have more flexibility in finding waterside locations for berthing, getting on a trailer,

Fig. 3. A 39-ft (12-m) glued-plywood lapstrake Longship—Design #572, built in 2001 by Hesse of Mulheim a.d.Ruhr in Germany. The relatively light weight of 3800 lb (1722 kg) allows for ready trailering. (*Photo by Susanne Altenburger*)

and exploring in shallow water areas where other craft cannot go. The technique of using plywood lapstrake can produce shapes and appearances that are more traditional but that have the advantages of light weight, improved strength, watertightness, and suitability for trailering (**Fig. 3**). Buoyant foam insulation and buoyant wood construction make it possible in many cases to produce full positive buoyancy (that is, unsinkability) even when completely flooded.

While plywood boat designs have been largely utilized to date in small professional craft shops and by homebuilders for recreational and smaller commercial craft, many of the concepts can be extended into other types of boats and also into the arena of large-scale production.

For background information *see* BUOYANCY; PLYWOOD; SHIP DESIGN; SHIPBUILDING in the McGraw-Hill Encyclopedia of Science & Technology.

Phil Bolger

Bibliography. P. C. Bolger, *Boats with An Open Mind*, International Marine/McGraw-Hill, 1993; H. I. Chapelle, *American Small Sailing Craft*, Norton, 1951; S. Devlin, *Devlin's Boatbuilding*, International Marine/McGraw-Hill, 1996; V. Gilpin, *The Good Little Ship*, Sutter House, 1952; T. J. Hill, *Ultralight Boatbuilding*, International Marine/Highmark Publishing, 1987; T. F. Jones, *New Plywood Boats*, Sheridan House, 2001; I. Oughtred, *Clinker Plywood Boatbuilding Manual*, Woodenboat Publications, 2001; R. Parker, *The Sharpie Book*, International Marine/McGraw-Hill, 1994; H. H. Payson, *Build the New Instant Boats*, International Marine, 1984; H. H. Payson, *Instant Boats*, International Marine, 1979.

Salt tolerance in plants

Excessive salinity affects about one-quarter of cultivated land and nearly half of irrigated land. Unfortunately, the most affected areas are also areas of high crop productivity, such as the Mediterranean basin, California, and southern Asia. These areas have optimal day length and temperatures, but rainfall is often limiting, necessitating irrigation (**Fig. 1***a*). Soluble salts in irrigation water plus those present in fertilizers contribute to the gradual accumulation of toxic levels of sodium ions (Na^+) in topsoil, adversely affecting many domesticated crops (Fig. 1*b*). Plants sensitive to salt may die or grow poorly. Sensitivity to salts such as sodium chloride (NaCl) varies among domesticated crop plants as well as in nondomesticated species. For example, fruit trees, cereals, and horticultural plants are extremely sensitive to NaCl. However, plants such as sugarbeet, cotton, and barley are slightly more tolerant, and mangroves and ice plants are extremely tolerant. The different degrees of salt sensitivity indicate that certain plants possess the necessary genetic information to survive in hostile saline environments such as those found in estuaries, where the sodium concentrations are high, ranging from 0.4 to 5 *M*.

The most productive approaches to identifying genes involved in salt tolerance have used two genetic model systems, namely the baker's yeast, *Saccharomyces cerevisiae*, and the tiny weed *Arabidopsis thaliana*. The DNA sequence of the entire genome for both *Arabidopsis* and yeast have been indentified, and scientists also now have the transgenic technologies that allow them to transfer genes between these two organisms. Thus, the identification of relevant genes involved in the adaptive responses of these organisms to salt stress has been dramatically accelerated. Investigations with these two model systems have led to important insights on how to produce salt-tolerant crops.

Sodium toxicity. When a plant encounters a high-salinity environment, there is a decrease in potassium (K^+) uptake and a simultaneous increase in sodium (Na^+) influx. High concentrations of sodium become toxic to important metabolic reactions that evolved in an intracellular environment where potassium is the major inorganic cation. Emerging evidence suggests that high intracellular sodium interferes with potassium uptake systems. So in order for a plant to grow in the presence of high sodium, it must deal with the cytotoxic effect of sodium and at the same time restore the required intracellular potassium levels. Some salt-tolerant plants avoid sodium's toxicity by transporting it into their vacuoles and sequestering it there. This detoxification process has received

Fig. 1. Pitfalls of artificial irrigation. (*a*) Agriculture in arid and semiarid regions depends on artificial irrigation. (*b*) Gradual accumulation of toxic levels of Na$^+$ in topsoil renders land useless.

a great deal of attention. An alternative cellular strategy, not mutually exclusive, to avoid sodium toxicity is either to increase sodium efflux systems or to reduce cellular sodium uptake.

Sodium sequestration. Plant physiologists described the mechanisms involved in the vacuolar Na$^+$ sequestration process more than 20 years ago. It was shown that the coordinated activity of a proton (H$^+$) pump and a proton/sodium (H$^+$/Na$^+$) exchanger are required to achieve the Na$^+$ sequestration into the vacuole. The role of the vacuolar H$^+$ pump is to accumulate H$^+$ into the vacuole; H$^+$ is then exchanged for Na$^+$ ions via a revolving door–like protein, the Na$^+$/H$^+$ exchanger. There are two H$^+$ pumps at the vacuolar membrane involved in the generation of this H$^+$ gradient, one dependent on ATP (H$^+$-ATPase) and the other dependent on inorganic pyrophosphate (H$^+$-PPase). Inorganic pyrophosphate, or PP$_i$, is produced as a by-product of a wide range of biosynthetic pathways. Its utilization as an energy donor for the activity of the vacuolar H$^+$-PPase allows ATP to be conserved and improves plant cell performance under a more demanding environment.

H$^+$/Na$^+$ exchanger. After the physiological characterization of the vacuolar detoxification mechanism, the search for the gene encoding the H$^+$/Na$^+$ exchanger began, but the initial search failed. A critical discovery was then made using yeast, which contributed to the final isolation of a plant gene encoding for an Na$^+$/H$^+$ exchanger. A gene involved in Na$^+$ sequestration into the yeast prevacuolar compartment was cloned and characterized. The sequence of this yeast Na$^+$/H$^+$ exchanger (*NHX1*) was then compared to the *Arabidopsis* genomic database, and the elusive plant Na$^+$/H$^+$ exchanger (*AtNHX1*) was finally discovered. Furthermore, the overexpression of this plant Na$^+$/H$^+$ exchanger was found to enhance salt tolerance in *Arabidopsis*, tomato, and canola. In each case, the plants accumulated more Na$^+$ in their vacuoles and actually prospered in high levels of salt. Na$^+$ accumulation occurred mainly in the green parts of the plant, but not in the fruit. These results imply that heightened activity of this Na$^+$/H$^+$ exchanger could enhance crop productivity.

H$^+$ pumps. An attractive alternative to improve vacuolar Na$^+$ sequestration would be to enhance the availability of H$^+$ in the vacuole. Salt-tolerant plants such as the ice plant *Mesembryanthemum crystallinum* naturally utilize high-level expression of both the vacuolar ATPase and the Na$^+$/H$^+$ exchanger to tolerate high-salt conditions. However, overexpression of the vacuolar ATPase is difficult mainly because this H$^+$ pump is composed of subunits encoded by at least 26 genes. Fortunately, the other vacuole H$^+$ pump, H$^+$-PPase, is a single subunit protein. Here again, yeast proved to be instrumental, as expression of a gain-of-function allele of the *Arabidopsis* vacuolar H$^+$-PPase gene (*AVP1-D*)

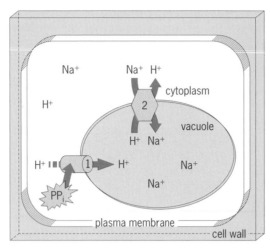

Fig. 2. *Arabidopsis* vacuolar H^+-PPase (AVP1), an H^+ pump that utilizes inorganic pyrophosphate (PP_i) as an energy source, provides increased H^+ to the vacuole (1). An H^+/Na^+ exchanger such as *AtNHX1* transports the H^+ out of the vacuole in exchange for Na^+ (2). By this mechanism Na^+ is removed from the cytoplasm and sequestered in the vacuole, and its cytotoxic effects are prevented.

suppressed the salt sensitivity of a yeast mutant lacking the plasma membrane sodium efflux pump. Transgenic *Arabidopsis* plants engineered to over-express *AVP1* exhibited increased tolerance to salt, and were capable of flowering and producing viable seeds in the presence of 0.25 *M* NaCl. *AVP1* transgenic plants are also drought-tolerant.

Mechanism. The enhanced salt tolerance of *AVP1* transgenic plants is most easily explained by an enhanced proton-driven uptake of solutes into vacuoles. Presumably, greater AVP1 activity in vacuolar membranes provides increased H^+ to drive the uptake of cations via H^+/cation exchangers into the vacuole (**Fig. 2**). These transport activities increase the membrane potential of the vacuole, thereby impeding further transport of cations. A compensatory transport of anions is needed in order to maintain electroneutrality so further exchange of Na^+ is possible. The resulting elevated vacuolar solute content is presumed to confer greater water retention, permitting plants to survive under drought conditions.

Cellular sodium uptake. To further improve salt tolerance in plants, an important concern relates to cellular Na^+ uptake mechanisms.

SOS1 Na^+/H^+ exchanger. Genetic studies with *Arabidopsis* uncovered an Na^+-driven signal transduction pathway involved in sodium uptake into cells. The main interactions are a putative plasma membrane Na^+/H^+ exchanger, SOS1; a serine/threonine protein kinase, SOS2; and a Ca^{2+}-binding protein, SOS3. An elegant study in yeast demonstrated that the SOS1 Na^+/H^+ exchanger, the SOS2 protein kinase and its associated Ca^{2+} sensor, SOS3, form a functional module involved in the control of cellular Na^+ homeostasis. SOS3's role is to shuttle SOS2 to the plasma membrane, where the SOS2/SOS3 complex activates the SOS1 exchanger. Interestingly, SOS1 expression has been localized in *Arabidopsis* to the epidermal cells at the root tip. This cell layer protects the root apical meristem, which consists of actively dividing cells lacking large vacuoles. Furthermore, the vacuolar Na^+/H^+ exchanger is not expressed at the root tip. So it appears that an important role of SOS1 is to prevent Na^+ uptake at the root tip level. SOS1 has also been localized to the cells surrounding the stele (the central vascular cylinder of roots and stems), suggesting that it is implicated in the Na^+ load of the vascular system.

Recently, a search for suppressors of the salt-sensitive phenotype of an *Arabidopsis* mutant in the *SOS3* gene yielded an important discovery. Researchers screened a tagged transform-DNA population in an *SOS3-1* salt-sensitive background and identified two allelic salt-tolerant mutations that disrupt the function of the *AtHKT1* gene. The wheat homolog encodes for a membrane transporter protein that moves K^+; however, the evidence presented by the researchers strongly suggested that in *A. thaliana* this gene product actually transports Na^+.

Other systems. Another group of proteins involved in Na^+ uptake are the channel proteins (membrane proteins that catalyze the net movement of millions of ions per minute following their electrochemical potential). There is also a body of evidence suggesting that nonselective cation channels (NSCCs) play a major role in Na^+ influx into root cells. Interestingly, these NSCCs are inhibited by calcium, a behavior consistent with earlier observations that addition of calcium reduces the stringency of a sodium stress in plants. Recently, another group of Na^+ channels involved in its uptake at the roots have been identified. This group of Na^+ channels is regulated via cyclic nucleotides.

Future directions. Recent research promoting salt tolerance in plants focuses on boosting the intracellular salt-sequestering mechanisms by transferring the gene for this phenotype from the model organism *A. thaliana* to selected crop species. A complementary approach focuses on the difficult task of reducing the net input of salt into the plants via interfering with the function of channels and transporters involved in sodium uptake without disturbing potassium uptake. An ideal scenario contemplates the generation of transgenic plants with an enhanced vacuolar salt sequestration capability and a reduced salt uptake. One remaining concern is that if low-quality (high-salt) waters are used to irrigate this new generation of salt-tolerant crops, history will surely repeat itself. This practice will eventually result in soils with enough salt to outstrip the protective mechanisms described above. Therefore, research must also focus on alternative irrigation practices that optimize the use of water, and on treatments to optimize its quality.

For background information *see* IRRIGATION; PLANT CELL; PLANT-WATER RELATIONS; PLANTS, SALINE ENVIRONMENTS OF; VACUOLE in the McGraw-Hill Encyclopedia of Science & Technology.

Roberto A. Gaxiola

Bibliography. R. A. Gaxiola, G. R. Fink, and K. D. Hirschi, Genetic manipulation of vacuolar proton pumps and transporters, *Plant Physiol.*, vol. 129, 2002; P. M. Hasegawa et al., Plant cellular and molecular responses to high salinity, in H. E. Gould (ed.), *Annu. Rev. Plant Physiol. Plant Mol. Biol.*, pp. 463–499, 2000; F. J. M. Maathuis and D. Sanders, Sodium uptake in *Arabidopsis* roots is regulated by cyclic nucleotides, *Plant Physiol.*, 127:1617–1625, 2001; A. Rus et al., AtHKT1 is a salt tolerance determinant that controls Na^+ entry into plant roots, *PNAS Early Ed.*, pp. 1–6, 2001; R. Serrano and R. Gaxiola, Microbial models and salt-stress tolerance in plants. *Crit. Rev. Plant Sci.*, 13:121–138, 1994; H. Shi et al., The putative plasma membrane Na^+/H^+ antiporter SOS1 controls long-distance Na^+ transport in plants, *Plant Cell*, 14:465–477, 2002; M. Stitt, Pyrophosphate as an energy donor in the cytosol of plant cells: An enigmatic alternative to ATP, *Bot. Acta*, 111:167–175, 1998; R. G. Zhen, E. J. Kim, and P. A. Rea, The molecular and biochemical basis of pyrophosphate-energized proton translocation at the vacuolar membrane, *The Plant Vacuole*, pp. 298–337, Academic Press, 1997.

SAR interferometry

Many important geophysical processes inaccessible to our direct observation have been studied by measuring subtle deformations of the Earth's surface. Orbital satellites can now provide precise measurements of surface changes for studying these processes worldwide. One major contribution in this area has been the development of interferometric synthetic aperture radar (InSAR), which can provide more spatially dense and accurate deformation measurements than have been possible previously with radar systems. The most important advances demonstrated to date have been related to tectonic (seismic and volcanic) processes, and to glacier and ice sheet motions mapped in the environmentally sensitive and diagnostic polar regions. Many other ground subsidence phenomena are under investigation, and promise continued significant results.

Detecting surface deformation. Geophysicists have been measuring crustal deformation for more than 100 years. Traditional methods are descended from techniques developed by surveyors, in which the surface is divided into many triangular patches. However, measurements could be obtained at only a few points for logistical reasons. Many spots are hard to get to, and the cost of sending people out for surveys forces compromises in the number of points, and hence the area, surveyed. By the 1980s, the development of the Global Positioning System (GPS) radically changed surveying by presenting the location of a ground receiver anywhere on Earth to a precision of better than 1 cm. But even GPS suffers the same vexing problems affecting traditional surveys. A person has to visit a site to place a receiver, and if a receiver is left behind, power must be supplied and data retrieved. This, in effect, limits the areas studied and the number of points where measurements are

acquired, which is why radar measurements have the potential to revolutionize crustal deformation investigations.

From their viewpoint high above the Earth, radar satellites can observe almost anywhere on the surface. The same advantages of immunity to darkness and cloud cover that spurred the initial development of radar for military reconnaissance are invaluable for geophysical investigations. At present, four civilian radar satellites are used for a variety of geophysical investigations, including studies of crustal deformation.

Today InSAR provides measurements with enough sensitivity, comprehensive coverage, and spatial density to allow the first peek at the details of crustal deformations similar to those expected from interseismic motions. Carried 800 km (500 mi) or more above the Earth on specialized satellites, interferometric radar instruments produce images of surface movements with better than 1 cm per year sensitivity over swaths 100 km (62 mi) or more in width, and at a resolution on the ground of 10 m (33 ft) or better.

InSAR technique. A radar sensor orbiting the Earth detects tiny changes on the ground by measuring very accurately changes in the time delay, or phase, of a radar echo. Radar systems form images by illuminating a fairly large portion of the surface, called the swath, with a series of pulses of microwave energy. By precise analysis of the reflected radio waves received back at the radar, the energy is redistributed according to the time delay and Doppler frequency shift of the pulse echoes, forming an "image" of the ground.

In the case of InSAR, a second radar image of the same ground area is acquired at a later time. If a comparison is made of the radar echoes from each

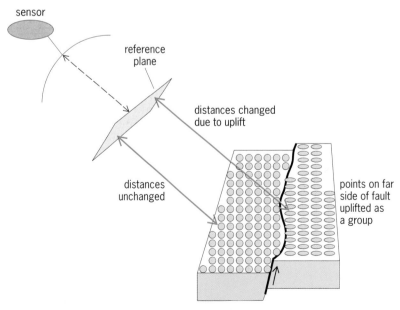

Fig. 1. Mechanism of phase shifts for surface displacements. If a point moves farther from the radar between observations, the time delay for its echo and its phase in the interferogram are increased.

point on the surface in each image, it is expected that the reflected signals in the second image will be the same as in the first image if the ground was unchanged between observations. But if the ground has shifted position over the time interval spanned by the images, the signal from the second image will be delayed in time proportionally to the difference in position (**Fig. 1**). The time delay is most sensitively measured by examining the phase of the echo signal, and can usually be determined to anywhere from 1/10 to 1/100 of a wavelength. Most radar satellites operate with wavelengths of a few centimeters, hence with a sensitivity of several millimeters or less.

It is quite difficult in practice to ensure that the radar platform returns to exactly the same position for the second observation. This is beyond the limits of navigation as currently available, so one must settle for returning only approximately to the same position. As a result, the surface will be viewed from a position near the initial position, resulting in some parallax distortion in every interferogram. Because an interferogram contains phase variations dependent on both topography and surface deformation, these effects must be separated if the interferograms are to be interpreted unambiguously. The topographic phase must be isolated and removed for deformation studies, and this can be done with either knowledge of the surface topography or additional satellite passes.

Deformation study examples. Perhaps the most obvious, and most devastating, form of deformation in the Earth's crust results from earthquakes, the sometimes-cataclysmic events that occur when stresses which have built up deep within the Earth's crust are released in a few seconds. Seismic waves carrying huge amounts of energy propagate in all directions from an earthquake's epicenter, and are recorded by seismometers. However, seismic techniques detect only the waves propagating through the crust after a fracture in the subsurface has occurred, with little or no warning of an earthquake until it happens. Clearly, if workers were able to

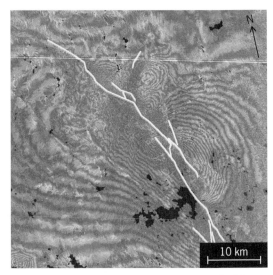

Fig. 2. Co-seismic interferogram of the magnitude-7.3 earthquake in Landers, CA, in 1992. The rich pattern of fringes shows 2.8-cm (1.1-in.) contours of surface displacement toward the radar, which can be interpreted to study the slip distribution of this event. (*NASA Jet Propulsion Laboratory*)

record deformations building up in the crust before any catastrophic rock failure, they not only would be able to better describe the physics of the earthquake but would also be closer to anticipating when such a failure might occur. Radar interferometry studies of earthquakes have already yielded detailed observations of crustal changes occurring during large earthquakes (**Fig. 2**). They have also detected finer-scale phenomena resulting from the flow of water through the pores of deep rocks due to the redistribution of the forces within the crust to a new equilibrium point after an earthquake. Studying such subsurface flows is important because they may indicate conditions leading to future fractures and seismic activity.

Earthquakes are not the only examples of ground motions that are the subject of interferometric investigation. Volcanoes, the surface venting of molten

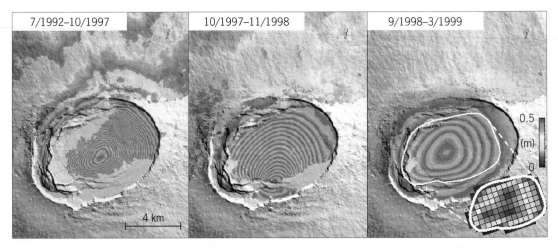

Fig. 3. Observed and subsequently modeled displacement field from the movement of magma beneath Sierra Negra volcano, Galápagos Islands. The inset at right is the inferred shape of the magma chamber. (*S. Jonsson, Stanford University*)

Fig. 4. Ice velocity measured at each point on the Petermann Glacier, Greenland. ma^{-1} = meters per year. (*Eric Rignot, NASA Jet Propulsion Laboratory*)

are significant inputs to global climate models. Because the polar regions are remote and inhospitable as well as large, glacier flow velocity measurements are an ideal application calling for space-borne radar.

Finally, surface subsidence phenomena such as those resulting from ground-water withdrawal are now allowing greater insight into resource management problems. In one study of Las Vegas Valley, the influence of faults on subsidence basins was conclusively demonstrated by the new, high-spatial-density measurements. Improved monitoring capabilities such as this one will allow improved use and conservation of resources such as water and oil.

Outlook. The application of radar interferometry as a technique for studying geophysical problems has been demonstrated by the scientific community. Many additional applications are in development, including measurements of subsidence from ground-water retrieval or from oil depletion. Still others likely remain to be discovered.

Today space-borne radar systems for scientific use are operated by the European Space Agency (the *Envisat* satellites), Canada (the *Radarsat* satellite), and Japan (*JERS-1*). Several new systems for free-flying interferometric radar satellites are under consideration by the U.S. space agency. Because interferometric data availability to the scientific community is a major factor in the advance of knowledge about many important geophysical problems, hopefully it will not be long before an optimized radar producing large amounts of crustal deformation data is in place.

For background information *see* DOPPLER EFFECT; EARTHQUAKE; FAULT AND FAULT STRUCTURES; GEODESY; INTERFEROMETRY; PLATE TECTONICS; RADAR; SEISMIC RISK; SYNTHETIC APERTURE RADAR (SAR); VOLCANO; VOLCANOLOGY in the McGraw-Hill Encyclopedia of Science & Technology.

Howard A. Zebker

Bibliography. F. Amelung et al., Sensing the ups and downs of Las Vegas: InSAR reveals structural control of land subsidence and aquifer-system deformation, *Geology*, 27(6):483–486, June 1999; D. Massonnet et al., The displacement field of the Landers earthquake mapped by radar interferometry, *Nature*, 364:138–142, 1993; H. A. Zebker et al., On the derivation of coseismic displacement fields using differential radar interferometry: The Landers earthquake, *J. Geophys. Res.*, 99:19,617–19,634, 1994.

rocks and gas from deep within the Earth, are another natural hazard that may be studied from minute changes in shape. Volcanic eruptions can threaten localities with lava, hot gases, and airborne debris, such as the eruption that buried Pompeii in Roman times. Explosions and mudflows are equally devastating, as seen by the destruction around Mount St. Helens in Washington state in 1980, or more recently by the massive mud and landslide damage caused by Mount Pinatubo in the Philippines. An example of a volcano application is shown in **Fig. 3**. A time series of InSAR measurements reveal variable deformation patterns in the Sierra Negra volcano, Galápagos, that are believed to be the result of the movement of magma beneath the volcano. The subsurface flow of magma forcing its way through existing rock layers distorts the crust, which we can measure from the deformation of the exposed surface. The deformation patterns are similar in the first and last periods, but a faulting event on the caldera rim dramatically altered its shape in the middle period. These patterns are diagnostic of changes in activity within the volcano.

Another area of active investigation using interferometric radar techniques is the measurement of the speed of moving glaciers in Antarctica and Greenland (**Fig. 4**). Whether or not ice is building up in the polar caps and how much is being discharged into the sea

Satellite radio

The concept of direct audio broadcasting from satellites to mobile and stationary receivers originated in the late 1980s as an outgrowth of direct television broadcasting from satellites to home receivers. There are currently two satellite radio systems (also known as satellite digital audio radio service) operating in the continental United States, while one is under construction to serve Japan and Korea, and another is in advanced planning stages to serve Europe.

The useful range of frequencies for radio transmission from satellites is 1–3 GHz, the most sought-after frequency band by all transmission services due to its superior propagation characteristics. Above 3 GHz, propagation losses and rain (precipitation) attenuation pose difficulties, and below 1 GHz, satellite antenna size and galactic noise (radio-frequency noise that originates outside the solar system) pose difficulties. The Federal Communications Commission (FCC) has allocated a frequency band of 2320–2345 MHz for satellite radio, which has been coordinated internationally. This frequency band cannot be used for any other service because the sensitivity, mobility, and antenna omnidirectionality of receivers require an interference-free environment. Of the available 25 MHz, a satellite radio system requires between 10 and 15 MHz bandwidth to support a reasonable number of audio programs. As a result, the FCC auctioned two 12.5-MHz-wide bands for satellite radio service, and granted licenses for two such systems in October 1997 to Sirius Satellite Radio Inc. and to XM Satellite Radio, Inc.

Technology. The technical challenge of satellite radio is in keeping service outages very infrequent and short. Service outages are caused by blockages, such as a building, structure, or mountain that obstructs the line-of-sight between a satellite and receiving antenna; by multipath, where received reflected signal components have sufficient amplitude and phase offset to corrupt (distort) the unreflected received signal; by foliage attenuation; and by interference, particularly the out-of-band emissions from transmitters in adjacent frequency bands.

The quality goal is to achieve continuity of service (that is, no outages) better than 99.9% of the time, excluding the time when a vehicle is indoors since the satellite transmissions do not substantially penetrate building walls. High service availability is accomplished by using high-power transmission satellites and by providing an unprecedented degree of transmission diversity in the system design.

Spatial diversity. This is accomplished by simultaneously broadcasting the same transmission from two satellites located in space so that their azimuths or elevation angles from the radio receiver are significantly different. Since the radio is designed to receive both transmissions, if the path from the radio to one of the satellites is blocked by a building or mountain, there will be no outage if the path to the other satellite is unobstructed.

Time diversity. This is accomplished by providing a 4–5-s offset either between transmissions from two satellites by a time delay or within each satellite transmission by a long interleaving span. If one or both transmissions are lost, the receiver continues to play using the portion of the transmission stored in a 4–5-s buffer memory, and no outage occurs if a transmission path is restored before the end of the stored signal. This technique is particularly effective in combating outages from roadway overpasses.

Frequency diversity. In this technique, two satellites transmit at different radio frequencies, several megahertz apart. Frequency diversity is effective in minimizing a form of multipath called frequency selective fading.

Modal diversity. Despite the many diversity techniques, it is impossible to provide high-quality service in dense urban areas since the blockage from buildings is overwhelming. However, this can be overcome by providing terrestrial repeaters. High-power broadcast transmitters located in dense urban areas are fed the same signal as transmitted from the satellite and then retransmit this signal in a frequency band between the two satellites' transmissions. A receiver with three channels, one for the terrestrial repeater and two for the diversity satellites, allows virtually uninterrupted service and seamless transition between satellite and terrestrial transmissions. The three signals, which are simultaneously received when available, are added together in a maximal ratio (diversity) combiner.

In addition to diversity, satellite elevation angle and the use of equalizers are important techniques for attaining high service availability.

Elevation angle. The elevation angle from the satellite to the radio is extremely important in mitigating blockage, multipath, and foliage attenuation. For geostationary orbits, the elevation angle is reduced as the location of the radio moves further north or south of the Equator. An alternative is to use a constellation of satellites in highly inclined, elliptical geosynchronous orbits so that high elevation angles can be provided to radios located at latitudes above 30°N (**Fig. 1**). In the Sirius geosynchronous satellite

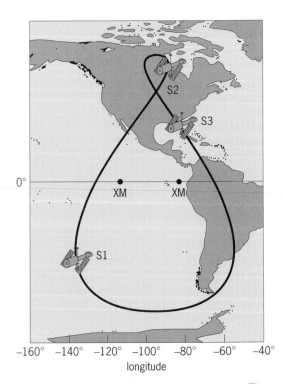

Fig. 1. Orbital locations of the XM geostationary satellites located at longitudes 85°W and 115°W, and the satellite ground track of the Sirius (S) geosynchronous satellite constellation.

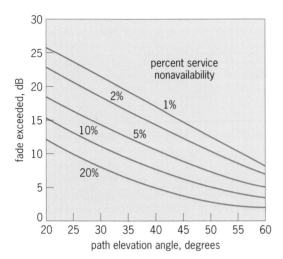

Fig. 2. Foliage attenuation.

constellation, three satellites follow each other at 8-h intervals and spend approximately 16 h north of the Equator and 8 h below.

The importance of elevation angle with regard to foliage attenuation is shown in **Fig. 2**. The difference between a 30° and a 60° elevation angle for a 99% service availability is over 13 dB, which means a satellite must transmit more than 20 times additional power at 30° than at 60° for equal service availability through foliage. **Figure 3** shows the importance of higher elevation angles for blockage reduction, where the blockage distance with a 60° elevation angle is only one-third of that with a 30° elevation angle. A high elevation angle also alleviates blockage outages from passing trucks.

Equalization. A technique for reducing outage from multipath is to have an equalizer in the receiver that compensates for a significant portion of the signal distortion in amplitude and phase caused by the multipath components. This is particularly effective in satellite radio for handling short multipath propagations that are caused, for example, by reflections from large, overhead roadway signs.

System design. For satellite radio, each satellite system generally provides 60 music channels and 40 voice channels. This mix can be changed and, if a market develops, one-way data channels can be substituted for one or more audio channels. The major elements of the system are the satellites, radios, and the broadcast studio/uplink (**Fig. 4**). The telemetry, tracking, and command (TT&C) subsystems that take care of the satellites are standard and use no new technology. Also, the terrestrial repeater network uses standard digital audio broadcasting (DAB) techniques.

Satellites. The satellites used are modifications of existing high-power communications satellites. The important technical modifications are conversion to 2.3-GHz transmitter operation, and concentration of the transmitter power to achieve a few megawatts (63–65 dBW) of effective isotropic radiated power (EIRP) over the relatively narrow transmission bandwidth (2.5–4.2 MHz). The high transmitter power

is achieved by paralleling many traveling-wave-tube amplifiers.

Radios. Radios have been produced for after-market installation in motor vehicles, boats, planes, and homes, as well as for installation during the assembly of motor vehicles. The receiver is a three-channel type with intelligent combining of the two satellite and terrestrial transmissions, when available. An application-specific integrated circuit (ASIC) chipset contains most of the required electronic circuits, excluding the antenna (omnidirectional with 3–5 dBi gain), radio-frequency amplifiers (typical system noise temperature of 160 K or −172°F), bulk memories, and power supply. The received digital signal is encrypted at the broadcast studio to prevent theft of service. In addition to having a decryptor in the receiver, each receiver has an embedded unique digital address. This allows the broadcast studio, through a service channel, to send messages and commands, which are recognized solely by the addressed receiver. Among other functions, this is used to turn subscriber service on and off.

Broadcast studio/uplink. These facilities include those used for generating the audio programming, as well as the resulting program signals' multiplexing, coding, modulation, and transmission (Fig. 4). The programming facilities are audio studios, using both recorded and live performances, which output in a digital form as a music or a voice channel. The channels are compressed, coded (the inner code is convolutional, the outer code is a Reed Solomon block code), multiplexed together using time division into one digital stream, modulated using quadrature phase shift keying, split into two identical signals, one of which is then time-delayed, translated to 7 GHz, and transmitted to the two active satellites. Other than the audio compression, the facilities and techniques are those used by newer communications satellite, terrestrial broadcast, and satellite television systems.

Audio compression. An audio compression technique, called perceptual audio coding (PAC), is the first extensive use of a technology developed over the past decade without which satellite radio would not

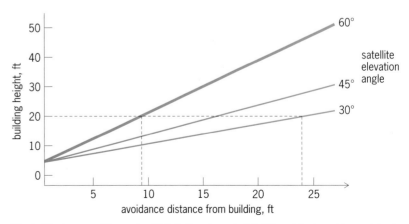

Fig. 3. Blockage avoidance. A vehicle (with antenna height 5 ft or 1.5 m) must be a minimal distance from a building to avoid blockage in the worse case. 1 ft = 0.3 m.

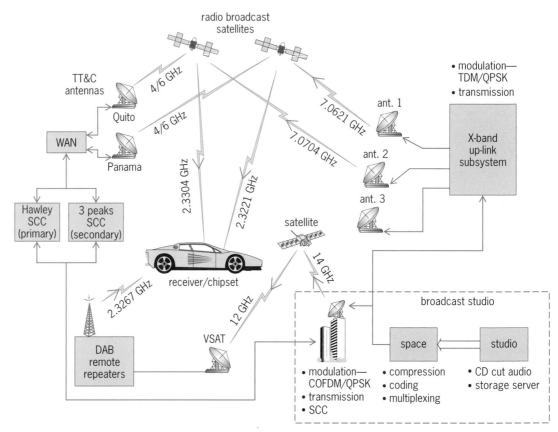

Fig. 4. Typical system for providing satellite radio service. TT&C = telemetry, tracking, and command; DAB = digital audio broadcasting; VSAT = very small aperture terminal; SCC = satellite control center; COFDM = coded othogonal frequency division modulation; QPSK = quadrature phase shift keying; TDM = time division modulation.

be practical or economic. It allows compact disk recordings (whose digital output is 1.2 mb/s) to be compressed to approximately 60 kb/s at the transmit studio and expanded in the radio receiver in a manner that the listener hears a music quality close to the uncompressed music. This is accomplished by compression/expansion algorithms which take advantage of the characteristics of the human ear (for example, its inability to hear certain sounds and artifacts). Similarly, a voice channel is compressed to approximately 25 kb/s.

Outlook. Satellite radio is in its infancy with regard to commercial success, which requires a few million subscribers for each system. New services and uses will unquestionably develop over the next several years. The possibilities of providing data, multimedia, and personalized services are already under investigation.

For background information *see* COMMUNICA-TIONS SATELLITE; DATA COMPRESSION; DIRECT BROADCASTING SATELLITE SYSTEMS; INFORMATION THEORY; MODULATION; RADIO BROADCASTING; RADIO SPECTRUM ALLOCATIONS in the McGraw-Hill Encyclopedia of Science & Technology.

Robert D. Briskman

Bibliography. R. D. Briskman and R. J. Prevaux, S-DARS broadcast from inclined, elliptical orbits, *52d International Astronautical Congress*, IAF-01-M.5.05, October 1-15, 2001; R. D. Briskman and S. P. Sharma, DARS satellite constellation performance, *AIAA 20th International Communications Satellite Systems Conference*, AIAA-2002-1967, May 12-15, 2002; Efficient high latitude service arc satellite mobile broadcasting systems, U.S. Patent and Trademark Office, 6,223,019, April 24, 2001; R. A. Michalski, An overview of the XM satellite radio system, *AIAA 20th International Communications Satellite Systems Conference*, AIAA-2002-1844, May 12-15, 2002; Mobile radio receivers using time diversity to avoid service outages in multichannel broadcast systems, U.S. Patent and Trademark Office, 5,592,471, January 7, 1997; Radio frequency broadcasting systems and methods using two low-cost geosynchronous satellites, U.S. Patent and Trademark Office, 5,319,673, June 7, 1994.

Satellites of outer planets

Each of the giant planets (Jupiter, Saturn, Uranus, and Neptune) hosts three types of natural satellites: regular satellites, collisional remnants, and irregular satellites. The regular satellites follow prograde orbits (in which they move in the same direction as the planets about the Sun) that are nearly circular and lie in the equatorial plane of their host at a distance of a few tens of planetary radii. Their sizes (about 1000 km or 600 mi) rival or exceed that of the Earth's Moon.

The smaller (about 10–100 km or 6–60 mi) collisional remnants also trace nearly circular, equatorial orbits, but they inhabit regions only a few planetary radii in extent and are often associated with planetary rings. At these distances, the more intense meteoroid flux, gravitationally focused by the planet, has collisionally disrupted presumably once-larger bodies. The sizes of the known irregular satellites overlap those of the collisional remnants, but the irregular satellites follow extended (hundreds of planetary radii) orbits with significant eccentricities and inclinations. These distinct orbital characteristics suggest different formation mechanisms: The regular satellites and the progenitors of the collisional remnant satellites are believed to have formed in a circumplanetary accretion disk, while the irregular satellites are generally thought to have been captured from heliocentric orbits. Although the regular satellites and collisional remnants have been and continue to be well studied by spacecraft missions, investigations of irregular satellites have been hampered by the small number of them that are known. However, in the past few years dozens more have been discovered, enlarging the known number from 11 to nearly 50. The larger number of examples of such bodies enables more detailed study of the mechanisms of their capture.

Search techniques. The increased rate of discovery of irregular satellites is primarily due to the availability of wide-field cameras on large telescopes, along with the computing facilities required to process and search the resulting data.

Irregular satellites are detected by being seen in reflected sunlight, at optical wavelengths. With their small sizes and large distances from the Sun, these bodies intercept little solar flux. Available evidence suggests that the surfaces of irregular satellites, as well as those of many other outer solar system bodies, are extremely dark, reflecting only a few percent of incident light. Earth-bound observers intercept even less of that reflected light. Thus, detecting distant irregular satellites requires large telescopes.

Furthermore, because the irregular satellites have extended orbits, large areas must be searched in order to find them. The most distant prograde orbits are limited by the Hill radius, the distance at which the gravity of the planet is balanced by the tidal perturbation from the Sun, given by Eq. (1),

$$R_H = a_p \left(\frac{m_p}{3M_\odot} \right)^{1/3} \qquad (1)$$

where m_p is the planet's mass, a_p is planet's semimajor axis, and $M_\odot$ is the Sun's mass. Although more distant stable retrograde orbits exist, all known irregular satellites orbit within one Hill radius. Viewed from Earth, the Hill radius subtends an angle of $4.8°$, $2.9°$, $1.5°$, and $1.5°$, respectively, for Jupiter, Saturn, Uranus, and Neptune. The photographic plates used in past searches could easily span a few degrees but were not sensitive enough to detect fainter satellites. Photographic media have been replaced by the much more sensitive charge-coupled device (CCD). A CCD is a solid-state silicon chip that detects and counts incident photons in an array of pixels, typically 2048 by 4096 pixels in size. These detectors have high quantum efficiency, high dynamic range, and excellent linearity, but their small sizes limit the typical field of view of an individual CCD to a few arcminutes. Searching the entire Hill sphere (the sphere within the Hill radius) of an outer planet with a single CCD is impractical. However, mosaic CCD cameras employ a grid of these devices to achieve wider detecting areas, tens of arcminutes on a side. With these cameras, such searches are now feasible.

Planetary satellites, as well as other solar system objects, are normally detected through their apparent motion on the sky. When an object is viewed near opposition (when the Earth lies on a line between the Sun and the object), this motion is principally due to parallax from the Earth's orbital motion around the Sun. The object's resulting apparent motion is in the retrograde direction, at a rate given by Eq. (2), where

$$\frac{d\theta}{dt} \approx \frac{148''/\text{h}}{\Delta} \qquad (2)$$

Δ is the distance from the Earth to the object in astronomical units. (An astronomical unit is the mean distance of the Earth from the Sun.) For the outer planets other than Jupiter, the intrinsic circumplanetary motion of a satellite is small in comparison to this apparent parallactic motion. Thus, satellites have a characteristic direction and rate of motion which, observed over the course of a single night, distinguishes them from background Kuiper belt objects or foreground asteroids and Centaurs.

Two techniques are used to detect the characteristic motion of irregular satellites. In the first, the blinked-image technique, a sequence of two to four (typically three) exposures of each field of view is taken. Each exposure is separated from the next by roughly an hour, enough time to clearly detect the apparent motion of a satellite. The large data sets produced by mosaic cameras cannot be efficiently examined by eye. Specialized software is used to identify candidate objects that move in a straight line at a constant rate. This can be done at the telescope in real time. Observers then confirm or reject the candidates by eye.

In the second approach, the pencil-beam technique, a long series of successive images of the same field is taken. The exposure time totals 3–6 h. The images are shifted and recombined at the rates and directions expected for satellites tracking their host planet. Objects moving at that rate and direction appear stationary with a circular profile; other objects appear trailed (see **illus.**). Again, the human operator examines the frames, looking for the point sources.

Regardless of the detection method used, subsequent observations over the course of several months are necessary to determine the circumplanetary orbits of the newly discovered satellites.

Recent searches. In September 1997, B. Gladman, P. Nicholson, and J. J. Kavelaars conducted a cursory search of the immediate vicinity of Uranus with the

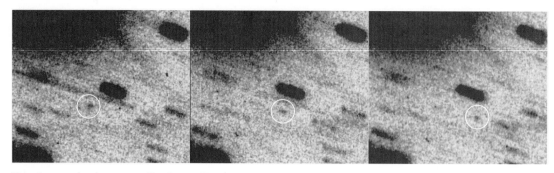

Three images showing a recent Uranian satellite candidate. The full data set has been subdivided into three groups which were shifted at the rate and direction of the motion of Uranus and then combined. The satellite candidate is indicated by the circle in each image and can be seen moving from left to right. The elongated features are stars that have been smeared out by the shifting process.

Palomar 5-m (200-in.) telescope, equipped with a single-chip CCD camera. This search examined four fields adjacent to Uranus, yielding the discovery of Sycorax and Caliban, the first two known irregular satellites of Uranus.

In July 1999, Gladman, Kavelaars, M. Holman, and J.-M. Petit conducted a more complete search of Uranus and Neptune with the Canada-France-Hawaii 3.6-m (194-in.) telescope (CFHT) with its mosaic CCD camera. This covered 6.5 square degrees around both Uranus and Neptune, encompassing the entire Hill sphere of each planet. This search yielded the discovery of three Uranian satellites: Setebos, Stephano, and Prospero, as well as about 40 Kuiper belt objects. No new Neptunian satellites were found.

Through the fall and winter 2000, this same team conducted a concerted search for Saturnian irregular satellites, using a variety of telescopes equipped with mosaic cameras. As before, a three-image technique was used to search the entire Hill sphere of Saturn. Twelve new Saturnian irregular moons were discovered, along with about 20 Kuiper belt objects.

During the period 2000–2002, S. S. Sheppard, D. C. Jewitt, Y. R. Fernandez, G. Magnier, and J. Kleyna conducted Jovian satellite searches with the University of Hawaii's 2.2-m (87-in.) telescope and mosaic CCD camera. These searches have, to date, yielded 22 satellites. One of these was 1975 J1, a satellite discovered 25 years earlier by C. Kowal but subsequently lost.

In July and August 2001, Holman and Kavelaars conducted a search for fainter satellites of Uranus and Neptune. This survey used the Cerro Tololo Inter-American Observatory's 4-m (158-in.) telescope and the CFHT. Unlike the previous searches which used the blinked-image technique, this search used the pencil-beam technique to detect fainter satellites. Three Uranian (see illus.) and two Neptunian satellite candidates were discovered. Follow-up observations were lost to poor weather; the orbits of all these candidates were not determined well enough to establish conclusively that the candidates were in bound satellite orbits.

Origins. Asteroids and comets can be temporarily captured into orbit about a planet. Comet Shoemaker/Levy 9, the fragments of which orbited Jupiter several times before finally colliding with the planet, provided a spectacular example of this phenomenon. However, aside from impacting the planet, such a temporarily captured body will eventually escape to heliocentric orbit unless enough orbital energy is dissipated or exchanged to render its circumplanetary orbit permanent.

Hypotheses for this process fall into four categories: (1) an increase in the mass of the planet through the accretion of nearby material, (2) a collision with an extant moon or between two temporarily captured objects, (3) gravitational interaction with an extant moon or another temporarily captured object, and (4) gas drag in extended envelopes or disks surrounding the still-forming planets.

A startling feature of the irregular satellites can be used to help distinguish among these possibilities. The orbits of the irregular satellites cluster in a number of tight groups. The members of each group share similar semimajor axes, eccentricities, and inclinations. This was seen earlier among the Jovian irregulars when only eight (four prograde and four retrograde) were known. Now this is seen to be common, occurring in the irregular satellite systems of Jupiter, Saturn, and Uranus. Furthermore, the variation among the orbits of the members of each group is consistent with a collisional dispersal of progenitor. The means of capture of the progenitor bodies has yet to be definitively established, although gas drag is most commonly accepted. The goal of future searches for irregular satellites, as well as continued study of the physical properties of those presently known, is to establish which of the capture mechanisms predominated.

For background information *see* ASTEROID; CHARGE-COUPLED DEVICES; COMET; JUPITER; KUIPER BELT; NEPTUNE; SATELLITE (ASTRONOMY); SATURN; URANUS in the McGraw-Hill Encyclopedia of Science & Technology.   Matthew J. Holman

Bibliography. B. Gladman et al., Discovery of 12 satellites of Saturn exhibiting orbital clustering, *Nature*, 412(6843):163–166, 2001; B. Gladman et al., NOTE: The discovery of Uranus XIX, XX, and XXI, *Icarus*, 147:320–324, 2000; S. J. Peale, Origin and evolution of the natural satellites, *Annu. Rev. Astron. Astrophys.*, 37:533–602, 1999; J. B. Pollack, J. A. Burns, and M. E. Tauber, Gas drag in primordial circumplanetary envelopes: A mechanism for satellite capture, *Icarus*, 37:587–611, 1979; S. S. Sheppard et al., Satellites of Jupiter, *Int. Astron. Union Circ.*, no. 7555, p. 1, 2001; S. S. Sheppard, D. C. Jewitt, and J. Kleyna, Satellites of Jupiter, *Int. Astron. Union Circ.*, no. 7900, p. 1, 2002.

Security printing

As a result of the recent proliferation of easily accessible electronic imaging hardware and software, printers specializing in the production of secure documents, packages, and labels (security printers) are now faced with new challenges and threats, but also opportunities. The ultimate goal of the security printer is to produce items in a way that deters counterfeiters, forgers, fraudsters, and terrorists from unauthorized copying or alterations of authentic items while maintaining the items' functionality, design, and esthetics. Counterfeiting, forgery, and the production of fake products ("knockoffs" of brand-name products) were recently defined in broadest terms as an infringement of property rights both real and intellectual, and it was estimated that worldwide they cost brand owners in excess of $260 billion dollars per year.

In past decades, security printing was a highly specialized field, since the reproduction process required specialty materials with limited availability, a large initial investment in specialty printing presses, and the experience and knowledge of printing craftspeople. These same limitations were also imposed on the would-be counterfeiters, and therefore most counterfeiting was done by organized crime, with banknotes (currency) being the favorite item to counterfeit due to their high return on investment.

However, with the advent of low-cost desktop computers, digital cameras, scanners, high-resolution ink jet and dye sublimation printers, and appropriate software, a new generation of counterfeiters was born and subsequently termed "digifeiters" by the U.S. Department of State Bureau of Consular Affairs and the U.S. Bureau of Engraving and Printing. Most of these counterfeiters had little knowledge of the printing process, but they were computer-literate. They no longer tried to make exact replicas of the original documents that could be identified as counterfeit only by forensic examination, but produced "look-alikes" that were just good enough to fool the general public. By and large, the digifeiters were neither members of organized crime nor terrorists, but students and individuals with ordinary occupations. Their counterfeiting activites generally were not focused on banknotes, but on event tickets, parking permits, store coupons, gift certificates, false driver licenses and personal identifications, and so forth.

Thus, today's security printer must design security documents, packages, and labels with layers of covert and overt deterrents to counterfeiting, using new concepts, new materials, and technologies that are not readily available to the would-be counterfeiter. However, these same counterfeiting deterrents must also be easily detected by the human eye (overt devices), for example, by a ticket taker at a special event, or they must be machine-readable (covert devices) only at the point of transaction.

Traditional security features. One of the oldest and perhaps the first device used for security printing is the watermark. A watermark is an image that is an integral part of the printing substrate (usually paper) produced during the manufacture of the substrate. It is defined as an optically variable device (OVD) because it changes appearance from a negative image when viewed with reflected light to a positive image when viewed with transmitted light. The U.S. Treasury Department selected the watermark as one of the counterfeiting deterrents to be used in the design of all the new currency denominations, starting with the one hundred dollar bill and ending with the five dollar bill.

The guilloche, or fine-line security pattern, consists of two or more bands of continuous, sinusoidal, overlapping, lacy line patterns that are usually present around the borders of security-printed documents such as titles of ownership, licenses to practice a profession, birth certificates, or financial instruments (for example, stocks and bonds). Sometimes these interwoven patterns are produced on a printing press using two single-pigment colored inks in a split ink fountain, thus allowing the two colors to mix and form a third color on the security-printed document. The idea behind using the guilloche patterns is to exceed the resolution limits of commercially available photocopy machines and thus prevent faithful reproduction of the original document. Today's sophisticated color copiers and digital cameras render this deterrent less effective than in the past. Still, most digital image capture devices break up the continuous lines of the guilloche into dot patterns, and the blended third color is often not reproducible by most of the common process colors found in today's color copying equipment.

The void pantograph is most often used to deter check forgery and counterfeiting of checks with commercially available photocopiers. With this approach, a hidden word (pantograph) becomes visible in a photocopy of a check, rendering it useless. For checks, the pantograph is the word "void." The principle behind the void pantagraph is that an image produced at a higher screen ruling than its surrounding camouflage background pattern will become visible as a result of increased contrast during the reproduction cycle or by using commercially available copy machines.

Trademark or spot colors are generally reproduced by special single-pigment printing inks and are very difficult to replicate with commercially available process color. Metallic inks result in photocopies that are easily distinguishable from the original document. Conventional fluorescent inks are covert in nature; that is, they appear to be a given color under normal lighting and viewing conditions, but change color and appear to self-luminesce when viewed under an ultraviolet light source.

Microtext, font size 15 to 90 micrometers, is usually printed as a repeating alphanumeric message and appears to be a continuous line of some geometric shape. Printers can cleverly design copy with signature lines or outline portraits or pictures with microline text. This is an excellent deterrent against the counterfeiting of documents, currency, and other financial instruments such as checks.

There are several postpress operations that the printer can use to provide additional layers of security by requiring special materials or specialized equipment not readily available to counterfeiters. These operations include embossing, die cutting, perforations, random numbering using alphanumerics, clear film lamination, and foil stamping.

Magnetic inks are made from conventional carbon black inks but contain particles of iron oxide. The iron oxide serves as a magnet and the resultant magnetic flux can be read with a machine that is equipped with magnetic ink character recognition detectors, or MICR systems. Magnetic inks, though still in use today on checks and banknotes, have lost much of their effectiveness as a counterfeiting deterrent because they are readily available as photocopy toners.

New technologies. New electronic imaging technologies have turned the previous art and craft of counterfeiting into an almost pedestrian activity that does not require great knowledge of the printing process, but computer literacy. Therefore, the printer must continually search for new technologies that can be effectively applied to the security printing processes to deter counterfeiting activities. The following are new technologies that may have fallen prey to digifeiters and some highly skilled counterfeiters to some degree but are still considered excellent counterfeiting deterrents and will hold up under forensic examination or are covert in nature and only machine-readable.

Optically variable devices. In general, the term "optically variable device" (OVD) refers to an object that changes its appearance as its spatial orientation is changed. That is, as it is rotated or tilted and the angle of observation or illumination is changed, either the observed content of the object changes or its color changes. These two types are classified as either noniridescent or iridescent diffractive optically variable devices (DOVDs), respectively. The noniridescent DOVD that is perhaps most familiar to the general public is the 3D hologram often found on credit cards. More advanced holograms, in which the image changes or appears to be in motion as the hologram is rotated or tilted, are known as kinegrams and pixelgrams. Both the kinegram and pixelgram appear to be three-dimensional, moving, or changing pictorials. The difference between a kinegram and a pixelgram is the manufacturing and creation process. The kinegram is created via a photographic process using lasers, whereas the pixelgram is computer-generated from pixels. Such holograms rely on em-

bossing highly reflective foils with fine line rulings in excess of 10,000 lines/cm (25,400 lines/in.) with the observed 3D image the result of Fraunhofer diffraction. DOVDs that change color with object orientation are generally produced by using multiple layers of high-refractive-index thin films that produce interfering light waves, Bragg diffraction, and the desired color shifts.

Planchets are small disks with a diameter of approximately one millimeter that are implanted between paper fibers during the paper-making process as security features. The color-shifting planchets on some of the Dutch guilder notes and the thin-film structures on some Canadian bank notes are DOVDs based on Bragg diffraction structures, whereas the color-shifting ink found on U.S. currency is the result of highly reflective microstructures oriented within the ink film itself, producing the desired Fresnel diffraction phenomena and resulting color shift.

More recently the development of nonmetallic holograms (thin film, high index of refraction, reduced metallic content materials) have given the security printer more options and opportunities to deter counterfeiting.

Ink technologies. Thermochromic inks (mixtures of specific lanthanide chelates synthesized with beta-diketone ligands) and photochromic inks (spiro-compounds and fulgides) are security printing inks that change color when they absorb heat or are exposed to high-energy light sources, respectively. They have been available for several decades, but only in recent times have ink formulators been able to suspend sufficient amounts of these materials in ink vehicles suitable for commercial printing processes. One attractive property associated with thermochromic or photochromic inks on security documents is that the changes are reversible. That is, once the heat or light is removed, the document returns to its original color or image. For example, the thermochromic image might change color or disappear by simply pressing on the image with a finger or thumb, and then revert to its original color or content when the digit is removed. This can be easily observed by bank tellers, retailers, and others. Another attractive feature of thermochromic and photochromic inks is that they are available only from a limited number of sources with distribution under tight control. Thermochromic and photochromic inks may also be used in combination with other types of security printing inks, such as the following:

Magnetic inks. Inks containing ferromagnetic particles are generally used in banknotes and checks; they allow for magnetic ink character recognition (MICR) and are detectable only by machines.

Erasable inks. This type of ink and paper substrate is often used to discourage the alteration of documents by mechanical means (for example, by scraping off ink images with a razor blade). They are easily removed but leave visual evidence of tampering.

Fugitive inks. These inks are reactive to either water or solvents and usually leave an unwanted stain on the document if alteration has been attempted.

Fluorescent inks. Visible fluorescent inks are often used in documents, labels, and packages to deter counterfeiting while maintaining visible information for the observer. The images produced by printing visible fluorescent inks appear visible to the observer under white light sources and are observed as very bright colors. They change their appearance under short or long wavelength ultraviolet (UV) and fluoresce, or glow.

Coin-reactive inks. These inks are invisible to the human eye under normal lighting conditions but produce an image when rubbed with a coin. That is, the inks contain a reagent that reacts to the metallic materials contained in the coin to form a visible compound.

Invisible fluorescent inks. These inks are more advanced than the visible fluorescent inks. They are covert security devices, invisible under normal viewing conditions, becoming visually detectable under either ultraviolet or infrared (IR) radiation.

Bleed-through inks. A bleed-through ink is a specialty ink that is invisible on the printed side of the document, but shows up as a colored image on the reverse side of the document. This is an excellent low-cost counterfeiting deterrent often used to secure gift certificates and retail store vouchers.

Micro taggents. Micro taggents are another security printing technology and have multiple applications. They are microscopic (10^{-6} m) particles that are color-coded and dispersed into the printing ink. They are visible only under magnification, and the color coding provides for unique signatures, thus allowing identification, authentication, and verification.

Digital watermarks. The modern-day counterpart to the traditional watermark is the digital watermark, a digital image embedded in the microstructure of an existing image file whose location and structure is known only to the creator of the original image file. The files are imaged onto a substrate such as paper to produce the desired image, but that image now contains a hidden watermark that is only machine-readable. To view the hidden digital watermark, one needs appropriate software and an image capture device for visual display and verification.

New substrates. Traditional printing has always been the process of transferring printing ink onto a porous paper (or board) substrate via a printing press. However, with today's advances in printing technologies, the printer can now transfer ink images onto nontraditional, nonporous substrates such as plastic film and foils. This allows the security printer to take advantage of the physical properties of these nonporous substrates, such as tear resistance, resistance to moisture, solvents, and UV, and heat or abrasion resistance. In addition, these materials can be transparent, translucent, or opaque. These optical features allow design of multilayer documents with see-through windows, interference filters, color filters, and so forth, thus providing additional layers of

sophisticated optical devices that help deter counterfeiting. Along with such nonporous materials, there have been several advances in traditional security paper substrates. These include such devices as visible and invisible microfluorescent threads, microtext printed on plastic threads and embedded in the paper substrate, and solvent/water-reactive coatings that leave tamper-evident marks which indicate attempts to alter or forge documents, labels, or packages.

For background information *see* DIFFRACTION; HOLOGRAPHY; INK; PAPER; PHOTOCOPYING PROCESSES; PRINTING; ULTRAVIOLET RADIATION in the McGraw-Hill Encyclopedia of Science & Technology.

Richard Warner

Bibliography. M. Buystead, Security inks: More than meets the eye, *Product Image Security Convention (PISEC) of the Americas*, no. 23, October 4, 2000; D. C. Gordon, The need for security print, *Graphic Arts Technical Foundation, Security Printing Conference*, no. 1, August 2000; D. Krysick, Brand owners beware: What piracy is really costing your firm, *Product Image Security Convention (PISEC)*, no. 17, October 23, 2002; B. Lalk-Menzel, Tuning up the automotive parts market, *Reconnaissance International, Authentication and Counterfeiting Protection*, no. 5, January 30, 2002; J. Mercer and C. Sara, Technology advancements in currency and security documents, *Graphic Arts Technical Foundation, TechAlert '99*, no. 1, February 2, 1999; F. W. Sears and M. W. Zemansky, *College Physics*, 3d ed., Addison-Wesley, Reading, MA, 1960; R. L. Van Renesse, *Optical Document Security*, 2d ed. Artech House, Boston, 1998.

Semiconductor factory automation

The latest generation of semiconductor factories incorporates very advanced automation systems primarily due to their unique manufacturing requirements. Besides being very large [15,000–20,000 m^2 (160,000–215,000 ft^2) cleanroom], they contain hundreds of pieces of equipment for producing some of the most complex products ever manufactured. The manufacturing process consists of 500–700 discrete steps, and often the same equipment is revisited many times in the production flow. The resulting complexity (tracking, identifying, transporting, storing, and process control) challenges factory designers, and equipment and automation system suppliers. The semiconductor industry's recent transition from 200-mm-diameter (8-in.) to 300-mm-diameter (12-in.) wafers necessitated an even higher degree of automation. The main driver was ergonomic constraints imposed by the weight of the 300-mm wafer carriers [>8 kg (18 lb)] coupled with a high rate of material movement. Automation systems are now required for moving and storing all work-in-process (WIP) material. In addition, this transition provided an opportunity for companies to integrate the changes in equipment and operational parameters

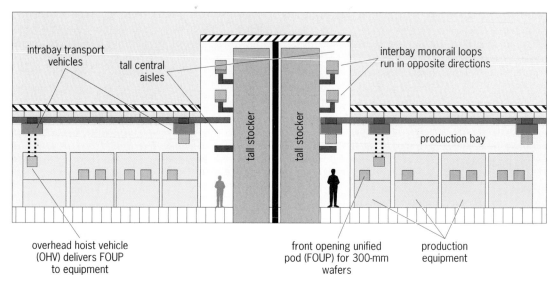

intrabay transport vehicles

tall central aisles

interbay monorail loops run in opposite directions

tall stocker

tall stocker

production bay

overhead hoist vehicle (OHV) delivers FOUP to equipment

front opening unified pod (FOUP) for 300-mm wafers

production equipment

Fig. 1. Cross-sectional view of a 300-mm fully automated factory showing tall central aisles for storage and multiple levels of interbay and intrabay transport systems.

into an overall factory design aimed at significantly improving productivity, manufacturing flexibility, and cost.

Automated material handling system. Central to such a factory is an automated material handling system (AMHS). It transports wafer carriers, called front opening unified pods (FOUPs), to production equipment for processing, as well as to and from automatic storage and retrieval systems, called stockers, that hold the work-in-process between sequential processing steps. The automated material handling system is operated as two different overhead monorail transportation systems that are physically connected through the stockers (**Fig. 1**). Interbay robotic vehicles provide long-distance transportation across the factory, and within a functional area the intrabay vehicles with automatic loading and unloading equip-

ment transport the FOUPs. This separation of transport functions reduces vehicle traffic congestion and eases recovery when a problem occurs. This is critical in a high-volume factory, where more than 3000 FOUPs per hour are moved by more than 250 robotic vehicles, 24 hours a day, 365 days a year. Integrated system reliability is critical to minimize chaos and manufacturing disruption from system failure. For example, a 5-min stoppage of the automated material handling system will result in more than 250 FOUPs being in the wrong location, and recovery is very complex. As a result, maintenance of an automated material handling system requires extensive planning and factory-wide coordination.

Interface standards. For full automation to be cost-effective, each major system was designed based on interface standardization. A 5-year effort, driven by the leading semiconductor manufacturers and coordinated through SEMATECH (a nonprofit industry consortium), convinced building designers, production equipment and automation suppliers, software providers, and semiconductor manufacturers to design, test, and accept systems around common and open (nonproprietary) software specifications and mechanical interface standards. **Figure 2** shows a highly simplified sketch of the standards that were fundamental to achieving interoperability of the different systems. Compliance with these standards has reduced risk, lowered costs, improved reliability, and increased production rates. The 200-mm wafer factory did not specify this level of standardization, and as a result, pervasive automation could not be reliably and cost-effectively achieved.

Computer-integrated manufacturing. Although the automated material handling system is the most visible element, there are many other breakthrough computer-integrated manufacturing (CIM) systems that leverage the Internet and manage production targets, material scheduling and dispatching, process

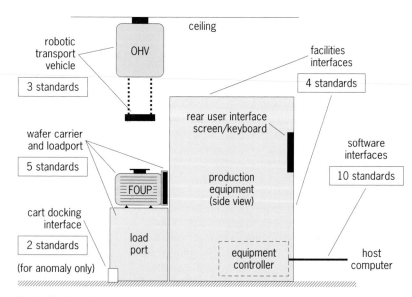

robotic transport vehicle

3 standards

wafer carrier and loadport

5 standards

cart docking interface

2 standards

(for anomaly only)

ceiling

OHV

facilities interfaces

4 standards

rear user interface screen/keyboard

software interfaces

10 standards

FOUP

production equipment (side view)

load port

equipment controller

host computer

Fig. 2. Number of nonproprietary (open) standards that were used to successfully create a fully automated semiconductor production line.

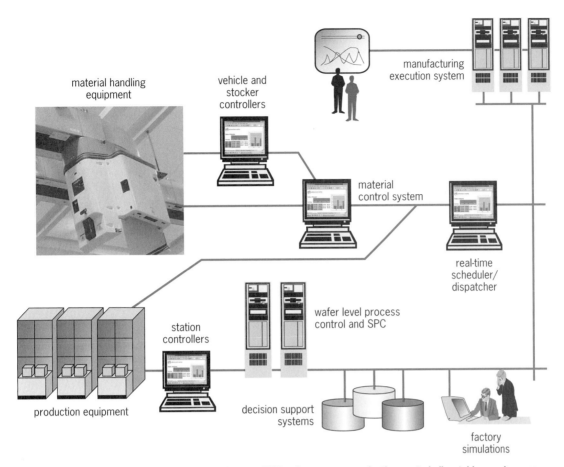

Fig. 3. High-level view of the integrated automation capabilities that manage production control, dispatching, and process control functions.

control systems for optimizing manufacturing yield, and other real-time decision support systems in the factory. Systems also control other critical manufacturing functions such as FOUP tracking, wafer-level tracking, equipment status tracking, preventive maintenance, and unscheduled repair actions. Dynamic factory simulations permit manufacturing personnel to estimate the possibility of capacity bottlenecks occurring, and allow them to take corrective action before a problem occurs on the production floor. **Figure 3** shows a conceptual sketch of some of the computer-integrated manufacturing capabilities.

The material controls system determines the optimum transport sequence to move the FOUP from its current location, and transport vehicles are scheduled to perform these moves. FOUPs are automatically scheduled to the next available equipment in its processing sequence as soon as a loadport of the destination equipment becomes available. An intrabay vehicle transports the FOUP to the assigned loadport, where its identification tag is automatically read and verified. The processing instruction is then loaded from the host computer, and processing is initiated without human intervention. During processing, advance process control (APC) systems provide real-time control functions that minimize run-to-run variability, automatically detect equip-

ment faults, and reduce rework. If an exception is detected, the equipment is shut down, and no new FOUPs are routed to that equipment. In addition, statistical process control (SPC) systems continuously monitor the entire line and dynamically change the inspection frequency and FOUP routing sequence at numerous points in the flow, depending upon process "health" and statistical process control limits. Statistical process control systems also put material on hold to prevent further processing if critical parameters are exceeded, and notify manufacturing personnel via paging. Once processing is completed, intrabay and interbay-transport vehicles move the FOUP to the closest upstream location. Real-time status tracking of all equipment loadports across the factory enables the automation systems to keep all production equipment running without interruption. This continuous mode of operation has greatly improved factory productivity.

Factory design attributes. A highly automated factory design is based on a vision of systems integration in which the factory layout and operational policies are integrated with the automated material handling system from the start. The entire factory—building structure, floor layout, and work-in-process management—is designed to provide rapid FOUP transport and storage. The layout is optimized to maximize output and streamline production equipment maintenance functions. The layout is a hybrid of job-shop (one function) and manufacturing cells (multiple functions) to optimize equipment change-outs, maintenance efficiency, and output. Support space, which is not directly used for production, is reduced to a minimum. For example, the automated material handling system occupies minimum space in the cleanroom, and is achieved by raising the cleanroom ceiling around areas where stockers are located, and stacking multiple levels of transportation rails (Fig. 1). Other facilities systems such as electrical, plumbing, utilities, bulk chemical distribution, and specialty gases are designed with flexibility and redundancy.

Automated factory and personnel. Despite the extensive automation, there is a very big role for manufacturing personnel. In older factories, where work-in-process movement was manual, layouts were optimized to help workers move material and operate equipment. As a result, operations were aligned to the production flow, and workstations were designed for ergonomic efficiency. On a new 300-mm line, there is no longer a need for workers to manually transport FOUPs from point to point, or load/unload and start/stop equipment all day. Automation systems now do that.

Aided extensively by computer information systems, the workers focus on equipment and manufacturing yield monitoring, troubleshooting and diagnosis, production line balancing, equipment maintenance and repair, spare-parts optimization, and new equipment installations. Traditional computer screens and user interfaces, which once were found on the front of the production equipment, are mostly gone, as that space is reserved for automated material handling system loading and unloading. Interfaces are located at the rear of the equipment and used mainly for maintenance and repair. Rear user interfaces (Fig. 2) reduce "people traffic" along the front side, reducing the space needed. Space reduction has enabled more production equipment to be installed in a cleanroom.

The use of remote diagnostics is being adopted in order to improve communication between factory personnel and equipment suppliers. Real-time collaboration between an equipment supplier's expert and a technician on the factory floor has reduced equipment installation and certification times. Using the Internet, an expert can log onto the factory equipment computer from an off-site location and collaborate with manufacturing personnel who are on the factory floor. This enables faster problem diagnosis and permits the downloading of new software fixes, as necessary, to bring the equipment online rapidly. In addition, productivity is enhanced when supplier technicians within a factory have access to important information stored within their own company's computers—schematics, technical and safety bulletins, parts lists, and up-to-date equipment manuals. The semiconductor industry is starting to benefit from remote diagnostics in manufacturing.

With reliable automation systems, semiconductor factories are achieving breakthrough production efficiencies. This path is not without high risks because such factory costs are in excess of $2.5 billion, but operating in an ever-changing industry, the potential rewards are enormous.

For background information *see* AUTOMATION; COMPUTER-AIDED DESIGN AND MANUFACTURING; COMPUTER-INTEGRATED MANUFACTURING; FLEXIBLE MANUFACTURING SYSTEM; INTEGRATED CIRCUITS; MANUFACTURING ENGINEERING; MATERIALS HANDLING; ROBOTICS in the McGraw-Hill Encyclopedia of Science & Technology.   Devadas Pillai

Bibliography. D. Pillai et al., Integration of 300-mm fab layouts and material handling automation, *Proceedings of 1999 International Symposium of Semiconductor Manufacturing*, October 11–13, 1999; D. Pillai and T. Abell, Accelerating 300-mm conversion using industry standards, *Proceedings of Semicon*, December 1, 1999; D. Pillai and S. Srinivasan, Material handling automation—Trends, vision and future plans, *Proceedings of 1996 International Symposium of Semiconductor Manufacturing*, October 1996; B. Sohn, D. Pillai, and N. Acker, 300-mm factory design for operational effectiveness, *Proceedings of the European IEEE/SEMI Semiconductor Manufacturing Conference*, April 2–3, 2000.

Semiconductor refrigerators

Solid-state cooling modules based on the thermoelectric Peltier effect are used to cool microprocessors, medical specimens, camping coolers, scientific instruments, and equipment in space satellites, among many other things. The cooling is produced at a junction of dissimilar conducting materials through which an electric current is passed, and as there are no moving parts the devices are vibration-free and reliable. Unfortunately, these modules are not nearly as efficient as vapor compression-expansion refrigerators, which are therefore preferred for nearly all cooling applications from domestic refrigerators and freezers to very large air-conditioning systems. New advanced materials having nanometer-scale internal structure may well improve Peltier modules and open the door to the universal use of thermoelectric cooling, free from gases which enhance the greenhouse effect if released into the atmosphere.

Peltier cooling. A Peltier-effect cooler is a solid-state heat pump that uses the flow of electrons and holes in semiconductors to generate a flow of heat from a cold plate to a hot plate. It is the exact inverse of the thermoelectric generator, in which the same flow of electrons produces a voltage between hot and cold junctions of dissimilar conducting materials (the Seeback effect), and thereby generates electric power. The geometry of a Peltier cooler is the same as that of a thermoelectric generator (**Fig. 1**). The simplest device consists of two blocks of

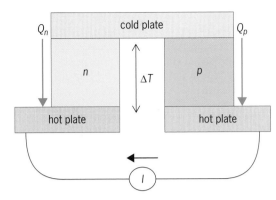

Fig. 1. Single thermoelectric cooler (couple). When a current flows in the circuit, electron and holes in the *n*- and *p*-type semiconductors carry heat (Q_n and Q_p) away from the cold plate, causing cooling ΔT.

semiconductor, one *p*-type and the other *n*-type, thermally anchored to a cold plate and a hot plate. A current *I* is made to pass through the two semiconductors, which are electrically connected in series. Practical coolers capable of pumping more heat are made by connecting several of these devices (couples) together (**Fig. 2**). Each branch, *n* and *p*, of the couple shown in Fig. 1 pumps a flow of heat *Q* that is related to the current *I* by the Peltier coefficient Π, Eqs. (1) and (2). Here the Peltier coefficients $\Pi_{n,p}$

$$Q_p = \Pi_p\, I \qquad (1)$$

$$Q_n = -\Pi_n\, I \qquad (2)$$

are related to the thermopower $S_{n,p}$ of the material and the average temperature *T* by the Kelvin-Onsager relation, Eq. (3).

$$\Pi_{n,p} = S_{n,p} T \qquad (3)$$

The efficiency of a refrigeration system is characterized by a coefficient of performance (COP), which is defined as Eq. (4). It has been shown that the

$$\mathrm{COP} = \frac{\text{heat extracted from the cold plate}}{\text{work absorbed}} \qquad (4)$$

thermodynamic efficiency of the thermoelectric cooler which has a temperature difference ΔT

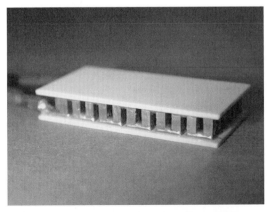

Fig. 2. Commercial Peltier cooler consisting of several couples connected together between aluminum oxide (Al_2O_3) plates.

across it is that of an ideal Carnot cycle if *S* is independent of the mean temperature *T* (as is usually approximately true); that is, the coefficient of performance is given by Eq. (5). However, this is true

$$\mathrm{COP} = \frac{T}{\Delta T} - \frac{1}{2} \qquad (5)$$

only if the heat conducted back from the hot to the cold side, as well as the heat generated by the electric current flowing through the resistance of the device (the Joule heat), can be neglected. Unfortunately, these two effects are far from negligible for usable temperature differences and heat flows, and are the root cause of the poor efficiency of existing devices.

The reverse heat flow is related to the thermal conductivities $K_{n,p}$ of the materials, and the Joule heating to their electrical conductivities $\sigma_{n,p}$. It can be shown that Eq. (6) relates the COP to the material

$$\mathrm{COP} = \frac{T \cdot (\sqrt{1 + Z \cdot T} - 1)}{\Delta T \cdot (\sqrt{1 + Z \cdot T} + 1)} - \frac{1}{2} \qquad (6)$$

parameters (*S*, κ and σ) and to *T* and ΔT. Here it is assumed that the *n*- and *p*-type semiconductors have the same conductivities κ and σ and that $S_n = -S_p$. The materials properties are collected in Eq. (7) into

$$Z = \frac{S^2 \cdot \sigma}{\kappa} \qquad (7)$$

a single parameter *Z*, called the figure of merit, a measure of the utility of a given thermoelectric material for cooling.

It is customary to use the dimensionless product *ZT* to characterize thermoelectric materials. Values for commercial materials, based on bismuth telluride (Bi_2Te_3) alloys, are on the order of $ZT = 0.9$ near room temperature. **Figure 3** shows a plot of Eq. (6), with the COP of refrigerators given as a function of *ZT* for two values of temperature differences encountered in commercial systems. It compares the efficiency of thermoelectric coolers with vapor-compression refrigeration systems that use tetrafluoroethane ($C_2H_2F_4$ or R134a) as the working fluid. Clearly, a material with $ZT > 2$ at room temperature must be developed for thermoelectric cooling to become competitive with vapor-compression systems.

Material optimization. Since tetrafluoroethane has been recognized as a greenhouse gas, a search for an environmentally friendlier refrigeration system is currently underway. Maximizing the figure of merit has been the subject of considerable research since the 1950s. Metals typically have a large density of electrons, which leads to a large electrical conductivity, but a small thermoelectric power *S*. Insulators typically have a large thermoelectric power but a low electrical conductivity. The optimum *Z* is obtained in semiconductors, with electron and hole densities of the order of 10^{19}–10^{20} cm^{-3}. Heat in such materials is mostly conducted by the lattice vibrations (phonons) rather than by the electrons as is

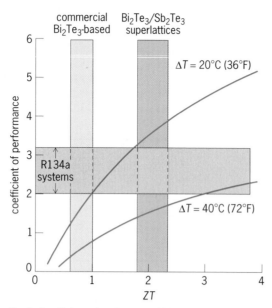

Fig. 3. Coefficient of performance (COP) of thermoelectric refrigerators as a function of the figure of merit *ZT* of the material, for two temperature differences, *ΔT*. The ranges of *ZT* of commercial materials and of a new nanostructured material are shown, and the corresponding achievable COPs can be read off from the portions of the COP-*ZT* curves which lie in these regions. The range of values of the COP of a tetrafluoroethane (R134a) vapor-compression system for similar temperature differences is also shown. All curves are shown for operation near room temperature ($T = 300$ K).

the case in metals. It is therefore advantageous to use semiconductors with high-atomic-number atoms and a complex lattice structure. Furthermore, the best semiconductors have an energy gap on the order of 0.2–0.3 eV. This limits the field to narrow-gap semiconductors such as Bi_2Te_3 or lead telluride (PbTe). Alloy scattering of phonons leads to a further reduction in the thermal conductivity and is beneficial as long as the mobility of the electrons does not decrease too much. As a result, optimal materials typically are solid solutions of Bi_2Te_3 and antimony telluride (Sb_2Te_3). This is the type of material that is labeled "commercial" in Fig. 3. While there has been progress in materials for thermoelectric generators, which operate at higher temperatures, progress in conventional materials operating near $T = 300$ K (80°F) has been slow. For example, over a narrow temperature range, adding cesium (Cs) to Bi_2Te_3 results in a small advantage.

Nanotechnologies. L. D. Hicks and M. S. Dresselhaus have suggested that low-dimensional structures, such as superlattices (alternating layers of two semiconductors) and quantum (nanoscale) wires, should show a large increase in figure of merit *ZT* over similar bulk materials. Their ideas are based on two effects.

First, under the right circumstances, lattice waves are scattered more than electrons by the interface between two dissimilar materials, resulting in a decrease in the thermal conductivity accompanied by a lesser decrease in the electrical conductivity. R. Venkatasubramanian has indeed demonstrated experimentally a figure of merit $ZT \approx 2.3$ on $Bi_2Te_3/$

Sb_2Te_3 superlattices. Thermoelectric superlattices are obtained in a geometry which is quite suitable for the cooling of electronic components. The resulting projected coefficient of performance, shown in Fig. 3, opens the door to thermoelectric coolers with efficiencies comparable to vapor-compression systems.

The second effect results from the fact that in quantum dots (cluster of atoms) and wires the spectrum of allowed energy levels is sharply confined to specific energy values. If the doping is controlled in such a way that most of the free electrons in the system have energies slightly above such a specific energy E_i, a relatively large density of electrons can be accommodated over a narrow energy range while maintaining a relatively small value of the Fermi energy (the difference between the Fermi level and E_i). As the thermopower S is inversely proportional to the Fermi energy, it is expected to be much larger in a low-dimensional form than in a three-dimensional form of a given material. Experimentally, a room-temperature *ZT* value of 2.0 has been reported by T. C. Harman and coworkers on nanostructured quantum-dot superlattices made from PbSnSeTe/PbTe. Both a reduced thermal conductivity and an enhanced Seebeck effect may be responsible for this remarkable result. Very strong enhancements of the thermopower S on silicon/germanium (Si/Ge) superlattices and on bismuth (Bi) nanowires have been reported. The latter results (**Fig. 4**) were obtained

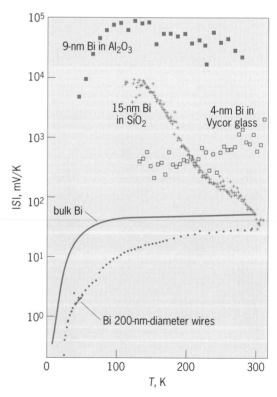

Fig. 4. Absolute value of the thermoelectric power *S* of bismuth (Bi) nanowires of the diameters indicated, and of pure bulk bismuth, as a function of temperature. The thermopower is most enhanced in composites with pore diameters around 9 nanometers. (*After J. P. Heremans et al., Thermoelectric power of bismuth nanocomposites, Phys. Rev. Lett., 88:216801, 2002*)

on bulk nanocomposite materials, prepared by introducing bismuth into porous host materials, such as silica gel, porous alumina, and Vycor glass, and suitable for large-scale applications. Unfortunately, the electrical resistance of these composites is still very high because the bismuth phase fills only a very small volume fraction of the composite.

Outlook. Thermoelectric cooling has the potential to replace vapor-compression refrigeration because it avoids the use of greenhouse gases and is compact, robust, and easily controlled. The efficiency of thermoelectric refrigeration should become comparable to that of conventional cooling technologies when nanoscale-engineered materials become available.

For background information *see* ARTIFICIALLY LAYERED STRUCTURES; BAND THEORY OF SOLIDS; CARNOT CYCLE; ELECTRICAL CONDUCTIVITY OF METALS; FREE-ELECTRON THEORY OF METALS; LATTICE VIBRATIONS; PELTIER EFFECT; PHONON; QUANTIZED ELECTRONIC STRUCTURE; REFRIGERATION; REFRIGERATION CYCLE; SEMICONDUCTOR; SEMICONDUCTOR HETEROSTRUCTURES; THERMOELECTRIC POWER GENERATORS; THERMOELECTRICITY in the McGraw-Hill Encyclopedia of Science & Technology.   Joseph Heremans

Bibliography. F. J. DiSalvo, Thermoelectric cooling and power generation, *Science*, 285:703–706, 1999; T. C. Harman et al., Quantum dot superlattice thermoelectric materials and devices, *Science*, 297:2229–2232, 2002; L. D. Hicks and M. S. Dresselhaus, Effect of quantum-well structures on the thermoelectric figure of merit, *Phys. Rev. B*, 47:12727–12731, 1993; L. D. Hicks and M. S. Dresselhaus, Thermoelectric figure of merit of a one-dimensional conductor, *Phys. Rev. B*, 47:16631–16634, 1993; B. C. Sales, Smaller is cooler, *Science*, 295:1248–1249, 2002; R. Venkatasubramanian et al., Thin-film thermoelectric devices with high room-temperature figures of merit, *Nature*, 413:597–602, 2001.

Ship design

As new technologies bring about advances in command, control, communications, computers, intelligence, surveillance, reconnaissance, and weapons systems (guns, missiles, and lasers), the complexity of designing a naval warship to carry these combat systems to sea is becoming more challenging. Even equipment associated with energy generation, conversion, and transmission for such purposes as propulsion and auxiliary power is on the verge of a revolution with the introduction of such concepts as superconducting motors and fuel cells. These technical advances are occurring ever more rapidly; indeed, many of these technology changes can happen within the time cycle during which a class of nominally identical ships is being built. In addition, shrinking product life cycles for current equipment make technology obsolescence one of the chief concerns of the navies of the United States and other countries.

Additional uncertainties that affect naval ship design are created when deciding what missions the ship is to perform over its life of perhaps 35 years. Whereas during World War II most destroyers were called upon to conduct fleet antisubmarine warfare, more recent destroyer duties include fleet anti-air warfare using long-range radars with missiles for ordnance instead of guns. Plans for the future include the ability to conduct naval gunfire support for land attacks similar to the shore bombardment previously carried out by battleships but with longer range. Such changes in missions can have a significant impact on ship conversions unless the ship was originally designed for such reconfiguration.

Finally, costs of new ships have escalated to the point where commercial-off-the-shelf (COTS) equipment is being utilized wherever possible to keep acquisition costs down. However, the use of COTS equipment entails reduced control over product support and replacement. If a particular manufacturer decides to stop production of a commercial product and use of a different supplier requires significant redesign and alteration for ship installation, the savings associated with using COTS equipment will be lost. Thus, the challenge in contemporary design is to accommodate change—for either technology insertion, mission reconfiguration, or alternate suppliers.

Modularity and standardization. Use of modularity and standardization in naval ship design, construction, and operation has been one of the more attractive concepts for addressing this challenge. The goals of modularity and standardization concepts have included the following:

1. Reduction in the time and cost of ship construction through:
   a. Procurement of equipment with a standard interface
   b. Modular packaging of equipment to ease outfitting
   c. Complete testing of equipment prior to ship installation
2. Reduction in the time and cost of mission reconfiguration through the use of modular mission packages.
3. Reduction in the time and cost of technology upgrades through the use of predefined interface standards for a specified functional area.

Achieving these goals results in a ship build time reduction of approximately 25% compared to onsite assembly and custom outfitting. More important to operations is the ability to command a ship with up-to-date technology and mission-relevant systems while benefitting from increased availability over the ship's life cycles of 30–35 years. Modernizations and conversions can occur in weeks instead of years.

Historical development. The first U.S. Navy program (1972 to 1978) to evaluate the advantages of modularity and standardization in ship design, construction, and operation was SEAMOD (Sea Systems Modification and Modernization by Modularity). It allowed for independent and parallel design,

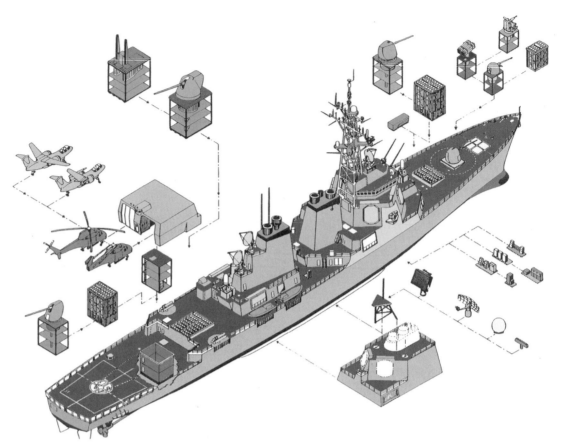

Fig. 1. Modular concept for the DDG 51 destroyer.

development, and acquisition of combat system payloads and platforms through the establishment of comprehensive interface design standards. This program was followed (1980–1985) by the Ship Systems Engineering Standards (SSES) program. SSES began development of modular interface standards for the next destroyer program, the DDG51 (**Fig. 1**). Only interface standards for the weapon modules (forward and aft) were completed in time to be built into the ship. Meanwhile in 1981 the German shipyard of Blohm & Voss completed construction of the first modular frigate using a concept called MEKO, which included SSES standards for its modular weapons. In 1986 the Royal Danish Navy began implementation of modularity concepts for a new class of patrol craft. This concept (STAN FLEX 300) uses modularity to quickly change missions of the craft. In a matter of days, the mission could be changed to one of four capabilities: surveillance, mine laying, missile launch, or mine countermeasures.

In 1992 the U.S. Navy reestablished a project on modularity and standardization called Affordability Through Commonality (ATC). In 1995 the Department of Defense established a special office at the Secretary of Defense level called the Open System Joint Task Force (OSJTF). The OSJTF was formed to promulgate the policy of Department of Defense Instruction 5000.2 requiring use of modularity and interface standards as a part of an open system ar-

chitecture for all defense weapon systems (Army, Air Force, Navy, and Marines). To implement the concept of open system architecture within the Navy, the ATC program (by this time formalized as a Program Management Office) expanded its efforts by establishing an integrated product team called Total Ship Open System Architecture.

Over time it has become clear that major defense systems (particularly ships) should be designed and constructed in a manner that provides ease of technology insertion to support transformation of new war-fighting operations against a yet-to-be-defined enemy. Modularity and standardization is now an accepted means to that end, and is being pursued by various navies and teams as new ship designs are developed.

Concepts. A module has been defined as "a compact assembly functioning as a component of a larger system." Modularity is often defined as "prepackaging of equipment to permit an entire assembly to be installed as a unit." Modularity can be applied in different ways. It could just be prepackaging of equipment without the use of any interface standards—solely for purposes of grouping equipment (such as pumps) for ease of ship installation and outfitting. This use of modularity could help streamline ship construction but may not accommodate future technologies since it is specific to the originally installed equipment only. Modularity can be used to divide any system into subassemblies (modules) for ease of repair and replacement of parts but this application only supports maintenance of that specific system. Modularity that improves both ship construction and maintenance while permitting easier technology upgrades involves development of an open system.

An open system is a system that has been partitioned into functional elements such that the elements and components (modules) within them represent the technical and functional building blocks of the system. These elements should be open in the sense that the software and hardware can be replaced by different or new products and technologies of like function and capacity without requiring changes to the system's software, services, and support structure, and can successfully operate when the different or new products and technologies are installed.

Standardization can be implemented in various degrees depending on the required outcome. The use of "standard hardware" brings with it the advantages of simplified logistic support (fewer spare parts to support equipment maintenance). However, this approach carries the risk of technology obsolescence, particularly for units or components with a high rate of technological change. In addition, dependence on a single supplier source can occur if not carefully managed. Standardization at the interface can ensure integration within the overall system while allowing the architecture of the equipment to change with technology. This use of standardization combined with modular open systems is called open systems architecture.

Thus open system architecture is a system design approach that establishes interface boundaries between the functional elements and the modular components within them. These interfaces will accommodate different commercial product designs or future military technologies that provide the same or improved functional capabilities. In the computer industry this approach is called plug-and-play—providing successful integration of constantly upgraded systems (both hardware and software). The goal for Navy ships is similar, but the development of interface standards is much more complex and extensive.

Interface standards development process. Development of interface standards for modular ships begins with the recognition that interface control can be established at different levels. The highest level is between the ship's hull and the various subsystems to be installed. What is important at this level is the ability to create a functional architecture so that partitioning between functional elements can take place, permitting establishment of natural interface points. **Figure 2** shows a typical breakdown of these functions aboard a surface combatant that

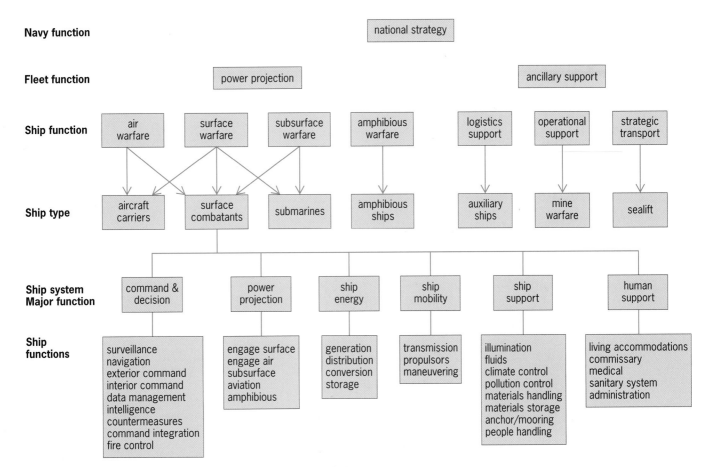

Fig. 2. Ship functional elements: reference model for functional relationships.

can be used to develop interface standards between functional elements and the ship. Grouping of equipment that performs like functions creates a basis for arrangement of functional element zones. A functional element zone is a contiguous area in the ship (one or more compartments) that contains ship-to-equipment interfaces for a given function. Such a zone can include multiple functions that line up with a single system (for example, "power projection-air/ surface" for a missile or gun module) or a function that has multiple systems (for example, "command integration" for numerous battle command work stations such as the Combat Information Center). The issues that have to be addressed at this level include assessment of ship missions over the life of the ship and extensive market surveillance of new technologies that could affect zone sizing and configuration. Scenarios need to be developed to decide how large to make each zone and how many zones are needed on the ship. Some functions (for example, climate control) are not allocated to a zone but are distributed throughout the ship. These distributed systems have ship-to-equipment interfaces also. The interfaces that are defined include physical characteristics (volume, weight, and center of gravity), electric power, heat rejection medium, data protocol (software), and any other parameter necessary for successful ship installation. These interface standards should be based upon the expected ship capabilities for the different mission roles (for example, land attack versus theatre ballistic missile defense) and technology insertion plans.

Once a consensus has been reached on standards for volume, weight, power, and heat rejection using known and projected technologies, they become "design to" targets for brand new systems not yet conceived. If the new system cannot meet the interfaces, then revision of the standards may be in order for new ships. However, if the developer can reasonably meet the standards built into the ship, then the new system can be backfitted (installed in a previously built ship) without requiring construction of a new hull or unaffordable major ripout and replacement. Implicit in this approach is the understanding that for new systems to be installed, old systems are better completely removed (significantly reducing general growth margins designed into ships based on historic trends).

The next level of interface control for modularity is within the equipment itself and is typically used for maintenance purposes. In the future, more emphasis will be placed on reducing on-site repairs with plans to reduce crew sizes by 50 to 90%. On-line monitoring and diagnostics will be used to replace entire subassemblies rather than "fix it in place." Interfaces for modular subassemblies may have to be more vendor-specific. However, interfaces for on-line monitoring should be standard.

The lowest level of interface control will be the most universally applied since it affects how connections are made regardless of the higher levels of modularity. These types of standards address structural connections, piping connections, electric

and electronic connectors (plugs and pins), keyboards (human interface), and so forth. Wide use of existing connector standards should be maximized so that true plug-and-play is possible. All three levels of interface standards have the same goal: ease of integration for alternative, replacement, or upgraded systems for a given function on the ship. The benefits and transition lessons of modularity and standardization should be traded among naval and commercial shipbuilding acquisition teams and other diverse industries.

Modularity with standard interfaces is in the best interest of the shipbuilders, the equipment suppliers, and the ultimate naval users. Its use in naval ship design, construction, and operation will increase in future ship acquisition programs as navies shift priorities to technology transformation and reduced life-cycle costs.

For background information *see* NAVAL ARMAMENT; NAVAL SURFACE SHIP; SHIP DESIGN in the McGraw-Hill Encyclopedia of Science & Technology.   Jack Abbott
Bibliography. J. W. Abbott, Modular payload ships in the U.S. Navy, *Trans. SNAME*, 85:350–395, 1977; M. L. Bosworth and J. J. Hough, Improvements in ship affordability, *Trans. SNAME*, 101:705–726, 1993; R. DeVries, K. T. Tompkins, and J. Vasilakos, Total ship open systems architecture, *Nav. Eng. J.*, 12(4): 59–77, July 2000.

Single-molecule optical imaging

Many scientific principles are based on macroscopic observations of group behavior of large numbers of molecules. However, recent advances in instrumentation have allowed the imaging of individual molecules at time scales characteristic of chemical transformations. Scientists can now follow step-by-step the detailed progression of single chemical or biochemical events, enabling the testing of established statistical concepts as well as the discovery of new phenomena associated with the random nature of distinct entities. The observation of a single deoxyribonucleic acid (DNA) molecule through a standard optical microscope was made almost 40 years ago. Since then, there has been an exponential growth in the number of reports on single-molecule imaging. These cover a large variety of molecule types as well as physical, chemical, and biological processes.

General principles. Almost all single-molecule optical imaging methods rely on lasers to excite fluorescence from the molecules. Lasers can produce high fluxes of photons in micrometer-scale spaces so that individual molecules can be forced to absorb and emit thousands of times to produce a detectable image. Large DNA or protein molecules can be labeled with many fluorophores (compounds that absorb light and subsequently emit light at a longer wavelength) to further facilitate detection. Imaging devices are now available with sensitivities capable of recording single photons. This combination is responsible for the success in making single-molecule imaging into a practical laboratory tool.

The typical molecule can be cycled between the ground and the excited states about 10^3 to 10^6 times before photodecomposition (light-induced chemical breakdown) sets in. Molecules can also be temporarily trapped in metastable states (excited stationary energy states) for long periods of time before recovering. The challenge is then to coax as many photons as possible from each molecule and to utilize the signal judiciously. For example, in order to follow molecular motion or chemical transformation, the total available photons should be spread out over the time frame of the event to be studied.

Imaging methods. There are two main approaches used to produce optical images. Either a single-point optical probe is scanned across a planar object or a two-dimensional array detector is placed at the focal plane containing the object. The image is essentially a collection of individual intensity measurements ordered according to the location where the photons originate. If the object (in this case, the molecule being imaged) is stationary, the two approaches are equivalent. However, for molecules in motion, array detectors are preferred, since scanning a single-point probe can take anywhere from milliseconds to many seconds. The integrating nature of array detectors means that time resolution can be as fine as the duration of the irradiating light source.

Spatial resolution is an important parameter in imaging molecules. If visible light and normal optics are used, the diffraction limit will restrict the ultimate resolution to 200 nanometers. However, it is possible to go below the diffraction limit if near-field imaging is employed. This method relies on spatial apertures to define the size of the light beam at the imaged plane. Although there is no lower theoretical limit to the diameter of a near-field aperture, the practical resolution is in the 10–50-nm range due to the rapidly decreasing light intensity that can be coupled to such small dimensions.

Optical imaging of molecules does not provide information about the shape of the molecules. Except for large DNA and protein molecules, optical methods do not have the subnanometer discrimination that is necessary to register structural features. The type of information that can be derived from single-molecule optical images includes spectroscopic characteristics, interactions with other molecules or with surfaces, molecular motion, and changes in the local environment.

Immobilized molecules. For stationary molecules, the signal-to-noise ratio can be enhanced by acquiring multiple images and then averaging them. By dispersing the molecule of interest at a low concentration in a host crystal, distinct entities can be identified and studied for essentially unlimited lengths of time. Some of the earliest single-molecule images were obtained in mixed crystals at cryogenic temperatures. In general, the lower temperature and the crystalline environment lead to sharper lines and, therefore, stronger absorption properties. Low temperature also helps to prevent photochemical decomposition. Both spectroscopic characteristics and photophysical phenomena have been reported that showed stochastic behavior from one molecule to the next. Such individualistic properties are naturally masked in traditional studies of ensembles of molecules.

Molecules can also be immobilized by deposition on a solid surface. Again, if the concentration is low enough, molecules will be randomly dispersed so that individual entities can be probed. Observation of molecules on surfaces can be accomplished by array detectors, near-field fluorescence, or confocal microscopy.

More relevant to biological systems are molecules immobilized within membranes. These are actually fluid structures, but over the time scale of acquiring an image they can be considered stationary. Additional insights can be obtained by acquiring successive images over time, revealing planar diffusion of the molecule in the membrane.

Chemical reactions can be studied for molecules immobilized on a surface. In one type of experiment, the molecule of interest is labeled with one type of fluorescent dye. The location of these molecules on the surface can thus be recorded. The reactant molecules in the solution above the surface are labeled with a second type of fluorescent dye. Reactions can be recognized by the appearance of a second color at the same surface location as the static molecule.

Partially immobilized molecules. Fixing the spatial location of a molecule facilitates tracking and detection. However, molecular transformations normally involve freely moving molecules. The compromise is to confine the molecule of interest to a small volume or to immobilize only one portion of the molecule. Dynamic events can then be monitored. With proper experimental design, these partially immobilized molecules can behave much like completely free species.

One of the most striking examples of imaging partially immobilized molecules is the study of molecular motors, in which the key question is how

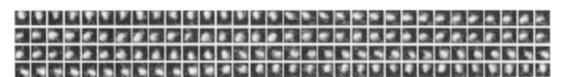

Fig. 1. Images of a single actin filament being rotated counterclockwise by the molecular motor F1-ATPase as it reacts with single molecules of ATP. The axis of rotation is the center of the field, which is 1.5 by 1.5 μm square. The sequence is obtained at 5-ms intervals from left to right in each row. (*From Y. Ishii and T. Yanagida, Single molecule detection in life science, Single Molecules, 1:5–16, 2000*)

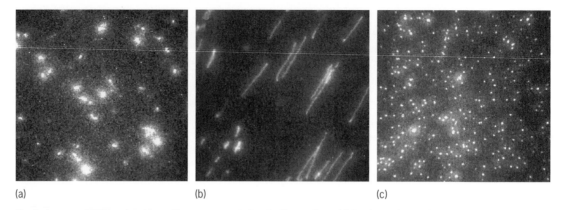

Fig. 2. Images of DNA molecules as they move near a fused-silica surface. (*a*) Freely moving molecules at pH 8.1; (*b*) completely adsorbed molecules at pH 4.5; and (*c*) precipitated molecules at pH 3.0. Each double-stranded DNA molecule used in these experiments contains 48,500 base pairs, enough genetic information to encode several proteins. When stretched out, as in (*b*), each molecule is 16 μm long. (*From S. H. Kang, M. R. Shortreed, and E. S. Yeung, Real-time dynamics of single-DNA molecules undergoing adsorption and desorption at liquid-solid interfaces, Anal. Chem., 73:1091–1099, 2001*)

chemical energy is converted into mechanical energy in biological systems. In the example depicted in **Fig. 1**, a fluorescent strand (actin filament) is attached to the axis of a single molecule of F_1-adenosine triphosphatase (ATPase). Rotation of the axis can be visualized in a movie recorded by a charge-coupled-device camera. Discrete motions of $120°$ steps can be recognized. By studying the concentration dependence of ATP in the surrounding solution, each of these rotation steps is shown to be the result of a single transformation of ATP to adenosine diphosphate (ADP). By changing the length of the fluorescent strand, the load can be varied, enabling the calculation of the force available in the molecular motor. The efficiency is found to be close to 100%.

Single molecules can also be trapped in small liquid pools inside a gel medium. These small volumes do not actually allow movements to be traced by microscopy with diffraction-limited optics. However, the intensity of fluorescence can be related to the distance of the molecule from a reference plane to follow its motion.

Molecules in free solution. For unconfined molecules, the experimental difficulty is in tracking them over time while they are undergoing physical and chemical changes. Molecular diffusion in solution is generally in the micrometer range for millisecond observation periods. If consecutive images are recorded, molecules in one image can be related to the corresponding molecules in a second image to follow their movement.

By using exposure times of 10–50 ms, molecules in solution would have moved several pixels in a particular image. However, fluorescence emission is continuous over this period. So, the integrated path of each molecule over the exposure time will be recorded, and can be used to calculate the diffusion coefficient. (An interesting finding is that motion is retarded when molecules approach charged surfaces such as fused silica.)

Another type of free-solution study involves large biomolecules such as DNA flowing past a fused-silica surface. At high pH, the molecules and the surface are negatively charged; thus they repel each other, allowing the molecules to move freely. Their shapes change continuously because the flexible coil winds and unwinds randomly (**Fig. 2***a*). At low pH, the molecules are adsorbed onto the surface. The interaction occurs at the two ends of the molecule. Therefore, the molecules are stretched out when both ends are finally fixed to the surface (Fig. 2*b*). At intermediate pH, the molecules are adsorbed only some of the time. This hybrid behavior explains how separation methods such as chromatography work. At very low pH, the charges are depleted within the molecule, and precipitation occurs as DNA condenses into tight particles (Fig. 2*c*).

Future applications. The ability to detect and follow the transformation of single molecules has opened up new areas of investigation, such as diffusion, structural changes, reactions, and adsorptive interactions. In the future, scientists may be able to utilize such information to help diagnose diseases. Specifically, imaging single molecules inside single cells may allow scientists to detect mutations or infections before they affect a person's health.

For background information *see* CONFOCAL MICROSCOPY; FLUORESCENCE; FLUORESCENCE MICROSCOPE; LASER; NANOTECHNOLOGY; OPTICAL MICROSCOPE in the McGraw-Hill Encyclopedia of Science & Technology.   Edward S. Yeung

Bibliography. Y. Ishii and T. Yanagida, Single molecule detection in life science, *Single Molecules*, 1:5–16, 2000; S. H. Kang, M. R. Shortreed, and E. S. Yeung, Real-time dynamics of single-DNA molecules undergoing adsorption and desorption at liquid-solid interfaces, *Anal. Chem.*, 73:1091–1099, 2001; A. D. Mehta et al., Single-molecule biomechanics with optical methods, *Science*, 283:1689–1695, 1999; W. E. Moerner and M. Orrit, Illuminating single molecules in condensed matter, *Science*, 283:1670–1676, 1999; X. Xu and E. S. Yeung, Direct measurement of single-molecule diffusion and photodecomposition in free solution, *Science*, 276:1106–1109, 1997; R. Yasuda et al., F_1-ATPase is a highly efficient molecular motor that rotates with discrete $120°$ steps, *Cell*, 93:1117–1124, 1998.

Single-site catalysts and resulting polyolefins

Polyolefins are plastics that are composed solely of carbon and hydrogen. Their basic units, ethylene and propylene, are easily obtained by cracking hydrocarbons. And because polyolefins are thermoplastics, they are easily processed. After use, polyolefin materials can be recycled, or they can be burned as a fuel since their combustion by-products are carbon dioxide and water. Except for low-density polyethylene (LDPE), which has a highly branched structure and is produced by a radical reaction at ethylene pressures of 1000–3000 bar (100–300 MPa), all polyolefins are synthesized at far lower pressures using catalysts.

In 2001, polyolefins such as polyethylene (PE), polypropylene (PP), and ethylene copolymers accounted for 95 million metric tons of the total 160 million metric tons of plastics produced worldwide. Polyethylene production alone, including high-density polyethylene (HDPE), low-density polyethylene, and linear low-density polyethylene (LLDPE), was 60 million metric tons, while 32 million metric tons of polypropylene were produced. Polyolefin growth is projected to increase at a rate of 4 million tons a year, such that in 2010 about 140 million metric tons of polyolefins will be produced. This increase is due largely to new catalysts which are able to tailor the polymer structure and, as a result, physical properties.

Classical catalysts. In 1953 at the Max-Planck-Institut in Mülheim, Karl Ziegler succeeded in polymerizing ethylene into high-density polyethylene at standard pressure and room temperature, based on the use of the catalyst titanium tetrachloride combined with diethylaluminum chloride. Some months later at the Polytechnic Institute in Milan, Giulio Natta demonstrated a catalyst system that was capable of polymerizing propylene into semicrystalline polypropylene. For their work, Ziegler and Natta shared the Nobel Prize for Chemistry in 1963. Modern Ziegler-Natta catalysts are mixtures of solid and liquid compounds, often containing $MgCl_2/TiCl_4/Al(C_2H_5)_3$ and, for propylene polymerization, different internal and external donors such as ethylbenzoate, silanes, or ethers to increase stereoregularity (tacticity). An important catalyst for ethylene polymerization is the Phillips catalyst, that is, chromium trioxide on a silica support. This catalyst is used in the gas-phase polymerization of ethylene, but is unable to produce polypropylene with methyl groups always on the same side of the chain (isotactic). As Ziegler-Natta catalysts are heterogeneous and complex systems with different active sites, the resulting polymer structure can be controlled only to a limited degree.

Metallocene catalysts. Metallocenes are "sandwich compounds" in which a π-bonded metal atom is situated between two aromatic ring systems (**Fig. 1**). This compound class initiated a more useful organometallic chemistry that did not play a role in the larger industrial processes in the past.

In contrast to Ziegler systems, metallocene catalysts have only one active site (single-site catalysts) and produce polymers with a narrow molecular weight distribution $M_w/M_n = 2$ (M_w and M_n are the weight average and number average molecular weights). Their catalytic activity is 10–100 times higher than that of the classical Ziegler-Natta systems. In addition, metallocene catalysts are soluble in hydrocarbons or liquid propylene, and their structure can be easily changed. These properties allow one to predict accurately the properties of the resulting polyolefins by knowing the structure of the catalyst used during their manufacture, as well as to control the resulting molecular weight and distribution, comonomer content, and tacticity by careful selection of the appropriate reactor conditions.

Metallocenes, in combination with the conventional aluminumalkyl cocatalysts used in Ziegler systems, are capable of polymerizing ethylene, but only at a very low activity. In 1977 in Hamburg, it was discovered that methylalumoxane (MAO) greatly improved catalysis with metallocenes, enhancing their activity, surprisingly, by a factor of 10,000. Methylaluminoxane is a compound in which aluminum and

$$CH_3-Al-O-Al-O-Al-O-Al-H_3C$$

Methylaluminoxane

oxygen atoms are arranged alternately and free valences are saturated by methyl substituents. It is prepared by the careful partial hydrolysis of trimethylaluminum and consists mainly of units of the basic structure $Al_4O_3Me_6$. As the aluminum atoms in this structure are coordinatively unsaturated, the basic units join, forming cluster compounds. These have molecular weights from 1200 to 1600 and are soluble in hydrocarbons. Metallocene catalysts, especially zirconocenes, treated with MAO can polymerize up to 100 tons of ethylene per gram of zirconium (Fig. 1). Such highly active catalysts can remain in the product. The insertion time (for the insertion

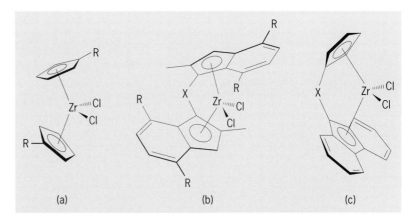

Fig. 1. Structures of metallocenes (in this case, zirconocenes). (a) Nonchiral structure produces atactic polypropylene. (b) Racemic mixture of this chiral structure produces isotactic polypropylene. (c) C_s-symmetric structure produces syndiotactic polypropylene. R = alkyl substitution [H, CH_3, C_2H_5, C_6H_5]; X = bridge [—CH_2—CH_2—, $(CH_3)_2Si$, $(CH_3)_2C$].

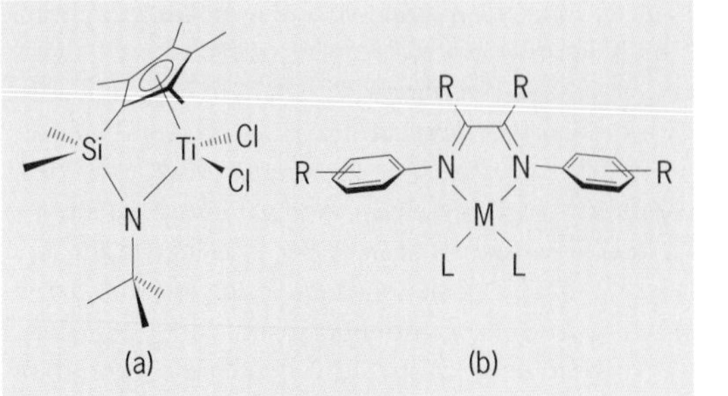

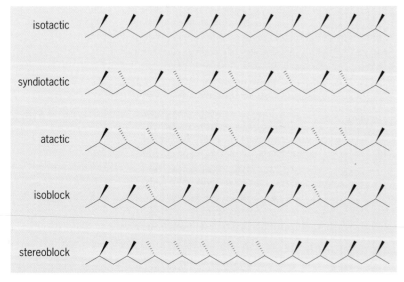

Fig. 2. Structures of (*a*) "half-sandwich" metallocenes, dimethylsilylamido(cyclopentadienyl)titanium compound for the production of linear low-density polyethylene (LLDPE) and (*b*) diimin complexes with M = Ni, Pd; R = H, alkyl; L = halogen.

of one molecule of ethylene into the growing chain) is only 10^{-5} s. A comparison to enzymes is not far-fetched. It is generally assumed that the function of MAO is to first undergo a fast ligand exchange reaction with the metallocene dichloride, thus producing the metallocene methyl and dimethylaluminum compounds. In the next step, either Cl^- or CH_3^- is abstracted from the metallocene compound by an aluminum center in MAO, thus forming a metallocene cation and an MAO anion. The alkylated metallocene cation represents the active center. Meanwhile, other weakly coordinating cocatalysts, such

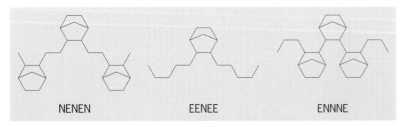

Fig. 3. Microstructures of polypropylenes.

Fig. 4. Structures of norbornene (N)/ethylene (E) copolymers. Alternating blocks can also occur.

as tetra(perfluorophenyl)borate anions, $[(C_6F_5)_4B]^-$, have been successfully used to activate metallocenes and other single-site catalysts. Polyolefins with different microstructures and characteristics can be custom-made by varying the ligands of the metallocene (Fig. 1). By combining different olefins and cycloolefins with one another, the range of characteristics can be further broadened. Conventional heterogeneous catalysts have not yet produced polyolefins with tailored microstructures or chemically uniform copolymers. Using metallocene catalysts, it was possible for the first time to produce polyethylenes, polypropylenes, and copolymers with narrow molecular-weight distribution, syndiotactic (alternating stereoregular structure) polypropylene, syndiotactic polystyrene, cyclopolymers of 1,5-hexadiene, and cycloolefin copolymers (COCs) with high catalytic activity.

Other single-site catalysts. "Half sandwich" metallocenes are highly active for the copolymerization of ethylene and 1-octene (**Fig. 2**). These catalysts produce long-chain branched polyolefins by incorporating oligomers with vinyl endgroups, which are formed during polymerization by β-hydrogen transfer. Long-branched copolymers of ethylene with 1-octene show elastic properties as long as the comonomer content is more than 20%. Other elastomers with different microstructures can be synthesized from dienes.

New palladium, nickel, iron, and cobalt complexes activated by MAO or borate cocatalysts are also active for the polymerization of olefins. Cationic Pd(II) and Ni(II) complexes are able to polymerize ethylene and other α-olefins when sterically bulky α-diimine ligands and noncoordinating counterions are used. The lower oxophilicity and presumed greater functional group tolerance of late-transition metals relative to early-transition metals make them likely targets for the development of catalysts for the copolymerization of ethylene with polar monomers under mild conditions.

Polypropylene. Propylene and long-chain olefins can be assembled in a stereoregular manner, such that the building blocks have a defined and recurring arrangement in the resulting polymer chain. The structural arrangement of polypropylene has a considerable influence on its functional properties. A random arrangement leads to amorphous (atactic) polypropylene which flows at room temperature, whereas stereoregular polypropylene (isotactic and syndiotactic) is crystalline having a melting point of 165°C (330°F). In addition to isotactic and atactic polypropylene, syndiotactic polypropylene as well as isoblock and stereoblock polypropylene have been made for the first time in large quantities and in high purity (**Fig. 3**). The block lengths of equal tacticity in isoblock polypropylene (meaning the position of the methyl groups in one direction) can be varied in a broad range on the nanoscale (4–100 units). This leads to microcrystalline polypropylene which is suitable for making transparent films. The development of applications for elastic

Comparison of some properties of polypropylene made by Ziegler-Natta and metallocene catalysts		
	Polypropylene from metallocene catalyst	Polypropylene from Ziegler-Natta catalyst
Melting point (°C)	161	162
M_w/M_n	2.5	5.8
Stress, tensile (N mm^{-2})	1620	1190
Hardness (N mm^{-2})	86	76
Extractable fraction (%)	0.1	2–4

stereoblock polypropylene has just begun. Polypropylenes made using metallocenes exhibit distinct differences to conventionally produced polypropylenes, such as narrow molar mass distributions, higher stiffness, and greater tensile strength (see **table**). This is caused not only by the uniform structure but also by the extremely low fractions of low-molecular-weight (oligomeric) products. These fractions amount to less than 0.1%, compared to 2–4% in Ziegler-Natta polypropylene.

Elastomers. One of the biggest impacts of single-site catalysts promises to be in the manufacture of elastomers with elastic properties similar to rubber. The copolymers of ethylene and propylene with a molar ratio of 1:0.5 up to 1:2 are of great industrial interest. These ethylene-propylene copolymers (EPM) show elastic properties. In addition, ethylene-propylene-diene terpolymers (EPDM), made by including 2–5 wt % of a diene as a third monomer, are elastomers. The diene, 5-ethylidene-2-norbornene (ENB) [norbornene = bicyclo[2.2.1]-hept-2-ene], is mainly used. Since there are no double bonds in the backbone of this polymer, it is stable to oxidation and photodegradation reactions.

Until recently, most processes for the production of EPM and EPDM rubber used soluble or highly dispersed vanadium catalysts. The elastomers produced by vanadium catalysts are pale yellow in color because of traces of remaining vanadium catalysts. Similar, less colored elastomers can be obtained with the single-site catalysts because the concentration of the single-site catalysts used for the polymerization is about a factor of 100 lower than the vanadium catalysts.

Cycloolefin copolymers. Single-site catalysts can be used to polymerize and copolymerize strained cyclic olefins such as cyclopentene or norbornene. The melting points for these homopolymers are extremely high, such as 400°C (750°F) for polycyclopentene, and as a result they may be used as engineering plastics. Copolymers of cyclic olefins with ethylene (COC) represent a new class of thermoplastic amorphous materials (**Fig. 4**). COCs are characterized by excellent transparency and very long life at high service temperatures. In addition they are chemically resistant and can be melt-processed. Due to their high carbon/hydrogen ratio, these polymers feature a high refractive index, for example, 1.53 for the ethene-norbornene copolymer at 50 mol % norbornene incorporation. Their stability against hydrolysis and chemical degradation, in combination with their stiffness, makes them desirable materials for optical applications such as compact discs, lenses, optical fibers, and films.

For background information see CATALYSIS; HETEROGENEOUS CATALYSIS; METALLOCENE CATALYST; METALLOCENES; POLYMER; POLYMERIZATION; POLYOLEFIN RESINS; STEREOSPECIFIC CATALYST in the McGraw-Hill Encyclopedia of Science & Technology.
W. Kaminsky

Bibliography. S. D. Ittel, L. K. Johnson, and M. Brookhart, Late-metal catalysts for ethylene homo- and copolymerization, *Chem. Rev.*, 100:1169–1203, 2000; W. Kaminsky, Highly active metallocene catalysts for olefin polymerization, *J. Chem. Soc., Dalton Trans.*, pp. 1413–1418, 1998; J. Scheirs and W. Kaminsky, *Metallocene Based Polyolefins*, vols. 1 and 2, Wiley, Chichester, 1999; K. B. Sinclair, Future trends in polyolefin materials, *Macromol. Symp.*, 173:237–261, 2001.

Space flight

In 2001, space flight continued its momentum of preceding years, with extraordinary activity in the exploration, utilization, and commercialization of space. However space endeavors did occur at a considerably reduced rate. Launch activity in 2001 reached its lowest point since 1963, with only 57 flights successfully placing payloads into orbit, compared to 81 in the preceding year. There were two launch failures (down from four in 2000).

The United States' National Aeronautics and Space Administration (NASA) continued to stand out with spectacular accomplishments in the advancing buildup and operation of the *International Space Station* (*ISS*), the successful launches of the Mars orbiter *Odyssey*, solar probe *Genesis*, and astronomy mission *Microwave Anisotropy Probe* (*MAP*), the landing of the *Near Earth Asteroid Rendezvous* (*NEAR*) mission on Eros 433, the successful arrival of Mars *Odyssey* at the Red Planet, and continuing exploration of the Jupiter system with the deep-space probes *Galileo* and *Cassini*, the latter while en route to Saturn.

In 2001, the commercial space market, while making headlines with the first paying space tourist flying on a Russian spaceship to the *ISS* for a week's stay, showed a dramatic decline from the strong growth trends of earlier years. Out of the 57 successful launches worldwide, only 22 (38%) were commercial launches (carrying 49 commercial payloads), compared to 40 (49%) in 2000 (**Table 1**). In the civil science satellite area, worldwide launches totaled 10, as compared to some 15 in the preceding year.

Russia's space program was marked by the end of an era, including the carefully controlled reentry and atmospheric destruction of the Earth-orbiting space station *Mir*, the only remaining symbol of once-mighty Soviet cosmonautics. But Russia also showed

TABLE 1. Successful launches in 2001 (Earth orbit and beyond)

Country	Number of launches (and attempts)
United States (NASA/DOD/Commercial)	23 (24)
Russia	23 (23)
Europe (*ESA/Arianespace*)	7 (8)
People's Republic of China	1 (1)
Japan	1 (1)
India	2 (2)
TOTAL	57 (59)

continued dependable participation in the buildup of the *ISS*. Europe's space activities in 2001 did not reach expected results in the transportation area, due to the unavailability of some scheduled commercial satellites and the failure of the tenth Ariane 5 launch vehicle.

During 2001, a total of eight crewed flights (up from seven in 2000) from the two major space-faring nations carried 44 humans into space (2000: 37), including five women (same as 2000), bringing the total number of people launched into space since 1958 (counting repeaters) to 915, including 94 women, or 415 individuals (35 female). Some significant space events in 2001 are listed in **Table 2**.

International Space Station

Goals of the *ISS* are to establish a permanent habitable residence and laboratory for science and research, and to maintain and support a human crew at this facility. The *ISS* will vastly expand the human experience of living and working in space, enable commercial development of space, and provide the capability for humans to perform long-duration space-based research in cell and developmental biology, plant biology, human physiology, fluid physics, combustion science, materials science, and fundamental physics. The *ISS* will also provide a platform for making observations of the Earth's surface and atmosphere, the Sun, and other astronomical objects. The experience and results obtained from using the *ISS* will guide the future direction of human exploration of space.

TABLE 2. Some significant space events in 2001

Designation	Date	Country	Event
Shenzhou 2	January 9	P. R. of China	Second crewless test flight and recovery, after 108 orbits, of an experimental crewed capsule for use by "taikonauts," with a monkey, a dog, a rabbit, and snails.
STS 98 (*Atlantis*)	February 7	United States	ISS mission 5A with the U.S. laboratory module *Destiny*. Docking at the station was on February 9, and lab installation at the node on February 10.
STS 102 (*Discovery*)	March 8	United States	ISS mission 5A.1, first "crew rotation" flight, carrying Expedition 2 crew, resupply and science racks, in multipurpose logistics module (MPLM) *Leonardo* (1st flight).
Mars Odyssey	April 7	United States	Launch of the 2001 Mars probe *Odyssey* on a Delta 2 for a 6-month, 286-million-mile voyage to the Red Planet. Arrived successfully on October 24.
GSat 1	April 18	India	First launch of new GSLV rocket with Russian-built 3d stage. Geosynchronous comsat *GSat 1* did not reach correct orbit due to 3d-stage engine underperformance.
STS-100 (*Endeavour*)	April 19	United States	ISS mission 6A, with the Canadian-built robot arm Canadarm2 and 2d MPLM, *Raffaello*, on its 1st flight. The cranelike manipulator was installed on April 22.
Soyuz TM-32/ISS 2S	April 28	Russia	Launch of 1st "taxi flight" to *ISS*, bringing a "fresh" Soyuz crew return vehicle (CRV) and carrying the world's first paying "space tourist," U.S. businessman Dennis Tito.
MAP	June 30	United States	NASA's *Microwave Anisotropy Mission*, launched on a Delta 2, to measure temperature fluctuations in the cosmic microwave background from the L2 libration point.
STS 104 (*Atlantis*)	July 12	United States	ISS mission 7A, carrying the joint airlock *Quest*, which was installed at the *ISS* node on July 14. Arrival of *Quest* marked end of *ISS* Phase 2, beginning of Phase 3.
Artemis	July 12	Europe	Launch of the 10th Ariane 5, with the technological comsat *Artemis* and broadcast satellite B-Sat2b. Both left in lower orbits than planned due to upper-stage failure.
Genesis	August 8	United States	Launch of interplanetary probe *Genesis* on a Delta 2 to the first Earth-Sun libration point L1 to collect samples of the solar wind and return them in September 2004.
STS 105 (*Discovery*)	August 10	United States	ISS mission 7A.1, 2d crew rotation, carrying *Leonardo* (2d flight) and replacing Expedition 2 crew with Expedition 3. Also conducted two spacewalks.
DC-1/ISS 4R	September 14	Russia	Launch of the Russian docking compartment DC 1 *Pirs* on a Soyuz-U. Installed at service module *Zvezda* on September 16. This also added a 2d airlock for spacewalks.
Soyuz TM-33/ISS 3S	October 21	Russia	Launch of 2d "taxi" flight to *ISS*, with new Soyuz CRV and a paying "guest" cosmonaut, researcher Claudie Haigneré from CNES/France. Returned on TM-32.
STS 108 (*Endeavour*)	December 5	United States	ISS mission UF-1, 1st utilization flight to *ISS*, with MPLM *Raffaello* and 4th expeditionary crew, to "rotate" with Expedition 3 after its 128-day stay in space.

The *ISS* is the largest and most complex international scientific project in history. The completed station will have a mass of about 520 tons (470 metric tons). It will measure 356 ft (108 m) across and 290 ft (88 m) long, with almost an acre (0.4 hectare) of solar panels to provide up to 110 kilowatts power to six state-of-the-art laboratories. Directed by the United States, the *ISS* draws upon the scientific and technological resources of 16 nations, also including Canada, Japan, Russia, the 11 nations of the European Space Agency (ESA), and Brazil.

The initial milestones for the *ISS* program, after the beginning of orbital assembly in 1998, included the first crewed logistics/supply flight of a space shuttle in May/June 1999, the arrival of the first long-duration station crew of U.S. Commander William Shepherd and Russian Pilot/Flight Engineers Yuri Gidzenko and Sergei Krikalev in November 2000, and the installation of the first set of U.S. solar array wings in December 2000. Buildup and early operations of the permanently crewed station continued through 2001 at rapid pace (**Fig. 1**).

In February 2001, the addition of the laboratory module *Destiny* made the *ISS* into the first long-term U.S. orbiting research laboratory in 27 years (*Skylab*, 1974); also, *ISS* day-to-day command and flight control transitioned from the Russian to the American segment. In March, the Expedition 1 crew was "rotated" with the new station crew of Russian Commander Yuri V. Usachev and U.S. Flight Engineers Susan Helms and James S. Voss, and the Italian-built multipurpose logistics module (MPLM) *Leonardo* ferried the first three science racks to the station. In April, the space station remote manipulator system (SSRMS) Canadarm2, the primary contribution by partner Canada, was successfully mounted

to the *ISS* (**Fig. 2**), while the second Italian MPLM *Raffaello* brought additional cargo and research equipment. In July, Canadarm2 was used to install the U.S. airlock module *Quest* at the node *Unity*, providing the station residents with their own "door" to space for EVAs (extravehicular activities), using both U.S. and Russian spacesuit systems (**Fig. 3***a*). In August, the Expedition 3 crew of U.S. Commander Frank Culbertson and Russian Flight Engineers Vladimir Dezhurov and Mikhail Tyurin arrived along with *Leonardo* on its second cargo run, bringing the total research rack number in the *ISS* lab to five. In September, the Russian docking compartment (DC-1) *Pirs* was brought from Baikonur, Kazakhstan, on a Soyuz rocket and attached to the service module *Zvezda*, to give the station a second airlock for spacewalks in Russian Orlan-M spacesuits (Fig. 3*b*). In December, the Expedition 4 crew of Russian Commander Yuri Onufrienko and U.S. Flight Engineers Carl E. Walz and Daniel W. Bursch rotated with Expedition 3, which returned to Earth after 128 days in space. By end-2000, 11 carriers had been launched to the *ISS*: six shuttles, two heavy Protons (FGB/*Zarya*, SM/*Zvezda*), and three Soyuz-U (Progress 1P, Progress 2P, Soyuz 2R). By end-2001, *ISS* missions totaled 24, of which 12 were flown by U.S. space shuttles, the other 12 by Russian Proton and Soyuz rockets.

STS 98. The February 7–20 flight of *Atlantis*, designated ISS-5A, was the seventh visit of the station by a space shuttle. *Atlantis* carried the U.S. laboratory module *Destiny* and a crew of five (Kenneth D. Cockrell, Mark L. Polansky, Robert L. Curbeam, Marsha S. Ivins, and Thomas D. Jones). Docking at the ISS PMA3 port took place on February 9, and on the following day the 28 × 14 ft (8.5 × 4.3 m)

Fig. 1. *International Space Station* (*ISS*) photographed from the space shuttle *Endeavour* during mission STS 108 in December 2001. Parts of Florida and the Bahamas are visible in the background. (*NASA*)

Fig. 2. Canadian astronaut Chris A. Hadfield working with Canadarm2, the new remote manipulator system being mounted on the *International Space Station*, during shuttle mission STS 100 in April 2001. Hadfield's feet are secured on a restraint attached to the shuttle's remote manipulator system arm. Both robot arms were built by Canada. (*NASA*)

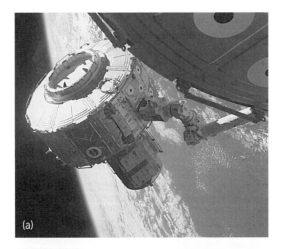

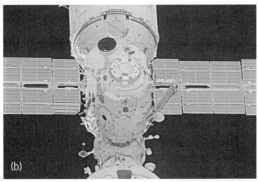

Fig. 3. Airlocks for the *International Space Station*. (a) *Quest* airlock being installed onto the starboard side of Unity node 1 during shuttle mission STS 104 in July 2001. Astronaut Susan J. Helms used controls onboard the station to maneuver the airlock into place with the Canadarm2 robot arm. (b) *Pirs* docking compartment (DC-1), which was installed on the service module *Zvedza* in September 2001, photographed from the shuttle *Endeavour* during mission STS 108 in December 2001. (*NASA*)

lab was installed at the node *Unity* by Ivins using the shuttle's RMS robot arm, assisted by spacewalkers Curbeam and Jones. Two more EVAs followed in the next 4 days as the *ISS* crew completed setup and activation of critical and noncritical lab systems.

STS 102. Mission ISS-5A.1, flown by *Discovery*, took place during March 8–21. The eighth visit to the space station carried resupply and systems/science racks for outfitting the U.S. lab *Destiny*, all packed in *Leonardo*, and a crew of seven, including the new *ISS* resident crew: James D. Wetherbee, James M. Kelly, Andrew S.W. Thomas, Paul W. Richards, Voss (up only), Helms (up only), and Usachev (up only). Docking on March 10 was delayed 64 min by a problem with *ISS* solar array latching. During the docked period, the MPLM was transferred to the *ISS* node nadir port, unloaded, filled with trash and discarded equipment, and returned to the shuttle. In two spacewalks on March 11 and 13, Helms and Voss, then Thomas and Richards, worked outside to support *ISS* assembly. In the first crew rotation, Usachev, Voss, and Helms became the new station crew, replacing Shepherd, Krikalev, and Gidzenko, who returned to Earth after 140 days in space (136 days in *ISS*).

STS 100. *Endeavour* flew on Mission ISS-6A, which lasted April 19–May 1. It carried the approximately 2-ton (1.8-metric-ton) space station remote manipulator system, the MPLM *Raffaello*, total mass loaded 4.5 tons (4.1 metric tons), and a crew of seven: four crew members from the United States. (Kent V. Rominger, Jeffrey S. Ashby, John L. Phillips, and Scott E. Parazynski) and three crew members from other countries [Umberto Guidoni (ESA/Italy), Yuri V. Lonchakov (Russia), and Chris A. Hadfield (Canada)]. *Endeavour* docked on April 21. The mission featured two EVAs by Parazynski and Hadfield, one on April 22 to support transfer and deployment of the SSRMS Canadarm2 from the shuttle payload bay to the *ISS* lab module (Fig. 2) and install a UHF (ultrahigh-frequency) antenna, the second on April 24 for external connections and removal of an early communications system antenna from the node. The MPLM was berthed at the node on April 24. The crew transferred two EXPRESS (Expedite Processing of Experiments to Space Station) payload racks and individual components from it to the *ISS* and loaded it with return cargo. *Raffaello* was returned to the Payload bay on April 27, as Mission Control Houston and the *ISS* crew struggled with some temporary computer breakdowns.

Soyuz TM-32. The April 28–May 6 Russian mission 2S was the first "taxi" flight to the *ISS*, bringing a fresh Soyuz crew return vehicle for the *ISS* crew, as Soyuz TM-31 was approaching its certified lifetime of 200 days. 2S was crewed by Talgat A. Musabaev and Yuri M. Baturin, and it also carried the first commercial space tourist, U.S. businessman Dennis Tito. After liftoff in Baikonur, the Soyuz capsule caught up with *ISS* in 34 orbits and docked smoothly at the *Zarya* nadir port on April 30. On May 5, the three visitors climbed into the "old" Soyuz TM-31, docked at the SM *Zvezda* aft end, and separated from the station. They made a "textbook landing" in Kazakhstan near Arkalyk.

STS 104. *Atlantis* on Mission ISS-7A, lasting July 12–24, carried a crew of five (Steven W. Lindsey, Charles O. Hobaugh, Michael L. Gernhardt, Janet L. Kavandi, and James F. Reilly) and the 6.5-ton (5.9-metric-ton) joint airlock *Quest*, which—after docking on July 13—was installed at the node's starboard berthing port, completing Phase II of the ISS program (Fig. 3a). Also installed were four high-pressure tanks with oxygen and nitrogen. These activities were supported by three spacewalks by Gernhardt and Reilly, the last one from the new airlock.

STS 105. In *ISS* assembly mission 7A.1 (August 10–22), *Discovery* linked up with the station on August 12 with a four-member crew (Scott J. Horowitz, Frederick W. Sturckow, Patrick G. Forrester, and Daniel T. Barry) plus the new Expedition 3 crew (Culbertson, Dezhurov, and Tyurin) on the second "crew rotation" mission. *Discovery* also brought equipment and supplies, carried in the MPLM *Leonardo* on its second flight, which was docked temporarily at the node for unloading and reloading with return cargo. Barry and Forrester conducted two spacewalks to install an ammonia servicer, materials experiment carriers, handrails, and cables. The shuttle landed at Kennedy Space Center with the Expedition 2 crew (Usachev, Voss, and Helms), which had spent 167 days 7 h 41 min in space.

DC-1 Pirs. The Russian docking compartment DC-1, mission 3R, was launched crewless on September 14 on a Soyuz-U rocket from Baikonur/Kazakhstan. The Stikovochniy Otsek No. 1 (SO1) linked up with the *ISS* on September 16. The new

16-ft-long (4.9-m) module, with a mass of 4 tons (3.6 metric tons), added a docking port for future Soyuz and Progress vehicles arriving at the station, plus a stowage area and an airlock for EVAs in Russian Orlan-M spacesuits (Fig. 3b). DC-1 was launched attached to a cargo ship named Progress M-SO1, a Soyuz-derived instrumentation and propulsion section of about 1.5 tons (1.35 metric tons), which was jettisoned in October, bringing the *ISS* mass to 152 tons (138 metric tons).

Soyuz TM-33. Soyuz 207, *ISS* mission 3S, was the second *ISS* "taxi" flight, lasting October 21–30. Its Franco-Russian "taksisty" crew was Viktor Afanasyev, Konstantin Kozeyev, and Claudie Haigneré, a French woman flying commercially. They brought a fresh Soyuz crew return vehicle to the station, good for another 200 days. Docking was on October 23 at the FGB *Zarya* nadir port. Crew assignment included the French Andromède (Andromeda) science mission, initiated by the French Ministry of Research and led by the French Space Agency CNES. Afanasyev, Kozeyev, and Haigneré departed in the old Soyuz TM-32 and landed in Kazakhstan under automatic control.

STS 108. On the December 5–17 mission, ISS-UF-1, *Endeavour* carried MPLM *Raffaello* with approximately 3 tons (2.7 metric tons) of cargo and four crew members—Dominic L. Gorie, Mark E. Kelly, Linda M. Godwin, and Daniel M. Tani—plus the fourth expeditionary crew of Onufrienko, Bursch, and Walz for the space station, to "rotate" with the Expedition 3 crew after their 128-day stay in space. It was the twelfth shuttle mission to the *ISS* and the first utilization flight (UF-1) of the *ISS* program. Docking occurred on December 7. The MPLM was transferred to the node nadir port by Godwin with the shuttle RMS on December 8. Tani and Godwin conducted an EVA on December 10, the twenty-sixth from a shuttle docked to *ISS*. After cargo unloading and replacement with discarded equipment and waste, *Raffaello* was returned to the shuttle cargo bay on December 14. Before its undocking on the following day, *Endeavour* conducted three reboosts of the station, with a total mean altitude increase of 7.6 nautical miles (14 km). Along with 12 Russian launches, UF-1 brought the total *ISS* missions count to 24. In addition to the above missions, Russia launched four crewless Progress logistics/resupply missions to the *ISS*: M-44 (3P) on February 26, M1-6 (4P) on May 20, M-45 (5P) on August 21, and M1-7 (6P) on November 26.

United States Space Activities

Launch activities in the United States in 2001 showed a distinct downturn from the previous year. There were 24 NASA, Department of Defense, and commercial launch attempts with 23 launches successful (2000: 30 out of 31).

Space shuttle. Six shuttle missions were conducted in 2001, one more than in 2000, all for supply, logistics, outfitting, crew rotation, and orbital assembly of the *ISS*. For the human space flight program, the year was particularly significant in that three of the shuttle missions involved crew rotation (replacement of resident crews on the *ISS*).

Advanced transportation systems activities. In the 5-year-old NASA/industry cooperative effort to develop a reusable space launch vehicle (RLV) to eventually take over launchings for a fraction of the cost of space transportation, 2001 brought some changes. On March 1, NASA announced that the X-33 and X-34 projects would not receive additional government funding, effectively ending these cooperative efforts with private industry to demonstrate in suborbital flight the technologies needed for an RLV. At the same time, NASA announced a new 5-year project, the Space Launch Initiative (SLI), also called the second-generation RLV program. On May 17, NASA awarded 22 contracts for developing the technologies that will be used to build an operational RLV before 2015.

NASA's Hyper-X program suffered a setback in 2001 when the first of three planned X-43 hypersonic test flights, the X-43A, ended in the intentional destruction of the research vehicle after its Pegasus booster rocket, used to accelerate the demonstrator to Mach 7 at 18 mi (29 km), went out of control early in the flight. The 12-ft-long (3.7-m), unpiloted, non-rocket-propelled X-43 vehicles, air-launched from a B-52 airplane, are powered by supersonic combustion ramjets (scramjets) on hydrogen fuel, after acceleration by the booster. The X-43C follow-on program continues. Slightly larger than X-43A, the X-43C will use flight-weight versions of the Air Force HyTech hydrocarbon scramjet engine, rocket-boosted to Mach 4 and then accelerating on its own power to Mach 7. The third demonstrator, the reusable X-43B, will be next, and it will be able to land on a runway after its Mach 7 flight following the B-52 air launch.

NASA is participating in an Air Force–led activity under a new National Hypersonic S&T Plan, formulated by the Office of the Secretary of Defense, to spearhead a much more focused combined government and industry effort to develop hypersonic technologies, which could enable new space transportation for NASA.

Specifically for the *ISS*, NASA continued work on a crew return vehicle to eventually take over the emergency lifeboat function for the space station from the currently chosen Russian Soyuz three-seater capsules. The CRV could provide a shirtsleeve environment for seven crew members. In 2001, NASA continued with full-scale flight testing of the X-38, the prototype test vehicle for the CRV, by dropping it from a B-52 and landing it under a large parafoil. (In 2002, NASA terminated the X-38 effort.)

Space sciences and astronomy. In 2001, the United States launched six civil science spacecraft, up four from the previous year. Since 1995, NASA has markedly increased the number of civil satellites it develops and launches due to the switch in development strategy, shortly after the loss in August 1993 of the *Mars Observer*, from large expensive satellites

to smaller and more numerous ones.

Hubble Space Telescope. Eleven years after it was placed in orbit, the Hubble Space Telescope (HST) continued to probe far beyond the solar system, producing imagery and data useful across a range of astronomical disciplines. Hubble is making discoveries at a rate that is unprecedented for a single observatory, and its contributions to astronomy and cosmology are wide-ranging. In 2001, astronomers using the HST measured the atmosphere of a planet outside our solar system.

Chandra Observatory. Launched on July 23, 1999, on shuttle mission STS 93, the massive 6.5-ton (5.8-metric-ton) *Chandra X-ray Observatory* uses a high-resolution camera, high-resolution mirrors, and a charge-coupled-device (CCD) imaging spectrometer to observe, via x-rays, some of the most violent phenomena in the universe which cannot be seen by Hubble's visual-range telescope. Throughout its second year of operation, *Chandra* continued to provide scientists with views of the high-energy universe never seen before, which promise to revolutionize astronomical and cosmological concepts. From the images, spectra and light curves created from *Chandra's* data streams, researchers have accumulated an impressive list of scientific firsts, including a flare from a brown dwarf star and possibly iron-line emissions in the x-ray afterglow of a gamma-ray burst. A number of technical problems had to be overcome, and thanks to the robust design of the observatory, their impact on its performance has been minimal. In a symposium "Two Years of Science with Chandra" on September 5–7, 2001, *Chandra's* contributions to virtually every astrophysics topic were presented, including stellar coronae, star formation, compact objects, black holes, quasars, supernova remnants, clusters of galaxies, solar system objects, and the resolution of the long-standing mystery of the origin of the celestial x-ray background. In September 2001, NASA formally extended the operational mission of *Chandra* from 5 years to 10 years, including the science grants that fund astronomers to analyze their data and publish their results.

Galileo. In 2001, *Galileo* continued to return unprecedented data on Jupiter and its satellites, particularly on its bizarre moon Io (**Fig. 4**). High-resolution images taken during several close passages of this intriguing satellite by the spacecraft are aiding analysis of the connection between volcanism and the rise and fall of mountains on Io. Few of Io's volcanoes resemble the crater-topped volcanic peaks seen on Earth and Mars; they are in relatively flat regions, not near mountains, but nearly half of the mountains on Io sit right beside volcanic craters. By the end of its observations of Io in early 2002, the spacecraft had discovered 74 of the 120 known Ionian hot spots, and the data will help scientists develop an understanding of how that distant moon resurfaces itself differently than the Earth does. Another important discovery of *Galileo* is the likelihood of a melted saltwater ocean under the moon Europa's icy crust, making it of great interest for future study of the possibility of extraterrestrial life. NASA has extended *Galileo's* original 2-year mission three times. By end-2001, *Galileo* was nearly out of the hydrazine propellant needed to keep its antenna pointed toward Earth and do maneuvers. Plans are for it to make its last flyby of a Jupiter moon in November 2002, when it passes close by Amalthea, then loop one last time away from Jupiter and finally perish in a fiery plunge into Jupiter's atmosphere in September 2003, to ensure that there is no chance the long-lived spacecraft might hit (and possibly contaminate) Europa.

Cassini. NASA's 6-ton (5.4-metric-ton) spacecraft *Cassini* continued its epic 6.7-year, 3.2-billion-kilometer) journey to the planet Saturn. During a final flyby with Jupiter on December 30, 2000, which boosted its velocity by 5000 mi/h (2.2 km/s), *Cassini* collected data on the giant planet—for example, bright auroras on Jupiter and its moon Io, and taking measurements on Jupiter's magnetosphere, which showed that the ionized-gas bubble encasing the planet is lopsided and leaky, with an unexpected abundance of high-energy particles bleeding out of one side, perhaps riding magnetic field lines attached to Jupiter at one end and waving loose on the other. Its readings also indicate that radiation belts very close to Jupiter could damage any future spacecraft there even more severely than previously estimated. The harshest radiation occurs within about 186,000 mi (300,000 km) of the giant planet, closer than the closest passages of the *Galileo* orbiter. The spacecraft is scheduled to enter orbit around the ringed planet Saturn on July 1, 2004. About 6 months after orbit insertion, it will release its piggybacked European-built *Huygens* probe for descent through the thick atmosphere of the moon Titan on January 14, 2005.

DS-1. NASA's *Deep Space 1* (*DS-1*) technology test satellite was launched on October 24, 1998. During a highly successful primary 1-year mission, it tested 12 advanced, high-risk technologies in space, including low-thrust xenon ion propulsion. Its mission was extended another 2 years, and on July 28, 1999, the *DS-1* flew past asteriod 9969/Braille. Camera problems limited the data received during this encounter. When the star tracker, used to navigate the spacecraft, became inoperable, the imaging camera was programmed to carry out the necessary navigation functions. On September 22, 2001, it flew a close encounter of Comet 19P/Borelly, coming within 1349 mi (2171 km) of the its solid core and returning the best images and other science data ever received from a comet. During its fully successful hyperextended mission, *DS-1* conducted further technology tests, until it was retired on December 18, 2001. Its ion propulsion system has provided the equivalent of about 9400-mi/h (4.2-km/s) velocity change to the spacecraft while consuming less than 154 lb (70 kg) of xenon propellant. The system has accumulated more than 640 days of thrust time.

Microwave Anisotropy Mission. NASA's *Microwave Anisotropy Mission* (*MAP*) was launched on June 30 on

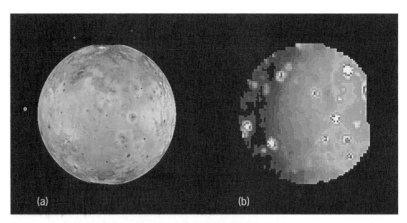

Fig. 4. Images of the same hemisphere of Jupiter's satellite Io from the *Galileo* spacecraft in (*a*) visible wavelengths and (*b*) the infrared wavelength of 5 micrometers. The infrared image serves as a thermal map in which hot eruption sites stand out dramatically, while the visible image serves to correlate the infrared data with geological features apparent in visible wavelengths. The infrared image was recorded when the left half of the hemisphere was in darkness and the right half in daylight. (*NASA/JPL/University of Arizona*)

a Delta 2. After executing several highly elliptical phasing orbits, *MAP* flew by the Moon, getting a gravitational assist to boost it to the second lagrangian libration point L2, from where its differential radiometers measure the temperature fluctuations of the cosmic microwave background radiation, with much higher resolution, sensitivity, and accuracy than the earlier *Cosmic Background Explorer* spacecraft launched in 1989. *See* UNIVERSE.

Genesis. The solar probe *Genesis* was launched on August 8, 2001, on a Delta 2 rocket and went into perfect orbit about the first Earth-Sun lagrangian libration point L1 on November 16. After the unconventional Lissajous orbit insertion (LOI), *Genesis* began the first of five "halo" loops around L1, which will last about 30 months. Science collection started officially on November 30, 2001, when the spacecraft opened its science canister. On December 3, it extended its collector arrays to catch atoms from the solar wind. After 29 months in orbit, the sample collectors will be restowed and returned to Earth, where the sample return capsule will be recovered in midair by helicopter over the Utah desert in September 2004.

ACE and Wind. The *Advanced Composition Explorer* (*ACE*) was launched on August 25, 1997, to the libration point L1. Positioned in a halo orbit around L1, where gravitational forces are in equilibrium, *ACE* in 2001 continued to observe, determine, and compare the isotopic and elemental composition of several distinct samples of matter, including the solar corona, the interplanetary medium, the local interstellar medium, and galactic matter. *Wind*, launched on November 1, 1994, as part of the International Solar-Terrestrial Project (ISTP), was first placed in a sunward, multiple double-lunar swingby orbit with a maximum apogee of 350 earth radii, followed by a halo orbit at the L1 point. Science objectives include measurements for magnetospheric and ionospheric studies, plasma processes occurring in the near-Earth solar wind, and comparison observations in the ecliptic plane for *Ulysses*.

Stardust. NASA's comet probe *Stardust* was launched on February 3, 1999, on a Delta 2 to begin its mission to intercept a comet and return closeup imagery to Earth. Also, for the first time ever, comet dust and interstellar dust particles will be collected during a close encounter with Comet Wild 2 in 2004 and returned to Earth for analysis. *Stardust's* trajectory is making three loops around the Sun before its closest approach to the comet in January 2004. All the collected samples, captured in an aerogel collector, will be retracted into a sample return capsule, which then will be returned to Earth via parachute for a soft landing at the U.S. Air Force's Utah Test and Training Range in 2006.

NEAR-Shoemaker. Launched on February 17, 1996, the *NEAR-Shoemaker* spacecraft entered orbit around the asteroid 433 Eros on February 14, 2000 (after a failure of the first of several rendezvous maneuvers on December 20, 1998, had changed plans), beginning its year-long orbit of the asteroid to determine its mass, structure, geology, composition, gravity, and magnetic field. In 2001, *NEAR-Shoemaker* became the first spacecraft to land on an asteroid. On February 12, the spacecraft was gradually lowered from its 22-mi (35-km) orbit until it touched down on the surface of Eros. Although designed as a purely orbiting mission, *NEAR-Shoemaker* survived the landing and continued operations on the asteroid until it was shut down on February 28.

Ulysses. With the European-built spacecraft and its scientific payload in excellent condition, *Ulysses* is in the middle of its current mission phase of studying the Sun's polar regions under conditions of high solar activity. *Ulysses* ended its south polar pass of the Sun on January 16, 2001, crossed the ecliptic on May 25, and started the second north polar pass on August 31. After reaching its maximum north solar latitude of 80.2° on October 13, it ended the second north polar pass on December 10. *Ulysses'* signals are transmitted to its operations center at NASA's Jet Propulsion Laboratory in Pasadena, California.

Mars exploration. After the stunning failures of two Mars probes in 1999, NASA's Mars exploration program rebounded in 2001. The Red Planet moved back into the focus of scientific inquiry, with new discoveries on the turbulent past of the planet's surface and atmosphere.

The 2001 *Mars Odyssey* probe was launched on April 7 and successfully reached Mars after a 6-month and 286-million-mile (460-million-kilometer) journey on October 24. Entering a highly elliptical orbit around the poles of the Red Planet, it began to change orbit parameters by aerobraking, reducing its ellipticity to become a circular orbit at 250 mi (400 km) by end of January 2002. The orbiter will circle Mars for at least 3 years, with the objective of conducting a detailed mineralogical analysis of the planet's surface from space and measuring the radiation environment. The mission has as its primary science goals to gather data to help determine whether the environment of Mars was ever conducive to life, to characterize the climate and geology of the planet, and to study potential radiation hazards to possible future astronaut missions. The orbiter will also act as a communications relay for future missions to Mars over a period of 5 years.

The *Mars Global Surveyor* (*MGS*) completed its primary mission at the end of January 2001 and entered an extended mission. The spacecraft has returned more data about the Red Planet than all other missions combined. After its arrival at Mars on September 11, 1997, *MGS* started a long series of aerobrake passes around the planet and, after reaching its operational orbit early in 1999, began its mapping mission in March. Since then, *MGS* has been transmitting a steady stream of high-resolution images of Mars, which showed that the Red Planet is a world constantly being reshaped by forces of nature including shifting sand dunes, monster dust devils, wind storms, frosts, and polar ice caps that grow and retreat with the seasons. In 2001, it sent back its one-hundred-thousandth image of the Martian surface and, in tandem with the Hubble Space Telescope, had a ringside seat to the largest global dust storm on the Martian surface seen in decades (**Fig. 5**).

Pioneer 10. The *Pioneer 10* continues on its epic voyage to the stars as contact with it is still maintained by NASA's Deep Space Network. *Pioneer 10* is currently at a distance of 7.6 billion miles (12.2 billion kilometers) from Earth and passing through the transitional region between the farthest traces of the Sun's atmosphere, the heliosphere, still noticeable at that distance, and interstellar space. Signals transmitted by the little spacecraft today need 11 h 17 min to reach Earth. On April 28, 2001, a signal was received from *Pioneer 10*, the first time since August 6, 2000, and it appears that the spacecraft now transmits only when contacted (two-way coherent mode), requiring 22 h 35 min of ground antenna time. On July 9, 2001, exactly 1 year after the last antenna pointing maneuver, radio data from *Pioneer 10* indicated that the maneuver had

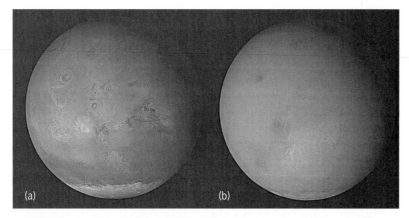

Fig. 5. Global views of Mars from the Mars orbiter camera onboard the *Mars Global Surveyor* (*a*) on June 10, 2001, and (*b*) on July 31, 2001, after the advent of a global dust storm which enshrouded the planet. Dust storm activity began to pick up in late June as southern winter transitioned to spring and cold air from the south polar cap moved northward toward the warmer air at the Martian equator. (*NASA/JPL/Malin Space Science Systems; images provided by Malin Space Science Systems; for more information, contact www.msss.com*)

indeed been successful, and another pointing maneuver was not necessary until the first quarter 2002.

Earth science. In 2001, NASA announced the creation of the first complete "biological record of Earth" by using data from NASA's Sea-viewing Wide Field-of-View sensor (SeaWiFS), aboard the *SeaStar* satellite, launched in 1997. Researchers also suggested that the Earth is becoming a greener greenhouse, determining that plant life in the northern latitudes has been growing more vigorously since 1981. In February 2001, NASA released a new map of Antarctica made from *Radarsat* data. Using the new maps and comparing them to maps produced in 1981, scientists will track Antarctic ice changes, a key to understanding our global environment and climate change. In 2001, NASA research also suggested that desert dust in the atmosphere over Africa might actually inhibit rainfall in the region, contributing to drought conditions.

Department of Defense space activities. U.S. military space organizations continued their efforts to make space a routine part of military operations across all service lines. One focus concerns plans for shifting the advanced technology base toward space in order to build a new technology foundation for more integrated air and space operations in the twenty-first century as space is increasingly dominant in military reconnaissance, communications, warning, navigation, missile defense, and weather-related areas. The distinction between space and missile activities is increasingly theoretical, as evidenced by missile interception tests made in 1999: a THAAD (Theater High-Altitude Area Defense) missile successfully intercepted a target missile outside the Earth's atmosphere on June 10 of that year. On December 4, 2001, a missile launched from the Marshall Islands successfully intercepted a Minuteman missile at 162 mi (260 km) altitude with an "Exoatmospheric Kill Vehicle," the third success in the context of the Ground-based Midcourse Defense (GMD).

In 2001, there were seven military space launches from Cape Canaveral Air Force Station, Florida, and Vandenberg Air Force Base, California: two Delta 2 rockets, two Atlas 2AS rockets, and three Titan 4B launch vehicles. Payloads included one Global Positioning System (GPS) navigation satellite, two large communication satellites (comsats), one large imaging spacecraft, one missile warning satellite, and two recon satellites.

Commercial space activities. In 2001, commercial space activities in the United States encountered serious industry difficulties due to a crisis in the communications space market caused by failures of satellite constellations for mobile telephony.

In addition to the financial crisis, some difficulties remained due to the export restrictions imposed on the U.S. industry on sensitive technologies. In general, commercial ventures continue to play a relatively minor role in U.S. space activities, amounting in 2001 to about 50% of commercial satellites and associated launch services worldwide.

Of the 24 total launch attempts by the United States in 2001 (versus 31 in 2000), 7 carried commercial payloads (NASA: 10; military: 7), as in 2000, with one failure. In the launch services area, Boeing launched seven Delta 2 vehicles, followed by Lockheed Martin with four Atlas 2A. The failed launch was an Orbital Science Corporation (OSC) Taurus with commercial payloads. Both sea launches of the Zenit 3SL rocket from the *Odyssey* launch platform floating at the Equator were successful, operated by a partnership of Boeing, RSC-Energia (Russia), NPO Yushnoye (Ukraine), and Kvaerner Group (Norway).

Russian Space Activities

Despite a slowly improving national economy, Russia in 2001 showed a pronounced slowdown in space operations from 2000. Its total of 23 successful launches (out of 23 attempts) was actually 11 less than the previous year's 34 (out of 36 attempts): eight Soyuz-U (two crewed), six Protons, three Tsiklons (modified from the former intercontinental ballistic missile [ICBM] SS-9), two Soyuz-FG, one Zenit 2, one Molniya, one Kosmos-3M, and one Start 1 (converted from the former Topol ICBM). The new Soyuz-FG rocket was launched for the first time on May 21; due to a new fuel injection system, it provides a 5% increase in thrust over the Soyuz-U, enhancing its lift capability by 440 lb (200 kg). This enables it to carry the new Soyuz-TMA spacecraft, which is heavier than the Soyuz-TM ship currently used to ferry crews to the *ISS*. Soyuz-TMA will be flown for the first time in October 2002.

In its partnership with the United States in the development of the *ISS*, Russia launched two crewed Soyuz "taxi" ships to provide the *ISS* with the periodically renewed crew return vehicle, and four automated Progress cargo ships. It also added a Russian airlock module, the DC 1 (Docking Module 1) *Pirs*, launched on a Soyuz rocket, to the Russian segment of the *ISS*.

Space station Mir. The year 2001 saw the end of *Mir*. Due to lack of financing, Russia had been forced to abandon its long-lived space station in August 1999 when its owner, RSC-Energia, found itself unable to fund continued crewed operation of the station. This left the station without a crew for the first time since a short crewless period 10 years earlier. On January 26, 2001, *Mir* was visited one last time by a crewless Progress tanker ship (MI-5), and on March 20, in a precise maneuver by the Progress propulsion system, the venerable 134-ton (122-metric-ton) space station was deorbited for a historic atmospheric reentry over the Pacific Ocean on March 23, with fiery debris streaking over the Fiji archipelago. Launched on February 20, 1986, in its 15 years of operation *Mir* circled Earth over 86,000 times, covering a distance of about 2.5 billion miles (4 billion kilometers). During 4591 days of human occupation, the complex hosted 125 cosmonauts and astronauts from 12 different countries and saw 78 spacewalks conducted from it. It supported 17 space expeditions, including 28 long-term crews. Its residents arrived via 31 spacecraft that docked with *Mir*, including nine U.S. space shuttles. Additionally, 64 crewless Progress cargo ships periodically ferried supplies, equipment, and propellants to *Mir*, which also served as a weightless laboratory for 23,000 scientific and medical experiments.

Commercial space activities. The Russian space program's major push to enter into the world's commercial arena by promoting its space products on the external market, driven by the need to survive in an era of severe reductions of public financing, suffered a setback in 2001. First launched in July 1965, the Proton heavy lifter, originally intended as a ballistic missile (UR500), by end-2001 had flown 209 times since 1980, with 13 failures (reliability: 0.938). Its launch rate in recent years has been as high as 13 per year. Of the six Protons launched in 2001 (2000: 14), two were launched for commercial customers (ASTRA 2C, PAS-10), and four others launched for the state, including military. From 1985 to 2001, 157 Proton and 381 Soyuz rockets were launched, with nine failures of the Proton and nine of the Soyuz, giving a combined reliability index of 0.966. By end-2001, the Soyuz rocket had flown 70 consecutive successful missions, including 11 with human crews on board.

Of the three launches of the Russian-Ukrainian Zenit 2 rocket, two were conducted from the ocean-based sea launch facility *Odyssey* (in which RSC-Energia has a 25% share), carrying the radio comsats XM2 "Rock" and XM1 "Roll."

In a new commercial venture, which replaced the former venture of selling services on board the *Mir* space station, Russia has now taken the initiative to market journeys to the *ISS* to "space tourists," beginning with Dennis Tito in April 2001, and paying guest cosmonauts such as Claudie Haigneré.

European Space Activities

Europe is positioned as world number 2 in research and development for space projects, but its efforts in 2001 remained modest compared to astronautics activities of NASA and the U.S. Department of Defense. A new European space strategy is emerging, as stated at the Council Meeting of ESA at ministerial level, held on November 15 and 16, 2001, at Edinburgh, Scotland, which strives to achieve an autonomous Europe in space through close cooperation and partnership between ESA and the European Commission. These are two very different institutional entities, and it will take considerable time to implement a joint European space policy, in which ESA is confirmed as the space agency for Europe.

For the European space program, launch successes in 2001 were less than expected because of the non-availability of some commercial spacecraft and the weak performance of the tenth Ariane 5 rocket.

In the launch vehicle area, Arianespace continued to operate a successful series of six Ariane 4 launches, two down from 2000 (due to satellite delivery delays), carrying seven commercial satellites for customers such as Italy, Turkey, United Kingdom, and the United States. At year's end, the Ariane 4 had flown 136 times, with seven failures (94.85% reliability) from its Kourou/French Guyana spaceport.

In 2001, the most significant events for ESA, the European intergovernmental organization comprising 14 nations, were the Edinburgh conference, with agreements on future developments including Ariane 5, a program to integrate eastern European countries, such as Rumania, Hungary, and Poland, in ESA, and the launch of *Artemis* on an Ariane 5 on July 12, along with the Japanese BSAT-2b Ku-band/video satellite.

In the human space flight area, while the *ISS* remains ESA's biggest ongoing program and its only engagement in the human space flight endeavor, European *ISS* contributions remain unchanged due to top-level agreement signed by previous governments of the participating nations. France has a large and active national space program, including bilateral (outside of ESA) activities with the United States and Russia. In Italy, the space agency ASI, created in 1988, participates in the *ISS* program through ESA but also has a protocol with NASA for the delivery of multipurpose logistics modules for the *ISS*. In Germany, the declining interest of the government in this field continued in 2001. Germany is the second major ESA contributor after France, but it has only a very small national space program.

ESA's science and communications research satellite *Artemis* was launched on July 12 on an Ariane 5, which sustained a failure in its upper stage (stage 2) by cutting off 80 seconds early. However, *Artemis* could ultimately be recovered and positioned at its proper location. The 1.65-ton (1.5-metric-ton) dry-mass satellite expands European capabilities in satellite communications, testing new technologies (such as laser communications), acting as a relay platform to improve existing services to other satellites and systems, and supporting the development of a European satellite navigation system. It will perform three specific functions: provide voice and data communications between mobile terminals, mainly for cars, trucks, trains or boats; broadcast accurate navigation information as an element of European Geostationary Navigation Overlay Service (EGNOS), a European satellite system designed to augment U.S. GPS navigation satellites and a similar Russian system known as the Global Orbiting Navigation Satellite System (GLONASS); and send high-data-rate communications directly between satellites in low Earth orbit and the ground. Its Semiconductor Laser Inter-Satellite Link Experiment (SILEX) laser communications device established the first liaison with the French *Spot 4* satellite on November 15, 2001, and 5 days later the first-ever image was transmitted between two satellites, when the "Pastel" terminal on *Spot 4* sent an Earth picture to the "Opale" terminal on *Artemis*, and thence to the ground, at a transfer rate of 50 Mb/s.

Asian Space Activities

China, India, and Japan have space programs capable of launch and satellite development and operations.

China. China's space program continued strong activities in 2001. After China separated its military and civil space programs in 1998 as part of a ministerial reform, the China National Space Administration (CNSA) became responsible for planning and development of space activities. Its top priority today is the development of piloted space flight (followed by applications satellites). After the launch and recovery, on November 21, 1999, of its first inhabitable (but still crewless) capsule "Shenzou," an 8-ton (7.2-metric-ton) modified version of the Russian Soyuz vehicle, China successfully launched and recovered Shenzou 2 on January 9, 2001, with several biological experiments and small animals on board, the only launch from the People's Republic in 2001. The launch vehicle was the new human-rated Long March 2F rocket. China's Long March (Chang Zheng, CZ) series of launch vehicles consists of 12 different versions, which by the end of 2001 had made 65 flights, sending 73 payloads (satellites and spacecraft) into space, with 90% success rate. China has three modern (but landlocked, thus azimuth-restricted) launch facilities: at Jinquan (Base 20, also known as Shuang Cheng-Tzu/East Wind) for low Earth orbit (LEO) missions, Taiyuan (Base 25) for Sun-synchronous missions, and Xichang (Base 27) for geostationary missions.

India. The Indian Space Research Organization (ISRO, created in 1969), part of the Department of Space (DOS), has intensified its development programs for satellites and launch vehicles. Main satellite programs are the INSAT (Indian National Satellite) telecommunications system, the IRS (Indian Remote Sensing) satellites for earth resources, and the new GSat series of large, up to 2.5-ton (2.3-metric-ton) experimental geostationary comsats. India's main launchers today are the PSLV (polar space launch vehicle) and the Delta 2 class GSLV (geostationary space launch vehicle). With one of its two launches in 2001 (April 18), India conducted the maiden flight of the GSLV-D1, equipped with a cryogenic third stage with the KVD 1 cryogenic rocket engine procured from Glavkosmos, Russia, carrying the 1.5-ton (1.35-metric-ton) *GSat 1*. Due to underperformance of the KVD 1 (0.5% thrust shortfall), *GSat 1* did not reach its correct geosynchronous orbit. The second launch (October 22) was a polar satellite launch vehicle with three satellites from India, Germany, and Belgium.

Japan. The central space development and operations organization in Japan is the National Space Development Agency (NASDA), spread over four centers: Tanegashima Space Center (major launch facility), Tsukuba Space Center (tracking and control), Kakuda Propulsion Center, and Earth Observation Center. NASDA developed the launchers N1, N2, H1, and H2. After seven test launches of the H2 until 1999, it was decided to focus efforts on the new, modified H2-A vehicle, an upgraded and more cost-effective version of the H-2. Its maiden flight took place in 2001 (August 29), carrying two technology development payloads (VEP-2 and LRE). The H-2A shows future growth capability toward increasing payloads and decreasing launch costs, but development funding for it may be increasingly difficult to obtain.

One area of great promise for Japan is the *ISS* program, in which the country is participating with a sizable 12.6% share. Its space budget in 2001 was comparable to that of the entire European (ESA) effort. Its contributions to the *ISS* are the Japanese experiment module (JEM), now called "Kibo" (Hope), along with its ancillary remote manipulator system and porchlike exposed facility, and the H-2 transfer vehicle (HTV), which will carry about 6.7 tons (6 metric tons) of provisions to the *ISS* once or twice a year, launched on an H2-A.

For background information *see* ASTEROID; COMMUNICATIONS SATELLITE; INFRARED ASTRONOMY; JUPITER; MARS; MILITARY SATELLITES; MOON; REMOTE SENSING; SATELLITE ASTRONOMY; SOLAR WIND; SPACE FLIGHT; SPACE PROBE; SPACE SHUTTLE; SPACE STATION; SPACE TECHNOLOGY; SUN; ULTRAVIOLET ASTRONOMY; X-RAY ASTRONOMY in the McGraw-Hill Encyclopedia of Science & Technology.

Jesco von Puttkamer

Bibliography. *Aerospace Daily*; *AIAA AEROSPACE AMERICA*; *Aviation Week & Space Technology*; European Space Agency, *Press Releases*; *European Space Directory 2002* (17th ed.); NASA Public Affairs Office, *News Releases*; *SPACE NEWS*.

Space nuclear technology

Space nuclear technology has been used for power generation, propulsion, and heating. It was first used in 1961 with the launch of the U.S. Navy's *Transit 4A* navigation satellite powered by a radioisotope thermoelectric generator (RTG), and both the United States and Russia have since launched spacecraft with radioisotope thermoelectric generators and nuclear reactors to generate power. No nuclear rockets have been launched, but there was extensive design and testing of such rockets in the United States in the 1950s and 1960s.

Radioisotope thermoelectric generators. These sources have powered satellites, *Apollo* lunar experiments, and deep space probes. The SNAP (Systems for Nuclear Auxiliary Power) 3B was the first such power source used in a United States spacecraft. It had 93 g (0.2 lb) of plutonium, which produced 2.7 watts electric to power the *Transit* navigation satellite. The most advanced radioisotope thermoelectric generators are in use for the *Galileo* mission, consisting of 54.4 kg (120 lb) of plutonium

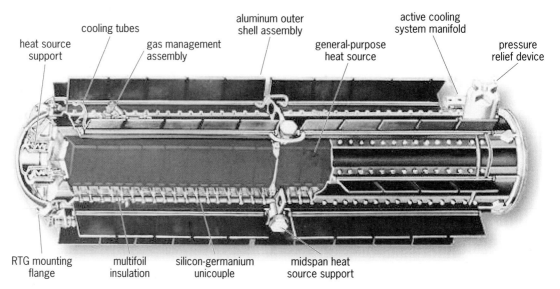

Fig. 1. Cutout drawing of a radioisotope thermoelectric generator (RTG). (*NASA*)

producing 290 We. Radioisotope thermoelectric generators use a radioisotope as a source of heat for a thermoelectric generator, which uses semiconductors to convert the heat directly to electricity (**Fig. 1**). There are no moving parts to wear out or lubricate. This makes the generators very reliable. Plutonium-238 has been the radioisotope of choice for radioisotope thermoelectric generators on United States spacecraft, although other fuels have been used. Plutonium-238 has a half-life of 87.75 years. This means that if a radioisotope thermoelectric generator starts out producing 100 We, in 87.75 years it will produce 50 W. The radioisotope thermoelectric generators aboard the two *Voyager* spacecraft, which were launched in 1977 and have left the solar system, are still producing power. Besides long life, other advantages of radioisotope thermoelectric generators are their high power density (power per unit mass) and their ability to operate independently of the Sun's energy. Thus, operation is not affected by the distance of the spacecraft from the Sun, whether there is shading caused by other parts of the spacecraft, or the angle of the Sun's light with the spacecraft's outer surface. This independence is the main reason that radioisotope thermoelectric generators are preferred for deep-space missions. Solar arrays would be too big to be practicable to reach even Jupiter. Radioisotope thermoelectric generators have an efficiency of roughly 8–9% in converting heat to electricity.

Radioisotope thermoelectric generators have some disadvantages, including the high cost of plutonium and the hazardous properties of this metal. Plutonium is not a naturally occurring element, and must be produced in nuclear reactors. Moreover, plutonium is toxic since it is a heavy metal, like lead, and is radioactive.

Dynamic isotope power systems. For power levels of up to about 1 kilowatt electric, the heat of radioisotope decay can be used to power a dynamic Rankine, Brayton, or Stirling power conversion device in a configuration known as a dynamic isotope power system (DIPS). Rankine devices change a liquid to a gas that turns a turbine to produce electricity (**Fig. 2***b*). Brayton devices use heat to expand a gas, such as helium, which turns a turbine (Fig. 2*c*). Stirling devices use heat to expand a gas to push a piston. All of these devices have the advantage of achieving approximately three times the efficiency of a thermoelectric generator. With the higher efficiency, they can produce the same power using less radioisotope fuel (lowering cost), or can produce higher power levels. Their disadvantage is that they have many moving parts, with consequent reduced reliability.

Reactors. Nuclear reactors in space are similar to terrestrial reactors, except that water is not used as the coolant. Water expands when it freezes, and that would lead to a loss of coolant due to ruptured pipes or radiators. Only one United States reactor has flown in space, the SNAP 10A, which was launched on an Atlas-Agena D vehicle on April 3, 1965. It was a zirconium hydride, uranium-235-powered reactor with control drums to raise and lower the power levels. Control drums are cylinders one-half of which have a material that absorbs neutrons while the other half reflects neutrons. (The neutrons cause the uranium nuclei to fission.) The SNAP 10A employed thermoelectric power conversion using silicon-germanium semiconductors. The power output was 533 W with an input of 43.8 kilowatts thermal, which yielded an efficiency of 1.22%. After 43 days the reactor shut itself down. This was theorized to have resulted from a failure in the voltage regulator in the Agena upper stage. At an orbit altitude of roughly 1300 km (800 mi), the reactor will reenter the atmosphere in 4000 years, and by then all the radioactive by-products will have decayed to safe levels.

Reactors are capable of achieving very high power outputs. When they are coupled with a Brayton- or

Rankine-cycle conversion device, megawatts of power can be generated. They have great potential for powering a lunar or Mars base. Since reactors are subcritical (not splitting atoms and producing heat) until they reach orbit, a reactor on the launch pad is less radioactive than a radioisotope thermoelectric generator.

Nuclear rockets. In 1955 Project Rover began to design and test nuclear rockets. In a chemical rocket the fuel burns with an oxidizer and the hot gases go through a nozzle. In a nuclear rocket the fuel, normally hydrogen, is heated by the reactor instead of a chemical reaction. Consequently the nuclear rocket is twice as efficient as a chemical rocket. This means that transit times for a mission to Mars are greatly reduced, making it ideal for a crewed mission. Further, the same rocket could take twice the payload for the same transit time. The United States tested many reactors. The most powerful was the NERVA, which achieved thrusts of 337 kilonewtons (75,000 lbf) at a specific impulse (efficiency) of 8085 m/s (825 s). By comparison the space shuttle main engines have a specific impulse of 4000 m/s (408 s).

Radioisotope heating units. Although not as well known as radioisotope thermoelectric generators or reactors, radioisotope heating units (RHUs) serve a vital purpose. They are small circular discs with plutonium in the middle. The heat of radioactive decay keeps parts of a spacecraft warm, such as boom joints or detectors at the end of the booms. If these parts are not at the correct temperature, they may not deploy (joints) or may not operate (detectors) because they are frozen. Heating them by using resistive heaters may require too much electrical power. This increases the mass of wiring, and thus radioisotope heating units solve many thermal design problems on deep-space probes.

Prospective applications. The National Aeronantics and Space Administration (NASA) is planning to use a radioisotope thermoelectric generator to power the 2009 Mars Smart Lander/Mobile Laboratory. It will be able to roam Mars day and night, searching for landing sites worth exploring.

Glenn Research Center is looking into Stirling engines to boost the power output and efficiency of spacecraft power systems starting in 2003. The new systems would use plutonium to heat four free-piston Stirling engines (FPSE), mounted in a "plus sign" design so that the movement of the pistons would cancel out any vibration.

Although radioisotope thermoelectric generators can generate enough power to power a spacecraft and its electric rocket, they cannot produce enough thrust to slow down the spacecraft to orbit an object, such as a planet or asteroid, for a long investigation. Nuclear reactors using a Brayton cycle are being designed to produce the tens of kilowatts needed for this mission, as are electric ion engines with a specific impulse of 88,200 m/s (9000 s).

Current scenarios for a crewed mission to Mars require approximately 7 months to transit to Mars, a year on the surface, and 7 months to come back

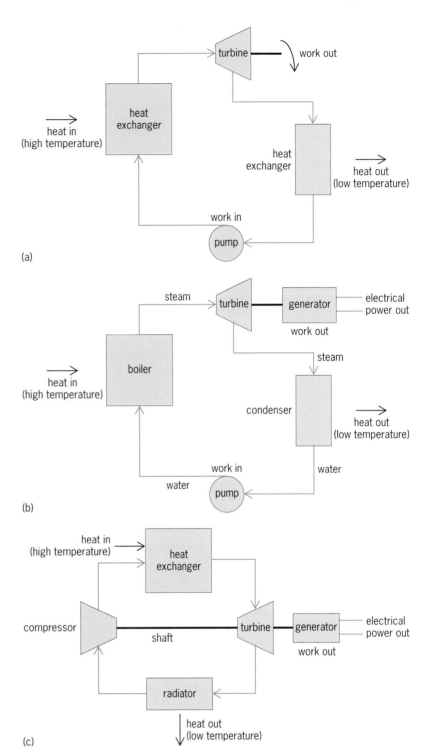

(a)

(b)

(c)

Fig. 2. Thermodynamic cycles. (*a*) Carnot cycle (conceptual). (*b*) Rankine cycle (ideal). (*c*) Brayton cycle (ideal).

to Earth. Many proposals have been made to make the total time shorter. The most promising is to use nuclear reactor rockets (1) to send large amounts of supplies to Mars for the crewed expedition, including fuel, or fuel-making devices, for the return mission; and (2) to speed the transit time to and from Mars, decreasing the amount of time the astronauts are exposed to cosmic rays and weightlessness. The reactor would be shielded from the astronauts and probably positioned at the end of a long boom to further minimize radiation exposure. Immediately behind the reactor would be the rocket nozzle. Fuel would be pumped to the reactor and heated, and the resulting hot gas would be sent though the nozzle.

Reactor rockets could be used to ferry supplies to a Moon base as well, or from a Moon base to Mars because of the greater efficiency of this rocket. Even a crewed trip to a satellite of Jupiter or Saturn is possible. The ship could use a combination of a hydrogen-fueled rocket to leave Earth's vicinity, and a nuclear electric rocket (in which the reactor would supply the electricity for the electric rocket and the spacecraft) to provide continuous thrust to Jupiter. At arrival the hydrogen reactor rocket would be reactivated to produce the high thrust needed to orbit Jupiter. A combination of aerobraking and rocket thrust might also be used. Hydrogen and helium taken from Jupiter's atmosphere would be used as fuel for the return trip.

Many designs for Moon or Mars bases have included nuclear reactors for power generation. To shield the astronauts from radiation, the reactor is located far away from the base or is buried, or both methods are used. Reactors are the only power supply that will have the megawatts of power needed to supply a base, particularly on Mars where sandstorms would constantly cover any solar arrays on the surface.

For background information *see* BRAYTON CYCLE; ELECTROTHERMAL PROPULSION; NUCLEAR BATTERY; NUCLEAR REACTOR; RANKINE CYCLE; ROCKET PROPULSION; SPACE POWER SYSTEMS; SPACE PROBE; SPECIFIC IMPULSE; STIRLING ENGINE; THERMOELECTRIC POWER GENERATOR in the McGraw-Hill Encyclopedia of Science & Technology.   Jeffrey C. Mitchell

Bibliography. J. A. Angelo and D. Buden, *Space Nuclear Power*, Orbit Book Co., Malabar, FL, 1985; A. K. Hyder et al., *Spacecraft Power Technologies*, Imperial College Press, London, 2000.

Stem cells

Stem cells are cells that have the ability to self-replicate and to give rise to specialized cells. Stem cells can be found at different stages of fetal development and are present in a wide range of adult tissues. Many of the terms used to distinguish stem cells are based on their origins and the cell types of their progeny.

There are three basic types of stem cells. Totipotent stem cells, meaning their potential is total, have the capacity to give rise to every cell type of the body and to form an entire organism. Pluripotent stem cells, such as embryonic stem cells, are capable of generating virtually all cell types of the body but are unable to form a functioning organism. Multipotent stem cells can give rise only to a limited number of cell types. For example, adult stem cells, also called organ- or tissue-specific stem cells, refer to multipotent stem cells found in specialized organs and tissues after birth. Their primary function is to replenish cells lost from normal turnover or disease in the specific organs and tissues in which they are found.

Totipotent and embryonic stem cells. Totipotent stem cells occur at the earliest stage of embryonic development. The union of sperm and egg creates a single totipotent cell. This cell divides into identical cells in the first hours after fertilization. All these cells have the potential to develop into a fetus when they are placed into the uterus. [To date, no such totipotent stem cell lines (primary cell cultures) have been developed.] The first differentiation of totipotent cells forms a hollow sphere of cells called the blastocyst, which has an outer layer of cells and an inner cell mass inside the sphere. The outer layer of cells will form the placenta and other supporting tissues during fetal development, whereas cells of the inner cell mass go on to form all three primary germ layers: ectoderm, mesoderm, and endoderm. The three germ layers are the embryonic source of all types of cells and tissues of the body. Embryonic stem cells are derived from the inner cell mass of the blastocyst. They retain the capacity to give rise to cells of all three germ layers. However, embryonic stem cells cannot form a complete organism because they are unable to generate the entire spectrum of cells and structures required for fetal development. Thus, embryonic stem cells are pluripotent, not totipotent, stem cells.

Embryonic germ cells. Embryonic germ (EG) cells differ from embryonic stem cells in the tissue sources from which they are derived, but appear to be similar to embryonic stem cells in their pluripotency. Human embryonic germ cell lines are established from the cultures of the primordial germ cells obtained from the gonadal ridge of late-stage embryos, a specific part that normally develops into the testes or the ovaries. Embryonic germ cells in culture, like cultured embryonic stem cells, form embryoid bodies, which are dense, multilayered cell aggregates consisting of partially differentiated cells. The embryoid body–derived cells have high growth potential. The cell lines generated from cultures of the embryoid body cells can give rise to cells of all three embryonic germ layers, indicating that embryonic germ cells may represent another source of pluripotent stem cells.

Growing mouse embryonic stem cells. Much of the knowledge about embryonic development and stem cells has been accumulated from basic research on mouse embryonic stem cells. The techniques for separating and culturing mouse embryonic stem cells from the inner cell mass of the blastocyst were first developed in the early 1980s. To maintain their growth potential and pluripotency, mouse embryonic stem cells can be grown on a feeder layer, usually consisting of mouse embryonic fibroblast cells. The feeder cells support embryonic stem cells by secreting a cytokine growth factor, the leukemia inhibitory factor, into the growth medium. Alternatively, purified leukemia inhibitory factor can be added to the growth medium without the use of a mouse embryonic feeder layer. (The leukemia inhibitory factor serves an essential growth factor to maintain embryonic stem cells in culture.) A line of embryonic stem cells can be generated from a single cell under culture conditions that keep embryonic stem cells in a proliferative and undifferentiated state. Embryonic stem cell lines can produce indefinite numbers of identical stem cells. When mouse embryonic stem cells are integrated into an embryo at the blastocyst stage, the introduced embryonic stem cells can contribute to cells in all tissues of the resulting mouse. In the absence of feeder cells and the leukemia inhibitory factor in cultures, embryonic stem cells undergo differentiation spontaneously. Many studies are focused on directing differentiation of embryonic stem cells in culture. The goal is to generate specific cell types. Formation of cell aggregates with three-dimensional structure during embryonic stem cell differentiation in culture may allow some of the cell-cell interaction to mimic that of in vivo development. The culture conditions can be designed to support and select specific cell types. With these experimental strategies, preliminary success has been achieved to generate some cell types, such as primitive types of vascular structures, blood cells, nerve cells, and pancreatic insulin-producing cells.

Growing human embryonic stem cells. Since 1998, research teams have succeeded in growing human embryonic stem cells in culture. Human embryonic stem cell lines have been established from the inner cell mass of human blastocysts that were produced through in vitro fertilization procedures. The techniques for growing human embryonic stem cells are similar to those used for growth of mouse embryonic stem cells. However, human embryonic stem cells must be grown on a mouse embryonic fibroblast feeder layer or in media conditioned by mouse embryonic fibroblasts (see **illus.**). There are a number of human embryonic stem lines being generated and maintained in laboratories in the United States and other nations, including Australia, Sweden, India, South Korea, and Israel. The National Institutes of Health has created a Human Embryonic Stem Cell Registry, which lists stem cell lines that have been developed and can be used for research. Human embryonic stem cell lines can be maintained in culture to generate indefinite numbers of identical stem cells for research. As with mouse embryonic stem cells, culture conditions have been designed to direct differentiation into specific cell types (for example, neural and hematopoietic cells).

Adult stem cells. Adult stem cells occur in mature tissues. Like all stem cells, adult stem cells can self-replicate. Their ability to self-renew can last throughout the lifetime of individual organisms. But unlike embryonic stem cells, it is usually difficult to expand adult stem cells in culture. Adult stem cells reside in specific organs and tissues, but account for a very small number of the cells in tissues. They are responsible for maintaining a stable state of the specialized

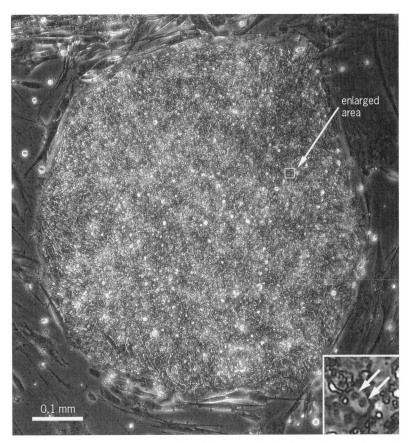

enlarged area

0.1 mm

A colony of the human embryonic stem cell line H9 growing in culture. The elongated cells surrounding the colony are part of the mouse embryonic fibroblast feeder layer on which the stem cells are grown. The inset shows an enlargement of the indicated area of the colony with arrows pointing to the two nuclei of a single stem cell. The H9 cell line meets the criteria for the use of human embryonic stem cells by researchers funded by the U.S. government. (*Courtesy of Clay Glennon*)

tissues. To replace lost cells, stem cells typically generate intermediate cells called precursor or progenitor cells, which are no longer capable of self-renewal. However, they continue undergoing cell divisions, coupled with maturation, to yield fully specialized cells. Such stem cells have been identified in many types of adult tissues, including bone marrow, blood, skin, gastrointestinal tract, dental pulp, retina of the eye, skeletal muscle, liver, pancreas, and brain. Adult stem cells are usually designated according to their source and their potential. Adult stem cells are multipotent because their potential is normally limited to one or more lineages of specialized cells. However, a special multipotent stem cell that can be found in bone marrow, called the mesenchymal stem cell, can produce all cell types of bone, cartilage, fat, blood, and connective tissues.

Blood stem cells. Blood stem cells, or hematopoietic stem cells, are the most studied type of adult stem cells. The concept of hematopoietic stem cells is not new, since it has been long realized that mature blood cells are constantly lost and destroyed. Billions of new blood cells are produced each day to make up the loss. This process of blood cell generation, called hematopoiesis, occurs largely in the bone marrow. The presence of hematopoietic stem cells in the bone marrow was first demonstrated in a mouse model in the early 1960s. The blood system of a mouse that has been subjected to heavy radiation can be restored by infusion of bone marrow. The stem cells responsible for reconstituting the blood system generate visible cell colonies on the spleen of the recipient mouse. Each of the spleen colonies consists of one or more types of blood cells, and all the cells in a colony are derived from a single cell. Self-renewal capacity of the colony-forming cells is demonstrated by their ability to form secondary spleen colonies. Such blood stem cells, known as colony forming unit–spleen cells, qualify as pluripotent hematopoietic stem cells because they can replicate and give rise to multiple types of mature blood cells.

Isolating blood stem cells. Like other adult stem cells, blood stem cells are rare and difficult to isolate. Only about 1 in 100,000 cells in the bone marrow is a stem cell. Scientists have used cell-sorting methods to enrich and purify blood stem cells. Stem cells differ from mature cells in their surface markers, which are specific protein molecules on the cell membrane that can be tagged with monoclonal antibodies. By using a set of surface markers, some expressed mainly on stem cells and others on mature blood cells, nearly pure populations of stem cells can be separated from bone marrow. The stem cells purified by this approach can engraft (begin to grow and function) and reconstitute the blood system in the recipient. In animal studies, as few as 30 purified stem cells can rescue a mouse that has been subjected to heavy radiation. Besides the bone marrow, a small number of blood stem cells can be found in circulating blood. In addition, stem cells in the bone marrow can be mobilized into the bloodstream by injecting the donor with certain growth factors or cytokines. This approach can result in a large number of stem cells circulating in peripheral blood, from which they can be collected and used for transplant therapy.

Umbilical cord blood. Another emerging source of blood stem cells is human umbilical cord blood. Umbilical cord blood is a small amount of blood remaining in the placenta and blood vessels of the umbilical cord. It is traditionally treated as a waste material after delivery of the newborn. However, since the recognition of the presence of blood stem cells in umbilical cord blood in the late 1980s, umbilical cord blood collection and banking has grown quickly. Similar to bone marrow, umbilical cord blood can be used as a source material of stem cells for transplant therapy. However, because of the limited number of stem cells in umbilical cord blood, most of the procedures are performed for young children of relatively low body weight. A current focus of study is to promote the growth of umbilical cord blood stem cells in culture in order to generate sufficient numbers of stem cells for adult recipients.

Neural stem cells. Neural stem cells, the multipotent stem cells that generate nerve cells, are a new focus in stem cell research. Active cellular turnover does not occur in the adult nervous system as it does in renewing tissues such as blood or skin. Because of this observation, it had been a dogma that the adult brain and spinal cord were unable to regenerate new nerve cells. However, since the early 1990s, neural stem cells have been isolated from the adult brain as well as fetal brain tissues. Stem cells in the adult brain are found in the areas called the subventricular zone and the ventricle zone. Brain ventricles are small cavities filled with cerebrospinal fluid. Another location of brain stem cells occurs in the hippocampus, a special structure of the cerebral cortex related to memory function. Stem cells isolated from these areas are able to divide and to give rise to nerve cells (neurons) and neuron-supporting cell types in culture.

Plasticity. Stem cell plasticity refers to the phenomenon of adult stem cells from one tissue generating the specialized cells of another tissue. The longstanding concept of adult organ-specific stem cells is that they are restricted to producing the cell types of their specific tissues. However, a series of recent studies have challenged the concept of tissue restriction of adult stem cells. Much of the experimental evidence is derived from transplant studies with blood stem cells. Bone marrow stem cells have been shown to contribute to liver, skeletal muscle, and cardiac cells in human recipients. In mouse models, purified blood stem cells have been demonstrated to generate cells in nonblood tissues, including the liver, gut, and skin. Although the stem cells appear able to cross their tissue-specific boundaries, crossing occurs generally at a low frequency and mostly only under conditions of host organ damage. The finding of stem cell plasticity is unorthodox and unexpected (since adult stem cells are considered to be organ/tissue-specific), but it carries significant implications for potential cell therapy. For example, if differentiation can be redirected, stem cells of abundant source and easy access, such as blood stem cells in bone marrow or umbilical cord blood, could be used to substitute stem cells in tissues that are difficult to isolate, such as heart and nervous system tissue.

Potential clinical applications. Stem cells hold great potential for developing cell therapies to treat a wide range of human diseases. Already in clinical use is blood stem cell transplant therapy, well known as bone marrow transplant therapy for the treatment of patients with certain types of blood diseases and cancers. The discovery of stem cells in various adult tissues, stem cell plasticity, and human embryonic stem cells brings new excitement and opportunities. Stem cells offer the possibility of cell replacement therapy for many human diseases, such as Parkinson's and Alzheimer's diseases, spinal cord injury, diabetes, heart disease, and arthritis, that result from loss or damage of cells in a specialized tissue of the body. Stem cell therapy might revolutionize the treatment and outcome of these diseases. Stem cell science is still in the very early stage. Much more research is required to understand the biological mechanisms that govern cell differentiation and to identify factors that direct cell specialization. Future cell therapy will depend largely on advances in the understanding of stem cell biology and the ability to harness the process of stem cell growth and differentiation.

For background information *see* CELL DIFFERENTIATION; EMBRYOLOGY; EMBRYONIC DIFFERENTIATION; GERM LAYERS; HEMATOPOIESIS; NEUROGENESIS; REGENERATION (BIOLOGY); TRANSPLANTATION BIOLOGY in the McGraw-Hill Encyclopedia of Science & Technology.   Chen Wang

Bibliography. J. Rossant, Stem cells from the mammalian blastocyst, *Stem Cells*, 19:447–482, 2001; G. J. Spangrude, S. Heimfeld, and I. L. Weissman, Purification and characterization of mouse hematopoietic stem cells, *Science*, 241:58–62, 1988; J. A. Thomson et al., Embryonic stem cell lines derived from human blastocysts, *Science*, 282:1145–1147, 1998; I. L. Weissman, D. J. Anderson, and F. Gage, Stem and progenitor cells: Origins, phenotypes, lineage commitment, and transdifferentiations, *Annu. Rev. Cell Develop. Biol.*, 17:387–403, 2001.

Stereo modeling

Stereo modeling is the process of creating a three-dimensional model of an object. The model can be in the form of a two-dimensional color picture, a three-dimensional rotating model on a computer screen, or an actual physical part.

From the moment of conceiving of a product, an inventor will want to transform it into a physical reality or at least the first prototype. A prototype is an original model used to evaluate form, fit, and function.

The start of a product's life cycle is an idea or concept. This is the stage at which prototyping is most common, sometimes starting with a simple pencil sketch. Soon, however, it becomes necessary to show a more detailed design to others, including marketing, engineering, and manufacturing personnel, and potential customers. Stereo modeling begins by using a computer-aided design (CAD) program to define geometry, surface texture, color, and size.

Conventionally, prototype fabrication is outsourced, for example, to a machine shop. Fully functional prototypes are expensive and take a long time to make. Stereo modeling allows for virtual and physical prototyping, techniques that are playing a bigger role in today's design and manufacturing world. Both of these depend on the creation of a digital product model. There are two methods for creating a computer model of an object: geometric construction using computer-aided design software, and scanning an existing object using lasers or cameras.

Virtual prototyping. Recent advances in three-dimensional computer graphics have revolutionized the way that products are designed. Almost all CAD modelers are based on Non-Uniform Rational B-Splines (NURBS). The power of NURBS allows the user to design smooth and free-form surfaces. Advanced shading techniques such as ray tracing, radiosity, and a combination of both, along with sophisticated texture mapping techniques, make the object on the screen look very realistic. Using these techniques, it is possible to quickly evaluate different material types, finishes, and lighting conditions, as well as the many available parameters to inspect the product visually.

Animation and virtual reality can also play a significant role in the virtual prototyping process. In particular, where kinematics and motion are involved, modeling the product in a dynamic system can show weaknesses and potential failures. Recent development of haptic feedback and data gloves with sensors of various types can aid in virtual prototyping of the product. Such virtual reality devices give the user a feel for holding or handling the part. Virtual reality devices and animation are excellent tools to give potential clients the feel and look of a prototype product.

Rapid prototyping. At some point it becomes desirable to create a physical model using traditional computerized numerical control machining or a technology called rapid prototyping. Rapid prototyping uses the CAD model to build a physical part in plastic, wax, or metal. All rapid prototyping technologies work by the same concept, that is, building one thin layer at a time. Some examples of the rapid prototyping machines include machines for stereolithography, fused deposition modeling, powder sintering, and laminated object modeling. The processes differ and so do the materials.

Stereolithography uses a liquid polymer resin and a laser to harden the resin. The selective laser sintering process uses lasers to sinter the powder material. A large variety of materials are used in the selective laser sintering process, from plastics to a metal called RapidSteel (a combination of copper and steel). The fused deposition modeling process makes parts using acrylonitrile-butadiene-styrene (ABS) plastics, casting wax, and medically approved nylon. Ceramic parts have been successfully produced in research labs by fused deposition. Although the working dimensions of the largest machines are limited to about $25 \times 25 \times 20$ in. ($64 \times 64 \times 51$ cm), they are big enough to accommodate most parts. There are new rapid prototyping machines, called desktop modelers, which are tabletop machines suitable for an office environment. They are intended for quick validation of a design. Rapid is a relative word, so a small model may take a few hours to produce. Compared to traditionally machined prototypes, this is a big improvement.

The rapid prototyping procedure is as follows:

1. The CAD model is converted to a faceted surface model (**Fig. 1**) consisting of small adjacent triangles. Each triangle is planar, and all triangles fit together to form a tight surface. This format is called stereolithography tessellation language (STL).

2. The STL file is mathematically sliced into uniformly thick layers (ranging from 0.005 to 0.020 in. or 0.013 to 0.05 cm, depending on the machine and desired accuracy). The planar nature of the triangles makes this mathematical operation easy and quick.

Fig. 1. Tessellated model.

3. Each slice (geometry) is transmitted to the rapid prototyping machine which lays down material on a base plate in the shape of the first slice. This process is repeated for each successive slice laid down.

Each rapid prototyping technique lays down material in layers, but each does it somewhat differently. Stereolithography uses a laser to harden a thin layer of photopolymer liquid in the shape of a layer, then lowers that hardened layer below the liquid surface, spreads a new thin liquid layer, hardens the next layer, and so on. In fused deposition modeling, molten material is extruded in the shape of a layer from a very small nozzle onto a plate. The plate lowers a distance of one layer thickness, and the process is repeated until the part is finished. In selective laser sintering, a thin layer of powder material is fused using a laser, the fused layer is lowered, and then a new layer of powder is appled, fused, and so on. **Figure 2** is a schematic representation of the selective laser sintering processes.

The models can also be created using three-dimensional laser scanning which measures the geometric location of as many as 10,000 points per square inch of surface area. The Partnership for Research in Stereo Modeling (PRISM) labs at Arizona State University have developed algorithms to accurately convert these "point clouds" to more efficient NURBS surfaces and then create the stereolithography tessellation language files of triangular facets for prototyping. In addition, algorithms have been created to intelligently classify the resulting shapes or features for further analysis.

The best situation is to produce not just an esthetic prototype but also a functional one. For example, it would be convenient to produce a metal turbine blade to test in an actual engine rather than produce a plastic version. Recently, with metal becoming an available option for rapid prototyping, it is possible to generate production metal parts, as well as the casting tooling. This saves the step of producing either a plastic or wax prototype to use as a master casting pattern, or of producing prototype casting molds for short runs of parts. If the material is acceptable, a custom part may be directly fabricated using rapid prototyping, specifically with selective laser sintering. Thus, a fourth F—fabrication—has been added to the list of form, fit, and function.

For background information *see* COMPUTER-AIDED DESIGN AND MANUFACTURING; COMPUTER GRAPHICS; MODEL THEORY; PROTOTYPE; VIRTUAL MANUFACTURING; VIRTUAL REALITY in the McGraw-Hill Encyclopedia of Science & Technology.   Anshuman Razdan;
Mark Henderson

Bibliography. K. G. Cooper, *Rapid Prototyping Technology*, Marcel Dekker, 2001; S. S. Dimov and D. T. Pham, *Rapid Manufacturing: The Technologies and Applications of Rapid Prototyping and Rapid Tooling*, Springer-Verlag, 2001; D. Kochan, *Solid Freeform Manufacturing*, Elsevier Science, 1993; T. Wohlers, *Wohlers Report 2002*, Wohlers Associates, Fort Collins, CO, 2002.

Stratospheric influences (weather and climate)

The stratosphere is the layer of Earth's atmosphere at altitudes between 8 and 30 mi (13 and 50 km). It is a stable region with few clouds and no storms. While the stratosphere is important for the environment at the Earth's surface (it contains the ozone layer that protects us from harmful ultraviolet radiation), it has been thought to have little influence on weather and climate near the ground. The density of air decreases rapidly with altitude, so in order to conserve their total energy, disturbances must strengthen when they propagate upward through the atmosphere and weaken when they propagate downward. Upward influences, therefore, are stronger than downward ones. While there has been sporadic interest in the idea that winds and temperatures in the stratosphere might influence weather

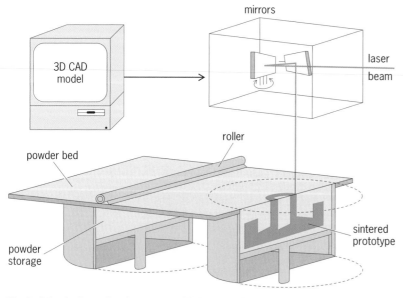

Fig. 2. Selective laser sintering process. (*University of Texas, 1995*)

and climate, only in the past few years has this idea found enough observational support to merit serious attention from meteorologists.

Stratospheric variability. Large-scale disturbances, called planetary waves, propagate from the lower atmosphere into the stratosphere. These waves have immense spatial scales, such that only a few wavelengths fit on a parallel of latitude. They reach the stratosphere when winds blow from west to east (are westerly) but are not too strong. In the summer, stratospheric winds blow from east to west (are easterly) at up to 130 mi/h (220 km/h) while winter winds are similarly strong but are westerly. Thus, planetary waves disturb the stratospheric circulation only in winter. The resulting distorted counterclockwise flow around the Pole in winter is called the polar vortex. Because the stratosphere varies significantly only in winter, it is in winter that any downward influence is expected. Wintertime variability in the stratosphere can be dramatic. When planetary waves reach large amplitudes and break, they decelerate the westerly winds. During stratospheric sudden warmings, the polar vortex is severely disrupted by breaking planetary waves and may break down completely. Warm air is mixed from low latitudes to the polar regions (thus the term "sudden warming"). These events, lasting for a week or two, typically occur late in the winter and, on average, in every second or third winter.

On climate time scales, increasing concentrations of atmospheric carbon dioxide and other greenhouse gases that have warmed the climate near the ground simultaneously have cooled the stratosphere. Ozone depletion, a consequence of the release of some synthetic chemicals, also has cooled the stratosphere.

The stratosphere has cooled more than 2°F (1°C) over the past 20 years, with the greatest cooling occurring near the Poles. This has strengthened the temperature contrast between low latitudes and the Pole, thereby strengthening the polar vortex.

Natural events and cycles also influence the stratosphere. Strong volcanic eruptions can produce a stratospheric haze layer that absorbs infrared radiation both from the Sun and the Earth's surface, warming the stratosphere at low latitudes and strengthening the polar vortex. The quasi-biennial oscillation (QBO) is a nearly periodic (roughly 2 years) fluctuation of stratospheric winds over the Equator. When equatorial winds are westerly, planetary waves can escape from high latitudes into the tropics, allowing the polar vortex to intensify.

Lower atmosphere variability—Arctic Oscillation. The dominant pattern of month-to-month fluctuations in sea-level barometric pressures over the Northern Hemisphere is the Arctic Oscillation, or AO (**Fig. 1***a*). When pressures are low over the Arctic, they are high over the North Atlantic and Europe and, to a lesser extent, over the North Pacific. The same pattern applies in its opposite phase, with high pressures over the Arctic and low pressures over the North Atlantic and Pacific oceans. The AO remains the leading pattern of variability during the summer, when the lower atmosphere and the stratosphere are uncoupled, and in computer models of the lower atmosphere, which do not include the stratosphere. Thus, the dominance of the AO pattern does not depend on the stratosphere. Its variability is sustained by interactions with synoptic weather systems, the highs and lows familiar from weather maps. These systems follow the jet streams, wavy

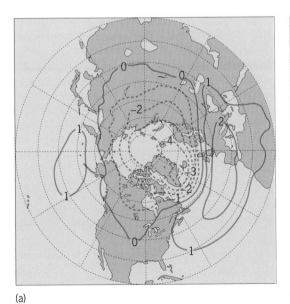

(a)

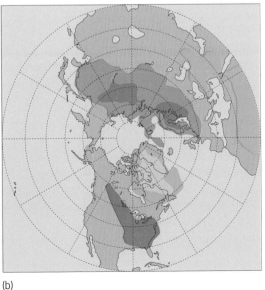

(b)

Fig. 1. Pressures and temperatures associated with the Arctic Oscillation. (*a*) Sea-level pressures (millibars). Values are those associated with a one standard deviation positive value in the AO index. (*b*) Surface temperatures (°F). Values are those associated with a one standard deviation positive value in the AO index. Dark color (northern Eurasia and eastern United States, with extension north-westward into Canada) indicates temperatures one or more degrees warmer than usual, lighter color (Labrador Sea and Greenland and Saharan Africa and east of the Mediterranean) indicates temperatures one or more degrees cooler than usual. (*NOAA-CIRES Climate Diagnostics Center, Boulder, CO: http://www.cdc.noaa.gov*)

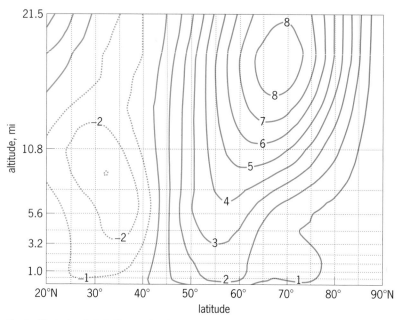

Fig. 2. Westerly winds (miles per hour) associated with the Arctic Oscillation. Values are those associated with a one standard deviation positive value in the AO index. Broken-line contours indicate negative (east-to-west) winds. *(NOAA-CIRES Climate Diagnostics Center, Boulder, CO: http://www.cdc.noaa.gov)*

bands of strong westerly winds at altitudes of 6 or 7 mi (10 or 11 km). The AO affects the locations of the jet streams, and the weather systems reinforce the AO by carrying momentum into the jet streams.

The AO also affects temperatures near the ground. The AO, in its positive phase, features strengthened westerly winds around the Arctic, especially over the North Atlantic. These winds carry relatively warm air from the North Atlantic over Scandinavia and northern Asia, and they carry cold air from Arctic Canada over the Labrador Sea, producing cooling (Fig. 1b).

Stratosphere–lower atmosphere connections. During the winter, the AO is strongly coupled to the

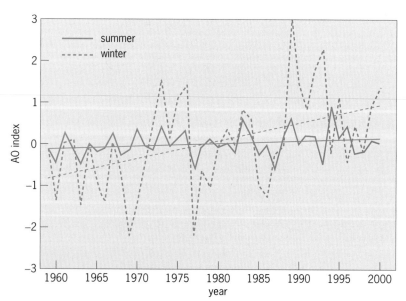

Fig. 3. History of the summer (June, July, August) and winter (December, January, February) AO index. The lines are best fits to linear trends. *(NOAA-CIRES Climate Diagnostics Center, Boulder, CO: http://www.cdc.noaa.gov)*

stratospheric polar vortex. When the AO index is positive, stronger-than-usual westerly winds are found at the Earth's surface between 45 and 65°N and throughout the polar vortex (**Fig. 2**). This simultaneous relationship does not reveal whether the source is primarily in the stratosphere or the troposphere, but the default assumption is that the lower atmosphere, the source of upward-propagating planetary waves, affects the stratosphere. However, when the AO index in February is correlated with winds in the preceding December and January, the strongest correlations are in the upper troposphere and lower stratosphere, implying that the strength of the polar vortex in early winter is useful for predicting the state of the AO later on. This statistical predictability extends to surface temperatures. A recent study found that cold waves in Chicago, New York, London, and Paris in the 60 days following the appearance of a weak polar vortex are nearly twice as likely as in the 60 days after the appearance of a strong vortex. The temperature pattern that follows a strong vortex is very similar to that associated with the AO (Fig. 1b).

The stratosphere also appears to influence the lower atmosphere on longer time scales. Surface temperature patterns associated with the QBO are similar to those associated with the AO, presumably because the QBO influences the polar vortex, which affects the AO. A similar pattern of temperatures appeared in the winter following the eruption of the Mount Pinatubo volcano in 1991. Over the past 40 years the AO index has increased (**Fig. 3**), but this trend is present only in the winter, when the troposphere and stratosphere are coupled. This trend has been accompanied by a tendency for the polar vortex to become more intense, and the frequency of sudden warmings has decreased. Computer modeling studies confirm that such a strengthening of the polar vortex can be transmitted to the troposphere. Two studies, however, found that, in global climate models, global warming can produce an increasing trend in the AO without the stratosphere being involved.

Mechanisms. Changes in the strength of the polar vortex cause changes in the upward propagation of planetary waves. When the vortex strengthens, planetary waves are deflected equatorward, and the deceleration of the vortex by the waves is reduced. Conversely, when the vortex weakens, more planetary waves enter the vortex, where they weaken it further. The force exerted by the waves on the vortex is eventually balanced by frictional forces at the ground, so that changes in surface winds mirror the changes in the strength of the vortex. Because the lower atmosphere is much more massive than the stratosphere, these changes in surface winds are weak. Observed changes in the stratospheric wave drag should change surface winds by only about 1 mi/h (1.6 km/h). The observed tropospheric signals are stronger than this, suggesting that the interactions between weather systems and the AO amplify the lower-atmospheric response to stratospheric forcing.

Given a sustained change in the strength of the polar vortex, computer models readily reproduce this sequence of events leading to downward influence, but transient fluctuations in the polar vortex have a more modest effect on the lower atmosphere. There are delays in the propagation of the signal down to the surface and in the subsequent adjustment of the lower atmospheric circulation. Moreover, the lower atmosphere produces its own strong variability in the AO mode independently of any forcing from the stratosphere. This was evident during the winter of 2001–2002, when fluctuations in the polar vortex failed to have the expected influence on the AO. Thus, while there is good evidence supporting stratospheric influences on the climate, stratospheric influences on the weather are less certain. There is an important distinction between these two problems. For the climate problem (year-to-year variations), changes originate in the stratosphere, produced by greenhouse gases, ozone depletion, volcanic debris, or the QBO. Within a single winter, however, changes in the stratosphere occur primarily because of changes in the lower atmospheric source of planetary waves. That the polar vortex is a useful statistical predictor of the subsequent state of the AO may mean only that it is a sensitive indicator of processes happening within the lower atmosphere.

Implications. The nature of stratospheric influences on the lower atmosphere has important implications for weather forecasting and for the study and prediction of climate change. If the influence of the polar vortex on the lower atmosphere is real (and significant), extended-range weather forecasting models will necessarily include a well-resolved stratosphere. This would approximately double the computer power requirments to run these models. In fact, the most convincing proof of a stratospheric effect on weather would be if the accuracy of computer-generated forecasts improves when the stratosphere is properly included in the models. For the climate problem, valid predictions of the regional impacts of global greenhouse warming may also require models that include the stratosphere. The computational burden here is even more severe, since global climate models also include detailed models of the ocean and ocean ice. These models already tax the capabilities of the most powerful computers.

For background information *see* ATMOSPHERIC GENERAL CIRCULATION; CLIMATE MODELING; CLIMATOLOGY; DYNAMIC METEOROLOGY; METEOROLOGY; MIDDLE-ATMOSPHERE DYNAMICS; STRATOSPHERE; WEATHER FORECASTING AND PREDICTION; WIND in the McGraw-Hill Encyclopedia of Science & Technology.   Walter A. Robinson

Bibliography. M. P. Baldwin and T. J. Dunkerton, Stratospheric harbingers of anomalous weather regimes, *Science*, vol. 294, 2001; D. L. Hartmann et al., Can ozone depletion and global warming interact to produce rapid climate change?, *Proc. Nat. Acad. Sci.*, vol. 97, 2000; L. M. Polvani and P. J. Kushner, Tropospheric response to stratospheric perturbations in a relatively simple general circulation model, *Geophys. Res. Lett.*, vol. 29, no. 7, 2002; D. T. Shindell et al., Simulation of recent northern winter climate trends by greenhouse-gas forcing, *Nature*, 399:452–455, 1999; D. W. J. Thompson et al., Stratospheric connection to Northern Hemisphere wintertime weather: Implications for prediction, *J. Climate*, vol. 15, 2002; D. W. J. Thompson and J. M. Wallace, Regional climate impacts of the Northern Hemisphere annular mode, *Science*, vol. 293, 2001; J. M. Wallace and D. W. J. Thompson, Annual modes and climate prediction, *Phys. Today*, February 2002.

Stress-function-morphology correlations in the brain

Stress is a highly individualized experience triggered by specific psychological determinants. The stress response consists of a cascade of neural and hormonal events that have short- and long-lasting consequences for the brain and body. Chronic reactivity to situations that are deemed novel or unpredictable or uncontrollable leads to secretion of stress hormones that access the brain and act negatively upon the hippocampus, a brain structure involved in learning and memory. Although this clinical picture might seem dismal for anyone exposed to various stressors on a daily basis, one must realize that since stress is psychologically defined, it is manageable through psychological coping strategies.

Prior to its application to biological systems, the term "stress" was used by engineers to explain forces that put strain on a structure. One could place strain on a piece of metal in such a way that it would break like glass when it reached its stress level. In 1936, Hans Selye borrowed the term from the field of engineering and redefined stress as a biological phenomenon representing the intersection of symptoms produced by a wide variety of noxious agents. For many years, Selye tested various stressors (such as fasting, operative injuries, and drug administration) that would produce morphological changes in the body that were representative of a stress response, such as enlargement of the adrenal gland, atrophy of the thymus, and gastric ulceration. Selye's view was that the determinants of the stress response are nonspecific; that is, many conditions can put strain on the organism and lead to disease in the same way that many different conditions can put strain on a piece of metal and break it like glass.

Not all researchers agreed with Selye's model, particularly with the notion that the determinants of the stress response are nonspecific. John Mason spent many years measuring stress hormone levels in humans subjected to various stressful conditions in order to define specific psychological characteristics that would make a condition stressful. This work was made possible in the early 1960s due to the development of new techniques that permitted scientists

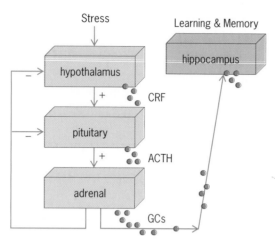

Schematic diagram of the hypothalamo-pituitary-adrenal axis and its relationship with learning and memory. ACTH = adrenocorticotropin; CRF = corticotropin-releasing factor; GCs = glucocorticoids.

to measure levels of hormones that are released during reactivity to stress.

HPA axis. The release of stress hormones is made possible through activation of an endocrine axis named the hypothalamo-pituitary-adrenal (HPA) axis. When a situation is interpreted as being stressful, the HPA axis is activated, and neurons in the hypothalamus, a structure located in the brain and called the "master gland," releases corticotropin-releasing hormone (CRH). The release of CRH triggers the subsequent secretion and release of another hormone called adrenocorticotropin (ACTH) from the pituitary gland, also located in the brain (**illus.**). ACTH travels through the blood to the adrenal glands, which are located above the kidneys, and triggers secretion of the so-called stress hormones. There are two main stress hormones, the corticosteroids (called corticosterone in animals, and cortisol in humans) and the catecholamines (adrenaline and noradrenaline). When these two hormones are secreted in response to stress, they act on the body to create a fight-or-flight response with symptoms such as an increase in heart rate and blood pressure.

By measuring the circulating levels of these hormones before and after individuals were exposed to various jobs or situations deemed to be stressful, Mason was able to define three main psychological determinants of a stress response in human beings. He showed that in order for a situation to be stressful, it has to be interpreted as being novel or unpredictable, or the individual must have the feeling that he or she does not have control over the situation. Further studies showed that these determinants were additive in that one determinant could trigger a stress reaction but more than one would trigger a stronger stress reaction. Furthermore, other studies showed that the individual's sense of control over the situation is the most important determinant in inducing a stress reaction.

With this knowledge, scientists started to explore the types of populations or individuals that could be

sensitive to stress as a function of these determinants. These populations or individuals included those who were exposed to traumatic events and suffered from posttraumatic stress disorder (PTSD), depressed patients who generally complained of having lost control over their emotions or lives, and retired elderly individuals who had a low sense of control due to their exposure to many novel and unpredictable situations.

Stress hormones and the brain. The study of the effects of stress on the function and morphology of the brain began when scientists discovered that the stress hormones released by the adrenal gland accessed the brain and acted on brain regions that are known to sustain memory function. Indeed, these hormones have the capacity to cross the blood-brain barrier (corticosteroids more than catecholamines) and bind to receptors in the brain. In 1968, scientists from Rockefeller University in New York discovered that the brain region containing the highest density of these receptors was the hippocampus, a brain structure which had been shown a few years earlier to be involved in learning and memory. A model was thus proposed in which chronic exposure to stress could trigger a long-term secretion of stress hormones which would eventually access the brain and act detrimentally on the hippocampus and lead to memory impairments and, eventually, to atrophy or shrinking of the hippocampus (illus.).

More than 30 years of research in this field has proven this original model. The majority of the animal studies performed to this day have shown that chronic exposure to high levels of stress hormones, particularly corticosteroids, leads to memory impairments and to atrophy of the hippocampus. Studies in humans have shown that in populations particularly susceptible to the effects of stress, long-term exposure to corticosteroids is correlated with both memory impairments and atrophy of the hippocampus.

Depression. In the 1980s it was reported that approximately 50% of patients suffering from major depression presented abnormally high levels of corticosteroids. Additional studies showed that depressed patients with high levels of corticosteroids presented memory impairments when compared to patients with normal circulating levels of corticosteroids. Given the capacity of corticosteroids to cross the blood-brain barrier and access the brain, further studies were performed to assess whether depressed patients presented an atrophy of the hippocampus. In 1996 a study reported that, indeed, depressed patients presented a significant atrophy of the hippocampus when compared to nondepressed individuals. This finding was recently confirmed by an independent study. Although it is interesting to relate the presence of high levels of corticosteroids to both memory impairments and atrophy of the hippocampus in depressed patients, it is noteworthy that in most studies performed to this day, levels of corticosteroids have not been shown to be correlated with measures of the volume of the hippocampus. It is therefore difficult to disentangle the effects of depression from those of corticosteroids on the hippocampal atrophy that is present in a significant proportion of depressed patients.

Posttraumatic stress disorder. The most powerful model to describe the acute and chronic effects of stress on the function and morphology of the brain is the model of posttraumatic stress disorder (PTSD). When humans are exposed to highly traumatic events, there is no doubt that an important stress reaction will be triggered, given the novelty, unpredictability, and uncontrollability of the events. Yet, only 3 to 20% of individuals exposed to a trauma will develop PTSD. Recent studies on the effects of PTSD on the function and morphology of the brain report that PTSD patients present a significant atrophy of the hippocampus, accompanied by severe memory impairments. A paradox exists in this literature since the hippocampal atrophy reported to exist in PTSD patients is accompanied by lower than normal levels of corticosteroids, instead of higher levels of corticosteroids as would be predicted based on previous data. Some scientists explain this finding on the grounds that the hippocampal atrophy observed in PTSD patients may have been induced near the time of exposure to the traumatic events, while measurements of corticosteroid levels are usually done many weeks, months, or years after exposure to trauma. Most of the studies on PTSD patients have shown that there exists an atrophy of the hippocampus that is accompanied by significant memory impairments.

Aging. Later life can be a time of frequent uncontrollable stress. The elderly often experience chronic illness and disability, the loss of friends and family members, as well as their own impending mortality. These events often represent novel and unpredictable situations for which the individual lacks a sense of control. Recent studies performed with elderly individuals report that about 30% of elders present a significant increase in stress hormone levels as years elapse, and those elders with high levels of corticosteroids show significant memory impairments. The high levels of stress hormones in some elderly individuals seem to be related to overreactivity to stressful situations. A recent study showed that memory of a list of words decreased significantly after exposure to a psychological stressor in aged humans who were highly reactive to the stressor when compared with aged humans who did not react to the stressor. Recent evidence reveals a significant 14% atrophy of the hippocampus in elderly persons with high levels of stress hormones and memory deficits. These data strongly support the idea that difficulties in dealing with the stress of aging are an important determinant for the occurrence of memory impairments during the later years of life.

For background information *see* ENDOCRINE MECHANISMS; HORMONE; PITUITARY GLAND; POSTTRAUMATIC STRESS DISORDER; STRESS (PSYCHOLOGY) in the McGraw-Hill Encyclopedia of Science & Technology. Sonia Lupien

Bibliography. G. Fink, *The Encyclopedia of Stress*, Academic Press, San Diego, 2000; B. S. McEwen and H. M. Schmeck, *The Hostage Brain*, Rockefeller University Press, New York, 1994; H. Selye, *The Stress of Life*, McGraw-Hill, New York, 1956.

Surgical consciousness monitor

The loss and return of consciousness induced by different drugs during surgical anesthesia offers a unique opportunity to study the brain mechanisms that are correlated with subjective awareness and conscious experience. In the last few years, there have been numerous studies of the changes in brain activity associated with the loss of consciousness caused by the use of surgical anesthetics. Such studies have used electroencephalography (EEG) and evoked potentials (general activity and activity elicited by stimulation of specific sensory receptors, respectively) to quantify brain electrical activity as well as functional brain imaging (positron emission tomography, single-photon emission computed tomography, and functional magnetic resonance imaging) to quantify blood flow, glucose metabolism, and oxygen consumption in different brain regions. Indices of other types of physiologic activity, such as respiratory sinus arrhythmia and the electrical currents generated in facial muscles, have also been shown to be sensitive to the depth of anesthesia. This research has resulted in the development of a number of clinical instruments intended to monitor the depth of anesthesia during surgery. Aside from their practical value, such instruments are of basic scientific interest. They provide evidence that consciousness, long considered by neuroscientists to be a scientifically inaccessible problem of interest only to philosophers, has reliable neurobiological correlates which allow it to be objectively measured.

Quantitative electroencephalography. Recordings from the surface of the scalp have long been known to demonstrate rhythmic voltage oscillations. It is now recognized that the power spectrum (the distribution of electrical signal intensity versus frequency) of this spontaneous electrical activity of the brain (EEG), recorded from the scalp of a normal healthy person resting with closed eyes, is regulated by a complex neuroanatomical homeostatic system. Quantitative electroencephalography (QEEG) routinely uses computer analysis to describe the power spectrum. The EEG spectrum is conventionally divided into frequency bands, which are defined as delta (0.5–3.5 Hz), theta (3.5–7.5 Hz), alpha (7.5–12.5 Hz), beta (12.5–25 Hz), and gamma (25–50Hz).

Normative age-regression equations have been defined that provide the mean value and standard deviation of the distribution of many different variables extracted from the power spectrum of the EEG recorded from any scalp electrode position for healthy individuals ranging in age from 6 to 97 years. Given the age of the subject, these equations accurately predict the power within various frequency bands for each region as well as the relationships among regions within or between the right and left hemispheres of the brain. After extraction of QEEG variables from any recording, these normative data permit the rescaling of each such measure from its physical dimensions (such as voltage and latency) to standard or Z-scores which can be evaluated statistically by using the method referred to as neurometrics.

These precise descriptions are independent of the ethnic or cultural background of the subject. QEEG has extremely high specificity as well as extremely high sensitivity to a wide variety of developmental, neurological, and psychiatric disorders. It also has excellent test-retest replicability within an individual and is exquisitely sensitive to changes of state. For these reasons, QEEG offers an ideal method to examine the effects on the brain of agents that alter consciousness, such as pharmacological agents and anesthetics. The waveshapes of evoked potentials from any region elicited by multimodal sensory stimuli are similarly predictable and sensitive.

Measuring the level of consciousness. Based upon conventional evaluation of EEG tracings, anesthesia induction has been reported to be accompanied by an increase of high-frequency beta EEG activity in frontal regions, spreading to more posterior regions with increased sedation and loss of consciousness. Conversely, low-frequency delta and theta EEG waves appear in posterior regions and migrate forward. This topographic pattern of frontal predominance or "anteriorization" of EEG power with loss of consciousness during anesthesia was first reported in monkeys and has since been consistently replicated in humans. Frontal and central increases of alpha as well as beta activity were proposed to be the most reliable indices of sedation with the intravenous administration of propofol.

In the last few years, a number of instruments have been developed that measure the depth of anesthesia using QEEG or evoked potential indices. These clinical monitors all rely on the stability and sensitivity of QEEG but differ with respect to the particular EEG rhythms or evoked potential waveshapes selected for monitoring, the scalp regions from which recordings are collected, the precise nature of the features objectively extracted from the raw data, and the invariance or lack thereof that has been demonstrated for the effects of various anesthetic agents upon the measure. However, they all provide practical clinical evidence that consciousness is a neurobiological phenomenon that can be objectively quantified and analyzed using electrophysiological variables.

Compressed spectral array. Using power spectral analysis of individual electrodes to quantify local EEG changes during anesthesia, graphic displays of power versus frequency have been computed and presented as sequential overlays, such as the compressed spectral array (CSA) or density spectral array (DSA). In this display mode, the fast Fourier transform algorithm is used to compute the power spectrum extracted from sequential EEG samples (each usually about 8 seconds long) recorded from a few, usually symmetrical scalp leads. The resulting curve of power versus frequency is encoded using a palette in which different hues of color or shades of gray represent different power levels. The evolution of the EEG spectrum, and therefore the depth of anesthesia, during induction, maintenance, and emergence of a patient from surgical anesthesia can thus be evaluated by the positions of vertical lines in the waterfall encoding various frequencies in the power spectrum. Clinical utility of this method is limited by the requirement that the user have experience with the distinctive frequency profiles induced in the EEG during induction with different pharmacological agents.

Median frequency/spectral edge. Global features have been extracted from the power spectrum provided by the fast Fourier transform algorithm, such as the median frequency or the spectral edge, which respectively define those frequencies below which one finds 50% or 95% of the EEG power. Such measures have been related to clinical signs or compared to analgesic end points. The use of these relatively crude features is based upon the hypothesis that with increasing depth of anesthesia the distribution of power in the EEG steadily shifts toward lower frequencies. Median frequency can be conceptualized as akin to the center of mass of the area of the curve outlining the power spectrum. Such methods can be considered as attempts to summarize the information in the CSA or DSA by a number representing only the point in the spectrum that satisfies the algebraic definition.

Entropy. Another approach has explored the utility of the entropy of the EEG to enable objective evaluation of the depth of anesthesia. This method treats the EEG power spectrum obtained prior to induction of anesthesia as a reference spectrum defining the "ground state" of the organized signal system represented by the QEEG. Since the ground state is homeostatically regulated, when the system conforms to that configuration, the QEEG contains no information and entropy is maximum. Deviations from the reference spectrum are considered to be information, or negative entropy.

Auditory index. It has long been known that the waveshape of the auditory evoked potential simplifies and becomes smaller with increasing depth of anesthesia. An evoked potential method to monitor anesthetic depth has been proposed which is based upon the 40-Hz steady-state auditory evoked potential. This method, sometimes referred to as the Auditory Index, quantifies the morphology of the auditory evoked potential. One version of this index measure essentially calculates the total length of the curve describing the evoked potential waveshape, as if it were a string. The longer the string, the lighter the anesthesia level; the shorter the string, the deeper the level of anesthesia. Several other versions of this attempt to simplify evaluation of evoked potential morphology have since been proposed and incorporated into anesthesia monitors.

Bispectral index. Another global measure, called the bispectral index, has undergone extensive investigation recently. The bispectral index monitor relies upon spectral analysis of the EEG recorded from one electrode position on the forehead. This monitor combines a variety of quantitative descriptors of the EEG into a multivariate number, the bispectral index, using a proprietary algorithm. This number is then scaled to range between 0 and 100. High correlations between this number and the state of consciousness have been reported in several studies.

Patient state index. A monitor called the Patient State Analyzer computes a different multivariate QEEG index called the Patient State Index to assess the depth of anesthesia. This instrument performs analyses of the EEGs recorded from an anterior/posterior array of electrodes sampling the activity of four brain regions; it extracts features describing not only the EEG power spectrum at each electrode but also some dynamic relationships between these regions, such as power gradient and coherence. A proprietary algorithm then evaluates these extracted features by computing a multivariate discriminant function to assess the probability that the patient is awake, which is scaled to range from 0 to 100. Significant relationships with level of consciousness and sensitivity to change in state have been demonstrated.

Although such derived measures correlate well with drug concentrations or clinical state, they provide relatively little insight into the underlying physiology of anesthesia or the brain mechanisms mediating consciousness. Nonetheless, their established clinical utility for assessment of the depth of anesthesia lends credibility to the assertion that a comprehensive description of the invariant and reversible changes in brain activity accompanying the loss and return of responsivity during the action of a wide variety of anesthetic agents can provide insight into the neurophysiology of consciousness. That is, the brain dynamic changes underlying these numbers imply a panoply of observable neurophysiological correlates of consciousness.

Neurophysiological theory of consciousness. Studies have shown that anesthetics cause loss of consciousness by (1) depressing the reticular formation; (2) causing thalamic inhibition via the nucleus reticularis; (3) blocking thalamo-cortical transmission in diffuse projection pathways; (4) preventing coincidence detection by pyramidal cells; (5) disrupting cortico-thalamo-cortical reverberations, leading to inhibition of certain brain regions; and (6) terminating resonance among brain regions. These observations of anesthetic effects together with findings in current neuroscience research have been used to construct a detailed neurophysiological theory of consciousness.

According to this theory, complex neuroanatomical and neurochemical homeostatic systems, probably genetically determined, regulate baseline levels of (1) local synchrony of neuronal ensembles,

(2) global interactions among brain regions, and (3) sampling of the electrophysiological signals at regular intervals. The interaction between brainstem, thalamus, and cortex plays a critical role in the regulation of brain rhythms. Pacemaker neurons distributed throughout thalamic regions oscillate in the alpha frequency range, modulating excitability of cells in the thalamo-cortical pathways. The nucleus reticularis (outer shell) of the thalamus can inhibit these pacemakers, slowing their oscillatory rhythms and decreasing the alpha frequency into the theta range. When unopposed, this inhibition can close the thalamic gates that permit afferent (sensory) inputs to reach the cortex.

However, sensory stimuli entering the ascending reticular activating system via collateral pathways cause influences from the brainstem reticular formation to inhibit the nucleus reticularis, thereby releasing its inhibitory actions upon the thalamus. According to the consciousness system model, information about complex, multimodal environmental events can then be transmitted via sensory-specific thalamo-cortical pathways and fractionated into projections upon axosomatic synapses (synapses between an axon and a cell body). These inputs depolarize membranes of cortical pyramidal neurons that are distributed among cell assemblies and function as feature detectors for particular attributes of complex multimodal stimuli. At about the same time, readout from subcortical regions encoding relevant recent and episodic memories reaches the cortex via nonsensory specific projections from the diffuse projection system to axodendritic synapses (synapses between an axon and a dendrite) of some of these cortical pyramidal cells. The pyramidal cells thus act as coincidence detectors between present inputs from the environment and past experiences as well as state of interoceptive systems, thereby converting fragmented sensations to fragments of percepts. In cells for which such specific and nonspecific inputs are concordant, cortico-thalamic discharge is markedly enhanced. The consequent coherent cortico-thalamic volley encoding the distributed fragments causes a cortico-thalamo-cortical loop to reverberate, binding the fragments into a unified perception.

The brain interactions that have been mathematically defined in large normative studies specify the most probable configuration of activity in the resting brain. When brain activity corresponds to this predictable setpoint, it contains no information and thus entropy is maximum. Information is encoded by nonrandom synchronization of neuronal ensembles or cell assemblies within a brain region rather than by discharges of dedicated cells. Since random neural activity is the most probable, deviations from the regulated setpoints constitute negative entropy and are consistently found during information processing and cognitive activity in many developmental, neurological, and psychiatric disorders; after administration of centrally active substances; in sleep; and during seizures which are accompanied by loss of consciousness, coma, and anesthesia.

When cortico-thalamo-cortical reverberation is adequate in magnitude and sustained for a critical duration, it causes resonance in the set of structures critically inhibited by anesthetics, namely the prefrontal, dorsolateral, medial frontal, and parasagittal cortices; anterior cingulate gyrus; basal ganglia; amygdala; and thalamus. It has been proposed that consciousness is the product of an electromagnetic field produced by this resonance.

Regions of local negative entropy are the building blocks of consciousness. Spatially distributed, essentially statistical information must be bound into a unified whole and transformed into a subjective experience.

Connectionistic theorists have attempted to explain perception as a converging hierarchy, from simple feature detectors to hypercomplex detectors of more complex combinations of attributes, finessing the question of the transformation from a hypercomplex detector to subjective experience. The inadequacy of connectionist concepts to account for this process points to the need for a paradigm shift. Integration of this fragmented information into Global Negative Entropy is postulated to produce consciousness, a property of a resonating electrical field.

For background information *see* ANESTHESIA; BRAIN; CONSCIOUSNESS; ELECTROENCEPHALOGRAPHY; INFORMATION THEORY (BIOLOGY); NERVOUS SYSTEM (VERTEBRATE); PERCEPTION; SENSATION in the McGraw-Hill Encyclopedia of Science & Technology.   E. Roy John; Leslie S. Prichep

Bibliography. M. T. Alkire, R. J. Haier, and J. H. Fallon, Toward a unified theory of narcosis: Brain imaging evidence for a thalamocoritical switch as the neurophysiologic basis of anesthesia-induced unconsciousness, *Conscious. Cognit.*, 9:370–386, 2000; J. Bosch-Bayard et al., 3D statistical parametric mapping of EEG source spectra by means of variable resolution electromagnetic tomography (VARETA), *Clin. EEG*, 32:47–61, 2001; D. Drover et al., Patient state index (PSI): Sensitivity to changes in anesthetic state and optimization of delivery and recovery from anesthesia, *Anesthesiology*, 97:82–89, 2002; E. R. John et al., Invariant reversible QEEG effects of anesthetics, *Conscious. Cognit.*, 10:165–183, 2001.

Sustainable materials and green chemistry

The conventional process for the production and use of materials has been to extract natural resources such as fossil fuel or minerals, refine them, modify them further through manufacturing, and then distribute them as products. At the end of their useful lives, the products are discarded, usually to a landfill or an incinerator. Based on current material practices, society faces a number of problems, including the dispersion of persistent toxics and other contaminants throughout the Earth, depletion of nonrenewable resources such as petroleum, destruction of biodiversity, and the depletion and contamination of aquifers and drinking water sources. There is a growing perception that these material practices are unsustainable.

Moving toward a sustainable materials management system first requires the recognition that current practices are unsustainable. The next step is to develop and implement a model of sustainability.

Sustainability. Sustainability and sustainable development can be problematic terms because they are overused and their meaning is not precise. The most commonly used definition for sustainable development comes from a report by the World Commission on Environment and Development—"To meet the needs of the present without compromising the ability of future generations to meet their own needs."

Some experts in this field say that sustainability is too limited a goal. They argue that practices not only should sustain but also should benefit and restore both human and environmental well-being. Regardless of the limits, sustainability is recognized as the first step toward ensuring survival of the growing human population and the Earth.

In 1989, a framework for sustainability called the The Natural Step emerged through the efforts of Karl-Henrik Robèrt, a leading Swedish oncologist. This framework provides a model and a set of system conditions that define a sustainable society based on the laws of thermodynamics and natural cycles. The Natural Step System Conditions consider rates and flows in order to avoid degradation, depletion, or pollution of the ecological system (**Fig. 1**).

Sustainable materials. Materials produced and used in society are diverse and evolving. There are approximately 75,000 chemicals now used commercially. Because no one formulation is uniquely sustainable, it is useful to provide an operational definition. A sustainable material is then a material that fits within the constraints of a sustainable material system. In order to be sustainable, the material must be appropriate for the system and the system must be appropriate for the material.

Two strategies have been identified to support a sustainable materials economy. One strategy, a process known as dematerialization, involves developing ways to use less material to provide the same service in order to satisfy human needs. A second is detoxification of materials used in products and industrial processes.

Dematerialization. Dematerialization means reducing the amount of material in a product without decreasing the quality of its function. Dematerialization reduces the flow of materials into and through the industrial/economic system, also known as the technical loop (Fig. 1). Strategies for dematerialization involve reducing the rate of mining of industrial metals, developing organic chemicals from biomass wastes rather than fossil fuels, and promoting recycling and secondary materials industries to keep materials in the technical loop. Designing products for repair, upgrade, or recycling, as well as substituting services for products (for example, leasing computers rather than selling new ones) support the need for fewer resources and help keep materials within the industrial/economic system. But dematerialization is effective only if the materials used can serve as biological or technical "nutrients"—meaning that their reintegration into natural or industrial/economic systems is beneficial or at least benign within the systems (as defined in this context by W. McDonough and M. Braungart).

Detoxification. The strategy of detoxification includes substituting benign alternatives for problematic chemicals (for example, chlorofluorocarbons, or CFCs); phasing-out persistent, bioaccumulative, and toxic pollutants [for example, mercury and its compounds, polychlorinated biphenyls (PCBs), and dioxins]; generating toxics on demand or just-in-time to avoid the need for storage and transportation; and designing new materials that are compatible with human health and the greater ecosystem. Chemicals that can be used and assimilated into natural systems without increasing harm are biological nutrients. The design of such materials is a component of the growing field of green chemistry, which links the design of chemical products and processes with their impacts on human health and the environment in order to create sustainable materials.

Green chemistry. Green chemistry is a tool for chemists, chemical engineers, and others who design materials to help move society toward the goal of sustainability. Design at the molecular level allows decisions to be made that impact how materials will be processed, used, and managed at the end of their life (**Fig. 2**).

Green chemistry focuses on eliminating hazard rather than risk. The term "hazard" includes any of the impacts identified earlier as consequences of an unsustainable materials system. Hazard may include acute (short-term) or chronic (long-term) human or ecological toxicity, safety, and the potential for damage to the ozone layer, water resources, or biodiversity. Risk is a function of the inherent hazard and probability of exposure. Traditionally, risk management focuses on controlling the potential for exposure. However, exposure control failures, such as the deadly accident in Bhopal, India, will occur. Exposure to a material with a high degree of inherent hazard may result in a high-risk situation. By addressing the inherent hazard of a material, it is possible to reduce risk and eliminate the need for exposure controls that can also be very expensive.

Examples of green chemistry. In recent years, the application of green chemistry has shown that materials can be environmentally compatible and can fit within a sustainable materials system through the design of chemical products and processes that reduce or eliminate the use and generation of hazardous substances.

Antifoulants. In 1998, Rohm and Haas Company received a Presidential Green Chemistry Challenge Award for designing the environmentally safe marine antifoulant called Sea-Nine™. Fouling, the unwanted growth of plants and animals on a ship's surface,

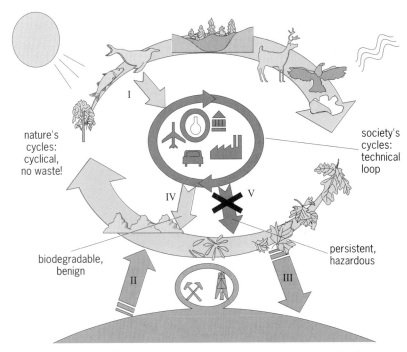

Fig. 1. Ecological aspects of The Natural Step System Conditions shown as the flow of materials in a closed system of two loops. The outer "biological" loop represents the cycling of materials within the Earth's ecosystems. In natural systems, there is essentially no waste, as all materials generated through living organisms become food or structure for other organisms. The inner "technical" loop represents cycling within the industrial/economic system. Arrow I represents the extraction of natural resources for use in the industrial/economic system. Arrows II and III represent extraction and resettling of materials from the Earth's crust—primarily fossil fuel and mined materials. Arrows IV and V represent materials that flow from the industrial/economic system to the greater ecosystem. The "persistent, hazardous" arrow represents chemicals or materials that cannot be safely assimilated into ecosystems, such as persistent, toxic, bioaccumulative, or otherwise hazardous materials. The "biodegradable, benign" arrow represents materials that can be assimilated without harm, either initially or after treatment. (*Larry Chalfan, Zero Waste Alliance, Portland, OR*)

costs the shipping industry approximately $3 billion a year. A significant portion of this cost is the increased fuel consumption needed to overcome hydrodynamic drag. The main compounds used worldwide to control fouling are organotin antifoulants, such as tributyltin oxide (TBTO). They are effective at preventing fouling, but have widespread environmental problems due to their persistence in the environment and the effects they cause, including acute toxicity, bioaccumulation, decreased reproductive viability, and increased shell thickness in shellfish. Rohm and Haas Company sought to develop an antifoulant that would prevent fouling from a wide variety of marine organisms without causing harm to nontarget organisms. Compounds from the 3-isothiazolone class were chosen. In particular, 4,5-dichloro-2-*n*-octyl-4-isothiazolin-3-one was selected as it was found to degrade extremely rapidly in seawater and even faster (1 h) in sediment. TBTO bioaccumulates as much as 10,000 times, while Sea-Nine™ bioaccumulation is essentially zero. Both TBTO and Sea-Nine™ were acutely toxic to marine organisms, but TBTO had widespread chronic toxicity, while Sea-Nine™ antifoulant showed no chronic toxicity.

Pest control. In 2001, EDEN Bioscience Corporation received a Presidential Green Chemistry Challenge

1. Prevention It is better to prevent waste than to treat or clean up waste after it has been created.

2. Atom Economy Synthetic methods should be designed to maximize the incorporation of all materials used in the process into the final product.

3. Less Hazardous Chemical Syntheses Wherever practicable, synthetic methods should be designed to use and generate substances that possess little or no toxicity to human health and the environment.

4. Designing Safer Chemicals Chemical products should be designed to effect their desired function while minimizing their toxicity.

5. Safer Solvents and Auxiliaries The use of auxiliary substances (such as solvents) should be made unnecessary wherever possible and innocuous when used.

6. Design For Energy Efficiency Energy requirements of chemical processes should be recognized for their environmental and economic impacts and should be minimized. If possible, synthetic methods should be conducted at ambient temperature and pressure.

7. Use of Renewable Feedstocks A raw material or feedstock should be renewable rather than depleting whenever technically and economically practicable.

8. Reduce Derivatives Unnecessary derivatization (use of blocking groups, protection/deprotection, temporary modification of physical/chemical processes) should be minimized or avoided if possible, because such steps require additional reagents and can generate waste.

9. Catalysis Catalytic reagents are superior to stoichiometric reagents because their chemoselectivity eliminates by-product formation.

10. Design for Degradation Chemical products should be designed so that at the end of their function they break down into innocuous degradation products and do not persist in the environment.

11. Real-time Analysis for Pollution Prevention Analytical methodologies need to be further developed to allow for real-time, in-process monitoring and control prior to the formation of hazardous substances.

12. Inherently Safer Chemistry for Accident Prevention Substances and the form of a substance used in a chemical process should be chosen to minimize the potential for chemical accidents, including releases, explosions, and fires.

Fig. 2. **Twelve principles of green chemistry.** (*Adapted from P. T. Anastas and J. C. Warner, Green Chemistry: Theory and Practice, p. 30, Oxford University Press, New York, 1998. By permission of Oxford University Press.*)

Award for their product, Messenger®, which is based on a new class of nontoxic, naturally occurring proteins called harpins. Harpins trigger a plant's natural defense systems to protect against disease and pests, and simultaneously activate certain plant growth systems without altering the plant's DNA. When applied to crops, harpins increase plant biomass, photosynthesis, nutrient uptake, and root development, leading to greater crop yield and quality.

The estimated annual losses to growers from pests is $300 billion worldwide. In order to be successful, growers have generally pursued two approaches to limit economic losses and increase yields: (1) use traditional chemical pesticides; or (2) grow crops that are genetically engineered for pest resistance. Each approach has consequences that have come under increasing criticism from a variety of sources. The use of harpins has been shown to have virtually no adverse effect on any of the organisms tested, including mammals, birds, honey bees, plants, fish, aquatic invertebrates, and algae. Harpins are fragile

molecules that are degraded rapidly by ultraviolet light and natural microorganisms; they have no potential to bioaccumulate or to contaminate surface- or ground-water resources. Unlike most agricultural chemicals, harpin-based products are produced in a water-based fermentation system that uses no harsh solvents or reagents, requires only modest energy inputs, and generates no hazardous chemical wastes.

Oxidation. Terrence J. Collins of Carnegie Mellon University received a Presidential Green Chemistry Challenge Award in 1999 for his work in the area of oxidation chemistry. Oxidation is used for bleaching wood pulp and textiles, as well as for disinfecting drinking water and wastewater. Many oxidation processes rely on chlorine chemistry which can form chlorinated pollutants, including dioxins. By developing a series of iron-based activators, called TAML™ (tetraamido-macrocyclic ligand), which contain no toxic functional groups and are effective with the natural oxidant hydrogen peroxide, Collins devised an environmentally benign oxidation technique with widespread application.

Research chemists tend to select simple designs and draw from the full range of elements from the periodic table, many of which are mined (relatively rare) and are persistent pollutants. Collins recognized that in nature selectivity is achieved through complex mechanisms using a limited set of elements available in the environment. He circumvented the problem of persistent pollutants in the environment by employing reagents and processes that mimic those found in nature.

Degradable polymers. In the 1990s, BASF developed a material called Savant™, made from nylon 6 fiber. Savant™ can be depolymerized and reused. BASF has initiated a take-back program for used carpet called 6ix Again. Recovered nylon 6 can be depolymerized and used in Savant™. Rather than downcycling it into a material with less value, the used nylon is "upcycled" into a product of high quality.

These examples show how innovative science and technology can support sustainability through the development of sustainable materials. Technology is not a panacea for sustainability, but it can provide innovative solutions when the challenges are defined by social choice to promote human and ecological well-being.

For background information *see* CONSERVATION OF RESOURCES; ECOLOGY, APPLIED; ENVIRONMENTAL MANAGEMENT; FOSSIL FUEL; HUMAN ECOLOGY; INDUSTRIAL ECOLOGY; MINERAL RESOURCES; RECYCLING TECHNOLOGY; SYSTEMS ECOLOGY; TOXICOLOGY in the McGraw-Hill Encyclopedia of Science & Technology.   Lauren Heine

Bibliography. P. T. Anastas and J. C. Warner, *Green Chemistry: Theory and Practice*, Oxford University Press, New York, 1998; K. G. Geiser, *Materials Matter: Toward a Sustainable Materials Policy*, MIT Press, Cambridge, MA, 2001; A. Grübler, *Technology and Global Change*, Cambridge University Press, Cambridge, 1998; W. McDonough and M. Braungart,

Cradle to Cradle, North Point Press, New York, 2002; W. McDonough and M. Braungart, The next industrial revolution, *Atlantic Mon.*, October 1998; World Commission on Environment and Development, *Our Common Future*, Oxford University Press, Oxford, 1987.

Thermohaline circulation changes

Covering some 71% of the Earth and absorbing about twice as much of the Sun's radiation as the atmosphere or the land surface, the oceans are a major component of the climate system. With their huge heat capacity, the oceans not only moderate temperature fluctuations but also play a dynamic role in transporting heat. Ocean currents move vast amounts of heat across the planet—roughly the same amount as the atmosphere does. But in contrast to the atmosphere, the oceans are confined by landmasses, so that their heat transport is more localized and channeled into specific regions.

One region that is strongly influenced by ocean currents is the North Atlantic. It is at the receiving end of a circulation system linking the Antarctic with the Arctic, known as the thermohaline circulation or the ocean conveyor belt (**Fig. 1**). The Gulf Stream and its extension toward Scotland play an important part in this system. The thermohaline circulation's driving forces are the temperature and salinity of sea water. These properties control the water density differences which ultimately drive the flow. The conveyor belt (loaded with heat) travels north, delivers the heat to the atmosphere, and then returns south at about 2–3 km (1–2 mi) below the sea surface as North Atlantic Deep Water (NADW). The heat transported to the northern Atlantic in this way is enormous, measuring around 10^{15} watts, the equivalent output of a half million large power-generating stations. This heat transport is the most important reason for the exceptionally warm climate of the North Atlantic region (**Fig. 2**). If locations in Europe are compared with similar latitudes on the North American continent, the effect becomes obvious. Bodö in Norway has an average temperature of $-2°C$ ($28°F$) in January and $14°C$ ($57°F$) in July, while Nome, on the Pacific coast of Alaska at the same latitude, is much colder, $-15°C$ ($5°F$) in January and $10°C$ ($50°F$) in July. Satellite images show how the warm current keeps much of the Greenland-Norwegian Sea free of ice in the winter, even when the rest of the Arctic Ocean, much farther south, is frozen.

During the past 100,000 years, this ocean circulation system has gone through many major and abrupt changes, which have been associated with large and abrupt changes in the surface climate. Since this discovery in the 1980s, scientists have been discussing the risk of future ocean circulation changes in response to anthropogenic global warming.

Past ocean circulation changes. During the last great Ice Age, lasting from 120,000 to 10,000 years

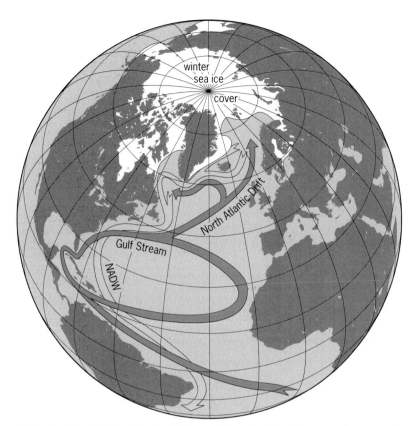

Fig. 1. Simplified sketch of the Atlantic thermohaline circulation. Warmer surface currents are shown in darker color and cold North Atlantic Deep Water (NADW) in lighter color. The thermohaline circulation heats the North Atlantic and northern Europe. It extends to the Greenland and Norwegian Seas, pushing back the winter sea ice margin.

before present, the climate was not just generally colder than the present climate but also was punctuated by abrupt transitions. The Greenland ice core data show over 20 warm events known as Dansgaard-Oeschger events. Dansgaard-Oeschger events typically start with an abrupt warming by around $10°C$ ($18°F$) within a few decades or less, followed by gradual cooling over several hundred or thousand years. While strongest in the northern Atlantic region, these events are reflected in many climate records around the world. The time interval between successive Dansgaard-Oeschger events is typically 1500 years or, with decreasing probability, 3000 or 4500 years.

A second, less frequent type of climate transition is known as the Heinrich event, which is associated with strong cooling of sea surface temperatures in the North Atlantic. Heinrich events involve the discharge of ice from the Laurentide Ice Sheet through the Hudson Strait, occurring in the colder phase of some Dansgaard-Oeschger cycles. They have a variable spacing of several thousand years. The icebergs released to the North Atlantic during Heinrich events leave telltale dropstones in the ocean sediments when they melt. Sediment data further suggest that Heinrich events shut down or at least drastically reduce the Atlantic thermohaline circulation.

At the end of the last glacial period, a particularly interesting abrupt climatic change took place,

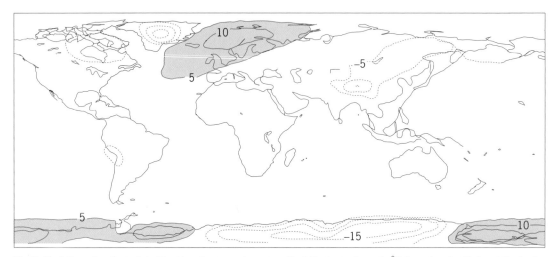

Fig. 2. Deviation of surface air temperature from zonal average. Deviations are shown in °C, based on the National Center for Atmospheric Research (NCAR) surface air temperature climatology. Regions that are too warm for their latitude, for example, in the northern Atlantic, correspond to regions of ocean deep-water formation. (*From S. Rahmstorf and A. Ganopolski, Climatic Change, 43(2):353–367, 1999; with permission of Kluwer Academic Publishers*)

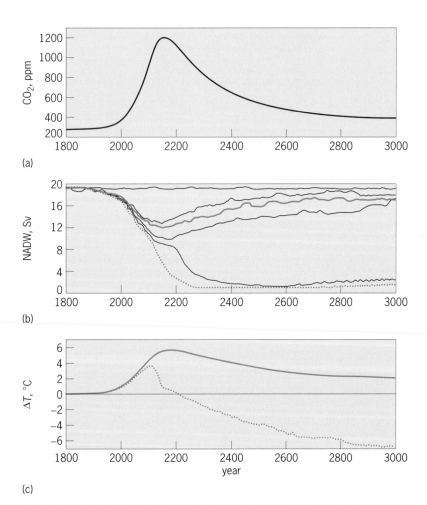

Fig. 3. Scenarios for future thermohaline circulation changes. (*a*) Assumed carbon dioxide concentration. (*b*) Response of the xthermohaline circulation. The scenarios differ in the amount of fresh water entering the northern Atlantic; in some cases the circulation recovers, but for large fresh-water input it collapses. (*c*) Temperature changes over the northern Atlantic for two scenarios. (*From S. Rahmstorf and A. Ganopolski, Climatic Change, 43(2):353–367, 1999; with permission of Kluwer Academic Publishers*)

called the Younger Dryas event (12,800–11,500 years before present). Conditions had already warmed to near-interglacial levels and continental ice sheets were retreating when, within decades, the climate in the North Atlantic region switched back to glacial conditions for more than a thousand years.

In recent years, simulations of these events with climate models have been increasingly realistic, and agree with many features seen in the paleoclimatic data. According to these simulations, two distinct changes in the thermohaline circulation played a key role in the observed abrupt climate changes.

The first was a thermohaline circulation shutdown that resulted from excessive amounts of fresh water entering the northern Atlantic, reducing surface salinity and density, and thereby inhibiting the deep mixing and sinking of water (deep-water renewal). This mechanism can explain the ocean response to Heinrich events (caused by ice-sheet instability) and the cold Younger Dryas event (caused by an influx of meltwater at the end of the glacial, when the surrounding continental ice sheets melted).

The second change was a latitude shift of the deep-water formation region, which could be triggered by more subtle changes in the fresh-water budget of the northern Atlantic. The abrupt warming during Dansgaard-Oeschger events can be explained as a shift of the convection site from the open Atlantic south of Iceland, to the Nordic Seas. The warm Atlantic waters were pushed north into the Nordic Seas, warming the surface waters and Greenland.

Possible future changes. Given the clear evidence for ocean circulation changes in the past and their dramatic impact on surface climate, it is natural to ask whether similar changes could happen in the future. The physical reasoning is simple. First, climatic warming will warm the surface waters of the ocean, reducing their density. Second, a warmer climate tends to be a wetter climate, and atmosphere models show enhanced precipitation over the northern

Atlantic catchment in global warming scenarios. Helped by fresh-water input from melting ice, this also reduces the density of the surface waters. Both factors—warming and freshening—tend to inhibit deep-water renewal and thus the thermohaline circulation.

A number of independent simulations with ocean-atmosphere models have revealed several possible scenarios.

The first scenario is simply a weakening of the thermohaline circulation by 15–50% during the coming 50–100 years. Most models show a weakening in this range. In the few scenarios that go beyond the year 2100, the circulation then recovers in many cases if atmospheric greenhouse gas content is stabilized.

A second scenario is a near-complete shutdown of the Atlantic thermohaline circulation, which occurs in some model scenarios when a critical threshold is crossed. This is similar to the Younger Dryas event and has been found in several models for scenarios with relatively high greenhouse gas content (for example, for a quadrupling of atmospheric carbon dioxide); the models typically show it occurring some time during the twenty-second century. A key control parameter is the amount of fresh water entering the northern Atlantic (**Fig. 3**).

A third scenario is a regional shutdown of deep-water renewal in one of the two main convection regions: the Labrador Sea or the Greenland-Norwegian Sea. This has some similarities with Dansgaard-Oeschger events. Several models have shown one of these possibilities for standard global warming scenarios, in some cases, as early as the year 2020.

Impacts and policy implications. Three types of impacts of such ocean circulation changes can be distinguished: those in the ocean (for example, impacts on marine ecosystems and fisheries), those on surface climate over land, and those at the land-sea margin (sea-level changes).

Little is known about the marine impacts, but several clues point at their being potentially severe. The high productivity of the northern Atlantic (as compared to the northern Pacific) has been attributed to the thermohaline circulation, which supplies nutrients and mild surface temperatures. Important fish stocks are highly temperature sensitive in their productivity, and spawning grounds are adapted to oceanographic conditions. Smaller, historical fluctuations in the path of the Gulf Stream have apparently caused mass casualties in fish and seabirds.

Climatic impacts over land will be felt most strongly near the northern Atlantic coasts (such as Scandinavia, Scotland, and Iceland), with reduced impact farther into the continents. A complete shutdown could lead to a regional cooling of up to 10°C (18°F), relative to the same situation without shutdown. Depending on the amount of greenhouse warming that has already occurred at the time of shutdown, this cooling would start from a warmer baseline than today.

The thermohaline circulation also affects regional sea level, causing the northern Atlantic to stand about 1 meter lower than the northern Pacific. A shutdown could lead to an additional sea-level rise by up to a meter around the northern Atlantic.

While the model simulations show physically plausible scenarios, supported by paleoclimatic evidence for similar changes in the past, there is currently no systematic way to assign probabilities to these scenarios. A substantial weakening of the circulation has to be considered likely. In contrast, a total shutdown is usually considered a low-probability and high-impact risk of global warming. A 2001 report of the Intergovernmental Panel on Climate Change (IPCC) states that a thermohaline circulation shutdown "presents a plausible, non-negligible risk," and could lead to "a sudden reversal of the warming trend" in regions bordering the North Atlantic, and that "the damage potential could be very high."

In short, the risk of thermohaline circulation changes adds uncertainty to the situation of policy makers who are trying to respond to existing information on global warming, and reduces the predictability of the climatic effects of anthropogenic emissions.

For background information *see* ARCTIC OCEAN; ATLANTIC OCEAN; CLIMATE HISTORY; CLIMATE MODELING; CLIMATE MODIFICATION; CLIMATIC PREDICTION; GLOBAL CLIMATE CHANGE; GULF STREAM; HEAT BALANCE, TERRESTRIAL ATMOSPHERIC; OCEAN CIRCULATION in the McGraw-Hill Encyclopedia of Science & Technology.   Stefan Rahmstorf

Bibliography. Intergovernmental Panel on Climate Change, *Climate Change 2001*, 3 vols., Cambridge University Press, Cambridge, 2001; S. Manabe and R. J. Stouffer, Century-scale effects of increased atmospheric CO_2 on the ocean-atmosphere system, *Nature*, 364:215–218, 1993; S. Rahmstorf, The thermohaline ocean circulation—A system with dangerous thresholds?, *Climatic Change*, 46:247–256, 2000; R. A. Wood et al., Changing spatial structure of the thermohaline circulation in response to atmospheric CO_2 forcing in a climate model, *Nature*, 399:572–575, 1999.

Time-lapse seismic reservoir monitoring

For many years, seismic exploration techniques have been used by geophysicists for imaging underground structures (identifying their general shapes) and, consequently, locating oil and gas reservoirs (hydrocarbon-bearing formations). This exploration was achieved first in two dimensions, using acoustic sensor arrays, and evolved to three dimensions (3D seismic) in the 1980s as computing power increased. Over the past 15 years, 3D seismic data have been used to characterize hydrocarbon-bearing formations in terms of thickness, porosity, fluid content, and so on. In the late 1990s, a new technique for reservoir monitoring and management called time-lapse seismic or 4D seismic was developed (the four dimensions being the three geometrical

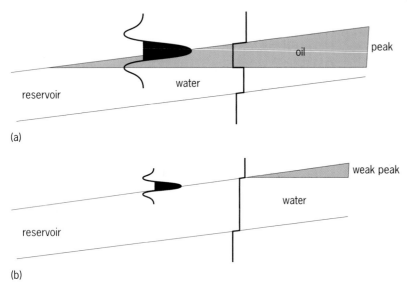

(a)

(b)

Fig. 1. Acoustic impedance profile, showing changes in acoustic impedance with reservoir flooding. (*a*) Initial. (*b*) After flooding.

dimensions plus time). By mid-2001, about 70 time-lapse seismic operations were under way throughout the world.

Time-lapse seismic consists of taking successive 3D seismic data surveys of the same area, using sensors to observe changes in seismic properties (usually acoustic impedance). Since acoustic impedance is the product of velocity (V) and density (ρ), the time-lapse signal is affected by incompressibility of the reservoir rock and the incompressibility of the pore fluids. This implies that soft rocks, such as sands, are perfect for time-lapse seismic, while stiff incompressible rocks, such as carbonates, are generally much more difficult. Distinguishable fluids typically have strong density differences (gas-oil, gas-water, oil-steam, and light oil-water), while heavy oils flooded by water may be very challenging to monitor. By interpreting the acoustic impedance changes caused by these materials, engineers can identify dynamic reservoir behavior, enabling them to efficiently manage and optimize hydrocarbon production (**Fig. 1**).

Feasibility. Before launching a time-lapse seismic survey, it must be determined if the physical properties of the reservoir rock are adequate to allow detection of production-related changes using seismic changes, and if a new survey can be done with sufficient repeatability.

Feasibility studies, including forward reservoir modeling, are mandatory to evaluate if time-lapse seismic can generate relevant information. In forward modeling, a reservoir fluid-flow simulator predicts likely changes in fluid distribution and pressure. These changes are translated to changes in wave propagation properties, and then seismic modeling predicts the likely seismic response.

Use of time-lapse seismic. Oil and gas field developments often require large capital investment, particularly offshore. As a result, a small increase in oil or

gas recovery may increase the return on investment significantly.

In the early oil and gas industry, hydrocarbons were produced using primary production methods (that is, by the natural reservoir pressure) with generally very poor recovery performance. Now, most reservoirs are produced by secondary methods, which displace the hydrocarbons with a fluid (sweeping fluid), typically water or gas. Secondary methods include (1) natural water drive, if there is sufficient influx from an existing aquifer; (2) artificial water drive, or waterflooding, where water is injected through wells located near the bottom of the reservoir; (3) natural gas drive, if a natural gas cap (a layer of free gas overlying an oil zone) can expand sufficiently; and (4) artificial gas drive, or gas flooding, where gas is injected through wells located near the top of the reservoir.

In all these cases, the sweeping of hydrocarbons is never totally efficient; the main reason is the heterogeneity of the underground formations, due to sedimentary deposition processes. As a result, the sweeping fluid may bypass hydrocarbons, which will not be recovered.

Time-lapse seismic allows engineers to identify a reservoir's remaining hydrocarbon reserves and make the decisions necessary to recover them, such as to optimize the injection/production scheme and flow rates, drill additional wells, or implement a new recovery mechanism.

For example, **Fig. 2** shows the seismic impedance data along the same cross-sectional line in an oil field produced by water drive. The strong changes in seismic impedance are caused by a rise in the water-oil contact level. Usually, the water-oil interface does not rise regularly (as a flat surface); it goes up faster in some areas and slower in others, bypassing undrained oil reserves.

After data acquisition (Fig. 2), 3D computational results provide an areal (*x-y*) image of drained zones (where water has replaced oil) and undrained zones (**Fig. 3**). Reservoir engineers can then drill additional wells to recover the oil from these undrained zones.

Analysis. Seismic processing requires considerable computing resources. For example, in the 1980s, the processing time for a typical 3D seismic survey was 18 months; it now is a couple of weeks. This is one reason why time-lapse seismic monitoring is now used.

The seismic response is a complex combination of various effects, some of them being relevant (signal) and many others being artifacts (noise). Seismic processing is used to improve the signal-to-noise ratio of these effects, such as geometrical effects (where multiple reflections/refractions occur in a large number of geological layers, in all directions). It is also used to account for rock property effects, since sound velocity may vary in large proportions as a function of the properties of the reservoir rocks and overlaying rocks.

The processed (clean) signal is a record of wave propagation properties, very often the acoustic

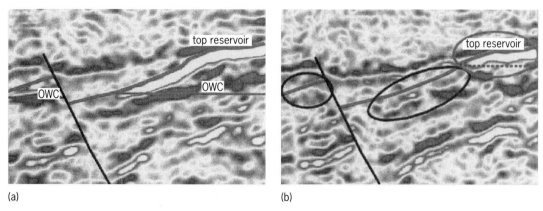

Fig. 2. Time-lapse seismic response changes caused by different positions of oil-water contact (OWC). (*a*) Oil-water contact level before production and (*b*) after 10 years' production. Zones with strong changes in seismic impedance are circled.

impedance, and must be translated into reservoir properties. The interpretive process of going from seismic signal to reservoir properties is known as seismic inversion. It is achieved by (1) empirically identifying the seismic attributes linked to specific properties of the reservoir (this is calibrated at the wells, where data exist for both seismic attributes and physical properties), or (2) establishing a strong

link between wave propagation properties and the reservoir rock properties (the rock physics model). The latter, more rigorous method may be difficult because a large number of parameters play a significant role, such as rock matrix stiffness, rock porosity, stress, fluid content, signal frequency, and so on.

The options for time-lapse seismic interpretation in particular are similar. A qualitative interpretation

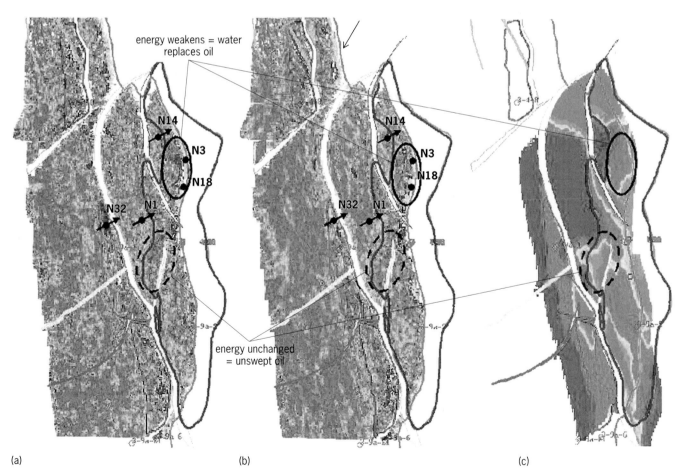

Fig. 3. Mapping of changes in oil saturation. (*a*) Using acoustic impedance, 1981. (*b*) Using acoustic impedance, 1996. (*c*) 1996 fluid saturation map deduced from (*b*).

is made by observing the changes of selected attributes, to visualize or to track the displacement of a water-oil or gas-oil contact, or to identify undrained (that is, unchanged) zones. A more rigorous quantitative interpretation is made by calculating the fluid content change (in terms of percent space occupied) with the help of an adequately calibrated rock physics model.

Two difficulties are associated with this second technique. First, the rock physics model has to be calibrated by laboratory experiments using actual core samples (which are not always available). This is very time consuming. Second, the seismic response is equally affected by fluid content and fluid pressure (which influences effective stress), and these change, often simultaneously, when time-lapse seismic monitoring is performed. As a result, resolution may be rather poor when circumstances are not very favorable. For these reasons, interpretation of time-lapse seismic monitoring is today mostly qualitative.

Repeatability. This issue is critical for the success of time-lapse seismic monitoring. Seismic surveys are never identical. The technology of seismic sources and seismic receivers is changing continuously, such that any given technology may be outdated within 5 years. In addition, acquisition parameters such as sensor pattern cannot be kept constant (due to positioning uncertainties, changes needed to accommodate new facilities, and so on). Even with permanently installed sensors, the problem is less severe but still exists, as coupling with the ground may change with time. In addition, processing should include cross equalization to correct for changes and normalize (make comparable) nonidentical surveys.

Outlook. Among the many challenges facing time-lapse seismic reservoir monitoring are the development of new inexpensive and reliable permanent sensors, both onshore and subsea; improvement in cross-equalization techniques to allow wider use of time-lapse seismic regardless of the difference between surveys; and development of quantitative interpretation methods. Another issue is how to use time-lapse seismic data in the history matching of reservoir models, an essential step in reservoir engineering.

For background information see ACOUSTIC IMPEDANCE; GEOPHYSICAL EXPLORATION; PETROLEUM ENHANCED RECOVERY; PETROLEUM GEOLOGY; PETROLEUM RESERVOIR ENGINEERING; SEISMIC EXPLORATION FOR OIL AND GAS; SEISMIC STRATIGRAPHY; SEISMOLOGY in the McGraw-Hill Encyclopedia of Science & Technology.   Alain Labastie

Bibliography. R. Behrens et al., *Practical Use of 4D in an Imperfect World*, SPE Pap. 71329, 2001; D. E. Lumley et al., *Practical Issues of 4D Seismic Reservoir Monitoring an Engineer Needs To Know*, SPE Pap. 53004, 1998; O. Yilmaz, Seismic data processing, *Investigations in Geophysics*, vol. 2, Society of Exploration Geophysicists Publications, Tulsa, 1987.

Transgenic plant vaccines

The use of vaccines in the last two centuries has led to dramatic reductions in many devastating infectious diseases. Certain diseases such as smallpox and polio have been nearly eradicated (although there is a fear that smallpox may resurface at the hands of bioterrorists). For most other diseases, however, no vaccines exist. Unfortunately, the development of new vaccines has been painstakingly difficult and expensive, and involves research that may span decades. In today's era of bioweapons, international travel, and exponential population growth, extra urgency exists to create new, safe, inexpensive, and easily administered vaccines.

In industrialized nations, children are required to endure approximately two dozen vaccine injections. However, current figures indicate that due to poor compliance rates, especially among undocumented immigrants, the United States has nearly 1 million unvaccinated children. The need for vaccination is most urgent for the tens of millions of people around the world for whom the cost of vaccines is too high or who live in areas that lack the equipment and personnel needed to deliver them. To increase the rate of vaccination among these groups, scientists have begun to explore the use of transgenic edible plants for the synthesis and delivery of oral vaccines. For the past 15 years, work has progressed toward development of plant-based vaccines that protect against a growing number of human and animal diseases (see **table**). In addition to saving lives, these vaccines have the potential to save billions of dollars that are currently lost annually due to health care expenditures, loss of work, and rampant disease in the livestock industry.

Ideal vaccine. To be most effective at preventing illness, a vaccine should trigger the immune system to generate long-lasting protective immunity against potential pathogenic invaders without causing adverse reactions. Because conventional vaccines are typically injected, they do not elicit the type of immune response that normally occurs when pathogens enter through mucosal routes (the eyes and digestive, urogenital, and respiratory tracts). Over 90% of infections begin at mucosal surfaces in humans, an area nearly equivalent to the surface of a basketball court. Interestingly, a vaccine delivered at one mucosal site (such as the intestine) will result in the generation of large amounts of secreted antibodies (S-IgA) that are released into all mucosal regions of the body. These S-IgA antibodies neutralize and block invasion of prospective pathogens or their toxins at their point of entry. Injected vaccines usually induce the production of antibody types (IgM and IgG) that lead to immune clearance of an invading disease agent once infection has begun.

A drawback of traditional vaccines is that since they contain live or weakened viruses or bacteria, or protein fragments of a pathogen, they must

Plant-based vaccines for infectious diseases	
Pathogen	Disease
Animal vaccines	
Canine parvovirus	Diarrhea in dogs
Foot-and-mouth disease virus	Debilitating vesicular disease of cloven-hoofed animals
Mannheimia haemolytica A1	Cattle shipping fever
Mink enteritis virus	Diarrhea in mink
Murine hepatitis virus	Liver disease in mice
Rabbit hemorrhagic disease virus	Fatal bleeding disease in rabbits
Rabies virus	Rabies
Swine-transmissible gastroenteritis virus	Diarrhea in pigs
Human vaccines	
Clostridium tetani	Tetanus
Cytomegalovirus	Congenital defects
Enterotoxigenic *E. coli*	Diarrhea
Hepatitis B virus	Jaundice
Hepatitis C virus	Liver cancer
Herpes simplex virus-2	Genital herpes
Human immunodeficiency virus	Acquired immune deficiency syndrome
Human papillomavirus 16	Genital warts, cervical cancer
Influenza virus	Flu
Measles virus	Measles
Norwalk virus	Diarrhea
Plasmodium protozoa	Malaria
Pseudomonas aeruginosa	Bacterial meningitis
Respiratory syncytial virus	Pneumonia
Rhinovirus 14	Common cold
Rotavirus	Diarrhea
Staphylococcus aureus	Food poisoning, pneumonia, sepsis
Streptococcus mutans	Dental caries (cavities)
Vibrio cholerae	Cholera (diarrhea)

be stored in toxic preservatives and maintained under refrigeration. In addition, there is a risk of developing allergies to proteins purified during vaccine harvest from animal or microbial hosts. Live vaccines are potentially deadly to patients with weak or compromised immune systems. Some newer vaccines contain only protein subunits of pathogens that are recognized by the immune system, rather than the whole organism. These proteins are usually synthesized in engineered bacteria or yeast, but require extensive purification and commonly require several booster immunizations to stimulate antibody-secreting memory B cells for long-term immunity.

Targeting mucosal surfaces may be the most effective form of vaccination, but most proteins are quickly degraded in the harsh environment surrounding these membranes, especially when delivered orally. Vaccine proteins synthesized inside plant cells, however, are protected naturally by the thick cellulose cell walls of plants, which can act as slow-release "capsules" when consumed.

Plant-based vaccine production. There are three primary methods used to transform plants into vaccine bioreactors. The most common technique is to utilize an engineered form of the soil bacterium *Agrobacterium tumefaciens* that normally causes crown gall tumors in plants. The genes in the bacterium's tumor-inducing (Ti) plasmid that result in tumor formation are removed and replaced with genes that code for proteins that stimulate an im-

mune response. Sterilized plant tissues (leaf or stem cuttings) are infected with the modified *Agrobacterium* strain, which is capable of transferring the foreign gene(s) into the plant cell nucleus. The DNA is then integrated into the plant genome, where it is transcribed and translated into the antigenic (antibody-generating) protein.

Biological transformation using *A. tumefaciens* has its limitations, however. Many plant species are not susceptible to infection by this bacterium, especially the cereal grains and other monocotyledonous plants. To genetically engineer important cereal crops, a physical transformation method known as "biolistic" or "particle bombardment" is used. DNA-coated microscopic metal (usually gold) particles are shot at plant tissues using a gas-pressurized projectile that is abruptly stopped just above the tissue, causing the DNA-coated metal particles to fly off and pierce the plant cells. A small percentage of the DNA adhering to the metal particles will become incorporated into the plant genome. This technique has recently been utilized for the insertion of DNA into genomes of chloroplast and chromoplast organelles. Most plant cells contain dozens of chloroplasts, each containing numerous copies of the plastid genome. Foreign genes inserted into the plastid genome can thus yield transformed plants that produce 10 to 1000 times more vaccine protein than plants with DNA integrated into nuclear genomes. An additional benefit is that because pollen grains do not have chloroplasts, the chance for cross-pollination of a wild-type species with pollen from a transformed plant is eliminated.

The third strategy used to manufacture vaccines in plants is to infect plants with genetically engineered viruses that contain vaccine-producing genes. The virus genome is modified by insertion of antigen-encoding genes into regions that code for either coat proteins or soluble proteins. When the virus replicates inside the plant cell, the fused gene products will be translated together with the viral proteins. Since plant viruses do not infect animals and are capable of replicating to high numbers in plant tissues, they are ideal vehicles for quickly generating large quantities of vaccine proteins that can be purified from infected leaf tissue. However, the transgene must not be too large or the encoded protein may interfere with viral protein assembly. In addition, the process of infecting and purifying plant tissues is laborious, and containment of the virus in a protected environment is essential.

Vaccine yield and dose reduction. The vaccines listed in the table have been tested in nonhuman animals and shown to generate significant levels of protective antibodies following one or more oral doses. Protection from a lethal dose of a disease agent in immunized animals has been demonstrated in several vaccines. As final evidence that plant-based vaccines are indeed feasible, vaccines against enterotoxigenic *Escherichia coli*, Hepatitis B virus, and Norwalk virus recently underwent human clinical trials. All three trials indicated considerable increases in disease-specific antibodies in most of the volunteers, suggesting that protection is likely should they encounter the disease agent.

A remaining obstacle in plant-based vaccination is production of large enough amounts of vaccine protein in individual plants so that the tissue dosage required for immune protection is reasonable for consumption. While efforts at generating increased vaccine protein yield in plants are underway, a new strategy being pursued is genetic fusion of antigens to binding proteins that target regions on the mucosal surface where antigens are recognized. Mucosal-associated lymphoid tissue (MALT) contains numerous M (microfold) cells on the surface that take up antigens from the environment and transport them to underlying dendritic cells, which become conditioned for activation of antigen-specific T cells. Activated effector T cells may differentiate further into two subsets: T_H1 cells for activation of cytotoxic T lymphocytes and macrophages for cell-mediated destruction, or T_H2 cells that stimulate B lymphocytes to become antibody-secreting plasma cells.

The nontoxic B subunit of cholera toxin (CTB), which binds to G_{M1} ganglioside receptors on gut cells, is one such example of a MALT-targeting molecule. Incidentally, CTB is also a fairly strong adjuvant (immune stimulator) when fused to an antigen protein. Furthermore, antibodies made against CTB in the fusion complex can protect against cholera. This concept was applied to generate the first multicomponent edible vaccine, in which CTB that was fused to a rotavirus protein was combined with the cholera toxin A_2 linker peptide and a cell-binding fimbrial adhesion protein of *E. coli*. Protection against all three diseases was observed in mice fed potatoes containing the multicomponent vaccine. The use of CTB fused to an antigen or autoantigen has lowered the dose requirement by as much as 5000-fold in certain vaccines.

Oral tolerance in autoimmune diseases. Recently, plants have been utilized for the production of autoantigens—self-proteins that are perceived as foreign by the immune system in individuals with autoimmunity. Several studies have shown that when an autoantigen is given orally, the immune system learns to ignore the presence of these proteins in a process known as oral tolerance. Immunotolerance is regulated by a subset of T_H2 cells (T_H3 and T_R1), which can actively suppress the lymphocytes that lead to autoimmune destruction (that is, T_H1 cells, cytotoxic T lymphocytes, and cytotoxic macrophages). The diabetes autoantigens insulin and glutamic acid decarboxylase (GAD) were fused to CTB and synthesized in transgenic potatoes, which were fed to a strain of mice that mimic the symptoms of type 1 diabetes. A slight suppression of diabetic symptoms was observed in mice fed transformed plants containing insulin or GAD alone. More dramatic improvement was seen after feeding plants containing insulin and GAD fused to CTB. At least eight other autoimmune diseases have shown oral tolerance responses when autoantigens were given orally to animals, although none of these autoantigens have been produced in plants as of yet.

Future applications. After the effective dose regime and safety of each edible vaccine have been established, it is envisioned that leaves, fruit, seeds, or tubers from these plants could be freeze-dried and delivered in capsules that could be stored unrefrigerated for long periods. Seeds could also be shipped worldwide, although concern over the uniformity of delivered doses and proper tracking of booster immunizations could, at least initially, limit distribution to facilities with trained personnel. Administration of plant-based vaccines raw or processed into juice, sauce, or powder could be a convenient means for vaccine delivery. However, processes that involve heating or cooking may destroy some plant-based vaccines. In addition, the amount fed must be carefully monitored to avoid "tolerizing" people against the vaccine by accidental overdose.

Future plant-based vaccines might carry antigenic proteins from several different pathogen species (multicomponent) or various antigens of the same species (multivalent) for broader coverage against infectious or autoimmune disease. Someday, immunizing children may be as simple as feeding them two or three doses of their favorite food.

For background information *see* BIOTECHNOLOGY; CELLULAR IMMUNOLOGY; GENETIC ENGINEERING;

VACCINATION in the McGraw-Hill Encyclopedia of Science & Technology.   James E. Carter III;
William H. R. Langridge

Bibliography. J. E. Carter III and W. H. R. Langridge, Plant-based vaccines for protection against infectious and autoimmune diseases, *Crit. Rev. Plant Sci.*, 21(2):93–109, 2002; H. Daniell, M. S. Khan, and L. Allison, Milestones in chloroplast genetic engineering: An environmentally friendly era in biotechnology, *Trends Plant Sci.*, 7:84–91, 2002; A. M. Faria and H. L. Weiner, Oral tolerance: Mechanisms and therapeutic applications, *Adv. Immunol.*, 73:153–264, 1999; S. Ruf et al., Stable genetic transformation of tomato plastids and expression of a foreign protein in fruit, *Nat. Biotechnol.*, 19:870–875, 2001; H. L. Weiner, The mucosal milieu creates tolerogenic dendritic cells and T_R1 and T_H3 regulatory cells, *Nat. Immunol.*, 2:671–672, 2001; J. Yu and W. H. R. Langridge, A plant-based multicomponent vaccine protects mice from enteric diseases, *Nat. Biotechnol.*, 19:548–552, 2001.

Transmissible spongiform encephalopathies

Transmissible spongiform encephalopathies (TSE) are a group of usually fatal neurodegenerative diseases affecting the brains of both animals and humans. The diseases are characterized by the cerebral accumulation of an abnormal form (structural isoform) of a protein, named prion protein (PrP; prion is an acronym for proteinaceous infectious agent). There is strong evidence that TSE diseases result solely from the accumulation of this abnormal prion protein (PrP) and that it is the conversion of the normal to the abnormal protein which triggers the disease process. However, another school of thought believes that in addition to the abnormal form of PrP there is a still-undiscovered component such as a nucleic acid, which could account for the many different strains of TSE disease.

Pathology. In TSE diseases, holes are frequently observed in the brain. This formation of holes, known as vacuolation, commonly occurs in the gray matter of the brain, where it often produces lesions in the nerve cell body itself. However, other pathological effects occur; one of the most consistently produced is deposits of the abnormal form of PrP not only in the brain but also in lymphoid tissue, where follicular dendritic cells in the germinal centers are involved. The normal form of PrP exists in an uninfected host, where its function has still to be determined. However, if a potential host becomes infected, the disease produces an alteration to the structure of the normal PrP into the abnormal form. Exactly how this occurs is not known, although there are several hypotheses (such as refolding and seeding models). In this state, the PrP can aggregate to form very large deposits in the brain that are

Immunorecognition of the disease-associated form of PrP in the dorsal motor vajus nucleus of the hindbrain of a sheep with natural scrapie.

sometimes observed encrusting blood vessels or as intra- or extracellular deposits with a granular appearance.

Animal diseases. One of the oldest animal forms of the disease is natural scrapie (see **illus.**), which occurs in sheep and has been recognized in the United Kingdom for at least 250 years, as well as being present in many countries throughout the world. In cattle, bovine spongiform encephalopathy (BSE) was first diagnosed in the mid-1980s and is considered by many to have originated from natural scrapie as a result of changes to the process of rendering animal remains. As these remains were included in many animal feedstuffs, the disease spread to other species, including zoo antelope and domestic cats. Although the incidence of BSE is now rapidly declining in the United Kingdom, it continues to threaten the rest of Europe and beyond.

Other examples of animal forms of disease include chronic wasting disease (CWD), which affects deer and elk in North America (and by all accounts seems to be on the increase) and transmissible mink encephalopathy (TME). A small number of outbreaks of TME have been confirmed in ranched mink, but there is no indication of an increased spread within the species.

Human diseases. It is now clear that BSE has been responsible for a new form of the human equivalent disease, variant Creutzfeldt-Jakob disease (vCJD), which has fatally infected more than 100 people in the United Kingdom. Currently, there are many studies being conducted involving BSE, including whether it could have transmitted to sheep. So far, however, there is no evidence of such an occurrence.

In people, vCJD and sporadic CJD (sCJD) are distinct, with vCJD affecting mostly younger victims and producing an extended clinical phase compared with a more rapid progression with sCJD. There are other associated disorders such as Gerstmann-Sträussler-Scheinker (GSS) syndrome and fatal familial insomnia (FFI), which occur even more rarely than the approximate one in a million for sCJD. In the Fore tribe of New Guinea, another related disease, kuru, probably arose and spread through the ritualistic cannibalism of affected individuals.

Latency and age of onset. Although it is now widely accepted that prions are the infectious agent in TSE diseases, they were known at one time as slow virus diseases. They can take many years to manifest as a clinical condition, and in some animal models this time span exceeds life expectancy. With BSE for example, the average age of affected cattle is 4–5 years; however, cases in cattle 8 years of age and older can occur depending on the timing and the amount of infectivity that they would have received. Natural scrapie normally occurs in 3–4-year-old sheep, but can appear much later with a clinical phase lasting up to 6 months. One of the critical differences between vCJD and sCJD is the age of onset, with the former appearing in much younger people, some in their teenage years, while the latter normally affects those over 60. The occurrence of vCJD in such young people is thought to be due to dietary habits and consumption of cheaper meat products. Undoubtedly, some of these products would have contained a proportion of mechanically recovered meat, which seems to have carried a higher risk of BSE infection from nervous tissue.

Experimental models of TSE also vary enormously in the length of disease. With some rodent models this can be 3 months or less, while in some ruminant models it can last nearly 7 years. Various elements are responsible for this, including host PrP genetics, size of dose, infecting source or strain of TSE, and route of challenge. From these studies it has emerged that infection by mouth is the least efficient route of transmission because it affords less opportunity for infectivity to reach sites of replication, such as peripheral lymphoid tissue and peripheral nerves, before progressing to the central nervous system. Whether this has helped minimize the number of people contracting BSE through infected food remains to be seen.

Transmission. Transmission by the ingestion of TSE-infected material has been fairly well researched, especially for some experimental and natural forms of disease in animals. It is certainly the most plausible explanation for the appearance of vCJD. For sCJD, some cases have arisen from tissues donated by infected but clinically normal individuals, such as corneal and dura mater grafts and cadavouric pituitary extract. However, of growing concern is the possibility that CJD could spread through contaminated blood products or even via improperly decontaminated instruments following surgery.

Little is known about the transmission of BSE between animals, although a possible low level of incidence has been suggested for the disease passing between an infected cow and her calf. Even this is not expected to perpetuate the disease, which should eventually die out between generations. Natural scrapie, however, is quite different. Ample evidence exists that transmission occurs horizontally by contact between infected and uninfected animals as well as vertically when an infected ewe passes the disease to her lamb, although the timing of this process is still under investigation. In all of this, the role of the placenta is thought to be crucial. Any attempts to eradicate natural scrapie are not going to be easy, and current efforts are focusing on the ovine PrP gene. It is well established from experimental and field studies that certain PrP genotypes are susceptible to scrapie (both the experimental and natural forms). Probably the most effective method of counteracting scrapie will be to alter the genetic frequencies of susceptible PrP alleles in favor of more resistant genotypes.

With CJD too, genetic predisposition is based on PrP gene alleles, which seem to govern susceptibility to the disease.

Diagnosis and prevention. The classic symptom of natural scrapie in sheep is the animal rubbing vigorously against an object, producing skin abrasions and wool loss. BSE-affected cattle, however, are much more likely to develop uncoordinated movements, often accompanied by aggressive behavior. In humans, there are also marked differences between the variant and sporadic forms of CJD, as the vCJD symptoms develop over a much longer time scale. In the later stages of the disease, the patient invariably suffers from behavioral and psychiatric disturbances and myoclonus (muscle spasms or twitches) and requires complete nursing care.

Clinical symptoms of TSE disease can occasionally extend beyond a year; vCJD is an example. Early verification of disease is crucial so that putative therapies, when they become available, can be implemented. One method of verifying TSE that has been used successfully in humans is magnetic resonance imaging of the brain, which has the benefit of being noninvasive. Invasive techniques, however, can still be used and include biopsy of tissues such as lymphoid (tonsil) or brain. Tissue recovery enables the disease-associated form of PrP to be visualized with anti-PrP antibodies in tissue sections, although TSE diseases themselves do not elicit an humoral response in the host. Tonsil biopsy was first developed in sheep to assess subclinical infection of natural scrapie, although its secondary use for diagnosing human TSE has not been fully substantiated.

The importance of reliable postmortem diagnosis, whether on animal or human remains, is clear and tends to concentrate on the recognition of disease-associated PrP. This may be accomplished through immunostaining affected tissue or by gel electrophoresis (separation of protein in silica gel according to electrical charge and size) of PrP protein fractions.

Monitoring randomly recovered tissues from slaughter houses to assess covert disease in a clinical animals is vital and is becoming routine.

Future research. The investigation of subclinical disease is a critical area of research not only because of the outcome to affected humans or animals but also because of the possibility of disease transmission from sources such as food or tissue/fluid donations. Studies are investigating the likelihood of a blood transmission from sheep with experimental and natural forms of the disease. Some early observations show that experimentally induced ovine BSE can be transmitted via whole-blood transfusion to ovine recipients.

It is evident that many questions involving the spread of TSE diseases remain and that much more work is required to formulate risk assessments for disease transmission between and within species. In the meantime, it is of the utmost importance that wherever natural TSE diseases exist, concerted action is taken in an effort to identify and eradicate them.

For background information *see* NERVOUS SYSTEM DISORDERS; PRION DISEASE; SCRAPIE in the McGraw-Hill Encyclopedia of Science & Technology.

James Foster

Bibliography. D. C. Bolton, M. P. McKinley, and S. B. Prusiner, Identification of a protein that purifies with the scrapie prion, *Science*, 218:1309–1311, 1982; M. E. Bruce et al., Transmissions to mice indicate that "new variant" CJD is caused by the BSE agent, *Nature*, 389:498–501, 1997; N. Hunter et al., Natural scrapie in a closed flock of Cheviot sheep occurs only in specific PrP genotypes, *Arch. Virol.*, 141:809–824, 1996; B. E. C. Schreuder, Preclinical test for prion diseases, *Vet. Rec.*, 381:563, 1996; J. W. Wilesmith et al., Bovine spongiform encephalopathy: Epidemiological studies, *Vet. Rec.*, 123:638–644, 1988.

Transporting single electrons

The manipulation of individual electrons has become possible as a result of the steady advances in nanolithography over the last 10 years. Today the transport of single electrons can be routinely achieved at very low temperatures in specially designed circuits having critical dimensions of several hundred nanometers or less. In a single-electron-transport device, electrons can be clocked through a circuit at a certain frequency. The resulting electrical current I_S through the circuit is the electron charge e times the clock frequency f. If the frequency is locked to a standard, a fundamental or quantum standard of current is generated. A quantum standard of current will be of great interest to the metrological community concerned with the derivation of electrical units from basic physical laws and dissemination of these for commercial calibrations. This is because a quantum standard of current would complete the "metrological triangle" of connections between the already existing electrical quantum standards of resistance and voltage, which are based on the quantum Hall effect and the Josephson effect respectively, and the new quantum standard of current.

In the Hall effect, a conductor carrying an electric current perpendicular to an applied magnetic field develops a voltage gradient in a direction perpendicular to both the current and the magnetic field. The ratio between the transverse voltage V_{trans} and the longitudinal current I_{long} is called the Hall resistance R_H. In the quantum Hall effect, the Hall resistance becomes quantized in a two-dimensional electron gas for a number of ranges of magnetic field applied to a device exhibiting this effect. Its value is given by Eq. (1), where i is a small integer depending on the

$$\frac{V_{\text{trans}}}{I_{\text{long}}} = R_H = \frac{R_K}{i} = \frac{h}{ie^2} \tag{1}$$

range of the magnetic field and h is Planck's constant. The quantity R_K is called the von Klitzing constant after its discoverer, Klaus von Klitzing, and is a quantum standard of resistance whose value seems to depend only on the values of h and e. In the Josephson effect, a superconducting tunnel junction produces a direct voltage when exposed to radio-frequency radiation. In this case the voltage V_J takes a quantized value given by Eq. (2), where n is an integer.

$$V_J = \frac{nf}{K_J} = \frac{nhf}{2e} \tag{2}$$

The quantity K_J is called the Josephson constant after Brian Josephson, who first predicted this effect in 1962. Closure of the metrological triangle implies checking the validity of the identity $I_S = 2V_J/R_H$. This would test whether the formulas for R_K and K_J are accurate to the uncertainty of the measurements, or need small correction terms which are not predicted by present theory (**Fig. 1**).

However, for such a check of the theory to be as rigorous as possible the quantum current standard should produce a very accurate current with at least the same or better accuracy as that for V_J or R_H, all being measured in consistent (usually SI) units. To date, the Josephson constant is known with a relative

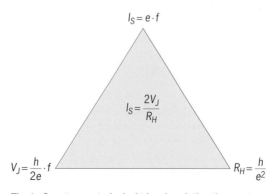

Fig. 1. Quantum metrological triangle, relating the quantum Hall resistance R_H, the voltage across a Josephson junction V_J, and the current through a single-electron-transport device I_S.

uncertainty of 4 parts in 10^7 and the von Klitzing constant with 2 parts in 10^7. Ideally an apparatus should be constructed in which the single-electron current is accurate to parts in 10^6 to 10^7.

Single-electron-tunneling device. One way of controlling the transport of single electrons is by using extremely small metallic circuits at very low temperatures of around 20 millikelvins. In these devices, small metallic islands are connected via ultrasmall tunnel junctions having very small capacitances C (smaller than 10^{-15} farad). The operation of these devices is based on Coulomb blockade: When the capacitance is small enough, the charging energy $e^2/2C$ can be made larger than the thermal fluctuations k_BT (where k_B is the Boltzmann constant). When the temperature T is low enough, tunneling of electrons onto the island is then blocked. By momentarily changing the energy of the island via a voltage applied to a small capacitively-coupled gate close to it, a single electron can be allowed to pass through the circuit. Applying an alternating voltage of frequency f results in a current of ef. Using this technique, electrons can be passed through the circuit with error rates as low as 1 in 10^8. However, the tunneling process is quite slow, and the operating frequency of these devices is limited to megahertz frequencies, producing a quantized current of the order of 1 picoampere. With this current, a sensitivity of 10^{-19} A would be required to check the theory, which is beyond the capability of present current-measuring techniques.

Rather than trying to measure this small current directly, metrologists use these devices to charge a capacitor. For example, a 1-pA current from a single-electron-tunneling device will charge a 1-pF capacitor to 1 V in 1 s. This voltage can be compared with the Josephson voltage, using another single-electron device as a detector. In this way, one defines a quantum standard of capacitance rather than current.

Acousto-electric current device. When a surface acoustic wave propagates on a piezoelectric substrate, a wave of electrostatic potential travels along with it and can interact with electrons in the substrate. The waves travel parallel to the surface, and their displacement amplitude decays rapidly away from the surface of the material so that they are confined to within approximately one wavelength of the surface. Recently, devices have been developed that use a surface acoustic wave to drive electrons through a narrow constriction. A situation can be created where each cycle of the wave pushes a single electron through this constriction, resulting in a current $I = ef_W$, where f_W is the frequency of the wave. This technique does not rely on electron tunneling and can be made to operate at much higher frequencies of the order of a few gigahertz, thereby creating nanoamperes of quantized current. In this case a direct comparison of the current with V_J and R_H might become possible with the required small uncertainty.

The basis for these surface-acoustic-wave devices is a GaAs-Al$_x$Ga$_{1-x}$As (gallium arsenide-aluminum gallium arsenide) heterostructure, identical to that used for making quantum Hall effect devices, which contains a two-dimensional electron gas just underneath the surface (at a depth of 80–100 nm) at the GaAs-AlGaAs interface. By means of electron beam lithography and subsequent evaporation of gold contacts or gates on the surface, a very small channel a few hundred nanometers wide is defined on the surface (**Fig. 2**). By applying a negative voltage with respect to the electron gas to these gates, the electrons are depleted from underneath the gates. Furthermore, by changing this voltage the channel can be varied smoothly in width or even completely closed.

Acoustic waves can be generated on the surface of a piezoelectric material by applying an alternating potential to suitable electrodes, also on the surface. The simplest design is an interdigitated transducer, which consists of interleaved pairs of fingers (Fig. 2) that are fabricated by means of electron beam lithography and metal evaporation techniques. The pitch of the fingers (that is, the distance between neighboring fingers) determines the wavelength λ_S and therefore the frequency of the wave, $f_W = v_{\text{sound}}/\lambda_S$, where v_{sound} is the sound velocity in the material (2700 m/s or 8400 ft/s in GaAs). The minimum attainable pitch (or maximum frequency) is limited by the capabilities of the nanolithography; the maximum frequency is presently set to a limit of about 5 GHz.

Quantized current generation. **Figure 3** shows the result of a typical acousto-electric current experiment. The current was measured with an electrometer between two contacts made to the layer containing the electron gas while the gate voltage was slowly varied. The quantum nature of the electron transport is immediately apparent from this data: The plateaus in the acousto-electric current coincide exactly with the passage of a small quantized number n ($= 1, 2, 3,$ or 4) of electrons per cycle of the acoustic wave through the constriction. As the width of the channel is varied by changing the gate voltage, n changes in a steplike fashion and $I_S = nef_W$.

For this experiment to work, the channel has to be just closed so that no normal free passage of electrons can occur which would destroy the quantized nature of the transport. In this situation the maxima of the acoustic-wave potential form a moving stream of zero-dimensional dots through the constriction. The term zero-dimensional means that there are no free degrees of movement left for the electrons: The electrons experience confinement in one direction by the heterostructure, in the transverse direction by the potential from the surface gate, and in the longitudinal direction by the acoustic-wave potential. In a similar way to the tunneling device, the Coulomb charging energy controls the number of electrons in these isolated dots. Unlike the tunneling device, however, accurately measured single-electron transport at high frequencies is possible because transport results from the electrons being moved along with

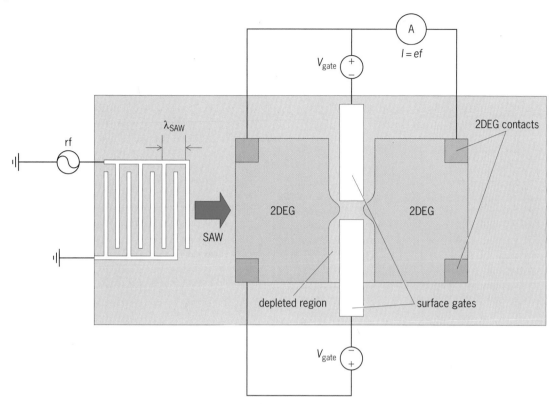

Fig. 2. Schematic layout of a surface-acoustic-wave (SAW) based single-electron transport device. 2DEG = two-dimensional electron gas.

the dots, so that relatively slow tunneling is not required.

Future challenges. In order that an experimental effect can constitute a metrological quantum standard, it needs to fulfil two important requirements. First, the measured parameter has to be an exact function of the fundamental constants: in this case e. If, for example, some of the transported quantum dots were empty or contained an excess number of electrons, the current would not be exactly ef. Second,

the measured quantity has to be stable over some finite range of the experimental parameters. In the case of the acoustic-wave device, this means that the current plateau has to be absolutely flat for some range of the gate voltage. From the data in Fig. 3 it can be seen that the current plateaus are slightly sloped, and therefore this last condition is not yet experimentally realized. Present research activities focus on studying why this slope occurs and what can be done to lessen it. If improvements can be made, this technique holds great promise as a quantum standard of current and as a research tool to study the metrological triangle and its implications. It is also clear that the technology described in this article may bear relevance to single-electron manipulation in general, for example, for information transmission, computing devices, and detecting and measuring very small currents.

For background information *see* ELECTRICAL UNITS AND STANDARDS; FUNDAMENTAL CONSTANTS; HALL EFFECT; JOSEPHSON EFFECT; QUANTIZED ELECTRONIC STRUCTURE (QUEST); SEMICONDUCTOR HETEROSTRUCTURES; SURFACE-ACOUSTIC-WAVE DEVICES; TUNNELING IN SOLIDS in the McGraw-Hill Encyclopedia of Science & Technology.   Jan-Theodoor Janssen

Bibliography. M. H. Devoret, D. Esteve, and C. Urbina, Single electron transfer in metallic nanostructures, *Nature*, 360:547, 1992; M. W. Keller et al., A capacitance standard based on counting electrons, *Science*, 285:1706–1709, 1999; J. M. Shilton

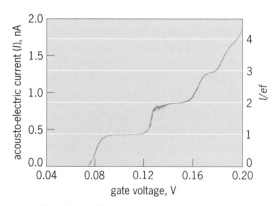

Fig. 3. Experimentally measured acousto-electric current in a surface-acoustic-wave-based single-electron transport device. Gate voltage is proportional to channel width. Right-hand scale measures current (*I*) in units of electron charge (*e*) times frequency (*f*). The frequency of the surface acoustic wave is 2699.32 MHz.

et al., High frequency single electron transport in a quasi-one-dimensional GaAs channel induced by surface acoustic waves, *J. Phys.: Condens. Matter*, 8:L531–L539, 1996; N. M. Zimmerman, A primer on electrical units in the Système International, *Amer. J. Phys.*, 66:324–331, 1998.

Tribology

Tribology is the science and technology of interacting surfaces in relative motion. It has three major subdivisions: friction, wear, and lubrication. Friction and wear are the principal consequences from rubbing two contacting surfaces, while lubrication controls and mitigates friction and wear.

In tribology, there are two types of surface contacts: conformal and counterformal. Conformal contacts, where the opposing surfaces are closely matched in shape over a large area, include plane sliders, thrust (axial) and journal (radial) bearings, computer read-write heads, and artificial hip joints. Counterformal contacts, where the contact area is small and the resulting pressure is high, include all rolling and sliding contacts in rolling bearings, gears, cams, and other powertrain components.

Rational understanding of lubricated conformal contacts began when the lubricant film behavior was first predicted by Osborne Reynolds a century ago. For counterformal contacts, the lubrication film behavior was not known until Duncan Dowson and Gordon R. Higginson solved the first elastohydrodynamic (EHD) problem for rollers almost a half century ago; that is, roller surfaces deform elastically, causing, between them, an increase in the lubricant versus viscosity and load-carrying capacity. In the last 20 years, many contributions have been made to predict the location and magnitude of the minimum film–to–roughness ratio in most lubricated contacts. While this is a great step forward in designing lubricated contacts, it is insufficient as a reliable failure predictor of these contacts because the surface roughness effect on lubrication has not been considered.

Recent developments have shown that the detailed film thickness and pressure distributions around the top areas of rough surfaces, called asperities, can now be readily simulated for counterformal elastohydrodynamic contacts. These powerful simulation tools, together with recent developments on superhard coatings and failure prediction models for surface pitting and scuffing failure, can now be integrated to form a virtual tribology system for designing advanced contacts in mechanical systems.

Mixed lubrication in rough EHD contacts. Aside from very high speed applications, most lubricated contacts operate in mixed lubrication, in which the load is partly supported at the asperities lubricated either by a very thin micro-EHD film or by a boundary (partial lubricating) film. The knowledge of the location and distribution of the asperity contact pressure, friction, and temperature is essential for making accurate failure predictions.

Recent developments on the simulation of mixed lubrication in rough EHD contacts show that the detailed features of asperity film thickness, pressure, friction, and temperature can now be obtained for a wide range of rolling and sliding speeds—even for very low speeds at which the load is largely supported by asperity contacts. Take, for example, a typical EHD point contact with a rough steel ball on a flat smooth steel surface lubricated with mineral oil, where the roughness on the moving steel ball is a typical, transversely oriented ground surface with a root-mean-square (rms) roughness height of 0.4 micrometer, the load is constant but the rolling velocity U is varied from 2500 to 0.001 mm/s, and the ratio of sliding speed to roll speed is held constant at 0.2. When the rolling velocity is reasonably high, only a small portion of the asperities are in contact. As the rolling velocity decreases, the asperity contact area increases. When the rolling velocity is 0.001 mm/s (nearly stationary), almost the entire area is in asperity contact.

Fatigue life prediction. Prediction of fatigue life for EHD contacts, such as gear teeth and rolling bearing contacts, usually requires a fast and accurate contact analysis. The results of this analysis are used to determine the stress in the component in order to estimate its fatigue life. Solution of the rough contact problems for monolithic or layered elastic solids generally requires the use of numerical methods.

For component life prediction, there are two important phases: crack initiation and propagation. If rolling bearing life is being considered, initiation is the most important phase with propagation occupying a relatively short time. On the other hand, if gears, which have higher sliding motion, are being considered, propagation can also have a significant influence in lifetime.

A review of the classical rolling contact fatigue life models has been given by E. V. Zaretsky. The contact fatigue calculation is based on a rolling contact fatigue (RCF) life integral over a stressed volume. If the probability of survival is specified, the number of cycles to failure can be approximated when the subsurface stresses are known.

Scuffing failure prediction. When the load increases in a sliding EHD contact, scuffing, a form of severe adhesive wear, can occur. Scuffing initiates whenever the interfacial shear stress at many asperitiy contacts exceeds the shear yield stress of the softer material. Presently, there are few rational models available to predict the scuffing failure.

The computer simulation of mixed lubrication in rough EHD contacts (described earlier) provides a very effective tool for studying the propagation of the scuffed asperities with increasing load and time. It is an effective tool for designing heavily loaded sliding tribological contacts such as spiral gears and cams.

Nanolayered superhard coatings. Hard titanium nitride (TiN) coatings can, in principle, be used to extend the life of machine components subject to rolling contact fatigue. A hard coating must be thick enough to shield the substrate against roughness-induced contact stress perturbations, thus reducing the risk of fatigue failure. Experimental studies have shown that the primary failure mechanism of TiN-coated rollers in RCF tests is spalling (surface pitting). Most sputter-deposited TiN coatings thicker than a few tens of nanometers have a columnar microstructure, which becomes coarser and develops intergranular voids with increasing thickness. These voids can be regarded as preexisting defects and become sites for crack initiation. Interfaces between columns are likely to be weak links, even in dense coatings, and can be regarded as preexisting defects, which become initiation sites for cracks.

Nanolayered coatings were developed with a twofold objective: (1) to establish the necessary deposition technique for TiN to suppress such coarse columnar growth and to maintain a fine equiaxed (equal dimensions in all directions) structure throughout the coating thickness, and (2) to evaluate if such coatings have better RCF life compared with conventional TiN coatings. For adequate adhesion, these coatings must have reasonably low internal stress. The strategy to produce a fine equiaxed microstructure is to interrupt periodically the growth of TiN by depositing nanometer-thick layers of a different material such as carbon nitride (CN_x) or silicon nitride (SiN_x). These TiN/CN_x and TiN/SiN_x multilayer coatings are deposited using reactive direct-current magnetron sputtering.

To provide an analytical explanation of these RCF experiments, a numerical approach was recently developed to obtain the stress distribution in cracked elastic solids. The analysis shows that in the single-layer case, a crack can propagate downward easily along the straight, uninterrupted column boundary. In multilayered cases, however, the column boundaries are interrupted by interfaces. Having propagated through one of the coating layers, the crack is forced to turn and start propagating along the interface. The crack will resume its downward propagation as soon as it encounters a column boundary in the next layer. Although the crack interruption is relatively small, it can hinder the mutual sliding of the crack faces, causing a slowing of crack growth. Results of this analysis are consistent with the increased life observed in experiments described above.

Virtual tribology. Virtual tribology is a methodology for creating and analyzing surface phenomena elements and systems by means of integrated advanced model-based simulations with modern information technology. The two important elements in virtual tribology are (1) contact simulation of the tribological performance for a given set of geometrical and operating conditions, and (2) failure prediction modules for determining the major modes of tribological failure such as surface fatigue and scuffing.

In virtual tribology, a tribological contact is designed by first using the appropriate contact simulation model to determine the tribological performance consisting of distributions of film thickness, lubricant and asperity contact pressure, friction, and temperature, and then, with the results, calculating the subsurface stress field, including the thermal stresses. The data can then be used to determine the limits of two major modes of failure: contact fatigue life and the probability of scuffing failure. If the results are not within the design limits, the contact geometry or other input conditions may be modified until they satisfy the requirements.

For background information *see* ANTIFRICTION BEARING; FRICTION; LUBRICANT; LUBRICATION; TRIBOLOGY; WEAR in the McGraw-Hill Encyclopedia of Science & Technology.   H. S. Cheng; Y. W. Chung; L. M. Keer; Q. Wang; D. Zhu

Bibliography. Y. H. Chen et al., Tribological properties and rolling contact fatigue lives of TiN/SiN_x multilayer coatings, *Surf. Coat. Technol.*, 154:152–161, 2002; B. J. Hamrock, *Fundamentals of Fluid Lubrication*, McGraw-Hill, New York, 1994; Y. Z. Hu and D. Zhu, A full numerical solution to the mixed lubrication in point contacts, *J. Tribol.*, 122:1–9, 2000; E. V. Zaretsky, J. V. Poplawski, and S. M. Peters, Comparison of life theories for rolling element bearings, *Tribol. Trans.*, 39:501–503, 1996.

Tsunamiites and seismites

Records of some of nature's most catastrophically powerful, short-lived phenomena are preserved in sediments and ancient sedimentary rocks called tsunamiites and seismites, which are important not only for reconstructing ancient events but also for evaluating future hazards. Tsunamiites (also spelled tsunamites) are composed of predominantly marine or lake sediments that were transported by huge water waves called tsunami, which are set into motion by earthquakes, massive landslides, volcanic explosions, and asteroid impacts. Tsunamiites also include continental sediments that were transported when tsunamis suddenly dislodged offshore sediment and mixed it with water to form turbidity currents—dense, turbid masses that flow down the slopes of large lakes and oceans and then commonly travel for hundreds of kilometers over the deep sea floor before being deposited. A seismite is a sediment or sedimentary rock that contains textures and structures produced by earthquake shaking; unlike a tsunamiite, the sediments in seismites were already accumulating when the disturbance occurred. By comparing their pre- and postearthquake features, seismites can be used to calculate the timing, frequency, and local intensities of historic or prehistoric earthquakes, the orientation of their stresses, and even the basin slopes on which the sediments were accumulating. Various seismite features may even provide estimates of the magnitude of the earthquake that produced them, if the distance to the epicenter and the depth of focus are reasonably well known.

Tsunamiites

Adjacent to beaches where high wave energies have concentrated abundant coarse sediment, tsunamiites brought onshore can consist mainly of sand or gravel and even boulders (**Fig. 1a**). A tsunamiite may be

(a)

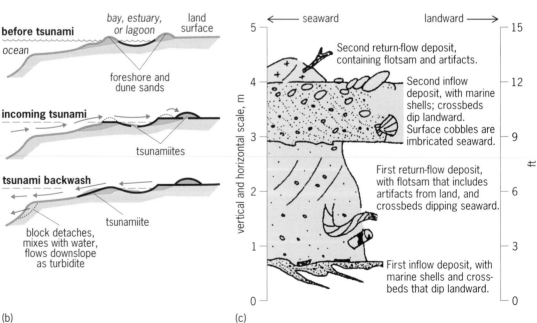

(b)   (c)

Fig. 1. Tsunamiites. (*a*) Cobbly gravel deposited on the backshore of the Hirahama coast in Japan by a tsunami in 1993. (*b*) Schematic diagram showing tsunamiites deposited by an incoming wave and its backwash, which also may dislodge offshore material to generate turbidity current. (*c*) Stratigraphy left by two tsunami waves and their return flows during the Hirahama tsunami of 1993. (*Parts a and c modified with permission from F. Nanayama et al., Sedimentary differences between the 1993 Hokkaido-nansei-oki tsunami and the 1959 Miyakojima typhoon at Taisei, southwestern Hokkaido, northern Japan, Sed. Geol., 135:255–264, 2000*)

indistinguishable from the deposits of a powerful storm; however, the seaward backwash of a storm surge is much more gradual and less violent than that of a tsunami. In addition, a tsunami may be propagated as more than one wave; thus the sediment fabric of a tsunamiite may document multiple reversals of flow (Fig. 1*b, c*).

Tsunamiites may be remarkably thin compared to their hazard significance. Near Seattle, Washington, widespread marshes more than 2 km (1.2 mi) inland are draped with fine sand containing marine fossils only 5–15 cm (2–6 in.) thick, documenting a major earthquake and tsunami about 1000 years ago. Modern tsunamiites record how high above sea level the tsunami rose, from which the magnitude of the earthquake can be estimated. The Seattle tsunamiite is draped over terrain with a vertical relief of 2 m, indicating an earthquake of magnitude 7.5 or greater.

Volcanic explosions can set huge tsunamis into motion (**Fig. 2**). When the Santorini volcano in the Mediterranean violently collapsed 3500 years ago, tsunamis deposited raised beaches of pumice as far away as Israel, 1000 km (620 mi) to the east. Concurrently, 600 km (370 mi) west of the volcano, 65 km³ (15.6 mi³) of homogeneous mud was suddenly deposited in waters 4000 m (13,000 ft) deep, covering an area of about 5000 km² (1930 mi²) and up to 24 m (79 ft) thick. The sediment, containing shallow-water carbonate minerals and fossils from the Gulf of Sirte off northern Africa, is interpreted as a tsunamiite or megaturbidite left by enormous turbidity currents that tsunamis triggered 800 km (500 mi) away from Santorini.

Large as the Santorini tsunami must have been, it is dwarfed by the waves generated when asteroids hit the ocean at typical velocities of over 70,000 km/h (43,500 mi/h). The impact of an asteroid 10–14 km (6–9 mi) in size at the end of the Cretaceous Period 65 million years ago is blamed for killing off half of Earth's species, including the dinosaurs. It is believed to have made the Chicxulub crater, 180 km (112 mi) in diameter, which is centered on the Yucatan coast of Mexico (**Fig. 3***a*). Large tsunamis left deposits at least 500 km (310 mi) inland, and as far from Chicxulub as northeastern Brazil. At numerous sites around the Gulf of Mexico and the Caribbean, sedimentary rocks 65 million years old with tsunamiite features are believed to be related to the end-Cretaceous asteroid because they contain microscopic glass droplets formed when rocks were melted by the heat of impact; quartz grains with their normal, invisible crystallographic structure cut across by microscopic "shock lamellae" from the enormous pressures of impact; and iridium, an element very rare on Earth but much more abundant in meteorites.

One particularly well-studied end-Cretaceous tsunamiite is the Peñalver Formation of northwestern Cuba, a limestone 180 m (590 ft) thick (Fig. 3*b*). Its basal 25 m (62 ft) is a coarse conglomerate of angular fragments, including boulders a meter in diame-

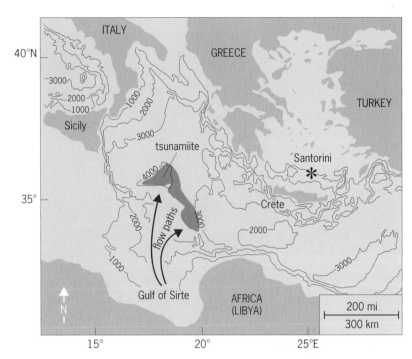

Fig. 2. Tsunamiites left in the deep Mediterranean by the Santorini explosion of 3500 years ago. (*Data from M. B. Cita and G. Aloisi, Deep-sea tsunami deposits triggered by the explosion of Santorini (3500 y BP), eastern Mediterranean, Sed. Geol., 135:181–203, 2000; and W. Heicke and F. Werner, The Augias megaturbidite in the central Ionian Sea (central Mediterranean) and its relation to the Holocene Santorini event, Sed. Geol., 135:205–218, 2000*)

ter, that were ripped out of the underlying carbonate layer while it was still soft. Despite the coarseness of the basal conglomerate, its fabric—the fact that it is mixed randomly with smaller-grained sediment—documents that the debris was quickly mixed with water and flowed as a liquid. Above this base, the formation becomes finer upward, from carbonate sand interbedded with 14 thin layers of conglomerates probably brought in by successive tsunamis to calcareous mudstone. Abundant water-escape structures in the middle member of the formation suggest that the material settled rapidly from high-density suspensions, much like the Santorini tsunamiite. Remarkably, although most carbonate sediments are produced by organisms, the limestone was undisturbed by burrowing animals, and its fossils are mainly forms reworked from the underlying rocks. This suggests that the limestones were violently resuspended and then quickly redeposited during a period of major biological catastrophe.

Seismites

The term "seismites" has been widely used since it was first proposed in 1969 to describe fault-graded beds (graded beds cut by faults) of mud that were accumulating in the quiet water of deep marine basins and were still relatively unconsolidated when earthquakes deformed them. Seismites centimeters to a meter (inches to several feet) thick also have been found in marsh and lake deposits. The term "seismite" refers only to sedimentary masses (such

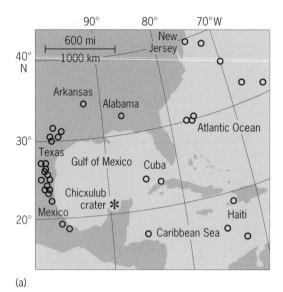

(a)

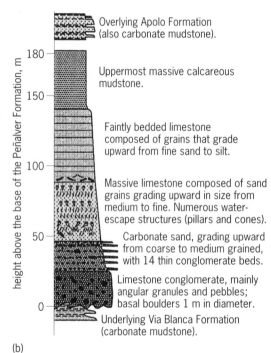

(b)

Fig. 3. Tsunamiites from the asteroid impact 65 million years ago. (*a*) Location of the Chicxulub impact site showing sites around and in the Gulf of Mexico and Caribbean Sea where tsunamiites from the impact have been recognized. Oceanic sites were cored by the Deep-Sea Drilling Project and Ocean Drilling Project. (*b*) Stratigraphy of the Peñalver Formation. (*Modified from H. Takayama et al., Origin of the Peñalver Formation in northwest Cuba and its relation to K/T boundary impact event, Sed. Geol., 135:295–320, 2000*)

as fault-graded beds) that were deformed without being moved any significant lateral distance. Thus, seismoturbidites, the deposits of turbidity currents that were triggered by earthquakes, are not seismites; they contain no original and fault-induced structures that could be used for evaluating seismic stresses and strains.

Homogeneous mud gradually changes in consistency downward as its own accumulating weight squeezes out water, making it more compact. Thus, from top to bottom, it responds to seismic shaking in liquid, plastic, and brittle fashion. Depending on the intensity of shaking, fault-graded or mixed beds may have a surface zone in which liquefaction and shaking has obliterated all depositional structures. Beneath it is a zone of somewhat compacted sediment fragments encased in a soupy matrix that may also have been intruded from below by plumose structures (**Fig. 4**). Next is a zone of more compacted mud, commonly broken by miniature step faults that may indicate how the basin floor originally sloped. A basal, relatively undisturbed zone of yet more compacted sediment may be cut by larger faults spaced a few meters apart. Several such paleoseismograms may be preserved in a single stratigraphic sequence. The ages of the earthquakes and their recurrence periods can be dated using radioactive isotopes, fossils, and archeological artifacts in the seismites and in the undisturbed deposits between them.

Seismite structures produced by weak shocks may simply be minor disruptions of laminae, or loop bedding (that is, laminate bundles pulled apart by tensile stresses). Among the most common seismite structures are convolute folds, typically about a meter long and a few meters high, encased in undeformed beds. Clearly, they were produced while still soft and close to the sea or lake floor.

Additional seismite features form in interbedded muds and sands. Shocks from earthquakes with magnitudes greater than 5 commonly liquefy water-saturated sands by breaking their grain-to-grain contacts. For the minute or so that the shaking lasts, the mixture of sand and water behaves as a slurry without strength. Driven by the weight of overlying deposits, the slurry rises up through vertical fissures in overlying sequences and is emplaced as sand dikes. The dikes may remain connected to their source beds, or may themselves serve as sources for subordinate, orthogonally oriented dikes that have no direct contact with the mother bed. Liquefaction also may cause water-saturated gravels to intrude overlying beds as irregular-shaped dikes, but gravels are less susceptible to liquefaction than sands, and such dikes may be fractured and faulted by continuing shocks after they are emplaced. Rising silts and sands may also escape entirely from their sources to form isolated, concave-upward pillow structures in overlying layers. Other masses of disturbed sediment can rise or sink, depending on their densities, and be emplaced as isolated pseudonodules.

Along fault scarps, alluvial fans accumulate gravels that are faulted, commonly more than once (**Fig. 5**). For example, a fault along the front of the Helan Mountains in north-central China experienced an earthquake of magnitude 8 in 1739 that caused 88 km (55 mi) of surface rupture and displaced the famous Great Wall of the Ming dynasty almost a meter vertically and 1.5 m (3.3 ft) laterally. Trenches dug across the fault scarp revealed faulted gravels and colluvial deposits produced not only by the 1739 event but by three older earthquakes as well that recurred at intervals of 2300–3000 years, as determined by radiocarbon dating.

For background information *see* EARTHQUAKE; FAULT AND FAULT STRUCTURES; SEDIMENTOLOGY;

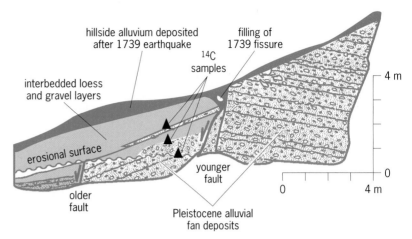

Fig. 5. Alluvial-fan seismite in China. (*Modified from Q. Deng and Y. Liao, Paleoseismology along the range-front fault of Helan Mountains, north central China, J. Geophys. Res., 101(B3):5873–5893, 1996*)

STRATIGRAPHY; TSUNAMI; TURBIDITY CURRENT; VOLCANO in the McGraw-Hill Encyclopedia of Science & Technology.   Kelvin S. Rodolfo

Bibliography. B. F. Atwater and A. L. Moore, A tsunami about 1000 years ago in Puget Sound, Washington, *Science*, 258:114–116, 1992; M. B. Cita and G. Aloisi, Deep-sea tsunami deposits triggered by the explosion of Santorini (3500 y BP), eastern Mediterranean, *Sed. Geol.*, 135:181–203; P. Claeys et al., Distribution of the Chicxulub ejecta at the Cretaceous-Tertiary boundary, *Geol. Soc. Amer. Spec. Pap.*, 359:55–69, 2002; Q. Deng and Y. Liao, Paleoseismology along the range-front fault of Helan Mountains, north central China, *J. Geophys. Res.*, 101(B3):5873–5893, 1996; W. Heicke and F. Werner, The Augias megaturbidite in the central Ionian Sea (central Mediterranean) and its relation to the Holocene Santorini event, *Sed. Geol.*, 135:205–218, 2000; A. Seilacher, Fault-graded beds interpreted as seismites, *Sedimentology*, 13:155-159, 1969; T. Shiki and T. Yamazaki, Tsunami-induced conglomerates in Miocene upper bathyal deposits, Chita Peninsula, central Japan, *Sed. Geol.*, 104:175–188, 1996.

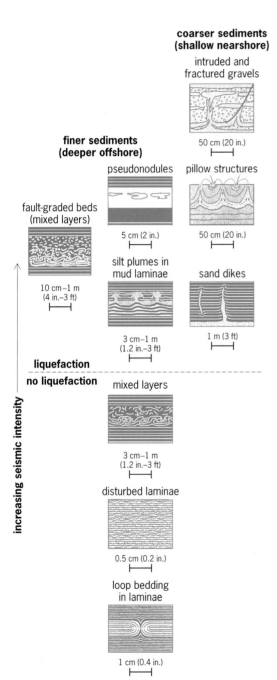

Fig. 4. Seismite features. (*Modified extensively from M. A. Rodriguez-Pascua et al., Soft-sediment sediment deformation structures in lacustrine sediments of the Prebetic Zone, SE Spain, and their potential use as indicators of earthquake magnitudes during the Late Miocene, Sed. Geol., 135:117–135, 2000*)

Turbulent transport and mixing

The vast majority of flows of interest in industrial, environmental, and biological systems are turbulent, and so turbulent mixing is a common phenomenon. One process of vital concern is the mixing and transport of pollutants released in inland and coastal waters and in the atmosphere. Turbulent mixing can also be a beneficial phenomenon, as in its application to create efficient and nonpolluting combustion systems and chemical reactors.

Molecular and turbulent diffusion. The mixing of fluids occurs by two distinct processes, termed molecular diffusion and turbulent diffusion. Molecular diffusion is present in both laminar and turbulent flows and even in still fluids and is the result of random motions of molecules. Turbulent diffusion occurs only in turbulent flows and is the result of random motions, stretching, distortions, and interactions of fluid entities called eddies.

Turbulent flows contain eddies with a wide range of sizes. Relatively large eddies, comparable to the extent of the flow or the size of apparatus, contain most of the turbulent kinetic energy, which they receive from the bulk fluid motion. Meanwhile, the process of an energy cascade transfers kinetic energy to smaller and smaller eddies until a size is reached at which friction among neighboring eddies with finite velocity differences converts fluid kinetic energy into heat. The smallest size η of eddies relevant to turbulence is called the Kolmogorov microscale; η is several orders of magnitude larger than intermolecular distances and so turbulent diffusion is completely decoupled from molecular diffusion.

Molecular diffusion tends to equalize local variations in temperature, species concentration, and momentum and is therefore more intense where strong gradients of such properties exist. A measure of diffusion of a substance contained in a fluid is the mass flux (mass crossing a certain area per unit time and area); it is related to the gradient of the substance concentration by Fick's law, which identifies the molecular diffusivity γ as the proportionality coefficient between these two properties. By analogy, a simple model of turbulent diffusion provides the turbulent mass flux as proportional to the mean, or time average, concentration gradient and identifies a proportionality coefficient as the turbulent, or eddy, diffusivity γ_T. Because turbulent diffusion is far more efficient in mixing fluids than molecular diffusion is, γ_T is typically several orders of magnitude larger than γ.

The characteristic scale at which molecular diffusion smears out concentration differences is called the Batchelor microscale, η_B; it is related to η as $\eta_B/\eta = (\gamma/\nu)^{1/2}$, where ν is the kinematic viscosity of the fluid. The ratio ν/γ is called the Schmidt number, Sc; in heat transfer, γ represents the thermal diffusivity and the ratio ν/γ is called the Prandtl number, Pr. Values of the Schmidt (or Prandtl) number comparable to unity indicate that the fine structure of the concentration (or temperature) field has a scale comparable to that of the velocity field; when $Sc \gg 1$, the concentration field has a much finer structure than the velocity field and, when $Sc \ll 1$, the opposite is true. For various common gases and vapors in air, the Schmidt number is in the range from 0.2 to 3; for liquid mixtures, the Schmidt number is as high as 10^3. Typical values of the Prandtl number are: for air and many common gases at room temperature, about 0.7; for water at room temperature, about 8; for mercury and melted metals, of the order of 10^{-2} to 10^{-3}; for engine oil at room temperature, of the order of 10^4.

Turbulence contorts, stretches, and distorts fluid volumes but does not, by itself, smear out concentration differences. In the absence of molecular diffusion, complete mixing of fluids would never occur, as each elementary fluid particle, however distorted it might become, would keep its initial concentration. The great contribution of turbulence in the mixing process is that it greatly increases the area of the interface that separates adjacent fluid volumes with different concentrations and, thus, enhances molecular diffusion. Indeed, the appearance of concentration fields in turbulent flows that have not been exposed much to molecular diffusion is quite patchy, with peak instantaneous local values of concentration far exceeding time-averaged or space-averaged values.

Simple and complex mixing processes. The simplest case of mixing is that of a passive scalar contaminant, which is transported and mixed by turbulence while itself having a negligible effect on the dynamics of the flow (see **illus.**). Far more complex are flows with chemical reactions, including combustion. These require the modeling of the chemical reactions and the effects of heat release and volume expansion of the reaction products. Combustion processes are customarily distinguished into premixed, in which a very thin flame front propagates through a mixture of fuel and oxidant, and non-premixed, or diffusion flames, in which the flame front separates fuel and oxidant. Turbulent mixing increases the contact area between the reactants and thus the combustion efficiency. Further complications of the mixing process are caused by body forces (buoyancy effects) and rotation (for example, in turbomachines and the planetary boundary layer). For example, stable density stratification (that is, in a flow with a heavier fluid located below a lighter one) impedes vertical mixing while enhancing horizontal mixing.

Research methods. The seminal work in turbulent transport and diffusion was a paper by G.I. Taylor in 1921, and the topic has since been the subject of

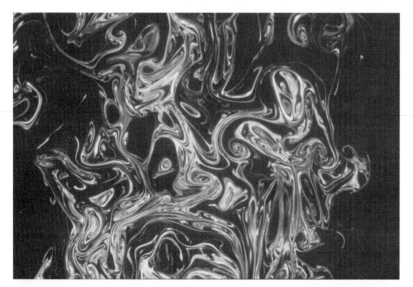

Flow visualization of passive scalar mixing in a uniformly sheared turbulent flow of water using laser-induced fluorescence. Water containing a fluorescent dye (fluorescein) was injected into the fully turbulent flow through a thin tube, posing only a small disturbance to the flow. The Schmidt number of the dye used is very large (about 2000), and this image shows little effect of molecular diffusion. The turbulent eddies responsible for mixing are clearly visible. (*Photograph by S. Marineau-Mes*)

intense research. Although understanding of turbulent diffusion processes and ability to predict them remain incomplete, progress has been steady, with significant advances accomplished in recent years, both in the development of suitable theoretical, numerical, and experimental methods of study and in the accumulation of knowledge and insight into specific phenomena and applications.

Direct numerical simulation (DNS). This technique has provided an impetus in the understanding of precise mixing and transport processes, including their effects on chemical reactions. Direct numerical simulation is a numerical method of solution of the "exact" (that is, not statistically averaged) dynamical equations of motion and the associated advection-diffusion equations for transported substances. It has been applied successfully to the mixing of passive scalars in homogeneous (that is, statistically uniform in space) turbulence, without mean shear or with a constant mean shear, providing details that are difficult or impossible to obtain by other theoretical, numerical, or experimental methods; examples include the study of lagrangian dynamics (that is, a description of fluid flow that follows the motion of fluid particles, rather than following fluid behavior and properties at fixed locations, as in the case of an eulerian description of flow) and the statistical determination of pressure fluctuations and their correlation to other flow variables. In recent years, direct numerical simulation has been extended to the study of more complex problems, notably the representation of chemical reactions and heat and mass release. A limitation of direct numerical simulation, which is not likely to be overcome in the near future, is its extreme requirement of computer resources (memory, storage, and central processing unit time), which prevents it from being extended to higher Reynolds numbers and to very complex geometrical configurations, as needed for the realistic solution of industrial and environmental problems.

Large eddy simulation (LES). This approach is more promising than direct numerical simulation as an engineering tool, since it can be applied to realistically large Reynolds numbers. This method provides solutions of equations that are filtered versions of the exact dynamic and transport equations, such that the phenomena that occur at the finest scales are not resolved but are modeled using various subgrid-scale models. Large eddy simulation can now be performed for flows with flames propagating in premixed, partially premixed, and non-premixed media as well as large-scale ecosystems. Progress in this approach is continuously being made, although at a pace slower than expected.

Experimental advances. On the experimental side, significant progress in recent years has been achieved in the development of visual and optical methods for the visualization and mapping of the random velocity, temperature, concentration, and pressure fields. Particle image velocimetry (PIV) provides simultaneous measurements of local velocity, in magnitude and direction, over a plane section and even over

a fluid volume, and can be used to produce velocity, strain, and vorticity isocontours. Laser-induced fluorescence (LIF) is based on the property of certain substances to emit radiation at a higher wavelength than that of the absorbed radiation. The latter technique has been applied to study mixing of fluorescent dyes in liquids (see illus.) as well as to identify the concentration of products of combustion of gases. Classical methods, for example hot-wire anemometry and cold-wire thermometry, have also been advanced and used to provide a wealth of information about the fine structure of flow and transported scalar fields.

New theories and applications. On the theoretical side, intense research has been devoted to the development of more efficient models of turbulence and chemical reactions, as well as to the testing of available models in new applications. New techniques and approaches are currently being applied toward solving the persisting problems of combustion efficiency, emission control, and pollutant dispersal. They are also employed to confront novel issues, for example the large-scale transport of oceanic plankton, and at a smaller scale, indoor transport of tobacco smoke and microorganisms from one person to another.

For background information *see* ANEMOMETER; COMPUTATIONAL FLUID DYNAMICS; DIFFUSION; DIMENSIONLESS GROUPS; FLUID FLOW; REYNOLDS NUMBER; TURBULENT FLOW in the McGraw-Hill Encyclopedia of Science & Technology.   Stavros Tavoularis

Bibliography. R. W. Bilger, Turbulent diffusion flames, *Annu. Rev. Fluid Mech.*, 21:101–135, 1989; A. Pollard and S. Candel (eds.), *IUTAM Symposium on Turbulent Mixing and Combustion*, Kluwer Academic Publishers, 2002; S. B. Pope, Turbulent premixed flames, *Annu. Rev. Fluid Mech.*, 19:237–270, 1987; P. J. W. Roberts and D. R. Webster, Turbulent diffusion, in *Environmental Fluid Mechanics—Theories and Applications*, ASCE, 2002; Z. Warhaft, Passive scalars in turbulent flows, *Annu. Rev. Fluid Mech.*, 32:203–240, 2000.

Ultracold collisions

With recent advances in laser cooling and trapping, atoms at temperatures less than 1 millikelvin (that is, one-thousandth of a degree above absolute zero) are now readily available for a variety of applications. These applications range from the production of Bose-Einstein condensates (coherent samples of atoms which behave as macroscopic quantum wavefunctions) to dramatic improvements in atomic clocks. Of particular importance are ultracold collisions, the study of interactions between atoms at these very low temperatures. These processes not only attract fundamental interest but also impact many of the other applications of laser cooling. For example, in a Bose-Einstein condensate the atomic collisional properties determine whether it will be

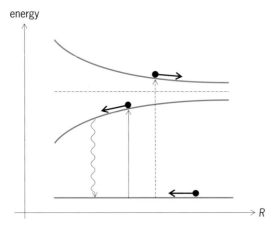

Fig. 1. Potential energies of interaction between two atoms as a function of their separation R. The lower curve corresponds to both atoms in their ground states and is essentially flat. The upper two curves correspond to one atom in the excited state. The solid vertical line indicates laser excitation to the attractive potential which draws the atoms into short range. The excitation may decay (wavy line), effectively terminating the collision. The broken vertical line indicates excitation to the repulsive curve which keeps the atoms apart.

stable or collapse upon itself. In laser-cooled atomic clocks, collisions cause undesirable frequency shifts, limiting their accuracy. Also, several proposed schemes for quantum computation with atoms rely on carefully controlled ultracold collisions. Future work on ultracold collisions will include molecules, where reactions and chemical processes are possible.

Atomic interactions. Although atoms are electrically neutral, they do interact with each other. Atomic energy levels are readily perturbed by the presence of a neighboring atom. If both atoms are in the ground state, the attractive van der Waals potential energy is short-range, varying as $1/R^6$, where R is the separation between the atoms. The situation is quite different for one ground-state atom and one excited-state atom (put there, for example, by laser excitation). In this case, the potential energy, which can be either attractive or repulsive, is much longer range, varying as $1/R^3$ (**Fig. 1**). At room temperature, atoms are moving with enough kinetic energy that a close encounter (for example, R less than 1 nm) is required for an observable effect. At ultracold temperatures, on the other hand, the atoms are

barely moving and their trajectories can be significantly altered even when the atoms are very far apart (for example, R greater than 100 nm).

Types of collisions. A myriad of collisional processes are possible in ultracold atoms. If the atoms are in their absolute lowest energy state, only elastic collisions are possible: the atoms simply bounce off each other, conserving energy. At low temperatures, the quantum de Broglie wavelength of the atoms is larger than the atomic size, and the scattering is quantum-mechanical (wavelike) in nature, with the cross section depending on details of the interatomic potential. These elastic collisions are important because they determine the rate at which a collection of ultracold atoms comes into thermal equilibrium. For example, in evaporative cooling the highest-energy atoms evaporate from the trap and the sample reequilibrates, via elastic collisions, at a lower temperature.

Hyperfine-changing collisions. Because atoms have many degrees of freedom, they can occupy a variety of internal energy states. For example, the electron and nucleus both have angular momentum (spin), and these can couple together in various ways. This causes the ground state of an alkali metal atom (for example, rubidium) to be split into two hyperfine levels (these are the states used in atomic clocks) separated typically by an energy corresponding to a few gigahertz. In the course of a collision, one or both of the atoms can change its hyperfine state. At low temperatures, only the exoergic (energy-releasing) process can occur. When this happens, the atoms can gain enough kinetic energy to escape from the trap (**Fig. 2**). This trap-loss mechanism can be important because laser cooling usually leaves atoms in the upper hyperfine level.

Collisions involving excited atoms. These can occur when laser light is tuned near the atomic resonance, as in many laser traps. These collisions can be particularly prevalent because of the long range of the potentials involved. The fact that the attractive interaction decreases only as $1/R^3$ means that the colliding atoms begin to "feel" each other at extremely long range. For example, rubidium atoms at a temperature of 0.2 millikelvin have an average kinetic energy equal to their attractive potential energy at a separation R of about 140 nm. This can lead to huge collision cross sections. However, an important mitigating

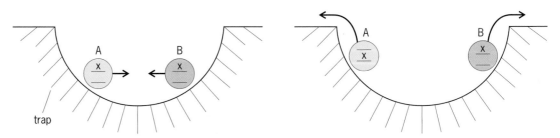

Fig. 2. Trap loss due to an inelastic hyperfine-changing collision. (*a*) The two colliding atoms, A and B, are initially in the upper energy level and moving very slowly. (*b*) After the collision, A ends up in the lower level. The released energy is shared by A and B, resulting in their ejection from the trap.

factor is the finite lifetime of the excited state. The long-range attraction occurs only when one of the colliding atoms is excited, a situation which lasts only for typically 30 ns. This is short compared to the time it takes for the atoms to actually come together, so in many cases the attraction is turned off in mid-collision. This "survival" of the excitation from long range, where it is created, to short range, where an observable inelastic process actually occurs, is one of the novel aspects of collisions at these very low energies.

Although there are many possible outcomes of a collision involving an excited atom, two are particularly important: fine-structure change and radiative escape. Excited states often have fine structure, whereby a single state becomes two states of slightly different energy depending on how the electron's spin angular momentum couples to its orbital angular momentum. Similar to the hyperfine-changing collisions discussed above, an atom can enter the collision in the higher energy fine-structure state and emerge in the lower one, converting the energy difference into kinetic energy. The energy released in such a fine-structure-changing collision is sufficient to escape from most laser traps. In radiative escape, the excited atom simply radiates back to the ground state after having rolled some distance down the attractive potential. The colliding atoms share the kinetic energy thus gained, which can be enough to eject them from the trap.

Photoassociation. Since two colliding atoms can be thought of as a transient molecule, it is not surprising that cold molecules can be formed in this way. In the process of photoassociation, the atoms collide in the presence of laser light which is resonant with a transition to an excited state of the molecule. In absorbing this light, the atom pair becomes bound. Since the resultant molecular state is excited, it will quickly decay, either reverting back into free atoms or forming a stable ground state of the molecule. This process of photoassociation is one of few techniques available for producing cold molecules, which unfortunately are not cooperative when it comes to laser cooling. The process of photoassociation has also enabled spectroscopy of novel states of molecules such as the pure-long-range states, where both the inner and outer turning points of the atomic vibration take place at very long range. In these peculiar molecules, the two atoms just do not get very close to each other. Photoassociative spectroscopy has also allowed precise measurements of various atomic and molecular properties such as dissociation energies, atomic lifetimes, and atomic scattering lengths.

Experimental techniques. Most experiments on ultracold collisions utilize the technique of trap loss. When two atoms collide and undergo an inelastic process, they can gain significant kinetic energy. The trap which is confining the atoms has a finite potential depth (typically corresponding to a temperature of less than 1 K), and if the kinetic energy per atom exceeds this depth, the atoms will escape. The loss rate due to collisions can be measured by loading up the trap and watching the number of trapped atoms decay over time. This is typically done by monitoring the fluorescence emitted by the atoms. Alternatively, a trap which is continuously loaded reaches an equilibrium between loading in and loss out. An additional loss rate due to collisions alters this balance, reducing the equilibrium number of trapped atoms. In some ultracold collisions (particularly with metastable rare-gas atoms), the product is an ion, which allows direct detection of the process.

Sample results. Ultracold collisions have been examined in most of the atoms which have been successfully trapped: alkali metals, alkaline earths, rare gases (in metastable states), and others. Two examples, shielding and time-resolved collisions, illustrate novel features arising in the ultracold domain. Since ultracold atoms are moving so slowly, they are easily manipulated. A pair of colliding atoms illuminated with light tuned above the atomic resonance can be excited to a repulsive molecular potential (Fig. 1). This occurs when the photon energy exactly matches the R-dependent energy of this repulsive state. Since the atoms have very little initial kinetic energy, they cannot further climb this potential hill and therefore turn around almost immediately. The excitation laser acts effectively as a shield, preventing the atoms from getting any closer to each other. This collisional suppression has been used to turn off inelastic processes which might otherwise eject atoms from a trap. The fact that the ultracold atoms are moving so slowly enables this shielding to work.

Collisions at room temperature happen very quickly. Typical velocities are 1000 m/s (3300 ft/s), and atoms must approach within about 1 nm for an observable collision to occur. This yields collision times on the order of 1 ps. With ultracold atoms, on the other hand, velocities are less than 1 m/s (3.3 ft/s) and the relevant length scales can be greater than 100 nm, resulting in collision durations approaching 1 μs. This has allowed collisions to be followed in real time by starting the collision with one laser pulse and probing it at a later time either with a second pulse or by direct observation of the collision product.

For background information *see* ATOMIC CLOCK; ATOMIC STRUCTURE AND SPECTRA; BOSE-EINSTEIN CONDENSATION; INTERMOLECULAR FORCES; LASER COOLING; PARTICLE TRAP; QUANTUM MECHANICS in the McGraw-Hill Encyclopedia of Science & Technology.   Phillip L. Gould

Bibliography. K. Burnett et al., Quantum encounters of the cold kind, *Nature*, 416:225–232, 2002; J. Glanz, The subtle flirtations of ultracold atoms, *Science*, 280:200–201, 1998; H. J. Metcalf and P. van der Straten, *Laser Cooling and Trapping*, Springer, New York, 1999; W. C. Stwalley and H. Wang, Photoassociation of ultracold atoms: A new spectroscopic technique, *J. Mol. Spectros.*, 195: 194–228, 1999; J. Weiner et al., Experiments and theory in cold and ultracold collisions, *Rev. Mod. Phys.*, 71:1–85, 1999.

Ultrahigh-density storage

Storage density in magnetic and optical recording has increased exponentially over the last 30 years. For magnetic recording, this has been achieved mainly by decreasing the medium sensor distance to tens of nanometers, and through new sensor technology based on the giant magnetoresistance effect. In optical recording, storage density is determined by the size of the optical spot that is bounded by the wavelength (λ) used and the numerical aperture (NA) of the objective lens that focuses the laser beam onto the data layer of the disk. Recently, nanometer-scale storage technology, with terabyte density, has been proposed.

Optical recording. The compact disk (CD) and digital versatile disk (DVD) are established optical recording technologies for cheap, mass-replicated distribution of content. A third optical recording format, called Blu-ray Disc (BD), was recently announced (**Fig. 1**). In contrast to CD and DVD, the BD development started with a phase-change-based rewritable medium, and will be followed by dye-based recordable and read-only memory (ROM) systems.

The BD format is based on a gallium nitride (blue) laser diode (405 nanometers) and an optical system with numerical aperture (NA) of 0.85. The NA is defined as $n \cdot \sin(\alpha)$, where n is the refractive index of the cover layer and α denotes the angular extent of the illuminating light cone. The scanning spot size is a function of λ/NA. For increasing NA, it is necessary to reduce the cover layer thickness accordingly to keep the sufficient margins for disc tilt with respect to the objective lens (Fig. 1). Extending the technology beyond BD in a conventional way would entail decreasing the wavelength. The technical feasibility of this path depends on the availability of a laser with a wavelength substantially shorter than 405 nm.

Research on diamond-based lasers at a wavelength around 250 nm is ongoing.

A second way to continue along the λ/NA path is to increase the numerical aperture. This can be done by focusing the laser beam inside a high-refractive-index lens, which increases the NA by a factor equal to the refractive index n of the lens. Because of total internal reflection at the lens-air boundary, it is not possible to increase the NA above 1 in a far-field optical system. However, an exponentially decreasing (evanescent) field is present that extends outside the lens. When a medium with high refractive index is brought to within the evanescent decay distance, the light from the lens can enter the medium, even when NA>1 (**Fig. 2**). For sufficient coupling efficiency (light transfer), the lens-to-medium distance must be smaller than one-tenth of the wavelength. To realize these small distances, one can use slider technology similar to those used in hard-disk drives or piezo-actuated heads. Another proposed solution is to embed high-refractive-index lenses in the medium itself to eliminate the small-gap requirement.

Multilayer storage. Because of the current limits of optical storage systems, the use of multilayer technology is an option for future high-density systems. While the extension of BD technology with up to four phase-change layers is feasible, true multilayer storage requires radical changes, especially in the disk materials. The challenge is to get a strong, selective interaction of the light with the addressed information layer, while keeping interaction with other layers at a minimum. One possibility is fluorescent multilayer technology (**Fig. 3**) in which the light emitted from the fluorescent medium has shifted to a slightly different wavelength than the incident laser light toward the red end of the spectrum. Only this fluorescent light, which is not absorbed by any of the other layers, is detected.

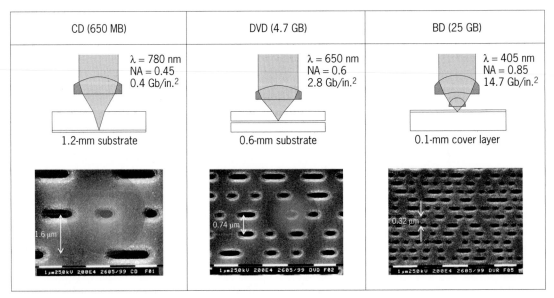

CD (650 MB)	DVD (4.7 GB)	BD (25 GB)
λ = 780 nm NA = 0.45 0.4 Gb/in.^{2}	λ = 650 nm NA = 0.6 2.8 Gb/in.^{2}	λ = 405 nm NA = 0.85 14.7 Gb/in.^{2}
1.2-mm substrate	0.6-mm substrate	0.1-mm cover layer

Fig. 1. Overview of optical recording formats.

Multilevel and 2D coding. Optical storage using multilevel approaches has recently witnessed a promising development. Multiple bits per bit cell can be stored by making effective use of the available signal-to-noise ratio. However, the number of bits that can be stored depends logarithmically on the number of levels available. Stringent tolerances are put on such a system, but the increasing power of signal processing electronics and techniques will enable the deployment of multilevel schemes in commercial products.

The progress in signal processing electronics also enables 2D-coding and -bit detection. These techniques are necessary for holographic storage but can also be applied to conventional storage systems. Holography potentially uses the full volume of the storage medium, with a data density scaling of $1/\lambda^3$.

Superresolution and domain expansion techniques. Optical superresolution (OSR) can be attained by adding an extra layer on top of the information layer to act as a mask aperture or a scattering structure, effectively creating a near-field probe.

Magnetic superresolution (MSR) techniques can be applied in magnetooptical recording systems, where bits as small as one-tenth of the spot size can be written by using laser pulsed–magnetic field modulation. Crescent-shaped magnetic domains are formed by switching both a laser and an external magnetic field at a high rate such that the circular domains largely overlap each other. This holds the promise of reaching a storage density of 100 gigabits per square inch (Gb/in.^{2}), while enjoying the advantages of a far-field optical system. However, straightforward detection of the crescent-shaped bits is hampered by large intersymbol interference (overlapping output pulses) and the limited optical resolution. The intersymbol interference problem can be overcome by applying the magnetically induced superresolution technique using a medium with two magnetic layers. In this technique, the lagging temperature distribution of the spot creates an "aperture" in an additional readout layer. Bits are copied from the recording layer through this aperture to the readout layer and appear in this layer as isolated bits (free from intersymbol interference), resulting in a low signal-to-noise ratio.

Recently, several solutions were proposed based on domain expansion techniques. The first one is domain wall displacement detection (DWDD). The technique is based on two layers that are exchange-coupled through an intermediate switching layer (**Fig. 4a**). At room temperature, the small crescent-shaped bits in the recording layer appear in the readout or displacement layer. In the area of the optical spot where the temperature exceeds the Curie temperature of the intermediate layer, the coupling between the recording and the displacement layer is eliminated. Then, the domain wall that is present in the "cold" part of the optical spot can move freely toward the high-temperature region to minimize its domain wall energy, thus increasing the total area of the domain.

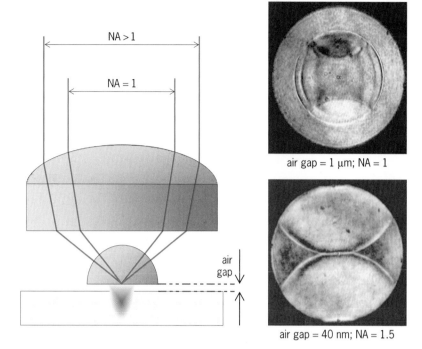

air gap = 1 μm; NA = 1

air gap = 40 nm; NA = 1.5

Fig. 2. Principle of near-field recording and two resulting images.

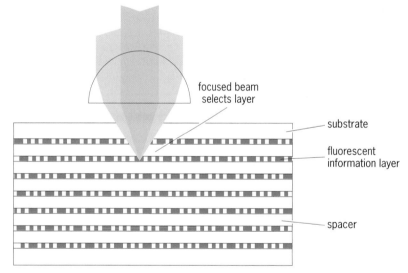

focused beam
selects layer

substrate

fluorescent
information layer

spacer

Fig. 3. Schematic drawing of a multilayer optical disk.

Another technique is the magnetically amplifying magnetooptic system (MAMMOS). It is based on magnetostatically coupled layers (Fig. 4b). A bit is copied in the heated region with increased magnetostatic coupling if the sum of the stray field and an applied external field is larger than the coercive (switching threshold) field. The domain expands in the readout layer to the full size of the optical spot. More recently, a technique without external field was proposed and is referred to as zero-field MAMMOS.

Both the MAMMOS and the DWDD technique need small coils to generate the recording field at high data rates. This small coil must be placed at a small distance from the recording material because

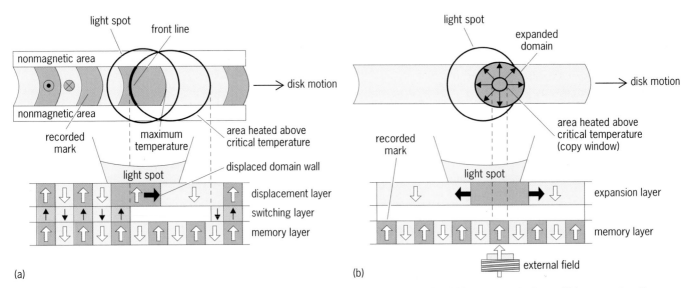

Fig. 4. Principles of (*a*) domain wall displacement detection (DWDD) and (*b*) the magnetically amplifying magnetooptic system (MAMMOS).

the field falls off exponentially as a function of this distance. In addition, thin cover layers are required, making the system sensitive to dust and scratches.

Magnetic storage. Currently, magnetic storage has the greatest density and data rate. Further areal density growth is limited by the thermal instability of the magnetization of the ever smaller magnetic grains in the medium (superparamagnetic effect), in combination with the limited possibilities to further improve write head designs and pole materials in order to enhance the write field strength. One way to postpone the onset of superparamagnetism is to use bits with their magnetization direction perpendicular to the recording surface. By using a soft magnetic underlayer (which acts as a magnetic mirror), the achievable field strength can be doubled, allowing the use of higher-coercivity materials and thereby increasing the stability of the recorded grains. It is expected that this approach may enable storage densities of 500 Gb/in.^{2} Presently, the lifetime of longitudinal recording is stretched by the use of antiferromagnetically coupled media where a three-atom-

thick layer of ruthenium is sandwiched between two magnetic layers.

A complementary approach is the use of patterned media. Here a bit is represented by a predetermined single magnetized domain instead of an ensemble of small grains. The individual magnetic domain volume can be much larger (factor of several hundred) than in standard recording, and very high densities beyond 500 Gb/in.^{2} are in principle possible. The largest obstacle to commercialization remains the cheap, homogeneous, and reliable manufacturing of these patterns over the surface of an entire disk.

A third way to increase the data density is hybrid, or thermally assisted, magnetic recording. During writing, the laser beam heats the recording material locally, thereby decreasing its coercivity to such an extent that the magnetic field of the recording head can switch the magnetization direction. Rapid cooling afterward effectively freezes the written bit in its current state. This technique allows the use of materials with extremely high coercivity values at ambient temperatures in which writing would normally not be possible.

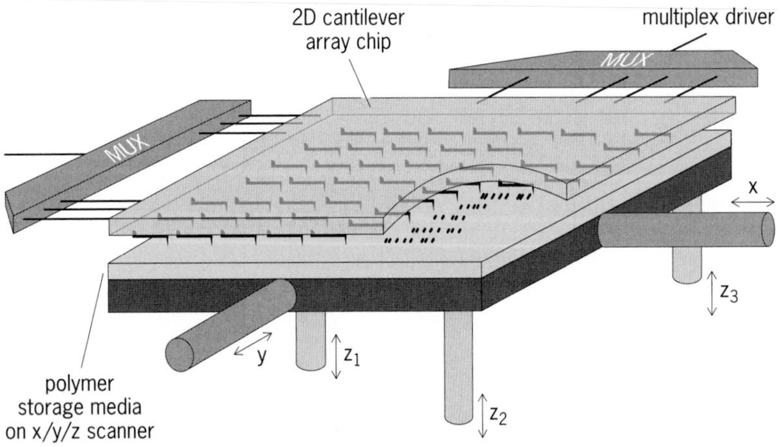

Nanoscale probe storage. A new approach that is being investigated is nanoscale probe storage (**Fig. 5**). In principle, storage on an atomic level is possible, for example, by using modified atomic force microscope setups in an integrated nano-electro-mechanical system (NEMS). Due to the limited scanning pitch of such NEMS devices and the small data rates of individual probes, large arrays of probes must be used in conjunction with parallel data addressing schemes. A prototype system, called Millipede, uses a 32 × 32 cantilever array, with each probe responsible for writing and reading a data page of 92 × 92 μm^2. Very high local densities of terabytes (1000 gigabytes) per square inch are possible, while the total capacity of such a system is limited by the array size. Important

Fig. 5. Schematic drawing of the Millipede probe storage concept. (©*1999 IEEE*)

issues to be solved include tip and medium wear, data rates, and overall system robustness, as well as a cost-effective, high-volume, high-yield fabrication process.

For background information *see* COMPACT DISK; COMPUTER STORAGE TECHNOLOGY; DIFFRACTION; MAGNETIC MATERIALS; MAGNETIC RECORDING; MAGNETORESISTANCE; OPTICAL INFORMATION SYSTEMS; OPTICAL RECORDING; VIDEO DISK in the McGraw-Hill Encyclopedia of Science & Technology.

Christopher Busch; André H.J. Immink

Bibliography. P. W. M. Blom et al., Spatial resolution of domain copying in a magnetic domain expansion readout disk, *IEEE Trans. Magnet.*, 37(5):3860–3864, 2001; R. Coehoorn et al., Hybrid recording, in G. C. Hadjipanayis (ed.), *Magnetic Storage Systems Beyond 2000*, pp. 571–583, Kluwer Academic, 2001; S. Furumiya et al., Wobble-address format of the blue-ray disc, *ISOM/ODS*, Hawaii, July 2002; H. Hieslmair et al., 34 GB multilevel-enabled rewritable system using blue laser and high NA optics, ISOM/ODS, Hawaii, July 2002; T. Kobayashi, M. Masuda, and T. Shiratori, Wall simulation for the domain wall displacement detection (I) and (II), *J. Magnet. Soc. Jap.*, 25 (no. 3, pt. 2):371–378, 2001; P. P. Vettiger et al., The "Millipede"—Nanotechnology entering data storage, *IEEE Trans. Nanotech.*, 1:39–55, 2002; R. Wood, The feasibility of magnetic recording at 1 terbit per square inch, *IEEE Trans. Magnet.*, 1:36–42, 2000; F. Zijp and Y. V. Martynov, Static tester for characterization of optical near-field coupling phenomena, *Proc. SPIE*, 4081:21–27, 2000.

Ultrawideband (UWB) systems

Ultrawideband, although considered a recent breakthrough in broadband wireless technology, has had a nearly 40-year history of technology development.

Development of technology. The origins of ultrawideband technology stem from work in time-domain electromagnetics begun in 1962 by Gerald F. Ross to describe fully the transient behavior of microwave networks through their characteristic impulse response. The concept was indeed simple. The conventional means of characterizing a linear, time-invariant system is by a swept frequency response (that is, amplitude and phase measurements versus frequency), a very tedious endeavor for broadband systems. Ross suggested that such a system could alternatively be fully characterized by its response to an impulse excitation—that is, the result of a single measurement. Mathematically, knowing the response to an impulse, the response to any arbitrary excitation could be readily determined by the convolution integral. However, two fundamental problems existed: how to generate a close approximation to a mathematically ideal impulse (an infinitely large, infinitesimally short-duration waveform), and how to actually measure the extremely short-duration

responses that would be expected from such excitations.

Fortuitously, in 1957 Leo Esaki invented the tunnel diode, the first known practical application of quantum physics. This device, with its extremely wide bandwidth (tens of gigahertz), not only permitted subnanosecond pulse generation essential for impulse excitation but also could be utilized as a sensitive thresholding device for the subsequent detection of such short-duration waveforms. In 1962, time-domain sampling oscilloscopes based upon the tunnel diode were introduced for high-speed triggering and detection, first enabling the capture and display of ultrawideband waveforms. Impulse measurement techniques were subsequently applied to the analysis of wideband radiating antenna elements, in which the impulse response is the radiated electromagnetic field. In doing so, it quickly became apparent that short-pulse radar and even communications systems could be developed using the same set of tools. However, it was not until the introduction of a low-cost short-pulse receiver in 1972 to replace the expensive time-domain sampling oscilloscope that system developments in ultrawideband radar and communications accelerated rapidly.

Early techniques for ultrawideband signal generation utilized the fast rise (or fall) times of a baseband-generated pulse to impulse- or shock-excite a wideband antenna, which in turn would generate an electromagnetic burst consisting of only a few radio-frequency cycles of energy (**Fig. 1**). Tunnel, step-recovery, and avalanche diodes were used to produce this excitation signal, while more modern techniques use the fast rise time of a semiconductor switch or gate. By varying the dimensions of the antenna, the frequency and bandwidth characteristics of the resulting ultrawideband pulse could be adjusted. More modern techniques for ultrawideband pulse generation utilize time-domain filtering techniques for spectral shaping.

Until the late 1980s, ultrawideband technology was alternatively referred to as baseband, carrier-free, or impulse; the term "ultrawideband" was not applied until approximately 1989, when ultrawideband theory, techniques, and many hardware approaches had experienced nearly 30 years of extensive development. Somewhat paralleling the development of spread-spectrum systems after World War II, much of the early (pre-1994) development of ultrawideband systems (particularly for communications applications) was classified. Indeed, the fact that these extremely short-duration pulses required unique techniques for detection made them of particular interest for low-probability-of-detection applications for the government and military.

Significance of technology. The early interest in short-pulse techniques was primarily concentrated in short-range radar applications. From first principles, the shorter a radar's pulse duration, the finer the resultant range resolution. Thus, with pulse durations measured in hundreds of picoseconds, resolutions of only a few inches (several centimeters) or

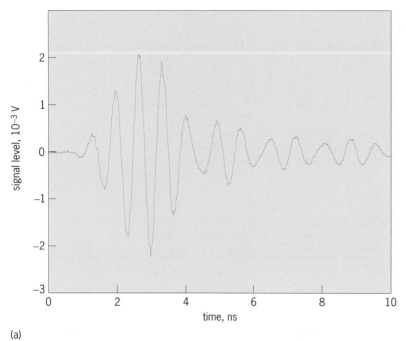

(a)

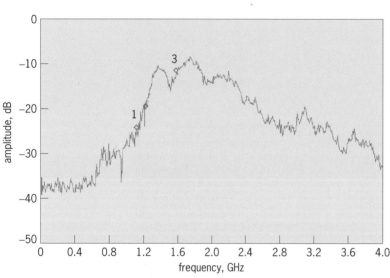

(b)

Fig. 1. Typical ultrawideband pulses in the time and frequency domains. (*a*) Typical ultrawideband transmit pulse in free space, with just a few cycles of radio-frequency energy. (*b*) Typical UWB power spectrum from impulse-excited wideband antenna. Center frequency $f_0 = 1.78$ GHz and bandwidth at -10 dB relative to peak amplitude is 1.12 GHz, giving a fractional bandwidth of 63%.

low-frequency wideband excitation translated into significantly enhanced material penetration capability. Ground-penetrating radar is used to locate buried objects, including humans in disasters such as building or mine collapse. Through-wall imaging is used for law enforcement activities.

The early interest in ultrawideband for communications, however, stemmed from the fact that short-pulse waveforms are extremely difficult to detect. Essentially, since the pulse bandwidth is spread over many hundreds of megahertz to gigahertz, a conventional (that is, narrowband) receiver will receive only a small slice of this spectral energy. For low-pulse-repetition-frequency (PRF) waveforms (that is, those with extremely low duty cycles), the total received energy is proportional to the ratio of the intercept receiver to ultrawideband spread bandwidths.

These low-duty-cycle waveforms have other unique properties as well. For example, one limiting factor affecting the performance of both mobile and indoor communications systems, particularly with narrowband systems, is the deleterious effect of multipath signal cancellation. In general, a received signal is the composite sum of the direct (or line-of-sight) signal from transmitter to receiver and a number of secondary reflections of the signal off objects between the transmitter and receiver. These "bounced" or multipath returns will arrive at the receiver later than the direct signal and, because of this time misalignment and possible phase inversion due to the reflection, will cause varying amounts of signal cancellation or distortion of the direct path. However, if the duration of the pulse is short enough, it is possible to distinguish in time between the direct and reflected multipath returns without causing any signal cancellation.

This capability is illustrated by the geometry of **Fig. 2**, in which two units, A and B, are attempting to communicate, but the signal also bounces off of a wall located 3 m (10 ft) away. With the speed of light at roughly 0.3 m (1 ft) per nanosecond, a signal reflection from the wall will arrive approximately 10 ns (3-m or 10-ft path differential) later than the direct path. If the signal's pulse duration is less than this 10-ns differential, the direct and reflected path can be fully resolved without mutual interference. Thus, short-pulse techniques become of particular interest for high-reliability communications in severe multipath channels. However, if the delay spread of the channel (that is, the time over which such multipath effects are dominant) exceeds the bit duration (reciprocal bit rate) of the ultrawideband communications system, intersymbol interference can occur and ultrawideband techniques become less effective.

Finally, because the time of arrival of a short-duration pulse can be very accurately measured using high-speed detection circuitry such as enabled by the Esaki diode, accurate time-of-flight or distance measurements can be accomplished, opening up the use of the technology for precision localization applications.

less were now possible. Such resolutions were orders of magnitude better than what could be achieved at that time, and significant research in the use of short-pulse techniques for radar applications continued.

From the time-scaling property of the Fourier transform relationship between time and frequency domains, the shorter the transmitted pulse the wider the instantaneous bandwidth. Thus, since short-pulse waveforms could be inexpensively produced directly at baseband (that is, without modulating a carrier frequency as in conventional radar), applications of ultrawideband to ground-penetrating radar and through-wall imaging followed quickly. Here,

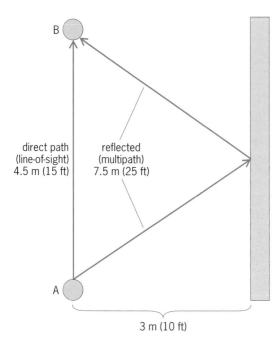

B

direct path
(line-of-sight)
4.5 m (15 ft)

reflected
(multipath)
7.5 m (25 ft)

A

3 m (10 ft)

Fig. 2. Multipath geometry.

Applications. Aside from ground-penetrating radar, only a handful of ultrawideband system designs have progressed beyond the laboratory stage. All fielded ultrawideband systems have, by necessity, been developed for the government or military, since no widespread commercial authorization for ultrawideband systems had existed until the recent Federal Communications Commission (FCC) Report and Order.

In the field of communications, most recently fielded ultrawideband systems have consisted of short-range (1–2 km or 0.6–1.2 mi), medium to high bit rate (128 kilobits per second to 6 megabits per second) systems for voice, data, or compressed video. Experimental work with longer-range (greater than 50 km or 30 mi), non-line-of-sight ultrawideband communications in the lower frequency bands has also been performed. However, since the release of the FCC Report and Order, high-data-rate (greater than 100 Mb/s), short-pulse systems have also been actively considered for various wireless networking applications.

Recent radar applications of ultrawideband have primarily concentrated in the areas of collision and obstacle avoidance, precision radar altimetry, and ground-penetrating radar, and in applications requiring lower-frequency radars for foliage penetration and for through-wall sensing.

Probably one of the most promising areas for ultrawideband technology is in the application to precision geolocation and positioning. Here, the extremely fine range resolution translates into precise time-of-flight measurements for three-dimensional (3D) triangulation, while the time-resolution property of short pulses enables operation in even the most severe of multipath conditions.

FCC Report and Order. As discussed above, a basic technique for generating ultrawideband waveforms is to impulse or step-excite a wideband antenna. Antennas, however, are very poor electrical filters; as a consequence, such shock-excited systems are very difficult to control spectrally and confine. However, unlicensed use of radio-frequency spectrum within the United States requires adherence to Part 15 of Title 47 of the Code of Federal Regulations. Part 15 devices must be designed so that their intentional emissions do not fall within certain restricted bands, several of which contain safety-of-life and safety-of-flight systems such as Global Positioning System (GPS) satellites. However, many proposed ultrawideband systems, with their inherently large spectral occupancy, overlapped these restricted regions.

To address this problem, the FCC issued a Notice of Inquiry in August 1998 and a Notice of Proposed Rule Making in June 2000. Among the key issues before the FCC were the impact of ultrawideband emissions on systems designated for flight safety, and the potential of ultrawideband interference to digital cellular systems (PCS) and satellite digital audio radio systems (SDARS) operating below 3.1 GHz. The National Telecommunications and Information Administration was tasked with obtaining test results to assess the potential for certain classes of ultrawideband systems to interfere with other government services.

On February 14, 2002, the FCC approved a First Report and Order to permit ultrawideband technology under Part 15 of its regulations. The Report and Order was precedent-setting in that, for the first time, the FCC had permitted intentional emissions to fall into previously restricted areas of the spectrum. The FCC waved restrictions on ultrawideband operation within certain restricted bands, but imposed additional constraints on the use of the technology for imaging, radar, and communications applications. These constraints included limitations on the field of operation and requirements for interagency coordination for the use of imaging and through-wall sensors; additional peak power constraints for all forms of ultrawideband operation; and operational restrictions on peer-to-peer indoor and handheld outdoor ultrawideband communications devices. Ultrawideband communications devices are restricted to intentional operation between 3.1 and 10.6 GHz; through-wall imaging and surveillance systems are restricted between 1.99 and 10.6 GHz (and used only by law enforcement, fire and rescue, and other designated organizations); and automotive radars are restricted to frequencies above 24.075 GHz. Ground-penetrating radar and through-wall imaging sensors were also permitted below 960 MHz.

For background information *see* ANTENNA (ELECTROMAGNETISM); FOURIER SERIES AND TRANSFORMS; GROUND-PROBING RADAR; RADAR; SPREAD SPECTRUM COMMUNICATION; TUNNEL DIODE; TUNNELING IN SOLIDS in the McGraw-Hill Encyclopedia of Science & Technology.   Robert J. Fontana

Bibliography. C. L. Bennett and G. F. Ross, Time-domain electromagnetics and its applications, *Proc. IEEE*, 66(3):299–318, 1978; J. Foerster et al., Ultra-wideband technology for short- or medium-range wireless communications, *Intel Technol. J.*, 2d Quarter, 2001; D. G. Leeper, Wireless data blaster, *Sci. Amer.*, May 2002; J. Taylor (ed.), *Introduction to Ultra-Wideband Radar Systems*, CRC Press, Boca Raton, FL, 1995; *2002 IEEE Conference on Ultra Wideband Systems and Technologies*, Institute of Electrical and Electronic Engineers, May 21–23, 2002; *Ultra-Wideband, Short-Pulse Electromagnetics 1, 2, 3*, and *4*, Plenum Press, New York, 1993, 1994, 1997, 1999.

Universe

One of the longstanding goals of modern cosmology has been to determine the global geometry of the universe. This is the geometry of the universe at very large scales (greater than about 2×10^8 light-years), at which the distribution of galaxies appears to be uniform. Determining the global geometry would answer the question of what is the curvature of space on the largest scales. (While the space-time of general relativity has four dimensions, it can be characterized by a curvature, just like a two-dimensional surface.) That is, is this space flat or curved? And, if curved, is the curvature positive (like a sphere) or negative (like a saddle-shaped surface)?

Moreover, a general relativistic model of an expanding universe specifies a relation between the universe's global geometry and its future evolution and eventual fate. This model was proposed in the 1920s by G. Lemaître and A. Friedmann, and its assumptions have finally been confirmed by observations made since the late 1980s. According to this model, if the curvature is positive, the universe is closed and will eventually stop expanding and collapse back upon itself. Similarly, if the curvature is negative, the universe is open and will expand forever, the density always decreasing as time goes on. The flat universe keeps expanding, but the expansion rate slows to zero asymptotically as time increases. Four recent experiments measured the curvature by observing and characterizing the anisotropies of the cosmic microwave background, and found the universe to have a flat geometry.

Cosmic microwave background. The cosmic microwave background is the relict radiation formed in the epoch when the temperature in the early universe dropped sufficiently (to about 4000 K, occurring approximately 300,000 years after the big bang) to allow the plasma of free electrons, protons, and helium ions to combine, leaving neutral atoms. During this epoch of recombination, the matter and radiation decoupled from each other and went on to cool at their own independent rates. The background radiation cooled as the universe expanded,

until today it is observed with a blackbody spectrum at a temperature of 2.725 K.

Measurement of curvature. The cosmic microwave background provides a unique opportunity to measure the curvature, independent of other methods. Imprinted upon the cosmic microwave background are small temperature fluctuations, or anisotropies, with peak values of the order of ±100 microkelvin, with an angular size of about 1° (warm or cold regions relative to the uniform 2.725 K large-scale background temperature). The fluctuations are due to oscillations that developed in the density of the plasma before the epoch of recombination, with the regions that are slightly overdense being slightly warmer than the surroundings and the underdense regions being slightly cooler. The size of the horizon during recombination (that is, the distance a light ray could have propagated from the beginning of the universe until that time) corresponds to the size of the largest fluctuations, with lower-amplitude fluctuations following at smaller angular scales. The spectrum of the observed fluctuations provides a unique signature for a number of cosmological parameters, among them the total mass density of the universe ρ.

The cosmological density parameter, $\Omega_{total} = \rho/\rho_{crit}$, is the observed mass density relative to the critical density ρ_{crit}, the density of a flat universe specified by the Friedmann-Lemaître model. (That is, if $\Omega_{total} = 1$, then $\rho = \rho_{crit}$, and the geometry is flat.) According to this model, this parameter determines the global geometry of the universe. If $\Omega_{total} > 1$, the large-scale curvature of space is positive and the universe is closed; if $\Omega_{total} < 1$, the large-scale curvature of space is negative and the universe is open.

Since the expected angular size of the horizon during recombination is known, corresponding to the size of the largest fluctuations in the cosmic microwave background, the global geometry of the universe can be determined by characterizing the angular size of the observed anisotropy in the cosmic microwave background. If $\Omega_{total} > 1$ and the large-scale curvature of space is positive, the geometry is analogous to that of a sphere. On a sphere (**Fig. 1a**), the sum of the three angles of a triangle is greater than 180° (the sum of the angles of a triangle on a flat surface); and likewise, when the large-scale curvature of space is positive, distant objects subtend larger angles than they would in a flat space. Thus, the apparent size of the horizon is larger than expected. Similarly, if $\Omega_{total} < 1$ and the large-scale curvature of space is negative, analogous to a saddle-shaped surface (Fig. 1b), the sum of the three angles of a triangle is less than 180°. In this case, distant objects subtend smaller angles than they would in a flat space, so that the apparent size of the horizon is less than expected. If the observed size of the fluctuations is the same as the expected size, $\Omega_{total} = 1$, and the universe is flat (Fig. 1c.)

The combined result of four different recent experiments was that $\Omega_{total} = 1.02 \pm 0.03$. This result

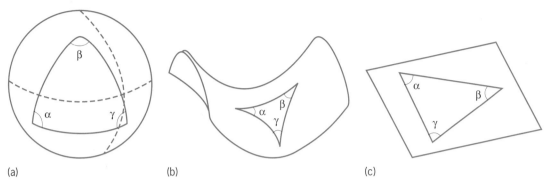

Fig. 1. Surface analogs of possible global geometries of the universe. (*a*) Closed geometry. Distant objects appear larger than expected and, in a triangle with angles α, β, γ, $\alpha + \beta + \gamma > 180°$. (*b*) Open geometry. Distant objects appear smaller than expected and $\alpha + \beta + \gamma < 180°$. (*c*) Flat geometry. Distant objects appear as expected and $\alpha + \beta + \gamma = 180°$.

implies that the universe has a flat geometry within the uncertainties of the measurements.

Experiments. While all the experiments observe the anisotropy in the cosmic microwave background, each individually has a unique instrumentation and observing strategy. There are three general requirements for any cosmic microwave background anisotropy experiment:

1. The detectors must be very sensitive. Since the signals of interest are very weak, a sensitive detector is necessary so that the observations can be carried out on a reasonable time scale.

2. The telescope used to observe the sky must be highly directional so that spurious noise signals from the local environment will not be mistaken for the signal of interest from the sky.

3. The observing location must minimize or eliminate the effect of the atmosphere.

All the experiments share these common traits, each having unique solutions to the general requirements.

Bolometric detector arrays. Two of the experiments, BOOMERanG (Balloon Observations of Millimetric Extragalactic Radiation and Geomagnetics) and MAXIMA (Millimeter Anisotropy Experiment Imaging Array), used arrays of bolometric detectors, essentially precision thermometers operating at subkelvin temperatures (less than 1 K). The radiation from the cosmic microwave background was detected by converting it to heat and measuring the resultant temperature rise. Remarkable as this may seem, bolometers are the most sensitive detectors available for observations of the cosmic microwave background. The BOOMERanG experiment used an array of 16 detectors operating at 0.3 K in four wavelength passbands from 0.75 to 3 mm. It used a long-duration balloon flight to accomplish the

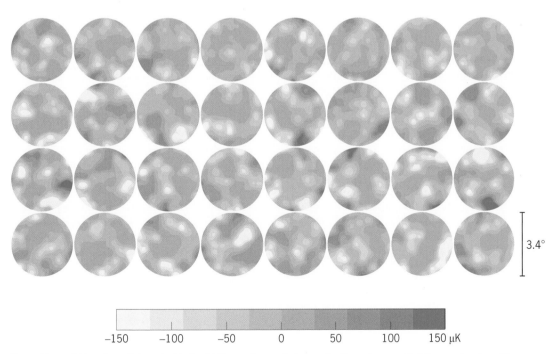

Fig. 2. Maps of 32 regions observed with the DASI experiment. By inspection it can be seen that the angular size of the warm and cool regions is of the order of 1°, as is expected for a universe with flat geometry.

observations, circumnavigating Antarctica in 10.5 days. The MAXIMA experiment was also balloon-based, but had a shorter flight of 12 hours, over North America. The detectors were more sensitive, operating at 0.1 K, so the results were comparable to the other experiments. Both balloon experiments had the unique advantage, along with the space-based experiments, that they could calibrate their sensitivity directly from the cosmic microwave background.

Telescope arrays. The DASI (Degree Angular Scale Interferometer) and VSA (Very Small Array) experiments use an array of small telescopes with near-quantum-limited amplifiers to boost the cosmic microwave background signal and interferometrically combine the outputs to generate a map of the anisotropy in the cosmic microwave background. The DASI experiment (**Fig. 2**), located at the South Pole, used 13 telescopes; and the VSA, located at the Teide Observatory on Tenerife in the Canary Islands, uses 14 telescopes. Both experiments work in 10 wavelength passbands between 8 and 11 mm, about three times longer than the wavelengths used in the bolometric experiments. All of the experiments generate fully sampled maps containing all the information available from the observations.

Space experiments. Currently the MAP (Microwave Anisotropy Probe) space mission of the National Aeronautics and Space Administration (NASA) is observing the cosmic microwave background. This experiment will observe the whole sky and provide a complete data set on angular scales greater than $0.25°$. The initial results should be announced in 2003. Further in the future, the Planck experiment of the European Space Agency (ESA) and NASA will provide the definitive cosmic microwave background data set, combining small angular resolution with large wavelength coverage over the whole sky. *See* SPACE FLIGHT.

For background information *see* BOLOMETER; COSMIC BACKGROUND RADIATION; COSMOLOGY; HORIZON; RELATIVITY; UNIVERSE in the McGraw-Hill Encyclopedia of Science & Technology.

Mark Dragovan

Bibliography. N. W. Halverson et al., Degree Angular Scale Interferometer first results: A measurement of the cosmic microwave angular power spectrum, *Astrophys. J.*, 568:38–45, 2002; A. T. Lee et al., A high spatial resolution analysis of the MAXIMA-1 cosmic microwave background anisotropy data, *Astrophys. J.*, 561:L1–L5, 2001; C. B. Netterfield et al., A measurement by BOOMERANG of multiple peaks in the angular power spectrum of the cosmic microwave background, *Astrophys. J.*, 571:604–614, 2001; R. A. Watson et al., First results from the Very Small Array, I. Observational methods, *Mon. Not. Roy. Astron. Soc.*, in press.

Uranium mining

Uranium (U) mining is the process of extracting uranium-bearing minerals or fluids from areas of the Earth's crust in which the concentration of uranium

TABLE 1. World uranium production by method in 2002

Production method	Production		Share of world production, %
	M lb U_3O_8	1000 mtU	
Open-pit mining	27.2	10.5	30
Underground mining	40.1	15.4	43
In situ leaching	15.9	6.1	17
By-product	9.5	3.7	10
Total	92.7	35.7	100

is sufficient to provide a reasonable balance between the cost of extraction and the value of the uranium produced. Mining methods for uranium production include open-pit mining, underground mining, and in situ leaching (ISL), that is, recovery by chemically dissolving uranium ore in permeable sandstone deposits. Uranium is also produced as a by-product of both copper and gold mining (**Table 1**). Unit measures for uranium production are usually given in terms of millions of pounds of uranium oxide (M lb U_3O_8), metric tons U_3O_8, or metric tons uranium (mtU).

Historically, most of the world's uranium production has been derived from conventional methods, such as open-pit mining for shallow deposits and underground mining for deeper deposits. Both methods produce substantial quantities of mining waste. Open-pit mining produces waste from material overlying the mining zone and from barren rock within the mining zone, while underground mining produces waste from the material removed to make the shafts and tunnels used to gain access to the mining zone. In both cases, mined uranium-bearing material is transported to a nearby recovery facility, or mill, where the uranium is concentrated into a salable product containing in excess of 70% uranium. This milling process produces large quantities of waste, called tailings, since most uranium ores contain only a few pounds of uranium per ton of material mined and processed.

In situ leaching has been increasingly used to recover uranium since the mid-1960s. In 2002, it was the sole means of uranium production in the United States. Other in situ leaching uranium producers include Kazakhstan, Uzbekistan, Australia, the Czech Republic, and Russia. The increased use of in situ leaching has been driven entirely by economics. Uranium can be recovered from deposits in permeable sandstones by in situ leaching methods at lower cost than by any other method. This low-cost recovery provides for a substantial increase in the uranium resource base since it is a means of economic production for many small or poor-quality deposits that cannot be mined profitably by any other means. Additional benefits include (1) far less surface and subsurface disturbance; (2) safer working conditions; and, most importantly, (3) negligible waste generation.

Uranium production. In situ leaching is a continuous process of mining and mineral concentration.

Mining. A wellfield consisting of a compact geometric pattern of injection and extraction wells is installed within the outlines of the mineralized area. Such wells might be arranged in square, hexagonal, or rectangular patterns, with a distance of 50–100 ft (15–30 m) between the injection and extraction wells. All wells are constructed with steel, plastic, or fiberglass pipe cemented in place from the surface to the mining zone in order to prevent leakage of the solution from the mining zone into overlying or underlying geologic formations. Perforated or slotted well screens are installed within the mining zone to allow the mining solutions to pass freely from the injection wells through the uranium mineralization and into the extraction wells (**Fig. 1**). Monitor wells surround the wellfield to make sure that leakage of the mining solutions is not occurring.

A solution of ground water fortified with uranium-dissolving chemicals (either alkaline or acidic, with a suitable oxidant) is circulated from the injection well through the mineralization to the extraction well. All United States in situ leaching operations use slightly alkaline solutions of carbon dioxide and oxygen, as such solutions have a relatively low impact on the quality of the ground water. In situ leaching operations in all other countries use acidic solutions which, despite mobilizing additional elements into the mining solutions, are more cost-effective.

Recovery. The uranium-bearing solutions are transferred via a large-diameter pipeline from the extraction wells to a central uranium recovery facility. There the uranium is adsorbed from solution using ion-exchange resin beads in a series of holding tanks.

Following recovery, a small portion, less than 1%, of the solution is removed from the process for disposal through evaporation, deep well injection, or land application. This discarded solution, called bleed, provides for a slightly negative pressure on the wellfield, which prevents the mining solutions from migrating outside the mining zone. Bleed is the sole substantive waste product of the in situ leaching process. The remaining process solution is refortified with uranium-dissolving chemicals, and then pumped back to injection wells for recirculation through the deposit.

Concentration. The adsorbed uranium is removed from the ion-exchange resin with a solution of sodium chloride, and the ion-exchange resin is regenerated by washing the chlorides out of the resin with a sulfate solution.

The uranium removed from the ion-exchange system is precipitated from solution by adjusting the acidity with sulfuric acid and by adding precipitating chemicals such as hydrogen peroxide, ammonia, or caustic soda (sodium hydroxide). Next, the water is removed from the uranium precipitate, and the precipitate is washed with clean water to remove dissolved contaminants such as chlorides. After washing, the precipitate is dried to less than 2% moisture to produce a uranium concentrate, which is packaged in U.S. Department of Transportation–approved 55-gallon (200-liter) steel drums for shipment.

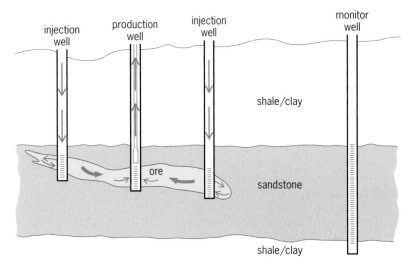

Components of a typical wellfield for in situ leaching of uranium ore.

Controlling parameters. Various technical and economic parameters control the applicability of in situ leaching to uranium production, for example, the mining solution and well flow rates, ore quality, mine depth, and uranium mineral solubility. These parameters may be quite different from mine to mine (**Table 2**).

Uranium minerals must exist within a permeable geologic formation, such as sandstone, in order to allow for the efficient circulation of the mining solutions through the mining zone. Economic flow rates for individual wells are typically in the range of 20–150 gal/min (1–10 L/s). In addition, the natural saturation, pressurization, and confinement of the mining zone between upper and lower formations of low permeability permit a high degree of control of mining solutions, and restrict the potential for those solutions to migrate outside the mining zone.

Uranium minerals must exist in sufficient concentrations in terms of both grade and thickness to offset the cost of extraction. Total uranium recovery from a mining zone usually falls in the range of 60–80%. In addition, the uranium minerals in the deposit must be easily soluble in weakly alkaline or acidic solutions since strong chemical solutions are costly and are likely to have negative impacts on the ground water.

Depth is an important economic parameter because of its influence on drilling and well installation costs. Currently, in situ leaching mines do not exceed 1800 ft (545 m).

Reclamation/restoration. Upon completion of the mining process, reclamation of the disturbed surface, as well as restoration of the subsurface, may proceed. The surface reclamation process includes removing pipelines, service roads, and well equipment, as well as reseeding the ground with native grasses and plants. Subsurface restoration includes the cementation of all wells to prevent future leakage and, perhaps, some degree of ground-water treatment to bring the ground water back to its premining condition. In most cases, premining concentrations of

TABLE 2. Key technical and operating parameters for several of the world's largest operating in situ leaching mines

	Units	Mine and location		
		Smith Ranch, U.S.	Beverley, Australia	Stepnoye, Kazakhstan
Leaching solution	—	Alkaline	Acidic	Acidic
Rated production capacity	M lb U_3O_8/yr 1000 mtU/yr	2.0 0.8	2.2 0.8	2.6 1.0
Production 2002	M lb U_3O_8 1000 mtU	1.0 0.4	1.8 0.7	2.2 0.8
Remaining reserves	M lb U_3O_8 1000 mtU	27.0 10.4	24.1 9.3	63.3 24.3
Solution flow	gal/min L/s	6000 380	4000 250	15,400 1000
Well depth	ft m	650 200	330 100	300–800 90–250
Ore grade	% U_3O_8 % U	0.10 0.08	0.18 0.15	0.04 0.03
Ore thickness	ft m	10 3.0	20 6.0	16 4.9
Well flow rate	gal/min L/s	20 1.3	160 10.0	40 2.5
Employees	—	60	60	800

radon, radium, and uranium in the ground water make it unfit for either human or animal consumption. Restoration of the ground-water constituents to premining levels has been a typical United States requirement, but seems to be giving way to a more realistic approach of return to class-of-use. Thus, potable ground water should be restored to potable classification, industrial ground water to industrial classification, and so on. Very poor quality waters may not require restoration under such guidelines.

Health and safety. Worker health and safety has been characteristically good for the in situ leaching process. Uranium production for nuclear fuel, in general, has had far lower human costs than those associated with the production of coal, oil, and gas for power plant fuels. In situ leaching production of uranium has a better health and safety record than open-pit and underground uranium production. Industrial accidents resulting in fatalities are rare during in situ leaching mining. In addition, in situ leaching methods avoid potential lung damage from dust, radon, and silica common to early under-ground mining and, with little large equipment in use and no blasting, also exceed safety norms for open-pit mines.

For background information *see* ION EXCHANGE; LEACHING; SOLUTION MINING; URANIUM in the McGraw-Hill Encyclopedia of Science & Technology.
Thomas C. Pool

Bibliography. P. D. Bush, Development considerations for the Honeymoon ISL Project, in *Uranium 2000—International Symposium on the Process Metallurgy of Uranium* (Saskatoon), September 9–15, 2000; J. Hunter, Highland in-situ leach mine, *Min. Mag.*, August 1991; D. E. Stover, Smith Ranch—North America's newest uranium mine, *Min. Mag.*, October 1977; D. Underhill, *Manual of Acid In Situ Leach Uranium Mining Technology*, IAEA-TECDOC-1239, International Atomic Energy Agency, Vienna, 2001; U.S. Nuclear Regulatory Commission, *Final Environmental Impact Statement To Construct and Operate the Crownpoint Uranium Solution Mining Project, Crownpoint, New Mexico*, NUREG-1508, 1997.

Vendobionts (Precambrian evolution)

The Vendobionta as a taxonomic group are based on a reinterpretation of the Ediacaran Fauna, vast fossil assemblages from the late Proterozoic age (600–543 million years ago) immediately preceding the end of the Precambrian Era. The Ediacaran Fauna was previously thought to contain only metazoan (multicellular) ancestors to numerous invertebrate groups. Because of their large sizes, segmentation, bilateral symmetry, and polarity, all the Ediacaran fossils were originally attributed to cnidarians (such as sea pens and jellyfish), annelid worms, and arthropods. However, a new interpretation has emerged for the majority of Ediacaran fossils, arising from functional incongruences which indicate that they were not related to these groups at all. *Charniodiscus*, for example, resembles modern sea pens in shape and erect attitude; but since its frond was a closed leaf, it would have been unsuited as a filter fan.

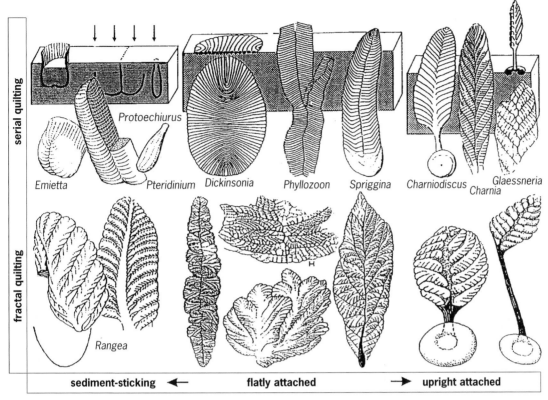

Fig. 1. Vendobiontan lifestyles. In spite of their simple quilted structure, vendobionts managed to adapt to a variety of lifestyles on and within soft sediments sealed by tough microbial biomats. (*From A. Seilacher, 1992*)

Similarly, *Dickinsonia* may be compared to a segmented worm. Yet its pancake shape—nearly 100 cm (39 in.) long and 20 cm (8 in.) wide but only 2–3 mm (0.8–1.2 in.) thick—allowed neither the winding nor the peristaltic modes of locomotion characteristic for worms. Nor does the superficially trilobite-like shape of *Spriggina* indicate a relationship since, unlike trilobita, *Spriggina* lacked a carapace. Other vendobionts resemble nothing so much as the leaves of present-day land plants (**Fig. 1**).

The present article summarizes the arguments why Vendobionta may represent not the ancestors of invertebrates but an extinct group of giant protists (single-celled organisms).

Constructional morphology. Differently shaped Ediacarans show a remarkably similar "quilted" construction; that is, they were contained in a flexible wall connected by septa at regular distances. This design can be explained fabricationally: either sausage-shaped chambers are added at the growing margin (serial quilting) or established chambers expand and become subdivided by secondary septa (fractal quilting). It can also be explained in a functional sense: the quilted construction increases the surface interacting with the environment relative to body volume, and at the same time strengthens the otherwise soft hydrostatic structure. If one accepts this architecture as the unifying character of a monophyletic group, symmetries and patterns previously attributed to phylogenetic relationships become in-

stead secondary results of different growth programs and lifestyles (Fig. 1).

Upright forms. Upright forms attached by the proximal end (the "head" in metazoan interpretations) developed a discoid holdfast. In addition, erect species strengthened the central axis either to withstand tensional stress (like kelp); or they elevated the frond into the water column on a stem that was consistent enough not to collapse during initial compaction. But how could discoidal holdfasts provide anchorage on muddy bottoms? The answer is found in specific sedimentary structures. They indicate that in Precambrian times sandy and muddy bottoms were generally sealed by tough microbial mats, which allowed attachment just as on rocky substrates. Most likely, erect vendobionts were not simply attached to the surface of the biomats but were anchored below them, because in felled individuals the holdfasts are never uprooted, while the surrounding bedding plane became lifted up like a tablecloth. In Newfoundland, all stemmed vendobionts were apparently felled in the same direction by the turbidity current which eventually smothered the whole community.

Carpetlike forms. Other Newfoundland vendobionts, shaped like spindles, tree leaves, or bushes, became neither aligned nor accumulated by the current, because they were sticking flatly to the biomat. Some individuals, however, became partly folded over like the corner of a carpet. They show that the

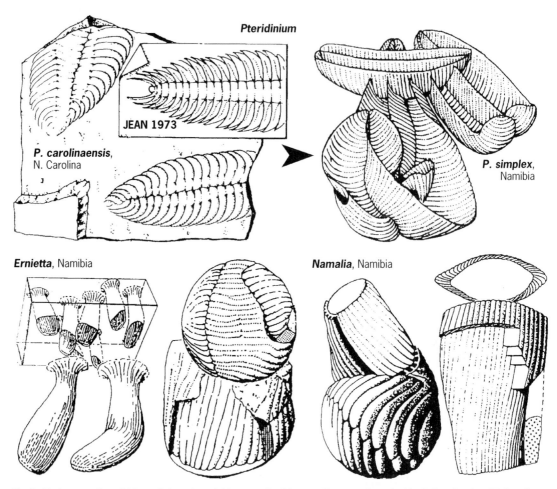

Fig. 2. Underground vendobionts. Infaunal vendobionts evolved from recliners, such as the North Carolina *Pteridinium*, by growing the quilts upward with sedimentation. The paleo-accident (upper right) of *P. simplex* demonstrates both the ability of these organisms to grow across their neighbors and the recovery of the victims by way of seemingly complicated growth programs. The sand inside the quilts of *Ernietta* and *Namalia* was probably used as an internal skeleton that subdivided the protoplasm into smaller-scale strands. (*Partly from D. Grazhdankin and A. Seilacher, 2002*)

attached side had exactly the same morphology as the exposed side.

While the majority of carpetlike vendobionts appear to have been sessile, a certain kind of mobility is recorded by a slab that M. Fedonkin recently discovered at the White Sea of Russia. In a series of nonoverlapping and equal-sized *Dickinsonia*-like impressions, only the last one shows the negative hyporelief preservation typical for carcasses. This suggests that the same organism serially digested the biomat, leaving a shallow impression of itself, and crept to new sites before it became buried alive.

Another variation on this lifestyle is revealed by J. Gehling's observation that when *Dickinsonia* is associated with *Phyllozoon* on the same bedding plane, either the one or the other is preserved only as a vague phantom. Since *Dickinsonia* always forms a negative hyporelief and *Phyllozoon* a positive hyporelief, the latter probably had a stationary lifestyle below the biomat.

Sediment-sticking forms. The third basic lifestyle prevails in sandstones whose sedimentary structures suggest a deltaic regime with relatively high rates of sedimentation. Here the vendobionts are found within the sand in three-dimensional preservation. This is due to a switch in lifestyle of originally carpetlike vendobionts, which responded to sedimentation by upward growth of the quilt tips. The most common representative of this guild, *Pteridinium*, resembled *Phyllozoon* except that it had three vanes along the median seam. In *P. carolinaensis* (originally described as a trilobite), two vanes spread in the bedding plane and were probably attached to a biomat, while the median vane, now folded over, stood vertically into the water column. In the three-dimensionally preserved *P. simplex*, however, the median vane stands upright and the lateral vanes curve upward as well. As the median seam is also slightly curved, the whole body attained the shape of a boat with the proximal end as the stern, the growing distal end as the bow, and the median vane as a separating wall.

In dense populations, the basic boat shape is commonly modified. When carefully dissecting such an assemblage, D. Grazhdankin not only could recognize several generations stacked on top of each other and separated by disturbance horizons, but he also discovered dramatic evidence of a paleo-accident:

the growing prow of one individual collided with two others and cut right through them. The two victims, with their bows amputated, responded by growing upward at the opposite stern end, and one of them proceeded to form a new horizontal boat at a higher level (**Fig. 2**). Such disfigurations had previously been explained by passive deformation of the organism during transport. If this were true, the overturned part should be concave-down; but it is again concave-up with the median vane on top, as in normal specimens. This acrobatic act was accomplished by a complete reorganization: by growing in a sharp fold, the previous median vane became the new right lateral vane, and the old right lateral vane turned into the median vane (Fig. 2).

Taxonomic position. If the vendobionts were not the ancestors of invertebrate animals, where else among modern organisms are their closest relatives? A major clue is their allometric segmentation relative to body size: whether being serially packed or fractally subdivided, all chambers maintain the same diameter throughout growth. This behavior is well known from various groups of larger foraminiferans. Small species grow isometrically by adding ever larger globular chambers to their calcareous shells, while oversized species (with centimetric dimensions, they are giants by protistan standards) maintain the same chamber diameter. Also, chambers tend to become sausage-shaped, subdivided into chamberlets by secondary septa, and filled with multinucleate protoplasm. The reason is probably that the metabolism of a single cell cannot be maintained if any point in this protoplasm exceeds a certain distance from the cell surface. Since the allometric quilting of vendobionts had a similar compartmentalizing effect, it had long been suspected that they also were giant unicells. There was only one irritating incongruence: vendobiontan quilts reach much larger diameters than the chambers and chamberlets of larger foraminiferans.

This dilemma can now be resolved by analogy with another kind of unicellular giant, the xenophyophores. Like amebas, radiolarians, and foraminiferans, they belong to the class Rhizopoda, which collect their food with naked pseudopodia. Today, xenophyophores are restricted to deep sea bottoms, where different species recline, stick in the mud, or elevate into the water column. Their allometrically chambered tests have soft walls reinforced by foreign particles (xenophyae); but, as in vendobionts, the chamber diameters are much larger than in foraminiferan tests. In this case the incongruence can be explained: xenophyophoran chambers contain only about 50% protoplasm; the remainder consists of aggregates of fine clay particles, which were probably taken up with the food. This aggregate portion, the stercomare, serves as a fill skeleton that subdivides the protoplasm into strands of permissible diameters. Vendobiont chambers contain no clay, but they were partly filled with loose sand. This is particularly obvious in sediment-sticking forms where the sand sank into the deeper parts of the

vertical quilts after death and kept them from collapsing, while the upper parts became compactionally deformed (Fig. 2). Since it would have been difficult for this sand to enter the closed quilts after death, it is more likely that the sand acted as a compartmentalizing fill skeleton in analogy to the xenophyophoran stercomare.

In conclusion, it is reasonable to assume that vendobionts are an extinct class of rhizopods that reached giant size by subdividing their multinucleate protoplasm by allometric quilts of membranous wall plus a sandy fill skeleton. The latter also allowed the wall to be perforated by pseudopodial pores without deflating.

The reinterpretation of the dominating Ediacaran body fossils, together with the recent interpretation of seemingly complex Ediacaran trace fossils as those chambered xenophyophores, dramatically reduces the number of Precambrian metazoans. What remains are simple worm burrows, rare impressions of polyps and sponges, and the death masks and radula scratches of a primitive mollusk—but no arthropods.

For background information *see* ANNELIDA; ARTHROPODA; COELENTERATA; EDIACARAN BIOTA; FORAMINIFERIDA; FOSSIL; GEOLOGIC TIME SCALE; PHYLOGENY in the McGraw-Hill Encyclopedia of Science & Technology.   Adolf Seilacher

Bibliography. M. F. Glaessner, *The Dawn of Animal Life: A Biohistoric Study*, Cambridge University Press, 1984; D. Grazhdankin and A. Seilacher, Underground Vendobionta from Namibia, *Paleontology*, 45:57–78, 2002; A. Seilacher, Vendobionta and Psammocorallia: Lost constructions of Precambrian evolution, *J. Geol. Soc., London*, 149:607–613, 1992.

Virtual musical instruments

Musical instruments can be simulated in real time by a computer program. For example, the acoustic response of a plucked guitar string can be calculated directly from its physical properties (mass, tension, length, and so forth) and the conditions of its excitation (pick position, pick hardness, and so forth). Such computational models provide extremely high quality virtual musical instruments, which are all-electronic while sounding entirely natural.

Physical models. Physical understanding of musical instruments is typically embodied in sets of differential equations specifying constraints on the possible acoustic motion of the physical system. Given an applied force f, the position x of a mass m at time t can be predicted by doubly integrating (up to time t) the acceleration a given by Newton's second law of motion, the differential equation $f = ma$.

Acoustically vibrating materials have elasticity as well as mass; that is, they behave like springs that "push back" when displaced. The ideal spring is described by Hooke's law, $f = -kx$, where the proportionality constant k is called the spring constant.

When a mass is attached to one end of a spring while the other end is rigidly fixed, a mass-spring oscillator is formed. It is described by differential equation (1), whose only solutions are sinusoidal

$$ma + kx = 0 \qquad (1)$$

motions of the form $A \sin(\omega t + p)$, where A is the amplitude, $\omega = \sqrt{k/m}$ is the radian frequency (2π times the number of oscillations per second), and p is the phase of the oscillation. The oscillation frequency ω is a property of the mass-spring oscillator and cannot be changed by the excitation conditions, but the phase is determined by exactly when the mass is set into motion, and the amplitude is determined by the initial displacement or velocity of the mass.

Acoustic differential equations. The differential equations used to describe vibrating strings, woodwind bores, the human vocal tract, horns, and the like are derived by applying Newton's second law and Hooke's law to differential volume elements (vanishingly small mathematical volumes) of the vibrating medium (string or air). For example, ideal vibrating strings (and acoustic tubes) are described by the one-dimensional lossless wave equation (2), where y

$$k\frac{\partial^2 y}{\partial x^2} = m\frac{\partial^2 y}{\partial t^2} \qquad (2)$$

denotes transverse string displacement (or longitudinal excess pressure in a tube), k is the string tension (or spring constant for air), and m is the mass per unit length along the string (or mass per unit volume in an acoustic tube). Finally, ∂ denotes a partial derivative, appropriate when differentiating with respect to one of two or more independent variables (time t and position x in this case). The wave equation is a statement of Newton's second law for the string on a microscopic scale: $k\partial^2 y/\partial x^2$ is the transverse restoring force on the string, while $m\partial^2 y/\partial t^2$ is the transverse acceleration on a differential element of the string.

Additional terms in the differential equation correspond to frictional forces. For example, adding a simple dynamic friction term to the differential equation for the mass-spring oscillator gives force equation (3), where v is the velocity of the mass

$$ma + kx + rv = 0 \qquad (3)$$

(now sliding on a surface exerting dynamic friction), and r is the dynamic friction coefficient. More generally, friction causes some energy of motion to be converted into heat. Friction (loss) nearly always increases with frequency in musical acoustics, and more terms in the differential equation are needed to impart this behavior to the model.

The stiffness of a piano string is a springlike force associated with bending the spring. It is modeled by a term proportional to the fourth derivative of string displacement with respect to position along the string axis, $\partial^4 y/\partial x^4$. Fixed wave shapes can propagate unchanged along ideal strings, while in a stiff string different frequency components propagate at different speeds, causing dispersion of the wave

shape. Friction terms cause propagating wave shapes to attenuate (decay toward zero). Waves get smoother as they decay, because the higher-frequency components decay faster than the low-frequency components.

Boundary conditions and forcing terms. As in the mass-spring oscillator, the differential equation describing a vibrating string or acoustic bore specifies a mathematical constraint on the space of possible vibrations. With the additional specification of boundary conditions and forcing terms, the equations can be solved numerically to obtain a unique solution. This solution specifies all details of the motion of the system, and it can therefore be used to compute the sound pressure at two ears in some location. In this way, natural-sounding virtual musical instruments may be synthesized.

Adding a forcing term to the differential equation for the mass-spring oscillator (with frictional damping) produces an equation of form (4), where $f(t)$

$$ma + rv + kx = f(t) \qquad (4)$$

is the force applied to the mass over time. Boundary conditions need not apply to the forced mass-spring oscillator because it is an ordinary differential equation, which involves differentiating functions of only a single variable (time). Alternatively, a plucked or struck mass may be modeled as an initial mass displacement or velocity, respectively, and no forcing function. Boundary conditions are needed for partial differential equations, which involve partial differentiation with respect to time and one or more spatial variables, and are used to describe distributed vibrating media such as strings and air. A common boundary condition for a vibrating string, for example, is that its end point at the "nut" of the instrument be rigidly terminated; that is, the boundary condition at the nut is defined as zero transverse displacement for all time t (at the value of x located on the boundary of the vibrating string).

Differential equations and boundary conditions are determined by the materials (type of wood or metal, properties of air) and the geometry of assembly (plate shape and thickness, string diameter and length, and so forth). In the course of playing a musical instrument, the performer may affect certain terms in the differential equations (for example, by bending a string to change its tension), or some boundary conditions (for example, by stopping a string at a particular fret along a guitar neck).

An exception is the piano, in which the differential equations and boundary conditions are essentially independent of the performance. The forcing function is typically defined as the force density along the string supplied by the felt-covered hammer; this force density is determined entirely by the hammer velocity, which is in turn determined by the integral of applied force during the stroke of the piano key.

Numerical solution. Any set of differential equations may be integrated numerically on a digital computer to obtain some quality of approximation to the ideal solution. Such a solution is generally not exact because numerical integration requires approximating infinitesimal differentials of the calculus by finite differences. For example, the first-order derivative with respect to time, $dx(t)/dt$, is usually approximated by a first-order time difference, expression (5), where T

$$\frac{x(t) - x(t - T)}{T} \qquad (5)$$

is the step size, chosen sufficiently small so that the approximation error lies within acceptable limits.

An example of numerical integration applied to the mass spring oscillator is obtained by writing its differential equation as (6); replacing $x(t)$ and $f(t)$ by

$$m\frac{d^2x(t)}{dt^2} + r\frac{dx(t)}{dt} + kx = f(t) \qquad (6)$$

their digitally sampled counterparts $x(nT)$ and $f(nT)$, where n is an integer; replacing the first time derivative $dx(t)/dt$ by a backward finite difference, expression (7); replacing $d^2x(t)/dt^2$ by a centered finite difference, expression (8); and solving for $x(nT + T)$

$$\frac{x(nT) - x(nT - T)}{T} \qquad (7)$$

$$\frac{x(nT + T) - 2x(nT) + x(nT - T)}{T^2} \qquad (8)$$

in terms of all other quantities. Then, starting at discrete time $n = 0$, given $x(0)$ and $x(-T)$, it is straightforward to compute $x(nT)$ for all $n = 1, 2, 3, \ldots$, given $f(nT)$.

Error audibility. In acoustic simulations for musical sound synthesis, the error that matters most is the audible error, not the error that is most naturally defined mathematically. As a result, the computations are arranged to yield zero audible error, even at a finite step size T. Since the bandwidth of human hearing is finite (nominally 20 Hz–20 kHz), sampling theory shows that it is usually a waste of computing power to use a step size T much less than 1/40,000 second, which is half of the smallest audible period. In particular, Shannon's sampling theorem proves that any band-limited signal $x(t)$ [such as any audio signal band-limited to the range of human hearing] can be exactly reconstructed from a set of uniform digital samples $x(nT)$, $n = \ldots, -2, -1, 0, 1, 2, \ldots$, provided the sampling rate $f_s = 1/T$ is higher than twice the highest frequency present in the signal. For audio signals, f_s must be greater than 40 kHz. Compact discs (CDs), for example, use $f_s = 44.1$ kHz.

Signal processing models. While numerical integration of the differential equations governing the motion of an acoustic system can provide a general solution, in principle, with an arbitrarily small approximation error, such a method does not readily yield a computational model that can execute in real time. For that goal, techniques from the field of digital signal processing have been applied to increase simulation speeds by many orders of magnitude while not significantly increasing the audible error.

Commutativity of LTI systems. One important principle used to speed up acoustic simulations is commutativity of linear time-invariant (LTI) systems. A system is generally defined as a processing operation normally having at least one input signal $x(t)$ and output signal $y(t)$. For a discrete-time system, the input and output signals are processed in sampled form, that is, $x(n)$ and $y(n)$, where $n = 0, 1, 2, \ldots$.

Time invariance means that the system itself does not change over time. A mass-spring oscillator is a time-invariant system provided the mass m and spring constant k are truly constants and do not change over time.

A linear time-invariant system is completely characterized by its transfer function, $H(z) = Y(z)/X(z)$, where $X(z)$ is the z transform of the input signal $x(n)$, and $Y(z)$ is the z transform of $y(n)$. The z transform is a generalization of the Fourier transform for discrete-time (sampled) signals. The Fourier transform measures the amount of each frequency present in a signal.

Commutativity means the same thing for linear time-invariant systems that it means in algebra; that is, the order of two operands can be interchanged. In algebra, multiplication of two real numbers a and b is commutative, that is, $ab = ba$. In linear systems theory, transfer functions are commutative; that is, $H_1(z)H_2(z) = H_2(z)H_1(z)$. The product of two transfer functions corresponds to feeding the output of one system as the input to the other. Thus, commutativity of linear time-invariant systems means that they can be interchanged. This basic principle has been used to simplify numerical simulation of musical instruments by many orders of magnitude.

Any linear differential equation with constant coefficients gives rise to a linear time-invariant simulation. In this case, the input signal is generally taken to be the forcing term, and the output signal is taken to be a simulated variable (string displacement or bore pressure) at a particular position over time. All the differential equations mentioned above satisfy these criteria.

Most differential equations describing vibrating systems in musical acoustics are linear time-invariant to a very good degree of approximation. Strongly nonlinear systems, whose nonlinearities must be taken into account before zero audible error can be achieved, include the sitar string and very loud horns. Time variation, on the other hand, is quite common, since normally system parameters (such as string or bore length) are varied over time to change the pitch of the tone produced. However, this normally does not invalidate a linear time-invariant model, because the changes are slow compared to a single cycle of vibration, and therefore the instruments can be modeled very effectively as piecewise time-invariant systems.

Lumping distributed losses. An important computational reduction made possible by commutativity of linear time-invariant systems is lumping of losses and dispersion in vibrating strings and acoustic tubes. When the numerical integration of the wave equation of a lossy, stiff system is regarded as a digital signal processing network, that network is linear time-invariant. Therefore, its series components can be commuted. The net effect is that all of the losses and dispersion in the string or bore can be concentrated at certain points without affecting simulation accuracy at those points. For example, if a string is excited at one end and observed at the other, it is possible to concentrate all of the losses near the observation end. If a new observation point is introduced, say, in the middle of the string, then for precise simulation a point of concentrated loss and dispersion should be introduced there as well. A point of concentrated loss or dispersion is implemented by a digital filter. Since most vibrating systems in the music world are close to lossless, these digital filters are usually very inexpensive computationally.

In summary, commutativity of linear time-invariant systems makes it possible to model lossy, dispersive strings and bores as exactly lossless, nondispersive (ideal) strings and bores, together with one or more digital filters implementing concentrated points of loss or dispersion. A wave travels unchanged along such a string until it reaches an observation point, where a digital filter attenuates and disperses it so that it looks (and sounds) identical to a full-blown numerical integration of the partial differential equation. This type of acoustic simulation is often called digital waveguide modeling.

Commuting strings and body resonators. A second use of commutativity in speeding up computational models of stringed musical instruments involves applying it on a larger scale to strings and body resonators, such as in guitars and pianos. In the schematic (9) of a

$$\text{excitation} \rightarrow \text{string} \rightarrow \text{body} \qquad (9)$$

guitar, the excitation is typically a pluck by a pick or finger. The string and body resonator are linear time-invariant to a high degree. Therefore they commute, and the guitar may instead be simulated as (10).

$$[\text{excitation} \rightarrow \text{body}] \rightarrow \text{string} \qquad (10)$$

Thus, the body resonator is "plucked" first, and the resulting signal is fed into the string. Since the excitation is a very simple signal (usually a single simple pulse), it is possible to cover the space of body excitation responses using a small set of stored tables. These tables take the place of a very large digital filter, which would otherwise be necessary to simulate the guitar body. Since the string is efficiently implemented as a digital waveguide, the overall simulation is so efficient that many different guitars can be simulated simultaneously in real time on a typical personal computer. This method of acoustic simulation is far faster than "brute force" numerical integration of the differential equations describing a guitar. For example, a digital waveguide string requires about three orders of magnitude less computation for the low E string of a guitar at the CD-quality sampling rate (44.1 kHz), and commuting the string and body yields another three orders of magnitude or so in

computational savings. Thus, commuted waveguide synthesis (for guitars) is on the order of a million times faster than basic numerical integration of the differential equations.

For background information *see* COMPACT DISK; CONTROL SYSTEMS; DIFFERENTIAL EQUATION; DIGITAL FILTER; FORCE; FORCED OSCILLATION; FOURIER SERIES AND TRANSFORMS; HARMONIC MOTION; LINEAR SYSTEM ANALYSIS; MUSICAL ACOUSTICS; MUSICAL INSTRUMENTS; NUMERICAL ANALYSIS; VIBRATION; Z TRANSFORM in the McGraw-Hill Encyclopedia of Science & Technology.   Julius O. Smith III

Bibliography. A. Askenfelt (ed.), *Five Lectures on the Acoustics of the Piano*, Royal Swedish Academy of Music, Stockholm, 1990; N. H. Fletcher and T. D. Rossing, *The Physics of Musical Instruments*, 2d ed., Springer-Verlag, New York, 1998; J. Strikwerda, *Finite Difference Schemes and Partial Differential Equations*, Wadsworth and Brooks, Pacific Grove, CA, 1989.

Virtual operant conditioning

Operant conditioning procedures that are used to shape animal behavior typically incorporate paradigms in which the animals are taught to produce specific actions in response to different sensory cues (for example, sounds and lights) in order to obtain rewards such as food and water. Such procedures are widely employed for studying animal behavior in the laboratory; outside the laboratory, they are often employed to train animals in useful tasks. Their efficacy depends on the ability of an animal to learn the relationship between its own response and external events such as cues and rewards. Because of this, traditional operant procedures are constrained by the need to physically deliver, and accurately time, cues and rewards. It is difficult, for example, to apply the traditional operant conditioning paradigm to freely moving animals (such as rats) outside particular laboratory environments, in areas where accurate delivery of cues and rewards cannot generally be guaranteed.

Virtual learning. One way to circumvent the physical limitations surrounding the delivery of cues and rewards is to use known properties of brain stimulation. It has long been known that mild electric stimulation of brain regions such as the medial forebrain bundle is rewarding, in that animals willingly learn to perform actions in order to obtain such stimulation. Similarly, it is also known that stimulation of many brain locations can cue the performance of learned actions in animals. For example, studies show that stimulation within the somatosensory cortex of the monkey brain can mimic normal touch sensations, and animals can learn to recognize such sensations as cues to perform certain actions.

Although knowledge of such phenomena has been well documented, studies thus far have been generally concerned with their underlying neural mechanisms; little thought has been given to the

Fig. 1. Rat with a backpack being navigated along a railway line.

potential of operant conditioning paradigms constructed wholly around virtual cues and rewards delivered by microstimulation of key areas of an animal's brain. The advantages of this virtual learning method are many: (1) cues and rewards can be delivered independent of any external physical apparatus, along with precise control of their timing and saliency; (2) the rewarding efficacy of medial forebrain bundle stimulation is relatively nonsatiating, and animals need not initiate consummatory behaviors to obtain them; and (3) additional richness of behavior can be obtained by delivering brain stimulation to the animal remotely via programmable wireless interfaces.

This method has been used to develop a behavioral model in which an operator is able to guide distant and freely moving animals in the same manner as "intelligent" robots. Specifically, using medial forebrain bundle stimulation as reward, rats have been trained to interpret stimulations within their somatosensory cortices as cues for directing their trajectory of motion. Brain stimulation was delivered remotely so that an operator was able to steer the rats over any arbitrarily specified route and over different real-world terrains (**Fig. 1**).

Methods. Rats were implanted with fine wire electrodes (100 micrometers in diameter) placed in three brain locations: the medial forebrain bundle and the right and left somatosensory cortical whisker representations (SI region). Five days later, a backpack containing a microcontroller, a radio-frequency receiver, and a battery was mounted on the rat. The outputs of the microcontroller, which functioned as a programmable stimulator, made connections with a skull-top adapter housing the ends of the implanted electrodes. This arrangement allowed an operator, who ran a simple program on a laptop computer connected to an ultrahigh-frequency transmitter, to directly deliver stimulation to any of the three implanted brain sites. Radio contact was achievable at distances of up to 500–700 m. Each stimulation consisted of a train of stimulus pulses, typically ten 5-volt, 0.5-millisecond biphasic pulses at 100 Hz. Stimulus currents were approximately 80 microamperes.

Training. The rats learned to navigate three-dimensional terrains within 10 days in daily 10-min sessions. In stage I, the animals were placed in an enclosed figure-8 maze where medial forebrain bundle stimulations (0.3–3 Hz) rewarded continuous forward locomotion. Within the first session, the rats learned to run continuously. In stage II, SI brain-stimulation cues for turning left or right were presented at all choice points in the maze. In order to issue a right-turn command, for example, the left brain whisker representation was stimulated. Since the facial whisker regions are mapped onto the opposite cortical hemisphere, the rat would be expected to perceive this stimulation as a touch to its right whiskers. Medial forebrain bundle rewards were immediately given for correct turns but were withheld for approximately 5 s after incorrect turns. Within a week, all animals performed with >99% turning accuracy.

In stage III, the animals were placed in large open spaces to test if they would follow commands in environments that lacked the rectilinear structure of the maze. All rats quickly generalized their task to their new surroundings. To gain medial forebrain bundle rewards, they ran forward and turned correctly and instantaneously on cue (latency 100–500 ms). Since the turn angles were not explicitly shaped, each animal developed its own characteristic angle of turn (from 20 to 90°, with some variation between the angles of left and right turns). Two or more sequential SI cues tended to summate, generating turns of successively greater turn angles. This allowed the operator to easily steer the rats over any prescribed path (**Fig. 2a**).

Performance. Stage IV evaluated the method's ability to navigate animals over three-dimensional structures. This was achieved by incorporating a curious property of medial forebrain bundle stimulation. It was found that medial forebrain bundle stimulation not only rewarded forward locomotion but also initiated further locomotion. (This property reflects the known priming effect of medial forebrain bundle stimulation, which produces motivational task-related actions.) Thus the rats would begin purposeful forward motion only when medial forebrain bundle stimulation commenced, indicating that medial forebrain bundle stimulation itself served as an effective cue—a go-forward command. On approaching objects such as a high step, go-forward medial forebrain bundle stimulations would persuade the rats to climb or to descend from it. As a rule, the number of stimulations required was proportional to the difficulty of the obstacle ahead. Thus, superimposing go-forward cues over the standard directional cues and rewards was sufficient to steer the rats through a wide variety of novel and difficult terrains (Fig. 2b).

Tests showed that rats could be easily steered through pipes and across elevated runways and ledges and could be made to climb or jump from any surface that offered sufficient footing (for example, trees). Of particular interest was the operator's

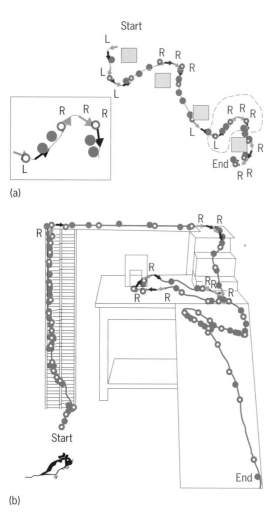

(a)

(b)

Fig. 2. Guided rat navigation using brain microstimulation. Both examples are sketches constructed from digitized video recordings. Unfilled circles indicate rat head positions at 1-s intervals; filled circles indicate positions at which medial forebrain bundle rewards were given; gray arrows indicate positions at which right (R) or left (L) directional cues were issued; black arrows indicate positions 0.5 s after directional commands. (a) A rat guided through a slalom course. The inset details the events that take place inside the broken-line enclosure. (b) A rat guided through a three-dimensional obstacle course: it was instructed to climb a vertical ladder, cross a narrow ledge, go down steps, thread through a hoop (book-end), and then walk/slide down a steep (70°) ramp.

ability to guide rats in systematically exploring large rubble piles of collapsed concrete structures. Finally, the animals were easily directed through environments that they would normally avoid, such as brightly lit wide-open outdoor arenas. The rats moved at speeds averaging approximately 0.3 m/s and worked continuously for periods up to the 1-h test limit.

Applications. The performance of the guided rats suggests that virtual learning methods using direct and instantaneous access to the central generators of cues and rewards, can exert powerful real-time control over behavior. It allows animals to be conditioned to perform tasks that may not be appropriate for traditional operant procedures, thus

expanding the scope of operant conditioning. The method gets its power by dissociating explicit variables such as cues and rewards from the physical variables normally associated with their delivery, lending a freedom from mechanical and parametric constraints on learning imposed by particular physical settings. Since virtual cues and rewards are perceived within a body-centered frame of reference, they may facilitate the learning of behaviors independent of external environmental contexts. The guided rat, for example, is able to generalize a minimal set of operator commands to its current environmental context, which may be novel, complex, and changing. It may also be possible to increase the "bandwidth" of conditionable sensory information by stimulating a multiplicity of sites in the brain, thus increasing the complexity of elicited behaviors. In this manner, commands other than go-forward or turn left or right (for example, stop, go-up/down, faster/slower) could also be interleaved into the program.

Virtual learning may be used to develop similar simple and powerful models for the study of almost any animal behavior. The guided rat, for instance, may have implications for new neurophysiological studies of directed animal navigation and spatial learning. The concept could also find use in more practical arenas such as robotics, representing a new extension for operant conditioning. As it stands, the guided rat is an effective mobile robot platform possessing several natural advantages over present-day mobile robots. By comparison, a living organism such as the rat has far greater maneuverability and navigation skills over unpredictable and complex terrains. Examples of real-world applications of such a technology could include search and rescue in areas of urban destruction, demining, and perhaps surveillance operations. For guided rats to be effective in such environments—which are unlikely to be in line-of-sight—information about their location and surroundings will be necessary. Suitable electronic sensor and navigation technologies (for example, miniature video cameras and global positioning systems) in addition to adequate wireless links will, therefore, play a role in their development. Interestingly, it may soon be possible to overcome many limitations of current electronic sensor technologies with the ability to remotely receive and accurately interpret brain sensory activity. For example, it may be possible to identify specific odors by their neural signatures in the olfactory regions of an animal's brain. With suitable sensory implants, the guided rat could then function not only as a mobile robot but also as a biological sensor.

For background information *see* BEHAVIORAL PSYCHOPHYSICS; BRAIN; CONDITIONED REFLEX; INSTRUMENTAL CONDITIONING; LEARNING MECHANISMS; MOTIVATION in the McGraw-Hill Encyclopedia of Science & Technology.   Sanjiv K. Talwar;
Shaohua Xu; John K. Chapin

Bibliography. J. A. Deutsch, Learning and electrical self-stimulation of the brain, *J. Theoret. Biol.*, 4:193–214, 1963; R. W. Doty, Electrical stimulation of the brain in behavioral context, *Ann. Rev. Psychol.*, 20:289–320, 1969; C. R. Gallistel, The incentive of brain-stimulation reward, *J. Comp. Physiol. Psychol.*, 69:713–721, 1969; M. E. Olds and J. L. Fobes, The central basis of motivation: Intracranial self-stimulation studies, *Ann. Rev. Psychol.*, 32:523–574, 1981; R. Romo et al., Sensing without touching: Psychophysical performance based on cortical microstimulation, *Neuron*, 26:273–278, 2000; B. F. Skinner, *The Behavior of Organisms: An Experimental Analysis*, Appleton-Century-Crofts, New York, 1938.

Wood composites

Composites are the fastest-growing area of wood products for housing and industrial applications. Most wood composites are a substitute for a solid wood product. The raw materials for wood composites include a wood base (fiber, particle, strand, or strip) combined with various adhesives, waxes, or other nonwood materials to produce a panel or lumber product. Both wood composite panels and composite lumber products can be used for structural or nonstructural purposes, depending upon the end use for which they are manufactured. Structural applications are those with specific strength requirements, such as wall sheathing, framing, decking, and flooring. Nonstructural applications involve the use of wood composites as substrates for decorative overlays, moldings, window and door parts, and other nonload-bearing uses.

Particleboard and medium-density fiberboard. The most important nonstructural panel composites are particleboard and medium-density fiberboard. Both are used extensively in furniture, cabinet manufacture, and flooring, forming the substrate over which various types of overlays are applied. These overlays are made of materials such as vinyl, melamine, foils, and paper, and can achieve an almost infinite number of finishes that imitate natural materials, such as wood and stone, or can produce any of a number of decorative effects. For these applications, a smooth, hard, durable panel face is essential, because the overlays can be extremely thin, allowing any underlying imperfections to show through. For this reason, composite manufacturers have continually focused on creating technologies that refine the surface of particleboard and medium-density fiberboard.

Particleboard production. Particleboard was created in Germany in the early 1930s, a result of the country's effort to use its timber supply more efficiently. Since then, the technology of particleboard production has advanced tremendously, although the basic materials remain the same. Particleboard is made from wood particles. These particles are combined with a synthetic resin or some suitable binder and bonded together under heat and pressure in a hot press. The average pressing temperature ranges from 300 to 340°F (149 to 171°C). The pressing cycle of particleboard manufacture is regressive: the cycle begins at 2500 pounds per square inch (psi) and is reduced to about 400 psi as the cycle ends. Each cycle takes only a few minutes, the length of time depending on the thickness of the panel being produced. Common thicknesses range from 1/4″ to 1-1/8″, in 1/16″ increments. The resulting panel consists of about 92% wood particles, 3% moisture content, and approximately 5% nonvolatile adhesive residues. Particleboard is produced in several industrial grades, floor underlayment, mobile home decking, and door core. Particleboard can be further processed by sanding, creating a smooth hard face.

Medium-density fiberboard production. The first production facility for medium-density fiberboard was established in Deposit, New York, in the late 1960s and is still producing medium-density fiberboard today. The creation of medium-density fiberboard was the result of a search to find a better substrate than particleboard. The basic technology for producing medium-density fiberboard already existed in the mechanical pulping process of paper manufacture. The union of this mechanical pulping process with some of the adhesives already in use in particleboard manufacture produced the desired substrate, medium-density fiberboard.

Medium-density fiberboard differs from particleboard primarily in the method of fiber preparation. Particleboard is made from ground wood particles, (which can vary in size), whereas medium-density fiberboard panels are made of wood fibers. The difference between a wood particle and a wood fiber is significant. The raw material for particleboard is made from a grinding process; however, medium-density fiberboard is the result of fibers derived from a "cooking" process that separates the cellulose fibers from lignin, the natural bonding agent in wood. Once the lignin is removed, the remaining cellulose fibers have extreme uniformity, providing a raw material from which a consistent and uniform panel, having an almost mirrorlike smooth face, can be produced. The heat and pressure ranges used in medium-density fiberboard hot presses are similar to those used in particleboard. Medium-density fiberboard is produced in varying density, ranging from 31 to 55 lb/ft³, with the density depending on the desired end use.

End uses. Particleboard and medium-density fiberboard are superior among solid wood substitutes. As elements in ready-to-assemble furniture, electronic case goods, kitchen cabinets, office furniture, and a host of other applications, they are unparalleled among wood composites (see **illus.**). Medium-density fiberboard, especially, is a versatile material; it is easily cut into complex shapes or profiled into moldings or decorative panels that have sharp edges and high machinability (are easily worked).

The wide range of overlays available to manufacturers can be used to create panels rivaling natural wood grains in appearance (so accurately that consumers have difficulty distinguishing natural graining from overlays). In addition, these composites provide unrivaled substrates for trendy, colorful

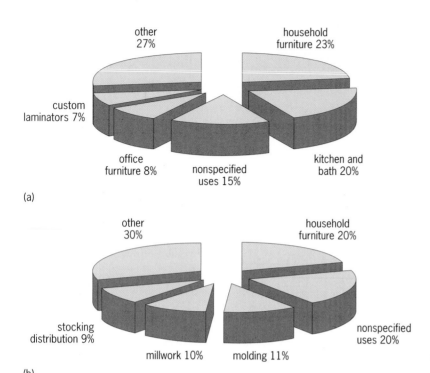

(a)

(b)

Primary end uses for (a) particleboard and (b) medium-density fiberboard in North America in 2000. (*Composite Panel Association*)

countertops, furniture, cabinets, and displays. New developments in overlay technology include processes to imitate stones, from smooth marble to rough cobblestone. In addition, complex pressed door faces are now created with new embossing and profiling techniques. These composites are popular among designers and modern consumers because they can be manipulated creatively, at a cost below that of solid wood.

Oriented strand board. Oriented strand board is the most important structural panel composite in the world market. Today's oriented strand board is at least a third-generation product that began in the early part of the twentieth century with prototypes of waferboard technology (developed in the Great Lakes area to create a viable commercial use for the high volume of aspen trees that grow abundantly there). A wafer is a thin flake of wood, about $1\frac{1}{8}$ in. wide and $2\frac{3}{8}$ in. long. Early experiments with wafer technology did not attract a suitable commercial response; however, in the late 1970s and early 1980s, technological advancements created a combination of wood wafers and suitable binders to overcome some of the early problems, such as warping, racking, edge swell, and moisture penetration. Once suitable adhesives and pressing techniques were devised, the product began to enter the structural panel market as a rival for sheathing plywood.

Production. The move from waferboard to oriented strand board was enabled by technological advancements in strand board production. Initial waferboard production techniques used random-shaped wood wafers and glued them together in a random pattern;

however, technicians eventually found that strands of wood about 1-1/8″ wide by 2-5/8″ long would bind together much more strongly. This discovery overcame much of the racking and warping of early waferboard production. Furthermore, it was discovered that if these strands of wood were oriented in layers at right angles to each other, the bond became significantly greater. Hence, the name "oriented strand board" reflects the production process.

Today's oriented strand board production technology uses even longer strands to create a stronger panel. Each panel of oriented strand board has at least five strand layers, oriented in alternating right-angle layers to each other. Most oriented strand board is manufactured with phenolic resins, although some manufacturers use an isocyanate resin for some specialty products. Oriented strand board is produced in hot presses at temperatures and pressures similar to those used in particleboard and medium-density fiberboard manufacture.

Commercial growth. In the 1980s, oriented strand board found commercial success in the North American construction markets. In the 1990s, it became a major rival for plywood, taking much of the market share from sheathing plywood. In 1999, oriented strand board production surpassed that of plywood in North America. Total production of oriented strand board in North America in 1990 was 7.649 billion square feet (3/8″ basis). In 2000, total North American oriented strand board production had risen to 20.650 billion square feet (3/8″ basis). In that same time span, annual production of plywood in North America fell from 23.216 billion square feet (1990) to 19.675 billion square feet (2000).

Benefits of composites. What makes composites so attractive and creates such an expanding array of end uses? First, they are extremely practical from an environmental perspective. Composites are made from a wide variety of renewable raw materials, such as waste wood products, recycled fiber, trees too small for other commercial applications, combinations of recycled wood and recycled plastic, and agricultural fiber (such as straw). Second, composites employ highly efficient, labor-saving processing techniques, enabling them to be cost-efficient and competitive with solid wood products. Third, some composites can be machined and profiled in numerous ways, enabling designers to customize them for a wide variety of home and office uses. Finally, composite technology has progressed to the point where composites simply do the job better than some of the solid wood competition. Thus, environmental sensitivity, higher-efficiency production, lower production costs, and wide end-use applicability have created a formula for success.

For background information *see* WOOD ENGINEERING DESIGN; WOOD PRODUCTS; WOOD PROPERTIES in the McGraw-Hill Encyclopedia of Science & Technology.   Sam Sherrill

Bibliography. *Panel Trends, 2002*, Composite Panel Association, Gaithersburg, MD, 2002; *Regional*

Production and Market Outlook for Structural Panels and Engineered Wood Products, 2002–2007, APA—The Engineered Wood Association, Tacoma, WA, 2002; *Wood Product Demand and the Environment,* Proceedings of an International Conference Sponsored by the Forest Products Research Society, Madison, WI, 1992; *Wood Products for Engineered Structures: Issues Affecting Growth and Acceptance of Engineered Wood Products,* Forest Products Research Society, Madison, WI, 1993.

Wood preservation

When wood is exposed to various environmental conditions, many degradation reactions (biological, ultraviolet, mechanical, moisture, and chemical) can occur. To protect wood from biological degradation, chemical preservatives are applied by nonpressure or pressure treatment. Penetration and retention of a chemical depend upon the wood species and the amount of heartwood (more difficult to treat) or sapwood (easier to treat). The objective of adding preservatives is to achieve long-term effectiveness for the wood product, thus sequestering (capturing and storing) carbon.

With the recent voluntary decision by United States and Canadian industries to phase out arsenic-containing pressure-treated wood for residential uses (for example, play structures, decks, picnic tables, landscaping timbers, residential fencing, patios, and walkways/boardwalks), alternative preservatives such as ammoniacal copper quat (ACQ) and copper azole (CBA) are replacing the most widely used chromated copper arsenate (CCA) treatments. By 2004, the U.S. Environmental Protection Agency (EPA) will not allow CCA products for any residential uses. However, it has not concluded that CCA-treated wood that is currently used in or near the home or that remains available in stores poses unreasonable risks to the public. Beyond these replacements for CCA may be wood protection systems based on nontoxic chemical modifications to prevent biological degradation. Chemical modification alters the chemical structure of the wood components, thereby reducing the biodegradability of the wood and increasing its dimensional stability when in contact with moisture.

Preservatives. Wood preservatives can be divided into (1) oil-type, such as creosote and petroleum solutions of pentachlorophenol, and (2) waterborne salts that are applied as solutions, such as CCA, ACQ, and CBA. The effectiveness of each preservative can vary greatly, depending upon its chemical composition, retention, depth of penetration, and ultimately the exposure conditions of the final product.

Exposure conditions. There are three exposure categories: (1) ground contact (high decay hazard; product is usually pressure-treated); (2) aboveground contact (low decay hazard; product is not usually pressure-treated), and (3) marine exposure (high decay hazard; product often needs a dual treatment).

Wood preservatives should always be used under ground (soil) contact and marine (salt-water) exposure conditions. Oil-borne preservatives such as creosote and solutions with heavy, less volatile petroleum oils often help protect wood from weathering; however, they may adversely influence its cleanliness, odor, color, paintability, and fire performance. Waterborne preservatives are often used when cleanliness and paintability of the treated wood are required. In seawater exposure, a dual treatment (waterborne copper-containing salt preservatives followed by creosote) is most effective against all types of marine borers.

Exposure conditions and length of product lifetime need to be considered when choosing a particular preservative treatment, process, and wood species. All these factors are considered by the consensus technical committees in setting reference levels required in the American Wood-Preservers' Association (AWPA), the American Society for Testing and Materials International (ASTM), and the Federal Specification Standards.

Efficacy. The efficacy of a particular preservative and treatment process depends on four basic requirements: toxicity, permanence, retention, and depth of penetration into the wood. Toxicity refers to a preservative's effectiveness against biological organisms, such as decay fungi, insects, and marine borers, that attack wood. The active ingredients in wood preservative formulations are many and varied, each has its own mode of action, and some of these modes are still unknown or unreported. In general, mechanisms of toxicity involve denaturation of proteins, inactivation of enzymes, cell membrane disruption (causing an increase in cell permeability), and inhibition of protein synthesis. Permanence refers to the resistance of the preservative to leaching, volatilization, and breakdown. Retention specifies the amount of preservative that must be impregnated into a specific volume of wood to meet standards and to ensure that the product will be effective against numerous biological agents (see **table**).

Evaluation of the efficacy of preservative-treated wood is performed first on small specimens in the laboratory and then on larger specimens in the field. The Forest Products Laboratory of the U.S. Department of Agriculture Forest Service has been conducting in-ground stake test studies on southern pine sapwood since 1938 in Saucier, Mississippi, and Madison, Wisconsin. These test sites expose the wood to decay and/or termite attack. A comparison of preservative-treated small wood panels exposed to a marine environment in Key West, Florida, has also been conducted. Such outdoor evaluations compare various preservatives and retention levels under each exposure condition at each individual site. The preservatives and treatments tested include creosotes, waterborne preservatives, dual treatments, chemical modification of wood, and various chemically modified polymers.

Retention levels of creosote and some waterborne preservatives for lumber, timbers, and plywood exposed to various conditions*

Preservative	Preservative retention, kg/m^3 (lb/ft^3)		
	Salt water†	Ground contact and fresh water	Above ground
Creosote	400 (25)	160 (10)	128 (8)
CCA (types I, II, or III)	40 (2.50)	6.4 (0.40)	4.0 (0.25)
ACQ (types B or D)	NR	6.4 (0.40)	4.0 (0.25)
CDDC as Cu	NR	3.2 (0.20)	1.6 (0.10)
CC	40 (2.50)	6.4 (0.40)	4.0 (0.25)
CBA (type A)	NR	NR	3.27 (0.20)

*Retention levels are those included in Federal Specification TT-W-571 and Commodity Standards of the American Wood-Preservers' Association. CCA = chromated copper arsenate, ACQ = ammoniacal copper quat, CDDC = copper bis(dimethyldithiocarbamate), Cu = copper, CC = ammoniacal copper citrate, CBA = copper azole, and NR = not recommended.
† Dual treatments are recommended when marine borer activity is known to be high.

Timber preparation and conditioning. Preparing timber for treatment involves carefully peeling the round or slabbed products to enable the wood to dry more quickly. Drying the wood before treatment opens up checks (small cracks) before the preservative is applied, thus increasing penetration and reducing the risk of checks opening up after treatment and exposing unpenetrated wood. Drying also helps to prevent decay, insect damage, and staining, but when treating with waterborne preservatives by certain diffusion methods, high moisture content levels may be permitted.

Treating plants that use pressure processes can condition green material (newly cut trees) by means other than air and kiln drying, thus avoiding a long delay and possible deterioration. When green wood is to be treated under pressure, one of several methods for conditioning may be selected. A steaming-and-vacuum process is used mainly for southern pines, and a boiling-under-vacuum (Boulton) process is used for Douglas-fir and sometimes hardwoods.

Heartwood of some softwood and hardwood species can be difficult to treat. Wood that is resistant to penetration by preservatives, such as Douglas-fir, western hemlock, western larch, and heartwood, may be incised before treatment to permit deeper and more uniform penetration. Incision involves passing the lumber or timbers through rollers that are equipped with teeth that sink into the wood to a predetermined depth, usually 13–19 mm ($^1/_2$–$^3/_4$ in.). The incisions open cell lumens along the grain, which improves penetration but can result in significant strength reduction. As much cutting and hole boring of the wood product as is possible should be done before the preservative treatment; otherwise untreated interiors will allow ready access of decay fungi or insects.

Treatment processes. There are two general types of wood preservation methods: pressure processes and nonpressure processes. During pressure processes, wood is impregnated with preservatives in a closed vessel above atmospheric pressure. In commercial practice, wood is put on cars or trams and run into a long steel cylinder, which is then closed and filled with preservative. Pressure forces are then applied until the desired amount of preservative has been absorbed into the wood.

Pressure processes. Three pressure processes are commonly used: full-cell, modified full-cell, and empty-cell. The full-cell process is used when the retention of a maximum quantity of preservative is desired. The steps include: sealing the wood in a treating cylinder and applying a vacuum for a half-hour or more to remove air from the cylinder and wood; admitting the preservative (at ambient or elevated temperature) to the cylinder without breaking the vacuum; applying pressure until the required retention is attained; and withdrawing the preservative from the cylinder. In addition, a short final vacuum may be applied to free the wood from dripping preservative.

The modified full-cell process is basically the same as the full-cell process except for the amount of initial vacuum and the occasional use of an extended final vacuum.

The goal of the empty-cell process is to obtain deep penetration with relatively low net retention of preservative; because a smaller amount of the chemical is used in this process, it is less costly and more environmentally friendly than full-cell processes. Two empty-cell processes (the Rueping and the Lowry) use the expansive force of compressed air to drive out part of the preservative absorbed during the pressure period. The Rueping empty-cell process is often called the empty-cell process with initial air. Air pressure is forced into the treating cylinder, which contains the wood, and then the preservative is forced into the cylinder. The air escapes into an equalizing or Rueping tank. The treating pressure is increased and maintained until the desired retention is attained. The preservative is drained, and a final vacuum is applied to remove surplus preservative. The Lowry process is the same as the Rueping except that there is no initial air pressure or vacuum applied. Hence, it is often called the empty-cell process without initial air pressure.

Nonpressure processes. The numerous nonpressure processes differ widely in their penetration and retention of a preservative. Nonpressure methods include surface applications of preservative by brushing or brief dipping; cold soaking in preservative oils or steeping in solutions of waterborne preservative; diffusion processes with waterborne preservatives; and vacuum treatment.

Purchasing and handling of treated wood. The EPA regulates pesticides, of which wood preservatives are one type. Preservatives that are not restricted by the EPA are available to the general consumer for nonpressure treatments, whereas the sale of others is restricted to only certified pesticide applicators. These preservatives can be used in only certain applications and are categorized as "restricted use." Restricted use refers to the chemical preservative, not to the treated wood product. The general consumer may buy and use wood products treated with restricted-use pesticides; the EPA does not consider treated wood a toxic substance, nor is it regulated as a pesticide.

Consumer Safety Information Sheets (EPA-approved) are available from retailers of treated wood products. The sheets provide users with information about the preservative and the use and disposal of treated-wood products. There are consumer information sheets for three major groups of wood preservatives: creosote pressure-treated wood, pentachlorophenol pressure-treated wood, and inorganic arsenical pressure-treated wood.

There are two important factors to consider when deciding which preservative-treated wood to choose, depending upon the intended end use of the wood: the grade or appearance of the lumber and the quality of the preservative treatment in the lumber. The U.S. Department of Commerce American Lumber Standard Committee (ALSC), an accrediting agency for treatment quality assurance, has an ink stamp or end tag for each grade stamp and quality mark. These marks indicate that the producer of the treated-wood product subscribes to an independent inspection agency. The stamp or end tag contains the type of preservative or active ingredient, the retention level, and the intended exposure conditions. Retention levels are usually provided in pounds of preservatives per cubic foot of wood and are specific to the type of preservative, wood species, and intended exposure conditions. (Note that mention of a chemical in this article does not constitute a recommendation; only chemicals registered by the EPA may be recommended.)

For background information *see* CREOSOTE; ENVIRONMENTAL TOXICOLOGY; WOOD DEGRADATION; WOOD PROPERTIES in the McGraw-Hill Encyclopedia of Science & Technology.   Rebecca E. Ibach

Bibliography. *Annual Book of ASTM Standards*, American Society for Testing and Materials, Section 4: Construction, and Volume 04.10: Wood, 2000; *AWPA 2001 Book of Standards*, American Wood-Preservers' Association, 2001; R. M. Rowell, Chemical modification of wood, *Handbook on Wood and Cellulosic Materials*, ed. by D. N.-S. Hon and N. Shiraishi, Marcel Dekker, New York, 1991; *Chromated Copper Arsenate (CCA)*, Canadian Pest Management Regulatory Agency, 2002; B. R. Johnson and D. I. Gutzmer, *Comparison of Preservative Treatments in Marine Exposure of Small Wood Panels*, USDA Forest Service, Forest Products Laboratory, FPL-RN-0258; D. I. Gutzmer and D. M. Crawford, *Comparison of Wood Preservatives in Stake Tests*, USDA Forest Service, Forest Products Laboratory, FPL-RN-02; *Fungicide: Pentachlorophenol*, U.S. Federal Supply Service, 1969; J. D. MacLean, Preservation of wood by pressure methods, *Agriculture Handbook 40*, USDA Forest Service, 1952; D. L. Cassens et al., *Selection and Use of Preservative-treated Wood*, Forest Products Society, 1995; *Whitman Announces Transition from Consumer Use of Treated Wood Containing Arsenic*, U.S. Environmental Protection Agency, 2002; R. A. Eaton and M. D. Hale, *Wood: Decay, Pests and Protection*, Chapman & Hall, New York, 1993; *Wood Handbook: Wood as an Engineering Material*, USDA Forest Service, Forest Products Laboratory, 1999; *Wood Preservation Treating Practices*, U.S. Federal Supply Service, 1968.

Contributors

Contributors

The affiliation of each Yearbook contributor is given, followed by the title of his or her article. An article title with the notation "in part" indicates that the author independently prepared a section of an article; "coauthored" indicates that two or more authors jointly prepared an article or section.

A

Abbatt, Prof. Jonathan. *Department of Chemistry, University of Toronto, Ontario, Canada.* AEROSOL-CLIMATE INTERACTIONS.

Abbott, Jack W. *President, AOC, Inc., Virginia.* SHIP DESIGN.

Ache, Dr. Barry. *Whitney Laboratory, St. Augustine, Florida.* CRUSTACEAN OLFACTORY ORGAN.

Albert, Dr. Victor A. *Natural History Museums and Botanical Garden, University of Oslo, Norway.* GENETICS OF FLOWER MORPHOLOGY.

Andrews, Prof. David. *Department of Mechanical Engineering, University College, London, United Kingdom.* NAVAL SURFACE SHIP.

Arlotta, Dr. Paola. *Research Fellow, Center for Nervous System Repair, Massachusetts General Hospital and Harvard Medical School, Boston.* NEUROGENESIS—coauthored.

Arya, Dr. Naveen. *University of Toronto, Ontario, Canada.* HEPATITIS C—coauthored.

Asher, Dr. David J. *Armagh Observatory, Armagh, United Kingdom, and Japan Spaceguard Association.* METEOR STORMS.

B

Bahn, Dr. Paul G. *Freelance archeologist, Yorkshire, England.* ORIGINS OF SYMBOLISM.

Bambach, Dr. Richard K. *Professor Emeritus, Virginia Technical, Blacksburg, and Associate of the Harvard Herbaria, Cambridge, Massachusetts.* PHANEROZOIC MARINE DIVERSITY.

Bank, Dr. Ruud A. *TNO Prevention and Health, Leiden, The Netherlands.* ADVANCED GLYCATION END PRODUCTS—coauthored.

Barker, Dr. Charles. *U.S. Geological Service, Denver Federal Center, Denver, Colorado.* COALBED METHANE.

Barraclough, Dr. Timothy G. *Royal Society University Research Fellow, Department of Biological Sciences, Impe-*rial College, Ascot, Berkshire, United Kingdom. PHYLOGENY AND SPECIATION PROCESSES.

Barthlott, Prof. Wilhelm. *Botanisches Insitut und Botanischer Garten, Universität Bonn, Germany.* EPICUTICULAR WAXES (BOTANY)—coauthored.

Basso, Dr. Federica. *Senior Fellow, Metabolic Diseases Branch, National Heart, Lung, and Blood Institute, National Institutes of Health, Bethesda, Maryland.* ABC LIPID TRANSPORTERS—coauthored.

Berezdivin, Dr. Robert. *Raytheon Information and Advanced Systems, Falls Church, Virginia.* MOBILE COMMUNICATIONS.

Bhunia, Dr. Arun K. *Associate Professor, Department of Food Science, Purdue University, West Lafayette, Indiana.* PATHOGEN DETECTION, FOOD-BORNE—coauthored.

Bingham, Prof. Carrol. *Department of Physics, University of Tennessee, Knoxville.* NUCLEAR DECAY—coauthored.

Bishop, Dr. David J. *Lucent Technologies, Murray Hill, New Jersey.* MICRO-OPTO-ELECTRO-MECHANICAL SYSTEMS.

Blair, Dr. David F. *Professor of Biology, University of Utah, Salt Lake City.* ROTARY MOTORS (BACTERIAL)—coauthored.

Bolger, Phil. *Gloucester, Massachusetts.* SAILING CRAFT.

Borengasser, Dr. Marcus. *Program Manager, GIS/Remote Sensing, Midwest Research Institute, Palm Bay, Florida.* HYPERSPECTRAL REMOTE SENSING.

Branham, Dr. Marc. *Postdoctoral Researcher, American Museum of Natural History, New York.* BIOLUMINESCENCE IN INSECTS—coauthored.

Briskman, Robert D. *Technical Executive, Sirius Satellite Radio, Inc., New York.* SATELLITE RADIO.

Broadley, R. Adam. *Newtown, Australia.* BIOLUMINESCENCE IN INSECTS—in part.

Brown, Dr. Timothy M. *National Center for Atmospheric Research, Boulder, Colorado.* EXTRASOLAR PLANETS—coauthored.

Bryant, Prof. Steven. *Assistant Professor, Department of Petroleum and Geosystems Engineering, University of Texas at Austin.* MICROBIAL ENHANCED OIL RECOVERY—coauthored.

Bud'ko, Dr. Sergey. *Associate Physicist, Ames Laboratory, Iowa State University, Ames.* MAGNESIUM DIBORIDE SUPERCONDUCTORS—coauthored.

Busch, Christopher. *Philips Research Laboratories, Eindhoven, The Netherlands.* ULTRAHIGH-DENSITY STORAGE—coauthored.

Byrne, Dr. Richard W. *Professor of Evolutionary Psychology, University of St. Andrews, Fife, Scotland.* APE COGNITION.

C

Canfield, Dr. Paul C. *Professor, Department of Physics and Astronomy, Senior Physicist, Ames Laboratory, Iowa State University, Ames.* MAGNESIUM DIBORIDE SUPERCONDUCTORS—coauthored.

Carter, Dr. James E., III. *Center for Molecular Biology and Gene Therapy, Loma Linda University, Loma Linda, California.* TRANSGENIC PLANT VACCINES—coauthored.

Cepollina, Dr. Frank. *Deputy Associate Director, HST Development Office, NASA.* HUBBLE SPACE TELESCOPE.

Chan, Arthur. *Center for Industrial and Medical Ultrasound, Department of Bioengineering and Applied Physics Laboratory, University of Washington, Seattle.* HIGH-INTENSITY FOCUSED ULTRASOUND—coauthored.

Chapin, John K. *Professor of Physiology, SUNY Downstate Medical Center, New York.* VIRTUAL OPERANT CONDITIONING—coauthored.

Chen, Prof. Mark. *Assistant Professor of Physics, Queen's University, Kingston, and Scholar, Canadian Institute for Advanced Research, Cosmology and Gravity Program, Toronto, Ontario, Canada.* NEUTRINO MASSES AND OSCILLATIONS.

Chen, Dr. Ruizhen. *Assistant Professor of Chemical Engineering, Virginia Commonwealth University, Richmond.* BIOCATALYSIS.

Cheng, Prof. Herbert. *Department of Mechanical Engineering, Northwestern University, Evanston, Illinois.* TRIBOLOGY—coauthored.

Chiappe, Dr. Luis M. *Curator and Chairman, Department of Vertebrate Paleontology, Natural History Museum of Los Angeles County, Los Angeles, California.* AVIAN EVOLUTION—coauthored.

Chopra, Dr. Prame. *Reader in Geophysics, Australian National University, Canberra.* GEOTHERMAL ENERGY.

Chung, Dr. Suh-Urk. *Physics Department, Brookhaven National Laboratory, Upton, New York.* EXOTIC MESONS.

Chung, Y. W. *Department of Mechanical Engineering, Northwestern University, Evanston, Illinois.* TRIBOLOGY—coauthored.

Conway Morris, Dr. Simon. *Professor of Evolutionary Palaeo Biology, University of Cambridge, United Kingdom.* DEUTEROSTOME EVOLUTION—coauthored.

Cook, Roger I. *Department of Biological Sciences, University of Warwick, Coventry, United Kingdom.* CIRCADIAN CLOCK (PLANTS)—coauthored.

Corcho, Dr. Oscar. *Universidad Politécnica de Madrid, Spain.* ONTOLOGY MARKUP LANGUAGES—coauthored.

Cordova, Prof. Carlos. *Assistant Professor, Geography Department, Oklahoma State University, Stillwater.* RECONSTRUCTING ENVIRONMENTAL HISTORY.

Crabtree, Prof. Robert H. *Chemistry Department, Yale University, New Haven, Connecticut.* C-H ACTIVATION.

Crum, Prof. Lawrence A. *Center for Industrial and Medical Ultrasound, Department of Bioengineering and Applied Physics Laboratory, University of Washington, Seattle.* HIGH-INTENSITY FOCUSED ULTRASOUND—coauthored.

D

Dalko, Dr. Peter I. *Ecole supérieure de physique et de chimie industrielles, Paris, France.* ORGANIC CATALYSTS.

Davidson, Dr. Nicholas O. *Professor of Medicine and Molecular Biology & Pharmacology, Washington University, St. Louis, Missouri.* RNA EDITING.

DeGroot, Dr. Jeroen. *TNO Prevention and Health, Leiden, The Netherlands.* ADVANCED GLYCATION END PRODUCTS—coauthored.

Detty, Dr. Michael R. *Department of Chemistry, State University of New York at Buffalo.* PHOTODYNAMIC THERAPY.

Dillingham, Dr. Mark S. *University of California, Davis.* DNA HELICASES—coauthored.

Dindia, Christine. *Environmental Studies Coordinator, Santa Clara University, Santa Clara, California.* HISTORICAL ECOLOGY.

Donoghue, Dr. Philip C. J. *University of Birmingham, School of Earth Sciences, Birmingham, United Kingdom.* EMERGENCE OF VERTEBRATES.

Dragovan, Dr. Mark. *Principal Scientist, Jet Propulsion Laboratory, Pasadena, California.* UNIVERSE.

Droser, Dr. Mary. *Department of Earth Sciences, University of California, Riverside.* ORDOVICIAN RADIATION.

Duan, Dr. Xiangfeng. *Department of Chemistry and Chemical Biology, Harvard University, Cambridge, Massachusetts.* NANOWIRE NANOCIRCUITS—coauthored.

Dyke, Dr. Gareth John. *Department of Zoology, University College, Dublin, Ireland.* AVIAN EVOLUTION—coauthored.

E

Egry, Prof. Ivan. *German Aerospace Center, Cologne, Germany.* MICROGRAVITY.

Elrad, Prof. Tzilla. *Research Professor, Computer Science Department, Illinois Institute of Technology, Chicago.* ASPECT-ORIENTED SOFTWARE DEVELOPMENT.

El-Shall, Dr. M. Samy. *Professor of Physical Chemistry, Virginia Commonwealth University, Richmond.* NANOPARTICLES.

Enger, Jonas. *Department of Physics, Göteborg University and Chalmers University of Technology, Göteborg, Sweden.* OPTICAL MANIPULATION OF MATTER—coauthored.

Erickson, Dr. John S. *Hewlett-Packard Laboratories, Norwich, Vermont.* DIGITAL OBJECT IDENTIFIER.

Ericsson, Mattias. *Department of Physics, Göteborg University and Chalmers University of Technology, Göteborg, Sweden.* OPTICAL MANIPULATION OF MATTER—coauthored.

F

Fontana, Dr. Robert J. *Multispectral Solutions, Inc., Germantown, Maryland.* ULTRAWIDEBAND (UWB) SYSTEMS.

Foster, Dr. J. T. *Institute for Animal Health, Neuropathogenesis Unit, Edinburgh, United Kingdom.* TRANSMISSIBLE SPONGIFORM ENCEPHALOPATHIES.

Fransen, Dr. Steven C. *Washington State University, Prosser.* RYEGRASS.

G

Gaska, Remis. *President and CEO, Sensor Electronic Technology, Latham, New York.* HIGH-BRIGHTNESS LIGHT-EMITTING DIODES—coauthored.

Gaxiola, Dr. Roberto A. *Associate Professor, Department of Plant Science, University of Connecticut, Storrs.* SALT TOLERANCE IN PLANTS.

Gido, Prof. Samuel P. *Department of Polymer Science and Engineering, University of Massachusetts, Amherst.* GRAFT COPOLYMERS—coauthored.

Girgrah, Dr. Nigel. *Assistant Professor of Medicine, University of Toronto, Ontario, Canada.* HEPATITIS C—coauthored.

Goldberg, Dr. Robert N. *National Institute of Standards & Technology, Gaithersburg, Maryland.* ENZYME CATALYSIS (THERMODYNAMICS).

Gómez del Campo, Dr. Jorge. *Oak Ridge National Laboratory, Oak Ridge, Tennessee.* NUCLEAR DECAY—coauthored.

Gómez-Pérez, Prof. Asunción. *Universidad Politécnica de Madrid, Spain.* ONTOLOGY MARKUP LANGUAGES—coauthored.

Gómez-Pinilla, Dr. Fernando. *University of California at Los Angeles.* EXERCISE AND THE BRAIN.

Gordon, Prof. Robert J. *Department of Chemistry, University of Illinois, Chicago.* LASER-CONTROLLED CHEMICAL REACTIONS.

Gould, Prof. Philip L. *Professor of Physics, University of Connecticut, Storrs.* ULTRACOLD COLLISIONS.

Graham, Dr. Anthony. *MRC Centre for Developmental Neurobiology, King's College, London, United Kingdom.* INNER EAR DEVELOPMENT.

Grant, Dr. Jon E. *University of Minnesota School of Medicine, Minneapolis.* BODY DYSMORPHIC DISORDER—coauthored.

Green, Larry. *Director, Antibody Technologies, Abgenix, Incorporated.* MONOCLONAL ANTIBODIES.

Groome, Dr. N. P. *School of Biological and Molecular Sciences, Oxford Brookes University, Oxford, United Kingdom.* INHIBIN.

H

Hajnal, Prof. J. V. *Imaging Sciences Department, Clinical Sciences Centre, Imperial College, London, United Kingdom.* DYNAMIC BRAIN ATLAS—coauthored.

Hanstorp, Prof. Dag. *Department of Physics, Göteborg University, and Chalmers University of Technology, Göteborg, Sweden.* OPTICAL MANIPULATION OF MATTER—coauthored.

Haridasan, Prof. Mundayatan. *Universidade de Brasilia, Brazil.* ALUMINUM-ACCUMULATING PLANTS—coauthored.

Harrison, Dr. Terry. *Department of Anthropology, New York University, New York.* HUMAN ORIGINS.

Hartkens, Prof. Thomas. *Computational Imaging Science Group, King's College, London, United Kingdom.* DYNAMIC BRAIN ATLAS—coauthored.

Harvey, Dr. Chris. *Research Fishery Biologist, Northwest Fisheries Science Center, National Marine Fisheries Service, Seattle, Washington.* INVASIVE SPECIES IMPACTS.

Hass-Klau, Prof. Carmen. *Environmental and Transport Planning, Brighton, United Kingdom.* LIGHT RAIL AND TRANSPORT POLICIES.

Heine, Dr. Lauren. *Director, Green Chemistry & Engineering, International Sustainable Development, Portland, Oregon.* SUSTAINABLE MATERIALS.

Henderson, Dr. Mark. *Arizona State University, Tempe.* STEREO MODELING—coauthored.

Heremans, Dr. Joseph. *Fellow, Delphi Research Labs, Shelby Township, Michigan.* SEMICONDUCTOR REFRIGERATORS.

Hill, Prof. Derek. *Computational Imaging Science Group, King's College, London, United Kingdom.* DYNAMIC BRAIN ATLAS—coauthored.

Hinds, Prof. Edward A. *Sussex Centre for Optical & Atomic Physics, University of Sussex, United Kingdom.* MANIPULATING COLD ATOMS.

Holden, Dr. Clare Janaki. *Wellcome Trust Research Fellow, Department of Anthropology, University College, London, United Kingdom.* EVOLUTION OF BANTU LANGUAGES.

Holman, Dr. Matthew J. *Astrophysicist, Harvard-Smithsonian Center for Astrophysics, Cambridge, Massachusetts.* SATELLITES OF OUTER PLANETS.

Huang, Yu. *Department of Chemistry and Chemical Biology, Harvard University, Cambridge, Massachusetts.* NANOWIRE NANOCIRCUITS—coauthored.

I

Ibach, Dr. Rebecca E. *Research Chemist, USDA Forest Service, Forest Products Laboratory, Madison, Wisconsin.* WOOD PRESERVATION.

Immink, Dr. André. *Philips Research Laboratories, Eindhoven, The Netherlands.* ULTRAHIGH-DENSITY STORAGE—coauthored.

J

Jackson Nielsen, Victoria B. *WellDynamics, Houston, Texas.* INTELLIGENT COMPLETION TECHNOLOGY.

Jaluria, Dr. Yogesh. *Board of Governors and Professor, Rutgers, The State University of New Jersey, Piscataway,* MATERIALS PROCESSING.

Jansen, Dr. Steven. *Postdoctoral Fellow of the Fund for Scientific Research—Flanders, and Laboratory of Plant Systematics, Katholieke Universiteit Leuven, Belgium.* ALUMINUM-ACCUMULATING PLANTS—coauthored.

Janssen, Dr. Jan-Theodoor. *Principal Research Scientist, National Physical Laboratory, Middlesex, United Kingdom.* TRANSPORTING SINGLE ELECTRONS.

John, Dr. E. Roy. *Director, Brain Research Laboratories, and Professor of Psychiatry, New York University School of Medicine, and Nathan S. Kline Institute of Psychiatric Research, Orangeburg, New York.* SURGICAL CONSCIOUSNESS MONITOR—coauthored.

Johnsson, Dr. Mats. *Department of Inorganic Chemistry, Arrhenius Laboratory, Stockholm University, Stockholm, Sweden.* CERAMIC WHISKERS—coauthored.

Jones, Edwin L., Jr. *Forensic Scientist, Ventura County Sheriff's Crime Laboratory, Ventura, California.* FORENSIC MICROSCOPY.

Joughin, Dr. Ian. *Jet Propulsion Laboratory, Pasadena, California.* ANTARCTIC ICE STREAM DYNAMICS—coauthored.

Joyce, Dr. Charles. *Senior Fellow, Metabolic Diseases Branch, National Heart, Lung, and Blood Institute, National Institutes of Health, Bethesda, Maryland.* ABC LIPID TRANSPORTERS—coauthored.

K

Kaminsky, Prof. Walter. *Institute of Technical & Macromolecular Chemistry, University of Hamburg, Germany.* SINGLE-SITE CATALYSTS AND RESULTING POLYOLEFINS.

Keer, L. M. *Department of Mechanical Engineering, Northwestern University, Evanston, Illinois.* TRIBOLOGY—coauthored.

Kelly, Dr. Colleen K. *School of Biological Sciences, University of Southampton, United Kingdom.* CLIMATE CHANGE AND PLANT ADAPTATION.

Kipphan, Dr. Helmut. *Chief Scientist/Technology Advisor, Heidelberger Druckmaschinen AG, Heidelberg, Germany.* ON-PRESS PLATE IMAGING.

Kisabeth, Dr. Robert. *Chair, Mayo Medical Laboratories, Mayo Clinic, Rochester, Minnesota.* PHARMACOGENOMICS—in part.

Koch, Dr. Kerstin. *Botanisches Insitut und Botanischer Garten, Universität Bonn, Germany.* EPICUTICULAR WAXES (BOTANY)—coauthored.

Koh, Dr. Carolyn Ann. *Reader in Chemistry, King's College, University of London, United Kingdom.* METHANE CLATHRATE.

Kojima, Dr. Seiji. *Department of Biology, University of Utah, Salt Lake City.* ROTARY MOTORS (BACTERIAL)—coauthored.

Kowalczykowski, Dr. Stephen C. *Professor, University of California at Davis.* DNA HELICASES—coauthored.

Kupinski, Dr. Matthew A. *Assistant Professor, Optical Sciences Center and Department of Radiology, University of Arizona, Tucson.* GAMMA-RAY IMAGING.

L

Labastie, Alain. *TotalFinaElf, France.* TIME-LAPSE SEISMIC RESERVOIR MONITORING.

Langridge, Dr. William H. R. *Professor, Center for Molecular Biology and Gene Therapy, Loma Linda University, Loma Linda, California.* TRANSGENIC PLANT VACCINES—coauthored.

Latham, Dr. David. *Harvard-Smithsonian Center for Astrophysics, Cambridge, Massachusetts.* EXTRASOLAR PLANETS—coauthored.

Lathrop, Amanda. *Graduate Research Assistant, Department of Food Science, Purdue University, West Lafayette, Indiana.* PATHOGEN DETECTION, FOOD-BORNE—coauthored.

Lentini, John J. *Applied Technical Services, Incorporated, Marietta, Georgia.* FORENSIC ARSON INVESTIGATION.

Lentz, Dr. Steven R. *Associate Professor of Internal Medicine, University of Iowa, Iowa City.* HOMOCYSTEINE.

Levy, Dr. Gary. *Professor of Medicine, University of Toronto, Ontario, Canada.* HEPATITIS C—coauthored.

Licinio, Dr. Julio. *Professor of Psychiatry and Medicine, and Director, Interdepartmental Clinical Pharmacology Center, UCLA School of Medicine, Los Angeles.* PHARMACOGENOMICS—coauthored.

Lieber, Prof. Charles M. *Mark Hyman Professor of Chemistry, Department of Chemistry & Chemical Biology, Division of Engineering and Applied Sciences, Harvard University, Cambridge, Massachusetts.* NANOWIRE NANOCIRCUITS—coauthored.

Linzey, Dr. Donald W. *Professor of Biology, Wytheville Community College, Wytheville, Virginia.* MIGRATION AND NAVIGATION (VERTEBRATES)—in part.

Lockhart, Thomas P. *Senior Project Manager, EniTecnologie, Milano, Italy.* MICROBIAL ENHANCED OIL RECOVERY—coauthored.

Lohmann, Prof. Catherine M. F. *Department of Biology, University of North Carolina, Chapel Hill.* MIGRATION AND NAVIGATION (VERTEBRATES)—coauthored.

Lohmann, Prof. Kenneth J. *Associate Professor of Biology, University of North Carolina, Chapel Hill.* MIGRATION AND NAVIGATION (VERTEBRATES)—coauthored.

Luo, Dr. Dan. *Department of Biological & Environmental Engineering, Cornell University, Ithaca, New York.* DNA DELIVERY SYSTEMS.

Lupien, Dr. Sonia J. *Department of Psychiatry, Douglas Hospital, McGill University, Montreal, Quebec, Canada.* STRESS-FUNCTION-MORPHOLOGY CORRELATIONS IN THE BRAIN.

M

Macklis, Dr. Jeffrey D. *Associate Professor of Neurology and Director, Center for Nervous System Repair, Massachusetts*

General Hospital and Harvard Medical School, Boston. NEUROGENESIS—coauthored.

Magavi, Dr. Sanjay S. *Research Fellow, Center for Nervous System Repair, Massachusetts General Hospital and Harvard Medical School, Boston.* NEUROGENESIS—coauthored.

Mahenthiralingham, Dr. Eshwar. *Lecturer, Cardiff School of Biosciences, Cardiff University, Cardiff, United Kingdom.* BURKHOLDERIA CEPACIA COMPLEX—coauthored.

Maheshwari, Prof. Ramesh. *Department of Biochemistry, Indian Institute of Science, Bangalore.* ENZYMES OF THERMOPHILIC FUNGI.

Mann, Prof. Michael E. *Department of Environmental Sciences, University of Virginia, Charlottesville.* RECONSTRUCTING TEMPERATURE VARIATIONS.

Martin, Prof. Bjorn. *Professor, Department of Plant and Soil Sciences, Oklahoma State University, Stillwater.* CARBON ISOTOPE DISCRIMINATION MEASUREMENT.

Mata-Toledo, Dr. Ramon A. *James Madison University, Harrisonburg, Virginia.* DATA MINING.

Mayberg, Dr. Helen. *Baycrest Centre for Geriatric Care, Rotman Research Institute, Toronto, Ontario, Canada.* NEURAL MODEL OF DEPRESSION.

Mays, Prof. Jimmy W. *Distinguished Professor, University of Tennessee, Knoxville, and Distinguished Scientist, Oak Ridge National Laboratory, Oak Ridge, Tennessee.* GRAFT COPOLYMERS—coauthored.

McEwen, Dr. Bruce F. *Wadsworth Center, New York State Department of Health, and Department of Biomedical Sciences, School of Public Health, State University of New York, Albany.* ELECTRON TOMOGRAPHY.

McGuirk, Dr. Jeffrey. *University of Colorado, Boulder.* ATOM INTERFEROMETER, MAGNETIC WAVEGUIDE.

McKleish, Prof. K. *Computational Imaging Science Group, King's College, London, United Kingdom.* DYNAMIC BRAIN ATLAS—coauthored.

Meehan, Dr. Richard. *Chief of Rheumatology, Associate Professor of Medicine, National Jewish Medical Research Center, Denver, Colorado.* DISEASE-MODIFYING ANTI-RHEUMATIC DRUGS.

Melton, Dr. Terry. *President/CEO, Mitotyping Technologies, State College, Pennsylvania.* FORENSIC MITOCHONDRIAL DNA ANALYSIS.

Millar, Dr. Andrew J. *Professor of Biological Sciences, University of Warwick, Coventry, United Kingdom.* CIRCADIAN CLOCK (PLANTS)—coauthored.

Mitchell, Dr. Jeffrey C. *Associate Professor, Florida Institute of Technology, Melbourne.* SPACE NUCLEAR TECHNOLOGY.

Muhlfelder, Dr. Barry. *Senior Research Physicist, Stanford University, Stanford, California.* GRAVITY PROBE B.

N

Neel, Dr. Maile. *David H. Smith Conservation Research Fellow, Department of Natural Resources Conservation, University of Massachusetts, Amherst.* GENETIC DIVERSITY IN NATURE RESERVES.

Neilan, Dr. Ruth E. *IGS Central Bureau, Jet Propulsion Laboratory, Pasadena, California.* INTERNATIONAL GPS SERVICE.

Neinhuis, Prof. Christopher. *Institut für Botanik, Technische Universität Dresden, Germany.* EPICUTICULAR WAXES (BOTANY)—coauthored.

Nüsslein, Dr. Klaus. *Assistant Professor, Department of Microbiology, University of Massachusetts, Amherst.* PATHOGEN DETECTION.

Nygren, Prof. Mats. *Department of Inorganic Chemistry, Arrhenius Laboratory, Stockholm University, Stockholm, Sweden.* CERAMIC WHISKERS—coauthored.

O

Ogren, Ingmar. *Tofs Corporation, Veddoe, Sweden.* MODELING LANGUAGES.

P

Pálfy, Dr. József. *Department of Paleontology, Hungarian Natural History Museum, Budapest.* END-TRIASSIC MASS EXTINCTION.

Phillips, Dr. Katharine. *Butler Hospital and Brown University, School of Medicine, Providence, Rhode Island.* BODY DYSMORPHIC DISORDER—coauthored.

Phillips, Mike. *Software Engineering Institute, Pittsburgh, Pennsylvania.* CAPABILITY MATURITY MODELING.

Pillai, Devadas D. *Intel Corporation, Chandler, Arizona.* SEMICONDUCTOR FACTORY AUTOMATION.

Pool, Thomas C. *International Nuclear, Inc., Golden, Colorado.* URANIUM MINING.

Prichep, Dr. Leslie S. *Associate Director, Brain Research Laboratories, and Professor of Psychiatry, New York University School of Medicine, and Nathan S. Kline Institute of Psychiatric Research, Orangeburg, New York.* SURGICAL CONSCIOUSNESS MONITOR—coauthored.

Q

Qui, Dr. Yin-Long. *Assistant Professor, Biology Department, University of Massachusetts, Amherst.* PHYLOGENY OF EARLY LAND PLANTS.

Quinn, Dr. Helen. *Stanford Linear Accelerator Center, Menlo Park, California.* CP SYMMETRY AND ITS VIOLATION.

R

Raboy, Dr. Victor. *Research Geneticist, USDA-Agricultural Research Service, Aberdeen, Idaho.* PHOSPHORUS—coauthored.

Rahmstorf, Dr. Stefan. *Potsdam Institute for Climate Impact Research, Potsdam, Germany.* THERMOHALINE CIRCULATION CHANGES.

Razdan, Dr. Anshuman. *Arizona State University, Tempe.* STEREO MODELING—coauthored.

Richards, Prof. Jeremy P. *Department of Earth and Atmospheric Sciences, University of Alberta, Edmonton, Alberta, Canada.* PROSPECTING (METALLOGENIC TRENDS).

Roberts, Dr. Victor. *President, Roberts Research & Consulting, Inc., Burnt Hills, New York.* RADIO-FREQUENCY LIGHTING.

Robinson, Prof. Walter A. *Professor of Atmospheric Sciences, University of Illinois at Urbana-Champaign.* STRATOSPHERIC INFLUENCES (WEATHER AND CLIMATE).

Rodolfo, Prof. Kelvin S. *Professor Emeritus, Department of Earth and Environmental Sciences, University of Illinois, Chicago.* TSUNAMIITES AND SEISMITES.

Romaine, Dr. C. Peter. *Professor of Plant Pathology, Pennsylvania State University, University Park.* BACTERIAL TRANSFORMATION OF FUNGI.

Rosing, Prof. Minik T. *Geological Museum, Copenhagen University, Copenhagen, Denmark.* EVIDENCE OF ARCHEAN LIFE.

Roth, Dr. G. Linn. *President, Locus, Inc., Madison, Wisconsin.* LORAN.

Rueckert, Prof. D. *Computer Science Department, Imperial College, London, United Kingdom.* DYNAMIC BRAIN ATLAS—coauthored.

S

Sage, Dr. Andrew P. *Founding Dean Emeritus and First American Bank Professor, University Professor, School of Information Technology and Engineering, George Mason University, Fairfax Station, Virginia.* KNOWLEDGE MANAGEMENT.

Santamarina-Fojo, Dr. Silvia. *Chief, Section of Molecular Biology, Metabolic Diseases Branch, National Heart, Lung, and Blood Institute, National Institutes of Health, Bethesda, Maryland.* ABC LIPID TRANSPORTERS—coauthored.

Sayre, Dr. Philip. *Associate Director, Risk Assessment Division, OPPT, U.S. Environmental Protection Agency, Washington, DC.* BURKHOLDERIA CEPACIA COMPLEX—coauthored.

Schetz, Prof. Joseph A. *Aerospace and Ocean Engineering Department, Virginia Polytechnic Institute and State University, Blacksburg.* HIGH-SPEED TRAIN AERODYNAMICS.

Schoenfisch, Dr. Mark H. *Assistant Professor, University of North Carolina, Chapel Hill.* NITRIC OXIDE BIOSENSORS—coauthored.

Schwendeman, Dr. Stephen P. *Associate Professor of Pharmaceutical Sciences, University of Michigan, Ann Arbor.* PROTEIN DRUG DELIVERY.

Seilacher, Dr. Adolf. *Institut und Museum für Geologie und Paläontologie, Eberhard-Karles-Universität Tübingen, Germany.* VENDOBIONTS (PRECAMBRIAN EVOLUTION).

Shaffer, Julie. *Director, Center for Imaging Excellence, Graphic Arts Technical Foundation, Sewickley, Pennsylvania.* DIGITAL WATERMARKING.

Shannon, Prof. Mark A. *Associate Professor, Department of Mechanical & Industrial Engineering, University of Illinois at Urbana-Champaign.* MESOSCOPIC MECHANICAL SYSTEMS.

Shaywitz, Dr. Bennett. *Yale University School of Medicine, Department of Pediatrics, New Haven, Connecticut.* DYSLEXIA—coauthored.

Shaywitz, Prof. Sally E. *Yale University School of Medicine, Department of Pediatrics, New Haven, Connecticut.* DYSLEXIA—coauthored.

Sheridon, Dr. Nicholas K. *Gyricon Media, Inc., Palo Alto, California.* ELECTRONIC PAPER.

Sherrill, Dr. Sam. *Executive Director, Crow Publications, Portland, Oregon.* WOOD COMPOSITES.

Shin, Jae Ho. *Research Assistant, University of North Carolina, Chapel Hill.* NITRIC OXIDE BIOSENSORS—coauthored.

Shindell, Dr. Drew T. *Lecturer, Department of Earth and Environmental Sciences, Columbia University, New York.* GLOBAL WARMING AND ATMOSPHERIC OZONE.

Shu, Prof. Degan. *Northwest University, Xi'an, China.* DEUTEROSTOME EVOLUTION—coauthored.

Shur, Prof. Michael S. *Professor, Department of Electrical, Computer, and Systems Engineering and Center for Integrated Electronics, Rensselaer Polytechnic Institute, Troy, New York.* HIGH-BRIGHTNESS LIGHT-EMITTING DIODES—coauthored.

Siddall, Dr. Mark E. *Associate Curator, Division of Invertebrate Zoology, American Museum of Natural History, New York.* LEECH EVOLUTION.

Simser, Brad. *Noranda Technology Centre, Pointe-Claire, Quebec, Canada.* MINE SEISMOLOGY.

Skinner, Dr. H. Catherine W. *Department of Geology & Geophysics, Yale University, New Haven, Connecticut.* MEDICAL GEOLOGY.

Smets, Prof. Erik. *Laboratory of Plant Systematics, Katholieke Universiteit Leuven, Belgium.* ALUMINUM-ACCUMULATING PLANTS—coauthored.

Smith, Dr. Julius O., III. *Center for Computer Research in Music and Acoustics, Department of Music, Stanford University, Stanford, California.* VIRTUAL MUSICAL INSTRUMENTS.

Smith, Prof. S. M. *Center for Functional Magnetic Resonance Imaging of the Brain, University of Oxford, United Kingdom.* DYNAMIC BRAIN ATLAS—coauthored.

Sonneborn, Dr. George. *Scientist, FUSE Project, NASA Goddard Space Flight Center, Greenbelt, Maryland.* FAR-ULTRAVIOLET ASTRONOMY.

Spaulding, Dr. Russell. *Manager of Optics, Vistakon Division of Johnson & Johnson Vision Care, Inc., Jacksonville, Florida.* CONTACT LENSES.

Spies, Dr. Maria. *University of California at Davis.* DNA HELICASES—coauthored.

Stanton, Prof. Anthony. *Director, Graphic Media Management, Carnegie Mellon University, Pittsburgh, Pennsylvania.* DIGITAL PHOTOGRAPHY.

Stewart, Dr. Brent S. *Senior Research Biologist, Hubbs-Sea World Research Institute, San Diego, California.* MIGRATION AND NAVIGATION (VERTEBRATES)—in part.

Swain, Dr. Greg M. *Associate Professor, Department of Chemistry, Michigan State University, East Lansing.* DIAMOND ELECTRODES (ELECTROCHEMISTRY).

T

Talwar, Dr. Sanjiv K. *Research Assistant Professor, SUNY Downstate Medical Center, New York.* VIRTUAL OPERANT CONDITIONING—coauthored.

Tavoularis, Prof. Stavros. *Department of Mechanical Engineering, University of Ottawa, Ontario, Canada.* TURBULENT TRANSPORT AND MIXING.

TeKoppele, Dr. Johan M. *TNO Prevention and Health, Leiden, The Netherlands.* ADVANCED GLYCATION END PRODUCTS—coauthored.

Teuber, Dr. M. *Swiss Federal Institute of Technology, Laboratory of Food Microbiology, Zurich.* ANTIBIOTIC RESISTANCE.

Thaut, Dr. Michael H. *Professor of Music and Professor of Neuroscience, and Director, School of the Arts, Colorado State University, Fort Collins.* NEUROMUSICOLOGY.

Theobald, Dr. David M. *Research Scientist, Natural Resource Ecology Laboratory, and Assistant Professor, Department of Natural Resources, Recreation and Tourism, Colorado State University, Fort Collins.* CONNECTED LANDSCAPES.

Tolbert, Thomas J. *Scripps Research Institute, La Jolla, California.* GLYCOPROTEIN SYNTHESIS—coauthored.

Trusler, Prof. J. P. Martin. *Professor of Thermophysics, Imperial College of Science, Technology and Medicine, London, United Kingdom.* POLYMER THERMODYNAMICS.

Tulaczyk, Prof. Slawek. *Department of Earth Sciences, University of California, Santa Cruz.* ANTARCTIC ICE STREAM DYNAMICS—coauthored.

Turner, Dr. Benjamin L. *USDA-Agricultural Research Service, Northwest Irrigation and Soils Research, Kimberly, Idaho.* PHOSPHORUS—coauthored.

U

Umstadter, Dr. Donald. *University of Michigan, Ann Arbor.* LASER-DRIVEN X-RAY SOURCES.

V

Verzijl, Dr. Nicole. *TNO Prevention and Health, Leiden, The Netherlands.* ADVANCED GLYCATION END PRODUCTS—coauthored.

Vestergaard Hau, Dr. Lene. *Lyman Laboratory, Department of Physics, Harvard University, Cambridge, Massachusetts.* FROZEN LIGHT.

Vezy, Shahram. *Center for Industrial and Medical Ultrasound, Department of Bioengineering and Applied Physics Laboratory, University of Washington, Seattle.* HIGH-INTENSITY FOCUSED ULTRASOUND—coauthored.

Vinckier, Stefan. *Laboratory of Plant Systematics, Institute of Botany and Microbiology, Katholieke Universiteit Leuven, Belgium.* ORBICULES (PLANT ANATOMY).

Vogel, Prof. Steven. *James B. Duke Professor, Duke University, Durham, North Carolina.* NATURAL AERODYNAMIC DEVICES.

Von Puttkamer, Dr. Jesco. *NASA Headquarters, Washington, DC.* SPACE FLIGHT.

W

Wang, Dr. Chen. *Mount Sinai Hospital, Pathology and Laboratory Medicine, Toronto, Ontario, Canada.* STEM CELLS.

Wang, Q. *Department of Mechanical Engineering, Northwestern University, Evanston, Illinois.* TRIBOLOGY—coauthored.

Warner, Richard D. *Senior Research Scientist (retired), Graphic Arts Technical Foundation, and President, R. D. Warner Consulting, Pennsylvania.* SECURITY PRINTING.

Weismer, Prof. Gary. *Professor and Chair of the Department of Communicative Disorders, University of Wisconsin—Madison.* ACOUSTIC PHONETICS.

Wen, Prof. Lianxing. *Assistant Professor of Geophysics, Department of Geosciences, State University of New York at Stony Brook.* INNER CORE ANISOTROPY AND HEMISPHERICITY.

Wenzel, Dr. John W. *Professor, Department of Entomology, Ohio State University, Columbus.* BIOLUMINESCENCE IN INSECTS—coauthored.

Wilkinson, Dr. John W. *Department of Biological Sciences, The Open University, Milton Keynes, United Kingdom, and International Coordinator, Declining Amphibian Population Task Force.* DECLINING AMPHIBIANS.

Williams, Dr. Mark. *Department of Crop and Soil Science, Oregon State University, Corvallis.* RHIZOSPHERE ECOLOGY.

Wiltschko, Dr. R. *Zoologisches Institut, J. W. Goethe-Universität, Frankfurt am Main, Germany.* MIGRATION AND NAVIGATION (VERTEBRATES)—coauthored.

Wiltschko, Dr. W. *Zoologisches Institut, J. W. Goethe-Universität, Frankfurt am Main, Germany.* MIGRATION AND NAVIGATION (VERTEBRATES)—coauthored.

Wong, Ma-Li. *Laboratory for Pharmacogenomics, Neuropsychiatric Institute, David Geffen School of Medicine, University of California, Los Angeles.* PHARMACOGENOMICS—coauthored.

Wong, Prof. Chi-Huey. *Ernest W. Hahn Chair in Chemistry, Scripps Research Institute, La Jolla, California.* GLYCOPROTEIN SYNTHESIS—coauthored.

Wu, Dr. Justina. *Senior Fellow, Metabolic Diseases Branch, National Heart, Lung, and Blood Institute, National Institutes of Health, Bethesda, Maryland.* ABC LIPID TRANSPORTERS—coauthored.

X

Xu, Shaohua. *SUNY Downstate Medical Center, New York.* VIRTUAL OPERANT CONDITIONING—coauthored.

Y

Yang, Dr. Wu Qiang. *Senior Lecturer, University of Manchester Institute of Science & Technology, Manchester, United Kingdom.* CAPACITANCE TOMOGRAPHY.

Yeung, Dr. Edward S. *Distinguished Professor in Liberal Arts & Sciences, Iowa State University, Ames.* SINGLE-MOLECULE OPTICAL IMAGING.

Young, Dr. Richard. *Department of Oceanography, University of Hawaii, Honolulu.* DEEP-SEA SQUID.

Z

Zahn, Dr. Jeffrey D. *Assistant Professor of Bioengineering, Pennsylvania State University, University Park.* BIO-MICRO-ELECTRO-MECHANICAL SYSTEMS FOR DRUG DELIVERY.

Zebker, Prof. Howard A. *Professor of Geophysics and Electrical Engineering, Stanford University, Stanford, California.* SAR INTERFEROMETRY.

Zeldin, Prof. Martel. *Department of Chemistry, Hobart and William Smith Colleges, Geneva, New York.* INORGANIC AND ORGANOMETALLIC POLYMERS.

Zhu, Prof. D. *Department of Mechanical Engineering, Northwestern University, Evanston, Illinois.* TRIBOLOGY—coauthored.

Žukauskas, Prof. Artūras. *Institute of Materials Science and Applied Research, Vilnius University, Vilnius, Lithuania.* HIGH-BRIGHTNESS LIGHT-EMITTING DIODES—coauthored.

Index

Asterisks indicate page references to article titles.